13th Conference of the European Chapter of the Association for Computational Linguistics 2012

(EACL 2012)

Avignon, France
23-27 April 2012

ISBN: 978-1-62276-042-8

Printed from e-media with permission by:

Curran Associates, Inc.
57 Morehouse Lane
Red Hook, NY 12571

Some format issues inherent in the e-media version may also appear in this print version.

Printed by Curran Associates, Inc. (2012)

Association for Computational Linguistics
209 N. Eighth Street
Stroudsburg, Pennsylvania 18360

Phone: 1-570-476-8006
Fax: 1-570-476-0860

acl@aclweb.org

Additional copies of this publication are available from:

Curran Associates, Inc.
57 Morehouse Lane
Red Hook, NY 12571 USA
Phone: 845-758-0400
Fax: 845-758-2634
Email: curran@proceedings.com
Web: www.proceedings.com

Preface: General Chair

Welcome to EACL 2012, the 13th Conference of the European Chapter of the Association for Computational Linguistics. We are happy that despite strong competition from other Computational Linguistics events and economic turmoil in many European countries, this EACL is comparable to the successful previous ones, both in terms of the number of papers submitted and in terms of attendance. We have a strong scientific program, including ten workshops, four tutorials, a demos session and a student research workshop. I am convinced that you will appreciate our program.

What does a General Chair at EACL have to do? Not much, it turns out. My job was to act as a liaison between the local organizing team, the scientific committees, and the EACL board, and to give advice when needed. Looking back at the thousands of e-mails I was copied on reminded me of the Jerome K. Jerome quote: "I like work. I can sit and look at it for hours". It has been an enjoyable experience to cooperate with the many people who made this conference happen, and to see them work. I have learned a lot from them.

The Program Committee at an ACL conference is a trained army of Area Chairs, Program Committee members, and additional reviewers. Mirella Lapata and Lluís Màrquez commanded this particular one. It is thanks to the voluntary peer reviewing work, year after year, of this large group of people, formed by the top researchers in our field, that you will find a high-quality program. It is thanks to Mirella and Lluís that you will not only find the quality we expect from EACL, but also innovation, coherence, breadth, and depth. I can't thank them enough for their work on all aspects of the scientific program and for their advice on virtually any other aspect of the organization. Many thanks also to Regina Barzilay, Raymond Mooney, and Martin Cooke for accepting to present an invited lecture and thereby increase the appeal of this event even more.

As in previous years, the selection of the workshops of all ACL conferences in the same year is coordinated in a single committee. For EACL, Kristiina Jokinen and Alessandro Moschitti collaborated with the NAACL and ACL chairs in reviewing and selecting the workshops. As EACL is the first conference of the three, they had to initiate the call for proposals and activate their colleagues long before they were planning to. Thanks to their professionalism and efficiency, the process went very smoothly, and the resulting workshops program reflects the diversity and maturity of the field. For even more variation during the first two days of the conference, we also have a strong tutorial program. Tutorial Chairs Lieve Macken and Eneko Agirre managed to attract an impressive list of high-quality submissions and performed a thorough and thoughtful review and selection. It is truly a pity only four could be accommodated in the program, but their quality and timeliness is inspiring. Many thanks to Kristiina, Alessandro, Lieve, and Eneko for making this important part of the scientific program such a success.

As is previous editions of EACL, the Student Research Workshop was organized by the student members of the EACL board: Pierre Lison, Mattias Nilsson, and Marta Recasens, with help from faculty advisor Laurence Danlos. Their task was a huge one: to organize a mini-conference within the conference. This included finding reviewers, selecting papers, setting up a program for the student session, finding mentors for the accepted papers, selecting a best paper award, ... The amount of work they did cannot be overestimated, and the result is brilliant. Thank you! To round of the scientific program, we have stimulating demonstration sessions, selected and coordinated by Demonstrations Chair Frédérique Segond. Thank you for showing so clearly the rapid progress application-oriented computational linguistics is making.

Thanks also to Gertjan van Noord and Caroline Sporleder for accepting the role of coordinators of the mentoring service. In the end, they didn't have to assign mentors, but it is important that such a service is available when needed.

For EACL 2012 we decided to switch to digital proceedings only. They were available before the conference from the website, during the conference on the memory stick you received with your registration material, and afterwards from the website and the ACL Anthology. An exception was made for the tutorial notes, which are available to participants on paper as well. I warned the Publications Chairs, Adrià de Gispert and Fabrice Lefèvre, beforehand that theirs was probably the most demanding and stressful task of the conference: making sure that huge volumes of material from so many sources are available in time and in the right format, incorporating last minute corrections, and handling unavoidable glitches in the publications software. It is a formidable task, but they completed it without flinching. We all owe them our gratitude.

EACL seems to follow economical crises, let us hope it does not become a habit. Both the previous conference in 2009 and the current one happened in grim economical times. Being a Sponsorship Chair is not a happy occasion in such times. Nevertheless, both the international ACL Sponsorship Committee (with Massimiliano Ciaramita as EACL member) and the local Sponsorship Chairs (Eric SanJuan and Stéphane Huet) left no stone unturned looking for sponsors. We would have ended up in a much worse financial situation if it hadn't been for their efforts. Thank you! And of course also many thanks to our sponsors who, despite the economic situation, decided to help us financially with the conference. I am convinced their investment will be rewarded.

Organizing large conferences like this is a complex undertaking, even with the help of extensive material (the ACL conference handbook). Whenever in doubt, I have had the opportunity to interact with the EACL Board, and occasionally with the ACL Board and with Priscilla Rasmussen. This has always been a pleasure. I have learned that the people running our associations are dedicated, know everything, and never sleep.

Last but not least, the local organizing team has had to carry the largest burden in the organization. The sheer number of tasks and actions the local organizers of a conference like EACL have to assume is astonishing. Marc El-Beze has been a wonderful chair and his team (Frederic Bechet, Yann Fernandez, Stéphane Huet, Tania Jimenez, Fabrice Lefevre, Georges Linares, Alexis Nasr, Eric SanJuan, and Iria Da Cunha) has done outstanding work. There is no beginning in mentioning the many tasks they had to fulfill for making this a top conference. I am very grateful for all the work they put in the event and for the stress-free and friendly cooperation. I am also grateful for the support of the University of Avignon.

I hope you will have many fond memories of EACL 2012, organized in these stunning surroundings in Avignon, both about the exciting scientific program and about the superb social program and local arrangements.

Walter Daelemans
General Chair
March 2012

Preface: Program Chairs

We are delighted to present you with this volume containing the papers accepted for presentation at the 13th Conference of the European Chapter of the Association for Computational Linguistics, held in Avignon, France, from April 23 till April 27 2012.

EACL 2012 received 326 submissions. We were able to accept 85 papers in total (an acceptance rate of 26%). 48 of the papers (14.7%) were accepted for oral presentation, and 34 (10.4%) for poster presentation. One oral paper was subsequently withdrawn after acceptance. The papers were selected by a program committee of 28 area chairs, from Asia, Europe, and North America, assisted by a panel of 471 reviewers. Each submission was reviewed by three reviewers, who were furthermore encouraged to discuss any divergences they might have, and the papers in each area were ranked by the area chairs. The final selection was made by the program co-chairs after an independent check of all reviews and discussions with the area chairs.

This year EACL introduced an author response period. Authors were able to read and respond to the reviews of their paper before the program committee made a final decision. They were asked to correct factual errors in the reviews and answer questions raised in the reviewers comments. The intention was to help produce more accurate reviews. In some cases, reviewers changed their scores in view of the authors response and the area chairs read all responses carefully prior to making recommendations for acceptance. Another new feature was to allow authors to include optional supplementary material in addition to the paper itself (e.g., code, data sets, and resources). Finally, in an attempt to eliminate any bias from the reviewing process we put in place a double-blind reviewing system where the identity of the authors was not revealed to the area chairs.

After the program was selected, each of the area chairs was asked to nominate the best paper from his or her area, or to explicitly decline to nominate any. This resulted in several nominations out of which three stood out and were further considered in more detail by an dedicated committee chaired by Stephen Clark. This independent committee selected the best paper of the conference, which will be also awarded with a prize sponsored by Google. The best paper and the other two finalists will be presented in plenary sessions at the conference.

In addition to the main conference program, EACL 2012 will feature the now traditional Student Research Workshop, 10 workshops, 4 tutorials and a demo session with 21 presentations. We are also fortunate to have three invited speakers, Martin Cooke, Ikerbasque (Basque Foundation for Science), Regina Barzilay, Massachusetts Institute of Technology, and Raymond Mooney, University of Texas at Austin. Martin Cooke will speak about "Speech Communication in the Wild", Regina Barzilay will discuss the topic of "Learning to Behave by Reading", and Raymond Mooney will present on "Learning Language from Perceptual Context".

First and foremost, we would like to thank the authors who submitted their work to EACL. The sheer number of submissions reflects how broad and active our field is. We are deeply indebted to the area chairs and the reviewers for their hard work. They enabled us to select an exciting program and to provide valuable feedback to the authors. We are grateful to our invited speakers who graciously agreed to give talks at EACL. Additional thanks to the Publications Chairs, Adrià de Gispert and Fabrice Lefèvre who put this volume together. We are grateful to Rich Gerber and the START team who always responded to our questions quickly, and helped us manage the large number of submissions smoothly. Thanks are due to the local organizing committee chair, Marc El-Beze for his cooperation with us over many organisational issues. We are also grateful to the Student Research Workshop chairs, Pierre Lison, Mattias Nilsson, and Marta Recasens, and the NAACL-HLT (Srinivas Bangalore, Eric Fosler-Lussier and Ellen Riloff) and ACL (Chin-Yew Lin and Miles Osborne) program chairs for their smooth collaboration in the handling of double submissions. Last but not least, we are indebted to the

General Chair, Walter Daelemans, for his guidance and support throughout the whole process.

We hope you enjoy the conference!

Mirella Lapata and Lluís Márquez

EACL 2012 Program Chairs

Organizing Committee

General Chair:

Walter Daelemans, University of Antwerp, Belgium

Programme Committee Chairs:

Mirella Lapata, University of Edinburgh, UK
Lluís Màrquez, Universitat Politècnica de Catalunya, Spain

Area Chairs:

Katja Filippova, Google
Min-Yen Kan, National University of Singapore
Charles Sutton, University of Edinburgh
Ivan Titov, Saarland University
Xavier Carreras, Universitat Politècnica de Catalunya (UPC)
Kenji Sagae, University of Southern California
Kallirroi Georgila, Institute for Creative Technologies, University of Southern California
Michael Strube, HITS gGmbH
Pascale Fung, The Hong Kong University of Science and Technology
Bing Liu, University of Illinois at Chicago
Theresa Wilson, Johns Hopkins University
David McClosky, Stanford University
Sebastian Riedel, University of Massachusetts
Phil Blunsom, University of Oxford
Mikel L. Forcada, Universitat d'Alacant
Christof Monz, University of Amsterdam
Sharon Goldwater, University of Edinburgh
Richard Wicentowski, Swarthmore College
Patrick Pantel, Microsoft Research
Hiroya Takamura, Tokyo Institute of Technology
Alexander Koller, University of Potsdam
Sebastian Padó, Universität Heidelberg
Maarten de Rijke, University of Amsterdam
Julio Gonzalo, UNED
Lori Levin, Carnegie Mellon University
Piek Vossen, VU University Amsterdam
Afra Alishahi, Tilburg University, The Netherlands
John Hale, Cornell University

Workshop Committee chairs:

Kristiina Jokinen, University of Helsinki, Finland
Alessandro Moschitti, University of Trento, Italy

Tutorials Committee chairs:

Eneko Agirre, University of the Basque Country, Spain
Lieve Macken, University College Ghent, Belgium

Student research workshop chairs:

Pierre Lison, University of Oslo, Norway
Mattias Nilsson, Uppsala University, Sweden
Marta Recasens, University of Barcelona, Spain

Student research workshop faculty advisor:

Laurence Danlos, Université Paris 7

System Demonstrations Committee:

Frédérique Segond

Publications Committee:

Adrià de Gispert, University of Cambridge, UK
Fabrice Lefèvre, University of Avignon, France

Sponsorship Committee:

Massimiliano Ciaramita

Mentoring service:

Caroline Sporleder, Saarland University, Germany
Gertjan van Noord, University of Groningen, The Netherlands

Local Organising Committee:

Marc El-Beze (Chair), University of Avignon, France
Frederic Bechet (Publicity chair), University Aix-Marseille 2, France
Yann Fernandez, University of Avignon, France
Stéphane Huet (Exhibits local chair), University of Avignon, France
Tania Jimenez, University of Avignon, France
Fabrice Lefevre, University of Avignon, France
Georges Linares, University of Avignon, France
Alexis Nasr, University Aix-Marseille 2, France
Eric SanJuan (Sponsorship local chair), University of Avignon, France
Iria Da Cunha, Pompeu Fabra University, Spain

Table of Contents

Conference Program

Wednesday April 25, 2012

(8:45) Session 1: Plenary Session

9:00 *Speech Communication in the Wild*
Martin Cooke

(10:30) Session 2a: Semantics

10:30 *Power-Law Distributions for Paraphrases Extracted from Bilingual Corpora*
Spyros Martzoukos and Christof Monz

10:55 *A Bayesian Approach to Unsupervised Semantic Role Induction*
Ivan Titov and Alexandre Klementiev

11:20 *Entailment above the word level in distributional semantics*
Marco Baroni, Raffaella Bernardi, Ngoc-Quynh Do and Chung-chieh Shan

11:45 *Evaluating Distributional Models of Semantics for Syntactically Invariant Inference*
Jackie Chi Kit Cheung and Gerald Penn

(10:30) Session 2b: Parsing

10:30 *Cross-Framework Evaluation for Statistical Parsing*
Reut Tsarfaty, Joakim Nivre and Evelina Andersson

10:55 *Dependency Parsing of Hungarian: Baseline Results and Challenges*
Richárd Farkas, Veronika Vincze and Helmut Schmid

11:20 *Dependency Parsing with Undirected Graphs*
Carlos Gómez-Rodríguez and Daniel Fernández-González

11:45 *The Best of BothWorlds – A Graph-based Completion Model for Transition-based Parsers*
Bernd Bohnet and Jonas Kuhn

Wednesday April 25, 2012 (continued)

15:15 *Compensating for Annotation Errors in Training a Relation Extractor*
Bonan Min and Ralph Grishman

(14:00) Session 3c: Machine Learning and Summarization

14:00 *Incorporating Lexical Priors into Topic Models*
Jagadeesh Jagarlamudi, Hal Daume III and Raghavendra Udupa

14:25 *DualSum: a Topic-Model based approach for update summarization*
Jean-Yves Delort and Enrique Alfonseca

14:50 *Large-Margin Learning of Submodular Summarization Models*
Ruben Sipos, Pannaga Shivaswamy and Thorsten Joachims

(16:10) Session 4: Posters (1) and Demos (1)

16:10 *A Probabilistic Model of Syntactic and Semantic Acquisition from Child-Directed Utterances and their Meanings*
Tom Kwiatkowski, Sharon Goldwater, Luke Zettlemoyer and Mark Steedman

16:10 *Active learning for interactive machine translation*
Jesús González-Rubio, Daniel Ortiz-Martínez and Francisco Casacuberta

16:10 *Adapting Translation Models to Translationese Improves SMT*
Gennadi Lembersky, Noam Ordan and Shuly Wintner

16:10 *Aspectual Type and Temporal Relation Classification*
Francisco Costa and António Branco

16:10 *Automatic generation of short informative sentiment summaries*
Andrea Glaser and Hinrich Schütze

16:10 *Bootstrapped Training of Event Extraction Classifiers*
Ruihong Huang and Ellen Riloff

16:10 *Bootstrapping Events and Relations from Text*
Ting Liu and Tomek Strzalkowski

Wednesday April 25, 2012 (continued)

16:10 *CLex: A Lexicon for Exploring Color, Concept and Emotion Associations in Language*
Svitlana Volkova, William B. Dolan and Theresa Wilson

16:10 *Extending the Entity-based Coherence Model with Multiple Ranks*
Vanessa Wei Feng and Graeme Hirst

16:10 *Generalization Methods for In-Domain and Cross-Domain Opinion Holder Extraction*
Michael Wiegand and Dietrich Klakow

16:10 *Skip N-grams and Ranking Functions for Predicting Script Events*
Bram Jans, Steven Bethard, Ivan Vulić and Marie-Francine Moens

16:10 *The Problem with Kappa*
David Martin Ward Powers

16:10 *User Edits Classification Using Document Revision Histories*
Amit Bronner and Christof Monz

16:10 *User Participation Prediction in Online Forums*
Zhonghua Qu and Yang Liu

16:10 *Inferring Selectional Preferences from Part-Of-Speech N-grams*
Hyeju Jang and Jack Mostow

16:10 *WebCAGe – A Web-Harvested Corpus Annotated with GermaNet Senses*
Verena Henrich, Erhard Hinrichs and Tatiana Vodolazova

Thursday April 26, 2012

	(9:00) Session 5: Plenary Session
9:00	*Learning to Behave by Reading* Regina Barzilay
	(10:30) Session 6a: Student Workshop
	(10:30) Session 6b: Student Workshop
	(10:30) Session 6c: Student Workshop
	(14:00) Session 7: EACL business meeting
	(14:50) Session 8: Plenary Session
14:50	*Lexical surprisal as a general predictor of reading time* Irene Fernandez Monsalve, Stefan L. Frank and Gabriella Vigliocco
15:15	*Spectral Learning for Non-Deterministic Dependency Parsing* Franco M. Luque, Ariadna Quattoni, Borja Balle and Xavier Carreras
	(16:10) Session 9: Posters (2) and Demos (2)
16:10	*Combining Tree Structures, Flat Features and Patterns for Biomedical Relation Extraction* Md. Faisal Mahbub Chowdhury and Alberto Lavelli
16:10	*Coordination Structure Analysis using Dual Decomposition* Atsushi Hanamoto, Takuya Matsuzaki and Jun'ichi Tsujii
16:10	*Cutting the Long Tail: Hybrid Language Models for Translation Style Adaptation* Arianna Bisazza and Marcello Federico
16:10	*Detecting Highly Confident Word Translations from Comparable Corpora without Any Prior Knowledge* Ivan Vulić and Marie-Francine Moens

Thursday April 26, 2012 (continued)

16:10	*Efficient parsing with Linear Context-Free Rewriting Systems* Andreas van Cranenburgh
16:10	*Evaluating language understanding accuracy with respect to objective outcomes in a dialogue system* Myroslava O. Dzikovska, Peter Bell, Amy Isard and Johanna D. Moore
16:10	*Experimenting with Distant Supervision for Emotion Classification* Matthew Purver and Stuart Battersby
16:10	*Feature-Rich Part-of-speech Tagging for Morphologically Complex Languages: Application to Bulgarian* Georgi Georgiev, Valentin Zhikov, Kiril Simov, Petya Osenova and Preslav Nakov
16:10	*Instance-Driven Attachment of Semantic Annotations over Conceptual Hierarchies* Janara Christensen and Marius Pasca
16:10	*Joint Satisfaction of Syntactic and Pragmatic Constraints Improves Incremental Spoken Language Understanding* Andreas Peldszus, Okko Buß, Timo Baumann and David Schlangen
16:10	*Learning How to Conjugate the Romanian Verb. Rules for Regular and Partially Irregular Verbs* Liviu P. Dinu, Vlad Niculae and Octavia-Maria Sulea
16:10	*Measuring Contextual Fitness Using Error Contexts Extracted from the Wikipedia Revision History* Torsten Zesch
16:10	*Perplexity Minimization for Translation Model Domain Adaptation in Statistical Machine Translation* Rico Sennrich
16:10	*Subcat-LMF: Fleshing out a standardized format for subcategorization frame interoperability* Judith Eckle-Kohler and Iryna Gurevych
16:10	*The effect of domain and text type on text prediction quality* Suzan Verberne, Antal van den Bosch, Helmer Strik and Lou Boves
16:10	*The Impact of Spelling Errors on Patent Search* Benno Stein, Dennis Hoppe and Tim Gollub

Thursday April 26, 2012 (continued)

16:10 *UBY - A Large-Scale Unified Lexical-Semantic Resource Based on LMF*
Iryna Gurevych, Judith Eckle-Kohler, Silvana Hartmann, Michael Matuschek, Christian M. Meyer and Christian Wirth

16:10 *Word Sense Induction for Novel Sense Detection*
Jey Han Lau, Paul Cook, Diana McCarthy, David Newman and Timothy Baldwin

Friday April 27, 2012

(9:00) Session 10: Plenary Session

9:00 *Learning Language from Perceptual Context*
Raymond Mooney

(10:30) Session 11a: Data Mining and Discourse

10:30 *Learning for Microblogs with Distant Supervision: Political Forecasting with Twitter*
Micol Marchetti-Bowick and Nathanael Chambers

10:55 *Learning from evolving data streams: online triage of bug reports*
Grzegorz Chrupala

11:20 *Towards a model of formal and informal address in English*
Manaal Faruqui and Sebastian Pado

11:45 *Character-based kernels for novelistic plot structure*
Micha Elsner

(10:30) Session 11b: Morphology

10:30 *Smart Paradigms and the Predictability and Complexity of Inflectional Morphology*
Grégoire Détrez and Aarne Ranta

10:55 *Probabilistic Hierarchical Clustering of Morphological Paradigms*
Burcu Can and Suresh Manandhar

11:20 *Modeling Inflection and Word-Formation in SMT*
Alexander Fraser, Marion Weller, Aoife Cahill and Fabienne Cap

11:45 *Identifying Broken Plurals, Irregular Gender, and Rationality in Arabic Text*
Sarah Alkuhlani and Nizar Habash

(10:30) Session 11c: Semantics

10:30 *Framework of Semantic Role Assignment based on Extended Lexical Conceptual Structure: Comparison with VerbNet and FrameNet*
Yuichiroh Matsubayashi, Yusuke Miyao and Akiko Aizawa

10:55 *Unsupervised Detection of Downward-Entailing Operators By Maximizing Classification Certainty*
Jackie Chi Kit Cheung and Gerald Penn

11:20 *Elliphant: Improved Automatic Detection of Zero Subjects and Impersonal Constructions in Spanish*
Luz Rello, Ricardo Baeza-Yates and Ruslan Mitkov

11:45 *Validation of sub-sentential paraphrases acquired from parallel monolingual corpora*
Houda Bouamor, Aurélien Max and Anne Vilnat

Friday April 27, 2012 (continued)

(14:00) Session 12a: Generation and Word Ordering

(14:00) Session 12b: Discourse and Dialogue

Friday April 27, 2012 (continued)

(14:00) Session 12c: Parsing and MT

14:00	*Composing extended top-down tree transducers* Aurelie Lagoutte, Fabienne Braune, Daniel Quernheim and Andreas Maletti
14:25	*Structural and Topical Dimensions in Multi-Task Patent Translation* Katharina Waeschle and Stefan Riezler
14:50	*Not as Awful as it Seems: Explaining German Case through Computational Experiments in Fluid Construction Grammar* Remi van Trijp

(15:45) Session 13: Plenary Session

15:45	*Managing Uncertainty in Semantic Tagging* Silvie Cinková, Martin Holub and Vincent Kríž
	Parallel and Nested Decomposition for Factoid Questions Aditya Kalyanpur, Siddharth Patwardhan, Branimir Boguraev, Jennifer Chu-Carroll and Adam Lally

Speech Communication in the Wild

Martin Cooke
Language and Speech Laboratory
University of the Basque Country
Ikerbasque (Basque Science Foundation)
m.cooke@ikerbasque.org

Abstract

Much of what we know about speech perception comes from laboratory studies with clean, canonical speech, ideal listeners and artificial tasks. But how do interlocutors manage to communicate effectively in the seemingly less-than-ideal conditions of everyday listening, which frequently involve trying to make sense of speech while listening in a non-native language, or in the presence of competing sound sources, or while multitasking? In this talk I'll examine the effect of real-world conditions on speech perception and quantify the contributions made by factors such as binaural hearing, visual information and prior knowledge to speech communication in noise. I'll present a computational model which trades stimulus-related cues with information from learnt speech models, and examine how well it handles both energetic and informational masking in a two-sentence separation task. Speech communication also involves listening-while-talking. In the final part of the talk I'll describe some ways in which speakers might be making communication easier for their interlocutors, and demonstrate the application of these principles to improving the intelligibility of natural and synthetic speech in adverse conditions.

Power-Law Distributions for Paraphrases Extracted from Bilingual Corpora

Spyros Martzoukos Christof Monz
Informatics Institute, University of Amsterdam
Science Park 904, 1098 XH Amsterdam, The Netherlands
{s.martzoukos, c.monz}@uva.nl

Abstract

We describe a novel method that extracts paraphrases from a bitext, for both the source and target languages. In order to reduce the search space, we decompose the phrase-table into sub-phrase-tables and construct separate clusters for source and target phrases. We convert the clusters into graphs, add smoothing/syntactic-information-carrier vertices, and compute the similarity between phrases with a random walk-based measure, the *commute time*. The resulting phrase-paraphrase probabilities are built upon the conversion of the commute times into artificial co-occurrence counts with a novel technique. The co-occurrence count distribution belongs to the power-law family.

1 Introduction

Paraphrase extraction has emerged as an important problem in NLP. Currently, there exists an abundance of methods for extracting paraphrases from monolingual, comparable and bilingual corpora (Madnani and Dorr, 2010; Androutsopoulos and Malakasiotis, 2010); we focus on the latter and specifically on the phrase-table that is extracted from a bitext during the training stage of Statistical Machine Translation (SMT). Bannard and Callison-Burch (2005) introduced the *pivoting* approach, which relies on a 2-step transition from a phrase, via its translations, to a paraphrase candidate. By incorporating the syntactic structure of phrases (Callison-Burch, 2005), the quality of the paraphrases extracted with pivoting can be improved. Kok and Brockett (2010) (henceforth KB) used a random walk framework to determine the similarity between phrases, which was shown to outperform pivoting with syntactic information, when multiple phrase-tables are used. In SMT, extracted paraphrases with associated pivot-based (Callison-Burch et al., 2006; Onishi et al., 2010) and cluster-based (Kuhn et al., 2010) probabilities have been found to improve the quality of translation. Pivoting has also been employed in the extraction of syntactic paraphrases, which are a mixture of phrases and non-terminals (Zhao et al., 2008; Ganitkevitch et al., 2011).

We develop a method for extracting paraphrases from a bitext for both the source and target languages. Emphasis is placed on the quality of the phrase-paraphrase probabilities as well as on providing a stepping stone for extracting syntactic paraphrases with equally reliable probabilities. In line with previous work, our method depends on the connectivity of the phrase-table, but the resulting construction treats each side separately, which can potentially be benefited from additional monolingual data.

The initial problem in harvesting paraphrases from a phrase-table is the identification of the search space. Previous work has relied on breadth first search from the query phrase with a depth of 2 (pivoting) and 6 (KB). The former can be too restrictive and the latter can lead to excessive noise contamination when taking shallow syntactic information features into account. Instead, we choose to cluster the phrase-table into separate source and target clusters and in order to make this task computationally feasible, we decompose the phrase-table into sub-phrase-tables. We propose a novel heuristic algorithm for the decomposition of the phrase-table (Section 2.1), and use a well-established co-clustering algorithm for clustering each sub-phrase-table (Section 2.2).

The underlying connectivity of the source and target clusters gives rise to a natural graph representation for each cluster (Section 3.1). The vertices of the graphs consist of phrases and features with a dual smoothing/syntactic-information-carrier role. The latter allow (a) re-distribution of the mass for phrases with no appropriate paraphrases and (b) the extraction of syntactic paraphrases. The proximity among vertices of a graph is measured by means of a random walk distance measure, the *commute time* (Aldous and Fill, 2001). This measure is known to perform well in identifying similar words on the graph of WordNet (Rao et al., 2008) and a related measure, the *hitting time* is known to perform well in harvesting paraphrases on a graph constructed from multiple phrase-tables (KB).

Generally in NLP, power-law distributions are typically encountered in the collection of counts during the training stage. The distances of Section 3.1 are converted into artificial co-occurrence counts with a novel technique (Section 3.2). Although they need not be integers, the main challenge is the type of the underlying distributions; it should ideally emulate the resulting count distributions from the phrase extraction stage of a monolingual parallel corpus (Dolan et al., 2004). These counts give rise to the desired probability distributions by means of relative frequencies.

2 Sub-phrase-tables & Clustering

2.1 Extracting Connected Components

For the decomposition of the phrase-table into sub-phrase-tables it is convenient to view the phrase-table as an undirected, unweighted graph P with the vertex set being the source and target phrases and the edge set being the phrase-table entries. For the rest of this section, we do not distinguish between source and target phrases, i.e. both types are treated equally as vertices of P. When referring to the size of a graph, we mean the number of vertices it contains.

A trivial initial decomposition of P is achieved by identifying all its *connected components* (components for brevity), i.e. the mutually disjoint connected subgraphs, $\{P_0, P_1, ..., P_n\}$. It turns out (see Section 4.1) that the largest component, say P_0, is of significant size. We call P_0 *giant* and it needs to be further decomposed. This is done by identifying all vertices such that, upon removal, the component becomes disconnected. Such vertices are called *articulation points* or *cut-vertices*. Cut-vertices of high connectivity degree are removed from the giant component (see Section 4.1). For the remaining vertices of the giant component, new components are identified and we proceed iteratively, while keeping track of the cut-vertices that are removed at each iteration, until the size of the largest component is less than a certain threshold θ (see Section 4.1).

Note that at each iteration, when removing cut-vertices from a giant component, the resulting collection of components may include graphs consisting of a single vertex. We refer to such vertices as *residues*. They are excluded from the resulting collection and are considered for separate treatment, as explained later in this section.

The cut-vertices need to be inserted appropriately back to the components: Starting from the last iteration step, the respective cut-vertices are added to all the components of P_0 which they used to 'glue' together; this process is performed iteratively, until there are no more cut-vertices to add. By 'addition' of a cut-vertex to a component, we mean the re-establishment of edges between the former and other vertices of the latter. The result is a collection of components whose total number of unique vertices is less than the number of vertices of the initial giant component P_0.

These remaining vertices are the residues. We then construct the graph R which consists of the residues together with *all* their translations (even those that are included in components of the above collection) and then identify its components $\{R_0, ..., R_m\}$. It turns out, that the largest component, say R_0, is giant and we repeat the decomposition process that was performed on P_0. This results in a new collection of components as well as new residues: The components need to be pruned (see Section 4.1) and the residues give rise to a new graph R' which is constructed in the same way as R. We proceed iteratively until the number of residues stops changing. For each remaining residue u, we identify its translations, and for each translation v we identify the largest component of which v is a member and add u to that component.

The final result is a collection $\mathcal{C} = \mathcal{D} \cup \mathcal{F}$, where $\mathcal{D}$ is the collection of components emerging from the entire iterative decomposition of P_0

and R, and $\mathcal{F} = \{P_1, ..., P_n\}$. Figure 1 shows the decomposition of a connected graph G_0; for simplicity we assume that only one cut-vertex is removed at each iteration and ties are resolved arbitrarily. In Figure 2 the residue graph is constructed and its two components are identified. The iterative insertion of the cut vertices is also depicted. The resulting two components together with those from R form the collection $\mathcal{D}$ for G_0.

The addition of cut-vertices into multiple components, as well as the construction method of the residue-based graph R, can yield the occurrences of a vertex in multiple components in $\mathcal{D}$. We exploit this property in two ways:

(a) In order to mitigate the risk of excessive decomposition (which implies greater risk of good paraphrases being in different components), as well as to reduce the size of $\mathcal{D}$, a conservative merging algorithm of components is employed. Suppose that the elements of $\mathcal{D}$ are ranked according to size in ascending order as $\mathcal{D} = \{D_1, ..., D_k, D_{k+1}, ..., D_{|\mathcal{D}|}\}$, where $|D_i| \leq \delta$, for $i = 1, ..., k$, and some threshold δ (see Section 4.1). Each component D_i with $i \in \{1, ..., k\}$ is examined as follows: For each vertex of D_i the number of its occurrences in $\mathcal{D}$ is inspected; this is done in order to identify an appropriate vertex b to act as a bridge between D_i and other components of which b is a member. Note that translations of a vertex b with smaller number of occurrences in $\mathcal{D}$ are less likely to capture their full spectrum of paraphrases. We thus choose a vertex b from D_i with the smallest number of occurrences in $\mathcal{D}$, resolving ties arbitrarily, and proceed with merging D_i with the largest component, say D_j with $j \in \{1, ..., |\mathcal{D}| - 1\}$, of which b is also a member. The resulting merged component $D_{j'}$ contains all vertices and edges of D_i and D_j and new edges, which are formed according to the rule: if u is a vertex of D_i and v is a vertex of D_j and (u, v) is a phrase-table entry, then (u, v) is an edge in $D_{j'}$. As long as no connected component has identified D_i as the component with which it should be merged, then D_i is deleted from the collection $\mathcal{D}$.

(b) We define an *idf*-inspired measure for each phrase pair (x, x') of the same type (source or target) as

$$idf(x, x') = \frac{1}{\log |\mathcal{D}|} \log \left(\frac{2c(x, x')|\mathcal{D}|}{c(x) + c(x')} \right), \quad (1)$$

where $c(x, x')$ is the number of components in which the phrases x and x' co-occur, and equivalently for $c(\cdot)$. The purpose of this measure is for pruning paraphrase candidates and its use is explained in Section 3.1. Note that $idf(x, x') \in [0, 1]$.

The merging process and the *idf* measure are irrelevant for phrases belonging to the components of $\mathcal{F}$, since the vertex set of each component of $\mathcal{F}$ is mutually disjoint with the vertex set of any other component in $\mathcal{C}$.

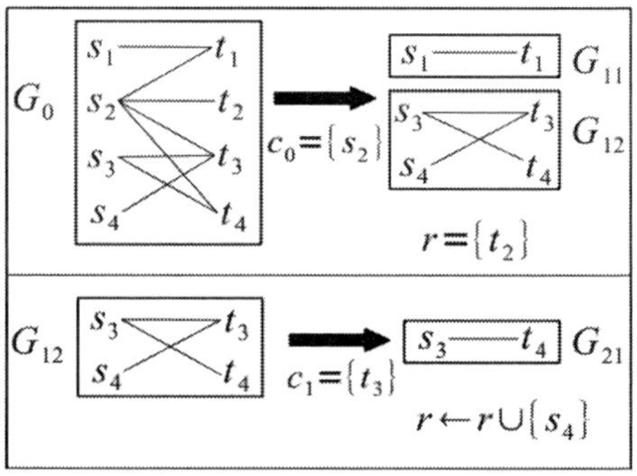

Figure 1: The decomposition of G_0 with vertices s_i and t_j: The cut-vertex of the ith iteration is denoted by c_i, and r collects the residues after each iteration. The task is completed in Figure 2.

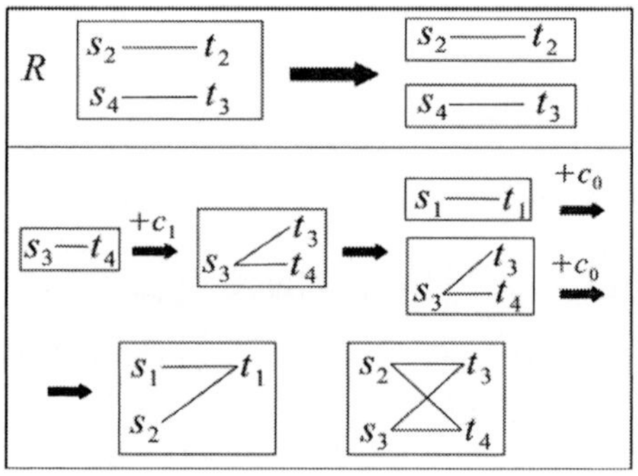

Figure 2: Top: Residue graph with its components (no further decomposition is required). Bottom: Adding cut-vertices back to their components.

2.2 Clustering Connected Components

The aim of this subsection is to generate separate clusters for the source and target phrases of each sub-phrase-table (component) $C \in \mathcal{C}$. For this purpose the Information-Theoretic Co-Clustering (ITC) algorithm (Dhillon et al., 2003) is employed, which is a general principled clustering algorithm that generates *hard* clusters (i.e. every element belongs to exactly one cluster) of two interdependent quantities and is known to perform well on high-dimensional and sparse data. In our case, the interdependent quantities are the source and target phrases and the sparse data is the phrase-table.

ITC is a search algorithm similar to K-means, in the sense that a cost function, is minimized at each iteration step and the number of clusters for both quantities are meta-parameters. The number of clusters is set to the most conservative initialization for both source and target phrases, namely to as many clusters as there are phrases. At each iteration, new clusters are constructed based on the identification of the argmin of the cost function for each phrase, which gradually reduces the number of clusters.

We observe that conservative choices for the meta-parameters often result in good paraphrases being in different clusters. To overcome this problem, the hard clusters are converted into soft (i.e. an element may belong to several clusters): One step before the stopping criterion is met, we modify the algorithm so that instead of assigning a phrase to the cluster with the smallest cost we select the bottom-X clusters ranked by cost. Additionally, only a certain number of phrases is chosen for soft clustering. Both selections are done conservatively with criteria based on the properties of the cost functions.

The formation of clusters leads to a natural refinement of the *idf* measure defined in eqn. (1): The quantity $c(x, x')$ is redefined as the number of components in which the phrases x and x' co-occur in at least one cluster.

3 Monolingual Graphs & Counts

We proceed with converting the clusters into directed, weighted graphs and then extract paraphrases for both the source and target side. For brevity we explain the process restricted to the source clusters of a sub-phrase-table, but the same method applies for the target side and for all sub-phrase-tables in the collection $\mathcal{C}$.

3.1 Monolingual graphs

Each source cluster is converted into a graph G as follows: The vertex set consists of the phrases of the cluster and an edge between s and s' exists, if (a) s and s' have at least one translation from the same target cluster, and (b) $idf(s, s')$ is greater than some threshold σ (see Section 4.1). If two phrases that satisfy condition (b) and have translations in more than one common target cluster, a distinct such edge is established. All edges are bi-directional with distinct weights for both directions.

Figure 3 depicts an example of such a construction; a link between a phrase s_i and a target cluster implies the existence of at least one translation for s_i in that cluster. We are not interested in the target phrases and they are thus not shown. For simplicity we assume that condition (b) is always satisfied and the extracted graph contains the maximum possible edges. Observe that phrases s_3 and s_4 have two edges connecting them, (due to target clusters T_c and T_d) and that the target cluster T_a is irrelevant to the construction of the graph, since s_1 is the only phrase with translations in it. This conversion of a source cluster into a graph G

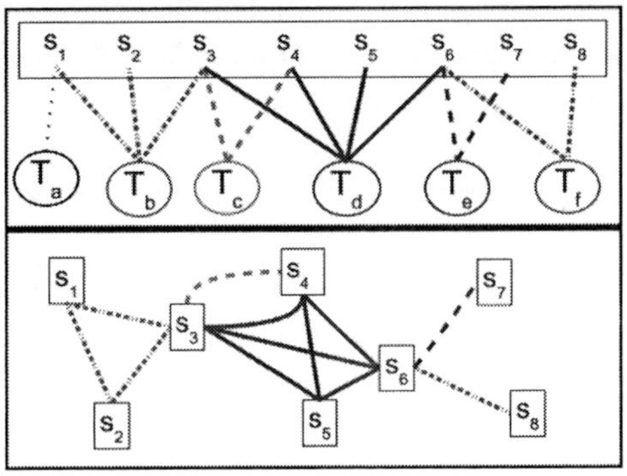

Figure 3: Top: A source cluster containing phrases s_1,..., s_8 and the associated target clusters T_a,..., T_f. Bottom: The extracted graph from the source cluster. All edges are bi-directional.

results in the formation of subgraphs in G, where each subgraph is generated by a target cluster. In general, if condition (b) is not always satisfied, then G need not be connected and each connected component is treated as a distinct graph.

Analogous to KB, we introduce *feature* vertices to G: For each phrase vertex s, its part-of-speech (POS) tag sequence and stem sequence are identified and inserted into G as new vertices with bi-directional weighted edges connected to s. If phrase vertices s and s' have the same POS tag sequence, then they are connected to the same POS tag feature vertex. Similarly for stem feature vertices. See Figure 4 for an example. Note that we do not allow edges between POS tag and stem fea-

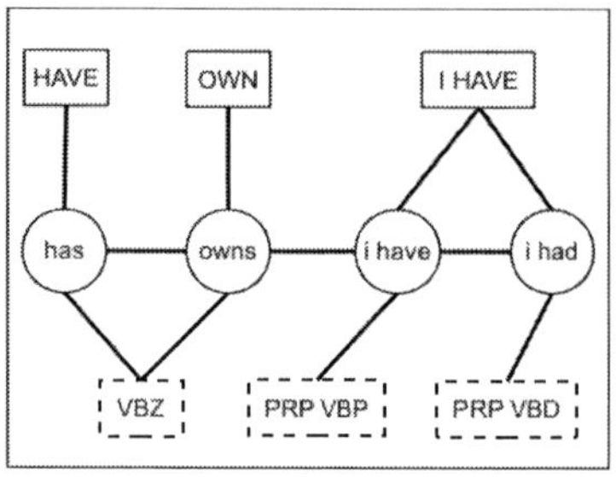

Figure 4: Adding feature vertices to the extracted graph (has) ⇌ (owns) ⇌ (i have) ⇌ (i had). Phrase, POS tag feature and stem feature vertices are drawn in circles, dotted rectangles and solid rectangles respectively. All edges are bidirectional.

ture vertices. The purpose of the feature vertices, unlike KB, is primarily for smoothing and secondarily for identifying paraphrases with the same syntactic information and this will become clear in the description of the computation of weights.

The set of all phrase vertices that are adjacent to s is written as $\Gamma(s)$, and referred to as the *neighborhood* of s. Let $n(s,t)$ denote the co-occurrence count of a phrase-table entry (s,t) (Koehn, 2009). We define the strength of s in the subgraph generated by cluster T as

$$n(s;T) = \sum_{t \in T} n(s,t), \tag{2}$$

which is simply a partial occurrence count for s. We proceed with computing weights for all edges of G:

Phrase⇌phrase weights: Inspired by the notion of *preferential attachment* (Yule, 1925), which is known to produce power-law weight distributions for evolving weighted networks (Barrat et al., 2004), we set the weight of a directed edge from s to s' to be proportional to the strengths of s' in all subgraphs in which both s and s' are members. Thus, in the random walk framework, s is more likely to visit a stronger (more reliable) neighbor. If $T_{s,s'} = \{T \mid s \text{ and } s' \text{ coexist in subgraph generated by } T\}$, then the weight $w(s \rightarrow s')$ of the directed edge from s to s' is given by

$$w(s \rightarrow s') = \sum_{T \in T_{s,s'}} n(s';T), \tag{3}$$

if $s' \in \Gamma(s)$ and 0 otherwise.

Phrase⇌feature weights: As mentioned above, feature vertices have the dual role of carrying syntactic information and smoothing. From eqn. (3) it can be deduced that, if for a phrase s, the amount of its outgoing weights is close to the amount of its incoming weights, then this is an indication that at least a significant part of its neighborhood is reliable; the larger the strengths, the more certain the indication. Otherwise, either s or a significant part of its neighborhood is unreliable. The amount of weight from s to its feature vertices should depend on this observation and we thus let

$$\text{net}(s) = \left| \sum_{s' \in \Gamma(s)} (w(s \rightarrow s') - w(s' \rightarrow s)) \right| + \epsilon, \tag{4}$$

where ϵ prevents net(s) from becoming 0 (see Section 4.1). The net weight of a phrase vertex s is distributed over its feature vertices as

$$w(s \rightarrow f_X) = < w(s \rightarrow s') > + \text{net}(s), \tag{5}$$

where the first summand is the average weight from s to its neighboring phrase vertices and $X = \text{POS}, \text{STEM}$. If s has multiple POS tag sequences, we distribute the weight of eqn. (5) relatively to the co-occurrences of s with the respective POS tag feature vertices. The quantity $< w(s \rightarrow s') >$ accounts for the basic smoothing and is augmented by a value net(s) that measures the reliability of s's neighborhood; the more unreliable the neighborhood, the larger the net weight and thus larger the overall weights to the feature vertices.

The choice for the opposite direction is trivial:

$$w(f_X \rightarrow s) = \frac{1}{|\{s' : (f_X, s') \text{ is an edge }\}|}, \tag{6}$$

where $X = \text{POS}, \text{STEM}$. Note the effect of eqns. (4)–(6) in the case where the neighborhood of s has unreliable strengths: In a random walk the feature vertices of s will be preferred and the resulting similarities between s and other phrase vertices will be small, as desired. Nonetheless, if the syntactic information is the same with any other phrase vertex in G, then the paraphrases will be captured.

The transition probability from *any* vertex u to *any* other vertex v in G, i.e., the probability of hopping from u to v in one step, is given by

$$p(u \to v) = \frac{w(u \to v)}{\sum_{v'} w(u \to v')}, \quad (7)$$

where we sum over all vertices adjacent to u in G. We can thus compute the similarity between *any* two vertices u and v in G by their commute time, i.e., the expected number of steps in a round trip, in a random walk from u to v and then back to u, which is denoted by $\kappa(u, v)$ (see Section 4.1 for the method of computation of κ). Since $\kappa(u, v)$ is a distance measure, the smaller its value, the more similar u and v are.

3.2 Counts

We convert the distance $\kappa(u, v)$ of a vertex pair u, v in a graph G into a co-occurrence count $n_G(u, v)$ with a novel technique: In order to assess the quality of the pair u, v with respect to G we compare $\kappa(u, v)$ with $\kappa(u, x)$ and $\kappa(v, x)$ for all other vertices x in G. We thus consider the average distance of u with the other vertices of G other than v, and similarly for v. This quantity is denoted by $\kappa(u; v)$ and $\kappa(v; u)$ respectively, and by definition it is given by

$$\kappa(i; j) = \sum_{\substack{x \in G \\ x \neq j}} \kappa(i, x) p_G(x|i) \quad (8)$$

where $p_G(x|i) \equiv p(x|G, i)$ is a yet unknown probability distribution with respect to G. The quantity $(\kappa(u; v) + \kappa(v; u))/2$ can then be viewed as the average distance of the pair u, v to the rest of the graph G. The co-occurrence count of u and v in G is thus defined by

$$n_G(u, v) = \frac{\kappa(u; v) + \kappa(v; u)}{2\kappa(u, v)}. \quad (9)$$

In order to calculate the probabilities $p_G(\cdot|\cdot)$ we employ the following heuristic: Starting with a uniform distribution $p_G^{(0)}(\cdot|\cdot)$ at timestep $t = 0$, we iterate

$$\kappa^{(t)}(i; j) = \sum_{\substack{x \in G \\ x \neq j}} \kappa(i, x) p_G^{(t)}(x|i) \quad (10)$$

$$n_G^{(t)}(u, v) = \frac{\kappa^{(t)}(u; v) + \kappa^{(t)}(v; u)}{2\kappa(u, v)} \quad (11)$$

$$p_G^{(t+1)}(v|u) = \frac{n_G^{(t)}(u, v)}{\sum_{x \in G} n_G^{(t)}(u, v)} \quad (12)$$

for all pairs of vertices u, v in G until convergence. Experimentally, we find that convergence is always achieved. After the execution of this iterative process we divide each count by the smallest count in order to achieve a lower bound of 1.

A pair u, v may appear in multiple graphs in the same sub-phrase-table C. The total co-occurrence count of u and v in C and the associated conditional probabilities are thus given by

$$n_C(u, v) = \sum_{G \in C} n_G(u, v) \quad (13)$$

$$p_C(v|u) = \frac{n_C(u, v)}{\sum_{x \in C} n_C(u, x)}. \quad (14)$$

A pair u, v may appear in multiple sub-phrase-tables and for the calculation of the final count $n(u, v)$ we need to average over the associated counts from all sub-phrase-tables. Moreover, we have to take into account the type of the vertices: For the simplest case where both u and v represent phrase vertices, their expected count is, by definition, given by

$$n(s, s') = \sum_{C} n_C(s, s') p(C|s, s'). \quad (15)$$

On the other hand, if at least one of u or v is a feature vertex, then we have to consider the phrase vertex that generates this feature: Suppose that u is the phrase vertex s='acquire' and v the POS tag vertex f='NN' and they co-occur in two sub-phrase-tables C and C' with positive counts $n_C(s, f)$ and $n_{C'}(s, f)$ respectively; the feature vertex f is generated by the phrase vertices 'ownership' in C and by 'possession' in C'. In that case, an interpolation of the counts $n_C(s, f)$ and $n_{C'}(s, f)$ as in eqn. (15) would be incorrect and a direct sum $n_C(s, f) + n_{C'}(s, f)$ would provide the true count. As a result we have

$$n(s, f) = \sum_{s'} \sum_{C} n_C(s, f(s')) p(C|s, f(s')), \quad (16)$$

where the first summation is over all phrase vertices s' such that $f(s') = f$. With a similar argument we can write

$$n(f, f') = \sum_{s, s'} \sum_{C} n_C(f(s), f(s')) \times \times p(C|f(s), f(s')). \quad (17)$$

For the interpolants, from standard probability we find

$$p(C|u,v) = \frac{p_C(v|u)p(C|u)}{\sum_{C'} p_{C'}(v|u)p(C'|u)}, \quad (18)$$

where the probabilities $p(C|u)$ can be computed by considering the likelihood function

$$\ell(u) = \prod_{i=1}^{N} p(x_i|u) = \prod_{i=1}^{N} \sum_{C} p_C(x_i|u)p(C|u)$$

and by maximizing the average log-likelihood $\frac{1}{N}\log \ell(u)$, where N is the total number of vertices with which u co-occurs with positive counts in all sub-phrase-tables.

Finally, the desired probability distributions are given by the relative frequencies

$$p(v|u) = \frac{n(u,v)}{\sum_x n(u,x)}, \quad (19)$$

for all pairs of vertices u, v.

4 Experiments

4.1 Setup

The data for building the phrase-table P is drawn from DE-EN bitexts crawled from `www.project-syndicate.org`, which is a standard resource provider for the WMT campaigns (News Commentary bitexts, see, e.g. (Callison-Burch et al., 2007)). The filtered bitext consists of 125K sentences; word alignment was performed running GIZA++ in both directions and generating the symmetric alignments using the 'grow-diag-final-and' heuristics. The resulting P has 7.7M entries, 30% of which are '1-1', i.e. entries (s,t) that satisfy $p(s|t) = p(t|s) = 1$. These entries are irrelevant for paraphrase harvesting for both the baseline and our method, and are thus excluded from the process.

The initial giant component P_0 contains 1.7M vertices (Figure 5), of which 30% become residues and are used to construct R. At each iteration of the decomposition of a giant component, we remove the top $0.5\% \cdot size$ cut-vertices ranked by degree of connectivity, where $size$ is the number of vertices of the giant component and set $\theta = 2500$ as the stopping criterion. The latter choice is appropriate for the subsequent step of co-clustering the components, for both time complexity and performance of the ITC algorithm.

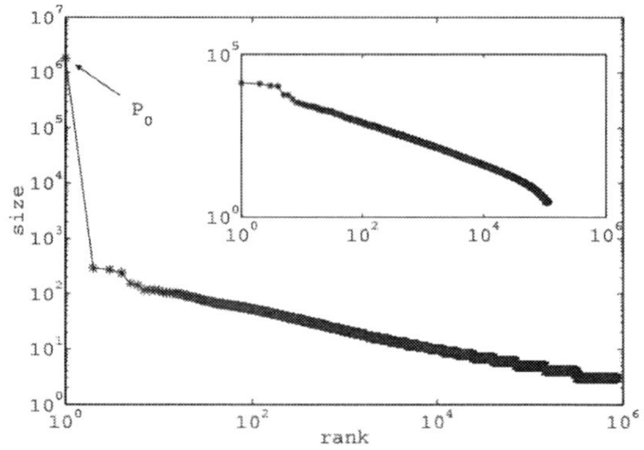

Figure 5: Log-log plot of ranked components according to their size (number of source and target phrases) for: (a) Components extracted from P. '1-1' components are not shown. (b) Components extracted from the decomposition of P_0.

In the components emerging from the decomposition of R_0, we observe an excessive number of cut-vertices. Note that vertices that consist these components can be of two types: i) former residues, i.e., residues that emerged from the decomposition of P_0, and ii) other vertices of P_0. Cut-vertices can be of either type. For each component, we remove cut-vertices that are not translations of the former residues of that component. Following this pruning strategy, the degeneracy of excessive cut-vertices does not reappear in the subsequent iterations of decomposing components generated by new residues, but the emergence of two giant components was observed: One consisting mostly of source type vertices and one of target type vertices. Without going into further details, the algorithm can extend to multiple giant components straightforwardly. For the merging process of the collection $\mathcal{D}$ we set $\delta = 5000$, to avoid the emergence of a giant component. The sizes of the resulting sub-phrase-tables are shown in Figure 6. For the ITC algorithm we use the smoothing technique discussed in (Dhillon and Guan, 2003) with $\alpha = 10^6$.

For the monolingual graphs, we set $\sigma = 0.65$ and discard graphs with more than 20 phrase vertices, as they contain mostly noise. Thus, the sizes of the graphs allow us to use analytical methods to compute the commute times: For a graph G, we form the *transition matrix* P, whose entries $P(u,v)$ are given by eqn. (7), and the *fundamen-*

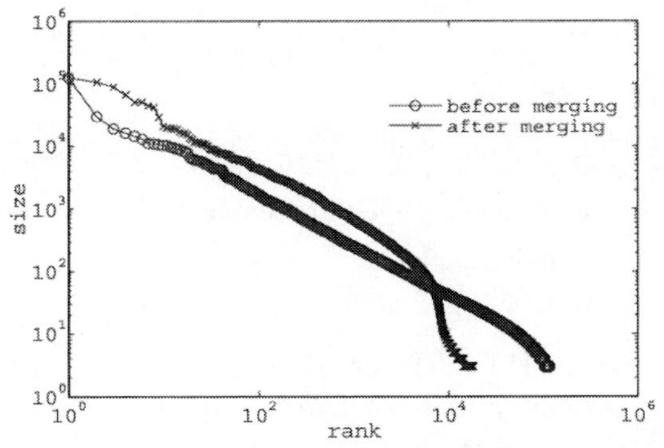

Figure 6: Log-log plot of ranked sub-phrase-tables according to their size (number of source and target phrases).

tal matrix (Grinstead and Snell, 2006; Boley et al., 2011) $Z = (I - P + \mathbf{1}\pi^T)^{-1}$, where I is the identity matrix, $\mathbf{1}$ denotes the vector of all ones and π is the vector of *stationary probabilities* (Aldous and Fill, 2001) which is such that $\pi^T P = \pi^T$ and $\pi^T \mathbf{1} = 1$ and can be computed as in (Hunter, 2000). The commute time between any vertices u and v in G is then given by (Grinstead and Snell, 2006)

$$\kappa(u, v) = (Z(v, v) - Z(u, v))/\pi(v) + \\ + \ (Z(u, u) - Z(v, u))/\pi(u). \qquad (20)$$

For the parameter of eqn. (4), an appropriate choice is $\epsilon = |\Gamma(s)| + 1$; for reliable neighborhoods, this quantity is insignificant. POS tags and lemmata are generated with TreeTagger[1].

Figure 7 depicts the most basic type of graph that can be extracted from a cluster; it includes two source phrase vertices a, b, of different syntactic information. Suppose that both a and b are highly reliable with strengths $n(a; T) = n(b; T) = 40$, for some target cluster T. The resulting conditional probabilities adequately represent the proximity of the involved vertices. On the other hand, the range of the co-occurrence counts is not compatible with that of the strengths. This is because i) there are no phrase vertices with small strength in the graph, and ii) eqn. (9) is essentially a comparison between a pair of vertices and the rest of the graph. To overcome this problem *inflation* vertices i_a and i_b of strength 1 with accompanying feature vertices are introduced to the graph. Figure 8 depicts the new graph, where the lengths of the edges represent the magnitude of commute times. Observe that the quality of the probabilities is preserved but the counts are inflated, as required.

In general, if a source phrase vertex s has at least one translation t such that $n(s, t) \geq 3$, then a triplet $(i_s, f(i_s), g(i_s))$ is added to the graph as in Figure 8. The inflation vertex i_s establishes edges with all other phrase and inflation vertices in the graph and weights are computed as in Section 3.1. The pipeline remains the same up to eqn. (13), where all counts that include inflation vertices are ignored.

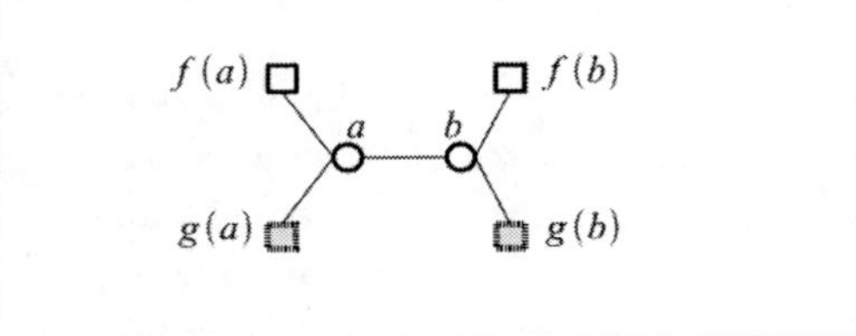

$n(a,b)$	$=2.0$	$p(b\|a)$	$=.20$
$n(a,f(a))$	$=2.6$	$p(f(a)\|a)$	$=.27$
$n(a,g(a))$	$=2.6$	$p(g(a)\|a)$	$=.27$
$n(a,f(b))$	$=1.3$	$p(f(b)\|a)$	$=.13$
$n(a,g(b))$	$=1.3$	$p(g(b)\|a)$	$=.13$

Figure 7: Top: A graph with source phrase vertices a and b, both of strength 40, with accompanying distinct POS sequence vertices $f(\cdot)$ and stem sequence vertices $g(\cdot)$. Bottom: The resulting co-occurrence counts and conditional probabilities for a.

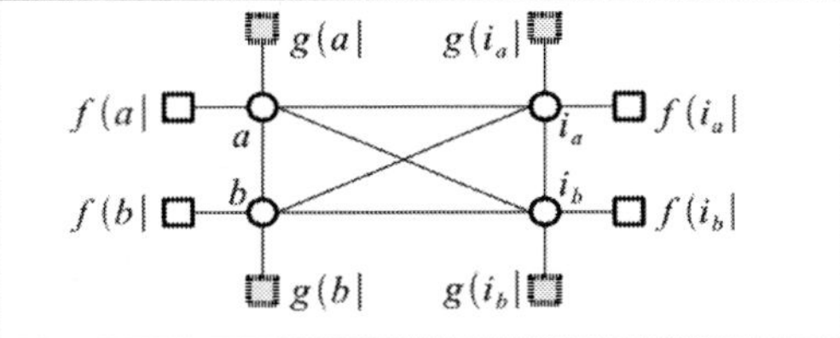

$n(a,b\|$	$=11.3$	$p(b)a\|$	$=.22$
$n(a,f(a\|\|$	$=13.5$	$p(f(a)a\|$	$=.26$
$n(a,g(a\|\|$	$=13.5$	$p(g(a)a\|$	$=.26$
$n(a,f(b\|\|$	$=6.7$	$p(f(b)a\|$	$=.13$
$n(a,g(b\|\|$	$=6.7$	$p(g(b)a\|$	$=.13$

Figure 8: The inflated version of Figure 7.

[1] http://www.ims.uni-stuttgart.de/projekte/corplex/TreeTagger/

4.2 Results

Our method generates conditional probabilities for any pair chosen from {phrase, POS sequence, stem sequence}, but for this evaluation we restrict ourselves to phrase pairs. For a phrase s, the quality of a paraphrase s' is assessed by

$$P(s'|s) \propto p(s'|s) + p(f_1(s')|s) + p(f_2(s')|s), \quad (21)$$

where $f_1(s')$ and $f_2(s')$ denote the POS tag sequence and stem sequence of s' respectively. All three summands of eqn. (21) are computed from eqn. (19). The baseline is given by pivoting (Bannard and Callison-Burch, 2005),

$$P(s'|s) = \sum_t p(t|s)p(s'|t), \quad (22)$$

where $p(t|s)$ and $p(s'|t)$ are the phrase-based relative frequencies of the translation model.

We select 150 phrases (an equal number for unigrams, bigrams and trigrams), for which we expect to see paraphrases, and keep the top-10 paraphrases for each phrase, ranked by the above measures. We follow (Kok and Brockett, 2010; Metzler et al., 2011) in the evaluation of the extracted paraphrases: Each phrase-paraphrase pair is manually annotated with the following options: 0) Different meaning; 1) (i) Same meaning, but potential replacement of the phrase with the paraphrase in a sentence ruins the grammatical structure of the sentence. (ii) Tokens of the paraphrase are morphological inflections of the phrase's tokens. 2) Same meaning. Although useful for SMT purposes, 'super/substrings of' are annotated with 0 to achieve an objective evaluation.

Both methods are evaluated in terms of the Mean Expected Precision (MEP) at k; the Expected Precision for each selected phrase s at rank k is computed by $E_s[p@k] = \frac{1}{k}\sum_{i=1}^{k} p_i$, where p_i is the proportion of positive annotations for item i. The desired metric is thus given by MEP@$k = \frac{1}{150}\sum_s E_s[p@k]$. The contribution to p_i can be restricted to perfect paraphrases only, which leads to a strict strategy for harvesting paraphrases. Table 1 summarizes the results of our evaluation and

Method	Lenient MEP			Strict MEP		
	@1	@5	@10	@1	@5	@10
Baseline	.58	.47	.41	.43	.33	.28
Graphs	.72	.61	.52	.53	.40	.33

Table 1: Mean Expected Precision (MEP) at k under lenient and strict evaluation criteria.

we deduce that our method can lead to improvements over the baseline.

An important accomplishment of our method is that the distribution of counts $n(u, v)$, (as given by eqns. (15)–(17)) for all vertices u and v, belongs to the power-law family (Figure 9). This is evidence that the monolingual graphs can simulate the phrase extraction process of a monolingual parallel corpus. Intuitively, we may think of the German side of the DE–EN parallel corpus as the 'English' approximation to a 'EN'–EN parallel corpus, and the monolingual graphs as the word alignment process.

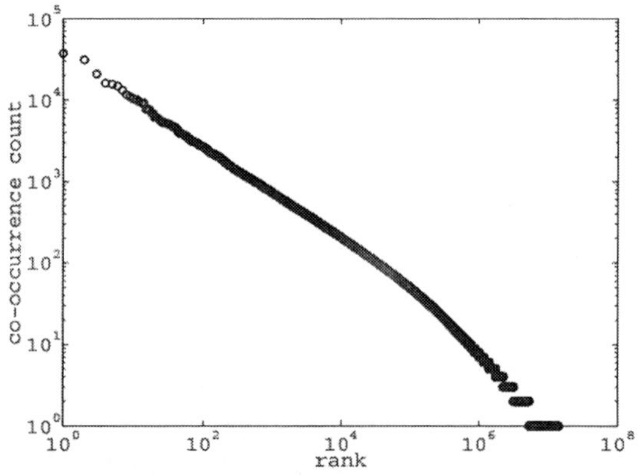

Figure 9: Log-log plot of ranked pairs of English vertices according to their counts

5 Conclusions & Future Work

We have described a new method that harvests paraphrases from a bitext, generates artificial co-occurrence counts for any pair chosen from {phrase, POS sequence, stem sequence}, and potentially identifies patterns for the syntactic information of the phrases. The quality of the paraphrases' ranked lists outperforms that of a standard baseline. The quality of the resulting conditional probabilities is promising and will be evaluated implicitly via an application to SMT.

This research was funded by the European Commission through the CoSyne project FP7-ICT- 4-248531.

References

David Aldous and James A. Fill. 2001. *Reversible Markov Chains and Random Walks on Graphs.* http://www.stat.berkeley.edu/~aldous/RWG/book.html

Ion Androutsopoulos and Prodromos Malakasiotis. 2010. *A Survey of Paraphrasing and Textual Entailment Methods.* Journal of Artificial Intelligence Research, 38:135–187.

Colin Bannard and Chris Callison-Burch. 2005. *Paraphrasing with Bilingual Parallel Corpora.* Proc. ACL, pp. 597–604.

Alain Barrat, Marc Barthlemy, and Alessandro Vespignani. 2004. *Modeling the Evolution of Weighted Networks.* Phys. Rev. Lett., 92.

Daniel Boley, Gyan Ranjan, and Zhi-Li Zhang. 2011. *Commute Times for a Directed Graph using an Asymmetric Laplacian.* Linear Algebra and its Applications, Issue 2, pp. 224–242.

Chris Callison-Burch. 2008. *Syntactic Constraints on Paraphrases Extracted from Parallel Corpora.* Proc. EMNLP, pp. 196–205.

Chris Callison-Burch, Cameron Fordyce, Philipp Koehn, Christof Monz, and Josh Schroeder. 2007 *(Meta-) Evaluation of Machine Translation.* Proc. Workshop on Statistical Machine Translation, pp. 136–158.

Chris Callison-Burch, Philipp Koehn, and Miles Osborne. 2006 *Improved statistical machine translation using paraphrases.* Proc. HLT/NAACL, pp. 17–24.

Inderjit S. Dhillon and Yuqiang Guan. 2003. *Information Theoretic Clustering of Sparse Co-Occurrence Data.* Proc. IEEE Int'l Conf. Data Mining, pp. 517–520.

Inderjit S. Dhillon, Subramanyam Mallela, and Dharmendra S. Modha. 2003. *Information-Theoretic Coclustering.* Proc. ACM SIGKDD Int'l Conf. Knowledge Discovery and Data Mining, pp. 89–98.

William Dolan, Chris Quirk, and Chris Brockett. 2004. *Unsupervised construction of large paraphrase corpora: Exploiting massively parallel news sources.* Proc. COLING, pp. 350-356.

Juri Ganitkevitch, Chris Callison-Burch, Courtney Napoles, and Benjamin Van Durme 2011. *Learning Sentential Paraphrases from Bilingual Parallel Corpora for Text-to-Text Generation.* Proc. EMNLP, pp. 1168–1179.

Charles Grinstead and Laurie Snell. 2006. *Introduction to Probability.* Second ed., American Mathematical Society.

Jeffrey J. Hunter. 2000. *A Survey of Generalized Inverses and their Use in Stochastic Modelling.* Res. Lett. Inf. Math. Sci., Vol. 1, pp. 25–36.

Philipp Koehn. 2009. *Statistical Machine Translation.* Cambridge University Press, Cambridge, UK.

Stanley Kok and Chris Brockett. 2010. *Hitting the Right Paraphrases in Good Time.* Proc. NAACL, pp.145–153.

Roland Kuhn, Boxing Chen, George Foster, and Evan Stratford. 2010. *Phrase Clustering for Smoothing TM Probabilities: or, how to Extract Paraphrases from Phrase Tables.* Proc. COLING, pp.608–616.

Nitin Madnani and Bonnie Dorr. 2010. *Generating Phrasal and Sentential Paraphrases: A Survey of Data-Driven Methods.* Computational Linguistics, 36(3):341–388.

Donald Metzler, Eduard Hovy, and Chunliang Zhang. 2011. *An Empirical Evaluation of Data-Driven Paraphrase Generation Techniques.* Proc. ACL:Short Papers, pp. 546–551.

Takashi Onishi, Masao Utiyama, and Eiichiro Sumita. 2010. *Paraphrase Lattice for Statistical Machine Translation.* Proc. ACL:Short Papers, pp. 1–5.

Delip Rao, David Yarowsky, and Chris Callison-Burch. 2008. *Affinity Measures based on the Graph Laplacian.* Proc. Textgraphs Workshop on Graph-based Algorithms for NLP at COLING, pp. 41–48.

George U. Yule. 1925. *A Mathematical Theory of Evolution, based on the Conclusions of Dr. J. C. Willis, F.R.S.* Philos. Trans. R. Soc. London, B 213, pp. 21–87.

Shiqi Zhao, Haifeng Wang, Ting Liu, and Sheng Li. 2008. *Pivot Approach for Extracting Paraphrase Patterns from Bilingual Corpora.* Proc. ACL, pp. 780–788.

A Bayesian Approach to Unsupervised Semantic Role Induction

Ivan Titov **Alexandre Klementiev**
Saarland University
Saarbrücken, Germany
{titov|aklement}@mmci.uni-saarland.de

Abstract

We introduce two Bayesian models for unsupervised semantic role labeling (SRL) task. The models treat SRL as clustering of syntactic signatures of arguments with clusters corresponding to semantic roles. The first model induces these clusterings independently for each predicate, exploiting the Chinese Restaurant Process (CRP) as a prior. In a more refined hierarchical model, we inject the intuition that the clusterings are similar across different predicates, even though they are not necessarily identical. This intuition is encoded as a distance-dependent CRP with a distance between two syntactic signatures indicating how likely they are to correspond to a single semantic role. These distances are automatically induced within the model and shared across predicates. Both models achieve state-of-the-art results when evaluated on PropBank, with the coupled model consistently outperforming the factored counterpart in all experimental set-ups.

1 Introduction

Semantic role labeling (SRL) (Gildea and Jurafsky, 2002), a shallow semantic parsing task, has recently attracted a lot of attention in the computational linguistic community (Carreras and Màrquez, 2005; Surdeanu et al., 2008; Hajič et al., 2009). The task involves prediction of predicate argument structure, i.e. both identification of arguments as well as assignment of labels according to their underlying *semantic role*. For example, in the following sentences:

(a) $[_{A0}$ Mary$]$ opened $[_{A1}$ the door$]$.

(b) $[_{A0}$ Mary$]$ is expected to open $[_{A1}$ the door$]$.

(c) $[_{A1}$ The door$]$ opened.

(d) $[_{A1}$ The door$]$ was opened $[_{A0}$ by Mary$]$.

Mary always takes an agent role ($A0$) for the predicate *open*, and *door* is always a patient ($A1$). SRL representations have many potential applications in natural language processing and have recently been shown to be beneficial in question answering (Shen and Lapata, 2007; Kaisser and Webber, 2007), textual entailment (Sammons et al., 2009), machine translation (Wu and Fung, 2009; Liu and Gildea, 2010; Wu et al., 2011; Gao and Vogel, 2011), and dialogue systems (Basili et al., 2009; van der Plas et al., 2011), among others. Though syntactic representations are often predictive of semantic roles (Levin, 1993), the interface between syntactic and semantic representations is far from trivial. The lack of simple deterministic rules for mapping syntax to shallow semantics motivates the use of statistical methods.

Although current statistical approaches have been successful in predicting shallow semantic representations, they typically require large amounts of annotated data to estimate model parameters. These resources are scarce and expensive to create, and even the largest of them have low coverage (Palmer and Sporleder, 2010). Moreover, these models are domain-specific, and their performance drops substantially when they are used in a new domain (Pradhan et al., 2008). Such domain specificity is arguably unavoidable for a semantic analyzer, as even the definitions of semantic roles are typically predicate specific, and different domains can have radically different distributions of predicates (and their senses). The necessity for a large amounts of human-annotated data for every language and domain is one of the major obstacles to the wide-spread adoption of semantic role representations.

These challenges motivate the need for unsupervised methods which, instead of relying on labeled data, can exploit large amounts of unlabeled texts. In this paper, we propose simple and efficient hierarchical Bayesian models for this task.

It is natural to split the SRL task into two stages: the identification of arguments (the *identification* stage) and the assignment of semantic roles (the *labeling* stage). In this and in much of the previous work on unsupervised techniques, the focus is on the labeling stage. Identification, though an important problem, can be tackled with heuristics (Lang and Lapata, 2011a; Grenager and Manning, 2006) or, potentially, by using a supervised classifier trained on a small amount of data. We follow (Lang and Lapata, 2011a), and regard the labeling stage as clustering of syntactic signatures of argument realizations for every predicate. In our first model, as in most of the previous work on unsupervised SRL, we define an independent model for each predicate. We use the Chinese Restaurant Process (CRP) (Ferguson, 1973) as a prior for the clustering of syntactic signatures. The resulting model achieves state-of-the-art results, substantially outperforming previous methods evaluated in the same setting.

In the first model, for each predicate we independently induce a linking between syntax and semantics, encoded as a clustering of syntactic signatures. The clustering implicitly defines the set of permissible *alternations*, or changes in the syntactic realization of the argument structure of the verb. Though different verbs admit different alternations, some alternations are shared across multiple verbs and are very frequent (e.g., passivization, example sentences (a) vs. (d), or dativization: *John gave a book to Mary* vs. *John gave Mary a book*) (Levin, 1993). Therefore, it is natural to assume that the clusterings should be similar, though not identical, across verbs.

Our second model encodes this intuition by replacing the CRP prior for each predicate with a distance-dependent CRP (dd-CRP) prior (Blei and Frazier, 2011) shared across predicates. The distance between two syntactic signatures encodes how likely they are to correspond to a single semantic role. Unlike most of the previous work exploiting distance-dependent CRPs (Blei and Frazier, 2011; Socher et al., 2011; Duan et al., 2007), we do not encode prior or external knowledge in the distance function but rather induce it automatically within our Bayesian model. The coupled dd-CRP model consistently outperforms the factored CRP counterpart across all the experimental settings (with gold and predicted syntactic parses, and with gold and automatically identified arguments).

Both models admit efficient inference: the estimation time on the Penn Treebank WSJ corpus does not exceed 30 minutes on a single processor and the inference algorithm is highly parallelizable, reducing inference time down to several minutes on multiple processors. This suggests that the models scale to much larger corpora, which is an important property for a successful unsupervised learning method, as unlabeled data is abundant.

The rest of the paper is structured as follows. Section 2 begins with a definition of the semantic role labeling task and discuss some specifics of the unsupervised setting. In Section 3, we describe CRPs and dd-CRPs, the key components of our models. In Sections 4 – 6, we describe our factored and coupled models and the inference method. Section 7 provides both evaluation and analysis. Finally, additional related work is presented in Section 8.

2 Task Definition

In this work, instead of assuming the availability of role annotated data, we rely only on automatically generated syntactic dependency graphs. While we cannot expect that syntactic structure can trivially map to a semantic representation (Palmer et al., 2005)[1], we can use syntactic cues to help us in both stages of unsupervised SRL. Before defining our task, let us consider the two stages separately.

In the argument identification stage, we implement a heuristic proposed in (Lang and Lapata, 2011a) comprised of a list of 8 rules, which use nonlexicalized properties of syntactic paths between a predicate and a candidate argument to iteratively discard non-arguments from the list of all words in a sentence. Note that inducing these rules for a new language would require some linguistic expertise. One alternative may be to annotate a small number of arguments and train a classifier with nonlexicalized features instead.

In the argument labeling stage, semantic roles are represented by clusters of arguments, and labeling a particular argument corresponds to deciding on its role cluster. However, instead of deal-

[1] Although it provides a strong baseline which is difficult to beat (Grenager and Manning, 2006; Lang and Lapata, 2010; Lang and Lapata, 2011a).

ing with argument occurrences directly, we represent them as predicate specific syntactic signatures, and refer to them as *argument keys*. This representation aids our models in inducing high purity clusters (of argument keys) while reducing their granularity. We follow (Lang and Lapata, 2011a) and use the following syntactic features to form the argument key representation:

- Active or passive verb voice (ACT/PASS).
- Argument position relative to predicate (LEFT/RIGHT).
- Syntactic relation to its governor.
- Preposition used for argument realization.

In the example sentences in Section 1, the argument keys for candidate arguments *Mary* for sentences (a) and (d) would be ACT:LEFT:SBJ and PASS:RIGHT:LGS->by,[2] respectively. While aiming to increase the purity of argument key clusters, this particular representation will not always produce a good match: e.g. *the door* in sentence (c) will have the same key as *Mary* in sentence (a). Increasing the expressiveness of the argument key representation by flagging intransitive constructions would distinguish that pair of arguments. However, we keep this particular representation, in part to compare with the previous work.

In this work, we treat the unsupervised semantic role labeling task as *clustering of argument keys*. Thus, argument occurrences in the corpus whose keys are clustered together are assigned the same semantic role. Note that some adjunct-like modifier arguments are already explicitly represented in syntax and thus do not need to be clustered (modifiers AM-TMP, AM-MNR, AM-LOC, and AM-DIR are encoded as 'syntactic' relations TMP, MNR, LOC, and DIR, respectively (Surdeanu et al., 2008)); instead we directly use the syntactic labels as semantic roles.

3 Traditional and Distance-dependent CRPs

The central components of our non-parametric Bayesian models are the Chinese Restaurant Processes (CRPs) and the closely related Dirichlet Processes (DPs) (Ferguson, 1973).

CRPs define probability distributions over partitions of a set of objects. An intuitive metaphor for describing CRPs is assignment of tables to restaurant customers. Assume a restaurant with a sequence of tables, and customers who walk into the restaurant one at a time and choose a table to join. The first customer to enter is assigned the first table. Suppose that when a client number i enters the restaurant, $i-1$ customers are sitting at each of the $k \in (1, \ldots, K)$ tables occupied so far. The new customer is then either seated at one of the K tables with probability $\frac{N_k}{i-1+\alpha}$, where N_k is the number customers already sitting at table k, or assigned to a new table with the probability $\frac{\alpha}{i-1+\alpha}$. The concentration parameter α encodes the granularity of the drawn partitions: the larger α, the larger the expected number of occupied tables. Though it is convenient to describe CRP in a sequential manner, the probability of a seating arrangement is invariant of the order of customers' arrival, i.e. the process is *exchangeable*. In our factored model, we use CRPs as a prior for clustering argument keys, as we explain in Section 4.

Often CRP is used as a part of the Dirichlet Process mixture model where each subset in the partition (each table) selects a parameter (a meal) from some base distribution over parameters. This parameter is then used to generate all data points corresponding to customers assigned to the table. The Dirichlet processes (DP) are closely connected to CRPs: instead of choosing meals for customers through the described generative story, one can equivalently draw a distribution G over meals from DP and then draw a meal for every customer from G. We refer the reader to Teh (2010) for details on CRPs and DPs. In our method, we use DPs to model distributions of arguments for every role.

In order to clarify how similarities between customers can be integrated in the generative process, we start by reformulating the traditional CRP in an equivalent form so that distance-dependent CRP (dd-CRP) can be seen as its generalization. Instead of selecting a table for each customer as described above, one can equivalently assume that a customer i chooses one of the previous customers c_i as a partner with probability $\frac{1}{i-1+\alpha}$ and sits at the same table, or occupies a new table with the probability $\frac{\alpha}{i-1+\alpha}$. The transitive closure of this seating-with relation determines the partition.

A generalization of this view leads to the definition of the distance-dependent CRP. In dd-CRPs,

[2] LGS denotes a logical subject in a passive construction (Surdeanu et al., 2008).

a customer i chooses a partner $c_i = j$ with the probability proportional to some non-negative score $d_{i,j}$ ($d_{i,j} = d_{j,i}$) which encodes a similarity between the two customers.[3] More formally,

$$p(c_i = j|D, \alpha) \propto \begin{cases} d_{i,j}, & i \neq j \\ \alpha, & i = j \end{cases} \quad (1)$$

where D is the entire similarity graph. This process lacks the exchangeability property of the traditional CRP but efficient approximate inference with dd-CRP is possible with Gibbs sampling. For more details on inference with dd-CRPs, we refer the reader to Blei and Frazier (2011).

Though in previous work dd-CRP was used either to encode prior knowledge (Blei and Frazier, 2011) or other external information (Socher et al., 2011), we treat D as a latent variable drawn from some prior distribution over weighted graphs. This view provides a powerful approach for coupling a family of distinct but similar clusterings: the family of clusterings can be drawn by first choosing a similarity graph D for the entire family and then re-using D to generate each of the clusterings independently of each other as defined by equation (1). In Section 5, we explain how we use this formalism to encode relatedness between argument key clusterings for different predicates.

4 Factored Model

In this section we describe the *factored* method which models each predicate independently. In Section 2 we defined our task as clustering of argument keys, where each cluster corresponds to a semantic role. If an argument key k is assigned to a role r ($k \in r$), all of its occurrences are labeled r.

Our Bayesian model encodes two common assumptions about semantic roles. First, we enforce the selectional restriction assumption: we assume that the distribution over potential argument fillers is sparse for every role, implying that 'peaky' distributions of arguments for each role r are preferred to flat distributions. Second, each role normally appears at most once per predicate occurrence. Our inference will search for a clustering which meets the above requirements to the maximal extent.

[3]It may be more standard to use a decay function $f : \mathcal{R} \rightarrow \mathcal{R}$ and choose a partner with the probability proportional to $f(-d_{i,j})$. However, the two forms are equivalent and using scores $d_{i,j}$ directly is more convenient for our induction purposes.

Our model associates two distributions with each predicate: one governs the selection of argument fillers for each semantic role, and the other models (and penalizes) duplicate occurrence of roles. Each predicate occurrence is generated independently given these distributions. Let us describe the model by first defining how the set of model parameters and an argument key clustering are drawn, and then explaining the generation of individual predicate and argument instances. The generative story is formally presented in Figure 1.

We start by generating a partition of argument keys B_p with each subset $r \in B_p$ representing a single semantic role. The partitions are drawn from CRP(α) (see the **Factored model** section of Figure 1) independently for each predicate. The crucial part of the model is the set of selectional preference parameters $\theta_{p,r}$, the distributions of arguments x for each role r of predicate p. We represent arguments by their syntactic heads,[4] or more specifically, by either their lemmas or word clusters assigned to the head by an external clustering algorithm, as we will discuss in more detail in Section 7.[5] For the agent role $A0$ of the predicate *open*, for example, this distribution would assign most of the probability mass to arguments denoting sentient beings, whereas the distribution for the patient role $A1$ would concentrate on arguments representing "openable" things (doors, boxes, books, etc).

In order to encode the assumption about sparseness of the distributions $\theta_{p,r}$, we draw them from the DP prior $DP(\beta, H^{(A)})$ with a small concentration parameter β, the base probability distribution $H^{(A)}$ is just the normalized frequencies of arguments in the corpus. The geometric distribution $\psi_{p,r}$ is used to model the number of times a role r appears with a given predicate occurrence. The decision whether to generate at least one role r is drawn from the uniform Bernoulli distribution. If 0 is drawn then the semantic role is not realized for the given occurrence, otherwise the number of additional roles r is drawn from the geometric distribution $Geom(\psi_{p,r})$. The Beta priors over ψ

[4]For prepositional phrases, we take as head the head noun of the object noun phrase as it encodes crucial lexical information. However, the preposition is not ignored but rather encoded in the corresponding argument key, as explained in Section 2.

[5]Alternatively, the clustering of arguments could be induced within the model, as done in (Titov and Klementiev, 2011).

Clustering of argument keys:	
Factored model:	
for each predicate $p = 1, 2, \ldots$:	
$B_p \sim CRP(\alpha)$	[partition of arg keys]
Coupled model:	
$D \sim NonInform$	[similarity graph]
for each predicate $p = 1, 2, \ldots$:	
$B_p \sim dd\text{-}CRP(\alpha, D)$	[partition of arg keys]
Parameters:	
for each predicate $p = 1, 2, \ldots$:	
for each role $r \in B_p$:	
$\theta_{p,r} \sim DP(\beta, H^{(A)})$	[distrib of arg fillers]
$\psi_{p,r} \sim Beta(\eta_0, \eta_1)$	[geom distr for dup roles]
Data Generation:	
for each predicate $p = 1, 2, \ldots$:	
for each occurrence l of p:	
for every role $r \in B_p$:	
if $[n \sim Unif(0, 1)] = 1$:	[role appears at least once]
GenArgument(p, r)	[draw one arg]
while $[n \sim \psi_{p,r}] = 1$:	[continue generation]
GenArgument(p, r)	[draw more args]
GenArgument(p, r):	
$k_{p,r} \sim Unif(1, \ldots, \lvert r \rvert)$	[draw arg key]
$x_{p,r} \sim \theta_{p,r}$	[draw arg filler]

Figure 1: Generative stories for the factored and coupled models.

can indicate the preference towards generating at most one argument for each role. For example, it would express the preference that a predicate *open* typically appears with a single agent and a single patient arguments.

Now, when parameters and argument key clusterings are chosen, we can summarize the remainder of the generative story as follows. We begin by independently drawing occurrences for each predicate. For each predicate role we independently decide on the number of role occurrences. Then we generate each of the arguments (see **GenArgument**) by generating an argument key $k_{p,r}$ uniformly from the set of argument keys assigned to the cluster r, and finally choosing its filler $x_{p,r}$, where the filler is either a lemma or a word cluster corresponding to the syntactic head of the argument.

5 Coupled Model

As we argued in Section 1, clusterings of argument keys implicitly encode the pattern of alternations for a predicate. E.g., passivization can be roughly represented with the clustering of the key `ACT:LEFT:SBJ` with `PASS:RIGHT:LGS->by` and `ACT:RIGHT:OBJ` with `PASS:LEFT:SBJ`. The set of permissible alternations is predicate-specific,[6] but nevertheless they arguably represent a small subset of all clusterings of argument keys. Also, some alternations are more likely to be applicable to a verb than others: for example, passivization and dativization alternations are both fairly frequent, whereas, locative-preposition-drop alternation (*Mary climbed up the mountain* vs. *Mary climbed the mountain*) is less common and applicable only to several classes of predicates representing motion (Levin, 1993). We represent this observation by quantifying how likely a pair of keys is to be clustered. These scores ($d_{i,j}$ for every pair of argument keys i and j) are induced automatically within the model, and treated as latent variables shared across predicates. Intuitively, if data for several predicates strongly suggests that two argument keys should be clustered (e.g., there is a large overlap between argument fillers for the two keys) then the posterior will indicate that $d_{i,j}$ is expected to be greater for the pair $\{i, j\}$ than for some other pair $\{i', j'\}$ for which the evidence is less clear. Consequently, argument keys i and j will be clustered even for predicates without strong evidence for such a clustering, whereas i' and j' will not.

One argument against coupling predicates may stem from the fact that we are using unlabeled data and may be able to obtain sufficient amount of learning material even for less frequent predicates. This may be a valid observation, but another rationale for sharing this similarity structure is the hypothesis that alternations may be easier to detect for some predicates than for others. For example, argument key clustering of predicates with very restrictive selectional restrictions on argument fillers is presumably easier than clustering for predicates with less restrictive and overlapping selectional restriction, as compactness of selectional preferences is a central assumption driving unsupervised learning of semantic roles. E.g., predicates *change* and *defrost* belong to the same Levin class (*change-of-state verbs*) and therefore admit similar alternations. However, the set of potential patients of *defrost* is sufficiently restricted,

[6]Or, at least specific to a class of predicates (Levin, 1993).

whereas the selectional restrictions for the patient of *change* are far less specific and they overlap with selectional restrictions for the agent role, further complicating the clustering induction task. This observation suggests that sharing clustering preferences across verbs is likely to help even if the unlabeled data is plentiful for every predicate.

More formally, we generate scores $d_{i,j}$, or equivalently, the full labeled graph D with vertices corresponding to argument keys and edges weighted with the similarity scores, from a prior. In our experiments we use a non-informative prior which factorizes over pairs (i.e. edges of the graph D), though more powerful alternatives can be considered. Then we use it, in a dd-CRP(α, D), to generate clusterings of argument keys for every predicate. The rest of the generative story is the same as for the factored model. The part relevant to this model is shown in the **Coupled model** section of Figure 1.

Note that this approach does not assume that the frequencies of syntactic patterns corresponding to alternations are similar, and a large value for $d_{i,j}$ does not necessarily mean that the corresponding syntactic frames i and j are very frequent in a corpus. What it indicates is that a large number of different predicates undergo the corresponding alternation; the frequency of the alternation is a different matter. We believe that this is an important point, as we do not make a restricting assumption that an alternation has the same distributional properties for all verbs which undergo this alternation.

6 Inference

An inference algorithm for an unsupervised model should be efficient enough to handle vast amounts of unlabeled data, as it can easily be obtained and is likely to improve results. We use a simple approximate inference algorithm based on greedy MAP search. We start by discussing MAP search for argument key clustering with the factored model and then discuss its extension applicable to the coupled model.

6.1 Role Induction

For the factored model, semantic roles for every predicate are induced independently. Nevertheless, search for a MAP clustering can be expensive, as even a move involving a single argument key implies some computations for all its occurrences in the corpus. Instead of more complex MAP search algorithms (see, e.g., (Daume III, 2007)), we use a greedy procedure where we start with each argument key assigned to an individual cluster, and then iteratively try to merge clusters. Each move involves (1) choosing an argument key and (2) deciding on a cluster to reassign it to. This is done by considering all clusters (including creating a new one) and choosing the most probable one.

Instead of choosing argument keys randomly at the first stage, we order them by corpus frequency. This ordering is beneficial as getting clustering right for frequent argument keys is more important and the corresponding decisions should be made earlier.[7] We used a single iteration in our experiments, as we have not noticed any benefit from using multiple iterations.

6.2 Similarity Graph Induction

In the coupled model, clusterings for different predicates are statistically dependent, as the similarity structure D is latent and shared across predicates. Consequently, a more complex inference procedure is needed. For simplicity here and in our experiments, we use the non-informative prior distribution over D which assigns the same prior probability to every possible weight $d_{i,j}$ for every pair $\{i, j\}$.

Recall that the dd-CRP prior is defined in terms of customers choosing other customers to sit with. For the moment, let us assume that this relation among argument keys is known, that is, every argument key k for predicate p has chosen an argument key $c_{p,k}$ to 'sit' with. We can compute the MAP estimate for all $d_{i,j}$ by maximizing the objective:

$$\arg\max_{d_{i,j},\, i \neq j} \sum_{p} \sum_{k \in \boldsymbol{K}_p} \log \frac{d_{k,c_{p,k}}}{\sum_{k' \in \boldsymbol{K}_p} d_{k,k'}},$$

where $\boldsymbol{K}_p$ is the set of all argument keys for the predicate p. We slightly abuse the notation by using $d_{i,i}$ to denote the concentration parameter α in the previous expression. Note that we also assume that similarities are symmetric, $d_{i,j} = d_{j,i}$. If the set of argument keys $\boldsymbol{K}_p$ would be the same for every predicate, then the optimal $d_{i,j}$ would

[7]This idea has been explored before for shallow semantic representations (Lang and Lapata, 2011a; Titov and Klementiev, 2011).

be proportional to the number of times either i selects j as a partner, or j chooses i as a partner.[8] This no longer holds if the sets are different, but the solution can be found efficiently using a numeric optimization strategy; we use the gradient descent algorithm.

We do not learn the concentration parameter α, as it is used in our model to indicate the desired granularity of semantic roles, but instead only learn $d_{i,j}$ $(i \neq j)$. However, just learning the concentration parameter would not be sufficient as the effective concentration can be reduced or increased arbitrarily by scaling all the similarities $d_{i,j}$ $(i \neq j)$ at once, as follows from expression (1). Instead, we enforce the normalization constraint on the similarities $d_{i,j}$. We ensure that the prior probability of choosing itself as a partner, averaged over predicates, is the same as it would be with uniform $d_{i,j}$ ($d_{i,j} = 1$ for every key pair $\{i, j\}$, $i \neq j$). This roughly says that we want to preserve the same granularity of clustering as it was with the uniform similarities. We accomplish this normalization in a post-hoc fashion by dividing the weights after optimization by $\sum_p \sum_{k,k' \in \boldsymbol{K}_p,\, k' \neq k} d_{k,k'} / \sum_p |\boldsymbol{K}_p|(|\boldsymbol{K}_p| - 1)$.

If D is fixed, partners for every predicate p and every k can be found using virtually the same algorithm as in Section 6.1: the only difference is that, instead of a cluster, each argument key iteratively chooses a partner.

Though, in practice, both the choice of partners and the similarity graphs are latent, we can use an iterative approach to obtain a joint MAP estimate of c_k (for every k) and the similarity graph D by alternating the two steps.[9]

Notice that the resulting algorithm is again highly parallelizable: the graph induction stage is fast, and induction of the seat-with relation (i.e. clustering argument keys) is factorizable over predicates.

One shortcoming of this approach is typical for generative models with multiple 'features': when such a model predicts a latent variable, it tends to ignore the prior class distribution and relies solely on features. This behavior is due to the over-simplifying independence assumptions. It is well known, for instance, that the posterior with Naive Bayes tends to be overconfident due to violated conditional independence assumptions (Rennie, 2001). The same behavior is observed here: the shared prior does not have sufficient effect on frequent predicates.[10] Though different techniques have been developed to discount the over-confidence (Kolcz and Chowdhury, 2005), we use the most basic one: we raise the likelihood term in power $\frac{1}{T}$, where the parameter T is chosen empirically.

7 Empirical Evaluation

7.1 Data and Evaluation

We keep the general setup of (Lang and Lapata, 2011a), to evaluate our models and compare them to the current state of the art. We run all of our experiments on the standard CoNLL 2008 shared task (Surdeanu et al., 2008) version of Penn Treebank WSJ and PropBank. In addition to gold dependency analyses and gold PropBank annotations, it has dependency structures generated automatically by the MaltParser (Nivre et al., 2007). We vary our experimental setup as follows:

- We evaluate our models on gold and automatically generated parses, and use either gold PropBank annotations or the heuristic from Section 2 to identify arguments, resulting in four experimental regimes.
- In order to reduce the sparsity of predicate argument fillers we consider replacing lemmas of their syntactic heads with word clusters induced by a clustering algorithm as a preprocessing step. In particular, we use Brown (*Br*) clustering (Brown et al., 1992) induced over RCV1 corpus (Turian et al., 2010). Although the clustering is hierarchical, we only use a cluster at the lowest level of the hierarchy for each word.

We use the purity (PU) and collocation (CO) metrics as well as their harmonic mean (F1) to measure the quality of the resulting clusters. Purity measures the degree to which each cluster contains arguments sharing the same gold role:

$$PU = \frac{1}{N} \sum_i \max_j |G_j \cap C_i|$$

where if C_i is the set of arguments in the i-th induced cluster, G_j is the set of arguments in the jth

[8] Note that weights $d_{i,j}$ are invariant under rescaling when the rescaling is also applied to the concentration parameter α.

[9] In practice, two iterations were sufficient.

[10] The coupled model without discounting still outperforms the factored counterpart in our experiments.

gold cluster, and N is the total number of arguments. Collocation evaluates the degree to which arguments with the same gold roles are assigned to a single cluster. It is computed as follows:

$$CO = \frac{1}{N} \sum_j \max_i |G_j \cap C_i|$$

We compute the aggregate PU, CO, and F1 scores over all predicates in the same way as (Lang and Lapata, 2011a) by weighting the scores of each predicate by the number of its argument occurrences. Note that since our goal is to evaluate the clustering algorithms, we *do not* include incorrectly identified arguments (i.e. mistakes made by the heuristic defined in Section 2) when computing these metrics.

We evaluate both factored and coupled models proposed in this work with and without Brown word clustering of argument fillers (*Factored, Coupled, Factored+Br, Coupled+Br*). Our models are robust to parameter settings, they were tuned (to an order of magnitude) on the development set and were the same for all model variants: $\alpha = 1.e\text{-}3$, $\beta = 1.e\text{-}3$, $\eta_0 = 1.e\text{-}3$, $\eta_1 = 1.e\text{-}10$, $T = 5$. Although they can be induced within the model, we set them by hand to indicate granularity preferences. We compare our results with the following alternative approaches. The syntactic function baseline (*SyntF*) simply clusters predicate arguments according to the dependency relation to their head. Following (Lang and Lapata, 2010), we allocate a cluster for each of 20 most frequent relations in the CoNLL dataset and one cluster for all other relations. We also compare our performance with the Latent Logistic classification (Lang and Lapata, 2010), Split-Merge clustering (Lang and Lapata, 2011a), and Graph Partitioning (Lang and Lapata, 2011b) approaches (labeled *LLogistic*, *SplitMerge*, and *GraphPart*, respectively) which achieve the current best unsupervised SRL results in this setting.

7.2 Results

7.2.1 Gold Arguments

Experimental results are summarized in Table 1. We begin by comparing our models to the three existing clustering approaches on gold syntactic parses, and using gold PropBank annotations to identify predicate arguments. In this set of experiments we measure the relative performance of argument clustering, removing the identification stage, and minimize the noise due to automatic syntactic annotations. All four variants of the models we propose substantially outperform other models: the coupled model with Brown clustering of argument fillers (*Coupled+Br*) beats the previous best model *SplitMerge* by 2.9% F1 score. As mentioned in Section 2, our approach specifically does not cluster some of the modifier arguments. In order to verify that this and argument filler clustering were not the only aspects of our approach contributing to performance improvements, we also evaluated our coupled model without Brown clustering and treating modifiers as regular arguments. The model achieves 89.2% purity, 74.0% collocation, and 80.9% F1 scores, still substantially outperforming all of the alternative approaches. Replacing gold parses with MaltParser analyses we see a similar trend, where *Coupled+Br* outperforms the best alternative approach *SplitMerge* by 1.5%.

	gold parses			auto parses		
	PU	CO	F1	PU	CO	F1
LLogistic	79.5	76.5	78.0	77.9	74.4	76.2
SplitMerge	88.7	73.0	80.1	86.5	69.8	77.3
GraphPart	88.6	70.7	78.6	87.4	65.9	75.2
Factored	88.1	77.1	82.2	85.1	71.8	77.9
Coupled	89.3	76.6	82.5	86.7	71.2	78.2
Factored+Br	86.8	78.8	82.6	83.8	74.1	78.6
Coupled+Br	88.7	78.1	**83.0**	86.2	72.7	**78.8**
SyntF	81.6	77.5	79.5	77.1	70.9	73.9

Table 1: Argument clustering performance with *gold argument identification*. Bold-face is used to highlight the best F1 scores.

7.2.2 Automatic Arguments

Results are summarized in Table 2.[11] The precision and recall of our re-implementation of the argument identification heuristic described in Section 2 on gold parses were 87.7% and 88.0%, respectively, and do not quite match 88.1% and 87.9% reported in (Lang and Lapata, 2011a). Since we could not reproduce their argument identification stage exactly, we are omitting their results for the two regimes, instead including the results for our two best models *Factored+Br* and *Coupled+Br*. We see a similar trend, where the coupled system consistently outperforms its factored counterpart, achieving 85.8% and 83.9% F1

[11]Note, that the scores are computed on correctly identified arguments only, and tend to be higher in these experiments probably because the complex arguments get discarded by the heuristic.

	gold parses			auto parses		
	PU	CO	F1	PU	CO	F1
Factored+Br	87.8	82.9	85.3	85.8	81.1	83.4
Coupled+Br	89.2	82.6	**85.8**	87.4	80.7	**83.9**
SyntF	83.5	81.4	82.4	81.4	79.1	80.2

Table 2: Argument clustering performance with *automatic argument identification*.

for gold and MaltParser analyses, respectively.

We observe that consistently through the four regimes, sharing of alternations between predicates captured by the coupled model outperforms the factored version, and that reducing the argument filler sparsity with clustering also has a substantial positive effect. Due to the space constraints we are not able to present detailed analysis of the induced similarity graph D, however, argument-key pairs with the highest induced similarity encode, among other things, passivization, benefactive alternations, near-interchangeability of some subordinating conjunctions and prepositions (e.g., *if* and *whether*), as well as, restoring some of the unnecessary splits introduced by the argument key definition (e.g., semantic roles for adverbials do not normally depend on whether the construction is passive or active).

8 Related Work

Most of SRL research has focused on the supervised setting (Carreras and Màrquez, 2005; Surdeanu et al., 2008), however, lack of annotated resources for most languages and insufficient coverage provided by the existing resources motivates the need for using unlabeled data or other forms of weak supervision. This work includes methods based on graph alignment between labeled and unlabeled data (Fürstenau and Lapata, 2009), using unlabeled data to improve lexical generalization (Deschacht and Moens, 2009), and projection of annotation across languages (Pado and Lapata, 2009; van der Plas et al., 2011). Semi-supervised and weakly-supervised techniques have also been explored for other types of semantic representations but these studies have mostly focused on restricted domains (Kate and Mooney, 2007; Liang et al., 2009; Titov and Kozhevnikov, 2010; Goldwasser et al., 2011; Liang et al., 2011).

Unsupervised learning has been one of the central paradigms for the closely-related area of relation extraction, where several techniques have been proposed to cluster semantically similar verbalizations of relations (Lin and Pantel, 2001; Banko et al., 2007). Early unsupervised approaches to the SRL problem include the work by Swier and Stevenson (2004), where the VerbNet verb lexicon was used to guide unsupervised learning, and a generative model of Grenager and Manning (2006) which exploits linguistic priors on syntactic-semantic interface.

More recently, the role induction problem has been studied in Lang and Lapata (2010) where it has been reformulated as a problem of detecting alterations and mapping non-standard linkings to the canonical ones. Later, Lang and Lapata (2011a) proposed an algorithmic approach to clustering argument signatures which achieves higher accuracy and outperforms the syntactic baseline. In Lang and Lapata (2011b), the role induction problem is formulated as a graph partitioning problem: each vertex in the graph corresponds to a predicate occurrence and edges represent lexical and syntactic similarities between the occurrences. Unsupervised induction of semantics has also been studied in Poon and Domingos (2009) and Titov and Klementiev (2010) but the induced representations are not entirely compatible with the PropBank-style annotations and they have been evaluated only on a question answering task for the biomedical domain. Also, the related task of unsupervised argument identification was considered in Abend et al. (2009).

9 Conclusions

In this work we introduced two Bayesian models for unsupervised role induction. They treat the task as a family of related clustering problems, one for each predicate. The first factored model induces each clustering independently, whereas the second model couples them by exploiting a novel technique for sharing clustering preferences across a family of clusterings. Both methods achieve state-of-the-art results with the coupled model outperforming the factored counterpart in all regimes.

Acknowledgements

The authors acknowledge the support of the MMCI Cluster of Excellence, and thank Hagen Fürstenau, Mikhail Kozhevnikov, Alexis Palmer, Manfred Pinkal, Caroline Sporleder and the anonymous reviewers for their suggestions, and Joel Lang for answering questions about their methods and data.

References

Omri Abend, Roi Reichart, and Ari Rappoport. 2009. Unsupervised argument identification for semantic role labeling. In *ACL-IJCNLP*.

Michele Banko, Michael J Cafarella, Stephen Soderland, Matt Broadhead, and Oren Etzioni. 2007. Open information extraction from the web. In *IJCAI*.

Roberto Basili, Diego De Cao, Danilo Croce, Bonaventura Coppola, and Alessandro Moschitti. 2009. Cross-language frame semantics transfer in bilingual corpora. In *CICLING*.

David M. Blei and Peter Frazier. 2011. Distance dependent chinese restaurant processes. *Journal of Machine Learning Research*, 12:2461–2488.

Peter F. Brown, Vincent Della Pietra, Peter V. deSouza, Jenifer C. Lai, and Robert L. Mercer. 1992. Class-based n-gram models for natural language. *Computational Linguistics*, 18(4):467–479.

Xavier Carreras and Lluís Màrquez. 2005. Introduction to the CoNLL-2005 Shared Task: Semantic Role Labeling. In *CoNLL*.

Hal Daume III. 2007. Fast search for dirichlet process mixture models. In *AISTATS*.

Koen Deschacht and Marie-Francine Moens. 2009. Semi-supervised semantic role labeling using the Latent Words Language Model. In *EMNLP*.

Jason Duan, Michele Guindani, and Alan Gelfand. 2007. Generalized spatial dirichlet process models. *Biometrika*, 94:809–825.

Thomas S. Ferguson. 1973. A Bayesian analysis of some nonparametric problems. *The Annals of Statistics*, 1(2):209–230.

Hagen Fürstenau and Mirella Lapata. 2009. Graph alignment for semi-supervised semantic role labeling. In *EMNLP*.

Qin Gao and Stephan Vogel. 2011. Corpus expansion for statistical machine translation with semantic role label substitution rules. In *ACL:HLT*.

Daniel Gildea and Daniel Jurafsky. 2002. Automatic labelling of semantic roles. *Computational Linguistics*, 28(3):245–288.

Dan Goldwasser, Roi Reichart, James Clarke, and Dan Roth. 2011. Confidence driven unsupervised semantic parsing. In *ACL*.

Trond Grenager and Christoph Manning. 2006. Unsupervised discovery of a statistical verb lexicon. In *EMNLP*.

Jan Hajič, Massimiliano Ciaramita, Richard Johansson, Daisuke Kawahara, Maria Antònia Martí, Lluís Màrquez, Adam Meyers, Joakim Nivre, Sebastian Padó, Jan Štěpánek, Pavel Straňák, Mihai Surdeanu, Nianwen Xue, and Yi Zhang. 2009. The CoNLL-2009 shared task: Syntactic and semantic dependencies in multiple languages. In *Proceedings of the 13th Conference on Computational Natural Language Learning (CoNLL-2009), June 4-5*.

Michael Kaisser and Bonnie Webber. 2007. Question answering based on semantic roles. In *ACL Workshop on Deep Linguistic Processing*.

Rohit J. Kate and Raymond J. Mooney. 2007. Learning language semantics from ambigous supervision. In *AAAI*.

Aleksander Kolcz and Abdur Chowdhury. 2005. Discounting over-confidence of naive bayes in high-recall text classification. In *ECML*.

Joel Lang and Mirella Lapata. 2010. Unsupervised induction of semantic roles. In *ACL*.

Joel Lang and Mirella Lapata. 2011a. Unsupervised semantic role induction via split-merge clustering. In *ACL*.

Joel Lang and Mirella Lapata. 2011b. Unsupervised semantic role induction with graph partitioning. In *EMNLP*.

Beth Levin. 1993. *English Verb Classes and Alternations: A Preliminary Investigation*. University of Chicago Press.

Percy Liang, Michael I. Jordan, and Dan Klein. 2009. Learning semantic correspondences with less supervision. In *ACL-IJCNLP*.

Percy Liang, Michael Jordan, and Dan Klein. 2011. Learning dependency-based compositional semantics. In *ACL: HLT*.

Dekang Lin and Patrick Pantel. 2001. DIRT – discovery of inference rules from text. In *KDD*.

Ding Liu and Daniel Gildea. 2010. Semantic role features for machine translation. In *Coling*.

J. Nivre, J. Hall, S. Kübler, R. McDonald, J. Nilsson, S. Riedel, and D. Yuret. 2007. The CoNLL 2007 shared task on dependency parsing. In *EMNLP-CoNLL*.

Sebastian Pado and Mirella Lapata. 2009. Cross-lingual annotation projection for semantic roles. *Journal of Artificial Intelligence Research*, 36:307–340.

Alexis Palmer and Caroline Sporleder. 2010. Evaluating FrameNet-style semantic parsing: the role of coverage gaps in FrameNet. In *COLING*.

M. Palmer, D. Gildea, and P. Kingsbury. 2005. The proposition bank: An annotated corpus of semantic roles. *Computational Linguistics*, 31(1):71–106.

Hoifung Poon and Pedro Domingos. 2009. Unsupervised semantic parsing. In *EMNLP*.

Sameer Pradhan, Wayne Ward, and James H. Martin. 2008. Towards robust semantic role labeling. *Computational Linguistics*, 34:289–310.

Jason Rennie. 2001. Improving multi-class text classification with Naive bayes. Technical Report AITR-2001-004, MIT.

M. Sammons, V. Vydiswaran, T. Vieira, N. Johri, M. Chang, D. Goldwasser, V. Srikumar, G. Kundu, Y. Tu, K. Small, J. Rule, Q. Do, and D. Roth. 2009. Relation alignment for textual entailment recognition. In *Text Analysis Conference (TAC)*.

Dan Shen and Mirella Lapata. 2007. Using semantic roles to improve question answering. In *EMNLP*.

Richard Socher, Andrew Maas, and Christopher Manning. 2011. Spectral chinese restaurant processes: Nonparametric clustering based on similarities. In *AISTATS*.

Mihai Surdeanu, Adam Meyers Richard Johansson, Lluís Màrquez, and Joakim Nivre. 2008. The CoNLL-2008 shared task on joint parsing of syntactic and semantic dependencies. In *CoNLL 2008: Shared Task*.

Richard Swier and Suzanne Stevenson. 2004. Unsupervised semantic role labelling. In *EMNLP*.

Yee Whye Teh. 2010. Dirichlet processes. In *Encyclopedia of Machine Learning*. Springer.

Ivan Titov and Alexandre Klementiev. 2011. A Bayesian model for unsupervised semantic parsing. In *ACL*.

Ivan Titov and Mikhail Kozhevnikov. 2010. Bootstrapping semantic analyzers from non-contradictory texts. In *ACL*.

Joseph Turian, Lev Ratinov, and Yoshua Bengio. 2010. Word representations: A simple and general method for semi-supervised learning. In *ACL*.

Lonneke van der Plas, Paola Merlo, and James Henderson. 2011. Scaling up automatic cross-lingual semantic role annotation. In *ACL*.

Dekai Wu and Pascale Fung. 2009. Semantic roles for SMT: A hybrid two-pass model. In *NAACL*.

Dekai Wu, Marianna Apidianaki, Marine Carpuat, and Lucia Specia, editors. 2011. *Proc. of Fifth Workshop on Syntax, Semantics and Structure in Statistical Translation*. ACL.

Entailment above the word level in distributional semantics

Marco Baroni
Raffaella Bernardi
University of Trento
name.surname@unitn.it

Ngoc-Quynh Do
Free University of Bozen-Bolzano
quynhdtn.hut@gmail.com

Chung-chieh Shan
Cornell University
University of Tsukuba
ccshan@post.harvard.edu

Abstract

We introduce two ways to detect entailment using distributional semantic representations of phrases. Our first experiment shows that the entailment relation between adjective-noun constructions and their head nouns (*big cat* $\models$ *cat*), once represented as semantic vector pairs, generalizes to lexical entailment among nouns (*dog* $\models$ *animal*). Our second experiment shows that a classifier fed semantic vector pairs can similarly generalize the entailment relation among quantifier phrases (*many dogs* $\models$ *some dogs*) to entailment involving unseen quantifiers (*all cats* $\models$ *several cats*). Moreover, nominal and quantifier phrase entailment appears to be cued by different distributional correlates, as predicted by the type-based view of entailment in formal semantics.

1 Introduction

Distributional semantics (DS) approximates linguistic meaning with vectors summarizing the contexts where expressions occur. The success of DS in lexical semantics has validated the hypothesis that semantically similar expressions occur in similar contexts (Landauer and Dumais, 1997; Lund and Burgess, 1996; Sahlgren, 2006; Schütze, 1997; Turney and Pantel, 2010). Formal semantics (FS) represents linguistic meanings as symbolic formulas and assemble them via composition rules. FS has successfully modeled quantification and captured inferential relations between phrases and between sentences (Montague, 1970; Thomason, 1974; Heim and Kratzer, 1998). The strengths of DS and FS have been complementary to date: On one hand, DS has induced large-scale semantic representations from corpora, but it has been largely limited to the lexical domain. On the other hand, FS has provided sophisticated models of sentence meaning, but it has been largely limited to hand-coded models that do not scale up to real-life challenges by learning from data.

Given these complementary strengths, we naturally ask if DS and FS can address each other's limitations. Two recent strands of research are bringing DS closer to meeting core FS challenges. One strand attempts to model compositionality with DS methods, representing both primitive and composed linguistic expressions as distributional vectors (Baroni and Zamparelli, 2010; Grefenstette and Sadrzadeh, 2011; Guevara, 2010; Mitchell and Lapata, 2010). The other strand attempts to reformulate FS's notion of logical inference in terms that DS can capture (Erk, 2009; Geffet and Dagan, 2005; Kotlerman et al., 2010; Zhitomirsky-Geffet and Dagan, 2010). In keeping with the lexical emphasis of DS, this strand has focused on inference at the word level, or *lexical entailment*, that is, discovering from distributional vectors of hyponyms (*dog*) that they entail their hypernyms (*animal*).

This paper brings these two strands of research together by demonstrating two ways in which the distributional vectors of composite expressions bear on inference. Here we focus on phrasal vectors harvested directly from the corpus rather than obtained compositionally. In a first experiment, we exploit the entailment properties of a class of composite expressions, namely adjective-noun constructions (ANs), to harvest training data for an entailment recognizer. The recognizer is then successfully applied to detect lexical entailment. In short, since almost all ANs entail the noun they contain (*red car* entails *car*), the distributional vectors of AN-N pairs can train a classifier to detect noun pairs that stand in the same relation (*dog* entails *animal*). With almost no manual effort, we achieve performance nearly identical with the state-of-the-art balAPinc measure that Kotlerman et al. (2010) crafted, which detects feature inclusion between the two nouns' occurrence contexts.

Our second experiment goes beyond lexical inference. We look at phrases built from a quantifying determiner[1] and a noun (QNs) and use their distributional vectors to recognize entailment relations of the form *many dogs* $\models$ *some dogs*, between two QNs sharing the same noun. It turns out that a classifier trained on a set of $Q_1N \models Q_2N$ pairs can recognize entailment in pairs with a new quantifier configuration. For example, we can train on *many dogs* $\models$ *some dogs* then correctly predict *all cats*$\models$*several cats*. Interestingly, on the QN entailment task, neither our classifier trained on AN-N pairs nor the balAPinc method beat baseline methods. This suggests that our successful QN classifiers tap into vector properties beyond such relations as feature inclusion that those methods for nominal entailment rely upon.

Together, our experiments show that corpus-harvested DS representations of composite expressions such as ANs and QNs contain sufficient information to capture and generalize their inference patterns. This result brings DS closer to the central concerns of FS. In particular, the QN study is the first to our knowledge to show that DS vectors capture semantic properties not only of content words, but of an important class of function words (quantifying determiners) deeply studied in FS but of little interest until now in DS.

Besides these theoretical implications, our results are of practical import. First, our AN study presents a novel, practical method for detecting lexical entailment that reaches state-of-the-art performance with little or no manual intervention. Lexical entailment is in turn fundamental for constructing ontologies and other lexical resources (Buitelaar and Cimiano, 2008). Second, our QN study demonstrates that phrasal entailment can be automatically detected and thus paves the way to apply DS to advanced NLP tasks such as recognizing textual entailment (Dagan et al., 2009).

[1]In the sequel we will simply refer to a "quantifying determiner" as a "quantifier".

2 Background

2.1 Distributional semantics above the word level

DS models such as LSA (Landauer and Dumais, 1997) and HAL (Lund and Burgess, 1996) approximate the meaning of a word by a vector that summarizes its distribution in a corpus, for example by counting co-occurrences of the word with other words. Since semantically similar words tend to share similar contexts, DS has been very successful in tasks that require quantifying semantic similarity among words, such as synonym detection and concept clustering (Turney and Pantel, 2010).

Recently, there has been a flurry of interest in DS to model meaning composition: How can we derive the DS representation of a composite phrase from that of its constituents? Although the general focus in the area is to perform algebraic operations on word semantic vectors (Mitchell and Lapata, 2010), some researchers have also directly examined the corpus contexts of phrases. For example, Baldwin et al. (2003) studied vector extraction for phrases because they were interested in the decomposability of multiword expressions. Baroni and Zamparelli (2010) and Guevara (2010) look at corpus-harvested phrase vectors to learn composition functions that should derive such composite vectors automatically. Baroni and Zamparelli, in particular, showed qualitatively that directly corpus-harvested vectors for AN constructions are meaningful; for example, the vector of *young husband* has nearest neighbors *small son*, *small daughter* and *mistress*. Following up on this approach, we show here quantitatively that corpus-harvested AN vectors are also useful for detecting entailment. We find moreover distributional vectors informative and useful not only for phrases made of content words (such as ANs) but also for phrases containing functional elements, namely quantifying determiners.

2.2 Entailment from formal to distributional semantics

Entailment in FS To characterize the conditions under which a sentence is true, FS begins with the lexical meanings of the words in the sentence and builds up the meanings of larger and larger phrases until it arrives at the meaning of the whole sentence. The meanings throughout this compositional process inhabit a variety of semantic domains, depending on the syntactic category of the expressions: typically, a sentence denotes a truth value (`true` or `false`) or truth conditions, a noun such as *cat* denotes a set of entities, and a quantifier phrase (QP) such as *all cats* denotes a set of sets of entities.

The entailment relation ($\models$) is a core notion of logic: it holds between one or more sentences and a sentence such that it cannot be that the former (antecedent) are true and the latter (consequent) is false. FS extends this notion from formal-logic sentences to natural-language expressions. By assigning meanings to parts of a sentence, FS allows defining entailment not only among sentences but also among words and phrases. Each semantic domain A has its own entailment relation $\models_A$. The entailment relation $\models_\text{S}$ among sentences is the logical notion just described, whereas the entailment relations $\models_\text{N}$ and $\models_\text{QP}$ among nouns and quantifier phrases are the inclusion relations among sets of entities and sets of sets of entities respectively. Our results in Section 5 show that DS needs to treat $\models_\text{N}$ and $\models_\text{QP}$ differently as well.

Empirical, corpus-based perspectives on entailment Until recently, the corpus-based research tradition has studied entailment mostly at the word level, with applied goals such as classifying lexical relations and building taxonomic WordNet-like resources automatically. The most popular approach, first adopted by Hearst (1992), extracts lexical relations from patterns in large corpora. For instance, from the pattern N_1 *such as* N_2 one learns that $N_2 \models N_1$ (from *insects such as beetles*, derive *beetles* $\models$ *insects*). Several studies have refined and extended this approach (Pantel and Ravichandran, 2004; Snow et al., 2005; Snow et al., 2006; Turney, 2008).

While empirically very successful, the pattern-based method is mostly limited to single content words (or frequent content-word phrases). We are interested in entailment between phrases, where it is not obvious how to use lexico-syntactic patterns and cope with data sparsity. For instance, it seems hard to find a pattern that frequently connects one QP to another it entails, as in *all beetles PATTERN many beetles*. Hence, we aim to find a more general method and investigate whether DS vectors (whether corpus-harvested or compositionally derived) encode the information needed to account for phrasal entailment in a way that can be captured and generalized to unseen phrase pairs.

Rather recently, the study of sentential entailment has taken an empirical turn, thanks to the development of benchmarks for entailment systems. The FS definition of entailment has been modified by taking common sense into account. Instead of a relation from the truth of the consequent to the truth of the antecedent in any circumstance, the applied view looks at entailment in terms of plausibility: $\phi \models \psi$ if a human who reads (and trusts) ϕ would most likely infer that ψ is also true. Entailment systems have been compared under this new perspective in various evaluation campaigns, the best known being the Recognizing Textual Entailment (RTE) initiative (Dagan et al., 2009).

Most RTE systems are based on advanced NLP components, machine learning techniques, and/or syntactic transformations (Zanzotto et al., 2007; Kouleykov and Magnini, 2005). A few systems exploit deep FS analysis (Bos and Markert, 2006; Chambers et al., 2007). In particular, the FS results about QP properties that affect entailment have been exploited by Chambers et al, who complement a core broad-coverage system with a Natural Logic module to trade lower recall for higher precision. For instance, they exploit the monotonicity properties of *no* that cause the following reversal in entailment direction: *some beetles* $\models$ *some insects* but *no insects* $\models$ *no beetles*.

To investigate entailment step by step, we address here a much simpler and clearer type of entailment than the more complex notion taken up by the RTE community. While RTE is outside our present scope, we do focus on QP entailment as Natural Logic does. However, our evaluation differs from Chambers et al.'s, since we rely on general-purpose DS vectors as our only resource, and we look at phrase pairs with different quantifiers but the same noun. For instance, we aim to predict that *all beetles* $\models$ *many beetles* but *few beetles* $\not\models$ *all beetles*. QPs, of course, have many well-known semantic properties besides entailment; we leave their analysis to future study.

Entailment in DS Erk (2009) suggests that it may not be possible to induce lexical entailment directly from a vector space representation, but it is possible to encode the relation in this space after it has been derived through other means. On the other hand, recent studies (Geffet and Dagan,

2005; Kotlerman et al., 2010; Weeds et al., 2004) have pursued the intuition that entailment is the asymmetric ability of one term to "substitute" for another. For example, *baseball* contexts are also *sport* contexts but not *vice versa*, hence *baseball* is "narrower" than *sport* and *baseball* $\models$ *sport*. On this view, entailment between vectors corresponds to inclusion of contexts or features, and can be captured by asymmetric measures of distribution similarity. In particular, Kotlerman et al. (2010) carefully crafted the balAPinc measure (see Section 3.5 below). We adopt this measure because it has been shown to outperform others in several tasks that require lexical entailment information.

Like Kotlerman et al., we want to capture the entailment relation between vectors of features. However, we are interested in entailment not only between words but also between phrases, and we ask whether the DS view of entailment as feature inclusion, which captures entailment between nouns, also captures entailment between QPs. To this end, we complement balAPinc with a more flexible supervised classifier.

3 Data and methods

3.1 Semantic space

We construct distributional semantic vectors from the 2.83-billion-token concatenation of the British National Corpus (`http://www.natcorp.ox.ac.uk/`), WackyPedia and ukWaC (`http://wacky.sslmit.unibo.it/`). We tokenize and POS-tag this corpus, then lemmatize it with TreeTagger (Schmid, 1995) to merge singular and plural instances of words and phrases (*some dogs* is mapped to *some dog*).

We process the corpus in two steps to compute *semantic vectors* representing our *phrases of interest*. We use *phrases of interest* as a general term to refer to both multiword phrases and single words, and more precisely to: those AN and QN sequences that are in the data sets (see next subsections), the adjectives, quantifiers and nouns contained in those sequences, and the most frequent (9.8K) nouns and (8.1K) adjectives in the corpus. The first step is to count the content words (more precisely, the most frequent 9.8K nouns, 8.1K adjectives, and 9.6K verbs in the corpus) that occur in the same sentence as phrases of interest. In the second step, following standard practice, the co-occurrence counts are converted into *pointwise mutual information* (PMI) scores (Church and Hanks, 1990). The result of this step is a sparse matrix (with both positive and negative entries) with 48K rows (one per phrase of interest) and 27K columns (one per content word).

3.2 The AN $\models$ N data set

To characterize entailment between nouns using their semantic vectors, we need data exemplifying which noun entails which. This section introduces one cheap way to collect such a training data set exploiting semantic vectors for composed expressions, namely AN sequences. We rely on the linguistic fact that ANs share a syntactic category and semantic type with plain common nouns (*big cat* shares syntactic category and semantic type with *cat*). Furthermore, most adjectives are *restrictive* in the sense that, for every noun N, the AN sequence entails the N alone (every *big cat* is a *cat*). From a distributional point of view, the vector for an N should by construction include the information in the vector for an AN, given that the contexts where the AN occurs are a subset of the contexts where the N occurs (*cat* occurs in all the contexts where *big cat* occurs). This ideal inclusion suggests that the DS notion of lexical entailment as feature inclusion (see Section 2.2 above) should be reflected in the AN $\models$ N pattern.

Because most ANs entail their head Ns, we can create positive examples of AN $\models$ N without any manual inspection of the corpus: simply pair up the semantic vectors of ANs and Ns. Furthermore, because an AN usually does not entail another N, we can create negative examples ($AN_1 \not\models N_2$) just by randomly permuting the Ns. Of course, such unsupervised data would be slightly noisy, especially because some of the most frequent adjectives are not restrictive.

To collect cleaner data and to be sure that we are really examining the phenomenon of entailment, we took a mere few moments of manual effort to select the 256 restrictive adjectives from the most frequent 300 adjectives in the corpus. We then took the Cartesian product of these 256 adjectives with the 200 concrete nouns in the BLESS data set (Baroni and Lenci, 2011). Those nouns were chosen to avoid highly polysemous words. From the Cartesian product, we obtain a total of 1246 AN sequences, such as *big cat*, that occur more than 100 times in the corpus. These AN sequences encompass 190 of the 256 adjectives and 128 of the 200 nouns.

The process results in 1246 positive instances of AN $\models$ N entailment, which we use as training data. To create a comparable amount of negative data, we randomly permuted the nouns in the positive instances to obtain pairs of $AN_1 \not\models N_2$ (e.g., *big cat* $\not\models$ *dog*). We manually double-checked that all positive and negative examples are correctly classified (2 of 1246 negative instances were removed, leaving 1244 negative training examples).

3.3 The lexical entailment $N_1 \models N_2$ data set

For testing data, we first listed all WordNet nouns in our corpus, then extracted hyponym-hypernym chains linking the first synsets of these nouns. For example, *pope* is found to entail *leader* because WordNet contains the chain *pope* $\rightarrow$ *spiritual_ leader* $\rightarrow$ *leader*. Eliminating the 20 hypernyms with more than 180 hyponyms (mostly very abstract nouns such as *entity*, *object*, and *quality*) yields 9734 hyponym-hypernym pairs, encompassing 6402 nouns. Manually double-checking these pairs leaves us with 1385 positive instances of $N_1 \models N_2$ entailment.

We created the negative instances of again 1385 pairs by inverting 33% of the positive instances (from *pope*$\models$*leader* to *leader*$\not\models$*pope*), and by randomly shuffling the words across the positive instances. We also manually double-checked these pairs to make sure that they are not hyponym-hypernym pairs.

3.4 The $Q_1N \models Q_2N$ data set

We study 12 quantifiers: *all, both, each, either, every, few, many, most, much, no, several, some*. We took the Cartesian product of these quantifiers with the 6402 WordNet nouns described in Section 3.3. From this Cartesian product, we obtain a total of 28926 QN sequences, such as *every cat*, that occur at least 100 times in the corpus. These are our QN phrases of interest to which the procedure in Section 3.1 assigns a semantic vector.

Also, from the set of quantifier pairs (Q_1, Q_2) where $Q_1 \neq Q_2$, we identified 13 clear cases where $Q_1 \models Q_2$ and 17 clear cases where $Q_1 \not\models Q_2$. These 30 cases are listed in the first column of Table 1. For each of these 30 quantifier pairs (Q_1, Q_2), we enumerate those WordNet nouns N such that semantic vectors are available for both Q_1N and Q_2N (that is, both sequences occur in at least 100 times). Each such noun then gives rise to an instance of entailment ($Q_1N \models Q_2N$ if $Q_1 \models Q_2$; example: *many dogs* $\models$ *several dogs*) or non-entailment ($Q_1N \not\models Q_2N$ if $Q_1 \not\models Q_2$; example: *many dogs* $\not\models$ *most dogs*). The number of QN pairs that each quantifier pair gives rise to in this way is listed in the second column of Table 1. As shown there, we have a total of 7537 positive instances and 8455 negative instances of QN entailment.

Quantifier pair	Instances	Correct
all $\models$ some	1054	1044 (99%)
all $\models$ several	557	550 (99%)
each $\models$ some	656	647 (99%)
all $\models$ many	873	772 (88%)
much $\models$ some	248	217 (88%)
every $\models$ many	460	400 (87%)
many $\models$ some	951	822 (86%)
all $\models$ most	465	393 (85%)
several $\models$ some	580	439 (76%)
both $\models$ some	573	322 (56%)
many $\models$ several	594	113 (19%)
most $\models$ many	463	84 (18%)
both $\models$ either	63	1 (2%)
Subtotal	*7537*	*5804 (77%)*
some $\not\models$ every	484	481 (99%)
several $\not\models$ all	557	553 (99%)
several $\not\models$ every	378	375 (99%)
some $\not\models$ all	1054	1043 (99%)
many $\not\models$ every	460	452 (98%)
some $\not\models$ each	656	640 (98%)
few $\not\models$ all	157	153 (97%)
many $\not\models$ all	873	843 (97%)
both $\not\models$ most	369	347 (94%)
several $\not\models$ few	143	134 (94%)
both $\not\models$ many	541	397 (73%)
many $\not\models$ most	463	300 (65%)
either $\not\models$ both	63	39 (62%)
many $\not\models$ no	714	369 (52%)
some $\not\models$ many	951	468 (49%)
few $\not\models$ many	161	33 (20%)
both $\not\models$ several	431	63 (15%)
Subtotal	*8455*	*6690 (79%)*
Total	*15992*	*12494 (78%)*

Table 1: Entailing and non-entailing quantifier pairs with number of instances per pair (Section 3.4) and $SVM_{pair\text{-}out}$ performance breakdown (Section 5).

3.5 Classification methods

We consider two methods to classify candidate pairs as entailing or non-entailing, the balAPinc measure of Kotlerman et al. (2010) and a standard Support Vector Machine (SVM) classifier.

balAPinc As discussed in Section 2.2, balAPinc is optimized to capture a relation of feature inclusion between the narrower (entailing) and broader (entailed) terms, while capturing other intuitions about the relative relevance of features. balAPinc averages two terms, APinc and LIN. APinc is given by:

$$\text{APinc}(u \models v) = \frac{\sum_{r=1}^{|F_u|}(P(r) \cdot rel'(f_r))}{|F_u|}$$

APinc is a version of the Average Precision measure from Information Retrieval tailored to lexical inclusion. Given vectors F_u and F_v representing the dimensions with positive PMI values in the semantic vectors of the candidate pair $u \models v$, the idea is that we want the features (that is, vector dimensions) that have larger values in F_u to also have large values in F_v (the opposite does not matter because it is u that should be included in v, not *vice versa*). The F_u features are ranked according to their PMI value so that f_r is the feature in F_u with rank r, i.e., r-th highest PMI. Then the sum of the product of the two terms $P(r)$ and $rel'(f_r)$ across the features in F_u is computed. The first term is the precision at r, which is higher when highly ranked u features are present in F_v as well. The relevance term $rel'(f_r)$ is higher when the feature f_r in F_u also appears in F_v with a high rank. (See Kotlerman et al. for how $P(r)$ and $rel'(f_r)$ are computed.) The resulting score is normalized by dividing by the entailing vector size $|F_u|$ (in accordance with the idea that having more v features should not hurt because the u features should be included in the v features, not *vice versa*).

To balance the potentially excessive asymmetry of APinc towards the features of the antecedent, Kotlerman et al. average it with LIN, the widely used symmetric measure of distributional similarity proposed by Lin (1998):

$$\text{LIN}(u, v) = \frac{\sum_{f \in F_u \cap F_v}[w_u(f) + w_v(f)]}{\sum_{f \in F_u} w_u(f) + \sum_{f \in F_v} w_v(f)}$$

LIN essentially measures feature vector overlap. The positive PMI values $w_u(f)$ and $w_v(f)$ of a feature f in F_u and F_v are summed across those features that are positive in both vectors, normalizing by the cumulative positive PMI mass in both vectors. Finally, balAPinc is the geometric average of APinc and LIN:

$$\text{balAPinc}(u \models v) = \sqrt{\text{APinc}(u \models v) \cdot \text{LIN}(u, v)}$$

To adapt balAPinc to recognize entailment, we must select a threshold t above which we classify a pair as entailing. In the experiments below, we explore two approaches. In balAPinc$_{\text{upper}}$, we optimize the threshold directly on the test data, by setting t to maximize the F-measure on the test set. This gives us an upper bound on how well balAPinc could perform on the test set (but note that optimizing F does not necessarily translate into a good accuracy performance, as clearly illustrated by Table 3 below). In balAPinc$_{\text{AN} \models \text{N}}$, we use the AN $\models$ N data set as training data and pick the t that maximizes F on this training set.

We use the balAPinc measure as a reference point because, on the evidence provided by Kotlerman et al., it is the state of the art in various tasks related to lexical entailment. We recognize however that it is somewhat complex and specifically tuned to capturing the relation of feature inclusion. Consequently, we also experiment with a more flexible classifier, which can detect other systematic properties of vectors in an entailment relation. We present this classifier next.

SVM Support vector machines are widely used high-performance discriminative classifiers that find the hyperplane providing the best separation between negative and positive instances (Cristianini and Shawe-Taylor, 2000). Our SVM classifiers are trained and tested using Weka 3 and LIBSVM 2.8 (Chang and Lin, 2011). We use the default polynomial kernel ($(u \cdot v/600)^3$) with ϵ (tolerance of termination criterion) set to 1.6. This value was tuned on the AN$\models$N data set, which we never use for testing. In the same initial tuning experiments on the AN$\models$N data set, SVM outperformed decision trees, naive Bayes, and k-nearest neighbors.

We feed each potential entailment pair to SVM by concatenating the two vectors representing the antecedent and consequent expressions.[2] However, for efficiency and to mitigate data sparseness, we reduce the dimensionality of the semantic vectors to 300 columns using Singular Value Decomposition (SVD) before feeding them to the classifier.[3] Because the SVD-reduced semantic

[2]We have tried also to represent a pair by subtracting and by dividing the two vectors. The concatenation operation gave more successful results.

[3]To keep a manageable parameter space, we picked 300 columns without tuning. This is the best value reported in many earlier studies, including classic LSA. Since SVD sometimes improves the semantic space (Landauer and Du-

vectors occupy a 300-dimensional space, the entailment pairs occupy a 600-dimensional space.

An SVM with a polynomial kernel takes into account not only individual input features but also their interactions (Manning et al., 2008, chapter 15). Thus, our classifier can capture not just properties of individual dimensions of the antecedent and consequent pairs, but also properties of their combinations (e.g., the product of the first dimensions of the antecedent and the consequent). We conjecture that this property of SVMs is fundamental to their success at detecting entailment, where relations between the antecedent and the consequent should matter more than their independent characteristics.

4 Predicting lexical entailment from AN $\models$ N evidence

Since the contexts of AN must be a subset of the contexts of N, semantic vectors harvested from AN phrases and their head Ns are by construction in an inclusion relation. The first experiment shows that these vectors constitute excellent training data to discover entailment between nouns. This suggests that the vector pairs representing entailment between nouns are also in an inclusion relation, supporting the conjectures of Kotlerman et al. (2010) and others.

Table 2 reports the results we obtained with $\text{balAPinc}_{\text{upper}}$, $\text{balAPinc}_{\text{AN} \models \text{N}}$ (Section 3.5) and $\text{SVM}_{\text{AN} \models \text{N}}$ (the SVM classifier trained on the AN $\models$ N data). As an upper bound for methods that generalize from AN $\models$ N, we also report the performance of SVM trained with 10-fold cross-validation on the $N_1 \models N_2$ data themselves ($\text{SVM}_{\text{upper}}$). Finally, we tried two baseline classifiers. The first baseline ($\text{fq}(N_1) < \text{fq}(N_2)$) guesses entailment if the first word is less frequent than the second. The second ($\cos(N_1, N_2)$) applies a threshold (determined on the test set) to the cosine similarity of the pair. The results of these baselines shown in Table 2 use SVD; those without SVD are similar. Both baselines outperformed more trivial methods such as random guessing or fixed response, but they performed significantly worse than SVM and balAPinc.

Both methods that generalize entailment from AN $\models$ N to $N_1 \models N_2$ perform well, with 70%

mais, 1997; Rapp, 2003; Schütze, 1997), we tried balAPinc on the SVD-reduced vectors as well, but results were consistently worse than with PMI vectors.

	P	R	F	Accuracy (95% C.I.)
$\text{SVM}_{\text{upper}}$	88.6	88.6	88.5	88.6 (87.3–89.7)
$\text{balAPinc}_{\text{AN} \models \text{N}}$	65.2	87.5	74.7	70.4 (68.7–72.1)
$\text{balAPinc}_{\text{upper}}$	64.4	90.0	75.1	70.1 (68.4–71.8)
$\text{SVM}_{\text{AN} \models \text{N}}$	69.3	69.3	69.3	69.3 (67.6–71.0)
$\cos(N_1, N_2)$	57.7	57.6	57.5	57.6 (55.8–59.5)
$\text{fq}(N_1) < \text{fq}(N_2)$	52.1	52.1	51.8	53.3 (51.4–55.2)

Table 2: Detecting lexical entailment. Results ranked by accuracy and expressed as percentages. 95% confidence intervals around accuracy calculated by binomial exact tests.

accuracy on the test set, which is balanced between positive and negative instances. Interestingly, the balAPinc decision thresholds tuned on the AN $\models$ N set and on the test data are very close (0.26 vs. 0.24), resulting in very similar performance for $\text{balAPinc}_{\text{AN} \models \text{N}}$ and $\text{balAPinc}_{\text{upper}}$. This suggests that the relation captured by balAPinc on the phrasal entailment training data is indeed the same that the measure captures when applied to lexical entailment data.

The success of this first experiment shows that the entailment relation present in the distributional representation of AN phrases and their head Ns transfers to lexical entailment (entailment among Ns). Most importantly, this result demonstrates that the semantic vectors of composite expressions (such as ANs) are useful for lexical entailment. Moreover, the result is in accordance with the view of FS, that ANs and Ns have the same semantic type, and thus they enter entailment relations of the same kind. Finally, the hypothesis that entailment among nouns is reflected by distributional inclusion among their semantic vectors (Kotlerman et al., 2010) is supported both by the successful generalization of the SVM classifier trained on AN $\models$ N pairs and by the good performance of the balAPinc measure.

5 Generalizing QN entailment

The second study is somewhat more ambitious, as it aims to capture and generalize the entailment relation between QPs (of shape QN) using only the corpus-harvested semantic vectors representing these phrases as evidence. We are thus first and foremost interested in testing whether these vectors encode information that can help a power-

	P	R	F	Accuracy (95% C.I.)
$\text{SVM}_{\text{pair-out}}$	76.7	77.0	76.8	78.1 (77.5–78.8)
$\text{SVM}_{\text{quantifier-out}}$	70.1	65.3	68.0	71.0 (70.3–71.7)
$\text{SVM}^{\text{Q}}_{\text{pair-out}}$	67.9	69.8	68.9	70.2 (69.5–70.9)
$\text{SVM}^{\text{Q}}_{\text{quantifier-out}}$	53.3	52.9	53.1	56.0 (55.2–56.8)
$\cos(\text{QN}_1, \text{QN}_2)$	52.9	52.3	52.3	53.1 (52.3–53.9)
$\text{balAPinc}_{\text{AN} \models \text{N}}$	46.7	5.6	10.0	52.5 (51.7–53.3)
$\text{SVM}_{\text{AN} \models \text{N}}$	2.8	42.9	5.2	52.4 (51.7–53.2)
$\text{fq}(\text{QN}_1) < \text{fq}(\text{QN}_2)$	51.0	47.4	49.1	50.2 (49.4–51.0)
$\text{balAPinc}_{\text{upper}}$	47.1	100	64.1	47.2 (46.4–47.9)

Table 3: Detecting quantifier entailment. Results ranked by accuracy and expressed as percentages. 95% confidence intervals around accuracy calculated by binomial exact tests.

ful classifier, such as SVM, to detect entailment.

To abstract away from lexical or other effects linked to a specific quantifier, we consider two challenging training and testing regimes. In the first ($\text{SVM}_{\text{pair-out}}$), we hold out one quantifier pair as testing data and use the other 29 pairs in Table 1 as training data. Thus, for example, the classifier must discover *all dogs* $\models$ *some dogs* without seeing any *all N* $\models$ *some N* instance in the training data. In the second ($\text{SVM}_{\text{quantifier-out}}$), we hold out one of the 12 quantifiers as testing data (that is, hold out every pair involving a certain quantifier) and use the rest as training data. For example, the quantifier must guess *all dogs* $\models$ *some dogs* without ever seeing *all* in the training data. We expect the second training regime to be more difficult, not just because there is less training data, but also because the trained classifier is tested on a quantifier that it has never encountered within any training QN sequence.[4]

Table 3 reports the results for $\text{SVM}_{\text{pair-out}}$ and $\text{SVM}_{\text{quantifier-out}}$, as well as for the methods we tried in the lexical entailment experiments. (As in the first study, the frequency- and cosine-based baselines are only slightly better overall than more trivial baselines.) We consider moreover an alternative approach that ignores the noun altogether and uses vectors for the quantifiers only (e.g., the decision about *all dogs* $\models$ *some dogs* considers the corpus-derived *all* and *some* vectors only). The models resulting from this Q-only strategy are marked with the superscript Q in the table.

The results confirm clearly that semantic vectors for QNs contain enough information to allow a classifier to detect entailment: $\text{SVM}_{\text{quantifier-out}}$ performs as well as the lexical entailment classifiers of our first study, and $\text{SVM}_{\text{pair-out}}$ does even better. This success is especially impressive given our challenging training and testing regimes.

In contrast to the first study, now $\text{SVM}_{\text{AN} \models \text{N}}$, the classifier trained on the AN $\models$ N data set, and balAPinc perform no better than the baselines. (Here $\text{balAPinc}_{\text{upper}}$ and $\text{balAPinc}_{\text{AN} \models \text{N}}$ pick very different thresholds: the first settling on a very low $t = 0.01$, whereas for the second $t = 0.26$.) As predicted by FS (see Section 2.2 above), noun-level entailment does not generalize to quantifier phrase entailment, since the two structures have different semantic types, corresponding to different kinds of entailment relations. Moreover, the failure of balAPinc suggests that, whatever evidence the SVMs rely upon, it is not simple feature inclusion.

Interestingly, even the Q vectors alone encode enough information to capture entailment above chance. Still, the huge drop in performance from $\text{SVM}^{\text{Q}}_{\text{pair-out}}$ to $\text{SVM}^{\text{Q}}_{\text{quantifier-out}}$ suggests that the Q-only method learned ad-hoc properties that do not generalize (e.g., "*all* entails every Q_2").

Tables 1 and 4 break down the SVM results by (pairs of) quantifiers. We highlight the remarkable dichotomy in Table 4 between the good performance on the universal-like quantifiers (*each, every, all, much*) and the poor performance on the existential-like ones (*some, no, both, either*).

In sum, the QN experiments show that semantic vectors contain enough information to detect a logical relation such as entailment not only between words, but also between phrases containing quantifiers that determine their entailment relation. While a flexible classifier such as SVM performs this task well, neither measuring feature inclusion nor generalizing nominal entailment works. SVMs are evidently tapping into other properties of the vectors.

[4] In our initial experiments, we added negative entailment instances by blindly permuting the nouns, under the assumption that $Q_1 N_1$ typically does not entail $Q_2 N_2$ when $Q_1 \neq Q_2$ and $N_1 \neq N_2$. These additional instances turned out to be much easier to classify: adding an equal proportion of them to the training data and testing data, such that the number of instances where $N_1 = N_2$ and where $N_1 \neq N_2$ is equal, reduced every error rate roughly by half. The reported results do not involve these additional instances.

Quantifier	Instances		Correct	
	$\models$	$\not\models$	$\models$	$\not\models$
each	656	656	649	637 (98%)
every	460	1322	402	1293 (95%)
much	248	0	216	0 (87%)
all	2949	2641	2011	2494 (81%)
several	1731	1509	1302	1267 (79%)
many	3341	4163	2349	3443 (77%)
few	0	461	0	311 (67%)
most	928	832	549	511 (60%)
some	4062	3145	1780	2190 (55%)
no	0	714	0	380 (53%)
both	636	1404	589	303 (44%)
either	63	63	2	41 (34%)
Total	*15074*	*16910*	*9849*	*12870 (71%)*

Table 4: Breakdown of results with leaving-one-quantifier-out ($SVM_{quantifier\text{-}out}$) training regime.

6 Conclusion

Our main results are as follows.

1. Corpus-harvested semantic vectors representing adjective-noun constructions and their heads encode a relation of entailment that can be exploited to train a classifier to detect lexical entailment. In particular, a relation of feature inclusion between the narrower antecedent and broader consequent terms captures both AN $\models$ N and $N_1 \models N_2$ entailment.

2. The semantic vectors of quantifier-noun constructions also encode information sufficient to learn an entailment relation that generalizes to QNs containing quantifiers that were not seen during training.

3. Neither the entailment information encoded in AN $\models$ N vectors nor the balAPinc measure generalizes well to entailment detection in QNs. This result suggests that QN vectors encode a different kind of entailment, as also suggested by type distinctions in Formal Semantics.

In future work, we want first of all to conduct an analysis of the features in the $Q_1N \models Q_2N$ vectors that are crucially exploited by our successful entailment recognizers, in order to understand which characteristics of entailment are encoded in these vectors.

Very importantly, instead of extracting vectors representing phrases directly from the corpus, we intend to derive them by compositional operations proposed in the literature (see Section 2.1 above). We will look for composition methods producing vector representations of composite expressions that are as good as (or better than) vectors directly extracted from the corpus at encoding entailment.

Finally, we would like to evaluate our entailment detection strategies for larger phrases and sentences, possibly containing multiple quantifiers, and eventually embed them as core components of an RTE system.

Acknowledgments

We thank the Erasmus Mundus EMLCT Program for the student and visiting scholar grants to the third and fourth author, respectively. The first two authors are partially funded by the ERC 2011 Starting Independent Research Grant supporting the COMPOSES project (nr. 283554). We are grateful to Gemma Boleda, Louise McNally, and the anonymous reviewers for valuable comments, and to Ido Dagan for important insights into entailment from an empirical point of view.

References

Timothy Baldwin, Colin Bannard, Takaaki Tanaka, and Dominic Widdows. 2003. An empirical model of multiword expression decomposability. In *Proceedings of the ACL 2003 Workshop on Multiword Expressions*, pages 89–96.

Marco Baroni and Alessandro Lenci. 2011. How we BLESSed distributional semantic evaluation. In *Proceedings of the Workshop on Geometrical Models of Natural Language Semantics*.

Marco Baroni and Roberto Zamparelli. 2010. Nouns are vectors, adjectives are matrices: Representing adjective-noun constructions in semantic space. In *Proceedings of EMNLP*, pages 1183–1193, Boston, MA.

Johan Bos and Katja Markert. 2006. When logical inference helps determining textual entailment (and when it doesn't. In *Proceedings of the Second PASCAL Challenges Workshop on Recognising Textual Entailment*.

Paul Buitelaar and Philipp Cimiano. 2008. *Bridging the Gap between Text and Knowledge*. IOS, Amsterdam.

Nathanael Chambers, Daniel Cer, Trond Grenager, David Hall, Chloe Kiddon, Bill MacCartney, Marie-Catherine de Marneffe, Daniel Ramage, Eric Yeh, and Christopher D. Manning. 2007. Learning alignments and leveraging natural logic. In *ACL-PASCAL Workshop on Textual Entailment and Paraphrasing*.

Chih-Chung Chang and Chih-Jen Lin. 2011. LIBSVM: A library for support vector machines. *ACM Transactions on Intelligent Systems and Technology*, 2(3):27:1–27:27.

Kenneth Church and Peter Hanks. 1990. Word association norms, mutual information, and lexicography. *Computational Linguistics*, 16(1):22–29.

Nello Cristianini and John Shawe-Taylor. 2000. *An introduction to Support Vector Machines and other kernel-based learning methods*. Cambridge University Press, Cambridge.

Ido Dagan, Bill Dolan, Bernardo Magnini, and Dan Roth. 2009. Recognizing textual entailment: rational, evaluation and approaches. *Natural Language Engineering*, 15:459–476.

Katrin Erk. 2009. Supporting inferences in semantic space: representing words as regions. In *Proceedings of IWCS*, pages 104–115, Tilburg, Netherlands.

Maayan Geffet and Ido Dagan. 2005. The distributional inclusion hypotheses and lexical entailment. In *Proceedings of ACL*, pages 107–114, Ann Arbor, MI.

Edward Grefenstette and Mehrnoosh Sadrzadeh. 2011. Experimental support for a categorical compositional distributional model of meaning. In *Proceedings of EMNLP*, pages 1395–1404, Edinburgh.

Emiliano Guevara. 2010. A regression model of adjective-noun compositionality in distributional semantics. In *Proceedings of the ACL GEMS Workshop*, pages 33–37, Uppsala, Sweden.

Marti Hearst. 1992. Automatic acquisition of hyponyms from large text corpora. In *Proceedings of COLING*, pages 539–545, Nantes, France.

Irene Heim and Angelika Kratzer. 1998. *Semantics in Generative Grammar*. Blackwell, Oxford.

Lili Kotlerman, Ido Dagan, Idan Szpektor, and Maayan Zhitomirsky-Geffet. 2010. Directional distributional similarity for lexical inference. *Natural Language Engineering*, 16(4):359–389.

Milen Kouleykov and Bernardo Magnini. 2005. Tree edit sistance for textual entailment. In *Proceedings of RALNP-2005, International Conference on Recent Advances in Natural Language Processing*, pages 271–278.

Thomas Landauer and Susan Dumais. 1997. A solution to Plato's problem: The latent semantic analysis theory of acquisition, induction, and representation of knowledge. *Psychological Review*, 104(2):211–240.

Dekang Lin. 1998. An information-theoretic definition of similarity. In *Proceedings of ICML*, pages 296–304, Madison, WI, USA.

Kevin Lund and Curt Burgess. 1996. Producing high-dimensional semantic spaces from lexical co-occurrence. *Behavior Research Methods*, 28:203–208.

Chris Manning, Prabhakar Raghavan, and Hinrich Schütze. 2008. *Introduction to Information Retrieval*. Cambridge University Press, Cambridge.

Jeff Mitchell and Mirella Lapata. 2010. Composition in distributional models of semantics. *Cognitive Science*, 34(8):1388–1429.

Richard Montague. 1970. Universal Grammar. *Theoria*, 36:373–398.

Patrick Pantel and Deepak Ravichandran. 2004. Automatically labeliing semantic classes. In *Proceedings of HLT-NAACL 2004*, pages 321–328.

Reinhard Rapp. 2003. Word sense discovery based on sense descriptor dissimilarity. In *Proceedings of the 9th MT Summit*, pages 315–322, New Orleans, LA.

Magnus Sahlgren. 2006. *The Word-Space Model*. Dissertation, Stockholm University.

Helmut Schmid. 1995. Improvements in part-of-speech tagging with an application to German. In *Proceedings of the EACL-SIGDAT Workshop*, Dublin, Ireland.

Hinrich Schütze. 1997. *Ambiguity Resolution in Natural Language Learning*. CSLI, Stanford, CA.

Rion Snow, Daniel Juravsky, and Andrew Y. Ng. 2005. Learning syntactic patterns for automatic hypernym discovery. In *Proceedings of NIPS 17*.

Rion Snow, Daniel Juravsky, and Andrew Y. Ng. 2006. Semantic taxonomy induction from heterogenous evidence. In *Proceedings of ACL 2006*, pages 801–808.

Richmond H. Thomason, editor. 1974. *Formal Philosophy: Selected Papers of Richard Montague*. Yale University Press, New York.

Peter Turney and Patrick Pantel. 2010. From frequency to meaning: Vector space models of semantics. *Journal of Artificial Intelligence Research*, 37:141–188.

Peter Turney. 2008. A uniform approach to analogies, synonyms, antonyms and associations. In *Proceedings of COLING*, pages 905–912, Manchester, UK.

Julie Weeds, David Weir, and Diana McCarthy. 2004. Characterising measures of lexical distributional similarity. In *Proceedings of the 20th International Conference of Computational Linguistics, COLING-2004*, pages 1015–1021.

Fabio M. Zanzotto, Marco Pennacchiotti, and Alessandro Moschitti. 2007. Shallow semantics in fast textual entailment rule learners. In *Proceedings of the ACL-PASCAL Workshop on Textual Entailment and Paraphrasing*.

Maayan Zhitomirsky-Geffet and Ido Dagan. 2010. Bootstrapping distributional feature vector quality. *Computational Linguistics*, 35(3):435–461.

Evaluating Distributional Models of Semantics for Syntactically Invariant Inference

Jackie CK Cheung and Gerald Penn
Department of Computer Science
University of Toronto
Toronto, ON, M5S 3G4, Canada
{jcheung,gpenn}@cs.toronto.edu

Abstract

A major focus of current work in distributional models of semantics is to construct phrase representations compositionally from word representations. However, the syntactic contexts which are modelled are usually severely limited, a fact which is reflected in the lexical-level WSD-like evaluation methods used. In this paper, we broaden the scope of these models to build sentence-level representations, and argue that phrase representations are best evaluated in terms of the inference decisions that they support, invariant to the particular syntactic constructions used to guide composition. We propose two evaluation methods in relation classification and QA which reflect these goals, and apply several recent compositional distributional models to the tasks. We find that the models outperform a simple lemma overlap baseline slightly, demonstrating that distributional approaches can already be useful for tasks requiring deeper inference.

1 Introduction

A number of unsupervised semantic models (Mitchell and Lapata, 2008, for example) have recently been proposed which are inspired at least in part by the distributional hypothesis (Harris, 1954)—that a word's meaning can be characterized by the contexts in which it appears. Such models represent word meaning as one or more high-dimensional vectors which capture the lexical and syntactic contexts of the word's occurrences in a training corpus.

Much of the recent work in this area has, following Mitchell and Lapata (2008), focused on the notion of compositionality as the litmus test of a truly semantic model. Compositionality is a natural way to construct representations of linguistic units larger than a word, and it has a long history in Montagovian semantics for dealing with argument structure and assembling rich semantical expressions of the kind found in predicate logic.

While compositionality may thus provide a convenient recipe for producing representations of propositionally typed phrases, it is not a necessary condition for a semantic representation. Rather, that distinction still belongs to the crucial ability to support inference. It is not the intention of this paper to argue for or against compositionality in semantic representations. Rather, our interest is in evaluating semantic models in order to determine their suitability for inference tasks. In particular, we contend that it is desirable and arguably necessary for a compositional semantic representation to support inference *invariantly*, in the sense that the particular syntactic construction that guided the composition should not matter relative to the representations of syntactically different phrases with the same meanings. For example, we can assert that *John threw the ball* and *The ball was thrown by John* have the same meaning for the purposes of inference, even though they differ syntactically.

An analogy can be drawn to research in image processing, in which it is widely regarded as important for the representations of images to be invariant to rotation and scaling. What we should want is a representation of sentence meaning that is invariant to diathesis, other regular syntactic alternations in the assignment of argument structure, and, ideally, even invariant to other meaning-preserving or near-preserving paraphrases.

Existing evaluations of distributional semantic models fall short of measuring this. One evaluation approach consists of lexical-level word substitution tasks which primarily evaluate a system's ability to disambiguate word senses within a controlled syntactic environment (McCarthy and Navigli, 2009, for example). Another approach is to evaluate parsing accuracy (Socher et al., 2010, for example), which is really a formalism-specific approximation to argument structure analysis. These evaluations may certainly be relevant to specific components of, for example, machine translation or natural language generation systems, but they tell us little about a semantic model's ability to support inference.

In this paper, we propose a general framework for evaluating distributional semantic models that build sentence representations, and suggest two evaluation methods that test the notion of structurally invariant inference directly. Both rely on determining whether sentences express the same semantic relation between entities, a crucial step in solving a wide variety of inference tasks like recognizing textual entailment, information retrieval, question answering, and summarization.

The first evaluation is a relation classification task, where a semantic model is tested on its ability to recognize whether a pair of sentences both contain a particular semantic relation, such as *Company X acquires Company Y*. The second task is a question answering task, the goal of which is to locate the sentence in a document that contains the answer. Here, the semantic model must match the question, which expresses a proposition with a missing argument, to the answer-bearing sentence which contains the full proposition.

We apply these new evaluation protocols to several recent distributional models, extending several of them to build sentence representations. We find that the models outperform a simple lemma overlap model only slightly, but that combining these models with the lemma overlap model can improve performance. This result is likely due to weaknesses in current models' ability to deal with issues such as named entities, coreference, and negation, which are not emphasized by existing evaluation methods, but it does suggest that distributional models of semantics can play a more central role in systems that require deep, precise inference.

2 Compositionality and Distributional Semantics

The idea of compositionality has been central to understanding contemporary natural language semantics from an historiographic perspective. The idea is often credited to Frege, although in fact Frege had very little to say about compositionality that had not already been repeated since the time of Aristotle (Hodges, 2005). Our modern notion of compositionality took shape primarily with the work of Tarski (1956), who was actually arguing that a central difference between formal languages and natural languages is that natural language is not compositional. This in turn was the "the contention that an important theoretical difference exists between formal and natural languages," that Richard Montague so famously rejected (Montague, 1974). Compositionality also features prominently in Fodor and Pylyshyn's (1988) rejection of early connectionist representations of natural language semantics, which seems to have influenced Mitchell and Lapata (2008) as well.

Logic-based forms of compositional semantics have long strived for syntactic invariance in meaning representations, which is known as the doctrine of the canonical form. The traditional justification for canonical forms is that they allow easy access to a knowledge base to retrieve some desired information, which amounts to a form of inference. Our work can be seen as an extension of this notion to distributional semantic models with a more general notion of representational similarity and inference.

There are many regular alternations that semantics models have tried to account for such as passive or dative alternations. There are also many lexical paraphrases which can take drastically different syntactic forms. Take the following example from Poon and Domingos (2009), in which the same semantic relation can be expressed by a transitive verb or an attributive prepositional phrase:

(1) *Utah <u>borders</u> Idaho.*
Utah <u>is next to</u> Idaho.

In distributional semantics, the original sentence similarity test proposed by Kintsch (2001) served as the inspiration for the evaluation performed by Mitchell and Lapata (2008) and most later work in the area. Intransitive verbs are given in the context of their syntactic subject, and candidate synonyms are ranked for their appropriateness. This method targets the fact that a synonym is appropriate for only some of the verb's senses, and the intended verb sense depends on the surrounding context. For example, *burn* and *beam* are both synonyms of *glow*, but given a particular subject, one of the synonyms (called the High similarity landmark) may be a more appropriate substitution than the other (the Low similarity landmark). So, if *the fire* is the subject, *glowed* is the High similarity landmark, and *beamed* the Low similarity landmark.

Fundamentally, this method was designed as a demonstration that compositionality in computing phrasal semantic representations does not interfere with the ability of a representation to synthesize non-compositional collocation effects that contribute to the disambiguation of homographs. Here, word-sense disambiguation is implicitly viewed as a very restricted, highly lexicalized case of inference for selecting the appropriate disjunct in the representation of a word's meaning.

Kintsch (2001) was interested in sentence similarity, but he only conducted his evaluation on a few hand-selected examples. Mitchell and Lapata (2008) conducted theirs on a much larger scale, but chose to focus only on this single case of syntactic combination, intransitive verbs and their subjects, in order to "factor out inessential degrees of freedom" to compare their various alternative models more equitably. This was not necessary—using the same, sufficiently large, unbiased but syntactically heterogeneous sample of evaluation sentences would have served as an adequate control—and this decision furthermore prevents the evaluation from testing the desired invariance of the semantic representation.

Other lexical evaluations suffer from the same problem. One uses the WordSim-353 dataset (Finkelstein et al., 2002), which contains human word pair similarity judgments that semantic models should reproduce. However, the word pairs are given without context, and homography is unaddressed. Also, it is unclear how reliable the similarity scores are, as different annotators may interpret the integer scale of similarity scores differently. Recent work uses this dataset mostly for parameter tuning. Another is the lexical paraphrase task of McCarthy and Navigli (2009), in which words are given in the context of the surrounding sentence, and the task is to rank a given list of proposed substitutions for that word. The list of substitutions as well as the correct rankings are elicited from annotators. This task was originally conceived as an applied evaluation of WSD systems, not an evaluation of phrase representations.

Parsing accuracy has been used as a preliminary evaluation of semantic models that produce syntactic structure (Socher et al., 2010; Wu and Schuler, 2011). However, syntax does not always reflect semantic content, and we are specifically interested in supporting syntactic invariance when doing semantic inference. Also, this type of evaluation is tied to a particular grammar formalism.

The existing evaluations that are most similar in spirit to what we propose are paraphrase detection tasks that do not assume a restricted syntactic context. Washtell (2011) collected human judgments on the general meaning similarity of candidate phrase pairs. Unfortunately, no additional guidance on the definition of "most similar in meaning" was provided, and it appears likely that subjects conflated lexical, syntactic, and semantic relatedness. Dolan and Brockett (2005) define paraphrase detection as identifying sentences that are in a bidirectional entailment relation. While such sentences do support exactly the same inferences, we are also interested in the inferences that can be made from similar sentences that are not paraphrases according to this strict definition — a situation that is more often encountered in end applications. Thus, we adopt a less restricted notion of paraphrasis.

3 An Evaluation Framework

We now describe a simple, general framework for evaluating semantic models. Our framework consists of the following components: a semantic model to be evaluated, pairs of sentences that are considered to have high similarity, and pairs of sentences that are considered to have low similarity.

In particular, the semantic model is a binary function, $s = \mathcal{M}(x, x')$, which returns a real-valued similarity score, s, given a pair of arbitrary linguistic units (that is, words, phrases, sentences, etc.), x and x'. Note that this formulation of the semantic model is agnostic to whether the models use compositionality to build a phrase representation from constituent representations, and even to the actual representation used. The model is tested by applying it to each element in the following two sets:

$$H = \{(h, h')|h \text{ and } h' \text{ are linguistic units with high similarity}\} \quad (2)$$

$$L = \{(l, l')|l \text{ and } l' \text{ are linguistic units with low similarity}\} \quad (3)$$

The resulting sets of similarity scores are:

$$\mathcal{S}^H = \{\mathcal{M}(h, h')|(h, h') \in H\} \quad (4)$$

$$\mathcal{S}^L = \{\mathcal{M}(l, l')|(l, l') \in L\} \quad (5)$$

The semantic model is evaluated according to its ability to separate $\mathcal{S}^H$ and $\mathcal{S}^L$. We will define specific measures of separation for the tasks that we propose shortly. While the particular definitions of "high similarity" and "low similarity" depend on the task, at the crux of both our evaluations is that two sentences are similar if they express the same semantic relation between a given entity pair, and dissimilar otherwise. This threshold for similarity is closely tied to the argument structure of the sentence, and allows considerable flexibility in the other semantic content that may be contained in the sentence, unlike the bidirectional paraphrase detection task. Yet it ensures that a consistent and useful distinction for inference is being detected, unlike unconstrained similarity judgments.

Also, compared to word similarity assessments or paraphrase elicitation, determining whether a sentence expresses a semantic relation is a much easier task cognitively for human judges. This binary judgment does not involve interpreting a numerical scale or coming up with an open-ended set of alternative paraphrases. It is thus easier to get reliable annotated data.

Below, we present two tasks that instantiate this evaluation framework and choice of similarity threshold. They differ in that the first is targeted towards recognizing declarative sentences or phrases, while the second is targeted towards a question answering scenario, where one argument in the semantic relation is queried.

3.1 Task 1: Relation Classification

The first task is a relation classification task. Relation extraction and recognition are central to a variety of other tasks, such as information retrieval, ontology construction, recognizing textual entailment and question answering.

In this task, the high and the low similarity sentence pairs are constructed in the following manner. First, a target semantic relation, such as *Company X acquires Company Y* is chosen, and entities are chosen for each slot in the relation, such as *Company X=Pfizer* and *Company Y=Rinat Neuroscience*. Then, sentences containing these entities are extracted and divided into two subsets. In one of them, E, the entities are in the target semantic relation, while in the other, NE, they are not. The evaluation sets H and L are then constructed as follows:

$$H = E \times E \setminus \{(e, e)|e \in E\} \quad (6)$$

$$L = E \times NE \quad (7)$$

In other words, the high similarity sentence pairs are all the pairs where both express the target semantic relation, except the pairs between a sentence and itself, while the low similarity pairs are all the pairs where exactly one of the two sentences expresses the target relation.

Several sentences expressing the relation *Pfizer acquires Rinat Neuroscience* are shown in Examples 8 to 10. These sentences illustrate the amount of syntactic and lexical variation that the semantic model must recognize as expressing the same semantic relation. In particular, besides recognizing synonymy or near-synonymy at the lexical level, models must also account for subcategorization differences, extra arguments or adjuncts, and part-of-speech differences due to nominalization.

(8) *Pfizer buys Rinat Neuroscience to extend neuroscience research and in doing so acquires a product candidate for OA.* (lexical difference)

(9) *A month earlier, Pfizer paid an estimated several hundred million dollars for biotech firm Rinat Neuroscience.* (extra argument, subcategorization)

(10) *Pfizer to Expand Neuroscience Research With Acquisition of Biotech Company Rinat Neuroscience* (nominalization)

Since our interest is to measure the models' ability to separate $\mathcal{S}^H$ and $\mathcal{S}^L$ in an unsupervised setting, standard supervised classification accuracy is not applicable. Instead, we employ the area under a ROC curve (AUC), which does not depend on choosing an arbitrary classification threshold. A ROC curve is a plot of the true positive versus false positive rate of a binary classifier as the classification threshold is varied. The area under a ROC curve can thus be seen as the performance of linear classifiers over the scores produced by the semantic model. The AUC can also be interpreted as the probability that a randomly chosen positive instance will have a higher similarity score than a randomly chosen negative instance. A random classifier is expected to have an AUC of 0.5.

3.2 Task 2: Restricted QA

The second task that we propose is a restricted form of question answering. In this task, the system is given a question q and a document $\mathcal{D}$ consisting of a list of sentences, in which one of the sentences contains the answer to the question. We define:

$$H = \{(q, d) | d \in \mathcal{D} \text{ and } d \text{ answers } q\} \tag{11}$$

$$L = \{(q, d) | d \in \mathcal{D} \text{ and } d \text{ does not answer } q\} \tag{12}$$

In other words, the sentences are divided into two subsets; those that contain the answer to q should be similar to q, while those that do not should be dissimilar. We also assume that only one sentence in each document contains the answer, so H contains only one sentence.

Unrestricted question answering is a difficult problem that forces a semantic representation to deal sensibly with a number of other semantic issues such as coreference and information aggregation which still seem to be out of reach for contemporary distributional models of meaning. Since our focus in this work is on argument structure semantics, we restrict the question-answer pairs to those that only require dealing with paraphrases of this type.

To do so, we semi-automatically restrict the question-answer pairs by using the output of an unsupervised clustering semantic parser (Poon and Domingos, 2009). The semantic parser clusters semantic sub-expressions derived from a dependency parse of the sentence, so that those sub-expressions that express the same semantic relations are clustered. The parser is used to answer questions, and the output of the parser is manually checked. We use only those cases that have thus been determined to be correct question-answer pairs. As a result of this restriction, this task is rather more like Task 1 in how it tests a model's ability to recognize lexical and syntactic paraphrases. This task also involves recognizing voicing alternations, which were automatically extracted by the semantic parser.

An example of a question-answer pair involving a voicing alternation that is used in this task is presented in Example 13.

(13) Q: *What does il-2 activate?*
A: *PI3K*
Sentence: *Phosphatidyl inositol 3-kinase (PI3K) is activated by IL-2.*

Since there is only one element in H and hence $\mathcal{S}^H$ for each question and document, we measure the separation between $\mathcal{S}^H$ and $\mathcal{S}^L$ using the rank of the score of answer-bearing sentence among the scores of all the sentences in the document. We normalize the rank so that it is between 0 (ranked least similar) and 1 (ranked most similar). Where ties occur, the sentence is ranked as if it were in the median position among the tied sentences. If the question-answer pairs are zero-indexed by i, $answer(i)$ is the index of the sentence containing the answer for the ith pair, and $length(i)$ is the number of sentences in the document, then the mean normalized rank score of a system is:

$$\overline{norm\_rank} = \mathop{\mathbf{E}}_{i}\left[1 - \frac{answer(i)}{length(i) - 1}\right] \tag{14}$$

4 Experiments

We drew a number of recent distributional semantic models to compare in this paper. We first describe the models and our reimplementation of them, before describing the tasks and the datasets used in detail and the results.

4.1 Distributional Semantic Models

We tested four recent distributional models and a lemma overlap baseline, which we now describe. We extended several of the models to compositionally construct phrase representations using component-wise vector addition and multiplication, as we note below. Since the focus of this paper is on evaluation methods for such models, we did not experiment with other compositionality operators. We do note, however, that component-wise operators have been popular in recent literature, and have been applied across unrestricted syntactic contexts (Mitchell and Lapata, 2009), so there is value in evaluating the performance of these operators in itself. The models were trained on the Gigaword corpus (2nd ed., ~2.3B words). All models use cosine similarity to measure the similarity between representations, except for the baseline model.

Lemma Overlap This baseline simply represents a sentence as the counts of each lemma present in the sentence after removing stop words. Let a sentence x consist of lemma-tokens $m_1, \ldots, m_{|x|}$. The similarity between two sentences is then defined as

$$\mathcal{M}(x, x') = \#In(x, x') + \#In(x', x) \quad (15)$$

$$\#In(x, x') = \sum_{i=1}^{|x|} \mathbf{1}_{x'}(m_i) \quad (16)$$

where $\mathbf{1}_{x'}(m_i)$ is an indicator function that returns 1 if $m_i \in x'$, and 0 otherwise. This definition accounts for multiple occurrences of a lemma.

M&L Mitchell and Lapata (2008) propose a framework for compositional distributional semantics using a standard term-context vector space word representation. A phrase is represented as a vector of context-word counts (actually, pmi-scaled values), which is derived compositionally by a function over constituent vectors, such as component-wise addition or multiplication. This model ignores syntactic relations and is insensitive to word-order.

E&P Erk and Padó (2008) introduce a structured vector space model which uses syntactic dependencies to model the selectional preferences of words. The vector representation of a word in context depends on the inverse selectional preferences of its dependents, and the selectional preferences of its head. For example, suppose *catch* occurs with a dependent *ball* in a direct object relation. The vector for *catch* would then be influenced by the inverse direct object preferences of *ball* (e.g. *throw, organize*), and the vector for *ball* would be influenced by the selectional preferences of *catch* (e.g. *cold, drift*). More formally, given words a and b in a dependency relation r, a distributional representation of a, v_a, the representation of a in context, a', is given by

$$a' = v_a \odot R_b(r^{-1}) \quad (17)$$

$$R_b(r) = \sum_{c: f(c,r,b) > \theta} f(c, r, b) \cdot v_c, \quad (18)$$

where $R_b(r)$ is the vector describing the selectional preference of word b in relation r, $f(c, r, b)$ is the frequency of this dependency triple, θ is a frequency threshold to weed out uncommon dependency triples (10 in our experiments), and $\odot$ is a vector combination operator, here component-wise multiplication. We extend the model to compute sentence representations from the contextualized word vectors using component-wise addition and multiplication.

TFP Thater et al. (2010)'s model is also sensitive to selectional preferences, but to two degrees. For example, the vector for *catch* might contain a dimension labelled (`OBJ,OBJ-1,throw`), which indicates the strength of connection between the two verbs through all of the co-occurring direct objects which they share. Unlike E&P, TFP's model encodes the selectional preferences in a single vector using frequency counts. We extend the model to the sentence level with component-wise addition and multiplication, and word vectors are contextualized by the dependency neighbours. We use a frequency threshold of 10 and a pmi threshold of 2 to prune infrequent word and dependencies.

D&L Dinu and Lapata (2010) (D&L) assume a global set of latent senses for all words, and models each word as a mixture over these latent senses. The vector for a word t_i in the context of a word c_j is modelled by

$$v(t_i, c_j) = P(z_1|t_i, c_j), ...P(z_K|t_i, c_j) \quad (19)$$

where $z_{1...K}$ are the latent senses. By making independence assumptions and decomposing probabilities, training becomes a matter of estimating the probability distributions $P(z_k|t_i)$ and $P(c_j|z_k)$ from data. While Dinu and Lapata (2010) describe two methods to do so, based on non-negative matrix factorization and latent Dirichlet allocation, the performances are similar, so we tested only the latent Dirichlet allocation method. Like the two previous models, we extend the model to build sentence representations

	Pfizer/Rinat N.	Yahoo/Inktomi	Besson/Paris	Antoinette/Vienna	Average
Overlap	0.7393	0.6007	0.7395	0.8914	0.7427
Models trained on the entire GigaWord					
M&L add	0.6196	0.5387	0.5259	0.7275	0.6029
M&L mult	0.9036	0.6099	0.6443	0.8467	0.7511
D&L add	0.9214	0.8168	0.6989	0.8932	**0.8326**
D&L mult	0.7732	0.6734	0.6527	0.7659	0.7163
Models trained on the AFP section					
E&P add	0.7536	0.4933	0.2780	0.6408	0.5414
E&P mult	0.5268	0.5328	0.5252	0.8421	0.6067
TFP add	0.4357	0.5325	0.8725	0.7183	0.6398
TFP mult	0.5554	0.5524	0.7283	0.6917	0.6320
M&L add	0.5643	0.5504	0.4594	0.7640	0.5845
M&L mult	0.8679	0.6324	0.4356	0.8258	0.6904
D&L add	0.8143	0.9062	0.6373	0.8664	**0.8061**
D&L mult	0.8429	0.7461	0.645	0.5948	0.7072

Table 1: Task 1 results in AUC scores. The values in bold indicate the best performing model for a particular training corpus. The expected random baseline performance is 0.5.

Entities: $\{X, Y\}$	+	N
Relation: acquires		
{Pfizer, Rinat Neuroscience}	41	50
{Yahoo, Inktomi}	115	433
Relation: was born in		
{Luc Besson, Paris}	6	126
{Marie Antoinette, Vienna}	39	105

Table 2: Task 1 dataset characteristics. N is the total number of sentences. + is the number of sentences that express the relation.

from the contextualized representations. We set the number of latent senses to 1200, and train for 600 Gibbs sampling iterations.

4.2 Training and Parameter Settings

We reimplemented these four models, following the parameter settings described by previous work where possible, though we also aimed for consistency in parameter settings between models (for example, in the number of context words). For the non-baseline models, we followed previous work and model only the 30000 most frequent lemmata. Context vectors are constructed using a symmetric window of 5 words, and their dimensions represent the 3000 most frequent lemmatized context words excluding stop words. Due to resource limitations, we trained the syntactic models over the AFP subset of Gigaword (~338M words). We also trained the other two models on just the AFP portion for comparison. Note that the AFP portion of Gigaword is three times larger than the BNC corpus (~100M words), on which several previous syntactic models were trained. Because our main goal is to test the general performance of the models and to demonstrate the feasibility of our evaluation methods, we did not further tune the parameter settings to each of the tasks, as doing so would likely only yield minor improvements.

4.3 Task 1

We used the dataset by Bunescu and Mooney (2007), which we selected because it contains multiple realizations of an entity pair in a target semantic relation, unlike similar datasets such as the one by Roth and Yih (2002). Controlling for the target entity pair in this manner makes the task more difficult, because the semantic model cannot make use of distributional information about the entity pair in inference. The dataset is separated into subsets depending on the target binary relation (*Company X acquires Company Y* or *Person X was born in Place Y*) and the entity pair (e.g., *Yahoo* and *Inktomi*) (Table 2).

The dataset was constructed semi-automatically using a Google search for the two entities in order with up to seven content words in between. Then, the extracted sentences were hand-labelled with whether they express the target relation. Because the order of the entities has been fixed, passive alternations do not appear

	Pure models		*Mixed models*	
	All	*Subset*	*All*	*Subset*
Overlap	**0.8770**	**0.7291**	0.8770	0.7291
Models trained on the entire GigaWord				
M&L add	0.7467	0.6106	0.8782	0.7523
M&L mult	0.5331	0.5690	0.8841	0.7678
D&L add	0.6552	0.5716	0.8791	0.7539
D&L mult	0.5488	0.5255	0.8841	0.7466
Models trained on the AFP section				
E&P add	0.4589	0.4516	0.8748	0.7375
E&P mult	0.5201	0.5584	0.8882	0.7719
TFP add	0.6887	0.6443	**0.8940**	**0.7871**
TFP mult	0.5210	0.5199	0.8785	0.7432
M&L add	0.7588	0.6206	0.8710	0.7371
M&L mult	0.5710	0.5540	0.8801	0.7540
D&L add	0.6358	0.5402	0.8713	0.7305
D&L mult	0.5647	0.5461	0.8856	0.7683

Table 3: Task 2 results, in normalized rank scores. *Subset* is the cases where lemma overlap does not achieve a perfect score. The two columns on the right indicate performance using the sum of the scores from the lemma overlap and the semantic model. The expected random baseline performance is 0.5.

in this dataset.

The results for Task 1 indicate that the D&L addition model performs the best (Table 1), though the lemma overlap model presents a surprisingly strong baseline. The syntax-modulated E&P and TFP models perform poorly on this task, even when compared to the other models trained on the AFP subset. The M&L multiplication model outperforms the addition model, a result which corroborates previous findings on the lexical substitution task. The same does not hold in the D&L latent sense space. Overall, some of the datasets (*Yahoo* and *Antoinette*) appear to be easier for the models than others (*Pfizer* and *Besson*), but more entity pairs and relations would be needed to investigate the models' variance across datasets.

4.4 Task 2

We used the question-answer pairs extracted by the Poon and Domingos (2009) semantic parser from the GENIA biomedical corpus that have been manually checked to be correct (295 pairs). Because our models were trained on newspaper text, they required adaptation to this specialized domain. Thus, we also trained the M&L, E&P and TFP models on the GENIA corpus, backing off to word vectors from the GENIA corpus when a word vector could not be found in the Gigaword-trained model. We could not do this for the D&L model, since the global latent senses that are found by latent Dirichlet allocation training do not have any absolute meaning that holds across multiple runs. Instead, we found the 5 words in the Gigaword-trained D&L model that were closest to each novel word in the GENIA corpus according to cosine similarity over the co-occurrence vectors of the words in the GENIA corpus, and took their average latent sense distributions as the vector for that word.

Unlike in Task 1, there is no control for the named entities in a sentence, because one of the entities in the semantic relation is missing. Also, distributional models have problems in dealing with named entities which are common in this corpus, such as the names of genes and proteins. To address these issues, we tested hybrid models where the similarity score from a semantic model is added to the similarity score from the lemma overlap model.

The results are presented in Table 3. Lemma overlap again presents a strong baseline, but the hybridized models are able to outperform simple lemma overlap. Unlike in Task 1, the E&P and TFP models are comparable to the D&L model, and the mixed TFP addition model achieves the best result, likely due to the need to more precisely distinguish syntactic roles in this task. The D&L addition model, which achieved the best performance in Task 1, does not perform as well in this task. This could be due to the domain adaptation procedure for the D&L model, which could not be reasonably trained on such a small, specialized corpus.

5 Related Work

Turney and Pantel (2010) survey various types of vector space models and applications thereof in computational linguistics. We summarize below a number of other word- or phrase-level distributional models.

Several approaches are specialized to deal with homography. The top-down *multi-prototype* approach determines a number of senses for each word, and then clusters the occurrences of the word (Reisinger and Mooney, 2010) into these senses. A prototype vector is created for each of these sense clusters. When a new occurrence of a word is encountered, it is represented as a combination of the prototype vectors, with the degree of influence from each prototype determined by the similarity of the new context to the existing sense contexts. In contrast, the bottom-up *exemplar*-based approach assumes that each occurrence of a word expresses a different sense of the word. The most similar senses of the word are activated when a new occurrence of it is encountered and combined, for example with a kNN algorithm (Erk and Padó, 2010).

The models we compared and the above work assume each dimension in the feature vector corresponds to a context word. In contrast, Washtell (2011) uses potential paraphrases directly as dimensions in his *expectation vectors*. Unfortunately, this approach does not outperform various context word-based approaches in two phrase similarity tasks.

In terms of the vector composition function, component-wise addition and multiplication are the most popular in recent work, but there exist a number of other operators such as tensor product and convolution product, which are reviewed by Widdows (2008). Instead of vector space representations, one could also use a matrix space representation with its much more expressive matrix operators (Rudolph and Giesbrecht, 2010). So far, however, this has only been applied to specific syntactic contexts (Baroni and Zamparelli, 2010; Guevara, 2010; Grefenstette and Sadrzadeh, 2011), or tasks (Yessenalina and Cardie, 2011).

Neural networks have been used to learn both phrase structure and representations. In Socher et al. (2010), word representations learned by neural network models such as (Bengio et al., 2006; Collobert and Weston, 2008) are fed as input into a recursive neural network whose nodes represent syntactic constituents. Each node models both the probability of the input forming a constituent and the phrase representation resulting from composition.

6 Conclusions

We have proposed an evaluation framework for distributional models of semantics which build phrase- and sentence-level representations, and instantiated two evaluation tasks which test for the crucial ability to recognize whether sentences express the same semantic relation. Our results demonstrate that compositional distributional models of semantics already have some utility in the context of more empirically complex semantic tasks than WSD-like lexical substitution tasks, in which compositional invariance is a requisite property. Simply computing lemma overlap, however, is a very competitive baseline, due to issues in these protocols with named entities and domain adaptivity. The better performance of the mixture models in Task 2 shows that such weaknesses can be addressed by hybrid semantic models. Future work should investigate more refined versions of such hybridization, as well as extend this idea to other semantic phenomena like coreference, negation and modality.

We also observe that no single model or composition operator performs best for all tasks and datasets. The latent sense mixture model of Dinu and Lapata (2010) performs well in recognizing semantic relations in general web text. Because of the difficulty of adapting it to a specialized domain, however, it does less well in biomedical question answering, where the syntax-based model of Thater et al. (2010) performs the best. A more thorough investigation of the factors that can predict the performance and/or invariance of a given composition operator is warranted.

In the future, we would like to evaluate other models of compositional semantics that have been recently proposed. We would also like to collect more comprehensive test data, to increase the external validity of our evaluations.

Acknowledgments

We would like to thank Georgiana Dinu and Stefan Thater for help with reimplementing their models. Saif Mohammad, Peter Turney, and the anonymous reviewers provided valuable comments on drafts of this paper. This project was supported by the Natural Sciences and Engineering Research Council of Canada.

References

Marco Baroni and Roberto Zamparelli. 2010. Nouns are vectors, adjectives are matrices: Representing adjective-noun constructions in semantic space. In *Proceedings of the 2010 Conference on Empirical Methods in Natural Language Processing*, pages 1183–1193.

Yoshua Bengio, Holger Schwenk, Jean-Sébastien Senécal, Fréderic Morin, and Jean-Luc Gauvain.

2006. Neural probabilistic language models. *Innovations in Machine Learning*, pages 137–186.

Razvan C. Bunescu and Raymond J. Mooney. 2007. Learning to extract relations from the web using minimal supervision. In *Proceedings of the 45th Annual Meeting of the Association for Computational Linguistics*, pages 576–583.

Ronan Collobert and Jason Weston. 2008. A unified architecture for natural language processing: Deep neural networks with multitask learning. In *Proceedings of the 25th International Conference on Machine Learning*, page 160–167.

Georgiana Dinu and Mirella Lapata. 2010. Measuring distributional similarity in context. In *Proceedings of the 2010 Conference on Empirical Methods in Natural Language Processing*, pages 1162–1172.

William B. Dolan and Chris Brockett. 2005. Automatically constructing a corpus of sentential paraphrases. In *Proceedings of the Third International Workshop on Paraphrasing*, pages 9–16.

Katrin Erk and Sebastian Padó. 2008. A structured vector space model for word meaning in context. In *Proceedings of the Conference on Empirical Methods in Natural Language Processing*, pages 897–906.

Katrin Erk and Sebastian Padó. 2010. Exemplar-based models for word meaning in context. In *Proceedings of the ACL 2010 Conference Short Papers*, pages 92–97.

Lev Finkelstein, Evgeniy Gabrilovich, Yossi Matias, Ehud Rivlin, Zach Solan, Gadi Wolfman, and Eytan Ruppin. 2002. Placing search in context: The concept revisited. *ACM Transactions on Information Systems*, 20(1):116–131.

Jerry A. Fodor and Zenon W. Pylyshyn. 1988. Connectionism and cognitive architecture: A critical analysis. *Cognition*, 28:3–71.

Edward Grefenstette and Mehrnoosh Sadrzadeh. 2011. Experimental support for a categorical compositional distributional model of meaning. In *Proceedings of the 2011 Conference on Empirical Methods in Natural Language Processing*, pages 1394–1404.

Emiliano Guevara. 2010. A regression model of adjective-noun compositionality in distributional semantics. In *Proceedings of the 2010 Workshop on GEometrical Models of Natural Language Semantics*, pages 33–37.

Zeller S. Harris. 1954. Distributional structure. *Word*, 10(23):146–162.

Wilfred Hodges. 2005. The interplay of fact and theory in separating syntax from meaning. In *Workshop on Empirical Challenges and Analytical Alternatives to Strict Compositionality*.

Walter Kintsch. 2001. Predication. *Cognitive Science*, 25(2):173–202.

Diana McCarthy and Roberto Navigli. 2009. The english lexical substitution task. *Language Resources and Evaluation*, 43(2):139–159.

Jeff Mitchell and Mirella Lapata. 2008. Vector-based models of semantic composition. In *Proceedings of ACL-08: HLT*, pages 236–244.

Jeff Mitchell and Mirella Lapata. 2009. Language models based on semantic composition. In *Proceedings of the 2009 Conference on Empirical Methods in Natural Language Processing*, pages 430–439.

Richard Montague. 1974. English as a formal language. *Formal Philosophy*, pages 188–221.

Hoifung Poon and Pedro Domingos. 2009. Unsupervised semantic parsing. In *Proceedings of the 2009 Conference on Empirical Methods in Natural Language Processing*, pages 1–10.

Joseph Reisinger and Raymond J. Mooney. 2010. Multi-prototype vector-space models of word meaning. In *Human Language Technologies: The 2010 Annual Conference of the North American Chapter of the Association for Computational Linguistics*.

Dan Roth and Wen-tau Yih. 2002. Probabilistic reasoning for entity & relation recognition. In *Proceedings of the 19th International Conference on Computational Linguistics*, pages 835–841.

Sebastian Rudolph and Eugenie Giesbrecht. 2010. Compositional matrix-space models of language. In *Proceedings of the 48th Annual Meeting of the Association for Computational Linguistics*, pages 907–916.

Richard Socher, Christopher D. Manning, and Andrew Y. Ng. 2010. Learning continuous phrase representations and syntactic parsing with recursive neural networks. *Proceedings of the Deep Learning and Unsupervised Feature Learning Workshop of NIPS 2010*, pages 1–9.

Alfred Tarski. 1956. The concept of truth in formalized languages. *Logic, Semantics, Metamathematics*, pages 152–278.

Stefan Thater, Hagen Fürstenau, and Manfred Pinkal. 2010. Contextualizing semantic representations using syntactically enriched vector models. In *Proceedings of the 48th Annual Meeting of the Association for Computational Linguistics*, pages 948–957.

Peter D. Turney and Patrick Pantel. 2010. From frequency to meaning: Vector space models of semantics. *Journal of Artificial Intelligence Research*, 37:141–188.

Justin Washtell. 2011. Compositional expectation: A purely distributional model of compositional semantics. In *Proceedings of the Ninth International Conference on Computational Semantics (IWCS 2011)*, pages 285–294.

Dominic Widdows. 2008. Semantic vector products: Some initial investigations. In *Second AAAI Symposium on Quantum Interaction*.

Stephen Wu and William Schuler. 2011. Structured composition of semantic vectors. In *Proceedings of the Ninth International Conference on Computational Semantics (IWCS 2011)*, pages 295–304.

Ainur Yessenalina and Claire Cardie. 2011. Compositional matrix-space models for sentiment analysis. In *Proceedings of the 2011 Conference on Empirical Methods in Natural Language Processing*, pages 172–182.

Cross-Framework Evaluation for Statistical Parsing

Reut Tsarfaty Joakim Nivre Evelina Andersson
Uppsala University, Box 635, 75126 Uppsala, Sweden
tsarfaty@stp.lingfil.uu.se, {joakim.nivre,evelina.andersson}@lingfil.uu.se

Abstract

A serious bottleneck of comparative parser evaluation is the fact that different parsers subscribe to different formal frameworks and theoretical assumptions. Converting outputs from one framework to another is less than optimal as it easily introduces noise into the process. Here we present a principled protocol for evaluating parsing results across frameworks based on function trees, tree generalization and edit distance metrics. This extends a previously proposed framework for cross-theory evaluation and allows us to compare a wider class of parsers. We demonstrate the usefulness and language independence of our procedure by evaluating constituency and dependency parsers on English and Swedish.

1 Introduction

The goal of statistical parsers is to recover a formal representation of the grammatical relations that constitute the argument structure of natural language sentences. The argument structure encompasses grammatical relationships between elements such as *subject, predicate, object*, etc., which are useful for further (e.g., semantic) processing. The parses yielded by different parsing frameworks typically obey different formal and theoretical assumptions concerning how to represent the grammatical relationships in the data (Rambow, 2010). For example, grammatical relations may be encoded on top of dependency arcs in a dependency tree (Mel'čuk, 1988), they may decorate nodes in a phrase-structure tree (Marcus et al., 1993; Maamouri et al., 2004; Sima'an et al., 2001), or they may be read off of positions in a phrase-structure tree using hard-coded conversion procedures (de Marneffe et al., 2006). This diversity poses a challenge to cross-experimental parser evaluation, namely: How can we evaluate the performance of these different parsers relative to one another?

Current evaluation practices assume a set of correctly annotated test data (or gold standard) for evaluation. Typically, every parser is evaluated with respect to its own formal representation type and the underlying theory which it was trained to recover. Therefore, numerical scores of parses across experiments are incomparable. When comparing parses that belong to different formal frameworks, the notion of a single gold standard becomes problematic, and there are two different questions we have to answer. First, what is an appropriate gold standard for cross-parser evaluation? And secondly, how can we alleviate the differences between formal representation types and theoretical assumptions in order to make our comparison sound – that is, to make sure that we are not comparing apples and oranges?

A popular way to address this has been to pick one of the frameworks and convert all parser outputs to its formal type. When comparing constituency-based and dependency-based parsers, for instance, the output of constituency parsers has often been converted to dependency structures prior to evaluation (Cer et al., 2010; Nivre et al., 2010). This solution has various drawbacks. First, it demands a conversion script that maps one representation type to another when some theoretical assumptions in one framework may be incompatible with the other one. In the constituency-to-dependency case, some constituency-based structures (e.g., coordination and ellipsis) do not comply with the single head assumption of dependency treebanks. Secondly, these scripts may be labor intensive to create, and are available mostly for English. So the evaluation protocol becomes language-dependent.

In Tsarfaty et al. (2011) we proposed a general protocol for handling annotation discrepancies when comparing parses across different dependency theories. The protocol consists of three phases: converting all structures into function trees, for each sentence, generalizing the different gold standard function trees to get their common denominator, and employing an evaluation measure based on tree edit distance (TED) which discards edit operations that recover theory-specific structures. Although the protocol is potentially applicable to a wide class of syntactic representation types, formal restrictions in the procedures effectively limit its applicability only to representations that are isomorphic to dependency trees.

The present paper breaks new ground in the ability to soundly compare the accuracy of different parsers relative to one another given that they employ different formal representation types and obey different theoretical assumptions. Our solution generally confines with the protocol proposed in Tsarfaty et al. (2011) but is re-formalized to allow for arbitrary linearly ordered labeled trees, thus encompassing constituency-based as well as dependency-based representations. The framework in Tsarfaty et al. (2011) assumes structures that are isomorphic to dependency trees, bypassing the problem of arbitrary branching. Here we lift this restriction, and define a protocol which is based on generalization and TED measures to soundly compare the output of different parsers.

We demonstrate the utility of this protocol by comparing the performance of different parsers for English and Swedish. For English, our parser evaluation across representation types allows us to analyze and precisely quantify previously encountered performance tendencies. For Swedish we show the first ever evaluation between dependency-based and constituency-based parsing models, all trained on the Swedish treebank data. All in all we show that our extended protocol, which can handle linearly-ordered labeled trees with arbitrary branching, can soundly compare parsing results across frameworks in a representation-independent and language-independent fashion.

2 Preliminaries: Relational Schemes for Cross-Framework Parse Evaluation

Traditionally, different statistical parsers have been evaluated using specially designated evaluation measures that are designed to fit their representation types. Dependency trees are evaluated using attachment scores (Buchholz and Marsi, 2006), phrase-structure trees are evaluated using ParsEval (Black et al., 1991), LFG-based parsers postulate an evaluation procedure based on f-structures (Cahill et al., 2008), and so on. From a downstream application point of view, there is no significance as to which formalism was used for generating the representation and which learning methods have been utilized. The bottom line is simply which parsing framework most accurately recovers a useful representation that helps to unravel the human-perceived interpretation.

Relational schemes, that is, schemes that encode the set of grammatical relations that constitute the predicate-argument structures of sentences, provide an interface to semantic interpretation. They are more intuitively understood than, say, phrase-structure trees, and thus they are also more useful for practical applications. For these reasons, relational schemes have been repeatedly singled out as an appropriate level of representation for the evaluation of statistical parsers (Lin, 1995; Carroll et al., 1998; Cer et al., 2010).

The annotated data which statistical parsers are trained on encode these grammatical relationships in different ways. Dependency treebanks provide a ready-made representation of grammatical relations on top of arcs connecting the words in the sentence (Kübler et al., 2009). The Penn Treebank and phrase-structure annotated resources encode partial information about grammatical relations as dash-features decorating phrase structure nodes (Marcus et al., 1993). Treebanks like Tiger for German (Brants et al., 2002) and Talbanken for Swedish (Nivre and Megyesi, 2007) explicitly map phrase structures onto grammatical relations using dedicated edge labels. The Relational-Realizational structures of Tsarfaty and Sima'an (2008) encode relational networks (sets of relations) projected and realized by syntactic categories on top of ordinary phrase-structure nodes.

Function trees, as defined in Tsarfaty et al. (2011), are linearly ordered labeled trees in which every node is labeled with the grammatical func-

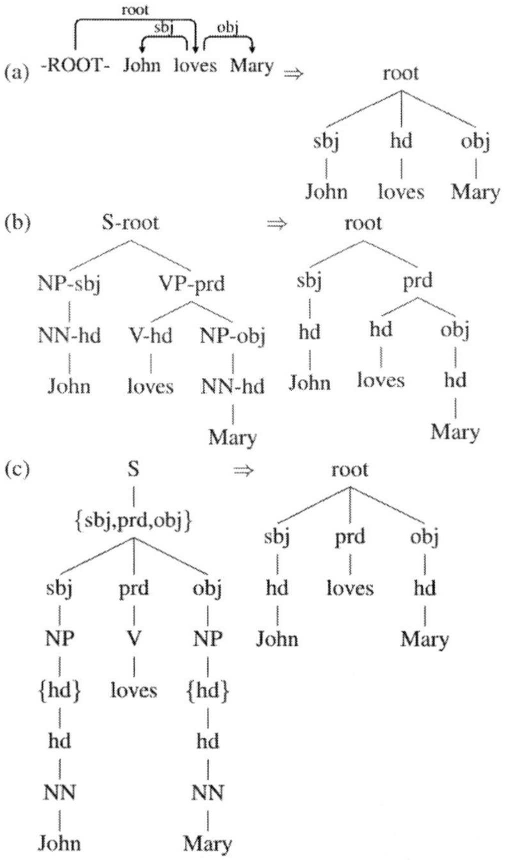

Figure 1: Deterministic conversion into function trees. The algorithm for extracting a function tree from a dependency tree as in (a) is provided in Tsarfaty et al. (2011). For a phrase-structure tree as in (b) we can replace each node label with its function (dash-feature). In a relational-realizational structure like (c) we can remove the projection nodes (sets) and realization nodes (phrase labels), which leaves the function nodes intact.

tion of the dominated span. Function trees benefit from the same advantages as other relational schemes, namely that they are intuitive to understand, they provide the interface for semantic interpretation, and thus may be useful for downstream applications. Yet they do not suffer from formal restrictions inherent in dependency structures, for instance, the single head assumption.

For many formal representation types there exists a fully deterministic, heuristics-free, procedure mapping them to function trees. In Figure 1 we illustrate some such procedures for a simple transitive sentence. Now, while all the structures at the right hand side of Figure 1 are of the same formal type (function trees), they have different tree structures due to different theoretical assumptions underlying the original formal frameworks.

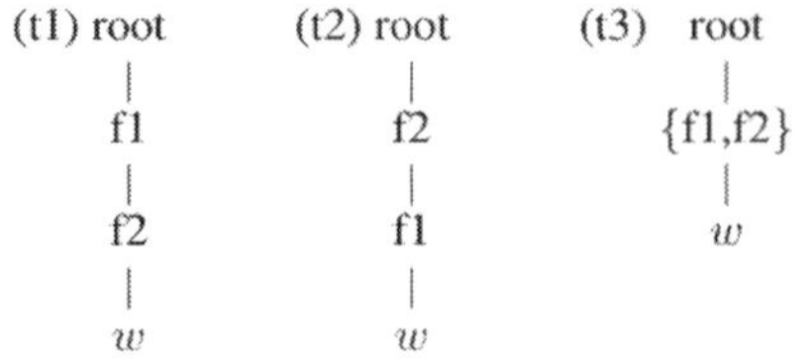

Figure 2: Unary chains in function trees

Once we have converted framework-specific representations into function trees, the problem of cross-framework evaluation can potentially be reduced to a cross-theory evaluation following Tsarfaty et al. (2011). The main idea is that once all structures have been converted into function trees, one can perform a formal operation called generalization in order to harmonize the differences between theories, and measure accurately the distance of parse hypotheses from the generalized gold. The generalization operation defined in Tsarfaty et al. (2011), however, cannot handle trees that may contain unary chains, and therefore cannot be used for arbitrary function trees.

Consider for instance (t1) and (t2) in Figure 2. According to the definition of subsumption in Tsarfaty et al. (2011), (t1) is subsumed by (t2) and vice versa, so the two trees should be identical – but they are not. The interpretation we wish to give to a function tree such as (t1) is that the word w has both the grammatical function f1 and the grammatical function f2. This can be graphically represented as a set of labels dominating w, as in (t3). We call structures such as (t3) *multi-function trees*. In the next section we formally define multi-function trees, and then use them to develop our protocol for cross-framework and cross-theory evaluation.

3 The Proposal: Cross-Framework Evaluation with Multi-Function Trees

Our proposal is a three-phase evaluation protocol in the spirit of Tsarfaty et al. (2011). First, we obtain a *formal* common ground for all frameworks in terms of multi-function trees. Then we obtain a *theoretical* common ground by means of tree-generalization on gold trees. Finally, we calculate TED-based scores that discard the cost of annotation-specific edits. In this section, we define multi-function trees and update the tree-generalization and TED-based metrics to handle multi-function trees that reflect different theories.

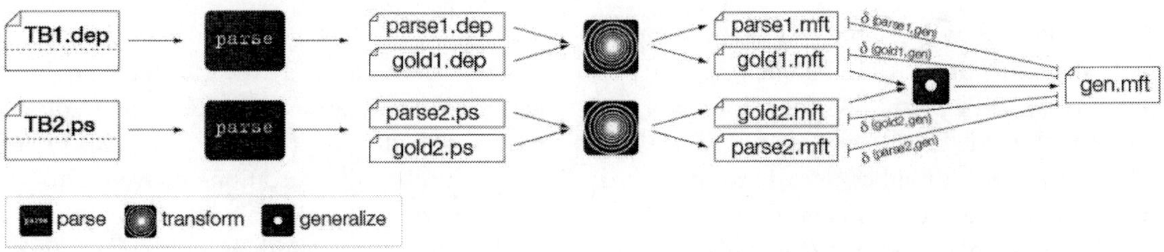

Figure 3: **The Evaluation Protocol.** Different formal frameworks yield different parse and gold formal types. All types are transformed into multi-function trees. All gold trees enter generalization to yield a new gold for each sentence. The different δ arcs represent the different edit scripts used for calculating the TED-based scores.

3.1 Defining Multi-Function Trees

An ordinary function tree is a linearly ordered tree $T = (V, A)$ with yield $w_1, ..., w_n$, where internal nodes are labeled with grammatical function labels drawn from some set $\mathcal{L}$. We use $span(v)$ and $label(v)$ to denote the yield and label, respectively, of an internal node v. A multi-function tree is a linearly ordered tree $T = (V, A)$ with yield $w_1, ..., w_n$, where internal nodes are labeled with *sets of* grammatical function labels drawn from $\mathcal{L}$ and where $v \neq v'$ implies $span(v) \neq span(v')$ for all internal nodes v, v'. We use $labels(v)$ to denote the label set of an internal node v.

We interpret multi-function trees as encoding sets of functional constraints over spans in function trees. Each node v in a multi-function tree represents a constraint of the form: for each $l \in labels(v)$, there should be a node v' in the function tree such that $span(v) = span(v')$ and $label(v') = l$. Whenever we have a conversion for function trees, we can efficiently collapse them into multi-function trees with no unary productions, and with label sets labeling their nodes. Thus, trees (t1) and (t2) in Figure 2 would both be mapped to tree (t3), which encodes the functional constraints encoded in either of them.

For dependency trees, we assume the conversion to function trees defined in Tsarfaty et al. (2011), where head daughters always get the label 'hd'. For PTB style phrase-structure trees, we replace the phrase-structure labels with functional dash-features. In relational-realization structures we remove projection and realization nodes. Deterministic conversions exist also for Tiger style treebanks and frameworks such as LFG, but we do not discuss them here.[1]

[1] All the conversions we use are deterministic and are defined in graph-theoretic and language-independent terms. We make them available at `http://stp.lingfil.uu.se/~tsarfaty/unipar/index.html`.

3.2 Generalizing Multi-Function Trees

Once we obtain multi-function trees for all the different gold standard representations in the system, we feed them to a generalization operation as shown in Figure 3. The goal of this operation is to provide a consensus gold standard that captures the linguistic structure that the different gold theories agree on. The generalization structures are later used as the basis for the TED-based evaluation. Generalization is defined by means of subsumption. A multi-function tree subsumes another one if and only if all the constraints defined by the first tree are also defined by the second tree. So, instead of demanding equality of labels as in Tsarfaty et al. (2011), we demand set inclusion:

> **T-Subsumption**, denoted $\sqsubseteq_t$, is a relation between multi-function trees that indicates that a tree π_1 is consistent with and more general than tree π_2. Formally: $\pi_1 \sqsubseteq_t \pi_2$ iff for every node $n \in \pi_1$ there exists a node $m \in \pi_2$ such that $span(n) = span(m)$ and $labels(n) \subseteq labels(m)$.
>
> **T-Unification**, denoted $\sqcup_t$, is an operation that returns the most general tree structure that contains the information from both input trees, and fails if such a tree does not exist. Formally: $\pi_1 \sqcup_t \pi_2 = \pi_3$ iff $\pi_1 \sqsubseteq_t \pi_3$ and $\pi_2 \sqsubseteq_t \pi_3$, and for all π_4 such that $\pi_1 \sqsubseteq_t \pi_4$ and $\pi_2 \sqsubseteq_t \pi_4$ it holds that $\pi_3 \sqsubseteq_t \pi_4$.
>
> **T-Generalization**, denoted $\sqcap_t$, is an operation that returns the most specific tree that is more general than both trees. Formally, $\pi_1 \sqcap_t \pi_2 = \pi_3$ iff $\pi_3 \sqsubseteq_t \pi_1$ and $\pi_3 \sqsubseteq_t \pi_2$, and for every π_4 such that $\pi_4 \sqsubseteq_t \pi_1$ and $\pi_4 \sqsubseteq_t \pi_2$ it holds that $\pi_4 \sqsubseteq_t \pi_3$.

The generalization tree contains all nodes that exist in both trees, and for each node it is labeled by the intersection of the label sets dominating the same span in both trees. The unification tree contains nodes that exist in one tree or another, and for each span it is labeled by the union of all label sets for this span in either tree. If we generalize two trees and one tree has no specification for labels over a span, it does not share anything with the label set dominating the same span in the other tree, and the label set dominating this span in the generalized tree is empty. If the trees do not agree on any label for a particular span, the respective node is similarly labeled with an empty set. When we wish to unify theories, then an empty set over a span is unified with any other set dominating the same span in the other tree, without altering it.

Digression: Using Unification to Merge Information From Different Treebanks In Tsarfaty et al. (2011), only the generalization operation was used, providing the common denominator of all the gold structures and serving as a common ground for evaluation. The unification operation is useful for other NLP tasks, for instance, combining information from two different annotation schemes or enriching one annotation scheme with information from a different one. In particular, we can take advantage of the new framework to enrich the node structure reflected in one theory with grammatical functions reflected in an annotation scheme that follows a different theory. To do so, we define the Tree-Labeling-Unification operation on multi-function trees.

> **TL-Unification**, denoted $\sqcup_{tl}$, is an operation that returns a tree that retains the structure of the first tree and adds labels that exist over its spans in the second tree. Formally: $\pi_1 \sqcup_{tl} \pi_2 = \pi_3$ iff for every node $n \in \pi_1$ there exists a node $m \in \pi_3$ such that $span(m) = span(n)$ and $labels(m) = labels(n) \cup labels(\pi_2, span(n))$.

Where $labels(\pi_2, span(n))$ is the set of labels of the node with yield $span(n)$ in π_2 if such a node exists and $\emptyset$ otherwise. We further discuss the TL-Unification and its use for data preparation in §4.

3.3 TED Measures for Multi-Function Trees

The result of the generalization operation provides us with multi-function trees for each of the sentences in the test set representing sets of constraints on which the different gold theories agree.

We would now like to use distance-based metrics in order to measure the gap between the gold and predicted theories. The idea behind distance-based evaluation in Tsarfaty et al. (2011) is that recording the edit operations between the native gold and the generalized gold allows one to discard their cost when computing the cost of a parse hypothesis turned into the generalized gold. This makes sure that different parsers do not get penalized, or favored, due to annotation specific decisions that are not shared by other frameworks.

The problem is now that TED is undefined with respect to multi-function trees because it cannot handle complex labels. To overcome this, we convert multi-function trees into *sorted function trees*, which are simply function trees in which any label set is represented as a unary chain of single-labeled nodes, and the nodes are sorted according to the canonical order of their labels.[2] In case of an empty set, a 0-length chain is created, that is, no node is created over this span. Sorted function trees prevent reordering nodes in a chain in one tree to fit the order in another tree, since it would violate the idea that the set of constraints over a span in a multi-function tree is unordered.

The edit operations we assume are **add-node**(l, i, j) and **delete-node**(l, i, j) where $l \in \mathcal{L}$ is a grammatical function label and $i < j$ define the span of a node in the tree. Insertion into a unary chain must confine with the canonical order of the labels. Every operation is assigned a cost. An edit script is a sequence of edit operations that turns a function tree π_1 into π_2, that is:

$$ES(\pi_1, \pi_2) = \langle e_1, \dots, e_k \rangle$$

Since all operations are anchored in spans, the sequence can be determined to have a unique order of traversing the tree (say, DFS). Different edit scripts then only differ in their set of operations on spans. The edit distance problem is finding the minimal cost script, that is, one needs to solve:

$$ES^*(\pi_1, \pi_2) = \min_{ES(\pi_1, \pi_2)} \sum_{e \in ES(\pi_1, \pi_2)} cost(e)$$

In the current setting, when using only add and delete operations on spans, there is only one edit script that corresponds to the minimal edit cost. So, finding the minimal edit script entails finding a single set of operations turning π_1 into π_2.

[2] The ordering can be alphabetic, thematic, etc.

We can now define δ for the ith framework, as the error of $parse_i$ relative to its native gold standard $gold_i$ and to the generalized gold gen. This is the edit cost minus the cost of the script turning $parse_i$ into gen intersected with the script turning $gold_i$ into gen. The underlying intuition is that if an operation that was used to turn $parse_i$ into gen is used to discard theory-specific information from $gold_i$, its cost should not be counted as error.

$$\delta(parse_i, gold_i, gen) = cost(ES^*(parse_i, gen))$$

$$-cost(ES^*(parse_i, gen) \cap ES^*(\text{gold}_i, \text{gen}))$$

In order to turn distance measures into parse-scores we now normalize the error relative to the size of the trees and subtract it from a unity. So the **Sentence Score** for parsing with framework i is:

$$score(parse_i, gold_i, gen) =$$

$$1 - \frac{\delta(parse_i, gold_i, gen)}{|parse_i| + |gen|}$$

Finally, **Test-Set Average** is defined by macro-avaraging over all sentences in the test-set:

$$1 - \frac{\sum_{j=1}^{|\text{testset}|} \delta(parse_{ij}, gold_{ij}, gen_j)}{\sum_{j=1}^{|\text{testset}|} |parse_{ij}| + |gen_j|}$$

This last formula represents the TEDEVAL metric that we use in our experiments.

A Note on System Complexity Conversion of a dependency or a constituency tree into a function tree is linear in the size of the tree. Our implementation of the generalization and unification operation is an exact, greedy, chart-based algorithm that runs in polynomial time ($O(n^2)$ in n the number of terminals). The TED software that we utilize builds on the TED efficient algorithm of Zhang and Shasha (1989) which runs in $O(|T_1||T_2| \min(d_1, n_1) \min(d_2, n_2))$ time where d_i is the tree degree (depth) and n_i is the number of terminals in the respective tree (Bille, 2005).

4 Experiments

We validate our cross-framework evaluation procedure on two languages, English and Swedish. For English, we compare the performance of two dependency parsers, MaltParser (Nivre et al., 2006) and MSTParser (McDonald et al., 2005), and two constituency-based parsers, the Berkeley parser (Petrov et al., 2006) and the Brown parser (Charniak and Johnson, 2005). All experiments use Penn Treebank (PTB) data. For Swedish, we compare MaltParser and MSTParser with two variants of the Berkeley parser, one trained on phrase structure trees, and one trained on a variant of the Relational-Realizational representation of Tsarfaty and Sima'an (2008). All experiments use the Talbanken Swedish Treebank (STB) data.

4.1 English Cross-Framework Evaluation

We use sections 02–21 of the WSJ Penn Treebank for training and section 00 for evaluation and analysis. We use two different native gold standards subscribing to different theories of encoding grammatical relations in tree structures:

∘ THE DEPENDENCY-BASED THEORY is the theory encoded in the basic Stanford Dependencies (SD) scheme. We obtain the set of basic stanford dependency trees using the software of de Marneffe et al. (2006) and train the dependency parsers directly on it.

∘ THE CONSTITUENCY-BASED THEORY is the theory reflected in the phrase-structure representation of the PTB (Marcus et al., 1993) enriched with function labels compatible with the Stanford Dependencies (SD) scheme. We obtain trees that reflect this theory by TL-Unification of the PTB multi-function trees with the SD multi-function trees (PTB$\sqcup_{tl}$SD) as illustrated in Figure 4.

The theory encoded in the multi-function trees corresponding to SD is different from the one obtained by our TL-Unification, as may be seen from the difference between the flat SD multi-function tree and the result of the PTB$\sqcup_{tl}$SD in Figure 4. Another difference concerns coordination structures, encoded as binary branching trees in SD and as flat productions in the PTB$\sqcup_{tl}$SD. Such differences are not only observable but also quantifiable, and using our redefined TED metric the cross-theory overlap is 0.8571.

The two dependency parsers were trained using the same settings as in Tsarfaty et al. (2011), using SVMTool (Giménez and Màrquez, 2004) to predict part-of-speech tags at parsing time. The two constituency parsers were used with default settings and were allowed to predict their own part-of-speech tags. We report three different evaluation metrics for the different experiments:

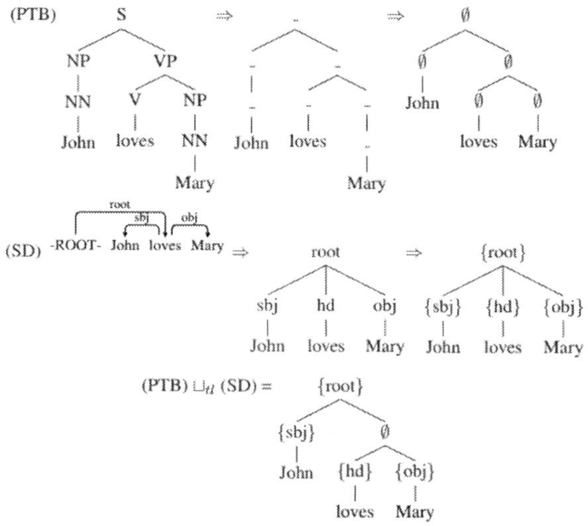

Figure 4: Conversion of PTB and SD tree to multi-function trees, followed by TL-Unification of the trees. Note that some PTB nodes remain without an SD label.

- LAS/UAS (Buchholz and Marsi, 2006)
- PARSEVAL (Black et al., 1991)
- TEDEVAL as defined in Section 3

We use LAS/UAS for dependency parsers that were trained on the same dependency theory. We use ParseEval to evaluate phrase-structure parsers that were trained on PTB trees in which dash-features and empty traces are removed. We use our implementation of TEDEVAL to evaluate parsing results across all frameworks under two different scenarios:[3] TEDEVAL SINGLE evaluates against the native gold multi-function trees. TEDEVAL MULTIPLE evaluates against the generalized (cross-theory) multi-function trees. Unlabeled TEDEVAL scores are obtained by simply removing all labels from the multi-function nodes, and using unlabeled edit operations. We calculate pairwise statistical significance using a shuffling test with 10K iterations (Cohen, 1995).

Tables 1 and 2 present the results of our cross-framework evaluation for English Parsing. In the left column of Table 1 we report ParsEval scores for constituency-based parsers. As expected, F-Scores for the Brown parser are higher than the F-Scores of the Berkeley parser. F-Scores are however not applicable across frameworks. In the rightmost column of Table 1 we report the LAS/UAS results for all parsers. If a parser yields a constituency tree, it is converted to and evaluated on SD. Here we see that MST outperforms Malt, though the differences for labeled dependencies are insignificant. We also observe here a familiar pattern from Cer et al. (2010) and others, where the constituency parsers significantly outperform the dependency parsers after conversion of their output into dependencies.

The conversion to SD allows one to compare results across formal frameworks, but not without a cost. The conversion introduces a set of annotation specific decisions which may introduce a bias into the evaluation. In the middle column of Table 1 we report the TEDEVAL metrics measured against the generalized gold standard for all parsing frameworks. We can now confirm that the constituency-based parsers significantly outperform the dependency parsers, and that this is not due to specific theoretical decisions which are seen to affect LAS/UAS metrics (Schwartz et al., 2011). For the dependency parsers we now see that Malt outperforms MST on labeled dependencies slightly, but the difference is insignificant.

The fact that the discrepancy in theoretical assumptions between different frameworks indeed affects the conversion-based evaluation procedure is reflected in the results we report in Table 2. Here the leftmost and rightmost columns report TEDEVAL scores against the own native gold (SINGLE) and the middle column against the generalized gold (MULTIPLE). Had the theories for SD and PTB$\sqcup_{tl}$SD been identical, TEDEVAL SINGLE and TEDEVAL MULTIPLE would have been equal in each line. Because of theoretical discrepancies, we see small gaps in parser performance between these cases. Our protocol ensures that such discrepancies do not bias the results.

4.2 Cross-Framework Swedish Parsing

We use the standard training and test sets of the Swedish Treebank (Nivre and Megyesi, 2007) with two gold standards presupposing different theories:

- THE DEPENDENCY-BASED THEORY is the dependency version of the Swedish Treebank. All trees are projectivized (STB-Dep).
- THE CONSTITUENCY-BASED THEORY is the standard Swedish Treebank with grammatical function labels on the edges of constituency structures (STB).

[3] Our TedEval software can be downloaded at http://stp.lingfil.uu.se/~tsarfaty/unipar/download.html.

Formalism	PS Trees	MF Trees	Dep Trees
Theory	**PTB $\sqcup_{lt}$ SD**	**(PTB $\sqcup_{lt}$ SD) $\sqcap_t$ SD**	**SD**
Metrics	PARSEVAL	TEDEVAL	ATTSCORES
MALT	N/A	U: 0.9525 L: *0.9088*	U: 0.8962 L: 0.8772
MST	N/A	U: *0.9549* L: 0.9049	U: *0.9059* L: *0.8795*
BERKELEY	F-Scores 0.9096	U: 0.9677 L: 0.9227	U: 0.9254 L: 0.9031
BROWN	F-Scores **0.9129**	U: **0.9702** L: **0.9264**	U: **0.9289** L: **0.9057**

Table 1: English cross-framework evaluation: Three measures as applicable to the different schemes. Boldface scores are highest in their column. Italic scores are the highest for dependency parsers in their column.

Formalism	PS Trees	MF Trees	Dep Trees
Theory	**PTB $\sqcup_{lt}$ SD**	**(PTB $\sqcup_{lt}$ SD) $\sqcap_t$ SD**	**SD**
Metrics	TEDEVAL SINGLE	TEDEVAL MULTIPLE	TEDEVAL SINGLE
MALT	N/A	U: 0.9525 L: *0.9088*	U: 0.9524 L: *0.9186*
MST	N/A	U: *0.9549* L: 0.9049	U: *0.9548* L: 0.9149
BERKELEY	U: 0.9645 L: 0.9271	U: 0.9677 L: 0.9227	U: 0.9649 L: 0.9324
BROWN	U: **0.9667** L: **0.9301**	U: **9702** L: **9264**	U: **0.9679** L: **0.9362**

Table 2: English cross-framework evaluation: TEDEVAL scores against gold and generalized gold. Boldface scores are highest in their column. Italic scores are highest for dependency parsers in their column.

Formalism	PS Trees	MF Trees	Dep Trees
Theory	**STB**	**STB $\sqcap_t$ Dep**	**Dep**
Metrics	PARSEVAL	TEDEVAL	ATTSCORE
MALT	N/A	U: 0.9266 L: **0.8225**	U: 0.8298 L: 0.7782
MST	N/A	U: 0.9275 L: 0.8121	U: **0.8438** L: **0.7824**
BKLY/STB-RR	F-Score **0.7914**	U: **0.9281** L: 0.7861	N/A
BKLY/STB-PS	F-Score 0.7855	N/A	N/A

Table 3: Swedish cross-framework evaluation: Three measures as applicable to the different schemes. Boldface scores are the highest in their column.

Formalism	PS Trees	MF Trees	Dep Trees
Theory	**STB**	**STB $\sqcap_t$ Dep**	**Dep**
Metrics	TEDEVAL SINGLE	TEDEVAL MULTIPLE	TEDEVAL SINGLE
MALT	N/A	U: 0.9266 L: **0.8225**	U: 0.9264 L: **0.8372**
MST	N/A	U: 0.9275 L: 0.8121	U: **0.9272** L: 0.8275
BKLY-STB-RR	U: **0.9239** L: **0.7946**	U: **0.9281** L: 0.7861	N/A

Table 4: Swedish cross-framework evaluation: TEDEVAL scores against the native gold and the generalized gold. Boldface scores are the highest in their column.

Because there are no parsers that can output the complete STB representation including edge labels, we experiment with two variants of this theory, one which is obtained by simply removing the edge labels and keeping only the phrase-structure labels (STB-PS) and one which is loosely based on the Relational-Realizational scheme of Tsarfaty and Sima'an (2008) but excludes the projection set nodes (STB-RR). RR trees only add function nodes to PS trees, and it holds that STB-PS$\sqcap_t$STB-RR=STB-PS. The overlap between the theories expressed in multi-function trees originating from STB-Dep and STB-RR is 0.7559. Our evaluation protocol takes into account such discrepancies while avoiding biases that may be caused due to these differences.

We evaluate MaltParser, MSTParser and two versions of the Berkeley parser, one trained on STB-PS and one trained on STB-RR. We use predicted part-of-speech tags for the dependency parsers, using the HunPoS tagger (Megyesi, 2009), but let the Berkeley parser predict its own tags. We use the same evaluation metrics and procedures as before. Prior to evaluating RR trees using ParsEval we strip off the added function nodes. Prior to evaluating them using TedEval we strip off the phrase-structure nodes.

Tables 3 and 4 summarize the parsing results for the different Swedish parsers. In the leftmost column of table 3 we present the constituency-based evaluation measures. Interestingly, the Berkeley RR instantiation performs better than when training the Berkeley parser on PS trees. These constituency-based scores however have a limited applicability, and we cannot use them to compare constituency and dependency parsers. In the rightmost column of Table 3 we report the LAS/UAS results for the two dependency parsers. Here we see higher performance demonstrated by MST on both labeled and unlabeled dependencies, but the differences on labeled dependencies are insignificant. Since there is no automatic procedure for converting bare-bone phrase-structure Swedish trees to dependency trees, we cannot use

LAS/UAS to compare across frameworks, and we use TEDEVAL for cross-framework evaluation.

Training the Berkeley parser on RR trees which encode a mapping of PS nodes to grammatical functions allows us to compare parse results for trees belonging to the STB theory with trees obeying the STB-Dep theory. For unlabeled TEDEVAL scores, the dependency parsers perform at the same level as the constituency parser, though the difference is insignificant. For labeled TEDEVAL the dependency parsers significantly outperform the constituency parser. When considering only the dependency parsers, there is a small advantage for Malt on labeled dependencies, and an advantage for MST on unlabeled dependencies, but the latter is insignificant. This effect is replicated in Table 4 where we evaluate dependency parsers using TEDEVAL against their own gold theories. Table 4 further confirms that there is a gap between the STB and the STB-Dep theories, reflected in the scores against the native and generalized gold.

5 Discussion

We presented a formal protocol for evaluating parsers across frameworks and used it to soundly compare parsing results for English and Swedish. Our approach follows the three-phase protocol of Tsarfaty et al. (2011), namely: (i) obtaining a formal common ground for the different representation types, (ii) computing the theoretical common ground for each test sentence, and (iii) counting only what counts, that is, measuring the distance between the common ground and the parse tree while discarding annotation-specific edits.

A pre-condition for applying our protocol is the availability of a relational interpretation of trees in the different frameworks. For dependency frameworks this is straightforward, as these relations are encoded on top of dependency arcs. For constituency trees with an inherent mapping of nodes onto grammatical relations (Merlo and Musillo, 2005; Gabbard et al., 2006; Tsarfaty and Sima'an, 2008), a procedure for reading relational schemes off of the trees is trivial to implement.

For parsers that are trained on and parse into bare-bones phrase-structure trees this is not so. Reading off the relational structure may be more costly and require interjection of additional theoretical assumptions via manually written scripts. Scripts that read off grammatical relations based on tree positions work well for configurational languages such as English (de Marneffe et al., 2006) but since grammatical relations are reflected differently in different languages (Postal and Perlmutter, 1977; Bresnan, 2000), a procedure to read off these relations in a language-independent fashion from phrase-structure trees does not, and should not, exist (Rambow, 2010).

The crucial point is that even when using external scripts for recovering a relational scheme for phrase-structure trees, our protocol has a clear advantage over simply scoring converted trees. Manually created conversion scripts alter the theoretical assumptions inherent in the trees and thus may bias the results. Our generalization operation and three-way TED make sure that theory-specific idiosyncrasies injected through such scripts do not lead to over-penalizing or over-crediting theory-specific structural variations.

Certain linguistic structures cannot yet be evaluated with our protocol because of the strict assumption that the labeled spans in a parse form a tree. In the future we plan to extend the protocol for evaluating structures that go beyond linearly-ordered trees in order to allow for non-projective trees and directed acyclic graphs. In addition, we plan to lift the restriction that the parse yield is known in advance, in order to allow for evaluation of joint parse-segmentation hypotheses.

6 Conclusion

We developed a protocol for comparing parsing results across different theories and representation types which is framework-independent in the sense that it can accommodate any formal syntactic framework that encodes grammatical relations, and it is language-independent in the sense that there is no language specific knowledge encoded in the procedure. As such, this protocol is adequate for parser evaluation in cross-framework and cross-language tasks and parsing competitions, and using it across the board is expected to open new horizons in our understanding of the strengths and weaknesses of different parsers in the face of different theories and different data.

Acknowledgments We thank David McClosky, Marco Khulmann, Yoav Goldberg and three anonymous reviewers for useful comments. We further thank Jennifer Foster for the Brown parses and parameter files. This research is partly funded by the Swedish National Science Foundation.

References

Philip Bille. 2005. A survey on tree edit distance and related. problems. *Theoretical Computer Science*, 337:217–239.

Ezra Black, Steven P. Abney, D. Flickenger, Claudia Gdaniec, Ralph Grishman, P. Harrison, Donald Hindle, Robert Ingria, Frederick Jelinek, Judith L. Klavans, Mark Liberman, Mitchell P. Marcus, Salim Roukos, Beatrice Santorini, and Tomek Strzalkowski. 1991. A procedure for quantitatively comparing the syntactic coverage of English grammars. In *Proceedings of the DARPA Workshop on Speech and Natural Language*, pages 306–311.

Sabine Brants, Stefanie Dipper, Silvia Hansen, Wolfgang Lezius, and George Smith. 2002. The Tiger treebank. In *Proceedings of TLT*.

Joan Bresnan. 2000. *Lexical-Functional Syntax*. Blackwell.

Sabine Buchholz and Erwin Marsi. 2006. CoNLL-X shared task on multilingual dependency parsing. In *Proceedings of CoNLL-X*, pages 149–164.

Aoife Cahill, Michael Burke, Ruth O'Donovan, Stefan Riezler, Josef van Genabith, and Andy Way. 2008. Wide-coverage deep statistical parsing using automatic dependency structure annotation. *Computational Linguistics*, 34(1):81–124.

John Carroll, Edward Briscoe, and Antonio Sanfilippo. 1998. Parser evaluation: A survey and a new proposal. In *Proceedings of LREC*, pages 447–454.

Daniel Cer, Marie-Catherine de Marneffe, Daniel Jurafsky, and Christopher D. Manning. 2010. Parsing to Stanford Dependencies: Trade-offs between speed and accuracy. In *Proceedings of LREC*.

Eugene Charniak and Mark Johnson. 2005. Coarse-to-fine n-best parsing and maxent discriminative reranking. In *Proceedings of ACL*.

Paul Cohen. 1995. *Empirical Methods for Artificial Intelligence*. The MIT Press.

Marie-Catherine de Marneffe, Bill MacCartney, and Christopher D. Manning. 2006. Generating typed dependency parses from phrase structure parses. In *Proceedings of LREC*, pages 449–454.

Ryan Gabbard, Mitchell Marcus, and Seth Kulick. 2006. Fully parsing the Penn treebank. In *Proceeding of HLT-NAACL*, pages 184–191.

Jesús Giménez and Lluís Màrquez. 2004. SVMTool: A general POS tagger generator based on support vector machines. In *Proceedings of LREC*.

Sandra Kübler, Ryan McDonald, and Joakim Nivre. 2009. *Dependency Parsing*. Number 2 in Synthesis Lectures on Human Language Technologies. Morgan & Claypool Publishers.

Dekang Lin. 1995. A dependency-based method for evaluating broad-coverage parsers. In *Proceedings of IJCAI-95*, pages 1420–1425.

Mohamed Maamouri, Ann Bies, Tim Buckwalter, and Wigdan Mekki. 2004. The Penn Arabic treebank: Building a large-scale annotated Arabic corpus. In *Proceedings of NEMLAR International Conference on Arabic Language Resources and Tools*.

Mitchell P. Marcus, Beatrice Santorini, and Mary Ann Marcinkiewicz. 1993. Building a large annotated corpus of English: The Penn Treebank. *Computational Linguistics*, 19:313–330.

Ryan McDonald, Fernando Pereira, Kiril Ribarov, and Jan Hajič. 2005. Non-projective dependency parsing using spanning tree algorithms. In *HLT '05: Proceedings of the conference on Human Language Technology and Empirical Methods in Natural Language Processing*, pages 523–530, Morristown, NJ, USA. Association for Computational Linguistics.

Beata Megyesi. 2009. The open source tagger HunPoS for Swedish. In *Proceedings of the 17th Nordic Conference of Computational Linguistics (NODALIDA)*, pages 239–241.

Igor Mel'čuk. 1988. *Dependency Syntax: Theory and Practice*. State University of New York Press.

Paola Merlo and Gabriele Musillo. 2005. Accurate function parsing. In *Proceedings of EMNLP*, pages 620–627.

Joakim Nivre and Beata Megyesi. 2007. Bootstrapping a Swedish Treebank using cross-corpus harmonization and annotation projection. In *Proceedings of TLT*.

Joakim Nivre, Johan Hall, and Jens Nilsson. 2006. Maltparser: A data-driven parser-generator for dependency parsing. In *Proceedings of LREC*, pages 2216–2219.

Joakim Nivre, Laura Rimell, Ryan McDonald, and Carlos Gómez-Rodríguez. 2010. Evaluation of dependency parsers on unbounded dependencies. In *Proceedings of COLING*, pages 813–821.

Slav Petrov, Leon Barrett, Romain Thibaux, and Dan Klein. 2006. Learning accurate, compact, and interpretable tree annotation. In *Proceedings of ACL*.

Paul M. Postal and David M. Perlmutter. 1977. Toward a universal characterization of passivization. In *Proceedings of the 3rd Annual Meeting of the Berkeley Linguistics Society*, pages 394–417.

Owen Rambow. 2010. The simple truth about dependency and phrase structure representations: An opinion piece. In *Proceedings of HLT-ACL*, pages 337–340.

Roy Schwartz, Omri Abend, Roi Reichart, and Ari Rappoport. 2011. Neutralizing linguistically problematic annotations in unsupervised dependency parsing evaluation. In *Proceedings of ACL*, pages 663–672.

Khalil Sima'an, Alon Itai, Yoad Winter, Alon Altman, and Noa Nativ. 2001. Building a Tree-Bank for Modern Hebrew Text. In *Traitement Automatique des Langues*.

Reut Tsarfaty and Khalil Sima'an. 2008. Relational-Realizational parsing. In *Proceedings of CoLing*.

Reut Tsarfaty, Joakim Nivre, and Evelina Andersson. 2011. Evaluating dependency parsing: Robust and heuristics-free cross-framework evaluation. In *Proceedings of EMNLP*.

Kaizhong Zhang and Dennis Shasha. 1989. Simple fast algorithms for the editing distance between trees and related problems. In *SIAM Journal of Computing*, volume 18, pages 1245–1262.

Dependency Parsing of Hungarian: Baseline Results and Challenges

Richárd Farkas[1], **Veronika Vincze**[2], **Helmut Schmid**[1]
[1]Institute for Natural Language Processing, University of Stuttgart
{farkas,schmid}@ims.uni-stuttgart.de
[2]Research Group on Artificial Intelligence, Hungarian Academy of Sciences
vinczev@inf.u-szeged.hu

Abstract

Hungarian is a stereotype of morphologically rich and non-configurational languages. Here, we introduce results on dependency parsing of Hungarian that employ a 80K, multi-domain, fully manually annotated corpus, the Szeged Dependency Treebank. We show that the results achieved by state-of-the-art data-driven parsers on Hungarian and English (which is at the other end of the configurational-non-configurational spectrum) are quite similar to each other in terms of attachment scores. We reveal the reasons for this and present a systematic and comparative linguistically motivated error analysis on both languages. This analysis highlights that addressing the language-specific phenomena is required for a further remarkable error reduction.

1 Introduction

From the viewpoint of syntactic parsing, the languages of the world are usually categorized according to their level of configurationality. At one end, there is English, a strongly configurational language while Hungarian is at the other end of the spectrum. It has very few fixed structures at the sentence level. Leaving aside the issue of the internal structure of NPs, most sentence-level syntactic information in Hungarian is conveyed by morphology, not by configuration (É. Kiss, 2002).

A large part of the methodology for syntactic parsing has been developed for English. However, parsing non-configurational and less configurational languages requires different techniques. In this study, we present results on Hungarian dependency parsing and we investigate this general issue in the case of English and Hungarian.

We employed three state-of-the-art data-driven parsers (Nivre et al., 2004; McDonald et al., 2005; Bohnet, 2010), which achieved (un)labeled attachment scores on Hungarian not so different from the corresponding English scores (and even higher on certain domains/subcorpora). Our investigations show that the feature representation used by the data-driven parsers is so rich that they can – without any modification – effectively learn a reasonable model for non-configurational languages as well.

We also conducted a systematic and comparative error analysis of the system's outputs for Hungarian and English. This analysis highlights the challenges of parsing Hungarian and suggests that the further improvement of parsers requires special handling of language-specific phenomena. We believe that some of our findings can be relevant for intermediate languages on the configurational-non-configurational spectrum.

2 Chief Characteristics of the Hungarian Morphosyntax

Hungarian is an **agglutinative language**, which means that a word can have hundreds of word forms due to inflectional or derivational affixation. A lot of grammatical information is encoded in morphology and Hungarian is a stereotype of morphologically rich languages. The Hungarian **word order is free** in the sense that the positions of the subject, the object and the verb are not fixed within the sentence, but word order is related to information structure, e.g. new (or emphatic) information (the focus) always precedes the verb and old information (the topic) precedes the focus position. Thus, the position relative to the verb has no predictive force as regards the syntactic function of the given argument: while in English, the noun phrase before the verb is most typically the subject, in Hungarian, it is the focus of the sentence, which itself can be the subject, object or any other argument (É. Kiss, 2002).

The grammatical function of words is determined by **case suffixes** as in *gyerek* "child" – *gyereknek* (child-DAT) "for (a/the) child". Hungarian nouns can have about 20 cases[1] which mark the relationship between the head and its arguments and adjuncts. Although there are postpositions in Hungarian, case suffixes can also express relations that are expressed by prepositions in English.

Verbs are inflected for person and number and the definiteness of the object. Since conjugational information is sufficient to deduce the pronominal subject or object, they are typically omitted from the sentence: *Várlak* (wait-1SG2OBJ) "I am waiting for you". This pro-drop feature of Hungarian leads to the fact that there are several **clauses without an overt subject or object**.

Another peculiarity of Hungarian is that the third person singular present tense indicative form of the copula is phonologically empty, i.e. there are apparently verbless sentences in Hungarian: *A ház nagy* (the house big) "The house is big". However, in other tenses or moods, the copula is present as in *A ház nagy lesz* (the house big will.be) "The house will be big".

There are two **possessive constructions** in Hungarian. First, the possessive relation is only marked on the possessed noun (in contrast, it is marked only on the possessor in English): *a fiú kutyája* (the boy dog-POSS) "the boy's dog". Second, both the possessor and the possessed bear a possessive marker: *a fiúnak a kutyája* (the boy-DAT the dog-POSS) "the boy's dog". In the latter case, the possessor and the possessed may not be adjacent within the sentence as in *A fiúnak látta a kutyáját* (the boy-DAT see-PAST3SGOBJ the dog-POSS-ACC) "He saw the boy's dog", which results in a non-projective syntactic tree. Note that in the first case, the form of the possessor coincides with that of a nominative noun while in the second case, it coincides with a dative noun.

According to these facts, a Hungarian parser must rely much more on morphological analysis than e.g. an English one since in Hungarian it is morphemes that mostly encode morphosyntactic information. One of the consequences of this is that Hungarian sentences are shorter in terms of word numbers than English ones. Based on the word counts of the Hungarian–English parallel corpus Hunglish (Varga et al., 2005), an English sentence contains 20.5% more words than its Hungarian equivalent. These extra words in English are most frequently prepositions, pronominal subjects or objects, whose parent and dependency label are relatively easy to identify (compared to other word classes). This train of thought indicates that the cross-lingual comparison of final parser scores should be conducted very carefully.

3 Related work

We decided to focus on **dependency parsing** in this study as it is a superior framework for non-configurational languages. It has gained interest in natural language processing recently because the representation itself does not require the words inside of constituents to be consecutive and it naturally represent discontinuous constructions, which are frequent in languages where grammatical relations are often signaled by morphology instead of word order (McDonald and Nivre, 2011). The two main efficient approaches for dependency parsing are the graph-based and the transition-based parsers. The graph-based models look for the highest scoring directed spanning tree in the complete graph whose nodes are the words of the sentence in question. They solve the machine learning problem of finding the optimal scoring function of subgraphs (Eisner, 1996; McDonald et al., 2005). The transition-based approaches parse a sentence in a single left-to-right pass over the words. The next transition in these systems is predicted by a classifier that is based on history-related features (Kudo and Matsumoto, 2002; Nivre et al., 2004).

Although the available **treebanks for Hungarian** are relatively big (82K sentences) and fully manually annotated, the studies on parsing Hungarian are rather limited. The Szeged (Constituency) Treebank (Csendes et al., 2005) con-

[1]Hungarian grammars and morphological coding systems do not agree on the exact number of cases, some rare suffixes are treated as derivational suffixes in one grammar and as case suffixes in others; see e.g. Farkas et al. (2010).

sists of six domains – namely, short business news, newspaper, law, literature, compositions and informatics – and it is manually annotated for the possible alternatives of words' morphological analyses, the disambiguated analysis and constituency trees. We are aware of only two articles on phrase-structure parsers which were trained and evaluated on this corpus (Barta et al., 2005; Iván et al., 2007) and there are a few studies on hand-crafted parsers reporting results on small own corpora (Babarczy et al., 2005; Prószéky et al., 2004).

The Szeged Dependency Treebank (Vincze et al., 2010) was constructed by first automatically converting the phrase-structure trees into dependency trees, then each of them was manually investigated and corrected. We note that the dependency treebank contains more information than the constituency one as linguistic phenomena (like discontinuous structures) were not annotated in the former corpus, but were added to the dependency treebank. To the best of our knowledge no parser results have been published on this corpus. Both corpora are available at `www.inf.u-szeged.hu/rgai/SzegedTreebank`.

The multilingual track of the CoNLL-2007 Shared Task (Nivre et al., 2007) addressed also the task of dependency parsing of Hungarian. The Hungarian corpus used for the shared task consists of automatically converted dependency trees from the Szeged Constituency Treebank. Several issues of the automatic conversion tool were reconsidered before the manual annotation of the Szeged Dependency Treebank was launched and the annotation guidelines contained instructions related to linguistic phenomena which could not be converted from the constituency representation – for a detailed discussion, see Vincze et al. (2010). Hence the annotation schemata of the CoNLL-2007 Hungarian corpus and the Szeged Dependency Treebank are rather different and the final scores reported for the former are not directly comparable with our reported scores here (see Section 5).

4 The Szeged Dependency Treebank

We utilize the Szeged Dependency Treebank (Vincze et al., 2010) as the basis of our experiments for Hungarian dependency parsing. It contains 82,000 sentences, 1.2 million words and 250,000 punctuation marks from six domains. The annotation employs 16 coarse grained POS tags, 95 morphological feature values and 29 dependency labels. 19.6% of the sentences in the corpus contain non-projective edges and 1.8% of the edges are non-projective[2], which is almost 5 times more frequent than in English and is the same as the Czech non-projectivity level (Buchholz and Marsi, 2006). Here we discuss two annotation principles along with our modifications in the dataset for this study which strongly influence the parsers' accuracies.

Named Entities (NEs) were treated as one token in the Szeged Dependency Treebank. Assuming a perfect phrase recogniser on the whitespace tokenised input for them is quite unrealistic. Thus we decided to split them into tokens for this study. The new tokens automatically got a *proper noun with default morphological features* morphological analysis except for the last token – the head of the phrase –, which inherited the morphological analysis of the original multiword unit (which can contain various grammatical information). This resulted in an N N N N POS sequence for *Kovács és társa kft.* "Smith and Co. Ltd." which would be annotated as N C N N in the Penn Treebank. Moreover, we did not annotate any internal structure of Named Entities. We consider the last word of multiword named entities as the head because of morphological reasons (the last word of multiword units gets inflected in Hungarian) and all the previous elements are attached to the succeeding word, i.e. the penultimate word is attached to the last word, the antepenultimate word to the penultimate one etc. The reasons for these considerations are that we believe that there are no downstream applications which can exploit the information of the internal structures of Named Entities and we imagine a pipeline where a Named Entity Recogniser precedes the parsing step.

Empty copula: In the verbless clauses (predicative nouns or adjectives) the Szeged Dependency Treebank introduces virtual nodes (16,000 items in the corpus). This solution means that a similar tree structure is ascribed to the same sentence in the present third person singular and all the other tenses / persons. A further argument for the use of a virtual node is that the virtual node is always present at the syntactic level

[2]Using the transitive closure definition of Nivre and Nilsson (2005).

corpus		Malt		MST		Mate	
		ULA	LAS	ULA	LAS	ULA	LAS
Hungarian	dev	88.3 (89.9)	85.7 (87.9)	86.9 (88.5)	80.9 (82.9)	89.7 (91.1)	86.8 (89.0)
	test	88.7 (90.2)	86.1 (88.2)	87.5 (89.0)	81.6 (83.5)	90.1 (91.5)	87.2 (89.4)
English	dev	87.8 (89.1)	84.5 (86.1)	89.4 (91.2)	86.1 (87.7)	91.6 (92.7)	88.5 (90.0)
	test	88.8 (89.9)	86.2 (87.6)	90.7 (91.8)	87.7 (89.2)	92.6 (93.4)	90.3 (91.5)

Table 1: Results achieved by the three parsers on the (full) Hungarian (Szeged Dependency Treebank) and English (CoNLL-2009) datasets. The scores in brackets are achieved with gold-standard POS tagging.

since it is overt in all the other forms, tenses and moods of the verb. Still, the state-of-the-art dependency parsers cannot handle virtual nodes. For this study, we followed the solution of the Prague Dependency Treebank (Hajič et al., 2000) and virtual nodes were removed from the gold standard annotation and all of their dependents were attached to the head of the original virtual node and they were given a dedicated edge label (Exd).

Dataset splits: We formed training, development and test sets from the corpus where each set consists of texts from each of the domains. We paid attention to the issue that a document should not be separated into different datasets because it could result in a situation where a part of the test document was seen in the training dataset (which is unrealistic because of unknown words, style and frequently used grammatical structures). As the fiction subcorpus consists of three books and the law subcorpus consists of two rules, we took half of one of the documents for the test and development sets and used the other part(s) for training there. This principle was followed at our cross-fold-validation experiments as well except for the law subcorpus. We applied 3 folds for cross-validation for the fiction subcorpus, otherwise we used 10 folds (splitting at documentary boundaries would yield a training fold consisting of just 3000 sentences).[3]

5 Experiments

We carried out experiments using three state-of-the-art parsers on the Szeged Dependency Treebank (Vincze et al., 2010) and on the English datasets of the CoNLL-2009 Shared Task (Hajič et al., 2009).

Tools: We employed a finite state automata-based **morphological analyser** constructed from the morphdb.hu lexical resource (Trón et al., 2006) and we used the MSD-style morphological code system of the Szeged TreeBank (Alexin et al., 2003). The output of the morphological analyser is a set of possible lemma–morphological analysis pairs. This set of possible morphological analyses for a word form is then used as possible alternatives – instead of open and closed tag sets – in a standard sequential POS tagger. Here, we applied the Conditional Random Fields-based Stanford POS tagger (Toutanova et al., 2003) and carried out 5-fold-cross POS training/tagging inside the subcorpora.[4] For the English experiments we used the predicted POS tags provided for the CoNLL-2009 shared task (Hajič et al., 2009).

As the **dependency parser** we employed three state-of-the-art data-driven parsers, a transition-based parser (Malt) and two graph-based parsers (MST and Mate parsers). The Malt parser (Nivre et al., 2004) is a transition-based system, which uses an arc-eager system along with support vector machines to learn the scoring function for transitions and which uses greedy, deterministic one-best search at parsing time. As one of the graph-based parsers, we employed the MST parser (McDonald et al., 2005) with a second-order feature decoder. It uses an approximate exhaustive search for unlabeled parsing, then a separate arc label classifier is applied to label each arc. The Mate parser (Bohnet, 2010) is an efficient second order dependency parser that models the interaction between siblings as well as grandchildren (Carreras, 2007). Its decoder works on labeled edges, i.e. it uses a single-step approach for obtaining labeled dependency trees. Mate uses a rich and

[3]Both the training/development/test and the cross-validation splits are available at `www.inf.u-szeged.hu/rgai/SzegedTreebank`.

[4]The JAVA implementation of the morphological analyser and the slightly modified POS tagger along with trained models are available at `http://www.inf.u-szeged.hu/rgai/magyarlanc`.

corpus	#sent.	length	CPOS	DPOS	ULA	all ULA	LAS	all LAS
newspaper	9189	21.6	97.2	96.5	88.0 (90.0)	+0.8	84.7 (87.5)	+1.0
short business	8616	23.6	98.0	97.7	93.8 (94.8)	+0.3	91.9 (93.4)	+0.4
fiction	9279	12.6	96.9	95.8	87.7 (89.4)	-0.5	83.7 (86.2)	-0.3
law	8347	27.3	98.3	98.1	90.6 (90.7)	+0.2	88.9 (89.0)	+0.2
computer	8653	21.9	96.4	95.8	91.3 (92.8)	-1.2	88.9 (91.2)	-1.6
composition	22248	13.7	96.7	95.6	92.7 (93.9)	+0.3	88.9 (91.0)	+0.3

Table 2: Domain results achieved by the Mate parser in cross-validation settings. The scores in brackets are achieved with gold-standard POS tagging. The 'all' columns contain the added value of extending the training sets with each of the five out-domain subcorpora.

well-engineered feature set and it is enhanced by a Hash Kernel, which leads to higher accuracy.

Evaluation metrics: We apply the Labeled Attachment Score (LAS) and Unlabeled Attachment Score (ULA), taking into account punctuation as well for evaluating dependency parsers and the accuracy on the main POS tags (CPOS) and a fine-grained morphological accuracy (DPOS) for evaluating the POS tagger. In the latter, the analysis is regarded as correct if the main POS tag and each of the morphological features of the token in question are correct.

Results: Table 1 shows the results got by the parsers on the whole Hungarian corpora and on the English datasets. The most important point is that scores are not different from the English scores (although they are not directly comparable). To understand the reasons for this, we manually investigated the set of firing **features** with the highest weights in the Mate parser. Although the assessment of individual feature contributions to a particular decoder decision is not straightforward, we observed that features encoding configurational information (i.e. the direction or length of an edge, the words or POS tag sequences/sets between the governor and the dependent) were frequently among the highest weighted features in English but were extremely rare in Hungarian. For instance, one of the top weighted features for a subject dependency in English was the '*there is no word between the head and the dependent*' feature while this never occurred among the top features in Hungarian.

As a control experiment, we trained the Mate parser only having access to the gold-standard POS tag sequences of the sentences, i.e. we switched off the lexicalization and detailed morphological information. The goal of this experiment was to gain an insight into the performance of the parsers which can only access configurational information. These parsers achieved worse results than the full parsers by 6.8 ULA, 20.3 LAS and 2.9 ULA, 6.4 LAS on the development sets of Hungarian and English, respectively. As expected, Hungarian suffers much more when the parser has to learn from configurational information only, especially when grammatical functions have to be predicted (LAS). Despite this, the results of Table 1 show that the parsers can practically eliminate this gap by learning from morphological features (and lexicalization). This means that the data-driven parsers employing a very rich feature set can learn a model which effectively captures the dependency structures using feature weights which are radically different from the ones used for English.

Another cause of the relatively high scores is that the **CPOS accuracy scores** on Hungarian and English are almost equal: 97.2 and 97.3, respectively. This also explains the small difference between the results got by gold-standard and predicted POS tags. Moreover, the parser can also exploit the morphological features as input in Hungarian.

The Mate parser outperformed the other two parsers on each of the four datasets. Comparing the two graph-based parsers Mate and MST, the gap between them was twice as big in LAS than in ULA in Hungarian, which demonstrates that the **one-step approach looking for the maximum labeled spanning tree** is more suitable for Hungarian than the two-step arc labeling approach of MST. This probably holds for other morphologically rich languages too as the decoder can exploit information from the labels of decoded arcs. Based on these results, we decided to use only Mate for our further experiments.

Table 2 provides an insight into the effect of **domain differences** on POS tagging and parsing scores. There is a noticeable difference between the "newspaper" and the "short business news" corpora. Although these domains seem to be close to each other at the first glance (both are news), they have different characteristics. On the one hand, short business news is a very narrow domain consisting of 2-3 sentence long financial short reports. It frequently uses the same grammatical structures (like "Stock indexes rose X percent at the Y Stock on Wednesday") and the lexicon is also limited. On the other hand, the newspaper subcorpus consists of full journal articles covering various domains and it has a fancy journalist style.

The effect of extending the training dataset with out-of-domain parses is not convincing. In spite of the ten times bigger training datasets, there are two subcorpora where they just harmed the parser, and the improvement on other subcorpora is less than 1 percent. This demonstrates well the domain-dependence of parsing.

The parser and the POS tagger react to domain difficulties in a similar way, according to the first four rows of Table 2. This observation holds for the scores of the parsers working with gold-standard POS tags, which suggests that domain difficulties harm POS tagging and parsing as well. Regarding the two last subcorpora, the compositions consist of very short and usually simple sentences and the training corpora are twice as big compared with other subcorpora. Both factors are probably the reasons for the good parsing performance. In the computer corpus, there are many English terms which are manually tagged with an "unknown" tag. They could not be accurately predicted by the POS tagger but the parser could predict their syntactic role.

Table 2 also tells us that the difference between CPOS and DPOS is usually less than 1 percent. This experimentally supports that the **ambiguity among alternative morphological analyses** is mostly present at the POS-level and the morphological features are efficiently identified by our morphological analyser. The most frequent morphological features which cannot be disambiguated at the word level are related to suffixes with multiple functions or the word itself cannot be unambiguously segmented into morphemes. Although the number of such ambiguous cases is low, they form important features for the parser, thus we will focus on the more accurate handling of these cases in future work.

Comparison to CoNLL-2007 results: The best performing participant of the CoNLL-2007 Shared Task (Nivre et al., 2007) achieved an ULA of 83.6 and LAS of 80.3 (Hall et al., 2007) on the Hungarian corpus. The difference between the top performing English and Hungarian systems were 8.14 ULA and 9.3 LAS. The results reported in 2007 were significantly lower and the gap between English and Hungarian is higher than our current values. To locate the sources of difference we carried out other experiments with Mate on the CoNLL-2007 dataset using the gold-standard POS tags (the shared task used gold-standard POS tags for evaluation).

First we trained and evaluated Mate on the original CoNLL-2007 datasets, where it achieved ULA 84.3 and LAS 80.0. Then we used the sentences of the CoNLL-2007 datasets but with the new, manual annotation. Here, Mate achieved ULA 88.6 and LAS 85.5, which means that the modified annotation schema and the less erroneous/noisy annotation caused an improvement of ULA 4.3 and LAS 5.5. The annotation schema changed a lot: coordination had to be corrected manually since it is treated differently after conversion, moreover, the internal structure of adjectival/participial phrases was not marked in the original constituency treebank, so it was also added manually (Vincze et al., 2010). The improvement in the labeled attachment score is probably due to the reduction of the label set (from 49 to 29 labels), which step was justified by the fact that some morphosyntactic information was doubly coded in the case of nouns (e.g. *házzal* (house-INS) "with the/a house") in the original CoNLL-2007 dataset – first, by their morphological case (Cas=ins) and second, by their dependency label (INS).

Lastly, as the CoNLL-2007 sentences came from the newspaper subcorpus, we can compare these scores with the ULA 90.0 and LAS 87.5 of Table 2. The ULA 1.5 and LAS 2.0 differences are the result of the bigger training corpus (9189 sentences on average compared to 6390 in the CoNLL-2007 dataset).

Hungarian			English		
	label	attachment		label	attachment
virtual nodes	31.5%	39.5%	multiword NEs	15.2%	17.6%
conjunctions and negation	–	11.2%	PP-attachment	–	15.9%
noun attachment	–	9.6%	non-canonical word order	6.4%	6.5%
more than 1 premodifier	–	5.1%	misplaced clause	–	9.7%
coordination	13.5%	16.5%	coordination	8.5%	12.5%
mislabeled adverb	16.3%	–	mislabeled adverb	40.1%	–
annotation errors	10.7%	6.8%	annotation errors	9.7%	8.5%
other	28.0%	11.3%	other	20.1%	29.3%
TOTAL	100%	100%	TOTAL	100%	100%

Table 3: The most frequent corpus-specific and general attachment and labeling error categories (based on a manual investigation of 200–200 erroneous sentences).

6 A Systematic Error Analysis

In order to discover specialties and challenges of Hungarian dependency parsing, we conducted an error analysis of parsed texts from the newspaper domain both in English and Hungarian. 200 randomly selected erroneous sentences from the output of Mate were investigated in both languages and we categorized the errors on the basis of the linguistic phenomenon responsible for the errors – for instance, when an error occurred because of the incorrect identification of a multiword Named Entity containing a conjunction, we treated it as a Named Entity error instead of a conjunction error –, i.e. our goal was to reveal the real linguistic sources of errors rather than deducing from automatically countable attachment/labeling statistics.

We used the parses based on gold-standard POS tagging for this analysis as our goal was to identify the challenges of parsing independently of the challenges of POS tagging. The error categories are summarized in Table 3 along with their relative contribution to attachment and labeling errors. This table contains the categories with over 5% relative frequency.[5]

The 200 sentences contained 429/319 and 353/330 attachment/labeling errors in Hungarian and English, respectively. In Hungarian, attachment errors outnumber label errors to a great extent whereas in English, their distribution is basically the same. This might be attributed to the higher level of non-projectivity (see Section 4) and to the more fine-grained label set of the English dataset (36 against 29 labels in English and Hungarian, respectively).

[5]The full tables are available at www.inf.u-szeged.hu/rgai/SzegedTreebank.

Virtual nodes: In Hungarian, the most common source of parsing errors was virtual nodes. As there are quite a lot of verbless clauses in Hungarian (see Section 2 on sentences without copula), it might be difficult to figure out the proper dependency relations within the sentence, since the verb plays the central role in the sentence, cf. Tesnière (1959). Our parser was not efficient in identifying the structure of such sentences, probably due to the lack of information for data-driven parsers (each edge is labeled as Exd while they have similar features to ordinary edges). We also note that the output of the current system with Exd labels does not contain too much information for downstream applications of parsing. The appropriate handling of virtual nodes is an important direction for future work.

Noun attachment: In Hungarian, the nominal arguments of infinitives and participles were frequently erroneously attached to the main verb. Take the following sentence: *A Horn-kabinet idején jól bevált módszerhez próbálnak meg visszatérni* (the Horn-government time-3SGPOSS-SUP well tried method-ALL try-3PL PREVERB return-INF) "They are trying to return to the well-tried method of the Horn government". In this sentence, *a Horn-kabinet idején* "during the Horn government" is a modifier of the past participle *bevált* "well-tried", however, it is attached to the main verb *próbálnak* "they are trying" by the parser. Moreover, *módszerhez* "to the method" is an argument of the infinitive *visszatérni* "to return", but the parser links it to the main verb. In free word order languages, the order of the arguments of the infinitive and the main verb may get mixed, which is called scrambling (Ross, 1986). This is not a common source of error in English as arguments cannot scramble.

Article attachment: In Hungarian, if there is an article before a prenominal modifier, it can belong to the head noun and to the modifier as well. In *a szoba ajtaja* (the room door-3SGPOSS) "the door of the room" the article belongs to the modifier but when the prenominal modifier cannot have an article (e.g. *a februárban induló projekt* (the February-INE starting project) "the project starting in February"), it is attached to the head noun (i.e. to *projekt* "project"). It was not always clear for the parser which parent to select for the article. In contrast, these cases are not problematic in English since the modifier typically follows the head and thus each article precedes its head noun.

Conjunctions or **negation words** – most typically the words *is* "too", *csak* "only/just" and *nem/sem* "not" – were much more frequently attached to the wrong node in Hungarian than in English. In Hungarian, they are ambiguous between being adverbs and conjunctions and it is mostly their conjunctive uses which are problematic from the viewpoint of parsing. On the other hand, these words have an important role in marking the information structure of the sentence: they are usually attached to the element in focus position, and if there is no focus, they are attached to the verb. However, sentences with or without focus can have similar word order but their stress pattern is different. Dependency parsers obviously cannot recognize stress patterns, hence conjunctions and negation words are sometimes erroneously attached to the verb in Hungarian.

English sentences with **non-canonical word order** (e.g. questions) were often incorrectly parsed, e.g. the noun following the main verb is the object in sentences like *Replied a salesman: 'Exactly.'*, where it is the subject that follows the verb for stylistic reasons. However, in Hungarian, morphological information is of help in such sentences, as it is not the position relative to the verb but the case suffix that determines the grammatical role of the noun.

In English, high or low **PP-attachment** was responsible for many parsing ambiguities: most typically, the prepositional complement which follows the head was attached to the verb instead of the noun or vice versa. In contrast, Hungarian is a head-after-dependent language, which means that dependents most often occur before the head. Furthermore, there are no prepositions in Hungarian, and grammatical relations encoded by prepositions in English are conveyed by suffixes or postpositions. Thus, if there is a modifier before the nominal head, it requires the presence of a participle as in: *Felvette a kirakatban levő ruhát* (take.on-PAST3SGOBJ the shop.window-INE being dress-ACC) "She put on the dress in the shop window". The English sentence is ambiguous (either the event happens in the shop window or the dress was originally in the shop window) while the Hungarian has only the latter meaning.[6]

General dependency parsing difficulties: There were certain structures that led to typical label and/or attachment errors in both languages. The most frequent one among them is **coordination**. However, it should be mentioned that syntactic ambiguities are often problematic even for humans to disambiguate without contextual or background semantic knowledge.

In the case of label errors, the relation between the given node and its parent was labeled incorrectly. In both English and Hungarian, one of the most common errors of this type was **mislabeled adverbs** and adverbial phrases, e.g. locative adverbs were labeled as ADV/MODE. However, the frequency rate of this error type is much higher in English than in Hungarian, which may be related to the fact that in the English corpus, there is a much more balanced distribution of adverbial labels than in the Hungarian one (where the categories MODE and TLOCY are responsible for 90% of the occurrences). Assigning the most frequent label of the training dataset to each adverb yields an accuracy of 82% in English and 93% in Hungarian, which suggests that there is a higher level of ambiguity for English adverbial phrases. For instance, the preposition *by* may introduce an adverbial modifier of manner (MNR) in *by creating a bill* and the agent in a passive sentence (LGS). Thus, labeling adverbs seems to be a more

[6]However, there exists a head-before-dependent version of the sentence (*Felvette a ruhát a kirakatban*), whose preferred reading is "She was in the shop window while dressing up", that is, the modifier belongs to the verb.

difficult task in English.[7]

Clauses were also often mislabeled in both languages, most typically when there was no overt conjunction between clauses. Another source of error was when **more than one modifier** occurred before a noun (5.1% and 4.2% of attachment errors in Hungarian and in English): in these cases, the first modifier could belong to the noun (*a brown Japanese car*) or to the second modifier (*a brown haired girl*).

Multiword Named Entities: As we mentioned in Section 4, members of multiword Named Entities had a proper noun POS-tag and an NE label in our dataset. Hence when parsing is based on gold standard POS-tags, their recognition is almost perfect while it is a frequent source or errors in the CoNLL-2009 corpus. We investigated the parse of our 200 sentences with predicted POS tags at NEs and found that this introduces several errors (about 5% of both attachment and labeling errors) in Hungarian. On the other hand, the results are only slightly worse in English, i.e. identifying the inner structure of NEs does not depend on whether the parser builds on gold standard or predicted POS-tags since function words like conjunctions or prepositions – which mark grammatical relations – are tagged in the same way in both cases. The relative frequency of this error type is much higher in English even when the Hungarian parser does not have access to the gold proper noun POS tags. The reason for this is simple: in the Penn Treebank the correct internal structure of the NEs has to be identified beyond the "phrase boundaries" while in Hungarian their members just form a chain.

Annotation errors: We note that our analysis took into account only sentences which contained at least one parsing error and we crawled only the dependencies where the gold standard annotation and the output of the parser did not match. Hence, the frequency of annotation errors is probably higher than we found (about 1% of the entire set of dependencies) during our investigation as there could be annotation errors in the "error-free" sentences and also in the investigated sentences where the parser agrees with that error.

[7]We would nevertheless like to point out that adverbial labels have a highly semantic nature, i.e. it could be argued that it is not the syntactic parser that should identify them but a semantic processor.

7 Conclusions

We showed that state-of-the-art dependency parsers achieve similar results – in terms of attachment scores – on Hungarian and English. Although the results with this comparison should be taken with a pinch of salt – as sentence lengths (and information encoded in single words) differ, domain differences and annotation schema divergences are uncatchable – we conclude that parsing Hungarian is just as hard a task as parsing English. We argued that this is due to the relatively good POS tagging accuracy (which is a consequence of the low ambiguity of alternative morphological analyses of a sentence and the good coverage of the morphological analyser) and the fact that data-driven dependency parsers employ a rich feature representation which enables them to learn different kinds of feature weight profiles.

We also discussed the domain differences among the subcorpora of the Szeged Dependency Treebank and their effect on parsing results. Our results support that there can be higher differences in parsing scores among domains in one language than among corpora from a similar domain but different languages (which again marks pitfalls of inter-language comparison of parsing scores).

Our systematic error analysis showed that handling the virtual nodes (mostly empty copula) is a frequent source of errors. We identified several phenomena which are not typically listed as Hungarian syntax-specific features but are challenging for the current data-driven parsers, however, they are not problematic in English (like the attachment of conjunctions and negation words and the attachment problem of nouns and articles). We concluded – based on our quantitative analysis – that a further notable error reduction is only achievable if distinctive attention is paid to these language-specific phenomena.

We intend to investigate the problem of virtual nodes in dependency parsing in more depth and to implement new feature templates for the Hungarian-specific challenges as future work.

Acknowledgments

This work was supported in part by the Deutsche Forschungsgemeinschaft grant SFB 732 and the NIH grant (project codename MASZEKER) of the Hungarian government.

References

Zoltán Alexin, János Csirik, Tibor Gyimóthy, Károly Bibok, Csaba Hatvani, Gábor Prószéky, and László Tihanyi. 2003. Annotated Hungarian National Corpus. In *Proceedings of the EACL*, pages 53–56.

Anna Babarczy, Bálint Gábor, Gábor Hamp, and András Rung. 2005. Hunpars: a rule-based sentence parser for Hungarian. In *Proceedings of the 6th International Symposium on Computational Intelligence*.

Csongor Barta, Dóra Csendes, János Csirik, András Hócza, András Kocsor, and Kornél Kovács. 2005. Learning syntactic tree patterns from a balanced Hungarian natural language database, the Szeged Treebank. In *Proceedings of 2005 IEEE International Conference on Natural Language Processing and Knowledge Engineering*, pages 225 – 231.

Bernd Bohnet. 2010. Top accuracy and fast dependency parsing is not a contradiction. In *Proceedings of the 23rd International Conference on Computational Linguistics (Coling 2010)*, pages 89–97.

Sabine Buchholz and Erwin Marsi. 2006. CoNLL-X Shared Task on Multilingual Dependency Parsing. In *Proceedings of the Tenth Conference on Computational Natural Language Learning (CoNLL-X)*, pages 149–164.

Xavier Carreras. 2007. Experiments with a higher-order projective dependency parser. In *Proceedings of the CoNLL Shared Task Session of EMNLP-CoNLL 2007*, pages 957–961.

Dóra Csendes, János Csirik, Tibor Gyimóthy, and András Kocsor. 2005. The Szeged Treebank. In *TSD*, pages 123–131.

Katalin É. Kiss. 2002. *The Syntax of Hungarian*. Cambridge University Press, Cambridge.

Jason M. Eisner. 1996. Three new probabilistic models for dependency parsing: an exploration. In *Proceedings of the 16th conference on Computational linguistics - Volume 1*, COLING '96, pages 340–345.

Richárd Farkas, Dániel Szeredi, Dániel Varga, and Veronika Vincze. 2010. MSD-KR harmonizáció a Szeged Treebank 2.5-ben [Harmonizing MSD and KR codes in the Szeged Treebank 2.5]. In *VII. Magyar Számítógépes Nyelvészeti Konferencia*, pages 349–353.

Jan Hajič, Alena Böhmová, Eva Hajičová, and Barbora Vidová-Hladká. 2000. The Prague Dependency Treebank: A Three-Level Annotation Scenario. In Anne Abeillé, editor, *Treebanks: Building and Using Parsed Corpora*, pages 103–127. Amsterdam:Kluwer.

Jan Hajič, Massimiliano Ciaramita, Richard Johansson, Daisuke Kawahara, Maria Antònia Martí, Lluís Màrquez, Adam Meyers, Joakim Nivre, Sebastian Padó, Jan Štěpánek, Pavel Straňák, Mihai Surdeanu, Nianwen Xue, and Yi Zhang. 2009. The CoNLL-2009 Shared Task: Syntactic and Semantic Dependencies in Multiple Languages. In *Proceedings of the Thirteenth Conference on Computational Natural Language Learning (CoNLL 2009): Shared Task*, pages 1–18.

Johan Hall, Jens Nilsson, Joakim Nivre, Gülsen Eryigit, Beáta Megyesi, Mattias Nilsson, and Markus Saers. 2007. Single Malt or Blended? A Study in Multilingual Parser Optimization. In *Proceedings of the CoNLL Shared Task Session of EMNLP-CoNLL 2007*, pages 933–939.

Szilárd Iván, Róbert Ormándi, and András Kocsor. 2007. Magyar mondatok SVM alapú szintaxis elemzése [SVM-based syntactic parsing of Hungarian sentences]. In *V. Magyar Számítógépes Nyelvészeti Konferencia*, pages 281–283.

Taku Kudo and Yuji Matsumoto. 2002. Japanese dependency analysis using cascaded chunking. In *Proceedings of the 6th Conference on Natural Language Learning - Volume 20*, COLING-02, pages 1–7.

Ryan McDonald and Joakim Nivre. 2011. Analyzing and integrating dependency parsers. *Computational Linguistics*, 37:197–230.

Ryan McDonald, Fernando Pereira, Kiril Ribarov, and Jan Hajic. 2005. Non-Projective Dependency Parsing using Spanning Tree Algorithms. In *Proceedings of Human Language Technology Conference and Conference on Empirical Methods in Natural Language Processing*, pages 523–530.

Joakim Nivre and Jens Nilsson. 2005. Pseudo-Projective Dependency Parsing. In *Proceedings of the 43rd Annual Meeting of the Association for Computational Linguistics (ACL'05)*, pages 99–106.

Joakim Nivre, Johan Hall, and Jens Nilsson. 2004. Memory-Based Dependency Parsing. In *HLT-NAACL 2004 Workshop: Eighth Conference on Computational Natural Language Learning (CoNLL-2004)*, pages 49–56.

Joakim Nivre, Johan Hall, Sandra Kübler, Ryan McDonald, Jens Nilsson, Sebastian Riedel, and Deniz Yuret. 2007. The CoNLL 2007 Shared Task on Dependency Parsing. In *Proceedings of the CoNLL Shared Task Session of EMNLP-CoNLL 2007*, pages 915–932.

Gábor Prószéky, László Tihanyi, and Gábor L. Ugray. 2004. Moose: A Robust High-Performance Parser and Generator. In *Proceedings of the 9th Workshop of the European Association for Machine Translation*.

John R. Ross. 1986. *Infinite syntax!* ABLEX, Norwood, NJ.

Lucien Tesnière. 1959. *Éléments de syntaxe structurale*. Klincksieck, Paris.

Kristina Toutanova, Dan Klein, Christopher D. Manning, and Yoram Singer. 2003. Feature-rich part-of-speech tagging with a cyclic dependency network. In *Proceedings of the 2003 Conference of the North American Chapter of the Association for Computational Linguistics on Human Language Technology - Volume 1*, pages 173–180.

Viktor Trón, Péter Halácsy, Péter Rebrus, András Rung, Eszter Simon, and Péter Vajda. 2006. Morphdb.hu: Hungarian lexical database and morphological grammar. In *Proceedings of 5th International Conference on Language Resources and Evaluation (LREC '06)*.

Dániel Varga, Péter Halácsy, András Kornai, Viktor Nagy, László Németh, and Viktor Trón. 2005. Parallel corpora for medium density languages. In *Proceedings of the RANLP*, pages 590–596.

Veronika Vincze, Dóra Szauter, Attila Almási, György Móra, Zoltán Alexin, and János Csirik. 2010. Hungarian Dependency Treebank. In *Proceedings of the Seventh Conference on International Language Resources and Evaluation (LREC'10)*.

Dependency Parsing with Undirected Graphs

Carlos Gómez-Rodríguez
Departamento de Computación
Universidade da Coruña
Campus de Elviña, 15071
A Coruña, Spain
carlos.gomez@udc.es

Daniel Fernández-González
Departamento de Informática
Universidade de Vigo
Campus As Lagoas, 32004
Ourense, Spain
danifg@uvigo.es

Abstract

We introduce a new approach to transition-based dependency parsing in which the parser does not directly construct a dependency structure, but rather an undirected graph, which is then converted into a directed dependency tree in a post-processing step. This alleviates error propagation, since undirected parsers do not need to observe the single-head constraint.

Undirected parsers can be obtained by simplifying existing transition-based parsers satisfying certain conditions. We apply this approach to obtain undirected variants of the planar and 2-planar parsers and of Covington's non-projective parser. We perform experiments on several datasets from the CoNLL-X shared task, showing that these variants outperform the original directed algorithms in most of the cases.

1 Introduction

Dependency parsing has proven to be very useful for natural language processing tasks. Data-driven dependency parsers such as those by Nivre et al. (2004), McDonald et al. (2005), Titov and Henderson (2007), Martins et al. (2009) or Huang and Sagae (2010) are accurate and efficient, they can be trained from annotated data without the need for a grammar, and they provide a simple representation of syntax that maps to predicate-argument structure in a straightforward way.

In particular, **transition-based** dependency parsers (Nivre, 2008) are a type of dependency parsing algorithms which use a model that scores transitions between parser states. Greedy deterministic search can be used to select the transition to be taken at each state, thus achieving linear or quadratic time complexity.

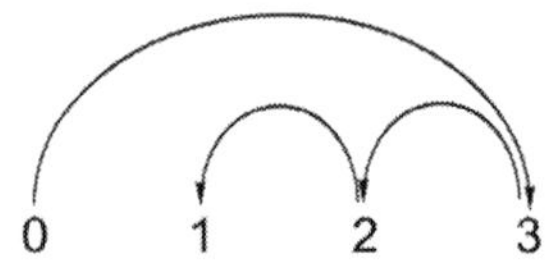

Figure 1: An example dependency structure where transition-based parsers enforcing the single-head constraint will incur in error propagation if they mistakenly build a dependency link $1 \rightarrow 2$ instead of $2 \rightarrow 1$ (dependency links are represented as arrows going from head to dependent).

It has been shown by McDonald and Nivre (2007) that such parsers suffer from **error propagation**: an early erroneous choice can place the parser in an incorrect state that will in turn lead to more errors. For instance, suppose that a sentence whose correct analysis is the dependency graph in Figure 1 is analyzed by any bottom-up or left-to-right transition-based parser that outputs dependency trees, therefore obeying the **single-head constraint** (only one incoming arc is allowed per node). If the parser chooses an erroneous transition that leads it to build a dependency link from 1 to 2 instead of the correct link from 2 to 1, this will lead it to a state where the single-head constraint makes it illegal to create the link from 3 to 2. Therefore, a single erroneous choice will cause two attachment errors in the output tree.

With the goal of minimizing these sources of errors, we obtain novel *undirected* variants of several parsers; namely, of the planar and 2-planar parsers by Gómez-Rodríguez and Nivre (2010) and the non-projective list-based parser described by Nivre (2008), which is based on Covington's algorithm (Covington, 2001). These variants work by collapsing the LEFT-ARC and

RIGHT-ARC transitions in the original parsers, which create right-to-left and left-to-right dependency links, into a single ARC transition creating an undirected link. This has the advantage that the single-head constraint need not be observed during the parsing process, since the directed notions of head and dependent are lost in undirected graphs. This gives the parser more freedom and can prevent situations where enforcing the constraint leads to error propagation, as in Figure 1.

On the other hand, these new algorithms have the disadvantage that their output is an undirected graph, which has to be post-processed to recover the direction of the dependency links and generate a valid dependency tree. Thus, some complexity is moved from the parsing process to this post-processing step; and each undirected parser will outperform the directed version only if the simplification of the parsing phase is able to avoid more errors than are generated by the post-processing. As will be seen in latter sections, experimental results indicate that this is in fact the case.

The rest of this paper is organized as follows: Section 2 introduces some notation and concepts that we will use throughout the paper. In Section 3, we present the undirected versions of the parsers by Gómez-Rodríguez and Nivre (2010) and Nivre (2008), as well as some considerations about the feature models suitable to train them. In Section 4, we discuss post-processing techniques that can be used to recover dependency trees from undirected graphs. Section 5 presents an empirical study of the performance obtained by these parsers, and Section 6 contains a final discussion.

2 Preliminaries

2.1 Dependency Graphs

Let $w = w_1 \dots w_n$ be an input string. A **dependency graph** for w is a directed graph $G = (V_w, E)$, where $V_w = \{0, \dots, n\}$ is the set of nodes, and $E \subseteq V_w \times V_w$ is the set of directed arcs. Each node in V_w encodes the position of a token in w, and each arc in E encodes a dependency relation between two tokens. We write $i \rightarrow j$ to denote a directed arc (i, j), which will also be called a **dependency link** from i to j.[1] We say that i is the **head** of j and, conversely, that j is a syntactic **dependent** of i.

[1]In practice, dependency links are usually **labeled**, but to simplify the presentation we will ignore labels throughout most of the paper. However, all the results and algorithms presented can be applied to labeled dependency graphs and will be so applied in the experimental evaluation.

Given a dependency graph $G = (V_w, E)$, we write $i \rightarrow^\star j \in E$ if there is a (possibly empty) directed path from i to j; and $i \leftrightarrow^\star j \in E$ if there is a (possibly empty) path between i and j in the undirected graph underlying G (omitting the references to E when clear from the context).

Most dependency-based representations of syntax do not allow arbitrary dependency graphs, instead, they are restricted to acyclic graphs that have at most one head per node. Dependency graphs satisfying these constraints are called dependency forests.

Definition 1 *A dependency graph G is said to be a **forest** iff it satisfies:*

1. *Acyclicity constraint: if $i \rightarrow^\star j$, then not $j \rightarrow i$.*
2. *Single-head constraint: if $j \rightarrow i$, then there is no $k \neq j$ such that $k \rightarrow i$.*

A node that has no head in a dependency forest is called a **root**. Some dependency frameworks add the additional constraint that dependency forests have only one root (or, equivalently, that they are connected). Such a forest is called a **dependency tree**. A dependency tree can be obtained from any dependency forest by linking all of its root nodes as dependents of a dummy root node, conventionally located in position 0 of the input.

2.2 Transition Systems

In the framework of Nivre (2008), transition-based parsers are described by means of a non-deterministic state machine called a **transition system**.

Definition 2 *A **transition system** for dependency parsing is a tuple $S = (C, T, c_s, C_t)$, where*

1. *C is a set of possible parser **configurations**,*
2. *T is a finite set of **transitions**, which are partial functions $t : C \rightarrow C$,*
3. *c_s is a total initialization function mapping each input string to a unique **initial configuration**, and*
4. *$C_t \subseteq C$ is a set of **terminal configurations**.*

To obtain a deterministic parser from a non-deterministic transition system, an **oracle** is used to deterministically select a single transition at each configuration. An oracle for a transition system $S = (C, T, c_s, C_t)$ is a function $o : C \rightarrow T$. Suitable oracles can be obtained in practice by training classifiers on treebank data (Nivre et al., 2004).

2.3 The Planar, 2-Planar and Covington Transition Systems

Our undirected dependency parsers are based on the planar and 2-planar transition systems by Gómez-Rodríguez and Nivre (2010) and the version of the Covington (2001) non-projective parser defined by Nivre (2008). We now outline these directed parsers briefly, a more detailed description can be found in the above references.

2.3.1 Planar

The planar transition system by Gómez-Rodríguez and Nivre (2010) is a linear-time transition-based parser for **planar** dependency forests, i.e., forests whose dependency arcs do not cross when drawn above the words. The set of planar dependency structures is a very mild extension of that of projective structures (Kuhlmann and Nivre, 2006).

Configurations in this system are of the form $c = \langle \Sigma, B, A \rangle$ where Σ and B are disjoint lists of nodes from V_w (for some input w), and A is a set of dependency links over V_w. The list B, called the **buffer**, holds the input words that are still to be read. The list Σ, called the **stack**, is initially empty and is used to hold words that have dependency links pending to be created. The system is shown at the top in Figure 2, where the notation $\Sigma \mid i$ is used for a stack with top i and tail Σ, and we invert the notation for the buffer for clarity (i.e., $i \mid B$ as a buffer with top i and tail B).

The system reads the input sentence and creates links in a left-to-right order by executing its four transitions, until it gets to a terminal configuration. A SHIFT transition moves the first (leftmost) node in the buffer to the top of the stack. Transitions LEFT-ARC and RIGHT-ARC create leftward or rightward link, respectively, involving the first node in the buffer and the topmost node in the stack. Finally, REDUCE transition is used to pop the top word from the stack when we have finished building arcs to or from it.

2.3.2 2-Planar

The 2-planar transition system by Gómez-Rodríguez and Nivre (2010) is an extension of the planar system that uses two stacks, allowing it to recognize 2-planar structures, a larger set of dependency structures that has been shown to cover the vast majority of non-projective structures in a number of treebanks (Gómez-Rodríguez and Nivre, 2010).

This transition system, shown in Figure 2, has configurations of the form $c = \langle \Sigma_0, \Sigma_1, B, A \rangle$, where we call Σ_0 the **active stack** and Σ_1 the **inactive stack**. Its SHIFT, LEFT-ARC, RIGHT-ARC and REDUCE transitions work similarly to those in the planar parser, but while SHIFT pushes the first word in the buffer to *both* stacks; the other three transitions only work with the top of the active stack, ignoring the inactive one. Finally, a SWITCH transition is added that makes the active stack inactive and vice versa.

2.3.3 Covington Non-Projective

Covington (2001) proposes several incremental parsing strategies for dependency representations and one of them can recover non-projective dependency graphs. Nivre (2008) implements a variant of this strategy as a transition system with configurations of the form $c = \langle \lambda_1, \lambda_2, B, A \rangle$, where λ_1 and λ_2 are **lists** containing partially processed words and B is the **buffer** list of unprocessed words.

The Covington non-projective transition system is shown at the bottom in Figure 2. At each configuration $c = \langle \lambda_1, \lambda_2, B, A \rangle$, the parser has to consider whether any dependency arc should be created involving the top of the buffer and the words in λ_1. A LEFT-ARC transition adds a link from the first node j in the buffer to the node in the head of the list λ_1, which is moved to the list λ_2 to signify that we have finished considering it as a possible head or dependent of j. The RIGHT-ARC transition does the same manipulation, but creating the symmetric link. A NO-ARC transition removes the head of the list λ_1 and inserts it at the head of the list λ_2 without creating any arcs: this transition is to be used where there is no dependency relation between the top node in the buffer and the head of λ_1, but we still may want to create an arc involving the top of the buffer and other nodes in λ_1. Finally, if we do not want to create any such arcs at all, we can execute a SHIFT transition, which advances the parsing process by removing the first node in the buffer B and inserting it at the head of a list obtained by concatenating

λ_1 and λ_2. This list becomes the new λ_1, whereas λ_2 is empty in the resulting configuration.

Note that the Covington parser has quadratic complexity with respect to input length, while the planar and 2-planar parsers run in linear time.

3 The Undirected Parsers

The transition systems defined in Section 2.3 share the common property that their LEFT-ARC and RIGHT-ARC have exactly the same effects except for the direction of the links that they create. We can take advantage of this property to define undirected versions of these transition systems, by transforming them as follows:

- Configurations are changed so that the arc set A is a set of undirected arcs, instead of directed arcs.
- The LEFT-ARC and RIGHT-ARC transitions in each parser are collapsed into a single ARC transition that creates an undirected arc.
- The preconditions of transitions that guarantee the single-head constraint are removed, since the notions of head and dependent are lost in undirected graphs.

By performing these transformations and leaving the systems otherwise unchanged, we obtain the undirected variants of the planar, 2-planar and Covington algorithms that are shown in Figure 3.

Note that the transformation can be applied to any transition system having LEFT-ARC and RIGHT-ARC transitions that are equal except for the direction of the created link, and thus collapsable into one. The above three transition systems fulfill this property, but not every transition system does. For example, the well-known arc-eager parser of Nivre (2003) pops a node from the stack when creating left arcs, and pushes a node to the stack when creating right arcs, so the transformation cannot be applied to it.[2]

[2]One might think that the arc-eager algorithm could still be transformed by converting each of its arc transitions into an undirected transition, without collapsing them into one. However, this would result into a parser that violates the acyclicity constraint, since the algorithm is designed in such a way that acyclicity is only guaranteed if the single-head constraint is kept. It is easy to see that this problem cannot happen in parsers where LEFT-ARC and RIGHT-ARC transitions have the same effect: in these, if a directed graph is not parsable in the original algorithm, its underlying undirected graph cannot not be parsable in the undirected variant.

3.1 Feature models

Some of the features that are typically used to train transition-based dependency parsers depend on the direction of the arcs that have been built up to a certain point. For example, two such features for the planar parser could be the POS tag associated with the head of the topmost stack node, or the label of the arc going from the first node in the buffer to its leftmost dependent.[3]

As the notion of head and dependent is lost in undirected graphs, this kind of features cannot be used to train undirected parsers. Instead, we use features based on undirected relations between nodes. We found that the following kinds of features worked well in practice as a replacement for features depending on arc direction:

- Information about the ith node linked to a given node (topmost stack node, topmost buffer node, etc.) on the left or on the right, and about the associated undirected arc, typically for $i = 1, 2, 3$,
- Information about whether two nodes are linked or not in the undirected graph, and about the label of the arc between them,
- Information about the first left and right "undirected siblings" of a given node, i.e., the first node q located to the left of the given node p such that p and q are linked to some common node r located to the right of both, and vice versa. Note that this notion of undirected siblings does not correspond exclusively to siblings in the directed graph, since it can also capture other second-order interactions, such as grandparents.

4 Reconstructing the dependency forest

The modified transition systems presented in the previous section generate undirected graphs. To obtain complete dependency parsers that are able to produce directed dependency forests, we will need a reconstruction step that will assign a direction to the arcs in such a way that the single-head constraint is obeyed. This reconstruction step can be implemented by building a directed graph with weighted arcs corresponding to both possible directions of each undirected edge, and then finding an optimum branching to reduce it to a directed

[3]These example features are taken from the default model for the planar parser in version 1.5 of MaltParser (Nivre et al., 2006).

Planar initial/terminal configurations:		$c_s(w_1 \dots w_n) = \langle [], [1 \dots n], \emptyset \rangle$, $C_f = \{\langle \Sigma, [], A \rangle \in C\}$
Transitions:	SHIFT	$\langle \Sigma, i\vert B, A \rangle \Rightarrow \langle \Sigma\vert i, B, A \rangle$
	REDUCE	$\langle \Sigma\vert i, B, A \rangle \Rightarrow \langle \Sigma, B, A \rangle$
	LEFT-ARC	$\langle \Sigma\vert i, j\vert B, A \rangle \Rightarrow \langle \Sigma\vert i, j\vert B, A \cup \{(j, i)\} \rangle$ only if $\nexists k \mid (k, i) \in A$ (single-head) and $i \leftrightarrow^* j \notin A$ (acyclicity).
	RIGHT-ARC	$\langle \Sigma\vert i, j\vert B, A \rangle \Rightarrow \langle \Sigma\vert i, j\vert B, A \cup \{(i, j)\} \rangle$ only if $\nexists k \mid (k, j) \in A$ (single-head) and $i \leftrightarrow^* j \notin A$ (acyclicity).
2-Planar initial/terminal configurations:		$c_s(w_1 \dots w_n) = \langle [], [], [1 \dots n], \emptyset \rangle$, $C_f = \{\langle \Sigma_0, \Sigma_1, [], A \rangle \in C\}$
Transitions:	SHIFT	$\langle \Sigma_0, \Sigma_1, i\vert B, A \rangle \Rightarrow \langle \Sigma_0\vert i, \Sigma_1\vert i, B, A \rangle$
	REDUCE	$\langle \Sigma_0\vert i, \Sigma_1, B, A \rangle \Rightarrow \langle \Sigma_0, \Sigma_1, B, A \rangle$
	LEFT-ARC	$\langle \Sigma_0\vert i, \Sigma_1, j\vert B, A \rangle \Rightarrow \langle \Sigma_0\vert i, \Sigma_1, j\vert B, A \cup \{j, i)\} \rangle$ only if $\nexists k \mid (k, i) \in A$ (single-head) and $i \leftrightarrow^* j \notin A$ (acyclicity).
	RIGHT-ARC	$\langle \Sigma_0\vert i, \Sigma_1, j\vert B, A \rangle \Rightarrow \langle \Sigma_0\vert i, \Sigma_1, j\vert B, A \cup \{(i, j)\} \rangle$ only if $\nexists k \mid (k, j) \in A$ (single-head) and $i \leftrightarrow^* j \notin A$ (acyclicity).
	SWITCH	$\langle \Sigma_0, \Sigma_1, B, A \rangle \Rightarrow \langle \Sigma_1, \Sigma_0, B, A \rangle$
Covington initial/term. configurations:		$c_s(w_1 \dots w_n) = \langle [], [], [1 \dots n], \emptyset \rangle$, $C_f = \{\langle \lambda_1, \lambda_2, [], A \rangle \in C\}$
Transitions:	SHIFT	$\langle \lambda_1, \lambda_2, i\vert B, A \rangle \Rightarrow \langle \lambda_1 \cdot \lambda_2\vert i, [], B, A \rangle$
	NO-ARC	$\langle \lambda_1\vert i, \lambda_2, B, A \rangle \Rightarrow \langle \lambda_1, i\vert \lambda_2, B, A \rangle$
	LEFT-ARC	$\langle \lambda_1\vert i, \lambda_2, j\vert B, A \rangle \Rightarrow \langle \lambda_1, i\vert \lambda_2, j\vert B, A \cup \{(j, i)\} \rangle$ only if $\nexists k \mid (k, i) \in A$ (single-head) and $i \leftrightarrow^* j \notin A$ (acyclicity).
	RIGHT-ARC	$\langle \lambda_1\vert i, \lambda_2, j\vert B, A \rangle \Rightarrow \langle \lambda_1, i\vert \lambda_2, j\vert B, A \cup \{(i, j)\} \rangle$ only if $\nexists k \mid (k, j) \in A$ (single-head) and $i \leftrightarrow^* j \notin A$ (acyclicity).

Figure 2: Transition systems for planar, 2-planar and Covington non-projective dependency parsing.

Undirected Planar initial/term. conf.:		$c_s(w_1 \dots w_n) = \langle [], [1 \dots n], \emptyset \rangle$, $C_f = \{\langle \Sigma, [], A \rangle \in C\}$
Transitions:	SHIFT	$\langle \Sigma, i\vert B, A \rangle \Rightarrow \langle \Sigma\vert i, B, A \rangle$
	REDUCE	$\langle \Sigma\vert i, B, A \rangle \Rightarrow \langle \Sigma, B, A \rangle$
	ARC	$\langle \Sigma\vert i, j\vert B, A \rangle \Rightarrow \langle \Sigma\vert i, j\vert B, A \cup \{\{i, j\}\} \rangle$ only if $i \leftrightarrow^* j \notin A$ (acyclicity).
Undirected 2-Planar initial/term. conf.:		$c_s(w_1 \dots w_n) = \langle [], [], [1 \dots n], \emptyset \rangle$, $C_f = \{\langle \Sigma_0, \Sigma_1, [], A \rangle \in C\}$
Transitions:	SHIFT	$\langle \Sigma_0, \Sigma_1, i\vert B, A \rangle \Rightarrow \langle \Sigma_0\vert i, \Sigma_1\vert i, B, A \rangle$
	REDUCE	$\langle \Sigma_0\vert i, \Sigma_1, B, A \rangle \Rightarrow \langle \Sigma_0, \Sigma_1, B, A \rangle$
	ARC	$\langle \Sigma_0\vert i, \Sigma_1, j\vert B, A \rangle \Rightarrow \langle \Sigma_0\vert i, \Sigma_1, j\vert B, A \cup \{\{i, j\}\} \rangle$ only if $i \leftrightarrow^* j \notin A$ (acyclicity).
	SWITCH	$\langle \Sigma_0, \Sigma_1, B, A \rangle \Rightarrow \langle \Sigma_1, \Sigma_0, B, A \rangle$
Undirected Covington init./term. conf.:		$c_s(w_1 \dots w_n) = \langle [], [], [1 \dots n], \emptyset \rangle$, $C_f = \{\langle \lambda_1, \lambda_2, [], A \rangle \in C\}$
Transitions:	SHIFT	$\langle \lambda_1, \lambda_2, i\vert B, A \rangle \Rightarrow \langle \lambda_1 \cdot \lambda_2\vert i, [], B, A \rangle$
	NO-ARC	$\langle \lambda_1\vert i, \lambda_2, B, A \rangle \Rightarrow \langle \lambda_1, i\vert \lambda_2, B, A \rangle$
	ARC	$\langle \lambda_1\vert i, \lambda_2, j\vert B, A \rangle \Rightarrow \langle \lambda_1, i\vert \lambda_2, j\vert B, A \cup \{\{i, j\}\} \rangle$ only if $i \leftrightarrow^* j \notin A$ (acyclicity).

Figure 3: Transition systems for undirected planar, 2-planar and Covington non-projective dependency parsing.

tree. Different criteria for assigning weights to arcs provide different variants of the reconstruction technique.

To describe these variants, we first introduce preliminary definitions. Let $U = (V_w, E)$ be an undirected graph produced by an undirected parser for some string w. We define the following sets of arcs:

$$A_1(U) = \{(i,j) \mid j \neq 0 \wedge \{i,j\} \in E\},$$
$$A_2(U) = \{(0,i) \mid i \in V_w\}.$$

Note that $A_1(U)$ represents the set of arcs obtained from assigning an orientation to an edge in U, except arcs whose dependent is the dummy root, which are disallowed. On the other hand, $A_2(U)$ contains all the possible arcs originating from the dummy root node, regardless of whether their underlying undirected edges are in U or not; this is so that reconstructions are allowed to link unattached tokens to the dummy root.

The reconstruction process consists of finding a minimum branching (i.e. a directed minimum spanning tree) for a weighted directed graph obtained from assigning a cost $c(i,j)$ to each arc (i,j) of the following directed graph:

$$D(U) = \{V_w, A(U) = A_1(U) \cup A_2(U)\}.$$

That is, we will find a dependency tree $T = (V_w, A_T \subseteq A(U))$ such that the sum of costs of the arcs in A_T is minimal. In general, such a minimum branching can be calculated with the Chu-Liu-Edmonds algorithm (Chu and Liu, 1965; Edmonds, 1967). Since the graph $D(U)$ has $O(n)$ nodes and $O(n)$ arcs for a string of length n, this can be done in $O(n \log n)$ if implemented as described by Tarjan (1977).

However, applying these generic techniques is not necessary in this case: since our graph U is acyclic, the problem of reconstructing the forest can be reduced to choosing a root word for each connected component in the graph, linking it as a dependent of the dummy root and directing the other arcs in the component in the (unique) way that makes them point away from the root.

It remains to see how to assign the costs $c(i,j)$ to the arcs of $D(U)$: different criteria for assigning scores will lead to different reconstructions.

4.1 Naive reconstruction

A first, very simple reconstruction technique can be obtained by assigning arc costs to the arcs in $A(U)$ as follows:

$$c(i,j) \begin{cases} 1 & \text{if } (i,j) \in A_1(U), \\ 2 & \text{if } (i,j) \in A_2(U) \wedge (i,j) \notin A_1(U). \end{cases}$$

This approach gives the same cost to all arcs obtained from the undirected graph U, while also allowing (at a higher cost) to attach any node to the dummy root. To obtain satisfactory results with this technique, we must train our parser to explicitly build undirected arcs from the dummy root node to the root word(s) of each sentence using arc transitions (note that this implies that we need to represent forests as trees, in the manner described at the end of Section 2.1). Under this assumption, it is easy to see that we can obtain the correct directed tree T for a sentence if it is provided with its underlying undirected tree U: the tree is obtained in $O(n)$ as the unique orientation of U that makes each of its edges point away from the dummy root.

This approach to reconstruction has the advantage of being very simple and not adding any complications to the parsing process, while guaranteeing that the correct directed tree will be recovered if the undirected tree for a sentence is generated correctly. However, it is not very robust, since the direction of all the arcs in the output depends on which node is chosen as sentence head and linked to the dummy root. Therefore, a parsing error affecting the undirected edge involving the dummy root may result in many dependency links being erroneous.

4.2 Label-based reconstruction

To achieve a more robust reconstruction, we use labels to encode a preferred direction for dependency arcs. To do so, for each pre-existing label X in the training set, we create two labels X_l and X_r. The parser is then trained on a modified version of the training set where leftward links originally labelled X are labelled X_l, and rightward links originally labelled X are labelled X_r. Thus, the output of the parser on a new sentence will be an undirected graph where each edge has a label with an annotation indicating whether the reconstruction process should prefer to link the pair of nodes with a leftward or a rightward arc. We can then assign costs to our minimum branching algorithm so that it will return a tree agreeing with as many such annotations as possible.

To do this, we call $A_{1+}(U) \subseteq A_1(U)$ the set of arcs in $A_1(U)$ that agree with the annotations, i.e., arcs $(i,j) \in A_1(U)$ where either $i < j$ and i, j is labelled X_r in U, or $i > j$ and i, j is labelled X_l in U. We call $A_{1-}(U)$ the set of arcs in $A_1(U)$ that disagree with the annotations, i.e., $A_{1-}(U) = A_1(U) \backslash A_{1+}(U)$. And we assign costs as follows:

$$c(i,j) \begin{cases} 1 & \text{if } (i,j) \in A_{1+}(U), \\ 2 & \text{if } (i,j) \in A_{1-}(U), \\ 2n & \text{if } (i,j) \in A_2(U) \wedge (i,j) \notin A_1(U). \end{cases}$$

where n is the length of the string.

With these costs, the minimum branching algorithm will find a tree which agrees with as many annotations as possible. Additional arcs from the root not corresponding to any edge in the output of the parser (i.e. arcs in $A_2(U)$ but not in $A_1(U)$) will be used only if strictly necessary to guarantee connectedness, this is implemented by the high cost for these arcs.

While this may be the simplest cost assignment to implement label-based reconstruction, we have found that better empirical results are obtained if we give the algorithm more freedom to create new arcs from the root, as follows:

$$c(i,j) \begin{cases} 1 & \text{if } (i,j) \in A_{1+}(U) \wedge (i,j) \notin A_2(U), \\ 2 & \text{if } (i,j) \in A_{1-}(U) \wedge (i,j) \notin A_2(U), \\ 2n & \text{if } (i,j) \in A_2(U). \end{cases}$$

While the cost of arcs from the dummy root is still $2n$, this is now so even for arcs that are in the output of the undirected parser, which had cost 1 before. Informally, this means that with this configuration the postprocessor does not "trust" the links from the dummy root created by the parser, and may choose to change them if it is convenient to get a better agreement with label annotations (see Figure 4 for an example of the difference between both cost assignments). We believe that the better accuracy obtained with this criterion probably stems from the fact that it is biased towards changing links from the root, which tend to be more problematic for transition-based parsers, while respecting the parser output for links located deeper in the dependency structure, for which transition-based parsers tend to be more accurate (McDonald and Nivre, 2007).

Note that both variants of label-based reconstruction have the property that, if the undirected parser produces the correct edges and labels for a given sentence, then the obtained directed tree is guaranteed to be correct (as it will simply be the tree obtained by decoding the label annotations).

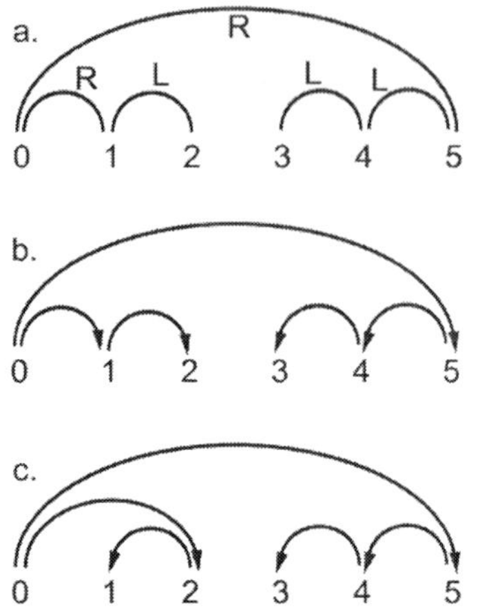

Figure 4: a) An undirected graph obtained by the parser with the label-based transformation, b) and c) The dependency graph obtained by each of the variants of the label-based reconstruction (note how the second variant moves an arc from the root).

5 Experiments

In this section, we evaluate the performance of the undirected planar, 2-planar and Covington parsers on eight datasets from the CoNLL-X shared task (Buchholz and Marsi, 2006).

Tables 1, 2 and 3 compare the accuracy of the undirected versions with naive and label-based reconstruction to that of the directed versions of the planar, 2-planar and Covington parsers, respectively. In addition, we provide a comparison to well-known state-of-the-art projective and non-projective parsers: the planar parsers are compared to the arc-eager projective parser by Nivre (2003), which is also restricted to planar structures; and the 2-planar parsers are compared with the arc-eager parser with pseudo-projective transformation of Nivre and Nilsson (2005), capable of handling non-planar dependencies.

We use SVM classifiers from the LIBSVM package (Chang and Lin, 2001) for all the languages except Chinese, Czech and German. In these, we use the LIBLINEAR package (Fan et al., 2008) for classification, which reduces training time for these larger datasets; and feature models adapted to this system which, in the case of German, result in higher accuracy than published results using LIBSVM.

The LIBSVM feature models for the arc-eager projective and pseudo-projective parsers are the same used by these parsers in the CoNLL-X shared task, where the pseudo-projective version of MaltParser was one of the two top performing systems (Buchholz and Marsi, 2006). For the 2-planar parser, we took the feature models from Gómez-Rodríguez and Nivre (2010) for the languages included in that paper. For all the algorithms and datasets, the feature models used for the undirected parsers were adapted from those of the directed parsers as described in Section 3.1.[4]

The results show that the use of undirected parsing with label-based reconstruction clearly improves the performance in the vast majority of the datasets for the planar and Covington algorithms, where in many cases it also improves upon the corresponding projective and non-projective state-of-the-art parsers provided for comparison. In the case of the 2-planar parser the results are less conclusive, with improvements over the directed versions in five out of the eight languages.

The improvements in LAS obtained with label-based reconstruction over directed parsing are statistically significant at the .05 level[5] for Danish, German and Portuguese in the case of the planar parser; and Czech, Danish and Turkish for Covington's parser. No statistically significant decrease in accuracy was detected in any of the algorithm/dataset combinations.

As expected, the good results obtained by the undirected parsers with label-based reconstruction contrast with those obtained by the variants with root-based reconstruction, which performed worse in all the experiments.

6 Discussion

We have presented novel variants of the planar and 2-planar transition-based parsers by Gómez-Rodríguez and Nivre (2010) and of Covington's non-projective parser (Covington, 2001; Nivre, 2008) which ignore the direction of dependency links, and reconstruction techniques that can be used to recover the direction of the arcs thus produced. The results obtained show that this idea of undirected parsing, together with the label-based reconstruction technique of Section 4.2, improves parsing accuracy on most of the tested dataset/algorithm combinations, and it can outperform state-of-the-art transition-based parsers.

The accuracy improvements achieved by relaxing the single-head constraint to mitigate error propagation were able to overcome the errors generated in the reconstruction phase, which were few: we observed empirically that the differences between the undirected LAS obtained from the undirected graph before the reconstruction and the final directed LAS are typically below 0.20%. This is true both for the naive and label-based transformations, indicating that both techniques are able to recover arc directions accurately, and the accuracy differences between them come mainly from the differences in training (e.g. having tentative arc direction as part of feature information in the label-based reconstruction and not in the naive one) rather than from the differences in the reconstruction methods themselves.

The reason why we can apply the undirected simplification to the three parsers that we have used in this paper is that their LEFT-ARC and RIGHT-ARC transitions have the same effect except for the direction of the links they create. The same transformation and reconstruction techniques could be applied to any other transition-based dependency parsers sharing this property. The reconstruction techniques alone could potentially be applied to any dependency parser (transition-based or not) as long as it can be somehow converted to output undirected graphs.

The idea of parsing with undirected relations between words has been applied before in the work on Link Grammar (Sleator and Temperley, 1991), but in that case the formalism itself works with undirected graphs, which are the final output of the parser. To our knowledge, the idea of using an undirected graph as an intermediate step towards obtaining a dependency structure has not been explored before.

Acknowledgments

This research has been partially funded by the Spanish Ministry of Economy and Competitiveness and FEDER (projects TIN2010-18552-C03-01 and TIN2010-18552-C03-02), Ministry of Education (FPU Grant Program) and Xunta de Galicia (Rede Galega de Recursos Lingüísticos para unha Soc. do Coñec.). The experiments were conducted with the help of computing resources provided by the Supercomputing Center of Galicia (CESGA). We thank Joakim Nivre for helpful input in the early stages of this work.

[4]All the experimental settings and feature models used are included in the supplementary material and also available at `http://www.grupolys.org/~cgomezr/exp/`.

[5]Statistical significance was assessed using Dan Bikel's randomized comparator: `http://www.cis.upenn.edu/~dbikel/software.html`

	Planar		UPlanarN		UPlanarL		MaltP	
Lang.	LAS(p)	UAS(p)	LAS(p)	UAS(p)	LAS(p)	UAS(p)	LAS(p)	UAS(p)
Arabic	**66.93 (67.34)**	**77.56 (77.22)**	65.91 (66.33)	77.03 (76.75)	66.75 (67.19)	77.45 (**77.22**)	66.43 (66.74)	77.19 (76.83)
Chinese	84.23 (84.20)	88.37 (88.33)	83.14 (83.10)	87.00 (86.95)	84.51* (84.50*)	88.37 (88.35*)	**86.42 (86.39)**	**90.06 (90.02)**
Czech	77.24 (77.70)	83.46 (83.24)	75.08 (75.60)	81.14 (81.14)	**77.60* (77.93*)**	**83.56* (83.41*)**	77.24 (77.57)	83.40 (83.19)
Danish	83.31 (82.60)	88.02 (86.64)	82.65 (82.45)	87.58 (86.67*)	**83.87* (83.83*)**	**88.94* (88.17*)**	83.31 (82.64)	88.30 (86.91)
German	84.66 (83.60)	87.02 (85.67)	83.33 (82.77)	85.78 (84.93)	**86.32* (85.67*)**	**88.62* (87.69*)**	86.12 (85.48)	88.52 (87.58)
Portug.	86.22 (83.82)	89.80 (86.88)	85.89 (83.82)	89.68 (87.06*)	86.52* (**84.83***)	**90.28* (88.03*)**	**86.60** (84.66)	90.20 (87.73)
Swedish	**83.01** (82.44)	88.53 (87.36)	81.20 (81.10)	86.50 (85.86)	82.95 (**82.66***)	88.29 (87.45*)	82.89 (82.44)	**88.61 (87.55)**
Turkish	62.70 (71.27)	73.67 (78.57)	59.83 (68.31)	70.15 (75.17)	**63.27* (71.63*)**	**73.93* (78.72*)**	62.58 (70.96)	73.09 (77.95)

Table 1: Parsing accuracy of the undirected planar parser with naive (UPlanarN) and label-based (UPlanarL) postprocessing in comparison to the directed planar (Planar) and the MaltParser arc-eager projective (MaltP) algorithms, on eight datasets from the CoNLL-X shared task (Buchholz and Marsi, 2006): Arabic (Hajič et al., 2004), Chinese (Chen et al., 2003), Czech (Hajič et al., 2006), Danish (Kromann, 2003), German (Brants et al., 2002), Portuguese (Afonso et al., 2002), Swedish (Nilsson et al., 2005) and Turkish (Oflazer et al., 2003; Atalay et al., 2003). We show labelled (LAS) and unlabelled (UAS) attachment score excluding and including punctuation tokens in the scoring (the latter in brackets). Best results for each language are shown in boldface, and results where the undirected parser outperforms the directed version are marked with an asterisk.

	2Planar		U2PlanarN		U2PlanarL		MaltPP	
Lang.	LAS(p)	UAS(p)	LAS(p)	UAS(p)	LAS(p)	UAS(p)	LAS(p)	UAS(p)
Arabic	**66.73 (67.19)**	**77.33 (77.11)**	66.37 (66.93)	77.15 (77.09)	66.13 (66.52)	76.97 (76.70)	65.93 (66.02)	76.79 (76.14)
Chinese	84.35 (84.32)	88.31 (88.27)	83.02 (82.98)	86.86 (86.81)	84.45* (84.42*)	88.29 (88.25)	86.42 (86.39)	90.06 (90.02)
Czech	77.72 (77.91)	83.76 (83.32)	74.44 (75.19)	80.68 (80.80)	78.00* (**78.59***)	84.22* (**84.21***)	**78.86** (78.47)	**84.54** (83.89)
Danish	**83.81** (83.61)	88.50 (87.63)	82.00 (81.63)	86.87 (85.80)	83.75 (**83.65***)	**88.62* (87.82*)**	83.67 (83.54)	88.52 (87.70)
German	86.28 (85.76)	88.68 (87.86)	82.93 (82.53)	85.52 (84.81)	86.52* (85.99*)	88.72* (87.92*)	**86.94 (86.62)**	**89.30 (88.69)**
Portug.	87.04 (**84.92**)	**90.82 (88.14)**	85.61 (83.45)	89.36 (86.65)	86.70 (84.75)	90.38 (87.88)	**87.08** (84.90)	90.66 (87.95)
Swedish	83.13 (**82.71**)	88.57 (**87.59**)	81.00 (80.71)	86.54 (85.68)	82.59 (82.25)	88.19 (87.29)	**83.39** (82.67)	**88.59** (87.38)
Turkish	61.80 (70.09)	72.75 (77.39)	58.10 (67.44)	68.03 (74.06)	61.92* (70.64*)	72.18 (77.46*)	**62.80 (71.33)**	**73.49 (78.44)**

Table 2: Parsing accuracy of the undirected 2-planar parser with naive (U2PlanarN) and label-based (U2PlanarL) postprocessing in comparison to the directed 2-planar (2Planar) and MaltParser arc-eager pseudo-projective (MaltPP) algorithms. The meaning of the scores shown is as in Table 1.

	Covington		UCovingtonN		UCovingtonL	
Lang.	LAS(p)	UAS(p)	LAS(p)	UAS(p)	LAS(p)	UAS(p)
Arabic	65.17 (65.49)	75.99 (**75.69**)	63.49 (63.93)	74.41 (74.20)	**65.61* (65.81*)**	**76.11*** (75.66)
Chinese	85.61 (85.61)	89.64 (89.62)	84.12 (84.02)	87.85 (87.73)	**86.28* (86.17*)**	**90.16* (90.04*)**
Czech	78.26 (77.43)	84.04 (83.15)	74.02 (74.78)	79.80 (79.92)	**78.42* (78.69*)**	**84.50* (84.16*)**
Danish	83.63 (82.89)	88.50 (87.06)	82.00 (81.61)	86.55 (85.51)	**84.27* (83.85*)**	**88.82* (87.75*)**
German	**86.70** (85.69)	**89.08** (87.78)	84.03 (83.51)	86.16 (85.39)	86.50 (**85.90***)	88.84 (**87.95***)
Portug.	84.73 (82.56)	89.10 (86.30)	83.83 (81.71)	87.88 (85.17)	**84.95* (82.70*)**	**89.18* (86.31*)**
Swedish	**83.53 (82.76)**	**88.91 (87.61)**	81.78 (81.47)	86.78 (85.96)	83.09 (82.73)	88.11 (87.23)
Turkish	64.25 (72.70)	74.85 (79.75)	63.51 (72.08)	74.07 (79.10)	**64.91* (73.38*)**	**75.46* (80.40*)**

Table 3: Parsing accuracy of the undirected Covington non-projective parser with naive (UCovingtonN) and label-based (UCovingtonL) postprocessing in comparison to the directed algorithm (Covington). The meaning of the scores shown is as in Table 1.

References

Susana Afonso, Eckhard Bick, Renato Haber, and Diana Santos. 2002. "Floresta sintá(c)tica": a treebank for Portuguese. In *Proceedings of the 3rd International Conference on Language Resources and Evaluation (LREC 2002)*, pages 1968–1703, Paris, France. ELRA.

Nart B. Atalay, Kemal Oflazer, and Bilge Say. 2003. The annotation process in the Turkish treebank. In *Proceedings of EACL Workshop on Linguistically Interpreted Corpora (LINC-03)*, pages 243–246, Morristown, NJ, USA. Association for Computational Linguistics.

Sabine Brants, Stefanie Dipper, Silvia Hansen, Wolfgang Lezius, and George Smith. 2002. The tiger treebank. In *Proceedings of the Workshop on Treebanks and Linguistic Theories, September 20-21*, Sozopol, Bulgaria.

Sabine Buchholz and Erwin Marsi. 2006. CoNLL-X shared task on multilingual dependency parsing. In *Proceedings of the 10th Conference on Computational Natural Language Learning (CoNLL)*, pages 149–164.

Chih-Chung Chang and Chih-Jen Lin, 2001. *LIBSVM: A Library for Support Vector Machines*. Software available at http://www.csie.ntu.edu.tw/~cjlin/libsvm.

K. Chen, C. Luo, M. Chang, F. Chen, C. Chen, C. Huang, and Z. Gao. 2003. Sinica treebank: Design criteria, representational issues and implementation. In Anne Abeillé, editor, *Treebanks: Building and Using Parsed Corpora*, chapter 13, pages 231–248. Kluwer.

Y. J. Chu and T. H. Liu. 1965. On the shortest arborescence of a directed graph. *Science Sinica*, 14:1396–1400.

Michael A. Covington. 2001. A fundamental algorithm for dependency parsing. In *Proceedings of the 39th Annual ACM Southeast Conference*, pages 95–102.

Jack Edmonds. 1967. Optimum branchings. *Journal of Research of the National Bureau of Standards*, 71B:233–240.

R.-E. Fan, K.-W. Chang, C.-J. Hsieh, X.-R. Wang, and C.-J. Lin. 2008. LIBLINEAR: A library for large linear classification. *Journal of Machine Learning Research*, 9:1871–1874.

Carlos Gómez-Rodríguez and Joakim Nivre. 2010. A transition-based parser for 2-planar dependency structures. In *Proceedings of the 48th Annual Meeting of the Association for Computational Linguistics*, ACL '10, pages 1492–1501, Stroudsburg, PA, USA. Association for Computational Linguistics.

Jan Hajič, Otakar Smrž, Petr Zemánek, Jan Šnaidauf, and Emanuel Beška. 2004. Prague Arabic Dependency Treebank: Development in data and tools. In *Proceedings of the NEMLAR International Conference on Arabic Language Resources and Tools*.

Jan Hajič, Jarmila Panevová, Eva Hajičová, Jarmila Panevová, Petr Sgall, Petr Pajas, Jan Štěpánek, Jiří Havelka, and Marie Mikulová. 2006. Prague Dependency Treebank 2.0. CDROM CAT: LDC2006T01, ISBN 1-58563-370-4. Linguistic Data Consortium.

Liang Huang and Kenji Sagae. 2010. Dynamic programming for linear-time incremental parsing. In *Proceedings of the 48th Annual Meeting of the Association for Computational Linguistics*, ACL '10, pages 1077–1086, Stroudsburg, PA, USA. Association for Computational Linguistics.

Matthias T. Kromann. 2003. The Danish dependency treebank and the underlying linguistic theory. In *Proceedings of the 2nd Workshop on Treebanks and Linguistic Theories (TLT)*, pages 217–220, Växjö, Sweden. Växjö University Press.

Marco Kuhlmann and Joakim Nivre. 2006. Mildly non-projective dependency structures. In *Proceedings of the COLING/ACL 2006 Main Conference Poster Sessions*, pages 507–514.

Andre Martins, Noah Smith, and Eric Xing. 2009. Concise integer linear programming formulations for dependency parsing. In *Proceedings of the Joint Conference of the 47th Annual Meeting of the ACL and the 4th International Joint Conference on Natural Language Processing of the AFNLP (ACL-IJCNLP)*, pages 342–350.

Ryan McDonald and Joakim Nivre. 2007. Characterizing the errors of data-driven dependency parsing models. In *Proceedings of the 2007 Joint Conference on Empirical Methods in Natural Language Processing and Computational Natural Language Learning (EMNLP-CoNLL)*, pages 122–131.

Ryan McDonald, Fernando Pereira, Kiril Ribarov, and Jan Hajič. 2005. Non-projective dependency parsing using spanning tree algorithms. In *Proceedings of the Human Language Technology Conference and the Conference on Empirical Methods in Natural Language Processing (HLT/EMNLP)*, pages 523–530.

Jens Nilsson, Johan Hall, and Joakim Nivre. 2005. MAMBA meets TIGER: Reconstructing a Swedish treebank from Antiquity. In Peter Juel Henrichsen, editor, *Proceedings of the NODALIDA Special Session on Treebanks*.

Joakim Nivre and Jens Nilsson. 2005. Pseudo-projective dependency parsing. In *Proceedings of the 43rd Annual Meeting of the Association for Computational Linguistics (ACL)*, pages 99–106.

Joakim Nivre, Johan Hall, and Jens Nilsson. 2004. Memory-based dependency parsing. In *Proceedings of the 8th Conference on Computational Natural Language Learning (CoNLL-2004)*, pages 49–56, Morristown, NJ, USA. Association for Computational Linguistics.

Joakim Nivre, Johan Hall, and Jens Nilsson. 2006. MaltParser: A data-driven parser-generator for dependency parsing. In *Proceedings of the 5th International Conference on Language Resources and Evaluation (LREC)*, pages 2216–2219.

Joakim Nivre. 2003. An efficient algorithm for projective dependency parsing. In *Proceedings of the 8th International Workshop on Parsing Technologies (IWPT)*, pages 149–160.

Joakim Nivre. 2008. Algorithms for Deterministic Incremental Dependency Parsing. *Computational Linguistics*, 34(4):513–553.

Kemal Oflazer, Bilge Say, Dilek Zeynep Hakkani-Tür, and Gökhan Tür. 2003. Building a Turkish treebank. In Anne Abeillé, editor, *Treebanks: Building and Using Parsed Corpora*, pages 261–277. Kluwer.

Daniel Sleator and Davy Temperley. 1991. Parsing English with a link grammar. Technical Report CMU-CS-91-196, Carnegie Mellon University, Computer Science.

R. E. Tarjan. 1977. Finding optimum branchings. *Networks*, 7:25–35.

Ivan Titov and James Henderson. 2007. A latent variable model for generative dependency parsing. In *Proceedings of the 10th International Conference on Parsing Technologies (IWPT)*, pages 144–155.

The Best of Both Worlds – A Graph-based Completion Model for Transition-based Parsers

Bernd Bohnet and **Jonas Kuhn**
University of Stuttgart
Institute for Natural Language Processing
{bohnet, jonas}@ims.uni-stuttgart.de

Abstract

Transition-based dependency parsers are often forced to make attachment decisions at a point when only partial information about the relevant graph configuration is available. In this paper, we describe a model that takes into account complete structures as they become available to rescore the elements of a beam, combining the advantages of transition-based and graph-based approaches. We also propose an efficient implementation that allows for the use of sophisticated features and show that the completion model leads to a substantial increase in accuracy. We apply the new transition-based parser on typologically different languages such as English, Chinese, Czech, and German and report competitive labeled and unlabeled attachment scores.

1 Introduction

Background. A considerable amount of recent research has gone into data-driven dependency parsing, and interestingly throughout the continuous process of improvements, two classes of parsing algorithms have stayed at the centre of attention, the transition-based (Nivre, 2003) vs. the graph-based approach (Eisner, 1996; McDonald et al., 2005).[1] The two approaches apply fundamentally different strategies to solve the task of finding the optimal labeled dependency tree over the words of an input sentence (where supervised machine learning is used to estimate the scoring parameters on a treebank).

The transition-based approach is based on the conceptually (and cognitively) compelling idea that machine learning, i.e., a model of linguistic experience, is used in exactly those situations when there is an attachment choice in an otherwise deterministic incremental left-to-right parsing process. As a new word is processed, the parser has to decide on one out of a small number of possible transitions (adding a dependency arc pointing to the left or right and/or pushing or popping a word on/from a stack representation). Obviously, the learning can be based on the feature information available at a particular snapshot in incremental processing, i.e., only surface information for the unparsed material to the right, but full structural information for the parts of the string already processed. For the completely processed parts, there are no principled limitations as regards the types of structural configurations that can be checked in feature functions.

The graph-based approach in contrast emphasizes the objective of exhaustive search over all possible trees spanning the input words. Commonly, dynamic programming techniques are used to decide on the optimal tree for each particular word span, considering all candidate splits into subspans, successively building longer spans in a bottom-up fashion (similar to chart-based constituent parsing). Machine learning drives the process of deciding among alternative candidate splits, i.e., feature information can draw on full structural information for the entire material in the span under consideration. However, due to the dynamic programming approach, the features cannot use arbitrarily complex structural configurations: otherwise the dynamic programming chart would have to be split into exponentially many special states. The typical feature models are based on combinations of edges (so-

[1]More references will be provided in sec. 2.

called second-order factors) that closely follow the bottom-up combination of subspans in the parsing algorithm, i.e., the feature functions depend on the presence of two specific dependency edges. Configurations not directly supported by the bottom-up building of larger spans are more cumbersome to integrate into the model (since the combination algorithm has to be adjusted), in particular for third-order factors or higher.

Empirically, i.e., when applied in supervised machine learning experiments based on existing treebanks for various languages, both strategies (and further refinements of them not mentioned here) turn out roughly equal in their capability of picking up most of the relevant patterns well; some subtle strengths and weaknesses are complementary, such that *stacking* of two parsers representing both strategies yields the best results (Nivre and McDonald, 2008): in training and application, one of the parsers is run on each sentence prior to the other, providing additional feature information for the other parser. Another successful technique to combine parsers is voting as carried out by Sagae and Lavie (2006).

The present paper addresses the question if and how a more integrated combination of the strengths of the two strategies can be achieved and implemented efficiently to warrant competitive results.

The main issue and solution strategy. In order to preserve the conceptual (and complexity) advantages of the transition-based strategy, the integrated algorithm we are looking for has to be transition-based at the top level. The advantages of the graph-based approach – a more globally informed basis for the decision among different attachment options – have to be included as part of the scoring procedure. As a prerequisite, our algorithm will require a memory for storing alternative analyses among which to choose. This has been previously introduced in transition-based approaches in the form of a beam (Johansson and Nugues, 2006): rather than representing only the best-scoring history of transitions, the k best-scoring alternative histories are kept around.

As we will indicate in the following, the mere addition of beam search does not help overcome a representational key issue of transition-based parsing: in many situations, a transition-based parser is forced to make an attachment decision for a given input word at a point where no or only partial information about the word's own dependents (and further decendents) is available. Figure 1 illustrates such a case.

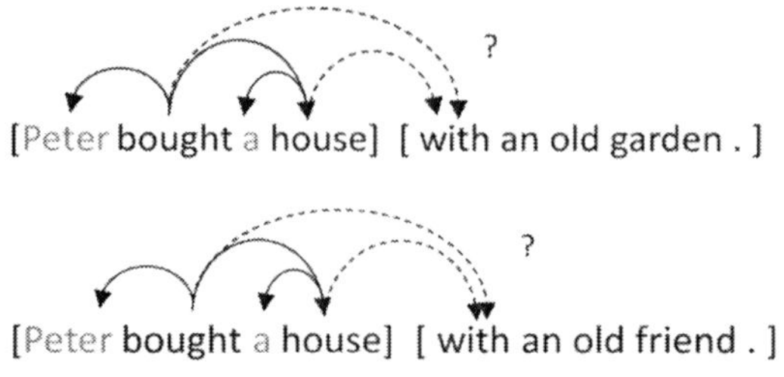

Figure 1: The left set of brackets indicates material that has been processed or is under consideration; on the right is the input, still to be processed. Access to information that is yet unavailable would help the parser to decide on the correct transition.

Here, the parser has to decide whether to create an edge between *house* and *with* or between *bought* and *with* (which is technically achieved by first popping *house* from the stack and then adding the edge). At this time, no information about the object of *with* is available; *with* fails to provide what we call a *complete factor* for the calculation of the scores of the alternative transitions under consideration. In other words, the model cannot make use of any evidence to distinguish between the two examples in Figure 1, and it is bound to get one of the two cases wrong.

Figure 2 illustrates the same case from the perspective of a graph-based parser.

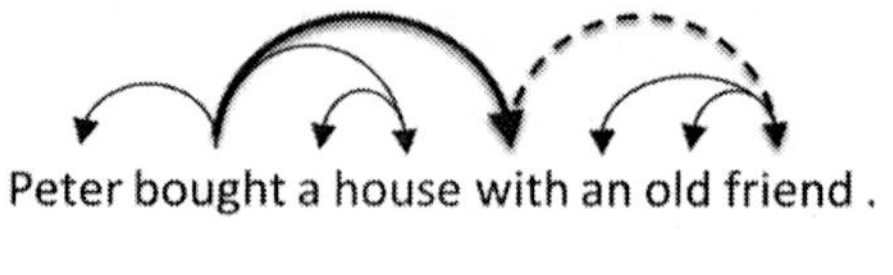

Figure 2: A second order model as used in graph-based parsers has access to the crucial information to build the correct tree. In this case, the parser condsiders the word *friend* (as opposed to *garden*, for instance) as it introduces the bold-face edge.

Here, the combination of subspans is performed at a point when their internal structure has been finalized, i.e., the attachment of *with* (to *bought* or *house*) is not decided until it is clear that *friend* is the object of *with*; hence, the semantically important lexicalization of *with*'s object informs the higher-level attachment decision through a so-called second order factor in the feature model.

Given a suitable amount of training data, the model can thus learn to make the correct decision. The dynamic-programming based graph-based parser is designed in such a way that any score calculation is based on complete factors for the subspans that are combined at this point.

Note that the problem for the transition-based parser cannot be remedied by beam search alone. If we were to keep the two options for attaching *with* around in a beam (say, with a slightly higher score for attachment to *house*, but with *bought* following narrowly behind), there would be no point in the further processing of the sentence at which the choice could be corrected: the transition-based parser still needs to make the decision that *friend* is attached to *with*, but this will not lead the parser to reconsider the decision made earlier on.

The strategy we describe in this paper applies in this very type of situation: whenever information is added in the transition-based parsing process, the scores of all the histories stored in the beam are *recalculated* based on a scoring model inspired by the graph-based parsing approach, i.e., taking complete factors into account as they become incrementally available. As a consequence the beam is reordered, and hence, the incorrect preference of an attachment of *with* to *house* (based on incomplete factors) can later be corrected as *friend* is processed and the complete second-order factor becomes available.[2]

The integrated transition-based parsing strategy has a number of advantages:
(1) We can integrate and investigate a number of third order factors, without the need to implement a more complex parsing model each time anew to explore the properties of such distinct model.
(2) The parser with completion model maintains the favorable complexity of transition-based parsers.
(3) The completion model compensates for the lower accuracy of cases when only incomplete information is available.
(4) The parser combines the two leading parsing paradigms in a single efficient parser **without** stacking the two approaches. Therefore the parser requires only one training phase (without jackknifing) and it uses only a single transition-based decoder.

[2]Since search is not exhaustive, there is of course a slight danger that the correct history drops out of the beam before complete information becomes available. But as our experiments show, this does not seem to be a serious issue empirically.

The structure of this paper is as follows. In Section 2, we discuss related work. In Section 3, we introduce our transition-based parser and in Section 4 the completion model as well as the implementation of third order models. In Section 5, we describe experiments and provide evaluation results on selected data sets.

2 Related Work

Kudo and Matsumoto (2002) and Yamada and Matsumoto (2003) carried over the idea for deterministic parsing by chunks from Abney (1991) to dependency parsing. Nivre (2003) describes in a more strict sense the first incremental parser that tries to find the most appropriate dependency tree by a sequence of local transitions. In order to optimize the results towards a more globally optimal solution, Johansson and Nugues (2006) first applied beam search, which leads to a substantial improvment of the results (cf. also (Titov and Henderson, 2007)). Zhang and Clark (2008) augment the beam-search algorithm, adapting the early update strategy of Collins and Roark (2004) to dependency parsing. In this approach, the parser stops and updates the model when the oracle transition sequence drops out of the beam. In contrast to most other approaches, the training procedure of Zhang and Clark (2008) takes the complete transition sequence into account as it is calculating the update. Zhang and Clark compare aspects of transition-based and graph-based parsing, and end up using a transition-based parser with a combined transition-based/second-order graph-based scoring model (Zhang and Clark, 2008, 567), which is similar to the approach we describe in this paper. However, their approach does not involve beam rescoring as the partial structures built by the transition-based parser are subsequently augmented; hence, there are cases in which our approach is able to differentiate based on higher-order factors that go unnoticed by the combined model of (Zhang and Clark, 2008, 567).

One step beyond the use of a beam is a dynamic programming approach to carry out a full search in the state space, cf. (Huang and Sagae, 2010; Kuhlmann et al., 2011). However, in this case one has to restrict the employed features to a set which fits to the elements composed by the dynamic programming approach. This is a trade-off between an exhaustive search and a unrestricted (rich) feature set and the question which provides a higher accuracy is still an open research question, cf. (Kuhlmann et al., 2011).

Parsing of non-projective dependency trees is an important feature for many languages. At first most algorithms were restricted to projective dependency trees and used pseudo-projective parsing (Kahane et al., 1998; Nivre and Nilsson, 2005). Later, additional transitions were introduced to handle non-projectivity (Attardi, 2006; Nivre, 2009). The most common strategy uses the *swap* transition (Nivre, 2009; Nivre et al., 2009), an alternative solution uses two planes and a *switch* transition to switch between the two planes (Gómez-Rodríguez and Nivre, 2010).

Since we use the scoring model of a graph-based parser, we briefly review releated work on graph-based parsing. The most well known graph-based parser is the MST (maximum spanning tree) parser, cf. (McDonald et al., 2005; McDonald and Pereira, 2006). The idea of the MST parser is to find the highest scoring tree in a graph that contains all possible edges. Eisner (1996) introduced a dynamic programming algorithm to solve this problem efficiently. Carreras (2007) introduced the left-most and right-most grandchild as factors. We use the factor model of Carreras (2007) as starting point for our experiments, cf. Section 4. We extend Carreras (2007) graph-based model with factors involving three edges similar to that of Koo and Collins (2010).

3 Transition-based Parser with a Beam

This section specifies the transition-based beam-search parser underlying the combined approach more formally. Sec. 4 will discuss the graph-based scoring model that we are adding.

The input to the parser is a word string x, the goal is to find the optimal set y of labeled edges $x_i \rightarrow_l x_j$ forming a dependency tree over x $\cup\{root\}$. We characterize the state of a transition-based parser as $\pi_i{=}\langle\sigma_i, \beta_i, y_i, h_i\rangle$, $\pi_i \in \Pi$, the set of possible states. σ_i is a stack of words from x that are still under consideration; β_i is the input buffer, the suffix of x yet to be processed; y_i the set of labeled edges already assigned (a partial labeled dependency tree); h_i is a sequence recording the history of transitions (from the set of operations Ω = {shift, left-arc$_l$, right-arc$_l$, reduce, swap}) taken up to this point.

(1) The initial state π_0 has an empty stack, the input buffer is the full input string x, and the edge set is empty. (2) The (partial) transition function $\tau(\pi_i, t) : \Pi \times \Omega \rightarrow \Pi$ maps a state and an operation t to a new state π_{i+1}. (3) Final states π_f are characterized by an empty input buffer and stack; no further transitions can be taken.

The transition function is informally defined as follows: The **shift** transition removes the first element of the input buffer and pushes it to the stack. The **left-arc**$_l$ transition adds an edge with label l from the first word in the buffer to the word on top of the stack, removes the top element from the stack and pushes the first element of the input buffer to the stack.
The **right-arc**$_l$ transition adds an edge from word on top of the stack to the first word in the input buffer and removes the top element of the input buffer and pushes that element onto the stack.
The **reduce** transition pops the top word from the stack.
The **swap** changes the order of the two top elements on the stack (possibly generating non-projkective trees).

When more than one operation is applicable, a scoring function assigns a numerical value (based on a feature vector and a weight vector trained by supervised machine learning) to each possible continuation. When using a beam search approach with beam size k, the highest-scoring k alternative states with the same length n of transition history h are kept in a set "beam$_n$".

In the beam-based parsing algorithm (cf. the pseudo code in Algorithm 1), all candidate states for the next set "beam$_{n+1}$" are determined using the transition function τ, but based on the scoring function, only the best k are preserved. (Final) states to which no more transitions apply are copied to the next state set. This means that once all transition paths have reached a final state, the overall best-scoring states can be read off the final "beam$_n$". The y of the top-scoring state is the predicted parse.

Under the plain transition-based scoring regime score$_T$, the score for a state π is the sum of the "local" scores for the transitions t_i in the state's history sequence:

$$\text{score}_T(\pi) = \sum_{i=0}^{|h|} w \cdot f(\pi_i, t_i)$$

Algorithm 1: Transition-based parser

// x is the input sentence, k is the beam size
$\sigma_0 = \emptyset, \beta_0 = x, y_0 = \emptyset, h = \emptyset$
$\pi_0 \leftarrow \langle \sigma_0, \beta_0, y_0, h_0 \rangle$ // initial parts of a state
$\text{beam}_0 \leftarrow \{\pi_0\}$ // create initial state
$n \leftarrow 0$ // iteration
repeat
  $n \leftarrow n + 1$
  for all $\pi_j \in \text{beam}_{n-1}$ **do**
    transitions $\leftarrow$ possible-applicable-transition (π_j)
    // if no transition is applicable keep state π_j:
    if transitions $= \emptyset$ **then** $\text{beam}_n \leftarrow \text{beam}_n \cup \{\pi_j\}$
    else for all $t_i \in$ transitions **do**
      // apply the transition i to state j
      $\pi \leftarrow \tau(\pi_j, t_i)$
      $\text{beam}_n \leftarrow \text{beam}_n \cup \{\pi\}$
    // end for
  // end for
  sort beam_n due to the **score**(π_j)
  $\text{beam}_n \leftarrow$ sublist $(\text{beam}_n, 0, k)$
until $\text{beam}_{n-1} = \text{beam}_n$ // beam changed?

w is the weight vector. Note that the features $f(\pi_i, t_i)$ can take into account all structural and labeling information available prior to taking transition t_i, i.e., the graph built so far, the words (and their part of speech etc.) on the stack and in the input buffer, etc. But if a larger graph configuration involving the next word evolves only later, as in Figure 1, this information is not taken into account in scoring. For instance, if the feature extraction uses the subcategorization frame of a word under consideration to compute a score, it is quite possible that some dependents are still missing and will only be attached in a future transition.

4 Completion Model

We define an augmented scoring function which can be used in the same beam-search algorithm in order to ensure that in the scoring of alternative transition paths, larger configurations can be exploited as they are completed in the incremental process. The feature configurations can be largely taken from graph-based approaches. Here, spans from the string are assembled in a bottom-up fashion, and the scoring for an edge can be based on structurally completed subspans ("factors").

Our completion model for scoring a state π_n incorporates factors for all configurations (matching the extraction scheme that is applied) that are present in the partial dependency graph y_n built up to this point, which is continuously augmented. This means if at a given point n in the transition path, complete information for a particular configuration (e.g., a third-order factor involving a head, its dependent and its grand-child dependent) is unavailable, scoring will ignore this factor at time n, but the configuration will inform the scoring later on, maybe at point $n+4$, when the complete information for this factor has entered the partial graph y_{n+4}.

We present results for a number of different second-order and third-order feature models.

Second Order Factors. We start with the model introduced by Carreras (2007). Figure 3 illustrates the factors used.

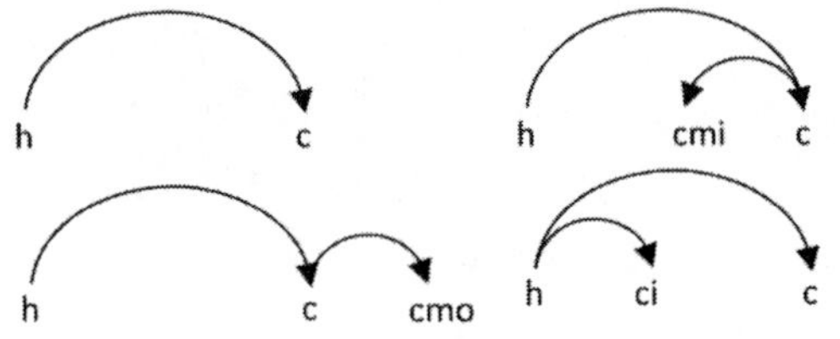

Figure 3: Model 2a. Second order factors of Carreras (2007). We omit the right-headed cases, which are mirror images. The model comprises a factoring into one first order part and three second order factors (2-4): 1) The head (h) and the dependent (c); 2) the head, the dependent and the left-most (or right-most) grandchild in between (cmi); 3) the head, the dependent and the right-most (or left-most) grandchild away from the head (cmo). 4) the head, the dependent and between those words the right-most (or left-most) sibling (ci).

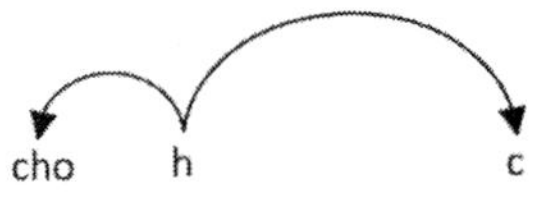

Figure 4: 2b. The left-most dependent of the head or the right-most dependent in the right-headed case.

Figure 4 illustrates a new type of factor we use, which includes the left-most dependent in the left-headed case and symmetricaly the right-most sibling in the right-head case.

Third Order Factors. In addition to the second order factors, we investigate combinations of third order factors. Figure 5 and 6 illustrate the third order factors, which are similar to the factors of Koo and Collins (2010). They restrict the factor to the innermost sibling pair for the *tri-siblings* and the outermost pair for the *grand-siblings*. We use the first two siblings of the dependent from the left side of the head for the tri-siblings and the first two dependents of the child for the grand-siblings. With these factors, we aim to capture non-projective edges and subcategorization information. Figure 7 illustrates a factor of a sequence of four nodes. All the right headed variants are symmetrically and left out for brevity.

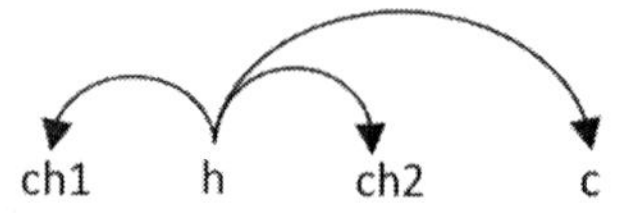

Figure 5: 3a. The first two children of the head, which do not include the edge between the head and the dependent.

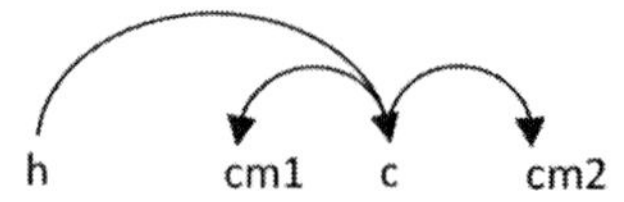

Figure 6: 3b. The first two children of the dependent.

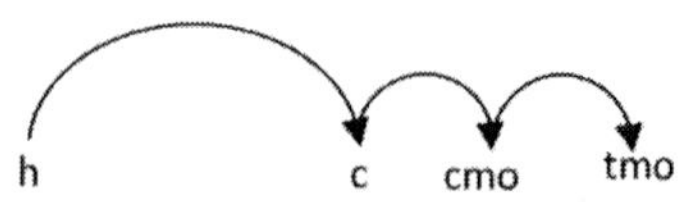

Figure 7: 3c. The right-most dependent of the right-most dependent.

Integrated approach. To obtain an integrated system for the various feature models, the scoring function of the transition-based parser from Section 3 is augmented by a family of scoring functions score_{G_m} for the completion model, where m is from 2a, 2b, 3a etc., x is the input string, and y is the (partial) dependency tree built so far:

$$\text{score}_{T_m}(\pi) = \text{score}_T(\pi) + \text{score}_{G_m}(x, y)$$

The scoring function of the completion model depends on the selected factor model G_m. The model G_{2a} comprises the edge factoring of Figure 3. With this model, we obtain the following scoring function.

$$\text{score}_{G_{2a}}(x,y) = \sum_{(h,c)\in y} w \cdot f_{first}(x,h,c)$$
$$+\sum_{(h,c,ci)\in y} w \cdot f_{sib}(x,h,c,ci)$$
$$+\sum_{(h,c,cmo)\in y} w \cdot f_{gra}(x,h,c,cmo)$$
$$+\sum_{(h,c,cmi)\in y} w \cdot f_{gra}(x,h,c,cmi)$$

The function f maps the input sentence x, and a subtree y defined by the indexes to a feature-vector. Again, w is the corresponding weight vector. In order to add the factor of Figure 4 to our model, we have to add the scoring function (2a) the sum:

(2b) $\text{score}_{G_{2b}}(x,y) = \text{score}_{G_{2a}}(x,y)$
$+\sum_{(h,c,cmi)\in y} w \cdot f_{gra}(x,h,c,cmi)$

In order to build a scoring function for combination of the factors shown in Figure 5 to 7, we have to add to the equation 2b one or more of the following sums:

(3a) $\sum_{(h,c,ch1,ch2)\in y} w \cdot f_{gra}(x,h,c,ch1,ch2)$

(3b) $\sum_{(h,c,cm1,cm2)\in y} w \cdot f_{gra}(x,h,c,cm1,cm2)$

(3c) $\sum_{(h,c,cmo,tmo)\in y} w \cdot f_{gra}(x,h,c,cmo,tmo)$

Feature Set. The feature set of the transition model is similar to that of Zhang and Nivre (2011). In addition, we use the cross product of morphologic features between the head and the dependent since we apply also the parser on morphologic rich languages.

The feature sets of the completion model described above are mostly based on previous work (McDonald et al., 2005; McDonald and Pereira, 2006; Carreras, 2007; Koo and Collins, 2010). The models denoted with + use all combinations of words before and after the head, dependent, sibling, grandchilrden, etc. These are respectively three-, and four-grams for the first order and second order. The algorithm includes these features only the words left and right do not overlap with the factor (e.g. the head, dependent, etc.). We use feature extraction procedure for second order, and third order factors. Each feature extracted in this procedure includes information about the position of the nodes relative to the other nodes of the part and a factor identifier.

Training. For the training of our parser, we use a variant of the perceptron algorithm that uses the Passive-Aggressive update function, cf. (Freund and Schapire, 1998; Collins, 2002; Crammer et al., 2006). The Passive-Aggressive perceptron uses an aggressive update strategy by modifying the weight vector by as much as needed to classify correctly the current example, cf. (Crammer et al., 2006). We apply a random function (hash function) to retrieve the weights from the weight vector instead of a table. Bohnet (2010) showed that the Hash Kernel improves parsing speed and accuracy since the parser uses additionaly negative features. Ganchev and Dredze (2008) used this technique for structured prediction in NLP to reduce the needed space, cf. (Shi et al., 2009). We use as weight vector size 800 million. After the training, we counted 65 millions non zero weights for English (penn2malt), 83 for Czech and 87 millions for German. The feature vectors are the union of features originating from the transition sequence of a sentence and the features of the factors over all edges of a dependency tree (e.g. G_{2a}, etc.). To prevent over-fitting, we use averaging to cope with this problem, cf. (Freund and Schapire, 1998; Collins, 2002). We calculate the error e as the sum of all attachment errors and label errors both weighted by 0.5. We use the following equations to compute the update.

loss: $l_t = e$-(score$_T(x_t^g, y_t^g)$-score$_T(x_t, y_t)$)

PA-update: $\tau_t = \frac{l_t}{||f_g - f_p||^2}$

We train the model to select the transitions and the completion model together and therefore, we use one parameter space. In order to compute the weight vector, we employ standard online learning with 25 training iterations, and carry out early updates, cf. Collins and Roark (2004; Zhang and Clark (2008).

Efficient Implementation. Keeping the scoring with the completion model tractable with millions of feature weights and for second- and third-order factors requires careful bookkeeping and a number of specialized techniques from recent work on dependency parsing.

We use two variables to store the scores (a) for complete factors and (b) for incomplete factors. The complete factors (first-order factors and higher-order factors for which further augmentation is structurally excluded) need to be calculated only once and can then be stored with the tree factors. The incomplete factors (higher-order factors whose node elements may still receive additional descendants) need to be dynamically recomputed while the tree is built.

The parsing algorithm only has to compute the scores of the factored model when the transition-based parser selects a left-arc or right-arc transition and the beam has to be sorted. The parser sorts the beam when it exceeds the maximal beam size, in order to discard superfluous parses or when the parsing algorithm terminates in order to select the best parse tree. The complexity of the transition-based parser is quadratic due to swap operation in the worse case, which is rare, and $O(n)$ in the best case, cf. (Nivre, 2009). The beam size B is constant. Hence, the complexity is in the worst case $O(n^2)$.

The parsing time is to a large degree determined by the feature extraction, the score calculation and the implementation, cf. also (Goldberg and Elhadad, 2010). The transition-based parser is able to parse 30 sentences per second. The parser with completion model processes about 5 sentences per second with a beam size of 80. Note, we use a rich feature set, a completion model with third order factors, negative features, and a large beam. [3]

We implemented the following optimizations:
(1) We use a parallel feature extraction for the beam elements. Each process extracts the features, scores the possible transitions and computes the score of the completion model. After the extension step, the beam is sorted and the best elements are selected according to the beam size.
(2) The calculation of each score is optimized (beyond the distinction of a static and a dynamic component): We calculate for each location determined by the last element $s_l \in \sigma_i$ and the first element of $b_0 \in \beta_i$ a numeric feature representation. This is kept fix and we add only the numeric value for each of the edge labels plus a value for the transition left-arc or right-arc. In this way, we create the features incrementally. This has some similarity to Goldberg and Elhadad (2010).
(3) We apply edge filtering as it is used in graph-based dependency parsing, cf. (Johansson and Nugues, 2008), i.e., we calculate the edge weights only for the labels that were found for the part-of-speech combination of the head and dependent in the training data.

5 Parsing Experiments and Discussion

The results of different parsing systems are often hard to compare due to differences in phrase structure to dependency conversions, corpus version, and experimental settings. For better comparison, we provide results on English for two commonly used data sets, based on two different conversions of the Penn Treebank. The first uses the Penn2Malt conversion based on the head-

[3] 6 core, 3.33 Ghz Intel Nehalem

	Section	Sentences	PoS Acc.
Training	2-21	39.832	97.08
Dev	24	1.394	97.18
Test	23	2.416	97.30

Table 1: Overview of the training, development and test data split converted to dependency graphs with head-finding rules of (Yamada and Matsumoto, 2003). The last column shows the accuracy of Part-of-Speech tags.

finding rules of Yamada and Matsumoto (2003). Table 1 gives an overview of the properties of the corpus. The annotation of the corpus does not contain non-projective links. The training data was 10-fold jackknifed with our own tagger.[4]. Table 1 shows the tagging accuracy.

Table 2 lists the accuracy of our transition-based parser with completion model together with results from related work. All results use predicted PoS tags. As a baseline, we present in addition results without the completion model and a graph-based parser with second order features (G_{2a}). For the Graph-based parser, we used 10 training iterations. The following rows denoted with T_a, T_{2a}, T_{2ab}, T_{2ab3a}, T_{2ab3b}, T_{2ab3bc}, and T_{2a3abc} present the result for the parser with completion model. The subscript letters denote the used factors of the completion model as shown in Figure 3 to 7. The parsers with subscribed plus (e.g. G_{2a+}) in addition use feature templates that contain one word left or right of the head, dependent, siblings, and grandchildren. We left those feature in our previous models out as they may interfere with the second and third order factors. As in previous work, we exclude punctuation marks for the English data converted with Penn2Malt in the evaluation, cf. (McDonald et al., 2005; Koo and Collins, 2010; Zhang and Nivre, 2011).[5] We optimized the feature model of our parser on section 24 and used section 23 for evaluation. We use a beam size of 80 for our transition-based parser and 25 training iterations.

The second English data set was obtained by using the *LTH* conversion schema as used in the CoNLL Shared Task 2009, cf. (Hajič et al., 2009). This corpus preserves the non-projectivity of the phrase structure annotation, it has a rich edge label set, and provides automatic assigned PoS tags. From the same data set, we selected the corpora for Czech and German. In all cases, we used the provided training, development, and test data split, cf. (Hajič et al., 2009). In contrast to the evaluation of the Penn2Malt conversion, we include punctuation marks for these corpora and follow in that the evaluation schema of the CoNLL Shared Task 2009. Table 3 presents the results as obtained for these data set.

Parser	UAS	LAS
(McDonald et al., 2005)	90.9	
(McDonald and Pereira, 2006)	91.5	
(Huang and Sagae, 2010)	92.1	
(Zhang and Nivre, 2011)	92.9	
(Koo and Collins, 2010)	93.04	
(Martins et al., 2010)	93.26	
T (baseline)	92.7	
G_{2a} (baseline)	92.89	
T_{2a}	92.94	91.87
T_{2ab}	93.16	92.08
T_{2ab3a}	93.20	92.10
T_{2ab3b}	93.23	92.15
T_{2ab3c}	93.17	92.10
$T_{2ab3abc+}$	93.39	92.38
G_{2a+}	93.1	
(Koo et al., 2008) †	93.16	
(Carreras et al., 2008) †	93.5	
(Suzuki et al., 2009) †	93.79	

Table 2: English **Attachment Scores** for the Penn2Malt conversion of the Penn Treebank for the test set. Punctuation is excluded from the evaluation. The results marked with † are not directly comparable to our work as they depend on additional sources of information (Brown Clusters).

The transition-based parser obtains higher accuracy scores for Czech but still lower scores for English and German. For Czech, the result of T is 1.59 percentage points higher than the top labeled score in the CoNLL shared task 2009. The reason is that T includes already third order features that are needed to determine some edge labels. The transition-based parser with completion model T_{2a} has even 2.62 percentage points higher accuracy and it could improve the results of the parser T by additional 1.03 percentage points. The results of the parser T are lower for English and German compared to the results of the graph-based parser G_{2a}. The completion model T_{2a} can reach a similar accuracy level for these two languages. The third order features let the transition-based parser reach higher scores than the graph-based parser. The third order features contribute for each language a relatively small improvement

[4]http://code.google.com/p/mate-tools/

[5]We follow Koo and Collins (2010) and ignore any token whose POS tag is one of the following tokens `` '' : , .

Parser	Eng.	Czech	German
(Gesmundo et al., 2009)†	88.79/-	80.38	87.29
(Bohnet, 2009)	89.88/-	80.11	87.48
T (Baseline)	89.52/92.10	81.97/87.26	87.53/89.86
G_{2a} (Baseline)	90.14/92.36	81.13/87.65	87.79/90.12
T_{2a}	90.20/92.55	83.01/88.12	88.22/90.36
T_{2ab}	90.26/92.56	83.22/88.34	88.31/90.24
T_{2ab3a}	90.20/90.51	83.21.88.30	88.14/90.23
T_{2ab3b}	90.26/92.57	83.22/88.35	88.50/90.59
$T_{2ab3abc}$	90.31/92.58	83.31/88.30	88.33/90.45
G_{2a+}	90.39/92.8	81.43/88.0	88.26/90.50
$T_{2ab3ab+}$	90.36/92.66	83.48/88.47	88.51/90.62

Table 3: **Labeled Attachment Scores** of parsers that use the data sets of the CoNLL shared task 2009. In line with previous work, punctuation is included. The parsers marked with † used a joint model for syntactic parsing and semantic role labelling. We provide more parsing results for the languages of CoNLL-X Shared Task at http://code.google.com/p/mate-tools/.

Parser	UAS	LAS
(Zhang and Clark, 2008)	84.3	
(Huang and Sagae, 2010)	85.2	
(Zhang and Nivre, 2011)	86.0	84.4
$T_{2ab3abc+}$	87.5	85.9

Table 4: Chinese **Attachment Scores** for the conversion of CTB 5 with head rules of Zhang and Clark (2008). We take the standard split of CTB 5 and use in line with previous work gold segmentation, POS-tags and exclude punctuation marks for the evaluation.

of the score. Small and statistically significant improvements provides the additional second order factor (2b).[6] We tried to determine the best third order factors or set of factors but we cannot denote such a factor which is the best for all languages. For German, we obtained a significant improvement with the factor (3b). We believe that this is due to the flat annotation of PPs in the German corpus. If we combine all third order factors we obtain for the Penn2Malt conversion a small improvement of 0.2 percentage points over the results of (2ab). We think that a more deep feature selection for third order factors may help to improve the actuary further.

In Table 4, we present results on the Chinese Treebank. To our knowledge, we obtain the best published results so far.

[6]The results of the baseline T compared to $T_{2ab3abc}$ are statistically significant ($p < 0.01$).

6 Conclusion and Future Work

The parser introduced in this paper combines advantageous properties from the two major paradigms in data-driven dependency parsing, in particular worst case quadratic complexity of transition-based parsing with a swap operation and the consideration of *complete* second and third order factors in the scoring of alternatives. While previous work using third order factors, cf. Koo and Collins (2010), was restricted to unlabeled and projective trees, our parser can produce labeled and non-projective dependency trees.

In contrast to parser stacking, which involves running two parsers in training and application, we use only the feature model of a graph-based parser but not the graph-based parsing algorithm. This is not only conceptually superior, but makes training much simpler, since no jackknifing has to be carried out. Zhang and Clark (2008) proposed a similar combination, without the rescoring procedure. Our implementation allows for the use of rich feature sets in the combined scoring functions, and our experimental results show that the "graph-based" completion model leads to an increase of between 0.4 (for English) and about 1 percentage points (for Czech). The scores go beyond the current state of the art results for typologically different languages such as Chinese, Czech, English, and German. For Czech, English (Penn2Malt) and German, these are to our knowlege the highest reported scores of a dependency parser that does not use additional sources of information (such as extra unlabeled training data for clustering). Note that the efficient techniques and implementation such as the Hash Kernel, the incremental calculation of the scores of the completion model, and the parallel feature extraction as well as the parallelized transition-based parsing strategy play an important role in carrying out this idea in practice.

References

S. Abney. 1991. Parsing by chunks. In *Principle-Based Parsing*, pages 257–278. Kluwer Academic Publishers.

G. Attardi. 2006. Experiments with a Multilanguage Non-Projective Dependency Parser. In *Tenth Conference on Computational Natural Language Learning (CoNLL-X)*.

B. Bohnet. 2009. Efficient Parsing of Syntactic and

Semantic Dependency Structures. In *Proceedings of the 13th Conference on Computational Natural Language Learning (CoNLL-2009)*.

B. Bohnet. 2010. Top accuracy and fast dependency parsing is not a contradiction. In *Proceedings of the 23rd International Conference on Computational Linguistics (Coling 2010)*, pages 89–97, Beijing, China, August. Coling 2010 Organizing Committee.

X. Carreras, M. Collins, and T. Koo. 2008. Tag, dynamic programming, and the perceptron for efficient, feature-rich parsing. In *Proceedings of the Twelfth Conference on Computational Natural Language Learning*, CoNLL '08, pages 9–16, Stroudsburg, PA, USA. Association for Computational Linguistics.

X. Carreras. 2007. Experiments with a Higher-order Projective Dependency Parser. In *EMNLP/CoNLL*.

M. Collins and B. Roark. 2004. Incremental parsing with the perceptron algorithm. In *ACL*, pages 111–118.

M. Collins. 2002. Discriminative Training Methods for Hidden Markov Models: Theory and Experiments with Perceptron Algorithms. In *EMNLP*.

K. Crammer, O. Dekel, S. Shalev-Shwartz, and Y. Singer. 2006. Online Passive-Aggressive Algorithms. *Journal of Machine Learning Research*, 7:551–585.

J. Eisner. 1996. Three New Probabilistic Models for Dependency Parsing: An Exploration. In *Proceedings of the 16th International Conference on Computational Linguistics (COLING-96)*, pages 340–345, Copenhaen.

Y. Freund and R. E. Schapire. 1998. Large margin classification using the perceptron algorithm. In *11th Annual Conference on Computational Learning Theory*, pages 209–217, New York, NY. ACM Press.

K. Ganchev and M. Dredze. 2008. Small statistical models by random feature mixing. In *Proceedings of the ACL-2008 Workshop on Mobile Language Processing*. Association for Computational Linguistics.

A. Gesmundo, J. Henderson, P. Merlo, and I. Titov. 2009. A Latent Variable Model of Synchronous Syntactic-Semantic Parsing for Multiple Languages. In *Proceedings of the 13th Conference on Computational Natural Language Learning (CoNLL-2009)*, Boulder, Colorado, USA., June 4-5.

Y. Goldberg and M. Elhadad. 2010. An efficient algorithm for easy-first non-directional dependency parsing. In *HLT-NAACL*, pages 742–750.

C. Gómez-Rodríguez and J. Nivre. 2010. A Transition-Based Parser for 2-Planar Dependency Structures. In *ACL*, pages 1492–1501.

J. Hajič, M. Ciaramita, R. Johansson, D. Kawahara, M. Antònia Martí, L. Màrquez, A. Meyers, J. Nivre, S. Padó, J. Štěpánek, P. Straňák, M. Surdeanu, N. Xue, and Y. Zhang. 2009. The CoNLL-2009 shared task: Syntactic and semantic dependencies in multiple languages. In *Proceedings of the Thirteenth Conference on Computational Natural Language Learning (CoNLL 2009): Shared Task*, pages 1–18, Boulder, United States, June.

L. Huang and K. Sagae. 2010. Dynamic programming for linear-time incremental parsing. In *Proceedings of the 48th Annual Meeting of the Association for Computational Linguistics*, pages 1077–1086, Uppsala, Sweden, July. Association for Computational Linguistics.

R. Johansson and P. Nugues. 2006. Investigating multilingual dependency parsing. In *Proceedings of the Shared Task Session of the Tenth Conference on Computational Natural Language Learning (CoNLL-X)*, pages 206–210, New York City, United States, June 8-9.

R. Johansson and P. Nugues. 2008. Dependency-based Syntactic–Semantic Analysis with PropBank and NomBank. In *Proceedings of the Shared Task Session of CoNLL-2008*, Manchester, UK.

S. Kahane, A. Nasr, and O. Rambow. 1998. Pseudo-projectivity: A polynomially parsable non-projective dependency grammar. In *COLING-ACL*, pages 646–652.

T. Koo and M. Collins. 2010. Efficient third-order dependency parsers. In *Proceedings of the 48th Annual Meeting of the Association for Computational Linguistics*, pages 1–11, Uppsala, Sweden, July. Association for Computational Linguistics.

Terry Koo, Xavier Carreras, and Michael Collins. 2008. Simple semi-supervised dependency parsing. pages 595–603.

T. Kudo and Y. Matsumoto. 2002. Japanese dependency analysis using cascaded chunking. In *proceedings of the 6th conference on Natural language learning - Volume 20*, COLING-02, pages 1–7, Stroudsburg, PA, USA. Association for Computational Linguistics.

M. Kuhlmann, C. Gómez-Rodríguez, and G. Satta. 2011. Dynamic programming algorithms for transition-based dependency parsers. In *ACL*, pages 673–682.

Andre Martins, Noah Smith, Eric Xing, Pedro Aguiar, and Mario Figueiredo. 2010. Turbo parsers: Dependency parsing by approximate variational inference. pages 34–44.

R. McDonald and F. Pereira. 2006. Online Learning of Approximate Dependency Parsing Algorithms. In *In Proc. of EACL*, pages 81–88.

R. McDonald, K. Crammer, and F. Pereira. 2005. Online Large-margin Training of Dependency Parsers. In *Proc. ACL*, pages 91–98.

J. Nivre and R. McDonald. 2008. Integrating Graph-Based and Transition-Based Dependency Parsers. In *ACL-08*, pages 950–958, Columbus, Ohio.

J. Nivre and J. Nilsson. 2005. Pseudo-projective dependency parsing. In *ACL*.

J. Nivre, M. Kuhlmann, and J. Hall. 2009. An improved oracle for dependency parsing with online reordering. In *Proceedings of the 11th International Conference on Parsing Technologies*, IWPT '09, pages 73–76, Stroudsburg, PA, USA. Association for Computational Linguistics.

J. Nivre. 2003. An Efficient Algorithm for Projective Dependency Parsing. In *8th International Workshop on Parsing Technologies*, pages 149–160, Nancy, France.

J. Nivre. 2009. Non-Projective Dependency Parsing in Expected Linear Time. In *Proceedings of the 47th Annual Meeting of the ACL and the 4th IJCNLP of the AFNLP*, pages 351–359, Suntec, Singapore.

K. Sagae and A. Lavie. 2006. Parser combination by reparsing. In *NAACL '06: Proceedings of the Human Language Technology Conference of the NAACL, Companion Volume: Short Papers on XX*, pages 129–132, Morristown, NJ, USA. Association for Computational Linguistics.

Q. Shi, J. Petterson, G. Dror, J. Langford, A. Smola, and S.V.N. Vishwanathan. 2009. Hash Kernels for Structured Data. In *Journal of Machine Learning*.

J. Suzuki, H. Isozaki, X. Carreras, and M Collins. 2009. An empirical study of semi-supervised structured conditional models for dependency parsing. In *EMNLP*, pages 551–560.

I. Titov and J. Henderson. 2007. A Latent Variable Model for Generative Dependency Parsing. In *Proceedings of IWPT*, pages 144–155.

H. Yamada and Y. Matsumoto. 2003. Statistical Dependency Analysis with Support Vector Machines. In *Proceedings of IWPT*, pages 195–206.

Y. Zhang and S. Clark. 2008. A tale of two parsers: investigating and combining graph-based and transition-based dependency parsing using beam-search. In *Proceedings of EMNLP*, Hawaii, USA.

Y. Zhang and J. Nivre. 2011. Transition-based dependency parsing with rich non-local features. In *Proceedings of the 49th Annual Meeting of the Association for Computational Linguistics: Human Language Technologies*, pages 188–193, Portland, Oregon, USA, June. Association for Computational Linguistics.

Answer Sentence Retrieval by Matching Dependency Paths Acquired from Question/Answer Sentence Pairs

Michael Kaisser
AGT Group (R&D) GmbH
Jägerstr. 41, 10117 Berlin, Germany
mkaisser@agtgermany.com

Abstract

In Information Retrieval (IR) in general and Question Answering (QA) in particular, queries and relevant textual content often significantly differ in their properties and are therefore difficult to relate with traditional IR methods, e.g. key-word matching. In this paper we describe an algorithm that addresses this problem, but rather than looking at it on a term matching/term reformulation level, we focus on the syntactic differences between questions and relevant text passages. To this end we propose a novel algorithm that analyzes dependency structures of queries and known relevant text passages and acquires transformational patterns that can be used to retrieve relevant textual content. We evaluate our algorithm in a QA setting, and show that it outperforms a baseline that uses only dependency information contained in the questions by 300% and that it also improves performance of a state of the art QA system significantly.

1 Introduction

It is a well known problem in Information Retrieval (IR) and Question Answering (QA) that queries and relevant textual content often significantly differ in their properties, and are therefore difficult to match with traditional IR methods. A common example is a user entering words to describe their information need that do not match the words used in the most relevant indexed documents. This work addresses this problem, but shifts focus from words to syntactic structures of questions and relevant pieces of text. To this end, we present a novel algorithm that analyses the dependency structures of known valid answer sentence and from these acquires patterns that can be used to more precisely retrieve relevant text passages from the underlying document collection. To achieve this, the position of key phrases in the answer sentence relative to the answer itself is analyzed and linked to a certain syntactic question type. Unlike most previous work that uses dependency paths for QA (see Section 2), our approach does not require a candidate sentence to be similar to the question in any respect. We learn valid dependency structures from the known answer sentences alone, and therefore are able to link a much wider spectrum of answer sentences to the question.

The work in this paper is presented and evaluated in a classical factoid Question Answering (QA) setting. The main reason for this is that in QA suitable training and test data is available in the public domain, e.g. via the Text REtrieval Conference (TREC), see for example (Voorhees, 1999). The methods described in this paper however can also be applied to other IR scenarios, e.g. web search. The necessary condition for our approach to work is that the user query is somewhat grammatically well formed; this kind of queries are commonly referred to as Natural Language Queries or NLQs.

Table 1 provides evidence that users indeed search the web with NLQs. The data is based on two query sets sampled from three months of user logs from a popular search engine, using two different sampling techniques. The "head" set samples queries taking query frequency into account, so that more common queries have a proportionally higher chance of being selected. The "tail" query set samples only queries that have been is-

Set	Head	Tail
Query #	15,665	12,500
how	1.33%	2.42%
what	0.77%	1.89%
define	0.34%	0.18%
is/are	0.25%	0.42%
where	0.18%	0.45%
do/does	0.14%	0.30%
can	0.14%	0.25%
why	0.13%	0.30%
who	0.12%	0.38%
when	0.09%	0.21%
which	0.03%	0.08%
Total	3.55%	6.86%

Table 1: Percentages of Natural Language queries in head and tail search engine query logs. See text for details.

sued less that 500 times during a three months period and it disregards query frequency. As a result, rare and frequent queries have the same chance of being selected. Doubles are excluded from both sets. Table 1 lists the percentage of queries in the query sets that start with the specified word. In most contexts this indicates that the query is a question, which in turn means that we are dealing with an NLQ. Of course there are many NLQs that start with words other than the ones listed, so we can expect their real percentage to be even higher.

2 Related Work

In IR the problem that queries and relevant textual content often do not exhibit the same terms is commonly encountered. Latent Semantic Indexing (Deerwester et al., 1900) was an early, highly influential approach to solve this problem. More recently, a significant amount of research is dedicated to query alteration approaches. (Cui et al., 2002), for example, assume that if queries containing one term often result in the selection of documents containing another term, then a strong relationship between the two terms exist. In their approach, query terms and document terms are linked via sessions in which users click on documents that are presented as results for the query. (Riezler and Liu, 2010) apply a Statistical Machine Translation model to parallel data consisting of user queries and snippets from clicked web documents and in such a way extract contextual expansion terms from the query rewrites.

We see our work as addressing the same fundamental problem, but shifting focus from query term/document term mismatch to mismatches observed between the grammatical structure of Natural Language Queries and relevant text pieces. In order to achieve this we analyze the queries' and the relevant contents' syntactic structure by using dependency paths.

Especially in QA there is a strong tradition of using dependency structures: (Lin and Pantel, 2001) present an unsupervised algorithm to automatically discover inference rules (essentially paraphrases) from text. These inference rules are based on dependency paths, each of which connects two nouns. Their paths have the following form:

N:subj:V←find→V:obj:N→solution→N:to:N

This path represents the relation "X finds a solution to Y" and can be mapped to another path representing e.g. "X solves Y." As such the approach is suitable to detect paraphrases that describe the relation between two entities in documents. However, the paper does not describe how the mined paraphrases can be linked to questions, and which paraphrase is suitable to answer which question type.

(Attardi et al., 2001) describes a QA system that, after a set of candidate answer sentences have been identified, matches their dependency relations against the question. Questions and answer sentences are parsed with MiniPar (Lin, 1998) and the dependency output is analyzed in order to determine whether relations present in a question also appear in a candidate sentence. For the question "Who killed John F. Kennedy", for example an answer sentence is expected to contain the answer as subject of the verb "kill", to which "John F. Kennedy" should be in object relation.

(Cui et al., 2005) describe a fuzzy dependency relation matching approach to passage retrieval in QA. Here, the authors present a statistical technique to measure the degree of overlap between dependency relations in candidate sentences with their corresponding relations in the question. Question/answer passage pairs from TREC-8 and TREC-9 evaluations are used as training data. As in some of the papers mentioned earlier, a statistical translation model is used, but this time to learn relatedness between paths. (Cui et al., 2004) apply the same idea to answer extraction. In each sentences returned by the IR module, all named entities of the expected answer types are treated as answer candidates. For questions with an unknown answer type, all NPs in the candidate sentence are considered. Then those paths in the answer sentence that are connected to an answer candidate are compared against the corresponding paths in the question, in a similar fashion as in (Cui et al., 2005). The candidate whose paths show the highest matching score is selected. (Shen and Klakow, 2006) also describe a method that is primarily based on similarity scores between dependency relation pairs. However, their algorithm computes the similarity of paths between key phrases, not between words. Furthermore, it takes relations in a path not as independent from each other, but acknowledges that they form a sequence, by comparing two paths with the help of an adaptation of the Dynamic Time Warping algorithm (Rabiner et al., 1991).

(Molla, 2006) presents an approach for the acquisition of question answering rules by applying graph manipulation methods. Questions are represented as dependency graphs, which are extended with information from answer sentences. These combined graphs can then be used to identify answers. Finally, in (Wang et al., 2007), a quasi-synchronous grammar (Smith and Eisner, 2006) is used to model relations between questions and answer sentences.

In this paper we describe an algorithm that learns possible syntactic answer sentence formulations for syntactic question classes from a set of example question/answer sentence pairs. Unlike the related work described above, it acknowledges that a) a valid answer sentence's syntax might be very different for the question's syntax and b) several valid answer sentence structures, which might be completely independent from each other, can exist for one and the same question.

To illustrate this consider the question "When was Alaska purchased?" The following four sentences all answer the given question, but only the first sentence is a straightforward reformulation of the question:

1. The United States purchased Alaska in 1867 from Russia.

2. Alaska was bought from Russia in 1867.

3. In 1867, the Russian Empire sold the Alaska territory to the USA.

4. The acquisition of Alaska by the United States of America from Russia in 1867 is known as "Seward's Folly".

The remaining three sentences introduce various forms of syntactic and semantic transformations. In order to capture a wide range of possible ways on how answer sentences can be formulated, in our model a candidate sentence is not evaluated according to its similarity with the question. Instead, its similarity to known answer sentences (which were presented to the system during training) is evaluated. This allows to us to capture a much wider range of syntactic and semantic transformations.

3 Overview of the Algorithm

Our algorithm uses input data containing pairs of the following:

NLQs/Questions NLQs that describe the users' information need. For the experiments carried out in this paper we use questions from the TREC QA track 2002-2006.

Relevant textual content This is a piece of text that is relevant to the user query in that it contains the information the user is searching for. In this paper, we use sentences extracted from the AQUAINT corpus (Graff, 2002) that contain the answer to the given TREC question.

In total, the data available to us for our experiments consists of 8,830 question/answer sentence pairs. This data is publicly available, see (Kaisser and Lowe, 2008). The algorithm described in this paper has three main steps:

Phrase alignment Key phrases from the question are paired with phrases from the answer sentences.

Pattern creation The dependency structures of queries and answer sentences are analyzed and patterns are extracted.

Pattern evaluation The patterns discovered in the last step are evaluated and a confidence score is assigned to each.

The acquired patterns can then be used during retrieval, where a question is matched against the antecedents describing the syntax of the question.

Input: (a) Query: "When was Alaska purchased?"
(b) Answer sentence: "The acquisition of Alaska happened in 1867."

Step 1: Question is segmented into key phrases and stop words:

```
When[1]+was[2]+NP[3]+VERB[4]
```

Step 2: Key question phrases are aligned with key answer sentence phrases:

[3]Alaska	→	Alaska
[4]purchased	→	acquisition
ANSWER	→	1867

Step 3: A pre-computed parse tree of the answer sentence is loaded:

1: The	(the, DT, 2)	[det]
2: acquisition	(acquisition, NN, 5)	[nsubj]
3: of	(of, IN, 2)	[prep]
4: Alaska	(Alaska, IN, 2)	[pobj]
5: happened	(happen, VBD, null)	[ROOT]
6: in	(in, IN, 5)	[prep]
7: 1867	(1867, CD, 6)	[pobj]

Step 4: Dependency paths from key question phrases to the answer are computed:
Alaska⇒1867: ⇑pobj⇑prep⇑nsubj⇓prep⇓pobj
acquisition⇒1867: ⇑nsubj⇓prep⇓pobj

Step 5: The resulting pattern is stored:

Query:	When[1]+was[2]+NP[3]+VERB[4]
Path 3:	⇑pobj⇑prep⇑nsubj⇓prep⇓pobj
Path 4:	⇑nsubj⇓prep⇓pobj

Figure 1: The pattern creation algorithm exemplified in five key steps for the query "When was Alaska purchased?" and the answer sentence "The acquisition of Alaska happened in 1867."

Note that one question can potentially match several patterns. The consequents contain descriptions of grammatical structures of potential answer sentences that can be used to identify and evaluate candidate sentences.

4 Phrase Alignment

The goal of this processing step is to align phrases from the question with corresponding phrases from the answer sentences in the training data. Consider the following example:

Query: "When was the Alaska territory purchased?"

Answer sentence: "The acquisition of what would become the territory of Alaska took place in 1867."

The mapping that has to be achieved is:

Query phrase	Answer Sentence phrase
"Alaska territory"	"territory of Alaska"
"purchased"	"acquisition"
ANSWER	"1867"

In our approach, this is a two step process. First we align on a word level, then the output of the word alignment process is used to identify and align phrases. Word Alignment is important in many fields of NLP, e.g. Machine Translation (MT) where words in parallel, bilingual corpora need to be aligned, see (Och and Ney, 2003) for a comparison of various statistical alignment models. In our case however we are dealing with a monolingual alignment problem which enables us to exploit clues not available for bilingual alignment: First of all, we can expect many query words to be present in the answer sentence, either with the exact same surface appearance or in some morphological variant. Secondly, there are tools available that tell us how semantically related two words are, most notably WordNet (Miller et al., 1993). For these reasons we implemented a bespoke alignment strategy, tailored towards our problem description.

This method is described in detail in (Kaisser, 2009). The processing steps described in the next sections build on its output. For reasons of brevity, we skip a detailed explanations in this paper and focus only on its key part: the alignment of words with very different surface structures. For more details we would like to point the reader to the aforementioned work.

In the above example, the alignment of "purchased" and "acquisition" is the most problematic, because the surface structures of the two words clearly are very different. For such cases we experimented with a number of alignment strategies based on WordNet. These approaches are similar in that each picks one word that has to be aligned from the question at a time and compares it to all of the non-stop words in the answer sentence. Each of the answer sentence words is assigned a value between zero and one expressing its relatedness to the question word. The highest scoring word, if above a certain threshold, is selected as the closest semantic match. Most of these approaches make use of WordNet::Similarity, a Perl software package that measures semantic similarity (or relatedness) between a pair of word senses by returning a numeric value that represents the degree to which they are similar or related (Pedersen et al., 2004). Additionally, we developed a custom-built method that assumes that two words are semantically related if any kind of pointer exists between any occurrence of the words root form in WordNet. For details of these experiments, please refer to (Kaisser, 2009). In our experiments the custom-built method performed best, and was therefore used for the experiments described in this paper. The main reasons for this are:

1. Many of the measures in the WordNet::Similarity package take only hyponym/hypernym relations into account. This makes aligning word of different parts of speech difficult or even impossible. However, such alignments are important for our needs.

2. Many of the measures return results, even if only a weak semantic relationship exists. For our purposes however, it is beneficial to only take strong semantic relations into account.

5 Pattern Creation

Figure 1 details our algorithm in its five key steps. In step 1 and 2 key phrases from the question are aligned to the corresponding phrases in the answer sentence, see Section 4 of this paper. Step 3 is concerned with retrieving the parse tree for the answer sentence. In our implementation all answer sentences in the training set have for performance reasons been parsed beforehand with the Stanford Parser (Klein and Manning, 2003b; Klein and Manning, 2003a), so at this point they are simply loaded from file. Step 4 is the key step in our algorithm. From the previous steps, we know where the key constituents from the question as well as the answer are located in the answer sentence. This enables us to compute the dependency paths in the answer sentences' parse tree that connect the answer with the key constituents. In our example the answer is "1867" and the key constituents are "acquisition" and "Alaska." Knowing the syntactic relationships (captured by their dependency paths) between the answer and the key phrases enables us to capture one syntactic possibility of how answer sentences to queries of the form `When+was+NP+VERB` can be formulated.

As can be seen in Step 5 a flat syntactic question representation is stored, together with numbers assigned to each constituent. The numbers for those constituents for which alignments in the answer sentence were sought and found are listed together with the resulting dependency paths. Path 3 for example denotes the path from constituent 3 (the NP "Alaska") to the answer. If no alignment could be found for a constituent, *null* is stored instead of a path. Should two or more alternative constituents be identified for one question constituent, additional patterns are created, so that each contains one of the possibilities. The described procedure is repeated for all question/answer sentence pairs in the training set and for each, one or more patterns are created.

It is worth to note that many TREC questions are fairly short and grammatically simple. In our training data we for example find 102 questions matching the pattern `When[1]+was[2]+NP[3]+VERB[4]`, which together list 382 answer sentences, and thus 382 potentially different answer sentence structures from which patterns can be gained. As a result, the amount of training examples we have available, is sufficient to achieve the performance described in Section 7. The algorithm described in this paper can of course also be used for more complicated NLQs, although in such a scenario a significantly larger amount of training data would have to be used.

6 Pattern Evaluation

For each created pattern, at least one matching example must exists: the sentence that was used to create it in the first place. However, we do not know how precise each pattern is. To this end, an additional processing step between pattern creation and application is needed: pattern evaluation. Similar approaches to ours have been described in the relevant literature, many of them concerned with bootstrapping, starting with (Ravichandran and Hovy, 2002). The general purpose of this step is to use the available data about questions and their correct answers to evaluate how often each created pattern returns a correct or an incorrect result. This data is stored with each pattern and the result of the equation, often called pattern precision, can be used during retrieval stage. Pattern precision in our case is defined as:

$$p = \frac{\#correct + 1}{\#correct + \#incorrect + 2} \quad (1)$$

We use Lucene to retrieve the top 100 paragraphs from the AQUAINT corpus by issuing a query that consists of the query's key words and all non-stop words in the answer. Then, all patterns are loaded whose antecedent matches the query that is currently being processed. After that, constituents from all sentences in the retrieved 100 paragraphs are aligned to the query's constituents in the same way as for the sentences during pattern creation, see Section 5. Now, the paths specified in these patterns are searched for in the paragraphs' parse trees. If they are all found, it is checked whether they all point to the same node and whether this node's surface structure is in some morphological form present in the answer strings associated with the question in our training data. If this is the case a variable in the pattern named *correct* is increased by 1, otherwise the variable *incorrect* is increased by 1. After the evaluation process is finished the final version of the pattern given as an example in Figure 1 now is:

Query:	When[1]+was[2]+NP[3]+VERB[4]
Path 3:	⇑pobj⇑prep⇑nsubj⇓prep⇓pobj
Path 4:	⇑nsubj⇓prep⇓pobj
Correct:	15
Incorrect:	4

The variables $correct$ and $incorrect$ are used during retrieval, where the score of an answer candidate ac is the sum of all scores of all matching patterns p:

$$score(ac) = \sum_{i=1}^{n} score(p_i) \quad (2)$$

where

$$score(p_i) = \begin{cases} \frac{correct_i + 1}{correct_i + incorrect_i + 2} & \text{if match} \\ 0 & \text{no match} \end{cases} \quad (3)$$

The highest scoring candidate is selected.

We would like to explicitly call out one property of our algorithm: It effectively returns two entities: a) a sentence that constitutes a valid response to the query, b) the head node of a phrase in that sentence that constitutes the answer. Therefore the algorithm can be used for sentence retrieval or for answer retrieval. It depends on the application which of the two behaviors is desired. In the next section, we evaluate its answer retrieval performance.

7 Experiments & Results

This section provides an evaluation of the algorithm described in this paper. The key questions we seek to answer are the following:

1. How does our method perform when compared to a baseline that extracts dependency paths from the question?

2. How much does the described algorithm improve performance of a state-of-the-art QA system?

3. What is the effect of training data size on performance? Can we expect that more training data would further improve the algorithm's performance?

7.1 Evaluation Setup

We use all factoid questions in TREC's QA test sets from 2002 to 2006 for evaluation for which a known answer exists in the AQUAINT corpus. Additionally, the data in (Lin and Katz, 2005) is used. In this paper the authors attempt to identify a much more complete set of relevant documents for a subset of TREC 2002 questions than TREC itself. We adopt a cross validation approach for our evaluation. Table 4 shows how the data is split into five folds.

In order to evaluate the algorithm's patterns we need a set of sentences to which they can be applied. In a traditional QA system architecture,

Test set	Number of Correct Answer Sentences										Mean	Med
	= 0	<= 1	<= 3	<= 5	<= 10	<= 25	<= 50	>= 75	>= 90	>= 100		
2002	0.203	0.396	0.580	0.671	0.809	0.935	0.984	0.0	0.0	0.0	6.86	2.0
2003	0.249	0.429	0.627	0.732	0.828	0.955	0.997	0.003	0.003	0.0	5.67	2.0
2004	0.221	0.368	0.539	0.637	0.799	0.936	0.985	0.0	0.0	0.0	6.51	3.0
2005	0.245	0.404	0.574	0.665	0.777	0.912	0.987	0.0	0.0	0.0	7.56	2.0
2006	0.241	0.389	0.568	0.665	0.807	0.920	0.966	0.006	0.0	0.0	8.04	3.0

Table 2: Fraction of sentences that contain correct answers in Evaluation Set 1 (approximation).

Test set	Number of Correct Answer Sentences										Mean	Med
	= 0	<= 1	<= 3	<= 5	<= 10	<= 25	<= 50	>= 75	>= 90	>= 100		
2002	0.0	0.074	0.158	0.235	0.342	0.561	0.748	0.172	0.116	0.060	33.46	21.0
2003	0.0	0.099	0.203	0.254	0.356	0.573	0.720	0.161	0.090	0.031	32.88	19.0
2004	0.0	0.073	0.137	0.211	0.328	0.598	0.779	0.142	0.069	0.034	30.82	20.0
2005	0.0	0.163	0.238	0.279	0.410	0.589	0.759	0.141	0.097	0.069	30.87	17.0
2006	0.0	0.125	0.207	0.281	0.415	0.596	0.727	0.173	0.122	0.088	32.93	17.5

Table 3: Fraction of sentences that contain correct answers in Evaluation Set 2 (approximation).

Fold	Training Data		Test Data	
	sets used	#	set	#
1	T03, T04, T05, T06	4565	T02	1159
2	T02, T04, T05, T06, Lin02	6174	T03	1352
3	T02, T03, T05, T06, Lin02	6700	T04	826
4	T02, T03, T04, T06, Lin02	6298	T05	1228
5	T02, T03, T04, T05, Lin02	6367	T06	1159

Table 4: Splits into training and tests sets of the data used for evaluation. T02 stands for TREC 2002 data etc. Lin02 is based on (Lin and Katz, 2005). The # rows show how many question/answer sentence pairs are used for training and for testing.

see e.g. (Prager, 2006; Voorhees, 2003), the document or passage retrieval step performs this function. This step is crucial to a QA system's performance, because it is impossible to locate answers in the subsequent answer extraction step if the passages returned during passage retrieval do not contain the answer in the first place. This also holds true in our case: the patterns cannot be expected to identify a correct answer if none of the sentences used as input contains the correct answer. We therefore use two different evaluation sets to evaluate our algorithm:

1. The first set contains for each question all sentences in the top 100 paragraphs returned by Lucene when using simple queries made up from the question's key words. It cannot be guaranteed that answers to every question are present in this test set.

2. For the second set, the query additionally list all known correct answers to the question as parts of one `OR` operator. This increases the chance that the evaluation set actually contains valid answer sentences significantly.

In order to provide a quantitative characterization of the two evaluation sets we estimated the number of correct answer sentences they contain. For each paragraph it was determined whether it contained one of the known answer strings and at least of one of the question key words. Tables 2 and 3 show for each evaluation set how many answers on average it contains per question. The column "= 0" for example shows the fraction of questions for which no valid answer sentence is contained in the evaluation set, while column ">= 90" gives the fraction of questions with 90 or more valid answer sentences. The last two columns show mean and median values.

7.2 Comparison with Baseline

As pointed out in Section 2 there is a strong tradition of using dependency paths in QA. Many relevant papers describe algorithms that analyze a question's grammatical structure and expect to find a similar structure in valid answer sentences, e.g. (Attardi et al., 2001), (Cui et al., 2005) or (Bouma et al., 2005) to name just a few. As already pointed out, a major contribution of our work is that we do not assume this similarity. In our approach valid answer sentences are allowed to have grammatical structures that are very different from the question and also very different from each other. Thus it is natural to compare our approach against a baseline that compares candidate sentences not against patterns that were gained from question/answer sentence pairs, but from questions alone. In order to create these patterns, we use a small trick: During the Pattern Creation step, see Section 5 and Figure 1, we replace the answer sentences in the input file with the questions, and assume that the question word indicates the position where the answer should be located.

Test set	Q number	Qs with patterns	> 1 correct	Overall correct	Accuracy overall	Acc. if pattern
2002	429	321	147	50	0.117	0.156
2003	354	237	76	22	0.062	0.093
2004	204	142	74	26	0.127	0.183
2005	319	214	97	46	0.144	0.215
2006	352	208	85	31	0.088	0.149
Sum	1658	1122	452	176	0.106	0.156

Table 5: Performance based on evaluation set 1.

Test set	Q number	Qs with patterns	> 1 correct	Overall correct	Accuracy overall	Acc. if pattern
2002	429	321	239	133	0.310	0.414
2003	354	237	149	88	0.248	0.371
2004	204	142	119	65	0.319	0.458
2005	319	214	161	92	0.288	0.429
2006	352	208	139	84	0.238	0.403
Sum	1658	1122	807	462	0.278	0.411

Table 6: Performance based on evaluation set 2.

Tables 5 and 6 show how our algorithm performs on evaluation sets 1 and 2, respectively. Tables 7 and 8 show how the baseline performs on evaluation sets 1 and 2, respectively. The tables' columns list the year of the TREC test set used, the number of questions in the set (we only use questions for which we know that there is an answer in the corpus), the number of questions for which one or more patterns exist, how often at least one pattern returned the correct answer, how often we get an overall correct result by taking all patterns and their confidence values into account, accuracy@1 of the overall system, and accuracy@1 computed only for those questions for which we have at least one pattern available (for all other questions the system returns no result.) As can be seen, on evaluation set 1 our method outperforms the baseline by 300%, on evaluation set 2 by 311%, taking accuracy if a pattern exists as a basis.

Test set	Q number	Qs with patterns	Min one correct	Overall correct	Accuracy overall	Acc. if pattern
2002	429	321	43	14	0.033	0.044
2003	354	237	28	10	0.028	0.042
2004	204	142	19	6	0.029	0.042
2005	319	214	21	7	0.022	0.033
2006	352	208	20	7	0.020	0.034
Sum	1658	1122	131	44	0.027	0.039

Table 7: Baseline performance based on evaluation set 1.

Many of the papers cited earlier that use an approach similar to our baseline approach of course report much better results than Tables 7 and 8. This however is not too surprising as the approach

Test set	Q number	Qs with patterns	Min one correct	Overall correct	Accuracy overall	Acc. if pattern
2002	429	321	77	37	0.086	0.115
2003	354	237	39	26	0.073	0.120
2004	204	142	25	15	0.074	0.073
2005	319	214	38	18	0.056	0.084
2006	352	208	34	16	0.045	0.077
Sum	1658	1122	213	112	0.068	0.100

Table 8: Baseline performance based on evaluation set 2.

described in this paper and the baseline approach do not make use of many techniques commonly used to increase performance of a QA system, e.g. TF-IDF fallback strategies, fuzzy matching, manual reformulation patterns etc. It was a deliberate decision from our side not to use any of these approaches. After all, this would result in an experimental setup where the performance of our answer extraction strategy could not have been observed in isolation. The QA system used as a baseline in the next section makes use of many of these techniques and we will see that our method, as described here, is suitable to increase its performance significantly.

7.3 Impact on an existing QA System

Tables 9 and 10 show how our algorithm increases performance of our QuALiM system, see e.g. (Kaisser et al., 2006). Section 6 in this paper describes via formulas 2 and 3 how answer candidates are ranked. This ranking is combined with the existing QA system's candidate ranking by simply using it as an additional feature that boosts candidates proportionally to their confidence score. The difference between both tables is that the first uses all 1658 questions in our test sets for the evaluation, whereas the second considers only those 1122 questions for which our system was able to learn a pattern. Thus for Table 10 questions which the system had no chance of answering due to limited training data are omitted. As can be seen, accuracy@1 increases by 4.9% on the complete test set and by 11.5% on the partial set.

Note that the QA system used as a baseline is at an advantage in at least two respects: a) It has important web-based components and as such has access to a much larger body of textual information. b) The algorithm described in this paper is an answer extraction approach only. For paragraph retrieval we use the same approach as for evaluation set 1, see Section 7.1. However, in more than 20% of the cases, this method returns not a single paragraph that contains both the answer and at least one question keyword. In such cases, the simple paragraph retrieval makes it close to impossible for our algorithm to return the correct answer.

Test Set	QuALiM	QASP	combined	increase
2002	0.503	0.117	0.524	4.2%
2003	0.367	0.062	0.390	6.2%
2004	0.426	0.127	0.451	5.7%
2005	0.373	0.144	0.389	4.2%
2006	0.341	0.088	0.358	5.0%
02-06	0.405	0.106	0.425	4.9%

Table 9: Top-1 accuracy of the QuALiM system on its own and when combined with the algorithm described in this paper. All increases are statistically significant using a sign test ($p < 0.05$).

Test Set	QuALiM	QASP	combined	increase
2002	0.530	0.156	0.595	12.3%
2003	0.380	0.093	0.430	13.3%
2004	0.465	0.183	0.514	10.6%
2005	0.388	0.214	0.421	8.4%
2006	0.385	0.149	0.428	11.3%
02-06	0.436	0.157	0.486	11.5%

Table 10: Top-1 accuracy of the QuALiM system on its own and when combined with the algorithm described in this paper, when only considering questions for which a pattern could be acquired from the training data. All increases are statistically significant using a sign test ($p < 0.05$).

7.4 Effect of Training Data Size

We now assess the effect of training data size on performance. Tables 5 and 6 presented earlier show that an average of 32.2% of the questions have no matching patterns. This is because the data used for training contained no examples for a significant subset of question classes. It can be expected that, if more training data would be available, this percentage would decrease and performance would increase. In order to test this assumption, we repeated the evaluation procedure detailed in this section several times, initially using data from only one TREC test set for training and then gradually adding more sets until all available training data had been used. The results for evaluation set 2 are presented in Figure 2. As can be seen, every time more data is added, performance increases. This strongly suggests that the point of diminishing returns, when adding additional training data no longer improves performance is not yet reached.

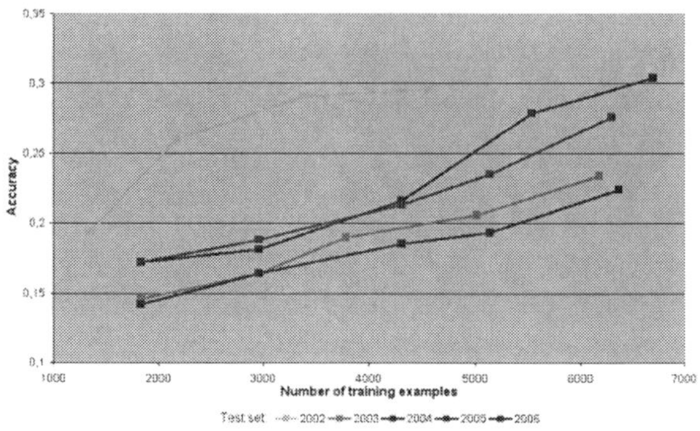

Figure 2: Effect of the amount of training data on system performance

8 Conclusions

In this paper we present an algorithm that acquires syntactic information about how relevant textual content to a question can be formulated from a collection of paired questions and answer sentences. Other than previous work employing dependency paths for QA, our approach does not assume that a valid answer sentence is similar to the question and it allows many potentially very different syntactic answer sentence structures. The algorithm is evaluated using TREC data, and it is shown that it outperforms an algorithm that merely uses the syntactic information contained in the question itself by 300%. It is also shown that the algorithm improves the performance of a state-of-the-art QA system significantly.

As always, there are many ways how we could imagine our algorithm to be improved. Combining it with fuzzy matching techniques as in (Cui et al., 2004) or (Cui et al., 2005) is an obvious direction for future work. We are also aware that in order to apply our algorithm on a larger scale and in a real world setting with real users, we would need a much larger set of training data. These could be acquired semi-manually, for example by using crowd-sourcing techniques. We are also thinking about fully automated approaches, or about using indirect human evidence, e.g. user clicks in search engine logs. Typically users only see the title and a short abstract of the document when clicking on a result, so it is possible to imagine a scenario where a subset of these abstracts, paired with user queries, could serve as training data.

References

Giuseppe Attardi, Antonio Cisternino, Francesco Formica, Maria Simi, and Alessandro Tommasi. 2001. PIQASso: Pisa Question Answering System. In *Proceedings of the 2001 Edition of the Text REtrieval Conference (TREC-01)*.

Gosse Bouma, Jori Mur, and Gertjan van Noord. 2005. Reasoning over Dependency Relations for QA. In *Proceedings of the IJCAI workshop on Knowledge and Reasoning for Answering Questions (KRAQ-05)*.

Hang Cui, Ji-Rong Wen, Jian-Yun Nie, and Wei-Ying Ma. 2002. Probabilistic query expansion using query logs. In *11th International World Wide Web Conference (WWW-02)*.

Hang Cui, Keya Li, Renxu Sun, Tat-Seng Chua, and Min-Yen Kan. 2004. National University of Singapore at the TREC-13 Question Answering Main Task. In *Proceedings of the 2004 Edition of the Text REtrieval Conference (TREC-04)*.

Hang Cui, Renxu Sun, Keya Li, Min-Yen Kan, and Tat-Seng Chua. 2005. Question Answering Passage Retrieval Using Dependency Relations. In *Proceedings of the 28th ACM-SIGIR International Conference on Research and Development in Information Retrieval (SIGIR-05)*.

Scott Deerwester, Susan Dumais, George Furnas, Thomas Landauer, and Richard Harshman. 1900. Indexing by Latent Semantic Analysis. *Journal of the American society for information science*, 41(6).

David Graff. 2002. The AQUAINT Corpus of English News Text.

Michael Kaisser and John Lowe. 2008. Creating a Research Collection of Question Answer Sentence Pairs with Amazon's Mechanical Turk. In *Proceedings of the Sixth International Conference on Language Resources and Evaluation (LREC-08)*.

Michael Kaisser, Silke Scheible, and Bonnie Webber. 2006. Experiments at the University of Edinburgh for the TREC 2006 QA track. In *Proceedings of the 2006 Edition of the Text REtrieval Conference (TREC-06)*.

Michael Kaisser. 2009. *Acquiring Syntactic and Semantic Transformations in Question Answering*. Ph.D. thesis, University of Edinburgh.

Dan Klein and Christopher D. Manning. 2003a. Accurate Unlexicalized Parsing. In *Proceedings of the 41st Meeting of the Association for Computational Linguistics (ACL-03)*.

Dan Klein and Christopher D. Manning. 2003b. Fast Exact Inference with a Factored Model for Natural Language Parsing. In *Advances in Neural Information Processing Systems 15*.

Jimmy Lin and Boris Katz. 2005. Building a Reusable Test Collection for Question Answering. *Journal of the American Society for Information Science and Technology (JASIST)*.

Dekang Lin and Patrick Pantel. 2001. Discovery of Inference Rules for Question-Answering. *Natural Language Engineering*, 7(4):343–360.

Dekang Lin. 1998. Dependency-based Evaluation of MINIPAR. In *Workshop on the Evaluation of Parsing Systems*.

George A. Miller, Richard Beckwith, Christiane Fellbaum, Derek Gross, and Katherine Miller. 1993. Introduction to WordNet: An On-Line Lexical Database. *Journal of Lexicography*, 3(4):235–244.

Diego Molla. 2006. Learning of Graph-based Question Answering Rules. In *Proceedings of HLT/NAACL 2006 Workshop on Graph Algorithms for Natural Language Processing*.

Franz Josef Och and Hermann Ney. 2003. A Systematic Comparison of Various Statistical Alignment Models. *Computational Linguistics*, 29(1):19–52.

Ted Pedersen, Siddharth Patwardhan, and Jason Michelizzi. 2004. WordNet::Similarity - Measuring the Relatedness of Concepts. In *Proceedings of the Nineteenth National Conference on Artificial Intelligence (AAAI-04)*.

John Prager. 2006. Open-Domain Question-Answering. *Foundations and Trends in Information Retrieval*, 1(2).

L. R. Rabiner, A. E. Rosenberg, and S. E. Levinson. 1991. Considerations in Dynamic Time Warping Algorithms for Discrete Word Recognition. In *Proceedings of IEEE Transactions on Acoustics, Speech and Signal Processing*.

Deepak Ravichandran and Eduard Hovy. 2002. Learning Surface Text Patterns for a Question Answering System. In *Proceedings of the 40th Annual Meeting of the Association for Computational Linguistics (ACL-02)*.

Stefan Riezler and Yi Liu. 2010. Query Rewriting using Monolingual Statistical Machine Translation. *Computational Linguistics*, 36(3).

Dan Shen and Dietrich Klakow. 2006. Exploring Correlation of Dependency Relation Paths for Answer Extraction. In *Proceedings of the 21st International Conference on Computational Linguistics and 44th Annual Meeting of the ACL (COLING/ACL-06)*.

David A. Smith and Jason Eisner. 2006. Quasisynchronous grammars: Alignment by Soft Projection of Syntactic Dependencies. In *Proceedings of the HLTNAACL Workshop on Statistical Machine Translation*.

Ellen M. Voorhees. 1999. Overview of the Eighth Text REtrieval Conference (TREC-8). In *Proceedings of the Eighth Text REtrieval Conference (TREC-8)*.

Ellen M. Voorhees. 2003. Overview of the TREC 2003 Question Answering Track. In *Proceedings of the 2003 Edition of the Text REtrieval Conference (TREC-03)*.

Mengqiu Wang, Noah A. Smith, and Teruko Mitamura. 2007. What is the Jeopardy model? A Quasisynchronous Grammar for QA. In *Proceedings of EMNLP-CoNLL 2007*.

Can Click Patterns across User's Query Logs Predict Answers to Definition Questions?

Alejandro Figueroa
Yahoo! Research Latin America
Blanco Encalada 2120, Santiago, Chile
afiguero@yahoo-inc.com

Abstract

In this paper, we examined click patterns produced by users of Yahoo! search engine when prompting definition questions. Regularities across these click patterns are then utilized for constructing a large and heterogeneous training corpus for answer ranking. In a nutshell, answers are extracted from clicked web-snippets originating from any class of web-site, including Knowledge Bases (KBs). On the other hand, non-answers are acquired from redundant pieces of text across web-snippets.

The effectiveness of this corpus was assessed via training two state-of-the-art models, wherewith answers to unseen queries were distinguished. These testing queries were also submitted by search engine users, and their answer candidates were taken from their respective returned web-snippets. This corpus helped both techniques to finish with an accuracy higher than 70%, and to predict over 85% of the answers clicked by users. In particular, our results underline the importance of non-KB training data.

1 Introduction

It is a well-known fact that definition queries are very popular across users of commercial search engines (Rose and Levinson, 2004). The essential characteristic of definition questions is their aim for discovering as much as possible descriptive information about the concept being defined (a.k.a. definiendum, pl. definienda). Some examples of this kind of query include "*Who is Benjamin Millepied?*" and "*Tell me about Bank of America*".

It is a standard practice of definition question answering (QA) systems to mine KBs (e.g., online encyclopedias and dictionaries) for reliable descriptive information on the definiendum (Sacaleanu et al., 2008). Normally, these pieces of information (i.e., nuggets) explain different facets of the definiendum (e.g., "*ballet choreographer*" and "*born in Bordeaux*"), and the main idea consists in projecting the acquired nuggets into the set of answer candidates afterwards. However, the performance of this category of method falls into sharp decline whenever few or no coverage is found across KBs (Zhang et al., 2005; Han et al., 2006). Put differently, this technique usually succeeds in discovering the most relevant facts about the most promiment sense of the definiendum. But it often misses many pertinent nuggets, especially those that can be paraphrased in several ways; and/or those regarding ancillary senses of the definiendum, which are hardly found in KBs.

As a means of dealing with this, current strategies try to construct general definition models inferred from a collection of definitions coming from the Internet or KBs (Androutsopoulos and Galanis, 2005; Xu et al., 2005; Han et al., 2006). To a great extent, models exploiting non-KB sources demand considerable annotation efforts, or when the data is obtained automatically, they benefit from empirical thresholds that ensure a certain degree of similarity to an array of KB articles. These thesholds attempt to trade-off the cleanness of the training material against its coverage. Moreover, gathering negative samples is also hard as it is not easy to find wide-coverage authoritative sources of non-descriptive information about a particular definiendum.

Our approach has different innovative aspects

compared to other research in the area of definition extraction. It is at the crossroads of query log analysis and QA systems. We study the click behavior of search engines' users with regard to definition questions. Based on this study, we propose a novel way of acquiring large-scale and heterogeneous training material for this task, which consists of:

- automatically obtaining positive samples in accordance with click patterns of search engine users. This aids in harvesting a host of descriptions from non-KB sources in conjunction with descriptive information from KBs.
- automatically acquiring negative data in consonance with redundancy patterns across snippets displayed within search engine results when processing definition queries.

In brief, our experiments reveal that these patterns can be effectively exploited for devising efficient models.

Given the huge amount of amassed data, we additionally contrast the performance of systems built on top of samples originated solely from KB, non-KB, and both combined. Our comparison corroborates that KBs yield massive trustworthy descriptive knowledge, but they do not bear enough diversity to discriminate all answering nuggets within any kind of text. Essentially, our experiments unveil that non-KB data is richer and therefore it is useful for discovering more descriptive nuggets than KB material. But its usage relies on its cleanness and on a negative set. Many people had these intuitions before, but to the best of our knowledge, we provide the first empirical confirmation and quantification.

The road-map of this paper is as follows: section 2 touches on related works; section 3 digs deeper into click patterns for definition questions, subsequently section 4 explains our corpus construction strategy; section 5 describes our experiments, and section 6 draws final conclusions.

2 Related Work

In recent years, definition QA systems have shown a trend towards the utilization of several discriminant and statistical learning techniques (Androutsopoulos and Galanis, 2005; Chen et al., 2006; Han et al., 2006; Fahmi and Bouma, 2006; Katz et al., 2007; Westerhout, 2009; Navigli and Velardi, 2010). Due to training, there is a pressing necessity for large-scale authoritative sources of descriptive and non-descriptive nuggets. In the same manner, there is a growing importance of strategies capable of extracting trustworthy and negative/positive samples from any type of text. Conventionally, these methods interpret descriptions as positive examples, whereas contexts providing non-descriptive information as negative elements. Four representative techniques are:

- centroid vector (Xu et al., 2003; Cui et al., 2004) collects an array of articles about the definiendum from a battery of predetermined KBs. These articles are then used to learn a vector of word frequencies, wherewith answer candidates are rated afterwards. Sometimes web-snippets together with a query reformulation method are exploited instead of pre-defined KBs (Chen et al., 2006).
- (Androutsopoulos and Galanis, 2005) gathered articles from KBs to score 250-characters windows carrying the definiendum. These windows were taken from the Internet, and accordingly, highly similar windows were interpreted as positive examples, while highly dissimilar as negative samples. For this purpose, two thresholds are used, which ensure the trustworthiness of both sets. However, they also cause the sets to be less diverse as not all definienda are widely covered across KBs. Indeed, many facets outlined within the 250-characters windows will not be detected.
- (Xu et al., 2005) manually labeled samples taken from an Intranet. Manual annotations are constrained to a small amount of examples, because it requires substantial human efforts to tag a large corpus, and disagreements between annotators are not uncommon.
- (Figueroa and Atkinson, 2009) capitalized on abstracts supplied by Wikipedia for building language models (LMs), thus there was no need for a negative set.

Our contribution is a novel technique for obtaining heterogeneous training material for definitional QA, that is to say, massive examples harvested from KBs and non-KBs. Fundamentally, positive examples are extracted from web snippets grounded on click patterns of users of a search engine, whereas the negative collection is acquired via redundancy patterns across web-snippets displayed to the user by the search engine. This data is capitalized by two state-of-the-art definition extractors, which are different in nature. In addition, our paper discusses the effect on the performance of different sorts (KBs and non-KBs) and amount of training data.

As for user clicks, they provide valuable relevance feedback for a variety of tasks, cf. (Radlinski et al., 2010). For instance, (Ji et al., 2009) extracted relevance information from clicked and non-clicked documents within aggregated search sessions. They modelled sequences of clicks as a means of learning to globally rank the relative relevance of all documents with respect to a given query. (Xu et al., 2010) improved the quality of training material for learning to rank approaches via predicting labels using clickthrough data. In our work, we combine click patterns across Yahoo! search query logs with QA techniques to build one-sided and two-sided classifiers for recognizing answers to definition questions.

3 User Click Analysis for Definition QA

In this section, we examine a collection of queries submitted to Yahoo! search engine during the period from December 2010 to March 2011. More specifically, for this analysis, we considered a log encompassing a random sample of 69,845,262 (23,360,089 distinct) queries. Basically, this log comprises the query sent by the user in conjunction with the displayed URLs and the information about the sequence of their clicks.

In the first place, we associate each query with a category in the taxonomy proposed by (Rose and Levinson, 2004), and in this way definition queries are selected. Secondly, we investigate user click patterns observed across these filtered definition questions.

3.1 Finding Definition Queries

According to (Broder, 2002; Lee et al., 2005; Dupret and Piwowarski, 2008), the intention of the user falls into at least two categories: navigational (e.g., "*google*") and informational (e.g., "*maximum entropy models*"). The former entails the desire of going to a specific site that the user has in mind, and the latter regards the goal of learning something by reading or viewing some content (Rose and Levinson, 2004). Navigational queries are hence of less relevance to definition questions, and for this reason, these were removed in congruence with the next three criteria:

- (Lee et al., 2005) pointed out that users will only visit the web site they bear in mind, when prompting navigational queries. Thus, these queries are characterized by clicking the same URL almost all the time (Lee et al., 2005). More precisely, we discarded queries that: a) appear more than four times in the query log; and which at the same time b) its most clicked URL represents more than 98% of all its clicks. Following the same idea, we additionally eliminated prompted URLs and queries where the clicked URL is of the form "www.search-query-without-spaces."

- By the same token, queries containing keywords such as "*homepage*", "*on-line*", and "*sign in*" were also removed.

- After the previous steps, many navigational queries (e.g., "*facebook*") still remained in the query log. We noticed that a substantial portion was signaled by several frequently and indistinctly clicked URLs. Take for instance "*facebook*": "www.facebook.com" and "www.facebook.com/login.php".

  With this in mind, we discarded entries embodied in a manually compiled black list. This list contains the 600 highest frequent cases.

A third category in (Rose and Levinson, 2004) regards resource queries, which we distinguished via keywords like "*image*", "*lyrics*" and "*maps*". Altogether, an amount of (35.67%) 24,916,610 (3,576,817 distinct) queries were seen as navigational and resource. Note that in (Rose and Levinson, 2004) both classes encompassed between 37%-38% of their query set.

Subsequently, we profited from the remaining 44,928,652 (informational) entries for detecting queries where the intention of the user is finding descriptive information about a topic (i.e., definiendum). In the taxonomy delineated by

(Rose and Levinson, 2004), informational queries are sub-categorized into five groups including list, locate, and definitional (directed and undirected). In practice, we filtered definition questions as follows:

1. We exploited an array of expressions that are commonly utilized in query analysis for classifying definition questions (Figueroa, 2010). E.g., "*Who is/was...*", "*What is/was a/an...*", "*define...*", and "*describe...*". Overall, these rules assisted in selecting 332,227 entries.

2. As stated in (Dupret and Piwowarski, 2008), informational queries are typified by the user clicking several documents. In light of that, we say that some definitional queries are characterized by multiple clicks, where at least one belongs to a KB. This aids in capturing the intention of the user when looking for descriptive knowledge and only entering noun phrases like "*thoracic outlet syndrome*":

www.medicinenet.com **en.wikipedia.org** health.yahoo.net www.livestrong.com
health.yahoo.net **en.wikipedia.org**
www.medicinenet.com www.mayoclinic.com **en.wikipedia.org**
www.nismat.org **en.wikipedia.org**

Table 1: Four distinct sequences of hosts clicked by users given the search query: "*thoracic outlet syndrome*".

In so doing, we manually compiled a list of 36 frequently clicked KB hosts (e.g., Wikipedia and Britannica encyclopedia). This filter produced 567,986 queries.

Unfortunately, since query logs stored by search engines are not publicly available due to privacy and legal concerns, there is no accessible training material to build models on top of annotated data. Thus, we exploited the aforementioned hand-crafted rules to connect queries to their respective category in this taxonomy.

3.2 User Click Patterns

In substance, the first filter recognizes the intention of the user by means of the formulation given by the user (e.g., "*What is a/the/an...*"). With regard to this filter, some interesting observations are as follows:

- In 40.27% of the entries, users did not visit any of the displayed web-sites. Consequently, we concluded that the information conveyed within the multiple snippets was often enough to answer the respective definition question. In other words, a significant fraction of the users were satisfied with a small set of brief, but quickly generated descriptions.

- In 2.18% of these cases, the search engine returned no results, and a few times users tried another paraphrase or query, due to useless results or misspellings.

- We also noticed that definition questions matched by these expressions are seldom related to more than one click, although informational queries produce several clicks, in general. In 46.44% of the cases, the user clicked a sole document, and more surprisingly, we observed that users are likely to click sources different from KBs, in contrast to the widespread belief in definition QA research. Users pick hits originating from small but domain-specific web-sites as a result of at least two effects: a) they are looking for minor or ancillary senses of the definiendum (e.g., "*ETA*" in "www.travel-industry-dictionary.com"); and more pertinent b) the user does not trust the information yielded by KBs and chooses more authoritative resources, for instance, when looking for reliable medical information (e.g., "*What is hypothyroidism?*", and "*What is mrsa infection?*").

While the first filter infers the intention of the user from the query itself, the second deduces it from the origin of the clicked documents. With regard to this second filter, clicking patterns are more disperse. Here, the first two clicks normally correspond to the top two/three ranked hits returned by the search engine, see also (Ji et al., 2009). Also, sequences of clicks signal that users normally visit only one site belonging to a KB, and at least one coming from a non-KB (see Table 1).

All in all, the insight gained in this analysis allows the construction of an heterogeneous corpus for definition question answering. Put differently, these user click patterns offer a way to obtain huge amounts of heterogeneous training material. In this way the heavy dependence of open-domain description identifiers on KB data can be alleviated.

4 Click-Based Corpus Acquisition

Since queries obtained by the previous two filters are not associated with the actual snippets seen by the users (due to storage limitations), snippets were recovered by means of submitting the queries to Yahoo! search engine.

After retrieval, we benefited from OpenNLP[1] for detecting sentence boundaries, tokenization and part-of-speech (POS) information. Here, we additionally interpreted truncations ("...") as sentence delimiters. POS tags were used to recognize and replace numbers with a placeholder (#CD#) as a means of creating sentence templates. We modified numbers as their value is just as often confusing as useful (Baeza-Yates and Ribeiro-Neto, 1999).

Along with numbers, sequences of full and partial matches of the definiendum were also substituted with placeholders, "#Q#" and "#QT#", respectively. To exemplify, consider this pre-processed snippet regarding "*Benjamin Millepied*" from "www.mashceleb.com":

```
#Q# / News &amp; Biography - MashCeleb
Latest news coverage of #Q#
#Q# ( born #CD# ) is a principal dancer
at New York City Ballet and a ballet
choreographer...
```

We benefit from these templates for building both a positive and a negative training set.

4.1 Negative Set

The negative set comprised templates appearing across all (clicked and unclicked) web-snippets, which at the same time, are related to more than five distinct queries. We hypothesize that these prominent elements correspond to non-informative, and thus non-descriptive, content as they appear within snippets across several questions. In other words: "*If it seems to answer every question, it will probably answer no question*". Take for instance:

```
Information about #Q# in the Columbia
Encyclopedia , Computer Desktop
Encyclopedia , computing dictionary
```

Conversely, templates that are more plausible to be answers are strongly related to their specific definition questions, and consequently, they are low in frequency and unlikely to be in the result set of a large number of queries. This negative set was expanded with templates coming from titles of snippets, which at the same time, have a frequency higher than four across all snippets (independent on which queries they appear). This process cooperated on gathering 1,021,571 different negative examples. In order to measure the precision of this process, we randomly selected and checked 1,000 elements, and we found an error of 1.3%.

4.2 Positive Set

As for the positive set, this was constructed only from the summary section of web-snippets clicked by the users. We constrained these snippets to bear a title template associated with at least two web-snippets clicked for two distinct queries. Some good examples are:

```
What is #Q# ?  Choices and Consequences.
Biology question :  What is an #Q# ?
```

Since clicks are linked with entire snippets, it is uncertain which sentences are genuine descriptions (see the previous example). Therefore, we removed those templates already contained in the negative set, along with those samples that matched an array of well-known hand-crafted rules. This set included:

a. sentences containing words such as "*ask*", "*report*", "*say*", and "*unless*" (Kil et al., 2005; Schlaefer et al., 2007);

b. sentences bearing several named entities (Schlaefer et al., 2006; Schlaefer et al., 2007), which were recognized by the number of tokens starting with a capital letter versus those starting with a lowercase letter;

c. statements of persons (Schlaefer et al., 2007); and

[1] http://opennlp.sourceforge.net

d. we also profited from about five hundred common expressions across web snippets including "*Picture of*", and "*Jump to : navigation , search*", as well as "*Recent posts*".

This process assisted in acquiring 881,726 different examples, where 673,548 came from KBs. Here, we also randomly selected 1,000 instances and manually checked if they were actual descriptions. The error of this set was 12.2%.

To put things into perspective, in contrast to other corpus acquisition approaches, the present method generated more than 1,800,000 positive and negative training samples combined, while the open-domain strategy of (Miliaraki and Androutsopoulos, 2004; Androutsopoulos and Galanis, 2005) ca. 20,000 examples, the close-domain technique of (Xu et al., 2005) about 3,000 and (Fahmi and Bouma, 2006) ca. 2,000.

5 Answering New Definition Queries

In our experiments, we checked the effectiveness of our user click-based corpus acquisition technique by studying its impact on two state-of-the-art systems. The first one is based on the **bi-term LMs** proposed by (Chen et al., 2006). This system requires only positive samples as training material. Conversely, our second system capitalizes on both positive and negative examples, and it is based on the **Maximum Entropy** (ME) models presented by (Fahmi and Bouma, 2006). These ME[2] models amalgamated bigrams and unigrams as well as two additional syntactic features, which were not applicable to our task (i.e, sentence position). We added to this model the sentence length as a feature in order to homologate the attributes used by both systems, therefore offering a good framework to assess the impact of our negative set. Note that (Fahmi and Bouma, 2006), unlike us, applied their models only to sentences observing some specific syntactic patterns.

With regard to the **test set**, this was constructed by manually annotating 113,184 sentence templates corresponding to 3,162 unseen definienda. In total, this array of unseen testing instances encompassed 11,566 different positive samples. In order to build a balanced testing collection, the same number of negative examples were randomly selected. Overall, our testing set contains 23,132 elements, and some illustrative annotations are shown in Table 2. It is worth highlighting that these examples signal that our models are considering pattern-free descriptions, that is to say, unlike other systems (Xu et al., 2003; Katz et al., 2004; Fernandes, 2004; Feng et al., 2006; Figueroa and Atkinson, 2009; Westerhout, 2009) which consider definitions aligning an array of well-known patterns (e.g., "*is a*" and "*also known as*"), our models disregard any class of syntactic constraint.

As to a **baseline** system, we accounted for the **centroid vector** (Xu et al., 2003; Cui et al., 2004). When implementing, we followed the blueprint in (Chen et al., 2006), and it was built for each *definiendum* from a maximum of 330 web snippets fetched by means of Bing Search. This baseline achieved a modest performance as it correctly classified 43.75% of the testing examples. In detail, 47.75% out of the 56.25% of the misclassified elements were a result of data-sparseness. This baseline has been widely used as a starting point for comparison purposes, however it is hard for this technique to discover diverse descriptive nuggets. This problem stems from the narrow-coverage of the centroid vector learned for the respective definienda (Zhang et al., 2005). In short, these figures support the necessity for more robust methods based on massive training material.

Experiments. We trained both models by systematically increasing the size of the training material by 1%. For this, we randomly split the training data into 100 equally sized packs, and systematically added one to the previously selected sets (i. e., 1%, 2%, 3%, . . . , 99%, 100%). We also experimented with: 1) positive examples originated solely from KBs; 2) positive samples harvested only from non-KBs; and eventually 3) all positive examples combined.

Figure 1 juxtaposes the outcomes accomplished by both techniques under the different configurations. These figures, compared with results obtained by the baseline, indicate the important contribution of our corpus to tackle data-sparseness. This contrast substantiates our claim that click patterns can be utilized as indicators of answers to definition questions. Since our models ignore definition patterns, they have the potential of detecting a wide diversity of descriptive information.

Further, the improvement of about 9%-10% by

[2]http://maxent.sourceforge.net/about.html

Label	Example/Template
+	Propylene #Q# is a type of alcohol made from fermented yeast and carbohydrates and is commonly used in a wide variety of products .
+	#Q# is aggressive behavior intended to achieve a goal .
+	In Hispanic culture , when a girl turns #CD# , a celebration is held called the #Q#, symbolizing the girl 's passage to womanhood .
+	Kirschwasser , German for " cherry water " and often shortened to #Q# in English-speaking countries , is a colorless brandy made from black ...
+	From the Gaelic 'dubhglas ' meaning #Q#, #QT# stream , or from the #QT# river .
+	Council Bluffs Orthopedic Surgeon Doctors physician directory - Read about #Q#, damage to any of the #CD# tendons that stabilize the shoulder joint .
+	It also occurs naturally in our bodies in fact , an average size adult manufactures up to #CD# grams of #Q# daily during normal metabolism .
-	Sterling Silver #Q# Hoop Earrings Overstockjeweler.com
-	I know V is the rate of reaction and the #Q# is hal ...
-	As sad and mean as that sounds , there is some truth to it , as #QT# as age their bodies do not function as well as they used to (in all respects) so there is a ...
-	If you 're new to the idea of Christian #Q#, what I call " the wild things of God ,
-	A look at the Biblical doctrine of the #QT# , showing the biblical basis for the teaching and including a discussion of some of the common objections .
-	#QT# is Users Choice (application need to be run at #QT# , but is not system critical) , this page shows you how it affects your Windows operating system .
-	Your doctor may recommend that you use certain drugs to help you control your #Q# .
-	Find out what is the full meaning of #Q# on Abbreviations.com !

Table 2: Samples of manual annotations (testing set).

means of exploiting our negative set makes its positive contribution clear. In particular, this supports our hypothesis that redundancy across web-snippets pertaining to several definition questions can be exploited as negative evidence. On the whole, this enhancement also suggests that ME models are a better option than LMs.

Furthermore, in the case of ME models, putting together evidence from KB and non-KBs betters the performance. Conversely, in the case of LMs, we do not observe a noticeable improvement when unifying both sources. We attribute this difference to the fact that non-KB data is noisier, and thus negative examples are necessary to cushion this noise. By and large, the outcomes show that the usage of descriptive information derived exclusively from KBs is not the best, but a cost-efficient solution.

Incidentally, Figure 1 reveals that more training data does not always imply better results. Overall, the best performance (ME-combined → 80.72%) was reaped when considering solely 32% of the training material. Hence, ME-KB finished with the best performance when accounting for about 215,500 positive examples (see Table 3). Adding more examples brought about a decline in accuracy. Nevertheless, this fraction (32%) is still larger than the data-sets considered by other open-domain Machine Learning approaches (Miliaraki and Androutsopoulos, 2004; Androutsopoulos and Galanis, 2005).

Best Conf. of	Accuracy	True positives	Positive examples
ME-combined	80.72%	88%	881,726
ME-KB	80.33%	89.37%	673,548
ME-N-KB	78.99%	93.38%	208,178

Table 3: Comparison of performance, the total amount and origin of training data, and the number of recognized descriptions.

In detail, when contrasting the confusion matrices of the best configurations accomplished by ME-combined (80.72%), ME-KB (80.33%) and ME-N-KB (78.99%), one can find that ME-combined correctly identified 88% of the answers (true positives), while ME-KB 89.37% and ME-N-KB 93.38% (see Table 3).

Interestingly enough, non-KB data only embodies 23.61% of all positive training material, but it still has the ability to recognize more answers. Despite of that, the other two strategies outperform ME-N-KB, because they are able

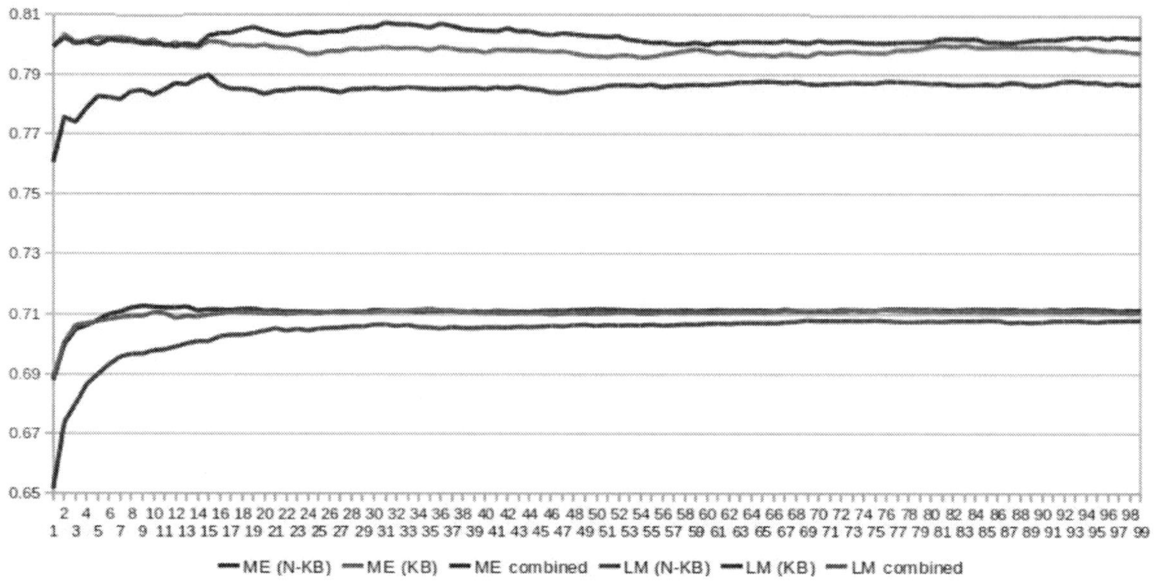

Figure 1: Results for each configuration (accuracy).

to correctly label more negative test examples. Given these figures, we can conclude that this is achieved by mitigating the impact of the noise in the training corpus by means of cleaner (KB) data.

We verified this synergy by inspecting the number of answers from non-KBs detected by the three top configurations in Table 3: ME-combined (9,086), ME-KB (9,230) and ME-N-KB (9,677). In like manner, we examined the confusion matrix for the best configuration (ME-combined → 80.72%): 1,388 (6%) positive examples were mislabeled as negative, while 3,071 (13.28%) negative samples were mistagged as positive.

In addition, we performed significance tests utilizing two-tailed paired t-test at 95% confidence interval on twenty samples. For this, we used only the top three configurations in Table 3 and each sample was determined by using boostrapping resampling. Each sample has the same size of the original test corpus. Overall, the tests implied that all pairs were statistically different from each other.

In summary, the results show that both negative examples and combining positive examples from heterogeneous sources are indispensable to tackle any class of text. However, it is vital to lessen the noise in non-KB data, since this causes a more adverse effect on the performance. Given the upperbound in accuracy, our outcomes indicate that cleanness and quality are more important than the size of the corpus. Our figures additionally suggest that more effort should go into increasing diversity than the number of training instances. In light of these observations, we also conjecture that a more reduced, but diverse and manually annotated, corpus might be more effective. In particular, a manually checked corpus distilled by inspecting click patterns across query logs of search engines.

Lastly, in order to evaluate how good a click predictor the three top ME-configurations are, we focused our attention only on the manually labeled positive samples (answers) that were clicked by the users. Overall, 86.33% (ME-combined), 88.85% (ME-KB) and 92.45% (ME-N-KB) of these responses were correctly predicted. In light of that, one can conclude that (clicked and non-clicked) answers to definition questions can be identified/predicted on the basis of user's click patterns across query logs.

From the viewpoint of search engines, web snippets are computed off-line, in general. In so doing, some methods select the spans of text bearing query terms with the potential of putting the document on top of the rank (Turpin et al., 2007; Tsegay et al., 2009). This helps to create an abridged version of the document that can quickly produce the snippet. This has to do with the trade-off between storage capacity, indexing, and retrieval speed. Ergo, our technique can help to determine whether or not a span of text is worth expanding, or in some cases whether or not it should be included in the snippet view of the document. In our instructive snippet, we now might have:

```
Benjamin Millepied / News &amp;
Biography - MashCeleb
Benjamin Millepied (born 1977) is a
principal dancer at New York City Ballet
and a ballet choreographer of
international reputation.  Millepied was
born in Bordeaux, France.  His...
```

Improving the results of informational (e.g., definition) queries, especially of less frequent ones, is key for competing commercial search engines as they are embodied in the non-navigational tail where these engines differ the most (Zaragoza et al., 2010).

6 Conclusions

This work investigates into the click behavior of commercial search engine users regarding definition questions. These behaviour patterns are then exploited as a corpus acquisition technique for definition QA, which offers the advantage of encompassing positive samples from heterogoneous sources. In contrast, negative examples are obtained in conformity to redundancy patterns across snippets, which are returned by the search engine when processing several definition queries. The effectiveness of these patterns, and hence of the obtained corpus, was tested by means of two models different in nature, where both were capable of achieving an accuracy higher than 70%.

As a future work, we envision that answers detected by our strategy can aid in determining some query expansion terms, and thus to devise some relevance feedback methods that can bring about an improvement in terms of the recall of answers. Along the same lines, it can cooperate on the visualization of the results by highlighting and/or extending truncated answers, that is more informative snippets, which is one of the holy grail of search operators, especially when processing informational queries.

NLP tools (e.g., parsers and name entity recognizers) can also be exploited for designing better training data filters and more discriminative features for our models that can assist in enhancing the performance, cf. (Surdeanu et al., 2008; Figueroa, 2010; Surdeanu et al., 2011). However, this implies that these tools have to be re-trained to cope with web-snippets.

Acknowledgements

This work was partially supported by R&D project FONDEF D09I1185. We also thank our reviewers for their interesting comments, which helped us to make this work better.

References

I. Androutsopoulos and D. Galanis. 2005. A practically Unsupervised Learning Method to Identify Single-Snippet Answers to Definition Questions on the web. In *HLT/EMNLP*, pages 323–330.

R. Baeza-Yates and B. Ribeiro-Neto. 1999. *Modern Information Retrieval*. Addison Wesley.

A. Broder. 2002. A Taxonomy of Web Search. *SIGIR Forum*, 36:3–10, September.

Y. Chen, M. Zhon, and S. Wang. 2006. Reranking Answers for Definitional QA Using Language Modeling. In *Coling/ACL-2006*, pages 1081–1088.

H. Cui, K. Li, R. Sun, T.-S. Chua, and M.-Y. Kan. 2004. National University of Singapore at the TREC 13 Question Answering Main Task. In *Proceedings of TREC 2004*. NIST.

Georges E. Dupret and Benjamin Piwowarski. 2008. A user browsing model to predict search engine click data from past observations. In *SIGIR '08*, pages 331–338.

Ismail Fahmi and Gosse Bouma. 2006. Learning to Identify Definitions using Syntactic Features. In *Proceedings of the Workshop on Learning Structured Information in Natural Language Applications*.

Donghui Feng, Deepak Ravichandran, and Eduard H. Hovy. 2006. Mining and Re-ranking for Answering Biographical Queries on the Web. In *AAAI*.

Aaron Fernandes. 2004. Answering Definitional Questions before they are Asked. Master's thesis, Massachusetts Institute of Technology.

A. Figueroa and J. Atkinson. 2009. Using Dependency Paths For Answering Definition Questions on The Web. In *WEBIST 2009*, pages 643–650.

Alejandro Figueroa. 2010. *Finding Answers to Definition Questions on the Web*. Phd-thesis, Universitaet des Saarlandes, 7.

K. Han, Y. Song, and H. Rim. 2006. Probabilistic Model for Definitional Question Answering. In *Proceedings of SIGIR 2006*, pages 212–219.

Shihao Ji, Ke Zhou, Ciya Liao, Zhaohui Zheng, Gui-Rong Xue, Olivier Chapelle, Gordon Sun, and Hongyuan Zha. 2009. Global ranking by exploiting user clicks. In *Proceedings of the 32nd international ACM SIGIR conference on Research and development in information retrieval*, SIGIR '09, pages 35–42, New York, NY, USA. ACM.

B. Katz, M. Bilotti, S. Felshin, A. Fernandes, W. Hildebrandt, R. Katzir, J. Lin, D. Loreto, G. Marton, F. Mora, and O. Uzuner. 2004. Answering multiple questions on a topic from heterogeneous resources. In *Proceedings of TREC 2004*. NIST.

B. Katz, S. Felshin, G. Marton, F. Mora, Y. K. Shen, G. Zaccak, A. Ammar, E. Eisner, A. Turgut, and L. Brown Westrick. 2007. CSAIL at TREC 2007 Question Answering. In *Proceedings of TREC 2007*. NIST.

Jae Hong Kil, Levon Lloyd, and Steven Skiena. 2005. Question Answering with Lydia (TREC 2005 QA track). In *Proceedings of TREC 2005*. NIST.

U. Lee, Z. Liu, and J. Cho. 2005. Automatic Identification of User Goals in Web Search. In *Proceedings of the 14th WWW conference*, WWW '05, pages 391–400.

S. Miliaraki and I. Androutsopoulos. 2004. Learning to identify single-snippet answers to definition questions. In *COLING '04*, pages 1360–1366.

Roberto Navigli and Paola Velardi. 2010. LearningWord-Class Lattices for Definition and Hypernym Extraction. In *Proceedings of the 48th Annual Meeting of the Association for Computational Linguistics (ACL 2010)*.

Filip Radlinski, Martin Szummer, and Nick Craswell. 2010. Inferring query intent from reformulations and clicks. In *Proceedings of the 19th international conference on World wide web*, WWW '10, pages 1171–1172, New York, NY, USA. ACM.

Daniel E. Rose and Danny Levinson. 2004. Understanding User Goals in Web Search. In *WWW*, pages 13–19.

B. Sacaleanu, G. Neumann, and C. Spurk. 2008. DFKI-LT at QA@CLEF 2008. In *In Working Notes for the CLEF 2008 Workshop*.

Nico Schlaefer, P. Gieselmann, and Guido Sautter. 2006. The Ephyra QA System at TREC 2006. In *Proceedings of TREC 2006*. NIST.

Nico Schlaefer, Jeongwoo Ko, Justin Betteridge, Guido Sautter, Manas Pathak, and Eric Nyberg. 2007. Semantic Extensions of the Ephyra QA System for TREC 2007. In *Proceedings of TREC 2007*. NIST.

Mihai Surdeanu, Massimiliano Ciaramita, and Hugo Zaragoza. 2008. Learning to Rank Answers on Large Online QA Collections. In *Proceedings of the 46th Annual Meeting of the Association for Computational Linguistics (ACL 2008)*, pages 719–727.

Mihai Surdeanu, Massimiliano Ciaramita, and Hugo Zaragoza. 2011. Learning to rank answers to non-factoid questions from web collections. *Computational Linguistics*, 37:351–383.

Yohannes Tsegay, Simon J. Puglisi, Andrew Turpin, and Justin Zobel. 2009. Document compaction for efficient query biased snippet generation. In *Proceedings of the 31th European Conference on IR Research on Advances in Information Retrieval*, ECIR '09, pages 509–520, Berlin, Heidelberg. Springer-Verlag.

Andrew Turpin, Yohannes Tsegay, David Hawking, and Hugh E. Williams. 2007. Fast generation of result snippets in web search. In *Proceedings of the 30th annual international ACM SIGIR conference on Research and development in information retrieval*, SIGIR '07, pages 127–134, New York, NY, USA. ACM.

Eline Westerhout. 2009. Extraction of definitions using grammar-enhanced machine learning. In *Proceedings of the EACL 2009 Student Research Workshop*, pages 88–96.

Jinxi Xu, Ana Licuanan, and Ralph Weischedel. 2003. TREC2003 QA at BBN: Answering Definitional Questions. In *Proceedings of TREC 2003*, pages 98–106. NIST.

J. Xu, Y. Cao, H. Li, and M. Zhao. 2005. Ranking Definitions with Supervised Learning Methods. In *WWW2005*, pages 811–819.

Jingfang Xu, Chuanliang Chen, Gu Xu, Hang Li, and Elbio Renato Torres Abib. 2010. Improving quality of training data for learning to rank using click-through data. In *Proceedings of the third ACM international conference on Web search and data mining*, WSDM '10, pages 171–180, New York, NY, USA. ACM.

H. Zaragoza, B. Barla Cambazoglu, and R. Baeza-Yates. 2010. We Search Solved? All Result Rankings the Same? In *Proceedings of CKIM'10*, pages 529–538.

Zhushuo Zhang, Yaqian Zhou, Xuanjing Huang, and Lide Wu. 2005. Answering Definition Questions Using Web Knowledge Bases. In *Proceedings of IJCNLP 2005*, pages 498–506.

Adaptation of Statistical Machine Translation Model for Cross-Lingual Information Retrieval in a Service Context

Vassilina Nikoulina
Xerox Research Center Europe
vassilina.nikoulina@xrce.xerox.com

Bogomil Kovachev
Informatics Institute
University of Amsterdam
B.K.Kovachev@uva.nl

Nikolaos Lagos
Xerox Research Center Europe
nikolaos.lagos@xrce.xerox.com

Christof Monz
Informatics Institute
University of Amsterdam
C.Monz@uva.nl

Abstract

This work proposes to adapt an existing general SMT model for the task of translating queries that are subsequently going to be used to retrieve information from a target language collection. In the scenario that we focus on access to the document collection itself is not available and changes to the IR model are not possible. We propose two ways to achieve the adaptation effect and both of them are aimed at tuning parameter weights on a set of parallel queries. The first approach is via a standard tuning procedure optimizing for BLEU score and the second one is via a reranking approach optimizing for MAP score. We also extend the second approach by using syntax-based features. Our experiments show improvements of 1-2.5 in terms of MAP score over the retrieval with the non-adapted translation. We show that these improvements are due both to the integration of the adaptation and syntax-features for the query translation task.

1 Introduction

Cross Lingual Information Retrieval (CLIR) is an important feature for any digital content provider in today's multilingual environment. However, many of the content providers are not willing to change existing well-established document indexing and search tools, nor to provide access to their document collection by a third-party external service. The work presented in this paper assumes such a context of use, where a query translation service allows translating queries posed to the search engine of a content provider into several target languages, without requiring changes to the undelying IR system used and without accessing, at translation time, the content provider's document set. Keeping in mind these constraints, we present two approaches on query translation optimisation.

One of the important observations done during the CLEF 2009 campaign (Ferro and Peters, 2009) related to CLIR was that the usage of Statistical Machine Translation (SMT) systems (eg. Google Translate) for query translation led to important improvements in the cross-lingual retrieval performance (the best CLIR performance increased from ~55% of the monolingual baseline in 2008 to more than 90% in 2009 for French and German target languages). However, general-purpose SMT systems are not necessarily adapted for query translation. That is because SMT systems trained on a corpus of standard parallel phrases take into account the phrase structure implicitly. The structure of queries is very different from the standard phrase structure: queries are very short and the word order might be different than the typical full phrase one. This problem can be seen as a problem of genre adaptation for SMT, where the genre is "query".

To our knowledge, no suitable corpora of parallel queries is available to train an adapted SMT system. Small corpora of parallel queries[1] however can be obtained (eg. CLEF tracks) or manually created. We suggest to use such corpora in order to adapt the SMT model parameters for query translation. In our approach the parameters of the SMT models are optimized on the basis of the parallel queries set. This is achieved either directly in the SMT system using the MERT (Minimum Error Rate Training) algorithm and optimiz-

[1] Insufficient for a full SMT system training (~500 entries)

ing according to the BLEU[2](Papineni et al., 2001) score, or via reranking the Nbest translation candidates generated by a baseline system based on new parameters (and possibly new features) that aim to optimize a retrieval metric.

It is important to note that both of the proposed approaches allow keeping the MT system independent of the document collection and indexing, and thus suitable for a query translation service. These two approaches can also be combined by using the model produced with the first approach as a baseline that produces the Nbest list of translations that is then given to the reranking approach.

The remainder of this paper is organized as follows. We first present related work addressing the problem of query translation. We then describe two approaches towards adapting an SMT system to the query-genre: tuning the SMT system on a parallel set of queries (Section 3.1) and adapting machine translation via the reranking framework (Section 3.2). We then present our experimental settings and results (Section 4) and conclude in section 5.

2 Related work

We may distinguish two main groups of approaches to CLIR: document translation and query translation. We concentrate on the second group which is more relevant to our settings. The standard query translation methods use different translation resources such as bilingual dictionaries, parallel corpora and/or machine translation. The aspect of disambiguation is important for the first two techniques.

Different methods were proposed to deal with disambiguation issues, often relying on the document collection or embedding the translation step directly into the retrieval model (Hiemstra and Jong, 1999; Berger et al., 1999; Kraaij et al., 2003). Other methods rely on external resources like query logs (Gao et al., 2010), Wikipedia (Jadidinejad and Mahmoudi, 2009) or the web (Nie and Chen, 2002; Hu et al., 2008). (Gao et al., 2006) proposes syntax-based translation models to deal with the disambiguation issues (NP-based, dependency-based). The candidate translations proposed by these models are then reranked with the model learned to minimize the translation error on the training data.

To our knowledge, existing work that use MT-based techniques for query translation use an out-of-the-box MT system, without adapting it for query translation in particular (Jones et al., 1999; Wu et al., 2008) (although some query expansion techniques might be applied to the produced translation afterwards (Wu and He, 2010)).

There is a number of works done for domain adaptation in Statistical Machine Translation. However, we want to distinguish between genre and domain adaptation in this work. Generally, genre can be seen as a sub-problem of domain. Thus, we consider genre to be the general style of the text e.g. conversation, news, blog, query (responsible mostly for the text structure) while the domain reflects more what the text is about – eg. social science, healthcare, history, so domain adaptation involves lexical disambiguation and extra lexical coverage problems. To our knowledge, there is not much work addressing explicitly the problem of genre adaptation for SMT. Some work done on domain adaptation could be applied to genre adaptation, such as incorporating available in-domain corpora in the SMT model: either monolingual (Bertoldi and Federico, 2009; Wu et al., 2008; Zhao et al., 2004; Koehn and Schroeder, 2007), or small parallel data used for tuning the SMT parameters (Zheng et al., 2010; Pecina et al., 2011).

3 Our approach

This work is based on the hypothesis that the general-purpose SMT system needs to be adapted for query translation. Although in (Ferro and Peters, 2009) it has been mentioned that using Google translate (general-purpose MT) for query translation allowed to CLEF participants to obtain the best CLIR performance, there is still 10% gap between monolingual and cross-lingual IR. We believe that, as in (Clinchant and Renders, 2007), more adapted query translation, possibly further combined with query expansion techniques, can lead to improved retrieval.

The problem of the SMT adaptation for query-genre translation has different quality aspects. On the one hand, we want our model to produce a "good" translation (well-formed and transmitting the information contained in the source query) of an input query. On the other hand, we want to obtain good retrieval performance using

[2]Standard MT evaluation metric

the proposed translation. These two aspects are not necessarily correlated: a bag-of-word translation can lead to good retrieval performance, even though it won't be syntactically well-formed; at the same time a well-formed translation can lead to worse retrieval if the wrong lexical choice is done. Moreover, often the retrieval demands some linguistic preprocessing (eg. lemmatisation, PoS tagging) which in interaction with badly-formed translations might bring some noise.

A couple of works studied the correlation between the standard MT evaluation metrics and the retrieval precision. Thus, (Fujii et al., 2009) showed a good correlation of the BLEU scores with the MAP scores for Cross-Lingual Patent Retrieval. However, the topics in patent search (long and well structured) are very different from standard queries. (Kettunen, 2009) also found a pretty high correlation ($0.8 - 0.9$) between standard MT evaluation metrics (METEOR(Banerjee and Lavie, 2005), BLEU, NIST(Doddington, 2002)) and retrieval precision for long queries. However, the same work shows that the correlation decreases ($0.6 - 0.7$) for short queries.

In this paper we propose two approaches to SMT adaptation for queries. The first one optimizes BLEU, while the second one optimizes Mean Average Precision (MAP), a standard metric in information retrieval. We'll address the issue of the correlation between BLEU and MAP in Section 4.

Both of the proposed approaches rely on the phrase-based SMT (PBMT) model (Koehn et al., 2003) implemented in the Open Source SMT toolkit MOSES (Koehn et al., 2007).

3.1 Tuning for genre adaptation

First, we propose to adapt the PBMT model by tuning the model's weights on a parallel set of queries. This approach addresses the first aspect of the problem, which is producing a "good" translation. The PBMT model combines different types of features via a log-linear model. The standard features include (Koehn, 2010, Chapter 5): language model, word penalty, distortion, different translation models, etc. The weights of these features are learned during the tuning step with the MERT (Och, 2003) algorithm. Roughly the MERT algorithm tunes feature weights one by one and optimizes them according to the BLEU score obtained.

Our hypothesis is that the impact of different features should be different depending on whether we translate a full sentence, or a query-genre entry. Thus, one would expect that in the case of query-genre the language model or the distortion features should get less importance than in the case of the full-sentence translation. MERT tuning on a genre-adapted parallel corpus should leverage this information from the data, adapting the SMT model to the query-genre. We would also like to note that the tuning approach (proposed for domain adaptation by (Zheng et al., 2010)) seems to be more appropriate for genre adaptation than for domain adaptation where the problem of lexical ambiguity is encoded in the translation model and re-weighting the main features might not be sufficient.

We use the MERT implementation provided with the Moses toolkit with default settings. Our assumption is that this procedure although not explicitly aimed at improving retrieval performance will nevertheless lead to "better" query translations when compared to the baseline. The results of this apporach allow us also to observe whether and to what extent changes in BLEU scores are correlated to changes in MAP scores.

3.2 Reranking framework for query translation

The second approach addresses the retrieval quality problem. An SMT system is usually trained to optimize the quality of the translation (eg. BLEU score for SMT), which is not necessarily correlated with the retrieval quality (especially for the short queries). Thus, for example, the word order which is crucial for translation quality (and is taken into account by most MT evaluation metrics) is often ignored by IR models. Our second approach follows (Nie, 2010, pp.106) argument that "the translation problem is an integral part of the whole CLIR problem, and unified CLIR models integrating translation should be defined". We propose integrating the IR metric (MAP) into the translation model optimisation step via the reranking framework.

Previous attempts to apply the reranking approach to SMT did not show significant improvements in terms of MT evaluation metrics (Och et al., 2003; Nikoulina and Dymetman, 2008). One of the reasons being the poor diversity of the Nbest list of the translations. However, we believe that this approach has more potential in the context of query translation.

First of all the average query length is ~5 words, which means that the Nbest list of the translations is more diverse than in the case of general phrase translation (average length 25-30 words).

Moreover, the retrieval precision is more naturally integrated into the reranking framework than standard MT evaluation metrics such as BLEU. The main reason is that the notion of Average Retrieval Precision is well defined for a single query translation, while BLEU is defined on the corpus level and correlates poorly with human quality judgements for the individual translations (Specia et al., 2009; Callison-Burch et al., 2009).

Finally, the reranking framework allows a lot of flexibility. Thus, it allows enriching the baseline translation model with new complex features which might be difficult to introduce into the translation model directly.

Other works applied the reranking framework to different NLP tasks such as Named Entities Extraction (Collins, 2001), parsing (Collins and Roark, 2004), and language modelling (Roark et al., 2004). Most of these works used the reranking framework to combine generative and discriminative methods when both approaches aim at solving the same problem: the generative model produces a set of hypotheses, and the best hypothesis is chosen afterwards via the discriminative reranking model, which allows to enrich the baseline model with the new complex and heterogeneous features. We suggest using the reranking framework to combine two different tasks: Machine Translation and Cross-lingual Information Retrieval. In this context the reranking framework doesn't only allow enriching the baseline translation model but also performing training using a more appropriate evaluation metric.

3.2.1 Reranking training

Generally, the reranking framework can be resumed in the following steps :

1. The baseline (generic-purpose) MT system generates a list of candidate translations $GEN(q)$ for each query q;

2. A vector of features $F(t)$ is assigned to each translation $t \in GEN(q)$;

3. The best translation $\hat{t}$ is chosen as the one maximizing the translation score, which is defined as a weighted linear combination of features: $\hat{t}(\lambda) = \arg\max_{t \in GEN(q)} \lambda \cdot F(t)$

As shown above the best translation is selected according to features' weights λ. In order to learn the weights λ maximizing the retrieval performance, an appropriate annotated training set has to be created. We use the CLEF tracks to create the training set. The retrieval scores annotations are based on the document relevance annotations performed by human annotators during the CLEF campaign.

The annotated training set is created out of queries $\{q_1, ..., q_K\}$ with an Nbest list of translations $GEN(q_i)$ of each query $q_i, i \in \{1..K\}$ as follows:

- A list of N (we take $N = 1000$) translations $(GEN(q_i))$ is produced by the baseline MT model for each query $q_i, i = 1..K$.

- Each translation $t \in GEN(q_i)$ is used to perform a retrieval from a target document collection, and an Average Precision score $(AP(t))$ is computed for each $t \in GEN(q_i)$ by comparing its retrieval to the relevance annotations done during the CLEF campaign.

The weights λ are learned with the objective of maximizing MAP for all the queries of the training set, and, therefore, are optimized for retrieval quality.

The weights optimization is done with the Margin Infused Relaxed Algorithm (MIRA)(Crammer and Singer, 2003), which was applied to SMT by (Watanabe et al., 2007; Chiang et al., 2008). MIRA is an online learning algorithm where each weights update is done to keep the new weights as close as possible to the old weights (first term), and score oracle translation (the translation giving the best retrieval score : $t_i^* = \arg\max_t AP(t)$) higher than each non-oracle translation (t_{ij}) by a margin at least as wide as the loss l_{ij} (second term):

$$\lambda = min_{\lambda'} \frac{1}{2} \|\lambda' - \lambda\|^2 + C \sum_{i=1}^{K} \max_{j=1..N} \left(l_{ij} - \lambda' \cdot (F(t_i^*) - F(t_{ij}) \right)$$

The loss l_{ij} is defined as the difference in the retrieval average precision between the oracle and non-oracle translations: $l_{ij} = AP(t_i^*) - AP(t_{ij})$. C is the regularization parameter which is chosen via 5-fold cross-validation.

3.2.2 Features

One of the advantages of the reranking framework is that new complex features can be easily integrated. We suggest to enrich the reranking model with different syntax-based features, such as:

- features relying on dependency structures: called therein *coupling* features (proposed by (Nikoulina and Dymetman, 2008));

- features relying on Part of Speech Tagging: called therein *PoS mapping* features.

By integrating the syntax-based features we have a double goal: showing the potential of the reranking framework with more complex features, and examining whether the integration of syntactic information could be useful for query translation.

Coupling features. The goal of the coupling features is to measure the similarity between source and target dependency structures. The initial hypothesis is that a better translation should have a dependency structure closer to the one of the source query.

In this work we experiment with two different *coupling* variants proposed in (Nikoulina and Dymetman, 2008), namely, Lexicalised and Label-specific coupling features.

The generic coupling features are based on the notion of "rectangles" that are of the following type : $((s_1, d_{s12}, s_2), (t_1, d_{t12}, t_2))$, where d_{s12} is an edge between source words s_1 and s_2, d_{t12} is an edge between target words t_1 and t_2, s_1 is aligned with t_1 and s_2 is aligned with t_2. Lexicalised features take into account the quality of lexical alignment, by weighting each rectangle (s_1, s_2, t_1, t_2) by a probability of aligning s_1 to t_1 and s_2 to t_2 (eg. $p(s_1|t_1)p(s_2|t_2)$ or $p(t_1|s_1)p(t_2|s_2)$).

The Label-Specific features take into account the nature of the aligned dependencies. Thus, the rectangles of the form (($s1$, subj, $s2$), ($t1$, subj, $t2$)) will get more weight than a rectangle (($s1$, subj, $s2$), ($t1$, nmod, $t2$)). The importance of each "rectangle" is learned on the parallel annotated corpus by introducing a collection of Label-Specific coupling features, each for a specific pair of source label and target label.

PoS mapping features. The goal of the PoS mapping features is to control the correspondence of Part Of Speech Tags between an input query and its translation. As the coupling features, the PoS mapping features rely on the word alignments between the source sentence and its translation[3]. A vector of sparse features is introduced where each component corresponds to a pair of PoS tags aligned in the training data. We introduce a generic PoS map variant, which counts a number of occurrences of a specific pair of PoS tags, and lexical PoS map variant, which weights down these pairs by a lexical alignment score ($p(s|t)$ or $p(t|s)$).

4 Experiments

4.1 Experimental basis

4.1.1 Data

To simulate parallel query data we used translation equivalent CLEF topics. The data set used for the first approach consists of the CLEF topic data from the following years and tasks: AdHoc-main track from 2000 to 2008; CLEF AdHoc-TEL track 2008; Domain Specific tracks from 2000 to 2008; CLEF robust tracks 2007 and 2008; GeoCLEf tracks 2005-2007. To avoid the issue of overlapping topics we removed duplicates. The created parallel queries set contained $500 - 700$ parallel entries (depending on the language pair, Table 1) and was used for Moses parameters tuning.

In order to create the training set for the reranking approach, we need to have access to the relevance judgements. We didn't have access to all relevance judgements of the previously desribed tracks. Thus we used only a subset of the previously extracted parallel set, which includes CLEF 2000-2008 topics from the AdHoc-main, AdHoc-TEL and GeoCLEF tracks.

The number of queries obtained altogether is shown in (Table 1).

4.1.2 Baseline

We tested our approaches on the CLEF AdHoc-TEL 2009 task (50 topics). This task dealt with monolingual and cross-lingual search in a library catalog. The monolingual retrieval is

[3] This alignment can be either produced by a toolkit like GIZA++(Och and Ney, 2003) or obtained directly by a system that produced the Nbest list of the translations (Moses).

Language pair	Number of queries
Total queries	
En - Fr, Fr - En	470
En - De, De - En	714
Annotated queries	
En - Fr, Fr - En	400
En - De, De - En	350

Table 1: Top: total number of parallel queries gathered from all the CLEF tasks (size of the tuning set). Bottom: number of queries extracted from the tasks for which the human relevance judgements were availble (size of the reranking training set).

performed with the lemur[4] toolkit (Ogilvie and Callan, 2001). The preprocessing includes lemmatisation (with the Xerox Incremental Parser-XIP (Aït-Mokhtar et al., 2002)) and filtering out the function words (based on XIP PoS tagging). Table 2 shows the performance of the monolingual retrieval model for each collection. The monolingual retrieval results are comparable to the CLEF AdHoc-TEL 2009 participants (Ferro and Peters, 2009). Let us note here that it is not the case for our CLIR results since we didn't exploit the fact that each of the collections could actually contain the entries in a language other than the official language of the collection.

The cross-lingual retrieval is performed as follows :

- the input query (eg. in English) is first translated into the language of the collection (eg. German);
- this translation is used to search the target collection (eg. Austrian National Library for German) .

The baseline translation is produced with Moses trained on Europarl. Table 2 reports the baseline performance both in terms of MT evaluation metrics (BLEU) and Information Retrieval evaluation metric MAP (Mean Average Precision).

The 1best MAP score corresponds to the case when the single translation is proposed for the retrieval by the query translation model. 5best MAP score corresponds to the case when the 5 top translations proposed by the translation service are concatenated and used for the retrieval. The 5best retrieval can be seen as a sort of query expansion, without accessing the document collection or any external resources.

Given that the query length is shorter than for a standard sentence, the 4-gramm BLEU (used for standart MT evaluation) might not be able to capture the difference between the translations (eg. English-German 4-gramm BLEU is equal to 0 for our task). For that reason we report both 3- and 4-gramm BLEU scores.

Note, that the French-English baseline retrieval quality is much better than the German-English. This is probably due to the fact that our German-English translation system doesn't use any decoumpounding, which results into many non-translated words.

4.2 Results

We performed the query-genre adaptation experiments for English-French, French-English, German-English and English-German language pairs.

Ideally, we would have liked to combine the two approaches we proposed: use the query-genre-tuned model to produce the Nbest list which is then reranked to optimize the MAP score. However, it was not possible in our experimental settings due to the small amount of training data available. We thus simply compare these two approaches to a baseline approach and comment on their respective performance.

4.2.1 Query-genre tuning approach

For the CLEF-tuning experiments we used the same translation model and language model as for the baseline (Europarl-based). The weights were then tuned on the CLEF topics described in section 4.1.1. We then tested the system obtained on 50 parallel queries from the CLEF AdHoc-TEL 2009 task.

Table 3 describes the results of the evaluation. We observe consistent 1-best MAP improvements, but unstable BLEU (3-gramm) (improvements for English-German, and degradation for other language pairs), although one would have expected BLEU to be improved in this experimental setting given that BLEU was the objective function for MERT. These results, on one side, confirm the remark of (Kettunen, 2009) that there is a correlation (although low) between BLEU and MAP scores. The unstable BLEU scores

[4]http://www.lemurproject.org/

	MAP		MAP 1-best	MAP 5-best	BLEU 4-gramm	BLEU 3-gramm
	Monolingual IR		Bilingual IR			
English	0.3159	French-English	0.1828	0.2186	0.1199	0.1568
		German-English	0.0941	0.0942	0.2351	0.2923
French	0.2386	English-French	0.1504	0.1543	0.2863	0.3423
German	0.2162	English-German	0.1009	0.1157	0.0000	0.1218

Table 2: Baseline MAP scores for monolingual and bilingual CLEF AdHoc TEL 2009 task.

	MAP 1-best	MAP 5-best	BLEU 4-gramm	BLEU 3-gramm
Fr-En	0.1954	0.2229	0.1062	0.1489
De-En	0.1018	0.1078	0.2240	0.2486
En-Fr	0.1611	0.1516	0.2072	0.2908
En-De	0.1062	0.1132	0.0000	0.1924

Table 3: BLEU and MAP performance on CLEF AdHoc TEL 2009 task for the genre-tuned model.

might also be explained by the small size of the test set (compared to a standard test set of 1000 full-sentences).

Secondly, we looked at the weights of the features both in the baseline model (Europarl-tuned) and in the adapted model (CLEF-tuned), shown in Table 4. We are unsure how suitable the sizes of the CLEF tuning sets are, especially for the pairs involving English and French. Nevertheless we do observe and comment on some patterns.

For the pairs involving English and German the distortion weight is much higher when tuning with CLEF data compared to tuning with Europarl data. The picture is reversed when looking at the two pairs involving English and French. This is to be expected if we interpret a high distortion weight as follows: "it is not encouraged to place source words that are near to each other far away from each other in the translation". Indeed, the local reorderings are much more frequent between English and French (e.g. white house = maison blanche), while the long-distance reorderings are more typcal between English and German.

The word penalty is consistenly higher over all pairs when tuning with CLEF data compared to tuning with Europarl data. We could see an explanation for this pattern in the smaller size of the CLEF sentences if we interpret higher word penalty as a preference for shorter translations. This can be explained both with the smaller average size of the queries and with the specific query structure: mostly content words and fewer function words when compared to the full sentence.

The language model weight is consistently though not drastically smaller when tuning with CLEF data. We suppose that this is due to the fact that a Europarl-base language model is not the best choice for translating query data.

4.2.2 Reranking approach

The reranking experiments include different features combinations. First, we experiment with the Moses features only in order to make this approach comparable with the first one. Secondly, we compare different syntax-based features combinations, as described in section 3.2.2. Thus, we compare the following reranking models (defined by the feature set): moses, lex (lexical coupling + moses features), lab (label-specific coupling + moses features), posmaplex (lexical PoS mapping + moses features), lab-lex (label-specific coupling + lexical coupling + moses features), lab-lex-posmap (label-specific coupling + lexical coupling features + generic PoS mapping). To reduce the size of feature-functions vectors we take only the 20 most frequent features in the training data for Label-specific coupling and PoS mapping features. The computation of the syntax features is based on the rule-based XIP parser, where some heuristics specific to query processing have been integrated into English and French (but not German) grammars (Brun et al., 2012).

The results of these experiments are illustrated

Lng pair	Tune set	DW	LM	$\phi(f\|e)$	$lex(f\|e)$	$\phi(e\|f)$	$lex(e\|f)$	PP	WP
Fr-En	Europarl	0.0801	0.1397	0.0431	0.0625	0.1463	0.0638	-0.0670	-0.3975
	CLEF	0.0015	0.0795	-0.0046	0.0348	0.1977	0.0208	-0.2904	0.3707
De-En	Europarl	0.0588	0.1341	0.0380	0.0181	0.1382	0.0398	-0.0904	-0.4822
	CLEF	0.3568	0.1151	0.1168	0.0549	0.0932	0.0805	0.0391	-0.1434
En-Fr	Europarl	0.0789	0.1373	0.0002	0.0766	0.1798	0.0293	-0.0978	-0.4002
	CLEF	0.0322	0.1251	0.0350	0.1023	0.0534	0.0365	-0.3182	-0.2972
En-De	Europarl	0.0584	0.1396	0.0092	0.0821	0.1823	0.0437	-0.1613	-0.3233
	CLEF	0.3451	0.1001	0.0248	0.0872	0.2629	0.0153	-0.0431	0.1214

Table 4: Feature weights for the query-genre tuned model. Abbreviations: DW - distortion weight, LM - language model weight, PP - phrase penalty, WP - word penalty, ϕ-phrase translation probability, lex-lexical weighting.

	Query Example	MAP	bleu1
Src1	Weibliche Märtyrer		
Ref	Female Martyrs		
T1	female martyrs	0.07	1
T2	Women martyr	0.4	0
Src 2	Genmanipulation am Menschen		
Ref	Human Gene Manipulation		
T1	On the genetic manipulation of people	0.044	0.167
T2	genetic manipulation of the human being	0.069	0.286
Src 3	Arbeitsrecht in der Europäischen Union		
Ref	European Union Labour Laws		
T1	Labour law in the European Union	0.015	0.5
T2	labour legislation in the European Union	0.036	0.5

Table 5: Some examples of queries translations (T1: baseline, T2: after reranking with lab-lex), MAP and 1-gramm BLEU scores for German-English.

in Figure 1. To keep the figure more readable, we report only on 3-gramm BLEU scores. When computing the 5best MAP score, the order in the Nbest list is defined by a corresponding reranking model. Each reranking model is illustrated by a single horizontal red bar. We compare the reranking results to the baseline model (vertical line) and also to the results of the first approach (yellow bar labelled MERT:moses) on the same figure.

First, we remark that the adapted models (query-genre tuning and reranking) outperform the baseline in terms of MAP (1best and 5 best) for French-English and German-English translations for most of the models. The only exception is posmaplex model (based on PoS tagging) for German which can be explained by the fact that the German grammar used for query processing was not adapted for queries as opposed to English and French grammars. However, we do not observe the same tendency for BLEU score, where only a few of the adapted models outperform the baseline, which confirms the hypothesis of the low correlation between BLEU and MAP scores in these settings. Table 5 gives some examples of the queries translations before (T1) and after (T2) reranking. These examples also illustrate different types of disagreement between MAP and 1-gramm BLEU[5] score.

The results for English-German and English-French look more confusing. This can be partly due to the more rich morphology of the target languages which may create more noise in the syntax structure. Reranking however improves over the 1-best MAP baseline for English-German, and 5-best MAP is also improved excluding the models involving PoS tagging for German (posmap, posmaplex, lab-lex-posmap). The results for English-French are more difficult to interpret. To find out the reason of such a behavior, we looked at the translations. We observed the following tokenization problem for French: the apostrophe is systematically separated, e.g. "*d ' aujourd ' hui*". This leads to both noisy pre-retrieval preprocessing (eg. *d* is tagged as a NOUN) and noisy syntax-based feature values, which might explain the unstable results.

Finally, we can see that the syntax-based features can be beneficial for the final retrieval quality: the models with syntax features can outperform the model basd on the moses features only. The syntax-based features leading to the most sta-

[5]The higher order BLEU scores are equal to 0 for most of the individual translations.

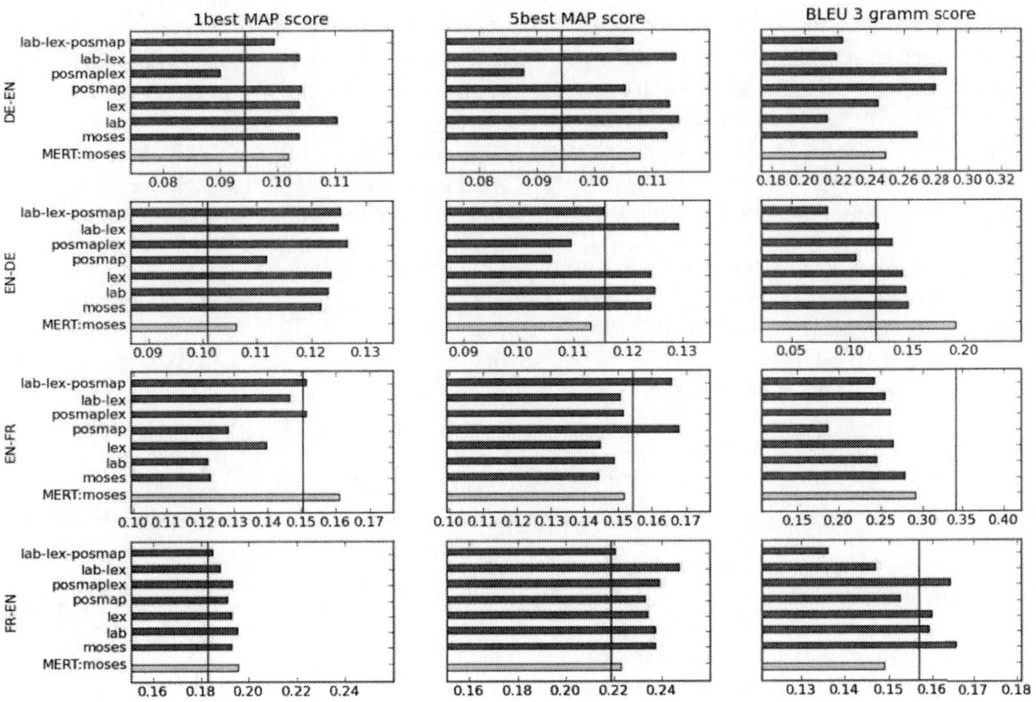

Figure 1: Reranking results. The vertical line corresponds to the baseline scores. The lowest bar (MERT:moses, in yellow): the results of the tuning approach, other bars(in red): the results of the reranking approach.

ble results seem to be lab-lex (combination of lexical and label-specific coupling): it leads to the best gains over 1-best and 5-best MAP for all language pairs excluding English-French. This is a surprising result given the fact that the underlying IR model doesn't take syntax into account in any way. In our opinion, this is probably due to the interaction between the pre-retrieval preprocessing (lemmatisation, PoS tagging) done with the linguistic tools which might produce noisy results when applied to the SMT outputs. The reranking with syntax-based features allows to choose a better-formed query for which the PoS tagging and lemmatisation tools produce less noise which leads to a better retrieval.

5 Conclusion

In this work we proposed two methods for query-genre adaptation of an SMT model: the first method addressing the translation quality aspect and the second one the retrieval precision aspect. We have shown that CLIR performance in terms of MAP is improved between 1-2.5 points. We believe that the combination of these two methods would be the most beneficial setting, although we were not able to prove this experimentally (due to the lack of training data). None of these methods require access to the document collection at test time, and can be used in the context of a query translation service. The combination of our adapted SMT model with other state-of-the art CLIR techniques (eg. query expansion with PRF) will be explored in future work.

Acknowledgements

This research was supported by the European Union's ICT Policy Support Programme as part of the Competitiveness and Innovation Framework Programme, CIP ICT-PSP under grant agreement nr 250430 (Project GALATEAS).

References

Salah Aït-Mokhtar, Jean-Pierre Chanod, and Claude Roux. 2002. Robustness beyond shallowness: incremental deep parsing. *Natural Language Engineering*, 8:121–144, June.

Satanjeev Banerjee and Alon Lavie. 2005. METEOR: an automatic metric for MT evaluation with improved correlation with human judgments. In *Proceedings of the ACL Workshop on Intrinsic and Extrinsic Evaluation Measures for Machine Translation and/or Summarization*, pages 65–72, Ann Arbor, Michigan, June. Association for Computational Linguistics.

Adam Berger, John Lafferty, and John La Erty. 1999. The weaver system for document retrieval. In *In Proceedings of the Eighth Text REtrieval Conference (TREC-8*, pages 163–174.

Nicola Bertoldi and Marcello Federico. 2009. Domain adaptation for statistical machine translation with monolingual resources. In *Proceedings of the Fourth Workshop on Statistical Machine Translation*, pages 182–189. Association for Computational Linguistics.

Caroline Brun, Vassilina Nikoulina, and Nikolaos Lagos. 2012. Linguistically-adapted structural query annotation for digital libraries in the social sciences. In *Proceedings of the 6th EACL Workshop on Language Technology for Cultural Heritage, Social Sciences, and Humanities*, Avignon, France, April.

Chris Callison-Burch, Philipp Koehn, Christof Monz, and Josh Schroeder. 2009. Findings of the 2009 Workshop on Statistical Machine Translation. In *Proceedings of the Fourth Workshop on Statistical Machine Translation*, pages 1–28, Athens, Greece, March. Association for Computational Linguistics.

David Chiang, Yuval Marton, and Philip Resnik. 2008. Online large-margin training of syntactic and structural translation features. In *Proceedings of the 2008 Conference on Empirical Methods in Natural Language Processing*, pages 224–233. Association for Computational Linguistics.

Stéphane Clinchant and Jean-Michel Renders. 2007. Query translation through dictionary adaptation. In *CLEF'07*, pages 182–187.

Michael Collins and Brian Roark. 2004. Incremental parsing with the perceptron algorithm. In *ACL '04: Proceedings of the 42nd Annual Meeting on Association for Computational Linguistics*.

Michael Collins. 2001. Ranking algorithms for named-entity extraction: boosting and the voted perceptron. In *ACL'02: Proceedings of the 40th Annual Meeting on Association for Computational Linguistics*, pages 489–496, Philadelphia, Pennsylvania. Association for Computational Linguistics.

Koby Crammer and Yoram Singer. 2003. Ultraconservative online algorithms for multiclass problems. *Journal of Machine Learning Research*, 3:951–991.

George Doddington. 2002. Automatic evaluation of Machine Translation quality using n-gram cooccurrence statistics. In *Proceedings of the second international conference on Human Language Technology Research*, pages 138–145, San Diego, California. Morgan Kaufmann Publishers Inc.

Nicola Ferro and Carol Peters. 2009. CLEF 2009 ad hoc track overview: TEL and persian tasks. In *Working Notes for the CLEF 2009 Workshop, Corfu, Greece*.

Atsushi Fujii, Masao Utiyama, Mikio Yamamoto, and Takehito Utsuro. 2009. Evaluating effects of machine translation accuracy on cross-lingual patent retrieval. In *Proceedings of the 32nd international ACM SIGIR conference on Research and development in information retrieval*, SIGIR '09, pages 674–675.

Jianfeng Gao, Jian-Yun Nie, and Ming Zhou. 2006. Statistical query translation models for cross-language information retrieval. 5:323–359, December.

Wei Gao, Cheng Niu, Jian-Yun Nie, Ming Zhou, Kam-Fai Wong, and Hsiao-Wuen Hon. 2010. Exploiting query logs for cross-lingual query suggestions. *ACM Trans. Inf. Syst.*, 28(2).

Djoerd Hiemstra and Franciska de Jong. 1999. Disambiguation strategies for cross-language information retrieval. In *Proceedings of the Third European Conference on Research and Advanced Technology for Digital Libraries*, pages 274–293.

Rong Hu, Weizhu Chen, Peng Bai, Yansheng Lu, Zheng Chen, and Qiang Yang. 2008. Web query translation via web log mining. In *Proceedings of the 31st annual international ACM SIGIR conference on Research and development in information retrieval*, SIGIR '08, pages 749–750. ACM.

Amir Hossein Jadidinejad and Fariborz Mahmoudi. 2009. Cross-language information retrieval using meta-language index construction and structural queries. In *Proceedings of the 10th cross-language evaluation forum conference on Multilingual information access evaluation: text retrieval experiments*, CLEF'09, pages 70–77, Berlin, Heidelberg. Springer-Verlag.

Gareth Jones, Sakai Tetsuya, Nigel Collier, Akira Kumano, and Kazuo Sumita. 1999. Exploring the use of machine translation resources for english-japanese cross-language information retrieval. In *In Proceedings of MT Summit VII Workshop on Machine Translation for Cross Language Information Retrieval*, pages 181–188.

Kimmo Kettunen. 2009. Choosing the best mt programs for clir purposes — can mt metrics be helpful? In *Proceedings of the 31th European Conference on IR Research on Advances in Information Retrieval*, ECIR '09, pages 706–712, Berlin, Heidelberg. Springer-Verlag.

Philipp Koehn and Josh Schroeder. 2007. Experiments in domain adaptation for statistical machine translation. In *Proceedings of the Second Workshop on Statistical Machine Translation*, StatMT

'07, pages 224–227. Association for Computational Linguistics.

Philipp Koehn, Franz Josef Och, and Daniel Marcu. 2003. Statistical phrase-based translation. In *NAACL '03: Proceedings of the 2003 Conference of the North American Chapter of the Association for Computational Linguistics on Human Language Technology*, pages 48–54, Morristown, NJ, USA. Association for Computational Linguistics.

Philipp Koehn, Hieu Hoang, Alexandra Birch, Chris Callison-Burch, Marcello Federico, Nicola Bertoldi, Brooke Cowan, Wade Shen, Christine Moran, Richard Zens, Chris Dyer, Ondřej Bojar, Alexandra Constantin, and Evan Herbst. 2007. Moses: open source toolkit for statistical machine translation. In *ACL '07: Proceedings of the 45th Annual Meeting of the ACL on Interactive Poster and Demonstration Sessions*, pages 177–180. Association for Computational Linguistics.

Philip Koehn. 2010. *Statistical Machine Translation*. Cambridge University Press.

Wessel Kraaij, Jian-Yun Nie, and Michel Simard. 2003. Embedding web-based statistical translation models in cross-language information retrieval. *Computational Linguistiques*, 29:381–419, September.

Jian-yun Nie and Jiang Chen. 2002. Exploiting the web as parallel corpora for cross-language information retrieval. *Web Intelligence*, pages 218–239.

Jian-Yun Nie. 2010. *Cross-Language Information Retrieval*. Morgan & Claypool Publishers.

Vassilina Nikoulina and Marc Dymetman. 2008. Experiments in discriminating phrase-based translations on the basis of syntactic coupling features. In *Proceedings of the ACL-08: HLT Second Workshop on Syntax and Structure in Statistical Translation (SSST-2)*, pages 55–60. Association for Computational Linguistics, June.

Franz Josef Och and Hermann Ney. 2003. A systematic comparison of various statistical alignment models. *Computational Linguistics*, 29(1):19–51.

Franz Josef Och, Daniel Gildea, Sanjeev Khudanpur, Anoop Sarkar, Kenji Yamada, Alex Fraser, Shankar Kumar, Libin Shen, David Smith, Katherine Eng, Viren Jain, Zhen Jin, and Dragomir Radev. 2003. Syntax for Statistical Machine Translation: Final report of John Hopkins 2003 Summer Workshop. Technical report, John Hopkins University.

Franz Josef Och. 2003. Minimum error rate training in statistical machine translation. In *ACL '03: Proceedings of the 41st Annual Meeting on Association for Computational Linguistics*, pages 160–167, Morristown, NJ, USA. Association for Computational Linguistics.

Paul Ogilvie and James P. Callan. 2001. Experiments using the lemur toolkit. In *TREC*.

K. Papineni, S. Roukos, T. Ward, and W. Zhu. 2001. Bleu: a method for automatic evaluation of machine translation.

Pavel Pecina, Antonio Toral, Andy Way, Vassilis Papavassiliou, Prokopis Prokopidis, and Maria Giagkou. 2011. Towards using web-crawled data for domain adaptation in statistical machine translation. In *Proceedings of the 15th Annual Conference of the European Associtation for Machine Translation*, pages 297–304, Leuven, Belgium. European Association for Machine Translation.

Brian Roark, Murat Saraclar, Michael Collins, and Mark Johnson. 2004. Discriminative language modeling with conditional random fields and the perceptron algorithm. In *Proceedings of the 42nd Annual Meeting of the Association for Computational Linguistics (ACL'04)*, July.

Lucia Specia, Marco Turchi, Nicola Cancedda, Marc Dymetman, and Nello Cristianini. 2009. Estimating the sentence-level quality of machine translation systems. In *Proceedings of the 13th Annual Conference of the EAMT*, page 28–35, Barcelona, Spain.

Taro Watanabe, Jun Suzuki, Hajime Tsukada, and Hideki Isozaki. 2007. Online large-margin training for statistical machine translation. In *Proceedings of the 2007 Joint Conference on Empirical Methods in Natural Language Processing and Computational Natural Language Learning (EMNLP-CoNLL)*, pages 764–773, Prague, Czech Republic. Association for Computational Linguistics.

Dan Wu and Daqing He. 2010. A study of query translation using google machine translation system. *Computational Intelligence and Software Engineering (CiSE)*.

Hua Wu, Haifeng Wang, and Chengqing Zong. 2008. Domain adaptation for statistical machine translation with domain dictionary and monolingual corpora. In *Proceedings of the 22nd International Conference on Computational Linguistics (Coling2008)*, pages 993–100.

Bing Zhao, Matthias Eck, and Stephan Vogel. 2004. Language model adaptation for statistical machine translation with structured query models. In *Proceedings of the 20th international conference on Computational Linguistics*, COLING '04. Association for Computational Linguistics.

Zhongguang Zheng, Zhongjun He, Yao Meng, and Hao Yu. 2010. Domain adaptation for statistical machine translation in development corpus selection. In *Universal Communication Symposium (IUCS), 2010 4th International*, pages 2–7. IEEE.

Computing Lattice BLEU Oracle Scores for Machine Translation

Artem Sokolov **Guillaume Wisniewski** **François Yvon**
LIMSI-CNRS & Univ. Paris Sud
BP-133, 91 403 Orsay, France
{firstname.lastname}@limsi.fr

Abstract

The search space of Phrase-Based Statistical Machine Translation (PBSMT) systems can be represented under the form of a directed acyclic graph (lattice). The quality of this search space can thus be evaluated by computing the best achievable hypothesis in the lattice, the so-called *oracle* hypothesis. For common SMT metrics, this problem is however NP-hard and can only be solved using heuristics. In this work, we present two new methods for efficiently computing BLEU oracles on lattices: the first one is based on a linear approximation of the corpus BLEU score and is solved using the FST formalism; the second one relies on integer linear programming formulation and is solved directly and using the Lagrangian relaxation framework. These new decoders are positively evaluated and compared with several alternatives from the literature for three language pairs, using lattices produced by two PBSMT systems.

1 Introduction

The search space of Phrase-Based Statistical Machine Translation (PBSMT) systems has the form of a very large directed acyclic graph. In several softwares, an approximation of this search space can be outputted, either as a n-*best list* containing the n top hypotheses found by the decoder, or as a phrase or word graph (*lattice*) which compactly encodes those hypotheses that have survived search space pruning. Lattices usually contain much more hypotheses than n-best lists and better approximate the search space.

Exploring the PBSMT search space is one of the few means to perform *diagnostic analysis* and to better understand the behavior of the system (Turchi et al., 2008; Auli et al., 2009). Useful diagnostics are, for instance, provided by looking at the best *(oracle)* hypotheses contained in the search space, *i.e*, those hypotheses that have the highest quality score with respect to one or several references. Such oracle hypotheses can be used for failure analysis and to better understand the bottlenecks of existing translation systems (Wisniewski et al., 2010). Indeed, the inability to faithfully reproduce reference translations can have many causes, such as scantiness of the translation table, insufficient expressiveness of reordering models, inadequate scoring function, non-literal references, over-pruned lattices, etc. Oracle decoding has several other applications: for instance, in (Liang et al., 2006; Chiang et al., 2008) it is used as a work-around to the problem of non-reachability of the reference in discriminative training of MT systems. Lattice reranking (Li and Khudanpur, 2009), a promising way to improve MT systems, also relies on oracle decoding to build the training data for a reranking algorithm.

For sentence level metrics, finding oracle hypotheses in n-best lists is a simple issue; however, solving this problem on lattices proves much more challenging, due to the number of embedded hypotheses, which prevents the use of brute-force approaches. When using BLEU, or rather sentence-level approximations thereof, the problem is in fact known to be NP-hard (Leusch et al., 2008). This complexity stems from the fact that the contribution of a given edge to the total *modified* n-gram precision can not be computed without looking at all other edges on the path. Similar (or worse) complexity result are expected for other metrics such as METEOR (Banerjee and Lavie, 2005) or TER (Snover et al., 2006). The exact computation of oracles under corpus level metrics, such as BLEU, poses supplementary combinatorial problems that will not be addressed in this work.

In this paper, we present two original methods for finding approximate oracle hypotheses on lattices. The first one is based on a linear approximation of the corpus BLEU, that was originally designed for efficient Minimum Bayesian Risk decoding on lattices (Tromble et al., 2008). The second one, based on Integer Linear Programming, is an extension to lattices of a recent work on failure analysis for phrase-based decoders (Wisniewski et al., 2010). In this framework, we study two decoding strategies: one based on a generic ILP solver, and one, based on Lagrangian relaxation.

Our contribution is also experimental as we compare the quality of the BLEU approximations and the time performance of these new approaches with several existing methods, for different language pairs and using the lattice generation capacities of two publicly-available state-of-the-art phrase-based decoders: Moses[1] and N-code[2].

The rest of this paper is organized as follows. In Section 2, we formally define the oracle decoding task and recall the formalism of finite state automata on semirings. We then describe (Section 3) two existing approaches for solving this task, before detailing our new proposals in sections 4 and 5. We then report evaluations of the existing and new oracles on machine translation tasks.

2 Preliminaries

2.1 Oracle Decoding Task

We assume that a *phrase-based* decoder is able to produce, for each source sentence $\mathbf{f}$, a *lattice* $L_\mathbf{f} = \langle Q, \Xi \rangle$, with $\# \{Q\}$ vertices (states) and $\# \{\Xi\}$ edges. Each edge carries a source phrase f_i, an associated output phrase e_i as well as a feature vector $\bar{h}_i$, the components of which encode various compatibility measures between f_i and e_i.

We further assume that $L_\mathbf{f}$ is a *word* lattice, meaning that each e_i carries a single word[3] and that it contains a unique initial state q_0 and a unique final state q_F. Let $\Pi_\mathbf{f}$ denote the set of all paths from q_0 to q_F in $L_\mathbf{f}$. Each path $\pi \in \Pi_\mathbf{f}$ corresponds to a possible translation $\mathbf{e}_\pi$. The job of a (conventional) decoder is to find the best path(s) in $L_\mathbf{f}$ using scores that combine the edges' feature vectors with the parameters $\bar{\lambda}$ learned during tuning.

In oracle decoding, the decoder's job is quite different, as we assume that at least a reference $\mathbf{r_f}$ is provided to evaluate the quality of each individual hypothesis. The decoder therefore aims at finding the path π^* that generates the hypothesis that best matches $\mathbf{r_f}$. For this task, only the output labels e_i will matter, the other informations can be left aside.[4]

Oracle decoding assumes the definition of a measure of the similarity between a reference and a hypothesis. In this paper we will consider sentence-level approximations of the popular BLEU score (Papineni et al., 2002). BLEU is formally defined for two parallel corpora, $\mathcal{E} = \{\mathbf{e}_j\}_{j=1}^J$ and $\mathcal{R} = \{\mathbf{r}_j\}_{j=1}^J$, each containing J sentences as:

$$n\text{-BLEU}(\mathcal{E}, \mathcal{R}) = BP \cdot \left(\prod_{m=1}^{n} p_m \right)^{1/n}, \quad (1)$$

where $BP = \min(1, e^{1-c_1(\mathcal{R})/c_1(\mathcal{E})})$ is the brevity penalty and $p_m = c_m(\mathcal{E}, \mathcal{R})/c_m(\mathcal{E})$ are *clipped* or *modified* m-gram precisions: $c_m(\mathcal{E})$ is the total number of word m-grams in $\mathcal{E}$; $c_m(\mathcal{E}, \mathcal{R})$ accumulates over sentences the number of m-grams in $\mathbf{e}_j$ that also belong to $\mathbf{r}_j$. These counts are clipped, meaning that a m-gram that appears k times in $\mathcal{E}$ and l times in $\mathcal{R}$, with $k > l$, is only counted l times. As it is well known, BLEU performs a compromise between precision, which is directly appears in Equation (1), and recall, which is indirectly taken into account via the brevity penalty. In most cases, Equation (1) is computed with $n = 4$ and we use BLEU as a synonym for 4-BLEU.

BLEU is defined for a pair of corpora, but, as an oracle decoder is working at the sentence-level, it should rely on an approximation of BLEU that can

[1] http://www.statmt.org/moses/

[2] http://ncode.limsi.fr/

[3] Converting a *phrase* lattice to a *word* lattice is a simple matter of redistributing a compound input or output over a linear chain of arcs.

[4] The algorithms described below can be straightforwardly generalized to compute oracle hypotheses under combined metrics mixing model scores and quality measures (Chiang et al., 2008), by weighting each edge with its model score and by using these weights down the pipe.

evaluate the similarity between a single hypothesis and its reference. This approximation introduces a discrepancy as gathering sentences with the highest (local) approximation may not result in the highest possible (corpus-level) BLEU score. Let BLEU$'$ be such a sentence-level approximation of BLEU. Then lattice oracle decoding is the task of finding an optimal path $\pi^*(\mathbf{f})$ among all paths $\Pi_{\mathbf{f}}$ for a given $\mathbf{f}$, and amounts to the following optimization problem:

$$\pi^*(\mathbf{f}) = \arg\max_{\pi \in \Pi_{\mathbf{f}}} \text{BLEU}'(\mathbf{e}_\pi, \mathbf{r}_{\mathbf{f}}). \tag{2}$$

2.2 Compromises of Oracle Decoding

As proved by Leusch et al. (2008), even with brevity penalty dropped, the problem of deciding whether a confusion network contains a hypothesis with clipped uni- and bigram precisions all equal to 1.0 is NP-complete (and so is the associated optimization problem of oracle decoding for 2-BLEU). The case of more general word and phrase lattices and 4-BLEU score is consequently also NP-complete. This complexity stems from chaining up of local unigram decisions that, due to the clipping constraints, have non-local effect on the bigram precision scores. It is consequently necessary to keep a possibly exponential number of non-recombinable hypotheses (characterized by counts for each n-gram in the reference) until very late states in the lattice.

These complexity results imply that any oracle decoder has to waive either the form of the objective function, replacing BLEU with better-behaved scoring functions, or the exactness of the solution, relying on approximate heuristic search algorithms.

In Table 1, we summarize different compromises that the existing (section 3), as well as our novel (sections 4 and 5) oracle decoders, have to make. The "target" and "target level" columns specify the targeted score. None of the decoders optimizes it directly: their objective function is rather the approximation of BLEU given in the "target replacement" column. Column "search" details the accuracy of the target replacement optimization. Finally, columns "clipping" and "brevity" indicate whether the corresponding properties of BLEU score are considered in the target substitute and in the search algorithm.

2.3 Finite State Acceptors

The implementations of the oracles described in the first part of this work (sections 3 and 4) use the common formalism of finite state acceptors (FSA) over different semirings and are implemented using the generic OpenFST toolbox (Allauzen et al., 2007).

A $(\oplus, \otimes)$-semiring $\mathbb{K}$ over a set K is a system $\langle K, \oplus, \otimes, \bar{0}, \bar{1}\rangle$, where $\langle K, \oplus, \bar{0}\rangle$ is a commutative monoid with identity element $\bar{0}$, and $\langle K, \otimes, \bar{1}\rangle$ is a monoid with identity element $\bar{1}$. $\otimes$ distributes over $\oplus$, so that $a \otimes (b \oplus c) = (a \otimes b) \oplus (a \otimes c)$ and $(b \oplus c) \otimes a = (b \otimes a) \oplus (c \otimes a)$ and element $\bar{0}$ annihilates K ($a \otimes \bar{0} = \bar{0} \otimes a = \bar{0}$).

Let $A = (\Sigma, Q, I, F, E)$ be a weighted finite-state acceptor with labels in Σ and weights in $\mathbb{K}$, meaning that the transitions (q, σ, q') in A carry a weight $w \in \mathbb{K}$. Formally, E is a mapping from $(Q \times \Sigma \times Q)$ into $\mathbb{K}$; likewise, initial I and final weight F functions are mappings from Q into $\mathbb{K}$. We borrow the notations of Mohri (2009): if $\xi = (q, a, q')$ is a transition in domain(E), $p(\xi) = q$ (resp. $n(\xi) = q'$) denotes its origin (resp. destination) state, $w(\xi) = \sigma$ its label and $E(\xi)$ its weight. These notations extend to paths: if π is a path in A, $p(\pi)$ (resp. $n(\pi)$) is its initial (resp. ending) state and $w(\pi)$ is the label along the path. A finite state transducer (FST) is an FSA with output alphabet, so that each transition carries a pair of input/output symbols.

As discussed in Sections 3 and 4, several oracle decoding algorithms can be expressed as shortest-path problems, provided a suitable definition of the underlying acceptor and associated semiring. In particular, quantities such as:

$$\bigoplus_{\pi \in \Pi(A)} E(\pi), \tag{3}$$

where the total weight of a successful path $\pi = \xi_1 \dots \xi_l$ in A is computed as:

$$E(\pi) = I(p(\xi_1)) \otimes \Big[\bigotimes_{i=1}^{l} E(\xi_i)\Big] \otimes F(n(\xi_l))$$

can be efficiently found by generic shortest distance algorithms over acyclic graphs (Mohri, 2002). For FSA-based implementations over semirings where $\oplus = \max$, the optimization problem (2) is thus reduced to Equation (3), while the oracle-specific details can be incorporated into in the definition of $\otimes$.

	oracle	target	target level	target replacement	search	clipping	brevity
existing	LM-2g/4g	2/4-BLEU	sentence	$P_2(\mathbf{e};\mathbf{r})$ or $P_4(\mathbf{e};\mathbf{r})$	exact	no	no
	PB	4-BLEU	sentence	partial log BLEU (4)	appr.	no	no
	PBℓ	4-BLEU	sentence	partial log BLEU (4)	appr.	no	yes
this paper	LB-2g/4g	2/4-BLEU	corpus	linear appr. lin BLEU (5)	exact	no	yes
	SP	1-BLEU	sentence	unigram count	exact	no	yes
	ILP	2-BLEU	sentence	uni/bi-gram counts (7)	appr.	yes	yes
	RLX	2-BLEU	sentence	uni/bi-gram counts (8)	exact	yes	yes

Table 1: Recapitulative overview of oracle decoders.

3 Existing Algorithms

In this section, we describe our reimplementation of two approximate search algorithms that have been proposed in the literature to solve the oracle decoding problem for BLEU. In addition to their approximate nature, none of them accounts for the fact that the count of each matching word has to be clipped.

3.1 Language Model Oracle (LM)

The simplest approach we consider is introduced in (Li and Khudanpur, 2009), where oracle decoding is reduced to the problem of finding the most likely hypothesis under a n-gram language model trained with the sole reference translation.

Let us suppose we have a n-gram language model that gives a probability $P(e_n|e_1 \dots e_{n-1})$ of word e_n given the $n-1$ previous words. The probability of a hypothesis $\mathbf{e}$ is then $P_n(\mathbf{e}|\mathbf{r}) = \prod_{i=1} P(e_{i+n}|e_i \dots e_{i+n-1})$. The language model can conveniently be represented as a FSA A_{LM}, with each arc carrying a negative log-probability weight and with additional ρ-type failure transitions to accommodate for back-off arcs.

If we train, for each source sentence $\mathbf{f}$, a separate language model $A_{LM}(\mathbf{r_f})$ using only the reference $\mathbf{r_f}$, oracle decoding amounts to finding a shortest (most probable) path in the weighted FSA resulting from the composition $L \circ A_{LM}(\mathbf{r_f})$ over the $(\min, +)$-semiring:

$$\pi^*_{LM}(\mathbf{f}) = \texttt{ShortestPath}(L \circ A_{LM}(\mathbf{r_f})).$$

This approach replaces the optimization of n-BLEU with a search for the most probable path under a simplistic n-gram language model. One may expect the most probable path to select frequent n-gram from the reference, thus augmenting n-BLEU.

3.2 Partial BLEU Oracle (PB)

Another approach is put forward in (Dreyer et al., 2007) and used in (Li and Khudanpur, 2009): oracle translations are shortest paths in a lattice L, where the weight of each path π is the sentence level $\log \mathrm{BLEU}(\pi)$ score of the corresponding complete or partial hypothesis:

$$\log \mathrm{BLEU}(\pi) = \frac{1}{4} \sum_{m=1\dots4} \log p_m. \quad (4)$$

Here, the brevity penalty is ignored and n-gram precisions are offset to avoid null counts: $p_m = (c_m(\mathbf{e}_\pi, \mathbf{r}) + 0.1)/(c_m(\mathbf{e}_\pi) + 0.1)$.

This approach has been reimplemented using the FST formalism by defining a suitable semiring. Let each weight of the semiring keep a set of tuples accumulated up to the current state of the lattice. Each tuple contains three words of recent history, a partial hypothesis as well as current values of the length of the partial hypothesis, n-gram counts (4 numbers) and the sentence-level $\log$ BLEU score defined by Equation (4). In the beginning each arc is initialized with a singleton set containing one tuple with a single word as the partial hypothesis. For the semiring operations we define one common $\otimes$-operation and two versions of the $\oplus$-operation:
• $L_1 \otimes_{PB} L_2$ – appends a word on the edge of L_2 to L_1's hypotheses, shifts their recent histories and updates n-gram counts, lengths, and current score; • $L_1 \oplus_{PB} L_2$ – merges all sets from L_1 and L_2 and recombinates those having the same recent history; • $L_1 \oplus_{PB\ell} L_2$ – merges all sets from L_1 and L_2 and recombinates those having the same recent history *and* the same hypothesis length.

If several hypotheses have the same recent history (and length in the case of $\oplus_{PB\ell}$), recombination removes all of them, but the one

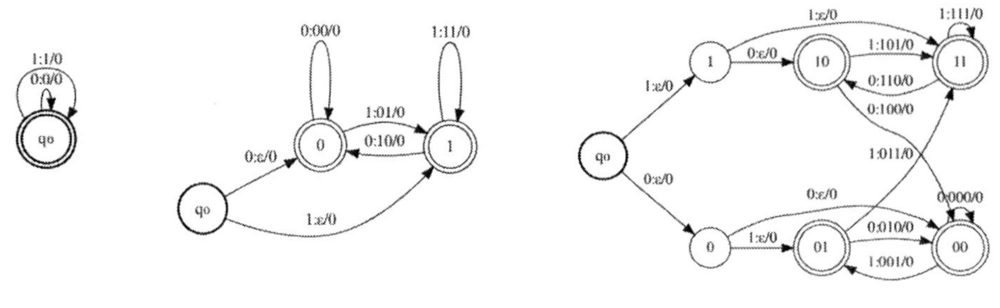

(a) Δ_1 (b) Δ_2 (c) Δ_3

Figure 1: Examples of the Δ_n automata for $\Sigma = \{0, 1\}$ and $n = 1 \ldots 3$. Initial and final states are marked, respectively, with bold and with double borders. Note that arcs between final states are weighted with 0, while in reality they will have this weight only if the corresponding n-gram does not appear in the reference.

with the largest current BLEU score. Optimal path is then found by launching the generic ShortestDistance(L) algorithm over one of the semirings above.

The $(\oplus_{PB\ell}, \otimes_{PB})$-semiring, in which the equal length requirement also implies equal brevity penalties, is more conservative in recombining hypotheses and should achieve final BLEU that is least as good as that obtained with the $(\oplus_{PB}, \otimes_{PB})$-semiring[5].

4 Linear BLEU Oracle (LB)

In this section, we propose a new oracle based on the linear approximation of the corpus BLEU introduced in (Tromble et al., 2008). While this approximation was earlier used for Minimum Bayes Risk decoding in lattices (Tromble et al., 2008; Blackwood et al., 2010), we show here how it can also be used to approximately compute an oracle translation.

Given five real parameters $\theta_{0\ldots4}$ and a word vocabulary Σ, Tromble et al. (2008) showed that one can approximate the *corpus*-BLEU with its first-order (linear) Taylor expansion:

$$\text{lin BLEU}(\boldsymbol{\pi}) = \theta_0 \, |\mathbf{e}_{\pi}| + \sum_{n=1}^{4} \theta_n \sum_{u \in \Sigma^n} c_u(\mathbf{e}_{\pi}) \delta_u(\mathbf{r}), \tag{5}$$

where $c_u(\mathbf{e})$ is the number of times the n-gram u appears in $\mathbf{e}$, and $\delta_u(\mathbf{r})$ is an indicator variable testing the presence of u in $\mathbf{r}$.

To exploit this approximation for oracle decoding, we construct four weighted FSTs Δ_n containing a (final) state for each possible $(n-1)$-gram, and all weighted transitions of the kind $(\sigma_1^{n-1}, \sigma_n : \sigma_1^n / \theta_n \times \delta_{\sigma_1^n}(\mathbf{r}), \sigma_2^n)$, where σs are in Σ, input word sequence σ_1^{n-1} and output sequence σ_2^n, are, respectively, the maximal prefix and suffix of an n-gram σ_1^n.

In supplement, we add auxiliary states corresponding to m-grams ($m < n-1$), whose functional purpose is to help reach one of the main $(n-1)$-gram states. There are $\frac{|\Sigma|^{n-1}-1}{|\Sigma|-1}, n > 1$, such supplementary states and their transitions are $(\sigma_1^k, \sigma_{k+1} : \sigma_1^{k+1}/0, \sigma_1^{k+1}), k = 1 \ldots n-2$. Apart from these auxiliary states, the rest of the graph (i.e., all final states) reproduces the structure of the well-known de Bruijn graph $B(\Sigma, n)$ (see Figure 1).

To actually compute the best hypothesis, we first weight all arcs in the input FSA L with θ_0 to obtain Δ_0. This makes each word's weight equal in a hypothesis path, and the total weight of the path in Δ_0 is proportional to the number of words in it. Then, by sequentially composing Δ_0 with other Δ_ns, we discount arcs whose output n-gram corresponds to a matching n-gram. The amount of discount is regulated by the ratio between θ_n's for $n > 0$.

With all operations performed over the $(\min, +)$-semiring, the oracle translation is then given by:

$$\boldsymbol{\pi}^*_{LB} = \texttt{ShortestPath}(\Delta_0 \circ \Delta_1 \circ \Delta_2 \circ \Delta_3 \circ \Delta_4).$$

We set parameters θ_n as in (Tromble et al., 2008): $\theta_0 = 1$, roughly corresponding to the brevity penalty (each word in a hypothesis adds up equally to the final path length) and $\theta_n = -(4p \cdot r^{n-1})^{-1}$, which are increasing discounts

[5] See, however, experiments in Section 6.

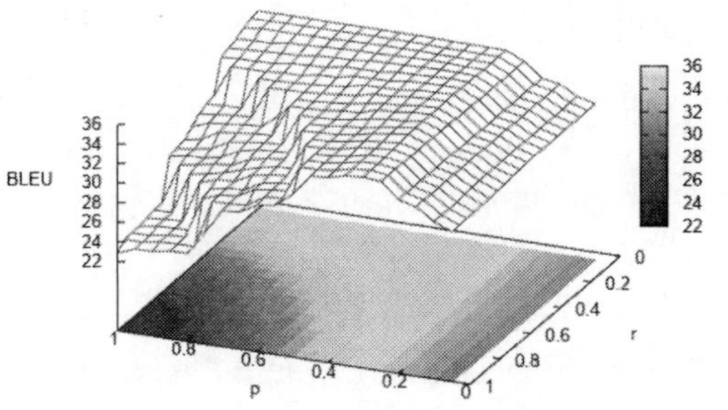

Figure 2: Performance of the LB-4g oracle for different combinations of p and r on WMT11 de2en task.

for matching n-grams. The values of p and r were found by grid search with a 0.05 step value. A typical result of the grid evaluation of the LB oracle for German to English WMT'11 task is displayed on Figure 2. The optimal values for the other pairs of languages were roughly in the same ballpark, with $p \approx 0.3$ and $r \approx 0.2$.

5 Oracles with n-gram Clipping

In this section, we describe two new oracle decoders that take n-gram clipping into account. These oracles leverage on the well-known fact that the shortest path problem, at the heart of all the oracles described so far, can be reduced straightforwardly to an Integer Linear Programming (ILP) problem (Wolsey, 1998). Once oracle decoding is formulated as an ILP problem, it is relatively easy to introduce additional constraints, for instance to enforce n-gram clipping. We will first describe the optimization problem of oracle decoding and then present several ways to efficiently solve it.

5.1 Problem Description

Throughout this section, abusing the notations, we will also think of an edge ξ_i as a binary variable describing whether the edge is "selected" or not. The set $\{0,1\}^{\#\{\Xi\}}$ of all possible edge assignments will be denoted by $\mathcal{P}$. Note that Π, the set of all paths in the lattice is a subset of $\mathcal{P}$: by enforcing some constraints on an assignment $\boldsymbol{\xi}$ in $\mathcal{P}$, it can be guaranteed that it will represent a path in the lattice. For the sake of presentation, we assume that each edge ξ_i generates a single word $w(\xi_i)$ and we focus first on finding the optimal hypothesis with respect to the sentence approximation of the 1-BLEU score.

As 1-BLEU is decomposable, it is possible to define, for every edge ξ_i, an associated reward, θ_i that describes the edge's local contribution to the hypothesis score. For instance, for the sentence approximation of the 1-BLEU score, the rewards are defined as:

$$\theta_i = \begin{cases} \Theta_1 & \text{if } w(\xi_i) \text{ is in the reference,} \\ -\Theta_2 & \text{otherwise,} \end{cases}$$

where Θ_1 and Θ_2 are two positive constants chosen to maximize the corpus BLEU score[6]. Constant Θ_1 (resp. Θ_2) is a reward (resp. a penalty) for generating a word in the reference (resp. *not* in the reference). The score of an assignment $\boldsymbol{\xi} \in \mathcal{P}$ is then defined as: $\text{score}(\boldsymbol{\xi}) = \sum_{i=1}^{\#\{\Xi\}} \xi_i \cdot \theta_i$. This score can be seen as a compromise between the number of common words in the hypothesis and the reference (accounting for recall) and the number of words of the hypothesis that do not appear in the reference (accounting for precision).

As explained in Section 2.3, finding the oracle hypothesis amounts to solving the shortest distance (or path) problem (3), which can be reformulated by a constrained optimization problem (Wolsey, 1998):

$$\begin{aligned} &\arg\max_{\boldsymbol{\xi} \in \mathcal{P}} \sum_{i=1}^{\#\{\Xi\}} \xi_i \cdot \theta_i \qquad (6) \\ &\text{s.t.} \sum_{\xi \in \Xi^-(q_F)} \xi = 1, \sum_{\xi \in \Xi^+(q_0)} \xi = 1 \\ &\sum_{\xi \in \Xi^+(q)} \xi - \sum_{\xi \in \Xi^-(q)} \xi = 0, \; q \in \mathcal{Q} \backslash \{q_0, q_F\} \end{aligned}$$

where q_0 (resp. q_F) is the initial (resp. final) state of the lattice and $\Xi^-(q)$ (resp. $\Xi^+(q)$) denotes the set of incoming (resp. outgoing) edges of state q. These *path constraints* ensure that the solution of the problem is a valid path in the lattice.

The optimization problem in Equation (6) can be further extended to take clipping into account. Let us introduce, for each word w, a variable γ_w that denotes the number of times w appears in the hypothesis clipped to the number of times, it appears in the reference. Formally, γ_w is defined by:

$$\gamma_w = \min \left\{ \sum_{\xi \in \Omega(w)} \xi, c_w(\mathbf{r}) \right\}$$

[6]We tried several combinations of Θ_1 and Θ_2 and kept the one that had the highest corpus 4-BLEU score.

where $\Omega(w)$ is the subset of edges generating w, and $\sum_{\xi \in \Omega(w)} \xi$ is the number of occurrences of w in the solution and $c_w(\mathbf{r})$ is the number of occurrences of w in the reference $\mathbf{r}$. Using the γ variables, we define a "clipped" approximation of 1-BLEU:

$$\Theta_1 \cdot \sum_w \gamma_w - \Theta_2 \cdot \left(\sum_{i=1}^{\#\{\Xi\}} \xi_i - \sum_w \gamma_w \right)$$

Indeed, the clipped number of words in the hypothesis that appear in the reference is given by $\sum_w \gamma_w$, and $\sum_{i=1}^{\#\{\Xi\}} \xi_i - \sum_w \gamma_w$ corresponds to the number of words in the hypothesis that do not appear in the reference or that are surplus to the clipped count.

Finally, the clipped lattice oracle is defined by the following optimization problem:

$$\arg\max_{\boldsymbol{\xi} \in \mathcal{P}, \gamma_w} \quad (\Theta_1 + \Theta_2) \cdot \sum_w \gamma_w - \Theta_2 \cdot \sum_{i=1}^{\#\{\Xi\}} \xi_i \tag{7}$$

$$\text{s.t.} \quad \gamma_w \geq 0, \gamma_w \leq c_w(\mathbf{r}), \gamma_w \leq \sum_{\xi \in \Omega(w)} \xi$$

$$\sum_{\xi \in \Xi^-(q_F)} \xi = 1, \sum_{\xi \in \Xi^+(q_0)} \xi = 1$$

$$\sum_{\xi \in \Xi^+(q)} \xi - \sum_{\xi \in \Xi^-(q)} \xi = 0, \; q \in Q \setminus \{q_0, q_F\}$$

where the first three sets of constraints are the linearization of the definition of γ_w, made possible by the positivity of Θ_1 and Θ_2, and the last three sets of constraints are the path constraints.

In our implementation we generalized this optimization problem to *bigram* lattices, in which each edge is labeled by the bigram it generates. Such bigram FSAs can be produced by composing the word lattice with Δ_2 from Section 4. In this case, the reward of an edge will be defined as a combination of the (clipped) number of unigram matches and bigram matches, and solving the optimization problem yields a 2-BLEU optimal hypothesis. The approach can be further generalized to higher-order BLEU or other metrics, as long as the reward of an edge can be computed locally.

The constrained optimization problem (7) can be solved efficiently using off-the-shelf ILP solvers[7].

[7] In our experiments we used Gurobi (Optimization, 2010) a commercial ILP solver that offers free academic license.

5.2 Shortest Path Oracle (SP)

As a trivial special class of the above formulation, we also define a Shortest Path Oracle (SP) that solves the optimization problem in (6). As no clipping constraints apply, it can be solved efficiently using the standard Bellman algorithm.

5.3 Oracle Decoding through Lagrangian Relaxation (RLX)

In this section, we introduce another method to solve problem (7) without relying on an external ILP solver. Following (Rush et al., 2010; Chang and Collins, 2011), we propose an original method for oracle decoding based on Lagrangian relaxation. This method relies on the idea of relaxing the clipping constraints: starting from an unconstrained problem, the counts clipping is enforced by incrementally strengthening the weight of paths satisfying the constraints.

The oracle decoding problem with clipping constraints amounts to solving:

$$\arg\min_{\boldsymbol{\xi} \in \Pi} \quad - \sum_{i=1}^{\#\{\Xi\}} \xi_i \cdot \theta_i \tag{8}$$

$$\text{s.t.} \quad \sum_{\xi \in \Omega(w)} \xi \leq c_w(\mathbf{r}), w \in \mathbf{r}$$

where, by abusing the notations, $\mathbf{r}$ also denotes the set of words in the reference. For sake of clarity, the path constraints are incorporated into the domain (the arg min runs over Π and not over $\mathcal{P}$). To solve this optimization problem we consider its dual form and use Lagrangian relaxation to deal with clipping constraints.

Let $\boldsymbol{\lambda} = \{\lambda_w\}_{w \in \mathbf{r}}$ be positive Lagrange multipliers, one for each different word of the reference, then the Lagrangian of the problem (8) is:

$$\mathcal{L}(\boldsymbol{\lambda}, \boldsymbol{\xi}) = - \sum_{i=1}^{\#\{\Xi\}} \xi_i \theta_i + \sum_{w \in \mathbf{r}} \lambda_w \left(\sum_{\xi \in \Omega(w)} \xi - c_w(\mathbf{r}) \right)$$

The dual objective is $\mathcal{L}(\boldsymbol{\lambda}) = \min_{\boldsymbol{\xi}} \mathcal{L}(\boldsymbol{\lambda}, \boldsymbol{\xi})$ and the dual problem is: $\max_{\boldsymbol{\lambda}, \boldsymbol{\lambda} \succeq 0} \mathcal{L}(\boldsymbol{\lambda})$. To solve the latter, we first need to work out the dual objective:

$$\boldsymbol{\xi}^* = \arg\min_{\boldsymbol{\xi} \in \Pi} \mathcal{L}(\boldsymbol{\lambda}, \boldsymbol{\xi})$$

$$= \arg\min_{\boldsymbol{\xi} \in \Pi} \sum_{i=1}^{\#\{\Xi\}} \xi_i \left(\lambda_{w(\xi_i)} - \theta_i \right)$$

where we assume that $\lambda_{w(\xi_i)}$ is 0 when word $w(\xi_i)$ is not in the reference. In the same way as in Section 5.2, the solution of this problem can be efficiently retrieved with a shortest path algorithm.

It is possible to optimize $\mathcal{L}(\boldsymbol{\lambda})$ by noticing that it is a concave function. It can be shown (Chang and Collins, 2011) that, at convergence, the clipping constraints will be enforced in the optimal solution. In this work, we chose to use a simple gradient descent to solve the dual problem. A subgradient of the dual objective is:

$$\frac{\partial \mathcal{L}(\boldsymbol{\lambda})}{\partial \lambda_w} = \sum_{\xi \in \Omega(w) \cap \xi^*} \xi - c_w(\mathbf{r}).$$

Each component of the gradient corresponds to the difference between the number of times the word w appears in the hypothesis and the number of times it appears in the reference. The algorithm below sums up the optimization of task (8). In the algorithm $\alpha^{(t)}$ corresponds to the step size at the tth iteration. In our experiments we used a constant step size of 0.1. Compared to the usual gradient descent algorithm, there is an additional projection step of $\boldsymbol{\lambda}$ on the positive orthant, which enforces the constraint $\boldsymbol{\lambda} \succeq 0$.

$\forall w, \lambda_w^{(0)} \leftarrow 0$
for $t = 1 \rightarrow T$ **do**
  $\boldsymbol{\xi}^{*(t)} = \arg\min_{\boldsymbol{\xi}} \sum_i \xi_i \cdot (\lambda_{w(\xi_i)} - \theta_i)$
  if *all clipping constraints are enforced*
  then optimal solution found
  else for $w \in \mathbf{r}$ **do**
    $n_w \leftarrow$ n. of occurrences of w in $\boldsymbol{\xi}^{*(t)}$
    $\lambda_w^{(t)} \leftarrow \lambda_w^{(t)} + \alpha^{(t)} \cdot (n_w - c_w(\mathbf{r}))$
    $\lambda_w^{(t)} \leftarrow \max(0, \lambda_w^{(t)})$

6 Experiments

For the proposed new oracles and the existing approaches, we compare the quality of oracle translations and the average time per sentence needed to compute them[8] on several datasets for 3 language pairs, using lattices generated by two open-source decoders: N-code and Moses[9] (Figures 3 and 4). Systems were trained on the data provided for the WMT'11 Evaluation task[10], tuned on the WMT'09 test data and evaluated on WMT'10 test set[11] to produce lattices. The BLEU test scores and oracle scores on 100-best lists with the approximation (4) for N-code and Moses are given in Table 2. It is not until considering 10,000-best lists that n-best oracles achieve performance comparable to the (mediocre) SP oracle.

	decoder	fr2en	de2en	en2de
test	N-code	27.88	22.05	15.83
	Moses	27.68	21.85	15.89
oracle	N-code	36.36	29.22	21.18
	Moses	35.25	29.13	22.03

Table 2: Test BLEU scores and oracle scores on 100-best lists for the evaluated systems.

To make a fair comparison with the ILP and RLX oracles which optimize 2-BLEU, we included 2-BLEU versions of the LB and LM oracles, identified below with the "-2g" suffix. The two versions of the PB oracle are respectively denoted as PB and PBℓ, by the type of the $\oplus$-operation they consider (Section 3.2). Parameters p and r for the LB-4g oracle for N-code were found with grid search and reused for Moses: $p = 0.25, r = 0.15$ (fr2en); $p = 0.175, r = 0.575$ (en2de) and $p = 0.35, r = 0.425$ (de2en). Correspondingly, for the LB-2g oracle: $p = 0.3, r = 0.15$; $p = 0.3, r = 0.175$ and $p = 0.575, r = 0.1$.

The proposed LB, ILP and RLX oracles were the best performing oracles, with the ILP and RLX oracles being considerably faster, suffering only a negligible decrease in BLEU, compared to the 4-BLEU-optimized LB oracle. We stopped RLX oracle after 20 iterations, as letting it converge had a small negative effect ($\sim$1 point of the corpus BLEU), because of the sentence/corpus discrepancy ushered by the BLEU score approximation.

Experiments showed consistently inferior performance of the LM-oracle resulting from the optimization of the sentence probability rather than BLEU. The PB oracle often performed comparably to our new oracles, however, with sporadic resource-consumption bursts, that are difficult to

[8]Experiments were run in parallel on a server with 64G of RAM and 2 Xeon CPUs with 4 cores at 2.3 GHz.

[9]As the ILP (and RLX) oracle were implemented in Python, we pruned Moses lattices to accelerate task preparation for it.

[10]http://www.statmt.org/wmt2011

[11]All BLEU scores are reported using the multi-bleu.pl script.

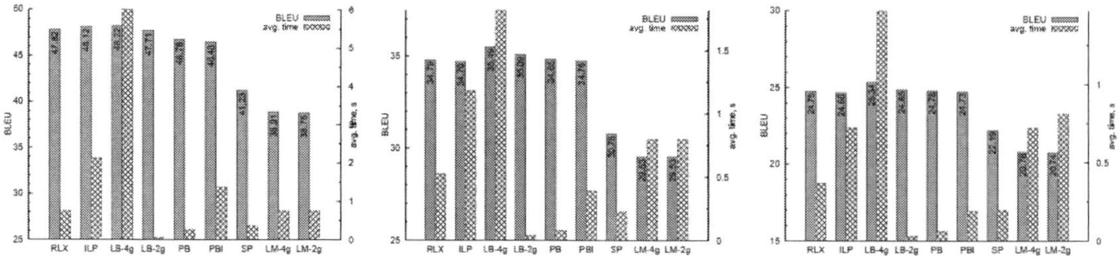

(a) fr2en (b) de2en (c) en2de

Figure 3: Oracles performance for N-code lattices.

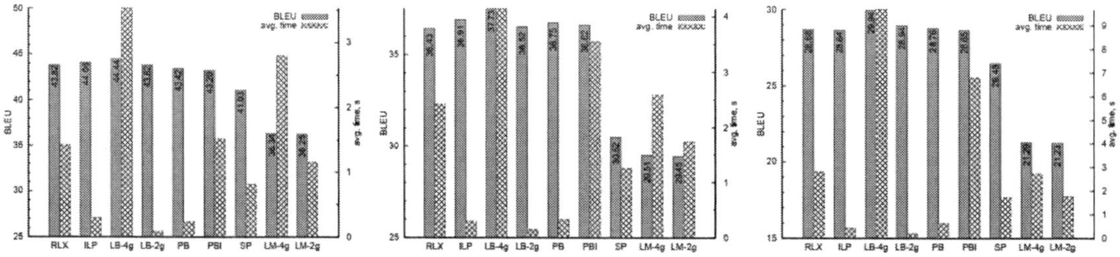

(a) fr2en (b) de2en (c) en2de

Figure 4: Oracles performance for Moses lattices pruned with parameter `-b 0.5`.

avoid without more cursory hypotheses recombination strategies and the induced effect on the translations quality. The length-aware PBℓ oracle has unexpectedly poorer scores compared to its length-agnostic PB counterpart, while it should, at least, stay even, as it takes the brevity penalty into account. We attribute this fact to the complex effect of clipping coupled with the lack of control of the process of selecting one hypothesis among several having the same BLEU score, length and recent history. Anyhow, BLEU scores of both of PB oracles are only marginally different, so the PBℓ's conservative policy of pruning and, consequently, much heavier memory consumption makes it an unwanted choice.

7 Conclusion

We proposed two methods for finding oracle translations in lattices, based, respectively, on a linear approximation to the corpus-level BLEU and on integer linear programming techniques. We also proposed a variant of the latter approach based on Lagrangian relaxation that does not rely on a third-party ILP solver. All these oracles have superior performance to existing approaches, in terms of the quality of the found translations, resource consumption and, for the LB-2g oracles, in terms of speed. It is thus possible to use better approximations of BLEU than was previously done, taking the corpus-based nature of BLEU, or clipping constrainst into account, delivering better oracles without compromising speed.

Using 2-BLEU and 4-BLEU oracles yields comparable performance, which confirms the intuition that hypotheses sharing many 2-grams, would likely have many common 3- and 4-grams as well. Taking into consideration the exceptional speed of the LB-2g oracle, in practice one can safely optimize for 2-BLEU instead of 4-BLEU, saving large amounts of time for oracle decoding on long sentences.

Overall, these experiments accentuate the acuteness of scoring problems that plague modern decoders: very good hypotheses exist for most input sentences, but are poorly evaluated by a linear combination of standard features functions. Even though the tuning procedure can be held responsible for part of the problem, the comparison between lattice and n-best oracles shows that the beam search leaves good hypotheses out of the n-best list until very high value of n, that are never used in practice.

Acknowledgments

This work has been partially funded by OSEO under the Quaero program.

References

Cyril Allauzen, Michael Riley, Johan Schalkwyk, Wojciech Skut, and Mehryar Mohri. 2007. OpenFst: A general and efficient weighted finite-state transducer library. In *Proc. of the Int. Conf. on Implementation and Application of Automata*, pages 11–23.

Michael Auli, Adam Lopez, Hieu Hoang, and Philipp Koehn. 2009. A systematic analysis of translation model search spaces. In *Proc. of WMT*, pages 224–232, Athens, Greece.

Satanjeev Banerjee and Alon Lavie. 2005. METEOR: An automatic metric for MT evaluation with improved correlation with human judgments. In *Proc. of the ACL Workshop on Intrinsic and Extrinsic Evaluation Measures for Machine Translation*, pages 65–72, Ann Arbor, MI, USA.

Graeme Blackwood, Adrià de Gispert, and William Byrne. 2010. Efficient path counting transducers for minimum bayes-risk decoding of statistical machine translation lattices. In *Proc. of the ACL 2010 Conference Short Papers*, pages 27–32, Stroudsburg, PA, USA.

Yin-Wen Chang and Michael Collins. 2011. Exact decoding of phrase-based translation models through lagrangian relaxation. In *Proc. of the 2011 Conf. on EMNLP*, pages 26–37, Edinburgh, UK.

David Chiang, Yuval Marton, and Philip Resnik. 2008. Online large-margin training of syntactic and structural translation features. In *Proc. of the 2008 Conf. on EMNLP*, pages 224–233, Honolulu, Hawaii.

Markus Dreyer, Keith B. Hall, and Sanjeev P. Khudanpur. 2007. Comparing reordering constraints for SMT using efficient BLEU oracle computation. In *Proc. of the Workshop on Syntax and Structure in Statistical Translation*, pages 103–110, Morristown, NJ, USA.

Gregor Leusch, Evgeny Matusov, and Hermann Ney. 2008. Complexity of finding the BLEU-optimal hypothesis in a confusion network. In *Proc. of the 2008 Conf. on EMNLP*, pages 839–847, Honolulu, Hawaii.

Zhifei Li and Sanjeev Khudanpur. 2009. Efficient extraction of oracle-best translations from hypergraphs. In *Proc. of Human Language Technologies: The 2009 Annual Conf. of the North American Chapter of the ACL, Companion Volume: Short Papers*, pages 9–12, Morristown, NJ, USA.

Percy Liang, Alexandre Bouchard-Côté, Dan Klein, and Ben Taskar. 2006. An end-to-end discriminative approach to machine translation. In *Proc. of the 21st Int. Conf. on Computational Linguistics and the 44th annual meeting of the ACL*, pages 761–768, Morristown, NJ, USA.

Mehryar Mohri. 2002. Semiring frameworks and algorithms for shortest-distance problems. *J. Autom. Lang. Comb.*, 7:321–350.

Mehryar Mohri. 2009. Weighted automata algorithms. In Manfred Droste, Werner Kuich, and Heiko Vogler, editors, *Handbook of Weighted Automata*, chapter 6, pages 213–254.

Gurobi Optimization. 2010. Gurobi optimizer, April. Version 3.0.

Kishore Papineni, Salim Roukos, Todd Ward, and Wei-Jing Zhu. 2002. BLEU: a method for automatic evaluation of machine translation. In *Proc. of the Annual Meeting of the ACL*, pages 311–318.

Alexander M. Rush, David Sontag, Michael Collins, and Tommi Jaakkola. 2010. On dual decomposition and linear programming relaxations for natural language processing. In *Proc. of the 2010 Conf. on EMNLP*, pages 1–11, Stroudsburg, PA, USA.

Matthew Snover, Bonnie Dorr, Richard Schwartz, Linnea Micciulla, and John Makhoul. 2006. A study of translation edit rate with targeted human annotation. In *Proc. of the Conf. of the Association for Machine Translation in the America (AMTA)*, pages 223–231.

Roy W. Tromble, Shankar Kumar, Franz Och, and Wolfgang Macherey. 2008. Lattice minimum bayes-risk decoding for statistical machine translation. In *Proc. of the Conf. on EMNLP*, pages 620–629, Stroudsburg, PA, USA.

Marco Turchi, Tijl De Bie, and Nello Cristianini. 2008. Learning performance of a machine translation system: a statistical and computational analysis. In *Proc. of WMT*, pages 35–43, Columbus, Ohio.

Guillaume Wisniewski, Alexandre Allauzen, and François Yvon. 2010. Assessing phrase-based translation models with oracle decoding. In *Proc. of the 2010 Conf. on EMNLP*, pages 933–943, Stroudsburg, PA, USA.

L. Wolsey. 1998. *Integer Programming*. John Wiley & Sons, Inc.

Toward Statistical Machine Translation without Parallel Corpora

Alexandre Klementiev Ann Irvine Chris Callison-Burch David Yarowsky
Center for Language and Speech Processing
Johns Hopkins University

Abstract

We estimate the parameters of a phrase-based statistical machine translation system from *monolingual* corpora instead of a *bilingual* parallel corpus. We extend existing research on bilingual lexicon induction to estimate *both* lexical and phrasal translation probabilities for MT-scale phrase-tables. We propose a novel algorithm to estimate reordering probabilities from monolingual data. We report translation results for an end-to-end translation system using these monolingual features alone. Our method only requires monolingual corpora in source and target languages, a small bilingual dictionary, and a small bitext for tuning feature weights. In this paper, we examine an idealization where a phrase-table is given. We examine the degradation in translation performance when bilingually estimated translation probabilities are removed and show that 80%+ of the loss can be recovered with monolingually estimated features alone. We further show that our monolingual features add 1.5 BLEU points when combined with standard bilingually estimated phrase table features.

1 Introduction

The parameters of statistical models of translation are typically estimated from large bilingual parallel corpora (Brown et al., 1993). However, these resources are not available for most language pairs, and they are expensive to produce in quantities sufficient for building a good translation system (Germann, 2001). We attempt an entirely different approach; we use cheap and plentiful monolingual resources to induce an end-to-end statistical machine translation system. In particular, we extend the long line of work on inducing translation lexicons (beginning with Rapp (1995)) and propose to use multiple independent cues present in monolingual texts to estimate lexical and phrasal translation probabilities for large, MT-scale phrase-tables. We then introduce a novel algorithm to estimate reordering features from monolingual data alone, and we report the performance of a phrase-based statistical model (Koehn et al., 2003) estimated using these monolingual features.

Most of the prior work on lexicon induction is motivated by the idea that it could be applied to machine translation but stops short of actually doing so. Lexicon induction holds the potential to create machine translation systems for languages which do not have extensive parallel corpora. Training would only require two large monolingual corpora and a small bilingual dictionary, if one is available. The idea is that intrinsic properties of monolingual data (possibly along with a handful of bilingual pairs to act as example mappings) can provide independent but informative cues to learn translations because words (and phrases) behave similarly across languages. This work is the first attempt to extend and apply these ideas to an end-to-end machine translation pipeline. While we make an explicit assumption that a table of phrasal translations is given a priori, we induce every other parameter of a full phrase-based translation system from monolingual data alone. The contributions of this work are:

- In Section 2.2 we analyze the challenges of using bilingual lexicon induction for statistical MT (performance on low frequency items, and moving from words to phrases).
- In Sections 3.1 and 3.2 we use multiple cues present in monolingual data to estimate lexical and phrasal translation scores.
- In Section 3.3 we propose a novel algorithm for estimating phrase reordering features from monolingual texts.
- Finally, in Section 5 we systematically drop feature functions from a phrase table and then replace them with monolingually estimated equivalents, reporting end-to-end translation quality.

2 Background

We begin with a brief overview of the standard phrase-based statistical machine translation model. Here, we define the parameters which we later replace with monolingual alternatives. We continue with a discussion of bilingual lexicon induction; we extend these methods to estimate the monolingual parameters in Section 3. This approach allows us to replace expensive/rare bilingual parallel training data with two large monolingual corpora, a small bilingual dictionary, and ≈2,000 sentence bilingual development set, which are comparatively plentiful/inexpensive.

2.1 Parameters of phrase-based SMT

Statistical machine translation (SMT) was first formulated as a series of probabilistic models that learn word-to-word correspondences from sentence-aligned bilingual parallel corpora (Brown et al., 1993). Current methods, including *phrase-based* (Och, 2002; Koehn et al., 2003) and *hierarchical* models (Chiang, 2005), typically start by word-aligning a bilingual parallel corpus (Och and Ney, 2003). They extract multi-word phrases that are consistent with the Viterbi word alignments and use these phrases to build new translations. A variety of parameters are estimated using the bitexts. Here we review the parameters of the standard phrase-based translation model (Koehn et al., 2007). Later we will show how to estimate them using monolingual texts instead. These parameters are:

- *Phrase pairs.* Phrase extraction heuristics (Venugopal et al., 2003; Tillmann, 2003; Och and Ney, 2004) produce a set of phrase pairs (e, f) that are consistent with the word alignments. In this paper we assume that the phrase pairs are given (without any scores), and we induce every other parameter of the phrase-based model from monolingual data.

- *Phrase translation probabilities.* Each phrase pair has a list of associated feature functions (FFs). These include phrase translation probabilities, $\phi(e|f)$ and $\phi(f|e)$, which are typically calculated via maximum likelihood estimation.

- *Lexical weighting.* Since MLE overestimates ϕ for phrase pairs with sparse counts, lexical weighting FFs are used to smooth. Average word translation probabilities, $w(e_i|f_j)$, are calculated via phrase-pair-internal word alignments.

- *Reordering model.* Each phrase pair (e, f) also has associated reordering parameters, $p_o(\text{orientation}|f, e)$, which indicate the distribution of its orientation with respect to the previously translated phrase. Orientations are *monotone, swap, discontinuous* (Tillman, 2004; Kumar and Byrne, 2004), see Figure 1.

- *Other features.* Other typical features are n-gram language model scores and a phrase penalty, which governs whether to use fewer longer phrases or more shorter phrases. These are not bilingually estimated, so we can re-use them directly without modification.

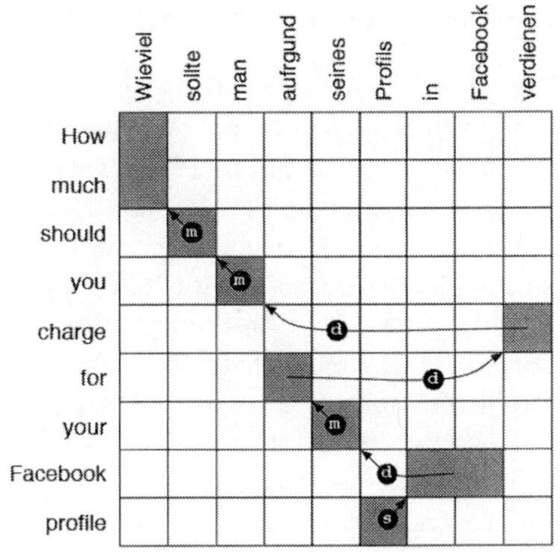

Figure 1: The reordering probabilities from the phrase-based models are estimated from bilingual data by calculating how often in the parallel corpus a phrase pair (f, e) is orientated with the preceding phrase pair in the 3 types of orientations (monotone, swapped, and discontinuous).

The features are combined in a log linear model, and their weights are set through minimum error rate training (Och, 2003). We use the same log linear formulation and MERT but propose alternatives derived directly from monolingual data for all parameters except for the phrase pairs themselves. Our pipeline still requires a small bitext of approximately 2,000 sentences to use as a development set for MERT parameter tuning.

2.2 Bilingual lexicon induction for SMT

Bilingual lexicon induction describes the class of algorithms that attempt to learn translations from monolingual corpora. Rapp (1995) was the first to propose using non-parallel texts to learn the translations of words. Using large, unrelated English and German corpora (with 163m and 135m words) and a small German-English bilingual dictionary (with 22k entires), Rapp (1999) demonstrated that reasonably accurate translations could be learned for 100 German nouns that were not contained in the seed bilingual dictionary. His algorithm worked by (1) building a context vector representing an unknown German word by counting its co-occurrence with all the other words in the German monolingual corpus, (2) projecting this German vector onto the vector space of English using the seed bilingual dictionary, (3) calculating the similarity of this sparse projected vector to vectors for English words that were constructed using the English monolingual corpus, and (4) outputting the English words with the highest similarity as the most likely translations.

A variety of subsequent work has extended the original idea either by exploring different measures of vector similarity (Fung and Yee, 1998) or by proposing other ways of measuring similarity beyond co-occurence within a context window. For instance, Schafer and Yarowsky (2002) demonstrated that word translations tend to co-occur *in time* across languages. Koehn and Knight (2002) used similarity *in spelling* as another kind of cue that a pair of words may be translations of one another. Garera et al. (2009) defined context vectors using *dependency relations* rather than adjacent words. Bergsma and Van Durme (2011) used the *visual similarity* of labeled web images to learn translations of nouns. Additional related work on learning translations from monolingual corpora is discussed in Section 6.

In this paper, we apply bilingual lexicon induction methods to statistical machine translation. Given the obvious benefits of not having to rely on scarce bilingual parallel training data, it is surprising that bilingual lexicon induction has not been used for SMT before now. There are several open questions that make its applicability to SMT uncertain. Previous research on bilingual lexicon induction learned translations only for a small number of high frequency words (e.g. 100

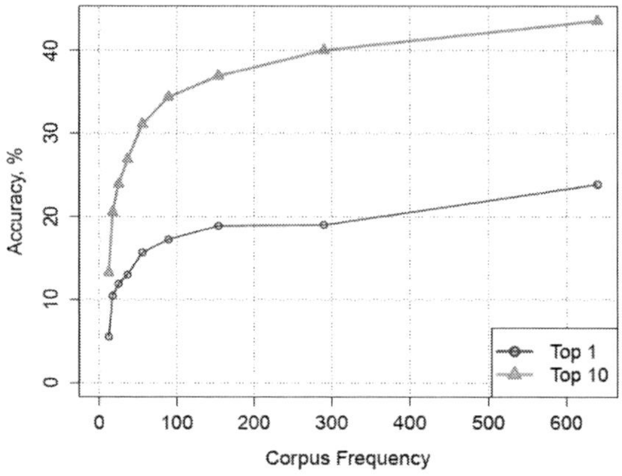

Figure 2: Accuracy of single-word translations induced using contextual similarity as a function of the source word corpus frequency. Accuracy is the proportion of the source words with at least one correct (bilingual dictionary) translation in the top 1 and top 10 candidate lists.

nouns in Rapp (1995), 1,000 most frequent words in Koehn and Knight (2002), or 2,000 most frequent nouns in Haghighi et al. (2008)). Although previous work reported high translation accuracy, it may be misleading to extrapolate the results to SMT, where it is necessary to translate a much larger set of words and phrases, including many low frequency items.

In a preliminary study, we plotted the accuracy of translations against the frequency of the source words in the monolingual corpus. Figure 2 shows the result for translations induced using contextual similarity (defined in Section 3.1). Unsurprisingly, frequent terms have a substantially better chance of being paired with a correct translation, with words that only occur once having a low chance of being translated accurately.[1] This problem is exacerbated when we move to multi-token phrases. As with phrase translation features estimated from parallel data, longer phrases are more sparse, making similarity scores less reliable than for single words.

Another impediment (not addressed in this paper) for using lexicon induction for SMT is the number of translations that must be learned. Learning translations for all words in the source language requires n^2 vector comparisons, since each word in the source language vocabulary must

[1] For a description of the experimental setup used to produce these translations, see Experiment 8 in Section 5.2.

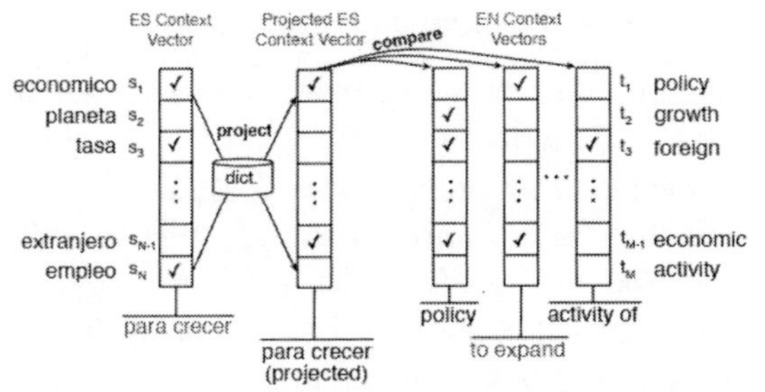

Figure 3: Scoring contextual similarity of *phrases*: first, contextual vectors are projected using a small seed dictionary and then compared with the target language candidates.

be compared against the vectors for all words in the target language vocabulary. The size of the n^2 comparisons hugely increases if we compare vectors for multi-word phrases instead of just words. In this work, we avoid this problem by assuming that a limited set of phrase pairs is given a priori (but without scores). By limiting ourselves to phrases in a phrase table, we vastly limit the search space of possible translations. This is an idealization because high quality translations are guaranteed to be present. However, as our lesion experiments in Section 5.1 show, a phrase table without accurate translation probability estimates is insufficient to produce high quality translations. We show that lexicon induction methods can be used to replace bilingual estimation of phrase- and lexical-translation probabilities, making a significant step towards SMT without parallel corpora.

3 Monolingual Parameter Estimation

We use bilingual lexicon induction methods to estimate the parameters of a phrase-based translation model from monolingual data. Instead of scores estimated from bilingual parallel data, we make use of cues present in monolingual data to provide multiple orthogonal estimates of similarity between a pair of phrases.

3.1 Phrasal similarity features

Contextual similarity. We extend the vector space approach of Rapp (1999) to compute similarity between *phrases* in the source and target languages. More formally, assume that $(s_1, s_2, \ldots s_N)$ and $(t_1, t_2, \ldots t_M)$ are (arbitrarily indexed) source and target vocabularies, respectively. A source phrase f is represented with an

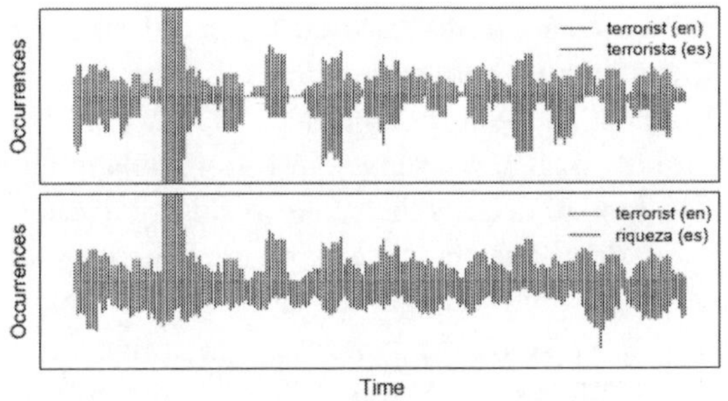

Figure 4: Temporal histograms of the English phrase *terrorist*, its Spanish translation *terrorista*, and *riqueza* (wealth) collected from monolingual texts spanning a 13 year period. While the correct translation has a good temporal match, the non-translation *riqueza* has a distinctly different signature.

N- and target phrase e with an M-dimensional vector (see Figure 3). The component values of the vector representing a phrase correspond to how often each of the words in that vocabulary appear within a two word window on either side of the phrase. These counts are collected using monolingual corpora. After the values have been computed, a contextual vector f is projected onto the English vector space using translations in a seed bilingual dictionary to map the component values into their appropriate English vector positions. This sparse projected vector is compared to the vectors representing all English phrases e. Each phrase pair in the phrase table is assigned a contextual similarity score $c(f, e)$ based on the similarity between e and the projection of f.

Various means of computing the component values and vector similarity measures have been proposed in literature (e.g. Rapp (1999), Fung and Yee (1998)). Following Fung and Yee (1998), we compute the value of the k-th component of f's contextual vector as follows:

$$w_k = n_{f,k} \times (log(n/n_k) + 1)$$

where $n_{f,k}$ and n_k are the number of times s_k appears in the context of f and in the entire corpus, and n is the maximum number of occurrences of any word in the data. Intuitively, the more frequently s_k appears with f and the less common it is in the corpus in general, the higher its component value. Similarity between two vectors is measured as the cosine of the angle between them.

Temporal similarity. In addition to contextual similarity, phrases in two languages may be scored in terms of their temporal similarity (Schafer and Yarowsky, 2002; Klementiev and Roth, 2006; Alfonseca et al., 2009). The intuition is that news stories in different languages will tend to discuss the same world events on the same day. The frequencies of translated phrases over time give them particular signatures that will tend to spike on the same dates. For instance, if the phrase *asian tsunami* is used frequently during a particular time span, the Spanish translation *maremoto asiático* is likely to also be used frequently during that time. Figure 4 illustrates how the temporal distribution of *terrorist* is more similar to Spanish *terrorista* than to other Spanish phrases. We calculate the temporal similarity between a pair of phrases $t(f, e)$ using the method defined by Klementiev and Roth (2006). We generate a temporal signature for each phrase by sorting the set of (time-stamped) documents in the monolingual corpus into a sequence of equally sized temporal bins and then counting the number of phrase occurrences in each bin. In our experiments, we set the window size to 1 day, so the size of temporal signatures is equal to the number of days spanned by our corpus. We use cosine distance to compare the normalized temporal signatures for a pair of phrases (f, e).

Topic similarity. Phrases and their translations are likely to appear in articles written about the same topic in two languages. Thus, topic or category information associated with monolingual data can also be used to indicate similarity between a phrase and its candidate translation. In order to score a pair of phrases, we collect their topic signatures by counting their occurrences in each topic and then comparing the resulting vectors. We again use the cosine similarity measure on the normalized topic signatures. In our experiments, we use interlingual links between Wikipedia articles to estimate topic similarity. We treat each linked article pair as a topic and collect counts for each phrase across all articles in its corresponding language. Thus, the size of a phrase topic signature is the number of article pairs with interlingual links in Wikipedia, and each component contains the number of times the phrase appears in (the appropriate side of) the corresponding pair. Our Wikipedia-based topic similarity feature, $w(f, e)$, is similar in spirit to polylingual topic models (Mimno et al., 2009), but it is scalable to full bilingual lexicon induction.

3.2 Lexical similarity features

In addition to the three phrase similarity features used in our model – $c(f, e), t(f, e)$ and $w(f, e)$ – we include four additional *lexical similarity features* for each of phrase pair. The first three lexical features $c_{lex}(f, e), t_{lex}(f, e)$ and $w_{lex}(f, e)$ are the lexical equivalents of the phrase-level *contextual, temporal* and *wikipedia topic* similarity scores. They score the similarity of individual words within the phrases. To compute these lexical similarity features, we average similarity scores over all possible word alignments across the two phrases. Because individual words are more frequent than multiword phrases, the accuracy of c_{lex}, t_{lex}, and w_{lex} tends to be higher than their phrasal equivalents (this is similar to the effect observed in Figure 2).

Orthographic / phonetic similarity. The final lexical similarity feature that we incorporate is $o(f, e)$, which measures the orthographic similarity between words in a phrase pair. Etymologically related words often retain similar spelling across languages with the same writing system, and low string edit distance sometimes signals translation equivalency. Berg-Kirkpatrick and Klein (2011) present methods for learning correspondences between the alphabets of two languages. We can also extend this idea to language pairs not sharing the same writing system since many cognates, borrowed words, and names remain phonetically similar. Transliterations can be generated for tokens in a source phrase (Knight and Graehl, 1997), with $o(f, e)$ calculating phonetic similarity rather than orthographic.

The three phrasal and four lexical similarity scores are incorporated into the log linear translation model as feature functions, replacing the bilingually estimated phrase translation probabilities ϕ and lexical weighting probabilities w. Our seven similarity scores are not the only ones that could be incorporated into the translation model. Various other similarity scores can be computed depending on the available monolingual data and its associated metadata (see, e.g. Schafer and Yarowsky (2002)).

3.3 Reordering

The remaining component of the phrase-based SMT model is the reordering model. We introduce a novel algorithm for estimating

Input: Source and target phrases f and e,
Source and target monolingual corpora C_f and C_e,
Phrase table pairs $T = \{(f^{(i)}, e^{(i)})\}_{i=1}^{N}$.
Output: Orientation features (p_m, p_s, p_d).

$S_f \leftarrow$ sentences containing f in C_f;
$S_e \leftarrow$ sentences containing e in C_e;
$(B_f, -, -) \leftarrow \text{CollectOccurs}(f, \cup_{i=1}^{N} f^{(i)}, S_f)$;
$(B_e, A_e, D_e) \leftarrow \text{CollectOccurs}(e, \cup_{i=1}^{N} e^{(i)}, S_e)$;
$c_m = c_s = c_d = 0$;
foreach *unique* f' *in* B_f **do**
  foreach *translation* e' *of* f' *in* T **do**
    $c_m = c_m + \#_{B_e}(e')$;
    $c_s = c_s + \#_{A_e}(e')$;
    $c_d = c_d + \#_{D_e}(e')$;
$c \leftarrow c_m + c_s + c_d$;
return $(\frac{c_m}{c}, \frac{c_s}{c}, \frac{c_d}{c})$

CollectOccurs(r, R, S)
  $B \leftarrow ()$; $A \leftarrow ()$; $D \leftarrow ()$;
  foreach *sentence* $s \in S$ **do**
    foreach *occurrence of phrase* r *in* s **do**
      $B \leftarrow B$ + (longest preceding r and in R);
      $A \leftarrow A$ + (longest following r and in R);
      $D \leftarrow D$ + (longest discontinuous w/ r and in R);
  return (B, A, D);

Figure 5: Algorithm for estimating reordering probabilities from monolingual data.

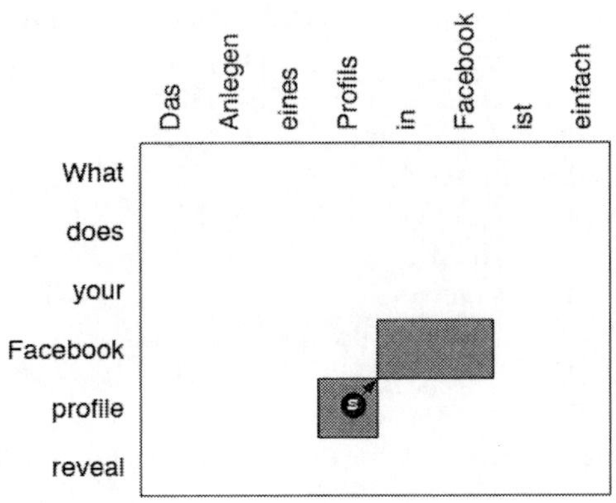

Figure 6: Collecting phrase orientation statistics for a English-German phrase pair (*"profile"*, *"Profils"*) from non-parallel sentences (the German sentence translates as *"Creating a Facebook profile is easy"*).

$p_o(\text{orientation}|f, e)$ from two monolingual corpora instead a bitext.

Figure 1 illustrates how the phrase pair orientation statistics are estimated in the standard phrase-based SMT pipeline. For a phrase pair like (f = *"Profils"*, e = *"profile"*), we count its orientation with the previously translated phrase pair (f' = *"in Facebook"*, e' = *"Facebook"*) across all translated sentence pairs in the bitext.

In our pipeline we do not have translated sentence pairs. Instead, we look for monolingual sentences in the source corpus which contain the source phrase that we are interested in, like f = *"Profils"*, and at least one other phrase that we have a translation for, like f' = *"in Facebook"*. We then look for all target language sentences in the target monolingual corpus that contain the translation of f (here e = *"profile"*) and any translation of f'. Figure 6 illustrates that it is possible to find evidence for $p_o(\text{swapped}|\textit{Profils}, \textit{profile})$, even from the non-parallel, non-translated sentences drawn from two independent monolingual corpora. By looking for foreign sentences containing pairs of adjacent foreign phrases (f, f') and English sentences containing their corresponding translations (e, e'), we are able to increment orientation counts for (f, e) by looking at whether e and e' are adjacent, swapped, or discontinuous. The orientations correspond directly to those shown in Figure 1.

One subtly of our method is that shorter and more frequent phrases (e.g. punctuation) are more likely to appear in multiple orientations with a given phrase, and therefore provide poor evidence of reordering. Therefore, we (a) collect the longest contextual phrases (which also appear in the phrase table) for reordering feature estimation, and (b) prune the set of sentences so that we only keep a small set of least frequent contextual phrases (this has the effect of dropping many function words and punctuation marks and and relying more heavily on multi-word content phrases to estimate the reordering).[2]

Our algorithm for learning the reordering parameters is given in Figure 5. The algorithm estimates a probability distribution over monotone, swap, and discontinuous orientations (p_m, p_s, p_d) for a phrase pair (f, e) from two monolingual corpora C_f and C_e. It begins by calling `CollectOccurs` to collect the longest matching phrase table phrases that precede f in source monolingual data (B_f), as well as those that precede (B_e), follow (A_e), and are discontinuous (D_e) with e in the target language data. For each unique phrase f' preceding f, we look up translations in the phrase table T. Next, we count[3] how

[2]The pruning step has an additional benefit of minimizing the memory needed for orientation feature estimations.

[3]$\#_L(x)$ returns the count of object x in list L.

Monolingual training corpora			
	Europarl	Gigaword	Wikipedia
date range	4/96-10/09	5/94-12/08	n/a
uniq shared dates	829	5,249	n/a
Spanish articles	n/a	3,727,954	59,463
English articles	n/a	4,862,876	59,463
Spanish lines	1,307,339	22,862,835	2,598,269
English lines	1,307,339	67,341,030	3,630,041
Spanish words	28,248,930	774,813,847	39,738,084
English words	27,335,006	1,827,065,374	61,656,646

Spanish-English phrase table	
Phrase pairs	3,093,228
Spanish phrases	89,386
English phrases	926,138
Spanish unigrams	13,216
Avg # translations	98.7
Spanish bigrams	41,426
Avg # translations	31.9
Spanish trigrams	34,744
Avg # translations	13.5

Table 1: Statistics about the monolingual training data and the phrase table that was used in all of the experiments.

many translations e' of f' appeared before, after or were discontinuous with e in the target language data. Finally, the counts are normalized and returned. These normalized counts are the values we use as estimates of $p_o(\text{orientation}|f, e)$.

4 Experimental Setup

We use the Spanish-English language pair to test our method for estimating the parameters of an SMT system from monolingual corpora. This allows us to compare our method against the normal bilingual training procedure. We expect bilingual training to result in higher translation quality because it is a more direct method for learning translation probabilities. We systematically remove different parameters from the standard phrase-based model, and then replace them with our monolingual equivalents. Our goal is to recover as much of the loss as possible for each of the deleted bilingual components.

The standard phrase-based model that we use as our top-line is the Moses system (Koehn et al., 2007) trained over the full Europarl v5 parallel corpus (Koehn, 2005). With the exception of maximum phrase length (set to 3 in our experiments), we used default values for all of the parameters. All experiments use a trigram language model trained on the English side of the Europarl corpus using SRILM with Kneser-Ney smoothing. To tune feature weights in minimum error rate training, we use a development bitext of 2,553 sentence pairs, and we evaluate performance on a test set of 2,525 single-reference translated newswire articles. These development and test datasets were distributed in the WMT shared task (Callison-Burch et al., 2010).[4] MERT was re-run for every experiment.

We estimate the parameters of our model from two sets of monolingual data, detailed in Table 1:

- First, we treat the two sides of the Europarl parallel corpus as independent, monolingual corpora. Haghighi et al. (2008) also used this method to show how well translations could be learned from monolingual corpora under ideal conditions, where the contextual and temporal distribution of words in the two monolingual corpora are nearly identical.

- Next, we estimate the features from truly monolingual corpora. To estimate the *contextual* and *temporal* similarity features, we use the Spanish and English Gigaword corpora.[5] These corpora are substantially larger than the Europarl corpora, providing 27x as much Spanish and 67x as much English for contextual similarity, and 6x as many paired dates for temporal similarity. *Topical* similarity is estimated using Spanish and English Wikipedia articles that are paired with interlanguage links.

To project context vectors from Spanish to English, we use a bilingual dictionary containing entries for 49,795 Spanish words. Note that end-to-end translation quality is robust to substantially reducing dictionary size, but we omit these experiments due to space constraints. The context vectors for words and phrases incorporate co-occurrence counts using a two-word window on either side.

The title of our paper uses the word *towards* because we assume that an inventory of phrase pairs is given. Future work will explore inducing the

[4]Specifcially, *news-test2008* plus *news-syscomb2009* for dev and *newstest2009* for test.

[5]We use the afp, apw and xin sections of the corpora.

	Exp	Phrase scores / orientation scores
1	B/B	bilingual / bilingual (Moses)
2	B/-	bilingual / distortion
3	-/B	none / bilingual
4	-/-	none / distortion
5, 12	-/M	none / mono
6, 13	t/-	temporal mono / distortion
7,14	o/-	orthographic mono / distortion
8, 15	c/-	contextual mono / distortion
16	w/-	Wikipedia topical mono / distortion
9, 17	M/-	all mono / distortion
10, 18	M/M	all mono / mono
11, 19	BM/B	bilingual + all mono / bilingual

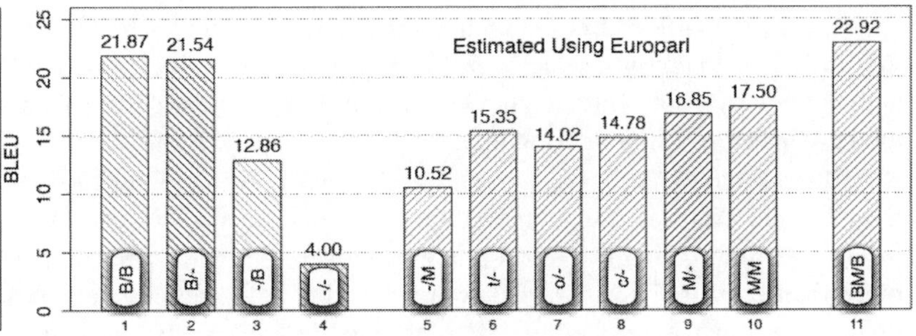

Figure 7: Much of the loss in BLEU score when bilingually estimated features are removed from a Spanish-English translation system (experiments 1-4) can be recovered when they are replaced with monolingual equivalents estimated from monolingual Europarl data (experiments 5-10). The labels indicate how the different types of parameters are estimated, the first part is for phrase-table features, the second is for reordering probabilities.

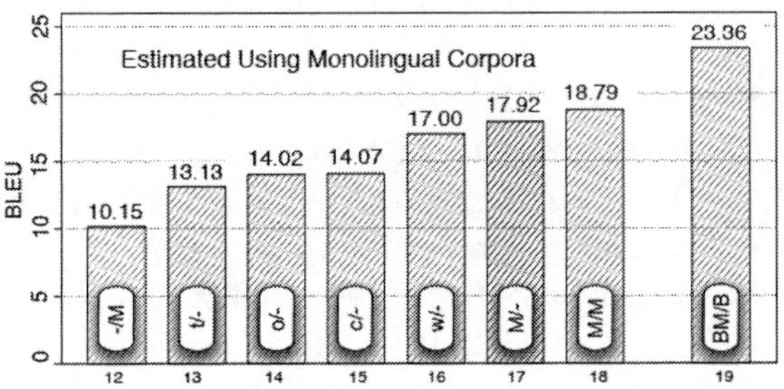

Figure 8: Performance of monolingual features derived from truly monolingual corpora. Over 82% of the BLEU score loss can be recovered.

phrase table itself from monolingual texts. Across all of our experiments, we use the phrase table that the bilingual model learned from the Europarl parallel corpus. We keep its phrase pairs, but we drop all of its scores. Table 1 gives details of the phrase pairs. In our experiments, we estimated similarity and reordering scores for more than 3 million phrase pairs. For each source phrase, the set of possible translations was constrained and likely to contain good translations. However, the average number of possible translations was high (ranging from nearly 100 translations for each unigram to 14 for each trigram). These contain a lot of noise and result in low end-to-end translation quality without good estimates of translation quality, as the experiments in Section 5.1 show.

Software. Because many details of our estimation procedures must be omitted for space, we distribute our full set of code along with scripts for running our experiments and output translations. These may be downed from `http://www.cs.jhu.edu/~anni/papers/lowresmt/`

5 Experimental Results

Figures 7 and 8 give experimental results. Figure 7 shows the performance of the standard phrase-based model when each of the bilingually estimated features are removed. It shows how much of the performance loss can be recovered using our monolingual features when they are estimated from the Europarl training corpus but treating each side as an independent, monolingual corpus. Figure 8 shows the recovery when using truly monolingual corpora to estimate the parameters.

5.1 Lesion experiments

Experiments 1-4 remove bilingually estimated parameters from the standard model. For Spanish-English, the relative contribution of the phrase-table features (which include the phrase translation probabilities ϕ and the lexical weights w) is greater than the reordering probabilities. When the reordering probability $p_o(\text{orientation}|f, e)$ is eliminated and replaced with a simple distance-based distortion feature that does not require a bitext to estimate, the score dips only marginally since word order in English and Spanish is similar. However, when both the reordering and the phrase table features are dropped, leaving only the LM feature and the phrase penalty, the resulting translation quality is abysmal, with the score dropping a total of over 17 BLEU points.

5.2 Adding equivalent monolingual features estimated using Europarl

Experiments 5-10 show how much our monolingual equivalents could recover when the monolingual corpora are drawn from the two sides of the bitext. For instance, our algorithm for estimating reordering probabilities from monolingual data (–/M) adds 5 BLEU points, which is 73% of the potential recovery going from the model (–/–) to the model with bilingual reordering features (–/B).

Of the **t**emporal, **o**rthographic, and **c**ontextual monolingual features the temporal feature performs the best. Together (**M/–**), they recover more than each individually. Combining monolingually estimated reordering and phrase table features (**M/M**) yields a total gain of 13.5 BLEU points, or over 75% of the BLEU score loss that occurred when we dropped all features from the phrase table. However, these results use "monolingual" corpora which have practically identical phrasal and temporal distributions.

5.3 Estimating features using *truly monolingual* corpora

Experiments 12-18 estimate all of the features from truly monolingual corpora. Our novel algorithm for estimating reordering holds up well and recovers 69% of the loss, only 0.4 BLEU points less than when estimated from the Europarl monolingual texts. The temporal similarity feature does not perform as well as when it was estimated using Europarl data, but the contextual feature does. The topic similarity using Wikipedia performs the strongest of the individual features.

Combining the monolingually estimated reordering features with the monolingually estimated similarity features (**M/M**) yields a total gain of **14.8 BLEU** points, or **over 82%** of the BLEU point loss that occurred when we dropped all features from the phrase table. This is equivalent to training the standard system on a bitext with roughly 60,000 lines or nearly 2 million words (learning curve omitted for space).

Finally, we supplement the standard bilingually estimated model parameters with our monolingual features (**BM/B**), and we see a **1.5 BLEU** point increase over the standard model. Therefore, our monolingually estimated scores capture some novel information not contained in the standard feature set.

6 Additional Related Work

Carbonell et al. (2006) described a data-driven MT system that used no parallel text. It produced translation lattices using a bilingual dictionary and scored them using an n-gram language model. Their method has no notion of translation similarity aside from a bilingual dictionary. Similarly, Sánchez-Cartagena et al. (2011) supplement an SMT phrase table with translation pairs extracted from a bilingual dictionary and give each a frequency of one for computing translation scores.

Ravi and Knight (2011) treat MT without parallel training data as a decipherment task and learn a translation model from monolingual text. They translate corpora of Spanish time expressions and subtitles, which both have a limited vocabulary, into English. Their method has not been applied to broader domains of text.

Most work on learning translations from monolingual texts only examine small numbers of frequent words. Huang et al. (2005) and Daumé and Jagarlamudi (2011) are exceptions that improve MT by mining translations for OOV items.

A variety of past research has focused on mining parallel or comparable corpora from the web (Munteanu and Marcu, 2006; Smith et al., 2010; Uszkoreit et al., 2010). Others use an existing SMT system to discover parallel sentences within independent monolingual texts, and use them to re-train and enhance the system (Schwenk, 2008; Chen et al., 2008; Schwenk and Senellart, 2009; Rauf and Schwenk, 2009; Lambert et al., 2011). These are complementary but orthogonal to our research goals.

7 Conclusion

This paper has demonstrated a novel set of techniques for successfully estimating phrase-based SMT parameters from *monolingual* corpora, potentially circumventing the need for large bitexts, which are expensive to obtain for new languages and domains. We evaluated the performance of our algorithms in a full end-to-end translation system. Assuming that a bilingual-corpus-derived phrase table is available, we were able utilize our monolingually-estimated features to recover over 82% of BLEU loss that resulted from removing the bilingual-corpus-derived phrase-table probabilities. We also showed that our monolingual features add 1.5 BLEU points when combined with standard bilingually estimated features. Thus our techniques have stand-alone efficacy when large bilingual corpora are not available and also make a significant contribution to combined ensemble performance when they are.

References

Enrique Alfonseca, Massimiliano Ciaramita, and Keith Hall. 2009. Gazpacho and summer rash: lexical relationships from temporal patterns of web search queries. In *Proceedings of EMNLP*.

Taylor Berg-Kirkpatrick and Dan Klein. 2011. Simple effective decipherment via combinatorial optimization. In *Proceedings of the 2011 Conference on Empirical Methods in Natural Language Processing (EMNLP-2011)*, Edinburgh, Scotland, UK.

Shane Bergsma and Benjamin Van Durme. 2011. Learning bilingual lexicons using the visual similarity of labeled web images. In *Proceedings of the International Joint Conference on Artificial Intelligence*.

Peter Brown, John Cocke, Stephen Della Pietra, Vincent Della Pietra, Frederick Jelinek, Robert Mercer, and Paul Poossin. 1988. A statistical approach to language translation. In *12th International Conference on Computational Linguistics (CoLing-1988)*.

Peter Brown, Stephen Della Pietra, Vincent Della Pietra, and Robert Mercer. 1993. The mathematics of machine translation: Parameter estimation. *Computational Linguistics*, 19(2):263–311, June.

Chris Callison-Burch, Philipp Koehn, Christof Monz, Kay Peterson, Mark Przybocki, and Omar Zaidan. 2010. Findings of the 2010 joint workshop on statistical machine translation and metrics for machine translation. In *Proceedings of the Workshop on Statistical Machine Translation*.

Jaime Carbonell, Steve Klein, David Miller, Michael Steinbaum, Tomer Grassiany, and Jochen Frey. 2006. Context-based machine translation. In *Proceedings of AMTA*.

Boxing Chen, Min Zhang, Aiti Aw, and Haizhou Li. 2008. Exploiting n-best hypotheses for SMT self-enhancement. In *Proceedings of ACL/HLT*, pages 157–160.

David Chiang. 2005. A hierarchical phrase-based model for statistical machine translation. In *Proceedings of ACL*.

Hal Daumé and Jagadeesh Jagarlamudi. 2011. Domain adaptation for machine translation by mining unseen words. In *Proceedings of ACL/HLT*.

Pascale Fung and Lo Yuen Yee. 1998. An IR approach for translating new words from nonparallel, comparable texts. In *Proceedings of ACL/CoLing*.

Nikesh Garera, Chris Callison-Burch, and David Yarowsky. 2009. Improving translation lexicon induction from monolingual corpora via dependency contexts and part-of-speech equivalences. In *Thirteenth Conference On Computational Natural Language Learning (CoNLL-2009)*, Boulder, Colorado.

Ulrich Germann. 2001. Building a statistical machine translation system from scratch: How much bang for the buck can we expect? In *ACL 2001 Workshop on Data-Driven Machine Translation*, Toulouse, France.

Aria Haghighi, Percy Liang, Taylor Berg-Kirkpatrick, and Dan Klein. 2008. Learning bilingual lexicons from monolingual corpora. In *Proceedings of ACL/HLT*.

Fei Huang, Ying Zhang, and Stephan Vogel. 2005. Mining key phrase translations from web corpora. In *Proceedings of EMNLP*.

Alexandre Klementiev and Dan Roth. 2006. Weakly supervised named entity transliteration and discovery from multilingual comparable corpora. In *Proceedings of the ACL/Coling*.

Kevin Knight and Jonathan Graehl. 1997. Machine transliteration. In *Proceedings of ACL*.

Philipp Koehn and Kevin Knight. 2002. Learning a translation lexicon from monolingual corpora. In *ACL Workshop on Unsupervised Lexical Acquisition*.

Philipp Koehn, Franz Josef Och, and Daniel Marcu. 2003. Statistical phrase-based translation. In *Proceedings of HLT/NAACL*.

Philipp Koehn, Hieu Hoang, Alexandra Birch, Chris Callison-Burch, Marcello Federico, Nicola Bertoldi, Brooke Cowan, Wade Shen, Christine Moran, Richard Zens, Chris Dyer, Ondrej Bojar, Alexandra Constantin, and Evan Herbst. 2007. Moses: Open source toolkit for statistical machine translation. In *Proceedings of the ACL-2007 Demo and Poster Sessions*.

Philipp Koehn. 2005. Europarl: A parallel corpus for statistical machine translation. In *Proceedings of the Machine Translation Summit*.

Shankar Kumar and William Byrne. 2004. Local phrase reordering models for statistical machine translation. In *Proceedings of HLT/NAACL*.

Patrik Lambert, Holger Schwenk, Christophe Servan, and Sadaf Abdul-Rauf. 2011. Investigations on translation model adaptation using monolingual data. In *Proceedings of the Workshop on Statistical Machine Translation*, pages 284–293, Edinburgh, Scotland, UK.

David Mimno, Hanna Wallach, Jason Naradowsky, David Smith, and Andrew McCallum. 2009. Polylingual topic models. In *Proceedings of EMNLP*.

Dragos Stefan Munteanu and Daniel Marcu. 2006. Extracting parallel sub-sentential fragments from non-parallel corpora. In *Proceedings of the ACL/Coling*.

Franz Josef Och and Hermann Ney. 2003. A systematic comparison of various statistical alignment models. *Computational Linguistics*, 29(1):19–51.

Franz Josef Och and Hermann Ney. 2004. The alignment template approach to statistical machine translation. *Computational Linguistics*, 30(4):417–449.

Franz Joseph Och. 2002. *Statistical Machine Translation: From Single-Word Models to Alignment Templates.* Ph.D. thesis, RWTH Aachen.

Franz Josef Och. 2003. Minimum error rate training for statistical machine translation. In *Proceedings of ACL.*

Reinhard Rapp. 1995. Identifying word translations in non-parallel texts. In *Proceedings of ACL.*

Reinhard Rapp. 1999. Automatic identification of word translations from unrelated English and German corpora. In *Proceedings of ACL.*

Sadaf Abdul Rauf and Holger Schwenk. 2009. On the use of comparable corpora to improve SMT performance. In *Proceedings of EACL.*

Sujith Ravi and Kevin Knight. 2011. Deciphering foreign language. In *Proceedings of ACL/HLT.*

Vctor M. Sánchez-Cartagena, Felipe Sánchez-Martnez, and Juan Antonio Pérez-Ortiz. 2011. Integrating shallow-transfer rules into phrase-based statistical machine translation. In *Proceedings of the XIII Machine Translation Summit.*

Charles Schafer and David Yarowsky. 2002. Inducing translation lexicons via diverse similarity measures and bridge languages. In *Proceedings of CoNLL.*

Holger Schwenk and Jean Senellart. 2009. Translation model adaptation for an Arabic/French news translation system by lightly-supervised training. In *MT Summit.*

Holger Schwenk. 2008. Investigations on large-scale lightly-supervised training for statistical machine translation. In *Proceedings of IWSLT.*

Jason R. Smith, Chris Quirk, and Kristina Toutanova. 2010. Extracting parallel sentences from comparable corpora using document level alignment. In *Proceedings of HLT/NAACL.*

Christoph Tillman. 2004. A unigram orientation model for statistical machine translation. In *Proceedings of HLT/NAACL.*

Christoph Tillmann. 2003. A projection extension algorithm for statistical machine translation. In *Proceedings of EMNLP.*

Jakob Uszkoreit, Jay M. Ponte, Ashok C. Popat, and Moshe Dubiner. 2010. Large scale parallel document mining for machine translation. In *Proceedings of CoLing.*

Ashish Venugopal, Stephan Vogel, and Alex Waibel. 2003. Effective phrase translation extraction from alignment models. In *Proceedings of ACL.*

Character-Based Pivot Translation for Under-Resourced Languages and Domains

Jörg Tiedemann
Department of Linguistics and Philology
Uppsala University, Uppsala/Sweden
jorg.tiedemann@lingfil.uu.se

Abstract

In this paper we investigate the use of character-level translation models to support the translation from and to under-resourced languages and textual domains via closely related pivot languages. Our experiments show that these low-level models can be successful even with tiny amounts of training data. We test the approach on movie subtitles for three language pairs and legal texts for another language pair in a domain adaptation task. Our pivot translations outperform the baselines by a large margin.

1 Introduction

Data-driven approaches have been extremely successful in most areas of natural language processing (NLP) and can be considered the main paradigm in application-oriented research and development. Research in machine translation is a typical example with the dominance of statistical models over the last decade. This is even enforced due to the availability of toolboxes such as Moses (Koehn et al., 2007) which make it possible to build translation engines within days or even hours for any language pair provided that appropriate training data is available. However, this reliance on training data is also the most severe limitation of statistical approaches. Resources in large quantities are only available for a few languages and domains. In the case of SMT, the dilemma is even more apparent as parallel corpora are rare and usually quite sparse. Some languages can be considered lucky, for example, because of political situations that lead to the production of freely available translated material on a large scale. A lot of research and development would not have been possible without the European Union and its language policies to give an example.

One of the main challenges of current NLP research is to port data-driven techniques to under-resourced languages, which refers to the majority of the world's languages. One obvious approach is to create appropriate data resources even for those languages in order to enable the use of similar techniques designed for *high-density* languages. However, this is usually too expensive and often impossible with the quantities needed. Another idea is to develop new models that can work with (much) less data but still make use of resources and techniques developed for other well-resourced languages.

In this paper, we explore pivot translation techniques for the translation from and to resource-poor languages with the help of intermediate resource-rich languages. We explore the fact that many poorly resourced languages are closely related to well equipped languages, which enables low-level techniques such as character-based translation. We can show that these techniques can boost the performance enormously, tested for several language pairs. Furthermore, we show that pivoting can also be used to overcome data sparseness in specific domains. Even high density languages are under-resourced in most textual domains and pivoting via in-domain data of another language can help to adapt statistical models. In our experiments, we observe that related languages have the largest impact in such a setup.

The remaining parts of the paper are organized as follows: First we describe the pivot translation approach used in this study. Thereafter, we discuss character-based translation models followed by a detailed presentation of our experimental results. Finally, we briefly summarize related work and conclude the paper with discussions and prospects for future work.

2 Pivot Models

Information from pivot languages can be incorporated in SMT models in various ways. The main principle refers to the combination of source-to-pivot and pivot-to-target translation models. In our setup, one of these models includes a resource-poor language (source or target) and the other one refers to a standard model with appropriate data resources. A condition is that we have at least some training data for the translation between pivot and the resource-poor language. However, for the original task (source-to-target translation) we do not require any data resources except for purposes of comparison.

We will explore various models for the translation between the resource-poor language and the pivot language and most of them are not compatible with standard phrase-based translation models. Hence, triangulation methods (Cohn and Lapata, 2007) for combining phrase tables are not applicable in our case. Instead, we explore a cascaded approach (also called "transfer method" (Wu and Wang, 2009)) in which we translate the input text in two steps using a linear interpolation for rescoring N-best lists. Following the method described in (Utiyama and Isahara, 2007) and (Wu and Wang, 2009), we use the best n hypotheses from the translation of source sentences s to pivot sentences p and combine them with the top m hypotheses for translating these pivot sentences to target sentences t:

$$\hat{t} \approx \underset{t}{argmax} \sum_{k=1}^{L} \alpha \lambda_k^{sp} h_k^{sp}(s,p) + (1-\alpha)\lambda_k^{pt} h_k^{pt}(p,t)$$

where h_k^{xy} are feature functions for model xy with appropriate weights λ_k^{xy}.[1] Basically, this means that we simply add the scores and, similar to related work, we assume that the feature weights can be set independently for each model using minimum error rate training (MERT) (Och, 2003). In our setup we added the parameter α that can be used to weight the importance of one model over the other. This can be useful as we do not consider the entire hypothesis space but only a small subset of N-best lists. In the simplest case, this weight is set to 0.5 making both models equally important. An alternative to fitting the interpolation weight would be to perform a global optimization procedure. However, a straightforward implementation of pivot-based MERT would be prohibitively slow due to the expensive two-step translation procedure over n-best lists.

A general condition for the pivot approach is to assume independent training sets for both translation models as already pointed out by (Bertoldi et al., 2008). In contrast to research presented in related work (see, for example, (Koehn et al., 2009)) this condition is met in our setup in which all data sets represent different samples over the languages considered (see section 4).[2]

3 Character-Based SMT

The basic idea behind character-based translation models is to take advantage of the strong lexical and syntactic similarities between closely related languages. Consider, for example, Figure 1. Related languages like Catalan and Spanish or Danish and Norwegian have common roots and, therefore, use similar concepts and express them in similar grammatical structures. Spelling conventions can still be quite different but those differences are often very consistent. The Bosnian-Macedonian example also shows that we do not have to require any alphabetic overlap in order to obtain character-level similarities.

Regularities between such closely related languages can be captured below the word level. We can also assume a more or less monotonic relation between the two languages which motivates the idea of translation models over character N-grams treating translation as a transliteration task (Vilar et al., 2007). Conceptually it is straightforward to think of phrase-based models on the character level. Sequences of characters can be used instead of word N-grams for both, translation and language models. Training can proceed with the same tools and approaches. The basic task is to

[1]Note, that we do not require the same feature functions in both models even though the formula above implies this for simplicity of representation.

[2]Note that different samples may still include common sentences.

Catalan - Spanish

Oko, comprova l'equip.
Oko, comprueba el equipo.

No hi ha constellació en la distància Visual.
No hay constelación en la distancia Visual.

Cap explosió estelar.
Ninguna explosión estelar.

Danish - Norwegian

Du ser forfærdelig ud.
- Du ser forferdelig ut.

Du kunnei det mindste have barberet dig.
Du kunne i det minste ha barbert deg.

Icelandic - Swedish

Barnið er dáið.
Barnet är dött.

Hann andaði aðeins í smástund.
Han andades bara en kort stund.

Svo andaði hann ekki meira.
Han andades aldrig igen.

Bosnian - Macedonian

Kako znate da se radi o jednoj životinji?
Како знете дека се работи за животно?

Ni ja ne verujem u zmajeve...
И јас не верувам во змејови . . .

Figure 1: Some examples of movie subtitle translations between closely related languages (either sharing parts of the same alphabet or not).

prepare the data to comply with the training procedures (see Figure 2).

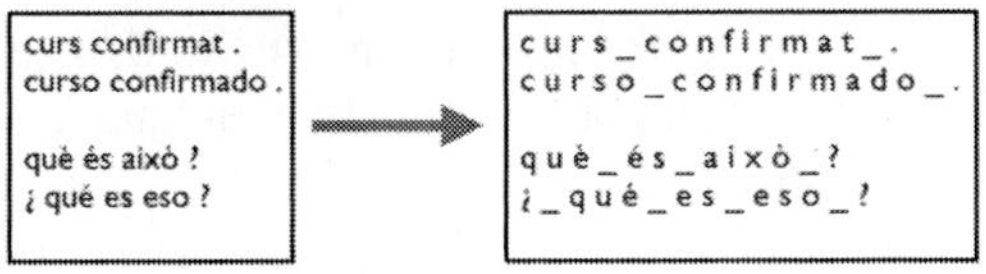

Figure 2: Data pre-processing for training models on the character level. Spaces are represented by '_' and each sentence is treated as one sequence of characters.

3.1 Character Alignment

One crucial difference is the alignment of characters, which is required instead of an alignment of words. Clearly, the traditional IBM word alignment models are not designed for this task especially with respect to distortion. However, the same generative story can still be applied in general. Vilar et al. (2007) explore a two-step procedure where words are aligned first (with the traditional IBM models) to divide sentence pairs into aligned segments of reasonable size and the characters are then aligned with the same algorithm.

An alternative is to use models designed for transliteration or related character-level transformation tasks. Many approaches are based on transducer models that resemble string edit operations such as insertions, deletions and substitutions (Ristad and Yianilos, 1998). Weighted finite state transducers (WFST's) can be trained on unaligned pairs of character sequences and have been shown to be very effective for transliteration tasks or letter-to-phoneme conversions (Jiampojamarn et al., 2007). The training procedure usually employs an expectation maximization (EM) procedure and the resulting transducer can be used to find the Viterbi alignment between characters according to the best sequence of edit operations applied to transform one string into the other. Extensions to this model are possible, for example the use of many-to-many alignments which have been shown to be very effective in letter-to-phoneme alignment tasks (Jiampojamarn et al., 2007).

One advantage of the edit-distance-based transducer models is that the alignments they predict are strictly monotonic and cannot easily be confused by spurious relations between characters over longer distances. Long distance alignments are only possible in connection with a series of insertions and deletions that usually increase the alignment costs in such a way that they are avoided if possible. On the other hand, IBM word alignment models also prefer monotonic alignments over non-monotonic ones if there is no good reason to do otherwise (i.e., there is frequent evidence of distorted alignments). However, the size of the vocabulary in a character-level model is very small (several orders of magnitude smaller than on the word level) and this may cause serious confusion of the word alignment model that very much relies on context-independent lexical translation probabilities. Hence, for character alignment, the lexical evidence is much less reliable without their context.

It is certainly possible to find a compromise between word-level and character-level models in order to generalize below word boundaries but avoiding alignment problems as discussed above. Morpheme-based translation models have been explored in several studies with similar motivations as in our approach, a better generalization from sparse training data (Fishel and Kirik, 2010; Luong et al., 2010). However, these approaches have the drawback that they require proper morphological analyses. Data-driven techniques exist even for morphology, but their use in SMT still needs to be shown (Fishel, 2009). The situation is comparable to the problems of integrating linguistically motivated phrases into phrase-based SMT (Koehn et al., 2003). Instead we opt for a more general approach to extend context to facilitate, especially, the alignment step. Figure 3 shows how we can transform texts into sequences of bigrams that can be aligned with standard approaches without making any assumptions about linguistically motivated segmentations.

cu ur rs so o_ _c co on nf fi ir rm ma ad do o_ _. ._

¿_ _q qu ué é_ _e es s_ _e es so o_ _? ?_

Figure 3: Two Spanish sentences as sequences of character bigrams with a final '_' marking the end of a sentence.

In this way we can construct a parallel corpus with slightly richer contextual information as input to the alignment program. The vocabulary remains small (for example, 1267 bigrams in the case of Spanish compared to 84 individual characters in our experiments) but lexical translation probabilities become now much more differentiated.

With this, it is now possible to use the alignment between bigrams to train a character-level translation system as we have the same number of bigrams as we have characters (and the first character in each bigram corresponds to the character at that position). Certainly, it is also possible to train a bigram translation model (and language model). This has the (one and only) advantage that one character of context across phrase boundaries (i.e. character N-grams) is used in the selection of translation alternatives from the phrase table.[3]

3.2 Tuning Character-Level Models

A final remark on training character-based SMT models is concerned with feature weight tuning. It certainly makes not much sense to compute character-level BLEU scores for tuning feature weights especially with the standard settings of matching relatively short N-grams. Instead we would still like to measure performance in terms of word-level BLEU scores (or any other MT evaluation metric used in minimum error rate training). Therefore, it is important to post-process character-translated development sets before adjusting weights. This is simply done by merging characters accordingly and replacing the place-holders with spaces again. Thereafter, MERT can run as usual.

3.3 Evaluation

Character-level translations can be evaluated in the same way as other translation hypotheses, for example using automatic measures such as BLEU, NIST, METEOR etc. The same simple post-processing as mentioned in the previous section can be applied to turn the character translations into "normal" text. However, it can be useful to look at some other measures as well that consider near matches on the character level instead of matching words and word N-grams only. Character-level models have the ability to produce strings that may be close to the reference and still do not match any of the words contained. They may generate non-words that include mistakes which look like spelling-errors or minor grammatical mistakes. Those words are usually close enough to the correct target words to be recognized by the user, which is often more acceptable than leaving foreign words untranslated. This is especially true as many unknown words represent important content words that bear a lot of information. The problem of unknown words is even more severe for morphologically rich language as many word forms are simply not part of (sparse) training data sets. Untranslated words are especially annoying when translating languages that use different writing systems. Consider, for example, the following subtitles in Macedonian (using Cyrillic letters) that have been translated from Bosnian (written in Latin characters):

reference: И чаша вино, како и секогаш.
word-based: И **čašu vina**, како секогаш.
char-based: И **чаша вино**, како секогаш.

reference: Во старото светилиште.
word-based: Во **starom svetilištu**.
char-based: Во **стар светилиштето**.

The underlined parts mark examples of character-level differences with respect to the reference translation. For the pivot translation approach, it is important that the translations generated in the first step can be handled by the second one. This means, that words generated by a character-based model should at least be valid input words for the second step, even though they might refer to erroneous inflections in that context. Therefore, we add another measure to our experimental results presented below – the number of unknown words with respect to the input language of the second step. This applies only to models that are used as the first step in pivot-based translations. For other models, we include a string similarity measure based on the longest common subsequence ratio (LCSR) (Stephen, 1992) in order to give an impression about the "closeness" of the system

[3]Using larger units (trigrams, for example) led to lower scores in our experiments (probably due to data sparseness) and, therefore, are not reported here.

output to the reference translations.

4 Experiments

We conducted a series of experiments to test the ideas of (character-level) pivot translation for resource-poor languages. We chose to use data from a collection of translated subtitles compiled in the freely available OPUS corpus (Tiedemann, 2009b). This collection includes a large variety of languages and contains mainly short sentences and sentence fragments, which suits character-level alignment very well. The selected settings represent translation tasks between languages (and domains) for which only very limited training data is available or none at all.

Below we present results from two general tasks:[4] (i) Translating between English and a resource-poor language (in both directions) via a pivot language that is close related to the resource-poor language. (ii) Translating between two languages in a domain for which no in-domain training data is available via a pivot language with in-domain data. We will start with the presentation of the first task and the character-based translation between closely related languages.

4.1 Task 1: Pivoting via Related Languages

We decided to look at resource-poor languages from two language families: Macedonian representing a Slavic language from the Balkan region, Catalan and Galician representing two Romance languages spoken mainly in Spain. There is only little or no data available for translating from or to English for these languages. However, there are related languages with medium or large amounts of training data. For Macedonian, we use Bulgarian (which also uses a Cyrillic alphabet) and Bosnian (another related language that mainly uses Latin characters) as the pivot language. For Catalan and Galician, the obvious choice was Spanish (however, Portuguese would, for example, have been another reasonable option for Galician). Table 1 lists the data available for training the various models. Furthermore, we reserved 2000 sentences for tuning parameters and another 2000 sentences for testing. For Galician, we only used 1000 sentences for each set due to the lack of additional data. We were especially careful when preparing the data to exclude all sentences from tuning and test sets that could be found in any pivot or direct translation model. Hence, all test sentences are unseen strings for all models presented in this paper (but they are not comparable with each other as they are sampled individually from independent data sets).

language pair	*#sent's*	*#words*
Galician – English	–	–
Galician – Spanish	2k	15k
Catalan – English	50k	400k
Catalan – Spanish	64k	500k
Spanish – English	30M	180M
Macedonian – English	220k	1.2M
Macedonian – Bosnian	12k	60k
Macedonian – Bulgarian	155k	800k
Bosnian – English	2.1M	11M
Bulgarian – English	14M	80M

Table 1: Training data for the translation task between closely related languages in the domain of movie subtitles. Number of sentences (#sent's) and number of words (#words) in thousands (k) and millions (M) (averages of source and target language).

The data sets represent several interesting test cases: Galician is the least supported language with extremely little training data for building our pivot model. There is no data for the direct model and, therefore, no explicit baseline for this task. There is 30 times more data available for Catalan-English, but still too little for a decent standard SMT model. Interesting here is that we have more or less the same amount of data available for the baseline and for the pivot translation between the related languages. The data set for Macedonian – English is by far the largest among the baseline models and also bigger than the sets available for the related pivot languages. Especially Macedonian – Bosnian is not well supported. The interesting questions is whether tiny amounts of pivot data can still be competitive. In all three cases, there is much more data available for the translation models between English and the pivot language.

In the following section we will look at the translation between related languages with various models and training setups before we consider the actual translation task via the bridge languages.

[4] In all experiments we use standard tools like Moses, Giza++, SRILM, mteval etc. Details about basic settings are omitted here due to space constraints but can be found in the supplementary material. The data sets are available from here: http://stp.lingfil.uu.se/~joerg/index.php?resources

Model	bs-mk		bg-mk		es-gl		es-ca	
	BLEU %	↑LCSR	BLEU %	↑LCSR	BLEU %	↑LCSR	BLEU %	↑LCSR
word-based	15.43	0.5067	14.66	0.6225	41.11	0.7966	62.73	0.8526
char – $WFST_{1:1}$	21.37++	0.6903	13.33−−	0.6159	36.94	0.7832	73.17++	0.8728
char – $WFST_{2:2}$	19.17++	0.6737	12.67−−	0.6190	43.39++	0.8083	70.64++	0.8684
char – IBM_{char}	23.17++	0.6968	14.57	0.6347	**45.21**++	**0.8171**	73.12++	0.8767
char – IBM_{bigram}	**24.84**++	**0.7046**	**15.01**++	**0.6374**	44.06++	0.8144	**74.21**++	**0.8803**

Table 2: Translating from a related pivot language to the target language. Bosnian (bs) / Bulgarian (bg) – Macedonian (mk); Galician (gl) / Catalan (ca) – Spanish (es). *Word-based* refers to standard phrase-based SMT models. All other models use phrases over character sequences. The $WFST_{x:y}$ models use weighted finite state transducers for character alignment with units that are at most x and y characters long, respectively. Other models use Viterbi alignments created by IBM model 4 using GIZA++ (Och and Ney, 2003) between characters (IBM_{char}) or bigrams (IBM_{bigram}). LCSR refers to the averaged longest common subsequence ratio between system translations and references. Results are significantly better ($p < 0.01^{++}$, $p < 0.05^{+}$) or worse ($p < 0.01^{--}$, $p < 0.05^{-}$) than the word-based baseline.

Model	mk-bs		mk-bg		gl-es		ca-es	
	BLEU %	↓UNK	BLEU %	↓UNK	BLEU %	↓UNK	BLEU %	↓UNK
word-based	14.22	17.83%	14.77	5.29%	43.22	10.18%	59.34	3.80%
char – $WFST_{1:1}$	21.74++	1.50%	16.04++	**0.77%**	50.24++	**1.17%**	62.87++	**0.45%**
char – $WFST_{2:2}$	19.19++	2.05%	15.32	0.96%	50.59++	1.28%	59.84	0.47%
char – IBM_{char}	24.15++	1.30%	17.12++	0.80%	**51.18**++	1.38%	64.35 ++	0.59%
char – IBM_{bigram}	**24.82**++	**1.00%**	**17.28**++	**0.77%**	50.70++	1.36%	**65.14**++	0.48%

Table 3: Translating from the source language to a related pivot language. UNK gives the proportion of unknown words with respect to the translation model from the pivot language to English.

4.1.1 Translating Related Languages

The main challenge for the translation models between related languages is the restriction to very limited parallel training data. Character-level models make it possible to generalize to very basic translation units leading to robust models in the sense of models without unknown events. The basic question is whether they provide reasonable translations with respect to given accepted references. Tables 2 and 3 give a comprehensive summary of various models for the languages selected in our experiments.

We can see that at least one character-based translation model outperforms the standard word-based model in all cases. This is true (and not very surprising) for the language pairs with very little training data but it is also the case for language pairs with slightly more reasonable data sets like Bulgarian-Macedonian. The automatic measures indicate decent translation performances at this stage which encourages their use in pivot translation that we will discuss in the next section.

Furthermore, we can also see the influence of different character alignment algorithms. Somewhat surprisingly, the best results are achieved with IBM alignment models that are not designed for this purpose. Transducer-based alignments produce consistently worse translation models (at least in terms of BLEU scores). The reason for this might be that the IBM models can handle noise in the training data more robustly. However, in terms of unknown words, WFST-based alignment is very competitive and often the best choice (but not much different from the best IBM based models). The use of character bigrams leads to further BLEU improvements for all data sets except Galician-Spanish. However, this data set is extremely small, which may cause unpredictable results. In any case, the differences between character-based alignments and bigram-based ones are rather small and our experiments do not lead to conclusive results.

4.1.2 Pivot Translation

In this section we now look at cascaded translations via the related pivot language. Tables 4 and 5 summarize the results for various settings.

As we can see, the pivot translations for Catalan and Galician outperform the baselines by a large margin. Here, the baselines are, of course, very weak due to the minimal amount of training data. Furthermore, the Catalan-English test set appears to be very easy considering the relatively high BLEU scores achieved even with tiny

Model *(BLEU in %)*	1x1	10x10
English – Catalan (baseline)	26.70	
English – (Spanish = Catalan)	8.38	
English – Spanish -word- Catalan	38.91++	39.59++
English – Spanish -char- Catalan	44.46++	**46.82**++
Catalan – English (baseline)	27.86	
(Catalan = Spanish) – English	9.52	
Catalan -word- Spanish – English	38.41++	38.65++
Catalan -char- Spanish – English	40.43++	**40.73**++
English – Galician (baseline)	—	
English – (Spanish = Galician)	7.46	
English – Spanish -word- Galician	20.55	20.76
English – Spanish -char- Galician	**21.12**	21.09
Galician – English (baseline)	—	
(Galician = Spanish) – English	5.76	
Galician -word- Spanish – English	13.16	13.20
Galician -char- Spanish – English	**16.04**	16.02

Table 4: Translating between Galician/Catalan and English via Spanish using a standard phrase-based SMT baseline, Spanish–English SMT models to translate from/to Catalan/Galician and pivot-based approaches using word-level models or character-level models (based on IBM_{bigram} alignments) with either one-best (1x1) or N-best lists (10x10 with $\alpha = 0.85$).

Model *(BLEU in %)*	1x1	10x10
English – Maced. (baseline)	11.04	
English – Bosn. -word- Maced.	7.33−−	7.64
English – Bosn. -char- Maced.	9.99	10.34
English – Bulg. -word- Maced.	12.49++	**12.62**++
English – Bulg. -char- Maced.	11.57++	11.59+
Maced. – English (baseline)	20.24	
Maced. -word- Bosn. – English	12.36−−	12.48−−
Maced. -char- Bosn. – English	18.73−	18.64−−
Maced. -word- Bulg. – English	19.62	19.74
Maced. -char- Bulg. – English	21.05	**21.10**

Table 5: Translating between Macedonian (Maced) and English via Bosnian (Bosn) / Bulgarian (Bulg).

amounts of training data for the baseline. Still, no test sentence appears in any training or development set for either direct translation or pivot models. From the results, we can also see that Catalan and Galician are quite different from Spanish and require language-specific treatment. Using a large Spanish – English model (with over 30% BLEU in both directions) to translate from or to Catalan or Galician is not an option. The experiments show that character-based pivot models lead to better translations than word-based pivot models (in terms of BLEU scores). This reflects the performance gains presented in Table 2. Rescoring of N-best lists, on the other hand, does not have a big impact on our results. However, we did not spend time optimizing the parameters of N-best size and interpolation weight.

The results from the Macedonian task are not as clear. This is especially due to the different setup in which the baseline uses more training data than any of the related language pivot models. However, we can still see that the pivot translation via Bulgarian clearly outperforms the baseline. For the case of translating to Macedonian via Bulgarian, the word-based model seems to be more robust than the character-level model. This may be due to a larger number of non-words generated by the character-based pivot model. In general, the BLEU scores are much lower for all models involved (even for the high-density languages), which indicates larger problems with the generation of correct output and intermediate translations.

Interesting is the fact that we can achieve almost the same performance as the baseline when translating via Bosnian even though we had much less training data at our disposal for the translation between Macedonian and Bosnian. In this setup, we can see that a character-based model was necessary in order to obtain the desired abstraction from the tiny amount of training data.

4.2 Task 2: Pivoting for Domain Adaptation

Sparse resources are not only a problem for specific languages but also for specific domains. SMT models are very sensitive to domain shifts and domain-specific data is often rare. In the following, we investigate a test case of translating between two languages (English and Norwegian) with reasonable amounts of data resources but in the wrong domain (movie subtitles instead of legal texts). Here again, we facilitate the translation process by a pivot language, this time with domain-specific data.

The task is to translate legal texts from Norwegian (Bokmål) to English and vice versa. The test set is taken from the English–Norwegian Parallel Corpus (ENPC) (Johansson et al., 1996) and contains 1493 parallel sentences (a selection of European treaties, directives and agreements). Otherwise, there is no training data available in this domain for English and Norwegian. Table 6 lists the other data resources we used in our study.

As we can see, there is decent amount of training data for English – Norwegian, but the domain is strikingly different. On the other hand, there

Language pair	*Domain*	#sent's	#words
English–Norwegian	subtitles	2.4M	18M
Norwegian–Danish	subtitles	1.5M	10M
Danish–English	DGT-TM	430k	9M

Table 6: Training data available for the domain adaptation task. DGT-TM refers to the translation memories provided by the JRC (Steinberger et al., 2006)

is in-domain data for other languages like Danish that may act as an intermediate pivot. Furthermore, we have out-of-domain data for the translation between pivot and Norwegian. The sizes of the training data sets for the pivot models are comparable (in terms of words). The in-domain pivot data is controlled and very consistent and, therefore, high quality translations can be expected. The subtitle data is noisy and includes various movie genres. It is important to mention that the pivot data still does not contain any sentence included in the English–Norwegian test set.

Table 7 summarizes the results of our experiments when using Danish and in-domain data as a pivot in translations from and to Norwegian.

Model (task: English – Norwegian)	BLEU
(step 1) English –dgt– Danish	52.76
(step 2) Danish –subs$_{wo}$– Norwegian	29.87
(step 2) Danish –subs$_{ch}$– Norwegian	29.65
(step 2) Danish –subs$_{bi}$– Norwegian	25.65
English –subs– Norwegian (baseline)	7.20
English –dgt– (Danish = Norwegian)	9.44++
English –dgt– Danish -subs$_{wo}$- Norwegian	17.49++
English –dgt– Danish -subs$_{ch}$- Norwegian	**17.61**++
English –dgt– Danish -subs$_{bi}$- Norwegian	14.07++

Model (task: Norwegian – English)	BLEU
(step 1) Norwegian –subs$_{wo}$– Danish	30.15
(step 1) Norwegian –subs$_{ch}$– Danish	27.81
(step 1) Norwegian –subs$_{bi}$– Danish	28.52
(step 2) Danish –dgt– English	57.23
Norwegian –subs– English (baseline)	11.41
(Norwegian = Danish) –dgt– English	13.21++
Norwegian –subs+dgtLM– English	13.33++
Norwegian –subs$_{wo}$– Danish –dgt– English	25.75++
(Norwegian –subs$_{ch}$– Danish –dgt– English	23.77++
Norwegian –subs$_{bi}$– Danish –dgt– English	**26.29**++

Table 7: Translating out-of-domain data via Danish. Models using in-domain data are marked with *dgt* and out-of-domain models are marked with *subs*. *subs+dgtLM* refers to a model with an out-of-domain translation model and an added in-domain language model. The subscripts *wo*, *ch* and *bi* refer to word, character and bigram models, respectively.

The influence of in-domain data in the translation process is enormous. As expected, the out-of-domain baseline does not perform well even though it uses the largest amount of training data in our setup. It is even outperformed by the in-domain pivot model when pretending that Norwegian is in fact Danish. For the translation into English, the in-domain language model helps a little bit (similar resources are not available for the other direction). However, having the strong in-domain model for translating to (and from) the pivot language improves the scores dramatically. The out-of-domain model in the other part of the cascaded translation does not destroy this advantage completely and the overall score is much higher than any other baseline.

In our setup, we used again a closely related language as a pivot. However, this time we had more data available for training the pivot translation model. Naturally, the advantages of the character-level approach diminishes and the word-level model becomes a better alternative. However, there can still be a good reason for the use of a character-based model as we can see in the success of the bigram model (–subs$_{bi}$–) in the translation from Norwegian to English (via Danish). A character-based model may generalize beyond domain-specific terminology which leads to a reduction of unknown words when applied to a new domain. Note that using a character-based model in step two could possibly cause more harm than using it in step one of the pivot-based procedure. Using n-best lists for a subsequent word-based translation in step two may fix errors caused by character-based translation simply by ignoring hypotheses containing them, which makes such a model more robust to noisy input.

Finally, as an alternative, we can also look at other pivot languages. The domain adaptation task is not at all restricted to closely related pivot languages especially considering the success of word-based models in the experiments above. Table 8 lists results for three other pivot languages.

Surprisingly, the results are much worse than for the Danish test case. Apparently, these models are strongly influenced by the out-of-domain translation between Norwegian and the pivot language. The only success can be seen with another closely related language, Swedish. Lexical and syntactic similarity seems to be important to create models that are robust enough for domain shifts in the cascaded translation setup.

Pivot=xx	*en–xx*	*xx–no*	*en–xx–no*
German	53.09	23.60	3.15−−
French	66.47	17.84	5.03−−
Swedish	52.62	24.79	**10.07**++
Pivot=xx	*no–xx*	*xx–en*	*no–xx–en*
German	15.02	53.02	5.52−−
French	17.69	65.85	8.78−−
Swedish	19.72	59.55	**16.35**++

Table 8: Alternative word-based pivot translations between Norwegian (no) and English (en).

5 Related Work

There is a wide range of pivot language approaches to machine translation and a number of strategies have been proposed. One of them is often called *triangulation* and usually refers to the combination of phrase tables (Cohn and Lapata, 2007). Phrase translation probabilities are merged and lexical weights are estimated by bridging word alignment models (Wu and Wang, 2007; Bertoldi et al., 2008). Cascaded translation via pivot languages are discussed by (Utiyama and Isahara, 2007) and are frequently used by various researchers (de Gispert and Mariño, 2006; Koehn et al., 2009; Wu and Wang, 2009) and commercial systems such as Google Translate. A third strategy is to generate or augment data sets with the help of pivot models. This is, for example, explored by (de Gispert and Mariño, 2006) and (Wu and Wang, 2009) (who call it the *synthetic method*). Pivoting has also been used for paraphrasing and lexical adaptation (Bannard and Callison-Burch, 2005; Crego et al., 2010). (Nakov and Ng, 2009) investigate pivot languages for resource-poor languages (but only when translating from the resource-poor language). They also use transliteration for adapting models to a new (related) language. Character-level SMT has been used for transliteration (Matthews, 2007; Tiedemann and Nabende, 2009) and also for the translation between closely related languages (Vilar et al., 2007; Tiedemann, 2009a).

6 Conclusions and Discussion

In this paper, we have discussed possibilities to translate via pivot languages on the character level. These models are useful to support under-resourced languages and explore strong lexical and syntactic similarities between closely related languages. Such an approach makes it possible to train reasonable translation models even with extremely sparse data sets. Moreover, character level models introduce an abstraction that reduce the number of unknown words dramatically. In most cases, these unknown words represent information-rich units that bear large portions of the meaning to be translated. The following illustrates this effect on example translations with and without pivot model:

Example: Catalan – English (via Spanish)

Reference:	I have to grade these papers.
Baseline:	Tincque qualificar these exàmens.
$Pivot_{word}$:	Tincque qualificar these tests.
$Pivot_{char}$:	I have to grade these papers.

Example: Macedonian – English (via Bulgarian)

Reference:	It's a simple matter of self-preservation.
Baseline:	It's simply a question of себесочувување.
$Pivot_{word}$:	That's a matter of себесочувување.
$Pivot_{char}$:	It's just a question of yourself.

Leaving unseen words untranslated is not only annoying (especially if the input language uses a different writing system) but often makes translations completely incomprehensible. Pivot translations will still not be perfect (see example two above), but can at least be more intelligible. Character-based models can even take care of tokenization errors as the one shown above ("Tincque" should be two words "Tinc que"). Fortunately, the generation of non-word sequences (observed as unknown words) does not seem to be a big problem and no special treatment is required to avoid such output. We would still like to address this issue in future work by adding a word level LM in character-based SMT. However, (Vilar et al., 2007) already showed that this did not have any positive effect in their character-based system. In a second study, we also showed that pivot models can be useful for adapting to a new domain. The use of in-domain pivot data leads to systems that outperform out-of-domain translation models by a large margin. Our findings point to many prospects for future work. For example, we would like to investigate combinations of character-based and word-based models. Character-based models may also be used for treating unknown words only. Multiple source approaches via several pivots is another possibility to be explored. Finally, we also need to further investigate the robustness of the approach with respect to other language pairs, data sets and learning parameters.

References

Colin Bannard and Chris Callison-Burch. 2005. Paraphrasing with bilingual parallel corpora. In *Proceedings of the 43rd Annual Meeting of the Association for Computational Linguistics (ACL'05)*, pages 597–604, Ann Arbor, Michigan, June. Association for Computational Linguistics.

Nicola Bertoldi, Madalina Barbaiani, Marcello Federico, and Roldano Cattoni. 2008. Phrase-Based Statistical Machine Translation with Pivot Languages. In *Proceedings of the International Workshop on Spoken Language Translation*, pages 143–149, Hawaii, USA.

Trevor Cohn and Mirella Lapata. 2007. Machine translation by triangulation: Making effective use of multi-parallel corpora. In *Proceedings of the 45th Annual Meeting of the Association of Computational Linguistics*, pages 728–735, Prague, Czech Republic, June. Association for Computational Linguistics.

Josep Maria Crego, Aurélien Max, and François Yvon. 2010. Local lexical adaptation in machine translation through triangulation: SMT helping SMT. In *Proceedings of the 23rd International Conference on Computational Linguistics (Coling 2010)*, pages 232–240, Beijing, China, August. Coling 2010 Organizing Committee.

A. de Gispert and J.B. Mariño. 2006. Catalan-english statistical machine translation without parallel corpus: Bridging through spanish. In *Proceedings of the 5th Workshop on Strategies for developing Machine Translation for Minority Languages (SALTMIL'06) at LREC*, pages 65–68, Genova, Italy.

Mark Fishel and Harri Kirik. 2010. Linguistically motivated unsupervised segmentation for machine translation. In *Proceedings of the International Conference on Language Resources and Evaluation (LREC)*, pages 1741–1745, Valletta, Malta.

Mark Fishel. 2009. Deeper than words: Morph-based alignment for statistical machine translation. In *Proceedings of the Conference of the Pacific Association for Computational Linguistics PacLing 2009*, Sapporo, Japan.

Sittichai Jiampojamarn, Grzegorz Kondrak, and Tarek Sherif. 2007. Applying many-to-many alignments and hidden markov models to letter-to-phoneme conversion. In *Human Language Technologies 2007: The Conference of the North American Chapter of the Association for Computational Linguistics; Proceedings of the Main Conference*, pages 372–379, Rochester, New York, April. Association for Computational Linguistics.

Stig Johansson, Jarle Ebeling, and Knut Hofland. 1996. Coding and aligning the English-Norwegian Parallel Corpus. In K. Aijmer, B. Altenberg, and M. Johansson, editors, *Languages in Contrast*, pages 87–112. Lund University Press.

Philipp Koehn, Franz Josef Och, and Daniel Marcu. 2003. Statistical phrase-based translation. In *Proceedings of the 2003 Conference of the North American Chapter of the Association for Computational Linguistics on Human Language Technology - Volume 1*, NAACL '03, pages 48–54, Stroudsburg, PA, USA. Association for Computational Linguistics.

Philipp Koehn, Hieu Hoang, Alexandra Birch, Chris Callison-Burch, Marcello Federico, Nicola Bertoldi, Brooke Cowan, Wade Shen, Christine Moran, Richard Zens, Chris Dyer, Ondrej Bojar, Alexandra Constantin, and Evan Herbst. 2007. Moses: Open source toolkit for statistical machine translation. In *Proceedings of the 45th Annual Meeting of the Association for Computational Linguistics Companion Volume Proceedings of the Demo and Poster Sessions*, pages 177–180, Prague, Czech Republic, June. Association for Computational Linguistics.

Philipp Koehn, Alexandra Birch, and Ralf Steinberger. 2009. 462 machine translation systems for europe. In *Proceedings of MT Summit XII*, pages 65–72, Ottawa, Canada.

Minh-Thang Luong, Preslav Nakov, and Min-Yen Kan. 2010. A hybrid morpheme-word representation for machine translation of morphologically rich languages. In *Proceedings of the 2010 Conference on Empirical Methods in Natural Language Processing*, pages 148–157, Cambridge, MA, October. Association for Computational Linguistics.

David Matthews. 2007. Machine transliteration of proper names. Master's thesis, School of Informatics, University of Edinburgh.

Preslav Nakov and Hwee Tou Ng. 2009. Improved statistical machine translation for resource-poor languages using related resource-rich languages. In *Proceedings of the 2009 Conference on Empirical Methods in Natural Language Processing*, pages 1358–1367, Singapore, August. Association for Computational Linguistics.

Franz Josef Och and Hermann Ney. 2003. A systematic comparison of various statistical alignment models. *Computational Linguistics*, 29(1):19–51.

Franz Josef Och. 2003. Minimum error rate training in statistical machine translation. In *Proceedings of the 41st Annual Meeting of the Association for Computational Linguistics*, pages 160–167, Sapporo, Japan, July. Association for Computational Linguistics.

Eric Sven Ristad and Peter N. Yianilos. 1998. Learning string edit distance. *IEEE Transactions on Pattern Recognition and Machine Intelligence*, 20(5):522–532, May.

Ralf Steinberger, Bruno Pouliquen, Anna Widiger, Camelia Ignat, Tomaž Erjavec, and Dan Tufiş. 2006. The JRC-Acquis: A multilingual aligned parallel corpus with 20+ languages. In *Proceedings of the 5th International Conference on Language Resources and Evaluation (LREC)*, pages 2142–2147.

Graham A. Stephen. 1992. String Search. Technical report, School of Electronic Engineering Science, University College of North Wales, Gwynedd.

Jörg Tiedemann and Peter Nabende. 2009. Translating transliterations. *International Journal of Computing and ICT Research*, 3(1):33–41.

Jörg Tiedemann. 2009a. Character-based PSMT for closely related languages. In *Proceedings of 13th Annual Conference of the European Association for Machine Translation (EAMT'09)*, pages 12 – 19, Barcelona, Spain.

Jörg Tiedemann. 2009b. News from OPUS - A collection of multilingual parallel corpora with tools and interfaces. In *Recent Advances in Natural Language Processing*, volume V, pages 237–248. John Benjamins, Amsterdam/Philadelphia.

Masao Utiyama and Hitoshi Isahara. 2007. A comparison of pivot methods for phrase-based statistical machine translation. In *Human Language Technologies 2007: The Conference of the North American Chapter of the Association for Computational Linguistics; Proceedings of the Main Conference*, pages 484–491, Rochester, New York, April. Association for Computational Linguistics.

David Vilar, Jan-Thorsten Peter, and Hermann Ney. 2007. Can we translate letters? In *Proceedings of the Second Workshop on Statistical Machine Translation*, pages 33–39, Prague, Czech Republic, June. Association for Computational Linguistics.

Hua Wu and Haifeng Wang. 2007. Pivot language approach for phrase-based statistical machine translation. In *Proceedings of the 45th Annual Meeting of the Association of Computational Linguistics*, pages 856–863, Prague, Czech Republic, June. Association for Computational Linguistics.

Hua Wu and Haifeng Wang. 2009. Revisiting pivot language approach for machine translation. In *Proceedings of the Joint Conference of the 47th Annual Meeting of the ACL and the 4th International Joint Conference on Natural Language Processing of the AFNLP*, pages 154–162, Suntec, Singapore, August. Association for Computational Linguistics.

Does more data always yield better translations?

Guillem Gascó, Martha-Alicia Rocha, Germán Sanchis-Trilles,
Jesús Andrés-Ferrer and Francisco Casacuberta
Departament de Sistemes Informàtics i Computació
Universitat Politècnica de València
Camí de Vera s/n, 46022 València, Spain
{ggasco,mrocha,gsanchis,jandres,fcn}@dsic.upv.es

Abstract

Nowadays, there are large amounts of data available to train statistical machine translation systems. However, it is not clear whether all the training data actually help or not. A system trained on a subset of such huge bilingual corpora might outperform the use of all the bilingual data. This paper studies such issues by analysing two training data selection techniques: one based on approximating the probability of an in-domain corpus; and another based on infrequent n-gram occurrence. Experimental results not only report significant improvements over random sentence selection but also an improvement over a system trained with the whole available data. Surprisingly, the improvements are obtained with just a small fraction of the data that accounts for less than 0.5% of the sentences. Afterwards, we show that a much larger room for improvement exists, although this is done under non-realistic conditions.

1 Introduction

Globalisation and the popularisation of the Internet have lead to a rapid increase in the amount of bilingual corpora available. Entities such as the European Union, the United Nations and other multinational organisations need to translate all the documentation they generate. Such translations happen every day and provide very large multilingual corpora, which are oftentimes difficult to process and significantly increase the computational requirements needed to train statistical machine translation (SMT) systems. For instance, the corpora made available for recent machine translation evaluations are in the order of 1 billion running words (Callison-Burch et al., 2010).

However, two main problems arise when attempting to use this huge pool of sentences for training SMT systems: firstly, a large portion of this data is obtained from domains that differ from that in which the SMT system is to be used or assessed; secondly, the use of all this data for training the system increases the computational training requirements. Despite the previous remarks, the *de facto* standard consists in training SMT systems with all the available data. This is due to the widespread misconception that the more data a system is trained with, the better its performance should be. Although the previous statement is theoretically true if all the data belongs to the same domain, this is not the case in the problems tackled by most of the SMT systems. For instance, enterprises often need to build on-demand systems (Yuste et al., 2010). In this case, since we are interested in translating some specific text, it is not clear whether training a system with all data yields better performance than training it with a wisely selected subset of bilingual sentences.

The *bilingual sentence selection (BSS)* task is stated as the problem of selecting the best subset of bilingual sentences from an available *pool of sentences*, with which to train a SMT system. This paper is concerned to BSS, and mainly two ideas are developed.

On the one hand, two BSS strategies that attempt to build better translation systems are analysed. Such strategies are able to improve state-of-the-art translation quality without the very high computational resources that are required when using the complete pool of sentences. Both techniques span through two orthogonal criteria when selecting bilingual sentences from the available pool: avoiding to introduce a bias in the original data distribution, and increasing the informativeness of the corpus.

On the other hand, we prove that among all possible subsets from the sentence pool, there is at least a small one that yields large improvements (up to 10 BLEU points) with respect to a system trained with all the data. In order to retrieve such subset, we had to use an oracle that employs information extracted from the reference translations only for the purpose of selecting bilingual sentences. However, references are not used at any stage within the translation system for obtaining the hypotheses. Note that although we are not able to achieve such an improvement without an oracle, this result restates the BSS problem as an interesting approach not only for reducing computational effort but also for significantly boosting performance. To our knowledge, no previous work has quantified the room of improvement in which BSS techniques could incur.

In order to assess the performance of the different BSS techniques, translation results are obtained by using a standard state-of-the-art SMT system (Koehn et al., 2007). The most recent literature defines the SMT problem (Papineni et al., 1998; Och and Ney, 2002) as follows: given an input sentence $\mathbf{f}$ from a certain source language, the purpose is to find an output sentence $\hat{\mathbf{e}}$ in a certain target language such that

$$\hat{\mathbf{e}} = \arg\max_{\mathbf{e}} \sum_{k=1}^{K} \lambda_k h_k(\mathbf{f}, \mathbf{e}) \qquad (1)$$

where $h_k(\mathbf{f}, \mathbf{e})$ is a score function representing an important feature for the translation of $\mathbf{f}$ into $\mathbf{e}$, as for example the language model of the target language, a reordering model or several translation models. λ_k are the log-linear combination weights.

The main contributions of this paper are:

- A BSS technique is analysed, which improves the results obtained with a random bilingual sentence selection strategy when the specific domain to be translated significantly differs from that of the pool of sentences.
- Another BSS technique is analysed that, using less than 0.5% of the sentences available, significantly improves over random selection, beating a system trained with all the pool of sentences.
- We prove, by means of an oracle, that a wise BSS technique can yield large improvements when compared with systems trained with all data available.

The remaining of the paper is structured as follows. Section 2 summarises the related work. Sections 3 and 4 present two BSS techniques, namely, probabilistic sampling and recovery of infrequent n-grams. In Section 5 experimental results are reported. Finally, the main results of the work and several future work directions are discussed in Section 6.

2 Related Work

Training data selection has been receiving an increasing amount of attention within the SMT community. For instance, in (Li et al., 2010; Gascó et al., 2010) several BSS techniques, similar to those analysed in this paper, have been applied for training MT systems when there are large training corpora available. However, neither such techniques have been formalised, nor its performance thoroughly analysed. A similar approach that gives weights to different subcorpora was proposed in (Matsoukas et al., 2009).

In (Lu et al., 2007), information retrieval methods are used in order to produce different submodels which are then weighted according to the sentence to be translated. In such work, authors define the baseline as the result obtained training only with the corpus that share the same domain of the test. Afterwards they claim that they are able to improve baseline translation quality by adding new sentences retrieved with their method. However, they neither compare their technique with random sentence selection, nor with a model trained with all the corpora.

Although the techniques that are applied for BSS are often very similar to those applied for active learning (AL), both problems are essentially different. Since the AL strategies assume that the pool of sentences are not translated, they are usually interested in finding the best monolingual subset of sentences to be translated by a human annotator. In contrast, in BSS, it is assumed that a fairly large amount of bilingual corpora is readily available, and the main goal consists in selecting only those sentences which will maximise system performance.

Some works have applied sentence selection in small scale AL frameworks. These works extend the training corpora at most with 5000 sentences. In (Ananthakrishnan et al., 2010), sentences are selected by means of discriminative techniques. In (Haffari et al., 2009) a technique is proposed for increasing the counts of phrases that are considered infrequent. Both works significantly differ from the current work not only on the framework, but also on the scale of the experiments, the proposed techniques and the obtained improvements. Similar ideas applied to adaptation problems have been proposed in (Moore and Lewis, 2010; Axelrod et al., 2011).

3 Probabilistic Sampling

As discussed in Section 2, BSS has inherently attached many meaningful links with AL techniques. Selecting samples for learning our models, incurs in a well-known difficulty in AL, the so-called *sample bias* problem (Dasgupta, 2009). This problem, which is spread to the BSS case, is summarised as the distortion introduced by the active strategy into the probability distribution underlying the training corpus. This bias forces the training algorithm to learn a distorted probability model which can significantly differ from the actual one.

In order to further analyse the sampling bias problem, consider the maximum likelihood estimation (MLE) of a probability model, $p_\theta(\mathbf{e}, \mathbf{f})$ for a given corpus of N data points,$\{(\mathbf{e}_n, \mathbf{f}_n)\}$, sampled from the actual probability distribution, $\Pr(\mathbf{e}, \mathbf{f})$. Recall that $\mathbf{e}$ denotes a target sentence whereas $\mathbf{f}$ stands for its source counterpart. MLE techniques aims at minimising the Kullback-Leibler divergence between the actual unknown probability distribution and the probability model (Bishop, 2006), defined as

$$\mathrm{KL}(\Pr \mid p_\theta) = \sum_{\mathbf{e},\mathbf{f}} \Pr(\mathbf{e}, \mathbf{f}) \log \left(\frac{\Pr(\mathbf{e}, \mathbf{f})}{p_\theta(\mathbf{e}, \mathbf{f})} \right) \tag{2}$$

When minimising, Eq. (2) is simplified to

$$\hat{\theta} = \arg\max_\theta \sum_{\mathbf{e},\mathbf{f}} \Pr(\mathbf{e}, \mathbf{f}) \log(p_\theta(\mathbf{e}, \mathbf{f})) \tag{3}$$

which is approximated by a sufficiently large dataset under the commonly hold assumption that it is independently and identically distributed according to $\Pr(\mathbf{e}, \mathbf{f})$ as

$$\hat{\theta} = \arg\max_\theta \sum_n \log(p_\theta(\mathbf{e}_n, \mathbf{f}_n)) \tag{4}$$

Therefore, by perturbing the sample $\{(\mathbf{e}_n, \mathbf{f}_n)\}$ with an active strategy, we are, in fact, modifying the approximation to Eq.(3) and learning a different underlying probability distribution.

In this section a statistical framework is proposed to build systems with BSS while avoiding the sample bias. The proposed approach relies in conserving the probability distribution of the task domain by wisely selecting the bilingual pairs to be used from the whole pool of sentences. Hence, it is mandatory to exclude sentences from the pool that distort the actual probability. In order to approximate the probability distribution, we assume that a small but representative corpus is available from the task domain. This corpus, referred henceforth as the *in-domain corpus*, provides a way to build an initial model which approximates the actual probability of the system. The pool of sentences will be oppositely denoted as the *out-of-domain corpus*.

The actual probability of the task domain, the so called *in-domain* probability, is approximated with the following model

$$p(\mathbf{e}, \mathbf{f}, |\mathbf{e}|, |\mathbf{f}|) = p(\mathbf{e}, \mathbf{f} \mid |\mathbf{e}|, |\mathbf{f}|) \cdot p(|\mathbf{e}|, |\mathbf{f}|) \tag{5}$$

where $p(|\mathbf{e}|, |\mathbf{f}|)$ denotes the in-domain length probability, and $p(\mathbf{e}, \mathbf{f} \mid |\mathbf{e}|, |\mathbf{f}|)$ the in-domain bilingual probability.

The length probability is estimated by MLE

$$p(|\mathbf{e}|, |\mathbf{f}|) = \frac{N(|\mathbf{e}| + |\mathbf{f}|)}{N} \tag{6}$$

where $N(|\mathbf{e}|+|\mathbf{f}|)$ is the number of bilingual pairs in the in-domain corpus such that their lengths sum up to $|\mathbf{e}|+|\mathbf{f}|$ and N denotes the total number of sentences. Note that no distinction is made between source and target lengths since the model is intended for sampling.

The complexity of the in-domain bilingual probability distribution, $p(\mathbf{e}, \mathbf{f} \mid |\mathbf{e}|, |\mathbf{f}|)$, requires a more sophisticated approximation

$$p(\mathbf{e}, \mathbf{f} / |\mathbf{e}|, |\mathbf{f}|) = \frac{\exp(\sum_k \gamma_k f_k(\mathbf{e}, \mathbf{f}))}{\mathcal{Z}} \tag{7}$$

being $\mathcal{Z}$ a normalisation constant; and where $f_k(\ldots)$ and γ_k are the features of the model and their respective parametric weights. Specifically, four logarithmic features were considered for this sampling technique: a direct and an inverse IBM model 4 (Brown et al., 1994); and both, source and target, 5-gram language models. All feature models are estimated in the in-domain corpus with standard techniques (Brown et al., 1994; Stolcke, 2002). As a first approach, the parameters of the log-linear model in Eq. (7), γ_k, were uniformly fixed to 1.

Once we have an appropriate model for the in-domain probability distribution, the proposed method randomly samples a given number of bilingual pairs from the out-of-domain corpora (the pool of sentences). The process of extending the in-domain corpus with additional bilingual pairs from the out-of-domain corpus is summarised as follows:

- Decide according to the in-domain length probability in Eq. (6), how many samples should be drawn for each length, i.e. divide the number of sentences to add into length dependent buckets.
- Randomly draw the number of samples specified in each bucket according to the in-domain bilingual probability in Eq. (7) among all the bilingual sentences that share the current bucket length.

Although the pool of sentences is typically large, it is not large enough to gather a significant amount of probability mass. Consequently, a small set of sentences accumulate most of the probability mass and tend to be selected multiple times. To avoid this awkward and undesired behaviour, the sampling is performed *without replacement*.

4 Infrequent n-gram Recovery

Another criterion when confronting the BSS task is to increase the informativeness of the training set. Thus, it seems important to choose sentences that provide information not seen in the training corpus. Note that this criterion is sometimes opposed to the one presented in Section 3.

The performance of phrase-based machine translation systems strongly relies in the quality of the phrases extracted from the training samples. In most of the cases, the inference of such phrases or rules is based on word alignments, which cannot be computed accurately when appearing rarely in the training corpus. The extreme case are the out-of-vocabulary words: words that do not appear in the training set, cannot be translated. Moreover, this problem can be extended to sequences of words (n-grams). Consider a 2-gram $f_i f_j$ appearing few or no times in the training set. Although f_i and f_j may appear separately in the training set, the system might not be able to infer the translation of the 2-gram $f_i f_j$, which may be different from the concatenation of the translations of both words separately.

When selecting sentences from the pool it is important to choose sentences that contain n-grams that have never been seen (or have been seen just a few times) in the training set. Such n-grams will be henceforth referred to as *infrequent n-grams* . An n-gram is considered infrequent when it appears less times than an infrequent threshold t. If the source language sentences to be translated are known beforehand, the set of infrequent n-grams can be reduced to those present in such sentences. Then, the technique consists in selecting from the pool those sentences which contain infrequent n-grams present in the source sentences to be translated.

Sentences in the pool are sorted by their infrequency score in order to select first the most informative. Let $\mathcal{X}$ the set of n-grams that appear in the sentences to be translated and $\mathbf{w}$ one of them; $C(\mathbf{w})$ the counts of $\mathbf{w}$ in the source language training set; and $N(\mathbf{w})$ the counts of $\mathbf{w}$ in the source sentence $\mathbf{f}$ to be scored. The infrequency score of $\mathbf{f}$ is:

$$i(\mathbf{f}) = \sum_{\mathbf{w} \in \mathcal{X}} \min(1, N(\mathbf{w})) \max(0, t - C(\mathbf{w})) \quad (8)$$

In order to avoid giving a high score to noisy sentences with a lot of occurrences of the same infrequent n-gram, only one occurrence of each n-gram is taken into account to compute the score. In addition, the score gives more importance to the n-grams with lowest counts in the training set. Although it could be possible to select the highest scored sentences, we updated the scores each time a sentence is selected. This decision was taken to avoid the selection of too many sentences with the same infrequent n-gram. First, sentences in the pool are scored using Equation (8). Then, in each iteration, the sentence $\mathbf{f}^*$ with the highest score is selected, added to the training set and removed from the pool. In addition, the counts of the n-grams present in $\mathbf{f}^*$ are updated and, hence, the scores of the rest of the sentences in the pool. Since rescoring the whole pool would incur in a very high computational cost, a suboptimal search strategy was followed, in which the search was constrained to a given set of highest scoring sentences. Here it was set to one million.

	$t=1$		$t=10$		$t=25$	
	tr	all	tr	all	tr	all
1-gr	11.6	1.3	40.5	3.5	59.9	5.1
2-gr	38	9.8	73.2	21.3	84.9	27.9
3-gr	66.8	33.5	91.1	55.7	96.4	64.9
4-gr	87.1	65.8	98.2	85.5	99.4	90.7

Table 1: Percentage of infrequent n-grams in the TED test set when considering only the TED training set (`tr`), and when adding the out-of-domain pool (`all`), for different infrequency thresholds t.

Table 1 shows the percentage of source language infrequent n-grams for the test of a relatively small corpus such as the TED corpus (for details see Section 5) when considering just the in-domain training set ($\approx 40K$ sentences) and the same percentage when adding the larger out of domain corpora. The percentages in the table have been computed separately for different values of the threshold t and for n-grams of order from 1 to 4. Note that the reduction in the number of infrequent n-grams is very high for the 1-grams but decreases progressively when considering n-grams of higher order. This indicates that the infrequent n-grams recovery technique should be very effective for lower order n-grams, but might have less effect for higher order n-grams. Therefore, and in order to lower the computational cost involved, the experiments carried out for this paper were performed considering only infrequent 1-grams, 2-grams and 3-grams.

5 Experiments

In the present Section, we first describe the experimental framework employed to assess the performance of the BSS techniques described. Then, results for the probabilistic sentence selection strategy are shown, followed by results obtained with the infrequent n-grams technique. Some example translations are shown and, finally, we also report experiments using the infrequent n-grams technique in Oracle mode, in order to establish the potential improvement for such technique and for BSS in general.

5.1 Experimental Setup

All experiments were carried out using the open-source SMT toolkit Moses (Koehn et al., 2007), in its standard non-monotonic configuration. The phrase tables were generated by means of symmetrised word alignments obtained with GIZA++ (Och and Ney, 2003). The language model used was a 5-gram with modified Kneser-Ney smoothing (Kneser and Ney, 1995), built with SRILM toolkit (Stolcke, 2002). The log-linear combination weights in Eq. (1) were optimised using Minimum Error Rate Training (Och and Ney, 2002) on the corresponding development sets.

Subset	Language	$\lvert S\rvert$	$\lvert W\rvert$	$\lvert V\rvert$
train	English	47.5K	747K	24.6K
	French		793K	31.7K
dev	English	571	9.2K	1.9K
	French		10.3K	2.2K
test	English	641	12.6K	2.4K
	French		12.8K	2.7K

Table 2: TED corpus main figures. K denotes thousands of elements. $|S|$ stands for number of sentences, $|W|$ for number of running words, and $|V|$ for vocabulary size.

Subset	Language	$\lvert S\rvert$	$\lvert W\rvert$	$\lvert V\rvert$
train	English	77.2K	1.71M	29.9K
	French		1.99M	48K
dev 08	English	2.1K	49.8K	8.7K
	French		55.4K	7.7K
test 09	English	2.5K	65.6K	8.9K
	French		72.5K	10.6K
test 10	English	2.5K	62K	8.9K
	French		70.5K	10.3K

Table 3: News Commentary corpus main figures.

Experiments were carried out on two corpora: TED (Paul et al., 2010) and News Commentary (NC) (Callison-Burch et al., 2010). TED is an English-French corpus composed of subtitles for a collection of public speeches on a variety of topics. The same partitions as in the IWSLT2010 evaluation task (Paul et al., 2010) have been used. Subtitles have been concatenated into complete sentences. NC is a slightly larger English-French corpus in the news domain. Main figures of both corpora are shown in Tables 2 and 3. As for the pool of sentences, three large corpora have been used: Europarl (Euro), United Nations (UN) and Gigaword (Giga), in the partition established for the 2010 workshop on SMT of the ACL (Callison-Burch et al., 2010). Sentences of length greater than 50 have been pruned. Table 4 shows the main figures of the tokenised and lowercased corpora.

When translating between some language pairs, there are words that remain invariable, like for example numbers or punctuation marks in the case of European languages. In fact, an easy and

Corpus	Language	$\|S\|$	$\|W\|$	$\|V\|$
Euro	English	1.25M	25.6M	81K
	French		28.2M	101K
UN	English	5M	94.4M	302K
	French		107M	283K
Giga	English	15.5M	303M	1.6M
	French		361M	1.6M

Table 4: Figures of the corpora used as sentence pool. M stands for millions of elements.

effective technique that is commonly used is to reproduce out-of-vocabulary words from the source sentence in the target hypothesis. However, invariable n-grams are usually infrequent as well, which implies that the infrequent n-grams technique would select sentences containing such n-grams, even though they do not provide further information. As a first approach, we exclude n-grams without any letter.

Baseline experiments have been carried out for TED and NC corpora using the corresponding training set. For comparison purposes, we also included results for a purely random sentence selection without replacement. In the plots, each point corresponding to random selection represent the average of 10 repetitions. Experiments using all data are also reported, although a 64GB machine was necessary, even with binarized phrase and distortion tables.

Experiments were conducted by selecting a fixed amount of sentences according to each one of the techniques described above. Then, these sentences were included into the training data and subsequent SMT systems were built for translating the test set.

Results are shown in terms of BLEU (Papineni et al., 2001), which is an accuracy metric that measures n-gram precision, with a penalty for sentences that are too short. Although it could be argued that improvements obtained might be due to a side effect of the brevity penalty, this was not found to be true: the BSS techniques (including random) and considering all data yielded very similar brevity penalties (± 0.005), within each corpus. In addition, TER scores (Snover et al., 2006) were also computed, but are omitted for clarity purposes and since they were found to be coherent with BLEU. TER is an error metric that computes the minimum number of edits required to modify the system hypotheses so that they match the references translations.

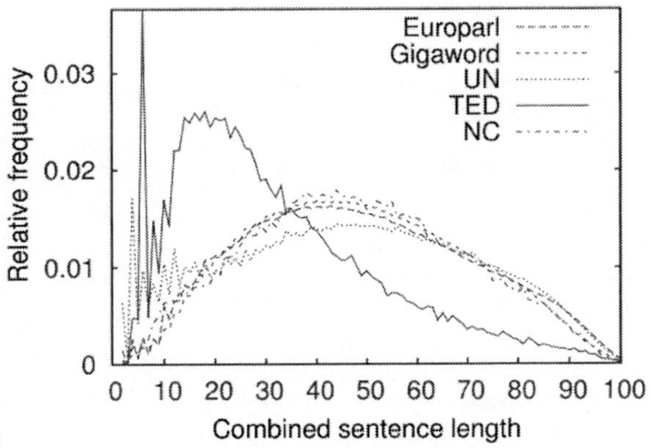

Figure 2: Combined length relative frequency.

5.2 Results for Probabilistic Sampling

In addition to the probabilistic sampling technique proposed in Section 3, we also analysed the effect of sampling only according to the combined source-reference length, with the purpose of establishing whether potential improvements were only due to the length component, or rather to the complete sampling model. Results for the 2009 test set are shown in Figure 1. Several things should be noted:

- Performing sentence selection only according to sentence lengths does not achieve better performance than random selection.
- Selecting sentences according to probabilistic sampling is able to improve random selection in the case of the TED corpus, but is not able to do so in the case of the NC corpus. Significance tests for the 500K case reported that the differences were significant in the case of the TED corpus, but not in the case of the NC corpus.
- In the case of the TED corpus, the performance achieved with the system built by sampling 500K sentences is only 0.5 BLEU points below the performance achieved by the system built with all the data available.

The explanation to the fact that probabilistic sampling is able to improve over random sampling only in the case of the TED corpus, but not in the case of NC, relies in the nature of the corpora. Although both of them belong to a very generic domain, their characteristics are very different. In fact, the NC data is very similar to the sentences in the pool, but, in contrast, the sentences present in the TED corpus have a much more different structure. This difference is illustrated in Figure 2, where the relative frequency of

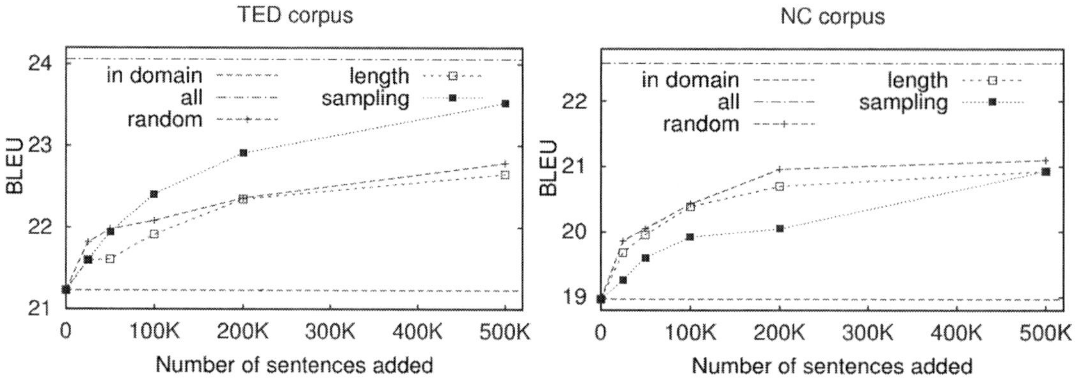

Figure 1: Effect of adding sentences over the BLEU score using the probabilistic sampling, length sampling and random selection techniques for the two corpora, TED and News Commentary. Horizontal lines represent the scores when using just the in domain training set and all the data available.

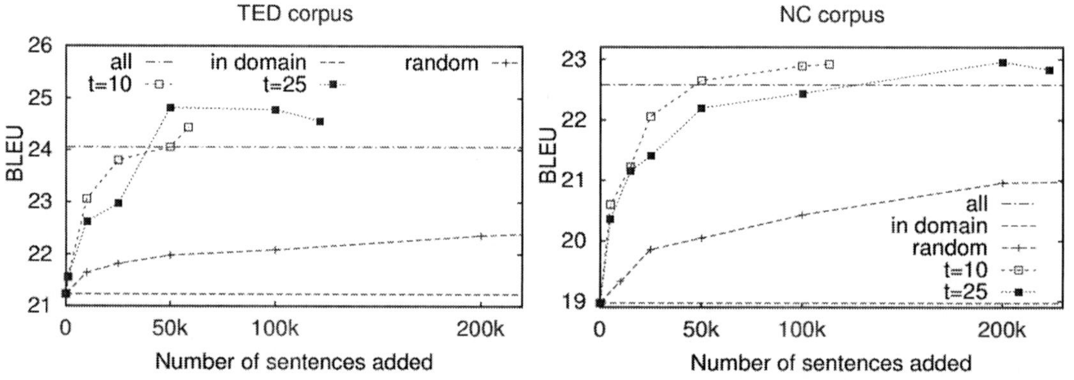

Figure 3: Effect of adding sentences over the BLEU score using the infrequent n-grams (with different thresholds) and random selection techniques for the two corpora, TED and News Commentary. Horizontal lines represent the scores when using just the in domain training set and all the data available.

each combined sentence length is shown. In this plot, it stands out clearly that the TED corpus has a very different length distribution than the other four corpora considered, whereas the NC corpus presents a very similar distribution. This implies that, when considering TED, an intelligent data selection strategy will have better chances to improve random selection than in the case of NC.

5.3 Results for Infrequent n-grams Recovery

Figure 3 shows the effect of adding sentences using the infrequent n-grams and the random selection techniques on the 2009 test set. Once all the infrequent n-grams have been covered t times, the infrequency score for all the sentences remaining in the pool is 0, and none of them can be selected. Hence, the number of sentences that can be selected for each t is limited. Although for clarity we only show results for $t = \{10, 25\}$, experiments have also been carried out for $t = \{1, 5, 10, 25\}$. Such results presented similar curves, although less sentences can be selected and hence improvements obtained are slightly lower. Several conclusions can be drawn:

- The translation quality provided by the infrequent n-grams technique is significantly better than the results achieved with random selection, comparing similar amount of sentences. Specifically, the improvements obtained are in the range of 3 BLEU points.
- Results for the TED corpus are more irregular. The best performance is achieved for $t = 25$ and 50K sentences added. In NC, the best result is for $t = 10$ and 112K.
- Selecting sentences with the infrequent n-grams technique provides better results than including all the available data. While using less than 0.5% of the data, improvements between 0.5 and 1 BLEU points are achieved.

When looking at Figure 3, one might suspect that t needs to be set specifically for a given test set, and that results from one set are not to be extrapolated to other test sets. For this reason, we selected the best configuration in Figure 3 and used it to build a new system for translating the unseen NC 2010 test set. Such experiment, with $t = 10$ and including all sentences with score greater than 0 ($\approx$ 110K), is shown in Table 5 and evidences that improvements are actually coherent among different test sets.

technique	BLEU	TER	#phrases
in-domain	19.0	65.2	5.1M
all data	22.7	60.8	1236M
infreq. $t = 10$	23.6	59.2	16.5M

Table 5: Effect of the infrequent n-gram recovery technique for an unseen test set, when setting $t = 10$ and number of phrases (parameters) of the models.

5.4 Oracle Results

In order to analyse the potential of BSS techniques, the infrequent n-grams recovery technique in Section 4 was implemented in oracle mode. In this way, sentences from the pool were selected according to the infrequent n-grams present in the *reference* translations of the test set. Note that test references were not included into the training data as such, but were rather used to establish which bilingual sentences within the pool were best suitable for training the SMT system. In this way, we were able to establish the potential for improvement of a BSS technique. Interestingly, the SMT system trained in this way achieved 31 BLEU points on the News Commentary 2009 test set, i.e. an 8 BLEU points improvement over the system trained with all the data available. This result would have beaten all the systems that took part in the 2009 Workshop on Machine translation (Callison-Burch et al., 2009). This result is really important: although we are aware that the sentences were selected in a non-realistic manner, it proves that an appropriate BSS technique would be able to boost SMT performance in a very significant manner. Similar results were obtained with the TED and NC 2010 test sets, with 10 and 7 points improvement, respectively.

5.5 Example Translations

Example translations are shown in Figure 4. In the first example, the baseline system is not able to translate *criticised*, which is considered out-of-vocabulary. Even though random selection is able to solve this problem (luckily), it does not achieve to translate it correctly, introducing a concordance error. A similar thing happens when using probabilistic sampling, where a grammatical error is also present, and only `Infr` and `All` are able to present a correct translation. This is not only casual, since, by ensuring that a given n-gram appears at least a certain number of times t, the odds of including all possible translations of *criticised* are incremented significantly. Note that, even if the `Infr` translation is different from the reference, it is equally correct. In the second example, the baseline translation is pretty much correct, but has a different meaning (something like "and one has music"). Similarly, when including all data the translation obtained by the system means "and some music". In this case, both random and probabilistic selection present grammatically incorrect sentences, and only `Infr` is able to provide a correct translation, although pretty literal and different from the reference.

Src	the budget has also been criticised by klaus .
Bsl	le budget a également été criticised par m. klaus .
Rdm	le budget a également été critiquées par m. klaus .
PS	le budget a également été critiquée par klaus .
All	le budget a également été critiqué par klaus .
Infr	le budget a également été critiqué par klaus .
Ref	klaus critique également le budget .
Src	and one has come from music .
Bsl	et un a de la musique .
Rdm	et on vient de musique .
PS	et on a viennent de musique .
All	et de la musique .
Infr	et un est venu de la musique .
Ref	et un vient du monde de la musique .

Figure 4: Examples of two translations for each of the SMT systems built: Src (source sentence), Bsl (baseline), Rdm (random selection), PS (probabilistic sampling), All (all the data available), Infr (Infrequent n-grams) and Ref (reference).

6 Discussion

Bilingual sentence selection (BSS) might be understood to be closely related to adaptation, even though both paradigms tackle problems which are, in essence, different. The goal of an adaptation technique is to *adapt model parameters*, which have been estimated on a large out-of-domain (or generic) data set, so that they are best suitable for dealing with a domain-specific test set. This adaptation process is ought to be achieved by means of a (potentially small) adaptation set, which belongs to the same domain as the test data. In contrast, BSS tackles with the problem of how to *select samples* from a large pool of training data, regardless of whether such pool of data is in-domain or out-of-domain. Hence, in one case we can assume to have a fairly well estimated translation model, which is to be adapted, whereas in BSS we still have full control over the estimation of such model and need not to aim at a specific domain, although it might often be so.

BSS is related with *instance weighting* (Jiang and Zhai, 2007; Foster et al., 2010). Adaptation and BSS can be considered to be orthogonal (yet complementary) problems under the instance weighting paradigm. In such case, instance weighting can be considered to span a complete paradigmatic space between both. At one end, there is sample selection (BSS for SMT), while at the other end there is adaptation. For instance, it is quite common to confront the adaptation problem by extracting different phrase-tables from different corpora, and then interpolate such tables. This technique could be also applied to promote the performance of the system built by means of BSS. However, this is left out as future work.

We thoroughly analysed two BSS approaches that obtain competitive results, while using a small fraction of the training data, although there is still much to be gained. For instance, oracle results have also been reported in this work, yielding improvements of up to 10 BLEU points. Even though the use of an oracle typically implies that the results obtained are not realistic, recall that the proposed oracle is special, in the sense that it only uses the reference sentences for the specific purpose of selecting training samples, but the references are not included into the training data as such. This is useful for assessing the potential behind BSS: ideally, if we were able to design a BSS strategy that, without using the references, would select exactly those training samples, we would be boosting system performance by 10 BLEU points. This re-states BSS as a compelling technique that has not yet received the attention it deserves.

BSS is not aimed at optimising computational requirements, but does so as a byproduct. This may seem despicable but it would allow to run more experiments with the same resources, use larger corpora or even more complex techniques, such as synchronous grammars or hierarchical models. For instance, the infrequent n-grams technique has beaten all the other systems using just a small fraction of the corpus, only 0.5%, and is yet able to outperform a system trained with all the data by 0.9 BLEU points and the random baseline by 3 points. This baseline has been proved to be difficult to beat by other works.

Preliminary experiments were performed in order to analyse the perplexity of the references, the number of out of vocabulary words (OoVs) and the ratio of target-source phrases. These experiments revealed that the improvements obtained are largely correlated with a decrease in perplexity and in the number of OoVs. On the one hand, reducing the amount of OoVs was mirrored by an important improvement in BLEU when the amount of additional data was small, and also entailed a decrease in perplexity. However, a reduction in perplexity by itself did not always imply significant improvements. Moreover, no real conclusion could be drawn from the analysis of target-source phrase ratio. Hence, we understand that the improvements obtained are provided mainly by a more specialised estimation of the model parameters. However, further experiments should still be conducted in order to verify this conclusion.

Acknowledgments

The research leading to these results has received funding from the European Union Seventh Framework Programme (FP7/2007-2013) under grant agreement nr. 287755. This work was also supported by the Spanish MEC/MICINN under the MIPRCV "Consolider Ingenio 2010" program (CSD2007-00018), and iTrans2 (TIN2009-14511) project. Also supported by the Spanish MITyC under the erudito.com (TSI-020110-2009-439) project and Instituto Tecnológico de León, DGEST-PROMEP y CONACYT, México.

References

Sankaranarayanan Ananthakrishnan, Rohit Prasad, David Stallard, and Prem Natarajan. 2010. Discriminative sample selection for statistical machine translation. In *Proc. of the EMNLP*, pages 626–635, Cambridge, MA, October.

Amittai Axelrod, Xiaodong He, and Jianfeng Gao. 2011. Domain adaptation via pseudo in-domain data selection. In *Proc of the EMNLP*, pages 355–362.

Christopher M. Bishop. 2006. *Pattern Recognition and Machine Learning*. Springer.

Peter F. Brown, Stephen Della Pietra, Vincent J. Della Pietra, and Robert L. Mercer. 1994. The mathematics of statistical machine translation: Parameter estimation. *Computational Linguistics*, 19(2):263–311.

Chris Callison-Burch, Philipp Koehn, Christof Monz, and Josh Schroeder. 2009. Findings of the 2009 Workshop on Statistical Machine Translation. In *Proc of the WSMT*, pages 1–28, Athens, Greece, March.

Chris Callison-Burch, Philipp Koehn, Christof Monz, Kay Peterson, Mark Przybocki, and Omar Zaidan. 2010. Findings of the 2010 joint Workshop on Statistical Machine Translation and Metrics for Machine Translation. In *Proc. of the MATR(ACL)*, pages 17–53, Uppsala, Sweden, July.

Sanjoy Dasgupta. 2009. The two faces of active learning. In *Proc. of The twentieth Conference on Algorithmic Learning Theory*, page 1, Porto (Portugal), October.

George Foster, Cyril Goutte, and Roland Kuhn. 2010. Discriminative instance weighting for domain adaptation in statistical machine translation. In *Proc. of the EMNLP*, pages 451–459, Cambridge, MA, October.

Guillem Gascó, Vicent Alabau, Jesús Andrés-Ferrer, Jesús González-Rubio, Martha-Alicia Rocha, Germán Sanchis-Trilles, Francisco Casacuberta, Jorge González, and Joan-Andreu Sánchez. 2010. ITI-UPV system description for IWSLT 2010. In *Proc. of the IWSLT 2010*, Paris, France, December.

Gholamreza Haffari, Maxim Roy, and Anoop Sarkar. 2009. Active learning for statistical phrase-based machine translation. In *Proc. of HLT/NAACL'09*, pages 415–423, Morristown, NJ, USA.

Jing Jiang and ChengXiang Zhai. 2007. Instance weighting for domain adaptation in NLP. In *Proc. of ACL'07*, pages 264–271.

Reinhard Kneser and Hermann Ney. 1995. Improved backing-off for m-gram language modeling. *Proc. of ICASSP*, II:181–184, May.

Philipp Koehn, Hieu Hoang, Alexandra Birch, Chris Callison-Burch, Marcello Federico, Nicola Bertoldi, Brooke Cowan, Wade Shen, Christie Moran, Richard Zens, Chris Dyer, Ontraj Bojar, Alexandra Constantin, and Evan Herbst. 2007. Moses: Open source toolkit for statistical machine translation. In *Proc. of ACL*, pages 177–180.

Zhifei Li, Chris Callison-Burch, Chris Dyer, Juri Ganitkevitch, Ann Irvine, Sanjeev Khudanpur, Lane Schwartz, Wren Thornton, Ziyuan Wang, Jonathan Weese, and Omar Zaidan. 2010. Joshua 2.0: A toolkit for parsing-based machine translation with syntax, semirings, discriminative training and other goodies. In *Proc. of the MATR(ACL)*, pages 139–143, Uppsala, Sweden, July.

Yajuan Lu, Jin Huang, and Qun Liu. 2007. Improving statistical machine translation performance by training data selection and optimization. In *Proc. of the EMNLP-CoNLL*, pages 343–350, Prague, Czech Republic, June.

Spyros Matsoukas, Antti-Veikko I. Rosti, and Bing Zhang. 2009. Discriminative corpus weight estimation for machine translation. In *Proc. of the EMNLP*, pages 708–717, Singapore, August.

Robert C. Moore and William Lewis. 2010. Intelligent selection of language model training data. In *ACL (Short Papers)*, pages 220–224.

Franz J. Och and Hermann Ney. 2002. Discriminative training and maximum entropy models for statistical machine translation. In *Proc. of ACL*, pages 295–302.

Franz J. Och and Hermann Ney. 2003. A systematic comparison of various statistical alignment models. In *Computational Linguistics*, volume 29, pages 19–51.

Kishore Papineni, Salim Roukos, and Todd Ward. 1998. Maximum likelihood and discriminative training of direct translation models. In *Proc. of ICASSP'98*, pages 189–192.

Kishore Papineni, Salim Roukos, Todd Ward, and Wei-Jing Zhu. 2001. Bleu: A method for automatic evaluation of machine translation. In *Technical Report RC22176 (W0109-022)*.

Michael Paul, Marcello Federico, and Sebastian Stker. 2010. Overview of the IWSLT 2010 evaluation campaign. In *Proc. of the IWSLT 2010*, Paris, France, December.

Matthew Snover, Bonnie Dorr, Richard Schwartz, Linnea Micciulla, and John Makhoul. 2006. A study of translation edit rate with targeted human annotation. In *Proc. of AMTA'06*.

Andreas Stolcke. 2002. SRILM – an extensible language modeling toolkit. In *Proc. of ICSLP*.

Elia Yuste, Manuel Herranz, Antonio Lagarda, Lionel Tarazón, Isaías Sánchez-Cortina, and Francisco Casacuberta. 2010. Pangeamt - putting open standards to work... well. In *Proc. of the AMTA2010*. Denver, CO, USA, November.

Recall-Oriented Learning of Named Entities in Arabic Wikipedia

Behrang Mohit* **Nathan Schneider†** **Rishav Bhowmick*** **Kemal Oflazer*** **Noah A. Smith†**
School of Computer Science, Carnegie Mellon University
*P.O. Box 24866, Doha, Qatar †Pittsburgh, PA 15213, USA
{behrang@,nschneid@cs.,rishavb@qatar.,ko@cs.,nasmith@cs.}cmu.edu

Abstract

We consider the problem of NER in Arabic Wikipedia, a semisupervised domain adaptation setting for which we have no labeled training data in the target domain. To facilitate evaluation, we obtain annotations for articles in four topical groups, allowing annotators to identify domain-specific entity types in addition to standard categories. Standard supervised learning on newswire text leads to poor target-domain recall. We train a sequence model and show that a simple modification to the online learner—a loss function encouraging it to "arrogantly" favor recall over precision—substantially improves recall and F_1. We then adapt our model with self-training on unlabeled target-domain data; enforcing the same recall-oriented bias in the self-training stage yields marginal gains.[1]

1 Introduction

This paper considers named entity recognition (NER) in text that is different from most past research on NER. Specifically, we consider Arabic Wikipedia articles with diverse topics beyond the commonly-used news domain. These data challenge past approaches in two ways:

First, Arabic is a morphologically rich language (Habash, 2010). Named entities are referenced using complex syntactic constructions (cf. English NEs, which are primarily sequences of proper nouns). The Arabic script suppresses most vowels, increasing lexical ambiguity, and lacks capitalization, a key clue for English NER.

Second, much research has focused on the use of *news* text for system building and evaluation. Wikipedia articles are not news, belonging instead to a wide range of domains that are not clearly delineated. One hallmark of this divergence between Wikipedia and the news domain is a difference in the distributions of named entities. Indeed, the classic named entity types (person, organization, location) may not be the most apt for articles in other domains (e.g., scientific or social topics). On the other hand, Wikipedia is a large dataset, inviting semisupervised approaches.

In this paper, we describe advances on the problem of NER in Arabic Wikipedia. The techniques are general and make use of well-understood building blocks. Our contributions are:

- A small corpus of articles annotated in a new scheme that provides more freedom for annotators to adapt NE analysis to new domains;
- An "arrogant" learning approach designed to boost recall in supervised training as well as self-training; and
- An empirical evaluation of this technique as applied to a well-established discriminative NER model and feature set.

Experiments show consistent gains on the challenging problem of identifying named entities in Arabic Wikipedia text.

2 Arabic Wikipedia NE Annotation

Most of the effort in NER has been focused around a small set of domains and general-purpose entity classes relevant to those domains—especially the categories PER(SON), ORG(ANIZATION), and LOC(ATION) (POL), which are highly prominent in news text. Arabic is no exception: the publicly available NER corpora—ACE (Walker et al., 2006), ANER (Benajiba et al., 2008), and OntoNotes (Hovy et al., 2006)—all are in the news domain.[2] However,

[1] The annotated dataset and a supplementary document with additional details of this work can be found at: http://www.ark.cs.cmu.edu/AQMAR

[2] OntoNotes contains news-related text. ACE includes some text from blogs. In addition to the POL classes, both corpora include additional NE classes such as facility, event, product, vehicle, etc. These entities are infrequent and may not be comprehensive enough to cover the larger set of pos-

	History	Science	Sports	Technology
dev:	Damascus	Atom	Raúl Gonzáles	Linux
	Imam Hussein Shrine	Nuclear power	Real Madrid	Solaris
test:	Crusades	Enrico Fermi	2004 Summer Olympics	Computer
	Islamic Golden Age	Light	Christiano Ronaldo	Computer Software
	Islamic History	Periodic Table	Football	Internet
	Ibn Tolun Mosque	Physics	Portugal football team	Richard Stallman
	Ummaya Mosque	Muhammad al-Razi	FIFA World Cup	X Window System

Claudio Filippone (PER) كلوديو فيلبون; Linux (SOFTWARE) لينكس; Spanish League (CHAMPIONSHIPS) الدوري الاسباني; proton (PARTICLE) بروتون; nuclear radiation (GENERIC-MISC) الاشعاع النووي; Real Zaragoza (ORG) ريال سرقسطة

Table 1: Translated titles of Arabic Wikipedia articles in our development and test sets, and some NEs with standard and article-specific classes. Additionally, Prussia and Amman were reserved for training annotators, and Gulf War for estimating inter-annotator agreement.

appropriate entity classes will vary widely by domain; occurrence rates for entity classes are quite different in news text vs. Wikipedia, for instance (Balasuriya et al., 2009). This is abundantly clear in technical and scientific discourse, where much of the terminology is domain-specific, but it holds elsewhere. Non-POL entities in the history domain, for instance, include important events (wars, famines) and cultural movements (*romanticism*). Ignoring such domain-critical entities likely limits the usefulness of the NE analysis.

Recognizing this limitation, some work on NER has sought to codify more robust inventories of general-purpose entity types (Sekine et al., 2002; Weischedel and Brunstein, 2005; Grouin et al., 2011) or to enumerate domain-specific types (Settles, 2004; Yao et al., 2003). Coarse, general-purpose categories have also been used for semantic tagging of nouns and verbs (Ciaramita and Johnson, 2003). Yet as the number of classes or domains grows, rigorously documenting and organizing the classes—even for a single language—requires intensive effort. Ideally, an NER system would refine the traditional classes (Hovy et al., 2011) or identify new entity classes when they arise in new domains, adapting to new data. For this reason, we believe it is valuable to consider NER systems that identify (but do not necessarily label) entity mentions, and also to consider annotation schemes that allow annotators more freedom in defining entity classes.

Our aim in creating an annotated dataset is to provide a testbed for *evaluation* of new NER models. We will use these data as development and testing examples, but not as training data. In §4 we will discuss our semisupervised approach to learning, which leverages ACE and ANER data as an annotated training corpus.

2.1 Annotation Strategy

We conducted a small annotation project on Arabic Wikipedia articles. Two college-educated native Arabic speakers annotated about 3,000 sentences from 31 articles. We identified four topical areas of interest—history, technology, science, and sports—and browsed these topics until we had found 31 articles that we deemed satisfactory on the basis of length (at least 1,000 words), cross-lingual linkages (associated articles in English, German, and Chinese[3]), and subjective judgments of quality. The list of these articles along with sample NEs are presented in table 1. These articles were then preprocessed to extract main article text (eliminating tables, lists, info-boxes, captions, etc.) for annotation.

Our approach follows ACE guidelines (LDC, 2005) in identifying NE boundaries and choosing POL tags. In addition to this traditional form of annotation, annotators were encouraged to articulate one to three *salient, article-specific* entity categories per article. For example, names of particles (e.g., *proton*) are highly salient in the Atom article. Annotators were asked to read the entire article first, and then to decide which non-traditional classes of entities would be important in the context of article. In some cases, annotators reported using heuristics (such as being proper

sible NEs (Sekine et al., 2002). Nezda et al. (2006) annotated and evaluated an Arabic NE corpus with an extended set of 18 classes (including temporal and numeric entities); this corpus has not been released publicly.

[3]These three languages have the most articles on Wikipedia. Associated articles here are those that have been manually hyperlinked from the Arabic page as cross-lingual correspondences. They are not translations, but if the associations are accurate, these articles should be topically similar to the Arabic page that links to them.

Token position agreement rate	92.6%	Cohen's κ: 0.86
Token agreement rate	88.3%	Cohen's κ: 0.86
Token F_1 between annotators	91.0%	
Entity boundary match F_1	94.0%	
Entity category match F_1	87.4%	

Table 2: Inter-annotator agreement measurements.

nouns or having an English translation which is conventionally capitalized) to help guide their determination of non-canonical entities and entity classes. Annotators produced written descriptions of their classes, including example instances.

This scheme was chosen for its flexibility: in contrast to a scenario with a fixed ontology, annotators required minimal training beyond the POL conventions, and did not have to worry about delineating custom categories precisely enough that they would extend straightforwardly to other topics or domains. Of course, we expect inter-annotator variability to be greater for these open-ended classification criteria.

2.2 Annotation Quality Evaluation

During annotation, two articles (Prussia and Amman) were reserved for training annotators on the task. Once they were accustomed to annotation, both independently annotated a third article. We used this 4,750-word article (Gulf War, حرب الخليج الثانية) to measure inter-annotator agreement. Table 2 provides scores for token-level agreement measures and entity-level F_1 between the two annotated versions of the article.[4]

These measures indicate strong agreement for locating and categorizing NEs both at the token and chunk levels. Closer examination of agreement scores shows that PER and MIS classes have the lowest rates of agreement. That the miscellaneous class, used for infrequent or article-specific NEs, receives poor agreement is unsurprising. The low agreement on the PER class seems to be due to the use of titles and descriptive terms in personal names. Despite explicit guidelines to exclude the titles, annotators disagreed on the inclusion of descriptors that disambiguate the NE (e.g., *the father* in جرج بوش الآب: George Bush, the father).

[4]The position and boundary measures ignore the distinctions between the POLM classes. To avoid artificial inflation of the token and token position agreement rates, we exclude the 81% of tokens tagged by both annotators as not belonging to an entity.

History: Gulf War, Prussia, Damascus, Crusades	
	WAR_CONFLICT • • •
Science: Atom, Periodic table	
THEORY •	CHEMICAL • •
NAME_ROMAN •	PARTICLE • •
Sports: Football, Raúl Gonzáles	
SPORT ○	CHAMPIONSHIP •
AWARD ○	NAME_ROMAN •
Technology: Computer, Richard Stallman	
COMPUTER_VARIETY ○	SOFTWARE •
	COMPONENT •

Table 3: Custom NE categories suggested by one or both annotators for 10 articles. Article titles are translated from Arabic. • indicates that both annotators volunteered a category for an article; ○ indicates that only one annotator suggested the category. Annotators were not given a predetermined set of possible categories; rather, category matches between annotators were determined by post hoc analysis. NAME_ROMAN indicates an NE rendered in Roman characters.

2.3 Validating Category Intuitions

To investigate the variability between annotators with respect to custom category intuitions, we asked our two annotators to independently read 10 of the articles in the data (scattered across our four focus domains) and suggest up to 3 custom categories for each. We assigned short names to these suggestions, seen in table 3. In 13 cases, both annotators suggested a category for an article that was essentially the same (•); three such categories spanned multiple articles. In three cases a category was suggested by only one annotator (○).[5] Thus, we see that our annotators were generally, but not entirely, consistent with each other in their creation of custom categories. Further, almost all of our article-specific categories correspond to classes in the extended NE taxonomy of (Sekine et al., 2002), which speaks to the reasonableness of both sets of categories—and by extension, our open-ended annotation process.

Our annotation of named entities outside of the traditional POL classes creates a useful resource for entity detection and recognition in new domains. Even the ability to detect non-canonical types of NEs should help applications such as QA and MT (Toral et al., 2005; Babych and Hartley, 2003). Possible avenues for future work include annotating and projecting non-canonical

[5]When it came to tagging NEs, one of the two annotators was assigned to each article. Custom categories only suggested by the other annotator were ignored.

NEs from English articles to their Arabic counterparts (Hassan et al., 2007), automatically clustering non-canonical types of entities into article-specific or cross-article classes (cf. Frietag, 2004), or using non-canonical classes to improve the (author-specified) article categories in Wikipedia.

Hereafter, we merge all article-specific categories with the generic MIS category. The proportion of entity mentions that are tagged as MIS, while varying to a large extent by document, is a major indication of the gulf between the news data (<10%) and the Wikipedia data (53% for the development set, 37% for the test set).

Below, we aim to develop entity detection models that generalize beyond the traditional POL entities. We do not address here the challenges of automatically *classifying* entities or inferring non-canonical groupings.

3 Data

Table 4 summarizes the various corpora used in this work.[6] Our NE-annotated Wikipedia subcorpus, described above, consists of several Arabic Wikipedia articles from four focus domains.[7] We do not use these for supervised training data; they serve only as development and test data. A larger set of Arabic Wikipedia articles, selected on the basis of quality heuristics, serves as unlabeled data for semisupervised learning.

Our out-of-domain labeled NE data is drawn from the ANER (Benajiba et al., 2007) and ACE-2005 (Walker et al., 2006) newswire corpora. Entity types in this data are POL categories (PER, ORG, LOC) and MIS. Portions of the ACE corpus were held out as development and test data; the remainder is used in training.

4 Models

Our starting point for statistical NER is a feature-based linear model over sequences, trained using the structured perceptron (Collins, 2002).[8]

In addition to lexical and morphological[9] features known to work well for Arabic NER (Benajiba et al., 2008; Abdul-Hamid and Darwish, 2010), we incorporate some additional features enabled by Wikipedia. We do not employ a gazetteer, as the construction of a broad-domain gazetteer is a significant undertaking orthogonal to the challenges of a new text domain like Wikipedia.[10] A descriptive list of our features is available in the supplementary document.

	words	*NEs*
Training		
ACE+ANER	212,839	15,796
Wikipedia (unlabeled, 397 docs)	1,110,546	—
Development		
ACE	7,776	638
Wikipedia (4 domains, 8 docs)	21,203	2,073
Test		
ACE	7,789	621
Wikipedia (4 domains, 20 docs)	52,650	3,781

Table 4: Number of words (entity mentions) in data sets.

We use a first-order structured perceptron; none of our features consider more than a pair of consecutive BIO labels at a time. The model enforces the constraint that NE sequences must begin with B (so the bigram $\langle O, I\rangle$ is disallowed).

Training this model on ACE and ANER data achieves performance comparable to the state of the art (F_1-measure[11] above 69%), but fares much worse on our Wikipedia test set (F_1-measure around 47%); details are given in §5.

4.1 Recall-Oriented Perceptron

By augmenting the perceptron's online update with a *cost* function term, we can incorporate a task-dependent notion of error into the objective, as with structured SVMs (Taskar et al., 2004; Tsochantaridis et al., 2005). Let $c(\boldsymbol{y}, \boldsymbol{y}')$ denote a measure of error when $\boldsymbol{y}$ is the correct label sequence but $\boldsymbol{y}'$ is predicted. For observed sequence $\boldsymbol{x}$ and feature weights (model parameters) $\mathbf{w}$, the structured hinge loss is $\ell_{hinge}(\boldsymbol{x}, \boldsymbol{y}, \mathbf{w}) =$

$$\max_{\boldsymbol{y}'} \left(\mathbf{w}^\top \mathbf{g}(\boldsymbol{x}, \boldsymbol{y}') + c(\boldsymbol{y}, \boldsymbol{y}')\right) - \mathbf{w}^\top \mathbf{g}(\boldsymbol{x}, \boldsymbol{y}) \quad (1)$$

The maximization problem inside the parentheses is known as *cost-augmented decoding*. If c fac-

[6] Additional details appear in the supplement.

[7] We downloaded a snapshot of Arabic Wikipedia (`http://ar.wikipedia.org`) on 8/29/2009 and preprocessed the articles to extract main body text and metadata using the `mwlib` package for Python (PediaPress, 2010).

[8] A more leisurely discussion of the structured perceptron and its connection to empirical risk minimization can be found in the supplementary document.

[9] We obtain morphological analyses from the MADA tool (Habash and Rambow, 2005; Roth et al., 2008).

[10] A gazetteer ought to yield further improvements in line with previous findings in NER (Ratinov and Roth, 2009).

[11] Though optimizing NER systems for F_1 has been called into question (Manning, 2006), no alternative metric has achieved widespread acceptance in the community.

tors similarly to the feature function $\mathbf{g}(\boldsymbol{x}, \boldsymbol{y})$, then we can increase penalties for $\boldsymbol{y}$ that have more local mistakes. This raises the learner's awareness about how it will be evaluated. Incorporating cost-augmented decoding into the perceptron leads to this decoding step:

$$\hat{\boldsymbol{y}} \leftarrow \arg\max_{\boldsymbol{y}'} \left(\mathbf{w}^\top \mathbf{g}(\boldsymbol{x}, \boldsymbol{y}') + c(\boldsymbol{y}, \boldsymbol{y}') \right), \quad (2)$$

which amounts to performing stochastic subgradient ascent on an objective function with the Eq. 1 loss (Ratliff et al., 2006).

In this framework, cost functions can be formulated to distinguish between different types of errors made during training. For a tag sequence $\boldsymbol{y} = \langle y_1, y_2, \ldots, y_M \rangle$, Gimpel and Smith (2010b) define word-local cost functions that differently penalize precision errors (i.e., $y_i = O \wedge \hat{y}_i \neq O$ for the ith word), recall errors ($y_i \neq O \wedge \hat{y}_i = O$), and entity class/position errors (other cases where $y_i \neq \hat{y}_i$). As will be shown below, a key problem in cross-domain NER is poor *recall*, so we will penalize recall errors more severely:

$$c(\boldsymbol{y}, \boldsymbol{y}') = \sum_{i=1}^{M} \begin{cases} 0 & \text{if } y_i = y'_i \\ \beta & \text{if } y_i \neq O \wedge y'_i = O \\ 1 & \text{otherwise} \end{cases} \quad (3)$$

for a penalty parameter $\beta > 1$. We call our learner the "recall-oriented" perceptron (ROP).

We note that Minkov et al. (2006) similarly explored the recall vs. precision tradeoff in NER. Their technique was to directly tune the weight of a single feature—the feature marking O (non-entity tokens); a lower weight for this feature will incur a greater penalty for predicting O. Below we demonstrate that our method, which is less coarse, is more successful in our setting.[12]

In our experiments we will show that injecting "arrogance" into the learner via the recall-oriented loss function substantially improves recall, especially for non-POL entities (§5.3).

4.2 Self-Training and Semisupervised Learning

As we will show experimentally, the differences between news text and Wikipedia text call for domain adaptation. In the case of Arabic Wikipedia, there is no available labeled training data. Yet the available *unlabeled* data is vast, so we turn to semisupervised learning.

Input: labeled data $\langle\langle \boldsymbol{x}^{(n)}, \boldsymbol{y}^{(n)} \rangle\rangle_{n=1}^{N}$; unlabeled data $\langle \bar{\boldsymbol{x}}^{(j)} \rangle_{j=1}^{J}$; supervised learner L; number of iterations T'
Output: $\mathbf{w}$
$\mathbf{w} \leftarrow L(\langle\langle \boldsymbol{x}^{(n)}, \boldsymbol{y}^{(n)} \rangle\rangle_{n=1}^{N})$
for $t = 1$ **to** T' **do**
  for $j = 1$ **to** J **do**
    $\hat{\boldsymbol{y}}^{(j)} \leftarrow \arg\max_{\boldsymbol{y}} \mathbf{w}^\top \mathbf{g}(\bar{\boldsymbol{x}}^{(j)}, \boldsymbol{y})$
  $\mathbf{w} \leftarrow L(\langle\langle \boldsymbol{x}^{(n)}, \boldsymbol{y}^{(n)} \rangle\rangle_{n=1}^{N} \cup \langle\langle \bar{\boldsymbol{x}}^{(j)}, \hat{\boldsymbol{y}}^{(j)} \rangle\rangle_{j=1}^{J})$

Algorithm 1: Self-training.

Here we adapt self-training, a simple technique that leverages a supervised learner (like the perceptron) to perform semisupervised learning (Clark et al., 2003; Mihalcea, 2004; McClosky et al., 2006). In our version, a model is trained on the labeled data, then used to label the unlabeled target data. We iterate between training on the hypothetically-labeled target data plus the original labeled set, and relabeling the target data; see Algorithm 1. Before self-training, we remove sentences hypothesized not to contain any named entity mentions, which we found avoids further encouragement of the model toward low recall.

5 Experiments

We investigate two questions in the context of NER for Arabic Wikipedia:

- **Loss function:** Does integrating a cost function into our learning algorithm, as we have done in the **recall-oriented perceptron** (§4.1), improve recall and overall performance on Wikipedia data?
- **Semisupervised learning for domain adaptation:** Can our models benefit from large amounts of unlabeled Wikipedia data, in addition to the (out-of-domain) labeled data? We experiment with a self-training phase following the fully supervised learning phase.

We report experiments for the possible combinations of the above ideas. These are summarized in table 5. Note that the recall-oriented perceptron can be used for the supervised learning phase, for the self-training phase, or both. This leaves us with the following combinations:

- **reg/none** (baseline): regular supervised learner.
- **ROP/none**: recall-oriented supervised learner.

[12]The distinction between the techniques is that our cost function adjusts the *whole* model in order to perform better at recall on the training data.

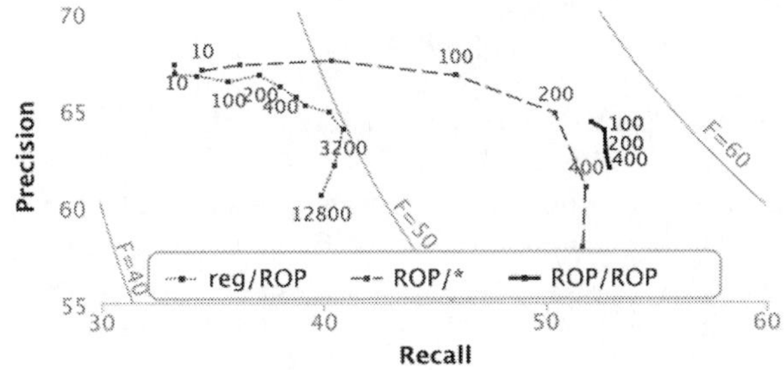

Figure 1: Tuning the recall-oriented cost parameter for different learning settings. We optimized for development set F_1, choosing penalty $\beta = 200$ for recall-oriented supervised learning (in the plot, ROP/*—this is regardless of whether a stage of self-training will follow); $\beta = 100$ for recall-oriented self-training following recall-oriented supervised learning (ROP/ROP); and $\beta = 3200$ for recall-oriented self-training following regular supervised learning (reg/ROP).

- **reg/reg**: standard self-training setup.
- **ROP/reg**: recall-oriented supervised learner, followed by standard self-training.
- **reg/ROP**: regular supervised model as the initial labeler for recall-oriented self-training.
- **ROP/ROP** (the "double ROP" condition): recall-oriented supervised model as the initial labeler for recall-oriented self-training. Note that the two ROPs can use different cost parameters.

For evaluating our models we consider the named entity *detection* task, i.e., recognizing which spans of words constitute entities. This is measured by per-entity precision, recall, and F_1.[13] To measure statistical significance of differences between models we use Gimpel and Smith's (2010) implementation of the paired bootstrap resampler of (Koehn, 2004), taking 10,000 samples for each comparison.

5.1 Baseline

Our baseline is the perceptron, trained on the POL entity boundaries in the ACE+ANER corpus (**reg/none**).[14] Development data was used to select the number of iterations (10). We performed 3-fold cross-validation on the ACE data and found wide variance in the *in-domain* entity detection performance of this model:

	P	R	F_1
fold 1	70.43	63.08	66.55
fold 2	87.48	81.13	84.18
fold 3	65.09	51.13	57.27
average	74.33	65.11	69.33

(Fold 1 corresponds to the ACE test set described in table 4.) We also trained the model to perform POL detection and classification, achieving nearly identical results in the 3-way cross-validation of ACE data. From these data we conclude that our baseline is on par with the state of the art for Arabic NER on ACE news text (Abdul-Hamid and Darwish, 2010).[15]

Here is the performance of the baseline entity detection model on our 20-article test set:[16]

	P	R	F_1
technology	60.42	20.26	30.35
science	64.96	25.73	36.86
history	63.09	35.58	45.50
sports	71.66	59.94	65.28
overall	66.30	35.91	46.59

Unsurprisingly, performance on Wikipedia data varies widely across article domains and is much lower than in-domain performance. Precision scores fall between 60% and 72% for all domains, but recall in most cases is far worse. Miscellaneous class recall, in particular, suffers badly (under 10%)—which partially accounts for the poor recall in science and technology articles (they have by far the highest proportion of MIS entities).

5.2 Self-Training

Following Clark et al. (2003), we applied self-training as described in Algorithm 1, with the perceptron as the supervised learner. Our unlabeled data consists of 397 Arabic Wikipedia articles (1 million words) selected at random from all articles exceeding a simple length threshold (1,000 words); see table 4. We used only one iteration ($T' = 1$), as experiments on development data showed no benefit from additional rounds. Several rounds of self-training hurt performance,

[13]Only entity spans that exactly match the gold spans are counted as correct. We calculated these scores with the `conlleval.pl` script from the CoNLL 2003 shared task.

[14]In keeping with prior work, we ignore non-POL categories for the ACE evaluation.

[15]Abdul-Hamid and Darwish report as their best result a macroaveraged F_1-score of 76. As they do not specify which data they used for their held-out test set, we cannot perform a direct comparison. However, our feature set is nearly a superset of their best feature set, and their result lies well within the range of results seen in our cross-validation folds.

[16]Our Wikipedia evaluations use models trained on POLM entity boundaries in ACE. Per-domain and overall scores are microaverages across articles.

	Self-training		
Supervised	**none**	**reg**	**ROP**
reg	66.3 35.9 46.59	66.7 35.6 46.41	59.2 40.3 47.97
ROP	60.9 44.7 **51.59**	59.8 46.2 **52.11**	58.0 47.4 **52.16**

Table 5: Entity detection precision, recall, and F_1 for each learning setting, microaveraged across the 24 articles in our Wikipedia test set. Rows differ in the supervised learning condition on the ACE+ANER data (regular vs. recall-oriented perceptron). Columns indicate whether this supervised learning phase was followed by self-training on unlabeled Wikipedia data, and if so which version of the perceptron was used for self-training.

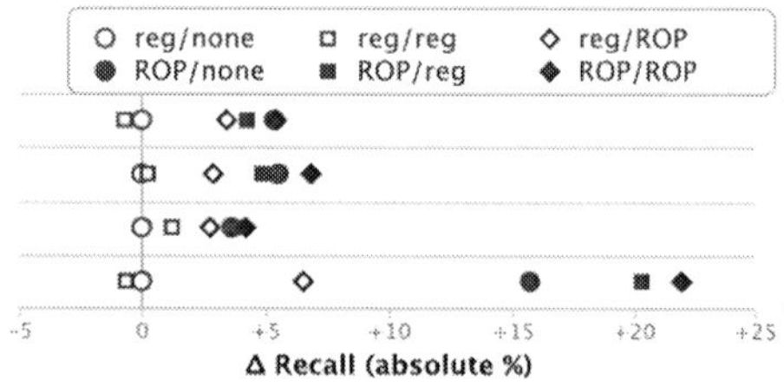

	entities	words	baseline recall
PER	1081	1743	49.95
ORG	286	637	23.92
LOC	1019	1413	61.43
MIS	1395	2176	9.30
overall	3781	5969	35.91

Figure 2: Recall improvement over baseline in the test set by gold NER category, counts for those categories in the data, and recall scores for our baseline model. Markers in the plot indicate different experimental settings corresponding to cells in table 5.

an effect attested in earlier research (Curran et al., 2007) and sometimes known as "semantic drift."

Results are shown in table 5. We find that standard self-training (the middle column) has very little impact on performance.[17] Why is this the case? We venture that poor baseline recall and the domain variability *within* Wikipedia are to blame.

5.3 Recall-Oriented Learning

The recall-oriented bias can be introduced in either or both of the stages of our semisupervised learning framework: in the supervised learning phase, modifying the objective of our baseline (§5.1); and within the self-training algorithm (§5.2).[18] As noted in §4.1, the aim of this approach is to discourage recall errors (false negatives), which are the chief difficulty for the news text–trained model in the new domain. We selected the value of the false positive penalty for cost-augmented decoding, β, using the development data (figure 1).

The results in table 5 demonstrate improvements due to the recall-oriented bias in both stages of learning.[19] When used in the supervised phase (bottom left cell), the recall gains are substantial—nearly 9% over the baseline. Integrating this bias within self-training (last column of the table) produces a more modest improvement (less than 3%) relative to the baseline. In both cases, the improvements to recall more than compensate for the amount of degradation to precision. This trend is robust: wherever the recall-oriented perceptron is added, we observe improvements in both recall and F_1. Perhaps surprisingly, these gains are somewhat additive: using the ROP in both learning phases gives a small (though not always significant) gain over alternatives (standard supervised perceptron, no self-training, or self-training with a standard perceptron). In fact, when the standard supervised learner is used, recall-oriented self-training succeeds despite the ineffectiveness of standard self-training.

Performance breakdowns by (gold) class, figure 2, and domain, figure 3, further attest to the robustness of the overall results. The most dramatic gains are in miscellaneous class recall—each form of the recall bias produces an improvement, and using this bias in both the supervised and self-training phases is clearly most successful for miscellaneous entities. Correspondingly, the technology and science domains (in which this class dominates—83% and 61% of mentions, ver-

[17] In neither case does regular self-training produce a significantly different F_1 score than no self-training.

[18] Standard Viterbi decoding was used to *label* the data within the self-training algorithm; note that cost-augmented decoding only makes sense in learning, not as a prediction technique, since it deliberately introduces errors relative to a correct output that must be provided.

[19] In terms of F_1, the worst of the 3 models with the ROP supervised learner significantly outperforms the best model with the regular supervised learner ($p < 0.005$). The improvements due to self-training are marginal, however: ROP self-training produces a significant gain only following regular supervised learning ($p < 0.05$).

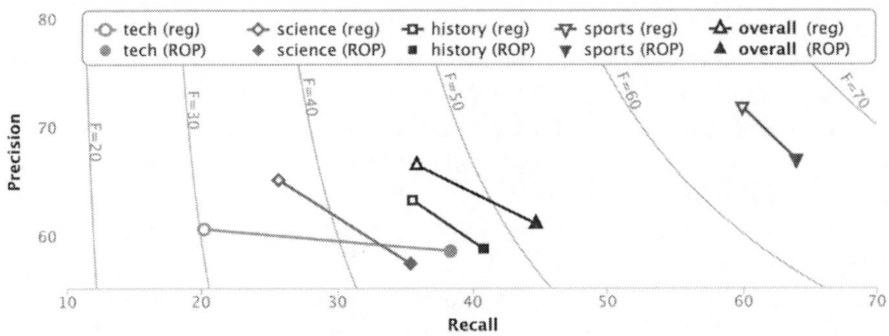

Figure 3: Supervised learner precision vs. recall as evaluated on Wikipedia test data in different topical domains. The regular perceptron (baseline model) is contrasted with ROP. No self-training is applied.

sus 6% and 12% for history and sports, respectively) receive the biggest boost. Still, the gaps between domains are not entirely removed.

Most improvements relate to the reduction of false negatives, which fall into three groups: (a) entities occurring infrequently or partially in the labeled training data (e.g. *uranium*); (b) domain-specific entities sharing lexical or contextual features with the POL entities (e.g. *Linux*, *titanium*); and (c) words with Latin characters, common in the science and technology domains. (a) and (b) are mostly transliterations into Arabic.

An alternative—and simpler—approach to controlling the precision-recall tradeoff is the Minkov et al. (2006) strategy of tuning a single feature weight subsequent to learning (see §4.1 above). We performed an oracle experiment to determine how this compares to recall-oriented learning in our setting. An oracle trained with the method of Minkov et al. outperforms the three models in table 5 that use the *regular* perceptron for the supervised phase of learning, but *underperforms* the supervised ROP conditions.[20]

Overall, we find that incorporating the recall-oriented bias in learning is fruitful for adapting to Wikipedia because the gains in recall outpace the damage to precision.

6 Discussion

To our knowledge, this work is the first suggestion that substantively modifying the *supervised* learning criterion in a resource-rich domain can reap benefits in subsequent *semisupervised* application in a new domain. Past work has looked at regularization (Chelba and Acero, 2006) and feature design (Daumé III, 2007); we alter the loss function. Not surprisingly, the double-ROP approach harms performance on the original domain (on ACE data, we achieve 55.41% F_1, far below the standard perceptron). Yet we observe that models can be prepared for adaptation even before a learner is exposed a new domain, sacrificing performance in the original domain.

The recall-oriented bias is not merely encouraging the learner to identify entities already seen in training. As recall increases, so does the number of new entity types recovered by the model: of the 2,070 NE types in the test data that were never seen in training, only 450 were ever found by the baseline, versus 588 in the reg/ROP condition, 632 in the ROP/none condition, and 717 in the double-ROP condition.

We note finally that our method is a simple extension to the standard structured perceptron; cost-augmented inference is often no more expensive than traditional inference, and the algorithmic change is equivalent to adding one additional feature. Our recall-oriented cost function is parameterized by a single value, β; recall is highly sensitive to the choice of this value (figure 1 shows how we tuned it on development data), and thus we anticipate that, in general, such tuning will be essential to leveraging the benefits of arrogance.

7 Related Work

Our approach draws on insights from work in the areas of NER, domain adaptation, NLP with Wikipedia, and semisupervised learning. As all are broad areas of research, we highlight only the most relevant contributions here.

Research in Arabic NER has been focused on compiling and optimizing the gazetteers and fea-

[20]Tuning the O feature weight to optimize for F_1 on our test set, we found that oracle precision would be 66.2, recall would be 39.0, and F_1 would be 49.1. The F_1 score of our best model is nearly 3 points higher than the Minkov et al.–style oracle, and over 4 points higher than the non-oracle version where the development set is used for tuning.

ture sets for standard sequential modeling algorithms (Benajiba et al., 2008; Farber et al., 2008; Shaalan and Raza, 2008; Abdul-Hamid and Darwish, 2010). We make use of features identified in this prior work to construct a strong baseline system. We are unaware of any Arabic NER work that has addressed diverse text domains like Wikipedia. Both the English and Arabic versions of Wikipedia have been used, however, as resources in service of traditional NER (Kazama and Torisawa, 2007; Benajiba et al., 2008). Attia et al. (2010) heuristically induce a mapping between Arabic Wikipedia and Arabic WordNet to construct Arabic NE gazetteers.

Balasuriya et al. (2009) highlight the substantial divergence between entities appearing in English Wikipedia versus traditional corpora, and the effects of this divergence on NER performance. There is evidence that models trained on Wikipedia data generalize and perform well on corpora with narrower domains. Nothman et al. (2009) and Balasuriya et al. (2009) show that NER models trained on both automatically and manually annotated Wikipedia corpora perform reasonably well on news corpora. The reverse scenario does not hold for models trained on news text, a result we also observe in Arabic NER. Other work has gone beyond the entity detection problem: Florian et al. (2004) additionally predict within-document entity coreference for Arabic, Chinese, and English ACE text, while Cucerzan (2007) aims to resolve every mention detected in English Wikipedia pages to a canonical article devoted to the entity in question.

The domain and topic diversity of NEs has been studied in the framework of domain adaptation research. A group of these methods use self-training and select the most informative features and training instances to adapt a source domain learner to the new target domain. Wu et al. (2009) bootstrap the NER leaner with a subset of unlabeled instances that bridge the source and target domains. Jiang and Zhai (2006) and Daumé III (2007) make use of some labeled target-domain data to tune or augment the features of the source model towards the target domain. Here, in contrast, we use labeled target-domain data only for tuning and evaluation. Another important distinction is that domain variation in this prior work is restricted to topically-related corpora (e.g. newswire vs. broadcast news), whereas in our work, major topical differences distinguish the training and test corpora—and consequently, their salient NE classes. In these respects our NER setting is closer to that of Florian et al. (2010), who recognize English entities in noisy text, (Surdeanu et al., 2011), which concerns information extraction in a topically distinct target domain, and (Dalton et al., 2011), which addresses English NER in noisy and topically divergent text.

Self-training (Clark et al., 2003; Mihalcea, 2004; McClosky et al., 2006) is widely used in NLP and has inspired related techniques that learn from automatically labeled data (Liang et al., 2008; Petrov et al., 2010). Our self-training procedure differs from some others in that we use all of the automatically labeled examples, rather than filtering them based on a confidence score.

Cost functions have been used in non-structured classification settings to penalize certain types of errors more than others (Chan and Stolfo, 1998; Domingos, 1999; Kiddon and Brun, 2011). The goal of optimizing our structured NER model for recall is quite similar to the scenario explored by Minkov et al. (2006), as noted above.

8 Conclusion

We explored the problem of learning an NER model suited to domains for which no labeled training data are available. A loss function to encourage recall over precision during supervised discriminative learning substantially improves recall and overall entity detection performance, especially when combined with a semisupervised learning regimen incorporating the same bias. We have also developed a small corpus of Arabic Wikipedia articles via a flexible entity annotation scheme spanning four topical domains (publicly available at `http://www.ark.cs.cmu.edu/AQMAR`).

Acknowledgments

We thank Mariem Fekih Zguir and Reham Al Tamime for assistance with annotation, Michael Heilman for his tagger implementation, and Nizar Habash and colleagues for the MADA toolkit. We thank members of the ARK group at CMU, Hal Daumé, and anonymous reviewers for their valuable suggestions. This publication was made possible by grant NPRP-08-485-1-083 from the Qatar National Research Fund (a member of the Qatar Foundation). The statements made herein are solely the responsibility of the authors.

References

Ahmed Abdul-Hamid and Kareem Darwish. 2010. Simplified feature set for Arabic named entity recognition. In *Proceedings of the 2010 Named Entities Workshop*, pages 110–115, Uppsala, Sweden, July. Association for Computational Linguistics.

Mohammed Attia, Antonio Toral, Lamia Tounsi, Monica Monachini, and Josef van Genabith. 2010. An automatically built named entity lexicon for Arabic. In Nicoletta Calzolari, Khalid Choukri, Bente Maegaard, Joseph Mariani, Jan Odijk, Stelios Piperidis, Mike Rosner, and Daniel Tapias, editors, *Proceedings of the Seventh Conference on International Language Resources and Evaluation (LREC'10)*, Valletta, Malta, May. European Language Resources Association (ELRA).

Bogdan Babych and Anthony Hartley. 2003. Improving machine translation quality with automatic named entity recognition. In *Proceedings of the 7th International EAMT Workshop on MT and Other Language Technology Tools*, EAMT '03.

Dominic Balasuriya, Nicky Ringland, Joel Nothman, Tara Murphy, and James R. Curran. 2009. Named entity recognition in Wikipedia. In *Proceedings of the 2009 Workshop on The People's Web Meets NLP: Collaboratively Constructed Semantic Resources*, pages 10–18, Suntec, Singapore, August. Association for Computational Linguistics.

Yassine Benajiba, Paolo Rosso, and José Miguel BenedíRuiz. 2007. ANERsys: an Arabic named entity recognition system based on maximum entropy. In Alexander Gelbukh, editor, *Proceedings of CICLing*, pages 143–153, Mexico City, Mexio. Springer.

Yassine Benajiba, Mona Diab, and Paolo Rosso. 2008. Arabic named entity recognition using optimized feature sets. In *Proceedings of the 2008 Conference on Empirical Methods in Natural Language Processing*, pages 284–293, Honolulu, Hawaii, October. Association for Computational Linguistics.

Philip K. Chan and Salvatore J. Stolfo. 1998. Toward scalable learning with non-uniform class and cost distributions: a case study in credit card fraud detection. In *Proceedings of the Fourth International Conference on Knowledge Discovery and Data Mining*, pages 164–168, New York City, New York, USA, August. AAAI Press.

Ciprian Chelba and Alex Acero. 2006. Adaptation of maximum entropy capitalizer: Little data can help a lot. *Computer Speech and Language*, 20(4):382–399.

Massimiliano Ciaramita and Mark Johnson. 2003. Supersense tagging of unknown nouns in WordNet. In *Proceedings of the 2003 Conference on Empirical Methods in Natural Language Processing*, pages 168–175.

Stephen Clark, James Curran, and Miles Osborne. 2003. Bootstrapping POS-taggers using unlabelled data. In Walter Daelemans and Miles Osborne, editors, *Proceedings of the Seventh Conference on Natural Language Learning at HLT-NAACL 2003*, pages 49–55.

Michael Collins. 2002. Discriminative training methods for hidden Markov models: theory and experiments with perceptron algorithms. In *Proceedings of the ACL-02 Conference on Empirical Methods in Natural Language Processing (EMNLP)*, pages 1–8, Stroudsburg, PA, USA. Association for Computational Linguistics.

Silviu Cucerzan. 2007. Large-scale named entity disambiguation based on Wikipedia data. In *Proceedings of the 2007 Joint Conference on Empirical Methods in Natural Language Processing and Computational Natural Language Learning (EMNLP-CoNLL)*, pages 708–716, Prague, Czech Republic, June.

James R. Curran, Tara Murphy, and Bernhard Scholz. 2007. Minimising semantic drift with Mutual Exclusion Bootstrapping. In *Proceedings of PACLING, 2007*.

Jeffrey Dalton, James Allan, and David A. Smith. 2011. Passage retrieval for incorporating global evidence in sequence labeling. In *Proceedings of the 20th ACM International Conference on Information and Knowledge Management (CIKM '11)*, pages 355–364, Glasgow, Scotland, UK, October. ACM.

Hal Daumé III. 2007. Frustratingly easy domain adaptation. In *Proceedings of the 45th Annual Meeting of the Association of Computational Linguistics*, pages 256–263, Prague, Czech Republic, June. Association for Computational Linguistics.

Pedro Domingos. 1999. MetaCost: a general method for making classifiers cost-sensitive. *Proceedings of the Fifth ACM SIGKDD International Conference on Knowledge Discovery and Data Mining*, pages 155–164.

Benjamin Farber, Dayne Freitag, Nizar Habash, and Owen Rambow. 2008. Improving NER in Arabic using a morphological tagger. In Nicoletta Calzolari, Khalid Choukri, Bente Maegaard, Joseph Mariani, Jan Odjik, Stelios Piperidis, and Daniel Tapias, editors, *Proceedings of the Sixth International Language Resources and Evaluation (LREC'08)*, pages 2509–2514, Marrakech, Morocco, May. European Language Resources Association (ELRA).

Radu Florian, Hany Hassan, Abraham Ittycheriah, Hongyan Jing, Nanda Kambhatla, Xiaoqiang Luo, Nicolas Nicolov, and Salim Roukos. 2004. A statistical model for multilingual entity detection and tracking. In Susan Dumais, Daniel Marcu, and Salim Roukos, editors, *Proceedings of the Human Language Technology Conference of the North*

American Chapter of the Association for Computational Linguistics: HLT-NAACL 2004, page 18, Boston, Massachusetts, USA, May. Association for Computational Linguistics.

Radu Florian, John Pitrelli, Salim Roukos, and Imed Zitouni. 2010. Improving mention detection robustness to noisy input. In *Proceedings of EMNLP 2010*, pages 335–345, Cambridge, MA, October. Association for Computational Linguistics.

Dayne Freitag. 2004. Trained named entity recognition using distributional clusters. In Dekang Lin and Dekai Wu, editors, *Proceedings of EMNLP 2004*, pages 262–269, Barcelona, Spain, July. Association for Computational Linguistics.

Kevin Gimpel and Noah A. Smith. 2010a. Softmax-margin CRFs: Training log-linear models with loss functions. In *Proceedings of the Human Language Technologies Conference of the North American Chapter of the Association for Computational Linguistics*, pages 733–736, Los Angeles, California, USA, June.

Kevin Gimpel and Noah A. Smith. 2010b. Softmax-margin training for structured log-linear models. Technical Report CMU-LTI-10-008, Carnegie Mellon University. `http://www.lti.cs.cmu.edu/research/reports/2010/cmulti10008.pdf`.

Cyril Grouin, Sophie Rosset, Pierre Zweigenbaum, Karn Fort, Olivier Galibert, and Ludovic Quintard. 2011. Proposal for an extension of traditional named entities: from guidelines to evaluation, an overview. In *Proceedings of the 5th Linguistic Annotation Workshop*, pages 92–100, Portland, Oregon, USA, June. Association for Computational Linguistics.

Nizar Habash and Owen Rambow. 2005. Arabic tokenization, part-of-speech tagging and morphological disambiguation in one fell swoop. In *Proceedings of the 43rd Annual Meeting of the Association for Computational Linguistics (ACL'05)*, pages 573–580, Ann Arbor, Michigan, June. Association for Computational Linguistics.

Nizar Habash. 2010. *Introduction to Arabic Natural Language Processing*. Morgan and Claypool Publishers.

Ahmed Hassan, Haytham Fahmy, and Hany Hassan. 2007. Improving named entity translation by exploiting comparable and parallel corpora. In *Proceedings of the Conference on Recent Advances in Natural Language Processing (RANLP '07)*, Borovets, Bulgaria.

Eduard Hovy, Mitchell Marcus, Martha Palmer, Lance Ramshaw, and Ralph Weischedel. 2006. OntoNotes: the 90% solution. In *Proceedings of the Human Language Technology Conference of the NAACL (HLT-NAACL)*, pages 57–60, New York City, USA, June. Association for Computational Linguistics.

Dirk Hovy, Chunliang Zhang, Eduard Hovy, and Anselmo Peas. 2011. Unsupervised discovery of domain-specific knowledge from text. In *Proceedings of the 49th Annual Meeting of the Association for Computational Linguistics: Human Language Technologies*, pages 1466–1475, Portland, Oregon, USA, June. Association for Computational Linguistics.

Jing Jiang and ChengXiang Zhai. 2006. Exploiting domain structure for named entity recognition. In *Proceedings of the Human Language Technology Conference of the NAACL (HLT-NAACL)*, pages 74–81, New York City, USA, June. Association for Computational Linguistics.

Jun'ichi Kazama and Kentaro Torisawa. 2007. Exploiting Wikipedia as external knowledge for named entity recognition. In *Proceedings of the 2007 Joint Conference on Empirical Methods in Natural Language Processing and Computational Natural Language Learning (EMNLP-CoNLL)*, pages 698–707, Prague, Czech Republic, June. Association for Computational Linguistics.

Chloe Kiddon and Yuriy Brun. 2011. That's what she said: double entendre identification. In *Proceedings of the 49th Annual Meeting of the Association for Computational Linguistics: Human Language Technologies*, pages 89–94, Portland, Oregon, USA, June. Association for Computational Linguistics.

Philipp Koehn. 2004. Statistical significance tests for machine translation evaluation. In Dekang Lin and Dekai Wu, editors, *Proceedings of EMNLP 2004*, pages 388–395, Barcelona, Spain, July. Association for Computational Linguistics.

LDC. 2005. ACE (Automatic Content Extraction) Arabic annotation guidelines for entities, version 5.3.3. Linguistic Data Consortium, Philadelphia.

Percy Liang, Hal Daumé III, and Dan Klein. 2008. Structure compilation: trading structure for features. In *Proceedings of the 25th International Conference on Machine Learning (ICML)*, pages 592–599, Helsinki, Finland.

Chris Manning. 2006. Doing named entity recognition? Don't optimize for F_1. `http://nlpers.blogspot.com/2006/08/doing-named-entity-recognition-dont.html`.

David McClosky, Eugene Charniak, and Mark Johnson. 2006. Effective self-training for parsing. In *Proceedings of the Human Language Technology Conference of the NAACL, Main Conference*, pages 152–159, New York City, USA, June. Association for Computational Linguistics.

Rada Mihalcea. 2004. Co-training and self-training for word sense disambiguation. In *HLT-NAACL 2004 Workshop: Eighth Conference on Computational Natural Language Learning (CoNLL-2004)*, Boston, Massachusetts, USA.

Einat Minkov, Richard Wang, Anthony Tomasic, and William Cohen. 2006. NER systems that suit user's preferences: adjusting the recall-precision trade-off for entity extraction. In *Proceedings of the Human Language Technology Conference of the NAACL, Companion Volume: Short Papers*, pages 93–96, New York City, USA, June. Association for Computational Linguistics.

Luke Nezda, Andrew Hickl, John Lehmann, and Sarmad Fayyaz. 2006. What in the world is a *Shahab*? Wide coverage named entity recognition for Arabic. In *Proccedings of LREC*, pages 41–46.

Joel Nothman, Tara Murphy, and James R. Curran. 2009. Analysing Wikipedia and gold-standard corpora for NER training. In *Proceedings of the 12th Conference of the European Chapter of the Association for Computational Linguistics (EACL 2009)*, pages 612–620, Athens, Greece, March. Association for Computational Linguistics.

PediaPress. 2010. mwlib. `http://code.pediapress.com/wiki/wiki/mwlib`.

Slav Petrov, Pi-Chuan Chang, Michael Ringgaard, and Hiyan Alshawi. 2010. Uptraining for accurate deterministic question parsing. In *Proceedings of the 2010 Conference on Empirical Methods in Natural Language Processing*, pages 705–713, Cambridge, MA, October. Association for Computational Linguistics.

Lev Ratinov and Dan Roth. 2009. Design challenges and misconceptions in named entity recognition. In *Proceedings of the Thirteenth Conference on Computational Natural Language Learning (CoNLL-2009)*, pages 147–155, Boulder, Colorado, June. Association for Computational Linguistics.

Nathan D. Ratliff, J. Andrew Bagnell, and Martin A. Zinkevich. 2006. Subgradient methods for maximum margin structured learning. In *ICML Workshop on Learning in Structured Output Spaces*, Pittsburgh, Pennsylvania, USA.

Ryan Roth, Owen Rambow, Nizar Habash, Mona Diab, and Cynthia Rudin. 2008. Arabic morphological tagging, diacritization, and lemmatization using lexeme models and feature ranking. In *Proceedings of ACL-08: HLT*, pages 117–120, Columbus, Ohio, June. Association for Computational Linguistics.

Satoshi Sekine, Kiyoshi Sudo, and Chikashi Nobata. 2002. Extended named entity hierarchy. In *Proceedings of LREC*.

Burr Settles. 2004. Biomedical named entity recognition using conditional random fields and rich feature sets. In Nigel Collier, Patrick Ruch, and Adeline Nazarenko, editors, *COLING 2004 International Joint workshop on Natural Language Processing in Biomedicine and its Applications (NLPBA/BioNLP) 2004*, pages 107–110, Geneva, Switzerland, August. COLING.

Khaled Shaalan and Hafsa Raza. 2008. Arabic named entity recognition from diverse text types. In *Advances in Natural Language Processing*, pages 440–451. Springer.

Mihai Surdeanu, David McClosky, Mason R. Smith, Andrey Gusev, and Christopher D. Manning. 2011. Customizing an information extraction system to a new domain. In *Proceedings of the ACL 2011 Workshop on Relational Models of Semantics*, Portland, Oregon, USA, June. Association for Computational Linguistics.

Ben Taskar, Carlos Guestrin, and Daphne Koller. 2004. Max-margin Markov networks. In Sebastian Thrun, Lawrence Saul, and Bernhard Schölkopf, editors, *Advances in Neural Information Processing Systems 16*. MIT Press.

Antonio Toral, Elisa Noguera, Fernando Llopis, and Rafael Muñoz. 2005. Improving question answering using named entity recognition. *Natural Language Processing and Information Systems*, 3513/2005:181–191.

Ioannis Tsochantaridis, Thorsten Joachims, Thomas Hofmann, and Yasemin Altun. 2005. Large margin methods for structured and interdependent output variables. *Journal of Machine Learning Research*, 6:1453–1484, September.

Christopher Walker, Stephanie Strassel, Julie Medero, and Kazuaki Maeda. 2006. ACE 2005 multilingual training corpus. LDC2006T06, Linguistic Data Consortium, Philadelphia.

Ralph Weischedel and Ada Brunstein. 2005. BBN pronoun coreference and entity type corpus. LDC2005T33, Linguistic Data Consortium, Philadelphia.

Dan Wu, Wee Sun Lee, Nan Ye, and Hai Leong Chieu. 2009. Domain adaptive bootstrapping for named entity recognition. In *Proceedings of the 2009 Conference on Empirical Methods in Natural Language Processing*, pages 1523–1532, Singapore, August. Association for Computational Linguistics.

Tianfang Yao, Wei Ding, and Gregor Erbach. 2003. CHINERS: a Chinese named entity recognition system for the sports domain. In *Proceedings of the Second SIGHAN Workshop on Chinese Language Processing*, pages 55–62, Sapporo, Japan, July. Association for Computational Linguistics.

Tree Representations in Probabilistic Models for Extended Named Entities Detection

Marco Dinarelli
LIMSI-CNRS
Orsay, France
marcod@limsi.fr

Sophie Rosset
LIMSI-CNRS
Orsay, France
rosset@limsi.fr

Abstract

In this paper we deal with Named Entity Recognition (NER) on transcriptions of French broadcast data. Two aspects make the task more difficult with respect to previous NER tasks: i) named entities annotated used in this work have a tree structure, thus the task cannot be tackled as a sequence labelling task; ii) the data used are more noisy than data used for previous NER tasks. We approach the task in two steps, involving Conditional Random Fields and Probabilistic Context-Free Grammars, integrated in a single parsing algorithm. We analyse the effect of using several tree representations. Our system outperforms the best system of the evaluation campaign by a significant margin.

1 Introduction

Named Entity Recognition is a traditinal task of the Natural Language Processing domain. The task aims at mapping words in a text into semantic classes, such like persons, organizations or localizations. While at first the NER task was quite simple, involving a limited number of classes (Grishman and Sundheim, 1996), along the years the task complexity increased as more complex class taxonomies were defined (Sekine and Nobata, 2004). The interest in the task is related to its use in complex frameworks for (semantic) content extraction, such like Relation Extraction applications (Doddington et al., 2004).

This work presents research on a Named Entity Recognition task defined with a new set of named entities. The characteristic of such set is in that named entities have a tree structure. As concequence the task cannot be tackled as a sequence labelling approach. Additionally, the use of noisy data like transcriptions of French broadcast data, makes the task very challenging for traditional NLP solutions. To deal with such problems, we adopt a two-steps approach, the first being realized with Conditional Random Fields (CRF) (Lafferty et al., 2001), the second with a Probabilistic Context-Free Grammar (PCFG) (Johnson, 1998). The motivations behind that are:

- Since the named entities have a tree structure, it is reasonable to use a solution coming from syntactic parsing. However preliminary experiments using such approaches gave poor results.

- Despite the tree-structure of the entities, trees are not as complex as syntactic trees, thus, before designing an ad-hoc solution for the task, which require a remarkable effort and yet it doesn't guarantee better performances, we designed a solution providing good results and which required a limited development effort.

- Conditional Random Fields are models robust to noisy data, like automatic transcriptions of ASR systems (Hahn et al., 2010), thus it is the best choice to deal with transcriptions of broadcast data. Once words have been annotated with basic entity constituents, the tree structure of named entities is simple enough to be reconstructed with relatively simple model like PCFG (Johnson, 1998).

The two models are integrated in a single parsing algorithm. We analyze the effect of the use of

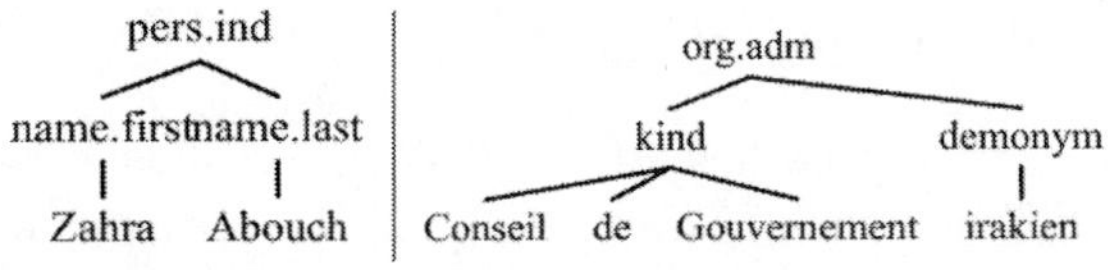

Figure 1: Examples of structured named entities annotated on the data used in this work

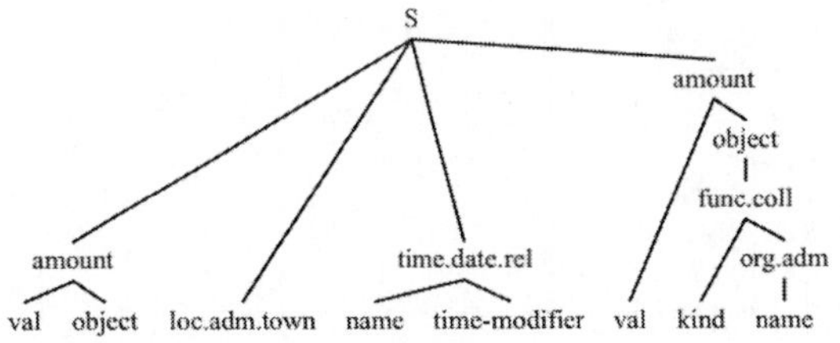

Figure 2: An example of named entity tree corresponding to entities of a whole sentence. Tree leaves, corresponding to sentence words have been removed to keep readability

several tree representations, which result in different parsing models with different performances. We provide a detailed evaluation of our models. Results can be compared with those obtained in the evaluation campaign where the same data were used. Our system outperforms the best system of the evaluation campaign by a significant margin.

The rest of the paper is structured as follows: in the next section we introduce the extended named entities used in this work, in section 3 we describe our two-steps algorithm for parsing entity trees, in section 4 we detail the second step of our approach based on syntactic parsing approaches, in particular we describe the different tree representations used in this work to encode entity trees in parsing models. In section 6 we describe and comment experiments, and finally, in section 7, we draw some conclusions.

2 Extended Named Entities

The most important aspect of the NER task we investigated is provided by the tree structure of named entities. Examples of such entities are given in figure 1 and 2, where words have been remove for readability issues and are: (*"90 persons are still present at Atambua. It's there that 3 employees of the High Conseil of United Nations for refugees have been killed yesterday morning"*):

> ***90 personnes*** *toujours présentes* ***à Atambua*** *c' est là qu'* ***hier matin*** *ont été tués* ***3 employés du haut commissariat des Nations unies*** *aux réfugiés ,* *le* ***HCR***

Words realizing entities in figure 2 are in bold, and they correspond to the tree leaves in the picture. As we see in the figures, entities can have complex structures. Beyond the use of subtypes, like *individual* in *person* (to give `pers.ind`), or *administrative* in *organization* (to give *org.adm*), entities with more specific content can be constituents of more general entities to form tree structures, like *name.first* and *name.last* for *pers.ind* or *val* (for value) and *object* for *amount*.

Quaero	training		dev	
# sentences	43,251		112	
	words	entities	words	entities
# tokens	1,251,432	245,880	2,659	570
# vocabulary	39,631	134	891	30
# components	–	133662	–	971
# components dict.	–	28	–	18
# OOV rate [%]	–	–	17.15	0

Table 1: Statistics on the training and development sets of the Quaero corpus

These named entities have been annotated on transcriptions of French broadcast news coming from several radio channels. The transcriptions constitute a corpus that has been split into training, development and evaluation sets.The evaluation set, in particular, is composed of two set of data, Broadcast News (BN in the table) and Broadcast Conversations (BC in the table). The evaluation of the models presented in this work is performed on the merge of the two data types. Some statistics of the corpus are reported in table 1 and 2. This set of named entities has been defined in order to provide more fine semantic information for entities found in the data, e.g. a person is better specified by first and last name, and is fully described in (Grouin, 2011) . In order to avoid confusion, entities that can be associated directly to words, like *name.first*, *name.last*, *val* and *object*, are called entity constituents, components or entity pre-terminals (as they are preterminals nodes in the trees). The other entities, like *pers.ind* or *amount*, are called entities or non-terminal entities, depending on the context.

3 Models Cascade for Extended Named Entities

Since the task of Named Entity Recognition presented here cannot be modeled as sequence labelling and, as mentioned previously, an approach

Quaero	test BN		test BC	
# sentences	1704		3933	
	words	entities	words	entities
# tokens	32945	2762	69414	2769
# vocabulary		28		28
# components	–	4128	–	4017
# components dict.	–	21	–	20
# OOV rate [%]	3.63	0	3.84	0

Table 2: Statistics on the test set of the Quaero corpus, divided in Broadcast News (BN) and Broadcast Conversations (BC)

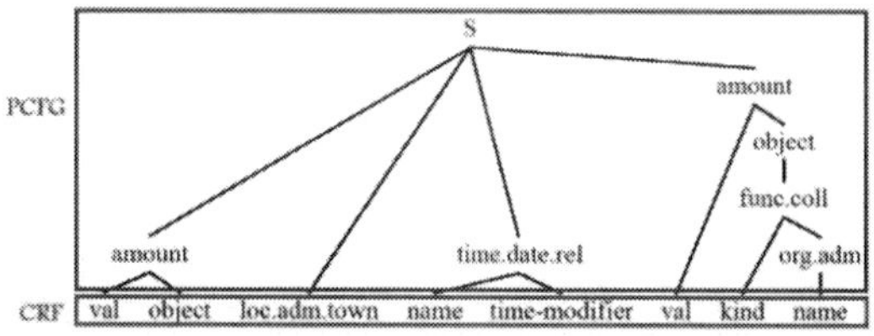

Figure 3: Processing schema of the two-steps approach proposed in this work: CRF plus PCFG

coming from syntactic parsing to perform named entity annotation in "one-shot" is not robust on the data used in this work, we adopt a two-steps. The first is designed to be robust to noisy data and is used to annotate entity components, while the second is used to parse complete entity trees and is based on a relatively simple model. Since we are dealing with noisy data, the hardest part of the task is indeed to annotate components on words. On the other hand, since entity trees are relatively simple, at least much simpler than syntactic trees, once entity components have been annotated in a first step, for the second step, a complex model is not required, which would also make the processing slower. Taking all these issues into account, the two steps of our system for tree-structured named entity recognition are performed as follows:

1. A CRF model (Lafferty et al., 2001) is used to annotate components on words.

2. A PCFG model (Johnson, 1998) is used to parse complete entity trees upon components, i.e. using components annotated by CRF as starting point.

This processing schema is depicted in figure 3. Conditional Random Fields are described shortly in the next subsection. PCFG models, constituting the main part of this work together with the analysis over tree representations, is described more in details in the next sections.

3.1 Conditional Random Fields

CRFs are particularly suitable for sequence labelling tasks (Lafferty et al., 2001). Beyond the possibility to include a huge number of features using the same framework as Maximum Entropy models (Berger et al., 1996), CRF models encode global conditional probabilities normalized at sentence level.

Given a sequence of N words $W_1^N = w_1, ..., w_N$ and its corresponding components sequence $E_1^N = e_1, ..., e_N$, CRF trains the conditional probabilities

$$P(E_1^N | W_1^N) =$$

$$\frac{1}{Z} \prod_{n=1}^{N} \exp\left(\sum_{m=1}^{M} \lambda_m \cdot h_m(e_{n-1}, e_n, w_{n-2}^{n+2}) \right) \quad (1)$$

where λ_m are the training parameters. $h_m(e_{n-1}, e_n, w_{n-2}^{n+2})$ are the feature functions capturing dependencies of entities and words. Z is the partition function:

$$Z = \sum_{\tilde{e}_1^N} \prod_{n=1}^{N} H(\tilde{e}_{n-1}, \tilde{e}_n, w_{n-2}^{n+2}) \quad (2)$$

which ensures that probabilities sum up to one. $\tilde{e}_{n-1}$ and $\tilde{e}_n$ are components for previous and current words, $H(\tilde{e}_{n-1}, \tilde{e}_n, w_{n-2}^{n+2})$ is an abbreviation for $\sum_{m=1}^{M} \lambda_m \cdot h_m(e_{n-1}, e_n, w_{n-2}^{n+2})$, i.e. the set of active feature functions at current position in the sequence.

In the last few years different CRF implementations have been realized. The implementation we refer in this work is the one described in (Lavergne et al., 2010), which optimize the following objective function:

$$-log(P(E_1^N | W_1^N)) + \rho_1 \|\lambda\|_1 + \frac{\rho_2}{2} \|\lambda\|_2^2 \quad (3)$$

$\|\lambda\|_1$ and $\|\lambda\|_2^2$ are the *l1* and *l2* regularizers (Riezler and Vasserman, 2004), and together in a linear combination implement the elastic net regularizer (Zou and Hastie, 2005). As mentioned in (Lavergne et al., 2010), this kind of regularizers are very effective for feature selection at training time, which is a very good point when dealing with noisy data and big set of features.

4 Models for Parsing Trees

The models used in this work for parsing entity trees refer to the models described in (Johnson, 1998), in (Charniak, 1997; Caraballo and Charniak, 1997) and (Charniak et al., 1998), and which constitutes the basis of the maximum entropy model for parsing described in (Charniak, 2000). A similar lexicalized model has been proposed also by Collins (Collins, 1997). All these models are based on a PCFG trained from data and used in a chart parsing algorithm to find the best parse for the given input. The PCFG model of (Johnson, 1998) is made of rules of the form:

- $X_i \Rightarrow X_j X_k$
- $X_i \Rightarrow w$

where X are non-terminal entities and w are terminal symbols (words in our case).[1] The probability associated to these rules are:

$$p_{i \to j,k} = \frac{P(X_i \Rightarrow X_j, X_k)}{P(X_i)} \quad (4)$$

$$p_{i \to w} = \frac{P(X_i \Rightarrow w)}{P(X_i)} \quad (5)$$

The models described in (Charniak, 1997; Caraballo and Charniak, 1997) encode probabilities involving more information, such as head words. In order to have a PCFG model made of rules with their associated probabilities, we extract rules from the entity trees of our corpus. This processing is straightforward, for example from the tree depicted in figure 2, the following rules are extracted:

S ⇒ amount loc.adm.town time.dat.rel amount
amount ⇒ val object
time.date.rel ⇒ name time-modifier
object ⇒ func.coll
func.coll ⇒ kind org.adm
org.adm ⇒ name

Using counts of these rules we then compute maximum likelihood probabilities of the Right Hand Side (RHS) of the rule given its Left Hand Side (LHS). Also binarization of rules, applied to have all rules in the form of 4 and 5, is straightforward and can be done with simple algorithms not discussed here.

[1]These rules are actually in Chomsky Normal Form, i.e. unary or binary rules only. A PCFG, in general, can have any rule, however, the algorithm we are discussing convert the PCFG rules into Chomsky Normal Form, thus for simplicity we provide directly such formulation.

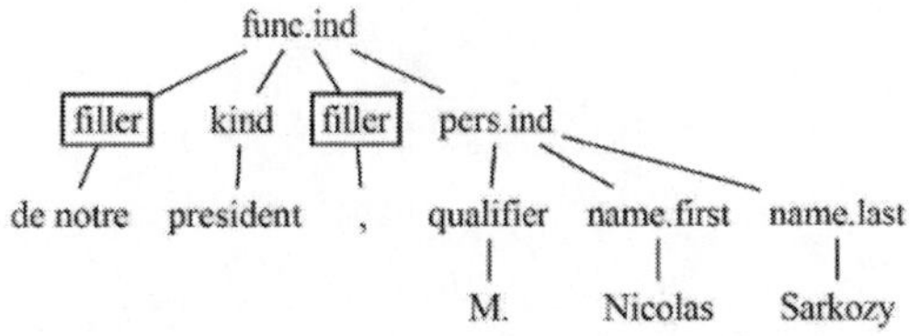

Figure 4: Baseline tree representations used in the PCFG parsing model

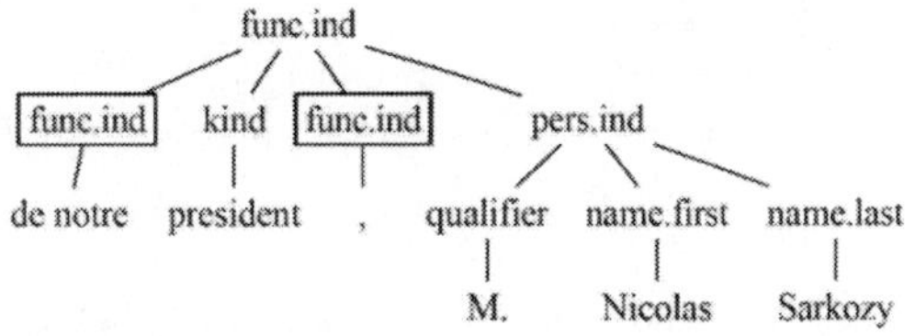

Figure 5: Filler-parent tree representations used in the PCFG parsing model

4.1 Tree Representations for Extended Named Entities

As discussed in (Johnson, 1998), an important point for a parsing algorithm is the representation of trees being parsed. Changing the tree representation can change significantly the performances of the parser. Since there is a large difference between entity trees used in this work and syntactic trees, from both meaning and structure point of view, it is worth performing an analysis with the aim of finding the most suitable representation for our task. In order to perform this analysis, we start from a named entity annotated on the words *de notre president , M. Nicolas Sarkozy(of our president, Mr. Nicolas Sarkozy)*. The corresponding named entity is shown in figure 4. As decided in the annotation guidelines, fillers can be part of a named entity. This can happen for complex named entities involving several words. The representation shown in figure 4 is the default representation and will be referred to as *baseline*. A problem created by this representation is the fact that fillers are present also outside entities. Fillers of named entities should be, in principle, distinguished from any other filler, since they may be informative to discriminate entities.

Following this intuition, we designed two different representations where entity fillers are con-

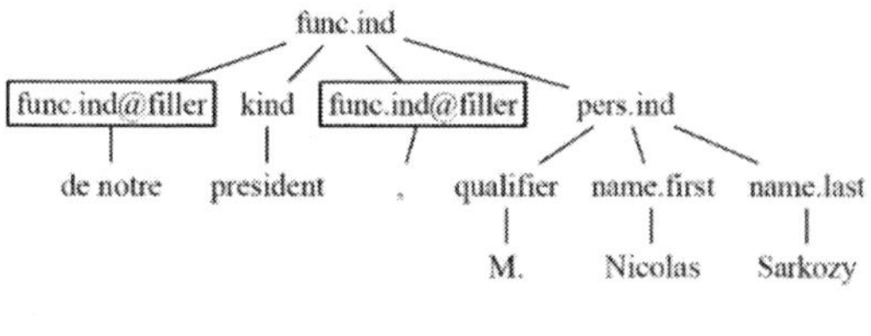

Figure 6: Parent-context tree representations used in the PCFG parsing model

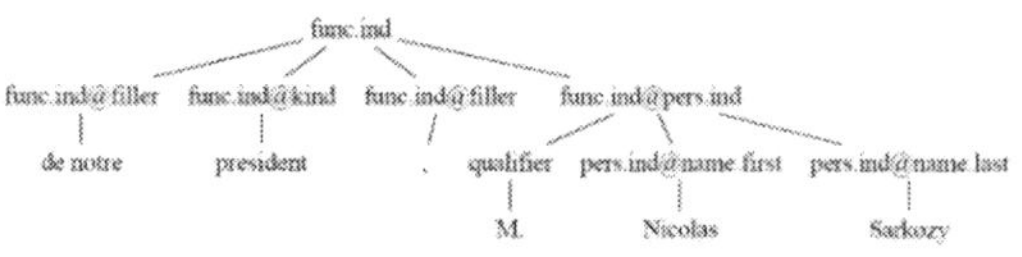

Figure 7: Parent-node tree representations used in the PCFG parsing model

textualized so that to be distinguished from the other fillers. In the first representation we give to the filler the same label of the parent node, while in the second representation we use a concatenation of the filler and the label of the parent node. These two representations are shown in figure 5 and 6, respectively. The first one will be referred to as *filler-parent*, while the second will be referred as *parent-context*. A problem that may be introduced by the first representation is that some entities that originally were used only for non-terminal entities will appear also as components, i.e. entities annotated on words. This may introduce some ambiguity.

Another possible contextualization can be to annotate each node with the label of the parent node. This representation is shown in figure 7 and will be referred to as *parent-node*. Intuitively, this representation is effective since entities annotated directly on words provide also the entity of the parent node. However this representation increases drastically the number of entities, in particular the number of components, which in our case are the set of labels to be learned by the CRF model. For the same reason this representation produces more rigid models, since label sequences vary widely and thus is not likely to match sequences not seen in the training data.

Finally, another interesting tree representation is a variation of the *parent-node* tree, where entity fillers are only distinguished from fillers not in an entity, using the label *ne-filler*, but they are not contextualized with entity information. This representation is shown in figure 8 and it will be

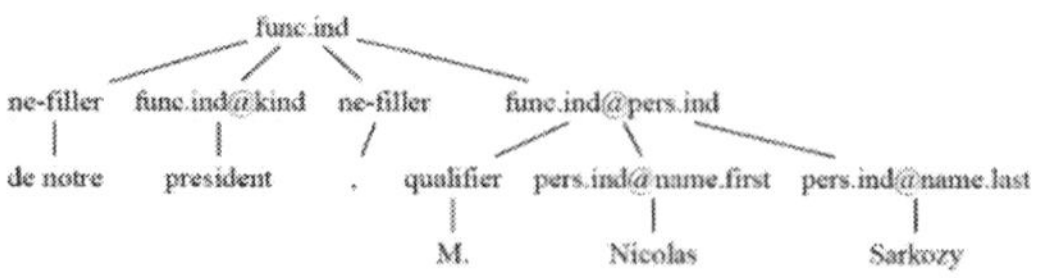

Figure 8: Parent-node-filler tree representations used in the PCFG parsing model

referred to as *parent-node-filler*. This representation is a good trade-off between contextual information and rigidity, by still representing entities as concatenation of labels, while using a common special label for entity fillers. This allows to keep lower the number of entities annotated on words, i.e. components.

Using different tree representations affects both the structure and the performance of the parsing model. The structure is described in the next section, the performance in the evaluation section.

4.2 Structure of the Model

Lexicalized models for syntactic parsing described in (Charniak, 2000; Charniak et al., 1998) and (Collins, 1997), integrate more information than what is used in equations 4 and 5. Considering a particular node in the entity tree, not including terminals, the information used is:

- s: the head word of the node, i.e. the most important word of the chunk covered by the current node
- h: the head word of the parent node
- t: the entity tag of the current node
- l: the entity tag of the parent node

The head word of the parent node is defined percolating head words from children nodes to parent nodes, giving the priority to verbs. They can be found using automatic approaches based on words and entity tag co-occurrence or mutual information. Using this information, the model described in (Charniak et al., 1998) is $P(s|h,t,l)$. This model being conditioned on several pieces of information, it can be affected by data sparsity problems. Thus, the model is actually approximated as an interpolation of probabilities:

$$P(s|h,t,l) = \lambda_1 P(s|h,t,l) + \lambda_2 P(s|c_h,t,l) + \lambda_3 P(s|t,l) + \lambda_4 P(s|t) \quad (6)$$

where $\lambda_i, i = 1, ..., 4$, are parameters of the model to be tuned, and c_h is the cluster of head words for a given entity tag t. With such model, when not all pieces of information are available to estimate reliably the probability with more conditioning, the model can still provide a probability with terms conditioned with less information. The use of head words and their percolation over the tree is called lexicalization. The goal of tree lexicalization is to add lexical information all over the tree. This way the probability of all rules can be conditioned also on lexical information, allowing to define the probabilities $P(s|h,t,l)$ and $P(s|c_h,t,l)$. Tree lexicalization reflects the characteristics of syntactic parsing, for which the models described in (Charniak, 2000; Charniak et al., 1998) and (Collins, 1997) were defined. Head words are very informative since they constitute keywords instantiating labels, regardless if they are syntactic constituents or named entities. However, for named entity recognition it doesn't make sense to give priority to verbs when percolating head words over the tree, even more because head words of named entities are most of the time nouns. Moreover, it doesn't make sense to give priority to the head word of a particular entity with respect to the others, all entities in a sentence have the same importance. Intuitively, lexicalization of entity trees is not straightforward as lexicalization of syntactic trees. At the same time, using not lexicalized trees doesn't make sense with models like 6, since all the terms involve lexical information. Instead, we can use the model of (Johnson, 1998), which define the probability of a tree τ as:

$$P(\tau) = \prod_{X \to \alpha} P(X \to \alpha)^{C_\tau(X \to \alpha)} \quad (7)$$

here the RHS of rules has been generalized with α, representing RHS of both unary and binary rules 4 and 5. $C_\tau(X \to \alpha)$ is the number of times the rule $X \to \alpha$ appears in the tree τ. The model 7 is instantiated when using tree representations shown in Fig. 4, 5 and 6. When using representations given in Fig. 7 and 8, the model is:

$$P(\tau|l) \quad (8)$$

where l is the entity label of the parent node. Although non-lexicalized models like 7 and 8 have shown less effective for syntactic parsing than their lexicalized couter-parts, there are evidences showing that they can be effective in our task. With reference to figure 4, considering the entity *pers.ind* instantiated by *Nicolas Sarkozy*, our algorithm detects first *name.first* for *Nicolas* and *name.last* for *Sarkozy* using the CRF model. As mentioned earlier, once the CRF model has detected components, since entity trees have not a complex structure with respect to syntactic trees, even a simple model like the one in equation 7 or 8 is effective for entity tree parsing. For example, once *name.first* and *name.last* have been detected by CRF, *pers.ind* is the only entity having *name.first* and *name.last* as children. Ambiguities, like for example for *kind* or *qualifier*, which can appear in many entities, can affect the model 7, but they are overcome by the model 8, taking the entity tag of the parent node into account. Moreover, the use of CRF allows to include in the model much more features than the lexicalized model in equation 6. Using features like word prefixes (P), suffixes (S), capitalization (C), morpho-syntactic features (MS) and other features indicated as F[2], the CRF model encodes the conditional probability:

$$P(t|w, P, S, C, MS, F) \quad (9)$$

where w is an input word and t is the corresponding component.

The probability of the CRF model, used in the first step to tag input words with components, is combined with the probability of the PCFG model, used to parse entity trees starting from components. Thus the structure of our model is:

$$P(t|w, P, S, C, MS, F) \cdot P(\tau) \quad (10)$$

or

$$P(t|w, P, S, C, MS, F) \cdot P(\tau|l) \quad (11)$$

depending if we are using the tree representation given in figure 4, 5 and 6 or in figure 7 and 8, respectively. A scale factor could be used to combine the two scores, but this is optional as CRFs can provide normalized posterior probabilities.

[2]The set of features used in the CRF model will be described in more details in the evaluation section.

5 Related Work

While the models used for named entity detection and the set of named entities defined along the years have been discussed in the introduction and in section 2, since CRFs and models for parsing constitute the main issue in our work, we discuss some important models here.

Beyond the models for parsing discussed in section 4, together with motivations for using or not in our work, another important model for syntactic parsing has been proposed in (Ratnaparkhi, 1999). Such model is made of four Maximum Entropy models used in cascade for parsing at different stages. Also this model makes use of head words, like those described in section 4, thus the same considerations hold, moreover it seems quite complex for real applications, as it involves the use of four different models together. The models described in (Johnson, 1998), (Charniak, 1997; Caraballo and Charniak, 1997), (Charniak et al., 1998), (Charniak, 2000), (Collins, 1997) and (Ratnaparkhi, 1999), constitute the main individual models proposed for constituent-based syntactic parsing. Later other approaches based on models combination have been proposed, like e.g. the reranking approach described in (Collins and Koo, 2005), among many, and also evolutions or improvements of these models.

More recently, approaches based on log-linear models have been proposed (Clark and Curran, 2007; Finkel et al., 2008) for parsing, called also "*Tree CRF*", using also different training criteria (Auli and Lopez, 2011). Using such models in our work has basically two problems: one related to scaling issues, since our data present a large number of labels, which makes CRF training problematic, even more when using "*Tree CRF*"; another problem is related to the difference between syntactic parsing and named entity detection tasks, as mentioned in sub-section 4.2. Adapting "*Tree CRF*" to our task is thus a quite complex work, it constitutes an entire work by itself, we leave it as feature work.

Concerning linear-chain CRF models, the one we use is a state-of-the-art implementation (Lavergne et al., 2010), as it implements the most effective optimization algorithms as well as state-of-the-art regularizers (see sub-section 3.1). Some improvement of linear-chain CRF have been proposed, trying to integrate higher order target-side features (Tang et al., 2006). An integration of the same kind of features has been tried also in the model used in this work, without giving significant improvements, but making model training much harder. Thus, this direction has not been further investigated.

6 Evaluation

In this section we describe experiments performed to evaluate our models. We first describe the settings used for the two models involved in the entity tree parsing, and then describe and comment the results obtained on the test corpus.

6.1 Settings

The CRF implementation used in this work is described in (Lavergne et al., 2010), named *wapiti*.[3] We didn't optimize parameters ρ_1 and ρ_2 of the elastic net (see section 3.1), although this improves significantly the performances and leads to more compact models, default values lead in most cases to very accurate models. We used a wide set of features in CRF models, in a window of $[-2, +2]$ around the target word:

- A set of standard features like word prefixes and suffixes of length from 1 to 6, plus some *Yes/No* features like *Does the word start with capital letter?*, etc.

- Morpho-syntactic features extracted from the output of the tool *tagger* (Allauzen and Bonneau-Maynard, 2008)

- Features extracted from the output of the semantic analyzer (Rosset et al., (2009)) provided by the tool *WMatch* (Galibert, 2009).

This analysis morpho-syntactic information as well as semantic information at the same level of named entities. Using two different sets of morpho-syntactic features results in more effective models, as they create a kind of agreement for a given word in case of match. Concerning the PCFG model, grammars, tree binarization and the different tree representations are created with our own scripts, while entity tree parsing is performed with the chart parsing algorithm described in (Johnson, 1998).[4]

[3]available at `http://wapiti.limsi.fr`

[4]available at `http://web.science.mq.edu.au/~mjohnson/Software.htm`

	CRF		PCFG
Model	# features	# labels	# rules
baseline	3,041,797	55	29,611
filler-parent	3,637,990	112	29,611
parent-context	3,605,019	120	29,611
parent-node	3,718,089	441	31,110
parent-node-filler	3,723,964	378	31,110

Table 3: Statistics showing the characteristics of the different models used in this work

6.2 Evaluation Metrics

All results are expressed in terms of Slot Error Rate (SER) (Makhoul et al., 1999) which has a similar definition of word error rate for ASR systems, with the difference that substitution errors are split in three types: i) correct entity type with wrong segmentation; ii) wrong entity type with correct segmentation; iii) wrong entity type with wrong segmentation; here, i) and ii) are given half points, while iii), as well as insertion and deletion errors, are given full points. Moreover, results are given using the well known $F1$ measure, defined as a function of precision and recall.

6.3 Results

In this section we provide evaluations of the models described in this work, based on combination of CRF and PCFG and using different tree representations of named entity trees.

6.3.1 Model Statistics

As a first evaluation, we describe some statistics computed from the CRF and PCFG models using the tree representations. Such statistics provide interesting clues of how difficult is learning the task and which performance we can expect from the model. Statistics for this evaluation are presented in table 3. Rows corresponds to the different tree representations described in this work, while in the columns we show the number of features and labels for the CRF models (**# features** and **# labels**), and the number of rules for PCFG models (# rules).

As we can see from the table, the number of rules is the same for the tree representations **baseline**, **filler-parent** and **parent-context**, and for the representations **parent-node** and **parent-node-filler**. This is the consequence of the contextualization applied by the latter representations, i.e. **parent-node** and **parent-node-filler** create several different labels depending from the context, thus the corresponding grammar

	DEV		TEST	
Model	SER	F1	SER	F1
baseline	20.0%	73.4%	14.2%	79.4%
filler-parent	16.2%	77.8%	12.5%	81.2%
parent-context	15.2%	78.6%	11.9%	81.4%
parent-node	6.6%	96.7%	5.9%	96.7%
parent-node-filler	6.8%	95.9%	5.7%	96.8%

Table 4: Results computed from oracle predictions obtained with the different models presented in this work

	DEV		TEST	
Model	SER	F1	SER	F1
baseline	33.5%	72.5%	33.4%	72.8%
filler-parent	31.3%	74.4%	33.4%	72.7%
parent-context	30.9%	74.6%	33.3%	72.8%
parent-node	31.2%	77.8%	31.4%	79.5%
parent-node-filler	28.7%	78.9%	30.2%	80.3%

Table 5: Results obtained with our combined algorithm based on CRF and PCFG

will have more rules. For example, the rule `pers.ind` ⇒ `name.first name.last` can appear as it is or contextualized with `func.ind`, like in figure 8. In contrast the other tree representations modify only fillers, thus the number of rules is not affected.

Concerning CRF models, as shown in table 3, the use of the different tree representations results in an increasing number of labels to be learned by CRF. This aspect is quite critical in CRF learning, as training time is exponential in the number of labels. Indeed, the most complex models, obtained with **parent-node** and **parent-node-filler** tree representations, took roughly 8 days for training. Additionally, increasing the number of labels can create data sparseness problems, however this problem doesn't seem to arise in our case since, apart the **baseline** model which has quite less features, all the others have approximately the same number of features, meaning that there are actually enough data to learn the models, regardless the number of labels.

6.3.2 Evaluations of Tree Representations

In this section we evaluate the models in terms of the evaluation metrics described in previous section, Slot Error Rate (SER) and F1 measure.

In order to evaluate PCFG models alone, we performed entity tree parsing using as input reference transcriptions, i.e. manual transcriptions and reference component annotations taken from development and test sets. This can be considered a kind of oracle evaluations and provides us an upper bound of the performance of the PCFG models. Results for this evaluation are reported in

Participant	SER
P1	48.9
P2	41.0
parent-context	33.3
parent-node	31.4
parent-node-filler	30.2

Table 6: Results obtained with our combined algorithm based on CRF and PCFG

table 4. As it can be intuitively expected, adding more contextualization in the trees results in more accurate models, the simplest model, **baseline**, has the worst oracle performance, **filler-parent** and **parent-context** models, adding similar contextualization information, have very similar oracle performances. Same line of reasoning applies to models **parent-node** and **parent-node-filler**, which also add similar contextualization and have very similar oracle predictions. These last two models have also the best absolute oracle performances. However, adding more contextualization in the trees results also in more rigid models, the fact that models are robust on reference transcriptions and based on reference component annotations, doesn't imply a proportional robustness on component sequences generated by CRF models.

This intuition is confirmed from results reported in table 5, where a real evaluation of our models is reported, using this time CRF output components as input to PCFG models, to parse entity trees. The results reported in table 5 show in particular that models using **baseline**, **filler-parent** and **parent-context** tree representations have similar performances, especially on test set. Models characterized by **parent-node** and **parent-node-filler** tree representations have indeed the best performances, although the gain with respect to the other models is not as much as it could be expected given the difference in the oracle performances discussed above. In particular the best absolute performance is obtained with the model **parent-node-filler**. As we mentioned in subsection 4.1, this model represents the best trade-off between rigidity and accuracy using the same label for all entity fillers, but still distinguishing between fillers found in entity structures and other fillers found in words not instantiating any entity.

6.3.3 Comparison with Official Results

As a final evaluation of our models, we provide a comparison of official results obtained at the 2011 evaluation campaign of extended named entity recognition (Galibert et al., 2011; 2) Results are reported in table 6, where the other two participants to the campaign are indicated as $P1$ and $P2$. These two participants $P1$ and $P2$, used a system based on CRF, and rules for deep syntactic analysis, respectively. In particular, $P2$ obtained superior performances in previous evaluation campaign on named entity recognition. The system we proposed at the evaluation campaign used a **parent-context** tree representation. The results obtained at the evaluation campaign are in the first three lines of Table 6. We compare such results with those obtained with the **parent-node** and **parent-node-filler** tree representations, reported in the last two rows of the same table. As we can see, the new tree representations described in this work allow to achieve the best absolute performances.

7 Conclusions

In this paper we have presented a Named Entity Recognition system dealing with extended named entities with a tree structure. Given such representation of named entities, the task cannot be modeled as a sequence labelling approach. We thus proposed a two-steps system based on CRF and PCFG. CRF annotate entity components directly on words, while PCFG apply parsing techniques to predict the whole entity tree. We motivated our choice by showing that it is not effective to apply techniques used widely for syntactic parsing, like for example tree lexicalization. We presented an analysis of different tree representations for PCFG, which affect significantly parsing performances.

We provided and discussed a detailed evaluation of all the models obtained by combining CRF and PCFG with the different tree representation proposed. Our combined models result in better performances with respect to other models proposed at the official evaluation campaign, as well as our previous model used also at the evaluation campaign.

Acknowledgments

This work has been funded by the project Quaero, under the program Oseo, French State agency for innovation.

References

Ralph Grishman and Beth Sundheim. 1996. Message Understanding Conference-6: a brief history. In *Proceedings of the 16th conference on Computational linguistics - Volume 1*, pages 466–471, Stroudsburg, PA, USA. Association for Computational Linguistics.

Satoshi Sekine and Chikashi Nobata. 2004. Definition, Dictionaries and Tagger for Extended Named Entity Hierarchy. In *Proceedings of LREC*.

G. Doddington, A. Mitchell, M. Przybocki, L. Ramshaw, S. Strassel, and R. Weischedel. 2004. The Automatic Content Extraction (ACE) Program–Tasks, Data, and Evaluation. *Proceedings of LREC 2004*, pages 837–840.

Cyril Grouin, Sophie Rosset, Pierre Zweigenbaum, Karn Fort, Olivier Galibert, Ludovic Quintard. 2011. Proposal for an extension or traditional named entities: From guidelines to evaluation, an overview. In *Proceedings of the Linguistic Annotation Workshop (LAW)*.

J. Lafferty, A. McCallum, and F. Pereira. 2001. Conditional random fields: Probabilistic models for segmenting and labeling sequence data. In *Proceedings of the Eighteenth International Conference on Machine Learning (ICML)*, pages 282–289, Williamstown, MA, USA, June.

Mark Johnson. 1998. Pcfg models of linguistic tree representations. *Computational Linguistics*, 24:613–632.

Stefan Hahn, Marco Dinarelli, Christian Raymond, Fabrice Lefèvre, Patrick Lehen, Renato De Mori, Alessandro Moschitti, Hermann Ney, and Giuseppe Riccardi. 2010. Comparing stochastic approaches to spoken language understanding in multiple languages. *IEEE Transactions on Audio, Speech and Language Processing (TASLP)*, 99.

Adam L. Berger, Stephen A. Della Pietra, and Vincent J. Della Pietra. 1996. A maximum entropy approach to natural language processing. *COMPUTATIONAL LINGUISTICS*, 22:39–71.

Thomas Lavergne, Olivier Cappé, and François Yvon. 2010. Practical very large scale CRFs. In *Proceedings the 48th Annual Meeting of the Association for Computational Linguistics (ACL)*, pages 504–513. Association for Computational Linguistics, July.

Stefan Riezler and Alexander Vasserman. 2004. Incremental feature selection and l1 regularization for relaxed maximum-entropy modeling. In *Proceedings of the International Conference on Empirical Methods for Natural Language Processing (EMNLP)*.

Hui Zou and Trevor Hastie. 2005. Regularization and variable selection via the Elastic Net. *Journal of the Royal Statistical Society B*, 67:301–320.

Eugene Charniak. 1997. Statistical parsing with a context-free grammar and word statistics. In *Proceedings of the fourteenth national conference on artificial intelligence and ninth conference on Innovative applications of artificial intelligence*, AAAI'97/IAAI'97, pages 598–603. AAAI Press.

Eugene Charniak. 2000. A maximum-entropy-inspired parser. In *Proceedings of the 1st North American chapter of the Association for Computational Linguistics conference*, pages 132–139, San Francisco, CA, USA. Morgan Kaufmann Publishers Inc.

Sharon A. Caraballo and Eugene Charniak. 1997. New figures of merit for best-first probabilistic chart parsing. *Computational Linguistics*, 24:275–298.

Michael Collins. 1997. Three generative, lexicalised models for statistical parsing. In *Proceedings of the 35th Annual Meeting of the Association for Computational Linguistics and Eighth Conference of the European Chapter of the Association for Computational Linguistics*, ACL '98, pages 16–23, Stroudsburg, PA, USA. Association for Computational Linguistics.

Eugene Charniak, Sharon Goldwater, and Mark Johnson. 1998. Edge-based best-first chart parsing. In *In Proceedings of the Sixth Workshop on Very Large Corpora*, pages 127–133. Morgan Kaufmann.

Alexandre Allauzen and Héléne Bonneau-Maynard. 2008. Training and evaluation of pos taggers on the french multitag corpus. In *Proceedings of the Sixth International Language Resources and Evaluation (LREC'08)*, Marrakech, Morocco, may.

Olivier Galibert. 2009. *Approches et méthodologies pour la réponse automatique à des questions adaptées à un cadre interactif en domaine ouvert*. Ph.D. thesis, Université Paris Sud, Orsay.

Rosset Sophie, Galibert Olivier, Bernard Guillaume, Bilinski Eric, and Adda Gilles. The LIMSI multilingual, multitask QAst system. In *Proceedings of the 9th Cross-language evaluation forum conference on Evaluating systems for multilingual and multimodal information access*, CLEF'08, pages 480–487, Berlin, Heidelberg, 2009. Springer-Verlag.

Azeddine Zidouni, Sophie Rosset, and Hervé Glotin. 2010. Efficient combined approach for named entity recognition in spoken language. In *Proceedings of the International Conference of the Speech Communication Assosiation (Interspeech)*, Makuhari, Japan

John Makhoul, Francis Kubala, Richard Schwartz, and Ralph Weischedel. 1999. Performance measures for information extraction. In *Proceedings of DARPA Broadcast News Workshop*, pages 249–252.

Adwait Ratnaparkhi. 1999. Learning to Parse Natural Language with Maximum Entropy Models. Journal of Machine Learning, vol. 34, issue 1-3, pages 151–175.

Michael Collins and Terry Koo. 2005. Discriminative Re-ranking for Natural Language Parsing. Journal of Machine Learning, vol. 31, issue 1, pages 25–70.

Clark, Stephen and Curran, James R. 2007. Wide-Coverage Efficient Statistical Parsing with CCG and Log-Linear Models. Journal of Computational Linguistics, vol. 33, issue 4, pages 493–552.

Finkel, Jenny R. and Kleeman, Alex and Manning, Christopher D. 2008. Efficient, Feature-based, Conditional Random Field Parsing. Proceedings of the Association for Computational Linguistics, pages 959–967, Columbus, Ohio.

Michael Auli and Adam Lopez 2011. Training a Log-Linear Parser with Loss Functions via Softmax-Margin. Proceedings of Empirical Methods for Natural Language Processing, pages 333–343, Edinburgh, U.K.

Tang, Jie and Hong, MingCai and Li, Juan-Zi and Liang, Bangyong. 2006. Tree-Structured Conditional Random Fields for Semantic Annotation. Proceedgins of the International Semantic Web Conference, pages 640–653, Edited by Springer.

Olivier Galibert; Sophie Rosset; Cyril Grouin; Pierre Zweigenbaum; Ludovic Quintard. 2011. Structured and Extended Named Entity Evaluation in Automatic Speech Transcriptions. IJCNLP 2011.

Marco Dinarelli, Sophie Rosset. Models Cascade for Tree-Structured Named Entity Detection IJCNLP 2011.

When Did *that* Happen? — Linking Events and Relations to Timestamps

Dirk Hovy*, **James Fan**, **Alfio Gliozzo**, **Siddharth Patwardhan** and **Chris Welty**
IBM T. J. Watson Research Center
19 Skyline Drive
Hawthorne, NY 10532
dirkh@isi.edu, {fanj,gliozzo,siddharth,welty}@us.ibm.com

Abstract

We present work on linking events and fluents (i.e., relations that hold for certain periods of time) to temporal information in text, which is an important enabler for many applications such as timelines and reasoning. Previous research has mainly focused on temporal links for events, and we extend that work to include fluents as well, presenting a common methodology for linking both events and relations to timestamps within the same sentence. Our approach combines tree kernels with classical feature-based learning to exploit context and achieves competitive F1-scores on event-time linking, and comparable F1-scores for fluents. Our best systems achieve F1-scores of 0.76 on events and 0.72 on fluents.

1 Introduction

It is a long-standing goal of NLP to process natural language content in such a way that machines can effectively reason over the entities, relations, and events discussed within that content. The applications of such technology are numerous, including intelligence gathering, business analytics, healthcare, education, etc. Indeed, the promise of *machine reading* is actively driving research in this area (Etzioni et al., 2007; Barker et al., 2007; Clark and Harrison, 2010; Strassel et al., 2010).

Temporal information is a crucial aspect of this task. For a machine to successfully understand natural language text, it must be able to associate time points and temporal durations with relations and events it discovers in text.

*The first author conducted this research during an internship at IBM Research.

In this paper we present methods to establish links between events (e.g. "bombing" or "election") or fluents (e.g. "spouseOf" or "employedBy") and temporal expressions (e.g. "last Tuesday" and "November 2008"). While previous research has mainly focused on temporal links for events only, we deal with both events and fluents with the same method. For example, consider the sentence below

> *Before his death in October, Steve Jobs led Apple for 15 years.*

For a machine reading system processing this sentence, we would expect it to link the fluent *CEO_of*(Steve_Jobs, Apple) to time duration "15 years". Similarly we expect it to link the event "death" to the time expression "October".

We do not take a strong "ontological" position on what events and fluents are, as part of our task these distinctions are made a priori. In other words, events and fluents are input to our temporal linking framework. In the remainder of this paper, we also do not make a strong distinction between relations in general and fluents in particular, and use them interchangeably, since our focus is only on the specific types of relations that represent fluents. While we only use binary relations in this work, there is nothing in the framework that would prevent the use of n-ary relations. Our work focuses on accurately identifying temporal links for eventual use in a machine reading context.

In this paper, we describe a single approach that applies to both fluents and events, using feature engineering as well as tree kernels. We show that we can achieve good results for both events and fluents using the same feature space, and advocate the versatility of our approach by achieving competitive results on yet another similar task with a different data set.

Our approach requires us to capture contextual properties of text surrounding events, fluents and time expressions that enable an automatic system to detect temporal linking within our framework. A common strategy for this is to follow standard feature engineering methodology and manually develop features for a machine learning model from the lexical, syntactic and semantic analysis of the text. A key contribution of our work in this paper is to demonstrate a shallow tree-like representation of the text that enables us to employ *tree kernel* models, and more accurately detect temporal linking. The feature space represented by such tree kernels is far larger than a manually engineered feature space, and is capable of capturing the contextual information required for temporal linking.

The remainder of this paper goes into the details of our approach for temporal linking, and presents empirical evidence for the effectiveness of our approach. The contributions of this paper can be summarized as follows:

1. We define a common methodology to link events and fluents to timestamps.
2. We use tree kernels in combination with classical feature-based approaches to obtain significant gains by exploiting context.
3. Empirical evidence illustrates that our framework for temporal linking is very effective for the task, achieving an F1-score of 0.76 on events and 0.72 on fluents/relations, as well as 0.65 for TempEval2, approaching state-of-the-art.

2 Related Work

Most of the previous work on relation extraction focuses on entity-entity relations, such as in the ACE (Doddington et al., 2004) tasks. Temporal relations are part of this, but to a lesser extent. The primary research effort in event temporality has gone into ordering events with respect to one another (e.g., Chambers and Jurafsky (2008)), and detecting their typical durations (e.g., Pan et al. (2006)).

Recently, TempEval workshops have focused on the temporal related issues in NLP. Some of the TempEval tasks overlap with ours in many ways. Our task is similar to task A and C of TempEval-1 (Verhagen et al., 2007) in the sense that we attempt to identify temporal relation between events and time expressions or document dates. However, we do not use a restricted set of events, but focus primarily on a single temporal relation t_{link} instead of named relations like BEFORE, AFTER or OVERLAP (although we show that we can incorporate these as well). Part of our task is similar to task C of TempEval-2 (Verhagen et al., 2010), determining the temporal relation between an event and a time expression in the same sentence. In this paper, we do apply our system to TempEval-2 data and compare our performance to the participating systems.

Our work is similar to that of Boguraev and Ando (2005), whose research only deals with temporal links between events and time expressions (and does not consider relations at all). They employ a sequence tagging model with manual feature engineering for the task and achieved state-of-the-art results on Timebank (Pustejovsky et al., 2003) data. Our task is slightly different because we include relations in the temporal linking, and our use of tree kernels enables us to explore a wider feature space very quickly.

Filatova and Hovy (2001) also explore temporal linking with events, but do not assume that events and time stamps have been provided by an external process. They used a heuristics-based approach to assign temporal expressions to events (also relying on the proximity as a base case). They report accuracy of the assignment for the correctly classified events, the best being 82.29%. Our best event system achieves an accuracy of 84.83%. These numbers are difficult to compare, however, since accuracy does not efficiently capture the performance of a system on a task with so many negative examples.

Mirroshandel et al. (2011) describe the use of syntactic tree kernels for event-time links. Their results on TempEval are comparable to ours. In contrast to them, we found, though, that syntactic tree kernels alone do not perform as well as using several flat tree representations.

3 Problem Definition

The task of linking events and relations to time stamps can be defined as the following: given a set of expressions denoting events or relation mentions in a document, and a set of time expressions in the same document, find all instances of the t_{link} relation between elements of the two input sets. The existence of a $t_{link}(e, t)$ means that e, which is an event or a relation mention, occurs within the temporal context specified by the time expression t.

Thus, our task can be cast as a binary relation classification task: for each possible pair of (event/relation, time) in a document, decide whether there exists a link between the two, and if so, express it in the data.

In addition, we make these assumptions about the data:

1. There does not exist a timestamp for every event/relation in a document. Although events and relations typically have temporal context, it may not be explicitly stated in a document.

2. Every event/relation has at most one time expression associated with it. This is a simplifying assumption, which in the case of relations we explore as future work.

3. Each temporal expression can be linked to one or more events or relations. Since multiple events or relations may happen for a given time, it is safe to assume that each temporal expression can be linked to more than one event/relation.

In general, the events/relations and their associated timestamps may occur within the same sentence or may occur across different sentences. In this paper, we focus on our effort and our evaluation on the same sentence linking task.

In order to solve the problem of temporal linking completely, however, it will be important to also address the links that hold between entities across sentences. We estimate, based on our data set, that across sentence links account for 41% of all correct event-time pairs in a document. For fluents, the ratio is much higher, more than 80% of the correct fluent-time links are across sentences. One of the main obstacles for our approach in the cross-sentence case is the very low ratio of positive to negative instances (3 : 100) in the set of all pairs in a document. Most pairs are not linked to one another.

4 Temporal Linking Framework

As previously mentioned, we approach the temporal linking problem as a classification task. In the framework of classification, we refer to each pair of (*event/relation, temporal expression*) occurring within a sentence as an instance. The goal is to devise a classifier that separates positive (i.e., linked) instances from negative ones, i.e., pairs where there is no link between the event/relation and the temporal expression in question. The latter case is far more frequent, so we have an inherent bias toward negative examples in our data.[1]

Note that the basis of the positive and negative links is the context around the target terms. It is impossible even for humans to determine the existence of a link based only on the two terms without their context. For instance, given just two words (e.g., "said" and "yesterday") there is no way to tell if it is a positive or a negative example. We need the context to decide.

Therefore, we base our classification models on contextual features drawn from lexical and syntactic analyses of the text surrounding the target terms. For this, we first define a feature-based approach, then we improve it by using tree kernels. These two subsections, plus the treatment of fluent relations, are the main contributions of this paper. In all of this work, we employ SVM classifiers (Vapnik, 1995) for machine learning.

4.1 Feature Engineering

A manual analysis of development data provided several intuitions about the kinds of features that would be useful in this task. Based on this analysis and with inspiration from previous work (cf. Boguraev and Ando (2005)) we established three categories of features whose description follows.

Features describing events or relations. We check whether the event or relation is phrasal, a verb, or noun, whether it is present tense, past tense, or progressive, the type assigned to the event/relation by the UIMA type system used for processing, and whether it includes certain trigger words, such as reporting verbs ("said", "reported", etc.).

[1] Initially, we employed an instance filtering method to address this, which proved to be ineffective and was subsequently left out.

Features describing temporal expressions. We check for the presence of certain trigger words (*last, next, old,* numbers, etc.) and the type of the expression (DURATION, TIME, or DATE) as specified by the UIMA type system.

Features describing context. We also include syntactic/structural features, such as testing whether the relation/event dominates the temporal expression, which one comes first in the sentence order, and whether either of them is dominated by a separate verb, preposition, "that" (which often indicates a subordinate sentence) or counterfactual nouns or verbs (which would negate the temporal link).

It is not surprising that some of the most informative features (event comes before temporal expression, time is syntactic child of event) are strongly correlated with the baselines. Less salient features include the test for certain words indicating the event is a noun, a verb, and if so which tense it has and whether it is a reporting verb.

4.2 Tree Kernel Engineering

We expect that there exist certain patterns between the entities of a temporal link, which manifest on several levels: some on the lexical level, others expressed by certain sequences of POS tags, NE labels, or other representations. Kernels provide a principled way of expanding the number of dimensions in which we search for a decision boundary, and allow us to easily model local sequences and patterns in a natural way (Giuliano et al., 2009). While it is possible to define a space in which we find a decision boundary that separates positive and negative instances with manually engineered features, these features can hardly capture the notion of context as well as those explored by a tree kernel.

Tree Kernels are a family of kernel functions developed to compute the similarity between tree structures by counting the number of subtrees they have in common. This generates a high-dimensional feature space that can be handled efficiently using dynamic programming techniques (Shawe-Taylor and Christianini, 2004). For our purposes we used an implementation of the Subtree and Subset Tree (SST) (Moschitti, 2006).

The advantages of using tree kernels are two-fold: thanks to an existing implementation (SVM^{light} with tree kernels, Moschitti (2004)), it is faster and easier than traditional feature engineering. The tree structure also allows us to use different levels of representations (POS, lemma, etc.) and combine their contributions, while at the same time taking into account the ordering of labels. We use POS, lemma, semantic type, and a representation that replaces each word with a concatenation of its features (capitalization, countable, abstract/concrete noun, etc.).

We developed a shallow tree representation that captures the context of the target terms, without encoding too much structure (which may prevent generalization). In essence, our tree structure induces behavior somewhat similar to a string kernel. In addition, we can model the tasks by providing specific markup on the generated tree. For example, in our experiment we used the labels EVENT (or equivalently RELATION) and TIMESTAMP to mark our target terms. In order to reduce the complexity of this comparison, we focus on the substring between event/relation and time stamp and the rest of the tree structure is truncated.

Figure 1 illustrates an example of the structure described so far for both lemmas and POS tags (note that the lowest level of the tree contains tokenized items, so their number can differ form the actual words, as in "attorney_general"). Similar trees are produced for each level of representations used, and for each instance (i.e., pair of time expressions and event/relation). If a sentence contains more than one event/relation, we create separate trees for each of them, which differ in the position of the EVENT/RELATION marks (at level 1 of the tree).

The tree kernel implicitly expands this structure into a number of substructures allowing us to capture sequential patterns in the data. As we will see, this step provides significant boosts to the task performance.

Curiously, using a full-parse syntactic tree as input representation did not help performance. This is in line with our finding that syntactic relations are less important than sequential patterns (see also Section 5.2). Therefore we adopted the "string kernel like" representation illustrated in Figure 1.

Scores of supporters of detained Egyptian opposition leader Nur demonstrated outside the attorney general's office in Cairo last Saturday, demanding he be freed immediately.

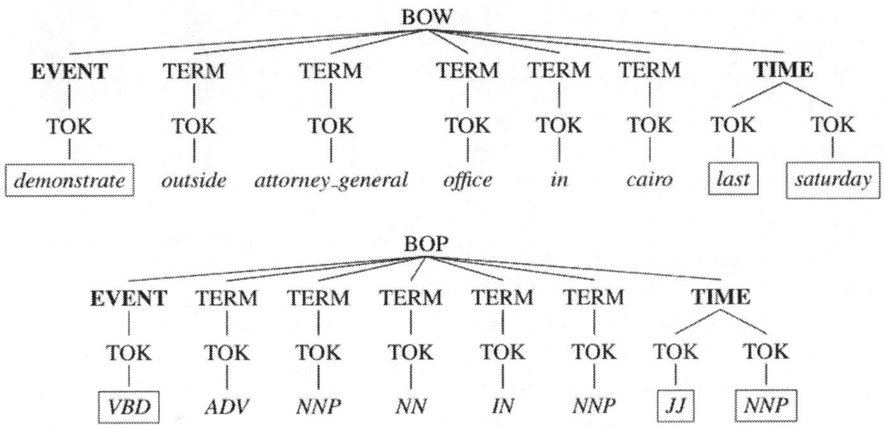

Figure 1: Input Sentence and Tree Kernel Representations for Bag of Words (BOW) and POS tags (BOP)

5 Evaluation

We now apply our models to real world data, and empirically demonstrate their effectiveness at the task of temporal linking. In this section, we describe the data sets that were used for evaluation, the baselines for comparison, parameter settings, and the results of the experiments.

5.1 Benchmark

We evaluated our approach in 3 different tasks:

1. Linking Timestamps and Events in the IC domain
2. Linking Timestamps and Relations in the IC domain
3. Linking Events to Temporal Expressions (TempEval-2, task C)

The first two data sets contained annotations in the intelligence community (IC) domain, i.e., mainly news reports about terrorism. It comprised 169 documents. This dataset has been developed in the context of the machine reading program (MRP) (Strassel et al., 2010). In both cases our goal is to develop a binary classifier to judge whether the event (or relation) overlaps with the time interval denoted by the timestamp. Success of this classification can be measured by precision and recall on annotated data.

We originally considered using accuracy as a measure of performance, but this does not correctly reflect the true performance of the system: given the skewed nature of the data (much smaller number of positive examples), we could achieve a high accuracy simply by classifying all instances as negative, i.e., not assigning a time stamp at all. We thus decided to report precision, recall and F1. Unless stated otherwise, results were achieved via 10-fold cross-validation (10-CV).

The number of instances (i.e., pairs of event and temporal expression) for each of the different cases listed above was (in brackets the ratio of positive to negative instances).

- events: 2046 (505 positive, 1541 negative)
- relations: 6526 (1847 positive, 4679 negative)

The size of the relation data set after filtering is 5511 (1847 positive, 3395 negative).

In order to increase the originally lower number of event instances, we made use of the annotated event-coreference as a sort of closure to add more instances: if events A and B corefer, and there is a link between A and time expression t, then there is also a link between B and t. This was not explicitly expressed in the data.

For the task at hand, we used gold standard annotations for timestamps, events and relations. The task was thus not the identification of these objects (a necessary precursor and a difficult task in itself), but the decision as to which events and time expressions could and should be linked.

We also evaluated our system on TempEval-2 (Verhagen et al., 2010) for better comparison to the state-of-the-art. TempEval-2 data included the task of linking events to temporal expressions (there called "task C"), using several link types (OVERLAP, BEFORE, AFTER, BEFORE-OR-OVERLAP, OVERLAP-OR-AFTER). This is a bit different from our settings as it required the implementation of a multi-class classifier. Therefore we trained three different binary classifiers (using the same feature set) for the first three of those types (for which there was sufficient training data) and we used a one-versus-all strategy to distinguish positive from negative examples. The output of the system is the category with the highest SVM decision score. Since we only use three labels, we incur an error every time the gold label is something else. Note that this is stricter than the evaluation in the actual task, which left contestants with the option of skipping examples their systems could not classify.

5.2 Baselines

Intuitively, one would expect temporal expressions to be close to the event they denote, or even syntactically related. In order to test this, we applied two baselines. In the first, each temporal expression was linked to the closest event (as measured in token distance). In the second, we attached each temporal expression to its syntactic head, if the head was an event. Results are reported in Figure 2.

While these results are encouraging for our task, it seems at first counter-intuitive that the syntactic baseline does worse than the proximity-based one. It does, however, reveal two facts: events are not always synonymous with syntactic units, and they are not always bound to temporal expressions through direct syntactic links. The latter makes even more sense given that the links can even occur across sentence boundaries. Parsing quality could play a role, yet seems far fetched to account for the difference.

More important than syntactic relations seem to be sequential patterns on different levels, a fact we exploit with the different tree representations used (POS tags, NE types, etc.).

For relations, we only applied the closest-relation baseline. Since relations consist of two or more arguments that occur in different, often separated syntactic constituents, a syntactic approach seems futile, especially given our experience with events. Results are reported in Figure 3.

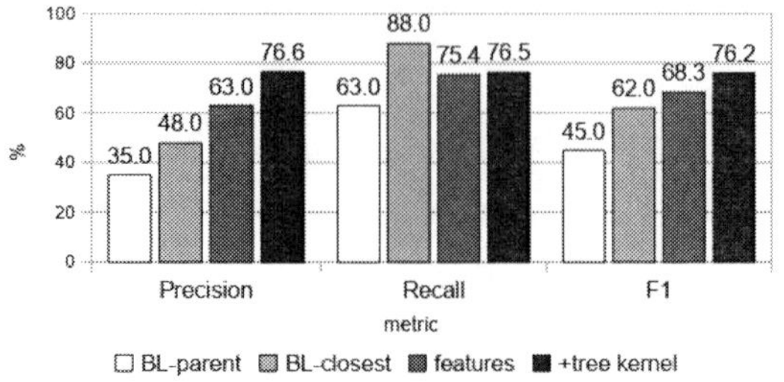

Figure 2: Performance on events

System	Accuracy
TRIOS	65%
this work	64.5%
JU-CSE, NCSU-indi TRIPS, USFD2	all 63%

Table 1: Comparison to Best Systems in TempEval-2

5.3 Events

Figure 2 shows the improvements of the feature-based approach over the two baseline, and the additional gain obtained by using the tree kernel. Both the features and tree kernels mainly improve precision, while the tree kernel adds a small boost in recall. It is remarkable, though, that the closest-event baseline has a very high recall value. This suggests that most of the links actually do occur between items that are close to one another. For a possible explanation for the low precision value, see the error analysis (Section 5.5).

Using a two-tailed t-test, we compute the significance in the difference between the F1-scores. Both the feature-based and the tree kernel approach improvements are statistically significant at $p < 0.001$ over the baseline scores.

Table 1 compares the performances of our system to the state-of-the-art systems on TempEval-2 Data, task C, showing that our approach is very competitive. The best systems there used sequential models. We attribute the competitive nature of our results to the use of tree kernels, which enables us to make use of contextual information.

5.4 Relations

In general, performance for relations is not as high as for events (see Figure 3). The reason here is two-fold: relations consist of two (or more) elements, which can be in various positions with respect to one another and the temporal expression, and each relation can be expressed in a number of

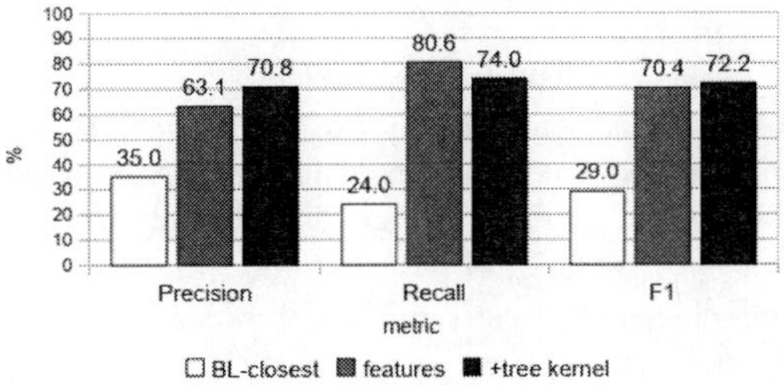

Figure 3: Performance on relations/fluents

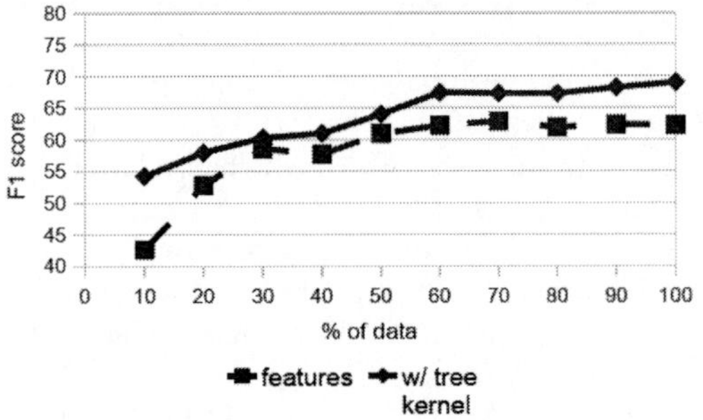

Figure 4: Learning curves for relation models

different ways.

Again, we perform significance tests on the difference in F1 scores and find that our improvements over the baseline are statistically significant at $p < 0.001$. The improvement of the tree kernel over the feature-based approach, however, are not statistically significant at the same value.

The learning curve over parts of the training data (exemplary shown here for relations, Figure 4)[2] indicates that there is another advantage to using tree kernels: the approach can benefit from more data. This is conceivably because it allows the kernel to find more common subtrees in the various representations the more examples it gets, while the feature space rather finds more instances that invalidate the expressiveness of features (i.e., it encounters positive and negative instances that have very similar feature vectors). The curve suggests that tree kernels could yield even better results with more data, while there is little to no expected gain using only features.

5.5 Error Analysis

Examining the misclassified examples in our data, we find that both feature-based and tree-kernel approaches struggle to correctly classify examples where time expression and event/relation are immediately adjacent, but unrelated, as in "the man arrested **last Tuesday told** the police ...", where *last Tuesday* modifies *arrested*. It limits the amount of context that is available to the tree kernels, since we truncate the tree representations to the words between those two elements. This case closely resembles the problem we see in the closest-event/relation baseline, which, as we have seen, does not perform too well. In this case, the incorrect event ("told") is as close to the time expression as the correct one ("arrested"), resulting in a false positive that affects precision. Features capturing the order of the elements do not seem help here, since the elements can be arranged in any order (i.e., temporal expression before or after the event/relation). The only way to solve this problem would be to include additional information about whether a time expression is already attached to another event/relation.

5.6 Ablations

To quantify the utility of each tree representation, we also performed all-but-one ablation tests, i.e., left out each of the tree representations in turn, ran 10-fold cross-validation on the data and observed the effect on F1. The larger the loss in F1, the more informative the left-out-representation. We performed ablations for both events and relations, and found that the ranking of the representations is the same for both.

In events and relations alike, leaving out POS trees has the greatest effect on F1, followed by the feature-bundle representation. Lemma and semantic type representation have less of an impact.

We hypothesize that the former two capture underlying regularities better by representing different words with the same label. Lemmas in turn are too numerous to form many recurring patterns, and semantic type, while having a smaller label alphabet, does not assign a label to every word, thus creating a very sparse representation that picks up more noise than signal.

In preliminary tests, we also used annotated dependency trees as input to the tree kernel, but found that performance improved when they were left out. This is at odds with work that clearly showed the value of syntactic tree kernels (Mirroshandel et al., 2011). We identify two potential causes—either our setup was not capable of correctly capturing and exploiting the information

[2]The learning curve for events looks similar and is omitted due to space constraints.

from the dependency trees, or our formulation of the task was not amenable to it. We did not investigate this further, but leave it to future work.

6 Conclusion and Future Work

We cast the problem of linking events and relations to temporal expressions as a classification task using a combination of features and tree kernels, with probabilistic type filtering. Our main contributions are:

- We showed that within-sentence temporal links for both events and relations can be approached with a common strategy.
- We developed flat tree representations and showed that these produce considerable gains, with significant improvements over different baselines.
- We applied our technique without great adjustments to an existing data set and achieved competitive results.
- Our best systems achieve F1 score of 0.76 on events and 0.72 on relations, and are effective at the task of temporal linking.

We developed the models as part of a machine reading system and are currently evaluating it in an end-to-end task.

Following tasks proposed in TempEval-2, we plan to use our approach for across-sentence classification, as well as a similar model for linking entities to the document creation date.

Acknowledgements

We would like to thank Alessandro Moschitti for his help with the tree kernel setup, and the reviewers who supplied us with very constructive feedback. Research supported in part by Air Force Contract FA8750-09-C-0172 under the DARPA Machine Reading Program.

References

Ken Barker, Bhalchandra Agashe, Shaw-Yi Chaw, James Fan, Noah Friedland, Michael Glass, Jerry Hobbs, Eduard Hovy, David Israel, Doo Soon Kim, Rutu Mulkar-Mehta, Sourabh Patwardhan, Bruce Porter, Dan Tecuci, and Peter Yeh. 2007. Learning by reading: A prototype system, performance baseline and lessons learned. In *Proceedings of the 22nd National Conference for Artificial Intelligence*, Vancouver, Canada, July.

Branimir Boguraev and Rie Kubota Ando. 2005. Timeml-compliant text analysis for temporal reasoning. In *Proceedings of IJCAI*, volume 5, pages 997–1003. IJCAI.

Nathanael Chambers and Dan Jurafsky. 2008. Unsupervised learning of narrative event chains. pages 789–797. Association for Computational Linguistics.

Peter Clark and Phil Harrison. 2010. Machine reading as a process of partial question-answering. In *Proceedings of the NAACL HLT Workshop on Formalisms and Methodology for Learning by Reading*, Los Angeles, CA, June.

George Doddington, Alexis Mitchell, Mark Przybocki, Lance Ramshaw, Stephanie Strassel, and Ralph Weischedel. 2004. The automatic content extraction program – tasks, data and evaluation. In *Proceedings of the LREC Conference*, Canary Islands, Spain, July.

Oren Etzioni, Michele Banko, and Michael Cafarella. 2007. Machine reading. In *Proceedings of the AAAI Spring Symposium Series*, Stanford, CA, March.

Elena Filatova and Eduard Hovy. 2001. Assigning time-stamps to event-clauses. In *Proceedings of the workshop on Temporal and spatial information processing*, volume 13, pages 1–8. Association for Computational Linguistics.

Claudio Giuliano, Alfio Massimiliano Gliozzo, and Carlo Strapparava. 2009. Kernel methods for minimally supervised wsd. *Computational Linguistics*, 35(4).

Seyed A. Mirroshandel, Mahdy Khayyamian, and Gholamreza Ghassem-Sani. 2011. Syntactic tree kernels for event-time temporal relation learning. *Human Language Technology. Challenges for Computer Science and Linguistics*, pages 213–223.

Alessandro Moschitti. 2004. A study on convolution kernels for shallow semantic parsing. In *Proceedings of the 42nd Annual Meeting on Association for Computational Linguistics*, pages 335–es. Association for Computational Linguistics.

Alessandro Moschitti. 2006. Making tree kernels practical for natural language learning. In *Proceedings of EACL*, volume 6.

Feng Pan, Rutu Mulkar, and Jerry R. Hobbs. 2006. Learning event durations from event descriptions. In *Proceedings of the 21st International Conference on Computational Linguistics and the 44th annual meeting of the Association for Computational Linguistics*, pages 393–400. Association for Computational Linguistics.

James Pustejovsky, Patrick Hanks, Roser Saurı, Andrew See, Robert Gaizauskas, Andrea Setzer, Dragomir Radev, Beth Sundheim, David Day, Lisa

Ferro, and Marcia Lazo. 2003. The TIMEBANK Corpus. In *Proceedings of Corpus Linguistics 2003*, pages 647–656.

John Shawe-Taylor and Nello Christianini. 2004. *Kernel Methods for Pattern Analysis*. Cambridge University Press.

Stephanie Strassel, Dan Adams, Henry Goldberg, Jonathan Herr, Ron Keesing, Daniel Oblinger, Heather Simpson, Robert Schrag, and Jonathan Wright. 2010. The DARPA Machine Reading Program-Encouraging Linguistic and Reasoning Research with a Series of Reading Tasks. In *Proceedings of LREC 2010*.

Vladimir Vapnik. 1995. *The Nature of Statistical Learning Theory*. Springer, New York, NY.

Marc Verhagen, Robert Gaizauskas, Frank Schilder, Mark Hepple, Graham Katz, and James Pustejovsky. 2007. Semeval-2007 task 15: Tempeval temporal relation identification. In *Proceedings of the 4th International Workshop on Semantic Evaluations*, pages 75–80. Association for Computational Linguistics.

Marc Verhagen, Roser Sauri, Tommaso Caselli, and James Pustejovsky. 2010. Semeval-2010 task 13: Tempeval-2. In *Proceedings of the 5th International Workshop on Semantic Evaluation*, pages 57–62. Association for Computational Linguistics.

Compensating for Annotation Errors in Training a Relation Extractor

Bonan Min
New York University
715 Broadway, 7th floor
New York, NY 10003 USA
min@cs.nyu.edu

Ralph Grishman
New York University
715 Broadway, 7th floor
New York, NY 10003 USA
grishman@cs.nyu.edu

Abstract

The well-studied supervised Relation Extraction algorithms require training data that is accurate and has good coverage. To obtain such a gold standard, the common practice is to do independent double annotation followed by adjudication. This takes significantly more human effort than annotation done by a single annotator. We do a detailed analysis on a snapshot of the ACE 2005 annotation files to understand the differences between single-pass annotation and the more expensive nearly three-pass process, and then propose an algorithm that learns from the much cheaper single-pass annotation and achieves a performance on a par with the extractor trained on multi-pass annotated data. Furthermore, we show that given the same amount of human labor, the better way to do relation annotation is not to annotate with high-cost quality assurance, but to annotate more.

1. Introduction

Relation Extraction aims at detecting and categorizing semantic relations between pairs of entities in text. It is an important NLP task that has many practical applications such as answering factoid questions, building knowledge bases and improving web search.

Supervised methods for relation extraction have been studied extensively since rich annotated linguistic resources, e.g. the Automatic Content Extraction[1] (ACE) training corpus, were released. We will give a summary of related methods in section 2. Those methods rely on accurate and complete annotation. To obtain high quality annotation, the common wisdom is to let two annotators independently annotate a corpus, and then asking a senior annotator to adjudicate the disagreements[2]. This annotation procedure roughly requires 3 passes[3] over the same corpus. Therefore it is very expensive. The ACE 2005 annotation on relations is conducted in this way.

In this paper, we analyzed a snapshot of ACE training data and found that each annotator missed a significant fraction of relation mentions and annotated some spurious ones. We found that it is possible to separate most missing examples from the vast majority of true-negative unlabeled examples, and in contrast, most of the relation mentions that are adjudicated as incorrect contain useful expressions for learning a relation extractor. Based on this observation, we propose an algorithm that purifies negative examples and applies transductive inference to utilize missing examples during the training process on the single-pass annotation. Results show that the extractor trained on single-pass annotation with the proposed algorithm has a performance that is close to an extractor trained on the 3-pass annotation. We further show that the proposed algorithm trained on a single-pass annotation on the complete set of documents has a higher performance than an extractor trained on 3-pass annotation on 90% of the documents in the same corpus, although the effort of doing a single-pass annotation over the entire set costs less than half that of doing 3 passes over 90% of the documents. From the perspective of learning a high-performance relation extractor, it suggests that a better way to do relation annotation is not to annotate with a high-cost quality assurance, but to annotate more.

---

[1] http://www.itl.nist.gov/iad/mig/tests/ace/

[2] The senior annotator also found some missing examples as shown in figure 1.

[3] In this paper, we will assume that the adjudication pass has a similar cost compared to each of the two first-passes. The adjudicator may not have to look at as many sentences as an annotator, but he is required to review all instances found by both annotators. Moreover, he has to be more skilled and may have to spend more time on each instance to be able to resolve disagreements.

2. Background

2.1 Supervised Relation Extraction

One of the most studied relation extraction tasks is the ACE relation extraction evaluation sponsored by the U.S. government. ACE 2005 defined 7 major entity types, such as PER (Person), LOC (Location), ORG (Organization). A relation in ACE is defined as an ordered pair of entities appearing in the same sentence which expresses one of the predefined relations. ACE 2005 defines 7 major relation types and more than 20 subtypes. Following previous work, we ignore sub-types in this paper and only evaluate on types when reporting relation classification performance. Types include General-affiliation (GEN-AFF), Part-whole (PART-WHOLE), Person-social (PER-SOC), etc. ACE provides a large corpus which is manually annotated with entities (with coreference chains between entity mentions annotated), relations, events and values. Each mention of a relation is tagged with a pair of entity mentions appearing in the same sentence as its arguments. More details about the ACE evaluation are on the ACE official website.

Given a sentence *s* and two entity mentions arg_1 and arg_2 contained in *s*, a candidate relation mention *r* with argument arg_1 preceding arg_2 is defined as $r=(s, arg_1, arg_2)$. The goal of Relation Detection and Classification (RDC) is to determine whether *r* expresses one of the types defined. If so, classify it into one of the types. Supervised learning treats RDC as a classification problem and solves it with supervised Machine Learning algorithms such as MaxEnt and SVM. There are two commonly used learning strategies (Sun et al., 2011). Given an annotated corpus, one could apply a **flat** learning strategy, which trains a single multi-class classifier on training examples labeled as one of the relation types or *not-a-relation*, and apply it to determine its type or output *not-a relation* for each candidate relation mention during testing. The examples of each type are the relation mentions that are tagged as instances of that type, and the *not-a-relation* examples are constructed from pairs of entities that appear in the same sentence but are not tagged as any of the types. Alternatively, one could apply a **hierarchical** learning strategy, which trains two classifiers, a binary classifier *RD* for relation detection and the other a multi-class classifier *RC* for relation classification. *RD* is trained by grouping tagged relation mentions of all types as positive instances and using all the *not-a-relation* cases (same as described above) as negative examples. *RC* is trained on the annotated examples with their tagged types. During testing, *RD* is applied first to identify whether an example expresses some relation, then RC is applied to determine the most likely type only if it is detected as correct by *RD*.

State-of-the-art supervised methods for relation extraction also differ from each other on data representation. Given a relation mention, feature-based methods (Miller et al., 2000; Kambhatla, 2004; Boschee et al., 2005; Grishman et al., 2005; Zhou et al., 2005; Jiang and Zhai, 2007; Sun et al., 2011) extract a rich list of structural, lexical, syntactic and semantic features to represent it; in contrast, the kernel based methods (Zelenko et al., 2003; Bunescu and Mooney, 2005a; Bunescu and Mooney, 2005b; Zhao and Grishman, 2005; Zhang et al., 2006a; Zhang et al., 2006b; Zhou et al., 2007; Qian et al., 2008) represent each instance with an object such as augmented token sequences or a parse tree, and used a carefully designed kernel function, e.g. subsequence kernel (Bunescu and Mooney, 2005b) or convolution tree kernel (Collins and Duffy, 2001), to calculate their similarity. These objects are usually augmented with features such as semantic features.

In this paper, we use the hierarchical learning strategy since it simplifies the problem by letting us focus on relation detection only. The relation classification stage remains unchanged and we will show that it benefits from improved detection. For experiments on both relation detection and relation classification, we use SVM[4] (Vapnik 1998) as the learning algorithm since it can be extended to support transductive inference as discussed in section 4.3. However, for the analysis in section 3.2 and the purification preprocess steps in section 4.2, we use a MaxEnt[5] model since it outputs probabilities[6] for its predictions. For the choice of features, we use the full set of features from Zhou et al. (2005) since it is reported to have a state-of-the-art performance (Sun et al., 2011).

2.2 ACE 2005 annotation

The ACE 2005 training data contains 599 articles

[4] SVM-Light is used. http://svmlight.joachims.org/

[5] OpenNLP MaxEnt package is used. http://maxent.sourceforge.net/about.html

[6] SVM also outputs a value associated with each prediction. However, this value cannot be interpreted as probability.

from newswire, broadcast news, weblogs, usenet newsgroups/discussion forum, conversational telephone speech and broadcast conversations. The annotation process is conducted as follows: two annotators working independently annotate each article and complete all annotation tasks (entities, values, relations and events). After two annotators both finished annotating a file, all discrepancies are then adjudicated by a senior annotator. This results in a high-quality annotation file. More details can be found in the documentation of ACE 2005 Multilingual Training Data V3.0.

Since the final release of the ACE training corpus only contains the final adjudicated annotations, in which all the traces of the two first-pass annotations are removed, we use a snapshot of almost-finished annotation, ACE 2005 Multilingual Training Data V3.0, for our analysis. In the remainder of this paper, we will call the two independent first-passes of annotation *fp1* and *fp2*. The higher-quality data done by merging *fp1* and *fp2* and then having disagreements adjudicated by the senior annotator is called *adj*. From this corpus, we removed the files that have not been completed for all three passes. On the final corpus consisting of 511 files, we can differentiate the annotations on which the three annotators have agreed and disagreed.

A notable fact of ACE relation annotation is that it is done with arguments from the list of annotated entity mentions. For example, in a relation mention *tyco's ceo and president dennis kozlowski* which expresses an *EMP-ORG* relation, the two arguments *tyco* and *dennis kozlowski* must have been tagged as entity mentions previously by the annotator. Since *fp1* and *fp2* are done on all tasks independently, their disagreement on entity annotation will be propagated to relation annotation; thus we need to deal with these cases specifically.

3. Analysis of data annotation

3.1 General statistics

As discussed in section 2, relation mentions are annotated with entity mentions as arguments, and the lists of annotated entity mentions vary in *fp1*, *fp2* and *adj*. To estimate the impact propagated from entity annotation, we first calculate the ratio of overlapping entity mentions between entities annotated in *fp1*/*fp2* with *adj*. We found that *fp1*/*fp2* each agrees with *adj* on around 89% of the entity mentions. Following up, we checked the relation mentions[7] from *fp1* and *fp2* against the adjudicated list of entity mentions from *adj* and found that 682 and 665 relation mentions respectively have at least one argument which doesn't appear in the list of adjudicated entity mentions.

Given the list of relation mentions with both arguments appearing in the list of adjudicated entity mentions, figure 1 shows the inter-annotator agreement of the ACE 2005 relation annotation. In this figure, the three circles represent the list of relation mentions in *fp1*, *fp2* and *adj*, respectively.

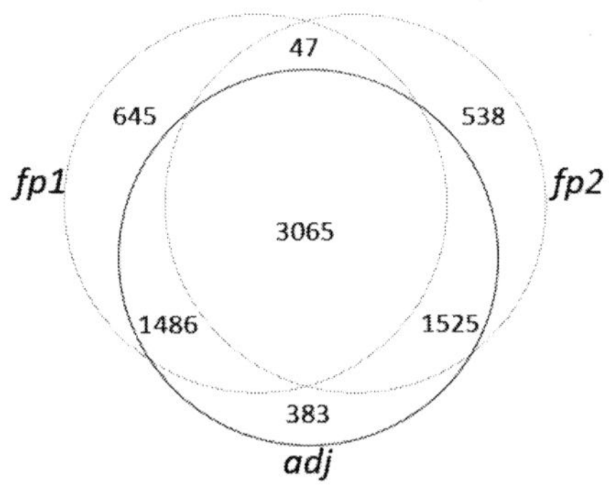

Figure 1. Inter-annotator agreement of ACE 2005 relation annotation. Numbers are the distinct relation mentions whose both arguments are in the list of adjudicated entity mentions.

It shows that each annotator missed a significant number of relation mentions annotated by the other. Considering that we removed 682/665 relation mentions from *fp1*/*fp2* because we generate this figure based on the list of adjudicated entity mentions, we estimate that *fp1* and *fp2* both missed around 18.3-28.5%[8] of the relation mentions. This clearly shows that both of the annotators missed a significant fraction of the relation mentions. They also annotated some spurious relation mentions (as adjudicated in *adj*), although the fraction is smaller (close to 10% of all relation mentions in *adj*).

ACE 2005 relation annotation guidelines (ACE English Annotation Guidelines for Relations, version 5.8.3) defined 7 syntactic classes and the *other* class. We plot the distribution of syntactic classes of the annotated

[7] This is done by selecting the relation mentions whose both arguments are in the list of adjudicated entity mentions.

[8] We calculate the lower bound by assuming that the 682 relation mentions removed from *fp1* are found in *fp2*, although with different argument boundary and headword tagged. The upper bound is calculated by assuming that they are all irrelevant and erroneous relation mentions.

relations in figure 2 (3 of the classes, accounting together for less than 10% of the cases, are omitted) and the *other* class. It seems that it is generally easier for the annotators to find and agree on relation mentions of the type *Preposition/PreMod/Possessives* but harder to find and agree on the ones belonging to *Verbal* and *Other*. The definition and examples of these syntactic classes can be found in the annotation guidelines.

In the following sections, we will show the analysis on *fp1* and *adj* since the result is similar for *fp2*.

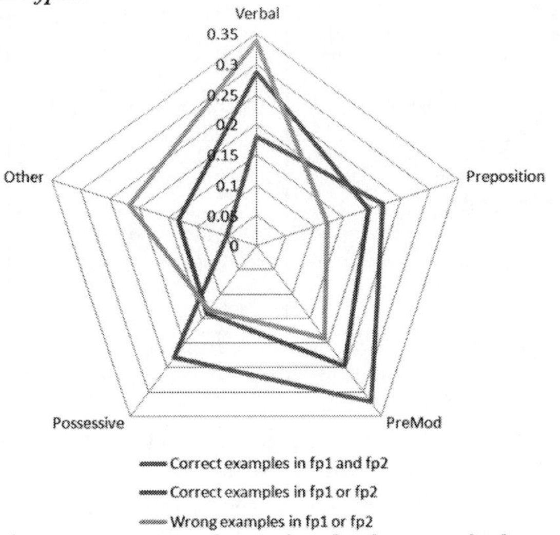

Figure 2. Percentage of examples of major syntactic classes.

3.2 Why the differences?

To understand what causes the missing annotations and the spurious ones, we need methods to find how similar/different the false positives are to true positives and also how similar/different the false negatives (missing annotations) are to true negatives. If we adopt a good similarity metric, which captures the structural, lexical and semantic similarity between relation mentions, this analysis will help us to understand the similarity/difference from an extraction perspective.

We use a state-of-the-art feature space (Zhou et al., 2005) to represent examples (including all correct examples, erroneous ones and untagged examples) and use MaxEnt as the weight learning model since it shows competitive performance in relation extraction (Jiang and Zhai, 2007) and outputs probabilities associated with each prediction. We train a MaxEnt model for relation detection on true positives and true negatives, which respectively are the subset of correct examples annotated by *fp1* (and adjudicated as correct ones) and negative examples that are not annotated in *adj*, and use it to make predictions on the mixed pool of correct examples, missing examples and spurious ones.

To illustrate how distinguishable the missing examples (false negatives) are from the true negative ones, 1) we apply the MaxEnt model on both false negatives and true negatives, 2) put them together and rank them by the model-predicted probabilities of being positive, 3) calculate their relative rank in this pool. We plot the Cumulative distribution of frequency (CDF) of the ranks (as percentages in the mixed pools) of false negatives in figure 3. We took similar steps for the spurious ones (false positives) and plot them in figure 3 as well (However, they are ranked by model-predicted probabilities of being negative).

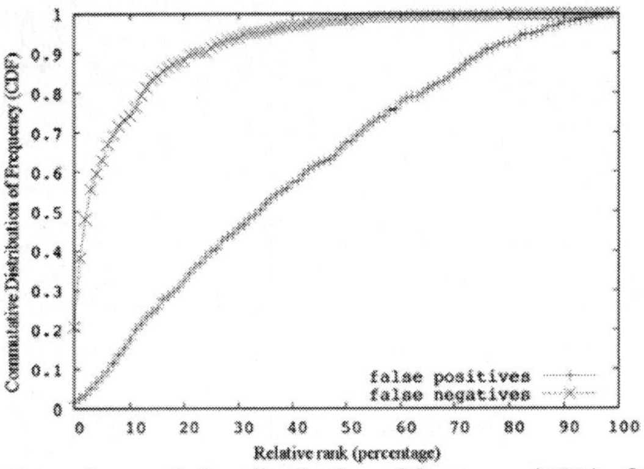

Figure 3: cumulative distribution of frequency (CDF) of the relative ranking of model-predicted probability of being positive for false negatives in a pool mixed of false negatives and true negatives; and the CDF of the relative ranking of model-predicted probability of being negative for false positives in a pool mixed of false positives and true positives.

For false negatives, it shows a highly skewed distribution in which around 75% of the false negatives are ranked within the top 10%. That means the missing examples are lexically, structurally or semantically similar to correct examples, and are distinguishable from the true negative examples. However, the distribution of false positives (spurious examples) is close to uniform (flat curve), which means they are generally indistinguishable from the correct examples.

3.3 Categorize annotation errors

The automatic method shows that the errors (spurious annotations) are very similar to the correct examples but provides little clue as to why that is the case. To understand their causes, we sampled 65 examples from *fp1* (10% of the 645 errors), read the sentences containing these

Category	Percentage	Example		
		Relation Type	Sampled text of spurious examples in *fp1*	Notes (examples are similar ones in *adj* for comparison)
Duplicate relation mention for coreferential entity mentions	49.2%	ORG-AFF	*... his budding friendship with US President George W. Bush in the face of ...*	*... his budding friendship with US President George W. Bush in the face of ...*
Correct	20%	PHYS	*Hundreds of thousands of demonstrators took to the streets in Britain...*	
		PER-SOC	*The dead included the quack doctor, 55-year-old Nityalila Naotia, his teenaged son and...*	(Symmetric relation) *The dead included the quack doctor, 55-year-old Nityalila Naotia, his teenaged son*
Argument not in list	15.4%	PER-SOC	*Putin had even secretly invited British Prime Minister Tony Blair, Bush's staunchest backer in the war on Iraq...*	
Violate reasonable reader rule	6.2%	PHYS	*"The amazing thing is they are going to turn San Francisco into ground zero for every criminal who wants to profit at their chosen profession", Paredes said.*	
Errors	6.1%	PART-WHOLE	*...a likely candidate to run Vivendi Universal's entertainment unit in the United States...*	Arguments are tagged reversed
		PART-WHOLE	*Khakamada argued that the United States would also need Russia's help "to make the new Iraqi government seem legitimate.*	Relation type error
illegal promotion through "blocked" categories	3%	PHYS	*Up to 20,000 protesters thronged the plazas and streets of San Francisco, where...*	*Up to 20,000 protesters thronged the plazas and streets of San Francisco, where...*

Table 1. Categories of spurious relation mentions in *fp1 (on a sample of 10%* of relation mentions), ranked by the percentage of the examples in each category. In the sample text, red text (also marked with dotted underlines) shows head words of the first arguments and the underlined text shows head words of the second arguments.

erroneous relation mentions and compared them to the correct relation mentions in the same sentence; we categorized these examples and show them in table 1. The most common type of error is *duplicate relation mention for coreferential entity mentions*. The first row in table 1 shows an example, in which there is a relation ORG-AFF tagged between *US* and *George W. Bush* in *adj*. Because *President* and *George W. Bush* are coreferential, the example *<US, President >* from *fp1* is adjudicated as incorrect. This shows that if a relation is expressed repeatedly across relation mentions whose arguments are coreferential, the adjudicator only tags one of the relation mentions as correct, although the other is correct too. This shared the same principle with another type of error *illegal promotion through "blocked" categories* [9] as defined in the annotation guideline. The second largest category is *correct*, by which we mean the example is a correct relation mention and the adjudicator made a mistake. The third largest category is *argument not in list*, by which we mean that at least one of the arguments is not in the list of adjudicated entity mentions.

Based on Table 1, we can see that as many as 72%-88% of the examples which are adjudicated as incorrect are actually correct if viewed from a relation learning perspective, since most of them contain informative expressions for tagging relations. The annotation guideline is designed to ensure high quality while not imposing too much burden on human annotators. To reduce annotation effort, it defined rules such as *illegal promotion through "blocked" categories*. The annotators' practice suggests that they are following another rule not to annotate *duplicate relation mention for coreferential entity mentions*. This follows the similar principle of reducing annotation effort but is not explicitly stated in the guideline: to avoid propagation of a relation through a coreference chain. However, these examples are useful for learning more ways to express a relation. Moreover, even for the erroneous examples (as shown in table 1 as *violate reasonable reader rule* and *errors*), most of them have some level of similar structures or semantics to the targeted relation. Therefore, it is very hard to distinguish them without human proofreading.

[9] For example, in sentence *Smith went to a hotel in Brazil*, *(Smith, hotel)* is a taggable PHYS Relation but *(Smith, Brazil)* is not, because to get the second relationship, one would have to "promote" *Brazil* through *hotel*. For the precise definition of annotation rules, please refer to ACE (Automatic Content Extraction) English Annotation Guidelines for Relations, version 5.8.3.

Exp #	Training data	Testing data	Detection (%)			Classification (%)		
			Precision	Recall	F1	Precision	Recall	F1
1	*fp1*	*adj*	83.4	60.4	70.0	75.7	54.8	63.6
2	*fp2*	*adj*	83.5	60.5	70.2	76.0	55.1	63.9
3	*adj*	*adj*	80.4	69.7	74.6	73.4	63.6	68.2

Table 2. Performance of RDC trained on *fp1*/*fp2*/*adj*, and tested on *adj*.

3.4 Why missing annotations and how many examples are missing?

For the large number of missing annotations, there are a couple of possible reasons. One reason is that it is generally easier for a human annotator to annotate correctly given a well-defined guideline, but it is hard to ensure completeness, especially for a task like relation extraction. Furthermore, the ACE 2005 annotation guideline defines more than 20 relation subtypes. These many subtypes make it hard for an annotator to keep all of them in mind while doing the annotation, and thus it is inevitable that some examples are missed.

Here we proceed to approximate the number of missing examples given limited knowledge. Let each annotator annotate n examples and assume that each pair of annotators agrees on a certain fraction p of the examples. Assuming the examples are equally likely to be found by an annotator, therefore the total number of unique examples found by k annotators is $\sum_{i=0}^{k}(1-p)^i n$. If we had an infinite number of annotators ($k \to \infty$), the total number of unique examples will be $\frac{n}{p}$, which is the upper bound of the total number of examples. In the case of the ACE 2005 relation mention annotation, since the two annotators annotate around 4500 examples and they agree on 2/3 of them, the total number of all positive examples is around 6750. This is close to the number of relation mentions in the adjudicated list: 6459. Here we assume the adjudicator is doing a more complex task than an annotator, resolving the disagreements and completing the annotation (as shown in figure 1).

The assumption of the calculation is a little crude but reasonable given the limited number of passes of annotation we have. Recent research (Ji et al, 2010) shows that, by adding annotators for IE tasks, the merged annotation tends to converge after having 5 annotators. To understand the annotation behavior better, in particular whether annotation will converge after adding a few annotators, more passes of annotation need to be collected. We leave this as future work.

4. Relation extraction with low-cost annotation

4.1 Baseline algorithm

To see whether a single-pass annotation is useful for relation detection and classification, we did 5-fold cross validation (5-fold CV) with each of *fp1*, *fp2* and *adj* as the training set, and tested on *adj*. The experiments are done with the same 511 documents we used for the analysis. As shown in table 2, we did 5-fold CV on *adj* for experiment 3. For fairness, we use settings similar to 5-fold CV for experiment 1 and 2. Take experiment 1 as an example: we split both of *fp1* and *adj* into 5 folds, use 4 folds from *fp1* as training data, and 1 fold from *adj* as testing data and does one train-test cycle. We rotate the folds (both training and testing) and repeat 5 times. The final results are averaged over the 5 runs. Experiment 2 was conducted similarly. In the reminder of the paper, 5-fold CV experiments are all conducted in this way.

Table 2 shows that a relation tagger trained on the single-pass annotated data *fp1* performs worse than the one trained on merged and adjudicated data *adj*, with 4.6 points lower F measure in relation detection, and 4.6 points lower relation classification. For detection, precision on *fp1* is 3 points higher than on *adj* but recall is much lower (close to 10 points). The recall difference shows that the missing annotations contain expressions that can help to find more correct examples during testing. The small precision difference indirectly shows that the spurious ones in *fp1* (as adjudicated) do not hurt precision. Performance on classification shows a similar trend because the relation classifier takes the examples predicted by the detector as correct as its input. Therefore, if there is an error, it gets propagated to this stage. Table 2 also shows similar performance differences between *fp2* and *adj*.

In the remainder of this paper, we will discuss a few algorithms to improve a relation tagger trained on single-pass annotated data[10]. Since we

[10] We only use *fp1* and *adj* in the following experiments because we observed that *fp1* and *fp2* are similar in general in the analysis, though a fraction of the annotation in *fp1*

already showed that most of the spurious annotations are not actually errors from an extraction perspective and table 2 shows that they do not hurt precision, we will only focus on utilizing the missing examples, in other words, training with an incomplete annotation.

4.2 Purify the set of negative examples

As discussed in section 2, traditional supervised methods find all pairs of entity mentions that appear within a sentence, and then use the pairs that are not annotated as relation mentions as the negative examples for the purpose of training a relation detector. It relies on the assumption that the annotators annotated all relation mentions and missed no (or very few) examples. However, this is not true for training on a single-pass annotation, in which a significant portion of relation mentions are left not annotated. If this scheme is applied, all of the correct pairs which the annotators missed belong to this "negative" category. Therefore, we need a way to purify the "negative" set of examples obtained by this conventional approach.

Li and Liu (2003) focuses on classifying documents with only positive examples. Their algorithm initially sets all unlabeled data to be negative and trains a Rocchio classifier, selects negative examples which are closer to the negative centroid than positive centroid as the purified negative examples, and then retrains the model. Their algorithm performs well for text classification. It is based on the assumption that there are fewer unannotated positive examples than negative ones in the unlabeled set, so true negative examples still dominate the set of noisy "negative" examples in the purification step.

Based on the same assumption, our purification process consists of the following steps:

1) Use annotated relation mentions as positive examples; construct all possible relation mentions that are not annotated, and initially set them to be negative. We call this noisy data set D.
2) Train a MaxEnt relation detection model M_{det} on D.
3) Apply M_{det} on all unannotated examples, and rank them by the model-predicted probabilities of being positive,
4) Remove the top N examples from D.

These preprocessing steps result in a purified data set D_{pure}. We can use D_{pure} for the normal training process of a supervised relation extraction algorithm.

The algorithm is similar to Li and Liu 2003. However, we drop a few noisy examples instead of choosing a small purified subset since we have relatively few false negatives compared to the entire set of unannotated examples. Moreover, after step 3, most false negatives are clustered within the small region of top ranked examples which has a high model-predicated probability of being positive. The intuition is similar to what we observed from figure 3 for false negatives since we also observed very similar distribution using the model trained with noisy data. Therefore, we can purify negatives by removing examples in this noisy subset.

However, the false negatives are still mixed with true negatives. For example, still slightly more than half of the top 2000 examples are true negatives. Thus we cannot simply flip their labels and use them as positive examples. In the following section, we will use them in the form of unlabeled examples to help train a better model.

4.3 Transductive inference on unlabeled examples

Transductive SVM (Vapnik, 1998; Joachims, 1999) is a semi-supervised learning method which learns a model from a data set consisting of both labeled and unlabeled examples. Compared to its popular antecedent SVM, it also learns a maximum margin classification hyperplane, but additionally forces it to separate a set of unlabeled data with large margin. The optimization function of Transductive SVM (TSVM) is the following:

$$\textit{Minimize over } (y_1^*, \ldots, y_n^*, \vec{w}, b, \xi_1, \ldots, \xi_n, \xi_1^*, \ldots, \xi_k^*):$$

$$\frac{1}{2}||\vec{w}||^2 + C\sum_{i=0}^{n}\xi_i + C^*\sum_{j=0}^{k}\xi_j^*$$

$$\begin{aligned} \textit{subject to:} \quad & \forall_{i=1}^{n} : y_i[\vec{w}\cdot\vec{x}_i + b] \geq 1 - \xi_i \\ & \forall_{j=1}^{k} : y_j^*[\vec{w}\cdot\vec{x}_j^* + b] \geq 1 - \xi_j^* \\ & \forall_{i=1}^{n} : \xi_i > 0 \\ & \forall_{j=1}^{k} : \xi_j^* > 0 \end{aligned}$$

Figure 4. TSVM optimization function for non-separable case (Joachims, 1999)

TSVM can leverage an unlabeled set of examples to improve supervised learning. As shown in section 3, a significant number of relation mentions are missing from the single-pass annotation data. Although it is not possible to find all missing annotations without human effort, we can improve the model by further

and *fp2* is different. Moreover, algorithms trained on them show similar performance.

utilizing the fact that some unannotated examples should have been annotated.

The purification process discussed in the previous section removes N examples which have a high density of false negatives. We further utilize the N examples as follows:

1) Construct a training corpus D_{hybrid} from D_{pure} by taking a random sample[11] of $N*(1-p)/p$ (p is the ratio of annotated examples to all examples; $p=0.05$ in *fp1*) negatively labeled examples in D_{pure} and setting them to be unlabeled. In addition, the N examples removed by the purification process are added back as unlabeled examples.
2) Train TSVM on D_{hybrid}.

The second step trained a model which replaced the detection model in the hierarchical detection-classification learning scheme we used. We will show in the next section that this improves the model.

5. Experiments

Experiments were conducted over the same set of documents on which we did analysis: the 511 documents which have completed annotation in all of the *fp1*, *fp2* and *adj* from the ACE 2005 Multilingual Training Data V3.0. To reemphasize, we apply the hierarchical learning scheme and we focus on improving relation detection while keeping relation classification unchanged (results show that its performance is improved because of the improved detection). We use SVM as our learning algorithm with the full feature set from Zhou et al. (2005).

Baseline algorithm: The relation detector is unchanged. We follow the common practice, which is to use annotated examples as positive ones and all possible untagged relation mentions as negative ones. We sub-sampled the negative data by ½ since that shows better performance.

+purify: This algorithm adds an additional purification preprocessing step (section 4.2) before the hierarchical learning RDC algorithm. After purification, the RDC algorithm is trained on the positive examples and purified negative examples. We set $N=2000$[12] in all experiments.

+tSVM: First, the same purification process of **+purify** is applied. Then we follow the steps described in section 4.3 to construct the set of unlabeled examples, and set all the rest of purified negative examples to be negative. Finally, we train TSVM on both labeled and unlabeled data and replace the relation detection in the RDC algorithm. The relation classification is unchanged.

Table 3 shows the results. All experiments are done with 5-fold cross validation[13] using testing data from *adj*. The first three rows show experiments trained on *fp1*, and the last row **(ADJ)** shows the unmodified RDC algorithm trained on *adj* for comparison. The purification of negative examples shows significant performance gain, 3.7% F1 on relation detection and 3.4% on relation classification. The precision decreases but recall increases substantially since the missing examples are not treated as negatives. Experiment shows that the purification process removes more than 60% of the false negatives. Transductive SVM further improved performance by a relatively small margin. This shows that the latent positive examples can help refine the model. Results also show that transductive inference can find around 17% of missing relation mentions. We notice that the performance of relation classification is improved since by improving relation detection, some examples that do not express a relation are removed. The classification performance on single-pass annotation is close to the one trained on *adj* due to the help from a better relation detector trained with our algorithm.

We also did 5-fold cross validation with a model trained on a fraction of the 4/5 (4 folds) of *adj* data (each experiment shown in table 4 uses 4 folds of *adj* documents for training since one fold is left for cross validation). The documents are sampled randomly. Table 4 shows results for varying training data size. Compared to the results shown in the "+tSVM" row of table 3, we can see that our best model trained on single-pass annotation outperforms SVM trained on 90% of the dual-pass, adjudicated data in both relation detection and classification, although it costs less than half the 3-pass annotation. This suggests that given the same amount of human effort for

[11] We included this large random sample so that the balance of positive to negative examples in the unlabeled set would be similar to that of the labeled data. The test data is not included in the unlabeled set.

[12] We choose 2000 because it is close to the number of relations missed from each single-pass annotation. In practice, it contains more than 70% of the false negatives, and it is less than 10% of the unannotated examples. To estimate how many examples are missing (section 3.4), one should perform multiple passes of independent annotation on a small dataset and measure inter-annotator agreements.

[13] Details about the settings for 5-fold cross validation are in section 4.1.

Algorithm	Detection (%)			Classification (%)		
	Precision	Recall	F1	Precision	Recall	F1
Baseline	83.4	60.4	70.0	75.7	54.8	63.6
+purify	76.8	70.9	73.7	69.8	64.5	67.0
+tSVM	76.4	72.1	**74.2**	69.4	65.2	**67.2**
ADJ (on *adj*)	80.4	69.7	74.6	73.4	63.6	68.2

Table 3. 5-fold cross-validation results. All are trained on *fp1* (except the last row showing the unchanged algorithm trained on *adj* for comparison), and tested on adj. McNemar's test show that the improvement from +purify to +tSVM, and from +tSVM to ADJ are statistically significant (with $p<0.05$).

Percentage of *adj* used	Detection (%)			Classification (%)		
	Precision	Recall	F1	Precision	Recall	F1
60% × 4/5	86.9	41.2	55.8	78.6	37.2	50.5
70% × 4/5	85.5	51.3	64.1	77.7	46.6	58.2
80% × 4/5	83.3	58.1	68.4	75.8	52.9	62.3
90% × 4/5	82.0	64.9	72.5	74.9	59.4	66.2

Table 4. Performance with SVM trained on a fraction of *adj*. It shows 5 fold cross validation results.

relation annotation, annotating more documents with single-pass offers advantages over annotating less data with high quality assurance (dual passes and adjudication).

6. Related work

Dligach et al. (2010) studied WSD annotation from a cost-effectiveness viewpoint. They showed empirically that, with same amount of annotation dollars spent, single-annotation is better than dual-annotation and adjudication. The common practice for quality control of WSD annotation is similar to Relation annotation. However, the task of WSD annotation is very different from relation annotation. WSD requires that every example must be assigned some tag, whereas that is not required for relation tagging. Moreover, relation tagging requires identifying two arguments and correctly categorizing their types.

The purified approach applied in this paper is related to the general framework of learning from positive and unlabeled examples. Li and Liu (2003) initially set all unlabeled data to be negative and train a Rocchio classifier, then select negative examples which are closer to the negative centroid than positive centroid as the purified negative examples. We share a similar assumption with Li and Liu (2003) but we use a different method to select negative examples since the false negative examples show a very skewed distribution, as described in section 5.2.

Transductive SVM was introduced by Vapnik (1998) and later refined in Joachims (1999). A few related methods were studied on the subtask of relation classification (the second stage of the hierarchical learning scheme) in Zhang (2005).

Chan and Roth (2011) observed the similar phenomenon that ACE annotators rarely duplicate a relation link for coreferential mentions. They use an evaluation scheme to avoid being penalized by the relation mentions which are not annotated because of this behavior.

7. Conclusion

We analyzed a snapshot of the ACE 2005 relation annotation and found that each single-pass annotation missed around 18-28% of relation mentions and contains around 10% spurious mentions. A detailed analysis showed that it is possible to find some of the false negatives, and that most spurious cases are actually correct examples from a system builder's perspective. By automatically purifying negative examples and applying transductive inference on suspicious examples, we can train a relation classifier whose performance is comparable to a classifier trained on the dual-annotated and adjudicated data. Furthermore, we show that single-pass annotation is more cost-effective than annotation with high quality assurance.

Acknowledgments

Supported by the Intelligence Advanced Research Projects Activity (IARPA) via Air Force Research Laboratory (AFRL) contract number FA8650-10-C-7058. The U.S. Government is authorized to reproduce and distribute reprints for Governmental purposes notwithstanding any copyright annotation thereon. The views and conclusions contained herein are those of the authors and should not be interpreted as necessarily representing the official policies or endorsements, either expressed or implied, of IARPA, AFRL, or the U.S. Government.

References

ACE. http://www.itl.nist.gov/iad/mig/tests/ace/

ACE (Automatic Content Extraction) English Annotation Guidelines for Relations, version 5.8.3. 2005. http://projects.ldc.upenn.edu/ace/.

ACE 2005 Multilingual Training Data V3.0. 2005. LDC2005E18. LDC Catalog.

Elizabeth Boschee, Ralph Weischedel, and Alex Zamanian. 2005. Automatic information extraction. In Proceedings of the International Conference on Intelligence Analysis.

Razvan C. Bunescu and Raymond J. Mooney. 2005a. A shortest path dependency kenrel for relation extraction. In Proceedings of HLT/EMNLP-2005.

Razvan C. Bunescu and Raymond J. Mooney. 2005b. Subsequence kernels for relation extraction. In Proceedings of NIPS-2005.

Yee Seng Chan and Dan Roth. 2011. Exploiting Syntactico-Semantic Structures for Relation Extraction. In Proceedings of ACL-2011.

Michael Collins and Nigel Duffy. Convolution Kernels for Natural Language. In Proceedings of NIPS-2001.

Dmitriy Dligach, Rodney D. Nielsen and Martha Palmer. 2010. To annotate more accurately or to annotate more. In Proceedings of Fourth Linguistic Annotation Workshop at ACL 2010

Ralph Grishman, David Westbrook and Adam Meyers. 2005. NYU's English ACE 2005 System Description. In Proceedings of ACE 2005 Evaluation Workshop

Scott Miller, Heidi Fox, Lance Ramshaw, and Ralph Weischedel. 2000. A novel use of statistical parsing to extract information from text In Proceedings of NAACL-2010.

Heng Ji, Ralph Grishman, Hoa Trang Dang and Kira Griffitt. 2010. An Overview of the TAC2010 Knowledge Base Population Track. In Proceedings of TAC-2010

Jing Jiang and ChengXiang Zhai. 2007. A systematic exploration of the feature space for relation extraction. In Proceedings of HLT-NAACL-2007.

Thorsten Joachims. 1999. Transductive Inference for Text Classification using Support Vector Machines. In Proceedings of ICML-1999.

Nanda Kambhatla. 2004. Combining lexical, syntactic, and semantic features with maximum entropy models for information extraction. In Proceedings of ACL-2004

Xiao-Li Li and Bing Liu. 2003. Learning to classify text using positive and unlabeled data. In Proceedings of IJCAI-2003.

Longhua Qian, Guodong Zhou, Qiaoming Zhu and Peide Qian. 2008. Exploiting constituent dependencies for tree kernel-based semantic relation extraction . In Proc. of COLING-2008.

Ang Sun, Ralph Grishman and Satoshi Sekine. 2011. Semi-supervised Relation Extraction with Large-scale Word Clustering. In Proceedings of ACL-2011.

Vladimir N. Vapnik. 1998. Statistical Learning Theory. John Wiley.

Dmitry Zelenko, Chinatsu Aone, and Anthony Richardella. 2003. Kernel methods for relation extraction. Journal of Machine Learning Research.

Min Zhang, Jie Zhang and Jian Su. 2006a. Exploring syntactic features for relation extraction using a convolution tree kernel, In Proceedings of HLT-NAACL-2006.

Min Zhang, Jie Zhang, Jian Su, and GuoDong Zhou. 2006b. A composite kernel to extract relations between entities with both flat and structured features. In Proceedings of COLING-ACL-2006.

Zhu Zhang. 2005. Mining Inter-Entity Semantic Relations Using Improved Transductive Learning. In Proceedings of ICJNLP-2005.

Shubin Zhao and Ralph Grishman, 2005. Extracting Relations with Integrated Information Using Kern el Methods. In Proceedings of ACL-2005.

Guodong Zhou, Jian Su, Jie Zhang and Min Zhang. 2005. Exploring various knowledge in relation extraction. In Proceedings of ACL-2005.

Guodong Zhou, Min Zhang, DongHong Ji, and QiaoMing Zhu. 2007. Tree kernel-based relation extraction with context-sensitive structured parse tree information. In Proceedings of EMNLP/CoNLL-2007.

Incorporating Lexical Priors into Topic Models

Jagadeesh Jagarlamudi
University of Maryland
College Park, USA
jags@umiacs.umd.edu

Hal Daumé III
University of Maryland
College Park, USA
hal@umiacs.umd.edu

Raghavendra Udupa
Microsoft Research
Bangalore, India
raghavu@microsoft.com

Abstract

Topic models have great potential for helping users understand document corpora. This potential is stymied by their purely unsupervised nature, which often leads to topics that are neither entirely meaningful nor effective in extrinsic tasks (Chang et al., 2009). We propose a simple and effective way to guide topic models to learn topics of specific interest to a user. We achieve this by providing *sets of seed words* that a user believes are representative of the underlying topics in a corpus. Our model uses these seeds to improve *both* topic-word distributions (by biasing topics to produce appropriate seed words) and to improve document-topic distributions (by biasing documents to select topics related to the seed words they contain). Extrinsic evaluation on a document clustering task reveals a significant improvement when using seed information, even over other models that use seed information naïvely.

1 Introduction

Topic models such as Latent Dirichlet Allocation (LDA) (Blei et al., 2003) have emerged as a powerful tool to analyze document collections in an unsupervised fashion. When fit to a document collection, topic models implicitly use document level co-occurrence information to group semantically related words into a single topic. Since the objective of these models is to maximize the probability of the observed data, they have a tendency to explain only the most obvious and superficial aspects of a corpus. They effectively sacrifice performance on rare topics to do a better job in modeling frequently occurring words. The user is then left with a skewed impression of the corpus, and perhaps one that does not perform well in extrinsic tasks.

To illustrate this problem, we ran LDA on the most frequent five categories of the Reuters-21578 (Lewis et al., 2004) text corpus. This document distribution is very skewed: more than half of the collection belongs to the most frequent category ("Earn"). The five topics identified by the LDA are shown in Table 1. A brief observation of the topics reveals that LDA has roughly allocated topics 1 & 2 for the most frequent class ("Earn") and one topic for the subsequent two frequent classes ("Acquisition" and "Forex") and merged the least two frequent classes ("Crude" and "Grain") into a single topic. The red colored words in topic 5 correspond to the "Crude" class and blue words are from the "Grain" class.

This leads to the situation where the topics identified by LDA are not in accordance with the underlying topical structure of the corpus. This is a problem not just with LDA: it is potentially a problem with any extension thereof that have focused on improving the semantic coherence of the words in each topic (Griffiths et al., 2005; Wallach, 2005; Griffiths et al., 2007), the document topic distributions (Blei and McAuliffe, 2008; Lacoste-Julien et al., 2008) or other aspects (Blei. and Lafferty., 2009).

We address this problem by providing some additional information to the model. Initially, along with the document collection, a user may provide higher level view of the document collection. For instance, as discussed in Section 4.4, when run on historical NIPS papers, LDA fails to find topics related to Brain Imaging, Cognitive Science or Hardware, even though we know from the call for

mln, dlrs, billion, year, pct, company, share, april, record, cts, quarter, march, earnings, stg, first, pay
mln, NUM, cts, loss, net, dlrs, shr, profit, revs, year, note, oper, avg, shrs, sales, includes
lt, company, shares, corp, dlrs, stock, offer, group, share, common, board, acquisition, shareholders
bank, market, dollar, pct, exchange, foreign, trade, rate, banks, japan, yen, government, rates, today
oil, tonnes, prices, mln, wheat, production, pct, gas, year, grain, crude, price, corn, dlrs, bpd, opec

Table 1: Topics identified by LDA on the frequent-5 categories of the Reuters corpus. The categories are Earn, Acquisition, Forex, Grain and Crude (in the order document frequency).

1	company, billion, quarter, shrs, earnings
2	acquisition, procurement, merge
3	exchange, currency, trading, rate, euro
4	grain, wheat, corn, oilseed, oil
5	natural, gas, oil, fuel, products, petrol

Table 2: An example for sets of seed words (*seed topics*) for the frequent-5 categories of the Reuters-21578 categorization corpus. We use them as running example in the rest of the paper.

papers that such topics should exist in the corpus. By allowing the user to provide some *seed words* related to these underrepresented topics, we encourage the model to find evidence of these topics in the data. Importantly, we *only* encourage the model to follow the seed sets and do *not* force it. So if it has compelling evidence in the data to overcome the seed information then it still has the freedom to do so. Our seeding approach in combination with the interactive topic modeling (Hu et al., 2011) will allow a user to both *explore* a corpus, and also guide the exploration towards the distinctions that he/she finds more interesting.

2 Incorporating Seeds

Our approach to allowing a user to guide the topic discovery process is to let him provide *seed information* at the level of word type. Namely, the user provides sets of seed words that are representative of the corpus. Table 2 shows an example of seed sets one might use for the Reuters corpus. This kind of supervision is similar to the seeding in bootstrapping literature (Thelen and Riloff, 2002) or prototype-based learning (Haghighi and Klein, 2006). Our reliance on seed sets is orthogonal to existing approaches that use external knowledge, which operate at the level of documents (Blei and McAuliffe, 2008), tokens (Andrzejewski and Zhu, 2009) or pair-wise constraints (Andrzejewski et al., 2009).

We build a model that uses the seed words in two ways: to improve both topic-word and document-topic probability distributions. For ease of exposition, we present these ideas separately and then in combination (Section 2.3). To improve topic-word distributions, we set up a model in which each topic prefers to generate words that are related to the words in a seed set (Section 2.1). To improve document-topic distributions, we encourage the model to select document-level topics based on the existence of input seed words in that document (Section 2.2).

Before moving on to the details of our models, we briefly recall the generative story of the LDA model and the reader is encouraged to refer to (Blei et al., 2003) for further details.

1. For each topic $k = 1 \cdots$ T,
   - choose $\phi_k \sim \text{Dir}(\beta)$.
2. For each document d, choose $\theta_d \sim \text{Dir}(\alpha)$.
   - For each token $i = 1 \cdots N_d$:
     (a) Select a topic $z_i \sim \text{Mult}(\theta_d)$.
     (b) Select a word $w_i \sim \text{Mult}(\phi_{z_i})$.

where T is the number of topics, α, β are hyperparameters of the model and ϕ_k and θ_d are topic-word and document-topic Multinomial probability distributions respectively.

2.1 Word-Topic Distributions (Model 1)

In regular topic models, each topic k is defined by a Multinomial distribution ϕ_k over words. We extend this notion and instead define a topic as a mixture of *two* Multinomial distributions: a "seed topic" distribution and a "regular topic" distribution. The seed topic distribution is constrained to *only* generate words from a corresponding seed set. The regular topic distribution may generate any word (*including* seed words). For example, seed topic 4 (in Table 2) can only generate the five words in its set. The word "oil" can be generated by seed topics 4 and 5, as well as any regular

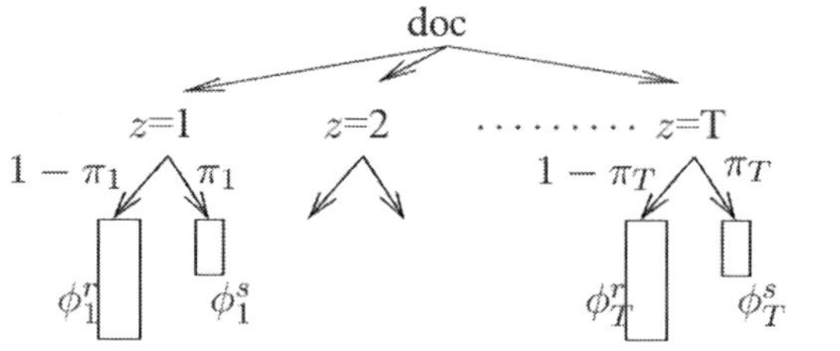

Figure 1: Tree representation of a document in Model 1.

topic. We want to emphasize that, like any regular topic, each seed topic is a *non*-uniform probability distribution over the words in its set. The user only inputs the sets of seed words and the model will infer their probability distributions.

For the sake of simplicity, we describe our model by assuming a one-to-one correspondence between seed and regular topics. This assumption can be easily relaxed by duplicating the seed topics when there are more regular topics. As shown in Fig. 1, each document is a mixture over T topics, where each of those topics is a mixture of a regular topic ($\phi^r_\cdot$) and its associated seed topic ($\phi^s_\cdot$) distributions. The parameter π_k controls the probability of drawing a word from the seed topic distribution versus the regular topic distribution. For our first model, we assume that the corpus is generated based on the following generative process (its graphical notation is shown in Fig. 2(a)):

1. For each topic k=1$\cdots$T,
   (a) Choose regular topic $\phi^r_k \sim \text{Dir}(\beta_r)$.
   (b) Choose *seed* topic $\phi^s_k \sim \text{Dir}(\beta_s)$.
   (c) Choose $\pi_k \sim \text{Beta}(1, 1)$.
2. For each document d, choose $\theta_d \sim \text{Dir}(\alpha)$.
   - For each token $i = 1 \cdots N_d$:
     (a) Select a topic $z_i \sim \text{Mult}(\theta_d)$.
     (b) Select an indicator $x_i \sim \text{Bern}(\pi_{z_i})$
     (c) if x_i is 0
       - Select a word $w_i \sim \text{Mult}(\phi^r_{z_i})$. // choose from regular topic
     (d) if x_i is 1
       - Select a word $w_i \sim \text{Mult}(\phi^s_{z_i})$. // choose from seed topic

The first step is to generate Multinomial distributions for both seed topics and regular topics. The seed topics are drawn in a way that *constrains* their distribution to only generate words in the corresponding seed set. Then, for each token in a document, we first generate a topic. After choosing a topic, we flip a (biased) coin to pick either the seed or the regular topic distribution. Once this distribution is selected we generate a word from it. It is important to note that although there are 2×T topic-word distributions in total, each document is still a mixture of *only* T topics (as shown in Fig. 1). This is crucial in relating seed and regular topics and is similar to the way topics and aspects are tied in TAM model (Paul and Girju, 2010).

To understand how this model gathers words related to seed words, consider a seed topic (say the fourth row in Table 2) with seed words {grain, wheat, corn, *etc.* }. Now by assigning all the related words such as "tonnes", "agriculture", "production" *etc.* to its corresponding *regular topic*, the model can potentially put high probability mass on topic $z = 4$ for agriculture related documents. Instead, if it places these words in another regular topic, say $z = 3$, then the document probability mass has to be distributed among topics 3 and 4 and as a result the model will pay a steeper penalty. Thus the model uses seed topic to gather related words into its associated regular topic and as a consequence the document-topic distributions also become focussed.

We have experimented with two ways of choosing the binary variable x_i (step 2b) of the generative story. In the first method, we fix this sampling probability to a constant value which is independent of the chosen topic (*i.e.* $\pi_i = \hat{\pi}$, $\forall i = 1 \cdots T$). And in the second method we learn the probability as well (Sec. 4).

2.2 Document-Topic distributions (Model 2)

In the previous model we used seed words to improve topic-word probability distributions. Here we propose a model to explore the use of seed words to improve document-topic probability distributions. Unlike the previous model, we will present this model in the general case where the number of seed topics is not equal to the number of regular topics. Hence, we associate each seed set (we refer seed set as group for conciseness) with a Multinomial distribution over the regular topics which we call group-topic distribution.

To give an overview of our model, first, we transfer the seed information from words onto

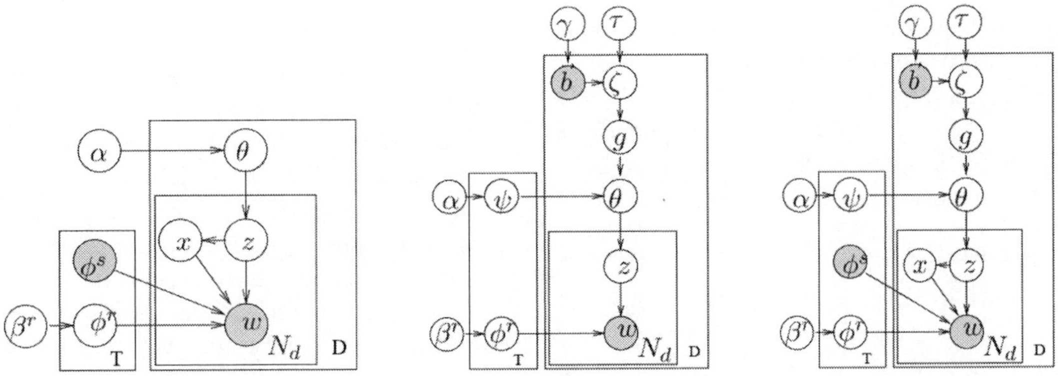

(a) Model 1 (b) Model 2 (c) SeededLDA

Figure 2: The graphical notation of all the three models. In Model 1 we use seed topics to improve the topic-word probability distributions. In Model 2, the seed topic information is first transfered to the document level based on the document tokens and then it is used to improve document-topic distributions. In the final, SeededLDA, model we combine both the models. In Model 1 and SeededLDA, we dropped the dependency of ϕ^s on hyper parameter β_s since it is observed. And, for clarity, we also dropped the dependency of x on π.

the documents that contain them. Then, the document-topic distribution is drawn in a two step process: we sample a seed set (g for group) and then use its group-topic distribution (ψ_g) as prior to draw the document-topic distribution (θ_d). We used this two step process, to allow flexible number of seed and regular topics, and to tie the topic distributions of all the documents within a group. We assume the following generative story and its graphical notation is shown in Fig. 2(b).

1. For each $k = 1 \cdots$ T,
   (a) Choose $\phi^r_k \sim \text{Dir}(\beta_r)$.
2. For each seed set $s = 1 \cdots$ S,
   (a) Choose group-topic distribution $\psi_s \sim \text{Dir}(\alpha)$. // the topic distribution for s^{th} group (seed set) – a vector of length T.
3. For each document d,
   (a) Choose a binary vector $\vec{b}$ of length S.
   (b) Choose a document-group distribution $\zeta^d \sim \text{Dir}(\tau\vec{b})$.
   (c) Choose a group variable $g \sim \text{Mult}(\zeta^d)$
   (d) Choose $\theta_d \sim \text{Dir}(\psi_g)$. // of length T
   (e) For each token $i = 1 \cdots N_d$:
      i. Select a topic $z_i \sim \text{Mult}(\theta_d)$.
      ii. Select a word $w_i \sim \text{Mult}(\phi^r_{z_i})$.

We first generate T topic-word distributions (ϕ_k) and S group-topic distributions (ψ_s). Then for each document, we generate a list of seed sets that are allowed for this document. This list is represented using the binary vector $\vec{b}$. This binary vector can be populated based on the document words and hence it is treated as an observed variable. For example, consider the (very short!) document "oil companies have merged". According to the seed sets from Table 2, we define a binary vector that denotes which seed topics contain words in this document. In this case, this vector $\vec{b} = \langle 1, 1, 0, 1, 1 \rangle$, indicating the presence of seeds from sets 1, 2, 4 and 5.[1] As discussed in (Williamson et al., 2010), generating binary vector is crucial if we want a document to talk about topics that are less prominent in the corpus.

The binary vector $\vec{b}$, that indicates which seeds exist in this document, defines a *mean* of a Dirichlet distribution from which we sample a *document-group* distribution, ζ^d (step 3b). We set the concentration of this Dirichlet to a hyperparamter τ, which we set by hand (Sec. 4); thus, $\zeta^d \sim \text{Dir}(\tau\vec{b})$. From the resulting multinomial, we draw a *group* variable g for this document. This group variable brings clustering structure among the documents by grouping the documents that are likely to talk about same seed set.

Once the group variable (g) is drawn, we choose the document-topic distribution (θ_d) from a Dirichlet distribution with the group's-topic distribution as the prior (step 3d). This step ensures that the topic distributions of documents within each group are related. The remaining sampling

[1] As a special case, if no seed word is found in the document, $\vec{b}$ is defined as the all-ones vector.

process proceeds like LDA. We sample a topic for each word and then generate a word from its corresponding topic-word distribution. Observe that, if the binary vector is all ones and if we set $\theta_d = \zeta^d$ then this model reduces to the LDA model with τ and β_r as the hyperparameters.

2.3 SeededLDA

Both of our models use seed words in different ways to improve topic-word and document-topic distributions respectively. We can combine both the above models easily. We refer to the combined model as SeededLDA and its generative story is as follows (its graphical notation is shown in Fig. 2(c)). The variables have same semantics as in the previous models.

1. For each k=1 $\cdots$ T,
   (a) Choose regular topic $\phi_k^r \sim \text{Dir}(\beta_r)$.
   (b) Choose *seed* topic $\phi_k^s \sim \text{Dir}(\beta_s)$.
   (c) Choose $\pi_k \sim \text{Beta}(1,1)$.
2. For each seed set $s = 1 \cdots$ S,
   (a) Choose group-topic distribution $\psi_s \sim \text{Dir}(\alpha)$.
3. For each document d,
   (a) Choose a binary vector $\vec{b}$ of length S.
   (b) Choose a document-group distribution $\zeta^d \sim \text{Dir}(\tau\vec{b})$.
   (c) Choose a group variable $g \sim \text{Mult}(\zeta^d)$.
   (d) Choose $\theta_d \sim \text{Dir}(\psi_g)$. // of length T
   (e) For each token $i = 1 \cdots N_d$:
      i. Select a topic $z_i \sim \text{Mult}(\theta_d)$.
      ii. Select an indicator $x_i \sim \text{Bern}(\pi_{z_i})$.
      iii. if x_i is 0
         - Select a word $w_i \sim \text{Mult}(\phi_{z_i}^r)$.
      iv. if x_i is 1
         - Select a word $w_i \sim \text{Mult}(\phi_{z_i}^s)$.

In the SeededLDA model, the process for generating group variable of a document is same as the one described in the Model 2. And like in the Model 2, we sample a document-topic probability distribution as a Dirichlet draw with the group-topic distribution of the chosen group as prior. Subsequently, we choose a topic for each token and then flip a biased coin. We choose either the seed or the regular topic based on the result of the coin toss and then generate a word from its distribution.

2.4 Automatic Seed Selection

In (Andrzejewski and Zhu, 2009; Andrzejewski et al., 2009), the seed information is provided manually. Here, we describe the use of feature selection techniques, prevalent in the classification literature, to automatically derive the seed sets. If we want the topicality structure identified by the LDA to align with the underlying class structure, then the seed words need to be representative of the underlying topicality structure. To enable this, we first take class labeled data (doesn't need to be multi-class labeled data unlike (Ramage et al., 2009)) and identify the discriminating features for each class. Then we choose these discriminating features as the initial sets of seed words. In principle, this is similar to the prototype driven unsupervised learning (Haghighi and Klein, 2006).

We use Information Gain (Mitchell, 1997) to identify the required discriminating features. The Information Gain (IG) of a word (w) in a class (c) is given by

$$IG(c, w) = H(c) - H(c|w)$$

where $H(c)$ is the entropy of the class and $H(c|w)$ is the conditional entropy of the class given the word. In computing Information Gain, we binarize the document vectors and consider whether a word occurs in any document of a given class or not. Thus obtained ranked list of words for each class are filtered for ambiguous words and then used as initial sets of seed words to be input to the model.

3 Related Work

Seed-based supervision is closely related to the idea of seeding in the bootstrapping literature for learning semantic lexicons (Thelen and Riloff, 2002). The goals are similar as well: growing a small set of seed examples into a much larger set. A key difference is the *type* of semantic information that the two approaches aim to capture: semantic lexicons are based on much more specific notions of semantics (*e.g.* all the country names) than the generic "topic" semantics of topic models. The idea of seeding has also been used in prototype-driven learning (Haghighi and Klein, 2006) and shown similar efficacies for these semi-supervised learning approaches.

LDAWN (Boyd-Graber et al., 2007) models sets of words for the word sense disambiguation task. It assumes that a topic is a distribution over synsets and relies on the Wordnet to obtain the synsets. The most related prior work is that of (Andrzejewski et al., 2009), who propose the use Dirichlet Forest priors to incorporate Must Link and Cannot Link constraints into the topic models. This work is analogous to constrained K-means clustering (Wagstaff et al., 2001; Basu et al., 2008). A must link between a pair word types represents that the model should encourage both the words to have either high or low probability in any particular topic. A cannot link between a word pair indicates both the words should not have high probability in a single topic. In the Dirichlet Forest approach, the constraints are first converted into trees with words as the leaves and edges having pre-defined weights. All the trees are joined to a dummy node to form a forest. The sampling for a word translates into a random walk on the forest: starting from the root and selecting one of its children based on the edge weights until you reach a leaf node.

While the Dirichlet Forest method requires supervision in terms of Must link and Cannot link information, the Topics In Sets (Andrzejewski and Zhu, 2009) model proposes a different approach. Here, the supervision is provided at the *token* level. The user chooses specific tokens and restrict them to occur only with in a specified list of topics. While this needs minimal changes to the inference process of LDA, it requires information at the level of tokens. The word type level seed information can be converted into token level information (like we do in Sec. 4) but this prevents their model from distinguishing the tokens based on the word senses.

Several models have been proposed which use supervision at the document level. Supervised LDA (Blei and McAuliffe, 2008) and DiscLDA (Lacoste-Julien et al., 2008) try to predict the category labels (*e.g.* sentiment classification) for the input documents based on a document labeled data. Of these models, the most related one to SeededLDA is the LabeledLDA model (Ramage et al., 2009). Their model operates on multi-class labeled corpus. Each document is assumed to be a mixture over a known subset of topics (classes) with each topic being a distribution over words. The process of generating document topic distribution in LabeledLDA is similar to the process of generating group distribution in our Model 2 (Sec. 2.2). However our model differs from LabeledLDA in the subsequent steps. Rather than using the group distribution directly, we sample a group variable and use it to constrain the document-topic distributions of all the documents within this group. Moreover, in their model the binary vector is observed directly in the form of document labels while, in our case, it is automatically populated based on the document tokens.

Interactive topic modeling brings the user into the loop, by allowing him/her to make suggestions on how to improve the quality of the topics at each iteration (Hu et al., 2011). In their approach, the authors use Dirichlet Forest method to incorporate the user's preferences. In our experiments (Sec. 4), we show that SeededLDA performs better than Dirichlet Forest method, so SeededLDA when used with their framework can allow an user to explore a document collection in a more meaningful manner.

4 Experiments

We evaluate different aspects of the model separately. Our experimental setup proceeds as follows: a) Using an existing model, we evaluate the effectiveness of automatically derived constraints indicating the potential benefits of adding seed words into the topic models. b) We evaluate each of our proposed models in different settings and compare with multiple baseline systems.

Since our aim is to overcome the dominance of majority topics by encouraging the topicality structure identified by the topic models to align with that of the document corpus, we choose extrinsic evaluation as the primary evaluation method. We use document clustering task and use frequent-5 categories of Reuters-21578 corpus (Lewis et al., 2004) and four classes from the 20 Newsgroups data set (*i.e.*'rec.autos', 'sci.electronics', 'comp.hardware' and 'alt.atheism'). For both the corpora we do the standard preprocessing of removing stopwords and infrequent words (Williamson et al., 2010).

For all the models, we use a Collapsed Gibbs sampler (Griffiths and Steyvers, 2004) for the inference process. We use the standard hyperparameters values $\alpha = 1.0$, $\beta = 0.01$ and $\tau = 1.0$ and run the sampler for 1000 iterations, but one can use techniques like slice sampling to estimate the hyperparameters (Johnson and Goldwater, 2009).

	Reuters		20 Newsgroups	
	F-measure	VI	F-measure	VI
LDA	0.64 (±.05)	1.26 (±.16)	0.77 (±.06)	0.9 (±.13)
Dirichlet Forest	**0.67*** (±.02)	**1.17** (±.11)	**0.79**(±.01)	**0.83***(±.03)
Δ over LDA	*(+4.68%)*	*(-7.1%)*	*(+2.6%)*	*(-7.8%)*

Table 3: The effect of adding constraints by Dirichlet Forest Encoding. For Variational Information (VI) a lower score indicates a better clustering. * indicates statistical significance at $p = 0.01$ as measured by the t-test. All the four improvements are significant at $p = 0.05$.

We run all the models with the same number of topics as the number of clusters. Then, for each document, we find the topic that has maximum probability in the posterior document-topic distribution and assign it to that cluster. The accuracy of the document clustering is measured in terms of F-measure and Variation of Information. F-measure is calculated based on the pairs of documents, *i.e.* if two documents belong to a cluster in both ground truth and the clustering proposed by the system then it is counted as correct, otherwise it is counted as wrong. Variational Information (VI) of two clusterings X and Y is given as (Meilă, 2007):

$$\text{VI}(X, Y) = H(X) + H(Y) - 2I(X, Y)$$

where $H(X)$ denotes the entropy of the clustering X and $I(X, Y)$ denotes the mutual information between the two clusterings. For VI, a lower value indicates a better clustering. All the accuracies are averaged over 25 different random initializations and all the significance results are measured using the t-test at $p = 0.01$.

4.1 Seed Extraction

The seeds were extracted automatically (Sec. 2.4) based on a small sample of labeled data other than the test data. We first extract 25 seeds words per each class and then remove the seed words that appear in more than one class. After this filtering, on an average, we are left with 9 and 15 words per each seed topic for Reuters and 20 Newsgroups corpora respectively.

We use the existing Dirichlet Forest method to evaluate the effectiveness of the automatically extracted seed words. The Must and Cannot links required for the supervision (Andrzejewski et al., 2009) are automatically obtained by adding a must-link between every pair of words belonging to the same seed set and a split constraint between every pair of words belonging to different sets. The accuracies are averaged over 25 different random initializations and are shown in Table 3. We have also indicated the relative performance gains compared to LDA. The significant improvement over the plain LDA demonstrates the effectiveness of the automatic extraction of seed words in topic models.

4.2 Document Clustering

In the next experiment, we compare our models with LDA and other baselines. The first baseline (maxCluster) simply counts the number of tokens in each document from each of the seed topics and assigns the document to the seed topic that has most tokens. This results in a clustering of documents based on the seed topic they are assigned to. This baseline evaluates the effectiveness of the seed words with respect to the underlying clustering. Apart from the maxCluster baseline, we use LDA and z-labels (Andrzejewski and Zhu, 2009) as our baselines. For z-labels, we treat all the tokens of a seed word in the same way. Table 4 shows the comparison of our models with respect to the baseline systems.[2] Comparing the performance of maxCluster to that of LDA, we observe that the seed words themselves do a poor job in clustering the documents.

We experimented with two variants of Model 1. In the first run (Model 1) we sample the π_k value, *i.e.* the probability of choosing a seed topic for each topic. While in the 'Model 1 ($\hat{\pi} = 0.7$)' run, we fix this probability to a constant value of 0.7 irrespective of the topic.[3] Though both the models

[2] The code used for LDA baseline in Tables 3 and 4 are different. For Table 3, we use the code available from http://pages.cs.wisc.edu/~andrzeje/research/df_lda.html. We use our own version for Table 4. We tried to produce a comparable baseline by running the former for more iterations and with different hyperparameters. In Table 3, we report their best results.

[3] We chose this value based on intuition; it is *not* tuned.

	Reuters		20 Newsgroups	
	F-measure	VI	F-measure	VI
maxCluster	0.53	1.75	0.58	1.44
LDA	0.66 (±.04)	1.2 (±.12)	0.76 (±.06)	0.9 (±.14)
z-labels	0.73 (±.01)	1.04 (±.01)	0.8 (±.00)	0.82 (±.01)
Δ over LDA	*(+10.6%)*	*(-13.3%)*	*(+5.26%)*	*(-8.8%)*
Model 1	0.69 (±.00)	1.13 (±.01)	0.8 (±.01)	0.81 (±.02)
Model 1 ($\hat{\pi} = 0.7$)	0.73 (±.00)	1.09 (±.01)	0.8 (±.01)	0.81 (±.02)
Model 2	0.66 (±.04)	1.22 (±.1)	0.77 (±.07)	0.85 (±.12)
SeededLDA	**0.76*** (±.01)	**0.99*** (±.03)	**0.81*** (±.01)	**0.75*** (±.02)
Δ over LDA	*(+15.5%)*	*(-17.5%)*	*(+6.58%)*	*(-16.7%)*

Table 4: Accuracies on document clustering task with different models. * indicates significant improvement compared to the z-labels approach, as measured by the t-test with $p = 0.01$. The relative performance gains are with respect to the LDA model and are provided for comparison with Dirichlet Forest method (in Table 3.)

performed better than LDA, fixing the probability gave better results. When we attempt to learn this value, the model chooses to explain some of the seed words by the regular topics. On the other hand, when π is fixed, it explains almost all the seed words based on the seed topics. The next row (Model 2) indicates the performance of our second model on the same data sets. The first model seems to be performing better than the second model, which is justifiable since the latter uses seed topics indirectly. Though the variants of Model 1 and Model 2 performed better than the LDA, they fell short of the z-labels approach.

Table 4 also shows the performance of our combined model (SeededLDA) on both the corpora. When the models are combined, the performance improves over each of them and is also better than the baseline systems. As explained before, our individual models improve both the topic-word and document-topic distributions respectively. But it turns out that the knowledge learnt by both the individual models is complementary to each other. As a result the combined model performed better than the individual models and other baseline systems. Comparing the last rows of Tables 4 and 3, we notice that the relative performance gains observed in the case of SeededLDA is significantly higher than the performance gains obtained by incorporating the constraints using the Dirichlet Forest method. Moreover, as indicated in the Table 4, SeededLDA achieves significant gains over the z-labels approach as well.

We have also provided the standard intervals for each of the approaches. A quick inspection of these intervals reveals the superior performance of SeededLDA compared to all the baselines. The standard deviation of the F-measures over different random initializations of our our model is about 1% for both the corpora while it is 4% and 6% for the LDA on Reuters and 20 Newsgroups corpora respectively. The reduction in the variance, across all the approaches that use seed information, shows the increased robustness of the inference process when using seed words. From the accuracies in both the tables, it is clear that SeededLDA model out-performs other models which try to incorporate seed information into the topic models.

4.3 Effect of Ambiguous Seeds

In the following experiment we study the effect of ambiguous seeds. We allow a seed word to occur in multiple seed sets. Table 6 shows the corresponding results. The performance drops when we add ambiguous seed words, but it is still higher than that of the LDA model. This suggests that the quality of the seed topics is determined by the discriminative power of the seed words rather than the number of seed words in each seed topic. The topics identified by the SeededLDA on Reuters corpus are shown in the Table 5. With the help of the seed sets, the model is able to split the 'Grain' and 'Crude' into two separate topics which were merged into a single topic by the plain LDA.

4.4 Qualitative Evaluation on NIPS papers

We ran LDA and SeededLDA models on the NIPS papers from 2001 to 2010. For this corpus, the seed words are chosen from the call for proposal.

group, offer, common, cash, agreement, shareholders, acquisition, stake, merger, board, sale
oil, price, prices, production, lt, gas, crude, 1987, 1985, bpd, opec, barrels, energy, first, petroleum
0, mln, cts, net, loss, 2, dlrs, shr, 3, profit, 4, 5, 6, revs, 7, 9, 8, year, note, 1986, 10, 0, sales
tonnes, wheat, mln, grain, week, corn, department, year, export, program, agriculture, 0, soviet, prices
bank, market, pct, dollar, exchange, billion, stg, today, foreign, rate, banks, japan, yen, rates, trade

Table 5: Topics identified by SeededLDA on the frequent-5 categories of Reuters corpus

	Reuters		20 Newsgroups	
	F	VI	F	VI
LDA	0.66	1.2	0.76	0.9
SeededLDA	**0.76**	**0.99**	**0.81**	**0.75**
SeededLDA (amb)	0.71	1.08	0.79	0.78

Table 6: Effect of ambiguous seed words on SeededLDA.

There are 10 major areas with sub areas under each of them. We ran both the models with 10 topics. For SeededLDA, the words in each of the areas are selected as seed words and we filter out the ambiguous seed words. Upon a qualitative observation of the output topics, we found that LDA has identified seven major topics and left out "Brain Imaging", "Cognitive Science and Artificial Intelligence" and "Hardware Technologies" areas. Not surprisingly, but reassuringly, these areas are underrepresented among the NIPS papers. On the other hand, SeededLDA successfully identifies all of the major topics. The topics identified by LDA and SeededLDA are shown in the supplementary material.

5 Discussion

In traditional topic models, a symmetric Dirichlet distribution is used as prior for topic-word distributions. A first attempt method to incorporate seed words into the model is to use an asymmetric Dirichlet distribution as prior for the topic-word distributions (also called as Informed priors). For example, to encourage Topic 5 to align with a seed set we can choose an asymmetric prior of the form $\vec{\beta}_5 = \{\beta, \cdots, \beta + c, \cdots, \beta\}$, *i.e.* we increase the component values corresponding to the seed words by a positive constant value. This favors the desired seed words to be drawn with a higher probability from this topic. But, it is argued elsewhere that words drawn from such distributions rarely pick words other than the seed words (Andrzejewski et al., 2009). Moreover, since, in our method each seed topic is a distribution over the seed words, the convex combination of regular and seed topics can be seen as adding different weights (c_i) to different components of the prior vector. Thus our Model 1 can be seen as an asymmetric generalization of the Informed priors.

For comparability purposes, in this paper, we experimented with same number of regular topics as the number of seed topics. But as explained in the modeling part, our model is general enough to handle situation with unequal number of seed and regular topics. In this case, we assume that the seed topics indicate a higher level of topicality structure of the corpus and associate each seed topic (or group) with a distribution over the regular topics. On the other hand, in many NLP applications, we tend to have *only* a partial information rather than high-level supervision. In such cases, one can create some empty seed sets and tweak the model 2 to output a 1 in the binary vector corresponding to these seed sets. In this paper, we used information gain to select the discriminating seed words. But in the real world applications, one can use publicly available ODP categorization data to obtain the higher level seed words and thus explore the corporal in a more meaningful way.

In this paper, we have explored two methods to incorporate lexical prior into the topic models, combining them into a single model that we call SeededLDA. From our experimental analysis, we found that automatically derived seed words can improve clustering performance significantly. Moreover, we found out that allowing a seed word to be shared across multiple sets of seed words degrades the performance.

6 Acknowledgments

We thank the anonymous reviewers for their helpful comments. This material is partially supported by the National Science Foundation under Grant No. IIS-1153487.

References

Andrzejewski, D. and Zhu, X. (2009). Latent dirichlet allocation with topic-in-set knowledge. In *Proceedings of the NAACL HLT 2009 Workshop on Semi-Supervised Learning for Natural Language Processing*, SemiSupLearn '09, pages 43–48, Morristown, NJ, USA. Association for Computational Linguistics.

Andrzejewski, D., Zhu, X., and Craven, M. (2009). Incorporating domain knowledge into topic modeling via dirichlet forest priors. In *ICML '09: Proceedings of the 26th Annual International Conference on Machine Learning*, pages 25–32, New York, NY, USA. ACM.

Basu, S., Ian, D., and Wagstaff, K. (2008). *Constrained Clustering : Advances in Algorithms, Theory, and Applications*. Chapman & Hall/CRC Pres.

Blei, D. and McAuliffe, J. (2008). Supervised topic models. In *Advances in Neural Information Processing Systems 20*, pages 121–128, Cambridge, MA. MIT Press.

Blei., D. M. and Lafferty., J. (2009). Topic models. In *Text Mining: Theory and Applications*. Taylor and Francis.

Blei, D. M., Ng, A. Y., and Jordan, M. I. (2003). Latent dirichlet allocation. *Journal of Maching Learning Research*, 3:993–1022.

Boyd-Graber, J., Blei, D. M., and Zhu, X. (2007). A topic model for word sense disambiguation. In *Empirical Methods in Natural Language Processing*.

Chang, J., Boyd-Graber, J., Wang, C., Gerrish, S., and Blei, D. M. (2009). Reading tea leaves: How humans interpret topic models. In *Neural Information Processing Systems*.

Griffiths, T., Steyvers, M., and Tenenbaum, J. (2007). Topics in semantic representation. *Psychological Review*, 114(2):211–244.

Griffiths, T. L. and Steyvers, M. (2004). Finding scientific topics. *Proceedings of National Academy of Sciences USA*, 101 Suppl 1:5228–5235.

Griffiths, T. L., Steyvers, M., Blei, D. M., and Tenenbaum, J. B. (2005). Integrating topics and syntax. In *Advances in Neural Information Processing Systems*, volume 17, pages 537–544.

Haghighi, A. and Klein, D. (2006). Prototype-driven learning for sequence models. In *Proceedings of the main conference on Human Language Technology Conference of the North American Chapter of the Association of Computational Linguistics*, HLT-NAACL '06, pages 320–327, Stroudsburg, PA, USA. Association for Computational Linguistics.

Hu, Y., Boyd-Graber, J., and Satinoff, B. (2011). Interactive topic modeling. In *Proceedings of the 49th Annual Meeting of the Association for Computational Linguistics: Human Language Technologies - Volume 1*, HLT '11, pages 248–257, Stroudsburg, PA, USA. Association for Computational Linguistics.

Johnson, M. and Goldwater, S. (2009). Improving nonparameteric bayesian inference: experiments on unsupervised word segmentation with adaptor grammars. In *Proceedings of Human Language Technologies: The 2009 Annual Conference of the North American Chapter of the Association for Computational Linguistics*, NAACL '09, pages 317–325, Stroudsburg, PA, USA. Association for Computational Linguistics.

Lacoste-Julien, S., Sha, F., and Jordan, M. (2008). DiscLDA: Discriminative learning for dimensionality reduction and classification. In *Proceedings of NIPS '08*.

Lewis, D. D., Yang, Y., Rose, T. G., and Li, F. (2004). Rcv1: A new benchmark collection for text categorization research. *J. Mach. Learn. Res.*, 5:361–397.

Meilă, M. (2007). Comparing clusterings—an information based distance. *J. Multivar. Anal.*, 98:873–895.

Mitchell, T. M. (1997). *Machine Learning*. McGraw-Hill, New York.

Paul, M. and Girju, R. (2010). A two-dimensional topic-aspect model for discovering multi-faceted topics. In *AAAI*.

Ramage, D., Hall, D., Nallapati, R., and Manning, C. D. (2009). Labeled LDA: a supervised topic model for credit attribution in multi-labeled corpora. In *Proceedings of the 2009 Conference on Empirical Methods in Natural Language Processing: Volume 1 - Volume 1*, EMNLP '09, pages 248–256, Morristown, NJ, USA. Association for Computational Linguistics.

Thelen, M. and Riloff, E. (2002). A bootstrapping method for learning semantic lexicons using extraction pattern contexts. In *In Proc. 2002 Conf. Empirical Methods in NLP (EMNLP)*.

Wagstaff, K., Cardie, C., Rogers, S., and Schrödl, S. (2001). Constrained k-means clustering with background knowledge. In *Proceedings of the Eighteenth International Conference on Machine Learning*, ICML '01, pages 577–584, San Francisco, CA, USA. Morgan Kaufmann Publishers Inc.

Wallach, H. M. (2005). Topic modeling: beyond bag-of-words. In *NIPS 2005 Workshop on Bayesian Methods for Natural Language Processing*.

Williamson, S., Wang, C., Heller, K. A., and Blei, D. M. (2010). The IBP compound dirichlet process and its application to focused topic modeling. In *ICML*, pages 1151–1158.

DualSum: a Topic-Model based approach for update summarization

Jean-Yves Delort
Google Research
Brandschenkestrasse 110
8002 Zurich, Switzerland
jydelort@google.com

Enrique Alfonseca
Google Research
Brandschenkestrasse 110
8002 Zurich, Switzerland
ealfonseca@google.com

Abstract

Update summarization is a new challenge in multi-document summarization focusing on summarizing a set of recent documents relatively to another set of earlier documents. We present an unsupervised probabilistic approach to model novelty in a document collection and apply it to the generation of update summaries. The new model, called DUALSUM, results in the second or third position in terms of the ROUGE metrics when tuned for previous TAC competitions and tested on TAC-2011, being statistically indistinguishable from the winning system. A manual evaluation of the generated summaries shows state-of-the art results for DUALSUM with respect to focus, coherence and overall responsiveness.

1 Introduction

Update summarization is the problem of extracting and synthesizing novel information in a collection of documents with respect to a set of documents assumed to be known by the reader. This problem has received much attention in recent years, as can be observed in the number of participants to the special track on update summarization organized by DUC and TAC since 2007. The problem is usually formalized as follows: Given two collections $\mathcal{A}$ and $\mathcal{B}$, where the documents in $\mathcal{A}$ chronologically precede the documents in $\mathcal{B}$, generate a summary of $\mathcal{B}$ under the assumption that the user of the summary has already read the documents in $\mathcal{A}$.

Extractive techniques are the most common approaches in multi-document summarization. Summaries generated by such techniques consist of sentences extracted from the document collection. Extracts can have coherence and cohesion problems, but they generally offer a good trade-off between linguistic quality and informativeness.

While numerous extractive summarization techniques have been proposed for multi-document summarization (Erkan and Radev, 2004; Radev et al., 2004; Shen and Li, 2010; Li et al., 2011), few techniques have been specifically designed for update summarization. Most existing approaches handle it as a redundancy removal problem, with the goal of producing a summary of collection $\mathcal{B}$ that is as dissimilar as possible from either collection $\mathcal{A}$ or from a summary of collection $\mathcal{A}$. A problem with this approach is that it can easily classify as redundant sentences in which novel information is mixed with existing information (from collection $\mathcal{A}$). Furthermore, while this approach can identify sentences that contain novel information, it cannot model explicitly what the novel information is.

Recently, Bayesian models have successfully been applied to multi-document summarization showing state-of-the-art results in summarization competitions (Haghighi and Vanderwende, 2009; Jin et al., 2010). These approaches offer clear and rigorous probabilistic interpretations that many other techniques lack. Furthermore, they have the advantage of operating in unsupervised settings, which can be used in real-world scenarios, across domains and languages. To our best knowledge, previous work has not used this approach for update summarization.

In this article, we propose a novel nonparametric Bayesian approach for update summarization. Our approach, which is a variation of Latent

Dirichlet Allocation (LDA) (Blei et al., 2003), aims to learn to distinguish between common information and novel information. We have evaluated this approach on the ROUGE scores and demonstrate that it produces comparable results to the top system in TAC-2011. Furthermore, our approach improves over that system when evaluated manually in terms of linguistic quality and overall responsiveness.

2 Related work

2.1 Bayesian approaches in Summarization

Most Bayesian approaches to summarization are based on topic models. These generative models represent documents as mixtures of latent topics, where a topic is a probability distribution over words. In TOPICSUM (Haghighi and Vanderwende, 2009), each word is generated by a single topic which can be a corpus-wide background distribution over common words, a distribution of document-specific words or a distribution of the core content of a given cluster. BAYESSUM (Daumé and Marcu, 2006) and the Special Words and Background model (Chemudugunta et al., 2006) are very similar to TOPICSUM.

A commonality of all these models is the use of collection and document-specific distributions in order to distinguish between the general and specific topics in documents. In the context of summarization, this distinction helps to identify the important pieces of information in a collection.

Models that use more structure in the representation of documents have also been proposed for generating more coherent and less redundant summaries, such as HIERSUM (Haghighi and Vanderwende, 2009) and TTM (Celikyilmaz and Hakkani-Tur, 2011). For instance, HIERSUM models the intuitions that first sentences in documents should contain more general information, and that adjacent sentences are likely to share specic content vocabulary. However, HIERSUM, which builds upon TOPICSUM, does not show a statistically signicant improvement in ROUGE over TOPICSUM.

A number of techniques have been proposed to rank sentences of a collection given a word distribution (Carbonell and Goldstein, 1998; Goldstein et al., 1999). The Kullback-Leibler divergence (KL) is a widely used measure in summarization. Given a target distribution T that we want a summary S to approximate, KL is commonly used as the scoring function to select the subset of sentences S^* that minimizes the KL divergence with T:

$$S^* = \underset{S}{\text{argmin}} KL(T, S) = \sum_{w \in \mathbf{V}} p_T(w) \log \frac{p_T(w)}{p_S(w)}$$

where w is a word from the vocabulary $\mathbf{V}$. This strategy is called KLSum. Usually, a smoothing factor τ is applied on the candidate distribution S in order to avoid the divergence to be undefined[1].

This objective function selects the most representative sentences of the collection, and at the same time it also diversifies the generated summary by penalizing redundancy. Since the problem of finding the subset of sentences from a collection that minimizes the KL divergence is NP-complete, a greedy algorithm is often used in practice[2]. Some variations of this objective function can be considered, such as penalizing sentences that contain document-specific topics (Mason and Charniak, 2011) or rewarding sentences appearing closer to the beginning of the document.

Wang et al. (2009) propose a Bayesian approach for summarization that does not use KL for reranking. In their model, Bayesian Sentence-based Topic Models, every sentence in a document is assumed to be associated to a unique latent topic. Once the model parameters have been calculated, a summary is generated by choosing the sentence with the highest probability for each topic.

While hierarchical topic modeling approaches have shown remarkable effectiveness in learning the latent topics of document collections, they are not designed to capture the novel information in a collection with respect to another one, which is the primary focus of update summarization.

2.2 Update Summarization

The goal of update summarization is to generate an *update summary* of a collection $\mathcal{B}$ of recent documents assuming that the users already read earlier documents from a collection $\mathcal{A}$. We refer

[1]In our experiments we set $\tau = 0.01$.

[2]In our experiments, we follow the same approach as in (Haghighi and Vanderwende, 2009) by greedily adding sentences to a summary so long as they decrease KL divergence.

to collection $\mathcal{A}$ as the *base collection* and to collection $\mathcal{B}$ as the *update collection*.

Update summarization is related to novelty detection which can be defined as the problem of determining whether a document contains new information given an existing collection (Soboroff and Harman, 2005). Thus, while the goal of novelty detection is to determine whether some information is new, the goal of update summarization is to extract and synthesize the novel information.

Update summarization is also related to contrastive summarization, i.e. the problem of jointly generating summaries for two entities in order to highlight their differences (Lerman and McDonald, 2009). The primary difference here is that update summarization aims to extract novel or updated information in the update collection with respect to the base collection.

The most common approach for update summarization is to apply a normal multi-document summarizer, with some added functionality to remove sentences that are redundant with respect to collection $\mathcal{A}$. This can be achieved using simple filtering rules (Fisher and Roark, 2008), Maximal Marginal Relevance (Boudin et al., 2008), or more complex graph-based algorithms (Shen and Li, 2010; Wenjie et al., 2008). The goal here is to boost sentences in $\mathcal{B}$ that bring out completely novel information. One problem with this approach is that it is likely to discard as redundant sentences in $\mathcal{B}$ containing novel information if it is mixed with known information from collection $\mathcal{A}$.

Another approach is to introduce specific features intended to capture the novelty in collection $\mathcal{B}$. For example, comparing collections $\mathcal{A}$ and $\mathcal{B}$, FastSum derives features for the collection $\mathcal{B}$ such as number of named entities in the sentence that already occurred in the old cluster or the number of new content words in the sentence not already mentioned in the old cluster that are subsequently used to train a Support Vector Machine classifier (Schilder et al., 2008). A limitation with this approach is there are no large training sets available and, the more features it has, the more it is affected by the sparsity of the training data.

3 DualSum

3.1 Model Formulation

The input for DUALSUM is a set of pairs of collections of documents $C = \{(\mathcal{A}_i, \mathcal{B}_i)\}_{i=1...m}$, where $\mathcal{A}_i$ is a base document collection and $\mathcal{B}_i$ is an update document collection. We use c to refer to a collection pair $(\mathcal{A}_c, \mathcal{B}_c)$.

In DUALSUM, documents are modeled as a bag of words that are assumed to be sampled from a mixture of latent topics. Each word is associated with a latent variable that specifies which topic distribution is used to generate it. Words in a document are assumed to be conditionally independent given the hidden topic.

As in previous Bayesian works for summarization (Daumé and Marcu, 2006; Chemudugunta et al., 2006; Haghighi and Vanderwende, 2009), DUALSUM not only learns collection-specific distributions, but also a general background distribution over common words, ϕ^G and a document-specific distribution ϕ^{cd} for each document d in collection pair c, which is useful to separate the specific aspects from the general aspects of c. The main novelty is that DUALSUM introduces specific machinery for identifying novelty.

To capture the differences between the base and the update collection for each pair c, DUALSUM learns two topics for every collection pair. The joint topic, $\phi^{\mathcal{A}_c}$ captures the common information between the two collections in the pair, i.e. the main event that both collections are discussing. The update topic, $\phi^{\mathcal{B}_c}$ focuses on the specific aspects that are specific of the documents inside the update collection.

In the generative model,

- For a document d in a collection $\mathcal{A}_c$, words can be originated from one of three different topics: ϕ^G, ϕ^{cd} and $\phi^{\mathcal{A}_c}$, the last one of which captures the main topic described in the collection pair.

- For a document d in a collection $\mathcal{B}_c$, words can be originated from one of four different topics: ϕ^G, ϕ^{cd}, $\phi^{\mathcal{A}_c}$ and $\phi^{\mathcal{B}_c}$. The last one will capture the most important updates to the main topic.

To make this representation easier, we can also state that both collections are generated from the four topics, but we constrain the topic probability

1. Sample $\phi^G \sim Dir(\lambda_G)$
2. For each collection pair $c = (\mathcal{A}_c, \mathcal{B}_c)$:
   - Sample $\phi^{\mathcal{A}_c} \sim Dir(\lambda_{\mathcal{A}})$
   - Sample $\phi^{\mathcal{B}_c} \sim Dir(\lambda_{\mathcal{B}})$
   - For each document d of type $u_{cd} \in \{\mathcal{A}, \mathcal{B}\}$:
     - Sample $\phi^{cd} \sim Dir(\lambda_D)$
     - If $(u_{cd} = \mathcal{A})$ sample $\psi^{cd} \sim Dir(\gamma^{\mathcal{A}})$
     - If $(u_{cd} = \mathcal{B})$ sample $\psi^{cd} \sim Dir(\gamma^{\mathcal{B}})$
     - For each word w in document d:
       (a) Sample a topic $z \sim Mult(\psi^{cd})$, $z \in \{G, cd, \mathcal{A}_c, \mathcal{B}_c\}$
       (b) Sample a word $w \sim Mult(\phi^z)$

Figure 1: Generative model in DUALSUM.

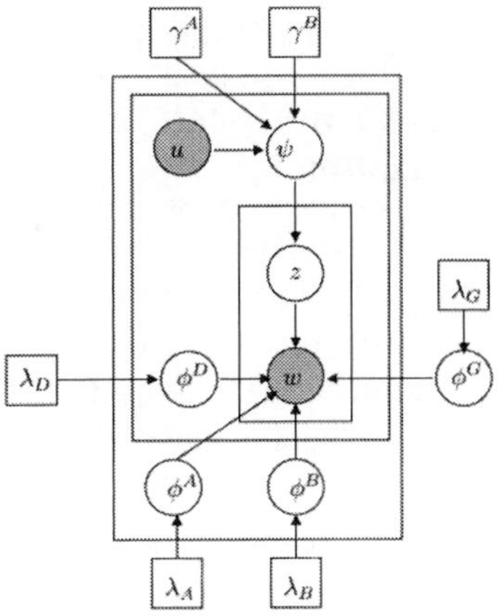

Figure 2: Graphical model representation of DUALSUM.

for $\phi^{\mathcal{B}_c}$ to be always zero when generating a base document.

We denote $u_{cd} \in \{A, B\}$ the type of a document d in pair c. This is an observed, Boolean variable stating whether the document d belongs to the base or the update collection inside the pair c.

The generation process of documents in DUALSUM is described in Figure 1, and the plate diagram corresponding to this generative story is shown in Figure 2. DUALSUM is an LDA-like model, where topic distributions are multinomial distributions over words and topics that are sampled from Dirichlet distributions. We use $\lambda = (\lambda_G, \lambda_D, \lambda_{\mathcal{A}}, \lambda_{\mathcal{B}})$ as symmetric priors for the Dirichlet distributions generating the word distributions. In our experiments, we set $\lambda_G = 0.1$ and $\lambda_D = \lambda_{\mathcal{A}} = \lambda_{\mathcal{B}} = 0.001$. A greater value is assigned to λ_G in order to reflect the intuition that there should be more words in the background than in the other distributions, so the mass is expected to be shared on a larger number of words.

Unlike for the word distributions, mixing probabilities are drawn from a Dirichlet distribution with asymmetric priors. The prior knowledge about the origin of words in the base and update collections is again encoded at the level the hyper-parameters. For example, if we set $\gamma^{\mathcal{A}} = (5, 3, 2, 0)$, this would reflect the intuition that, on average, in the base collections, 50% of the words originate from the background distribution, 30% from the document-specific distribution, and 20% from the joint topic. Similarly, if we set $\gamma^{\mathcal{B}} = (5, 2, 2, 1)$, the prior reflects the assumption that, on average, in the update collections, 50% of the words originate from the background distribution, 20% from the document-specific distribution, 20% from the joint topic, and 10% from the novel, update topic[3]. The priors we have actually used are reported in Section 4.

3.2 Learning and inference

In order to find the optimal model parameters, the following equation needs to be computed:

$$p(\mathbf{z}, \psi, \phi | \mathbf{w}, \mathbf{u}) = \frac{p(\mathbf{z}, \psi, \phi, \mathbf{w}, \mathbf{u})}{p(\mathbf{w}, \mathbf{u})}$$

Omitting hyper-parameters for notational simplicity, the joint distribution over the observed variables is:

$$\begin{aligned} p(\mathbf{w}, \mathbf{u}) = {} & p(\phi^G) \times \\ & \prod_c p(\phi^{\mathcal{A}_c}) p(\phi^{\mathcal{B}_c}) \times \\ & \prod_d p(u_{cd}) p(\phi^{cd}) \int_\Delta p(\psi^{cd} | u_{cd}) d\psi^{cd} \times \\ & \prod_n \sum_{cdn} p(w_{cdn} | z_{cdn}) p(z_{cdn} | \psi^{cd}) \end{aligned}$$

where Δ denotes the 4-dimensional simplex[4]. Since this equation is intractable, we need to perform approximate inference in order to estimate the model parameters. A number of Bayesian statistical inference techniques can be used to address this problem.

[3] To highlight the difference between asymmetric and symmetric priors we put the indices in superscript and subscript respectively.

[4] Remember that, for base documents, words cannot be generated by the update topic, so Δ denotes the 3-dimensional simplex for base documents.

Variational approaches (Blei et al., 2003) and collapsed Gibbs sampling (Griffiths and Steyvers, 2004) are common techniques for approximate inference in Bayesian models. They offer different advantages: the variational approach is arguably faster computationally, but the Gibbs sampling approach is in principal more accurate since it asymptotically approaches the correct distribution (Porteous et al., 2008). In this section, we provide details on a collapsed Gibbs sampling strategy to infer the model parameters of DUALSUM for a given dataset.

Collapsed Gibbs sampling is a particular case of Markov Chain Monte Carlo (MCMC) that involves repeatedly sampling a topic assignment for each word in the corpus. A single iteration of the Gibbs sampler is completed after sampling a new topic for each word based on the previous assignment. In a collapsed Gibbs sampler, the model parameters are integrated out (or collapsed), allowing to only sample $\mathbf{z}$. Let us call w_{cdn} the n-th word in document d in collection c, and z_{cdn} its topic assignment. For Gibbs sampling, we need to calculate $p(z_{cdn}|\mathbf{w}, \mathbf{u}, \mathbf{z_{-cdn}})$ where $\mathbf{z_{-cdn}}$ denotes the random vector of topic assignments except the assignment z_{cdn}.

$$p(z_{cdn} = j|\mathbf{w}, \mathbf{u}, \mathbf{z_{-cdn}}, \gamma^{\mathcal{A}}, \gamma^{\mathcal{B}}, \lambda) \propto \frac{n^{(w_{cdn})}_{-cdn,j} + \lambda_j}{\sum_{v=1}^{V} n^{(v)}_{-cdn,j} + V\lambda_j} \frac{n^{(cd)}_{-cdn,j} + \gamma_j^{u_{cd}}}{\sum_{k\in K}(n^{(cd)}_{-cdn,k} + \gamma_k^{u_{cd}})}$$

where $K = \{G, cd, \mathcal{A}_c, \mathcal{B}_c\}$, $n^{(v)}_{-cdn,j}$ denotes the number of times word v is assigned to topic j excluding current assignment of word w_{cdn} and $n^{(cd)}_{-cdn,k}$ denotes the number of words in document d of collection c that are assigned to topic j excluding current assignment of word w_{cdn}.

After each sampling iteration, the model parameters can be estimated using the following formulas[5].

$$\phi_w^k = \frac{n_k^{(w)} + \lambda_k}{\sum_{v=1}^{V} n_k^{(v)} + V\lambda_k}$$

$$\psi_k^{cd} = \frac{n_k^{(cd)} + \lambda_k}{\sum n^{(cd)} + V\lambda_k}$$

[5]The interested reader is invited to consult (Wang, 2011) for more details on using Gibbs sampling for LDA-like models

where $k \in K$, $n_k^{(v)}$ denotes the number of times word v is assigned to topic k, and $n_k^{(cd)}$ denotes the number of words in document d of collection c that are assigned to topic k.

By the strong law of large numbers, the average of sample parameters should converge towards the true expected value of the model parameter. Therefore, good estimates of the model parameters can be obtained averaging over the sampled values. As suggested by Gamerman and Lopes (2006), we have set a lag (20 iterations) between samples in order to reduce auto-correlation between samples. Our sampler also discards the first 100 iterations as burn-in period in order to avoid averaging from samples that are still strongly influenced by the initial assignment.

4 Experiments in Update Summarization

The Bayesian graphical model described in the previous section can be run over a set of news collections to learn the background distribution, a joint distribution for each collection, an update distribution for each collection and the document-specific distributions. Once this is done, one of the learned collections can be used to generate the summary that best approximates this collection, using the greedy algorithm described by Haghighi and Vanderwende (2009). Still, there are some parameters that can be defined and which affects the results obtained:

- DUALSUM's choice of hyper-parameters affects how the topics are learned.
- The documents can be represented with n-grams of different lengths.
- It is possible to generate a summary that approximates the joint distribution, the update-only distribution, or a combination of both.

This section describes how these parameters have been tuned.

4.1 Parameter tuning

We use the TAC 2008 and 2009 update task datasets as training set for tuning the hyper-parameters for the model, namely the pseudo-counts for the two Dirichlet priors that affects the topic mix assignment for each document. By performing a grid search over a large set of possible hyper-parameters, these have been fixed to

$\gamma^{\mathcal{A}} = (90, 190, 50, 0)$ and $\gamma^{\mathcal{B}} = (90, 170, 45, 25)$ as the values that produced the best ROUGE-2 score on those two datasets.

Regarding the base collection, this can be interpreted as setting as prior knowledge that roughly 27% of the words in the original dataset originate from the background distribution, 58% from the document-specific distributions, and 15% from the topic of the original collection. We remind the reader that the last value in $\gamma^{\mathcal{A}}$ is set to zero because, due to the problem definition, the original collection must have no words generated from the update topic, which reflects the most recent developments that are still not present in the base collections $\mathcal{A}$.

Regarding the update set, 27% of the words are assumed to originate again from the background distribution, 51% from the document-specific distributions, 14% from an topic in common with the original collection, and 8% from the update-specific topic. One interesting fact to note from these settings is that most of the words belong to topics that are specific to single documents (58% and 51% respectively for both sets $\mathcal{A}$ and $\mathcal{B}$) and to the background distribution, whereas the joint and update topics generate a much smaller, limited set of words. This helps these two distributions to be more focused.

The other settings mentioned at the beginning of this section have been tuned using the TAC-2010 dataset, which we reserved as our development set. Once the different document-specific and collection-specific distributions have been obtained, we have to choose the target distribution T to with which the possible summaries will be compared using the KL metric. Usually, the human-generated update summaries not only include the terms that are very specific about the last developments, but they also include a little background regarding the developing event. Therefore, we try, for KLSum, a simple mixture between the joint topic ($\phi^{\mathcal{A}}$) and the update topic ($\phi^{\mathcal{B}}$).

Figure 3 shows the ROUGE-2 results obtained as we vary the mixture weight between the joint $\phi^{\mathcal{A}}$ distribution and the update-specific $\phi^{\mathcal{B}}$ distribution. As can be seen at the left of the curve, using only the update-specific model, which disregards the generic words about the topic described, produces much lower results. The results improve as the relative weight of the joined topic model

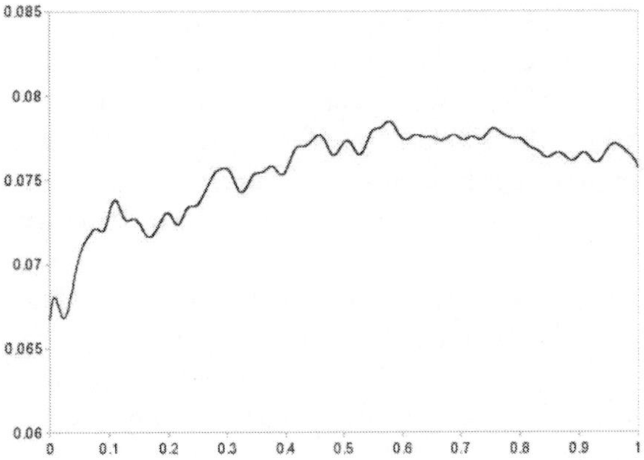

Figure 3: Variation in ROUGE-2 score in the TAC-2010 dataset as we change the mixture weight for the joined topic model between 0 and 1.

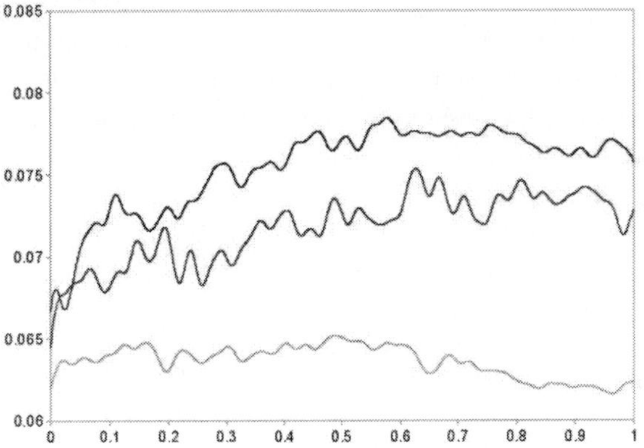

Figure 4: Effect of the mixture weight in ROUGE-2 scores (TAC-2010 dataset). Results are reported using bigrams (above, blue), unigrams (middle, red) and trigrams (below, yellow).

increases until it plateaus at a maximum around roughly the interval [0.6, 0.8], and from that point performance slowly degrades as at the right part of the curve the update model is given very little importance in generating the summary. Based on these results, from this point onwards, the mixture weight has been set to 0.7. Note that using only the joint distribution (setting the mixture weight to 1.0) also produces reasonable results, hinting that it successfully incorporates the most important n-grams from across the base and the update collections at the same time.

A second parameter is the size of the n-grams for representing the documents. The original implementations of SumBasic (Nenkova and Vanderwende, 2005) and TopicSum (Haghighi and Vanderwende, 2009) were defined over single words (unigrams). Still, Haghighi and Vanderwende (2009) report some improvements in the ROUGE-2 score when representing words as a bag of bigrams, and Darling (2010) mention similar improvements when running SUMBASIC with bigrams. Figure 4 shows the effect on the ROUGE-2 curve when we switch to using unigrams and trigrams. As stated in previous work, using bigrams has better results than using unigrams. Using trigrams was worse than either of them. This is probably because trigrams are too specific and the document collections are small, so the models are more likely to suffer from data sparseness.

4.2 Baselines

DUALSUM is a modification of TOPICSUM designed specifically for the case of update summarization, by modifying TOPICSUM's graphical model in a way that captures the dependency between the joint and the update collections. Still, it is important to discover whether the new graphical model actually improves over simpler applications of TOPICSUM to this task. The three baselines that we have considered are:

- Running TOPICSUM on the set of collections containing only the update documents. We call this run $\text{TOPICSUM}_{\mathcal{B}}$.
- Running TOPICSUM on the set of collections containing both the base and the update documents. Contrary to the previous run, the topic model for each collection in this run will contain information relevant to the base events. We call this run $\text{TOPICSUM}_{\mathcal{A}\cup\mathcal{B}}$.
- Running TOPICSUM twice, once on the set of collections containing the update documents, and the second time on the set of collections containing the base documents. Then, for each collection, the obtained base and update models are combined in a mixture model using a mixture weight between zero and one. The weight has been tuned using TAC-2010 as development set. We call this run $\text{TOPICSUM}_{\mathcal{A}}$+$\text{TOPICSUM}_{\mathcal{B}}$.

4.3 Automatic evaluation

DUALSUM and the three baselines[6] have been automatically evaluated using the TAC-2011 dataset. Table 1 shows the ROUGE results obtained. Because of the non-deterministic nature of Gibbs sampling, the results reported here are the average of five runs for all the baselines and for DUALSUM. DUALSUM outperforms two of the baselines in all three ROUGE metrics, and it also outperforms $\text{TOPICSUM}_{\mathcal{B}}$ on two of the three metrics.

The top three systems in TAC-2011 have been included for comparison. The results between these three systems, and between them and DUALSUM, are all indistinguishable at 95% confidence. Note that the best baseline, $\text{TOPICSUM}_{\mathcal{B}}$, is quite competitive, with results that are indistinguishable to the top participants in this year's evaluation. Note as well that, because we have five different runs for our algorithms, whereas we just have one output for the TAC participants, the confidence intervals in the second case were slightly bigger when checking for statistical significance, so it is slightly harder for these systems to assert that they outperform the baselines with 95% confidence. These results would have made DUALSUM the second best system for ROUGE-1 and ROUGE-SU4, and the third best system in terms of ROUGE-2.

The supplementary materials contain a detailed example of the the topic model obtained for the background in the TAC-2011 dataset, and the base and update models for collection D1110. As expected, the top unigrams and bigrams are all closed-class words and auxiliary verbs. Because trigrams are longer, background trigrams actually include some content words (e.g. *university* or *director*). Regarding the models for $\phi^{\mathcal{A}}$ and $\phi^{\mathcal{B}}$, the base distribution contains words related to the original event of an earthquake in Sichuan province (China), and the update distribution focuses more on the official (updated) death toll numbers. It can be noted here that the tokenizer we used is very simple (splitting tokens separated with white-spaces or punctuation) so that numbers such as 7.9 (the magnitude of the earthquake) and 12,000 or 14,000 are divided into two tokens. We thought this might be a for the bigram-based system to produce better results, but we ran the summarizers with a numbers-aware tokenizer and the statistical differences between versions still hold.

[6] Using the settings obtained in the previous section, having been optimized on the datasets from previous TAC competitions.

Method	R-1	R-2	R-SU4
TOPICSUM$_{\mathcal{B}}$	0.3442	0.0868	0.1194
TOPICSUM$_{\mathcal{A}\cup\mathcal{B}}$	0.3385	0.0809	0.1159
TOPICSUM$_{\mathcal{A}}$+TOPICSUM$_{\mathcal{B}}$	0.3328	0.0770	0.1125
DUALSUM	$0.3575^{\ddagger\dagger*}$	$0.0924^{\dagger*}$	$0.1285^{\ddagger\dagger*}$
TAC-2011 best system (Peer 43)	$0.3559^{\dagger*}$	$0.0958^{\dagger*}$	$0.1308^{\ddagger\dagger*}$
TAC-2011 2nd system (Peer 25)	$0.3582^{\dagger*}$	0.0926^{*}	$0.1276^{\dagger*}$
TAC-2011 3rd system (Peer 17)	$0.3558^{\dagger*}$	0.0886	$0.1279^{\dagger*}$

Table 1: Results on the TAC-2011 dataset. ‡, † and * indicate that a result is significantly better than TOPICSUM$_{\mathcal{B}}$, TOPICSUM$_{\mathcal{A}\cup\mathcal{B}}$ and TOPICSUM$_{\mathcal{A}}$+TOPICSUM$_{\mathcal{B}}$, respectively ($p < 0.05$).

4.4 Manual evaluation

While the ROUGE metrics provides an arguable estimate of the informativeness of a generated summary, it does not account for other important aspects such as the readability or the overall responsiveness. To evaluate such aspects, a manual evaluation is required. A fairly standard approach for manual evaluation is through pairwise comparison (Haghighi and Vanderwende, 2009; Celikyilmaz and Hakkani-Tur, 2011).

In this approach, raters are presented with pairs of summaries generated by two systems and they are asked to say which one is best with respect to some aspects. We followed a similar approach to compare DualSum with Peer 43 - the best system with respect to ROUGE-2, on the TAC 2011 dataset. For each collection, raters were presented with three summaries: a reference summary randomly chosen from the model summaries, and the summaries generated by Peer 43 and DualSum. They were asked to read the summaries and say which one of the two generated summaries is best with respect to: 1) Overall responsiveness: which summary is best overall (both in terms of content and fluency), 2) Focus: which summary contains less irrelevant details, 3) Coherence: which summary is more coherent and 4) Non-redundancy: which summary repeats less the same information. For each aspect, the rater could also reply that both summary were of the same quality.

For each of the 44 collections in TAC-2011, 3 ratings were collected from raters[7]. Results are reported in Table 2. DualSum outperforms Peer 43 in three aspects, including *Overall Responsiveness*, which aggregates all the other scores and can be considered the most important one. Regarding *Non-redundancy*, DualSum and Peer 43 obtain similar results but the majority of raters found no difference between the two systems. Fleiss κ has been used to measure the inter-rater agreement. For each aspect, we observe $\kappa \sim 0.2$ which corresponds to a slight agreement; but if we focus on tasks where the 3 ratings reflect a preference for either of the two systems, then $\kappa \sim 0.5$, which indicates moderate agreement.

Aspect	Best system		
	Peer 43	Same	DualSum
Overall Responsiveness	39	25	**68**
Focus	41	22	**69**
Coherence	39	30	**63**
Non-redundancy	40	**53**	39

Table 2: Results of the side-by-side manual evaluation.

4.5 Efficiency and applicability

The running time for summarizing the TAC collections with DualSum, averaged over a hundred runs, is 4.97 minutes, using one core (2.3 GHz). Memory consumption was 143 MB.

It is important to note as well that, while TOPICSUM incorporates an additional layer to model topic distributions at the sentence level, we noted early in our experiments that this did not improve the performance (as evaluated with ROUGE) and consequently relaxed that assumption in DualSum. This resulted in a simplification of the model and a reduction of the sampling time.

While five minutes is fast enough to be able to experiment and tune parameters with the TAC collections, it would be quite slow for a real-time summarization system able to generate summaries on request. As can be seen from the plate diagram in Figure 2, all the collections are generated independently from each other. The only exception, for which it is necessary to have all

[7] In total 132 raters participated to the task via our own crowdsourcing platform, not mentioned yet for blind review.

the collections available at the same time during Gibbs sampling, is the background distribution, which is estimated from all the collections simultaneously, roughly representing 27% of the words, that should appear distributed across all documents.

The good news is that this background distribution will contain closed-class words in the language, which are domain-independent (see supplementary material for examples). Therefore, we can generate this distribution from one of the TAC datasets only once, and then it can be reused. Fixing the background distribution to a pre-computed value requires a very simple modification of the Gibbs sampling implementation, which just needs to adjust at each iteration the collection and document-specific models, and the topic assignment for the words.

Using this modified implementation, it is now possible to summarize a single collection independently. The summarization of a single collection of the size of the TAC collections is reduced on average to only three seconds on the same hardware settings, allowing the use of this summarizer in an on-line application.

5 Conclusions

The main contribution of this paper is DUALSUM, a new topic model that is specifically designed to identify and extract novelty from pairs of collections.

It is inspired by TOPICSUM (Haghighi and Vanderwende, 2009), with two main changes: Firstly, while TOPICSUM can only learn the main topic of a collection, DUALSUM focuses on the differences between two collections. Secondly, while TOPICSUM incorporates an additional layer to model topic distributions at the sentence level, we have found that relaxing this assumption and modeling the topic distribution at document level does not decrease the ROUGE scores and reduces the sampling time.

The generated summaries, tested on the TAC-2011 collection, would have resulted on the second and third position in the last summarization competition according to the different ROUGE scores. This would make DUALSUM statistically indistinguishable from the top system with 0.95 confidence.

We also propose and evaluate the applicability of an alternative implementation of Gibbs sampling to on-line settings. By fixing the background distribution we are able to summarize a distribution in only three seconds, which seems reasonable for some on-line applications.

As future work, we plan to explore the use of DUALSUM to generate more general contrastive summaries, by identifying differences between collections whose differences are not of temporal nature.

Acknowledgments

The research leading to these results has received funding from the European Union's Seventh Framework Programme (FP7/2007-2013) under grant agreement number 257790. We would also like to thank Yasemin Altun and the anonymous reviewers for their useful comments on the draft of this paper.

References

David M. Blei, Andrew Y. Ng, and Michael I. Jordan. 2003. Latent dirichlet allocation. *J. Mach. Learn. Res.*, 3:993–1022, March.

Florian Boudin, Marc El-Bèze, and Juan-Manuel Torres-Moreno. 2008. A scalable MMR approach to sentence scoring for multi-document update summarization. In *Coling 2008: Companion volume: Posters*, pages 23–26, Manchester, UK, August. Coling 2008 Organizing Committee.

J. Carbonell and J. Goldstein. 1998. The use of mmr, diversity-based reranking for reordering documents and producing summaries. In *Proceedings of the 21st annual international ACM SIGIR conference on Research and development in information retrieval*, pages 335–336. ACM.

Asli Celikyilmaz and Dilek Hakkani-Tur. 2011. Discovery of topically coherent sentences for extractive summarization. In *Proceedings of the 49th Annual Meeting of the Association for Computational Linguistics: Human Language Technologies*, pages 491–499, Portland, Oregon, USA, June. Association for Computational Linguistics.

Chaitanya Chemudugunta, Padhraic Smyth, and Mark Steyvers. 2006. Modeling general and specific aspects of documents with a probabilistic topic model. In *NIPS*, pages 241–248.

W.M. Darling. 2010. Multi-document summarization from first principles. In *Proceedings of the third Text Analysis Conference, TAC-2010*. NIST.

Hal Daumé, III and Daniel Marcu. 2006. Bayesian query-focused summarization. In *Proceedings of the 21st International Conference on Computational Linguistics and the 44th annual meeting of the Association for Computational Linguistics*, ACL-2006, pages 305–312, Stroudsburg, PA, USA. Association for Computational Linguistics.

Günes Erkan and Dragomir R. Radev. 2004. Lexrank: graph-based lexical centrality as salience in text summarization. *J. Artif. Int. Res.*, 22:457–479, December.

S. Fisher and B. Roark. 2008. Query-focused supervised sentence ranking for update summaries. In *Proceedings of the first Text Analysis Conference, TAC-2008*.

Dani Gamerman and Hedibert F. Lopes. 2006. *Markov Chain Monte Carlo: Stochastic Simulation for Bayesian Inference*. Chapman and Hall/CRC.

Jade Goldstein, Mark Kantrowitz, Vibhu Mittal, and Jaime Carbonell. 1999. Summarizing text documents: sentence selection and evaluation metrics. In *Proceedings of the 22nd annual international ACM SIGIR conference on Research and development in information retrieval*, SIGIR '99, pages 121–128, New York, NY, USA. ACM.

T. L. Griffiths and M. Steyvers. 2004. Finding scientific topics. *Proceedings of the National Academy of Sciences*, 101(Suppl. 1):5228–5235, April.

A. Haghighi and L. Vanderwende. 2009. Exploring content models for multi-document summarization. In *Proceedings of Human Language Technologies: The 2009 Annual Conference of the North American Chapter of the Association for Computational Linguistics*, pages 362–370. Association for Computational Linguistics.

Feng Jin, Minlie Huang, and Xiaoyan Zhu. 2010. The thu summarization systems at tac 2010. In *Proceedings of the third Text Analysis Conference, TAC-2010*.

Kevin Lerman and Ryan McDonald. 2009. Contrastive summarization: an experiment with consumer reviews. In *Proceedings of Human Language Technologies: The 2009 Annual Conference of the North American Chapter of the Association for Computational Linguistics, Companion Volume: Short Papers*, NAACL-Short '09, pages 113–116, Stroudsburg, PA, USA. Association for Computational Linguistics.

Xuan Li, Liang Du, and Yi-Dong Shen. 2011. Graph-based marginal ranking for update summarization. In *Proceedings of the Eleventh SIAM International Conference on Data Mining*. SIAM / Omnipress.

Rebecca Mason and Eugene Charniak. 2011. Extractive multi-document summaries should explicitly not contain document-specific content. In *Proceedings of the Workshop on Automatic Summarization for Different Genres, Media, and Languages*, WASDGML '11, pages 49–54, Stroudsburg, PA, USA. Association for Computational Linguistics.

A. Nenkova and L. Vanderwende. 2005. The impact of frequency on summarization. *Microsoft Research, Redmond, Washington, Tech. Rep. MSR-TR-2005-101*.

Ian Porteous, David Newman, Alexander Ihler, Arthur Asuncion, Padhraic Smyth, and Max Welling. 2008. Fast collapsed Gibbs sampling for latent Dirichlet allocation. In *KDD '08: Proceeding of the 14th ACM SIGKDD international conference on Knowledge discovery and data mining*, pages 569–577, New York, NY, USA, August. ACM.

Dragomir R. Radev, Hongyan Jing, Malgorzata Styś, and Daniel Tam. 2004. Centroid-based summarization of multiple documents. *Inf. Process. Manage.*, 40:919–938, November.

Frank Schilder, Ravikumar Kondadadi, Jochen L. Leidner, and Jack G. Conrad. 2008. Thomson reuters at tac 2008: Aggressive filtering with fastsum for update and opinion summarization. In *Proceedings of the first Text Analysis Conference, TAC-2008*.

Chao Shen and Tao Li. 2010. Multi-document summarization via the minimum dominating set. In *Proceedings of the 23rd International Conference on Computational Linguistics*, COLING '10, pages 984–992, Stroudsburg, PA, USA. Association for Computational Linguistics.

Ian Soboroff and Donna Harman. 2005. Novelty detection: the trec experience. In *Proceedings of the conference on Human Language Technology and Empirical Methods in Natural Language Processing*, HLT '05, pages 105–112, Stroudsburg, PA, USA. Association for Computational Linguistics.

Dingding Wang, Shenghuo Zhu, Tao Li, and Yihong Gong. 2009. Multi-document summarization using sentence-based topic models. In *Proceedings of the ACL-IJCNLP 2009 Conference Short Papers*, ACLShort '09, pages 297–300, Stroudsburg, PA, USA. Association for Computational Linguistics.

Yi Wang. 2011. Distributed gibbs sampling of latent dirichlet allocation: The gritty details.

Li Wenjie, Wei Furu, Lu Qin, and He Yanxiang. 2008. Pnr2: ranking sentences with positive and negative reinforcement for query-oriented update summarization. In *Proceedings of the 22nd International Conference on Computational Linguistics - Volume 1*, COLING '08, pages 489–496, Stroudsburg, PA, USA. Association for Computational Linguistics.

Large-Margin Learning of Submodular Summarization Models

Ruben Sipos
Dept. of Computer Science
Cornell University
Ithaca, NY 14853 USA
rs@cs.cornell.edu

Pannaga Shivaswamy
Dept. of Computer Science
Cornell University
Ithaca, NY 14853 USA
pannaga@cs.cornell.edu

Thorsten Joachims
Dept. of Computer Science
Cornell University
Ithaca, NY 14853 USA
tj@cs.cornell.edu

Abstract

In this paper, we present a supervised learning approach to training submodular scoring functions for extractive multi-document summarization. By taking a structured prediction approach, we provide a large-margin method that directly optimizes a convex relaxation of the desired performance measure. The learning method applies to all submodular summarization methods, and we demonstrate its effectiveness for both pairwise as well as coverage-based scoring functions on multiple datasets. Compared to state-of-the-art functions that were tuned manually, our method significantly improves performance and enables high-fidelity models with number of parameters well beyond what could reasonably be tuned by hand.

1 Introduction

Automatic document summarization is the problem of constructing a short text describing the main points in a (set of) document(s). Example applications range from generating short summaries of news articles, to presenting snippets for URLs in web-search. In this paper we focus on extractive multi-document summarization, where the final summary is a subset of the sentences from multiple input documents. In this way, extractive summarization avoids the hard problem of generating well-formed natural-language sentences, since only existing sentences from the input documents are presented as part of the summary.

A current state-of-the-art method for document summarization was recently proposed by Lin and Bilmes (2010), using a submodular scoring function based on inter-sentence similarity. On the one hand, this scoring function rewards summaries that are similar to many sentences in the original documents (i.e. promotes coverage). On the other hand, it penalizes summaries that contain sentences that are similar to each other (i.e. discourages redundancy). While obtaining the exact summary that optimizes the objective is computationally hard, they show that a greedy algorithm is guaranteed to compute a good approximation. However, their work does not address how to select a good inter-sentence similarity measure, leaving this problem as well as selecting an appropriate trade-off between coverage and redundancy to manual tuning.

To overcome this problem, we propose a supervised learning method that can learn both the similarity measure as well as the coverage/reduncancy trade-off from training data. Furthermore, our learning algorithm is not limited to the model of Lin and Bilmes (2010), but applies to all monotone submodular summarization models. Due to the diminishing-returns property of monotone submodular set functions and their computational tractability, this class of functions provides a rich space for designing summarization methods. To illustrate the generality of our approach, we also provide experiments for a coverage-based model originally developed for diversified information retrieval (Swaminathan et al., 2009).

In general, our method learns a parameterized monotone submodular scoring function from supervised training data, and its implementation is available for download.[1] Given a set of documents and their summaries as training examples,

[1] http://www.cs.cornell.edu/~rs/sfour/

we formulate the learning problem as a structured prediction problem and derive a maximum-margin algorithm in the structural support vector machine (SVM) framework. Note that, unlike other learning approaches, our method does not require a heuristic decomposition of the learning task into binary classification problems (Kupiec et al., 1995), but directly optimizes a structured prediction. This enables our algorithm to directly optimize the desired performance measure (e.g. ROUGE) during training. Furthermore, our method is not limited to linear-chain dependencies like (Conroy and O'leary, 2001; Shen et al., 2007), but can learn any monotone submodular scoring function.

This ability to easily train summarization models makes it possible to efficiently tune models to various types of document collections. In particular, we find that our learning method can reliably tune models with hundreds of parameters based on a training set of about 30 examples. This increases the fidelity of models compared to their hand-tuned counterparts, showing significantly improved empirical performance. We provide a detailed investigation into the sources of these improvements, identifying further directions for research.

2 Related work

Work on extractive summarization spans a large range of approaches. Starting with unsupervised methods, one of the widely known approaches is Maximal Marginal Relevance (MMR) (Carbonell and Goldstein, 1998). It uses a greedy approach for selection and considers the trade-off between relevance and redundancy. Later it was extended (Goldstein et al., 2000) to support multi-document settings by incorporating additional information available in this case. Good results can be achieved by reformulating this as a knapsack packing problem and solving it using dynamic programing (McDonald, 2007). Alternatively, we can use annotated phrases as textual units and select a subset that covers most concepts present in the input (Filatova and Hatzivassiloglou, 2004) (which can also be achieved by our coverage scoring function if it is extended with appropriate features).

A popular stochastic graph-based summarization method is LexRank (Erkan and Radev, 2004). It computes sentence importance based on the concept of eigenvector centrality in a graph of sentence similarities. Similarly, TextRank (Mihalcea and Tarau, 2004) is also graph based ranking system for identification of important sentences in a document by using sentence similarity and PageRank (Brin and Page, 1998). Sentence extraction can also be implemented using other graph based scoring approaches (Mihalcea, 2004) such as HITS (Kleinberg, 1999) and positional power functions. Graph based methods can also be paired with clustering such as in CollabSum (Wan et al., 2007). This approach first uses clustering to obtain document clusters and then uses graph based algorithm for sentence selection which includes inter and intra-document sentence similarities. Another clustering-based algorithm (Nomoto and Matsumoto, 2001) is a diversity-based extension of MMR that finds diversity by clustering and then proceeds to reduce redundancy by selecting a representative for each cluster.

The manually tuned sentence pairwise model (Lin and Bilmes, 2010; Lin and Bilmes, 2011) we took inspiration from is based on budgeted submodular optimization. A summary is produced by maximizing an objective function that includes coverage and redundancy terms. Coverage is defined as the sum of sentence similarities between the selected summary and the rest of the sentences, while redundancy is the sum of pairwise intra-summary sentence similarities. Another approach based on submodularity (Qazvinian et al., 2010) relies on extracting important keyphrases from citation sentences for a given paper and using them to build the summary.

In the supervised setting, several early methods (Kupiec et al., 1995) made independent binary decisions whether to include a particular sentence in the summary or not. This ignores dependencies between sentences and can result in high redundancy. The same problem arises when using learning-to-rank approaches such as ranking support vector machines, support vector regression and gradient boosted decision trees to select the most relevant sentences for the summary (Metzler and Kanungo, 2008).

Introducing some dependencies can improve the performance. One limited way of introducing dependencies between sentences is by using a linear-chain HMM. The HMM is assumed to produce the summary by having a chain transitioning between summarization and non-summarization states (Conroy and O'leary, 2001) while traversing the sentences in a document. A more expressive approach is using a CRF for sequence labeling (Shen et al., 2007) which can utilize larger and not necessarily independent feature spaces. The disadvantage of using linear chain models, however, is that they represent the summary as a sequence of sentences. Dependencies between sentences that are far away from each other cannot be modeled efficiently. In contrast to such linear chain models, our approach on submodular scoring functions can model long-range dependencies. In this way our method can use properties of the whole summary when deciding which sentences to include in it.

More closely related to our work is that of Li et al. (2009). They use the diversified retrieval method proposed in Yue and Joachims (2008) for document summarization. Moreover, they assume that subtopic labels are available so that additional constraints for diversity, coverage and balance can be added to the structural SVM learning problem. In contrast, our approach does not require the knowledge of subtopics (thus allowing us to apply it to a wider range of tasks) and avoids adding additional constraints (simplifying the algorithm). Furthermore, it can use different submodular objective functions, for example word coverage and sentence pairwise models described later in this paper.

Another closely related work also takes a max-margin discriminative learning approach in the structural SVM framework (Berg-Kirkpatrick et al., 2011) or by using MIRA (Martins and Smith, 2009) to learn the parameters for summarizing a set of documents. However, they do not consider submodular functions, but instead solve an Integer Linear Program (ILP) or an approximation thereof. The ILP encodes a compression model where arbitrary parts of the parse trees of sentences in the summary can be cut and removed. This allows them to select parts of sentences and yet preserve some gramatical structure. Their work focuses on learnirig a particular compression model based on ILP inference, while our work explores learning a general and large class of sentence selection models using submodular optimization. The third notable approach uses SEARN (Daumé, 2006) to learn parameters for joint summarization and compression model, however it uses vine-growth model and employs search to to find the best policy which is then used to generate a summary.

A specific subclass of submodular (but not monotone) functions are defined by Determinantal Point Processes (DPPs) (Kulesza and Taskar, 2011). While they provide an elegant probabilistic interpretation of the resulting summarization models, the lack of monotonicity means that no efficient approximation algorithms are known for computing the highest-scoring summary.

3 Submodular document summarization

In this section, we illustrate how document summarization can be addressed using submodular set functions. The set of documents to be summarized is split into a set of individual sentences $x = \{s_1, ..., s_n\}$. The summarization method then selects a subset $\hat{y} \subseteq x$ of sentences that maximizes a given scoring function $F_x : 2^x \to \mathbb{R}$ subject to a budget constraint (e.g. less than B characters).

$$\hat{y} = \arg\max_{y \subseteq x} F_x(y) \qquad s.t.\ |y| \leq B \quad (1)$$

In the following we restrict the admissible scoring functions F to be submodular.

Definition 1. *Given a set x, a function $F : 2^x \to \mathbb{R}$ is submodular iff for all $u \in U$ and all sets s and t such that $s \subseteq t \subseteq x$, we have,*

$$F(s \cup \{u\}) - F(s) \geq F(t \cup \{u\}) - F(t).$$

Intuitively, this definition says that adding u to a subset s of t increases f at least as much as adding it to t. Using two specific submodular functions as examples, the following sections illustrate how this diminishing returns property naturally reflects the trade-off between maximizing coverage while minimizing redundancy.

3.1 Pairwise scoring function

The first submodular scoring function we consider was proposed by Lin and Bilmes (2010) and is based on a model of pairwise sentence similarities. It scores a summary y using the following function, which Lin and Bilmes (2010) show is submodular:

$$F_x(y) = \sum_{i \in x \setminus y, j \in y} \sigma(i,j) - \lambda \sum_{i,j \in y : i \neq j} \sigma(i,j). \quad (2)$$

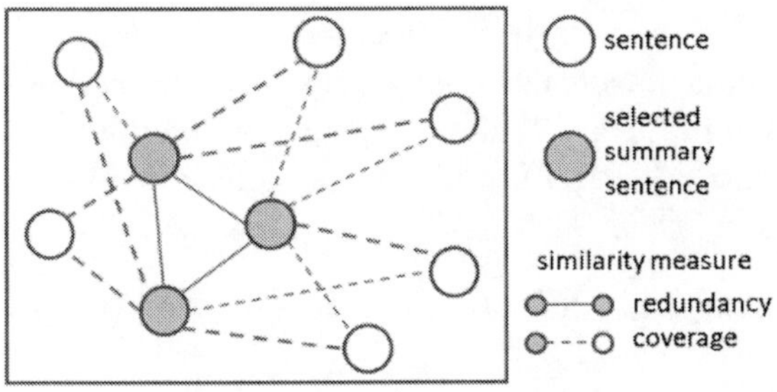

Figure 1: Illustration of the pairwise model. Not all edges are shown for clarity purposes. Edge thickness denotes the similarity score.

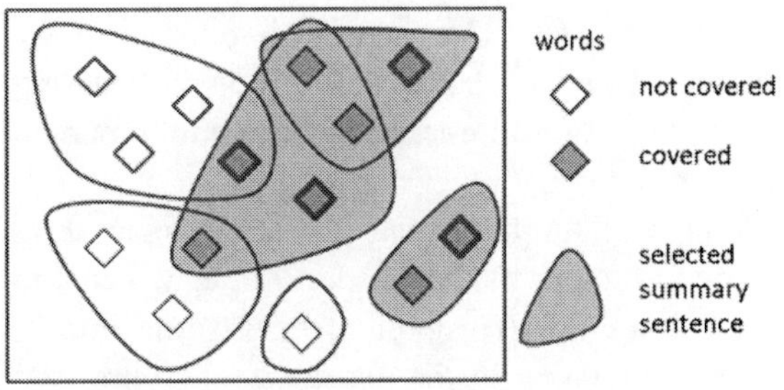

Figure 2: Illustration of the coverage model. Word border thickness represents importance.

In the above equation, $\sigma(i, j) \geq 0$ denotes a measure of similarity between pairs of sentences i and j. The first term in Eq. 2 is a measure of how similar the sentences included in summary y are to the other sentences in x. The second term penalizes y by how similar its sentences are to each other. $\lambda > 0$ is a scalar parameter that trades off between the two terms. Maximizing $F_x(y)$ amounts to increasing the similarity of the summary to excluded sentences while minimizing repetitions in the summary. An example is illustrated in Figure 1. In the simplest case, $\sigma(i, j)$ may be the TFIDF (Salton and Buckley, 1988) cosine similarity, but we will show later how to learn sophisticated similarity functions.

3.2 Coverage scoring function

A second scoring function we consider was first proposed for diversified document retrieval (Swaminathan et al., 2009; Yue and Joachims, 2008), but it naturally applies to document summarization as well (Li et al., 2009). It is based on a notion of word coverage, where each word v has some importance weight $\omega(v) \geq 0$. A summary y covers a word if at least one of its sentences contains the word. The score of a summary is then simply the sum of the word weights its covers (though we could also include a concave discount function that rewards covering a word multiple times (Raman et al., 2011)):

$$F_x(y) = \sum_{v \in V(y)} \omega(v). \quad (3)$$

In the above equation, $V(y)$ denotes the union of all words in y. This function is analogous to a maximum coverage problem, which is known to be submodular (Khuller et al., 1999).

An example of how a summary is scored is illustrated in the Figure 2. Analogous to the definition of similarity $\sigma(i, j)$ in the pairwise model, the choice of the word importance function $\omega(v)$ is crucial in the coverage model. A simple heuristic is to weigh words highly that occur in many sentences of x, but in few other documents (Swaminathan et al., 2009). However, we will show in the following how to learn $\omega(v)$ from training data.

Algorithm 1 Greedy algorithm for finding the best summary $\hat{y}$ given a scoring function $F_x(y)$.

Parameter: $r > 0$.
$\hat{y} \leftarrow \emptyset$
$A \leftarrow x$
while $A \neq \emptyset$ **do**
  $k \leftarrow \arg\max_{l \in A} \frac{F_x(\hat{y} \cup \{l\}) - F_x(\hat{y})}{(c_l)^r}$
  if $c_k + \sum_{i \in \hat{y}} c_i \leq B$ **and** $F_x(\hat{y} \cup \{k\}) - F_x(\hat{y}) \geq 0$ **then**
    $\hat{y} \leftarrow \hat{y} \cup \{k\}$
  end if
  $A \leftarrow A \backslash \{k\}$
end while

3.3 Computing a Summary

Computing the summary that maximizes either of the two scoring functions from above (i.e. Eqns. (2) and (3)) is NP-hard (McDonald, 2007). However, it is known that the greedy algorithm 1 can achieve a $1 - 1/e$ approximation to the optimum solution for any linear budget constraint (Lin and Bilmes, 2010; Khuller et al., 1999). Even further, this algorithm provides a $1 - 1/e$ approximation for any monotone submodular scoring function.

The algorithm starts with an empty summarization. In each step, a sentence is added to the summary that results in the maximum relative increase of the objective. The increase is relative to the amount of budget that is used by the added sentence. The algorithm terminates when the budget B is reached.

Note that the algorithm has a parameter r in the denominator of the selection rule, which Lin and Bilmes (2010) report to have some impact on performance. In the algorithm, c_i represents the cost of the sentence (i.e., length). Thus, the algorithm actually selects sentences with large marginal unity relative to their length (trade-off controlled by the parameter r). Selecting r to be less than 1 gives more importance to "information density" (i.e. sentences that have a higher ratio of score increase per length). The $1 - \frac{1}{e}$ greedy approximation guarantee holds despite this additional parameter (Lin and Bilmes, 2010). More details on our choice of r and its effects are provided in the experiments section.

4 Learning algorithm

In this section, we propose a supervised learning method for training a submodular scoring function to produce desirable summaries. In particular, for the pairwise and the coverage model, we show how to learn the similarity function $\sigma(i,j)$ and the word importance weights $\omega(v)$ respectively. In particular, we parameterize $\sigma(i,j)$ and $\omega(v)$ using a linear model, allowing that each depends on the full set of input sentences x:

$$\sigma_x(i,j) = \mathbf{w}^T \phi_x^p(i,j) \qquad \omega_x(v) = \mathbf{w}^T \phi_x^c(v). \quad (4)$$

In the above equations, $\mathbf{w}$ is a weight vector that is learned, and $\phi_x^p(i,j)$ and $\phi_x^c(v)$ are feature vectors. In the pairwise model, $\phi_x^p(i,j)$ may include feature like the TFIDF cosine between i and j or the number of words from the document titles that i and j share. In the coverage model, $\phi_x^c(v)$ may include features like a binary indicator of whether v occurs in more than 10% of the sentences in x or whether v occurs in the document title.

We propose to learn the weights following a large-margin framework using structural SVMs (Tsochantaridis et al., 2005). Structural SVMs learn a discriminant function

$$h(x) = \arg\max_{y \in \mathcal{Y}} \mathbf{w}^\top \Psi(x,y) \quad (5)$$

that predicts a structured output y given a (possibly also structured) input x. $\Psi(x,y) \in \mathbb{R}^N$ is called the joint feature-map between input x and output y. Note that both submodular scoring function in Eqns. (2) and (3) can be brought into the form $\mathbf{w}^T \Psi(x,y)$ for the linear parametrization in Eq. (6) and (7):

$$\Psi^p(x,y) = \sum_{i \in x \setminus y, j \in y} \phi_x^p(i,j) - \lambda \sum_{i,j \in y: i \neq j} \phi_x^p(i,j), \quad (6)$$

$$\Psi^c(x,y) = \sum_{v \in V(y)} \phi_x^c(v). \quad (7)$$

After this transformation, it is easy to see that computing the maximizing summary in Eq. (1) and the structural SVM prediction rule in Eq. (5) are equivalent.

To learn the weight vector $\mathbf{w}$, structural SVMs require training examples $(x^1, y^1), \ldots, (x^n, y^n)$ of input/output pairs. In document summarization, however, the "correct" extractive summary is typically not known. Instead, training documents x^i are typically annotated with multiple manual (non-extractive) summaries (denoted by Y^i). To determine a single extractive target summary y^i for training, we find the extractive summary that (approximately) optimizes ROUGE score – or some other loss function $\Delta(Y^i, y)$ – with respect to Y^i.

$$y^i = \operatorname*{argmin}_{y \in \mathcal{Y}} \Delta(Y^i, y) \quad (8)$$

We call the y^i determined in this way the "target" summary for x^i. Note that y^i is a greedily constructed approximate target summary based on its proximity to Y^i via Δ. Because of this, we will learn a model that can predict approximately good summaries y^i from x_i. However, we believe that most of the score difference between manual summaries and y^i (as explored in the experiments section) is due to it being an extractive summary and not due to greedy construction.

Following the structural SVM approach, we can now formulate the problem of learning $\mathbf{w}$ as the following quadratic program (QP):

$$\min_{\mathbf{w}, \xi \geq 0} \frac{1}{2} \|\mathbf{w}\|^2 + \frac{C}{n} \sum_{i=1}^{n} \xi_i \quad (9)$$

$$\text{s.t. } \mathbf{w}^\top \Psi(x^i, y^i) - \mathbf{w}^\top \Psi(x^i, \hat{y}^i) \geq \Delta(\hat{y}^i, Y^i) - \xi_i, \ \forall \hat{y}^i \neq y^i, \ \forall 1 \leq i \leq n.$$

The above formulation ensures that the scoring function with the target summary (i.e. $\mathbf{w}^\top \Psi(x^i, y^i)$) is larger than the scoring function

Algorithm 2 Cutting-plane algorithm for solving the learning optimization problem.

Parameter: desired tolerance $\epsilon > 0$.
$\forall i : \mathcal{W}_i \leftarrow \emptyset$
repeat
  for $\forall i$ **do**
    $\hat{y} \leftarrow \arg\max_{y} w^T \Psi(x^i, y) + \Delta(Y^i, y)$
    if $w^T \Psi(x^i, y^i) + \epsilon \leq w^T \Psi(x^i, \hat{y}) + \Delta(Y^i, \hat{y}) - \xi_i$ **then**
      $\mathcal{W}_i \leftarrow \mathcal{W}_i \cup \{\hat{y}\}$
      $w \leftarrow$ solve QP (9) using constraints $\mathcal{W}_i$
    end if
  end for
until no $\mathcal{W}_i$ has changed during iteration

for any other summary $\hat{y}^i$ (i.e., $\mathbf{w}^\top \Psi(x^i, \hat{y}^i)$). The objective function learns a large-margin weight vector $\mathbf{w}$ while trading it off with an upper bound on the empirical loss. The two quantities are traded off with a parameter $C > 0$.

Even though the QP has exponentially many constraints in the number of sentences in the input documents, it can be solved approximately in polynomial time via a cutting plane algorithm (Tsochantaridis et al., 2005). The steps of the cutting-plane algorithm are shown in Algorithm 2. In each iteration of the algorithm, for each training document x^i, a summary $\hat{y}^i$ which most violates the constraint in (9) is found. This is done by finding

$$\hat{y} \leftarrow \arg\max_{y \in \mathcal{Y}} w^T \Psi(x^i, y) + \Delta(Y^i, y),$$

for which we use a variant of the greedy algorithm in Figure 1. After a violating constraint for each training example is added, the resulting quadratic program is solved. These steps are repeated until all the constraints are satisfied to a required precision ϵ.

Finally, special care has to be taken to appropriately define the loss function Δ given the disparity of Y^i and y^i. Therefore, we first define an intermediate loss function

$$\Delta_R(Y, \hat{y}) = \max(0, 1 - ROUGE1_F(Y, \hat{y})),$$

based on the ROUGE-1 F score. To ensure that the loss function is zero for the target label as defined in (8), we normalized the above loss as below:

$$\Delta(Y^i, \hat{y}) = \max(0, \Delta_R(Y^i, \hat{y}) - \Delta_R(Y^i, y^i)),$$

The loss Δ was used in our experiments. Thus training a structural SVM with this loss aims to maximize the ROUGE-1 F score with the manual summaries provided in the training examples, while trading it off with margin. Note that we could also use a different loss function (as the method is not tied to this particular choice), if we had a different target evaluation metric. Finally, once a $\mathbf{w}$ is obtained from structural SVM training, a predicted summary for a test document x can be obtained from (5).

5 Experiments

In this section, we empirically evaluate the approach proposed in this paper. Following Lin and Bilmes (2010), experiments were conducted on two different datasets (DUC '03 and '04). These datasets contain document sets with four manual summaries for each set. For each document set, we concatenated all the articles and split them into sentences using the tool provided with the '03 dataset. For the supervised setting we used 10 resamplings with a random 20/5/5 ('03) and 40/5/5 ('04) train/test/validation split. We determined the best C value in (9) using the performance on each validation set and then report average performence over the corresponding test sets. Baseline performance (the approach of Lin and Bilmes (2010)) was computed using all 10 test sets as a single test set. For all experiments and datasets, we used $r = 0.3$ in the greedy algorithm as recommended in Lin and Bilmes (2010) for the '03 dataset. We find that changing r has only a small influence on performance.[2]

The construction of features for learning is organized by word groups. The most trivial group is simply all words (*basic*). Considering the properties of the words themselves, we constructed several features from properties such as capitalized words, non-stop words and words of certain length (*cap+stop+len*). We obtained another set of features from the most frequently occuring words in all the articles (*minmax*). We also considered the position of a sentence (containing

[2]Setting r to 1 and thus eliminating the non-linearity does lower the score (e.g. to 0.38466 for the pairwise model on DUC '03 compared with the results on Figure 3).

the word) in the article as another feature (*location*). All those word groups can then be further refined by selecting different thresholds, weighting schemes (e.g. TFIDF) and forming binned variants of these features.

For the pairwise model we use cosine similarity between sentences using only words in a given word group during computation. For the word coverage model we create separate features for covering words in different groups. This gives us fairly comparable feature strength in both models. The only further addition is the use of different word coverage levels in the coverage model. First we consider how well does a sentence cover a word (e.g. a sentence with five instances of the same word might cover it better than another with only a single instance). And secondly we look at how important it is to cover a word (e.g. if a word appears in a large fraction of sentences we might want to be sure to cover it). Combining those two criteria using different thresholds we get a set of features for each word. Our coverage features are motivated from the approach of Yue and Joachims (2008). In contrast, the hand-tuned pairwise baseline uses only TFIDF weighted cosine similarity between sentences using all words, following the approach in Lin and Bilmes (2010).

The resulting summaries are evaluated using ROUGE version 1.5.5 (Lin and Hovy, 2003). We selected the ROUGE-1 F measure because it was used by Lin and Bilmes (2010) and because it is one of the commonly used performance scores in recent work. However, our learning method applies to other performance measures as well. Note that we use the ROUGE-1 F measure both for the loss function during learning, as well as for the evaluation of the predicted summaries.

5.1 How does learning compare to manual tuning?

In our first experiment, we compare our supervised learning approach to the hand-tuned approach. The results from this experiment are summarized in Figure 3. First, supervised training of the pairwise model (Lin and Bilmes, 2010) resulted in a statistically significant ($p \leq 0.05$ using paired t-test) increase in performance on both datasets compared to our reimplementation of the manually tuned pairwise model. Note that our reimplementation of the approach of Lin and Bilmes (2010) resulted in slightly different performance numbers than those reported in Lin and Bilmes (2010) – better on DUC '03 and somewhat lower on DUC '04, if evaluated on the same selection of test examples as theirs. We conjecture that this is due to small differences in implementation and/or preprocessing of the dataset. Furthermore, as authors of Lin and Bilmes (2010) note in their paper, the '03 and '04 datasets behave quite differently.

model	dataset	ROUGE-1 F (stderr)
pairwise	DUC '03	**0.3929** (0.0074)
coverage		**0.3784** (0.0059)
hand-tuned		0.3571 (0.0063)
pairwise	DUC '04	**0.4066** (0.0061)
coverage		0.3992 (0.0054)
hand-tuned		0.3935 (0.0052)

Figure 3: Results obtained on DUC '03 and '04 datasets using the supervised models. Increase in performance over the hand-tuned is statistically significant ($p \leq 0.05$) for the pairwise model on the both datasets, but only on DUC '03 for the coverage model.

Figure 3 also reports the performance for the coverage model as trained by our algorithm. These results can be compared against those for the pairwise model. Since we are using features of comparable strength in both approaches, as well as the same greedy algorithm and structural SVM learning method, this comparison largely reflects the quality of models themselves. On the '04 dataset both models achieve the same performance while on '03 the pairwise model performs significantly ($p \leq 0.05$) better than the coverage model.

Overall, the pairwise model appears to perform slightly better than the coverage model with the datasets and features we used. Therefore, we focus on the pairwise model in the following.

5.2 How fast does the algorithm learn?

Hand-tuned approaches have limited flexibility. Whenever we move to a significantly different collection of documents we have to reinvest time to retune it. Learning can make this adaptation to a new collection more automatic and faster – especially since training data has to be collected even for manual tuning.

Figure 4 evaluates how effectively the learning algorithm can make use of a given amount of training data. In particular, the figure shows the

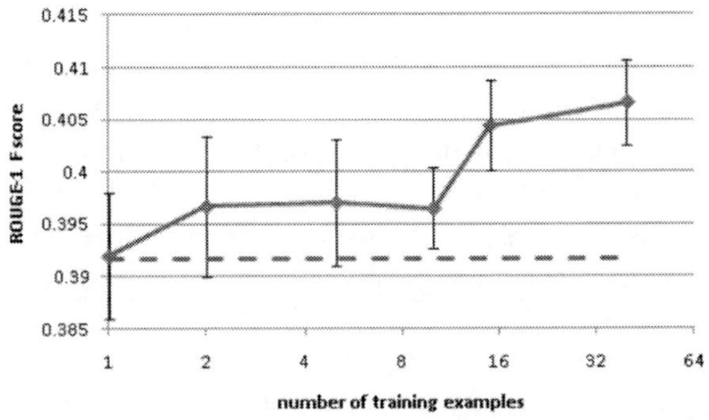

Figure 4: Learning curve for the pairwise model on DUC '04 dataset showing ROUGE-1 F scores for different numbers of learning examples (logarithmic scale). The dashed line represents the preformance of the hand-tuned model.

learning curve for our approach. Even with very few training examples, the learning approach already outperforms the baseline. Furthermore, at the maximum number of training examples available to us the curve still increases. We therefore conjecture that more data would further improve performance.

5.3 Where is room for improvement?

To get a rough estimate of what is actually achievable in terms of the final ROUGE-1 F score, we looked at different "upper bounds" under various scenarios (Figure 5). First, ROUGE score is computed by using four manual summaries from different assessors, so that we can estimate inter-subject disagreement. If one computes the ROUGE score of a held-out summary against the remaining three summaries, the resulting performance is given in the row labeled *human* of Figure 5. It provides a reasonable estimate of human performance.

Second, in extractive summarization we restrict summaries to sentences from the documents themselves, which is likely to lead to a reduction in ROUGE. To estimate this drop, we use the greedy algorithm to select the extractive summary that maximizes ROUGE on the test documents. The resulting performance is given in the row *extractive* of Figure 5. On both dataset, the drop in performance for this (approximately[3]) optimal extractive summary is about 10 points of ROUGE.

Third, we expect some drop in performance, since our model may not be able to fit the optimal extractive summaries due to a lack of expressiveness. This can be estimated by looking at training set performance, as reported in row *model fit* of Figure 5. On both datasets, we see a drop of about 5 points of ROUGE performance. Adding more and better features might help the model fit the data better.

Finally, a last drop in performance may come from overfitting. The test set ROUGE scores are given in the row *prediction* of Figure 5. Note that the drop between training and test performance is rather small, so overfitting is not an issue and is well controlled in our algorithm. We therefore conclude that increasing model fidelity seems like a promising direction for further improvements.

bound	dataset	ROUGE-1 F
human	DUC '03	0.56235
extractive		0.45497
model fit		0.40873
prediction		0.39294
human	DUC '04	0.55221
extractive		0.45199
model fit		0.40963
prediction		0.40662

Figure 5: Upper bounds on ROUGE-1 F scores: agreement between manual summaries, greedily computed best extractive summaries, best model fit on the train set (using the best C value) and the test scores of the pairwise model.

5.4 Which features are most useful?

To understand which features affected the final performance of our approach, we assessed the strength of each set of our features. In particular, we looked at how the final test score changes when we removed certain features groups (described in the beginning of Section 5) as shown in Figure 6.

The most important group of features are the *basic* features (pure cosine similarity between sentences) since removing them results in the largest drop in performance. However, other features play a significant role too (i.e. only the basic ones are not enough to achieve good perfor-

[3]We compared the greedy algorithm with exhaustive search for up to three selected sentences (more than that would take too long). In about half the cases we got the same solution, in other cases the soultion was on average about 1% below optimal confirming that greedy selection works quite well.

mance). This confirms that performance can be improved by adding richer fatures instead of using only a single similarity score as in Lin and Bilmes (2010). Using learning for these complex model is essential, since hand-tuning is likely to be intractable.

The second most important group of features considering the drop in performance (i.e. *location*) looks at positions of sentences in the articles. This makes intuitive sense because the first sentences in news articles are usually packed with information. The other three groups do not have a significant impact on their own.

removed group	ROUGE-1 F
none	0.40662
basic	**0.38681**
all except basic	**0.39723**
location	**0.39782**
sent+doc	0.39901
cap+stop+len	0.40273
minmax	0.40721

Figure 6: Effects of removing different feature groups on the DUC '04 dataset. Bold font marks significant difference ($p \leq 0.05$) when compared to the full pariwise model. The most important are basic similarity features including all words (similar to (Lin and Bilmes, 2010)). The last feature group actually lowered the score but is included in the model because we only found this out later on DUC '04 dataset.

5.5 How important is it to train with multiple summaries?

While having four manual summaries may be important for computing a reliable ROUGE score for evaluation, it is not clear whether such an approach is the most efficient use of annotator resources for training. In our final experiment, we trained our method using only a single manual summary for each set of documents. When using only a single manual summary, we arbitrarily took the first one out of the provided four reference summaries and used only it to compute the target label for training (instead of using average loss towards all four of them). Otherwise, the experimental setup was the same as in the previous subsections, using the pairwise model.

For DUC '04, the ROUGE-1 F score obtained using only a single summary per document set was 0.4010, which is slightly but not significantly lower than the 0.4066 obtained with four summaries (as shown on Figure 3). Similarly, on DUC '03 the performance drop from 0.3929 to 0.3838 was not significant as well.

Based on those results, we conjecture that having more documents sets with only a single manual summary is more useful for training than fewer training examples with better labels (i.e. multiple summaries). In both cases, we spend approximately the same amount of effort (as the summaries are the most expensive component of the training data), however having more training examples helps (according to the learning curve presented before) while spending effort on multiple summaries appears to have only minor benefit for training.

6 Conclusions

This paper presented a supervised learning approach to extractive document summarization based on structual SVMs. The learning method applies to all submodular scoring functions, ranging from pairwise-similarity models to coverage-based approaches. The learning problem is formulated into a convex quadratic program and was then solved approximately using a cutting-plane method. In an empirical evaluation, the structural SVM approach significantly outperforms conventional hand-tuned models on the DUC '03 and '04 datasets. A key advantage of the learning approach is its ability to handle large numbers of features, providing substantial flexibility for building high-fidelity summarization models. Furthermore, it shows good control of overfitting, making it possible to train models even with only a few training examples.

Acknowledgments

We thank Claire Cardie and the members of the Cornell NLP Seminar for their valuable feedback. This research was funded in part through NSF Awards IIS-0812091 and IIS-0905467.

References

T. Berg-Kirkpatrick, D. Gillick and D. Klein. *Jointly Learning to Extract and Compress.* In Proceedings of ACL, 2011.

S. Brin and L. Page. *The Anatomy of a Large-Scale*

Hypertextual Web Search Engine. In Proceedings of WWW, 1998.

J. Carbonell and J. Goldstein. *The use of MMR, diversity-based reranking for reordering documents and producing summaries.* In Proceedings of SIGIR, 1998.

J. M. Conroy and D. P. O'leary. *Text summarization via hidden markov models.* In Proceedings of SIGIR, 2001.

H. Daumé III. *Practical Structured Learning Techniques for Natural Language Processing.* Ph.D. Thesis, 2006.

G. Erkan and D. R. Radev. *LexRank: Graph-based Lexical Centrality as Salience in Text Summarization.* In Journal of Artificial Intelligence Research, Vol. 22, 2004, pp. 457–479.

E. Filatova and V. Hatzivassiloglou. *Event-Based Extractive Summarization.* In Proceedings of ACL Workshop on Summarization, 2004.

T. Finley and T. Joachims. *Training structural SVMs when exact inference is intractable.* In Proceedings of ICML, 2008.

D. Gillick and Y. Liu. *A scalable global model for summarization.* In Proceedings of ACL Workshop on Integer Linear Programming for Natural Language Processing, 2009.

J. Goldstein, V. Mittal, J. Carbonell, and M. Kantrowitz. *Multi-document summarization by sentence extraction.* In Proceedings of NAACL-ANLP, 2000.

S. Khuller, A. Moss and J. Naor. *The budgeted maximum coverage problem.* In Information Processing Letters, Vol. 70, Issue 1, 1999, pp. 39–45.

J. M. Kleinberg. *Authoritative sources in a hyperlinked environment.* In Journal of the ACM, Vol. 46, Issue 5, 1999, pp. 604-632.

A. Kulesza and B. Taskar. *Learning Determinantal Point Processes.* In Proceedings of UAI, 2011.

J. Kupiec, J. Pedersen, and F. Chen. *A trainable document summarizer.* In Proceedings of SIGIR, 1995.

L. Li, Ke Zhou, G. Xue, H. Zha, and Y. Yu. *Enhancing Diversity, Coverage and Balance for Summarization through Structure Learning.* In Proceedings of WWW, 2009.

H. Lin and J. Bilmes. 2010. *Multi-document summarization via budgeted maximization of submodular functions.* In Proceedings of NAACL-HLT, 2010.

H. Lin and J. Bilmes. 2011. *A Class of Submodular Functions for Document Summarization.* In Proceedings of ACL-HLT, 2011.

C. Y. Lin and E. Hovy. *Automatic evaluation of summaries using N-gram co-occurrence statistics.* In Proceedings of NAACL, 2003.

F. T. Martins and N. A. Smith. *Summarization with a joint model for sentence extraction and compression.* In Proceedings of ACL Workshop on Integer Linear Programming for Natural Language Processing, 2009.

R. McDonald. 2007. *A Study of Global Inference Algorithms in Multi-document Summarization.* In Advances in Information Retrieval, Lecture Notes in Computer Science, 2007, pp. 557–564.

D. Metzler and T. Kanungo. *Machine learned sentence selection strategies for query-biased summarization.* In Proceedings of SIGIR, 2008.

R. Mihalcea. 2004. *Graph-based ranking algorithms for sentence extraction, applied to text summarization.* In Proceedings of the ACL on Interactive poster and demonstration sessions, 2004.

R. Mihalcea and P. Tarau. *Textrank: Bringing order into texts.* In Proceedings of EMNLP, 2004.

T. Nomoto and Y. Matsumoto. *A new approach to unsupervised text summarization.* In Proceedings of SIGIR, 2001.

V. Qazvinian, D. R. Radev, and A. Özgür. 2010. *Citation Summarization Through Keyphrase Extraction.* In Proceedings of COLING, 2010.

K. Raman, T. Joachims and P. Shivaswamy. *Structured Learning of Two-Level Dynamic Rankings.* In Proceedings of CIKM, 2011.

G. Salton and C. Buckley. *Term-weighting approaches in automatic text retrieval.* In Information processing and management, 1988, pp. 513–523.

D. Shen, J. T. Sun, H. Li, Q. Yang, and Z. Chen. *Document summarization using conditional random fields.* In Proceedings of IJCAI, 2007.

A. Swaminathan, C. V. Mathew and D. Kirovski. *Essential Pages.* In Proceedings of WI-IAT, IEEE Computer Society, 2009.

I. Tsochantaridis, T. Hofmann, T. Joachims and Y. Altun. *Large margin methods for structured and interdependent output variables.* In Journal of Machine Learning Research, Vol. 6, 2005, pp. 1453-1484.

X. Wan, J. Yang, and J. Xiao. *Collabsum: Exploiting multiple document clustering for collaborative single document summarizations.* In Proceedings of SIGIR, 2007.

Y. Yue and T. Joachims. *Predicting diverse subsets using structural svms.* In Proceedings of ICML, 2008.

A Probabilistic Model of Syntactic and Semantic Acquisition from Child-Directed Utterances and their Meanings

Tom Kwiatkowski[*][†] tomk@cs.washington.edu
Sharon Goldwater[*] sgwater@inf.ed.ac.uk
Luke Zettlemoyer[†] lsz@cs.washington.edu
Mark Steedman[*] steedman@inf.ed.ac.uk

[*] ILCC, School of Informatics
University of Edinburgh
Edinburgh, EH8 9AB, UK

[†]Computer Science & Engineering
University of Washington
Seattle, WA, 98195, USA

Abstract

This paper presents an incremental probabilistic learner that models the acquistion of syntax and semantics from a corpus of child-directed utterances paired with possible representations of their meanings. These meaning representations approximate the contextual input available to the child; they do not specify the meanings of individual words or syntactic derivations. The learner then has to infer the meanings and syntactic properties of the words in the input along with a parsing model. We use the CCG grammatical framework and train a non-parametric Bayesian model of parse structure with online variational Bayesian expectation maximization. When tested on utterances from the CHILDES corpus, our learner outperforms a state-of-the-art semantic parser. In addition, it models such aspects of child acquisition as "fast mapping," while also countering previous criticisms of statistical syntactic learners.

1 Introduction

Children learn language by mapping the utterances they hear onto what they believe those utterances mean. The precise nature of the child's prelinguistic representation of meaning is not known. We assume for present purposes that it can be approximated by compositional logical representations such as (1), where the meaning is a logical expression that describes a relationship $have$ between the person you refers to and the object $another(x, cookie(x))$:

$$\begin{array}{rl} \text{Utterance}: & \text{you have another cookie} \\ \text{Meaning}: & have(you, another(x, cookie(x))) \end{array} \quad (1)$$

Most situations will support a number of plausible meanings, so the child has to learn in the face of *propositional uncertainty*[1], from a set of contextually afforded meaning candidates, as here:

$$\begin{array}{rl} \text{Utterance}: & \text{you have another cookie} \\ \text{Candidate Meanings} & \left\{ \begin{array}{c} have(you, another(x, cookie(x))) \\ eat(you, your(x, cake(x))) \\ want(i, another(x, cookie(x))) \end{array} \right. \end{array}$$

The task is then to learn, from a sequence of such (utterance, meaning-candidates) pairs, the correct lexicon and parsing model. Here we present a probabilistic account of this task with an emphasis on cognitive plausibility.

Our criteria for plausibility are that the learner must not require any language-specific information prior to learning and that the learning algorithm must be strictly *incremental*: it sees each training instance sequentially and exactly once. We define a Bayesian model of parse structure with Dirichlet process priors and train this on a set of (utterance, meaning-candidates) pairs derived from the CHILDES corpus (MacWhinney, 2000) using online variational Bayesian EM.

We evaluate the learnt grammar in three ways. First, we test the accuracy of the trained model in parsing unseen utterances onto gold standard annotations of their meaning. We show that it outperforms a state-of-the-art semantic parser (Kwiatkowski et al., 2010) when run with similar training conditions (i.e., neither system is given the corpus based initialization originally used by Kwiatkowski et al.). We then examine the learning curves of some individual words, showing that the model can learn word meanings on the basis of a single exposure, similar to the *fast mapping* phenomenon observed in children (Carey and Bartlett, 1978). Finally, we show that our

[1]Similar to *referential uncertainty* but relating to propositions rather than referents.

learner captures the step-like learning curves for word order regularities that Thornton and Tesan (2007) claim children show. This result counters Thornton and Tesan's criticism of statistical grammar learners—that they tend to exhibit gradual learning curves rather than the abrupt changes in linguistic competence observed in children.

1.1 Related Work

Models of syntactic acquisition, whether they have addressed the task of learning both syntax and semantics (Siskind, 1992; Villavicencio, 2002; Buttery, 2006) or syntax alone (Gibson and Wexler, 1994; Sakas and Fodor, 2001; Yang, 2002) have aimed to learn a single, correct, deterministic grammar. With the exception of Buttery (2006) they also adopt the Principles and Parameters grammatical framework, which assumes detailed knowledge of linguistic regularities[2]. Our approach contrasts with all previous models in assuming a very general kind of linguistic knowledge and a probabilistic grammar. Specifically, we use the probabilistic Combinatory Categorial Grammar (CCG) framework, and assume only that the learner has access to a small set of general combinatory schemata and a functional mapping from semantic type to syntactic category. Furthermore, this paper is the first to evaluate a model of child syntactic-semantic acquisition by parsing unseen data.

Models of child word learning have focused on semantics only, learning word meanings from utterances paired with either sets of concept symbols (Yu and Ballard, 2007; Frank et al., 2008; Fazly et al., 2010) or a compositional meaning representation of the type used here (Siskind, 1996). The models of Alishahi and Stevenson (2008) and Maurits et al. (2009) learn, as well as word-meanings, orderings for verb-argument structures but not the full parsing model that we learn here.

Semantic parser induction as addressed by Zettlemoyer and Collins (2005, 2007, 2009), Kate and Mooney (2007), Wong and Mooney (2006, 2007), Lu et al. (2008), Chen et al. (2010), Kwiatkowski et al. (2010, 2011) and Börschinger et al. (2011) has the same task definition as the one addressed by this paper. However, the learning approaches presented in those previous papers are not designed to be cognitively plausible, using batch training algorithms, multiple passes over the data, and language specific initialisations (lists of noun phrases and additional corpus statistics), all of which we dispense with here. In particular, our approach is closely related that of Kwiatkowski et al. (2010) but, whereas that work required careful initialisation and multiple passes over the training data to learn a discriminative parsing model, here we learn a generative parsing model without either.

[2]This linguistic use of the term "parameter" is distinct from the statistical use found elsewhere in this paper.

1.2 Overview of the approach

Our approach takes, as input, a corpus of (utterance, meaning-candidates) pairs $\{(s_i, \{m\}_i) : i = 1, \ldots, N\}$, and learns a CCG lexicon Λ and the probability of each *production* $a \rightarrow b$ that could be used in a parse. Together, these define a probabilistic parser that can be used to find the most probable meaning for any new sentence.

We learn both the lexicon and production probabilities from allowable parses of the training pairs. The set of allowable parses $\{t\}$ for a single (utterance, meaning-candidates) pair consists of those parses that map the utterance onto one of the meanings. This set is generated with the functional mapping $\mathcal{T}$:

$$\{t\} = \mathcal{T}(s, m), \qquad (2)$$

which is defined, following Kwiatkowski et al. (2010), using only the CCG combinators and a mapping from semantic type to syntactic category (presented in in Section 4).

The CCG lexicon Λ is learnt by reading off the lexical items used in all parses of all training pairs. Production probabilities are learnt in conjunction with Λ through the use of an incremental parameter estimation algorithm, online Variational Bayesian EM, as described in Section 5.

Before presenting the probabilistic model, the mapping $\mathcal{T}$, and the parameter training algorithm, we first provide some background on the meaning representations we use and on CCG.

2 Background

2.1 Meaning Representations

We represent the meanings of utterances in first-order predicate logic using the lambda-calculus. An example logical expression (henceforth also referred to as a lambda expression) is:

$$like(eve, mummy) \qquad (3)$$

which expresses a logical relationship $like$ between the entity eve and the entity $mummy$. In Section 6.1 we will see how logical expressions like this are created for a set of child-directed utterances (to use in training our model).

The lambda-calculus uses λ operators to define functions. These may be used to represent functional meanings of utterances but they may also be used as a 'glue language', to compose elements of first order logical expressions. For example, the function $\lambda x \lambda y.like(y, x)$ can be combined with the object $mummy$ to give the phrasal meaning $\lambda y.like(y, mummy)$ through the lambda-calculus operation of *function application*.

2.2 CCG

Combinatory Categorial Grammar (CCG; Steedman 2000) is a strongly lexicalised linguistic formalism that tightly couples syntax and semantics. Each CCG lexical item in the lexicon Λ is a triple, written as word $\vdash$ syntactic category : *logical expression*. Examples are:

$$\begin{aligned} \text{You} &\vdash \mathsf{NP} : you \\ \text{read} &\vdash \mathsf{S\backslash NP/NP} : \lambda x \lambda y.read(y, x) \\ \text{the} &\vdash \mathsf{NP/N} : \lambda f.the(x, f(x)) \\ \text{book} &\vdash \mathsf{N} : \lambda x.book(x) \end{aligned}$$

A full CCG category $\mathsf{X} : h$ has syntactic category X and logical expression h. Syntactic categories may be atomic (e.g., S or NP) or complex (e.g., $(\mathsf{S\backslash NP})/\mathsf{NP}$). Slash operators in complex categories define functions from the range on the right of the slash to the result on the left in much the same way as lambda operators do in the lambda-calculus. The direction of the slash defines the linear order of function and argument.

CCG uses a small set of *combinatory rules* to concurrently build syntactic parses and semantic representations. Two example combinatory rules are forward (>) and backward (<) *application*:

$$\begin{array}{llcll} X/Y : f & Y : g & \Rightarrow & X : f(g) & (>) \\ Y : g & X\backslash Y : f & \Rightarrow & X : f(g) & (<) \end{array}$$

Given the lexicon above, the phrase "You read the book" can be parsed using these rules, as illustrated in Figure 1 (with additional notation discussed in the following section)..

CCG also includes combinatory rules of forward (> **B**) and backward (< **B**) *composition*:

$$\begin{array}{ll} X/Y : f \;\; Y/Z : g \Rightarrow X/Z : \lambda x.f(g(x)) & (> \mathbf{B}) \\ Y\backslash Z : g \;\; X\backslash Y : f \Rightarrow X\backslash Z : \lambda x.f(g(x)) & (< \mathbf{B}) \end{array}$$

3 Modelling Derivations

The objective of our learning algorithm is to learn the correct parameterisation of a probabilistic model $P(s, m, t)$ over (utterance, meaning, derivation) triples. This model assigns a probability to each of the *grammar productions* $a \rightarrow b$ used to build the derivation tree t. The probability of any given CCG derivation t with sentence s and semantics m is calculated as the product of all of its production probabilities.

$$P(s, m, t) = \prod_{a \rightarrow b \in t} P(b|a) \qquad (4)$$

For example, the derivation in Figure 1 contains 13 productions, and its probability is the product of the 13 production probabilities. Grammar productions may be either *syntactic*—used to build a syntactic derivation tree, or *lexical*—used to generate logical expressions and words at the leaves of this tree.

A syntactic production $\mathsf{C_h} \rightarrow \mathcal{R}$ expands a head node $\mathsf{C_h}$ into a result $\mathcal{R}$ that is either an ordered pair of syntactic parse nodes $\langle \mathsf{C_l}, \mathsf{C_r} \rangle$ (for a binary production) or a single parse node (for a unary production). Only two unary syntactic productions are allowed in the grammar: $\mathsf{START} \rightarrow \mathsf{A}$ to generate A as the top syntactic node of a parse tree and $\mathsf{A} \rightarrow [\mathsf{A}]_{\mathsf{lex}}$ to indicate that A is a leaf node in the syntactic derivation and should be used to generate a logical expression and word. Syntactic derivations are built by recursively applying syntactic productions to non-leaf nodes in the derivation tree. Each syntactic production $\mathsf{C_h} \rightarrow \mathcal{R}$ has conditional probability $P(\mathcal{R}|\mathsf{C_h})$. There are 3 binary and 5 unary syntactic productions in Figure 1.

Lexical productions have two forms. *Logical expressions* are produced from leaf nodes in the syntactic derivation tree $\mathsf{A_{lex}} \rightarrow m$ with conditional probability $P(m|\mathsf{A_{lex}})$. *Words* are then produced from these logical expressions with conditional probability $P(w|m)$. An example logical production from Figure 1 is $[\mathsf{NP}]_{\mathsf{lex}} \rightarrow you$. An example word production is $you \rightarrow$ You.

Every production $a \rightarrow b$ used in a parse tree t is chosen from the set of productions that could be used to expand a head node a. If there are a finite K productions that could expand a then a K-dimensional *Multinomial distribution* parameterised by θ_a can be used to model the categorical

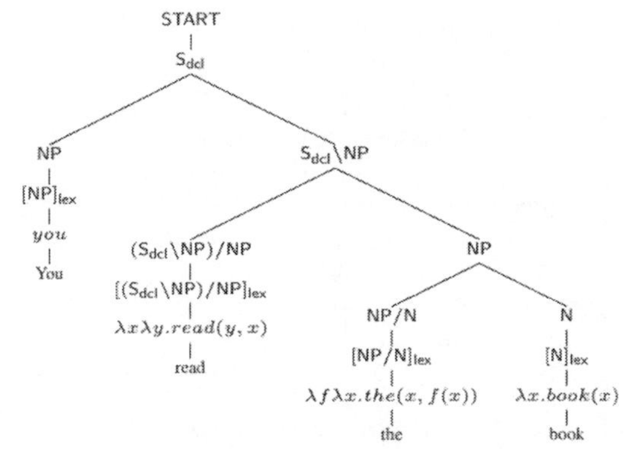

Figure 1: Derivation of sentence `You read the book` with meaning $read(you, the(x, book(x)))$.

choice of production:

$$b \sim \text{Multinomial}(\theta_a) \quad (5)$$

However, before training a model of language acquisition the dimensionality and contents of both the syntactic grammar and lexicon are unknown. In order to maintain a probability model with cover over the countably infinite number of possible productions, we define a Dirichlet Process (DP) prior for each possible production head a. For the production head a, $DP(\alpha_a, H_a)$ assigns some probability mass to all possible production targets $\{b\}$ covered by the base distribution H_a.

It is possible to use the DP as an infinite prior from which the parameter set of a finite dimensional Multinomial may be drawn provided that we can choose a suitable partition of $\{b\}$. When calculating the probability of an (s, m, t) triple, the choice of this partition is easy. For any given production head a there is a finite set of usable production targets $\{b_1, \ldots, b_{k-1}\}$ in t. We create a partition that includes one entry for each of these along with a final entry $\{b_k, \ldots\}$ that includes all other ways in which a could be expanded in different contexts. Then, by applying the distribution G_a drawn from the DP to this partition, we get a parameter vector θ_a that is equivalent to a draw from a k dimensional Dirichlet distribution:

$$G_a \sim DP(\alpha_a, H_a) \quad (6)$$

$$\begin{aligned} \theta_a &= (G_a(b_1), \ldots, G_a(b_{k-1}), G_a(\{b_k, \ldots\}) \\ &\sim \text{Dir}(\alpha_a H(b_1), \ldots, \alpha_a H_a(b_{k-1}), \quad (7) \\ &\qquad \alpha_a H_a(\{b_k, \ldots\})) \end{aligned}$$

Together, Equations 4-7 describe the joint distribution $P(\mathbf{X}, \mathbf{S}, \theta)$ over the observed training data $\mathbf{X} = \{(s_i, \{m\}_i) : i = 1, \ldots, N\}$, the latent variables $\mathbf{S}$ (containing the productions used in each parse t) and the parsing parameters θ.

4 Generating Parses

The previous section defined a parameterisation over parses assuming that the CCG lexicon Λ was known. In practice Λ is empty prior to training and must be populated with the lexical items from parses t consistent with training pairs $(s, \{m\})$.

The set of allowed parses $\{t\}$ is defined by the function $\mathcal{T}$ from Equation 2. Here we review the *splitting procedure* of Kwiatkowski et al. (2010) that is used to generate CCG lexical items and describe how it is used by $\mathcal{T}$ to create a packed chart representation of all parses $\{t\}$ that are consistent with s and at least one of the meaning representations in $\{m\}$. In this section we assume that s is paired at each point with only a single meaning m. Later we will show how $\mathcal{T}$ is used multiple times to create the set of parses consistent with s and a set of candidate meanings $\{m\}$.

The splitting procedure takes as input a CCG category $\mathsf{X}{:}h$, such as $\mathsf{NP} : a(x, cookie(x))$, and returns a set of *category splits*. Each category split is a pair of CCG categories $(\mathsf{C_l} : m_l, \mathsf{C_r} : m_r)$ that can be recombined to give $\mathsf{X} : h$ using one of the CCG combinators in Section 2.2. The CCG category splitting procedure has two parts: *logical splitting* of the category semantics h; and *syntactic splitting* of the syntactic category X. Each logical split of h is a pair of lambda expressions (f, g) in the following set:

$$\{(f, g) \mid h = f(g) \vee h = \lambda x.f(g(x))\}, \quad (8)$$

which means that f and g can be recombined using either *function application* or *function composition* to give the original lambda expression h. An example split of the lambda expression $h = a(x, cookie(x))$ is the pair

$$(\lambda y.a(x, y(x)), \lambda x.cookie(x)), \quad (9)$$

where $\lambda y.a(x, y(x))$ applied to $\lambda x.cookie(x)$ returns the original expression $a(x, cookie(x))$.

Syntactic splitting assigns linear order and syntactic categories to the two lambda expressions f and g. The initial syntactic category X is split by a reversal of the CCG application combinators in Section 2.2 if f and g can be recombined to give

Syntactic Category	Semantic Type	Example Phrase
$\mathsf{S_{dcl}}$	$\langle ev, t\rangle$	I took it $\vdash \mathsf{S_{dcl}}{:}\lambda e.took(i, it, e)$
$\mathsf{S_t}$	t	I'm angry $\vdash \mathsf{S_t}{:}angry(i)$
$\mathsf{S_{wh}}$	$\langle e, \langle ev, t\rangle\rangle$	Who took it? $\vdash \mathsf{S_{wh}}{:}\lambda x \lambda e.took(x, it, e)$
$\mathsf{S_q}$	$\langle ev, t\rangle$	Did you take it? $\vdash \mathsf{S_q}{:}\lambda e.Q(take(you, it, e))$
N	$\langle e, t\rangle$	cookie $\vdash \mathsf{N}{:}\lambda x.cookie(x)$
NP	e	John $\vdash \mathsf{NP}{:}john$
PP	$\langle ev, t\rangle$	on John $\vdash \mathsf{PP}{:}\lambda e.on(john, e)$

Figure 2: Atomic Syntactic Categories.

h with function application:

$$\{(X/Y : f \;\; Y : g), \qquad (Y : g \;\; : X\backslash Y : f) | h = f(g)\} \tag{10}$$

or by a reversal of the CCG composition combinators if f and g can be recombined to give h with function composition:

$$\{(X/Z : f \;\; Z/Y : g, \qquad (Z\backslash Y : g \;\; : X\backslash Z : f) | h = \lambda x.f(g(x))\} \tag{11}$$

Unknown category names in the result of a split (Y in (10) and Z in (11)) are labelled via a functional mapping cat from semantic type T to syntactic category:

$$\mathtt{cat}(T) = \begin{cases} \mathtt{Atomic}(T) & \text{if } T \in \text{Figure 2} \\ \mathtt{cat}(T_1)/\mathtt{cat}(T_2) & \text{if } T = \langle T_1, T_2\rangle \\ \mathtt{cat}(T_1)\backslash\mathtt{cat}(T_2) & \text{if } T = \langle T_1, T_2\rangle \end{cases}$$

which uses the Atomic function illustrated in Figure 2 to map semantic-type to basic CCG syntactic category. As an example, the logical split in (9) supports two CCG category splits, one for each of the CCG application rules.

$$(\mathsf{NP/N}{:}\lambda y.a(x, y(x)),\; \mathsf{N}{:}\lambda x.cookie(x)) \tag{12}$$

$$(\mathsf{N}{:}\lambda x.cookie(x),\; \mathsf{NP\backslash N}{:}\lambda y.a(x, y(x))) \tag{13}$$

The parse generation algorithm $\mathcal{T}$ uses the function split to generate all CCG category pairs that are an allowed split of an input category $\mathsf{X}{:}h$:

$$\{(\mathsf{C_l}{:}m_l, \mathsf{C_r}{:}m_r)\} = \mathtt{split}(\mathsf{X}{:}h),$$

and then packs a chart representation of $\{t\}$ in a top-down fashion starting with a single cell entry $\mathsf{C_m} : m$ for the top node shared by all parses $\{t\}$. For the utterance and meaning in (1) the top parse node, spanning the entire word-string, is

$$\mathsf{S}{:}have(you, another(x, cookie(x))).$$

$\mathcal{T}$ cycles over all cell entries in increasingly small spans and populates the chart with their splits. For any cell entry $\mathsf{X}{:}h$ spanning more than one word $\mathcal{T}$ generates a set of pairs representing the splits of $\mathsf{X}{:}h$. For each split $(\mathsf{C_l}{:}m_l, \mathsf{C_r}{:}m_r)$ and every binary partition $(w_{i:k}, w_{k:j})$ of the word-span $\mathcal{T}$ creates two new cell entries in the chart: $(\mathsf{C_l} : m_l)_{i:k}$ and $(\mathsf{C_r}{:}m_r)_{k:j}$.

Input : Sentence $[w_1, \ldots, w_n]$, top node $\mathsf{C_m}{:}m$
Output: Packed parse chart Ch containing $\{t\}$
$\mathtt{Ch} = [\,[\{\}_1, \ldots, \{\}_n]_1, \;\ldots\;, [\{\}_1, \ldots, \{\}_n]_n\,]$
$\mathtt{Ch}[1][n-1] = \mathsf{C_m}{:}m$
for $i = n, \ldots, 2;\; j = 1 \ldots (n-i)+1$ **do**
  for $\mathsf{X}{:}h \in \mathtt{Ch}[j][i]$ **do**
    for $(\mathsf{C_l}{:}m_l, \mathsf{C_r}{:}m_r) \in \mathtt{split}(\mathsf{X}{:}h)$ **do**
      for $k = 1, \ldots, i-1$ **do**
        $\mathtt{Ch}[j][k] \leftarrow \mathsf{C_l}{:}m_l$
        $\mathtt{Ch}[j+k][i-k] \leftarrow \mathsf{C_r}{:}m_r$

Algorithm 1: Generating $\{t\}$ with $\mathcal{T}$.

Algorithm 1 shows how the learner uses $\mathcal{T}$ to generate a packed chart representation of $\{t\}$ in the chart Ch. The function $\mathcal{T}$ massively overgenerates parses for any given natural language. The probabilistic parsing model introduced in Section 3 is used to choose the best parse from the overgenerated set.

5 Training

5.1 Parameter Estimation

The probabilistic model of the grammar describes a distribution over the observed training data $\mathbf{X}$, latent variables $\mathbf{S}$, and parameters θ. The goal of training is to estimate the posterior distribution:

$$p(\mathbf{S}, \theta | \mathbf{X}) = \frac{p(\mathbf{S}, \mathbf{X}|\theta)p(\theta)}{p(\mathbf{X})} \tag{14}$$

which we do with online Variational Bayesian Expectation Maximisation (oVBEM; Sato (2001), Hoffman et al. (2010)). oVBEM is an online

Bayesian extension of the EM algorithm that accumulates observation pseudocounts $n_{a \to b}$ for each of the productions $a \to b$ in the grammar. These pseudocounts define the posterior over production probabilities as follows:

$$(\theta_{a \to b_1}, \ldots, \theta_{a \to b_{\{k,\ldots\}}})) \mid \mathbf{X}, \mathbf{S} \sim \tag{15}$$

$$\text{Dir}(\alpha H(b_1) + n_{a \to b_1}, \ldots, \sum_{j=k}^{\infty} \alpha H(b_j) + n_{a \to b_j})$$

These pseudocounts are computed in two steps:

oVBE-step For the training pair $(s_i, \{m\}_i)$ which supports the set of parses $\{t\}$, the expectation $E_{\{t\}}[a \to b]$ of each production $a \to b$ is calculated by creating a packed chart representation of $\{t\}$ and running the inside-outside algorithm. This is similar to the E-step in standard EM apart from the fact that each production is scored with the current *expectation* of its parameter weight $\hat{\theta}^{i-1}_{a \to b}$, where:

$$\hat{\theta}^{i-1}_{a \to b} = \frac{e^{\Psi\left(\alpha_a H_a(a \to b) + n^{i-1}_{a \to b}\right)}}{e^{\Psi\left(\sum^{K}_{\{b'\}} \alpha_a H_a(a \to b') + n^{i-1}_{a \to b'}\right)}} \tag{16}$$

and Ψ is the digamma function (Beal, 2003).

oVBM-step The expectations from the oVBE step are used to update the pseudocounts in Equation 15 as follows,

$$n^{i}_{a \to b} = n^{i-1}_{a \to b} + \eta_i (N \times E_{\{t\}}[a \to b] - n^{i-1}_{a \to b}) \tag{17}$$

where η_i is the learning rate and N is the size of the dataset.

5.2 The Training Algorithm

Now the training algorithm used to learn the lexicon Λ and pseudocounts $\{n_{a \to b}\}$ can be defined. The algorithm, shown in Algorithm 2, passes over the training data only once and one training instance at a time. For each $(s_i, \{m\}_i)$ it uses the function $\mathcal{T}$ $|\{m\}_i|$ times to generate a set of consistent parses $\{t\}'$. The lexicon is populated by using the `lex` function to read all of the lexical items off from the derivations in each $\{t\}'$. In the parameter update step, the training algorithm updates the pseudocounts associated with each of the productions $a \to b$ that have ever been seen during training according to Equation (17).

Only non-zero pseudocounts are stored in our model. The count vector is expanded with a new entry every time a new production is used. While

Input : Corpus $D = \{(s_i, \{m\}_i) | i = 1, \ldots, N\}$, Function $\mathcal{T}$, Semantics to syntactic category mapping `cat`, function `lex` to read lexical items off derivations.
Output: Lexicon Λ, Pseudocounts $\{n_{a \to b}\}$.
$\Lambda = \{\}, \ \{t\} = \{\}$
for $i = 1, \ldots, N$ **do**
  $\{t\}_i = \{\}$
  for $m' \in \{m\}_i$ **do**
    $\mathsf{C}_{m'} = \mathtt{cat}(m')$
    $\{t\}' = \mathcal{T}(s_i, \mathsf{C}_{m'} : m')$
    $\{t\}_i = \{t\}_i \cup \{t\}', \ \{t\} = \{t\} \cup \{t\}'$
    $\Lambda = \Lambda \cup \mathtt{lex}(\{t\}')$
  for $a \to b \in \{t\}$ **do**
    $n^{i}_{a \to b} = n^{i-1}_{a \to b} + \eta_i (N \times E_{\{t\}_i}[a \to b] - n^{i-1}_{a \to b})$

Algorithm 2: Learning Λ and $\{n_{a \to b}\}$

the parameter update step cycles over all productions in $\{t\}$ it is not neccessary to store $\{t\}$, just the set of productions that it uses.

6 Experimental Setup

6.1 Data

The Eve corpus, collected by Brown (1973), contains $14,124$ English utterances spoken to a single child between the ages of 18 and 27 months. These have been hand annotated by Sagae et al. (2004) with labelled syntactic dependency graphs. An example annotation is shown in Figure 3.

While these annotations are designed to represent syntactic information, the parent-child relationships in the parse can also be viewed as a proxy for the predicate-argument structure of the semantics. We developed a template based deterministic procedure for mapping this predicate-argument structure onto logical expressions of the type discussed in Section 2.1. For example, the dependency graph in Figure 3 is automatically transformed into the logical expression

$$\lambda e.have(you, another(y, cookie(y)), e) \wedge on(the(z, table(z)), e), \tag{18}$$

where e is a Davidsonian event variable used to deal with adverbial and prepositional attachments. The deterministic mapping to logical expressions uses 19 templates, three of which are used in this example: one for the verb and its arguments, one for the prepositional attachment and one (used twice) for the quantifier-noun constructions.

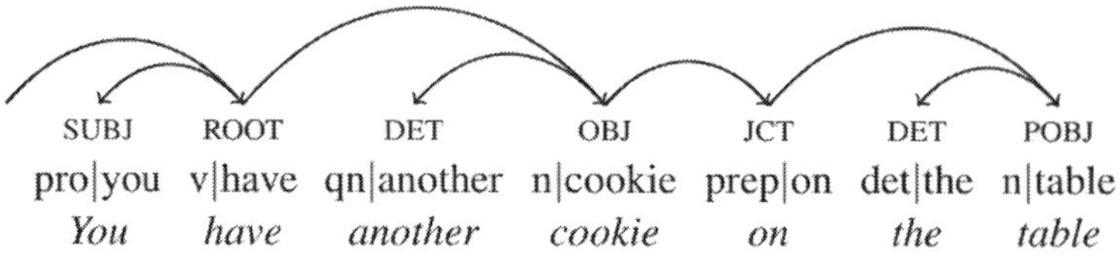

Figure 3: Syntactic dependency graph from Eve corpus.

This mapping from graph to logical expression makes use of a predefined dictionary of allowed, typed, logical constants. The mapping is successful for 31% of the child-directed utterances in the Eve corpus[3]. The remaining data is mostly accounted for by one-word utterances that have no straightforward interpretation in our typed logical language (e.g. *what; okay; alright; no; yeah; hmm; yes; uhhuh; mhm; thankyou*), missing verbal arguments that cannot be properly guessed from the context (largely in imperative sentences such as *drink the water*), and complex noun constructions that are hard to match with a small set of templates (e.g. as *top to a jar*). We also remove the small number of utterances containing more than 10 words for reasons of computational efficiency (see discussion in Section 8).

Following Alishahi and Stevenson (2010), we generate a context set $\{m\}_i$ for each utterance s_i by pairing that utterance with its correct logical expression along with the logical expressions of the preceding and following $(|\{m\}_i|-1)/2$ utterances.

6.2 Base Distributions and Learning Rate

Each of the production heads a in the grammar requires a base distribution H_a and concentration parameter α_a. For word-productions the base distribution is a geometric distribution over character strings and spaces. For syntactic-productions the base distribution is defined in terms of the new category to be named by `cat` and the probability of splitting the rule by reversing either the *application* or *composition* combinators.

Semantic-productions' base distributions are defined by a probabilistic branching process conditioned on the type of the syntactic category. This distribution prefers less complex logical expressions. All concentration parameters are set to 1.0. The learning rate for parameter updates is $\eta_i = (0.8 + i)^{-0.5}$.

[3]Data available at www.tomkwiat.com/resources.html

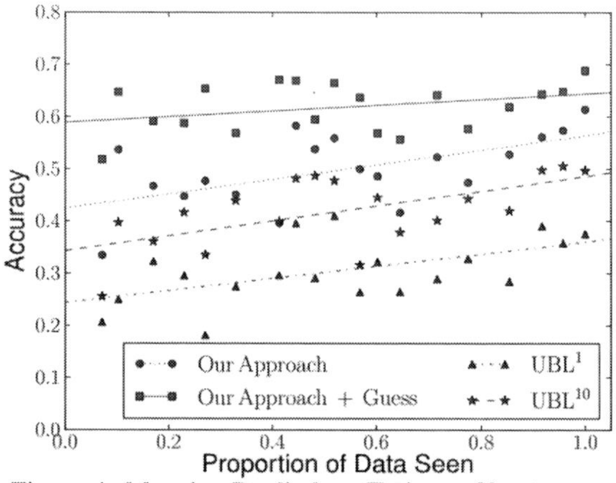

Figure 4: Meaning Prediction: Train on files $1, \ldots, n$ test on file $n + 1$.

7 Experiments

7.1 Parsing Unseen Sentences

We test the parsing model that is learnt by training on the first i files of the longitudinally ordered Eve corpus and testing on file $i + 1$, for $i = 1 \ldots 19$. For each utterance s' in the test file we use the parsing model to predict a meaning m^* and compare this to the target meaning m'. We report the proportion of utterances for which the prediction m^* is returned correctly both with and without word-meaning guessing. When a word has never been seen at training time our parser has the ability to 'guess' a typed logical meaning with placeholders for constant and predicate names.

For comparison we use the UBL semantic parser of Kwiatkowski et al. (2010) trained in a similar setting—i.e., with no language specific initialisation[4]. Figure 4 shows accuracy for our approach with and without guessing, for UBL

[4]Kwiatkowski et al. (2010) initialise lexical weights in their learning algorithm using corpus-wide alignment statistics across words and meaning elements. Instead we run UBL with small positive weight for all lexical items. When run with Giza++ parameter initialisations, UBL^{10} achieves 48.1% across folds compared to 49.2% for our approach.

when run over the training data once (UBL[1]) and for UBL when run over the training data 10 times (UBL[10]) as in Kwiatkowski et al. (2010). Each of the points represents accuracy on one of the 19 test files. All of these results are from parsers trained on utterances paired with a single candidate meaning. The lines of best fit show the upward trend in parser performance over time.

Despite only seeing each training instance once, our approach, due to its broader lexical search strategy, outperforms both versions of UBL which performs a greedy search in the space of lexicons and requires initialisation with co-occurence statistics between words and logical constants to guide this search. These statistics are not justified in a model of language acquisition and so they are not used here. The low performance of all systems is due largely to the sparsity of the data with 32.9% of all sentences containing a previously unseen word.

7.2 Word Learning

Due to the sparsity of the data, the training algorithm needs to be able to learn word-meanings on the basis of very few exposures. This is also a desirable feature from the perspective of modelling language acquisition as Carey and Bartlett (1978) have shown that children have the ability to learn word meanings on the basis of one, or very few, exposures through the process of *fast mapping*.

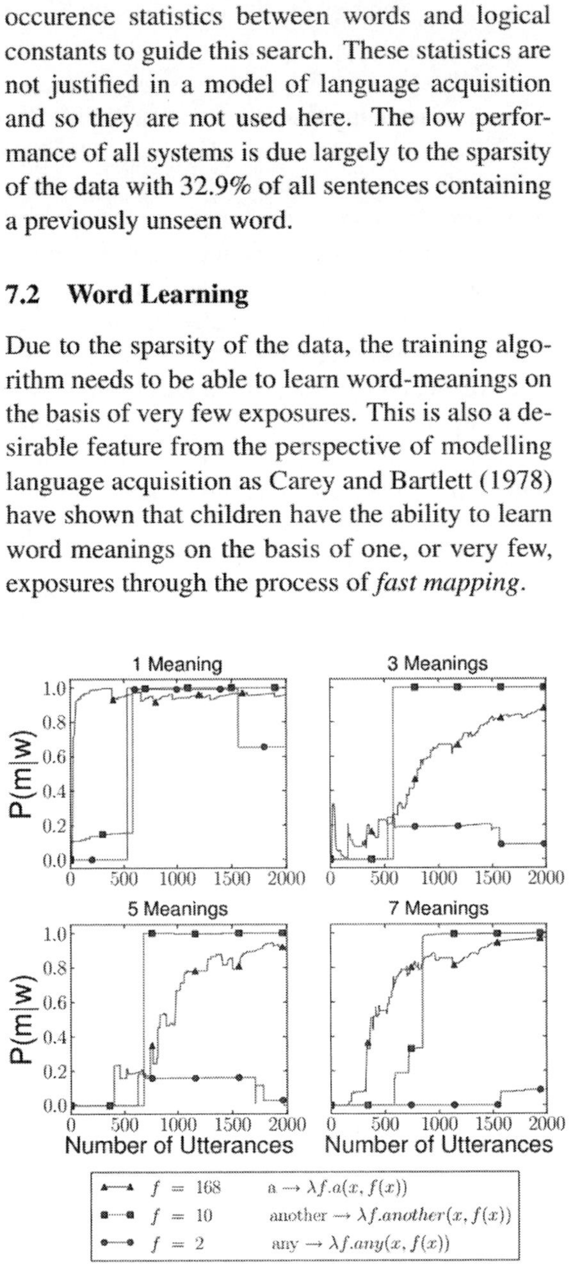

Figure 5: Learning quantifiers with frequency *f*.

Figure 5 shows the posterior probability of the correct meanings for the quantifiers 'a', 'another' and 'any' over the course of training with 1, 3, 5 and 7 candidate meanings for each utterance[5]. These three words are all of the same class but have very different frequencies in the training subset shown (168, 10 and 2 respectively). In all training settings, the word 'a' is learnt gradually from many observations but the rarer words 'another' and 'any' are learnt (when they are learnt) through large updates to the posterior on the basis of few observations. These large updates result from a *syntactic bootstrapping* effect (Gleitman, 1990). When the model has great confidence about the derivation in which an unseen lexical item occurs, the pseudocounts for that lexical item get a large update under Equation 17. This large update has a greater effect on rare words which are associated with small amounts of probability mass than it does on common ones that have already accumulated large pseudocounts. The fast learning of rare words later in learning correlates with observations of word learning in children.

7.3 Word Order Learning

Figure 6 shows the posterior probability of the correct SVO word order learnt from increasing amounts of training data. This is calculated by summing over all lexical items containing transitive verb semantics and sampling in the space of parse trees that could have generated them. With no propositional uncertainty in the training data the correct word order is learnt very quickly and stabilises. As the amount of propositional uncertainty increases, the rate at which this rule is learnt decreases. However, even in the face of ambiguous training data, the model can learn the correct word-order rule. The distribution over word orders also exhibits initial uncertainty, followed by a sharp convergence to the correct analysis. This ability to learn syntactic regularities abruptly means that our system is not subject to the criticisms that Thornton and Tesan (2007) levelled at statistical models of language acquisition—that their learning rates are too gradual.

[5]The term 'fast mapping' is generally used to refer to noun learning. We chose to examine quantifier learning here as there is a greater variation in quantifier frequencies. Fast mapping of nouns is also achieved.

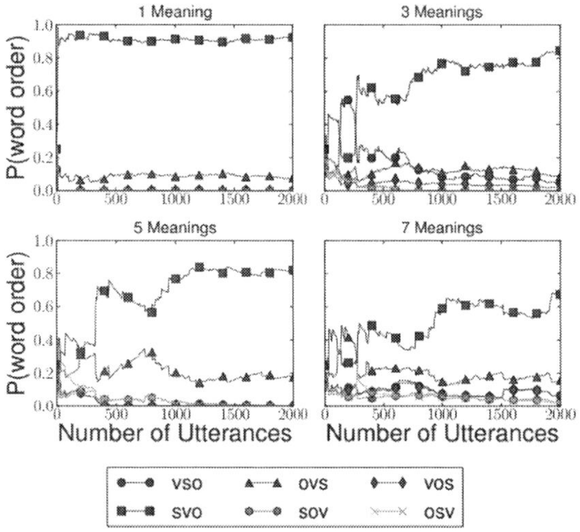

Figure 6: Learning SVO word order.

8 Discussion

We have presented an incremental model of language acquisition that learns a probabilistic CCG grammar from utterances paired with one or more potential meanings. The model assumes no language-specific knowledge, but does assume that the learner has access to language-universal correspondences between syntactic and semantic types, as well as a Bayesian prior encouraging grammars with heavy reuse of existing rules and lexical items. We have shown that this model not only outperforms a state-of-the-art semantic parser, but also exhibits learning curves similar to children's: lexical items can be acquired on a single exposure and word order is learnt suddenly rather than gradually.

Although we use a Bayesian model, our approach is different from many of the Bayesian models proposed in cognitive science and language acquisition (Xu and Tenenbaum, 2007; Goldwater et al., 2009; Frank et al., 2009; Griffiths and Tenenbaum, 2006; Griffiths, 2005; Perfors et al., 2011). These models are intended as *ideal observer* analyses, demonstrating what would be learned by a probabilistically optimal learner. Our learner uses a more cognitively plausible but approximate online learning algorithm. In this way, it is similar to other cognitively plausible approximate Bayesian learners (Pearl et al., 2010; Sanborn et al., 2010; Shi et al., 2010).

Of course, despite the incremental nature of our learning algorithm, there are still many aspects that could be criticized as cognitively implausible. In particular, it generates all parses consistent with each training instance, which can be both memory- and processor-intensive. It is unlikely that children do this once they have learnt at least some of the target language. In future, we plan to investigate more efficient parameter estimation methods. One possibility would be an approximate oVBEM algorithm in which the expectations in Equation 17 are calculated according to a high probability subset of the parses $\{t\}$. Another option would be particle filtering, which has been investigated as a cognitively plausible method for approximate Bayesian inference (Shi et al., 2010; Levy et al., 2009; Sanborn et al., 2010).

As a crude approximation to the context in which an utterance is heard, the logical representations of meaning that we present to the learner are also open to criticism. However, Steedman (2002) argues that children do have access to structured meaning representations from a much older apparatus used for planning actions and we wish to eventually ground these in sensory input.

Despite the limitations listed above, our approach makes several important contributions to the computational study of language acquisition. It is the first model to learn syntax and semantics concurrently; previous systems (Villavicencio, 2002; Buttery, 2006) learnt categorial grammars from sentences where all word meanings were known. Our model is also the first to be evaluated by parsing sentences onto their meanings, in contrast to the work mentioned above and that of Gibson and Wexler (1994), Siskind (1992) Sakas and Fodor (2001), and Yang (2002). These all evaluate their learners on the basis of a small number of predefined syntactic parameters.

Finally, our work addresses a misunderstanding about statistical learners—that their learning curves must be gradual (Thornton and Tesan, 2007). By demonstrating sudden learning of word order and fast mapping, our model shows that statistical learners can account for sudden changes in children's grammars. In future, we hope to extend these results by examining other learning behaviors and testing the model on other languages.

9 Acknowledgements

We thank Mark Johnson for suggesting an analysis of learning rates. This work was funded by the ERC Advanced Fellowship 24952 GramPlus and EU IP grant EC-FP7-270273 Xperience.

References

Alishahi and Stevenson, S. (2008). A computational model for early argument structure acquisition. *Cognitive Science*, 32:5:789–834.

Alishahi, A. and Stevenson, S. (2010). Learning general properties of semantic roles from usage data: a computational model. *Language and Cognitive Processes*, 25:1.

Beal, M. J. (2003). Variational algorithms for approximate Bayesian inference. Technical report, Gatsby Institute, UCL.

Börschinger, B., Jones, B. K., and Johnson, M. (2011). Reducing grounded learning tasks to grammatical inference. In *Proceedings of the 2011 Conference on Empirical Methods in Natural Language Processing*, pages 1416–1425, Edinburgh, Scotland, UK. Association for Computational Linguistics.

Brown, R. (1973). *A First Language: the Early Stages*. Harvard University Press, Cambridge MA.

Buttery, P. J. (2006). Computational models for first language acquisition. Technical Report UCAM-CL-TR-675, University of Cambridge, Computer Laboratory.

Carey, S. and Bartlett, E. (1978). Acquring a single new word. *Papers and Reports on Child Language Development*, 15.

Chen, D. L., Kim, J., and Mooney, R. J. (2010). Training a multilingual sportscaster: Using perceptual context to learn language. *J. Artif. Intell. Res. (JAIR)*, 37:397–435.

Fazly, A., Alishahi, A., and Stevenson, S. (2010). A probabilistic computational model of cross-situational word learning. *Cognitive Science*, 34(6):1017–1063.

Frank, M., Goodman, S., and Tenenbaum, J. (2009). Using speakers referential intentions to model early cross-situational word learning. *Psychological Science*, 20(5):578–585.

Frank, M. C., Goodman, N. D., and Tenenbaum, J. B. (2008). A bayesian framework for cross-situational word-learning. *Advances in Neural Information Processing Systems 20*.

Gibson, E. and Wexler, K. (1994). Triggers. *Linguistic Inquiry*, 25:355–407.

Gleitman, L. (1990). The structural sources of verb meanings. *Language Acquisition*, 1:1–55.

Goldwater, S., Griffiths, T. L., and Johnson, M. (2009). A Bayesian framework for word segmentation: Exploring the effects of context. *Cognition*, 112(1):21–54.

Griffiths, T. L., . T. J. B. (2005). Structure and strength in causal induction. *Cognitive Psychology*, 51:354–384.

Griffiths, T. L. and Tenenbaum, J. B. (2006). Optimal predictions in everyday cognition. *Psychological Science*.

Hoffman, M., Blei, D. M., and Bach, F. (2010). Online learning for latent dirichlet allocation. In *NIPS*.

Kate, R. J. and Mooney, R. J. (2007). Learning language semantics from ambiguous supervision. In *Proceedings of the 22nd Conference on Artificial Intelligence (AAAI-07)*.

Kwiatkowski, T., Zettlemoyer, L., Goldwater, S., and Steedman, M. (2010). Inducing probabilistic CCG grammars from logical form with higher-order unification. In *Proceedings of the Conference on Emperical Methods in Natural Language Processing*.

Kwiatkowski, T., Zettlemoyer, L., Goldwater, S., and Steedman, M. (2011). Lexical generalization in ccg grammar induction for semantic parsing. In *Proceedings of the Conference on Emperical Methods in Natural Language Processing*.

Levy, R., Reali, F., and Griffiths, T. (2009). Modeling the effects of memory on human online sentence processing with particle filters. In *Advances in Neural Information Processing Systems 21*.

Lu, W., Ng, H. T., Lee, W. S., and Zettlemoyer, L. S. (2008). A generative model for parsing natural language to meaning representations. In *Proceedings of The Conference on Empirical Methods in Natural Language Processing*.

MacWhinney, B. (2000). *The CHILDES project: tools for analyzing talk*. Lawrence Erlbaum, Mahwah, NJ u.a. EN.

Maurits, L., Perfors, A., and Navarro, D. (2009). Joint acquisition of word order and word reference. In *Proceedings of the 31th Annual Conference of the Cognitive Science Society*.

Pearl, L., Goldwater, S., and Steyvers, M. (2010). How ideal are we? Incorporating human limitations into Bayesian models of word segmentation. pages 315–326, Somerville, MA. Cascadilla Press.

Perfors, A., Tenenbaum, J. B., and Regier, T. (2011). The learnability of abstract syntactic principles. *Cognition*, 118(3):306 – 338.

Sagae, K., MacWhinney, B., and Lavie, A. (2004). Adding syntactic annotations to transcripts of parent-child dialogs. In *Proceedings of the 4th International Conference on Language Resources and Evaluation*. Lisbon, LREC.

Sakas, W. and Fodor, J. D. (2001). The structural triggers learner. In Bertolo, S., editor, *Language Acquisition and Learnability*, pages 172–233. Cambridge University Press, Cambridge.

Sanborn, A. N., Griffiths, T. L., and Navarro, D. J. (2010). Rational approximations to rational models: Alternative algorithms for category learning. *Psychological Review.*

Sato, M. (2001). Online model selection based on the variational bayes. *Neural Computation*, 13(7):1649–1681.

Shi, L., Griffiths, T. L., Feldman, N. H., and Sanborn, A. N. (2010). Exemplar models as a mechanism for performing bayesian inference. *Psychonomic Bulletin & Review*, 17(4):443–464.

Siskind, J. M. (1992). *Naive Physics, Event Perception, Lexical Semantics, and Language Acquisition*. PhD thesis, Massachusetts Institute of Technology.

Siskind, J. M. (1996). A computational study of cross-situational techniques for learning word-to-meaning mappings. *Cognition*, 61(1-2):1–38.

Steedman, M. (2000). *The Syntactic Process*. MIT Press, Cambridge, MA.

Steedman, M. (2002). Plans, affordances, and combinatory grammar. *Linguistics and Philosophy*, 25.

Thornton, R. and Tesan, G. (2007). Categorical acquisition: Parameter setting in universal grammar. *Biolinguistics*, 1.

Villavicencio, A. (2002). The acquisition of a unification-based generalised categorial grammar. Technical Report UCAM-CL-TR-533, University of Cambridge, Computer Laboratory.

Wong, Y. W. and Mooney, R. (2006). Learning for semantic parsing with statistical machine translation. In *Proceedings of the Human Language Technology Conference of the NAACL.*

Wong, Y. W. and Mooney, R. (2007). Learning synchronous grammars for semantic parsing with lambda calculus. In *Proceedings of the Association for Computational Linguistics.*

Xu, F. and Tenenbaum, J. B. (2007). Word learning as Bayesian inference. *Psychological Review*, 114:245–272.

Yang, C. (2002). *Knowledge and Learning in Natural Language*. Oxford University Press, Oxford.

Yu, C. and Ballard, D. H. (2007). A unified model of early word learning: Integrating statistical and social cues. *Neurocomputing*, 70(13-15):2149 – 2165.

Zettlemoyer, L. S. and Collins, M. (2005). Learning to map sentences to logical form: Structured classification with probabilistic categorial grammars. In *Proceedings of the Conference on Uncertainty in Artificial Intelligence.*

Zettlemoyer, L. S. and Collins, M. (2007). Online learning of relaxed CCG grammars for parsing to logical form. In *Proc. of the Joint Conference on Empirical Methods in Natural Language Processing and Computational Natural Language Learning.*

Zettlemoyer, L. S. and Collins, M. (2009). Learning context-dependent mappings from sentences to logical form. In *Proceedings of The Joint Conference of the Association for Computational Linguistics and International Joint Conference on Natural Language Processing.*

Active learning for interactive machine translation

Jesús González-Rubio and **Daniel Ortiz-Martínez** and **Francisco Casacuberta**
D. de Sistemas Informáticos y Computación
U. Politècnica de València
C. de Vera s/n, 46022 Valencia, Spain
{jegonzalez,dortiz,fcn}@dsic.upv.es

Abstract

Translation needs have greatly increased during the last years. In many situations, text to be translated constitutes an unbounded stream of data that grows continually with time. An effective approach to translate text documents is to follow an interactive-predictive paradigm in which both the system is guided by the user and the user is assisted by the system to generate error-free translations. Unfortunately, when processing such unbounded data streams even this approach requires an overwhelming amount of manpower. Is in this scenario where the use of active learning techniques is compelling. In this work, we propose different active learning techniques for interactive machine translation. Results show that for a given translation quality the use of active learning allows us to greatly reduce the human effort required to translate the sentences in the stream.

1 Introduction

Translation needs have greatly increased during the last years due to phenomena such as globalization and technologic development. For example, the European Parliament[1] translates its proceedings to 22 languages in a regular basis or Project Syndicate[2] that translates editorials into different languages. In these and many other examples, data can be viewed as an incoming unbounded stream since it grows continually with time (Levenberg et al., 2010). Manual translation of such streams of data is extremely expensive given the huge volume of translation required, therefore various automatic machine translation methods have been proposed.

However, automatic *statistical machine translation* (SMT) systems are far from generating error-free translations and their outputs usually require human post-editing in order to achieve high-quality translations. One way of taking advantage of SMT systems is to combine them with the knowledge of a human translator in the *interactive-predictive machine translation* (IMT) framework (Foster et al., 1998; Langlais and Lapalme, 2002; Barrachina et al., 2009), which is a particular case of the computer-assisted translation paradigm (Isabelle and Church, 1997). In the IMT framework, a state-of-the-art SMT model and a human translator collaborate to obtain high-quality translations while minimizing required human effort.

Unfortunately, the application of either post-editing or IMT to data streams with massive data volumes is still too expensive, simply because manual supervision of all instances requires huge amounts of manpower. For such massive data streams the need of employing *active learning* (AL) is compelling. AL techniques for IMT selectively ask an oracle (e.g. a human translator) to supervise a small portion of the incoming sentences. Sentences are selected so that SMT models estimated from them translate new sentences as accurately as possible. There are three challenges when applying AL to unbounded data streams (Zhu et al., 2010). These challenges can be instantiated to IMT as follows:

1. The pool of candidate sentences is dynamically changing, whereas existing AL algorithms are dealing with static datasets only.

[1] http://www.europarl.europa.eu
[2] http://project-syndicate.org

2. Concepts such as optimum translation and translation probability distribution are continually evolving whereas existing AL algorithms only deal with constant concepts.

3. Data volume is unbounded which makes impractical to batch-learn one single system from all previously translated sentences. Therefore, model training must be done in an incremental fashion.

In this work, we present a proposal of AL for IMT specifically designed to work with stream data. In short, our proposal divides the data stream into blocks where AL techniques for static datasets are applied. Additionally, we implement an incremental learning technique to efficiently train the base SMT models as new data is available.

2 Related work

A body of work has recently been proposed to apply AL techniques to SMT (Haffari et al., 2009; Ambati et al., 2010; Bloodgood and Callison-Burch, 2010). The aim of these works is to build one single optimal SMT model from manually translated data extracted from static datasets. None of them fit in the setting of data streams.

Some of the above described challenges of AL from unbounded streams have been previously addressed in the MT literature. In order to deal with the evolutionary nature of the problem, Nepveu et al. (2004) propose an IMT system with dynamic adaptation via cache-based model extensions for language and translation models. Pursuing the same goal for SMT, Levenberg et al., (2010) study how to bound the space when processing (potentially) unbounded streams of parallel data and propose a method to incrementally retrain SMT models. Another method to efficiently retrain a SMT model with new data was presented in (Ortiz-Martínez et al., 2010). In this work, the authors describe an application of the online learning paradigm to the IMT framework.

To the best of our knowledge, the only previous work on AL for IMT is (González-Rubio et al., 2011). There, the authors present a naïve application of the AL paradigm for IMT that do not take into account the dynamic change in probability distribution of the stream. Nevertheless, results show that even that simple AL framework halves the required human effort to obtain a certain translation quality.

In this work, the AL framework presented in (González-Rubio et al., 2011) is extended in an effort to address all the above described challenges. In short, we propose an AL framework for IMT that splits the data stream into blocks. This approach allows us to have more context to model the changing probability distribution of the stream (challenge 2) and results in a more accurate sampling of the changing pool of sentences (challenge 1). In contrast to the proposal described in (González-Rubio et al., 2011), we define sentence sampling strategies whose underlying models can be updated with the newly available data. This way, the sentences to be supervised by the user are chosen taking into account previously supervised sentences. To efficiently retrain the underlying SMT models of the IMT system (challenge 3), we follow the online learning technique described in (Ortiz-Martínez et al., 2010). Finally, we integrate all these elements to define an AL framework for IMT with an objective of obtaining an optimum balance between translation quality and human user effort.

3 Interactive machine translation

IMT can be seen as an evolution of the SMT framework. Given a sentence $\mathbf{f}$ from a source language to be translated into a sentence $\mathbf{e}$ of a target language, the fundamental equation of SMT (Brown et al., 1993) is defined as follows:

$$\hat{\mathbf{e}} = \arg\max_{\mathbf{e}} Pr(\mathbf{e} \mid \mathbf{f}) \tag{1}$$

where $Pr(\mathbf{e} \mid \mathbf{f})$ is usually approximated by a log linear translation model (Koehn et al., 2003). In this case, the decision rule is given by the expression:

$$\hat{\mathbf{e}} = \arg\max_{\mathbf{e}} \left\{ \sum_{m=1}^{M} \lambda_m h_m(\mathbf{e}, \mathbf{f}) \right\} \tag{2}$$

where each $h_m(\mathbf{e}, \mathbf{f})$ is a feature function representing a statistical model and λ_m its weight.

In the IMT framework, a human translator is introduced in the translation process to collaborate with an SMT model. For a given source sentence, the SMT model fully automatically generates an initial translation. The human user checks this translation, from left to right, correcting the first

source ($\mathbf{f}$): Para ver la lista de recursos
desired translation ($\hat{\mathbf{e}}$): To view a listing of resources

inter.-0	$\mathbf{e}_p$	
	$\mathbf{e}_s$	*To view the resources list*
inter.-1	$\mathbf{e}_p$	To view
	k	a
	$\mathbf{e}_s$	*list of resources*
inter.-2	$\mathbf{e}_p$	To view a list
	k	i
	$\mathbf{e}_s$	*ng resources*
inter.-3	$\mathbf{e}_p$	To view a listing
	k	o
	$\mathbf{e}_s$	*f resources*
accept	$\mathbf{e}_p$	To view a listing of resources

Figure 1: IMT session to translate a Spanish sentence into English. The desired translation is the translation the human user have in mind. At interaction-0, the system suggests a translation ($\mathbf{e}_s$). At interaction-1, the user moves the mouse to accept the first eight characters "To view " and presses the a key (k), then the system suggests completing the sentence with "*list of resources*" (a new $\mathbf{e}_s$). Interactions 2 and 3 are similar. In the final interaction, the user accepts the current translation.

error. Then, the SMT model proposes a new extension taking the correct prefix, $\mathbf{e}_p$, into account. These steps are repeated until the user accepts the translation. Figure 1 illustrates a typical IMT session. In the resulting decision rule, we have to find an extension $\mathbf{e}_s$ for a given prefix $\mathbf{e}_p$. To do this we reformulate equation (1) as follows, where the term $Pr(\mathbf{e}_p \mid \mathbf{f})$ has been dropped since it does not depend on $\mathbf{e}_s$:

$$\hat{\mathbf{e}}_s = \arg\max_{\mathbf{e}_s} Pr(\mathbf{e}_p, \mathbf{e}_s \mid \mathbf{f}) \quad (3)$$

$$\approx \arg\max_{\mathbf{e}_s} p(\mathbf{e}_s \mid \mathbf{f}, \mathbf{e}_p) \quad (4)$$

The search is restricted to those sentences $\mathbf{e}$ which contain $\mathbf{e}_p$ as prefix. Since $\mathbf{e} \equiv \mathbf{e}_p\, \mathbf{e}_s$, we can use the same log-linear SMT model, equation (2), whenever the search procedures are adequately modified (Barrachina et al., 2009).

4 Active learning for IMT

The aim of the IMT framework is to obtain high-quality translations while minimizing the required human effort. Despite the fact that IMT may reduce the required effort with respect to post-editing, it still requires the user to supervise all the translations. To address this problem, we propose to use AL techniques to select only a small number of sentences whose translations are worth to be supervised by the human expert.

This approach implies a modification of the user-machine interaction protocol. For a given source sentence, the SMT model generates an initial translation. Then, if this initial translation is classified as incorrect or "worth of supervision", we perform a conventional IMT procedure as in Figure 1. If not, we directly return the initial automatic translation and no effort is required from the user. At the end of the process, we use the new sentence pair $(\mathbf{f}, \mathbf{e})$ available to refine the SMT models used by the IMT system.

In this scenario, the user only checks a small number of sentences, thus, final translations are not error-free as in conventional IMT. However, results in previous works (González-Rubio et al., 2011) show that this approach yields important reduction in human effort. Moreover, depending on the definition of the sampling strategy, we can modify the ratio of sentences that are interactively translated to adapt our system to the requirements of a specific translation task. For example, if the main priority is to minimize human effort, our system can be configured to translate all the sentences without user intervention.

Algorithm 1 describes the basic algorithm to implement AL for IMT. The algorithm receives as input an initial SMT model, M, a sampling strategy, S, a stream of source sentences, F, and the block size, B. First, a block of B sentences, X, is extracted from the data stream (line 3). From this block, we sample those sentences, Y, that are worth to be supervised by the human expert (line 4). For each of the sentences in X, the current SMT model generates an initial translation, $\hat{\mathbf{e}}$, (line 6). If the sentence has been sampled as worthy of supervision, $\mathbf{f} \in Y$, the user is required to interactively translate it (lines 8–13) as exemplified in Figure 1. The source sentence $\mathbf{f}$ and its human-supervised translation, $\mathbf{e}$, are then used to retrain the SMT model (line 14). Otherwise, we directly output the automatic translation $\hat{\mathbf{e}}$ as our final translation (line 17).

Most of the functions in the algorithm denote different steps in the interaction between the human user and the machine:

- `translate(`M`,f)`: returns the most probable automatic translation of $\mathbf{f}$ given by M.
- `validPrefix(e)`: returns the prefix of $\mathbf{e}$

```
input    : M (initial SMT model)
           S (sampling strategy)
           F (stream of source sentences)
           B (block size)
auxiliar : X (block of sentences)
           Y (sentences worth of supervision)
begin
    repeat
        X = getSentsFromStream(B, F);
        Y = S(X, M);
        foreach f ∈ X do
            ê = translate(M, f);
            if f ∈ Y then
                e = ê;
                repeat
                    e_p = validPrefix(e);
                    ê_s = genSuffix(M, f, e_p);
                    e = e_p ê_s;
                until validTranslation(e) ;
                M = retrain(M, (f, e));
                output(e);
            else
                output(ê);
    until True ;
end
```

Algorithm 1: Pseudo-code of the proposed algorithm to implement AL for IMT from unbounded data streams.

validated by the user as correct. This prefix includes the correction k.

- `genSuffix(`$M,\mathbf{f},\mathbf{e}_\mathrm{p}$`)`: returns the suffix of maximum probability that extends prefix $\mathbf{e}_\mathrm{p}$.
- `validTranslation(e)`: returns *True* if the user considers the current translation to be correct and *False* otherwise.

Apart from these, the two elements that define the performance of our algorithm are the sampling strategy $\mathrm{S}(X, M)$ and the `retrain(`$M,(\mathbf{f},\mathbf{e})$`)` function. On the one hand, the sampling strategy decides which sentences should be supervised by the user, which defines the human effort required by the algorithm. Section 5 describes our implementation of the sentence sampling to deal with the dynamic nature of data streams. On the other hand, the `retrain(·)` function incrementally trains the SMT model with each new training pair $(\mathbf{f}, \mathbf{e})$. Section 6 describes the implementation of this function.

5 Sentence sampling strategies

A good sentence sampling strategy must be able to select those sentences that along with their correct translations improve most the performance of the SMT model. To do that, the sampling strategy have to correctly discriminate "informative" sentences from those that are not. We can make different approximations to measure the informativeness of a given sentence. In the following sections, we describe the three different sampling strategies tested in our experimentation.

5.1 Random sampling

Arguably, the simplest sampling approach is random sampling, where the sentences are randomly selected to be interactively translated. Although simple, it turns out that random sampling perform surprisingly well in practice. The success of random sampling stem from the fact that in data stream environments the translation probability distributions may vary significantly through time. While general AL algorithms ask the user to translate informative sentences, they may significantly change probability distributions by favoring certain translations, consequently, the previously human-translated sentences may no longer reveal the genuine translation distribution in the current point of the data stream (Zhu et al., 2007). This problem is less severe for static data where the candidate pool is fixed and AL algorithms are able to survey all instances. Random sampling avoids this problem by randomly selecting sentences for human supervision. As a result, it always selects those sentences with the most similar distribution to the current sentence distribution in the data stream.

5.2 n-gram coverage sampling

One technique to measure the informativeness of a sentence is to directly measure the amount of new information that it will add to the SMT model. This sampling strategy considers that sentences with rare n-grams are more informative. The intuition for this approach is that rare n-grams need to be seen several times in order to accurately estimate their probability.

To do that, we store the counts for each n-gram present in the sentences used to train the SMT model. We assume that an n-gram is accurately represented when it appears A or more times in the training samples. Therefore, the score for a given sentence **f** is computed as:

$$C(\mathbf{f}) = \frac{\sum_{n=1}^{N} |\mathcal{N}_n^{<A}(\mathbf{f})|}{\sum_{n=1}^{N} |\mathcal{N}_n(\mathbf{f})|} \quad (5)$$

where $\mathcal{N}_n(\mathbf{f})$ is the set of n-grams of size n in $\mathbf{f}$, $\mathcal{N}_n^{<A}(\mathbf{f})$ is the set of n-grams of size n in $\mathbf{f}$ that are inaccurately represented in the training data and N is the maximum n-gram order. In the experimentation, we assume $N = 4$ as the maximum n-gram order and a value of 10 for the threshold A. This sampling strategy works by selecting a given percentage of the highest scoring sentences.

We update the counts of the n-grams seen by the SMT model with each new sentence pair. Hence, the sampling strategy is always up-to-date with the last training data.

5.3 Dynamic confidence sampling

Another technique is to consider that the most informative sentence is the one the current SMT model translates worst. The intuition behind this approach is that an SMT model can not generate good translations unless it has enough information to translate the sentence.

The usual approach to compute the quality of a translation hypothesis is to compare it to a reference translation, but, in this case, it is not a valid option since reference translations are not available. Hence, we use confidence estimation (Gandrabur and Foster, 2003; Blatz et al., 2004; Ueffing and Ney, 2007) to estimate the probability of correctness of the translations. Specifically, we estimate the quality of a translation from the confidence scores of their individual words.

The confidence score of a word e_i of the translation $\mathbf{e} = e_1 \ldots e_i \ldots e_I$ generated from the source sentence $\mathbf{f} = f_1 \ldots f_j \ldots f_J$ is computed as described in (Ueffing and Ney, 2005):

$$C_w(e_i, \mathbf{f}) = \max_{0 \le j \le |\mathbf{f}|} p(e_i|f_j) \quad (6)$$

where $p(e_i|f_j)$ is an IBM model 1 (Brown et al., 1993) bilingual lexicon probability and f_0 is the empty source word. The confidence score for the full translation **e** is computed as the ratio of its words classified as correct by the word confidence measure. Therefore, we define the confidence-based informativeness score as:

$$C(\mathbf{e}, \mathbf{f}) = 1 - \frac{|\{e_i \mid C_w(e_i, \mathbf{f}) > \tau_w\}|}{|\mathbf{e}|} \quad (7)$$

Finally, this sampling strategy works by selecting a given percentage of the highest scoring sentences.

We dynamically update the confidence sampler each time a new sentence pair is added to the SMT model. The incremental version of the EM algorithm (Neal and Hinton, 1999) is used to incrementally train the IBM model 1.

6 Retraining of the SMT model

To retrain the SMT model, we implement the online learning techniques proposed in (Ortiz-Martínez et al., 2010). In that work, a state-of-the-art log-linear model (Och and Ney, 2002) and a set of techniques to incrementally train this model were defined. The log-linear model is composed of a set of feature functions governing different aspects of the translation process, including a language model, a source sentence–length model, inverse and direct translation models, a target phrase–length model, a source phrase–length model and a distortion model.

The incremental learning algorithm allows us to process each new training sample in constant time (i.e. the computational complexity of training a new sample does not depend on the number of previously seen training samples). To do that, a set of sufficient statistics is maintained for each feature function. If the estimation of the feature function does not require the use of the well-known expectation–maximization (EM) algorithm (Dempster et al., 1977) (e.g. n-gram language models), then it is generally easy to incrementally extend the model given a new training sample. By contrast, if the EM algorithm is required (e.g. word alignment models), the estimation procedure has to be modified, since the conventional EM algorithm is designed for its use in batch learning scenarios. For such models, the incremental version of the EM algorithm (Neal and Hinton, 1999) is applied. A detailed description of the update algorithm for each of the models in the log-linear combination is presented in (Ortiz-Martínez et al., 2010).

7 Experiments

We carried out experiments to assess the performance of the proposed AL implementation for IMT. In each experiments, we started with an initial SMT model that is incrementally updated

corpus	use	sentences	words (Spa/Eng)
Europarl	train	731K	15M/15M
	devel.	2K	60K/58K
News Commentary	test	51K	1.5M/1.2M

Table 1: Size of the Spanish–English corpora used in the experiments. K and M stand for thousands and millions of elements respectively.

with the sentences selected by the current sampling strategy. Due to the unavailability of public benchmark data streams, we selected a relatively large corpus and treated it as a data stream for AL. To simulate the interaction with the user, we used the reference translations in the data stream corpus as the translation the human user would like to obtain. Since each experiment is carried out under the same conditions, if one sampling strategy outperforms its peers, then we can safely conclude that this is because the sentences selected to be translated are more informative.

7.1 Training corpus and data stream

The training data comes from the Europarl corpus as distributed for the shared task in the NAACL 2006 workshop on statistical machine translation (Koehn and Monz, 2006). We used this data to estimate the initial log-linear model used by our IMT system (see Section 6). The weights of the different feature functions were tuned by means of minimum error–rate training (Och, 2003) executed on the Europarl development corpus. Once the SMT model was trained, we use the News Commentary corpus (Callison-Burch et al., 2007) to simulate the data stream. The size of these corpora is shown in Table 1. The reasons to choose the News Commentary corpus to carry out our experiments are threefold: first, its size is large enough to simulate a data stream and test our AL techniques in the long term; second, it is out-of-domain data which allows us to simulate a real-world situation that may occur in a translation company, and, finally, it consists in editorials from eclectic domain: general politics, economics and science, which effectively represents the variations in the sentence distributions of the simulated data stream.

7.2 Assessment criteria

We want to measure both the quality of the generated translations and the human effort required to obtain them.

We measure translation quality with the well-known BLEU (Papineni et al., 2002) score.

To estimate human user effort, we simulate the actions taken by a human user in its interaction with the IMT system. The first translation hypothesis for each given source sentence is compared with a single reference translation and the longest common character prefix (LCP) is obtained. The first non-matching character is replaced by the corresponding reference character and then a new translation hypothesis is produced (see Figure 1). This process is iterated until a full match with the reference is obtained. Each computation of the LCP would correspond to the user looking for the next error and *moving the pointer* to the corresponding position of the translation hypothesis. Each character replacement, on the other hand, would correspond to a *keystroke* of the user.

Bearing this in mind, we measure the user effort by means of the keystroke and mouse-action ratio (KSMR) (Barrachina et al., 2009). This measure has been extensively used to report results in the IMT literature. KSMR is calculated as the number of keystrokes plus the number of mouse movements divided by the total number of reference characters. From a user point of view the two types of actions are different and require different types of effort (Macklovitch, 2006). In any case, as an approximation, KSMR assumes that both actions require a similar effort.

7.3 Experimental results

In this section, we report results for three different experiments. First, we studied the performance of the sampling strategies when dealing with the sampling bias problem. In the second experiment, we carried out a typical AL experiment measuring the performance of the sampling strategies as a function of the percentage of the corpus used to retrain the SMT model. Finally, we tested our AL implementation for IMT in order to study the tradeoff between required human effort and final translation quality.

7.3.1 Dealing with the sampling bias

In this experiment, we want to study the performance of the different sampling strategies when

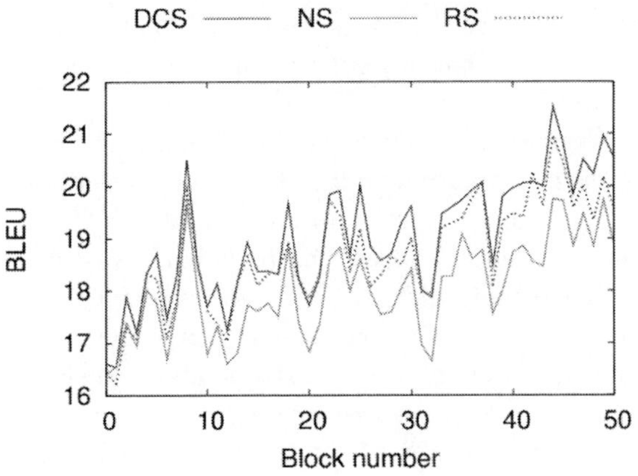

Figure 2: Performance of the AL methods across different data blocks. Block size 500. Human supervision 10% of the corpus.

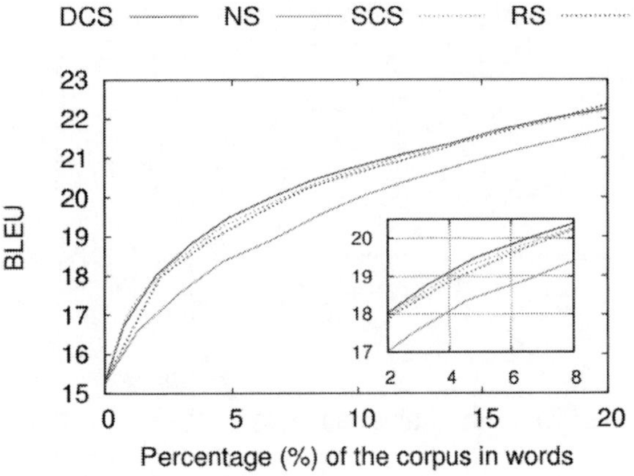

Figure 3: BLEU of the initial automatic translations as a function of the percentage of the corpus used to retrain the model.

dealing with the sampling bias problem. Figure 2 shows the evolution of the translation quality, in terms of BLEU, across different data blocks for the three sampling strategies described in section 5, namely, dynamic confidence sampling (DCS), n-gram coverage sampling (NS) and random sampling (RS). On the one hand, the x-axis represents the data blocks number in their temporal order. On the other hand, the y-axis represents the BLEU score when automatically translating a block. Such translation is obtained by the SMT model trained with translations supervised by the user up to that point of the data stream. To fairly compare the different methods, we fixed the percentage of words supervised by the human user (10%). In addition to this, we used a block size of 500 sentences. Similar results were obtained for other block sizes.

Results in Figure 2 indicate that the performances for the data blocks fluctuate and fluctuations are quite significant. This phenomenon is due to the eclectic domain of the sentences in the data stream. Additionally, the steady increase in performance is caused by the increasing amount of data used to retrain the SMT model.

Regarding the results for the different sampling strategies, DCS consistently outperformed RS and NS. This observation asserts that for concept drifting data streams with constant changing translation distributions, DCS can adaptively ask the user to translate sentences to build a superior SMT model. On the other hand, NS obtains worse results that RS. This result can be explained by the fact that NS is independent of the target language and just looks into the source language, while DCS takes into account both the source sentence and its automatic translation. Similar phenomena has been reported in a previous work on AL for SMT (Haffari et al., 2009).

7.3.2 AL performance

We carried out experiments to study the performance of the different sampling strategies. To this end, we compare the quality of the initial automatic translations generated in our AL implementation for IMT (line 6 in Algorithm 1). Figure 3 shows the BLEU score of these initial translations represented as a function of the percentage of the corpus used to retrain the SMT model. The percentage of the corpus is measured in number of running words.

In Figure 3, we present results for the three sampling strategies described in section 5. Additionally, we also compare our techniques with the AL technique for IMT proposed in (González-Rubio et al., 2011). Such technique is similar to DCS but it does not update the IBM model 1 used by the confidence sampler with the newly available human-translated sentences. This technique is referred to as static confidence sampler (SCS).

Results in Figure 3 indicate that the performance of the retrained SMT models increased as more data was incorporated. Regarding the sampling strategies, DCS improved the results obtained by the other sampling strategies. NS obtained by far the worst results, which confirms the results shown in the previous experiment. Finally,

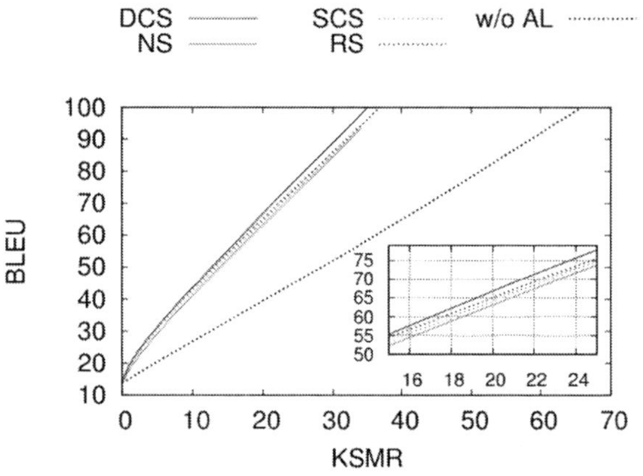

Figure 4: Quality of the data stream translation (BLEU) as a function of the required human effort (KSMR). w/o AL denotes a system with no retraining.

as it can be seen, SCS obtained slightly worst results than DCS showing the importance of dynamically adapting the underlying model used by the sampling strategy.

7.3.3 Balancing human effort and translation quality

Finally, we studied the balance between required human effort and final translation error. This can be useful in a real-world scenario where a translation company is hired to translate a stream of sentences. Under these circumstances, it would be important to be able to predict the effort required from the human translators to obtain a certain translation quality.

The experiment simulate this situation using our proposed IMT system with AL to translate the stream of sentences. To have a broad view of the behavior of our system, we repeated this translation process multiple times requiring an increasing human effort each time. Experiments range from a fully-automatic translation system with no need of human intervention to a system where the human is required to supervise all the sentences. Figure 4 presents results for SCS (see section 7.3.2) and the sentence selection strategies presented in section 5. In addition, we also present results for a static system without AL (w/o AL). This system is equal to SCS but it do not perform any SMT retraining.

Results in Figure 4 show a consistent reduction in required user effort when using AL. For a given human effort the use of AL methods allowed to obtain twice the translation quality. Regarding the different AL sampling strategies, DCS obtains the better results but differences with other methods are slight.

Varying the sentence classifier, we can achieve a balance between final translation quality and required human effort. This feature allows us to adapt the system to suit the requirements of the particular translation task or to the available economic or human resources. For example, if a translation quality of 60 BLEU points is satisfactory, then the human translators would need to modify only a 20% of the characters of the automatically generated translations.

Finally, it should be noted that our IMT systems with AL are able to generate new suffixes and retrain with new sentence pairs in tenths of a second. Thus, it can be applied in real time scenarios.

8 Conclusions and future work

In this work, we have presented an AL framework for IMT specially designed to process data streams with massive volumes of data. Our proposal splits the data stream in blocks of sentences of a certain size and applies AL techniques individually for each block. For this purpose, we implemented different sampling strategies that measure the informativeness of a sentence according to different criteria.

To evaluate the performance of our proposed sampling strategies, we carried out experiments comparing them with random sampling and the only previously proposed AL technique for IMT described in (González-Rubio et al., 2011). According to the results, one of the proposed sampling strategies, specifically the dynamic confidence sampling strategy, consistently outperformed all the other strategies.

The results in the experimentation show that the use of AL techniques allows us to make a tradeoff between required human effort and final translation quality. In other words, we can adapt our system to meet the translation quality requirements of the translation task or the available human resources.

As future work, we plan to investigate on more sophisticated sampling strategies such as those based in information density or query-by-committee. Additionally, we will conduct experiments with real users to confirm the results obtained by our user simulation.

Acknowledgements

The research leading to these results has received funding from the European Union Seventh Framework Programme (FP7/2007-2013) under grant agreement n° 287576. Work also supported by the EC (FEDER/FSE) and the Spanish MEC under the MIPRCV Consolider Ingenio 2010 program (CSD2007-00018) and iTrans2 (TIN2009-14511) project and by the Generalitat Valenciana under grant ALMPR (Prometeo/2009/01).

References

Vamshi Ambati, Stephan Vogel, and Jaime Carbonell. 2010. Active learning and crowd-sourcing for machine translation. In *Proc. of the conference on International Language Resources and Evaluation*, pages 2169–2174.

Sergio Barrachina, Oliver Bender, Francisco Casacuberta, Jorge Civera, Elsa Cubel, Shahram Khadivi, Antonio Lagarda, Hermann Ney, Jesús Tomás, Enrique Vidal, and Juan-Miguel Vilar. 2009. Statistical approaches to computer-assisted translation. *Computational Linguistics*, 35:3–28.

John Blatz, Erin Fitzgerald, George Foster, Simona Gandrabur, Cyril Goutte, Alex Kulesza, Alberto Sanchis, and Nicola Ueffing. 2004. Confidence estimation for machine translation. In *Proc. of the international conference on Computational Linguistics*, pages 315–321.

Michael Bloodgood and Chris Callison-Burch. 2010. Bucking the trend: large-scale cost-focused active learning for statistical machine translation. In *Proc. of the Association for Computational Linguistics*, pages 854–864.

Peter F. Brown, Vincent J. Della Pietra, Stephen A. Della Pietra, and Robert L. Mercer. 1993. The mathematics of statistical machine translation: parameter estimation. *Computational Linguistics*, 19:263–311.

Chris Callison-Burch, Cameron Fordyce, Philipp Koehn, Christof Monz, and Josh Schroeder. 2007. (Meta-) evaluation of machine translation. In *Proc. of the Workshop on Statistical Machine Translation*, pages 136–158.

Arthur Dempster, Nan Laird, and Donald Rubin. 1977. Maximum likelihood from incomplete data via the EM algorithm. *Journal of the Royal Statistical Society.*, 39(1):1–38.

George Foster, Pierre Isabelle, and Pierre Plamondon. 1998. Target-text mediated interactive machine translation. *Machine Translation*, 12:175–194.

Simona Gandrabur and George Foster. 2003. Confidence estimation for text prediction. In *Proc. of the Conference on Computational Natural Language Learning*, pages 315–321.

Jesús González-Rubio, Daniel Ortiz-Martínez, and Francisco casacuberta. 2011. An active learning scenario for interactive machine translation. In *Proc. of the 13thInternational Conference on Multimodal Interaction*. ACM.

Gholamreza Haffari, Maxim Roy, and Anoop Sarkar. 2009. Active learning for statistical phrase-based machine translation. In *Proc. of the North American Chapter of the Association for Computational Linguistics*, pages 415–423.

Pierre Isabelle and Kenneth Ward Church. 1997. Special issue on new tools for human translators. *Machine Translation*, 12(1-2):1–2.

Philipp Koehn and Christof Monz. 2006. Manual and automatic evaluation of machine translation between european languages. In *Proc. of the Workshop on Statistical Machine Translation*, pages 102–121.

Philipp Koehn, Franz Josef Och, and Daniel Marcu. 2003. Statistical phrase-based translation. In *Proceedings of the 2003 Conference of the North American Chapter of the Association for Computational Linguistics on Human Language Technology - Volume 1*, pages 48–54.

Philippe Langlais and Guy Lapalme. 2002. Trans Type: development-evaluation cycles to boost translator's productivity. *Machine Translation*, 17:77–98.

Abby Levenberg, Chris Callison-Burch, and Miles Osborne. 2010. Stream-based translation models for statistical machine translation. In *Proc. of the North American Chapter of the Association for Computational Linguistics*, pages 394–402, Los Angeles, California, June.

Elliott Macklovitch. 2006. TransType2: the last word. In *Proc. of the conference on International Language Resources and Evaluation*, pages 167–17.

Radford Neal and Geoffrey Hinton. 1999. A view of the EM algorithm that justifies incremental, sparse, and other variants. *Learning in graphical models*, pages 355–368.

Laurent Nepveu, Guy Lapalme, Philippe Langlais, and George Foster. 2004. Adaptive language and translation models for interactive machine translation. In *Proc, of EMNLP*, pages 190–197, Barcelona, Spain, July.

Franz Och and Hermann Ney. 2002. Discriminative training and maximum entropy models for statistical machine translation. In *Proc. of the Association for Computational Linguistics*, pages 295–302.

Franz Och. 2003. Minimum error rate training in statistical machine translation. In *Proc. of the Association for Computational Linguistics*, pages 160–167.

Daniel Ortiz-Martínez, Ismael García-Varea, and Francisco Casacuberta. 2010. Online learning for interactive statistical machine translation. In *Proc. of the North American Chapter of the Association for Computational Linguistics*, pages 546–554.

Kishore Papineni, Salim Roukos, Todd Ward, and Wei-Jing Zhu. 2002. BLEU: a method for automatic evaluation of machine translation. In *Proc. of the Association for Computational Linguistics*, pages 311–318.

Nicola Ueffing and Hermann Ney. 2005. Application of word-level confidence measures in interactive statistical machine translation. In *Proc. of the European Association for Machine Translation conference*, pages 262–270.

Nicola Ueffing and Hermann Ney. 2007. Word-level confidence estimation for machine translation. *Computational Linguistics*, 33:9–40.

Xingquan Zhu, Peng Zhang, Xiaodong Lin, and Yong Shi. 2007. Active learning from data streams. In *Proc. of the 7th IEEE International Conference on Data Mining*, pages 757–762. IEEE Computer Society.

Xingquan Zhu, Peng Zhang, Xiaodong Lin, and Yong Shi. 2010. Active learning from stream data using optimal weight classifier ensemble. *Transactions on Systems, Man and Cybernetics Part B*, 40:1607–1621, December.

Adapting Translation Models to Translationese Improves SMT

Gennadi Lembersky
Dept. of Computer Science
University of Haifa
31905 Haifa, Israel
glembers@campus.haifa.ac.il

Noam Ordan
Dept. of Computer Science
University of Haifa
31905 Haifa, Israel
noam.ordan@gmail.com

Shuly Wintner
Dept. of Computer Science
University of Haifa
31905 Haifa, Israel
shuly@cs.haifa.ac.il

Abstract

Translation models used for statistical machine translation are compiled from parallel corpora; such corpora are manually translated, but the direction of translation is usually unknown, and is consequently ignored. However, much research in Translation Studies indicates that the direction of translation matters, as translated language (*translationese*) has many unique properties. Specifically, phrase tables constructed from parallel corpora translated in the same direction as the translation task perform better than ones constructed from corpora translated in the opposite direction.

We reconfirm that this is indeed the case, but emphasize the importance of using also texts translated in the 'wrong' direction. We take advantage of information pertaining to the direction of translation in constructing phrase tables, by adapting the translation model to the special properties of translationese. We define entropy-based measures that estimate the correspondence of target-language phrases to translationese, thereby eliminating the need to annotate the parallel corpus with information pertaining to the direction of translation. We show that incorporating these measures as features in the phrase tables of statistical machine translation systems results in consistent, statistically significant improvement in the quality of the translation.

1 Introduction

Much research in Translation Studies indicates that translated texts have unique characteristics that set them apart from original texts (Toury, 1980; Gellerstam, 1986; Toury, 1995). Known as *translationese*, translated texts (in any language) constitute a genre, or a dialect, of the target language, which reflects both artifacts of the translation process and traces of the original language from which the texts were translated. Among the better-known properties of translationese are *simplification* and *explicitation* (Baker, 1993, 1995, 1996): translated texts tend to be shorter, to have lower type/token ratio, and to use certain discourse markers more frequently than original texts. Incidentally, translated texts are so markedly different from original ones that automatic classification can identify them with very high accuracy (van Halteren, 2008; Baroni and Bernardini, 2006; Ilisei et al., 2010; Koppel and Ordan, 2011).

Contemporary Statistical Machine Translation (SMT) systems use parallel corpora to train *translation models* that reflect source- and target-language phrase correspondences. Typically, SMT systems ignore the direction of translation used to produce those corpora. Given the unique properties of translationese, however, it is reasonable to assume that this direction may affect the quality of the translation. Recently, Kurokawa et al. (2009) showed that this is indeed the case. They train a system to translate between French and English (and vice versa) using a French-translated-to-English parallel corpus, and then an English-translated-to-French one. They find that in translating into French the latter parallel corpus yields better results, whereas for translating into English it is better to use the former.

Usually, of course, the translation direction of a parallel corpus is unknown. Therefore, Kurokawa et al. (2009) train an SVM-based classifier to predict which side of a bi-text is the origin and which one is the translation, and only use the subset of the corpus that corresponds to the translation direction of the task in training their translation model.

We use these results as our departure point, but improve them in two major ways. First, we demonstrate that the other subset of the corpus, reflecting translation in the 'wrong' direction, is also important for the translation task, and must not be ignored; second, we show that explicit information on the direction of translation of the parallel corpus, whether manually-annotated or machine-learned, is not mandatory. This is achieved by casting the problem in the framework of domain adaptation: we use domain-adaptation techniques to direct the SMT system toward producing output that better reflects the properties of translationese. We show that SMT systems adapted to translationese produce better translations than vanilla systems trained on exactly the same resources. We confirm these findings using an automatic evaluation metric, BLEU (Papineni et al., 2002), as well as through a qualitative analysis of the results.

Our departure point is the results of Kurokawa et al. (2009), which we successfully replicate in Section 3. First (Section 4), we explain *why* translation quality improves when the parallel corpus is translated in the 'right' direction. We do so by showing that the subset of the corpus that was translated in the direction of the translation task (the 'right' direction, henceforth *source-to-target*, or $S \rightarrow T$) yields *phrase tables* that are better suited for translation of the original language than the subset translated in the reverse direction (the 'wrong' direction, henceforth *target-to-source*, or $T \rightarrow S$). We use several statistical measures that indicate the better quality of the phrase tables in the former case.

Then (Section 5), we explore ways to build a translation model that is adapted to the unique properties of translationese. We first show that using the entire parallel corpus, including texts that are translated both in the 'right' and in the 'wrong' direction, improves the quality of the results. Furthermore, we show that the direction of translation used for producing the parallel corpus can be approximated by defining several entropy-based measures that correlate well with translationese, and, consequently, with the quality of the translation.

Specifically, we use the entire corpus, create a single, unified phrase table and then use the statistical measures mentioned above, and in particular *cross-entropy*, as a clue for selecting phrase pairs from this table. The benefit of this method is that not only does it yield the best results, but it also eliminates the need to directly predict the direction of translation of the parallel corpus. The main contribution of this work, therefore, is a methodology that improves the quality of SMT by building translation models that are adapted to the nature of translationese.

2 Related Work

Kurokawa et al. (2009) are the first to address the direction of translation in the context of SMT. Their main finding is that using the $S \rightarrow T$ portion of the parallel corpus results in mucqqh better translation quality than when the $T \rightarrow S$ portion is used for training the translation model. We indeed replicate these results here (Section 3), and view them as a baseline. Additionally, we show that the $T \rightarrow S$ portion is also important for machine translation and thus should not be discarded. Using information-theory measures, and in particular *cross-entropy*, we gain statistically significant improvements in translation quality beyond the results of Kurokawa et al. (2009). Furthermore, we eliminate the need to (manually or automatically) detect the direction of translation of the parallel corpus.

Lembersky et al. (2011) also investigate the relations between translationese and machine translation. Focusing on the *language* model (LM), they show that LMs trained on translated texts yield better translation quality than LMs compiled from original texts. They also show that perplexity is a good discriminator between original and translated texts.

Our current work is closely related to research in domain-adaptation. In a typical domain adaptation scenario, a system is trained on a large corpus of "general" (out-of-domain) training material, with a small portion of in-domain training texts. In our case, the translation model is trained on a large parallel corpus, of which some (generally unknown) subset is "in-domain" ($S \rightarrow T$), and some other subset is "out-of-domain" ($T \rightarrow S$). Most existing adaptation methods focus on selecting in-domain data from a general domain corpus. In particular, perplexity is used to score the sentences in the general-domain corpus according to an in-domain language model. Gao et al. (2002) and Moore and Lewis (2010) apply this method to language modeling, while Foster et al. (2010) and Axelrod et al. (2011) use it on the translation model. Moore and Lewis (2010) suggest a slightly different approach, using cross-entropy *difference* as a ranking function.

Domain adaptation methods are usually applied at the corpus level, while we focus on an adaptation of the *phrase table* used for SMT. In this sense, our work follows Foster et al. (2010), who weigh out-of-domain phrase pairs according to their relevance to the target domain. They use multiple features that help distinguish between phrase pairs in the general domain and those in the specific domain. We rely on features that are motivated by the findings of Translation Studies, having established their relevance through a comparative analysis of the phrase tables. In particular, we use measures such as translation model entropy, inspired by Koehn et al. (2009). Additionally, we apply the method suggested by Moore and Lewis (2010) using perplexity *ratio* instead of cross-entropy difference.

3 Experimental Setup

The tasks we focus on are translation between French and English, in both directions. We use the Hansard corpus, containing transcripts of the Canadian parliament from 1996–2007, as the source of all parallel data. The Hansard is a bilingual French–English corpus comprising approximately 80% English-original texts and 20% French-original texts. Crucially, each sentence pair in the corpus is annotated with the direction of translation. Both English and French are lower-cased and tokenized using MOSES (Koehn et al., 2007). Sentences longer than 80 words are discarded.

To address the effect of the corpus size, we compile six subsets of different sizes (250K, 500K, 750K, 1M, 1.25M and 1.5M parallel sentences) from each portion (English-original and French-original) of the corpus. Additionally, we use the *devtest* section of the Hansard corpus to randomly select French-original and English-original sentences that are used for tuning (1,000 sentences each) and evaluation (5,000 sentences each). French-to-English MT systems are tuned and tested on French-original sentences and English-to-French systems on English-original ones.

To replicate the results of Kurokawa et al. (2009) and set up a baseline, we train twelve French-to-English and twelve English-to-French phrase-based (PB-) SMT systems using the MOSES toolkit (Koehn et al., 2007), each trained on a different subset of the corpus. We use GIZA++ (Och and Ney, 2000) with *grow-diag-final* alignment, and extract phrases of length up to 10 words. We prune the resulting phrase tables as in Johnson et al. (2007), using at most 30 translations per source phrase and discarding singleton phrase pairs.

We construct English and French 5-gram language models from the English and French subsections of the Europarl-V6 corpus (Koehn, 2005), using interpolated modified Kneser-Ney discounting (Chen, 1998) and no cut-off on all n-grams. Europarl consists of a large number of subsets translated from various languages, and is therefore unlikely to be biased towards a specific source language. The reordering model used in all MT systems is trained on the union of the 1.5M French-original and the 1.5M English-original subsets, using *msd-bidirectional-fe* reordering. We use the MERT algorithm (Och, 2003) for tuning and BLEU (Papineni et al., 2002) as our evaluation metric. We test the statistical significance of the differences between the results using the bootstrap resampling method (Koehn, 2004).

A word on notation: We use 'English-original' (EO) and 'French-original' (FO) to refer to the subsets of the corpus that are translated from English to French and from French to English, respectively. The translation tasks are English-to-French (E2F) and French-to-English (F2E). We thus use '$S \rightarrow T$' when the FO corpus is used for the F2E task or when the EO corpus is used for the E2F task; and '$T \rightarrow S$' when the FO corpus is used for the E2F task or when the EO corpus is used for the F2E task.

Table 1 depicts the BLEU scores of the baseline systems. The data are consistent with the findings of Kurokawa et al. (2009): systems trained on $S \rightarrow T$ parallel texts outperform systems trained on $T \rightarrow S$ texts, even when the latter are much larger. The difference in BLEU score can be as high as 3 points.

4 Analysis of the Phrase Tables

The baseline results suggest that $S \rightarrow T$ and $T \rightarrow S$ phrase tables differ substantially, presumably due to the different characteristics of original

Task: French-to-English		
Corpus subset	$S \rightarrow T$	$T \rightarrow S$
250K	34.35	31.33
500K	35.21	32.38
750K	36.12	32.90
1M	35.73	33.07
1.25M	36.24	33.23
1.5M	36.43	33.73
Task: English-to-French		
Corpus subset	$S \rightarrow T$	$T \rightarrow S$
250K	27.74	26.58
500K	29.15	27.19
750K	29.43	27.63
1M	29.94	27.88
1.25M	30.63	27.84
1.5M	29.89	27.83

Table 1: BLEU scores of baseline systems

and translated texts. In this section we explain the better translation quality in terms of the better quality of the respective phrase tables, as defined by a number of statistical measures. We first relate these measures to the unique properties of translationese.

Translated texts tend to be simpler than original ones along a number of criteria. Generally, translated texts are not as rich and variable as original ones, and in particular, their type/token ratio is lower. Consequently, we expect $S \rightarrow T$ phrase tables (which are based on a parallel corpus whose source is original texts, and whose target is translationese) to have more unique source phrases and a lower number of translations per source phrase. A large number of unique source phrases suggests better coverage of the source text, while a small number of translations per source phrase means a lower phrase table entropy. Entropy-based measures are well-established tools to assess the quality of a phrase table. Phrase table entropy captures the amount of uncertainty involved in choosing candidate translation phrases (Koehn et al., 2009).

Given a source phrase s and a phrase table T with translations t of s whose probabilities are $p(t|s)$, the entropy H of s is:

$$H(s) = -\sum_{t \in T} p(t|s) \times log_2 p(t|s) \qquad (1)$$

There are two major flavors of the phrase table entropy metric: Lambert et al. (2011) calculate the average entropy over all translation options for each source phrase (henceforth, *phrase table entropy* or *PtEnt*), whereas Koehn et al. (2009) search through all possible segmentations of the source sentence to find the optimal covering set of test sentences that minimizes the average entropy of the source phrases in the covering set (henceforth, *covering set entropy* or *CovEnt*).

We also propose a metric that assesses the quality of the *source* side of a phrase table. The metric finds the minimal covering set of a given text in the source language using source phrases from a particular phrase table, and outputs the average length of a phrase in the covering set (henceforth, *covering set average length* or *CovLen*).

Lembersky et al. (2011) show that *perplexity* distinguishes well between translated and original texts. Moreover, perplexity reflects the degree of 'relatedness' of a given phrase to original language or to translationese. Motivated by this observation, we design two cross-entropy-based measures to assess how well each phrase table fits the genre of translationese. Since MT systems are evaluated against human translations, we believe that this factor may have a significant impact on translation performance. The cross-entropy of a text $T = w_1, w_2, \cdots w_N$ according to a language model L is:

$$H(T, L) = -\frac{1}{N}\sum_{i=1}^{N} log_2 L(w_i) \qquad (2)$$

We build language models of translated texts as follows. For English translationese, we extract 170,000 French-original sentences from the English portion of Europarl, and 3,000 English-translated-from-French sentences from the Hansard corpus (disjoint from the training, development and test sets, of course). We use each corpus to train a trigram language model with interpolated modified Kneser-Ney discounting and no cut-off. All out-of-vocabulary words are mapped to a special token, $\langle unk \rangle$. Then, we interpolate the Hansard and Europarl language models to minimize the perplexity of the target side of the development set ($\lambda = 0.58$). For French translationese, we use 270,000 sentences from Europarl and 3,000 sentences from Hansard, $\lambda = 0.81$. Finally, we compute the cross-entropy of each target phrase in the phrase tables according to these language models.

As with the entropy-based measures, we define two cross-entropy metrics: *phrase table cross-entropy* or *PtCrEnt* calculates the average cross-entropy over weighted cross-entropies of all translation options for each source phrase, and *covering set cross-entropy* or *CovCrEnt* finds the optimal covering set of test sentences that minimizes the weighted cross-entropy of the source phrase in the covering set. Given a phrase table T and a language model L, the weighted cross-entropy W for a source phrase s is:

$$W(s, L) = -\sum_{t \in T} H(t, L) \times p(t|s) \quad (3)$$

where $H(t, L)$ is the cross-entropy of t according to a language model L.

Table 2 depicts various statistical measures computed on the phrase tables corresponding to our 24 SMT systems.[1] The data meet our preliminary expectations: $S \rightarrow T$ phrase tables have more unique source phrases, but fewer translation options per source phrase. They have lower entropy and cross-entropy, but higher covering set length.

In order to asses the correspondence of each measure to translation quality, we compute the correlation of BLEU scores from Table 1 with each of the measures specified in Table 2; we compute the correlation coefficient R^2 (the square of Pearson's product-moment correlation coefficient) by fitting a simple linear regression model. Table 3 lists the results. Only the *covering set cross-entropy* measure shows stability over the French-to-English and English-to-French translation tasks, with R^2 equals to 0.56 and 0.54, respectively. Other measures are sensitive to the translation task: *covering set entropy* has the highest correlation with BLEU ($R^2 = 0.94$) when translating French-to-English, but it drops to 0.46 for the reverse task. The *covering set average length* measure shows similar behavior: R^2 drops from 0.75 in French-to-English to 0.56 in English-to-French. Still, the correlation of these measures with BLEU is high.

Consequently, we use the three best measures, namely *covering set entropy*, *cross-entropy* and *average length*, as indicators of better translations, more similar to translationese. Crucially,

Measure	R^2 (FR–EN)	R^2 (EN-FR)
AvgTran	0.06	0.22
PtEnt	0.03	0.19
CovEnt	**0.94**	0.46
PtCrEnt	0.33	0.44
CovCrEnt	0.56	0.54
CovLen	0.75	**0.56**

Table 3: Correlation of BLEU scores with phrase table statistical measures

these measures are computed directly on the phrase table, and do not require reference translations or meta-information pertaining to the direction of translation of the parallel phrase.

5 Translation Model Adaptation

We have thus established the fact that $S \rightarrow T$ phrase tables have an advantage over $T \rightarrow S$ ones that stems directly from the different characteristics of original and translated texts. We have also identified three statistical measures that explain most of the variability in translation quality. We now explore ways for taking advantage of the *entire* parallel corpus, including translations in *both* directions, in light of the above findings. Our goal is to establish the best method to address the issue of different translation direction components in the parallel corpus.

First, we simply take the union of the two subsets of the parallel corpus. We create three different mixtures of FO and EO: 500K sentences each of FO and EO ('MIX1'), 500K sentences of FO and 1M sentences of EO ('MIX2'), and 1M sentences of FO and 500K sentences of EO ('MIX3'). We use these corpora to train French-to-English and English-to-French MT systems, evaluating their quality on the evaluation sets described in Section 3. We use the same Moses configuration as well as the same language and reordering models as in Section 3.

Table 4 reports the results, comparing them to the results obtained for the baseline MT systems trained on individual French-original and English-original bi-texts (see Section 3).[2] Note that the mixed corpus includes many more sentences than each of the baseline models; this is a

[1]The phrase tables were pruned, retaining only phrases that are included in the evaluation set.

[2]Recall that when translating from French to English, $S \rightarrow T$ means that the bi-text is French-original; when translating from English to French, $S \rightarrow T$ means it is English-original.

Set	Total	Source	AvgTran	PtEnt	CovEnt	PtCrEnt	CovCrEnt	CovLen
Task: French-to-English								
$S \rightarrow T$								
250K	231K	69K	3.35	0.86	0.36	3.94	1.64	2.44
500K	360K	86K	4.21	0.98	0.35	3.52	1.30	2.64
750K	461K	96K	4.81	1.05	0.35	3.24	1.10	2.77
1M	544K	103K	5.27	1.10	0.34	3.09	0.99	2.85
1.25M	619K	109K	5.66	1.14	0.34	2.98	0.91	2.92
1.5M	684K	114K	6.01	1.18	0.33	2.90	0.85	2.97
$T \rightarrow S$								
250K	199K	55K	3.65	0.92	0.45	4.00	1.87	2.25
500K	317K	69K	4.56	1.05	0.43	3.57	1.52	2.42
750K	405K	78K	5.19	1.12	0.43	3.39	1.35	2.53
1M	479K	85K	5.66	1.16	0.42	3.21	1.21	2.61
1.25M	545K	90K	6.07	1.20	0.41	3.11	1.12	2.67
1.5M	602K	94K	6.43	1.24	0.41	3.04	1.07	2.71
Task: English-to-French								
Set	Total	Source	AvgTran	PtEnt	CovEnt	PtCrEnt	CovCrEnt	CovLen
$S \rightarrow T$								
250K	224K	49K	4.52	1.07	0.63	3.48	1.88	2.08
500K	346K	61K	5.64	1.21	0.59	3.08	1.49	2.25
750K	437K	68K	6.39	1.29	0.57	2.91	1.33	2.33
1M	513K	74K	6.95	1.34	0.55	2.75	1.18	2.41
1.25M	579K	78K	7.42	1.38	0.54	2.63	1.09	2.46
1.5M	635K	81K	7.83	1.41	0.53	2.58	1.03	2.50
$T \rightarrow S$								
250K	220K	46K	4.75	1.12	0.63	3.62	2.09	2.02
500K	334K	57K	5.82	1.24	0.60	3.24	1.70	2.16
750K	421K	64K	6.54	1.31	0.58	2.97	1.48	2.25
1M	489K	69K	7.10	1.36	0.57	2.84	1.35	2.32
1.25M	550K	73K	7.56	1.40	0.55	2.74	1.25	2.37
1.5M	603K	76K	7.92	1.43	0.55	2.66	1.17	2.41

Table 2: Statistic measures computed on the phrase tables: total size, in tokens ('Total'); the number of unique source phrases ('Source'); the average number of translations per source phrase ('AvgTran'); phrase table entropy ('PtEnt') and covering set entropy ('CovEnt'); phrase table cross-entropy ('PtCrEnt') and covering set cross-entropy ('CovCrEnt'); and the covering set average length ('CovLen')

realistic scenario, in which one can opt either to use the entire parallel corpus, or only its $S \rightarrow T$ subset. Even with a corpus several times as large, however, the 'mixed' MT systems perform only slightly better than the $S \rightarrow T$ ones. On one hand, this means that one can train MT systems on $S \rightarrow T$ data only, at the expense of only a minor loss in quality. On the other hand, it is obvious that the $T \rightarrow S$ component also contributes to translation quality. We now look at ways to better utilize this portion.

We compute the measures established in the previous section on phrase tables trained on the MIX corpora, and compare them with the same measures computed for phrase tables trained on the relevant $S \rightarrow T$ corpus for both translation tasks. Table 5 displays the figures for the MIX1 corpus: Phrase tables trained on mixed corpora have higher covering set average length, similar covering set entropy, but significantly worse covering set cross-entropy. Consequently, improving covering set cross-entropy has the greatest potential for improving translation quality. We therefore use this feature to 'encourage' the decoder to

Task: French-to-English			
System	**MIX1**	**MIX2**	**MIX3**
Union	**35.27**	**35.36**	**35.94**
$S \to T$	35.21	35.21	35.73
$T \to S$	32.38	33.07	32.38
Task: English-to-French			
System	**MIX1**	**MIX2**	**MIX3**
Union	**29.27**	**30.01**	**29.44**
$S \to T$	29.15	29.94	29.15
$T \to S$	27.19	27.19	27.88

Table 4: Evaluation of the MIX systems

select translation options that are more related to the genre of translated texts.

French-to-English		
Measure	MIX1	$S \to T$
CovLen	2.78	2.64
CovEnt	0.37	0.35
CovCrEnt	1.58	1.10
English-to-French		
Measure	MIX1	$S \to T$
CovLen	2.40	2.25
CovEnt	0.55	0.58
CovCrEnt	2.09	1.48

Table 5: Statistical measures computed for mixed vs. source-to-target phrase tables

We do so by adding to each phrase pair in the phrase tables an additional factor, as a measure of its fitness to the genre of translationese. We experiment with two such factors. First, we use the language models described in Section 4 to compute the cross-entropy of each translation option according to this model. We add cross-entropy as an additional score of a translation pair that can be tuned by MERT (we refer to this system as *CrEnt*). Since cross-entropy is 'the lower the better' metric, we adjust the range of values used by MERT for this score to be negative. Second, following Moore and Lewis (2010), we define an adapting feature that not only measures how close phrases are to translated language, but also how far they are from original language, and use it as a factor in a phrase table (this system is referred to as *PplRatio*). We build two additional language models of original texts as follows. For original English, we extract 135,000 English-original sentences from the English portion of Europarl, and 2,700 English-original sentences from the Hansard corpus. We train a trigram language model with interpolated modified Kneser-Ney discounting on each corpus and we interpolate both models to minimize the perplexity of the source side of the development set for the English-to-French translation task ($\lambda = 0.49$). For original French, we use 110,000 sentences from Europarl and 2,900 sentences from Hansard, $\lambda = 0.61$. Finally, for each target phrase t in the phrase table we compute the ratio of the perplexity of t according to the original language model L_o and the perplexity of t with respect to the translated model L_t (see Section 4). In other words, the factor F is computed as follows:

$$F(t) = \frac{H(t, L_o)}{H(t, L_t)} \quad (4)$$

We apply these techniques to the French-to-English and English-to-French phrase tables built from the mixed corpora and use each phrase table to train an SMT system. Table 6 summarizes the performance of these systems. All systems outperform the corresponding Union systems. 'CrEnt' systems show significant improvements ($p < 0.05$) on balanced scenarios ('MIX1') and on scenarios biased towards the $S \to T$ component ('MIX2' in the French-to-English task, 'MIX3' in English-to-French). 'PplRatio' systems exhibit more consistent behavior, showing small, but statistically significant improvement ($p < 0.05$) in all scenarios.

Task: French-to-English			
System	**MIX1**	**MIX2**	**MIX3**
Union	35.27	35.36	35.94
CrEnt	35.54	35.45	**36.75**
PplRatio	**35.59**	**35.78**	36.22
Task: English-to-French			
System	**MIX1**	**MIX2**	**MIX3**
Union	29.27	30.01	29.44
CrEnt	29.47	**30.44**	29.45
PplRatio	**29.65**	30.34	**29.62**

Table 6: Evaluation of MT Systems

Note again that all systems in the same column are trained on exactly the same corpus and have exactly the same phrase tables. The only difference is an additional factor in the phrase table that "encourages" the decoder to select translation options that are closer to translated texts than to original ones.

6 Analysis

In order to study the effect of the adaptation qualitatively, rather than quantitatively, we focus on several concrete examples. We compare translations produced by the 'Union' (henceforth *baseline*) and by the 'PplRatio' (henceforth *adapted*) French-English SMT systems. We manually inspect 200 sentences of length between 15 and 25 from the French-English evaluation set.

In many cases, the adapted system produces more fluent and accurate translations. In the following examples, the baseline system generates common translations of French words that are adequate for a wider context, whereas the adapted system chooses less common, but more suitable translations:

Source *J'ai eu cette perception et j'étais* ***assez*** *certain que ça allait se faire.*

Baseline *I had that perception and I was* ***enough*** *certain it was going do.*

Adapted *I had that perception and I was* ***quite*** *certain it was going do.*

Source ***J'attends*** *donc que vous en demandiez la permission, monsieur le Président.*

Baseline ***I look*** *so that you seek permission, mr. chairman.*

Adapted ***I await****, then, that you seek permission, mr. chairman.*

In quite a few cases, the baseline system leaves out important words from the source sentence, producing ungrammatical, even illegible translations, whereas the adapted system generates good translations. Careful traceback reveals that the baseline system 'splits' the source sentence into phrases differently (and less optimally) than the adapted system. Apparently, when the decoder is coerced to select translation options that are more adapted to translationese, it tends to select source phrases that are more related to original texts, resulting in more successful coverage of the source sentence:

Source *Pourtant, lorsqu' on les avait présentés, c'était pour corriger les problèmes liés au PCSRA.*

Baseline *Yet when they had presented, it was to correct the problems the CAIS program.*

Adapted *Yet when they had presented, it was to correct the problems* ***associated*** *with CAIS.*

Source *Cependant, je pense qu'il est prématuré* ***de le faire actuellement****, étant donné que le ministre a lancé cette tournée.*

Baseline *However, I think it is premature* ***to the right now****, since the minister launched this tour.*

Adapted *However, I think it is premature* ***to do so now****, given that the minister has launched this tour.*

Finally, there are often cultural differences between languages, specifically the use of a 24-hour clock (common in French) vs. a 12-hour clock (common in English). The adapted system is more consistent in translating the former to the latter:

Source *On avait décidé de poursuivre la séance jusqu' à* ***18 heures****, mais on n'aura pas le temps de faire un autre tour de table.*

Baseline *We had decided to continue the meeting until* ***18 hours****, but we will not have the time to do another round.*

Adapted *We had decided to continue the meeting until* ***6 p.m.****, but we won't have the time to do another round.*

Source *Vu qu'il est* ***17h 20****, je suis d'accord pour qu'on ne discute pas de ma motion immédiatement.*

Baseline *Seen that it is* ***17h 20****, I agree that we are not talking about my motion immediately.*

Adapted *Given that it is* ***5:20****, I agree that we are not talking about my motion immediately.*

In (human) translation circles, translating *out of* one's mother tongue is considered unprofessional, even unethical (Beeby, 2009). Many professional associations in Europe urge translators to work exclusively into their mother tongue (Pavlović, 2007). The two kinds of automatic systems built in this paper reflect only partly the human situation, but they do so in a crucial way. The $S \rightarrow T$ systems learn examples from many human translators who follow the decree according to which translation should be made *into* one's native tongue. The $T \rightarrow S$ systems are flipped directions of humans' input and output. The $S \rightarrow T$ direction proved to be more fluent, accurate and even more culturally sensitive. This has to do with fact that the translators 'cover' the source texts more fully, having a better 'translation model'.

7 Conclusion

Phrase tables trained on parallel corpora that were translated in the same direction as the translation task perform better than ones trained on corpora translated in the opposite direction. Nonetheless, even 'wrong' phrase tables contribute to the translation quality. We analyze both 'correct' and 'wrong' phrase tables, uncovering a great deal of difference between them. We use insights from Translation Studies to explain these differences; we then adapt the translation model to the nature of translationese.

We incorporate information-theoretic measures that correlate well with translationese into phrase tables as an additional score that can be tuned by MERT, and show a statistically significant improvement in the translation quality over all baseline systems. We also analyze the results qualitatively, showing that SMT systems adapted to translationese tend to produce more coherent and fluent outputs than the baseline systems. An additional advantage of our approach is that it does not require an annotation of the translation direction of the parallel corpus. It is completely generic and can be applied to any language pair, domain or corpus.

This work can be extended in various directions. We plan to further explore the use of two phrase tables, one for each direction-determined subset of the parallel corpus. Specifically, we will interpolate the translation models as in Foster and Kuhn (2007), including a *maximum a posteriori* combination (Bacchiani et al., 2006). We also plan to upweight the $S \rightarrow T$ subset of the parallel corpus and train a single phrase table on the concatenated corpus. Finally, we intend to extend this work by combining the translation-model adaptation we present here with the language-model adaptation suggested by Lembersky et al. (2011) in a unified system that is more tuned to generating translationese.

Acknowledgments

We are grateful to Cyril Goutte, George Foster and Pierre Isabelle for providing us with an annotated version of the Hansard corpus. This research was supported by the Israel Science Foundation (grant No. 137/06) and by a grant from the Israeli Ministry of Science and Technology.

References

Amittai Axelrod, Xiaodong He, and Jianfeng Gao. Domain adaptation via pseudo in-domain data selection. In *Proceedings of the 2011 Conference on Empirical Methods in Natural Language Processing*, pages 355–362. Association for Computational Linguistics, July 2011. URL http://www.aclweb.org/anthology/D11-1033.

Michiel Bacchiani, Michael Riley, Brian Roark, and Richard Sproat. MAP adaptation of stochastic grammars. *Computer Speech and Language*, 20:41–68, January 2006. ISSN 0885-2308. doi: 10.1016/j.csl.2004.12.001. URL http://dl.acm.org/citation.cfm?id=1648820.1648854.

Mona Baker. Corpus linguistics and translation studies: Implications and applications. In Gill Francis Mona Baker and Elena Tognini-Bonelli, editors, *Text and technology: in honour of John Sinclair*, pages 233–252. John Benjamins, Amsterdam, 1993.

Mona Baker. Corpora in translation studies: An overview and some suggestions for future research. *Target*, 7(2):223–243, September 1995.

Mona Baker. Corpus-based translation studies: The challenges that lie ahead. In Gill Francis Mona Baker and Elena Tognini-Bonelli, editors, *Terminology, LSP and Translation. Studies in language engineering in honour of Juan C. Sager*, pages 175–186. John Benjamins, Amsterdam, 1996.

Marco Baroni and Silvia Bernardini. A new approach to the study of Translationese: Machine-learning the difference between original and translated text. *Literary and Linguistic Computing*, 21(3):259–274, September 2006. URL http://llc.oxfordjournals.org/cgi/content/short/21/3/259?rss=1.

Alison Beeby. Direction of translation (directionality). In Mona Baker and Gabriela Saldanha, editors, *Routledge Encyclopedia of Translation Studies*, pages 84–88. Routledge (Taylor and Francis), New York, 2nd edition, 2009.

Stanley F. Chen. An empirical study of smoothing techniques for language modeling. Technical report 10-98, Computer Science Group, Harvard University, November 1998.

George Foster and Roland Kuhn. Mixture-model adaptation for SMT. In *Proceedings of the Second Workshop on Statistical Machine Translation*, pages 128–135. Association for Computational Linguistics, June 2007. URL http://www.aclweb.org/anthology/W/W07/W07-0717.

George Foster, Cyril Goutte, and Roland Kuhn. Discriminative instance weighting for domain adaptation in statistical machine translation. In

Proceedings of the 2010 Conference on Empirical Methods in Natural Language Processing, pages 451–459, Stroudsburg, PA, USA, 2010. Association for Computational Linguistics. URL http://dl.acm.org/citation.cfm?id=1870658.1870702.

Jianfeng Gao, Joshua Goodman, Mingjing Li, and Kai-Fu Lee. Toward a unified approach to statistical language modeling for Chinese. *ACM Transactions on Asian Language Information Processing*, 1:3–33, March 2002. ISSN 1530-0226. doi: http://doi.acm.org/10.1145/595576.595578. URL http://doi.acm.org/10.1145/595576.595578.

Martin Gellerstam. Translationese in Swedish novels translated from English. In Lars Wollin and Hans Lindquist, editors, *Translation Studies in Scandinavia*, pages 88–95. CWK Gleerup, Lund, 1986.

Iustina Ilisei, Diana Inkpen, Gloria Corpas Pastor, and Ruslan Mitkov. Identification of translationese: A machine learning approach. In Alexander F. Gelbukh, editor, *Proceedings of CICLing-2010: 11th International Conference on Computational Linguistics and Intelligent Text Processing*, volume 6008 of *Lecture Notes in Computer Science*, pages 503–511. Springer, 2010. ISBN 978-3-642-12115-9. URL http://dx.doi.org/10.1007/978-3-642-12116-6.

Howard Johnson, Joel Martin, George Foster, and Roland Kuhn. Improving translation quality by discarding most of the phrasetable. In *Proceedings of the Joint Conference on Empirical Methods in Natural Language Processing and Computational Natural Language Learning (EMNLP-CoNLL)*, pages 967–975. Association for Computational Linguistics, June 2007. URL http://www.aclweb.org/anthology/D/D07/D07-1103.

Philipp Koehn. Statistical significance tests for machine translation evaluation. In *Proceedings of EMNLP 2004*, pages 388–395, Barcelona, Spain, July 2004. Association for Computational Linguistics.

Philipp Koehn. Europarl: A Parallel Corpus for Statistical Machine Translation. In *Conference Proceedings: the tenth Machine Translation Summit*, pages 79–86, Phuket, Thailand, 2005. AAMT. URL http://mt-archive.info/MTS-2005-Koehn.pdf.

Philipp Koehn, Hieu Hoang, Alexandra Birch, Chris Callison-Burch, Marcello Federico, Nicola Bertoldi, Brooke Cowan, Wade Shen, Christine Moran, Richard Zens, Chris Dyer, Ondrej Bojar, Alexandra Constantin, and Evan Herbst. Moses: Open source toolkit for statistical machine translation. In *Proceedings of the 45th Annual Meeting of the Association for Computational Linguistics Companion Volume Proceedings of the Demo and Poster Sessions*, pages 177–180, Prague, Czech Republic, June 2007. Association for Computational Linguistics. URL http://www.aclweb.org/anthology/P07-2045.

Philipp Koehn, Alexandra Birch, and Ralf Steinberger. 462 machine translation systems for Europe. In *Machine Translation Summit XII*, 2009.

Moshe Koppel and Noam Ordan. Translationese and its dialects. In *Proceedings of the 49th Annual Meeting of the Association for Computational Linguistics: Human Language Technologies*, pages 1318–1326, Portland, Oregon, USA, June 2011. Association for Computational Linguistics. URL http://www.aclweb.org/anthology/P11-1132.

David Kurokawa, Cyril Goutte, and Pierre Isabelle. Automatic detection of translated text and its impact on machine translation. In *Proceedings of MT-Summit XII*, 2009.

Patrik Lambert, Holger Schwenk, Christophe Servan, and Sadaf Abdul-Rauf. Investigations on translation model adaptation using monolingual data. In *Proceedings of the Sixth Workshop on Statistical Machine Translation*, pages 284–293. Association for Computational Linguistics, July 2011. URL http://www.aclweb.org/anthology/W11-2132.

Gennadi Lembersky, Noam Ordan, and Shuly Wintner. Language models for machine translation: Original vs. translated texts. In *Proceedings of the 2011 Conference on Empirical Methods in Natural Language Processing*, pages 363–374, Edinburgh, Scotland, UK, July 2011. Association for Computational Linguistics. URL http://www.aclweb.org/anthology/D11-1034.

Robert C. Moore and William Lewis. Intelligent selection of language model training data. In *Proceedings of the ACL 2010 Conference, Short Papers*, pages 220–224, Stroudsburg, PA, USA, 2010. Association for Computational Linguistics. URL http://dl.acm.org/citation.cfm?id=1858842.1858883.

Franz Josef Och. Minimum error rate training in statistical machine translation. In *ACL '03: Proceedings of the 41st Annual Meeting on Association for Computational Linguistics*, pages 160–167, Morristown, NJ, USA, 2003. Association for Computational Linguistics. doi: http://dx.doi.org/10.3115/1075096.1075117.

Franz Josef Och and Hermann Ney. Improved statistical alignment models. In *ACL '00: Proceedings of the 38th Annual Meeting on Association for Computational Linguistics*, pages 440–447, Morristown,

NJ, USA, 2000. Association for Computational Linguistics. doi: http://dx.doi.org/10.3115/1075218.1075274.

Kishore Papineni, Salim Roukos, Todd Ward, and Wei-Jing Zhu. BLEU: a method for automatic evaluation of machine translation. In *ACL '02: Proceedings of the 40th Annual Meeting on Association for Computational Linguistics*, pages 311–318, Morristown, NJ, USA, 2002. Association for Computational Linguistics. doi: http://dx.doi.org/10.3115/1073083.1073135.

Nataša Pavlović. Directionality in translation and interpreting practice. Report on a questionnaire survey in Croatia. *Forum*, 5(2):79–99, 2007.

Gideon Toury. *In Search of a Theory of Translation*. The Porter Institute for Poetics and Semiotics, Tel Aviv University, Tel Aviv, 1980.

Gideon Toury. *Descriptive Translation Studies and beyond*. John Benjamins, Amsterdam / Philadelphia, 1995.

Hans van Halteren. Source language markers in EUROPARL translations. In *COLING '08: Proceedings of the 22nd International Conference on Computational Linguistics*, pages 937–944, Morristown, NJ, USA, 2008. Association for Computational Linguistics. ISBN 978-1-905593-44-6.

Aspectual Type and Temporal Relation Classification

Francisco Costa
Universidade de Lisboa
fcosta@di.fc.ul.pt

António Branco
Universidade de Lisboa
Antonio.Branco@di.fc.ul.pt

Abstract

In this paper we investigate the relevance of aspectual type for the problem of temporal information processing, i.e. the problems of the recent TempEval challenges.

For a large list of verbs, we obtain several indicators about their lexical aspect by querying the web for expressions where these verbs occur in contexts associated with specific aspectual types.

We then proceed to extend existing solutions for the problem of temporal information processing with the information extracted this way. The improved performance of the resulting models shows that (i) aspectual type can be data-mined with unsupervised methods with a level of noise that does not prevent this information from being useful and that (ii) temporal information processing can profit from information about aspectual type.

1 Introduction

Extracting the temporal information present in a text is relevant to many natural language processing applications, including question-answering, information extraction, and even document summarization, as summaries may be more readable if they follow a chronological order.

Recent evaluation campaigns have focused on the extraction of temporal information from written text. TempEval (Verhagen et al., 2007), in 2007, and more recently TempEval-2 (Verhagen et al., 2010), in 2010, were concerned with this problem. Additionally, they provided data that can be used to develop and evaluate systems that can automatically temporally tag natural language text. These data are annotated according to the TimeML (Pustejovsky et al., 2003) scheme.

Figure 1 shows a small and slightly simplified fragment of the data from TempEval, with TimeML annotations. There, event terms, such as the term referring to the event of releasing the tapes, are annotated using `EVENT` tags. States (such as the situations denoted by verbs like *want* or *love*) are also considered events. Temporal expressions, such as *today*, are enclosed in `TIMEX3` tags. The attribute `value` of time expressions holds a normalized representation of the date or time they refer to (e.g. the word *today* denotes the date `1998-01-14` in this example). The `TLINK` elements at the end describe temporal relations between events and temporal expressions. For instance, the event of the plane going down is annotated as temporally preceding the date denoted by the temporal expression *today*.

The major tasks of these two TempEval evaluation challenges were about guessing the type of temporal relations, i.e. the value of the `relType` attribute of the `TLINK` elements in Figure 1, all other annotations being given. Temporal relation classification is also the most interesting problem in temporal information processing. The other relevant tasks (identifying and normalizing temporal expressions and events) have a longer research history and show better evaluation results.

TempEval was organized in three tasks (TempEval-2 has four additional ones, that are not relevant to this work): task A was concerned with classifying temporal relations holding between an event and a time mentioned in the same sentence (although they could be syntactically unrelated, as the temporal relation represented by the `TLINK` with the `lid` with the value `l1` in Figure 1); task

```
<s>In Washington <TIMEX3 tid="t53" type="DATE"
value="1998-01-14">today</TIMEX3>, the Federal
Aviation Administration <EVENT eid="e1"
class="OCCURRENCE" stem="release"
aspect="NONE" tense="PAST" polarity="POS"
pos="VERB">released</EVENT> air traffic control tapes from
<TIMEX3 tid="t54" type="TIME"
value="1998-XX-XXTNI">the night</TIMEX3> the TWA
Flight eight hundred <EVENT eid="e2"
class="OCCURRENCE" stem="go" aspect="NONE"
tense="PAST" polarity="POS"
pos="VERB">went</EVENT> down.</s>
<TLINK lid="l1" relType="BEFORE" eventID="e2"
relatedToTime="t53"/>
<TLINK lid="l2" relType="OVERLAP"
eventID="e2" relatedToTime="t54"/>
```

Figure 1: Sample of the data annotated for TempEval, corresponding to the fragment: *In Washington today, the Federal Aviation Administration released air traffic control tapes from the night the TWA Flight eight hundred went down.*

	Task		
	A	B	C
Best system	0.62	0.80	0.55
Average of all participants	0.56	0.74	0.51
Majority class baseline	0.57	0.56	0.47

Table 1: Results for English in TempEval (F-measure), from Verhagen et al. (2009)

B focused on the temporal relation between events and the document's creation time, which is also annotated in TimeML (not shown in that Figure); and task C was about classifying the temporal relation between the main events of two consecutive sentences. The possible values for the type of temporal relation are BEFORE, AFTER and OVERLAP.[1]

Table 1 shows the results of the first TempEval evaluation. The results of TempEval-2 are fairly similar (Verhagen et al., 2010), but the data used are similar but not identical.

The best system in TempEval for tasks A and B (Puşcaşu, 2007) combined statistical and knowledge based methods to propagate temporal constraints along parse trees coming from a syntactic parser. The best system for task C (Min et al., 2007) also combined rule-based and machine learning approaches. It employed sophisticated NLP to compute some of the features used; more specifically it used syntactic features.

Our goal with this work is to evaluate the impact of information about aspectual type on these tasks. The TimeML annotations include an attribute `class` for EVENTs that encodes some aspectual information, distinguishing between stative (annotated with the value STATE) and non-stative events (value OCCURRENCE). This attribute is relevant to the classification problem at hand, i.e. it is a useful feature for machine learned classifiers for the TempEval tasks (although this `class` attribute encodes other kinds of information as well). However, aspectual distinctions can be more fine-grained than a mere binary distinction, and so far no system has explored this sort of information to help improve the solutions to temporal relation classification.

In this paper we work with Portuguese, but in principle there is no reason to believe that our findings would not apply to other languages that display similar aspectual phenomena, such as English. Some of the details, such as the material in Section 4.2, are however language specific and would need adaptation.

2 Aspectual Type

Distinctions of aspectual type (also referred to as situation type, lexical aspect or *Aktionsart*) of the sort of Vendler (1967) and Dowty (1979) are expected to improve the existing solutions to the problem of temporal relation classification. The major aspectual distinctions are between (i) states (e.g. *to hate beer, to know the answer, to own a car, to stink*), (ii) processes, also called activities (*to work, to eat ice cream, to grow, to play the piano*), (iii) culminated processes, also called accomplishments (*to paint a picture, to burn down, to deliver a sermon*) and (iv) culminations, also called achievements (*to explode, to win the game, to find the key*). States and processes are atelic situations in that they do not make salient a specific instant in time. Culminated processes and culminations are telic situations: they have an intrinsic, instantaneous endpoint, called the culmination (e.g. in the case of *to paint a picture*, it is the moment when the picture is ready; in the case of *to explode*, it is the moment of the explosion).

There are several reasons to think aspectual

[1]There are the additional disjunctive values BEFORE-OR-OVERLAP, OVERLAP-OR-AFTER and VAGUE, employed when the annotators could not make a more specific decision, but these affect a small number of instances.

type is relevant to temporal information processing. First, these distinctions are related to how long events last: culminations are punctual, whereas states can be very prolonged in time. States are thus more likely to temporally overlap other temporal entities than culminations, for instance.

Second, there are grammatical consequences on how events are anchored in time. Consider the following examples, from Ritchie (1979) and Moens and Steedman (1988):

(1) When they built the 59th Street bridge, they used the best materials.

(2) When they built that bridge, I was still a young lad.

The situation of building the bridge is a culminated processed, composed by the process of actively building a bridge followed by the culmination of the bridge being finished. In sentence (1), the event described in the main clause (that of using the best materials) is a process, but in sentence (2) it is a state (the state of being a young lad). Even though the two clauses in each sentence are connected by *when*, the temporal relations holding between the events of each clause are different. On the one hand, in sentence (1) the event of using the best materials (a process) overlaps with the process of actively building the bridge and precedes the culmination of finishing the bridge. On the other hand, in sentence (2) the event of being a young lad (which is a state) overlaps with both the process of actively building the bridge and the culmination of the bridge being built. This difference is arguably caused by the different aspectual types of the main events of each sentence.

As another example, states overlap with temporal location adverbials, as in (3), while culminations are included in them, as in (4).

(3) He was happy last Monday.

(4) He reached the top of Mount Everest last Monday.

In other cases, differences in aspectual type can disambiguate ambiguous linguistic material. For instance, the preposition *in* is ambiguous as it can be used to locate events in the future but also to measure the duration of culminated processes; it is thus ambiguous with culminated processes, as in *he will read the book in three days* but not with other aspectual types, as in *he will be living there in three days*.

A factor related to aspectual class, that is not trivial to account for, is the phenomenon of aspectual shift, or aspectual coercion (Moens and Steedman, 1988; de Swart, 1998; de Swart, 2000). Many linguistic contexts pose constraints on aspectual type. This does not mean, however, that clashes of aspectual type cause ungrammaticality. What often happens is that phrases associated with an incompatible aspectual type get their type changed in order to be of the required type, causing a change in meaning.

For instance, the progressive construction combines with processes. When it combines with e.g. a culminated process, the culmination is stripped off from this culminated process, which is thus converted into a process. The result is that a sentence like (5) does not say that the bridge was finished (the event has no culmination), whereas one such as (6) does say this (the event has a culmination).

(5) They were building that bridge.

(6) They built that bridge.

Aspectual type is not a property of just words, but phrases as well. For example, while the progressive construction just mentioned combines with processes, the resulting phrase behaves as a state (cf. the sentence *When they built the 59th Street bridge, they were using the best materials* and what was mentioned above about *when* clauses).

3 Strategy

Aspectual type is hard to annotate. This is partly because of what was just mentioned: it is not a property of just words, but rather phrases, and different phrases with the same head word can have different aspectual types; however annotation schemes like TimeML annotate the head word as denoting events, not full phrases or clauses.

For this reason, our strategy is to obtain aspectual type information from unannotated data. Because these data are gradient—an event-denoting word can be associated with different aspectual types, depending on word sense—we do not aim to extract categorical information, but rather numeric values for each event term that reflect associations to aspectual types. These may be seen as values that are indicative of the frequencies in which an event term denotes a state, or a process, etc.

In order to extract these indicators, we resort to a methodology sometimes referred to as Google Hits: large amounts of queries are sent to a web search engine (not necessarily Google), and the number of search results (the number of web pages that match the query) is recorded and taken as a measure of the frequency of the queried expression.

This methodology is not perfect, since multiple occurrences of the queried expression in the same web page are not reflected in the hit count, and in many cases the hit counts reported by search engines are just estimates and might not be very accurate. Additionally, uncarefully formulated queries can match expressions that are syntactically and semantically very different from what was intended. In any case, it has the advantages of being based on a very large amount of data and not requiring any manual annotation, which can introduce errors.

3.1 The Web as a Very Large Corpus

Hearst (1992) is one of the earliest studies where specific textual patterns are used to extract lexico-semantic information from very large corpora. The author's goal was to extract hyponymy relations. With the same goal, Kozareva et al. (2008) apply similar textual patterns to the web.

The web has been used as a corpus by many other authors with the purpose of extracting syntactic or semantic properties of words or relations between them, e.g. Ravichandran and Hovy (2002), Etzioni et al. (2004), etc. Some of this work is specially relevant to the problem of temporal information processing. VerbOcean (Chklovski and Pantel, 2004) is a database of web mined relations between verbs. Among other kinds of relations, it includes typical precedence relations, e.g. *sleeping* happens before *waking up*. This type of information has in fact been used by some of the participating systems of TempEval-2 (Ha et al., 2010), with good results.

More generally, there is a large body of work focusing on lexical acquisition from corpora. Just as an example, Mayol et al. (2005) learn subcategorization frames of verbs from large amounts of data. Relevant to our work is that of Siegel and McKeown (2000). The authors guess the aspectual type of verbs by searching for specific patterns in a one million word corpus that has been syntactically parsed. They extract several linguistic indicators and combine them with machine learning algorithms. The indicators that they extract are naturally different from ours, since they have access to syntactic structure and we do not, but our data are based on a much larger corpus.

3.2 Textual Patterns as Indicators of Aspectual Type

Because of aspectual shift phenomena (see Section 2), full syntactic parsing is necessary in order to determine the aspectual type of a natural language expression. However, this can be approximated by frequencies: it is natural to expect that e.g. stative verbs occur more frequently in stative contexts than non-stative verbs, even if there may be errors in determining these contexts if syntactic parsing is not a possibility.

If one uses Google Hits, syntactic information is not accessible. In return for its impreciseness, Google Hits have the advantage of being based on very large amounts of data.

4 Scope and Approach

In this study we focus exclusively on verbs, but events can be denoted by words belonging to other parts-of-speech. This limitation is linked to the fact that the textual patterns that are used to search for specific aspectual contexts are sensitive to part-of-speech (i.e. what may work for a verb may not work equally well for a noun).

In order to assess whether aspectual type information is relevant to the problem of temporal relation classification, our approach is to check whether incorporating that kind of information into existing solutions for this problem can improve their performance. TimeML annotated data, such as those used for TempEval, can be used to train machine learned classifiers. These can then be augmented with attributes encoding aspectual type information and their performance compared to the original classifiers.

Additionally, we work with Portuguese data. This is because our work is part of an effort to implement a temporal processing system for Portuguese. We briefly describe the data next.

```
<s>Em Washington, <TIMEX3 tid="t53" type="DATE"
value="1998-01-14">hoje</TIMEX3>, a Federal Aviation
Administration <EVENT eid="e1" class="OCCURRENCE"
stem="publicar" aspect="NONE" tense="PPI"
polarity="POS" pos="VERB">publicou</EVENT>
gravações do controlo de tráfego aéreo da <TIMEX3
tid="t54" type="TIME"
value="1998-XX-XXTNI">noite</TIMEX3> em que o voo
TWA800 <EVENT eid="e2" class="OCCURRENCE"
stem="cair" aspect="NONE" tense="PPI"
polarity="POS" pos="VERB">caiu</EVENT>.</s>
<TLINK lid="l1" relType="BEFORE" eventID="e2"
relatedToTime="t53"/>
<TLINK lid="l2" relType="OVERLAP"
eventID="e2" relatedToTime="t54"/>
```

Figure 2: Sample of the Portuguese data adapted from the TempEval data, corresponding to the fragment: *Em Washington, hoje, a Federal Aviation Administration publicou gravações do controlo de tráfego aéreo da noite em que o voo TWA800 caiu.*

4.1 Data

Our experiments used TimeBankPT (Costa and Branco, 2010; Costa and Branco, 2012; Costa, to appear). This corpus is an adaptation of the original TempEval data to Portuguese, obtained by translating it and then adapting the annotations. Figure 2 shows the Portuguese equivalent to the sample presented above in Figure 1. The two corpora are quite similar, but there is of course the language difference. TimeBankPT contains a few corrections to the data (mostly the temporal relations), but these corrections only changed around 1.2% of the total number of annotated temporal relations (Costa and Branco, 2012). Although we did not test our results on English data, we speculate that our results carry over to other languages.

Just like the original English corpus for TempEval, it is divided in a training part and a testing part. The numbers (sentences, words, annotated events, time expressions and temporal relations) are fairly similar for the two corpora (the English one and the Portuguese one).

4.2 Extracting the Aspectual Indicators

We extracted the 4,000 most common verbs from a 180 million word corpus of Portuguese newspaper text, CETEMPúblico. Because this corpus is not annotated, we used a part-of-speech tagger and morphological analyzer (Barreto et al., 2006; Silva, 2007) to detect verbs and to obtain their dictionary form. We then used an inflection tool (Branco et al., 2009) to generate the specific verb forms that are used in the queries. They are mostly third person singular forms of several different tenses.

The indicators that we used are ratios of Google Hits. They compare two queries.

Several indicators were tested. We provide examples with the verb *fazer* "do" for the queries being compared by each indicator. The name of each indicator reflects the aspectual type being tested, i.e. states should present high values for State Indicators 1 and 2, processes should show high values for Process Indicators 1–4, etc.

- State Indicator 1 (Indicator **S1**) is about imperfective and perfective past forms of verbs. It compares the number of hits a for an imperfective form *fazia* "did" to the number of hits b for a perfective form *fez* "did": $\frac{a}{a+b}$. Assuming the imperfective past constrains the entire clause to be a state, and the perfective past constrains it to be telic, the higher this value the more frequently the verb appears in stative clauses in a past tense.[2]

- State Indicator 2 (Indicator **S2**) is about the co-occurrence with *acaba de* "has just finished". It compares the number of hits a for *acaba de fazer* "has just finished doing" to the number of hits b for *fazer* "to do": $\frac{b}{a+b}$. In Portuguese, this construction does not seem to be felicitous with states.

- Process Indicator 1 (Indicator **P1**) is about past progressive forms and simple past forms (both imperfective). It compares the number of hits a for *fazia* "did" to the number of hits b for *estava a fazer* "was doing": $\frac{b}{a+b}$. Assuming the progressive construction is a function from processes to states (see Section 2), the higher this value, the more likely the verb can occur with the interpretation of a process.

[2] We expect this frequency to be indicative of states because states can appear in the imperfective past tense with their interpretation unchanged, whereas non-stative events have their interpretation shifted to a stative one in that context (e.g. they get a habitual reading). In order to refer to an event occurring in the past with an on-going interpretation, non-stative verbs require the progressive construction to be used in Portuguese, whereas states do not. Therefore, states should occur more freely in the simple imperfective past.

- Process Indicator 2 (Indicator **P2**) is about past progressive forms vs. simple past forms (perfective). It compares the number of hits a for *fez* "did" to the number of hits b for *esteve a fazer* "was doing": $\frac{b}{a+b}$. Similarly to the previous indicator, this one tests the frequency of a verb appearing in a context typical of processes.

- Process Indicator 3 (Indicator **P3**) is about the occurrence of *for* Adverbials. It compares the number of hits a for *fez* "did" to the number of hits b for *fez durante muito tempo* "did for a long time": $\frac{b}{a+b}$. This number is also intended to be an indication of how frequent a verb can be used with the interpretation of a process. Note that Portuguese allows modifiers to occur freely between a verb and its complements, so this test should work for transitive verbs (or any other subcategorization frame involving complements), not just intransitive ones.

- Process Indicator 4 (Indicator **P4**) is about the co-occurrence of a verb with *parar de* "to stop". It compares the number of hits a for *parou de fazer* "stopped doing" to the number of hits b for *fazer* "to do": $\frac{a}{a+b}$. Just like the English verbs *stop* and *finish* are sensitive to the aspectual type of their complement, so is the Portuguese verb *parar*, which selects for processes.

- Atelicity Indicator 1 (Indicator **A1**) is about comparing *in* and *for* adverbials. It compares the number of hits a for *fez num instante* "did in an instant" to the number of hits b for *fez durante muito tempo* "did for a long time": $\frac{b}{a+b}$. Processes can be modified by *for* adverbials, whereas culminated processes are modified by *in* adverbials. This indicator tests the occurrence of a verb in contexts that require these aspectual types.

- Atelicity Indicator 2 (Indicator **A2**) is about comparing *for* Adverbials with *suddenly*. It compares the number of hits a for *fez de repente* "did suddenly" to the number of hits b for *fez durante muito tempo* "did for a long time": $\frac{b}{a+b}$. *De repente* "suddenly" seems to modify culminations, so this indicator compares process readings with culmination readings.

- Culmination Indicator1 (Indicator **C1**) is about differentiating culminations and culminated processes. It compares the number of hits a for *fez de repente* "did suddenly" to the number of hits b for *fez num instante* "did in an instant": $\frac{a}{a+b}$.

For each of the 4,000 verbs, the necessary queries required by these indicators were generated and then sent to a search engine. The queries were enclosed in quotes, so as to guarantee exact matches. The number of hits was recorded for each query.

We had some problems with outliers for a few rather infrequent verbs. These could show very extreme values for some indicators. In order to minimize their impact, for each indicator we homogenized the 100 highest values that were found. More specifically, for each indicator, each one of the highest 100 values was replaced by the 100th highest value. The bottom 100 values were similarly changed. This way the top 99 values and the bottom 99 values are replaced by the 100th highest value and the 100th lowest value respectively.

Each indicator ranges between 0 and 1 in theory. In practice, we seldom find values close to the extremes, as this would imply that some queries would have close to 0 hits, which does not occur very often (after all, we intentionally used queries for which we would expect large hit counts, as these are more likely to be representative of true language use). For this reason, each indicator is scaled so that its minimum (actual) value is 0 and its maximum (actual) value is 1.

5 Evaluation

As mentioned before, in order to assess the usefulness of these aspectual indicators for the tasks of temporal relation classification, we checked whether they can improve machine learned classifiers trained for this problem. We next describe the classifiers that were used as the bases for comparison.

5.1 Experimental Setup

In order to obtain bases for comparison, we trained machine learned classifiers on the Portuguese corpus TimeBankPT, that is adapted from the TempEval data (see Section 4.1). We took inspiration in the work of Hepple et al. (2007).

This was one of the participating systems of TempEval. It used machine learning algorithms implemented in Weka (Witten and Frank, 1999). For our experiments, we used Weka's implementation of the C4.5 algorithm, `trees.J48` (Quinlan, 1993), the RIPPER algorithm as implemented by Weka's `rules.JRip` (Cohen, 1995), a nearest neighbors classifier, `lazy.KStar` (Cleary and Trigg, 1995), a Naïve Bayes classifier, namely Weka's `bayes.NaiveBayes` (John and Langley, 1995), and a support vector classifier, Weka's `functions.SMO` (Platt, 1998) . We chose these algorithms as they are representative of a wide range of machine learning approaches.

Recall that the tasks of TempEval are to guess the type of temporal relations. Each train or test instance thus corresponds to a temporal relation, i.e. a `TLINK` element in the TimeML annotations (see Figures 1 and 2). The classification problem is to determine the value of the attribute `relType` of TimeML `TLINK` elements. These temporal relations relate an event (referred by the `eventID` attribute of `TLINK` elements) to another temporal entity, that can be a time (pointed to by the `relatedToTime` attribute), in the case of tasks A and B, or, in the case of task C, another event (given by the `relatedToEvent` attribute).

As for the features that were employed, we also took inspiration in the approach of Hepple et al. (2007). These authors used as classifier attributes two types of features. The first group of features corresponds to TimeML attributes: for instance the value of the `aspect` attribute of `EVENT` elements, for the events involved in the temporal relation to be classified. The second group of features corresponds to simple features that can be computed with string manipulation and do not require any kind of natural language processing.

Table 2 shows the features that were tried and employed.

The *event* features correspond to attributes of `EVENT` elements, with the exception of the `event-string` feature, which takes as value the character data inside the corresponding TimeML `EVENT` element. In a similar spirit, the *timex3* features are taken from the attributes of `TIMEX3` elements with the same name. The `tlink-relType` feature is the class attribute and corresponds to the `relType` attribute of the TimeML `TLINK` element that represents the temporal relation to be classified. The *order* features are the attributes computed from the document's textual content. The feature `order-event-first` encodes whether the event terms precedes in the text the time expression it is related to by the temporal relation to classify. The classifier attribute `order-event-between` describes whether any other event is mentioned in the text between the two expressions for the entities that are in the temporal relation, and similarly `order-timex3-between` is about whether there is an intervening temporal expression. Finally, `order-adjacent` is true iff both `order-timex3-between` and `order-event-between` are false (even if other linguistic material occurs between the expressions denoting the two entities in the temporal relation).

	Task		
Attribute	A	B	C
event-aspect	×	✓	✓
event-polarity	✓	✓	✓
event-POS	×	×	✓
event-stem	×	✓	×
event-string	✓	×	×
event-class	✓	×	✓
event-tense	✓	✓	✓
order-event-first	✓	N/A	N/A
order-event-between	✓	N/A	N/A
order-timex3-between	×	N/A	N/A
order-adjacent	✓	N/A	N/A
timex3-mod	✓	×	N/A
timex3-type	×	×	N/A
tlink-relType	✓	✓	✓

Table 2: Feature combinations used in the classifiers used as comparison bases. Features inspired by the ones used by Hepple et al. (2007) in TempEval.

In order to arrive at the final set of features (marked with a check mark in Table 2), we performed exhaustive search on all possible combinations of these features for each task, using the Naïve Bayes algorithm. They were compared using 10-fold cross-validation on the training data. The feature combinations shown in Table 2 are the optimal combinations arrived at in this way.

These are the classifiers that we used for the

comparison with the aspectual type indicators. We chose this straightforward approach because it forms a basis for comparison that is easily reproducible: the algorithm implementations that were used are part of freely available software, and the features that were employed are easily computed from the annotated data, with no need to run any natural language processing tools whatsoever.

As mentioned before in Section 4.1, the data used are organized in a training set and an evaluation set. The training part is around 60K words long, the test data containing around 9K words. When tested on held-out data, these classifiers present the scores shown in italics in Table 3.

These results are fairly similar to the scores that the system of Hepple et al. (2007) obtained in TempEval with English data: 0.59 for task A, 0.73 for task B, and 0.54 for task C. They are also not very far from the best results of TempEval. As such they represent interesting bases for comparison, as improving their performance is likely to be relevant to the best systems that have been developed for temporal information processing.

	Task		
Classifier	A	B	C
`trees.J48`	*0.57*	*0.77*	*0.53*
With best indicator			**0.55**
`rules.JRip`	*0.60*	*0.76*	*0.51*
With best indicator	**0.61**		**0.54**
`lazy.KStar`	*0.54*	*0.70*	*0.52*
With best indicator		**0.73**	**0.53**
`bayes.NaiveBayes`	*0.50*	*0.76*	*0.53*
With best indicator	**0.53**		**0.54**
`functions.SMO`	*0.55*	*0.79*	*0.54*
With best indicator	**0.56**		**0.55**

Table 3: Evaluation on held-out test data of classifiers trained on full train data. Values for the classifiers used as comparison bases are in italics. Boldface highlights improvements resulting from incorporating aspectual indicators as classifier features, and missing values represent no improvement.

5.2 Results and Discussion

After obtaining the bases for comparison described above, we proceeded to check whether the aspectual type indicators described in Section 4.2 can improve these results.

For each aspectual indicator, we implemented a classifier feature that encodes its value for the event term in the temporal relation (if it is not a verb, this value is missing). In the case of task C, two features are added for each indicator, one for each event term.

We extended each of these classifiers with one of these features at a time (two in the case of task C), and checked whether it improved the results on the test data. So for instance, in order to test Indicator S1, we extended each of these classifiers with a feature that encodes the value that this indicator presents for the term that denotes the event present in the temporal relation to be classified. In the case of task C, two classifier features are added, one for each event term, and both for the same Indicator S1. For instance, for the (training) instance corresponding to the `TLINK` in Figure 2 with the `lid` attribute that has the value `l1`, the classifier feature for Indicator S1 has the value that was computed for the verb *cair* "go down", since this is the `stem` of the word that denotes the event that is the first argument of this temporal relation. After adding each of these features, we retrained the classifiers on the training data and tested them on the held-out test data. In order to keep the evaluation manageable, we did not test combinations of multiple indicators.

Table 3 shows the overall results. For task A, the best indicators were **P4** (with `JRip`), **A1** (`NaiveBayes`) and **S1** (`SMO`). For task B the best one was **P4** (`KStar`). For task C, the best indicators were **P3** (`J48`), **A1** and **P3** (`JRip`), **C1** (`KStar`), **A1** (`NaiveBayes`) and **P2** (`SMO`). Each of the indicators **S2**, **P1** and **A2** either does not improve the results or does so but not as much as another, better indicator for the same task and algorithm.

It seems clear from Table 3 that some tasks benefit from these indicators more than others. In particular, task C shows consistent improvements whereas task B is hardly affected. Since task C is about relations involving two events, the classifiers may be picking up the sort of linguistic generalizations mentioned in Section 2 about *when* clauses.

`J48` and `JRip` produce human-readable models. We checked how these classifiers are taking advantage of the aspectual indicators. For task C, the induced models are generally associating high values of the indicators **A1** and **P3** with overlap relations and low values of these indicators with other types of relations. This is expected. On the one end, high values for these indicators are associated with atelicity (i.e. the endpoint of the corresponding event is not presented). On the other hand, both indicators are based on queries containing the phrase *durante muito tempo* "for a long time", which, in addition to picking up events that can be modified by *for* adverbials, more specifically pick up events that happen *for a long time* and are thus likely to overlap other events.

For task A, `JRip` also associates high values of the indicator **P4**—which constitute evidence that the corresponding events are processes (which are atelic)—with overlap relations. This is a specially interesting result, considering that the queries on which this indicator is based reflect a purely aspectual constraint.

6 Concluding Remarks

In this paper, we evaluated the relevance of information about aspectual type for temporal processing tasks.

Temporal information processing has received substantial attention recently with the two TempEval challenges in 2007 and 2010. The most interesting problem of temporal information processing, that of temporal relation classification, is still affected by high error rates.

Even though a very substantial part of the semantics literature on tense and aspect focuses on aspectual type, solutions to the problem of automatic temporal relation classification have not incorporated this sort of semantic information. In part this is expected, as aspectual type is very interconnected with syntax (cf. the discussion about aspectual coercion in Section 2), and the phenomenon of aspect shift can make it hard to compute even when syntactic information is available.

Our contribution with this paper is to incorporate this sort of information in existing machine learned classifiers that tackle this problem. Even though these classifiers do not have access to syntactic information, aspectual type information seemed to be useful in improving the performance of these models. We hypothesize that combining aspectual type information with information about syntactic structure can further improve the problems of temporal information processing, but we leave that research to future work.

An interesting question that we hope will be addressed by future work is how these results extend to other languages. We cannot provide an answer to this question, as we do not have the data. However, this experiment can be replicated for any language that has (i) TimeML annotated data, (ii) a reasonable size of documents on the Web and a search engine capable of separating them from the documents in other languages and (iii) an aspectual system similar enough that the question being addressed in this paper makes sense (and useful patterns for queries can be constructed, even if not entirely identical to the ones that we used). The second criterion is met by many, many languages. The third one also seems to affect many languages, as the existing literature on aspectual phenomena indicates that these phenomena are quite widespread. The second criterion is, at the moment, the hardest to fulfill as not many languages have data with rich annotations about time (i.e. including events and temporal relations). We speculate that our results can extend to English, although a different set of query patterns may have to be used in order to extract the aspectual indicators that are employed. We believe this because the two languages largely overlap when it comes to aspectual phenomena.

References

Florbela Barreto, António Branco, Eduardo Ferreira, Amália Mendes, Maria Fernanda Nascimento, Filipe Nunes, and João Silva. 2006. Open resources and tools for the shallow processing of Portuguese: the TagShare project. In *Proceedings of LREC 2006*.

António Branco, Francisco Costa, Eduardo Ferreira, Pedro Martins, Filipe Nunes, João Silva, and Sara Silveira. 2009. LX-Center: a center of online linguistic services. In *Proceedings of the Demo Session, ACL-IJCNLP2009*, Singapore.

Timothy Chklovski and Patrick Pantel. 2004. VerbOcean: Mining the Web for fine-grained semantic verb relations. In *In Proceedings of EMNLP-2004*, Barcelona, Spain.

John G. Cleary and Leonard E. Trigg. 1995. K*: An instance-based learner using an entropic distance measure. In *12th International Conference on Machine Learning*, pages 108–114.

William W. Cohen. 1995. Fast effective rule induction. In *Proceedings of the Twelfth International Conference on Machine Learning*, pages 115–123.

Francisco Costa and António Branco. 2010. Temporal information processing of a new language: Fast porting with minimal resources. In *Proceedings of ACL 2010*.

Francisco Costa and António Branco. 2012. TimeBankPT: A TimeML annotated corpus of Portuguese. In *Proceedings of LREC2012*.

Francisco Costa. to appear. *Processing Temporal Information in Unstructured Documents*. Ph.D. thesis, Universidade de Lisboa, Lisbon.

Henriëtte de Swart. 1998. Aspect shift and coercion. *Natural Language and Linguistic Theory*, 16:347–385.

Henriëtte de Swart. 2000. Tense, aspect and coercion in a cross-linguistic perspective. In *Proceedings of the Berkeley Formal Grammar conference*, Stanford. CSLI Publications.

David R. Dowty. 1979. *Word Meaning and Montague Grammar: the Semantics of Verbs and Times in Generative Semantics and Montague's PTQ*. Reidel, Dordrecht.

Oren Etzioni, Michael Cafarella, Doug Downey, Stanley Kok, Ana-Maria Popescu, Tal Shaked, , Stephen Soderland, Daniel S. Weld, and Alexander Yates. 2004. Web-scale information extraction in KnowItAll. In *Proceedings of the 13th International Conference on World Wide Web*.

Eun Young Ha, Alok Baikadi, Carlyle Licata, and James C. Lester. 2010. NCSU: Modeling temporal relations with Markov logic and lexical ontology. In *Proceedings of SemEval 2010*.

Marti A. Hearst. 1992. Automatic acquisition of hyponyms from large text corpora. In *Proceedings of the 14th Conference on Computational Linguistics*, volume 2, pages 539–545, Nantes, France.

Mark Hepple, Andrea Setzer, and Rob Gaizauskas. 2007. USFD: Preliminary exploration of features and classifiers for the TempEval-2007 tasks. In *Proceedings of SemEval-2007*, pages 484–487, Prague, Czech Republic. Association for Computational Linguistics.

George H. John and Pat Langley. 1995. Estimating continuous distributions in Bayesian classifiers. In *Eleventh Conference on Uncertainty in Artificial Intelligence*, pages 338–345, San Mateo.

Zornitsa Kozareva, Ellen Riloff, and Eduard Hovy. 2008. Semantic class learning from the web with hyponym pattern linkage graphs. In *Proceedings of ACL-08: HLT*, pages 1048–1056, Columbus, Ohio. Association for Computational Linguistics.

Laia Mayol, Gemma Boleda, and Toni Badia. 2005. Automatic acquisition of syntactic verb classes with basic resources. *Language Resources and Evaluation*, 39(4):295–312.

Congmin Min, Munirathnam Srikanth, and Abraham Fowler. 2007. LCC-TE: A hybrid approach to temporal relation identification in news text. pages 219–222.

Marc Moens and Mark Steedman. 1988. Temporal ontology and temporal reference. *Computational Linguistics*, 14(2):15–28.

John Platt. 1998. Fast training of support vector machines using sequential minimal optimization. In Bernhard Schölkopf, Chris Burges, and Alexander J. Smola, editors, *Advances in Kernel Methods—Support Vector Learning*.

Georgiana Puşcaşu. 2007. WVALI: Temporal relation identification by syntactico-semantic analysis. In *Proceedings of SemEval-2007*, pages 484–487, Prague, Czech Republic. Association for Computational Linguistics.

James Pustejovsky, José Castaño, Robert Ingria, Roser Saurí, Robert Gaizauskas, Andrea Setzer, and Graham Katz. 2003. TimeML: Robust specification of event and temporal expressions in text. In *IWCS-5, Fifth International Workshop on Computational Semantics*.

John Ross Quinlan. 1993. *C4.5: Programs for Machine Learning*. Morgan Kaufmann, San Mateo, CA.

Deepak Ravichandran and Eduard Hovy. 2002. Learning surface text patterns for a question answering system. In *Proceedings of ACL 2002*.

Graeme D. Ritchie. 1979. Temporal clauses in English. *Theoretical Linguistics*, 6:87–115.

Eric V. Siegel and Kathleen McKeown. 2000. Learning methods to combine linguistic indicators: Improving aspectual classification and revealing linguistic insights. *Computational Linguistics*, 24(4):595–627.

João Ricardo Silva. 2007. Shallow processing of Portuguese: From sentence chunking to nominal lemmatization. Master's thesis, Faculdade de Ciências da Universidade de Lisboa, Lisbon, Portugal.

Zeno Vendler. 1967. Verbs and times. *Linguistics in Philosophy*, pages 97–121.

Marc Verhagen, Robert Gaizauskas, Frank Schilder, Mark Hepple, and James Pustejovsky. 2007. SemEval-2007 Task 15: TempEval temporal relation identification. In *Proceedings of SemEval-2007*.

Marc Verhagen, Robert Gaizauskas, Frank Schilder, Mark Hepple, Jessica Moszkowicz, and James Pustejovsky. 2009. The TempEval challenge: identifying temporal relations in text. Language Resources and Evaluation.

Marc Verhagen, Roser Saurí, Tommaso Caselli, and James Pustejovsky. 2010. SemEval-2010 task 13: TempEval-2. In *Proceedings of SemEval-2010*.

Ian H. Witten and Eibe Frank. 1999. *Data Mining: Practical Machine Learning Tools and Techniques with Java Implementations*. Morgan Kaufmann, San Francisco.

Automatic generation of short informative sentiment summaries

Andrea Glaser and Hinrich Schütze
Institute for Natural Language Processing
University of Stuttgart, Germany
glaseraa@ims.uni-stuttgart.de

Abstract

In this paper, we define a new type of summary for sentiment analysis: a single-sentence summary that consists of a *supporting sentence* that conveys the overall sentiment of a review as well as a convincing reason for this sentiment. We present a system for extracting supporting sentences from online product reviews, based on a simple and unsupervised method. We design a novel comparative evaluation method for summarization, using a crowdsourcing service. The evaluation shows that our sentence extraction method performs better than a baseline of taking the sentence with the strongest sentiment.

1 Introduction

Given the success of work on sentiment analysis in NLP, increasing attention is being focused on how to present the results of sentiment analysis to the user. In this paper, we address an important use case that has so far been neglected: quick scanning of short summaries of a body of reviews with the purpose of finding a subset of reviews that can be studied in more detail. This use case occurs in companies that want to quickly assess, perhaps on a daily basis, what consumers think about a particular product. One-sentence summaries can be quickly scanned – similar to the summaries that search engines give for search results – and the reviews that contain interesting and new information can then be easily identified. Consumers who want to quickly scan review summaries to pick out a few reviews that are helpful for a purchasing decision are a similar use case.

For a one-sentence summary to be useful in this context, it must satisfy two different "information needs": it must convey the sentiment of the review, but it must also provide a specific reason for that sentiment, so that the user can make an informed decision as to whether reading the entire review is likely to be worth the user's time – again similar to the purpose of the summary of a web page in search engine results.

We call a sentence that satisfies these two criteria a *supporting sentence*. A supporting sentence contains information on the sentiment as well as a specific reason for why the author arrived at this sentiment. Examples for supporting sentences are *"The picture quality is very good"* or *"The battery life is 2 hours"*. Non-supporting sentences contain opinions without such reasons such as *"I like the camera"* or *"This camera is not worth the money"*.

To address use cases of sentiment analysis that involve quick scanning and selective reading of large numbers of reviews, we present a simple unsupervised system in this paper that extracts one supporting sentence per document and show that it is superior to a baseline of selecting the sentence with the strongest sentiment.

One problem we faced in our experiments was that standard evaluations of summarization would have been expensive to conduct for this study. We therefore used crowdsourcing to perform a new type of comparative evaluation method that is different from training set and gold standard creation, the dominant way crowdsourcing has been used in NLP so far.

In summary, our contributions in this paper are as follows. We define supporting sentences, a new type of sentiment summary that is appropriate in situations where both the sentiment of a review and a good reason for that sentiment need to be conveyed succinctly. We present a simple unsupervised method for extracting supporting sentences and show that it is superior to a baseline in a novel crowdsourcing-based evaluation.

In the next section, we describe related work that is relevant to our new approach. In Section 3 we present the approach we use to identify supporting sentences. Section 4 describes the feature representation of sentences and the classification method. In Section 5 we give an overview of the crowdsourcing evaluation. Section 6 discusses our experimental results. In Sections 7 and 8, we present our conclusions and plans for future work.

2 Related Work

Both sentiment analysis (Pang and Lee, 2008; Liu, 2010) and summarization (Nenkova and McKeown, 2011) are important subfields of NLP. The work most relevant to this paper is work on summarization methods that addresses the specific requirements of summarization in sentiment analysis. There are two lines of work in this vein with goals similar to ours: (i) aspect-based and pro/con-summarization and (ii) approaches that extract summary sentences from reviews.

An aspect is a component or attribute of a product such as *"battery"*, *"lens cap"*, *"battery life"*, and *"picture quality"* for cameras. Aspect-oriented summarization (Hu and Liu, 2004; Zhuang et al., 2006; Kim and Hovy, 2006) collects sentiment assessments for a given set of aspects and returns a list of pros and cons about every aspect for a review or, in some cases, on a per-sentence basis.

Aspect-oriented summarization and pro/con-summarization differ in a number of ways from supporting sentence summarization. First, aspects and pros&cons are taken from a fixed inventory. The inventory is typically small and does not cover the full spectrum of relevant information. Second, in its most useful form, aspect-oriented summarization requires classification of phrases and sentences according to the aspect they belong to; e.g., *"The camera is very light"* has to be recognized as being relevant to the aspect *"weight"*. Developing a component that assigns phrases and sentences to their corresponding categories is time-consuming and has to be redone for each domain. Any such component will make mistakes and undetected or incorrectly classified aspects can result in bad summaries.

Our approach enables us to find strong supporting sentences even if the reason given in that sentence does not fit well into the fixed inventory. No manual work like the creation of an aspect inventory is necessary and there are no requirements on the format of the reviews such as author-provided pros and cons.

Aspect-oriented summarization also differs in that it does not differentiate along the dimension of quality of the reason given for a sentiment. For example, *"I don't like the zoom"* and *"The zoom range is too limited"* both give reasons for why a camera gets a negative evaluation, but only the latter reason is informative. In our work, we evaluate the quality of the reason given for a sentiment.

The use case we address in this paper requires a short, easy-to-read summary. A well-formed sentence is usually easier to understand than a pro/con table. It also has the advantage that the information conveyed is accurately representing what the user wanted to say – this is not the case for a presentation that involves several complex processing steps and takes linguistic material out of the context that may be needed to understand it correctly.

Berend (2011) performs a form of pro/con summarization that does not rely on aspects. However, most of the problems of aspect-based pro/con summarization also apply to this paper: no differentiation between good and bad reasons, the need for human labels to train a classifier, and inferior readability compared to a well-formed sentence.

Two previous approaches that have attempted to extract sentences from reviews in the context of summarization are (Beineke et al., 2004) and (Arora et al., 2009). Beineke et al. (2004) train a classifier on rottentomatoes.com summary sentences provided by review authors. These sentences sometimes contain a specific reason for the overall sentiment of the review, but sometimes they are just catchy lines whose purpose is to draw moviegoers in to read the entire review; e.g., *"El Bulli barely registers a pulse stronger than a book's"* (which does not give a specific reason for why the movie does not register a strong pulse).

Arora et al. (2009) define two classes of sentences: qualified claims and bald claims. A qualified claim gives the reader more details (e.g., *"This camera is small enough to fit easily in a coat pocket"*) while a bald claim is open to interpretation (e.g., *"This camera is small"*). Qualified/bald is a dimension of classification of sentiment statements that is to some extent orthogonal to quality of reason. Qualified claims do not have to contain a reason and bald claims can contain an informative reason. For example, *"I didn't like the camera, but I suspect it will be a great camera for first timers"* is classified as a qualified claim, but the sentence does not give a good reason for the sentiment of the document. Both dimensions (qualified/bald, high-quality/low-quality reason) are important and can be valuable components of a complete sentiment analysis system.

Apart from the definition of the concept of supporting sentence, which we believe to be more appropriate for the application we have in mind than rottentomatoes.com summary sentences and qualified claims, there are two other important differences of our approach to these two papers. First, we directly evaluate the quality of the reasons in a crowdsourcing experiment. Second, our approach is unsupervised and does not require manual annotation of a training set of supporting sentences.

As we will discuss in Section 5, we propose a novel evaluation measure for summarization based on crowdsourcing in this paper. The most common use of crowdsourcing in NLP is to have workers label a training set and then train a supervised classifier on this training set. In contrast, we use crowdsourcing to directly evaluate the relative quality of the automatic summaries generated by the unsupervised method we propose.

3 Approach

Our approach is based on the following three premises.

(i) *A good supporting sentence conveys both the review's sentiment and a supporting fact.* We make this assumption because we want the sentence to be self-contained. If it only describes a fact about a product without evaluation, then it does not on its own explain which sentiment is conveyed by the article and why.

(ii) *Supporting facts are most often expressed by noun phrases.* We call a noun phrase that expresses a supporting fact a *keyphrase*. We are not assuming that *all* important words in the supporting sentence are nominal; the verb will be needed in many cases to accurately convey the reason for the sentiment expressed. However, it is a fairly safe assumption that part of the information is conveyed using noun phrases since it is difficult to convey specific information without using specific noun phrases. Adjectives are often important when expressing a reason, but frequently a noun is also mentioned or one would need to resolve a pronoun to make the sentence a self-contained supporting sentence. In a sentence like *"It's easy to use"* it is not clear what the adjective is referring to.

(iii) *Noun phrases that express supporting facts tend to be domain-specific; they can be automatically identified by selecting noun phrases that are frequent in the domain – either in relative terms (compared to a generic corpus) or in absolute terms.* By making this assumption we may fail to detect supporting sentences that are worded in an original way using ordinary words. However, in a specific domain there is usually a lot of redundancy and most good reasons occur many times and are expressed by similar words.

Based on these assumptions, we select the supporting sentence in two steps. In the first step, we determine the n sentences with the strongest sentiment within every review by classifying the polarity of the sentences (where n is a parameter). In the second step, we select one of the n sentences as the best supporting sentence by means of a weighting function.

Step 1: Sentiment Classification

In this step, we apply a sentiment classifier to all sentences of the review to classify sentences as positive or negative. We then select the n sentences with the highest probability of conforming with the overall sentiment of the document. For example, if the document's polarity is negative, we select the n sentences that are most likely to be negative according to the sentiment classifier. We restrict the set of n sentences to sentences with the "right" sentiment because even an excellent supporting sentence is not a good characterization of the content of the review if it contradicts the overall assessment given by the review. Only in cases where there are fewer than n sentences with the correct sentiment, we also select sentences with the "wrong" sentence to obtain a minimum of n sentences for each review.

Step 2: Weighting Function

Based on premises (ii) and (iii) above, we score a sentence based on the number of noun phrases that *occur with high absolute and relative frequency* in the domain. We only consider simple nouns and compound nouns consisting of two nouns in this paper. In general, compound nouns are more informative and specific. A compound noun may refer to a specific reason even if the head noun does not (e.g., *"life"* vs. *"battery life"*). This means that we need to compute scores in a way that allows us to give higher weight to compound nouns than to simple nouns.

In addition, we also include counts of nouns and compounds in the scoring that do not have high absolute/relative frequency because frequency heuristics identify keyphrases with only moderate accuracy. However, theses nouns and compounds are given a lower weight.

This motivates a scoring function that is a weighted sum of four variables: number of simple nouns with high frequency, number of infrequent simple nouns, number of compound nouns with high frequency, and number of infrequent compound nouns. High frequency is defined as follows. Let $f_{dom}(p)$ be the domain-specific absolute frequency of phrase p, i.e., the frequency in the review corpus, and $f_{wiki}(p)$ the frequency of p in the English Wikipedia. We view the distribution of terms in Wikipedia as domain-independent and define the relative frequency as in Equation 1.

$$f_{rel}(p) = \frac{f_{dom}(p)}{f_{wiki}(p)} \tag{1}$$

We do not consider nouns and compound nouns that do not occur in Wikipedia for computing the relative frequency. A noun (resp. compound noun) is deemed to be of high frequency if it is one of the $k\%$ nouns (resp. compound nouns) with the highest $f_{dom}(p)$ and at the same time is one of the $k\%$ nouns (resp. compound nouns) with the highest $f_{rel}(p)$ where k is a parameter.

Based on these definitions, we define four different sets: F_1 (the set of nouns with high frequency), I_1 (the set of infrequent nouns), F_2 (the set of compounds with high frequency), and I_2 (the set of infrequent compounds). An infrequent noun (resp. compound) is simply defined as a noun (resp. compound) that does not meet the frequency criterion.

We define the score s of a sentence with n tokens $t_1 \dots t_n$ (where the last token t_n is a punctuation mark) as follows:

$$\begin{aligned} s = \sum_{i=1}^{n-1} \; & w_{f_2} \cdot [\![(t_i, t_{i+1}) \in F_2]\!] \\ & + w_{i_2} \cdot [\![(t_i, t_{i+1}) \in I_2]\!] \\ & + w_{f_1} \cdot [\![t_i \in F_1]\!] \\ & + w_{i_1} \cdot [\![t_i \in I_1]\!] \end{aligned} \tag{2}$$

where $[\![\phi]\!] = 1$ if ϕ is true and $[\![\phi]\!] = 0$ otherwise. Note that a noun in a compound will contribute to the overall score in two different summands.

The weights w_{f_2}, w_{i_2}, w_{f_1}, and w_{i_1} are determined using logistic regression. The training set for the regression is created in an unsupervised fashion as follows. From each set of n sentences (one per review), we select the two highest scoring, i.e., the two sentences that were classified with the highest confidence. The two classes in the regression problem are then the top ranked sentences vs. the sentences at rank 2. Since taking all sentences turned out to be too noisy, we eliminate sentence pairs where the top sentence is better than the second sentence on almost all of the set counts (i.e., count of members of F_1, I_1, F_2, and I_2). Our hypothesis in setting up this regression was that the sentence with the strongest sentiment often does not give a good reason. Our experiments confirm that this hypothesis is true.

The weights w_{f_2}, w_{i_2}, w_{f_1}, and w_{i_1} estimated by the regression are then used to score sentences according to Equation 2.

We give the same weight to all keyphrase compounds (and the same weight to all keyphrase nouns) – in future work one could attempt to give higher weights to keyphrases with higher absolute or relative frequency. In this paper, our goal is to establish a simple baseline for the task of extraction of supporting sentences.

After computing the overall weight for each sentence in a review, the sentence with the highest weight is chosen as the supporting sentence – the sentence that is most informative for explaining the overall sentiment of the review.

4 Experiments

4.1 Data

We use part of the Amazon dataset from Jindal and Liu (2008). The dataset consists of more than 5.8 million consumer-written reviews of several products, taken from the Amazon website. For our experiment we used the digital camera domain and extracted 15,340 reviews covering a total of 740 products. See table 1 for key statistics of the data set.

Type	Number
Brands	17
Products	740
Documents (all)	15,340
Documents (cleaned)	11,624
Documents (train)	9,880
Documents (test)	1,744
Short test documents	147
Long test documents	1,597
Average number of sents	13.36
Median number of sents	10

Table 1: Key statistics of our dataset

In addition to the review text, authors can give an overall rating (a number of stars) to the product. Possible ratings are 5 (very positive), 4 (positive), 3 (neutral), 2 (negative), and 1 (very negative). We unify ratings of 4 and 5 to "positive" and ratings of 1 and 2 to "negative" to obtain polarity labels for binary classification. Reviews with a rating of 3 are discarded.

4.2 Preprocessing

We tokenized and part-of-speech (POS) tagged the corpus using TreeTagger (Schmid, 1994). We split each review into individual sentences by using the sentence boundaries given by TreeTagger. One problem with user-written reviews is that they are often not written in coherent English, which results in wrong POS tags. To address some of these problems, we cleaned the corpus after the tokenization step. We separated word-punctuation clusters (e.g., *word...word*) and removed emoticons, html tags, and all sentences with three or fewer tokens, many of which were a result of wrong tokenization. We excluded all reviews with fewer than five sentences. Short reviews are often low-quality and do not give good reasons. The cleaned corpus consists of 11,624 documents. Finally, we split the corpus into training set (85%) and test set (15%) as shown in Table 1. The average number of sentences of a review is 13.36 sentences, the median number of sentences is 10.

4.3 Sentiment Classification

We first build a sentence sentiment classifier by training the Stanford maximum entropy classifier (Manning and Klein, 2003) on the sentences in the training set. Sentences occurring in positive (resp. negative) reviews are labeled positive (resp. negative). We use a simple bag-of-words representation (without punctuation characters and frequent stop words). Propagating labels from documents to sentences creates a noisy training set because some sentences have sentiment different from the sentiment in their documents; however, there is no alternative because we need per-sentence classification decisions, but do not have per-sentence human labels.

The accuracy of the classifier is 88.4% on "propagated" sentence labels.

We use the sentence classifier in two ways. First, it defines our *baseline* BL for extracting supporting sentences: the baseline simply proposes the sentence with the highest sentiment score that is compatible with the sentiment of the document as the supporting sentence.

Second, the sentence classifier selects a subset of candidate sentences that is then further processed using the scoring function in Equation 2. This subset consists of the $n = 5$ sentences with the highest sentiment scores of the "right" polarity – that is, if the document is positive (resp. negative), then the $n = 5$ sentences with the highest positive (resp. negative) scores are selected.

4.4 Determining Frequencies and Weights

The absolute frequency of nouns and compound nouns simply is computed as their token frequency in the training set. For computing the relative frequency (as described in Section 3, Equation 1), we use the 20110405 dump of the English Wikipedia.

In the product review corpora we studied, the percentage of high-frequency keyphrase compound nouns was higher than that of simple nouns. We therefore use two different thresholds for absolute and relative frequency. We define F_1 as the set of nouns that are in the top $k_n = 2.5\%$ for both absolute and relative frequencies; and F_2 as the set of compounds that are in the top $k_p = 5\%$ for both absolute and relative frequencies. These thresholds are set to obtain a high density of good keyphrases with few false positives. Below the threshold there are still other good keyphrases, but they cannot be separated easily from non-keyphrases.

Sentences are scored according to Equation 2. Recall that the parameters w_{f_2}, w_{i_2}, w_{f_1}, and w_{i_1} are determined using logistic regression. The obtained parameter values (see table 2) indicate the relative importance of the four different types of terms. Compounds are the most important term and even those with a frequency below the threshold k_p still provide more detailed information than simple nouns above the threshold k_n; the value of w_{i_2} is approximately twice the value w_{f_1} for this reason. Non-keyphrase nouns are least important and are weighted with only a very small value of $w_{i_1} = 0.01$.

Phrase	Par	Value
keyphrase compounds	w_{f_2}	1.07
non-keyphrase compounds	w_{i_2}	0.89
keyphrase nouns	w_{f_1}	0.46
non-keyphrase nouns	w_{i_1}	0.01

Table 2: Weight settings

The scoring function with these parameter values is applied to the $n = 5$ selected sentences of the review. The highest scoring sentence is then selected as the supporting sentence proposed by our system.

For 1380 of the 1744 reviews, the sentence selected by our system is different from the baseline sentence; however, there are 364 cases (20.9%) where the two are the same. Only the 1380 cases where the two methods differ are included in the crowdsourcing evaluation to be described in the next section. As we will show below, our system selects better supporting sentences than the baseline in most cases. So if baseline and our system agree, then it is even more likely that the sentence selected by both is a good supporting sentence. However, there could also be cases where the $n = 5$ sentences selected by the sentiment classifier are all bad supporting sentences or cases where the document does not contain any good supporting sentences.

5 Comparative Evaluation with Amazon Mechanical Turk

One standard way to evaluate summarization systems is to create hand-edited summaries and to compute some measure of similarity (e.g., word or n-gram overlap) between automatic and human summaries. An alternative for extractive summaries is to classify all sentences in the document with respect to their appropriateness as summary sentences. An automatic summary can then be scored based on its ability to correctly identify good summary sentences. Both of these methods require a large annotation effort and are most likely too complex to be outsourced to a crowdsourcing service because the creation of manual summaries requires skilled writers. For the second type of evaluation, ranking sentences according to a criterion is a lot more time consuming than making a binary decision – so ranking the 13 or 14 sentences that a review contains on average for the entire test set would be a significant annotation effort. It would also be difficult to obtain consistent and repeatable annotation in crowdsourcing on this task due to its subtlety.

We therefore designed a novel evaluation methodology in this paper that has a much smaller startup cost. It is well known that relative judgments are easier to make on difficult tasks than absolute judgments. For example, much recent work on relevance ranking in information retrieval relies on relative relevance judgments (one document is more relevant than another) rather than absolute relevance judgments. We adopt this general idea and only request such relative judgments on supporting sentences from annotators. Unlike a complete ranking of the sentences (which would require $m(m-1)/2$ judgments where m is the length of the review), we choose a setup where we need to only elicit a single relative judgment per review, one relative judgment on a sentence pair (consisting of the baseline sentence and the system sentence) for each of the 1380 reviews selected in the previous section. This is a manageable annotation task that can be run on a crowdsourcing service in a short time and at little cost.

We use Amazon Mechanical Turk (AMT) for this annotation task. The main advantage of AMT is that cost per annotation task is very low, so that we can obtain large annotated datasets for an af-

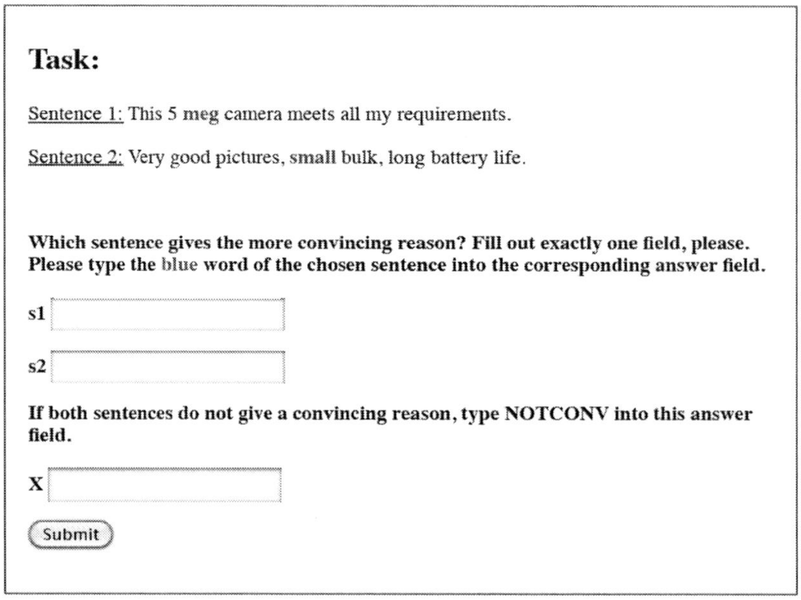

Figure 1: AMT interface for annotators

fordable price. The disadvantage is the level of quality of the annotation which will be discussed at the end of this section.

5.1 Task Design

We created a HIT (Human Intelligence Task) template including detailed annotation guidelines. Every HIT consists of a pair of sentences. One sentence is the baseline sentence; the other sentence is the system sentence, i.e., the sentence selected by the scoring function. The two sentences are presented in random order to avoid bias.

The workers are then asked to evaluate the relative quality of the sentences by selecting one of the following three options:

1. Sentence 1 has the more convincing reason
2. Sentence 2 has the more convincing reason
3. Neither sentence has a convincing reason

If both sentences contain reasons, the worker has to compare the two reasons and choose the sentence with the more convincing reason.

Each HIT was posted to three different workers to make it possible to assess annotator agreement. Every worker can process each HIT only once so that the three assignments are always done by three different people.

Based on the worker annotations, we compute a gold standard score for each sentence. This score is simply the number of times it was rated better than its competitor. The score can be 0, 1, 2 or 3. HITs for which the worker chooses the option "Neither sentence has a convincing reason" are ignored when computing sentence scores.

The sentence with the higher score is then selected as the best supporting sentence for the corresponding review.

In cases of ties, we posted the sentence pair one more time for one worker. If one of the two sentences has a higher score after this reposting, we choose it as the winner. Otherwise we label this sentence pair "no decision" or "N-D".

5.2 Quality of AMT Annotations

Since our crowdsourcing based evaluation is novel, it is important to investigate if human annotators perform the annotation consistently and reproducibly.

The Fleiss' κ agreement score for the final experiment is 0.17. AMT workers only have the instructions given by the requesters. If they are not clear enough or too complicated, workers can misunderstand the task, which decreases the quality of the answers. There are also AMT workers who spam and give random answers to tasks. Moreover, ranking sentences according to the quality of the given reason is a subjective task. Even if the sentence contains a reason, it might not be convincing for the worker.

To ensure a high level of quality for our dataset,

	Experiment	# Docs	BL	SY	N-D	B=S
1	AMT, first pass	1380	27.4	57.9	14.7	-
2	AMT, second pass	203	46.8	45.8	7.4	-
3	AMT final	1380	34.3	**64.6**	1.1	-
4	AMT+[B=S]	1744	27.1	**51.1**	0.9	20.9

Table 3: AMT evaluation results. Numbers are percentages or counts. BL = baseline, SY = system, N-D = no decision, B=S = same sentence selected by baseline and system

we took some precautions. To force workers to actually read the sentences and not just click a few boxes, we randomly marked one word of each sentence blue. The worker had to type the word of their preferred sentence into the corresponding answer field or NOTCONV into the special field if neither sentence was convincing. Figure 1 shows our AMT interface design.

For each answer field we have a gold standard (the words we marked blue and the word NOTCONV) which enables us to look for spam. The analysis showed that some workers mistyped some words, which however only indicates that the worker actually typed the word instead of copying it from the task. Some workers submitted inconsistent answers, for instance, they typed a random word or filled out all three answer fields. In such cases we reposted this HIT again to receive a correct answer.

After the task, we counted how often a worker said that neither sentence is convincing since a high number indicates that the worker might have only copied the word for several sentence pairs without checking the content of the sentences. We also analyzed the time a worker needed for every HIT. Since no task was done in less than 10 seconds, the possibility of just copying the word was rather low.

6 Results and discussion

The results of the AMT experiment are shown in table 3. As described above, each of the 1380 sentence pairs was evaluated by three workers. Workers rated the system sentence as better for 57.9% of the reviews, and the baselines sentence as better for 27.4% of the reviews; for 14.7% of reviews, the scores of the two sentences were tied (line 1 of Table 3). The 203 reviews in this category were reposted one more time (as described in Section 5). The responses were almost perfectly evenly split: about 47% of workers preferred the baseline system, 46% the system sentence; 7.4% of the responses were undecided (line 2). Line 3 presents the consolidated results where the 14.7% ties on line 1 are replaced by the ratings obtained on line 2 in the second pass.

The consolidated results (line 3) show that our system is clearly superior to the baseline of selecting the sentence with the strongest sentiment. Our system selected a better supporting sentence for 64.6% of the reviews; the baseline selected a better sentence for 34.3% of the reviews. These results exclude the reviews where baseline and system selected the same sentence. If we assume that these sentences are also acceptable sentences (since they score well on the traditional sentiment metrics as well as on our new content keyword metric), then our system finds a good supporting sentence for 72.0% of reviews (51.1+20.9) whereas the baseline does so for only 48.0% (27.1+20.9).

6.1 Error Analysis

Our error analysis revealed that a significant proportion of system sentences that were worse than baseline sentences did contain a reason. However, the baseline sentence also contained a reason and was rated better by AMT annotators. Examples (1) and (2) show two such cases. The first sentence is the baseline sentence (BL) which was rated better. The system sentence (SY) contains a similar or different reason. Since rating reasons is a very subjective task, it is impossible to define which of these two sentences contains the better reason and depends on how the workers think about it.

(1) BL: *The best thing is that everything is just so easily displayed and one doesn't need a manual to start getting the work done.*

SY: *The zoom is incredible, the video was so clear that I actually thought of making a 15 min movie.*

(2) BL: *The colors are horrible, indoor shots are horrible, and too much noise.*

SY: *Who cares about 8 mega pixels and 1600 iso when it takes such bad quality pictures.*

In example (3) the system sentence is an incomplete sentence consisting of only two noun phrases. These cut-off sentences are mainly caused by incorrect usage of grammar and punctuation by the reviewers which results in wrongly determined sentence boundaries in the preprocessing step.

(3) BL: *Gives peace of mind to have it fit perfectly.*

SY: *battery and SD card.*

In some cases, the two sentences that were presented to the worker in the evaluation had a different polarity. This can have two reasons: (i) due to noisy training input, the classifier misclassified some of the sentences, and (ii) for short reviews we also used sentences with the non-conforming polarity. Sentences with different polarity often confused the workers and they tended to prefer the positive sentence even if the negative one contained a more convincing reason as can be seen in example (4).

(4) BL: *It shares same basic commands and setup, so the learning curve was minimal.*

SY: *I was not blown away by the image quality, and as others have mentioned, the flash really is weak.*

A general problem with our approach is that the weighting function favors sentences with many noun phrases. The system sentence in example (5) contains many noun phrases, including some highly frequent nouns (e.g., *"lens"*, *"battery"*), but there is no convincing reason and the baseline sentence has been selected by the workers.

(5) BL: *I have owned my cd300 for about 3 weeks and have already taken 700 plus pictures.*

SY: *It has something to do with the lens because the manual says it only happens to the 300 and when I called Sony tech support the guy tried to tell me the battery was faulty and it wasn't.*

Finally, there are a number of cases where our assumption that good supporting sentences contain keyphrases is incorrect. For example, sentence (6) does not contain any keyphrases indicative of good reasons. The information that makes it a good supporting sentence is mainly expressed using verbs and particles.

(6) *I have had an occasional problem with the camera not booting up and telling me to turn it off and then on again.*

7 Conclusion

In this work, we presented a system that extracts supporting sentences, single-sentence summaries of a document that contain a convincing reason for the author's opinion about a product. We used an unsupervised approach that extracts keyphrases of the given domain and then weights these keyphrases to identify supporting sentences. We used a novel comparative evaluation methodology with the crowdsourcing framework Amazon Mechanical Turk to evaluate this novel task since no gold standard is available. We showed that our keyphrase-based system performs better than a baseline of extracting the sentence with the highest sentiment score.

8 Future work

Our method failed for some of the about 35% of reviews where it did not find a convincing reason because of the noisiness of reviews. Reviews are user-generated content and contain grammatically incorrect sentences and are full of typographical errors. This problem makes it hard to perform preprocessing steps like part-of-speech tagging and sentence boundary detection correctly and reliably. We plan to address these problems in future work by developing a more robust processing pipeline.

Acknowledgments

This work was supported by Deutsche Forschungsgemeinschaft (Sonderforschungsbereich 732, Project D7) and in part by the IST Programme of the European Community, under the PASCAL2 Network of Excellence, IST-2007-216886. This publication only reflects the authors' views.

References

Shilpa Arora, Mahesh Joshi, and Carolyn P. Rosé. 2009. Identifying types of claims in online customer reviews. In *Proceedings of Human Language Technologies: The 2009 Annual Conference of the North American Chapter of the Association for Computational Linguistics, Companion Volume: Short Papers*, NAACL-Short '09, pages 37–40, Stroudsburg, PA, USA. Association for Computational Linguistics.

Philip Beineke, Trevor Hastie, Christopher Manning, and Shivakumar Vaithyanathan. 2004. Exploring sentiment summarization. In *Proceedings of the AAAI Spring Symposium on Exploring Attitude and Affect in Text: Theories and Applications*. AAAI Press. AAAI technical report SS-04-07.

Gábor Berend. 2011. Opinion expression mining by exploiting keyphrase extraction. In *Proceedings of 5th International Joint Conference on Natural Language Processing*, pages 1162–1170, Chiang Mai, Thailand, November. Asian Federation of Natural Language Processing.

Minqing Hu and Bing Liu. 2004. Mining and summarizing customer reviews. In *Proceedings of the Tenth ACM SIGKDD international conference on Knowledge discovery and data mining*, KDD '04, pages 168–177, New York, NY, USA. ACM.

Nitin Jindal and Bing Liu. 2008. Opinion spam and analysis. In *WSDM '08: Proceedings of the international conference on Web search and web data mining*, pages 219–230, New York, NY, USA. ACM.

Soo-Min Kim and Eduard Hovy. 2006. Automatic identification of pro and con reasons in online reviews. In *Proceedings of the COLING/ACL on Main conference poster sessions*, COLING-ACL '06, pages 483–490, Stroudsburg, PA, USA. Association for Computational Linguistics.

Bing Liu. 2010. Sentiment analysis and subjectivity. *Handbook of Natural Language Processing*, 2nd ed.

Christopher Manning and Dan Klein. 2003. Optimization, maxent models, and conditional estimation without magic. In *Proceedings of the 2003 Conference of the North American Chapter of the Association for Computational Linguistics on Human Language Technology: Tutorials - Volume 5*, NAACL-Tutorials '03, pages 8–8, Stroudsburg, PA, USA. Association for Computational Linguistics.

Ani Nenkova and Kathleen McKeown. 2011. Automatic summarization. *Foundations and Trends in Information Retrieval*, 5(2-3):103–233.

Bo Pang and Lillian Lee. 2008. Opinion mining and sentiment analysis. *Foundations and Trends in Information Retrieval*, 2(1-2):1–135.

Helmut Schmid. 1994. Probabilistic part-of-speech tagging using decision trees. In *Proceedings of the International Conference on New Methods in Language Processing*, Manchester, UK.

Li Zhuang, Feng Jing, and Xiao-Yan Zhu. 2006. Movie review mining and summarization. In *Proceedings of the 15th ACM international conference on Information and knowledge management*, CIKM '06, pages 43–50, New York, NY, USA. ACM.

Bootstrapped Training of Event Extraction Classifiers

Ruihong Huang and Ellen Riloff
School of Computing
University of Utah
Salt Lake City, UT 84112
{huangrh,riloff}@cs.utah.edu

Abstract

Most event extraction systems are trained with supervised learning and rely on a collection of annotated documents. Due to the domain-specificity of this task, event extraction systems must be retrained with new annotated data for each domain. In this paper, we propose a bootstrapping solution for event role filler extraction that requires minimal human supervision. We aim to rapidly train a state-of-the-art event extraction system using a small set of "seed nouns" for each event role, a collection of relevant (in-domain) and irrelevant (out-of-domain) texts, and a semantic dictionary. The experimental results show that the bootstrapped system outperforms previous weakly supervised event extraction systems on the MUC-4 data set, and achieves performance levels comparable to supervised training with 700 manually annotated documents.

1 Introduction

Event extraction systems process stories about domain-relevant events and identify the role fillers of each event. A key challenge for event extraction is that recognizing role fillers is inherently contextual. For example, a PERSON can be a perpetrator or a victim in different contexts (e.g., *"John Smith assassinated the mayor"* vs. *"John Smith was assassinated"*). Similarly, any COMPANY can be an acquirer or an acquiree depending on the context.

Many supervised learning techniques have been used to create event extraction systems using gold standard "answer key" event templates for training (e.g., (Freitag, 1998a; Chieu and Ng, 2002; Maslennikov and Chua, 2007)). However, manually generating answer keys for event extraction is time-consuming and tedious. And more importantly, event extraction annotations are highly domain-specific, so new annotations must be obtained for each domain.

The goal of our research is to use bootstrapping techniques to automatically train a state-of-the-art event extraction system without human-generated answer key templates. The focus of our work is the TIER event extraction model, which is a multi-layered architecture for event extraction (Huang and Riloff, 2011). TIER's innovation over previous techniques is the use of four different classifiers that analyze a document at increasing levels of granularity. TIER progressively zooms in on event information using a pipeline of classifiers that perform document-level classification, sentence classification, and noun phrase classification. TIER outperformed previous event extraction systems on the MUC-4 data set, but relied heavily on a large collection of 1,300 documents coupled with answer key templates to train its four classifiers.

In this paper, we present a bootstrapping solution that exploits a large unannotated corpus for training by using *role-identifying nouns* (Phillips and Riloff, 2007) as seed terms. Phillips and Riloff observed that some nouns, by definition, refer to entities or objects that play a specific role in an event. For example, "assassin", "sniper", and "hitman" refer to people who play the role of PERPETRATOR in a criminal event. Similarly, "victim", "casualty", and "fatality" refer to people who play the role of VICTIM, by virtue of their lexical semantics. Phillips and Riloff called these words *role-identifying nouns* and used them to learn extraction patterns. Our research also uses *role-identifying nouns* to learn extraction patterns, but the role-identifying nouns and patterns are then used to create training data for event extraction classifiers. Each classifier is then self-trained in a bootstrapping loop.

Our weakly supervised training procedure requires a small set of "seed nouns" for each event role, and a collection of relevant (in-domain) and irrelevant (out-of-domain) texts. No answer key templates or annotated texts are needed. The seed nouns are used to automatically generate a set of *role-identifying patterns*, and then the nouns, patterns, and a semantic dictionary are used to label training instances. We also propagate the event role labels across coreferent noun phrases within a document to produce additional training instances. The automatically labeled texts are used to train three components of TIER: its two types of sentence classifiers and its noun phrase classifiers. To create TIER's fourth component, its document genre classifier, we apply heuristics to the output of the sentence classifiers.

We present experimental results on the MUC-4 data set, which is a standard benchmark for event extraction research. Our results show that the bootstrapped system, TIER_{lite}, outperforms previous weakly supervised event extraction systems and achieves performance levels comparable to supervised training with 700 manually annotated documents.

2 Related Work

Event extraction techniques have largely focused on detecting event "triggers" with their arguments for extracting role fillers. Classical methods are either pattern-based (Kim and Moldovan, 1993; Riloff, 1993; Soderland et al., 1995; Huffman, 1996; Freitag, 1998b; Ciravegna, 2001; Califf and Mooney, 2003; Riloff, 1996; Riloff and Jones, 1999; Yangarber et al., 2000; Sudo et al., 2003; Stevenson and Greenwood, 2005) or classifier-based (e.g., (Freitag, 1998a; Chieu and Ng, 2002; Finn and Kushmerick, 2004; Li et al., 2005; Yu et al., 2005)).

Recently, several approaches have been proposed to address the insufficiency of using only local context to identify role fillers. Some approaches look at the broader sentential context around a potential role filler when making a decision (e.g., (Gu and Cercone, 2006; Patwardhan and Riloff, 2009)). Other systems take a more global view and consider discourse properties of the document as a whole to improve performance (e.g., (Maslennikov and Chua, 2007; Ji and Grishman, 2008; Liao and Grishman, 2010; Huang and Riloff, 2011)). Currently, the learning-based event extraction systems that perform best all use supervised learning techniques that require a large number of texts coupled with manually-generated annotations or answer key templates.

A variety of techniques have been explored for weakly supervised training of event extraction systems, primarily in the realm of pattern or rule-based approaches (e.g., (Riloff, 1996; Riloff and Jones, 1999; Yangarber et al., 2000; Sudo et al., 2003; Stevenson and Greenwood, 2005)). In some of these approaches, a human must manually review and "clean" the learned patterns to obtain good performance. Research has also been done to learn extraction patterns in an unsupervised way (e.g., (Shinyama and Sekine, 2006; Sekine, 2006)). But these efforts target open domain information extraction. To extract domain-specific event information, domain experts are needed to select the pattern subsets to use.

There have also been weakly supervised approaches that use more than just local context. (Patwardhan and Riloff, 2007) uses a semantic affinity measure to learn primary and secondary patterns, and the secondary patterns are applied only to event sentences. The event sentence classifier is self-trained using seed patterns. Most recently, (Chambers and Jurafsky, 2011) acquire event words from an external resource, group the event words to form event scenarios, and group extraction patterns for different event roles. However, these weakly supervised systems produce substantially lower performance than the best supervised systems.

3 Overview of TIER

The goal of our research is to develop a weakly supervised training process that can successfully train a state-of-the-art event extraction system for a new domain with minimal human input. We decided to focus our efforts on the TIER event extraction model because it recently produced better performance on the MUC-4 data set than prior learning-based event extraction systems (Huang and Riloff, 2011). In this section, we briefly give an overview of TIER's architecture and its com-

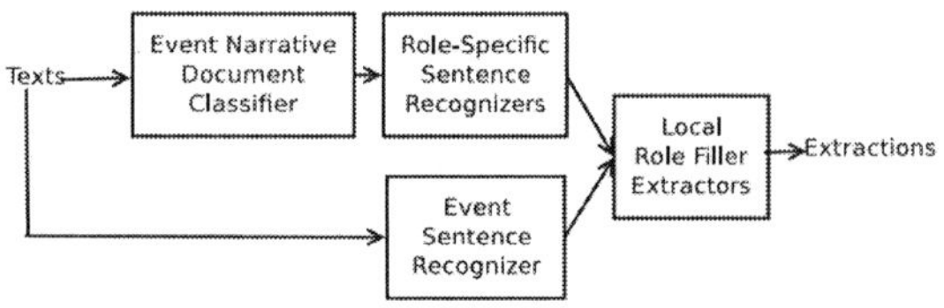

Figure 1: TIER Overview

ponents.

TIER is a multi-layered architecture for event extraction, as shown in Figure 1. Documents pass through a pipeline where they are analyzed at different levels of granularity, which enables the system to gradually "zoom in" on relevant facts. The pipeline consists of a document genre classifier, two types of sentence classifiers, and a set of noun phrase (role filler) classifiers.

The lower pathway in Figure 1 shows that all documents pass through an *event sentence classifier*. Sentences labeled as event descriptions then proceed to the noun phrase classifiers, which are responsible for identifying the role fillers in each sentence. The upper pathway in Figure 1 involves a document genre classifier to determine whether a document is an "event narrative" story (i.e., an article that primarily discusses the details of a domain-relevant event). Documents that are classified as event narratives warrant additional scrutiny because they most likely contain a lot of event information. Event narrative stories are processed by an additional set of *role-specific sentence classifiers* that look for role-specific contexts that will not necessarily mention the event. For example, a victim may be mentioned in a sentence that describes the aftermath of a crime, such as transportation to a hospital or the identification of a body. Sentences that are determined to have "role-specific" contexts are passed along to the noun phrase classifiers for role filler extraction. Consequently, event narrative documents pass through both the lower pathway and the upper pathway. This approach creates an event extraction system that can discover role fillers in a variety of different contexts by considering the type of document being processed.

TIER was originally trained with supervised learning using 1,300 texts and their corresponding answer key templates from the MUC-4 data set (MUC-4 Proceedings, 1992). Human-generated answer key templates are expensive to produce because the annotation process is both difficult and time-consuming. Furthermore, answer key templates for one domain are virtually never reusable for different domains, so a new set of answer keys must be produced from scratch for each domain. In the next section, we present our weakly supervised approach for training TIER's event extraction classifiers.

4 Bootstrapped Training of Event Extraction Classifiers

We adopt a two-phase approach to train TIER's event extraction modules using minimal human-generated resources. The goal of the first phase is to automatically generate positive training examples using *role-identifying* seed nouns as input. The seed nouns are used to automatically generate a set of *role-identifying patterns* for each event role. Each set of patterns is then assigned a set of semantic constraints (selectional restrictions) that are appropriate for that event role. The semantic constraints consist of the role-identifying seed nouns as well as general semantic classes that constrain the event role (e.g., a victim must be a HUMAN). A noun phrase will satisfy the semantic constraints if its head noun is in the seed noun list or if it has the appropriate semantic type (based on dictionary lookup). Each pattern is then matched against the unannotated texts, and if the extracted noun phrase satisfies its semantic constraints, then the noun phrase is automatically labeled as a role filler.

The second phase involves bootstrapped training of TIER's classifiers. Using the labeled instances generated in the first phase, we iteratively train three of TIER's components: the two types of sentential classifiers and the noun phrase classifiers. For the fourth component, the document classifier, we apply heuristics to the output of the sentence classifiers to assess the density of relevant sentences in a document and label high-density stories as event narratives. In the following sections, we present the details of each of these steps.

4.1 Automatically Labeling Training Data

Finding seeding instances of high precision and reasonable coverage is important in bootstrapping. However, this is especially challenging for event extraction task because identifying role fillers is inherently contextual. Furthermore, role

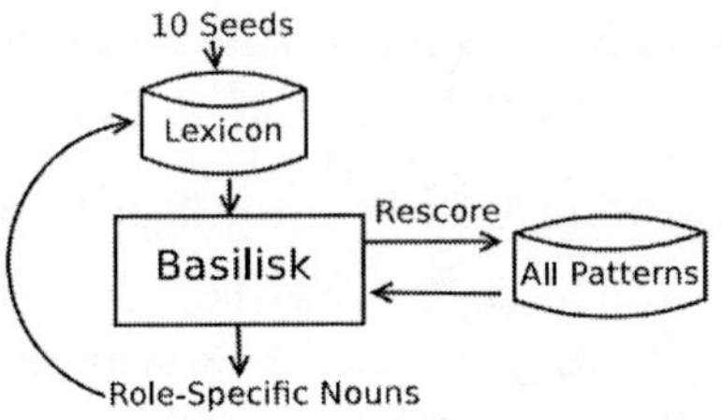

Figure 2: Using Basilisk to Induce Role-Identifying Patterns

fillers occur sparsely in text and in diverse contexts.

In this section, we explain how we generate *role-identifying patterns* automatically using seed nouns, and we discuss why we add semantic constraints to the patterns when producing labeled instances for training. Then, we discuss the coreference-based label propagation that we used to obtain additional training instances. Finally, we give examples to illustrate how we create training instances.

4.1.1 Inducing Role-Identifying Patterns

The input to our system is a small set of manually-defined *seed nouns* for each event role. Specifically, the user is required to provide 10 *role-identifying nouns* for each event role. (Phillips and Riloff, 2007) defined a noun as being "role-identifying" if its lexical semantics reveal the role of the entity/object in an event. For example, the words "assassin" and "sniper" are people who participate in a violent event as a PERPETRATOR. Therefore, the entities referred to by role-identifying nouns are probable role fillers.

However, treating every context surrounding a role-identifying noun as a role-identifying pattern is risky. The reason is that many instances of role-identifying nouns appear in contexts that do not describe the event. But, if one pattern has been seen to extract many role-identifying nouns and seldomly seen to extract other nouns, then the pattern likely represents an event context.

As (Phillips and Riloff, 2007) did, we use Basilisk to learn patterns for each event role. Basilisk was originally designed for semantic class learning (e.g., to learn nouns belonging to semantic categories, such as *building* or *human*). As shown in Figure 2, beginning with a small set of seed nouns for each semantic class, Basilisk learns additional nouns belonging to the same semantic class. Internally, Basilisk uses extraction patterns automatically generated from unannotated texts to assess the similarity of nouns. First, Basilisk assigns a score to each pattern based on the number of seed words that co-occur with it. Basilisk then collects the noun phrases extracted by the highest-scoring patterns. Next, the head noun of each noun phrase is assigned a score based on the set of patterns that it co-occurred with. Finally, Basilisk selects the highest-scoring nouns, automatically labels them with the semantic class of the seeds, adds these nouns to the lexicon, and restarts the learning process in a bootstrapping fashion.

For our work, we give Basilisk *role-identifying seed nouns* for each event role. We run the bootstrapping process for 20 iterations and then harvest the 40 best patterns that Basilisk identifies for each event role. We also tried using the additional role-identifying nouns learned by Basilisk, but found that these nouns were too noisy.

4.1.2 Using the Patterns to Label NPs

The induced *role-identifying patterns* can be matched against the unannotated texts to produce labeled instances. However, relying solely on the pattern contexts can be misleading. For example, the pattern context *<subject> caused damage* will extract some noun phrases that are weapons (e.g., *the bomb*) but some noun phrases that are not (e.g., *the tsunami*).

Based on this observation, we add selectional restrictions to each pattern that requires a noun phrase to satisfy certain semantic constraints in order to be extracted and labeled as a positive instances for an event role. The selectional restrictions are satisfied if the head noun is among the *role-identifying seed nouns* or if the semantic class of the head noun is compatible with the corresponding event role. In the previous example, *tsunami* will not be extracted as a weapon because it has an incompatible semantic class (EVENT), but *bomb* will be extracted because it has a compatible semantic class (WEAPON).

We use the semantic class labels assigned by the Sundance parser (Riloff and Phillips, 2004) in our experiments. Sundance looks up each noun in a semantic dictionary to assign the semantic class labels. As an alternative, general resources (e.g., WordNet (Miller, 1990)) or a semantic tagger (e.g., (Huang and Riloff, 2010)) could be used.

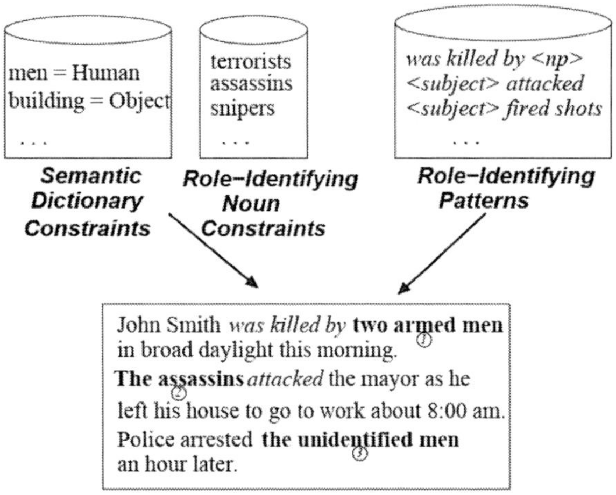

Figure 3: Automatic Training Data Creation

4.1.3 Propagating Labels with Coreference

To enrich the automatically labeled training instances, we also propagate the event role labels across coreferent noun phrases within a document. The observation is that once a noun phrase has been identified as a role filler, its coreferent mentions in the same document likely fill the same event role since they are referring to the same real world entity.

To leverage these coreferential contexts, we employ a simple head noun matching heuristic to identify coreferent noun phrases. This heuristic assumes that two noun phrases that have the same head noun are coreferential. We considered using an off-the-shelf coreference resolver, but decided that the head noun matching heuristic would likely produce higher precision results, which is important to produce high-quality labeled data.

4.1.4 Examples of Training Instance Creation

Figure 3 illustrates how we label training instances automatically. The text example shows three noun phrases that are automatically labeled as perpetrators. Noun phrases #1 and #2 occur in role-identifying pattern contexts (*was killed by <np>* and *<subject> attacked*) and satisfy the semantic constraints for perpetrators because "men" has a compatible semantic type and "assassins" is a role-identifying noun for perpetrators.

Noun phrase #3 ("the unidentified men") does not occur in a pattern context, but it is deemed to be coreferent with "two armed men" because they have the same head noun. Consequently, we propagate the perpetrator label from noun phrase #1 to noun phrase #3.

4.2 Creating TIER$_{lite}$ with Bootstrapping

In this section, we explain how the labeled instances are used to train TIER's classifiers with bootstrapping. In addition to the automatically labeled instances, the training process depends on a text corpus that consists of both relevant (in-domain) and irrelevant (out-of-domain) documents. Positive instances are generated from the relevant documents and negative instances are generated by randomly sampling from the irrelevant documents.

The classifiers are all support vector machines (SVMs), implemented using the SVMlin software (Keerthi and DeCoste, 2005). When applying the classifiers during bootstrapping, we use a sliding confidence threshold to determine which labels are reliable based on the values produced by the SVM. Initially, we set the threshold to be 2.0 to identify highly confident predictions. But if fewer than k instances pass the threshold, then we slide the threshold down in decrements of 0.1 until we obtain at least k labeled instances or the threshold drops below 0, in which case bootstrapping ends. We used k=10 for both sentence classifiers and k=30 for the noun phrase classifiers.

The following sections present the details of the bootstrapped training process for each of TIER's components.

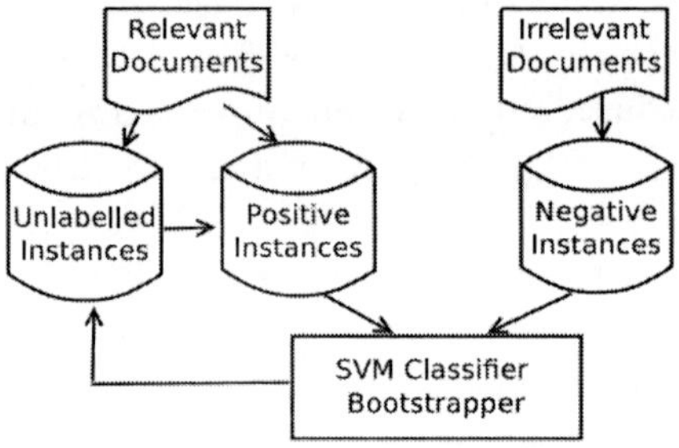

Figure 4: The Bootstrapping Process

4.2.1 Noun Phrase Classifiers

The mission of the noun phrase classifiers is to determine whether a noun phrase is a plausible event role filler based on the local features surrounding the noun phrase (NP). A set of classifiers is needed, one for each event role.

As shown in Figure 4, to seed the classifier training, the positive noun phrase instances are generated from the relevant documents following Section 4.1. The negative noun phrase instances are drawn randomly from the irrelevant documents. Considering the sparsity of role fillers in texts, we set the negative:positive ratio to be 10:1. Once the classifier is trained, it is applied to the unlabeled noun phrases in the relevant documents. Noun phrases that are assigned role filler labels by the classifier with high confidence (using the sliding threshold) are added to the set of positive instances. New negative instances are drawn randomly from the irrelevant documents to maintain the 10:1 (negative:positive) ratio.

We extract features from each noun phrase (NP) and its surrounding context. The features include the NP head noun and its premodifiers. We also use the Stanford NER tagger (Finkel et al., 2005) to identify Named Entities within the NP. The context features include four words to the left of the NP, four words to the right of the NP, and the lexico-syntactic patterns generated by AutoSlog to capture expressions around the NP (see (Riloff, 1993) for details).

4.2.2 Event Sentence Classifier

The event sentence classifier is responsible for identifying sentences that describe a relevant event. Similar to the noun phrase classifier training, positive training instances are selected from the relevant documents and negative instances are drawn from the irrelevant documents. All sentences in the relevant documents that contain one or more labeled noun phrases (belonging to any event role) are labeled as positive training instances. We randomly sample sentences from the irrelevant documents to obtain a negative:positive training instance ratio of 10:1. The bootstrapping process is then identical to that of the noun phrase classifiers. The feature set for this classifier consists of unigrams, bigrams and AutoSlog's lexico-syntactic patterns surrounding all noun phrases in the sentence.

4.2.3 Role-Specific Sentence Classifiers

The role-specific sentence classifiers are trained to identify the contexts specific to each event role. All sentences in the relevant documents that contain at least one labeled noun phrase for the appropriate event role are used as positive instances. Negative instances are randomly sampled from the irrelevant documents to maintain the negative:positive ratio of 10:1. The bootstrapping process and feature set are the same as for the event sentence classifier.

The difference between the two types of sentence classifiers is that the event sentence classifier uses positive instances from all event roles, while each role-specific sentence classifiers only uses the positive instances for one particular event role. The rationale is similar as in the supervised setting (Huang and Riloff, 2011); the event sentence classifier is expected to generalize over all event roles to identify event mention contexts, while the role-specific sentence classifiers are expected to learn to identify contexts specific to individual roles.

4.2.4 Event Narrative Document Classifier

TIER also uses an event narrative document classifier and only extracts information from role-specific sentences within event narrative documents. In the supervised setting, TIER uses heuristic rules derived from answer key templates to identify the event narrative documents in the training set, which are used to train an event narrative document classifier. The heuristic rules require that an event narrative should have a high density of relevant information and tend to mention the relevant information within the first several sentences.

In our weakly supervised setting, we use the information density heuristic directly instead of training an event narrative classifier. We approximate the relevant information density heuristic by computing the ratio of relevant sentences (both event sentences and role-specific sentences) out of all the sentences in a document. Thus, the event narrative labeller only relies on the output of the two sentence classifiers. Specifically, we label a document as an event narrative if $\geq 50\%$ of the sentences in the document are relevant (i.e., labeled positively by either sentence classifier).

5 Evaluation

In this section, we evaluate our bootstrapped system, TIER_{lite}, on the MUC-4 event extraction data set. First, we describe the IE task, the data set, and the weakly supervised baseline systems that we use for comparison. Then we present the results of our fully bootstrapped system TIER_{lite}, the weakly supervised baseline systems, and two fully supervised event extraction systems, TIER and GLACIER. In addition, we analyze the performance of TIER$_{lite}$ using different configurations to assess the impact of its components.

5.1 IE Task and Data

We evaluated the performance of our systems on the MUC-4 terrorism IE task (MUC-4 Proceedings, 1992) about Latin American terrorist events. We used 1,300 texts (DEV) as our training set and 200 texts (TST3+TST4) as the test set. All the documents have answer key templates. For the training set, we used the answer keys to separate the documents into relevant and irrelevant subsets. Any document containing at least one relevant event was considered to be relevant.

PerpInd	PerpOrg	Target	Victim	Weapon
129	74	126	201	58

Table 1: # of Role Fillers in the MUC-4 Test Set

Following previous studies, we evaluate our system on five MUC-4 string event roles: *perpetrator individuals* (PerpInd), *perpetrator organizations* (PerpOrg), *physical targets*, *victims*, and *weapons*. Table 1 shows the distribution of role fillers in the MUC-4 test set. The complete IE task involves the creation of answer key templates, one template per event[1]. Our work focuses on extracting individual role fillers and not template generation, so we evaluate the accuracy of the role fillers irrespective of which template they occur in.

We used the same *head noun* scoring scheme as previous systems, where an extraction is correct if its head noun matches the head noun in the answer key[2]. Pronouns were discarded from both the system responses and the answer keys since no coreference resolution is done. Duplicate extractions were conflated before being scored, so they count as just one hit or one miss.

5.2 Weakly Supervised Baselines

We compared the performance of our system with three previous weakly supervised event extraction systems.

AutoSlog-TS (Riloff, 1996) generates lexicosyntactic patterns exhaustively from unannotated texts and ranks them based on their frequency and probability of occurring in relevant documents. A human expert then examines the patterns and manually selects the best patterns for each event role. During testing, the patterns are matched against unseen texts to extract event role fillers.

PIPER (Patwardhan and Riloff, 2007; Patwardhan, 2010) learns extraction patterns using a semantic affinity measure, and it distinguishes between primary and secondary patterns and applies them selectively. (Chambers and Jurafsky, 2011) (C+J) created an event extraction system by acquiring event words from WordNet (Miller, 1990), clustering the event words into different event scenarios, and grouping extraction patterns for different event roles.

5.3 Performance of TIER$_{lite}$

Table 2 shows the seed nouns that we used in our experiments, which were generated by sorting the nouns in the corpus by frequency and manually identifying the first 10 role-identifying nouns for each event role.[3] Table 3 shows the number of training instances (noun phrases) that were automatically labeled for each event role using our training data creation approach (Section 4.1).

Event Role	Seed Nouns
Perpetrator Individual	terrorists assassins criminals rebels murderers death_squads guerrillas member members individuals
Perpetrator Organization	FMLN ELN FARC MRTA M-19 Front Shining_Path Medellin_Cartel The_Extraditables Army_of_National_Liberation
Target	houses residence building home homes offices pipeline hotel car vehicles
Victim	victims civilians children jesuits Galan priests students women peasants Romero
Weapon	weapons bomb bombs explosives rifles dynamite grenades device car_bomb

Table 2: Role-Identifying Seed Nouns

PerpInd	PerpOrg	Target	Victim	Weapon
296	157	522	798	248

Table 3: # of Automatically Labeled NPs

Table 4 shows how our bootstrapped system TIER$_{lite}$ compares with previous weakly supervised systems and two supervised systems, its supervised counterpart TIER (Huang and Riloff, 2011) and a model that jointly considers local and sentential contexts, GLACIER (Patwardhan

[1]Documents may contain multiple events per article.

[2]For example, "armed men" will match "5 armed men".

[3]We only found 9 weapon terms among the high-frequency terms.

Weakly Supervised Baselines						
	PerpInd	PerpOrg	Target	Victim	Weapon	Average
AUTOSLOG-TS (1996)	33/49/40	52/33/41	54/59/56	49/54/51	38/44/41	45/48/46
PIPER$_{Best}$ (2007)	39/48/43	55/31/40	37/60/46	44/46/45	47/47/47	44/46/45
C+J (2011)	-	-	-	-	-	44/36/40
Supervised Models						
GLACIER (2009)	51/58/54	34/45/38	43/72/53	55/58/56	57/53/55	48/57/52
TIER (2011)	48/57/52	46/53/50	51/73/60	56/60/58	53/64/58	51/62/56
Weakly Supervised Models						
TIER$_{lite}$	47/51/49	60/39/47	37/65/47	39/53/45	53/55/54	47/53/50

Table 4: Performance of the Bootstrapped Event Extraction System (Precision/Recall/F-score)

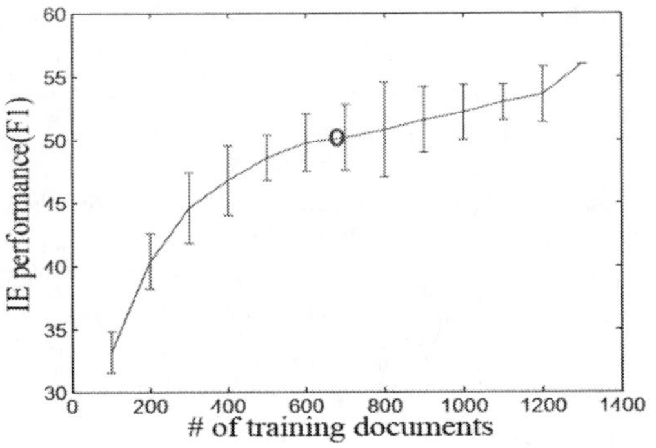

Figure 5: The Learning Curve of Supervised TIER

and Riloff, 2009). We see that TIER$_{lite}$ outperforms all three weakly supervised systems, with slightly higher precision and substantially more recall. When compared to the supervised systems, the performance of TIER$_{lite}$ is similar to GLACIER, with comparable precision but slightly lower recall. But the supervised TIER system, which was trained with 1,300 annotated documents, is still superior, especially in recall.

Figure 5 shows the learning curve for TIER when it is trained with fewer documents, ranging from 100 to 1,300 in increments of 100. Each data point represents five experiments where we randomly selected k documents from the training set and averaged the results. The bars show the range of results across the five runs. Figure 5 shows that TIER's performance increases from an F score of 34 when trained on just 100 documents up to an F score of 56 when training on 1,300 documents. The circle shows the performance of our bootstrapped system, TIER$_{lite}$, which achieves an F score comparable to supervised training with about 700 manually annotated documents.

5.4 Analysis

Table 6 shows the effect of the coreference propagation step described in Section 4.1.3 as part of training data creation. Without this step, the performance of the bootstrapped system yields an F score of 41. With the benefit of the additional training instances produced by coreference propagation, the system yields an F score of 53. The new instances produced by coreference propagation seem to substantially enrich the diversity of the set of labeled instances.

Seeding	P/R/F
wo/Coref	45/38/41
w/Coref	47/53/50

Table 6: Effects of Coreference Propagation

In the evaluation section, we saw that the supervised event extraction systems achieve higher recall than the weakly supervised systems. Although our bootstrapped event extraction system TIER$_{lite}$ produces higher recall than previous weakly supervised systems, a substantial recall gap still exists.

Considering the pipeline structure of the event extraction system, as shown in Figure 1, the noun phrase extractors are responsible for identifying all candidate role fillers. The sentential classifiers and the document classifier effectively serve as filters to rule out candidates from irrelevant contexts. Consequently, there is no way to recover missing recall (role fillers) if the noun phrase extractors fail to identify them.

Since the noun phrase classifiers are so central to the performance of the system, we compared the performance of the bootstrapped noun phrase classifiers directly with their supervised conterparts. The results are shown in Table 5. Both sets of classifiers produce low precision when used in isolation, but their precision levels are compara-

	PerpInd	PerpOrg	Target	Victim	Weapon	Average
Supervised Classifier	25/67/36	26/78/39	34/83/49	32/72/45	30/75/43	30/75/42
Bootstrapped Classifier	30/54/39	37/53/44	30/71/42	28/63/39	36/57/44	32/60/42

Table 5: Evaluation of Bootstrapped Noun Phrase Classifiers (Precision/Recall/F-score)

ble. The TIER pipeline architecture is successful at eliminating many of the false hits. However, the recall of the bootstrapped classifiers is consistently lower than the recall of the supervised classifiers. Specifically, the recall is about 10 points lower for three event roles (*PerpInd*, *Target* and *Victim*) and 20 points lower for the other two event roles (*PerpOrg* and *Weapon*). These results suggest that our bootstrapping approach to training instance creation does not fully capture the diversity of role filler contexts that are available in the supervised training set of 1,300 documents. This issue is an interesting direction for future work.

6 Conclusions

We have presented a bootstrapping approach for training a multi-layered event extraction model using a small set of "seed nouns" for each event role, a collection of relevant (in-domain) and irrelevant (out-of-domain) texts and a semantic dictionary. The experimental results show that the bootstrapped system, TIER_{lite}, outperforms previous weakly supervised event extraction systems on a standard event extraction data set, and achieves performance levels comparable to supervised training with 700 manually annotated documents. The minimal supervision required to train such a model increases the portability of event extraction systems.

7 Acknowledgments

We gratefully acknowledge the support of the National Science Foundation under grant IIS-1018314 and the Defense Advanced Research Projects Agency (DARPA) Machine Reading Program under Air Force Research Laboratory (AFRL) prime contract no. FA8750-09-C-0172. Any opinions, findings, and conclusions or recommendations expressed in this material are those of the authors and do not necessarily reflect the view of the DARPA, AFRL, or the U.S. government.

References

M.E. Califf and R. Mooney. 2003. Bottom-up Relational Learning of Pattern Matching rules for Information Extraction. *Journal of Machine Learning Research*, 4:177–210.

Nathanael Chambers and Dan Jurafsky. 2011. Template-Based Information Extraction without the Templates. In *Proceedings of the 49th Annual Meeting of the Association for Computational Linguistics: Human Language Technologies (ACL-11)*.

H.L. Chieu and H.T. Ng. 2002. A Maximum Entropy Approach to Information Extraction from Semi-Structured and Free Text. In *Proceedings of the 18th National Conference on Artificial Intelligence*.

F. Ciravegna. 2001. Adaptive Information Extraction from Text by Rule Induction and Generalisation. In *Proceedings of the 17th International Joint Conference on Artificial Intelligence*.

J. Finkel, T. Grenager, and C. Manning. 2005. Incorporating Non-local Information into Information Extraction Systems by Gibbs Sampling. In *Proceedings of the 43rd Annual Meeting of the Association for Computational Linguistics*, pages 363–370, Ann Arbor, MI, June.

A. Finn and N. Kushmerick. 2004. Multi-level Boundary Classification for Information Extraction. In *In Proceedings of the 15th European Conference on Machine Learning*, pages 111–122, Pisa, Italy, September.

Dayne Freitag. 1998a. Multistrategy Learning for Information Extraction. In *Proceedings of the Fifteenth International Conference on Machine Learning*. Morgan Kaufmann Publishers.

Dayne Freitag. 1998b. Toward General-Purpose Learning for Information Extraction. In *Proceedings of the 36th Annual Meeting of the Association for Computational Linguistics*.

Z. Gu and N. Cercone. 2006. Segment-Based Hidden Markov Models for Information Extraction. In *Proceedings of the 21st International Conference on Computational Linguistics and 44th Annual Meeting of the Association for Computational Linguistics*, pages 481–488, Sydney, Australia, July.

Ruihong Huang and Ellen Riloff. 2010. Inducing Domain-specific Semantic Class Taggers from (Almost) Nothing. In *Proceedings of The 48th Annual Meeting of the Association for Computational Linguistics (ACL 2010)*.

Ruihong Huang and Ellen Riloff. 2011. Peeling Back the Layers: Detecting Event Role Fillers in Secondary Contexts. In *Proceedings of the 49th Annual*

Meeting of the Association for Computational Linguistics: Human Language Technologies (ACL-11).

S. Huffman. 1996. Learning Information Extraction Patterns from Examples. In Stefan Wermter, Ellen Riloff, and Gabriele Scheler, editors, *Connectionist, Statistical, and Symbolic Approaches to Learning for Natural Language Processing*, pages 246–260. Springer-Verlag, Berlin.

H. Ji and R. Grishman. 2008. Refining Event Extraction through Cross-Document Inference. In *Proceedings of ACL-08: HLT*, pages 254–262, Columbus, OH, June.

S. Keerthi and D. DeCoste. 2005. A Modified Finite Newton Method for Fast Solution of Large Scale Linear SVMs. *Journal of Machine Learning Research*.

J. Kim and D. Moldovan. 1993. Acquisition of Semantic Patterns for Information Extraction from Corpora. In *Proceedings of the Ninth IEEE Conference on Artificial Intelligence for Applications*, pages 171–176, Los Alamitos, CA. IEEE Computer Society Press.

Y. Li, K. Bontcheva, and H. Cunningham. 2005. Using Uneven Margins SVM and Perceptron for Information Extraction. In *Proceedings of Ninth Conference on Computational Natural Language Learning*, pages 72–79, Ann Arbor, MI, June.

Shasha Liao and Ralph Grishman. 2010. Using Document Level Cross-Event Inference to Improve Event Extraction. In *Proceedings of the 48st Annual Meeting on Association for Computational Linguistics (ACL-10)*.

M. Maslennikov and T. Chua. 2007. A Multi-Resolution Framework for Information Extraction from Free Text. In *Proceedings of the 45th Annual Meeting of the Association for Computational Linguistics*.

G. Miller. 1990. Wordnet: An On-line Lexical Database. *International Journal of Lexicography*, 3(4).

MUC-4 Proceedings. 1992. *Proceedings of the Fourth Message Understanding Conference (MUC-4)*. Morgan Kaufmann.

S. Patwardhan and E. Riloff. 2007. Effective Information Extraction with Semantic Affinity Patterns and Relevant Regions. In *Proceedings of 2007 the Conference on Empirical Methods in Natural Language Processing (EMNLP-2007)*.

S. Patwardhan and E. Riloff. 2009. A Unified Model of Phrasal and Sentential Evidence for Information Extraction. In *Proceedings of 2009 the Conference on Empirical Methods in Natural Language Processing (EMNLP-2009)*.

S. Patwardhan. 2010. *Widening the Field of View of Information Extraction through Sentential Event Recognition*. Ph.D. thesis, University of Utah.

W. Phillips and E. Riloff. 2007. Exploiting Role-Identifying Nouns and Expressions for Information Extraction. In *Proceedings of the 2007 International Conference on Recent Advances in Natural Language Processing (RANLP-07)*, pages 468–473.

E. Riloff and R. Jones. 1999. Learning Dictionaries for Information Extraction by Multi-Level Bootstrapping. In *Proceedings of the Sixteenth National Conference on Artificial Intelligence*.

E. Riloff and W. Phillips. 2004. An Introduction to the Sundance and AutoSlog Systems. Technical Report UUCS-04-015, School of Computing, University of Utah.

E. Riloff. 1993. Automatically Constructing a Dictionary for Information Extraction Tasks. In *Proceedings of the 11th National Conference on Artificial Intelligence*.

E. Riloff. 1996. Automatically Generating Extraction Patterns from Untagged Text. In *Proceedings of the Thirteenth National Conference on Artificial Intelligence*, pages 1044–1049.

Satoshi Sekine. 2006. On-demand information extraction. In *Proceedings of Joint Conference of the International Committee on Computational Linguistics and the Association for Computational Linguistics (COLING/ACL-06*.

Y. Shinyama and S. Sekine. 2006. Preemptive Information Extraction using Unrestricted Relation Discovery. In *Proceedings of the Human Language Technology Conference of the North American Chapter of the Association for Computational Linguistics*, pages 304–311, New York City, NY, June.

S. Soderland, D. Fisher, J. Aseltine, and W. Lehnert. 1995. CRYSTAL: Inducing a conceptual dictionary. In *Proc. of the Fourteenth International Joint Conference on Artificial Intelligence*, pages 1314–1319.

M. Stevenson and M. Greenwood. 2005. A Semantic Approach to IE Pattern Induction. In *Proceedings of the 43rd Annual Meeting of the Association for Computational Linguistics*, pages 379–386, Ann Arbor, MI, June.

K. Sudo, S. Sekine, and R. Grishman. 2003. An Improved Extraction Pattern Representation Model for Automatic IE Pattern Acquisition. In *Proceedings of the 41st Annual Meeting of the Association for Computational Linguistics (ACL-03)*.

R. Yangarber, R. Grishman, P. Tapanainen, and S. Huttunen. 2000. Automatic Acquisition of Domain Knowledge for Information Extraction. In *Proceedings of the Eighteenth International Conference on Computational Linguistics (COLING 2000)*.

K. Yu, G. Guan, and M. Zhou. 2005. Resumé Information Extraction with Cascaded Hybrid Model. In *Proceedings of the 43rd Annual Meeting of the Association for Computational Linguistics*, pages 499–506, Ann Arbor, MI, June.

Bootstrapping Events and Relations from Text

Ting Liu
ILS, University at Albany, USA
tliu@albany.edu

Tomek Strzalkowski
ILS, University at Albany, USA
Polish Academy of Sciences
tomek@albany.edu

Abstract

In this paper, we describe a new approach to semi-supervised adaptive learning of *event extraction* from text. Given a set of examples and an un-annotated text corpus, the BEAR system (Bootstrapping Events And Relations) will automatically learn how to recognize and understand descriptions of complex semantic relationships in text, such as events involving multiple entities and their roles. For example, given a series of descriptions of bombing and shooting incidents (e.g., in newswire) the system will learn to extract, with a high degree of accuracy, other *attack*-type events mentioned elsewhere in text, irrespective of the form of description. A series of evaluations using the ACE data and event set show a significant performance improvement over our baseline system.

1 Introduction

We constructed a semi-supervised machine learning process that effectively exploits statistical and structural properties of natural language discourse in order to rapidly acquire rules to detect mentions of events and other complex relationships in text, extract their key attributes, and construct template-like representations. The learning process exploits descriptive and structural redundancy, which is common in language; it is often critical for achieving successful communication despite distractions, different contexts, or incompatible semantic models between a speaker/writer and a hearer/reader. We also take advantage of the high degree of referential consistency in discourse (e.g., as observed in word sense distribution by (Gale, et al. 1992), and arguably applicable to larger linguistic units), which enables the reader to efficiently correlate different forms of description across coherent spans of text.

The method we describe here consists of two steps: (1) supervised acquisition of initial extraction rules from an annotated training corpus, and (2) self-adapting unsupervised multi-pass bootstrapping by which the system learns new rules as it reads un-annotated text using the rules learnt in the first step and in the subsequent learning passes. When a sufficient quantity and quality of text material is supplied, the system will learn many ways in which a specific class of events can be described. This includes the capability to detect individual event mentions using a system of context-sensitive triggers and to isolate pertinent attributes such as agent, object, instrument, time, place, etc., as may be specific for each type of event. This method produces an accurate and highly adaptable event extraction that significantly outperforms current information extraction techniques both in terms of accuracy and robustness, as well as in deployment cost.

2 Learning by bootstrapping

As a semi-supervised machine learning method, bootstrapping can start either with a set of predefined rules or patterns, or with a collection of training examples (seeds) annotated by a domain expert on a (small) data set. These are normally related to a target application domain and may be regarded as initial "teacher instructions" to the learning system. The training set enables the system to derive initial extraction rules, which are applied to un-annotated text data in order to produce a much larger set of examples. The examples found by the initial rules will occur in a variety of linguistic contexts, and some of these contexts may provide support for creating *alternative extraction rules*. When the new rules are subsequently applied to the text corpus, additional instances of the target concepts will be identified, some of which will be positive and some not. As this process continues to iterate over, the system acquires more extraction rules, fanning out from the seed set until no new rules can be learned.

Thus defined, bootstrapping has been used in natural language processing research, notably in word sense disambiguation (Yarowsky, 1995). Strzalkowski and Wang (1996) were first to demonstrate that the technique could be applied to adaptive learning of named entity extraction rules. For example, given a "naïve" rule for identifying company names in text, e.g., "capitalized NP followed by *Co.*", their system would first find a large number of (mostly) positive instances of company names, such as "*Henry Kauffman Co.*" From the context surrounding each of these instances it would isolate alternative indicators, such as "*the president of*", which is noted to occur in front of many company names, as in "*The president of American Electric Automobile Co. …*". Such alternative indicators give rise to new extraction rules, e.g., "*president of* + CNAME". The new rules find more entities, including company names that do not end with *Co.*, and the process iterates until no further rules are found. The technique achieved a very high performance (95% precision and 90% recall), which encouraged more research in IE area by using bootstrapping techniques. Using a similar approach, (Thelen and Riloff, 2002) generated new syntactic patterns by exploiting the context of known seeds for learning semantic categories.

In Snowball (Agichtein and Gravano, 2000) and Yangarber's IE system (2000), bootstrapping technique was applied for extraction of binary relations, such as Organization-Location, e.g., between *Microsoft* and *Redmond, WA*. Then, Xu (2007) extended the method for more complex relations extraction by using sentence syntactic structure and a data driven pattern generation. In this paper, we describe a different approach on building event patterns and adapting to the different structures of unseen events.

3 Bootstrapping applied to event learning

Our objective in this project was to expand the bootstrapping technique to learn extraction of events from text, irrespective of their form of description, a property essential for successful adaptability to new domains and text genres. The major challenge in advancing from entities and binary relations to event learning is the complexity of structures involved that not only consist of multiple elements but their linguistic context may now extend well beyond a few surrounding words, even past sentence boundaries. These considerations guided the design of the BEAR system (Bootstrapping Events And Relations), which is described in this paper.

3.1 Event representation

An event description can vary from very concise, newswire-style to very rich and complex as may be found in essays and other narrative forms. The system needs to recognize any of these forms and to do so we need to distill each description to a basic event pattern. This pattern will capture the heads of key phrases and their dependency structure while suppressing modifiers and certain other non-essential elements. Such skeletal representations cannot be obtained with keyword analysis or linear processing of sentences at word level (e.g., Agichtein and Gravano, 2000), because such methods cannot distinguish a phrase head from its modifier. A shallow dependency parser, such as Minipar (Lin, 1998), that recognizes dependency relations between words is quite sufficient for deriving head-modifier relations and thus for construction of event templates. Event templates are obtained by stripping the parse tree of modifiers while preserving the basic dependency structure as shown in Figure 1, which is a stripped down parse tree of, "*Also Monday, Israeli soldiers **fired** on four diplomatic vehicles in the northern Gaza town of Beit Hanoun, said diplomats*"

The model proposed here represents a significant advance over the current methods for relation extraction, such as the SVO model (Yangarber, et al. 2000) and its extension, e.g., the chain model (Sudo, et al. 2001) and other related variants (Riloff, 1996) all of which lack the expressive power to accurately recognize and represent complex event descriptions and to support successful machine learning. While Sudo's subtree model (2003) overcomes some of the limitations of the chain models and is thus conceptually closer to our method, it nonetheless lacks efficiency required for practical applications.

We represent complex relations as tree-like structures anchored at an *event trigger* (which is usually but not necessarily the main verb) with branches extending to the event attributes (which are usually named entities). Unlike the singular concepts (i.e., named entities such as 'person' or

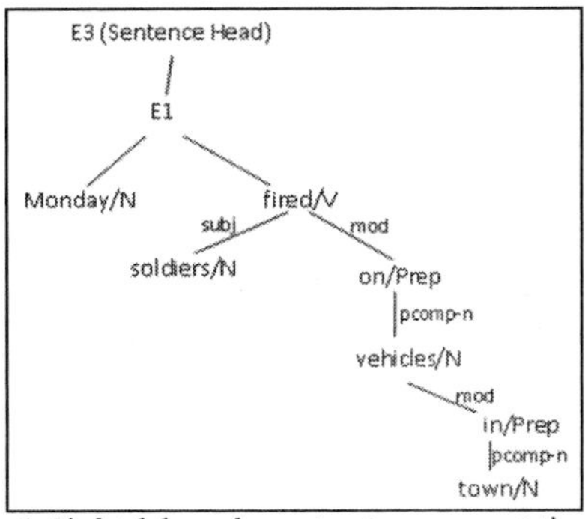

Figure 1. Skeletal dependency structure representation of an event mention.

'location') or linear relations (i.e., tuples such as 'Gates – CEO – Microsoft'), an event description consists of elements that form non-linear dependencies, which may not be apparent in the word order and therefore require syntactic and semantic analysis to extract. Furthermore, an arrangement of these elements in text can vary greatly from one event mention to the next, and there is usually other intervening material involved. Consequently, we construe event representation as a collection of *paths* linking the trigger to the attributes through the nodes of a parse tree[1].

To create an event pattern (which will be part of an extraction rule), we generalize the dependency paths that connect the event trigger with each of the event key attributes (the *roles*). A dependency path consists of lexical and syntactic relations (POS and phrase dependencies), as well as semantic relations, such as entity tags (e.g., Person, Company, etc.) of event roles and word sense designations (based on Wordnet senses) of event triggers. In addition to the trigger-role paths (which we shall call the *sub-patterns*), an event pattern also contains the following:

- Event Type and Subtype – which is inherited from seed examples;
- Trigger class – an instance of the trigger must be found in text before any patterns are applied;
- Confidence score – expected accuracy of the pattern established during training process;
- Context profile – additional features collected from the context surrounding the event description, including references of other types of events near this event, in the same sentence, same paragraph, or adjacent paragraphs.

We note that the trigger-attribute sub-patterns are defined over phrase structures rather than over linear text, as shown in Figure 2. In order to compose a complete event pattern, sub-patterns are collected across multiple mentions of the same-type event.

Attacker: <N(subj, PER): Attacker> <V(fire): trigger>
Place: <V(fire): trigger> <Prep> <N> <Prep(in)> <N(GPE): Place>
Target: <V(fire): trigger> <Prep(on)> <N(VEH): Target>
Time-Within:<N(timex2): Time-Within><SentHead><V(fire): trigger>

Figure 2. Trigger-attribute sub-patterns for key roles in a *Conflict-Attack* event pattern.

[1] Details of how to derive the skeletal tree representation are described in (Liu, 2009).

[2] t – the type of the event, w_pos – the lemma of a word and its POS.

[3] In this figure we omit the parse tree trimming step which was explained in the previous section.

3.2 Designating the sense of event triggers

An event trigger may have multiple senses but only one of them is for the event representation. If the correct sense can be determined, we would be able to use its synonyms and hyponym as alternative event triggers, thus enabling extraction of more events. This, in turn, requires sense disambiguation to be performed on the event triggers.

In MUC evaluations, participating groups (Yangarber and Grishman, 1998) used human experts to decide the correct sense of event triggers and then manually added correct synonyms to generalize event patterns. Although accurate, the process is time consuming and not portable to new domains.

We developed a new approach for utilizing Wordnet to decide the correct sense of an event trigger. The method is based on the hypothesis that event triggers will share same sense when represent same type of event. For example, when the verbs, *attack, assail, strike, gas, bomb*, are trigger words of Conflict-Attack event, they share same sense. This process is described in the following steps:

1) From training corpus, collect all triggers, which specify the lemma, POS tag, the type of event and get all possible senses of them from Wordnet.
2) Order the triggers by the *trigger frequency* TrF(t, w_pos),[2] which is calculated by dividing number of times each word (w_pos) is used as a trigger for the event of type (t) by the total number of times this word occurs in the training corpus. Clearly, the greater trigger frequency of a word, the more discriminative it is as a trigger for the given type of event. When the senses of the triggers with high accuracy are defined, they can be the reference for the triggers in low accuracy.
3) From the top of the trigger list, select the first none-sense defined trigger (Tr1)
4) Again, beginning from the top of the trigger list, for every trigger Tr2 (other than Tr1), we look for a pair of compatible senses between Tr1 and Tr2. To do so, traverse Synonym, Hypernym, and Hyponym links starting from the sense(s) of Tr2 (use either the sense already assigned to Tr2 if has or all its possible senses) and see whether there are paths which can reach the senses of Tr1. If such converging paths exist, the compatible senses

[2] t – the type of the event, w_pos – the lemma of a word and its POS.

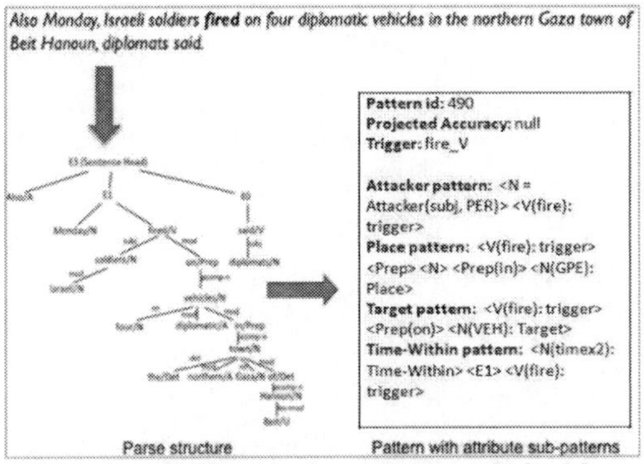

Figure 3. A Conflict-Attack event pattern derived from a positive example in the training corpus

are identified and assigned to Tr1 and Tr2 (if Tr2's sense wasn't assigned before). Then go back to step 3. However, if no such path exist between Tr1 senses with other triggers senses, the first sense listed in Wordnet will be assigned to Tr1

This algorithm tries to assign the most proper sense to every trigger for one type of event. For example, the sense of *fire* as trigger of Conflict-Attack event is "start firing a weapon"; while it is used in Personal-End_Position, its sense is "terminate the employment of". After the trigger sense is defined, we can expand event triggers by adding their synonyms and hyponyms during the event extraction.

3.3 Deriving initial rules from seed examples

Extraction rules are construed as transformations from the event patterns derived from text onto a formal representation of an event. The initial rules are derived from a manually annotated training text corpus (seed data), supplied as part of an application task. Each rule contains the type of events it extracts, trigger, a list of role sub-patterns, and the confidence score obtained through a validation process (see section 3.6). Figure 3 shows an extraction pattern for the Conflict-Attack event derived from the training corpus (but not validated yet)[3].

3.4 Learning through pattern mutation

Given an initial set of extraction rules, a variety of pattern mutation techniques are applied to derive new patterns and new rules. This is done by selecting elements of previously learnt patterns, based on the history of partial matches and combining them into new patterns. This form of learning, which also includes conditional rule relaxation, is particularly useful for rapid adaptation of extraction capability to slightly altered, partly ungrammatical, or otherwise variant data.

The basic idea is as follows: the patterns acquired in prior learning iterations (starting with those obtained from the seed examples) are matched against incoming text to extract new events. Along the way there will be a number of partial matches, i.e., when no existing pattern fully matches a span of text. This may simply mean that no event is present; however, depending upon the degree of the partial match we may also consider that a novel structural variant was found. BEAR would automatically test this hypothesis by attempting to construe a new pattern, out of the elements of existing patterns, in order to achieve a full match. If a match is achieved, the new "mutated" pattern will be added to BEAR learned collection, subject to a validation step. The validation step (discussed later in this paper) is to assure that the added pattern would not introduce an unacceptable drop in overall system precision. Specific pattern mutation techniques include the following:

- Adding a role subpattern: When a pattern matches an event mention while there is a sufficient linguistic evidence (e.g., presence of certain types of named entities) that additional roles may be present in text, then appropriate role subpatterns can be "imported" from other, non-matching patterns (Figure 4).
- Replacing a role subpattern: When a pattern matches but for one role, the system can replace this role subpattern by another subpattern for the same role taken from a different pattern for the same event type.
- Adding or replacing a trigger: When a pattern matches but for the trigger, a new trigger can be added if it either is already present in another pattern for the same event type or the synonym/hyponym/hypernym of the trigger (found in section 3.2).

We should point out that some of the same effects can be obtained by making patterns more general, i.e., adding "optional" attributes (i.e., optional sub-patterns), etc. Nonetheless, the pattern mutation is more efficient because it will automatically learn such generalization on an as-needed basis in an entirely data-driven fashion, while also maintaining high precision of the resulting pattern set. It is thus a more general method. Figure 4 illustrated the use of the elements combination technique. In this example,

[3] In this figure we omit the parse tree trimming step which was explained in the previous section.

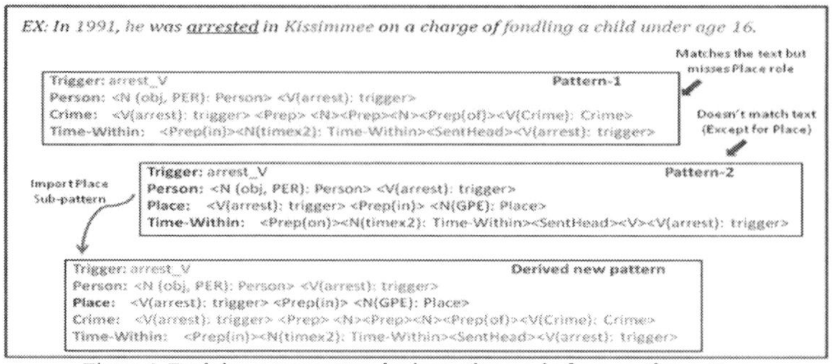

Figure 4. Deriving a new pattern by importing a role from another pattern

neither of the two existing patterns can fully match the new event description; however, by combining the first pattern with the Place role sub-pattern from the second pattern we obtain a new pattern that fully matches the text. While this adjustment is quite simple, it is nonetheless performed automatically and without any human assistance. The new pattern is then "learned" by BEAR, subject to a verification step explained in a later section.

3.5 Learning by exploiting structural duality

As the system reads through new text extracting more events using already learnt rules, each extracted event mention is analyzed for presence of alternative trigger elements that can consistently predict the presence of a subset of events that includes the current one. Subsequently, an alternative sub-pattern structure will be built with branches extending from the new trigger to the already identified attributes, as shown schematically in Figure 5.

In this example, a *Conflict-Attack*-type event is extracted using a pattern (shown in Figure 5A) anchored at the "*bombing*" trigger. Nonetheless, an alternative trigger structure is discovered, which is anchored at "an attack" NP, as shown on the right side of Figure 5. This "discovery" is based upon seeing the new trigger repeatedly – it needs to "explain" a subset of previously seen events to be adopted. The new trigger will prompt BEAR to derive additional event patterns, by computing alternative trigger-attribute paths in the dependency tree. The new pattern (shown in Figure 5B) is of course subject to confidence validation, after which it will be immediately applied to extract more events.

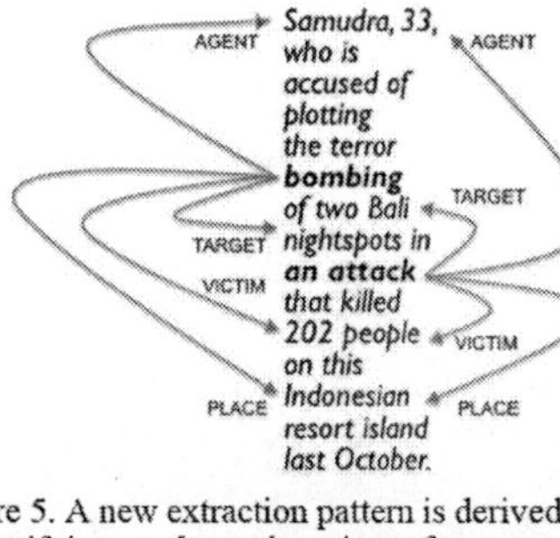

Figure 5. A new extraction pattern is derived by identifying an alternative trigger for an event.

Another way of getting at this kind of structural duality is to exploit co-referential consistency within coherent spans of discourse, e.g., a single news article or a similar document. Such documents may contain references to multiple events, but when the same type of event is mentioned along with the same attributes, it is more likely than not in reference to the same event.
This hypothesis is a variant of an argument advanced in (Gale, et al. 2000) that a polysemous word used multiple times within a single document, is consistently used in the same sense. So if we extract an event mention (of type T) with trigger *t* in one part of a document, and then find that *t* occurs in another part of the same document, then we may assume that this second occurrence of *t* has the same sense as the first. Since *t* is a trigger for an event of type T, we can hypothesize its subsequent occurrences indicate additional mentions of type T events that were not extracted by any of the existing patterns. Our objective is to exploit these unextracted mentions and then automatically generate additional event patterns.

Indeed, Ji (2008) showed that trigger co-occurrence helps finding new mentions of the

Pattern ID: 1207
Type: Conflict **Subtype:** Attack
Trigger: bombing_N
Target: <N(bombing): trigger> <Prep(of)> <N(FAC): Target>
Attacker: <N(PER): Attacker> <V> <N(bombing): trigger>
Time-Within: <N(bombing): trigger> <Prep> <N> <Prep> <N> <E0> <V> <N(timex2): Time-within>

Figure 5A. A pattern with the *bombing* trigger matches the event mention in Fig. 5.

Pattern ID: 1286
Type: Conflict **Subtype:** Attack
Trigger: attack_N
Target: <N(FAC): Target> <Prep(in)> <N(attack): trigger>
Attacker: <N(PER): Attacker> <V> <N> <Prep> <N> <Prep(in)> <N(attack): trigger>
Time-Within: <N(attack): trigger> <E0> <V> <N(timex2): Time-within>

Figure 5B. A new pattern is derived for event in Fig 5, with an *attack* as the trigger.

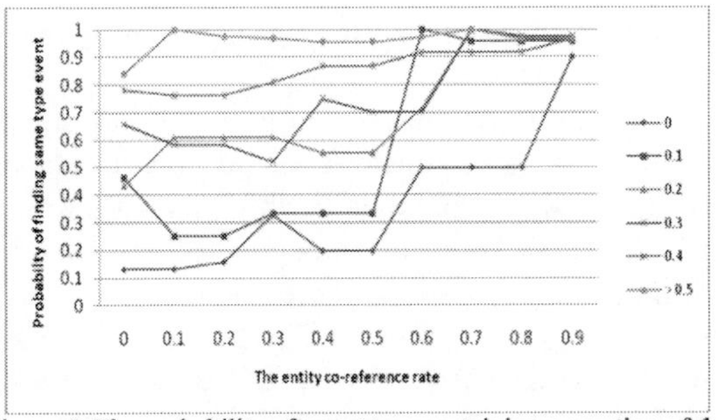

Figure 6. The probability of a sentence containing a mention of the same type of event within a single document

same event; however, we found that if using entity co-reference as another factor, more new mentions could be identified when the trigger has low projected accuracy (Liu, 2009; Yu Hong, et al. 2011). Our experiments (Figure 6[4]), which compared the triggers and the roles across all event mentions within each document on ACE training corpus, showed that when the trigger accuracy is 0.5 or higher, each of its occurrences within the document indicates an event mention of the same type with a very high probability (mostly > 0.9). For triggers with lower accuracy, this high probability is only achieved when the two mentions share at least 60% of their roles, in addition to having a common trigger. Thus our approach uses co-occurrence of both trigger and event argument for detecting new event mentions.

In Figure 7, an End-Position event is extracted from left sentence (L), with "***resign***" as the trigger and "***Capek***" and "***UBS***" assigned Person and Entity roles, respectively[5]. The right sentence (R), taken from the same document, contains the same trigger word, "***resigned***" and also the same

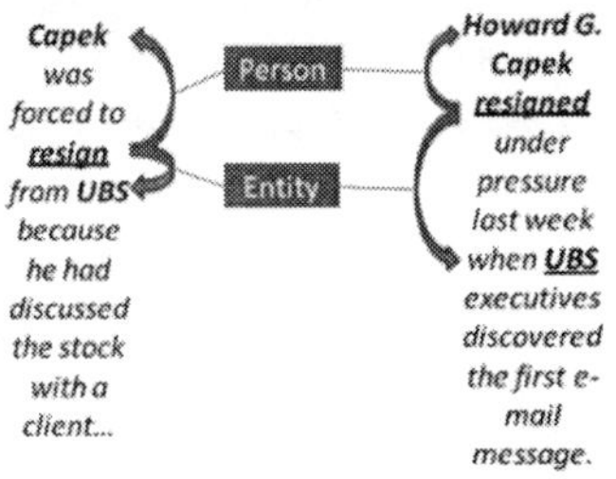

Figure 7. Two event mentions have different triggers and sub-patterns structures

Pattern ID: -1
Type: Personnel **Subtype:** End-Position
Trigger: resign_V
Person: <N(PER, subj): Person> <V(resign): trigger>
Entity: <V(resign):trigger> <E0> <N(ORG): Entity> <N> <V>

Figure 7A. A new pattern for *End-Position* learned by exploiting event co-reference.

[4] The X-axis is the percentage of entities coreferred between the EVMs (Event mentions) and the SEs (Sentences); while the Y-axis shows the probability that the SE contains a mention that is the same type as the EVM.

[5] Entity is the employer in the event

entities, "***Howard G. Capek***" and "***UBS***". The projected accuracy of *resign*_V as an End-Position trigger is 0.88. With 100% argument overlap rate, we estimate the probability that sentence R contains an event mention of the same type as sentence L (and in fact co-referential mention) at 97% (We set 80% as the threshold). Thus a new event mention is found and a new pattern for End-Position is automatically derived from R, as shown in Figure 7A.

3.6 Pattern validation

Extraction patterns are validated after each learning cycle against the already annotated data. In the first supervised learning step, patterns accuracy is tested against the training corpus based on the similarity between the extracted events and human annotated events:

- *A Full match* is achieved when the event type is correctly identified and all its roles are correctly matched. A full credit is added to the pattern score.
- *A Partial match* is achieved when the event type is correctly identified but only a subset of roles is correctly extracted. A partial score, which is the ratio of the matched roles to the whole roles, is added.
- *A False Alarm* occurs when a wrong type of event is extracted (including when no event is present in text). No credit is added to the pattern score.

In the subsequent steps, the validation is extended over parts of the unannotated corpus. In Riloff (1996) and Sudo et al. (2001), the pattern accuracy is mainly dependent on its occurrences in the relevant documents[6] vs. the whole corpus. However, one document may contain multiple types of events, thus we set a more restricted validation measure on new rules:

- *Good Match* If a new rule "rediscovers" already extracted events of the same type, then it will be counted as either a *Full Match* or *Partial Match* based on previous rules
- *Possible Match* If an already extracted event of same type of a rule contains same entities and trigger as the candidate extracted by the rule. This candidate is a possible match, so it will get a partial

[6] If a document contains same type of events extracted from previous steps, the document is a relevant document to the pattern.

Event id: 27
from: sample
Projected Accuracy: 0.1765
Adjusted Projected Accuracy: 0.91
Type: Justice **Subtype:** Arrest-Jail
Trigger: capture
Person sub-pattern: <N(obj, PER): Person> <V(capture): trigger>
Co-occurrence ratio: {para_Conflict_Demonstrate=100%, …}
Mutually exclusive ratio: {sent_Conflict_Attack=100%, para_Conflict_Attack=96.3%, …}

Figure 8. An *Arrest-Jail* pattern with context profile information

score based on the statistics result from Figure 6.

- *False Alarm* If a new rule picks up an already extracted event in different type

Thus, event patterns are validated for overall expected precision by calculating the ratio of positive matches to all matches against known events. This produces pattern confidence scores, which are used to decide if a pattern is to be learned or not. Learning only the patterns with sufficiently high confidence scores helps to guard the bootstrapping process from spinning off track; nonetheless, the overall objective is to maximize the performance of the resulting set of extraction rules, particularly by expanding its recall rate.

For the patterns where the projected accuracy score falls under the cutoff threshold, we may still be able to make some "repairs" by taking into account their context profile. To do so, we applied a similar approach as (Liao, 2010), which showed that some types of events can appeared frequently with each other. We collected all the matches produced by such a failed pattern and created a list of all other events that occur in their immediate vicinity: in the same sentence, as well as the sentences before and after it[7]. These other events, of different types and detected by different patterns, may be seen as co-occurring near the target event: these that co-occur near positive matches of our pattern will be added to the *positive context support* of this pattern; conversely, events co-occurring near false alarms will be added to the *negative context support* for this pattern. By collecting such contextual information, we can find contextually-based indicators and non-indicators for occurrence of event mentions. When these extra constraints are included in a previously failed pattern, its projected accuracy is expected to increase, in some cases above the threshold.

For example, the pattern in Figure 8 has an initially low projected accuracy score; however, we find that positive matches of this pattern show a very high (100% in fact) degree of correlation with mentions of *Demonstrate* events. Therefore, limiting the application of this pattern to situations where a *Justice-Arrest-Jail* event is mentioned in a nearby text improves its projected accuracy to 91%, which is well above the required threshold.

In addition to the confidence rate of each new pattern, we also calculate projected accuracy of each of the role sub-patterns, because they may be used in the process of detecting new patterns, and it will be necessary to score partial matches, as a function confidence weights for pattern components. To validate a sub-pattern we apply it to the training corpus and calculate its projected accuracy score by dividing the number of correctly matched roles by the total number of matches returned. The projected accuracy score will tell us how well a sub-pattern can distinguish a specific event role from other information, when used independently from other elements of the complete pattern.

Figure 9 shows three sub-pattern examples. The first sub-pattern extracts the *Victim* role in a *Life-Die* event with very high projected accuracy. This sub-pattern is also a good candidate for generations of additional patterns for this type of event, a process which we describe in section D. The second sub-pattern was built to extract the *Attacker* role in Conflict-Attack events, but it has very low projected accuracy. The third one shows another *Attacker* sub-pattern whose projected accuracy score is 0.417 after the first step

Victim pattern: <N(obj, PER): Victim> <V(kill): trigger> *(Life-Die)*
Projected Accuracy: 0.9390243902439024
Number of negative matches: 5
Number of Positive matches: 77

Attacker pattern: <N(subj, PE/PER/ORG): Attacker> <V> <V(use): trigger> *(Conflict-Attack)*
Projected Accuracy: 0.025210084033613446
Number of negative matches: 116
Number of positive matches: 3

Attacker pattern: <N(subj, GPE/PER): Attacker> <V(attack): trigger> *(Conflict-Attack)*
Projected Accuracy: 0.4166666666666667
Number of negative matches: 7
Number of positive matches: 5

categories of positive matches:	GPE: 4 GPE_Nation: 4 PER: 1 PER_Individual: 1
categories of negative matches:	GPE: 1 GPE_Nation: 1 PER: 6 PER_Group: 1 PER_Individual: 5

Figure 9. sub-patterns with projected accuracy scores

[7] If a known event is detected in the same sentence (sent_…), the same paragraph (para_…), or an adjacent paragraph (adj_para_...) as the candidate event, it becomes an element of the pattern context support.

Table 1. Sub-patterns whose projected accuracy is significantly increased after noisy samples are removed

Sub-patterns	Projected Accuracy	Additional constraints	Revised Accuracy
Movement-Transport:			
<N(obj, PER/VEH): Artifact> <V(send): trigger>	0.475	removing PER	0.667
<V(bring): trigger> <N(obj)> <Prep = to> <N(FAC/GPE): Destination>	0.375	removing GPE	1.0
...			
Conflict Attack:			
<N(PER/ORG/GPE):Attacker><N(attack):trigger>	0.682	removing PER	0.8
<N(subj,GPE/PER):Attacker><V(attack): trigger>	0.417	removing GPE	0.8
<N(obj,VEH/PER/FAC):Target><V(target):trigger>	0.364	removing PER_Individual	0.667
...			

in validation process. This is quite low; however, it can be repaired by constraining its entity type to GPE. This is because we note that with a GPE entity, the subpattern is 80% on target, while with PER entity it is 85% a false alarm. After this sub-pattern is restricted to GPE its projected accuracy becomes 0.8.

Table 1 lists example sub-patterns for which the projected accuracy increases significantly after adding more constrains. When the projected accuracy of a sub-pattern is improved, all patterns containing this sub-pattern will also improve their projected accuracy. If the adjusted projected accuracy rises above the predefined threshold, the repaired pattern will be saved.

In the following section, we will discuss the experiments conducted to evaluate the performance of the techniques underlying BEAR: how effectively it can learn and how accurately it can perform its extraction task.

4 Evaluation

We test the system learning effectiveness by comparing its performance immediately following the first iteration (i.e., using rules derived from the training data) with its performance after N cycles of unsupervised learning. We split ACE training corpus[8] randomly into 5 folders and trained BEAR on the four folders and evaluated it on the left one. Then, we did 5 fold cross validation. Our experiments showed that BEAR reached the best cross-validated score, 66.72%, when pattern accuracy threshold is set at 0.5. The highest score of single run is 67.62%. In the following of this section, we will use results of one single run to display the learning behavior of BEAR.

In Figure 10, X-axis shows values of the learning threshold (in descending order), while Y-axis is the average F-score achieved by the automatically learned patterns for all types of events against the test corpus. The red (lower) line represents BEAR's base run immediately after the first iteration (supervised learning step); the blue (upper) line represents BEAR's performance after an additional 10 unsupervised learning cycles[9] are completed. We note that the final performance of the bootstrapped system steadily increases as the learning threshold is lowered, peaking at about 0.5 threshold value, and then declines as the threshold value is further decreased, although it remains solidly above the base run. Analyzing more closely a few selected points on this chart we note, for example, that the base run at threshold of 0 has F-score of 34.5%, which represents 30.42% recall, 40% precision. On the other end of the curve, at the threshold of 0.9, the base run precision is 91.8% but recall at only 21.5%, which produces F-score of 34.8%. It is interesting to observe that at neither of these two extremes the system learning effectiveness is particularly good, and is significantly less than at

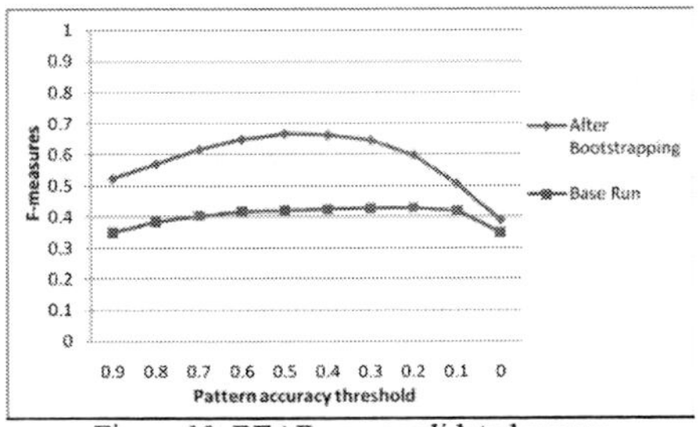

Figure 10. BEAR cross-validated scores

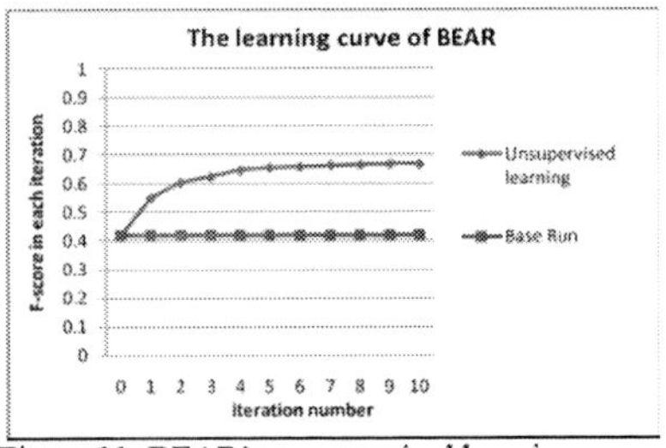

Figure 11. BEAR's unsupervised learning curve.

[8] ACE training data contains 599 documents from news, weblog, usenet, and conversational telephone speech. Total 33 types of events are defined in ACE corpus.

[9] The learning process for one type of event will stop when no new patterns can be generated, so the number of learning cycles for each event type is different. The highest number of learning cycles is 10 and lowest one is 2.

the median threshold of 0.5 (based on the experiments conducted thus far), where the system performance improves from 42% to 66.86% F-score, which represents 83.9% precision and 55.57% recall.

Figure 11 explains BEAR's learning effectiveness at what we determined empirically to be the optimal confidence threshold (0.5) for pattern acquisition. We note that the performance of the system steadily increases until it reaches a plateau after about 10 learning cycles.

Figure 12 and Figure 13 show a detailed breakdown of BEAR extraction performance after 10 learning cycles for different types of events. We note that while precision holds steady across the event types, recall levels vary significantly. The main reason for low recall in some types of events is the failure to find a sufficient number of high-confidence patterns. This may point to limitations of the current pattern discovery methods and may require new ways of reaching outside of the current feature set.

In the previous section we described several learning methods that BEAR uses to discover, validate and adapt new event extraction rules. Some of them work by manipulating already learnt patterns and adapting them to new data in order to create new patterns, and we shall call these *pattern-mutation methods* (PMM). Other described methods work by exploiting a broader linguistic context in which the events occur, or *context-based methods* (CBM). CB methods look for structural duality in text surrounding the events and thus discover alternative extraction patterns.

In Table 2, we report the results of running BEAR with each of these two groups of learning methods separately and then in combination to

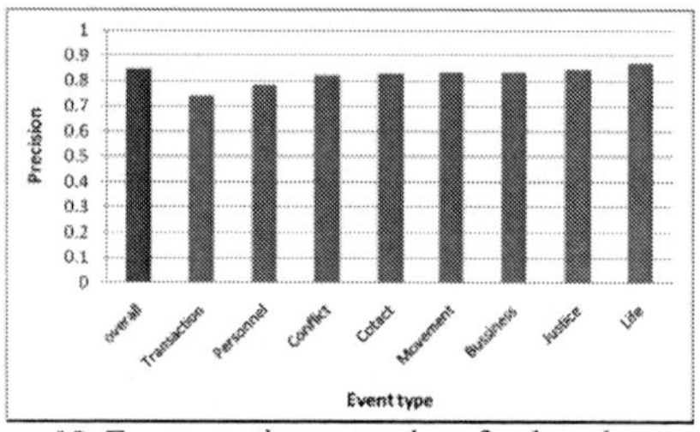

Figure 12. Event mention extraction after learning: precision for each type of event

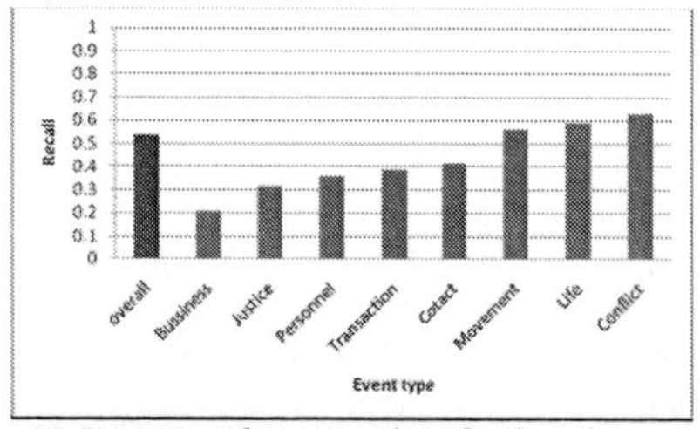

Figure 13. Event mention extraction after learning: recall for each type of event

Table 2. BEAR performance following different selections of learning steps

	Precision	Recall	F-score
Base1	0.89	0.22	0.35
Base2	0.87	0.28	0.42
All	0.84	0.56	0.67
PMM	0.84	0.48	0.61
CBM	0.86	0.37	0.52

see how they contribute to the end performance. Base1 and Base2 showed the result without and with adding trigger synonyms in event extraction. By introducing trigger synonyms, 27% more good events were extracted at the first iteration and thus, BEAR had more resources to use in the unsupervised learning steps.

The ALL is the combination of PMM and CBM, which demonstrate both methods have the contribution to the final results. Furthermore, as explained before, new extraction rules are learned in each iteration cycle based on what was learned in prior cycles and that new rules are adopted only after they are tested for their projected accuracy (confidence score), so that the overall precision of the resulting rule set is maintained at a high level relative to the base run.

5 Conclusion and future work

In this paper, we presented a semi-supervised method for learning new event extraction patterns from un-annotated text. The techniques described here add significant new tools that increase capabilities of information extraction technology in general, and more specifically, of systems that are built by purely supervised methods or from manually designed rules. Our evaluation using ACE dataset demonstrated that that bootstrapping can be effectively applied to learning event extraction rules for 33 different types of events and that the resulting system can outperform supervised system (base run) significantly.

Some follow-up research issues include:

- New techniques are needed to recognize event descriptions that still evade the current pattern derivation techniques, especially for the events defined in *Personnel*, *Business*, and *Transactions* classes.
- Adapting the bootstrapping method to extract events in a different language, e.g. Chinese or Arabic.
- Expanding this method to extraction of larger "scenarios", i.e., groups of correlated events that form coherent "stories" often described in larger sections of text, e.g., an event and its immediate consequences.

References

Agichtein, E. and Gravano, L. 2000. Snowball: Extracting Relations from Large Plain-Text Collections. In *Proceedings of the Fifth ACM International Conference on Digital Libraries*

Gale, W. A., Church, K. W., and Yarowsky, D. 1992. One sense per discourse. In *Proceedings of the workshop on Speech and Natural Language*, 233-237. Harriman, New York: Association for Computational Linguistics.

Hong, Y., Zhang, J., Ma, B., Yao, J., Zhou, G., and Zhu, Q,. 2011. Using Cross-Entity Inference to Improve Event Extraction. In *Proceedings of the Annual Meeting of the Association of Computational Linguistics (ACL 2011)*. Portland, Oregon, USA.

Ji, H. and Grishman, R. 2008. Refining Event Extraction Through Unsupervised Cross-document Inference. In *Proceedings of the Annual Meeting of the Association of Computational Linguistics (ACL 2008)*.Ohio, USA.

Liao, S. and Grishman R. 2010. Using Document Level Cross-Event Inference to Improve Event Extraction. *In Proc. ACL-2010,* pages 789-797, Uppsala, Sweden, July.

Lin, D. 1998. Dependency-based evaluation of MINIPAR. In *Workshop on the Evaluation of Parsing System,* Granada, Spain.

Liu Ting. 2009. BEAR: Bootstrap Event and Relations from Text. Ph.D. Thesis

Riloff, E. 1996. Automatically Generating Extraction Patterns from Untagged Text. In *Proceedings of the Thirteenth National Conference on Artificial Intelligence*, pages 1044–1049. The AAAI Press/MIT Press.

Sudo, K., Sekine, S., Grishman, R. 2001. Automatic Pattern Acquisition for Japanese Information Extraction. In *Proceedings of Human Language Technology Conference (HLT2001)*.

Sudo, K., Sekine, S., Grishman, R. 2003. An improved extraction pattern representation model for automatic IE pattern acquisition. *Proceedings of ACL 2003* , 224 – 231. Tokyo.

Strzalkowski, T., and Wang, J. 1996. A self-learning universal concept spotter. In *Proceedings of the 16th conference on Computational linguistics - Volume 2*, 931-936, Copenhagen, Denmark: Association for Computational Linguistics

Thelen, M., Riloff, E. 2002. A bootstrapping method for learning semantic lexicons using extraction pattern contexts. In *Proceedings of the ACL-02 conference on Empirical methods in natural language processing - Volume 10*. 214-222. Morristown, NJ: Association for Computational Linguistics

Xu, F., Uszkoreit, H., & Li, H. (2007). A seed-driven bottom-up machine learning framework for extracting relations of various complexity. In Proc. of the 45th Annual Meeting of the Association of Comp. Linguistics, pp. 584–591, Prague, Czech Republic.

Yangarber, R., and Grishman, R. 1998. NYU: Description of the Proteus/PET System as Used for MUC-7 ST. In *Proceedings of the 7th conference on Message understanding*.

Yangarber, R., Grishman, R., Tapanainen, P., and Huttunen, S. 2000. Unsupervised discovery of scenario-level patterns for information extraction. In *Proceedings of the Sixth Conference on Applied Natural Language Processing, (ANLP-NAACL 2000)*, 282-289

Yarowsky, D. 1995. Unsupervised word sense disambiguation rivaling supervised methods. In *Proceedings of the 33rd annual meeting on Association for Computational Linguistics*, 189-196, Cambridge, Massachusetts: Association for Computational Linguistics

CLex: A Lexicon for Exploring Color, Concept and Emotion Associations in Language

Svitlana Volkova
Johns Hopkins University
3400 North Charles
Baltimore, MD 21218, USA
svitlana@jhu.edu

William B. Dolan
Microsoft Research
One Microsoft Way
Redmond, WA 98052, USA
billdol@microsoft.com

Theresa Wilson
HLTCOE
810 Wyman Park Drive
Baltimore, MD 21211, USA
taw@jhu.edu

Abstract

Existing concept-color-emotion lexicons limit themselves to small sets of basic emotions and colors, which cannot capture the rich pallet of color terms that humans use in communication. In this paper we begin to address this problem by building a novel, color-emotion-concept association lexicon via crowdsourcing. This lexicon, which we call CLEX, has over 2,300 color terms, over 3,000 affect terms and almost 2,000 concepts. We investigate the relation between color and concept, and color and emotion, reinforcing results from previous studies, as well as discovering new associations. We also investigate cross-cultural differences in color-emotion associations between US and India-based annotators.

1 Introduction

People typically use color terms to describe the visual characteristics of objects, and certain colors often have strong associations with particular objects, *e.g., blue - sky, white - snow*. However, people also take advantage of color terms to strengthen their messages and convey emotions in natural interactions (Jacobson and Bender, 1996; Hardin and Maffi, 1997). Colors are both indicative of and have an effect on our feelings and emotions. Some colors are associated with positive emotions, *e.g., joy, trust* and *admiration* and some with negative emotions, *e.g., aggressiveness, fear, boredom* and *sadness* (Ortony et al., 1988).

Given the importance of color and visual descriptions in conveying emotion, obtaining a deeper understanding of the associations between colors, concepts and emotions may be helpful for many tasks in language understanding and generation. A detailed set of color-concept-emotion associations (*e.g., brown - darkness - boredom; red - blood - anger*) could be quite useful for sentiment analysis, for example, in helping to understand what emotion a newspaper article, a fairy tale, or a tweet is trying to evoke (Alm et al., 2005; Mohammad, 2011b; Kouloumpis et al., 2011). Color-concept-emotion associations may also be useful for textual entailment, and for machine translation as a source of paraphrasing.

Color-concept-emotion associations also have the potential to enhance human-computer interactions in many real- and virtual-world domains, *e.g.,* online shopping, and avatar construction in gaming environments. Such knowledge may allow for clearer and hopefully more natural descriptions by users, for example searching for *a sky-blue shirt* rather than *blue* or *light blue shirt*. Our long term goal is to use color-emotion-concept associations to enrich dialog systems with information that will help them generate more appropriate responses to users' different emotional states.

This work introduces a new lexicon of color-concept-emotion associations, created through crowdsourcing. We call this lexicon CLEX[1]. It is comparable in size to only two known lexicons: WORDNET-AFFECT (Strapparava and Valitutti, 2004) and EMOLEX (Mohammad and Turney, 2010). In contrast to the development of these lexicons, we do not restrict our annotators to a particular set of emotions. This allows us to

[1] Available for download at: http://research.microsoft.com/en-us/downloads/
Questions about the data and the access process may be sent to svitlana@jhu.edu

collect more linguistically rich color-concept annotations associated with mood, cognitive state, behavior and attitude. We also do not have any restrictions on color naming, which helps us to discover a rich lexicon of color terms and collocations that represent various hues, darkness, saturation and other natural language collocations.

We also perform a comprehensive analysis of the data by investigating several questions including: What affect terms are evoked by a certain color, *e.g.,* positive *vs.* negative? What concepts are frequently associated with a particular color? What is the distribution of part-of-speech tags over concepts and affect terms in the data collected without any preselected set of affect terms and concepts? What affect terms are strongly associated with a certain concept or a category of concepts and is there any correlation with a semantic orientation of a concept?

Finally, we share our experience collecting the data using crowdsourcing, describe advantages and disadvantages as well as the strategies we used to ensure high quality annotations.

2 Related Work

Interestingly, some color-concept associations vary by culture and are influenced by the traditions and beliefs of a society. As shown in (Sable and Akcay, 2010) *green* represents *danger* in Malaysia, *envy* in Belgium, *love* and *happiness* in Japan; *red* is associated with *luck* in China and Denmark, but with *bad luck* in Nigeria and Germany and reflects *ambition* and *desire* in India.

Some expressions involving colors share the same meaning across many languages. For instance, *white heat or red heat* (the state of high physical and mental tension), *blue-blood* (an aristocrat, royalty), *white-collar or blue collar* (office clerks). However, there are some expressions where color associations differ across languages, *e.g.,* British or Italian *black eye* becomes *blue* in Germany, *purple* in Spain and *black-butter* in France; your French, Italian and English neighbors are *green with envy* while Germans are *yellow with envy* (Bortoli and Maroto, 2001).

There has been little academic work on constructing color-concept and color-emotion lexicons. The work most closely related to ours collects concept-color (Mohammad, 2011c) and concept-emotion (EMOLEX) associations, both relying on crowdsourcing. His project involved collecting color and emotion annotations for 10,170 word-sense pairs from Macquarie Thesaurus[2]. They analyzed their annotations, looking for associations with the 11 basic color terms from Berlin and Key (1988). The set of emotion labels used in their annotations was restricted to the set of 8 basic emotions proposed by Plutchik (1980). Their annotators were restricted to the US, and produced 4.45 annotations per word-sense pair on average.

There is also a commercial project from Cymbolism[3] to collect concept-color associations. It has 561,261 annotations for a restricted set of 256 concepts, mainly nouns, adjectives and adverbs.

Other work on collecting emotional aspect of concepts includes WordNet-Affect (WNA) (Strapparava and Valitutti, 2004), the General Enquirer (GI) (Stone et al., 1966), Affective Forms of English Words (Bradley and Lang, 1999) and Elliott's Affective Reasoner (Elliott, 1992).

The WNA lexicon is a set of affect terms from WordNet (Miller, 1995). It contains emotions, cognitive states, personality traits, behavior, attitude and feelings, *e.g., joy, doubt, competitive, cry, indifference, pain.* Total of 289 affect terms were manually extracted, but later the lexicon was extended using WordNet semantic relationships. WNA covers 1903 affect terms - 539 nouns, 517 adjectives, 238 verbs and 15 adverbs.

The General Enquirer covers 11,788 concepts labeled with 182 category labels including certain affect categories (*e.g., pleasure, arousal, feeling, pain*) in addition to positive/negative semantic orientation for concepts[4].

Affective Forms of English Words is a work which describes a manually collected set of normative emotional ratings for 1K English words that are rated in terms of emotional arousal (ranging from *calm* to *excited*), affective valence (ranging from *pleasant* to *unpleasant*) and dominance (ranging from *in control* to *dominated*).

Elliott's Affective Reasoner is a collection of programs that is able to reason about human emotions. The system covers a set of 26 emotion categories from Ortony et al (1988).

Kaya (2004) and Strapparava and Ozbal (2010) both have worked on inferring emotions associated with colors using semantic similarity. Their

[2]http://www.macquarieonline.com.au

[3]http://www.cymbolism.com/

[4]http://www.wjh.harvard.edu/~inquirer/

research found that Americans perceive *red* as excitement, *yellow* as cheer, *purple* as dignity and associate *blue* with comfort and security. Other research includes that geared toward discovering culture-specific color-concept associations (Gage, 1993) and color preference, for example, in children *vs.* adults (Ou et al., 2011).

3 Data Collection

In order to collect color-concept and color-emotion associations, we use Amazon Mechanical Turk[5]. It is a fast and relatively inexpensive way to get a large amount of data from many cultures all over the world.

3.1 MTurk and Data Quality

Amazon Mechanical Turk is a crowdsourcing platform that has been extensively used for obtaining low-cost human annotations for various linguistic tasks over the last few years (Callison-Burch, 2009). The quality of the data obtained from non-expert annotators, also referred to as workers or turkers, was investigated by Snow et al (2008). Their empirical results show that the quality of non-expert annotations is comparable to the quality of expert annotations on a variety of natural language tasks, but the cost of the annotation is much lower.

There are various quality control strategies that can be used to ensure annotation quality. For instance, one can restrict a "crowd" by creating a pilot task that allows only workers who passed the task to proceed with annotations (Chen and Dolan, 2011). In addition, new quality control mechanisms have been recently introduced *e.g., Masters*. They are groups of workers who are trusted for their consistent high quality annotations, but to employ them costs more.

Our task required direct natural language input from workers and did not include any multiple choice questions (which tend to attract more cheating). Thus, we limited our quality control efforts to (1) checking for empty input fields and (2) blocking copy/paste functionality on a form. We did not ask workers to complete any qualification tasks because it is impossible to have gold standard answers for color-emotion and color-concept associations. In addition, we limited our crowd to a set of trusted workers who had been consistently working on similar tasks for us.

[5]http://www.mturk.com

3.2 Task Design

Our task was designed to collect a linguistically rich set of color terms, emotions, and concepts that were associated with a large set of colors, specifically the 152 RGB values corresponding to facial features of cartoon human avatars. In total we had 36 colors for hair/eyebrows, 18 for eyes, 27 for lips, 26 for eye shadows, 27 for facial mask and 18 for skin. These data is necessary to achieve our long-term goal which is to model natural human-computer interactions in a virtual world domain such as the avatar editor.

We designed two MTurk tasks. For Task 1, we showed a swatch for one RGB value and asked 50 workers to name the color, describe emotions this color evokes and define a set of concepts associated with that color. For Task 2, we showed a particular facial feature and a swatch in a particular color, and asked 50 workers to name the color and describe the concepts and emotions associated with that color. Figure 1 shows what would be presented to worker for Task 2.

Q1. How would you name this color?
Q2. What emotion does this color evoke?
Q3. What concepts do you associate with it?

Figure 1: Example of MTurk Task 2. Task 1 is the same except that only a swatch is given.

The design that we suggested has a minor limitation in that a color swatch may display differently on different monitors. However, we hope to overcome this issue by collecting 50 annotations per RGB value. The example color $\xrightarrow{e}$ emotion $\xrightarrow{c}$ concept associations produced by different annotators a_i are shown below:

- [R=222, G=207, B=186] (a_1) light golden yellow $\xrightarrow{e}$ purity, happiness $\xrightarrow{c}$ butter cookie, vanilla; (a_2) gold $\xrightarrow{e}$ cheerful, happy $\xrightarrow{c}$ sun, corn; (a_3) golden $\xrightarrow{e}$ sexy $\xrightarrow{c}$ beach, jewelery.

- [R=218, G=97, B=212] (a_4) pinkish purple $\xrightarrow{e}$ peace, tranquility, stressless $\xrightarrow{c}$ justin bieber's headphones, someday perfume; (a_5) pink $\xrightarrow{e}$ happiness $\xrightarrow{c}$ rose, bougainvillea.

In addition, we collected data about workers' gender, age, native language, number of years of experience with English, and color preferences. This data is useful for investigating variance in annotations for color-emotion-concept associations among workers from different cultural and linguistic backgrounds.

4 Data Analysis

We collected 15,200 annotations evenly divided between the two tasks over 12 days. In total, 915 workers (41% male, 51% female and 8% who did not specify), mainly from India and United States, completed our tasks as shown in Table 1. 18% workers produced 20 or more annotations. They spent 78 seconds on average per annotation with an average salary rate \$2.3 per hour (\$0.05 per completed task).

Country	Annotations
India	7844
United States	5824
Canada	187
United Kingdom	172
Colombia	100

Table 1: Demographic information about annotators: top 5 countries represented in our dataset.

In total, we collected 2,315 unique color terms, 3,397 unique affect terms, and 1,957 unique concepts for the given 152 RGB values. In the sections below we discuss our findings on color naming, color-emotion and color-concept associations. We also give a comparison of annotated affect terms and concepts from CLEX and other existing lexicons.

4.1 Color Terms

Berlin and Kay (1988) state that as languages evolve they acquire new color terms in a strict chronological order. When a language has only two colors they are white (light, warm) and black (dark, cold). English is considered to have 11 basic colors: *white, black, red, green, yellow, blue, brown, pink, purple, orange and gray*, which is known as the B&K order.

In addition, colors can be distinguished along at most three independent dimensions of hue (*olive, orange*), darkness (*dark, light, medium*), saturation (*grayish, vivid*), and brightness (*deep, pale*) (Mojsilovic, 2002). Interestingly, we observe these dimensions in CLEX by looking for B&K color terms and their frequent collocations. We present the top 10 color collocations for the B&K colors in Table 2. As can be seen, color terms truly are distinguished by darkness, saturation and brightness terms *e.g., light, dark, greenish, deep*. In addition, we find that color terms are also associated with color-specific collocations, *e.g., sky blue, chocolate brown, pea green, salmon pink, carrot orange*. These collocations were produced by annotators to describe the color of particular RGB values. We investigate these color-concept associations in more details in Section 4.3.

In total, the CLEX has 2,315 unique color

Color	Co-occurrences	$\sum$
white	off, antique, half, dark, black, bone, milky, pale, pure, silver	0.62
black	light, blackish brown, brownish, brown, jet, dark, green, off, ash, blackish grey	0.43
red	dark, light, dish brown, brick, orange, brown, indian, dish, crimson, bright	0.59
green	dark, light, olive, yellow, lime, forest, sea, dark olive, pea, dirty	0.54
yellow	light, dark, green, pale, golden, brown, mustard, orange, deep, bright	0.63
blue	light, sky, dark, royal, navy, baby, grey, purple, cornflower, violet	0.55
brown	dark, light, chocolate, saddle, reddish, coffee, pale, deep, red, medium	0.67
pink	dark, light, hot, pale, salmon, baby, deep, rose, coral, bright	0.55
purple	light, dark, deep, blue, bright, medium, pink, pinkish, bluish, pretty	0.69
orange	light, burnt, red, dark, yellow, brown, brownish, pale, bright, carrot	0.68
gray	dark, light, blue, brown, charcoal, leaden, greenish, grayish blue, pale, grayish brown	0.62

Table 2: Top 10 color term collocations for the 11 B&K colors; co-occurrences are sorted by frequency from left to right in a decreasing order; $\sum_1^{10} p(\bullet \mid color)$ is a total estimated probability of the top 10 co-occurrences.

Agreement	Color Term	
% of overall	Exact match	0.492
agreement	Substring match	0.461
Free-marginal	Exact match	0.458
Kappa	Substring match	0.424

Table 3: Inter-annotator agreement on assigning names to RGB values: 100 annotators, 152 RGB values and 16 color categories including 11 B&K colors, 4 additional colors and none of the above.

names for the set of 152 RGB values. The inter-annotator agreement rate on color naming is shown in Table 3. We report free-marginal Kappa (Randolph, 2005) because we did not force annotators to assign certain number of RGB values to a certain number of color terms. Additionally, we report inter-annotator agreement for an exact string match *e.g., purple, green* and a substring match *e.g., pale yellow = yellow = golden yellow.*

4.2 Color-Emotion Associations

In total, the CLEX lexicon has 3,397 unique affect terms representing feelings *(calm, pleasure)*, emotions *(joy, love, anxiety)*, attitudes *(indifference, caution)*, and mood *(anger, amusement)*. The affect terms in CLEX include the 8 basic emotions from (Plutchik, 1980): *joy, sadness, anger, fear, disgust, surprise, trust and anticipation*[6]

CLEX is a very rich lexicon because we did not restrict our annotators to any specific set of affect terms. A wide range of parts-of-speech are represented, as shown in the first column in Table 4. For instance, the term *love* is represented by other semantically related terms such as: *lovely, loved, loveliness, loveless, love-able* and the term *joy* is represented as *enjoy, enjoyable, enjoyment, joyful, joyfulness, overjoyed.*

POS	Affect Terms, %	Concepts, %
Nouns	79	52
Adjectives	12	29
Adverbs	3	5
Verbs	6	12

Table 4: Main syntactic categories for affect terms and concepts in CLEX.

The manually constructed portion of WORDNET-AFFECT includes 101 positive and 188 negative affect terms (Strapparava and Valitutti, 2004). Of this set, 41% appeared at least once in CLEX. We also looked specifically at the set of terms labeled as emotions in the WORDNET-AFFECT hierarchy. Of these, 12 are positive emotions and 10 are negative emotions.

We found that 9 out of 12 positive emotion terms (except *self-pride*, *levity* and *fearlessness*) and 9 out of 10 negative emotion terms (except *ingratitude*) also appear in CLEX as shown in Table 5. Thus, we can conclude that annotators do not associate any colors with *self-pride, levity, fearlessness* and *ingratitude*. In addition, some emotions were associated more frequently with colors than others. For instance, positive emotions like *calmness, joy, love* are more frequent in CLEX than *expectation* and *ingratitude*; negative emotions like *sadness, fear* are more frequent than *shame, humility* and *daze*.

Positive	Freq.	Negative	Freq.
calmness	1045	sadness	356
joy	527	fear	250
love	482	anxiety	55
hope	147	despair	19
affection	86	compassion	10
enthusiasm	33	dislike	8
liking	5	shame	5
expectation	3	humility	3
gratitude	3	daze	1

Table 5: WORDNET-AFFECT positive and negative emotion terms from CLEX. Emotions are sorted by frequency in decreasing order from the total 27,802 annotations.

Next, we analyze the color-emotion associations in CLEX in more detail and compare them with the only other publicly-available color-emotion lexicon, EMOLEX. Recall that EMOLEX (Mohammad, 2011a) has 11 B&K colors associated with 8 basic positive and negative emotions from (Plutchik, 1980). Affect terms in CLEX are not labeled as conveying positive or negative emotions. Instead, we use the overlapping 289 affect terms between WORDNET-AFFECT and CLEX and propagate labels from WORDNET-AFFECT to the corresponding affect terms in CLEX. As a result we discover positive and negative affect term associations with the 11 B&K colors. Table 6 shows the percentage of positive and negative affect term associations with colors for both CLEX and EMOLEX.

[6]The set of 8 Plutchik's emotions is a superset of emotions from (Ekman, 1992).

	Positive		Negative	
	CLEX	EL	CLEX	EL
white	**2.5**	**20.1**	0.3	2.9
black	0.6	3.9	**9.3**	**28.3**
red	1.7	8.0	**8.2**	**21.6**
green	**3.3**	**15.5**	2.7	4.7
yellow	**3.0**	**10.8**	0.7	6.9
blue	**5.9**	**12.0**	1.6	4.1
brown	6.5	4.8	**7.6**	**9.4**
pink	**5.6**	**7.8**	1.1	1.2
purple	**3.1**	**5.7**	1.8	2.5
orange	1.6	**5.4**	**1.7**	3.8
gray	1.0	5.7	**3.6**	**14.1**

Table 6: The percentage of affect terms associated with B&K colors in CLEX and EMOLEX (similar color-emotion associations are shown in bold).

The percentage of color-emotion associations in CLEX and EMOLEX differs because the set of affect terms in CLEX consists of 289 positive and negative affect terms compared to 8 affect terms in EMOLEX. Nevertheless, we observe the same pattern as (Mohammad, 2011a) for negative emotions. They are associated with *black, red* and *gray* colors, except *yellow* becomes a color of positive emotions in CLEX. Moreover, we found the associations with the color *brown* to be ambiguous as it was associated with both positive and negative emotions. In addition, we did not observe strong associations between *white* and positive emotions. This may be because *white* is the color of *grief* in India. The rest of the positive emotions follow the EMOLEX pattern and are associated with *green, pink, blue* and *purple* colors.

Next, we perform a detailed comparison between CLEX and EMOLEX color-emotion associations for the 11 B&K colors and the 8 basic emotions from (Plutchik, 1980) in Table 7. Recall that annotations in EMOLEX are done by workers from the USA only. Thus, we report two numbers for CLEX - annotations from workers from the USA (C_A) and all annotations (C). We take EMOLEX results from (Mohammad, 2011c). We observe a strong correlation between CLEX and EMOLEX affect lexicons for some color-emotion associations. For instance, *anger* has a strong association with *red* and *brown*, *anticipation* with *green*, *fear* with *black*, *joy* with *pink*, *sadness* with *black, brown* and *gray*, *surprise* with *yellow* and *orange*, and finally, *trust* is associated with *blue* and *brown*. Nonetheless, we also found a disagreement in color-emotion associations between CLEX and EMOLEX. For instance *anticipation* is associated with *orange* in CLEX compared to *white, red* or *yellow* in EMOLEX. We also found quite a few inconsistent associations with the *disgust* emotion. This inconsistency may be explained by several reasons: (a) EMOLEX associates emotions with colors through concepts, but CLEX has color-emotion associations obtained directly from annotators; (b) CLEX has 3,397 affect terms compared to 8 basic emotions in EMOLEX. Therefore, it may be introducing some ambiguous color-emotion associations.

Finally, we investigate cross-cultural differences in color-emotion associations between the two most representative groups of our annotators: US-based and India-based. We consider the 8 Plutchik's emotions and allow associations with all possible color terms (rather than only 11 B&K colors). We show top 5 colors associated with emotions for two groups of annotators in Figure 2. For example, we found that US-based annotators associate *pink* with *joy*, *dark brown* with *trust vs.* India-based annotators who associate *yellow* with *joy* and *blue* with *trust*.

4.3 Color-Concept Associations

In total, workers annotated the 152 RGB values with 37,693 concepts which is on average 2.47 concepts compared to 1.82 affect term per annotation. CLEX contains 1,957 unique concepts including 1,667 nouns, 23 verbs, 28 adjectives, and 12 adverbs. We investigate an overlap of concepts by part-of-speech tag between CLEX and other lexicons including EMOLEX (EL), Affective Norms of English Words (AN), General Inquirer (GI). The results are shown in Table 8.

Finally, we generate concept clusters associated with *yellow, white* and *brown* colors in Figure 3. From the clusters, we observe the most frequent k concepts associated with these colors have a correlation with either positive or negative emotion. For example, *white* is frequently associated with *snow, milk, cloud* and all of these concepts evolve positive emotions. This observation helps resolve the ambiguity in color-emotion associations we found in Table 7.

5 Conclusions

We have described a large-scale crowdsourcing effort aimed at constructing a rich color-emotion-

		white	*black*	*red*	*green*	*yellow*	*blue*	*brown*	*pink*	*purple*	*orange*	*grey*
	C	-	3.6	**43.4**	0.3	0.3	0.3	3.3	0.6	0.3	1.5	2.1
anger	C_A	-	3.8	**40.6**	0.8	-	-	4.5	-	0.8	2.3	0.8
	E_A	2.1	30.7	**32.4**	5.0	5.0	2.4	6.6	0.5	2.3	2.5	9.9
	C	0.3	**24.0**	0.3	0.6	0.3	4.2	**11.4**	0.3	2.2	0.3	**10.3**
sadness	C_A	-	**22.2**	-	0.6	-	5.3	**9.4**	-	4.1	-	**12.3**
	E_A	3.0	**36.0**	**18.6**	3.4	5.4	5.8	7.1	0.5	1.4	2.1	**16.1**
	C	0.8	**43.0**	**8.9**	2.0	1.2	0.4	6.1	0.4	0.8	0.4	2.0
fear	C_A	-	**29.5**	**10.5**	3.2	1.1	-	3.2	-	1.1	1.1	4.2
	E_A	4.5	**31.8**	**25.0**	3.5	6.9	3.0	6.1	1.3	2.3	3.3	11.8
	C	-	2.3	1.1	**11.2**	1.1	1.1	**24.7**	1.1	3.4	1.1	-
disgust	C_A	-	-	-	**14.8**	1.8	-	**33.3**	-	1.8	-	-
	E_A	2.0	**33.7**	**24.9**	4.8	5.5	1.9	9.7	1.1	1.8	3.5	10.5
	C	1.0	0.2	0.2	3.4	5.7	4.2	4.2	**9.1**	4.4	4.0	0.6
joy	C_A	0.9	-	0.3	3.3	4.5	4.8	2.7	**10.6**	4.2	3.9	0.6
	E_A	**21.8**	2.2	7.4	14.1	13.4	11.3	3.1	11.1	6.3	5.8	2.8
	C	-	-	1.2	3.5	1.2	**17.4**	8.1	1.2	1.2	5.8	1.2
trust	C_A	-	-	3.0	**6.1**	3.0	3.0	**9.1**	-	-	3.0	3.0
	E_A	22.0	6.3	8.4	**14.2**	8.3	**14.4**	5.9	5.5	4.9	3.8	5.8
	C	-	-	-	3.3	6.7	6.7	3.3	3.3	6.7	**13.3**	3.3
surprise	C_A	-	-	-	-	5.6	5.6	-	5.6	**11.1**	**11.1**	-
	E_A	11.0	13.4	**21.0**	8.3	13.5	5.2	3.4	5.2	4.1	5.6	8.8
	C	-	-	-	5.3	5.3	-	5.3	5.3	-	**15.8**	5.3
anticipation	C_A	-	-	-	-	-	-	-	10.0	-	10.0	10.0
	E_A	16.2	7.5	11.5	**16.2**	10.7	9.5	5.7	5.9	3.1	4.9	8.4

Table 7: The percentage of the 8 basic emotions associated with 11 B&K colors in CLEX *vs.* EMOLEX, *e.g.*, *sadness* is associated with *black* by 36% of annotators in EMOLEX(E_A), 22.1% in CLEX(C_A) by US-based annotators only and 24% in CLEX(C) by all annotators; we report zero associations by "-".

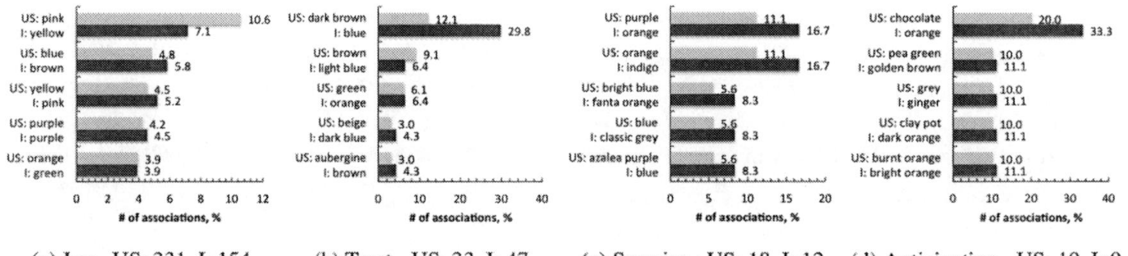

(a) Joy - US: 331, I: 154 (b) Trust - US: 33, I: 47 (c) Surprise - US: 18, I: 12 (d) Anticipation - US: 10, I: 9

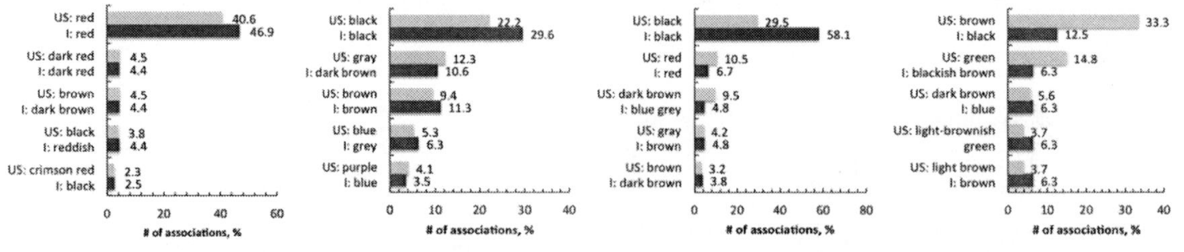

(e) Anger - US: 133, I: 160 (f) Sadness - US: 171, I: 142 (g) Fear - US: 95, I: 105 (h) Disgust - US: 54, I: 16

Figure 2: Apparent cross-cultural differences in color-emotion associations between US- and India-based annotators. 10.6% of US workers associated *joy* with *pink*, while 7.1% India-based workers associated *joy* with *yellow* (based on 331 *joy* associations from the US and from 154 India).

(a) Yellow (b) Brown (c) White

Figure 3: Concept clusters of color-concept associations for ambiguous colors: *yellow, white, brown*.

concept association lexicon, CLEX. This lexicon links concepts, color terms and emotions to specific RGB values. This lexicon may help to disambiguate objects when modeling conversational interactions in many domains. We have examined the association between color terms and positive or negative emotions.

Our work also investigated cross-cultural differences in color-emotion associations between India- and US-based annotators. We identified frequent color-concept associations, which suggests that concepts associated with a particular color may express the same sentiment as the color.

Our future work includes applying statistical inference for discovering a hidden structure of concept-emotion associations. Moreover, automatically identifying the strength of association between a particular concept and emotions is another task which is more difficult than just identifying the polarity of the word. We are also interested in using a similar approach to investigate the way that colors are associated with concepts and emotions in languages other than English.

CLEX∩AN		CLEX∩EL		CLEX∩GI	
Noun	287	Noun	574	Noun	708
Verb	4	Verb	13	Verb	17
Adj	28	Adj	53	Adj	66
Adv	1	Adv	2	Adv	3
	320		**642**		**794**
AN\CLEX		EL\CLEX		GI\CLEX	
	712		**7,445**		**11,101**
CLEX\AN		CLEX\EL		CLEX\GI	
	1,637		**1,315**		**1,163**

Table 8: An overlap of concepts by part-of-speech tag between CLEX and existing lexicons. CLEX∩GI stands for the intersection of sets, CLEX\GI denotes the difference of sets.

Acknowledgments

We are grateful to everyone in the NLP group at Microsoft Research for helpful discussion and feedback especially Chris Brocket, Piali Choudhury, and Hassan Sajjad. We thank Natalia Rud from Tyumen State University, Center of Linguistic Education for helpful comments and suggestions.

References

Cecilia Ovesdotter Alm, Dan Roth, and Richard Sproat. 2005. Emotions from text: machine learning for text-based emotion prediction. In *Proceedings of the conference on Human Language Technology and Empirical Methods in Natural Language Processing*, HLT '05, pages 579–586, Stroudsburg, PA, USA. Association for Computational Linguistics.

Brent Berlin and Paul Kay. 1988. *Basic Color Terms: their Universality and Evolution*. Berkley: University of California Press.

M. Bortoli and J. Maroto. 2001. Translating colors in web site localisation. In *In The Proceedings of European Languages and the Implementation of Communication and Information Technologies (Elicit)*.

M. Bradley and P. Lang. 1999. Affective forms for english words (anew): Instruction manual and affective ranking.

Chris Callison-Burch. 2009. Fast, cheap, and creative: evaluating translation quality using amazon's mechanical turk. In *EMNLP '09: Proceedings of the 2009 Conference on Empirical Methods in Natural Language Processing*, pages 286–295, Stroudsburg, PA, USA. Association for Computational Linguistics.

David L. Chen and William B. Dolan. 2011. Building a persistent workforce on mechanical turk for multilingual data collection. In *Proceedings of The 3rd Human Computation Workshop (HCOMP 2011)*, August.

Paul Ekman. 1992. An argument for basic emotions. *Cognition & Emotion*, 6(3):169–200.

Clark Davidson Elliott. 1992. *The affective reasoner: a process model of emotions in a multi-agent system*. Ph.D. thesis, Evanston, IL, USA. UMI Order No. GAX92-29901.

J. Gage. 1993. Color and culture: Practice and meaning from antiquity to abstraction, univ. of calif.

C. Hardin and L. Maffi. 1997. *Color Categories in Thought and Language*.

N. Jacobson and W. Bender. 1996. Color as a determined communication. *IBM Syst. J.*, 35:526–538, September.

N. Kaya. 2004. Relationship between color and emotion: a study of college students. *College Student Journal*.

Efthymios Kouloumpis, Theresa Wilson, and Johanna Moore. 2011. Twitter sentiment analysis: The good the bad and the OMG! In *Proc. ICWSM*.

George A. Miller. 1995. Wordnet: A lexical database for english. *Communications of the ACM*, 38:39–41.

Saif M. Mohammad and Peter D. Turney. 2010. Emotions evoked by common words and phrases: using mechanical turk to create an emotion lexicon. In *Proceedings of the NAACL HLT 2010 Workshop on Computational Approaches to Analysis and Generation of Emotion in Text*, CAAGET '10, pages 26–34, Stroudsburg, PA, USA. Association for Computational Linguistics.

Saif Mohammad. 2011a. Colourful language: Measuring word-colour associations. In *Proceedings of the 2nd Workshop on Cognitive Modeling and Computational Linguistics*, pages 97–106, Portland, Oregon, USA, June. Association for Computational Linguistics.

Saif Mohammad. 2011b. From once upon a time to happily ever after: Tracking emotions in novels and fairy tales. In *Proceedings of the 5th ACL-HLT Workshop on Language Technology for Cultural Heritage, Social Sciences, and Humanities*, pages 105–114, Portland, OR, USA, June. Association for Computational Linguistics.

Saif M. Mohammad. 2011c. Even the abstract have colour: consensus in word-colour associations. In *Proceedings of the 49th Annual Meeting of the Association for Computational Linguistics: Human Language Technologies: short papers - Volume 2*, HLT '11, pages 368–373, Stroudsburg, PA, USA. Association for Computational Linguistics.

Aleksandra Mojsilovic. 2002. A method for color naming and description of color composition in images. In *Proc. IEEE Int. Conf. Image Processing*, pages 789–792.

Andrew Ortony, Gerald L. Clore, and Allan Collins. 1988. *The Cognitive Structure of Emotions*. Cambridge University Press, July.

Li-Chen Ou, M. Ronnier Luo, Pei-Li Sun, Neng-Chung Hu, and Hung-Shing Chen. 2011. Age effects on colour emotion, preference, and harmony. *Color Research and Application*.

R. Plutchik, 1980. *A general psychoevolutionary theory of emotion*, pages 3–33. Academic press, New York.

Justus J. Randolph. 2005. Author note: Free-marginal multirater kappa: An alternative to fleiss fixed-marginal multirater kappa.

P. Sable and O. Akcay. 2010. Color: Cross cultural marketing perspectives as to what governs our response to it. In *In The Proceedings of ASSBS*, volume 17.

Rion Snow, Brendan O'Connor, Daniel Jurafsky, and Andrew Y. Ng. 2008. Cheap and fast—but is it good?: evaluating non-expert annotations for natural language tasks. In *Proceedings of the Conference on Empirical Methods in Natural Language Processing*, EMNLP '08, pages 254–263, Stroudsburg, PA, USA. Association for Computational Linguistics.

Philip J. Stone, Dexter C. Dunphy, Marshall S. Smith, and Daniel M. Ogilvie. 1966. *The General Inquirer: A Computer Approach to Content Analysis*. MIT Press.

Carlo Strapparava and Gozde Ozbal. 2010. The color of emotions in text. *COLING*, pages 28–32.

C. Strapparava and A. Valitutti. 2004. Wordnet-affect: an affective extension of wordnet. In *In: Proceedings of the 4th International Conference on Language Resources and Evaluation (LREC 2004), Lisbon*, pages 1083–1086.

Extending the Entity-based Coherence Model with Multiple Ranks

Vanessa Wei Feng
Department of Computer Science
University of Toronto
Toronto, ON, M5S 3G4, Canada
weifeng@cs.toronto.edu

Graeme Hirst
Department of Computer Science
University of Toronto
Toronto, ON, M5S 3G4, Canada
gh@cs.toronto.edu

Abstract

We extend the original entity-based coherence model (Barzilay and Lapata, 2008) by learning from more fine-grained coherence preferences in training data. We associate multiple ranks with the set of permutations originating from the same source document, as opposed to the original pairwise rankings. We also study the effect of the permutations used in training, and the effect of the coreference component used in entity extraction. With no additional manual annotations required, our extended model is able to outperform the original model on two tasks: *sentence ordering* and *summary coherence rating*.

1 Introduction

Coherence is important in a well-written document; it helps make the text semantically meaningful and interpretable. Automatic evaluation of coherence is an essential component of various natural language applications. Therefore, the study of coherence models has recently become an active research area. A particularly popular coherence model is the entity-based local coherence model of Barzilay and Lapata (B&L) (2005; 2008). This model represents local coherence by transitions, from one sentence to the next, in the grammatical role of references to entities. It learns a pairwise ranking preference between alternative renderings of a document based on the probability distribution of those transitions. In particular, B&L associated a lower rank with automatically created permutations of a source document, and learned a model to discriminate an original text from its permutations (see Section 3.1 below). However, coherence is matter of degree rather than a binary distinction, so a model based only on such pairwise rankings is insufficiently fine-grained and cannot capture the subtle differences in coherence between the permuted documents.

Since the first appearance of B&L's model, several extensions have been proposed (see Section 2.3 below), primarily focusing on modifying or enriching the original feature set by incorporating other document information. By contrast, we wish to refine the learning procedure in a way such that the resulting model will be able to evaluate coherence on a more fine-grained level. Specifically, we propose a concise extension to the standard entity-based coherence model by learning not only from the original document and its corresponding permutations but also from ranking preferences among the permutations themselves.

We show that this can be done by assigning a suitable objective score for each permutation indicating its dissimilarity from the original one. We call this a *multiple-rank model* since we train our model on a multiple-rank basis, rather than taking the original pairwise ranking approach. This extension can also be easily combined with other extensions by incorporating their enriched feature sets. We show that our multiple-rank model outperforms B&L's basic model on two tasks, *sentence ordering* and *summary coherence rating*, evaluated on the same datasets as in Barzilay and Lapata (2008).

In *sentence ordering*, we experiment with different approaches to assigning dissimilarity scores and ranks (Section 5.1.1). We also experiment with different entity extraction approaches

	Manila	Miles	Island	Quake	Baco
1	–	–	X	X	–
2	S	–	O	–	–
3	X	X	X	X	X

Table 1: A fragment of an entity grid for five entities across three sentences.

(Section 5.1.2) and different distributions of permutations used in training (Section 5.1.3). We show that these two aspects are crucial, depending on the characteristics of the dataset.

2 Entity-based Coherence Model

2.1 Document Representation

The original entity-based coherence model is based on the assumption that a document makes repeated reference to elements of a set of entities that are central to its topic. For a document d, an entity grid is constructed, in which the columns represent the entities referred to in d, and rows represent the sentences. Each cell corresponds to the grammatical role of an entity in the corresponding sentence: subject (S), object (O), neither (X), or nothing (–). An example fragment of an entity grid is shown in Table 1; it shows the representation of three sentences from a text on a Philippine earthquake. B&L define a local transition as a sequence $\{S, O, X, -\}^n$, representing the occurrence and grammatical roles of an entity in n adjacent sentences. Such transition sequences can be extracted from the entity grid as continuous subsequences in each column. For example, the entity "Manila" in Table 1 has a bigram transition $\{S, X\}$ from sentence 2 to 3. The entity grid is then encoded as a feature vector $\mathbf{\Phi}(d) = (p_1(d), p_2(d), \ldots, p_m(d))$, where $p_t(d)$ is the probability of the transition t in the entity grid, and m is the number of transitions with length no more than a predefined optimal transition length k. $p_t(d)$ is computed as the number of occurrences of t in the entity grid of document d, divided by the total number of transitions of the same length in the entity grid.

For entity extraction, Barzilay and Lapata (2008) had two conditions: **Coreference+** and **Coreference−**. In **Coreference+**, entity coreference relations in the document were resolved by an automatic coreference resolution tool (Ng and Cardie, 2002), whereas in **Coreference−**, nouns are simply clustered by string matching.

2.2 Evaluation Tasks

Two evaluation tasks for Barzilay and Lapata (2008)'s entity-based model are *sentence ordering* and *summary coherence rating*.

In sentence ordering, a set of random permutations is created for each source document, and the learning procedure is conducted on this synthetic mixture of coherent and incoherent documents. Barzilay and Lapata (2008) experimented on two datasets: news articles on the topic of earthquakes (*Earthquakes*) and narratives on the topic of aviation accidents (*Accidents*). A training data instance is constructed as a pair consisting of a source document and one of its random permutations, and the permuted document is always considered to be less coherent than the source document. The entity transition features are then used to train a support vector machine ranker (Joachims, 2002) to rank the source documents higher than the permutations. The model is tested on a different set of source documents and their permutations, and the performance is evaluated as the fraction of correct pairwise rankings in the test set.

In summary coherence rating, a similar experimental framework is adopted. However, in this task, rather than training and evaluating on a set of synthetic data, system-generated summaries and human-composed reference summaries from the Document Understanding Conference (DUC 2003) were used. Human annotators were asked to give a coherence score on a seven-point scale for each item. The pairwise ranking preferences between summaries generated from the same input document cluster (excluding the pairs consisting of two human-written summaries) are used by a support vector machine ranker to learn a discriminant function to rank each pair according to their coherence scores.

2.3 Extended Models

Filippova and Strube (2007) applied Barzilay and Lapata's model on a German corpus of newspaper articles with manual syntactic, morphological, and NP coreference annotations provided. They further clustered entities by semantic relatedness as computed by the WikiRelated! API (Strube and Ponzetto, 2006). Though the improvement was not significant, interestingly, a short subsection in their paper described their approach to extending pairwise rankings to longer rankings, by supplying the learner with rankings of all renderings as computed by Kendall's τ, which is one of our extensions considered in this paper. Although Filippova and Strube simply discarded this idea because it hurt accuracies when tested on their data, we found it a promising direction for further exploration. Cheung and Penn (2010) adapted the standard entity-based coherence model to the same German corpus, but replaced the original linguistic dimension used by Barzilay and Lapata (2008) — grammatical role — with topological field information, and showed that for German text, such a modification improves accuracy.

For English text, two extensions have been proposed recently. Elsner and Charniak (2011) augmented the original features used in the standard entity-based coherence model with a large number of entity-specific features, and their extension significantly outperformed the standard model on two tasks: *document discrimination* (another name for *sentence ordering*), and *sentence insertion*. Lin et al. (2011) adapted the entity grid representation in the standard model into a discourse role matrix, where additional discourse information about the document was encoded. Their extended model significantly improved ranking accuracies on the same two datasets used by Barzilay and Lapata (2008) as well as on the *Wall Street Journal* corpus.

However, while enriching or modifying the original features used in the standard model is certainly a direction for refinement of the model, it usually requires more training data or a more sophisticated feature representation. In this paper, we instead modify the learning approach and propose a concise and highly adaptive extension that can be easily combined with other extended features or applied to different languages.

3 Experimental Design

Following Barzilay and Lapata (2008), we wish to train a discriminative model to give the correct ranking preference between two documents in terms of their degree of coherence. We experiment on the same two tasks as in their work: *sentence ordering* and *summary coherence rating*.

3.1 Sentence Ordering

In the standard entity-based model, a discriminative system is trained on the pairwise rankings between source documents and their permutations (see Section 2.2). However, a model learned from these pairwise rankings is not sufficiently fine-grained, since the subtle differences between the permutations are not learned. Our major contribution is to further differentiate among the permutations generated from the same source documents, rather than simply treating them all as being of the same degree of coherence.

Our fundamental assumption is that there exists a canonical ordering for the sentences of a document; therefore we can approximate the degree of coherence of a document by the similarity between its actual sentence ordering and that canonical sentence ordering. Practically, we automatically assign an objective score for each permutation to estimate its dissimilarity from the source document (see Section 4). By learning from all the pairs across a source document and its permutations, the effective size of the training data is increased while no further manual annotation is required, which is favorable in real applications when available samples with manually annotated coherence scores are usually limited. For r source documents each with m random permutations, the number of training instances in the standard entity-based model is therefore $r \times m$, while in our multiple-rank model learning process, it is $r \times \binom{m+1}{2} \approx \frac{1}{2} r \times m^2 > r \times m$, when $m > 2$.

3.2 Summary Coherence Rating

Compared to the standard entity-based coherence model, our major contribution in this task is to show that by automatically assigning an objective score for each machine-generated summary to estimate its dissimilarity from the human-generated summary from the same input document cluster, we are able to achieve performance competitive with, or even superior to, that of B&L's model without knowing the true coherence score given by human judges.

Evaluating our multiple-rank model in this task is crucial, since in summary coherence rating, the coherence violations that the reader might encounter in real machine-generated texts can be more precisely approximated, while the sentence ordering task is only partially capable of doing so.

4 Dissimilarity Metrics

As mentioned previously, the subtle differences among the permutations of the same source document can be used to refine the model learning process. Considering an original document $\boldsymbol{d}$ and one of its permutations, we call $\sigma = (1, 2, \ldots, N)$ the *reference ordering*, which is the sentence ordering in $\boldsymbol{d}$, and $\pi = (o_1, o_2, \ldots, o_N)$ the *test ordering*, which is the sentence ordering in that permutation, where N is the number of sentences being rendered in both documents.

In order to approximate different degrees of coherence among the set of permutations which bear the same content, we need a suitable metric to quantify the dissimilarity between the test ordering π and the reference ordering σ. Such a metric needs to satisfy the following criteria: (1) It can be automatically computed while being highly correlated with human judgments of coherence, since additional manual annotation is certainly undesirable. (2) It depends on the particular sentence ordering in a permutation while remaining independent of the entities within the sentences; otherwise our multiple-rank model might be trained to fit particular probability distributions of entity transitions rather than true coherence preferences.

In our work we use three different metrics: *Kendall's τ distance*, *average continuity*, and *edit distance*.

Kendall's τ distance: This metric has been widely used in evaluation of sentence ordering (Lapata, 2003; Lapata, 2006; Bollegala et al., 2006; Madnani et al., 2007)[1]. It measures the disagreement between two orderings σ and π in terms of the number of inversions of adjacent sentences necessary to convert one ordering into another. Kendall's τ distance is defined as

$$\tau = \frac{2m}{N(N-1)},$$

where m is the number of sentence inversions necessary to convert σ to π.

Average continuity (AC): Following Zhang (2011), we use average continuity as the second dissimilarity metric. It was first proposed by Bollegala et al. (2006). This metric estimates the quality of a particular sentence ordering by the number of correctly arranged continuous sentences, compared to the reference ordering. For example, if $\pi = (\ldots, 3, 4, 5, 7, \ldots, o_N)$, then $\{3, 4, 5\}$ is considered as continuous while $\{3, 4, 5, 7\}$ is not. Average continuity is calculated as

$$AC = \exp\left(\frac{1}{n-1}\sum_{i=2}^{n}\log\left(P_i + \alpha\right)\right),$$

where $n = \min(4, N)$ is the maximum number of continuous sentences to be considered, and $\alpha = 0.01$. P_i is the proportion of continuous sentences of length i in π that are also continuous in the reference ordering σ. To represent the *dissimilarity* between the two orderings π and σ, we use its complement $AC' = 1 - AC$, such that the larger AC' is, the more dissimilar two orderings are[2].

Edit distance (ED): Edit distance is a commonly used metric in information theory to measure the difference between two sequences. Given a test ordering π, its edit distance is defined as the minimum number of edits (i.e., insertions, deletions, and substitutions) needed to transform it into the reference ordering σ. For permutations, the edits are essentially movements, which can be considered as equal numbers of insertions and deletions.

5 Experiments

5.1 Sentence Ordering

Our first set of experiments is on sentence ordering. Following Barzilay and Lapata (2008), we use all transitions of length ≤ 3 for feature extraction. In addition, we explore three specific aspects in our experiments: rank assignment, entity extraction, and permutation generation.

5.1.1 Rank Assignment

In our multiple-rank model, pairwise rankings between a source document and its permutations are extended into a longer ranking with multiple ranks. We assign a rank to a particular permutation, based on the result of applying a chosen dissimilarity metric from Section 4 (τ, AC, or ED) to the sentence ordering in that permutation.

We experiment with two different approaches to assigning ranks to permutations, while each

[1] Filippova and Strube (2007) found that their performance dropped when using this metric for longer rankings; but they were using data in a different language and with manual annotations, so its effect on our datasets is worth trying nonetheless.

[2] We will refer to AC' as AC from now on.

source document is always assigned a zero (the highest) rank.

In the **raw** option, we rank the permutations directly by their dissimilarity scores to form a full ranking for the set of permutations generated from the same source document.

Since a full ranking might be too sensitive to noise in training, we also experiment with the **stratified** option, in which C ranks are assigned to the permutations generated from the same source document. The permutation with the smallest dissimilarity score is assigned the same (zero, the highest) rank as the source document, and the one with the largest score is assigned the lowest $(C-1)$ rank; then ranks of other permutations are uniformly distributed in this range according to their raw dissimilarity scores. We experiment with 3 to 6 ranks (the case where $C = 2$ reduces to the standard entity-based model).

5.1.2 Entity Extraction

Barzilay and Lapata (2008)'s best results were achieved by employing an automatic coreference resolution tool (Ng and Cardie, 2002) for extracting entities from a source document, and the permutations were generated only afterwards — entity extraction from a permuted document depends on knowing the correct sentence order and the oracular entity information from the source document — since resolving coreference relations in permuted documents is too unreliable for an automatic tool.

We implement our multiple-rank model with full coreference resolution using Ng and Cardie's coreference resolution system, and entity extraction approach as described above — the **Coreference+** condition. However, as argued by Elsner and Charniak (2011), to better simulate the real situations that human readers might encounter in machine-generated documents, such oracular information should not be taken into account. Therefore we also employ two alternative approaches for entity extraction: (1) use the same automatic coreference resolution tool on permuted documents — we call it the **Coreference±** condition; (2) use no coreference resolution, i.e., group head noun clusters by simple string matching — B&L's **Coreference−** condition.

5.1.3 Permutation Generation

The quality of the model learned depends on the set of permutations used in training. We are not aware of how B&L's permutations were generated, but we assume they are generated in a perfectly random fashion.

However, in reality, the probabilities of seeing documents with different degrees of coherence are not equal. For example, in an essay scoring task, if the target group is (near-) native speakers with sufficient education, we should expect their essays to be less incoherent — most of the essays will be coherent in most parts, with only a few minor problems regarding discourse coherence. In such a setting, the performance of a model trained from permutations generated from a uniform distribution may suffer some accuracy loss.

Therefore, in addition to the set of permutations used by Barzilay and Lapata (2008) (PS_{BL}), we create another set of permutations for each source document (PS_M) by assigning most of the probability mass to permutations which are mostly similar to the original source document. Besides its capability of better approximating real-life situations, training our model on permutations generated in this way has another benefit: in the standard entity-based model, all permuted documents are treated as incoherent; thus there are many more incoherent training instances than coherent ones (typically the proportion is 20:1). In contrast, in our multiple-rank model, permuted documents are assigned different ranks to further differentiate the different degrees of coherence within them. By doing so, our model will be able to learn the characteristics of a coherent document from those near-coherent documents as well, and therefore the problem of lacking coherent instances can be mitigated.

Our permutation generation algorithm is shown in Algorithm 1, where $\alpha = 0.05$, $\beta = 5.0$, $MAX\_NUM = 50$, and K and K' are two normalization factors to make $p(swap\_num)$ and $p(i, j)$ proper probability distributions. For each source document, we create the same number of permutations as PS_{BL}.

5.2 Summary Coherence Rating

In the summary coherence rating task, we are dealing with a mixture of multi-document summaries generated by systems and written by humans. Barzilay and Lapata (2008) did not assume

Algorithm 1 Permutation Generation.

Input: $S_1, S_2, \ldots, S_N$; $\sigma = (1, 2, \ldots, N)$
  Choose a number of sentence swaps
    swap_num with probability $e^{-\alpha \times swap\_num}/K$
  for $i = 1 \rightarrow swap\_num$ **do**
    Swap a pair of sentence (S_i, S_j)
      with probability $p(i, j) = e^{-\beta \times |i-j|}/K'$
  end for
Output: $\pi = (o_1, o_2, \ldots, o_N)$

a simple binary distinction among the summaries generated from the same input document cluster; rather, they had human judges give scores for each summary based on its degree of coherence (see Section 3.2). Therefore, it seems that the subtle differences among incoherent documents (system-generated summaries in this case) have already been learned by their model.

But we wish to see if we can replace human judgments by our computed dissimilarity scores so that the original supervised learning is converted into unsupervised learning and yet retain competitive performance. However, given a summary, computing its dissimilarity score is a bit involved, due to the fact that we do not know its correct sentence order. To tackle this problem, we employ a simple sentence alignment between a system-generated summary and a human-written summary originating from the same input document cluster. Given a system-generated summary $D_s = (S_{s1}, S_{s2}, \ldots, S_{sn})$ and its corresponding human-written summary $D_h = (S_{h1}, S_{h2}, \ldots, S_{hN})$ (here it is possible that $n \neq N$), we treat the sentence ordering $(1, 2, \ldots, N)$ in D_h as σ (the original sentence ordering), and compute $\pi = (o_1, o_2, \ldots, o_n)$ based on D_s. To compute each o_i in π, we find the most similar sentence $S_{hj}, j \in [1, N]$ in D_h by computing their cosine similarity over all tokens in S_{hj} and S_{si}; if all sentences in D_h have zero cosine similarity with S_{si}, we assign -1 to o_i.

Once π is known, we can compute its "dissimilarity" from σ using a chosen metric. But because now π is not guaranteed to be a permutation of σ (there may be repetition or missing values, i.e., -1, in π), Kendall's τ cannot be used, and we use only *average continuity* and *edit distance* as dissimilarity metrics in this experiment.

The remaining experimental configuration is the same as that of Barzilay and Lapata (2008), with the optimal transition length set to ≤ 2.

6 Results

6.1 Sentence Ordering

In this task, we use the same two sets of source documents (*Earthquakes* and *Accidents*, see Section 3.1) as Barzilay and Lapata (2008). Each contains 200 source documents, equally divided between training and test sets, with up to 20 permutations per document. We conduct experiments on these two domains separately. For each domain, we accompany each source document with two different sets of permutations: the one used by B&L (PS_{BL}), and the one generated from our model described in Section 5.1.3 (PS_M). We train our multiple-rank model and B&L's standard two-rank model on each set of permutations using the SVM^{rank} package (Joachims, 2006), and evaluate both systems on their test sets. Accuracy is measured as the fraction of correct pairwise rankings for the test set.

6.1.1 Full Coreference Resolution with Oracular Information

In this experiment, we implement B&L's fully-fledged standard entity-based coherence model, and extract entities from permuted documents using oracular information from the source documents (see Section 5.1.2).

Results are shown in Table 2. For each test situation, we list the best accuracy (in *Acc* columns) for each chosen dissimilarity metric, with the corresponding rank assignment approach. *C* represents the number of ranks used in stratifying raw scores ("*N*" if using **raw** configuration, see Section 5.1.1 for details). Baselines are accuracies trained using the standard entity-based coherence model[3].

Our model outperforms the standard entity-based model on both permutation sets for both datasets. The improvement is not significant when trained on the permutation set PS_{BL}, and is achieved only with one of the three metrics;

[3]There are discrepancies between our reported accuracies and those of Barzilay and Lapata (2008). The differences are due to the fact that we use a different parser: the Stanford dependency parser (de Marneffe et al., 2006), and might have extracted entities in a slightly different way than theirs, although we keep other experimental configurations as close as possible to theirs. But when comparing our model with theirs, we always use the exact same set of features, so the absolute accuracies do not matter.

Condition: Coreference+					
Perms	Metric	*Earthquakes*		*Accidents*	
		C	Acc	*C*	Acc
PS_{BL}	τ	3	79.5	3	82.0
	AC	4	85.2	3	**83.3**
	ED	3	**86.8**	6	82.2
	Baseline		85.3		83.2
PS_M	τ	3	**86.8**	3	**85.2***
	AC	3	**85.6**	1	**85.4***
	ED	*N*	**87.9***	4	**86.3***
	Baseline		85.3		81.7

Table 2: Accuracies (%) of extending the standard entity-based coherence model with multiple-rank learning in sentence ordering using **Coreference+** option. Accuracies which are significantly better than the baseline ($p < .05$) are indicated by *.

Condition: Coreference±					
Perms	Metric	*Earthquakes*		*Accidents*	
		C	Acc	*C*	Acc
PS_{BL}	τ	3	71.0	3	73.3
	AC	3	***76.8**	3	**74.5**
	ED	4	***77.4**	6	**74.4**
	Baseline		71.7		73.8
PS_M	τ	3	**55.9**	3	51.5
	AC	4	**53.9**	6	49.0
	ED	4	**53.9**	5	52.3
	Baseline		49.2		**53.2**

Table 3: Accuracies (%) of extending the standard entity-based coherence model with multiple-rank learning in sentence ordering using **Coreference±** option. Accuracies which are significantly better than the baseline ($p < .05$) are indicated by *.

but when trained on PS_M (the set of permutations generated from our biased model), our model's performance significantly exceeds B&L's[4] for all three metrics, especially as their model's performance drops for dataset *Accidents*.

From these results, we see that in the ideal situation where we extract entities and resolve their coreference relations based on the oracular information from the source document, our model is effective in terms of improving ranking accuracies, especially when trained on our more realistic permutation sets PS_M.

6.1.2 Full Coreference Resolution without Oracular Information

In this experiment, we apply the same automatic coreference resolution tool (Ng and Cardie, 2002) on not only the source documents but also their permutations. We want to see how removing the oracular component in the original model affects the performance of our multiple-rank model and the standard model. Results are shown in Table 3.

First we can see when trained on PS_M, running full coreference resolution significantly hurts performance for both models. This suggests that, in real-life applications, where the distribution of training instances with different degrees of coherence is skewed (as in the set of permutations generated from our model), running full coreference resolution is not a good option, since it almost makes the accuracies no better than random guessing (50%).

Moreover, considering training using PS_{BL}, running full coreference resolution has a different influence for the two datasets. For *Earthquakes*, our model significantly outperforms B&L's while the improvement is insignificant for *Accidents*. This is most probably due to the different way that entities are realized in these two datasets. As analyzed by Barzilay and Lapata (2008), in dataset *Earthquakes*, entities tend to be referred to by pronouns in subsequent mentions, while in dataset *Accidents*, literal string repetition is more common.

Given a balanced permutation distribution as we assumed in PS_{BL}, switching distant sentence pairs in *Accidents* may result in very similar entity distribution with the situation of switching closer sentence pairs, as recognized by the automatic tool. Therefore, compared to *Earthquakes*, our multiple-rank model may be less powerful in indicating the dissimilarity between the sentence orderings in a permutation and its source document, and therefore can improve on the baseline only by a small margin.

6.1.3 No Coreference Resolution

In this experiment, we do not employ any coreference resolution tool, and simply cluster head

[4]Following Elsner and Charniak (2011), we use the Wilcoxon Sign-rank test for significance.

Condition: Coreference−					
Perms	Metric	*Earthquakes*		*Accidents*	
		C	Acc	C	Acc
PS_{BL}	τ	4	82.8	N	**82.0**
	AC	3	78.0	3	****84.2**
	ED	N	78.2	3	***82.7**
	Baseline		**83.7**		80.1
PS_M	τ	3	****86.4**	N	****85.7**
	AC	4	***84.4**	N	****86.6**
	ED	5	****86.7**	N	****84.6**
	Baseline		82.6		77.5

Table 4: Accuracies (%) of extending the standard entity-based coherence model with multiple-rank learning in sentence ordering using **Coreference−** option. Accuracies which are significantly better than the baseline are indicated by * ($p < .05$) and ** ($p < .01$).

nouns by string matching. Results are shown in Table 4.

Even with such a coarse approximation of coreference resolution, our model is able to achieve around 85% accuracy in most test cases, except for dataset *Earthquakes*, training on PS_{BL} gives poorer performance than the standard model by a small margin. But such inferior performance should be expected, because as explained above, coreference resolution is crucial to this dataset, since entities tend to be realized through pronouns; simple string matching introduces too much noise into training, especially when our model wants to train a more fine-grained discriminative system than B&L's. However, we can see from the result of training on PS_M, if the permutations used in training do not involve swapping sentences which are too far away, the resulting noise is reduced, and our model outperforms theirs. And for dataset *Accidents*, our model consistently outperforms the baseline model by a large margin (with significance test at $p < .01$).

6.1.4 Conclusions for Sentence Ordering

Considering the particular dissimilarity metric used in training, we find that *edit distance* usually stands out from the other two metrics. *Kendall's τ distance* proves to be a fairly weak metric, which is consistent with the findings of Filippova and Strube (2007) (see Section 2.3). Figure 1 plots the testing accuracies as a function of different

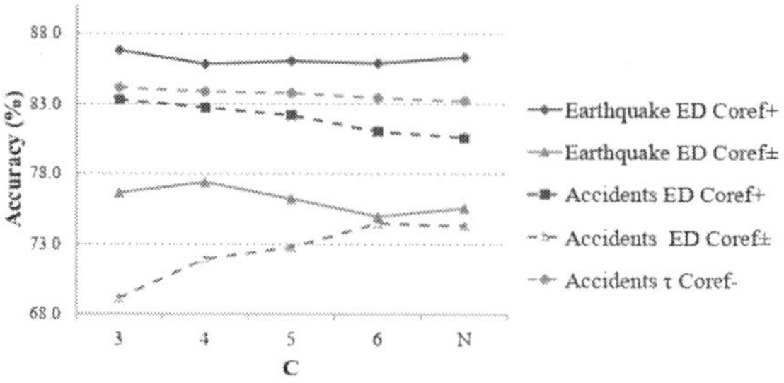

Figure 1: Effect of C on testing accuracies in selected *sentence ordering* experimental configurations.

choices of C's with the configurations where our model outperforms the baseline model. In each configuration, we choose the dissimilarity metric which achieves the best accuracy reported in Tables 2 to 4 and the PS_{BL} permutation set. We can see that the dependency of accuracies on the particular choice of C is not consistent across all experimental configurations, which suggests that this free parameter C needs careful tuning in different experimental setups.

Combining our multiple-rank model with simple string matching for entity extraction is a robust option for coherence evaluation, regardless of the particular distribution of permutations used in training, and it significantly outperforms the baseline in most conditions.

6.2 Summary Coherence Rating

As explained in Section 3.2, we employ a simple sentence alignment between a system-generated summary and its corresponding human-written summary to construct a test ordering π and calculate its dissimilarity between the reference ordering σ from the human-written summary. In this way, we convert B&L's supervised learning model into a fully unsupervised model, since human annotations for coherence scores are not required. We use the same dataset as Barzilay and Lapata (2008), which includes multi-document summaries from 16 input document clusters generated by five systems, along with reference summaries composed by humans.

In this experiment, we consider only *average continuity (AC)* and *edit distance (ED)* as dissimilarity metrics, with **raw** configuration for rank assignment, and compare our multiple-rank model with the standard entity-based model using either full coreference resolution[5] or no resolution

[5]We run the coreference resolution tool on all documents.

Entities	Metric	Same	Full
Coreference+	*AC*	**82.5**	***72.6**
	ED	**81.3**	****73.0**
	Baseline	78.8	70.9
Coreference−	*AC*	76.3	72.0
	ED	78.8	71.7
	Baseline	**80.0**	**72.3**

Table 5: Accuracies (%) of extending the standard entity-based coherence model with multiple-rank learning in summary rating. Baselines are results of standard entity-based coherence model. Accuracies which are significantly better than the corresponding baseline are indicated by * ($p < .05$) and ** ($p < .01$).

for entity extraction. We train both models on the ranking preferences (144 in all) among summaries originating from the same input document cluster using the SVM^{rank} package (Joachims, 2006), and test on two different test sets: *same-cluster test* and *full test*. *Same-cluster* test is the one used by Barzilay and Lapata (2008), in which only the pairwise rankings (80 in all) between summaries originating from the same input document cluster are tested; we also experiment with *full test*, in which pairwise rankings (1520 in all) between all summary pairs excluding two human-written summaries are tested.

Results are shown in Table 5. **Coreference+** and **Coreference−** denote the configuration of using full coreference resolution or no resolution separately. First, clearly for both models, performance on *full test* is inferior to that on *same-cluster* test, but our model is still able to achieve performance competitive with the standard model, even if our fundamental assumption about the existence of canonical sentence ordering in documents with same content may break down on those test pairs not originating from the same input document cluster. Secondly, for the baseline model, using the **Coreference−** configuration yields better accuracy in this task (80.0% vs. 78.8% on *same-cluster test*, and 72.3% vs. 70.9% on *full test*), which is consistent with the findings of Barzilay and Lapata (2008). But our multiple-rank model seems to favor the **Coreference+** configuration, and our best accuracy even exceeds B&L's best when tested on the same set: 82.5% vs. 80.0% on *same-cluster test*, and 73.0% vs. 72.3% on *full test*.

When our model performs poorer than the baseline (using **Coreference−** configuration), the difference is not significant, which suggests that our multiple-rank model with unsupervised score assignment via simple cosine matching can remain competitive with the standard model, which requires human annotations to obtain a more fine-grained coherence spectrum. This observation is consistent with Banko and Vanderwende (2004)'s discovery that human-generated summaries look quite extractive.

7 Conclusions

In this paper, we have extended the popular coherence model of Barzilay and Lapata (2008) by adopting a multiple-rank learning approach. This is inherently different from other extensions to this model, in which the focus is on enriching the set of features for entity-grid construction, whereas we simply keep their original feature set intact, and manipulate only their learning methodology. We show that this concise extension is effective and able to outperform B&L's standard model in various experimental setups, especially when experimental configurations are most suitable considering certain dataset properties (see discussion in Section 6.1.4).

We experimented with two tasks: *sentence ordering* and *summary coherence rating*, following B&L's original framework. In sentence ordering, we also explored the influence of removing the oracular component in their original model and dealing with permutations generated from different distributions, showing that our model is robust for different experimental situations. In summary coherence rating, we further extended their model such that their original supervised learning is converted into unsupervised learning with competitive or even superior performance.

Our multiple-rank learning model can be easily adapted into other extended entity-based coherence models with their enriched feature sets, and further improvement in ranking accuracies should be expected.

Acknowledgments

This work was financially supported by the Natural Sciences and Engineering Research Council of Canada and by the University of Toronto.

References

Michele Banko and Lucy Vanderwende. 2004. Using n-grams to understand the nature of summaries. In *Proceedings of Human Language Technologies and North American Association for Computational Linguistics 2004: Short Papers*, pages 1–4.

Regina Barzilay and Mirella Lapata. 2005. Modeling local coherence: An entity-based approach. In *Proceedings of the 42rd Annual Meeting of the Association for Computational Linguistics (ACL 2005)*, pages 141–148.

Regina Barzilay and Mirella Lapata. 2008. Modeling local coherence: an entity-based approach. *Computational Linguistics*, 34(1):1–34.

Danushka Bollegala, Naoaki Okazaki, and Mitsuru Ishizuka. 2006. A bottom-up approach to sentence ordering for multi-document summarization. In *Proceedings of the 21st International Conference on Computational Linguistics and 44th Annual Meeting of the Association for Computational Linguistics*, pages 385–392.

Jackie Chi Kit Cheung and Gerald Penn. 2010. Entity-based local coherence modelling using topological fields. In *Proceedings of the 48th Annual Meeting of the Association for Computational Linguistics (ACL 2010)*, pages 186–195.

Marie-Catherine de Marneffe, Bill MacCartney, and Christopher D. Manning. 2006. Generating typed dependency parses from phrase structure parses. In *Proceedings of the 5th International Conference on Language Resources and Evaluation (LREC 2006)*.

Micha Elsner and Eugene Charniak. 2011. Extending the entity grid with entity-specific features. In *Proceedings of the 49th Annual Meeting of the Association for Computational Linguistics (ACL 2011)*, pages 125–129.

Katja Filippova and Michael Strube. 2007. Extending the entity-grid coherence model to semantically related entities. In *Proceedings of the Eleventh European Workshop on Natural Language Generation (ENLG 2007)*, pages 139–142.

Thorsten Joachims. 2002. Optimizing search engines using clickthrough data. In *Proceedings of the 8th ACM SIGKDD International Conference on Knowledge Discovery and Data Mining (KDD 2002)*, pages 133–142.

Thorsten Joachims. 2006. Training linear SVMs in linear time. In *Proceedings of the 12th ACM SIGKDD International Conference on Knowledge Discovery and Data Mining (KDD 2006)*, pages 217–226.

Mirella Lapata. 2003. Probabilistic text structuring: Experiments with sentence ordering. In *Proceedings of the 41st Annual Meeting of the Association for Computational Linguistics (ACL 2003)*, pages 545–552.

Mirella Lapata. 2006. Automatic evaluation of information ordering: Kendall's tau. *Computational Linguistics*, 32(4):471–484.

Ziheng Lin, Hwee Tou Ng, and Min-Yen Kan. 2011. Automatically evaluating text coherence using discourse relations. In *Proceedings of the 49th Annual Meeting of the Association for Computational Linguistics (ACL 2011)*, pages 997–1006.

Nitin Madnani, Rebecca Passonneau, Necip Fazil Ayan, John M. Conroy, Bonnie J. Dorr, Judith L. Klavans, Dianne P. O'Leary, and Judith D. Schlesinger. 2007. Measuring variability in sentence ordering for news summarization. In *Proceedings of the Eleventh European Workshop on Natural Language Generation (ENLG 2007)*, pages 81–88.

Vincent Ng and Claire Cardie. 2002. Improving machine learning approaches to coreference resolution. In *Proceedings of the 40th Annual Meeting on Association for Computational Linguistics (ACL 2002)*, pages 104–111.

Michael Strube and Simone Paolo Ponzetto. 2006. Wikirelate! Computing semantic relatedness using Wikipedia. In *Proceedings of the 21st National Conference on Artificial Intelligence*, pages 1219–1224.

Renxian Zhang. 2011. Sentence ordering driven by local and global coherence for summary generation. In *Proceedings of the ACL 2011 Student Session*, pages 6–11.

Generalization Methods for In-Domain and Cross-Domain Opinion Holder Extraction

Michael Wiegand and **Dietrich Klakow**
Spoken Language Systems
Saarland University
D-66123 Saarbrücken, Germany
{Michael.Wiegand|Dietrich.Klakow}@lsv.uni-saarland.de

Abstract

In this paper, we compare three different generalization methods for in-domain and cross-domain opinion holder extraction being simple unsupervised word clustering, an induction method inspired by distant supervision and the usage of lexical resources. The generalization methods are incorporated into diverse classifiers. We show that generalization causes significant improvements and that the impact of improvement depends on the type of classifier and on how much training and test data differ from each other. We also address the less common case of opinion holders being realized in patient position and suggest approaches including a novel (linguistically-informed) extraction method how to detect those opinion holders without labeled training data as standard datasets contain too few instances of this type.

1 Introduction

Opinion holder extraction is one of the most important subtasks in sentiment analysis. The extraction of sources of opinions is an essential component for complex real-life applications, such as opinion question answering systems or opinion summarization systems (Stoyanov and Cardie, 2011). Common approaches designed to extract opinion holders are based on data-driven methods, in particular supervised learning.

In this paper, we examine the role of generalization for opinion holder extraction in both in-domain and cross-domain classification. Generalization may not only help to compensate the availability of labeled training data but also conciliate domain mismatches.

In order to illustrate this, compare for instance (1) and (2).

(1) Malaysia did not agree to such treatment of Al-Qaeda soldiers as they were prisoners-of-war and should be accorded treatment as provided for under the Geneva Convention.
(2) Japan wishes to build a $21 billion per year aerospace industry centered on commercial satellite development.

Though both sentences contain an opinion holder, the lexical items vary considerably. However, if the two sentences are compared on the basis of some higher level patterns, some similarities become obvious. In both cases the opinion holder is an entity denoting a person and this entity is an agent[1] of some predictive predicate (i.e. *agree* in (1) and *wishes* in (2)), more specifically, an expression that indicates that the agent utters a subjective statement. Generalization methods ideally capture these patterns, for instance, they may provide a domain-independent lexicon for those predicates. In some cases, even higher order features, such as certain syntactic constructions may vary throughout the different domains. In (1) and (2), the opinion holders are agents of a predictive predicate, whereas the opinion holder *her daughters* in (3) is a patient[2] of *embarrasses*.

(3) Mrs. Bennet does what she can to get Jane and Bingley together and embarrasses her daughters by doing so.

If only sentences, such as (1) and (2), occur in the training data, a classifier will not correctly extract the opinion holder in (3), unless it obtains additional knowledge as to which predicates take opinion holders as patients.

[1]By *agent* we always mean constituents being labeled as *A0* in PropBank (Kingsbury and Palmer, 2002).

[2]By *patient* we always mean constituents being labeled as *A1* in PropBank.

In this work, we will consider three different generalization methods being simple unsupervised word clustering, an induction method and the usage of lexical resources. We show that generalization causes significant improvements and that the impact of improvement depends on how much training and test data differ from each other. We also address the issue of opinion holders in patient position and present methods including a novel extraction method to detect these opinion holders without any labeled training data as standard datasets contain too few instances of them.

In the context of generalization it is also important to consider different classification methods as the incorporation of generalization may have a varying impact depending on how robust the classifier is by itself, i.e. how well it generalizes even with a standard feature set. We compare two state-of-the-art learning methods, conditional random fields and convolution kernels, and a rule-based method.

2 Data

As a labeled dataset we mainly use the MPQA 2.0 corpus (Wiebe et al., 2005). We adhere to the definition of opinion holders from previous work (Wiegand and Klakow, 2010; Wiegand and Klakow, 2011a; Wiegand and Klakow, 2011b), i.e. every source of a *private state* or a *subjective speech event* (Wiebe et al., 2005) is considered an opinion holder.

This corpus contains almost exclusively news texts. In order to divide it into different domains, we use the topic labels from (Stoyanov et al., 2004). By inspecting those topics, we found that many of them can grouped to a cluster of news items discussing human rights issues mostly in the context of combating global terrorism. This means that there is little point in considering every single topic as a distinct (sub)domain and, therefore, we consider this cluster as one single domain ETHICS.[3] For our cross-domain evaluation, we want to have another topic that is fairly different from this set of documents. By visual inspection, we found that the topic discussing issues regarding the International Space Station would suit our purpose. It is henceforth called SPACE.

[3]The cluster is the union of documents with the following MPQA-topic labels: *axisofevil*, *guantanamo*, *humanrights*, *mugabe* and *settlements*.

Domain	# Sentences	# Holders in sentence (average)
ETHICS	5700	0.79
SPACE	628	0.28
FICTION	614	1.49

Table 1: Statistics of the different domain corpora.

In addition to these two (sub)domains, we chose some text type that is not even news text in order to have a very distant domain. Therefore, we had to use some text not included in the MPQA corpus. Existing text collections containing product reviews (Kessler et al., 2010; Toprak et al., 2010), which are generally a popular resource for sentiment analysis, were not found suitable as they only contain few distinct opinion holders. We finally used a few summaries of fictional work (two Shakespeare plays and one novel by Jane Austen[4]) since their language is notably different from that of news texts and they contain a large number of different opinion holders (therefore opinion holder extraction is a meaningful task on this text type). These texts make up our third domain FICTION. We manually labeled it with opinion holder information by applying the annotation scheme of the MPQA corpus.

Table 1 lists the properties of the different domain corpora. Note that ETHICS is the largest domain. We consider it our primary (source) domain as it serves both as a training and (in-domain) test set. Due to their size, the other domains only serve as test sets (target domains).

For some of our generalization methods, we also need a large unlabeled corpus. We use the North American News Text Corpus (LDC95T21).

3 The Different Types of Generalization

3.1 Word Clustering (Clus)

The simplest generalization method that is considered in this paper is word clustering. By that, we understand the automatic grouping of words occurring in similar contexts. Such clusters are usually computed on a large unlabeled corpus. Unlike lexical features, features based on clusters are less sparse and have been proven to significantly improve data-driven classifiers in related tasks, such as named-entity recognition (Turian et

[4]available at: `www.absoluteshakespeare.com/guides/{othello|twelfth_night}/summary/{othello|twelfth_night}_summary.htm`
`www.wikisummaries.org/Pride_and_Prejudice`

I.	Madrid, Dresden, Bordeaux, Istanbul, Caracas, Manila, ...
II.	Toby, Betsy, Michele, Tim, Jean-Marie, Rory, Andrew, ...
III.	detest, resent, imply, liken, indicate, suggest, owe, expect, ...
IV.	disappointment, unease, nervousness, dismay, optimism, ...
V.	remark, baby, book, saint, manhole, maxim, coin, batter, ...

Table 2: Some automatically induced clusters.

ETHICS	SPACE	FICTION
1.47	2.70	11.59

Table 3: Percentage of opinion holders as patients.

al., 2010). Such a generalization is, in particular, attractive as it is cheaply produced. As a state-of-the-art clustering method, we consider Brown clustering (Brown et al., 1992) as implemented in the SRILM-toolkit (Stolcke, 2002). We induced 1000 clusters which is also the configuration used in (Turian et al., 2010).[5]

Table 2 illustrates a few of the clusters induced from our unlabeled dataset introduced in Section (§) 2. Some of these clusters represent location or person names (e.g. I. & II.). This exemplifies why clustering is effective for named-entity recognition. We also find clusters that intuitively seem to be meaningful for our task (e.g. III. & IV.) but, on the other hand, there are clusters that contain words that with the exception of their part of speech do not have anything in common (e.g. V.).

3.2 Manually Compiled Lexicons (Lex)

The major shortcoming of word clustering is that it lacks any task-specific knowledge. The opposite type of generalization is the usage of manually compiled lexicons comprising predicates that indicate the presence of opinion holders, such as *supported*, *worries* or *disappointed* in (4)-(6).

(4) I always *supported* this idea. holder:agent.
(5) This *worries* me. holder:patient
(6) He *disappointed* me. holder:patient

We follow Wiegand and Klakow (2011b) who found that those predicates can be best obtained by using a subset of Levin's verb classes (Levin, 1993) and the strong subjective expressions of the Subjectivity Lexicon (Wilson et al., 2005). For those predicates it is also important to consider in which argument position they usually take an opinion holder. Bethard et al. (2004) found the majority of holders are agents (4). A certain number of predicates, however, also have opinion holders in patient position, e.g. (5) and (6).

Wiegand and Klakow (2011b) found that many of those latter predicates are listed in one of Levin's verb classes called *amuse verbs*. While on the evaluation on the entire MPQA corpus, opinion holders in patient position are fairly rare (Wiegand and Klakow, 2011b), we may wonder whether the same applies to the individual domains that we consider in this work. Table 3 lists the proportion of those opinion holders (computed manually) based on a random sample of 100 opinion holder mentions from those corpora. The table shows indeed that on the domains from the MPQA corpus, i.e. ETHICS and SPACE, those opinion holders play a minor role but there is a notably higher proportion on the FICTION-domain.

3.3 Task-Specific Lexicon Induction (Induc)

3.3.1 Distant Supervision with Prototypical Opinion Holders

Lexical resources are potentially much more expressive than word clustering. This knowledge, however, is usually manually compiled, which makes this solution much more expensive. Wiegand and Klakow (2011a) present an intermediate solution for opinion holder extraction inspired by *distant supervision* (Mintz et al., 2009). The output of that method is also a lexicon of predicates but it is automatically extracted from a large unlabeled corpus. This is achieved by collecting predicates that frequently co-occur with prototypical opinion holders, i.e. common nouns such as *opponents* (7) or *critics* (8), if they are an agent of that predicate. The rationale behind this is that those nouns act very much like actual opinion holders and therefore can be seen as a proxy.

(7) Opponents *say* these arguments miss the point.
(8) Critics *argued* that the proposed limits were unconstitutional.

This method reduces the human effort to specifying a small set of such prototypes.

Following the best configuration reported in (Wiegand and Klakow, 2011a), we extract 250 verbs, 100 nouns and 100 adjectives from our unlabeled corpus (§2).

3.3.2 Extension for Opinion Holders in Patient Position

The downside of using prototypical opinion holders as a proxy for opinion holders is that it

[5]We also experimented with other sizes but they did not produce a better overall performance.

anguish*, astonish, astound, concern, convince, daze, delight, disenchant*, disappoint, displease, disgust, disillusion, dissatisfy, distress, embitter*, enamor*, engross, enrage, entangle*, excite, fatigue*, flatter, fluster, flummox*, frazzle*, hook*, humiliate, incapacitate*, incense, interest, irritate, obsess, outrage, perturb, petrify*, sadden, sedate*, shock, stun, tether*, trouble

Table 4: Examples of the automatically extracted verbs taking opinion holders as patients (*: not listed as *amuse verb*).

is limited to agentive opinion holders. Opinion holders in patient position, such as the ones taken by *amuse verbs* in (5) and (6), are not covered. Wiegand and Klakow (2011a) show that considering less restrictive contexts significantly drops classification performance. So the natural extension of looking for predicates having prototypical opinion holders in patient position is not effective. Sentences, such as (9), would mar the result.

(9) They criticized their opponents.

In (9) the prototypical opinion holder *opponents* (in the patient position) is not a true opinion holder.

Our novel method to extract those predicates rests on the observation that the past participle of those verbs, such as *shocked* in (10), is very often identical to some predicate adjective (11) having a similar if not identical meaning. For the predicate adjective, the opinion holder is, however, its subject/agent and not its patient.

(10) He had $shocked_{verb}$ me. holder:patient
(11) I was $shocked_{adj}$. holder:agent

Instead of extracting those verbs directly (10), we take the detour via their corresponding predicate adjectives (11). This means that we collect all those verbs (from our large unlabeled corpus (§2)) for which there is a predicate adjective that coincides with the past participle of the verb.

To increase the likelihood that our extracted predicates are meaningful for opinion holder extraction, we also need to check the semantic type in the relevant argument position, i.e. make sure that the agent of the predicate adjective (which would be the patient of the corresponding verb) is an entity likely to be an opinion holder. Our initial attempts with prototypical opinion holders were too restrictive, i.e. the number of prototypical opinion holders co-occurring with those adjectives was too small. Therefore, we widen the semantic type of this position from prototypical opinion holders to persons. This means that we allow personal pronouns (i.e. *I*, *you*, *he*, *she* and *we*) to appear in this position. We believe that this relaxation can be done in that particular case, as adjectives are much more likely to convey opinions a priori than verbs (Wiebe et al., 2004).

An intrinsic evaluation of the predicates that we thus extracted from our unlabeled corpus is difficult. The 250 most frequent verbs exhibiting this special property of coinciding with adjectives (this will be the list that we use in our experiments) contains 42% entries of the *amuse verbs* (§3.2). However, we also found many other potentially useful predicates on this list that are not listed as *amuse verbs* (Table 4). As *amuse verbs* cannot be considered a complete golden standard for all predicates taking opinion holders as patients, we will focus on a task-based evaluation of our automatically extracted list (§6).

4 Data-driven Methods

In the following, we present the two supervised classifiers we use in our experiments. Both classifiers incorporate the same levels of representations, including the same generalization methods.

4.1 Conditional Random Fields (CRF)

The supervised classifier most frequently used for information extraction tasks, in general, are conditional random fields (CRF) (Lafferty et al., 2001). Using CRF, the task of opinion holder extraction is framed as a tagging problem in which given a sequence of observations $x = x_1 x_2 \dots x_n$ (words in a sentence) a sequence of output tags $y = y_1 y_2 \dots y_n$ indicating the boundaries of opinion holders is computed by modeling the conditional probability $P(x|y)$.

The features we use (Table 5) are mostly inspired by Choi et al. (2005) and by the ones used for plain support vector machines (SVMs) in (Wiegand and Klakow, 2010). They are organized into groups. The basic group *Plain* does not contain any generalization method. Each other group is dedicated to one specific generalization method that we want to examine (*Clus*, *Induc* and *Lex*). Apart from considering generalization features indicating the presence of generalization types, we also consider those types in conjunction with semantic roles. As already indicated above, semantic roles are especially important for the detection of opinion holders. Unfortunately, the cor-

Group	Features
Plain	Token features: unigrams and bigrams POS/chunk/named-entity features: unigrams, bigrams and trigrams Constituency tree path to nearest predicate Nearest predicate Semantic role to predicate+lexical form of predicate
Clus	Cluster features: unigrams, bigrams and trigrams Semantic role to predicate+cluster-id of predicate Cluster-id of nearest predicate
Induc	Is there predicate from induced lexicon within window of 5 tokens? Semantic role to predicate, if predicate is contained in induced lexicon Is nearest predicate contained in induced lexicon?
Lex	Is there predicate from manually compiled lexicons within window of 5 tokens? Semantic role to predicate, if predicate is contained in manually compiled lexicons Is nearest predicate contained in manually compiled lexicons?

Table 5: Feature set for CRF.

responding feature from the *Plain* feature group that also includes the lexical form of the predicate is most likely a sparse feature. For the opinion holder *me* in (10), for example, it would correspond to *A1_shock*. Therefore, we introduce for each generalization method an additional feature replacing the sparse lexical item by a generalization label, i.e. *Clus*: *A1_CLUSTER-35265*, *Induc*: *A1_INDUC-PRED* and *Lex*: *A1_LEX-PRED*.[6]

For this learning method, we use CRF++.[7] We choose a configuration that provides good performance on our source domain (i.e. ETHICS).[8] For semantic role labeling we use SWIRL[9], for chunk parsing CASS (Abney, 1991) and for constituency parsing Stanford Parser (Klein and Manning, 2003). Named-entity information is provided by Stanford Tagger (Finkel et al., 2005).

4.2 Convolution Kernels (CK)

Convolution kernels (CK) are special kernel functions. A kernel function $K : X \times X \rightarrow \mathbb{R}$ computes the similarity of two data instances x_i and x_j ($x_i \wedge x_j \in X$). It is mostly used in SVMs that estimate a hyperplane to separate data instances from different classes $H(\vec{x}) = \vec{w} \cdot \vec{x} + b = 0$ where $w \in \mathbb{R}^n$ and $b \in \mathbb{R}$ (Joachims, 1999). In convolution kernels, the structures to be compared within the kernel function are not vectors comprising manually designed features but the underlying discrete structures, such as syntactic parse trees or part-of-speech sequences. Since they are directly provided to the learning algorithm, a classifier can be built without taking the effort of implementing an explicit feature extraction.

We take the best configuration from (Wiegand and Klakow, 2010) that comprises a combination of three different tree kernels being two tree kernels based on constituency parse trees (one with *predicate* and another with *semantic scope*) and a tree kernel encoding predicate-argument structures based on semantic role information. These representations are illustrated in Figure 1. The resulting kernels are combined by plain summation.

In order to integrate our generalization methods into the convolution kernels, the input structures, i.e. the linguistic tree structures, have to be augmented. For that we just add additional nodes whose labels correspond to the respective generalization types (i.e. *Clus*: CLUSTER-*ID*, *Induc*: INDUC-PRED and *Lex*: LEX-PRED). The nodes are added in such a way that they (directly) dominate the leaf node for which they provide a generalization.[10] If several generalization methods are used and several of them apply for the same lexical unit, then the (vertical) order of the generalization nodes is LEX-PRED $\succ$ INDUC-PRED $\succ$ CLUSTER-ID.[11] Figure 2 illustrates the predicate argument structure from Figure 1 augmented with INDUC-PRED and CLUSTER-IDs.

For this learning method, we use the SVMLight-TK toolkit.[12] Again, we tune the parameters to our source domain (ETHICS).[13]

5 Rule-based Classifiers (RB)

Finally, we also consider rule-based classifiers (RB). The main difference towards CRF and CK is that it is an unsupervised approach not requiring training data. We re-use the framework by Wiegand and Klakow (2011b). The candidate set are all noun phrases in a test set. A candidate is classified as an opinion holder if all of the following

[6]Predicates in patient position are given the same generalization label as the predicates in agent position. Specially marking them did not result in a notable improvement.

[7]`http://crfpp.sourceforge.net`

[8]The soft margin parameter $-c$ is set to 1.0 and all features occurring less than 3 times are removed.

[9]`http://www.surdeanu.name/mihai/swirl`

[10]Note that even for the configuration *Plain* the trees are already augmented with named-entity information.

[11]We chose this order as it roughly corresponds to the specificity of those generalization types.

[12]`disi.unitn.it/moschitti`

[13]The cost parameter $-j$ (Morik et al., 1999) was set to 5.

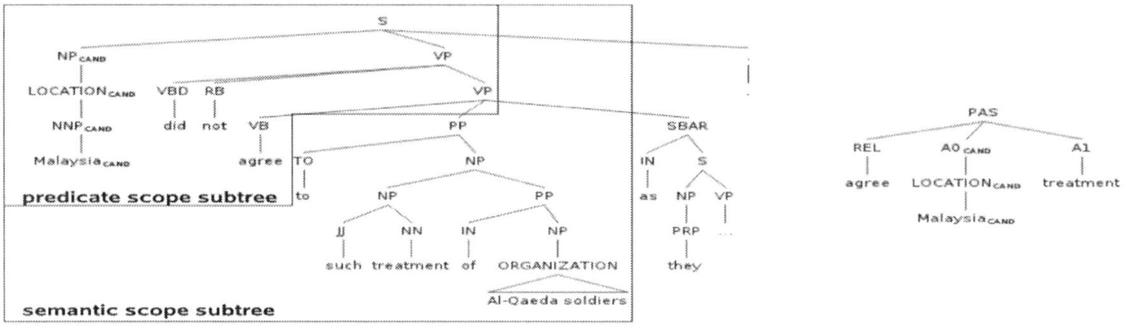

Figure 1: The different structures (*left*: constituency trees, *right*: predicate argument structure) derived from Sentence (1) for the opinion holder candidate *Malaysia* used as input for convolution kernels (CK).

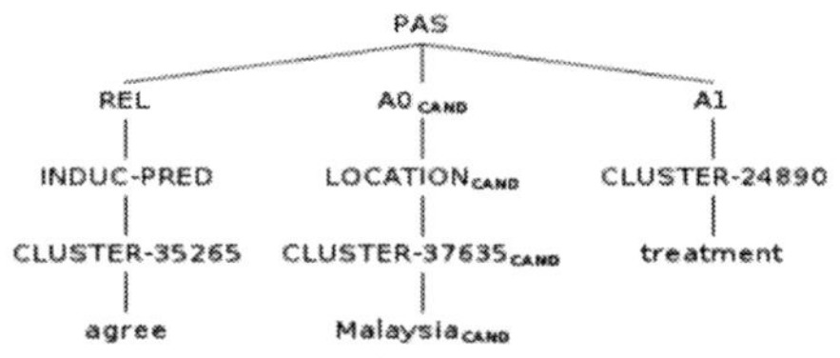

Figure 2: Predicate argument structure augmented with generalization nodes.

conditions hold:

- The candidate denotes a person or group of persons.
- There is a predictive predicate in the same sentence.
- The candidate has a pre-specified semantic role in the event that the predictive predicate evokes (*default: agent-role*).

The set of predicates is obtained from a given lexicon. For predicates that take opinion holders as patients, the default agent-role is overruled.

We consider several classifiers that differ in the lexicon they use. RB-Lex uses the combination of the manually compiled lexicons presented in §3.2. RB-Induc uses the predicates that have been automatically extracted from a large unlabeled corpus using the methods presented in §3.3. RB-Induc+Lex considers the union of those lexicons. In order to examine the impact of modeling opinion holders in patient position, we also introduce two versions of each lexicon. AG just considers predicates in agentive position while AG+PT also considers predicates that take opinion holders as patients. For example, RB-Induc$_{AG+PT}$ is a classifier that uses automatically extracted predicates in order to detect opinion holders in both agent and patient argument position, i.e. RB-Induc$_{AG+PT}$ also covers our novel extraction method for patients (§3.3.2).

The output of clustering will exclusively be evaluated in the context of learning-based methods, since there is no straightforward way of incorporating this output into a rule-based classifier.

	Features				
	Induc		**Lex**		**Induc+Lex**
Domains	**AG**	**AG+PT**	**AG**	**AG+PT**	**AG+PT**
ETHICS	50.77	50.99	52.22	52.27	**53.07**
SPACE	45.81	46.55	47.60	**48.47**	45.20
FICTION	46.59	49.97	54.84	59.35	**63.11**

Table 6: F-score of the different rule-based classifiers.

6 Experiments

CK and RB have an instance space that is different from the one of CRF. While CRF produces a prediction for every word token in a sentence, CK and RB only produce a prediction for every noun phrase. For evaluation, we project the predictions from RB and CK to word token level in order to ensure comparability. We evaluate the sequential output with precision, recall and F-score as defined in (Johansson and Moschitti, 2010; Johansson and Moschitti, 2011).

6.1 Rule-based Classifier

Table 6 shows the cross-domain performance of the different rule-based classifiers. RB-Lex performs better than RB-Induc. In comparison to the domains ETHICS and SPACE the difference is larger on FICTION. Presumably, this is due to the fact that the predicates in *Induc* are extracted from a news corpus (§2). Thus, *Induc* may slightly suffer from a domain mismatch. A combination of the two classifiers, i.e. RB-Lex+Induc, results in a notable improvement in the FICTION-domain. The approaches that also detect opinion holders as patients (AG+PT) including our novel approach (§3.3.2) are effective. A notable improvement can

		Training Size (%)				
Features	**Alg.**	**5**	**10**	**20**	**50**	**100**
Plain	CRF	32.14	35.24	41.03	51.05	55.13
	CK	42.15	46.34	51.14	56.39	59.52
+Clus	CRF	33.06	37.11	43.47	52.05	56.18
	CK	42.02	45.86	51.11	56.59	59.77
+Induc	CRF	37.28	42.31	46.54	54.27	56.71
	CK	46.26	49.35	53.26	57.28	60.42
+Lex	CRF	40.69	43.91	48.43	55.37	58.46
	CK	46.45	50.59	53.93	58.63	61.50
+Clus+Induc	CRF	37.27	42.19	47.35	54.95	57.14
	CK	45.14	48.20	52.39	57.37	59.97
+Clus+Lex	CRF	40.52	44.29	49.32	55.44	58.80
	CK	45.89	49.35	53.56	58.74	61.43
+Lex+Induc	CRF	**42.23**	**45.92**	49.96	55.61	58.40
	CK	**47.46**	**51.44**	**54.80**	58.74	**61.58**
All	CRF	41.56	45.75	**50.39**	**56.24**	**59.08**
	CK	46.18	50.10	54.04	**58.92**	61.44

Table 7: F-score of in-domain (ETHICS) learning-based classifiers.

only be measured on the FICTION-domain since this is the only domain with a significant proportion of those opinion holders (Table 3).

6.2 In-Domain Evaluation of Learning-based Methods

Table 7 shows the performance of the learning-based methods CRF and CK on an in-domain evaluation (ETHICS-domain) using different amounts of labeled training data. We carry out a 5-fold cross-validation and use $n\%$ of the training data in the training folds. The table shows that CK is more robust than CRF. The fewer training data are used the more important generalization becomes. CRF benefits much more from generalization than CK. Interestingly, the CRF configuration with the best generalization is usually as good as plain CK. This proves the effectiveness of CK. In principle, *Lex* is the strongest generalization method while *Clus* is by far the weakest. For *Clus*, systematic improvements towards no generalization (even though they are minor) can only be observed with CRF. As far as combinations are concerned, either *Lex+Induc* or *All* performs best. This in-domain evaluation proves that opinion holder extraction is different from named-entity recognition. Simple unsupervised generalization, such as word clustering, is not effective and popular sequential classifiers are less robust than margin-based tree-kernels.

Table 8 complements Table 7 in that it compares the learning-based methods with the best rule-based classifier and also displays precision and recall. RB achieves a high recall, whereas the learning-based methods always excel RB in precision.[14] Applying generalization to the learning-based methods results in an improvement of both recall and precision if few training data are used. The impact on precision decreases, however, the more training data are added. There is always a significant increase in recall but learning-based methods may not reach the level of RB even though they use the same resources. This is a side-effect of preserving a much higher precision. It also explains why learning-based methods with generalization may have a lower F-score than RB.

6.3 Out-of-Domain Evaluation of Learning-based Methods

Table 9 presents the results of out-of-domain classifiers. The complete ETHICS-dataset is used for training. Some properties are similar to the previous experiments: CK always outperforms CRF. RB provides a high recall whereas the learning-based methods maintain a higher precision. Similar to the in-domain setting using few labeled training data, the incorporation of generalization increases both precision and recall. Moreover, a combination of generalization methods is better than just using one method on average, although *Lex* is again a fairly robust individual generalization method. Generalization is more effective in this setting than on the in-domain evaluation using all training data, in particular for CK, since the training and test data are much more different from each other and suitable generalization methods partly close that gap.

There is a notable difference in precision between the SPACE- and FICTION-domain (and also the source domain ETHICS (Table 8)). We strongly assume that this is due to the distribution of opinion holders in those datasets (Table 1). The FICTION-domain contains much more opinion holders, therefore the chance that a predicted opinion holder is correct is much higher.

With regard to recall, a similar level of performance as in the ETHICS-domain can only be achieved in the SPACE-domain, i.e. CK achieves a recall of 60%. In the FICTION-domain, however, the recall is much lower (best recall of CK is below 47%). This is no surprise as the SPACE-domain is more similar to the source domain than

[14]The reason for RB having a high recall is extensively discussed in (Wiegand and Klakow, 2011b).

the FICTION-domain since ETHICS and SPACE are news texts. FICTION contains more out-of-domain language. Therefore, RB (which exclusively uses domain-independent knowledge) outperforms both learning-based methods including the ones incorporating generalization. Similar results have been observed for rule-based classifiers from other tasks in cross-domain sentiment analysis, such as subjectivity detection and polarity classification. High-level information as it is encoded in a rule-based classifier generalizes better than learning-based methods (Andreevskaia and Bergler, 2008; Lambov et al., 2009).

We set up another experiment exclusively for the FICTION-domain in which we combine the output of our best learning-based method, i.e. CK, with the prediction of a rule-based classifier. The combined classifier will predict an opinion holder, if either classifier predicts one. The motivation for this is the following: The FICTION-domain is the only domain to have a significant proportion of opinion holders appearing as patients. We want to know how much of them can be recognized with the best out-of-domain classifier using training data with only very few instances of this type and what benefit the addition of using various RBs which have a clearer notion of these constructions brings about. Moreover, we already observed that the learning-based methods have a bias towards preserving a high precision and this may have as a consequence that the generalization features incorporated into CK will not receive sufficiently large weights. Unlike the SPACE-domain where a sufficiently high recall is already achieved with CK (presumably due to its stronger similarity towards the source domain) the FICTION-domain may be more severely affected by this bias and evidence from RB may compensate for this.

Table 10 shows the performance of those combined classifiers. For all generalization types considered, there is, indeed, an improvement by adding information from RB resulting in a large boost in recall. Already the application of our induction approach *Induc* results in an increase of more than 8% points compared to plain CK. The table also shows that there is always some improvement if RB considers opinion holders as patients (AG+PT). This can be considered as some evidence that (given the available data we use) opinion holders in patient position can only be effectively extracted with the help of RBs. It is also

		CRF			*CK*		
Size	**Feat.**	**Prec**	**Rec**	**F1**	**Prec**	**Rec**	**F1**
10	Plain	52.17	26.61	35.24	58.26	38.47	46.34
	All	62.85	35.96	45.75	63.18	41.50	50.10
50	Plain	59.85	44.50	51.05	59.60	53.50	56.39
	All	62.99	50.80	56.24	61.91	56.20	58.92
100	Plain	64.14	48.33	55.13	62.38	56.91	59.52
	All	**64.75**	54.32	**59.08**	**63.81**	59.24	**61.44**
	RB	47.38	**60.32**	53.07	47.38	**60.32**	53.07

Table 8: Comparison of best RB with learning-based approaches on in-domain classification.

Algorithms	**Generalization**	**Prec**	**Rec**	**F**
CK (Plain)		66.90	41.48	51.21
CK	Induc	67.06	45.15	53.97
CK+RB$_{AG}$	Induc	60.22	54.52	57.23
CK+RB$_{AG+PT}$	Induc	61.09	58.14	59.58
CK	Lex	69.45	46.65	55.81
CK+RB$_{AG}$	Lex	67.36	59.02	62.91
CK+RB$_{AG+PT}$	Lex	68.25	63.28	65.67
CK	Induc+Lex	**69.73**	46.17	55.55
CK+RB$_{AG}$	Induc+Lex	61.41	65.56	63.42
CK+RB$_{AG+PT}$	Induc+Lex	62.26	**70.56**	**66.15**

Table 10: Combination of out-of-domain CK and rule-based classifiers on FICTION (i.e. distant domain).

further evidence that our novel approach to extract those predicates (§3.3.2) is effective.

The combined approach in Table 10 not only outperforms CK (discussed above) but also RB (Table 6). We manually inspected the output of the classifiers to find also cases in which CK detect opinion holders that RB misses. CK has the advantage that it is not only bound to the relationship between candidate holder and predicate. It learns further heuristics, e.g. that sentence-initial mentions of persons are likely opinion holders. In (12), for example, this heuristics fires while RB overlooks this instance as *to give someone a share of advice* is not part of the lexicon.

(12) She later *gives* Charlotte her *share of advice* on running a household.

7 Related Work

The research on opinion holder extraction has been focusing on applying different data-driven approaches. Choi et al. (2005) and Choi et al. (2006) explore conditional random fields, Wiegand and Klakow (2010) examine different combinations of convolution kernels, while Johansson and Moschitti (2010) present a re-ranking approach modeling complex relations between multiple opinions in a sentence. A comparison of

	SPACE (similar target domain)						FICTION (distant target domain)					
	CRF			CK			CRF			CK		
Features	**Prec**	**Rec**	**F1**	**Prec**	**Rec**	**F1**	**Prec**	**Rec**	**F1**	**Prec**	**Rec**	**F1**
Plain	47.32	48.62	47.96	45.89	57.07	50.87	68.58	28.96	40.73	66.90	41.48	51.21
+Clus	49.00	48.62	48.81	49.23	57.64	53.10	71.85	32.21	44.48	67.54	41.21	51.19
+Induc	42.92	49.15	45.82	46.66	**60.45**	52.67	71.59	34.77	46.80	67.06	45.15	53.97
+Lex	49.65	49.07	49.36	49.60	59.88	54.26	71.91	35.83	47.83	69.45	46.65	55.81
+Clus+Induc	46.61	48.78	47.67	48.65	58.20	53.00	71.32	35.88	47.74	67.46	42.17	51.90
+Lex+Induc	48.75	50.87	49.78	49.92	58.76	53.98	**74.02**	37.37	49.67	69.73	46.17	55.55
+Clus+Lex	49.72	50.87	50.29	**53.70**	59.32	**56.37**	73.41	37.15	49.33	70.59	43.98	54.20
All	**49.87**	51.03	**50.44**	51.68	58.76	54.99	72.00	37.44	49.26	**70.61**	44.83	54.84
best RB	41.72	**57.80**	48.47	41.72	57.80	48.47	63.26	**62.96**	**63.11**	63.26	**62.96**	**63.11**

Table 9: Comparison of best RB with learning-based approaches on out-of-domain classification.

those methods has not yet been attempted. In this work, we compare the popular state-of-the-art learning algorithms conditional random fields and convolution kernels for the first time. All these data-driven methods have been evaluated on the MPQA corpus. Some generalization methods are incorporated but unlike this paper they are neither systematically compared nor combined. The role of resources that provide the knowledge of argument positions of opinion holders is not covered in any of these works. This kind of knowledge should be directly learnt from the labeled training data. In this work, we found, however, that the distribution of argument positions of opinion holders varies throughout the different domains and, therefore, cannot be learnt from any arbitrary out-of-domain training set.

Bethard et al. (2004) and Kim and Hovy (2006) explore the usefulness of semantic roles provided by FrameNet (Fillmore et al., 2003). Bethard et al. (2004) use this resource to acquire labeled training data while in (Kim and Hovy, 2006) FrameNet is used within a rule-based classifier mapping frame-elements of frames to opinion holders. Bethard et al. (2004) only evaluate on an artificial dataset (i.e. a subset of sentences from FrameNet and PropBank (Kingsbury and Palmer, 2002)). The only realistic test set on which Kim and Hovy (2006) evaluate their approach are news texts. Their method is compared against a simple rule-based baseline and, unlike this work, not against a robust data-driven algorithm.

(Wiegand and Klakow, 2011b) is similar to (Kim and Hovy, 2006) in that a rule-based approach is used relying on the relationship towards predictive predicates. Diverse resources are considered for obtaining such words, however, they are only evaluated on the entire MPQA corpus.

The only cross-domain evaluation of opinion holder extraction is reported in (Li et al., 2007) using the MPQA corpus as a training set and the NTCIR collection as a test set. A low cross-domain performance is obtained and the authors conclude that this is due to the very different annotation schemes of those corpora.

8 Conclusion

We examined different generalization methods for opinion holder extraction. We found that for in-domain classification, the more labeled training data are used, the smaller is the impact of generalization. Robust learning methods, such as convolution kernels, benefit less from generalization than weaker classifiers, such as conditional random fields. For cross-domain classification, generalization is always helpful. Distant domains are problematic for learning-based methods, however, rule-based methods provide a reasonable recall and can be effectively combined with the learning-based methods. The types of generalization that help best are manually compiled lexicons followed by an induction method inspired by distant supervision. Finally, we examined the case of opinion holders as patients and also presented a novel automatic extraction method that proved effective. Such dedicated extraction methods are important as common labeled datasets (from the news domain) do not provide sufficient training data for these constructions.

Acknowledgements

This work was funded by the German Federal Ministry of Education and Research (Software-Cluster) under grant no. "01IC10S01". The authors thank Alessandro Moschitti, Benjamin Roth and Josef Ruppenhofer for their technical support and interesting discussions.

References

Steven Abney. 1991. Parsing By Chunks. In Robert Berwick, Steven Abney, and Carol Tenny, editors, *Principle-Based Parsing*. Kluwer Academic Publishers, Dordrecht.

Alina Andreevskaia and Sabine Bergler. 2008. When Specialists and Generalists Work Together: Overcoming Domain Dependence in Sentiment Tagging. In *Proceedings of the Annual Meeting of the Association for Computational Linguistics: Human Language Technologies (ACL/HLT)*, Columbus, OH, USA.

Steven Bethard, Hong Yu, Ashley Thornton, Vasileios Hatzivassiloglou, and Dan Jurafsky. 2004. Extracting Opinion Propositions and Opinion Holders using Syntactic and Lexical Cues. In *Computing Attitude and Affect in Text: Theory and Applications*. Springer-Verlag.

Peter F. Brown, Peter V. deSouza, Robert L. Mercer, Vincent J. Della Pietra, and Jenifer C. Lai. 1992. Class-based n-gram models of natural language. *Computational Linguistics*, 18:467–479.

Yejin Choi, Claire Cardie, Ellen Riloff, and Siddharth Patwardhan. 2005. Identifying Sources of Opinions with Conditional Random Fields and Extraction Patterns. In *Proceedings of the Conference on Human Language Technology and Empirical Methods in Natural Language Processing (HLT/EMNLP)*, Vancouver, BC, Canada.

Yejin Choi, Eric Breck, and Claire Cardie. 2006. Joint Extraction of Entities and Relations for Opinion Recognition. In *Proceedings of the Conference on Empirical Methods in Natural Language Processing (EMNLP)*, Sydney, Australia.

Charles. J. Fillmore, Christopher R. Johnson, and Miriam R. Petruck. 2003. Background to FrameNet. *International Journal of Lexicography*, 16:235 – 250.

Jenny Rose Finkel, Trond Grenager, and Christopher Manning. 2005. Incorporating Non-local Information into Information Extraction Systems by Gibbs Sampling. In *Proceedings of the Annual Meeting of the Association for Computational Linguistics (ACL)*, Ann Arbor, MI, USA.

Thorsten Joachims. 1999. Making Large-Scale SVM Learning Practical. In B. Schölkopf, C. Burges, and A. Smola, editors, *Advances in Kernel Methods - Support Vector Learning*. MIT Press.

Richard Johansson and Alessandro Moschitti. 2010. Reranking Models in Fine-grained Opinion Analysis. In *Proceedings of the International Conference on Computational Linguistics (COLING)*, Beijing, China.

Richard Johansson and Alessandro Moschitti. 2011. Extracting Opinion Expressions and Their Polarities – Exploration of Pipelines and Joint Models. In *Proceedings of the Annual Meeting of the Association for Computational Linguistics (ACL)*, Portland, OR, USA.

Jason S. Kessler, Miriam Eckert, Lyndsay Clarke, and Nicolas Nicolov. 2010. The ICWSM JDPA 2010 Sentiment Corpus for the Automotive Domain. In *Proceedings of the International AAAI Conference on Weblogs and Social Media Data Challange Workshop (ICWSM-DCW)*, Washington, DC, USA.

Soo-Min Kim and Eduard Hovy. 2006. Extracting Opinions, Opinion Holders, and Topics Expressed in Online News Media Text. In *Proceedings of the ACL Workshop on Sentiment and Subjectivity in Text*, Sydney, Australia.

Paul Kingsbury and Martha Palmer. 2002. From TreeBank to PropBank. In *Proceedings of the Conference on Language Resources and Evaluation (LREC)*, Las Palmas, Spain.

Dan Klein and Christopher D. Manning. 2003. Accurate Unlexicalized Parsing. In *Proceedings of the Annual Meeting of the Association for Computational Linguistics (ACL)*, Sapporo, Japan.

John Lafferty, Andrew McCallum, and Fernando Pereira. 2001. Conditional Random Fields: Probabilistic Models for Segmenting and Labeling Sequence Data. In *Proceedings of the International Conference on Machine Learning (ICML)*.

Dinko Lambov, Gaël Dias, and Veska Noncheva. 2009. Sentiment Classification across Domains. In *Proceedings of the Portuguese Conference on Artificial Intelligence (EPIA)*, Aveiro, Portugal. Springer-Verlag.

Beth Levin. 1993. *English Verb Classes and Alternations: A Preliminary Investigation*. University of Chicago Press.

Yangyong Li, Kalina Bontcheva, and Hamish Cunningham. 2007. Experiments of Opinion Analysis on the Corpora MPQA and NTCIR-6. In *Proceedings of the NTCIR-6 Workshop Meeting*, Tokyo, Japan.

Mike Mintz, Steven Bills, Rion Snow, and Dan Jurafsky. 2009. Distant Supervision for Relation Extraction without Labeled Data. In *Proceedings of the Joint Conference of the Annual Meeting of the Association for Computational Linguistics and the International Joint Conference on Natural Language Processing of the Asian Federation of Natural Language Processing (ACL/IJCNLP)*, Singapore.

Katharina Morik, Peter Brockhausen, and Thorsten Joachims. 1999. Combining Statistical Learning with a Knowledge-based Approach - A Case Study in Intensive Care Monitoring. In *Proceedings the International Conference on Machine Learning (ICML)*.

Andreas Stolcke. 2002. SRILM - An Extensible Language Modeling Toolkit. In *Proceedings of the In-*

ternational Conference on Spoken Language Processing (ICSLP), Denver, CO, USA.

Veselin Stoyanov and Claire Cardie. 2011. Automatically Creating General-Purpose Opinion Summaries from Text. In *Proceedings of Recent Advances in Natural Language Processing (RANLP)*, Hissar, Bulgaria.

Veselin Stoyanov, Claire Cardie, Diane Litman, and Janyce Wiebe. 2004. Evaluating an Opinion Annotation Scheme Using a New Multi-Perspective Question and Answer Corpus. In *Proceedings of the AAAI Spring Symposium on Exploring Attitude and Affect in Text*, Menlo Park, CA, USA.

Cigdem Toprak, Niklas Jakob, and Iryna Gurevych. 2010. Sentence and Expression Level Annotation of Opinions in User-Generated Discourse. In *Proceedings of the Annual Meeting of the Association for Computational Linguistics (ACL)*, Uppsala, Sweden.

Joseph Turian, Lev Ratinov, and Yoshua Bengio. 2010. Word Representations: A Simple and General Method for Semi-supervised Learning. In *Proceedings of the Annual Meeting of the Association for Computational Linguistics (ACL)*, Uppsala, Sweden.

Janyce Wiebe, Theresa Wilson, Rebecca Bruce, Matthew Bell, and Melanie Martin. 2004. Learning Subjective Language. *Computational Linguistics*, 30(3).

Janyce Wiebe, Theresa Wilson, and Claire Cardie. 2005. Annotating Expressions of Opinions and Emotions in Language. *Language Resources and Evaluation*, 39(2/3):164–210.

Michael Wiegand and Dietrich Klakow. 2010. Convolution Kernels for Opinion Holder Extraction. In *Proceedings of the Human Language Technology Conference of the North American Chapter of the ACL (HLT/NAACL)*, Los Angeles, CA, USA.

Michael Wiegand and Dietrich Klakow. 2011a. Prototypical Opinion Holders: What We can Learn from Experts and Analysts. In *Proceedings of Recent Advances in Natural Language Processing (RANLP)*, Hissar, Bulgaria.

Michael Wiegand and Dietrich Klakow. 2011b. The Role of Predicates in Opinion Holder Extraction. In *Proceedings of the RANLP Workshop on Information Extraction and Knowledge Acquisition (IEKA)*, Hissar, Bulgaria.

Theresa Wilson, Janyce Wiebe, and Paul Hoffmann. 2005. Recognizing Contextual Polarity in Phrase-level Sentiment Analysis. In *Proceedings of the Conference on Human Language Technology and Empirical Methods in Natural Language Processing (HLT/EMNLP)*, Vancouver, BC, Canada.

Skip N-grams and Ranking Functions for Predicting Script Events

Bram Jans
KU Leuven
Leuven, Belgium
bram.jans@gmail.com

Steven Bethard
University of Colorado Boulder
Boulder, Colorado, USA
steven.bethard@colorado.edu

Ivan Vulić
KU Leuven
Leuven, Belgium
ivan.vulic@cs.kuleuven.be

Marie Francine Moens
KU Leuven
Leuven, Belgium
sien.moens@cs.kuleuven.be

Abstract

In this paper, we extend current state-of-the-art research on unsupervised acquisition of scripts, that is, stereotypical and frequently observed sequences of events. We design, evaluate and compare different methods for constructing models for script event prediction: given a partial chain of events in a script, predict other events that are likely to belong to the script. Our work aims to answer key questions about how best to (1) identify representative event chains from a source text, (2) gather statistics from the event chains, and (3) choose ranking functions for predicting new script events. We make several contributions, introducing skip-grams for collecting event statistics, designing improved methods for ranking event predictions, defining a more reliable evaluation metric for measuring predictiveness, and providing a systematic analysis of the various event prediction models.

1 Introduction

There has been recent interest in automatically acquiring world knowledge in the form of *scripts* (Schank and Abelson, 1977), that is, frequently recurring situations that have a stereotypical sequence of events, such as a visit to a restaurant. All of the techniques so far proposed for this task share a common sub-task: given an event or partial chain of events, predict other events that belong to the same script (Chambers and Jurafsky, 2008; Chambers and Jurafsky, 2009; Chambers and Jurafsky, 2011; Manshadi et al., 2008; McIntyre and Lapata, 2009; McIntyre and Lapata, 2010; Regneri et al., 2010). Such a model can then serve as input to a system that identifies the order of the events within that script (Chambers and Jurafsky, 2008; Chambers and Jurafsky, 2009) or that generates a story using the selected events (McIntyre and Lapata, 2009; McIntyre and Lapata, 2010).

In this article, we analyze and compare techniques for constructing models that, given a partial chain of events, predict other events that belong to the script. In particular, we consider the following questions:

- How should representative chains of events be selected from the source text?
- Given an event chain, how should statistics be gathered from it?
- Given event n-gram statistics, which ranking function best predicts the events for a script?

In the process of answering these questions, this article makes several contributions to the field of script and narrative event chain understanding:

- We explore for the first time the use of skip-grams for collecting narrative event statistics, and show that this approach performs better than classic n-gram statistics.
- We propose a new method for ranking events given a partial script, and show that it performs substantially better than ranking methods from prior work.
- We propose a new evaluation procedure (using Recall@N) for the cloze test, and advocate its usage instead of *average rank* used previously in the literature.
- We provide a systematic analysis of the interactions between the choices made when constructing an event prediction model.

Section 2 gives an overview of the prior work related to this task. Section 3 lists and briefly describes different approaches that try to provide answers to the three questions posed in this introduction, while Section 4 presents the results of our experiments and reports on our findings. Finally, Section 5 provides a conclusive discussion along with ideas for future work.

2 Prior Work

Our work is primarily inspired by the work of Chambers and Jurafsky, which combined a dependency parser with coreference resolution to collect event script statistics and predict script events (Chambers and Jurafsky, 2008; Chambers and Jurafsky, 2009). For each document in their training corpus, they used coreference resolution to identify all the entities, and a dependency parser to identify all verbs that had an entity as either a subject or object. They defined an event as a verb plus a dependency type (either subject or object), and collected for each entity, the chain of events that it participated in. They then calculated pointwise mutual information (PMI) statistics over all the pairs of events that occurred in the event chains in their corpus. To predict a new script event given a partial chain of events, they selected the event with the highest sum of PMIs with all the events in the partial chain.

The work of McIntyre and Lapata followed in this same paradigm, (McIntyre and Lapata, 2009; McIntyre and Lapata, 2010), collecting chains of events by looking at entities and the sequence of verbs for which they were a subject or object. They also calculated statistics over the collected event chains, though they considered both event bigram and event trigram counts. Rather than predicting an event for a script however, they used these simple counts to predict the next event that should be generated for a children's story.

Manshadi and colleagues were concerned about the scalability of running parsers and coreference over a large collection of story blogs, and so used a simplified version of event chains – just the main verb of each sentence (Manshadi et al., 2008). Rather than rely on an ad-hoc summation of PMIs, they apply language modeling techniques (specifically, a smoothed 5-gram model) over the sequence of events in the collected chains. However, they only tested these language models on sequencing tasks (e.g. is the real sequence better than a random sequence?) rather than on prediction tasks (e.g. which event should follow these events?).

In the current article, we attempt to shed some light on these previous works by comparing different ways of collecting and using event chains.

3 Methods

Models that predict script events typically have three stages. First, a large corpus is processed to find event chains in each of the documents. Next, statistics over these event chains are gathered and stored. Finally, the gathered statistics are used to create a model that takes as input a partial script and produces as output a ranked list of events for that script. The following sections give more details about each of these stages and identify the decisions that must be made in each step, and an overview of the whole process with an example source text is displayed in Figure 1.

3.1 Identifying Event Chains

Event chains are typically defined as a sequence of actions performed by some actor. Formally, an event chain C for some actor a, is a partially ordered set of events (v, d) where each v is a verb that has the actor a as its dependency d. Following prior work (Chambers and Jurafsky, 2008; Chambers and Jurafsky, 2009; McIntyre and Lapata, 2009; McIntyre and Lapata, 2010), these event chains are identified by running a coreference system and a dependency parser. Then for each entity identified by the coreference system, all verbs that have a mention of that entity as one of their dependencies are collected[1]. The event chain is then the sequence of (verb, dependency-type) tuples. For example, given the sentence *A Crow was sitting on a branch of a tree when a Fox observed her*, the event chain for the *Crow* would be (*sitting*, SUBJECT), (*observed*, OBJECT).

Once event chains have been identified, the most appropriate event chains for training the model must be selected. The goal of this process is to select the subset of the event chains identified by the coreference system and the dependency parser that look to be the most reliable. Both the coreference system and the dependency parser make some errors, so not all event chains are necessarily useful for training a model. The three strategies we consider for this selection process are:

[1] Also following prior work, we consider only the dependencies *subject* and *object*.

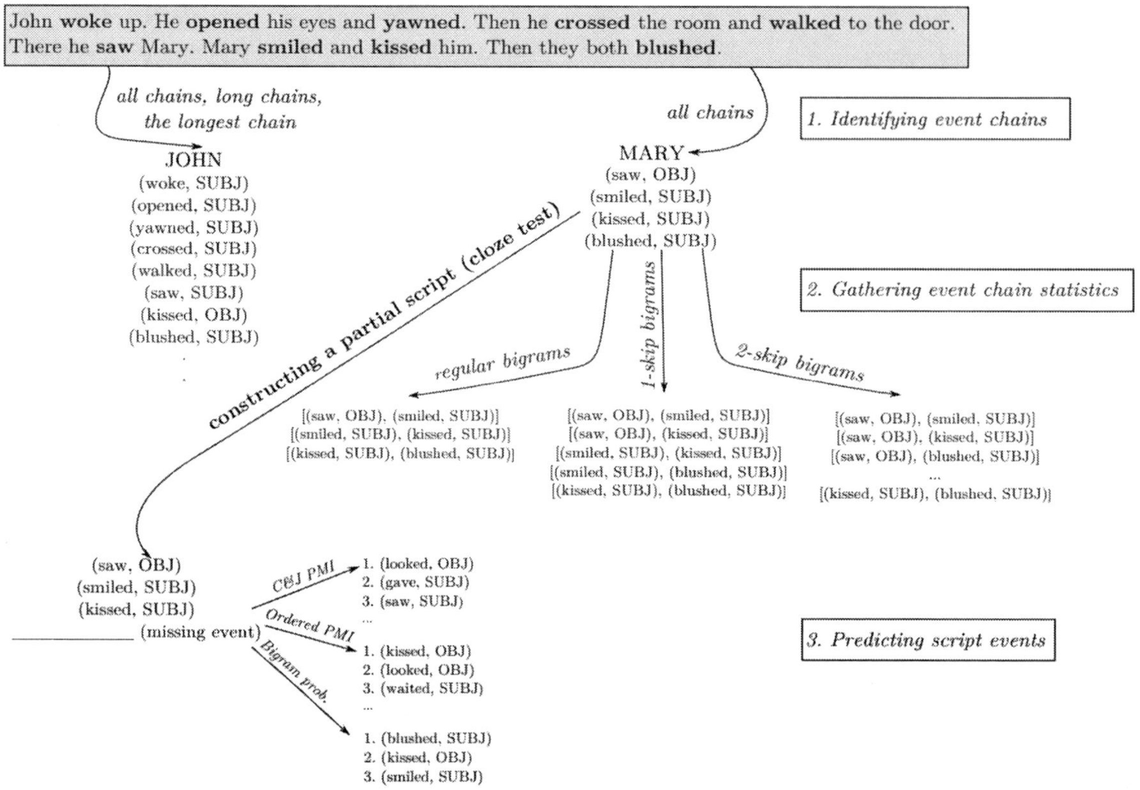

Figure 1: An overview of the whole linear work flow showing the three key steps – identifying event chains, collecting statistics out of the chains and predicting a missing event in a script. The figure also displays how a partial script for evaluation (Section 4.3) is constructed. We show the whole process for Mary's event chain only, but the same steps are followed for John's event chain.

- Select **all event chains**, that is, all sequences of two or more events linked by common actors. This strategy will produce the largest number of event chains to train a model from, but it may produce noisier training data as the very short chains included by this strategy may be less likely to represent real scripts.
- Select all **long event chains** consisting of 5 or more events. This strategy will produce a smaller number of event chains, but as they are longer, they may be more likely to represent scripts.
- Select only the **longest event chain**. This strategy will produce the smallest number of event chains from a corpus. However, they may be of higher quality, since this strategy looks for the key actor in each story, and only uses the events that are tied together by that key actor. Since this is the single actor that played the largest role in the story, its actions may be the most likely to represent a real script.

3.2 Gathering Event Chain Statistics

Once event chains have been collected from the corpus, the statistics necessary for constructing the event prediction model must be gathered. Following prior work (Chambers and Jurafsky, 2008; Chambers and Jurafsky, 2009; Manshadi et al., 2008; McIntyre and Lapata, 2009; McIntyre and Lapata, 2010), we focus on gathering statistics about the n-grams of events that occur in the collected event chains. Specifically, we look at strategies for collecting bigram statistics, the most common type of statistics gathered in prior work. We consider three strategies for collecting bigram statistics:

- **Regular bigrams**. We find all pairs of events that are adjacent in an event chain and collect the number of times each event pair was observed. For example, given the chain of events (*saw*, SUBJ), (*kissed*, OBJ), (*blushed*, SUBJ), we would extract the two event bigrams: ((*saw*, SUBJ), (*kissed*, OBJ)) and ((*kissed*, OBJ), (*blushed*, SUBJ)). In addition to the event pair counts, we also collect the number of times each event was observed individually, to allow for various conditional probability calculations. This strategy follows the classic approach for most language models.

- **1-skip bigrams**. We collect pairs of events that occur with 0 or 1 events intervening between them. For example, given the chain (*saw*, SUBJ), (*kissed*, OBJ), (*blushed*, SUBJ), we would extract three bigrams: the two regular bigrams ((*saw*, SUBJ), (*kissed*, OBJ)) and ((*kissed*, OBJ), (*blushed*, SUBJ)), plus the 1-skip-bigram, ((*saw*, SUBJ), (*blushed*, SUBJ)). This approach to collecting n-gram statistics is sometimes called *skip-gram* modeling, and it can reduce data sparsity by extracting more event pairs per chain (Guthrie et al., 2006). It has not previously been applied in the task of predicting script events, but it may be quite appropriate to this task because in most scripts it is possible to skip some events in the sequence.

- **2-skip bigrams**. We collect pairs of events that occur with 0, 1 or 2 intervening events, similar to what was done in the 1-skip bigrams strategy. This will extract even more pairs of events from each chain, but it is possible the statistics over these pairs of events will be noisier.

3.3 Predicting Script Events

Once statistics over event chains have been collected, it is possible to construct the model for predicting script events. The input of this model will be a partial script c of n events, where $c = c_1 c_2 \ldots c_n = (v_1, d_1), (v_2, d_2), \ldots, (v_n, d_n)$, and the output of this model will be a ranked list of events where the highest ranked events are the ones most likely to belong to the event sequence in the script. Thus, the key issue for this model is to define the function f for ranking events. We consider three such ranking functions:

- **Chambers & Jurafsky PMI**. Chambers and Jurafsky (2008) define their event ranking function based on pointwise mutual information. Given a partial script c as defined above, they consider each event $e = (v', d')$ collected from their corpus, and score it as the sum of the pointwise mutual informations between the event e and each of the events in the script:

$$f(e, c) = \sum_i^n \log \frac{P(c_i, e)}{P(c_i)P(e)}$$

Chambers and Jurafsky's description of this score suggests that it is unordered, such that $P(a, b) = P(b, a)$. Thus the probabilities must be defined as:

$$P(e_1, e_2) = \frac{C(e_1, e_2) + C(e_2, e_1)}{\sum_{e_i} \sum_{e_j} C(e_i, e_j)}$$

$$P(e) = \frac{C(e)}{\sum_{e'} C(e')}$$

where $C(e_1, e_2)$ is the number of times that the ordered event pair (e_1, e_2) was counted in the training data, and $C(e)$ is the number of times that the event e was counted.

- **Ordered PMI**. A variation on the approach of Chambers and Jurafsky is to have a score that takes the order of the events in the chain into account. In this scenario, we assume that in addition to the partial script of events, we are given an insertion point, m, where the new event should be added. The score is then defined as:

$$f(e, c) = \sum_{k=1}^{m} \log \frac{P(c_k, e)}{P(c_k)P(e)} + \sum_{k=m+1}^{n} \log \frac{P(e, c_k)}{P(e)P(c_k)}$$

where the probabilities are defined as:

$$P(e_1, e_2) = \frac{C(e_1, e_2)}{\sum_{e_i} \sum_{e_j} C(e_i, e_j)}$$

$$P(e) = \frac{C(e)}{\sum_{e'} C(e')}$$

This approach uses pointwise mutual information but also models the event chain in the order it was observed.

- **Bigram probabilities**. Finally, a natural ranking function, which has not been applied to the script event prediction task (but has been applied to related tasks (Manshadi et al., 2008)) is to use the bigram probabilities of language modeling rather than pointwise mutual information scores. Again, given an insertion point m for the event in the script, we define the score as:

$$f(e, c) = \sum_{k=1}^{m} \log P(e|c_k) + \sum_{k=m+1}^{n} \log P(c_k|e)$$

where the conditional probability is defined as[2]:

$$P(e_1|e_2) = \frac{C(e_1, e_2)}{C(e_2)}$$

This approach scores an event based on the probability that it was observed following all the events before it in the chain and preceding all the events after it in the chain. This approach most directly models the event chain in the order it was observed.

4 Experiments

Our experiments aimed to answer three questions: Which event chains are worth keeping? How should event bigram counts be collected? And which ranking method is best for predicting script events? To answer these questions we use two corpora, the Reuters Corpus and the Andrew Lang Fairy Tale Corpus, to evaluate our three different chain selection methods, {*all chains, long chains, the longest chain*}, our three different bigram counting methods, {*regular bigrams, 1-skip bigrams, 2-skip bigrams*}, and our three different ranking methods, {*Chambers & Jurafsky PMI, ordered PMI, bigram probabilities*}.

4.1 Corpora

We consider two corpora for evaluation:

- **Reuters Corpus, Volume 1** [3] (Lewis et al., 2004) – a large collection of 806,791 news stories written in English concerning a number of different topics such as politics, economics, sports, etc., strongly varying in length, topics and narrative structure.
- **Andrew Lang Fairy Tale Corpus** [4] – a small collection of 437 children stories with an average length of 125 sentences, and used previously for story generation by McIntyre and Lapata (2009).

In general, the Reuters Corpus is much larger and allows us to see how well script events can be predicted when a lot of data is available, while the Andrew Lang Fairy Tale Corpus is much smaller, but has a more straightforward narrative structure that may make identifying scripts simpler.

4.2 Corpus Processing

Constructing a model for predicting script events requires a corpus that has been parsed with a dependency parser, and whose entities have been identified via a coreference system. We therefore processed our corpora by (1) filtering out non-narrative articles, (2) applying a dependency parser, (3) applying a coreference resolution system and (4) identifying event chains via entities and dependencies.

First, articles that had no narrative content were removed from the corpora. In the Reuters Corpus, we removed all files solely listing stock exchange values, interest rates, etc., as well as all articles that were simply summaries of headlines from different countries or cities. After removing these files, the Reuters corpus was reduced to 788,245 files. Removing files from the Fairy Tale corpus was not necessary – all 437 stories were retained.

We then applied the Stanford Parser (Klein and Manning, 2003) to identify the dependency structure of each sentence in each article in the corpus. This parser produces a constitutent-based syntactic parse tree for each sentence, and then converts this tree to a collapsed dependency structure via a set of tree patterns.

Next we applied the OpenNLP coreference engine[5] to identify the entities in each article, and the noun phrases that were mentions of each entity.

Finally, to identify the event chains, we took each of the entities proposed by the coreference system, walked through each of the noun phrases associated with that entity, retrieved any *subject*

[2]Note that predicted bigram probabilities are calculated in this way for both classic language modeling and skip-gram modeling. In skip-gram modeling, skips in the n-grams are only used to increase the size of the training data; prediction is performed exactly as in classic language modeling.

[3]http://trec.nist.gov/data/reuters/reuters.html

[4]http://www.mythfolklore.net/andrewlang/

[5]http://incubator.apache.org/opennlp/

or *object* dependencies that linked a verb to that noun phrase, and created an event chain from the sequence of (verb, dependency-type) tuples in the order that they appeared in the text.

4.3 Evaluation Metrics

We follow the approach of Chambers and Jurafsky (2008), evaluating our models for predicting script events in a *narrative cloze* task. The narrative cloze task is inspired by the classic psychological cloze task in which subjects are given a sentence with a word missing and asked to fill in the blank (Taylor, 1953). Similarly, in the narrative cloze task, the system is given a sequence of events from a script where one event is missing, and asked to predict the missing event. The difficulty of a cloze task depends a lot on the context around the missing item – in some cases it may be quite predictable, but in many cases there is no single correct answer, though some answers are more probable than others. Thus, performing well on a cloze task is more about ranking the missing event highly, and not about proposing a single "correct" event.

In this way, narrative cloze is like perplexity in a language model. However, where perplexity measures how good the model is at predicting a script event given the previous events in the script, narrative cloze measures how good the model is at predicting what is missing between events in the script. Thus narrative cloze is somewhat more appropriate to our task, and at the same time simplifies comparisons to prior work.

Rather than manually constructing a set of scripts on which to run the cloze test, we follow Chambers and Jurafsky in reserving a section of our parsed corpora for testing, and then using the event chains from that section as the scripts for which the system must predict events. Given an event chain of length n, we run n cloze tests, with a different one of the n events removed each time to create a *partial script* from the remaining $n-1$ events (see Figure 1). Given a partial script as input, an accurate event prediction model should rank the missing event highly in the *guess list* that it generates as output.

We consider two approaches to evaluating the guess lists produced in response to narrative cloze tests. Both are defined in terms of a test collection C, consisting of $|C|$ partial scripts, where for each partial script c with missing event e, $rank_{sys}(c)$ is the rank of e in the system's guess list for c.

- **Average rank**. The average rank of the missing event across all of the partial scripts:

$$\frac{1}{|C|}\sum_{c\in C} rank_{sys}(c)$$

  This is the evaluation metric used by Chambers and Jurafsky (2008).

- **Recall@N**. The fraction of partial scripts where the missing event is ranked N or less[6] in the guess list.

$$\frac{1}{|C|}|\{c : c \in C \wedge rank_{sys}(c) \leq N\}|$$

  In our experiments we use $N = 50$, but results are roughly similar for lower and higher values of N.

Recall@N has not been used before for evaluating models that predict script events, however we suggest that it is a more reliable metric than Average rank. When calculating the average rank, the length of the guess lists will have a significant influence on results. For instance, if a small model is trained with only a small vocabulary of events, its guess lists will usually be shorter than a larger model, but if both models predict the missing event at the bottom of the list, the larger model will get penalized more. Recall@N does not have this issue – it is not influenced by length of the guess lists.

An alternative evaluation metric would have been mean average precision (MAP), a metric commonly used to evaluate information retrieval. Mean average precision reduces to mean reciprocal rank (MRR) when there's only a single answer as in the case of narrative cloze, and would have scored the ranked lists as:

$$\frac{1}{|C|}\sum_{c\in C}\frac{1}{rank_{sys}(c)}$$

Note that mean reciprocal rank has the same issues with guess list length that average rank does. Thus, since it does not aid us in comparing to prior work, and it has the same deficiencies as average rank, we do not report MRR in this article.

[6]Rank 1 is the event that the system predicts is most probable, so we want the missing event to have the smallest rank possible.

	2-skip + bigram prob.	
Chain selection	**Av. rank**	**Recall@50**
all chains	**502**	**0.5179**
long chains	549	0.4951
the longest chain	546	0.4984

Table 1: Chain selection methods for the Reuters corpus - comparison of average ranks and Recall@50.

	2-skip + bigram prob.	
Chain selection	**Av. rank**	**Recall@50**
all chains	1650	0.3376
long chains	**452**	**0.3461**
the longest chain	1534	0.3376

Table 2: Chain selection methods for the Fairy Tale corpus - comparison of average ranks and Recall@50.

	all chains + bigram prob.	
Bigram selection	**Av. rank**	**Recall@50**
regular bigrams	789	0.4886
1-skip bigrams	630	0.4951
2-skip bigrams	**502**	**0.5179**

Table 3: Event bigram selection methods for the Reuters corpus - comparison of average ranks and Recall@50.

	all chains + bigram prob.	
Bigram selection	**Av. rank**	**Recall@50**
regular bigrams	2363	0.3227
1-skip bigrams	1690	**0.3418**
2-skip bigrams	**1650**	0.3376

Table 4: Event bigram selection methods for the Fairy Tales corpus - comparison of average ranks and Recall@50.

4.4 Results

We considered all 27 combinations of our chain selection methods, bigram counting methods, and ranking methods: {*all chains, long chains, the longest chain*}x{*regular bigrams, 1-skip bigrams, 2-skip bigrams*}x{*Chambers & Jurafsky PMI, ordered PMI, bigram probabilities*}. The best among these 27 combinations for the Reuters corpus was {*all chains*}x{*2-skip bigrams*}x{*bigram probabilities*} achieving an average rank of 502 and a Recall@50 of 0.5179.

Since viewing all the combinations at once would be confusing, instead the following sections investigate each decision (selection, counting, ranking) one at a time. While one decision is varied across its three choices, the other decisions are held to their values in the best model above.

4.4.1 Identifying Event Chains

We first try to answer the question: How should representative chains of events be selected from the source text? Tables 1 and 2 show performance when we vary the strategy for selecting event chains, while fixing the counting method to *2-skip bigrams*, and fixing the ranking method to *bigram probabilities*.

For the Reuters collection, we see that using *all chains* gives a lower average rank and a higher Recall@50 than either of the strategies that select a subset of the event chains. The explanation is probably simple: using *all chains* produces more than 700,000 bigrams from the Reuters corpus, while using only the long chains produces only around 300,000. So more data is better data for predicting script events.

For the Fairy Tale collection, *long chains* gives the lowest average rank and highest Recall@50. In this collection, there is apparently some benefit to filtering the shorter event chains, probably because the collection is small enough that the noise introduced from dependency and coreference errors plays a larger role.

4.4.2 Gathering Event Chain Statistics

We next try to answer the question: Given an event chain, how should statistics be gathered from it? Tables 3 and 4 show performance when we vary the strategy for counting event pairs, while fixing the selecting method to *all chains*, and fixing the ranking method to *bigram probabilities*.

For the Reuters corpus, *2-skip bigrams* achieves the lowest average rank and the highest Recall@50. For the Fairy Tale corpus, *1-skip bigrams* and *2-skip bigrams* perform similarly, and both have lower average rank and higher Recall@50 than *regular bigrams*.

Skip-grams probably outperform regular n-grams on both of these corpora because the skip-grams provide many more event pairs over which to calculate statistics: in the Reuters corpus, *regular bigrams* extracts 737,103 bigrams, while *2-skip bigrams* extracts 1,201,185 bigrams. Though skip-grams have not been applied to predicting script events before, it seems that they are a good fit, and better capture statistics about narrative event chains than regular n-grams do.

	all bigrams + 2-skip	
Ranking method	**Av. rank**	**Recall@50**
C&J PMI	2052	0.1954
ordered PMI	3584	0.1694
bigram prob.	**502**	**0.5179**

Table 5: Ranking methods for the Reuters corpus - comparison of average ranks and Recall@50.

	all bigrams + 2-skip	
Ranking method	**Av. rank**	**Recall@50**
C&J PMI	**1455**	0.1975
ordered PMI	2460	0.0467
bigram prob.	1650	**0.3376**

Table 6: Ranking methods for the Fairy Tale corpus - comparison of average ranks and Recall@50.

4.4.3 Predicting Script Events

Finally, we try to answer the question: Given event n-gram statistics, which ranking function best predicts the events for a script? Tables 5 and 6 show performance when we vary the strategy for ranking event predictions, while fixing the selection method to *all chains*, and fixing the counting method to *2-skip bigrams*.

For both Reuters and the Fairy Tale corpus, Recall@50 identifies *bigram probabilities* as the best ranking function by far. On the Reuters corpus the *Chambers & Jurafsky PMI* ranking method achieves Recall@50 of only 0.1954, while *bigram probabilities* ranking method achieves 0.5179. The gap is also quite large on the Fairy Tales corpus: 0.1975 vs. 0.3376.

On the Reuters corpus, average rank also identifies *bigram probabilities* as the best ranking function, yet for the Fairy Tales corpus, *Chambers & Jurafsky PMI* and *bigram probabilities* have similar average ranks. This inconsistency is probably due to the flaws in the average rank evaluation measure that were discussed in Section 4.3 – the measure is overly sensitive to the length of the guess list, particularly when the missing event is ranked lower, as it is likely to be when training on a smaller corpus like the Fairy Tales corpus.

5 Discussion

Our experiments have led us to several important conclusions. First, we have introduced *skip-grams* and proved their utility for acquiring script knowledge – our models that employ skip bigrams score consistently higher on event prediction. By following the intuition that events do not have to appear strictly one after another to be closely semantically related, skip-grams decrease data sparsity and increase the size of the training data.

Second, our novel *bigram probabilities* ranking function outperforms the other ranking methods. In particular, it outperforms the state-of-the-art pointwise mutual information method introduced by Chambers and Jurafsky (2008), and it does so by a large margin, more than doubling the Recall@50 on the Reuters corpus. The key insight here is that, when modeling events in a script, a language-model-like approach better fits the task than a mutual information approach.

Third, we have discussed why Recall@N is a better and more consistent evaluation metric than *Average rank*. However, both evaluation metrics suffer from the strictness of the narrative cloze test, which accepts only one event being the correct event, while it is sometimes very difficult, even for humans, to predict the missing events, and sometimes more solutions are possible and equally correct. In future research, our goal is to design a better evaluation framework which is more suitable for this task, where credit can be given for proposed script events that are appropriate but not identical to the ones observed in a text.

Fourth, we have observed some differences in results between the Reuters and the Fairy Tale corpora. The results for Reuters are consistently better (higher Recall@50, lower average rank), although fairy tales contain a plainer narrative structure, which should be more appropriate to our task. This again leads us to the conclusion that more data (even with more noise as in Reuters) leads to a greater coverage of events, better overall models and, consequently, to more accurate predictions. Still, the Reuters corpus seems to be far from a perfect corpus for research in the automatic acquisition of scripts, since only a small portion of the corpus contains true narratives. Future work must therefore gather a large corpus of true narratives, like fairy tales and children's stories, whose simple plot structures should provide better learning material, both for models predicting script events, and for related tasks like automatic storytelling (McIntyre and Lapata, 2009).

One of the limitations of the work presented here is that it takes a fairly linear, n-gram-based approach to characterizing story structure. We think such an approach is useful because it forms a natural baseline for the task (as it does in many other tasks such as named entity tagging and language modeling). However, story structure is seldom strictly linear, and future work should consider models based on grammatical or discourse links that can capture the more complex nature of script events and story structure.

Acknowledgments

We would like to thank the anonymous reviewers for their constructive comments. This research was carried out as a master thesis in the framework of the TERENCE European project (EU FP7-257410).

References

Nathanael Chambers and Dan Jurafsky. 2008. Unsupervised learning of narrative event chains. In *Proceedings of the 46th Annual Meeting of the Association for Computational Linguistics: Human Language Technologies*, pages 789–797.

Nathanael Chambers and Dan Jurafsky. 2009. Unsupervised learning of narrative schemas and their participants. In *Proceedings of the Joint Conference of the 47th Annual Meeting of the Association for Computational Linguistics and the 4th International Joint Conference on Natural Language Processing of the AFNLP*, pages 602–610.

Nathanael Chambers and Dan Jurafsky. 2011. Template-based information extraction without the templates. In *Proceedings of the 49th Annual Meeting of the Association for Computational Linguistics: Human Language Technologies*, pages 976–986.

David Guthrie, Ben Allison, W. Liu, Louise Guthrie, and Yorick Wilks. 2006. A closer look at skip-gram modelling. In *Proceedings of the Fifth international Conference on Language Resources and Evaluation (LREC)*, pages 1222–1225.

Dan Klein and Christopher D. Manning. 2003. Accurate unlexicalized parsing. In *Proceedings of the 41st Annual Meeting of the Association for Computational Linguistics*, pages 423–430.

David D. Lewis, Yiming Yang, Tony G. Rose, and Fan Li. 2004. RCV1: a new benchmark collection for text categorization research. *Journal of Machine Learning Research*, 5:361–397.

Mehdi Manshadi, Reid Swanson, and Andrew S. Gordon. 2008. Learning a probabilistic model of event sequences from internet weblog stories. In *Proceedings of the Twenty-First International Florida Artificial Intelligence Research Society Conference*.

Neil McIntyre and Mirella Lapata. 2009. Learning to tell tales: A data-driven approach to story generation. In *Proceedings of the Joint Conference of the 47th Annual Meeting of the Association for Computational Linguistics and the 4th International Joint Conference on Natural Language Processing of the AFNLP*, pages 217–225.

Neil McIntyre and Mirella Lapata. 2010. Plot induction and evolutionary search for story generation. In *Proceedings of the 48th Annual Meeting of the Association for Computational Linguistics*, pages 1562–1572.

Michaela Regneri, Alexander Koller, and Manfred Pinkal. 2010. Learning script knowledge with web experiments. In *Proceedings of the 48th Annual Meeting of the Association for Computational Linguistics*, pages 979–988.

Roger C. Schank and Robert P. Abelson. 1977. *Scripts, plans, goals, and understanding: an inquiry into human knowledge structures*. Lawrence Erlbaum Associates.

Wilson L. Taylor. 1953. Cloze procedure: a new tool for measuring readibility. *Journalism Quarterly*, 30:415–433.

The Problem with Kappa

David M W Powers
Centre for Knowledge & Interaction Technology, CSEM
Flinders University
David.Powers@flinders.edu.au

Abstract

It is becoming clear that traditional evaluation measures used in Computational Linguistics (including Error Rates, Accuracy, Recall, Precision and F-measure) are of limited value for unbiased evaluation of systems, and are not meaningful for comparison of algorithms unless both the dataset and algorithm parameters are strictly controlled for skew (Prevalence and Bias). The use of techniques originally designed for other purposes, in particular Receiver Operating Characteristics Area Under Curve, plus variants of Kappa, have been proposed to fill the void.

This paper aims to clear up some of the confusion relating to evaluation, by demonstrating that the usefulness of each evaluation method is highly dependent on the assumptions made about the distributions of the dataset and the underlying populations. The behaviour of a number of evaluation measures is compared under common assumptions.

Deploying a system in a context which has the opposite skew from its validation set can be expected to approximately negate Fleiss Kappa and halve Cohen Kappa but leave Powers Kappa unchanged. For most *performance* evaluation purposes, the latter is thus most appropriate, whilst for comparison of *behaviour*, Matthews Correlation is recommended.

Introduction

Research in Computational Linguistics usually requires some form of quantitative evaluation. A number of traditional measures borrowed from Information Retrieval (Manning & Schütze, 1999) are in common use but there has been considerable critical evaluation of these measures themselves over the last decade or so (Entwisle & Powers, 1998, Flach, 2003, Ben-David. 2008).

Receiver Operating Analysis (ROC) has been advocated as an alternative by many, and in particular has been used by Fürnkranz and Flach (2005), Ben-David (2008) and Powers (2008) to better understand both learning algorithms relationship and the between the various measures, and the inherent biases that make many of them suspect. One of the key advantages of ROC is that it provides a clear indication of chance level performance as well as a less well known indication of the relative cost weighting of positive and negative cases for each possible system or parameterization represented.

ROC Area Under the Curve (Fig. 1) has been also used as a performance measure but averages over the false positive rate (Fallout) and is thus a function of cost that is dependent on the classifier rather than the application. For this reason it has come into considerable criticism and a number of variants and alternatives have been proposed (e.g. AUK, Kaymak et. Al, 2010 and H-measure, Hand, 2009). An AUC curve that is at least as good as a second curve at all points, is said to dominate it and indicates that the first classifier is equal or better than the second for all plotted values of the parameters, and all cost ratios. However AUC being greater for one classifier than another does not have such a property – indeed deconvexities within or intersections of ROC curves are both prima facie evidence that fusion of the parameterized classifiers will be useful (cf. Provost and Facett, 2001; Flach and Wu, 2005).

AUK stands for Area under Kappa, and represents a step in the advocacy of Kappa (Ben-David, 2008ab) as an alternative to the traditional measures and ROC AUC. Powers (2003,2007) has also proposed a Kappa-like measure (Informedness) and analysed it in terms of ROC, and there are many more, Warrens (2010) analyzing the relationships between some of the others.

Systems like RapidMiner (2011) and Weka (Witten and Frank, 2005) provide almost all of the measures we have considered, and many more besides. This encourages the use of multiple measures, and indeed it is now becoming routine to display tables of multiple results for each system, and this is in particular true for the frameworks of some of the challenges and competitions brought to the communities (e.g. 2nd i2b2 Challenge in NLP for Clinical Data, 2011; 2nd Pascal Challenge on HTC, 2011)).

This use of multiple statistics is no doubt in response to the criticism levelled at the evaluation mechanisms used in earlier generations of competitions and the above mentioned critiques, but the proliferation of alternate measures in some ways merely compounds the problem. Researchers have the temptation of choosing those that favour their system as they face the dilemma of what to do about competing (and often disagreeing) evaluation measures that they do not completely understand. These systems and competitions also exhibit another issue, the tendency to macro-averages over multiple classes, even of measures that are not denominated in class (e.g. that are proportions of predicted labels rather than real classes, as with Precision).

This paper is directed at better understanding some of these new and old measures as well as providing recommendations as to which measures are appropriate in which circumstances.

What's in a Kappa?

In this paper we focus on the Kappa family of measures, as well as some closely related statistics named for other letters of the Greek alphabet, and some measures that we will show behave as Kappa measures although they were not originally defined as such. These include Informedness, Gini Coefficient and single point ROC AUC, which are in fact all equivalent to DeltaP' in the dichotomous case, which we deal with first, and to the other Kappas when the marginal prevalences (or biases) match.

1.1 Two classes and non-negative Kappa.

Kappa was originally proposed (Cohen, 1960) to compare human ratings in a binary, or dichotomous, classification task. Cohen (1960) recognized that Rand Accuracy did not take chance into account and therefore proposed to subtract off the chance level of Accuracy and then renormalize to the form of a probability:

$$K(Acc) = [Acc - E(Acc)] / [1 - E(Acc)] \quad (1)$$

This leaves the question of how to estimate the expected Accuracy, E(Acc). Cohen (1960) made the assumption that raters would have different distributions that could be estimated as the products of the corresponding marginal coefficients of the contingency table:

	+ve Class	−ve Class	
+ve Prediction	A=TP	B=FP	PP
−ve Prediction	C=FN	D=TN	PN
Notation	RP	RN	N

Table 1. Statistical and IR Contingency Notation

In order to discuss this further it is important to discuss our notational conventions, and it is noted that in statistics, the letters A-D (upper case or lower case) are conventionally used to label the cells, and their sums may be used to label the marginal cells. However in the literature on ROC analysis, which we follow here, it is usual to talk about true and false positives (that is positive predictions that are correct or incorrect), and conversely true and false negatives. Often upper case is used to indicate counts in the contingency table, which sum to the number of instances, N. In this case lower case letters are used to indicate probabilities, which means that the corresponding upper case values in the contingency table are all divided by N, and n=1.

Statistics relative to (the total numbers of items in) the real classes are called Rates and have the number (or proportion) of Real Positives (RP) or Real Negatives (RN) in the denominator. In this notation, we have Recall = TPR = TP/RP.

Conversely statistics relative to the (number of) predictions are called Accuracies, so relative to the predictions that label instances positively, Predicted Positives (PP), we have Precision = TPA = TP/PP.

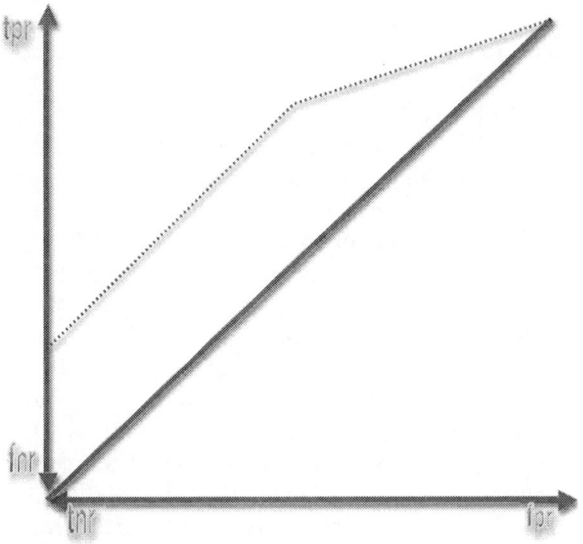

Figure 1. Illustration of ROC Analysis. The solid diagonal represents chance performance for different rates of guessing positive or negative labels. The dotted line represent the convex hull enclosing the results of different systems, thresholds or parameters tested. The (0,0) and (1,1) points represent guessing always negative and always positive and are always nominal systems in a ROC curve. The points along any straight line segment of a convex hull are achievable by probabilistic interpolation of the systems at each end, the gradient represents the cost ratio and all points along the segment, including the endpoints have the same effective cost benefit. AUC is the area under the curve joining the systems with straight edges and AUCH is the area under the convex hull where points within it are ignored. The height above the chance line of any point represents DeltaP', the Gini Coefficient and also the Dichotomous Informedness of the corresponding system, and also corresponds to twice the area of the triangle between it and the chance line, and thus 2AUC-1 where AUC is calculated on this single point curve (not shown) joining it to (0,0) and (1,1). The (1,0) point represents perfect performance with 100% True Positive Rate and 0% False Negative Rate.

The accuracy of all our predictions, positive or negative, is given by Rand Accuracy = (TF+TN)/N = tf+tn, and this is what is meant in general by the unadorned term Accuracy, or the abbreviation Acc.

Rand Accuracy is the weighted average of Precision and Inverse Precision (probability that negative predictions are correctly labeled), where the weighting is made according to the number of predictions made for the corresponding labels. Rand Accuracy is also the weighted average of Recall and Inverse Recall (probability that negative instances are correctly predicted), where the weighting is made according to the number of instances in the corresponding classes.

The marginal probabilities rp and pp are also known as Prevalence (the class prevalence of positive instances) and Bias (the label bias to positive predictions), and the corresponding probabilities of negative classes and labels are the Inverse Prevalence and Inverse Bias respectively. In the ROC literature, the ratios of negative to positive classes is often referred to as the class ratio or skew. We can similarly also refer to a label ratio, prediction ratio or prediction skew. Note that optimal performance can only be achieved if class skew = label skew.

The Expected True Positives and Expected True Negatives for Cohen Kappa, as well as Chi-squared significance, are estimated as the product of Bias and Prevalence, and the product of Inverse Bias and Inverse Prevalence, resp., where traditional uses of Kappa for agreement of human raters, the contingency table represents one rater as providing the classification to be predicted by the other rater. Cohen assumes that their distribution of ratings are independent, as reflected both by the margins and the contingencies: ETP = RP*PP; ETN = RN*NN. This gives us E(Acc) = (ETP+ETN)/N=etp+etn.

By contrast the two rater two class form of Fleiss (1981) Kappa, also known as Scott Pi, assumes that both raters are labeling independently using the same distribution, and that the margins reflect this potential variation. The expected number of positives is thus effectively estimated as the average of the two raters' counts, so that EP = (RP+PP)/2, and EN = (RN+PN)/2, ETP = EP^2 and ETN = EN^2.

1.2 Inverting Kappa

The definition of Kappa in Eqn (1) can be seen to be applicable to arbitrary definitions of Expected Accuracy, and in order to discover how other measures relate to the family of Kappa measures it is useful to invert Kappa to discover the implicit definition of Expected Accuracy that allows a measure to be interpreted as a form of Kappa. We simply make E(Acc) the subject by multiplying out Eqn (1) to a common denominator and associating factors of E(Acc):

$$K(Acc) = [Acc - E(Acc)] / [1 - E(Acc)] \quad (1)$$

$$E(Acc) = [Acc - K(Acc)] / [1 - K(Acc)] \quad (2)$$

Note that for a given value of Acc the function connecting E(Acc) and K(Acc) is its own inverse:

$$E(Acc) = f_{Acc}(K(Acc)) \quad (3)$$

$$K(Acc) = f_{Acc}(E(Acc)) \quad (4)$$

For the future we will tend to drop the Acc argument or subscript when it is clear, and we will also subscript E and K with the name or initial of the corresponding definition of Expectation and thus Kappa (viz. Fleiss and Cohen so far).

Note that given Acc and E(Acc) are in the range of 0..1 as probabilities, Kappa is also restricted to this range, and takes the form of a probability.

1.3 Multiclass multirater Kappa

Fleiss (1981) and others sought to generalize the Cohen (1960) definition of Kappa to handle both multiple class (not just positive/negative) and multiple raters (not just two – one of which we have called real and the other prediction). Fleiss in fact generalized Scott's (1955) Pi in both senses, not Cohen Kappa. The Fleiss Kappa is not formulated as we have done here for exposition, but in terms of pairings (agreements) amongst the raters, who are each assumed to have rated the same number of items, N, but not necessarily all. Krippendorf's (1970, 1978) effectively generalizes further by dealing with arbitrary numbers of raters assessing different numbers of items.

Light (1971) and Hubert (1977) successfully generalized Cohen Kappa. Another approach to estimating E(Acc) was taken by Bennett et al (1955) which basically assumed all classes were equilikely (effectively what use of Accuracy, F-Measure etc. do, although they don't subtract off the chance component).

The Bennett Kappa was generalized by Randolph (2005), but as our starting point is that we need to take the actual margins into account, we do not pursue these further. However, Warrens (2010a) shows that, under certain conditions, Fleiss Kappa is a lower bound of both the Hubert generalization of Cohen Kappa and the Randolph generalization of Bennet Kappa, which is itself correspondingly an upper bound of both the Hubert and the Light generalizations of Cohen Kappa. Unfortunately the conditions are that there is some agreement between the class and label skews (viz. the prevalence and bias of each class/label). Our focus in this paper is the behaviour of the various Kappa measures as we move from strongly matched to strongly mismatched biases.

Cohen (1968) also introduced a weighted variant of Kappa. We have also discussed cost weighting in the context of ROC, and Hand (2009) seeks to improve on ROC AUC by introducing a beta distribution as an estimated cost profile, but we will not discuss them further here as we are more interested in the effectiveness of the classifer overall rather than matching a particular cost profile, and are skeptical about any generic cost distribution. In particular the beta distribution gives priority to central tendency rather than boundary conditions, but boundary conditions are frequently encountered in optimization. Similarly Kaymak et al.'s (2010) proposal to replace AUC by AUK corresponds to a Cohen Kappa reweighting of ROC that eliminates many of its useful properties, without any expectation that the measure, as an integration across a surrogate cost distribution, has any validity for system selection. Introducing alternative weights is also allowed in the definition of F-Measure, although in practice this is almost invariably employed as the equally weighted harmonic mean of Recall and Precision. Introducing additional weight or distribution parameters, just multiplies the confusion as to which measure to believe.

Powers (2003) derived a further multiclass Kappa-like measure from first principles, dubbing it Informedness, based on an analogy of Bookmaker associating costs/payoffs based on the odds. This is then proven to measure the proportion of time (or probability) a decision is informed versus random, based on the same assumptions re expectation as Cohen Kappa, and we will thus call it Powers Kappa, and derive an formulation of the corresponding expectation.

Powers (2007) further identifies that the dichotomous form of Powers Kappa is equivalent to the Gini cooefficient as a deskewed version of the weighted Relative Accuracy proposed by Flach (2003) based on his analysis and deskewing of common evaluation measures in the ROC paradigm. Powers (2007) also identifies that Dichotomous Informedness is equivalent to an empirically derived psychological measure called DeltaP' (Perruchet et al. 2004). DeltaP' (and its dual DeltaP) were derived based on analysis of human word association data – the combination of this empirical observation with the place of DeltaP' as the dichotomous case of

Powers' 'Informedness' suggests that human association is in some sense optimal. Powers (2007) also introduces a dual of Informedness that he names Markedness, and shows that the geometric mean of Informedness and Markedness is Matthews Correlation, the nominal analog of Pearson Correlation.

Powers' Informedness is in fact a variant of Kappa with some similarities to Cohen Kappa, but also some advantages over both Cohen and Fleiss Kappa due to its asymmetric relation with Recall, in the dichotomous form of Powers (2007),

Informedness = Recall + InverseRecall – 1
= (Recall – Bias) / (1 – Prevalence).

If we think of Kappa as assessing the relationship between two raters, Powers' statistic is not evenhanded and the Informedness and Markedness duals measure the two directions of prediction, normalizing Recall and Precision. In fact, the relationship with Correlation allows these to be interpreted as regression coefficients for the prediction function and its inverse.

1.4 Kappa vs Correlation

It is often asked why we don't just use Correlation to measure. In fact, Castellan (1996) uses Tetrachoric Correlation, another generalization of Pearson Correlation that assumes that the two class variables are given by underlying normal distributions. Uebersax (1987), Hutchison (1993) and Bonnet and Price (2005) each compare Kappa and Correlation and conclude that there does not seem to be any situation where Kappa would be preferable to Correlation. However all the Kappa and Correlation variants considered were symmetric, and it is thus interesting to consider the separate regression coefficients underlying it that represent the Powers Kappa duals of Informedness and Markedness, which have the advantage of separating out the influences of Prevalence and Bias (which then allows macro-averaging, which is not admissable for any symmetric form of Correlation or Kappa, as we will discuss shortly). Powers (2007) regards Matthews Correlation as an appropriate measure for symmetric situations (like rater agreement) and generalizes the relationships between Correlation and Significance to the Markedness and Informedness Measures. The differences between Informedness and Markedness, which relate to mismatches in Prevalence and Bias, mean that the pair of numbers provides further information about the nature of the relationship between the two classifications or raters, whilst the ability to take the geometric mean (of macro-averaged) Informedness and Markedness means that a single Correlation can be provided when appropriate.

Our aim now is therefore to characterize Informedness (and hence as its dual Markedness) as a Kappa measure in relation to the families of Kappa measures represented by Cohen and Fleiss Kappa in the dichotomous case. Note that Warrens (2011) shows that a linearly weighted versions of Cohen's (1968) Kappa is in fact a weighted average of dichotomous Kappas. Similarly Powers (2003) shows that his Kappa (Informedness) has this property. Thus it is appropriate to consider the dichotomous case, and from this we can generalize as required.

1.5 Kappa vs Determinant

Warrens (2010c) discusses another commonly used measure, the Odds Ratio ad/bc (in Epidemiology rather than Computer Science or Computational Linguistics). Closely related to this is the Determinant of the Contingency Matrix dtp = ad-bc = etp-etn (in the Chi-Sqr, Cohen and Powers sense based on independent marginal probabilities). Both show whether the odds favour positives over negatives more for the first rater (real) than the second (predicted) – for the ratio it is if it is greater than one, for the difference it is if it is greater than 0. Note that taking logs of all coefficients would maintain the same relationship and that the difference of the logs corresponds to the log of the ratio, mapping into the information domain.

Warrens (2010c) further shows (in cost-weighted form) that Cohen Kappa is given by the following (in the notation of this paper, but preferring the notations Prevalence and Inverse Prevalence to rp and rn for clarity):

K_C = dtp/[(Prev*IBias+Bias*IPrev)/2]. (5)

Based on the previous characterization of Fleiss Kappa, we can further characterize it by

K_F = dtp/[(Prev+Bias)*(IBias+IPrev)/4]. (6)

Powers (2007) also showed corresponding formulations for Bookmaker Informedness (B, or Powers Kappa = K_P), Markedness and Matthews Correlation:

B = dtp/[(Prev*IPrev)]. (7)

M = dtp/[(Bias*IBias)]. (8)

C = dtp/[√(Prev*IPrev*Bias*IBias)]. (9)

These elegant dichotomous forms are straightforward, with the independence assumptions on Bias and Prevalence clear in

Cohen Kappa, the arithmetic means of Bias and Prevalence clear in Fleiss Kappa, and the geometric means of Bias and Prevalence in the Matthews Correlation. Further the independence of Bias is apparent for Powers Kappa in the Informedness form, and independence of Prevalence is clear in the Markedness direction.

Note that the names Powers uses suggest that we are measuring something about the information conveyed by the prediction about the class in the case of Informedness, and the information conveyed to the predictor by the class state in the case of Markedness. To the extent that Prevalence and Bias can be controlled independently, Informedness and Markedness are independent and Correlation represents the joint probability of information being passed in both directions! Powers (2007) further proposes using log formulations of these measures to take them into the information domain, as well as relating them to mutual information, G-squared and chi-squared significance.

1.6 Kappa vs Concordance

The pairwise approach used by Fleiss Kappa and its relatives does not assume raters use a common distribution, but does assume they are using the same set, and number of categories. When undertaking comparison of unconstrained ratings or unsupervised learning, this constraint is removed and we need to use a measure of concordance to compare clusterings against each other or against a Gold Standard. Some of the concordance measures use operators in probability space and relate closely to the techniques here, whilst others operate in information space. See Pfitzner et al. (2009) for reviews of clustering comparison/concordance.

A complete coverage of evaluation would also cover significance and the multiple testing problem, but we will confine our focus in this paper to the issue of choice of Kappa or Correlation statistic, as well as addressing some issues relating to the use of macro-averaging. In this paper we are regarding the choice of Bias as under the control of the experimenter, as we have a focus on learned or hand crafted computational linguistics systems. In fact, when we are using bootstrapping techniques or dealing with multiple real samples or different subjects or ecosystems, Prevalence may also vary. Thus the simple marginal assumptions of Cohen or Powers statistics are the appropriate ones.

1.7 Averaging

We now consider the issue of dealing with multiple measures and results of multiple classifiers by averaging. We first consider averages of some of the individual measures we have seen. The averages need not be arithmetic means, or may represent means over the Prevalences and Biases.

We will be punctuating our theoretical discussions and explanations with empirical demonstrations where we use 1:1 and 4:1 prevalence versus matching and mismatching bias to generate the chance level contingency based on marginal independence. We then mix in a proportion of informed decisions, with the remaining decisions made by chance.

Table 2 compares Accuracy and F-Measure for an informed decision percentage of 0, 100, 15 and -15. Note that Powers Kappa or 'Informedness' purports to recover this proportion or probability.

F-Measure is one of the most common measures in Computational Linguistics and Information Retrieval, being a Harmonic Mean of Recall and Precision, which in the common unweighted form also is interpretable with respect to a mean of Prevalence and Bias:

$$F = tp / [(Prev+Bias)/2] \quad (10)$$

Note that like Recall and Precision, F-Measure ignores totally cell D corresponding to tn. This is an issue when Prevalence and Bias are uneven or mismatched. In Information Retrieval, it is often justified on the basis that the number of irrelevant documents is large and not precisely known, but in fact this is due to lack of knowledge of the number of relevant documents, which affects Recall. In fact if tn is large with respect to both rp and pp, and thus with respect to components tp, fp and fn, then both tn/pn and tn/rn approach 0 as tn increases without bound.

As discussed earlier, Rand Accuracy is a prevalence (real class) weighted average of Precision and Inverse Precision, as well as a bias (prediction label) weighted average of Recall and Inverse Precision. It reflects the D (tn) cell unlike F, and while it does not remove the effect of chance it does not have the positive bias of F.

$$Acc = tp + fp \quad (11)$$

We also point out that the differences between the various Kappas shown in Determinant normalized form in Eqns (5-9) vary only in the way prevalences and biases are averaged together in the normalizing denominator.

Informed		1:1/1:1	4:1/4:1	4:1/1:4
0%	Acc	50%	68%	32%
	F	50%	80%	32%
100%	Acc	100%	100%	100%
	F	100%	100%	100%
15%	Acc	57.5%	72.8%	42.2%
	F	57.5%	83%	46.97%
-15%	Acc	42.5%	57.8%	27.2%
	F	42.5%	72%	27.2%

Table 2. Accuracy and F-Measure for different mixes of prevalence and bias skew (odds ratio shown) as well as different proportions of correct (informed) answers versus guessing – negative proportions imply that the informed decisions are deliberately made incorrectly (oracle tells me what to do and I do the opposite).

From Table 2 we note that the first set of statistics notes the chance level varies from the 50% expected for Bias=Prevalence=50%. This is in fact the E(Acc) used in calculating Cohen Kappa. Where Prevalences and Biases are equal and balanced, all common statistics agree – Recall = Precision = Accuracy = F, and they are interpretable with respect to this 50% chance level. All the Kappas will also agree, as the different averages of the identical prevalences and biases all come down to 50% as well. So subtracting 50% from 57.5% and normalizing (dividing) by the average effective prevalence of 50%, we return 15% informed decisions in all cases (as seen in detail in Table 3).

However, F-measure gives an inflated estimate when it focus on the more prevalent positive class, with corresponding bias in the chance component.

Worse still is the strength of the Acc and F scores under conditions of matched bias and prevalence when the deviation from chance is -15% - that is making the wrong decision 15% of the time and guessing the rest of the time. In academic terms, if we bump these rates up to ±25% F-factor gives a High Distinction for guessing 75% of the time and putting the right answer for the other 25%, a Distinction for 100% guessing, and a Credit for guessing 75% of the time and putting a *wrong* answer for the other 25%! In fact, the Powers Kappa corresponds to the methodology of multiple choice marking, where for questions with k+1 choices, a right answer gets 1 mark, and a wrong answer gets $-^{1}/_{k}$ so that guessing achieves an expected mark of 0. Cohen Kappa achieves a very similar result for unbiased guessing strategies.

We now turn to macro-averaging across multiple classifiers or raters. The Area Under the Curve measures are all of this form, whether we are talking about ROC, Kappa, Recall-Precision curves or whatever. The controversy over these averages, and macro-averaging in general, relates to one of two issues: 1. The averages are not in general over the appropriate units or denominators of the individual statistics; or 2. The averages are over a classifier determined cost function rather than an externally or standardly defined cost function. AUK and H-Measure seek to address these issues as discussed earlier. In fact they both boil down to averaging with an inappropriate distribution of weights.

Commonly macro-averaging averages across classes as average statistics derived for each class weighted by the cardinality of the class (viz. prevalence). In our review above, we cited four examples, but we will refer only to WEKA (Witten et al., 2005) here as a commonly used system and associated text book that employs and advocates macro-averaging. WEKA averages over tpr, fpr, Recall (yes redundantly), Precision, F-Factor and ROC AUC. Only the average over tpr=Recall is actually meaningful, because only it has the number of members of the class, or its prevalence, as its denominator. Precision needs to be macro-averaged over the number of predictions for each class, in which case it is equivalent to micro-averaging.

Other micro-averaged statistics are also shown, including Kappa (with the expectation determined from ZeroR – predicting the majority class, leading to a Cohen-like Kappa).

AUC will be pointwise for classifiers that don't provide any probabilistic information associated with label prediction, and thus don't allow varying a threshold for additional points on the ROC or other threshold curves. In the case where multiple threshold points are available, ROC AUC cannot be interpreted as having any relevance to any particular classifier, but is an average over a range of classifiers. Even then it is not so meaningful as AUCH, which should be used as classifiers on the convex hull are usually available. The AUCH measure will then dominate any individual classifiers, as if the convex hull is not the same as the single classifier it must include points that are above the classifier curve and thus its enclosed area totally includes the area that is enclosed by the individual classifier.

Macroaveraging of the curve based on each class in turn as the Positive Class, and weighted by the size of the positive class, is not meaningful as effectively shown by Powers (2003) for the special case of the single point curve given its equivalence to Powers Kappa.

In fact Markedness does admit averaging over classes, whilst Informedness requires averaging over predicted labels, as does Precision. The other Kappa and Correlations are more complex (note the demoninators in Eqns 5-9) and how they might be meaningfully macro-averaged is an open question. However, microaveraging can always be done quickly and easily by simply summing all the contingency tables (the true contingency tables are tables of counts, not probabilities, as shown in Table 1).

Macroaveraging should never be done except for the special cases of Recall and Markedness when it is equivalent to micro-average, which is only slightly more expensive/complicated to do.

Comparison of Kappas

We now turn to explore the different definitions of Kappas, using the same approach employed with Accuracy and F-Factor in Table 1: We will consider 0%, 100%, 15% and -15% informed decisions, with random decisions modelled on the basis of independent Bias and Prevalence.

This clearly biases against the Fleiss family of Kappas, which is entirely appropriate. As pointed out by Entwisle & Powers (1998) the practice of deliberately skewing bias to achieve better statistics is to be deprecated – they used the real-life example of a CL researcher choosing to say water was always a noun because it was a noun more often than not. With Cohen or Powers' measures, any actual power of the system to determine PoS, however weak, would be reflected in an improvement in the scores versus any random choice, whatever the distribution. Recall that choosing one answer all the time corresponds to the extreme points of the chance line in the ROC curve.

Studies like Fitzgibbon et al (2007) and Leibbrandt and Powers (2012) show divergences amongst the conventional and debiased measures, but it is tricky to prove which is better.

Kappa in the Limit

It is however straightforward to derive limits for the various Kappas and Expectations under extreme and central conditions of bias and prevalence, including both match and mismatch. The 36 theoretical results match the mixture model results in Table 3, however, due to space constraints, formal treatment will be limited to two of the more complex cases that both relate to Fleiss Kappa with its mismatch to the marginal independence assumptions we prefer. These will provide informedness of probability B plus a remaining proportion 1-B of random responses exhibiting extreme bias versus both neutral and contrary prevalence. Note that we consider only $|B|<1$ as all Kappas give Acc=1 and thus K=1 for B=1, and only Powers Kappa is designed to work for B<1, giving K= -1 for B= -1.

Recall that the general calculation of Expected Accuracy is

$$E(Acc) = etp+etn \qquad (11)$$

For Fleiss Kappa we must calculate the expected values of the correct contingencies as discussed previously with expected probabilities

$$ep = (rp+pp)/2 \quad \& \quad en = (rn+pn)/2 \qquad (12)$$

$$etp = ep^2 \quad \& \quad etn = en^2 \qquad (13)$$

We first consider cases where prevalence is extreme and the chance component exhibits inverse bias. We thus consider limits as $rp \rightarrow 0$, $rn \rightarrow 1$, $pp \rightarrow 1\text{-}B$, $pn \rightarrow B$. This gives us (assuming $|B|<1$)

$$E_F(Acc) = ({}^1/_4+B^2/_4+B/_2)^2+({}^1/_4+B^2/_4-B/_2)^2$$
$$= (1+B^2)/2 \qquad (14)$$

$$K_F(Acc) = (1-B)^2/[B^2-2] \qquad (15)$$

We second consider cases where the prevalence is balanced and chance extreme, with $rp \rightarrow 0.5$, $rn \rightarrow 0.5$, $pp \rightarrow 1\text{-}B$, $pn \rightarrow B$, giving

$$E_F(Acc) = {}^1/_2 + (B-{}^1/_2)^2/2$$
$$= {}^5/_8 + B(B-1)/2 \qquad (16)$$

$$K_F(Acc)=[(B-{}^1/_2)-(B-{}^1/_2)^2/2]/[{}^1/_2-(B-{}^1/_2)^2/2] \qquad (17)$$
$$=[B-{}^5/_8+B(B-1)/2]/[1-({}^5/_8+B(B-1)/2)$$

Conclusions

The asymmetric Powers Informedness gives the clearest measure of the predictive value of a system, while the Matthews Correlation (as geometric mean with the Powers Markedness dual) is appropriate for comparing equally valid classifications or ratings into an agreed number of classes. Concordance measures should be used if number of classes is not agreed or specified.

For mismatch cases (15) Fleiss is always negative for $|B|<1$) and thus fails to adequately reward good performance under these marginal conditions. For the chance case (17), the first form we provide shows that the deviation from matching Prevalence is a driver in a Kappa-like function. Cohen on the other hand (Table 3) tends to apply multiply the weight given to error in even mild prevalence-bias mismatch conditions. None of the symmetric Kappas designed for raters are suitable for classifiers.

	1:1 1:1	4:1 4:1	4:1 1:4	1:1 1:1	4:1 4:1	4:1 1:4	1:1 1:1	4:1 4:1	4:1 1:4
Informedness	**0%**	**0%**	**0%**	**0%**	**0%**	**0%**	**0%**	**0%**	**0%**
Prevalence	50%	80%	80%	50%	80%	80%	50%	20%	20%
Iprevalence	50%	20%	20%	50%	20%	20%	50%	80%	80%
Bias	50%	80%	20%	50%	80%	20%	50%	20%	80%
Ibias	50%	20%	80%	50%	20%	80%	50%	80%	20%
SkewR	100%	25%	25%	100%	25%	25%	100%	400%	400%
SkewP	100%	25%	400%	100%	25%	400%	100%	400%	25%
OddsRatio	100%	100%	6%	100%	100%	6%	100%	100%	1600%
ePowers	50%	68%	32%	50%	68%	32%	50%	68%	32%
eCohen	50%	68%	32%	50%	68%	32%	50%	68%	32%
eFleiss	50%	68%	50%	50%	68%	50%	50%	68%	50%
kPowers	**0%**	**0%**	**0%**	**0%**	**0%**	**0%**	**0%**	**0%**	**0%**
kCohen	**0%**	**0%**	**0%**	**0%**	**0%**	**0%**	**0%**	**0%**	**0%**
kFleiss	**0%**	**0%**	-36%	**0%**	**0%**	-36%	**0%**	**0%**	-36%
Informedness	**100%**	**100%**	**100%**	**100%**	**100%**	**100%**	**100%**	**100%**	**100%**
Prevalence	50%	80%	80%	50%	80%	80%	50%	20%	20%
Iprevalence	50%	20%	20%	50%	20%	20%	50%	80%	80%
Bias	50%	80%	80%	50%	80%	80%	50%	20%	20%
Ibias	50%	20%	20%	50%	20%	20%	50%	80%	80%
SkewR	100%	25%	25%	100%	25%	25%	100%	400%	400%
SkewP	100%	25%	25%	100%	25%	25%	100%	400%	400%
OddsRatio	100%	100%	100%	100%	100%	100%	100%	100%	100%
ePowers	50%	68%	68%	50%	68%	68%	50%	68%	68%
aCohen	50%	68%	68%	50%	68%	68%	50%	68%	68%
aFleiss	50%	68%	68%	50%	68%	68%	50%	68%	68%
kPowers	**100%**	**100%**	**100%**	**100%**	**100%**	**100%**	**100%**	**100%**	**100%**
kCohen	**100%**	**100%**	**100%**	**100%**	**100%**	**100%**	**100%**	**100%**	**100%**
kFleiss	**100%**	**100%**	**100%**	**100%**	**100%**	**100%**	**100%**	**100%**	**100%**
Informedness	**15%**	**15%**	**15%**	**99%**	**99%**	**99%**	**99%**	**99%**	**99%**
Prevalence	50%	80%	80%	50%	80%	80%	50%	20%	20%
Iprevalence	50%	20%	20%	50%	20%	20%	50%	80%	80%
Bias	50%	80%	29%	50%	80%	79%	50%	20%	79%
Ibias	50%	20%	71%	50%	20%	21%	50%	80%	21%
SkewR	100%	25%	25%	100%	25%	25%	100%	400%	400%
SkewP	100%	25%	245%	100%	25%	26%	100%	400%	26%
OddsRatio	100%	100%	6%	100%	100%	6%	100%	100%	1600%
ePowers	50%	68%	32%	50%	68%	32%	50%	68%	32%
eCohen	50%	68%	37%	50%	68%	68%	50%	68%	32%
eFleiss	50%	68%	50%	50%	68%	68%	50%	68%	50%
kPowers	**15%**	**15%**	**15%**	**99%**	**99%**	**99%**	**1%**	**1%**	**1%**
kCohen	**15%**	**15%**	8%	**99%**	**99%**	98%	**1%**	**1%**	0%
kFleiss	**15%**	**15%**	-17%	**99%**	**99%**	98%	**1%**	**1%**	-35%
Informedness	**-15%**	**-15%**	**-15%**	**-99%**	**-99%**	**-99%**	**-99%**	**-99%**	**-99%**
Prevalence	50%	80%	20%	50%	80%	80%	50%	20%	20%
Iprevalence	50%	20%	80%	50%	20%	20%	50%	80%	80%
Bias	50%	71%	80%	50%	21%	20%	50%	21%	80%
Ibias	50%	29%	20%	50%	79%	80%	50%	79%	20%
SkewR	100%	25%	400%	100%	25%	25%	100%	400%	400%
SkewP	100%	41%	25%	100%	385%	400%	100%	385%	25%
OddsRatio	100%	65%	1038%	100%	25%	25%	100%	104%	1542%
ePowers	50%	63%	37%	50%	50%	50%	50%	68%	32%
eCohen	50%	63%	32%	50%	32%	32%	50%	68%	32%
eFleiss	50%	63%	50%	50%	50%	50%	50%	68%	50%
kPowers	**-15%**	**-15%**	**-15%**	**-99%**	**-99%**	**-99%**	**-1%**	**-1%**	-1%
kCohen	**-15%**	-13%	-7%	**-99%**	-47%	-47%	**-1%**	-1%	0%
kFleiss	**-15%**	-14%	-46%	**-99%**	-99%	-99%	**-1%**	-1%	-37%

Table 3. Empirical Results for Accuracy and Kappa for Fleiss/Scott, Cohen and Powers. Shaded cells indicate misleading results, which occur for both Cohen and Fleiss Kappas.

References

2nd i2b2 Workshop on Challenges in Natural Language Processing for Clinical Data (2008). http://gnode1.mib.man.ac.uk/awards.html (accessed 4 November 2011)

2nd Pascal Challenge on Hierarchical Text Classification http://lshtc.iit.demokritos.gr/node/48 (accessed 4 November 2011)

N. Ailon. and M. Mohri (2010) Preference-based learning to rank. Machine Learning 80:189-211.

A. Ben-David. (2008a). About the relationship between ROC curves and Cohen's kappa. Engineering Applications of AI, 21:874–882, 2008.

A. Ben-David (2008b). Comparison of classification accuracy using Cohen's Weighted Kappa, Expert Systems with Applications 34 (2008) 825–832

Y. Benjamini and Y. Hochberg (1995). "Controlling the false discovery rate: a practical and powerful approach to multiple testing". Journal of the Royal Statistical Society. Series B (Methodological) 57 (1), 289–300.

D. G. Bonett & R.M. Price, (2005). Inferential Methods for the Tetrachoric Correlation Coefficient, Journal of Educational and Behavioral Statistics 30:2, 213-225

J. Carletta (1996). Assessing agreement on classification tasks: the kappa statistic. Computational Linguistics 22(2):249-254

N. J. Castellan, (1966). On the estimation of the tetrachoric correlation coefficient. Psychometrika, 31(1), 67-73.

J. Cohen (1960). A coefficient of agreement for nominal scales. Educational and Psychological Measurement, 1960:37-46.

J. Cohen (1968). Weighted kappa: Nominal scale agreement with provision for scaled disagreement or partial credit. Psychological Bulletin 70:213-20.

B. Di Eugenio and M. Glass (2004), The Kappa Statistic: A Second Look., Computational Linguistics 30:1 95-101.

J. Entwisle and D. M. W. Powers (1998). "The Present Use of Statistics in the Evaluation of NLP Parsers", pp215-224, NeMLaP3/CoNLL98 Joint Conference, Sydney, January 1998

Sean Fitzgibbon, David M. W. Powers, Kenneth Pope, and C. Richard Clark (2007). *Removal of EEG noise and artefact using blind source separation.* Journal of Clinical Neurophysiology 24(3):232-243, June 2007

P. A. Flach (2003). The Geometry of ROC Space: Understanding Machine Learning Metrics through ROC Isometrics, Proceedings of the Twentieth International Conference on Machine Learning (ICML-2003), Washington DC, 2003, pp. 226-233.

J. L. Fleiss (1981). Statistical methods for rates and proportions (2nd ed.). New York: Wiley.

A. Fraser & D. Marcu (2007). Measuring Word Alignment Quality for Statistical Machine Translation, Computational Linguistics 33(3):293-303.

J. Fürnkranz & P. A. Flach (2005). ROC 'n' Rule Learning – Towards a Better Understanding of Covering Algorithms, Machine Learning 58(1):39-77.

D. J. Hand (2009). Measuring classifier performance: a coherent alternative to the area under the ROC curve. Machine Learning 77:103-123.

T. P. Hutchinson (1993). Focus on Psychometrics. Kappa muddles together two sources of disagreement: tetrachoric correlation is preferable. Research in Nursing & Health 16(4):313-6, 1993 Aug.

U. Kaymak, A. Ben-David and R. Potharst (2010), AUK: a sinple alternative to the AUC, Technical Report, Erasmus Research Institute of Management, Erasmus School of Economics, Rotterdam NL.

K. Krippendorff (1970). Estimating the reliability, systematic error, and random error of interval data. Educational and Psychological Measurement, 30 (1),61-70.

K. Krippendorff (1978). Reliability of binary attribute data. Biometrics, 34 (1), 142-144.

J. Lafferty, A. McCallum. & F. Pereira. (2001). Conditional Random Fields: Probabilistic Models for Segmenting and Labeling Sequence Data. Proceedings of the 18th International Conference on Machine Learning (ICML-2001), San Francisco, CA: Morgan Kaufmann, pp. 282-289.

R. Leibbrandt & D. M. W. Powers, Robust Induction of Parts-of-Speech in Child-Directed Language by Co-Clustering of Words and Contexts. (2012). EACL Joint Workshop of ROBUS (Robust Unsupervised and Semi-supervised Methods in NLP) and UNSUP (Unsupervised Learning in NLP).

P. J. G. Lisboa, A. Vellido & H. Wong (2000). Bias reduction in skewed binary classfication with Bayesian neural networks. Neural Networks 13:407-410.

R. Lowry (1999). Concepts and Applications of Inferential Statistics. (Published on the web as http:// faculty.vassar.edu/lowry/webtext.html.)

C. D. Manning, and H. Schütze (1999). Foundations of Statistical Natural Language Processing. MIT Press, Cambridge, MA.

J. H McDonald, (2007). The Handbook of Biological Statistics. (Course handbook web published as http: //udel.edu/~mcdonald/statpermissions.html)

J.C. Nunnally and Bernstein, I.H. (1994). Psychometric Theory (Third ed.). McGraw-Hill.

K. Pearson and D. Heron (1912). On Theories of Association. J. Royal Stat. Soc. LXXV:579-652

P. Perruchet and R. Peereman (2004). The exploitation of distributional information in syllable processing, J. Neurolinguistics 17:97–119.

D. Pfitzner, R. E. Leibbrandt and D. M. W. Powers (2009). Characterization and evaluation of similarity measures for pairs of clusterings, Knowledge and Information Systems, 19:3, 361-394

D. M. W. Powers (2003), Recall and Precision versus the Bookmaker, Proceedings of the International Conference on Cognitive Science (ICSC-2003), Sydney Australia, 2003, pp. 529-534. (See http:// david.wardpowers.info/BM/index.htm.)

D. M. W. Powers (2008), Evaluation Evaluation, The 18th European Conference on Artificial Intelligence (ECAI'08)

D. M W Powers, (2007/2011) Evaluation: From Precision, Recall and F-Factor to ROC, Informedness, Markedness & Correlation, School of Informatics and Engineering, Flinders University, Adelaide, Australia, TR SIE-07-001, Journal of Machine Learning Technologies 2:1 37-63. https://dl-web.dropbox.com/get/Public/201101-Evaluation_JMLT_Postprint-Colour.pdf?w=abcda988

D. M. W. Powers, 2012. The Problem of Area Under the Curve. International Conference on Information Science and Technology, ICIST2012, in press.

D. M. W. Powers and A. Atyabi, 2012. The Problem of Cross-Validation: Averaging and Bias, Repetition and Significance, SCET2012, in press.

F. Provost and T. Fawcett. Robust classification for imprecise environments. Machine Learning, 44:203–231, 2001.

RapidMiner (2011). http://rapid-i.com (accessed 4 November 2011).

L. H. Reeker, (2000), Theoretic Constructs and Measurement of Performance and Intelligence in Intelligent Systems, PerMIS 2000. (See http://www.isd.mel.nist.gov/research_areas/ research_engineering/PerMIS_Workshop/ accessed 22 December 2007.)

W. A. Scott (1955). Reliability of content analysis: The case of nominal scale coding. *Public Opinion Quarterly, 19*, 321-325.

D. R. Shanks (1995). Is human learning rational? Quarterly Journal of Experimental Psychology, 48A, 257-279.

T. Sellke, Bayarri, M.J. and Berger, J. (2001), Calibration of P-values for testing precise null hypotheses, American Statistician 55, 62-71. (See http:// www.stat.duke.edu/%7Eberger/papers.html#p-value accessed 22 December 2007.)

P. J. Smith, Rae, DS, Manderscheid, RW and Silbergeld, S. (1981). Approximating the moments and distribution of the likelihood ratio statistic for multinomial goodness of fit. Journal of the American Statistical Association 76:375,737-740.

R. R. Sokal, Rohlf FJ (1995) Biometry: The principles and practice of statistics in biological research, 3rd ed New York: WH Freeman and Company.

J. Uebersax (1987). Diversity of decision-making models and the measurement of interrater agreement. Psychological Bulletin 101, 140–146.

J. Uebersax (2009) http://ourworld.compuserve.com/ homepages/jsuebersax/agree.htm accessed 24 February 2011.

M. J. Warrens (2010a), Inequalities between multi-rater kappas. Advances in Data Analysis and Classification 4:271-286.

M. J. Warrens (2010b). A formal proof of a paradox associated with Cohen's kappa. Journal of Classificaiton 27:322-332.

M. J. Warrens (2010c). A Kraemer-type rescaling that transforms the Odds Ratio into the Weighted Kappa Coefficient. Psychometrika 75:2 328-330.

M. J. Warrens (2011). Cohen's linearly wieghted Kappa is a weighted average of 2x2 Kappas. Psychometrika 76:3, 471-486.

D. A. Williams (1976). Improved Likelihood Ratio Tests for Complete Contingency Tables, Biometrika 63:33-37.

I. H. Witten & E. Frank, (2005). Data mining (2nd ed.). London: Academic Press.

User Edits Classification Using Document Revision Histories

Amit Bronner
Informatics Institute
University of Amsterdam
a.bronner@uva.nl

Christof Monz
Informatics Institute
University of Amsterdam
c.monz@uva.nl

Abstract

Document revision histories are a useful and abundant source of data for natural language processing, but selecting relevant data for the task at hand is not trivial. In this paper we introduce a scalable approach for automatically distinguishing between factual and fluency edits in document revision histories. The approach is based on supervised machine learning using language model probabilities, string similarity measured over different representations of user edits, comparison of part-of-speech tags and named entities, and a set of adaptive features extracted from large amounts of unlabeled user edits. Applied to contiguous edit segments, our method achieves statistically significant improvements over a simple yet effective edit-distance baseline. It reaches high classification accuracy (88%) and is shown to generalize to additional sets of unseen data.

1 Introduction

Many online collaborative editing projects such as Wikipedia[1] keep track of complete revision histories. These contain valuable information about the evolution of documents in terms of content as well as language, style and form. Such data is publicly available in large volumes and constantly growing. According to Wikipedia statistics, in August 2011 the English Wikipedia contained 3.8 million articles with an average of 78.3 revisions per article. The average number of revision edits per month is about 4 million in English and almost 11 million in total for all languages.[2]

Exploiting document revision histories has proven useful for a variety of natural language processing (NLP) tasks, including sentence compression (Nelken and Yamangil, 2008; Yamangil and Nelken, 2008) and simplification (Yatskar et al., 2010; Woodsend and Lapata, 2011), information retrieval (Aji et al., 2010; Nunes et al., 2011), textual entailment recognition (Zanzotto and Pennacchiotti, 2010), and paraphrase extraction (Max and Wisniewski, 2010; Dutrey et al., 2011).

The ability to distinguish between factual changes or edits, which alter the meaning, and fluency edits, which improve the style or readability, is a crucial requirement for approaches exploiting revision histories. The need for an automated classification method has been identified (Nelken and Yamangil, 2008; Max and Wisniewski, 2010), but to the best of our knowledge has not been directly addressed. Previous approaches have either applied simple heuristics (Yatskar et al., 2010; Woodsend and Lapata, 2011) or manual annotations (Dutrey et al., 2011) to restrict the data to the type of edits relevant to the NLP task at hand. The work described in this paper shows that it is possible to automatically distinguish between factual and fluency edits. This is very desirable as it does not rely on heuristics, which often generalize poorly, and does not require manual annotation beyond a small collection of training data, thereby allowing for much larger data sets of revision histories to be used for NLP research.

In this paper, we make the following novel contributions:

We address the problem of automated classification of user edits as factual or fluency edits

[1] http://www.wikipedia.org

[2] Average for the 5 years period between August 2006 and August 2011. The count includes edits by registered users, anonymous users, software bots and reverts. Source: http://stats.wikimedia.org.

by defining the scope of user edits, extracting a large collection of such user edits from the English Wikipedia, constructing a manually labeled dataset, and setting up a classification baseline.

A set of features is designed and integrated into a supervised machine learning framework. It is composed of language model probabilities and string similarity measured over different representations, including part-of-speech tags and named entities. Despite their relative simplicity, the features achieve high classification accuracy when applied to contiguous edit segments.

We go beyond labeled data and exploit large amounts of unlabeled data. First, we demonstrate that the trained classifier generalizes to thousands of examples identified by user comments as specific types of fluency edits. Furthermore, we introduce a new method for extracting features from an evolving set of unlabeled user edits. This method is successfully evaluated as an alternative or supplement to the initial supervised approach.

2 Related Work

The need for user edits classification is implicit in studies of Wikipedia edit histories. For example, Viegas et al. (2004) use revision size as a simplified measure for the change of content, and Kittur et al. (2007) use metadata features to predict user edit conflicts.

Classification becomes an explicit requirement when exploiting edit histories for NLP research. Yamangil and Nelken (2008) use edits as training data for sentence compression. They make the simplifying assumption that all selected edits retain the core meaning. Zanzotto and Pennacchiotti (2010) use edits as training data for textual entailment recognition. In addition to manually labeled edits, they use Wikipedia user comments and a co-training approach to leverage unlabeled edits. Woodsend and Lapata (2011) and Yatskar et al. (2010) use Wikipedia comments to identify relevant edits for learning sentence simplification.

The work by Max and Wisniewski (2010) is closely related to the approach proposed in this paper. They extract a corpus of rewritings, distinguish between weak semantic differences and strong semantic differences, and present a typology of multiple subclasses. Spelling corrections are heuristically identified but the task of automatic classification is deferred. Follow-up work by Dutrey et al. (2011) focuses on automatic paraphrase identification using a rule based approach and manually annotated examples.

Wikipedia vandalism detection is a user edits classification problem addressed by a yearly competition (since 2010) in conjunction with the CLEF conference (Potthast et al., 2010; Potthast and Holfeld, 2011). State-of-the-art solutions involve supervised machine learning using various content and metadata features. Content features use spelling, grammar, character- and word-level attributes. Many of them are relevant for our approach. Metadata features allow detection by patterns of usage, time and place, which are generally useful for the detection of online malicious activities (West et al., 2010; West and Lee, 2011). We deliberately refrain from using such features.

A wide range of methods and approaches has been applied to the similar tasks of textual entailment and paraphrase recognition, see Androutsopoulos and Malakasiotis (2010) for a comprehensive review. These are all related because paraphrases and bidirectional entailments represent types of fluency edits.

A different line of research uses classifiers to predict sentence-level fluency (Zwarts and Dras, 2008; Chae and Nenkova, 2009). These could be useful for fluency edits detection. Alternatively, user edits could be a potential source of human-produced training data for fluency models.

3 Definition of User Edits Scope

Within our approach we distinguish between *edit segments*, which represent the comparison (diff) between two document revisions, and *user edits*, which are the input for classification.

An *edit segment* is a contiguous sequence of deleted, inserted or equal words. The difference between two document revisions (v_i, v_j) is represented by a sequence of edit segments E. Each edit segment $(\delta, w_1^m) \in E$ is a pair, where $\delta \in \{deleted, inserted, equal\}$ and w_1^m is a m-word substring of v_i, v_j or both (respectively).

A *user edit* is a minimal set of sentences overlapping with deleted or inserted segments. Given the two sets of revision sentences (S_{v_i}, S_{v_j}), let

$$\phi(\delta, w_1^m) = \{s \in S_{v_i} \cup S_{v_j} \mid w_1^m \cap s \neq \emptyset\} \quad (1)$$

be the subset of sentences overlapping with a given edit segment, and let

$$\psi(s) = \{(\delta, w_1^m) \in E \mid w_1^m \cap s \neq \emptyset\} \quad (2)$$

be the subset of edit segments overlapping with a given sentence.

A user edit is a pair $(pre \subseteq S_{v_i}, post \subseteq S_{v_j})$ where

$$\forall s \in pre \cup post \;\; \forall \delta \in \{deleted, inserted\} \;\; \forall w_1^m$$
$$(\delta, w_1^m) \in \psi(s) \rightarrow \phi(\delta, w_1^m) \subseteq pre \cup post \quad (3)$$
$$\exists s \in pre \cup post \;\; \exists \delta \in \{deleted, inserted\} \;\; \exists w_1^m$$
$$(\delta, w_1^m) \in \psi(s) \quad (4)$$

Table 1 illustrates different types of edit segments and user edits. The term *replaced segment* refers to adjacent deleted and inserted segments. Example (1) contains a replaced segment because the deleted segment ("*1700s*") is adjacent to the inserted segment ("*18th century*"). Example (2) contains an inserted segment ("*and largest professional*"), a replaced segment ("*(est.*" → "*established in*") and a deleted segment (")"). User edits of both examples consist of a single *pre* sentence and a single *post* sentence because deleted and inserted segments do not cross any sentence boundary. Example (3) contains a replaced segment (". *He*" → "*who*"). In this case the deleted segment (". *He*") overlaps with two sentences and therefore the user edit consists of two *pre* sentences.

(1) Revisions 368209202 & 378822230	
pre	("By the mid **1700s**, Medzhybizh was the seat of power in Podilia Province.")
post	("By the mid **18th century**, Medzhybizh was the seat of power in Podilia Province.")
diff	(equal , "By the mid") , (**deleted**, "1700s") , (**inserted** , "18th century") , (equal , ", Medzhybizh was the seat of power in Podilia Province.")
(2) Revisions 148109085 & 149440273	
pre	("Original Society of Teachers of the Alexander Technique **(est.** 1958**)**.")
post	("Original **and largest professional** Society of Teachers of the Alexander Technique **established in** 1958.")
diff	(equal , "Original") , (**inserted** , "and largest professional") , (equal , "Society of Teachers of the Alexander Technique") , (**deleted** , "(est.") , (**inserted** , " established in") , (equal , "1958") , (**deleted** , ")") , (equal , ".")
(3) Revisions 61406809 & 61746002	
pre	("Fredrik Modin is a Swedish ice hockey left winger**.**" , "**He** is known for having one of the hardest slap shots in the NHL.")
post	("Fredrik Modin is a Swedish ice hockey left winger **who** is known for having one of the hardest slap shots in the NHL.")
diff	(equal , "Fredrik Modin is a Swedish ice hockey left winger") , (**deleted** , ". He") , (**inserted** , "who") , (equal , "is known for having one of the hardest slap shots in the NHL.")

Table 1: Examples of user edits and the corresponding edit segments (revision numbers correspond to the English Wikipedia).

4 Features for Edits Classification

We design a set of features for supervised classification of user edits. The design is guided by two main considerations: simplicity and interoperability. Simplicity is important because there are potentially hundreds of millions of user edits to be classified. This amount continues to grow at rapid pace and a scalable solution is required. Interoperability is important because millions of user edits are available in multiple languages. Wikipedia is a flagship project, but there are other collaborative editing projects. The solution should preferably be language- and project-independent. Consequently, we refrain from deeper syntactic parsing, Wikipedia-specific features, and language resources that are limited to English.

Our basic intuition is that longer edits are likely to be factual and shorter edits are likely to be fluency edits. The **baseline method** is therefore character-level edit distance (Levenshtein, 1966) between pre- and post-edited text.

Six feature categories are added to the baseline. Most features take the form of threefold counts referring to deleted, inserted and equal elements of each user edit. For instance, example (1) in Table 1 has one deleted token, two inserted tokens and 14 equal tokens. Many features use string similarity calculated over alternative representations.

Character-level features include counts of deleted, inserted and equal characters of different types, such as word & non-word characters or digits & non-digits. Character types may help identify edits types. For example, the change of digits may suggest a factual edit while the change of non-word characters may suggest a fluency edit.

Word-level features count deleted, inserted and equal words using three parallel representations: original case, lower case, and lemmas. Word-level edit distance is calculated for each representation. Table 2 illustrates how edit distance may vary across different representations.

Rep.	*User Edit*		*Dist*
Words	pre	Branch lines were built in Kenya	4
	post	A branch line was built in Kenya	
Lowcase	pre	branch lines were built in kenya	3
	post	a branch line was built in kenya	
Lemmas	pre	branch line be build in Kenya	1
	post	a branch line be build in Kenya	
PoS tags	pre	NN NNS VBD VBN IN NNP	2
	post	DT NN NN VBD VBN IN NNP	
NE tags	pre	LOCATION	0
	post	LOCATION	

Table 2: Word- and tag-level edit distance measured over different representations (example from Wikipedia revisions 2678278 & 2682972).

Fluency edits may shift words, which sometimes may be slightly modified. Fluency edits may also add or remove words that already appear in context. Optimal calculation of edit distance with shifts is computationally expensive (Shapira and Storer, 2002). Translation error rate (TER) provides an approximation but it is designed for the needs of machine translation evaluation (Snover et al., 2006). To have a more sensitive estimation of the degree of edit, we compute the minimal character-level edit distance between every pair of words that belong to different edit segments. For each pair of edit segments (δ, w_1^m), (δ', w'^k_1) overlapping with a user edit, if $\delta \neq \delta'$ we compute:

$$\forall w \in w_1^m : \min_{w' \in w'^k_1} \mathit{EditDist}(w, w') \quad (5)$$

Binned counts of the number of words with a minimal edit distance of 0, 1, 2, 3 or more characters are accumulated per edit segment type (equal, deleted or inserted).

Part-of-speech (PoS) features include counts of deleted, inserted and equal PoS tags (per tag) and edit distance at the tag level between PoS tags before and after the edit. Similarly, **named-entity (NE) features** include counts of deleted, inserted and equal NE tags (per tag, excluding *OTHER*) and edit distance at the tag level between NE tags before and after the edit. Table 2 illustrates the edit distance at different levels of representation. We assume that a deleted NE tag, e.g. *PERSON* or *LOCATION*, could indicate a factual edit. It could however be a fluency edit where the NE is replaced by a co-referent like "*she*" or "*it*". Even if we encounter an inserted *PRP* PoS tag, the features do not capture the explicit relation between the deleted NE tag and the inserted PoS tag. This is an inherent weakness of these features when compared to parsing-based alternatives.

An additional set of counts, NE values, describes the number of deleted, inserted and equal normalized values of numeric entities such as numbers and dates. For instance, if the word "100" is replaced by "200" and the respective numeric values 100.0 and 200.0 are normalized, the counts of deleted and inserted NE values will be incremented and suggest a factual edit. If on the other hand "100" is replaced by "hundred" and the latter is normalized as having the numeric value 100.0, then the count of equal NE values will be incremented, rather suggesting a fluency edit.

Acronym features count deleted, inserted and equal acronyms. Potential acronyms are extracted from word sequences that start with a capital letter and from words that contain multiple capital letters. If, for example, "UN" is replaced by "United Nations", "MicroSoft" by "MS" or "Jean Pierre" by "J.P", the count of equal acronyms will be incremented, suggesting a fluency edit.

The last category, **language model (LM) features**, takes a different approach. These features look at n-gram based sentence probabilities before and after the edit, with and without normalization with respect to sentence lengths. The ratio of the two probabilities, $\hat{P}_{ratio}(pre, post)$ is computed as follows:

$$\hat{P}(w_1^m) \approx \prod_{i=1}^{m} P(w_i | w_{i-n+1}^{i-1}) \quad (6)$$

$$\hat{P}_{norm}(w_1^m) = \hat{P}(w_1^m)^{\frac{1}{m}} \quad (7)$$

$$\hat{P}_{ratio}(pre, post) = \frac{\hat{P}_{norm}(post)}{\hat{P}_{norm}(pre)} \quad (8)$$

$$\log \hat{P}_{ratio}(pre, post) = \log \frac{\hat{P}_{norm}(post)}{\hat{P}_{norm}(pre)} \quad (9)$$

$$= \log \hat{P}_{norm}(post) - \log \hat{P}_{norm}(pre)$$

$$= \frac{1}{|post|} \log \hat{P}(post) - \frac{1}{|pre|} \log \hat{P}(pre)$$

Where $\hat{P}$ is the sentence probability estimated as a product of n-gram conditional probabilities and $\hat{P}_{norm}$ is the sentence probability normalized by the sentence length. We hypothesize that the relative change of normalized sentence probabilities is related to the edit type. As an additional feature, the number of out of vocabulary (OOV) words before and after the edit is computed. The intuition

	Dataset	*Labeled Subset*
Number of User Edits:		
	923,820 (100%)	2,008 (100%)
Edit Segments Distribution:		
Replaced	535,402 (57.96%)	1,259 (62.70%)
Inserted	235,968 (25.54%)	471 (23.46%)
Deleted	152,450 (16.5%)	278 (13.84%)
Character-level Edit Distance Distribution:		
1	202,882 (21.96%)	466 (23.21%)
2	81,388 (8.81%)	198 (9.86%)
3-10	296,841 (32.13%)	645 (32.12%)
11-100	342,709 (37.10%)	699 (34.81%)
Word-level Edit Distance Distribution:		
1	493,095 (53.38%)	1,008 (54.18%)
2	182,770 (19.78%)	402 (20.02%)
3	77,603 (8.40%)	161 (8.02%)
4-10	170,352 (18.44%)	357 (17.78%)
Labels Distribution:		
Fluency	-	1,008 (50.2%)
Factual	-	1,000 (49.8%)

Table 3: Dataset of nearly 1 million user edits with single deleted, inserted or replaced segments, of which 2K are labeled. The labels are almost equally distributed. The distribution over edit segment types and edit distance intervals is detailed.

is that unknown words are more likely to be indicative of factual edits.

5 Experiments

5.1 Experimental Setup

First, we extract a large amount of user edits from revision histories of the English Wikipedia.[3] The extraction process scans pairs of subsequent revisions of article pages and ignores any revision that was reverted due to vandalism. It parses the Wikitext and filters out markup, hyperlinks, tables and templates. The process analyzes the clean text of the two revisions[4] and computes the difference between them.[5] The process identifies the overlap between edit segments and sentence boundaries and extracts user edits. Features are calculated and user edits are stored and indexed. LM features are calculated against a large English 4-gram language model built by SRILM (Stolcke, 2002) with modified interpolated Kneser-Ney smoothing using the AFP and Xinhua portions of the English Gigaword corpus (LDC2003T05).

We extract a total of 4.3 million user edits of which 2.52 million (almost 60%) are insertions and deletions of complete sentences. Although these may include fluency edits such as sentence reordering or rewriting from scratch, we assume that the large majority is factual. Of the remaining 1.78 million edits, the majority (64.5%) contains single deleted, inserted or replaced segments. We decide to focus on this subset because sentences with multiple non-contiguous edit segments are more likely to contain mixed cases of unrelated factual and fluency edits, as illustrated by example (2) in Table 1. Learning to classify contiguous edit segments seems to be a reasonable way of breaking down the problem into smaller parts. We filter out user edits with edit distance longer than 100 characters or 10 words that we assume to be factual. The resulting dataset contains 923,820 user edits: 58% replaced segments, 25.5% inserted segments and 16.5% deleted segments.

Manual labeling of user edits is carried out by a group of annotators with near native or native level of English. All annotators receive the same written guidelines. In short, fluency labels are assigned to edits of letter case, spelling, grammar, synonyms, paraphrases, co-referents, language and style. Factual labels are assigned to edits of dates, numbers and figures, named entities, semantic change or disambiguation, addition or removal of content. A random set of 2,676 instances is labeled: 2,008 instances with a majority agreement of at least two annotators are selected as training set, 270 instances are held out as development set, 164 trivial fluency corrections of a single letter's case and 234 instances with no clear agreement among annotators are excluded. The last group (8.7%) emphasizes that the task is, to a limited extent, subjective. It suggests that automated classification of certain user edits would be difficult. Nevertheless, inter-rater agreement between annotators is high to very high. Kappa values between 0.74 to 0.84 are measured between six pairs of annotators, each pair annotated a common subset of at least 100 instances. Table 3 describes the resulting dataset, which we also make available to the research community.[6]

[3]Dump of all pages with complete edit history as of January 15, 2011 (342GB bz2), http://dumps.wikimedia.org.

[4]Tokenization, sentence split, PoS & NE tags by Stanford CoreNLP, http://nlp.stanford.edu/software/corenlp.shtml.

[5]Myers' $O(ND)$ difference algorithm (Myers, 1986), http://code.google.com/p/google-diff-match-patch.

[6]Available for download at `http://staff.`

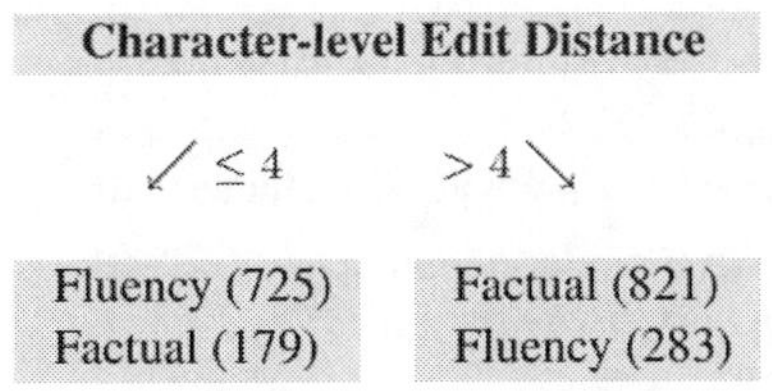

Figure 1: A decision tree that uses character-level edit distance as a sole feature. The tree correctly classifies 76% of the labeled user edits.

Feature set	SVM	RF	Logit
Baseline	76.26%	76.26%	76.34%
+ Char-level	83.71%†	84.45%†	84.01%†
+ Word-level	78.38%$^{\dagger\vee}$	81.38%$^{\dagger\wedge}$	78.13%$^{\dagger\vee}$
+ PoS	76.58%$^{\vee}$	76.97%	78.35%$^{\dagger\wedge}$
+ NE	82.71%†	83.12%†	82.38%†
+ Acronyms	76.55%	76.61%	76.96%
+ LM	76.20%	77.42%	76.52%
All Features	**87.14%**$^{\dagger\wedge}$	**87.14%**†	**85.64%**$^{\dagger\vee}$

Table 4: Classification accuracy using the baseline, each feature set added to the baseline, and all features combined. Statistical significance at $p < 0.05$ is indicated by † w.r.t the baseline (using the same classifier), and by $^{\wedge}$ w.r.t to another classifier marked by $^{\vee}$ (using the same features). Highest accuracy per classifier is marked in bold.

5.2 Feature Analysis

We experiment with three classifiers: Support Vector Machines (SVM), Random Forests (RF) and Logistic Regression (Logit).[7] SVMs (Cortes and Vapnik, 1995) and Logistic Regression (or Maximum Entropy classifiers) are two widely used machine learning techniques. SVMs have been applied to many text classification problems (Joachims, 1998). Maximum Entropy classifiers have been applied to the similar tasks of paraphrase recognition (Malakasiotis, 2009) and textual entailment (Hickl et al., 2006). Random Forests (Breiman, 2001) as well as other decision tree algorithms are successfully used for classifying Wikipedia edits for the purpose of vandalism detection (Potthast et al., 2010; Potthast and Holfeld, 2011).

Experiments begin with the edit-distance baseline. Then each one of the feature groups is separately added to the baseline. Finally, all features are evaluated together. Table 4 reports the percentage of correctly classified edits (classifiers' accuracy), and Table 5 reports the fraction of correctly classified edits per type. All results are for 10-fold cross validation. Statistical significance against the baseline and between classifiers is calculated at $p < 0.05$ using paired t-test.

Feature set	SVM *flu. / fac.*	RF *flu. / fac.*	Logit *flu. / fac.*
Baseline	0.85 / 0.67	0.74 / 0.79	0.85 / 0.67
+ Char-level	0.85 / 0.82	0.83 / 0.86	0.86 / 0.82
+ Word-level	0.88 / 0.69	0.81 / 0.82	0.86 / 0.70
+ PoS	0.85 / 0.68	0.78 / 0.76	0.84 / 0.72
+ NE	0.86 / 0.79	0.79 / 0.87	0.87 / 0.78
+ Acronyms	0.87 / 0.66	0.83 / 0.70	0.86 / 0.68
+ LM	0.85 / 0.67	0.79 / 0.76	0.84 / 0.69
All Features	0.88 / 0.86	0.86 / 0.88	0.87 / 0.84

Table 5: Fraction of correctly classified edits per type: fluency edits (left) and factual edits (right), using the baseline, each feature set added to the baseline, and all features combined.

The first interesting result is the highly predictive power of the single-feature baseline. It confirms the intuition that longer edits are mainly factual. Figure 1 shows that the edit distance of 72% of the user edits labeled as fluency is between 1 to 4, while the edit distance of 82% of those labeled as factual is greater than 4. The cut-off value is found by a single-node decision tree that uses edit distance as a sole feature. The tree correctly classifies 76% of the instances. This result implies that the actual challenge is to correctly classify short factual edits and long fluency edits.

Character-level features and named-entity features lead to significant improvements over the baseline for all classifiers. Their strength lies in their ability to identify short factual edits such as changes of numeric values or proper names. Word-level features also significantly improve the baseline but their contribution is smaller. PoS and acronym features lead to small statistically-insignificant improvements over the baseline.

The poor contribution of LM features is surprising. It might be due to the limited context of n-grams, but it might be that LM probabilities are not a good predictor for the task. Removing LM features from the set of all features

science.uva.nl/~abronner/uec/data.

[7]Using Weka classifiers: SMO (SVM), RandomForest & Logistic (Hall et al., 2009). Classifier's parameters are tuned using the held-out development set.

Fluency Edits Misclassified as Factual	
Equivalent or redundant in context	14
Paraphrases	13
Equivalent numeric patterns	7
Replacing first name with last name	4
Acronyms	4
Non specific adjectives or adverbs	3
Other	5

Factual Edits Misclassified as Fluency	
Short correction of content	35
Opposites	3
Similar names	3
Noise (unfiltered vandalism)	3
Other	6

Table 6: Error types based on manual examination of 50 fluency edit misclassifications and 50 factual edit misclassifications.

Correctly Classified Fluency Edits
"Adventure education ~~makes intentional use of~~ **intentionally uses** challenging experiences for learning."
"He served as president from October 1 , 1985 ~~and retired~~ **through his retirement** on June 30 , 2002."
"In 1973, he ~~helped organize~~ **assisted in organizing** his first ever visit to the West."

Correctly Classified Factual Edits
"Over the course of the next ~~two years~~ **five months**, the unit completed a series of daring raids."
"**Scottish born** David Tennant has reportedly said he would like his Doctor to wear a kilt."
"This family joined the strip ~~in late 1990~~ **around March 1991**."

Table 7: Examples of correctly classified user edits. Deleted segments are struck out, inserted are bold (revision numbers are omitted for brevity).

leads to a small decrease in classification accuracy, namely 86.68% instead of 87.14% for SVM. This decrease is not statistically significant.

The highest accuracy is achieved by both SVM and RF and there are few significant differences among the three classifiers. The fraction of correctly classified edits per type (Table 5) reveals that for SVM and Logit, most fluency edits are correctly classified by the baseline and most improvements over the baseline are attributed to better classification of factual edits. This is not the case for RF, where the fraction of correctly classified factual edits is higher and the fraction of correctly classified fluency edits is lower. This insight motivates further experimentation. Repeating the experiment with a meta-classifier that uses a majority voting scheme, achieves an improved accuracy of 87.58%. This improvement is not statistically significant.

5.3 Error Analysis

To have better understanding of errors made by the classifier, 50 fluency edit misclassifications and 50 factual edit misclassifications are randomly selected and manually examined. The errors are grouped into categories as summarized in Table 6. These explain certain limitations of the classifier and suggest possible improvements.

Fluency edit misclassifications: 14 instances (28%) are phrases (often co-referents) that are either equivalent or redundant in the given context. For example: "*in 1986*" $\rightarrow$ "*that year*", "*when she returned*" $\rightarrow$ "*when Ruffa returned*" and "*the core member of the group are*" $\rightarrow$ "*the core members are*". 13 (26%) are paraphrases misclassified as factual edits. Examples are: "*made cartoons*" $\rightarrow$ "*produced animated cartoons*" and "*with the implication that they are similar to*" $\rightarrow$ "*implying a connection to*". 7 modify numeric patterns that do not change the meaning such as the year "*37*" $\rightarrow$ "*1937*". 4 replace a first name of a person with the last name. 4 contain acronyms, e.g. "*Display PostScript*" $\rightarrow$ "*Display PostScript (or DPS)*". Acronym features are correctly identified but the classifier fails to recognize a fluency edit. 3 modify adjectives or adverbs that do not change the meaning such as "*entirely*" and "*various*".

Factual edit misclassifications: the big majority, 35 instances (70%), could be characterized as short corrections, often replacing a similar word, that make the content more accurate or more precise. Examples (context is omitted): "*city*" $\rightarrow$ "*village*", "*emigrated*" $\rightarrow$ "*immigrated*" and "*electrical*" $\rightarrow$ "*electromagnetic*". 3 are opposites or antonyms such as "*previous*" $\rightarrow$ "*next*" and "*lived*" $\rightarrow$ "*died*". 3 are modifications of similar person or entity names, e.g. "*Kelly*" $\rightarrow$ "*Kate*". 3 are instances of unfiltered vandalism, i.e. noisy examples. Other misclassifications include verb tense modifications such as "*is*" $\rightarrow$ "*was*" and "*consists*" $\rightarrow$ "*consisted*". These are difficult to

Comment	Test Set Size	Classified as Fluency Edits
"grammar"	1,122	88.9%
"spelling"	2,893	97.6%
"typo"	3,382	91.6%
"copyedit"	3,437	68.4%
Random set	5,000	49.4%

Table 8: Classifying unlabeled data selected by user comments that suggest a fluency edit. The SVM classifier is trained using the labeled data. User comments are not used as features.

classify because the modification of verb tense in a given context is sometimes factual and sometimes a fluency edit.

These findings agree with the feature analysis. Fluency edit misclassifications are typically longer phrases that carry the same meaning while factual edit misclassifications are typically single words or short phrases that carry different meaning. The main conclusion is that the classifier should take into account explicit content and context. Putting aside the consideration of simplicity and interoperability, features based on co-reference resolution and paraphrase recognition are likely to improve fluency edits classification, and features from language resources that describe synonymy and antonymy relations are likely to improve factual edits classification. While this conclusion may come at no surprise, it is important to highlight the high classification accuracy that is achieved without such capabilities and resources. Table 7 presents several examples of correct classification produced by our classifier.

6 Exploiting Unlabeled Data

We extracted a large set of user edits but our approach has been limited to a restricted number of labeled examples. This section attempts to find whether the classifier generalizes beyond labeled data and whether unlabeled data could be used to improve classification accuracy.

6.1 Generalizing Beyond Labeled Data

The aim of the next experiment is to test how well the supervised classifier generalizes beyond the labeled test set. The problem is the availability of test data. There is no shared task for user edits classification and no common test set to evaluate against. We resort to Wikipedia user comments. It is a problematic option because it is unreliable. Users may add a comment when submitting an edit, but it is not mandatory. The comment is a free text with no predefined structure. It could be meaningful or nonsense. The comment is per revision. It may refer to one, some or all edits submitted for a given revision. Nevertheless, we identify several keywords that represent certain types of fluency edits: *"grammar"*, *"spelling"*, *"typo"*, and *"copyedit"*. The first three clearly indicate grammar and spelling corrections. The last indicates a correction of format and style, but also of accuracy of the text. Therefore it only represents a bias towards fluency edits.

We extract unlabeled edits whose comment is equal to one of the keywords and construct a test set per keyword. An additional test set consists of randomly selected unlabeled edits with any comment. The five test sets are classified by the SVM classifier trained using the labeled data and the set of all features. To remove any doubt, user comments are not part of any feature of the classifier.

The results in Table 8 show that most unlabeled edits whose comments are *"grammar"*, *"spelling"* or *"typo"* are indeed classified as fluency edits. The classification of edits whose comment is *"copyedit"* is biased towards fluency edits, but as expected the result is less distinct. The classification of the random set is balanced, as expected.

Replaced by	Frequency	Edit class
"second"	144	Factual
"First"	38	Fluency
"last"	31	Factual
"1st"	22	Fluency
"third"	22	Factaul

Table 9: User edits replacing the word *"first"* with another single word: most frequent 5 out of 524.

Replaced by	Frequency	Replaced by	Frequency
"Adams"	7	*"Squidward"*	6
"Joseph"	7	*"Alexander"*	5
"Einstein"	6	*"Davids"*	5
"Galland"	6	*"Haim"*	5
"Lowe"	6	*"Hickes"*	5

Table 10: Fluency edits replacing the word *"He"* with proper noun: most frequent 10 out of 1,381.

Feature set	**SVM**	**RF**	**Logit**
Baseline	76.26%	76.26%	76.34%
All Features	87.14%$^{\dagger\wedge}$	87.14%†	85.64%$^{\dagger\vee}$
Unlabeled only	78.11%$^{\vee}$	83.49%$^{\dagger\wedge}$	78.78%$^{\dagger\vee}$
Base + unlabeled	80.86%$^{\dagger\vee}$	85.45%$^{\dagger\wedge}$	81.83%$^{\dagger\vee}$
All + unlabeled	87.23%	**88.35%**$^{\ddagger\dagger\wedge}$	85.92%$^{\vee}$

Table 11: Classification accuracy using features from unlabeled data. The first two rows are identical to Table 4. Statistical significance at $p < 0.05$ is indicated by: † w.r.t the baseline; ‡ w.r.t all features excluding features from unlabeled data; and $^{\wedge}$ w.r.t to another classifier marked by $^{\vee}$ (using the same features). The best result is marked in bold.

6.2 Features from Unlabeled Data

The purpose of the last experiment is to exploit unlabeled data in order to extract additional features for the classifier. The underlying assumption is that reoccurring patterns may indicate whether a user edit is factual or a fluency edit.

We could assume that fluency edits would reoccur across many revisions, while factual edits would only appear in revisions of specific documents. However, this assumption does not necessarily hold. Table 9 gives a simple example of single word replacements for which the most reoccurring edit is actually factual and other factual and fluency edits reoccur in similar frequencies.

Finding user edits reoccurrence is not trivial. We could rely on exact matches of surface forms, but this may lead to data sparseness issues. Fluency edits that exchange co-referents and proper nouns, as illustrated by the example in Table 10, may reoccur frequently but this fact could not be revealed by exact matching of specific proper nouns. On the other hand, using a bag of word approach may find too many unrelated edits.

We introduce a two-step method that measures the reoccurrence of edits in unlabeled data using exact and approximate matching over multiple representations. The method provides a set of frequencies that is fed into the classifier and allows for learning subtle patterns of reoccurrence. Staying consistent with our initial design considerations, the method is simple and interoperable.

Given a user edit $(pre, post)$, the method does not compare pre with $post$ in any way. It only compares pre with pre-edited sentences of other unlabeled edits and $post$ with post-edited sentences of other unlabeled edits. The first step is to select candidates using a bag of words approach. The second step is a comparison of the user edit with each one of the candidates while incrementing counts of similarity measures. These account for exact matches between different representations (original and low case, lemmas, PoS and NE tags) as well as for approximate matches using character- and word-level edit distance between those representations. An additional feature is the number of distinct documents in the candidate set.

We compute the set of features for the labeled dataset based on the unlabeled data. The number of candidates is set to 1,000 per user edit. We re-train the classifiers using five configurations: *Baseline* and *All Features* are identical to the first experiment. *Unlabeled only* uses the new feature set without any other feature. *Base + Unlabeled* adds the new feature set to the baseline. *All + Unlabeled* uses all available features. All results are for 10-fold cross validation with statistical significance at $p < 0.05$ by paired t-test, see Table 11.

We find that features extracted from unlabeled data outperform the baseline and lead to statistically significant improvements when added to it. The combination of all features allows Random Forests to achieve the highest statistically significant accuracy level of 88.35%.

7 Conclusions

This work addresses the task of user edits classification as factual or fluency edits. It adopts a supervised machine learning approach and uses character- and word- level features, part-of-speech tags, named entities, language model probabilities, and a set of features extracted from large amounts of unlabeled data. Our experiments with contiguous user edits extracted from revision histories of the English Wikipedia achieve high classification accuracy and demonstrate generalization to data beyond labeled edits.

Our approach shows that machine learning techniques can successfully distinguish between user edit types, making them a favorable alternative to heuristic solutions. The simple and adaptive nature of our method allows for application to large and evolving sets of user edits.

Acknowledgments. This research was funded in part by the European Commission through the CoSyne project FP7-ICT-4-248531.

References

A. Aji, Y. Wang, E. Agichtein, and E. Gabrilovich. 2010. Using the past to score the present: Extending term weighting models through revision history analysis. In *Proceedings of the 19th ACM international conference on Information and knowledge management*, pages 629–638.

I. Androutsopoulos and P. Malakasiotis. 2010. A survey of paraphrasing and textual entailment methods. *Journal of Artificial Intelligence Research*, 38(1):135–187.

L. Breiman. 2001. Random forests. *Machine learning*, 45(1):5–32.

J. Chae and A. Nenkova. 2009. Predicting the fluency of text with shallow structural features: case studies of machine translation and human-written text. In *Proceedings of the 12th Conference of the European Chapter of the Association for Computational Linguistics*, pages 139–147.

C. Cortes and V. Vapnik. 1995. Support-vector networks. *Machine learning*, 20(3):273–297.

C. Dutrey, D. Bernhard, H. Bouamor, and A. Max. 2011. Local modifications and paraphrases in Wikipedia's revision history. *Procesamiento del Lenguaje Natural*, Revista no 46:51–58.

M. Hall, E. Frank, G. Holmes, B. Pfahringer, P. Reutemann, and I.H. Witten. 2009. The WEKA data mining software: an update. *ACM SIGKDD Explorations Newsletter*, 11(1):10–18.

A. Hickl, J. Williams, J. Bensley, K. Roberts, B. Rink, and Y. Shi. 2006. Recognizing textual entailment with LCCs GROUNDHOG system. In *Proceedings of the Second PASCAL Challenges Workshop*.

T. Joachims. 1998. Text categorization with support vector machines: Learning with many relevant features. *Machine Learning: ECML-98*, pages 137–142.

A. Kittur, B. Suh, B.A. Pendleton, and E.H. Chi. 2007. He says, she says: Conflict and coordination in Wikipedia. In *Proceedings of the SIGCHI conference on Human factors in computing systems*, pages 453–462.

V.I. Levenshtein. 1966. Binary codes capable of correcting deletions, insertions, and reversals. *Soviet Physics Doklady*, 10(8):707–710.

P. Malakasiotis. 2009. Paraphrase recognition using machine learning to combine similarity measures. In *Proceedings of the ACL-IJCNLP 2009 Student Research Workshop*, pages 27–35.

A. Max and G. Wisniewski. 2010. Mining naturally-occurring corrections and paraphrases from Wikipedia's revision history. In *Proceedings of LREC*, pages 3143–3148.

E.W. Myers. 1986. An $O(ND)$ difference algorithm and its variations. *Algorithmica*, 1(1):251–266.

R. Nelken and E. Yamangil. 2008. Mining Wikipedia's article revision history for training computational linguistics algorithms. In *Proceedings of the AAAI Workshop on Wikipedia and Artificial Intelligence: An Evolving Synergy*, pages 31–36.

S. Nunes, C. Ribeiro, and G. David. 2011. Term weighting based on document revision history. *Journal of the American Society for Information Science and Technology*, 62(12):2471–2478.

M. Potthast and T. Holfeld. 2011. Overview of the 2nd international competition on Wikipedia vandalism detection. *Notebook for PAN at CLEF 2011*.

M. Potthast, B. Stein, and T. Holfeld. 2010. Overview of the 1st international competition on Wikipedia vandalism detection. *Notebook Papers of CLEF*, pages 22–23.

D. Shapira and J. Storer. 2002. Edit distance with move operations. In *Combinatorial Pattern Matching*, pages 85–98.

M. Snover, B. Dorr, R. Schwartz, L. Micciulla, and J. Makhoul. 2006. A study of translation edit rate with targeted human annotation. In *Proceedings of Association for Machine Translation in the Americas*, pages 223–231.

A. Stolcke. 2002. SRILM-an extensible language modeling toolkit. In *Proceedings of the international conference on spoken language processing*, volume 2, pages 901–904.

F.B. Viegas, M. Wattenberg, and K. Dave. 2004. Studying cooperation and conflict between authors with history flow visualizations. In *Proceedings of the SIGCHI conference on Human factors in computing systems*, pages 575–582.

A.G. West and I. Lee. 2011. Multilingual vandalism detection using language-independent & ex post facto evidence. *Notebook for PAN at CLEF 2011*.

A.G. West, S. Kannan, and I. Lee. 2010. Detecting Wikipedia vandalism via spatio-temporal analysis of revision metadata. In *Proceedings of the Third European Workshop on System Security*, pages 22–28.

K. Woodsend and M. Lapata. 2011. Learning to simplify sentences with quasi-synchronous grammar and integer programming. In *Proceedings of the 2011 Conference on Empirical Methods in Natural Language Processing*, pages 409–420.

E. Yamangil and R. Nelken. 2008. Mining Wikipedia revision histories for improving sentence compression. In *Proceedings of ACL-08: HLT, Short Papers*, pages 137–140.

M. Yatskar, B. Pang, C. Danescu-Niculescu-Mizil, and L. Lee. 2010. For the sake of simplicity: Unsupervised extraction of lexical simplifications from Wikipedia. In *Human Language Technologies: The 2010 Annual Conference of the North American Chapter of the Association for Computational Linguistics*, pages 365–368.

F.M. Zanzotto and M. Pennacchiotti. 2010. Expanding textual entailment corpora from Wikipedia using co-training. In *Proceedings of the 2nd Workshop on Collaboratively Constructed Semantic Resources, COLING 2010*.

S. Zwarts and M. Dras. 2008. Choosing the right translation: A syntactically informed classification approach. In *Proceedings of the 22nd International Conference on Computational Linguistics-Volume 1*, pages 1153–1160.

User Participation Prediction in Online Forums

Zhonghua Qu and **Yang Liu**
The University of Texas at Dallas
{qzh,yangl@hlt.utdallas.edu}

Abstract

Online community is an important source for latest news and information. Accurate prediction of a user's interest can help provide better user experience. In this paper, we develop a recommendation system for online forums. There are a lot of differences between online forums and formal media. For example, content generated by users in online forums contains more noise compared to formal documents. Content topics in the same forum are more focused than sources like news websites. Some of these differences present challenges to traditional word-based user profiling and recommendation systems, but some also provide opportunities for better recommendation performance. In our recommendation system, we propose to (a) use latent topics to interpolate with content-based recommendation; (b) model latent user groups to utilize information from other users. We have collected three types of forum data sets. Our experimental results demonstrate that our proposed hybrid approach works well in all three types of forums.

1 Introduction

Internet is an important source of information. It has become a habit of many people to go to the internet for latest news and updates. However, not all articles are equally interesting for different users. In order to intelligently predict interesting articles for individual users, personalized news recommendation systems have been developed. There are in general two types of approaches upon which recommendation systems are built. Content based recommendation systems use the textual information of news articles and user generated content to rank items. Collaborative filtering, on the other hand, uses co-occurrence information from a collection of users for recommendation.

During the past few years, online community has become a large part of internet. More often, latest information and knowledge appear at online community earlier than other formal media. This makes it a favorable place for people seeking timely update and latest information. Online community sites appear in many forms, for example, online forums, blogs, and social networking websites. Here we focus our study on online forums. It is very helpful to build an automatic system to suggest latest information a user would be interested in. However, unlike formal news media, user generated content in forums is usually less organized and not well formed. This presents a great challenge to many existing news article recommendation systems. In addition, what makes online forums different from other media is that users of online communities are not only the information consumers but also active providers as participants. Therefore in this study we develop a recommendation system to account for these characteristics of forums. We propose several improvements over previous work:

- Latent topic interpolation: This is to address the issue with the word-based content representation. In this paper we used Latent Dirichlet Allocation (LDA), a generative multinomial mixture model, for topic inference inside threads. We build a system based on words and latent topics, and linearly interpolate their results.

- User modeling: We model users' participation inside threads as latent user groups. Each latent group is a multinomial distribution on users. Then LDA is used to infer the group mixture inside each thread, based on which the probability of a user's participation can be derived.

- Hybrid system: Since content and user-based methods rely on different information sources, we combine the results from them for further improvement.

We have evaluated our proposed method using three data sets collected from three representative forums. Our experimental results show that in all forums, by using latent topics information, system can achieve better accuracy in predicting threads for recommendation. In addition, by modeling latent user groups in thread participation, further improvement is achieved in the hybrid system. Our analysis also showed that each forum has its nature, resulting in different optimal parameters in the different forums.

2 Related Work

Recommendation systems can help make information retrieving process more intelligent. Generally, recommendation methods are categorized into two types (Adomavicius and Tuzhilin, 2005), content-based filtering and collaborative filtering.

Systems using content-based filtering use the content information of recommendation items a user is interested in to recommend new items to the user. For example, in a news recommendation system, in order to recommend appropriate news articles to a user, it finds the most prominent features (e.g., key words, tags, category) in the document that a user likes, then suggests similar articles based on this "personal profile". In Fabs system (Balabanovic and Shoham, 1997), Skyskill & Webert system (Pazzani et al., 1997), documents are represented using a set of most important words according to a weighting measure. The most popular measure of word "importance" is TF-IDF (term frequency, inverse document frequency) (Salton and Buckley, 1988), which gives weights to words according to its "informativeness". Then, base on this "personal profile" a ranking machine is applied to give a ranked recommendation list. In Fabs system, Rocchio' algorithm (Rocchio, 1971) is used to learn the average TF-IDF vector of highly rated documents. Skyskill & Webert's system uses Naive Bayes classifiers to give the probability of documents being liked. Winnow's algorithm (Littlestone, 1988), which is similar to perception algorithm, has been shown to perform well when there are many features. An adaptive framework is introduced in (Li et al., 2010) using forum comments for news recommendation. In (Wu et al., 2010), a topic-specific topic flow model is introduced to rank the likelihood of user participating in a thread in online forums.

Collaborative-filtering based systems, unlike content-based systems, predict the recommending items using co-occurrence information between users. For example, in a news recommendation system, in order to recommend an article to user c, the system tries to find users with similar taste as c. Items favored by similar users would be recommended. Grundy (Rich, 1979) is known to be one of the first collaborative-filtering based systems. Collaborative filtering systems can be either model based or memory based (Breese et al., 1998). Memory-based algorithms, such as (Delgado and Ishii, 1999; Nakamura and Abe, 1998; Shardanand and Maes, 1995), use a utility function to measure the similarity between users. Then recommendation of an item is made according to the sum of the utility values of active users that participate in it. Model-based algorithms, on the other hand, try to formulate the probability function of one item being liked statistically using active user information. (Ungar et al., 1998) clustered similar users into groups for recommendation. Different clustering methods have been experimented, including K-means and Gibbs Sampling. Other probabilistic models have also been used to model collaborative relationships, including a Bayesian model (Chien and George, 1999), linear regression model (Sarwar et al., 2001), Gaussian mixture models (Hofmann, 2003; Hofmann, 2004). In (Blei et al., 2001) a collaborative filtering application is discussed using LDA. However in this model, re-estimation of parameters for the whole system is needed when a new item comes in. In this paper, we formulate users' participation differently using the LDA mixture model.

Some previous work has also evaluated using a hybrid model with both content and collaborative features and showed outstanding performance. For example, in (Basu et al., 1998), hybrid features are used to make recommendation using inductive learning.

3 Forum Data

We have collected data from three forums in this study.[1] Ubuntu community forum is a technical support forum; World of Warcraft (WoW) forum is about gaming; Fitness forum is about how to live a healthy life. These three forums are quite representative of online forums on the internet. Using three different types of forums for task evaluation helps to demonstrate the robustness of our proposed method. In addition, it can show how the same method could have substantial performance difference on forums of different nature. Users' behaviors in these three forums are very different. Casual forums like "Wow gaming" have much more posts in each thread. However its posts are the shortest in length. This is because discussions inside these types of forums are more like casual conversation, and there is not much requirement on the user's background, and thus there is more user participation. In contrast, technical forums like "Ubuntu" have fewer average posts in each thread, and have the longest post length. This is because a Question and Answer (QA) forum tends to be very goal oriented. If a user finds the thread is unrelated, then there will be no motivation for participation.

Inside forums, different boards are created to categorize the topics allowed for discussion. From the data we find that users tend to participate in a few selected boards of their choices. To create a data set for user interest prediction in this study, we pick the most popular boards in each forum. Even within the same board, users tend to participate in different threads base on their interest. We use a user's participation information as an indication whether a thread is interesting to a user or not. Hence, our task is to predict the user participation in forum threads. Note this approach could introduce some bias toward negative instances in terms of user interests. A users' absence from a thread does not necessarily mean the user is not interested in that thread; it may be a result of the user being offline by that time or the thread is too behind in pages. As a matter of fact, we found most users read only the threads on the first page during their time of visit of a forum. This makes participation prediction an even harder task than interest prediction.

In online forums, threads are ordered by the time stamp of their last participating post. Provided with the time stamp for each post, we can calculate the order of a thread on its board during a user's participation. Figure 1 shows the distribution of post location during users' participation. We found that most of the users read only the posts on the first page. In order to minimize the false negative instances from the data set, we did thread location filtering. That is, we want to filter out messages that actually interest the user but do not have the user's participation because they are not on the first page. For any user, only those threads appearing in the first 10 entries on a page during a user's visit are included in the data set.

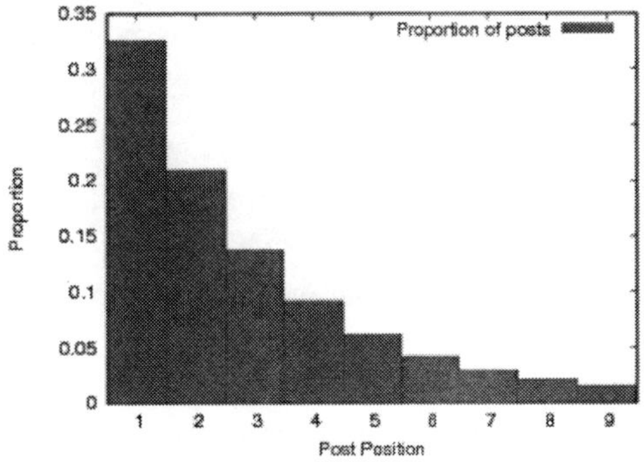

Figure 1: Thread position during users' participation.

In the pre-processing step of the experiment, first we use online status filtering discussed above to remove threads that a user does not see while offline. The statistics of the boards we have used in each forum are shown in Table 1. The statistics are consistent with the full forum statistics. For example, users in technical forums tend to post less than casual forums. We define active users as those who have participated in 10 or more threads. Column "Part. @300" shows the average number

[1]Please contact the authors to obtain the data.

of threads the top 300 users have participated in. "Filt. Threads@300" shows the average number of threads after using online filtering with a window of 10. Thread participation in "Ubuntu" forum is very sparse for each user, having only 10.01% participating threads for each user after filtering. "Fitness" and "Wow Forum" have denser participation, at 18.97% and 13.86% respectively.

4 Interesting Thread Prediction

In the task of interesting thread prediction, the system generates a ranked list of threads a user is likely to be interested in based on users' past history of thread participation. Here, instead of predicting the true interestedness, we predict the participation of the user, which is a sufficient condition for interestedness. This approach is also used by (Wu et al., 2010) for their task evaluation. In this section, we describe our proposed approaches for thread participation prediction.

4.1 Content-based Filtering

In the content-based filtering approach, only content of a thread is used as features for prediction. Recommendation through content-based filtering has its deep root in information retrieval. Here we use a Naive Bayes classifier for ranking the threads using information based on the words and the latent topic analysis.

4.1.1 Naive Bayes Classification

In (Pazzani et al., 1997) Naive Bayesian classifier showed outstanding performance in web page recommendation compared to several other classifiers. A Naive Bayes classifier is a generative model in which words inside a document are assumed to be conditionally independent. That is, given the class of a document, words are generated independently. The posterior probability of a test instance in Naive Bayes classifier takes the following form:

$$P(C_i|f_{1..k}) = \frac{1}{Z}P(C_i)\prod_j P(f_j|C_i) \quad (1)$$

where Z is the class label independent normalization term, $f_{1..k}$ is the bag-of-word feature vector for the document. Naive Bayes classifier is known for not having a well calibrated posterior probability (Bennett, 2000). (Pavlov et al., 2004) showed that normalization by document length yielded good empirical results in approximating a well calibrated posterior probability for Naive Bayes classifier. The normalized Naive Bayes classifier they used is as follows:

$$P(C_i|f_{1..k}) = \frac{1}{Z}P(C_i)\prod_j P(f_j|C_i)^{\frac{1}{|f|}} \quad (2)$$

In this equation, the probability of generating each word is normalized by the length of the feature vector $|f|$. The posterior probability $P(interested|f_{1..k})$ from (normalized) Naive Bayes classifier is used for recommendation item ranking.

4.1.2 Latent Topics based Interpolation

Because of noisy forum writing and limited training data, the above bag-of-word model used in naive Bayes classifier may suffer from data sparsity issues. We thus propose to use latent topic modeling to alleviate this problem. Latent Dirichlet Allocation (LDA) is a generative model based on latent topics. The major difference between LDA and previous methods such as probabilistic Latent Semantic Analysis (pLSA) is that LDA can efficiently infer topic composition of new documents, regardless of the training data size (Blei et al., 2001). This makes it ideal for efficiently reducing the dimension of incoming documents.

In an online forum, words contained in threads tend to be very noisy. Irregular words, such as abbreviation, misspelling and synonyms, are very common in an online environment. From our experiments, we observe that LDA seems to be quite robust to these phenomena and able to capture word relationship semantically. To illustrate the words inside latent topics in the LDA model inferred from online forums, we show in Table 2 the top words in 3 out of 20 latent topics inferred from "Ubuntu" forum according to its multinomial distribution. We can see that variations of the same words are grouped into the same topic.

Since each post could be very short and LDA is generally known not to work well with short documents, we concatenated the content of posts inside each thread to form documents. In order to build a valid evaluation configuration, only posts before the first time the testing user participated are used for model fitting and inference.

Forum Name	Threads	Posts	Active Users	Part. @300	Filt. Threads @300
Ubuntu	185,747	940,230	1,700	464.72	4641.25
Fitness	27,250	529,201	2,808	613.15	3231.04
Wow Gaming	34,187	1,639,720	19,173	313.77	2264.46

Table 1: Data statistics after filtering.

Topic 1	Topic 2	Topic 3
lol'd	wine	email
lol.	Wine	mail
imo.	game	Thunderbird
,'	fixme	evolution
-,-	stub	send
lulz.	not	emails
lmao.	WINE	gmail
rofl.	play	postfix

Table 2: Example of LDA topics that capture words with different variations.

After model fitting for LDA, the topic distributions on new threads can be inferred using the model. Compared to the original bag-of-word feature vector, the topic distribution vector is not only more robust against noise, but also closer to human interpretation of words. For example in topic 3 in Table 2, people who care about "Thunderbird", an email client, are also very likely to show interest in "postfix", which is a Linux email service. These closely related words, however, might not be captured using the bag-of-word model since that would require the exact words to appear in the training set.

In order to take advantage of the topic level information while not losing the "fine-grained" word level feature, we use the topic distribution as additional features in combination with the bag-of-word features. To tune the contribution of topic level features in classifiers like Naive Bayes classifiers, we normalize the topic level feature to a length of $L_t = \gamma|f|$ and bag-of-word feature to $L_w = (1-\gamma)|f|$. γ is a tuning parameter from 0 to 1 that determines the proportion of the topic information used in the features. $|f|$ is from the original bag-of-word feature vector. The final feature vector for each thread can be represented as:

$$F = L_w w_1, ..., L_w w_k \cup L_t\theta_1, ..., L_t\theta_T \quad (3)$$

where $\theta_1, ..., \theta_t$ is the multinomial distribution of topics for the thread.

4.2 Collaborative Filtering

Collaborative filtering techniques make prediction using information from similar users. It has advantages over content-based filtering in that it can correctly predict items that are vastly different in content but similar in concepts indicated by users' participation.

In some previous work, clustering methods were used to partition users into several groups, Then, predictions were made using information from users in the same group. However, in the case of thread recommendation, we found that users' interest does not form clean clusters. Figure 2 shows the mutual information between users after doing an average-link clustering on their pairwise mutual information. In a clean clustering, intra-cluster mutual information should be high, while inter-cluster mutual information is very low. If so, we would expect that the figure shows clear rectangles along the diagonal. Unfortunately, from this figure it appears that users far away in the hierarchy tree still have a lot of common thread participation. Here, we propose to model user similarity based on latent user groups.

4.2.1 Latent User Groups

In this paper, we model users' participation inside threads as an LDA generative model. We model each user group as a multinomial distribution. Users inside each group are assumed to have common interests in certain topic(s). A thread in an online forum typically contains several such topics. We could model a user's participation in a thread as a mixture of several different user groups. Since one thread typically attracts a subset of user groups, it is reasonable to add a Dirichlet prior on the user group mixture.

The generative process is the same as the LDA used above for topic modeling, except now users

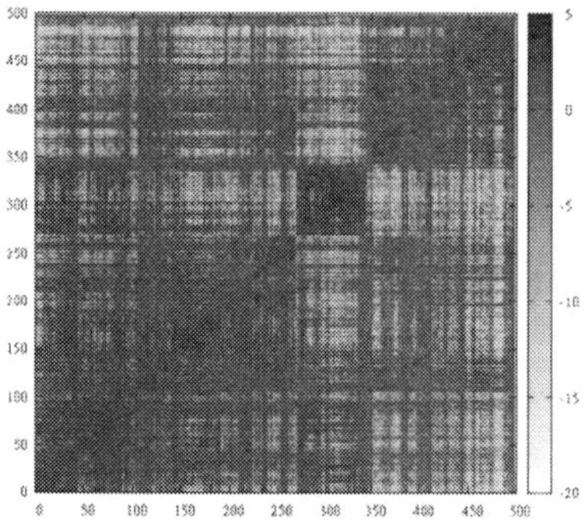

Figure 2: Mutual information between users in Average Link Hierarchical clustering.

are 'words' and user groups are 'topics'. Using LDA to model user participation can be viewed as soft-clustering of users in a sense that one user could appear in multiple groups at the same time. The generative process for participating users is as follows.

1. Choose $\theta \sim Dir(\alpha)$
2. For each of N participating users, u_n:
   (a) Choose a group $z_n \sim Multinomial(\theta)$
   (b) Choose a user $u_n \sim p(u_n|z_n)$

One thing worth noting is that in LDA model a document is assumed to consist of many words. In the case of modeling user participation, a thread typically has far fewer users than words inside a document. This could potentially cause problem during variable estimation and inference. However, we show that this approach actually works well in practice (experimental results in Section 5).

4.2.2 Using Latent User Groups for Prediction

For an incoming new thread, first the latent group distribution is inferred using collapsed Gibbs Sampling (Griffiths and Steyvers, 2004). The posterior probability of a user u_i participating in thread j given the user group distribution is as follows.

$$P(u_i|\theta_j, \phi) = \sum_{k \in T} P(u_i|\phi_k)P(k|\theta_j) \quad (4)$$

In the equation, ϕ_k is the multinomial distribution of users in group k, T is the number of latent user groups, and θ_j is the group composition in thread j after inference using the training data. In general, the probability of user u_i appearing in thread j is proportional to the membership probabilities of this user in the groups that compose the participating users.

4.3 Hybrid System

Up to this point we have two separate systems that can generate ranked recommendation lists based on different factors of threads. In order to generate the final ranked list, we give each item a score according to the ranked lists from the two systems. Then the two scores are linearly interpolated using a tuning parameter λ as shown in Equation 5. The final ranked list is generated accordingly.

$$\begin{aligned} C_i = &(1-\lambda)Score_{content} \\ &+ \lambda Score_{collaborative} \end{aligned} \quad (5)$$

We propose several different rescoring methods to generate the scores in the above formula for the two individual systems.

- **Posterior:** The posterior probabilities of each item from the two systems are used directly as the score.

$$Score_{dir} = p(c_{like}|item_i) \quad (6)$$

  This way the confidence of "how likely" an item is interesting is preserved. However, the downside is that the two different systems have different calibration on its posterior probability, which could be problematic when directly adding them together.

- **Linear rescore:** To counter the problem associated with posterior probability calibration, we use linear rescoring based on the ranked list:

$$Score_{lin} = 1 - \frac{pos_i}{N} \quad (7)$$

  In the formula, pos_i is the position of item i in the ranked list, and N is the total number of items being ranked. The resulting score is between 0 and 1, 1 being the first item on the list and 0 being the last.

- **Sigmoid rescore:** In a ranked list, usually items on the top and bottom of the list have higher confidence than those in the middle. That is to say more "emphasis" should be put on both ends of the list. Hence we use a sigmoid function on the $Score_{linear}$ to capture this.

$$Score_{sig} = \frac{1}{1 + e^{-l(Score_{lin} - 0.5)}} \quad (8)$$

A sigmoid function is relatively flat on both ends while being steep in the middle. In the equation, l is a tuning parameter that decides how "flat" the score of both ends of the list is going to be. Determining the best value for l is not a trivial problem. Here we empirically assign $l = 10$.

5 Experiment and Evaluation

In this section, we evaluate our approach empirically on the three forum data sets described in Section 3. We pick the top 300 most active users from each forum for the evaluation. Among the 300 users, 100 of them are randomly selected as the development set for parameter tuning, while the rest is test set. All the data sets are filtered using an online filter as previously described, with a window size of 10 threads.

Threads are tokenized into words and filtered using a simple English stop word list. All words are then ordered by their occurrences multiplied by their inverse document frequencies (IDF).

$$idf_w = log \frac{|D|}{|\{d : w \in d\}|} \quad (9)$$

The top 4,000 words from this list are then used to form the vocabulary.

We used standard mean average precision (MAP) as the evaluation metric. This standard information retrieval evaluation metric measures the quality of the returned rank lists from a system. Entries higher in the rank are more accurate than lower ones. For an interesting thread recommendation system, it is preferable to provide a short and high-quality list of recommendation; therefore, instead of reporting full-range MAP, we report MAP on top 10 relevant threads (MAP@10). The reason why we picked 10 as the number of relevant document for MAP evaluation is that users might not have time to read too many posts, even if they are relevant.

During evaluation, a 3-fold cross-validation is performed for each user in the test set. In each fold, MAP@10 score is calculated from the ranked list generated by the system. Then the average from all the folds and all the users is computed as the final result.

To make a proper evaluation configuration, for each user, only posts up to the first participation of the testing user are used for the test set.

5.1 Content-based Results

Here we evaluate the performance of interest thread prediction using only features from text. First we use the ranking model with latent topic information only on the development set to determine an optimal number of topics. Empirically, we use hyper parameter $\beta = 0.1$ and $\alpha = 1/K$ (K is the number of topics). We use the performance of content-based recommendation directly to determine the optimal topic number K. We varied the latent topic number K from 10 to 100, and found that the best performance was achieved using 30 topics in all three forums. Hence we use $K = 30$ for content based recommendation unless otherwise specified.

Next, we show how topic information can help content-based recommendation achieve better results. We tune the parameter γ described in Section 4.1.2 and show corresponding performances. We compare the performance using Naive Bayes classifier, before and after normalization. The MAP@10 results on the test set are shown in Figure 3 for three forums. When $\gamma = 0$, no latent topic information is used, and when $\gamma = 1$, latent topics are used without any word features.

When using Naive Bayes classifier without normalization, we find relatively larger performance gain from adding topic information for the γ values of close to 0. This phenomenon is probably because of the poor posterior probabilities of the Naive Bayes classifier, which are close to either 1 or 0.

For normalized Naive Bayes classifier, interpolating with latent topics based ranking yields performance improvement compared to word-based results consistently for the three forums. In "Wow Gaming" corpus, the optimal performance is achieved with a relatively high γ value (at around 0.5), and it is even higher for the "Fitness" forum.

This means that the system relies more on the latent topics information. This is because in these forums, casual conversation contains more irregular words, causing more severe data sparsity problem than others.

Between the two naive Bayes classifiers, we can see that using normalized probabilities outperforms the original one in "Wow Gaming" and "Ubuntu" forums. This observation is consistent with previous work (e.g., (Pavlov et al., 2004)). However, we found that in "Fitness Forum", the performance degrades with normalization. Further work is still needed to understand why this is the case.

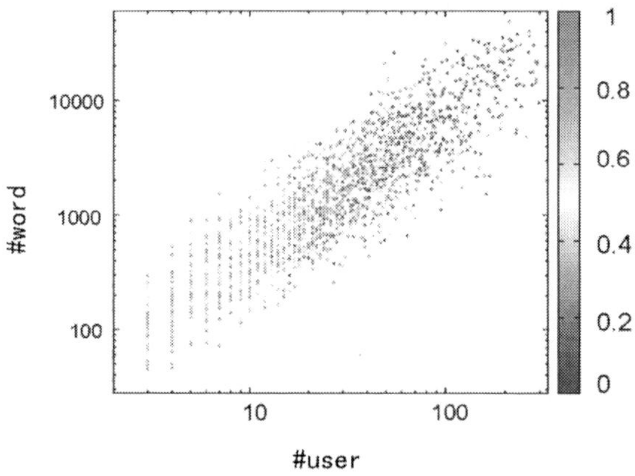

Figure 5: Position of items with different #users and #words in a ranked list. (red=0 being higher on the ranked list and green being lower)

5.2 Latent User Group Classification

In this section, collaborative filtering using latent user groups is evaluated. First, participating users from the training set are used to estimate an LDA model. Then, users participating in a thread are used to infer the topic distribution of the thread. Candidate threads are then sorted by the probability of a target user's participation according to Equation 4. Note that all the users in the forum are used to estimate the latent user groups, but only the top 300 active users are used in evaluation. Here, we vary the number of latent user groups G from 5 to 100. Hyper parameters were set empirically: $\alpha = 1/G, \beta = 0.1$.

Figure 4 shows the MAP@10 results using different numbers of latent groups for the three forums. We compare the performance using latent groups with a baseline using SVM ranking. In the baseline system, users' participation in a thread is used as a binary feature. LibSVM with radius based function (RBF) kernel is used to estimate the probability of a user's participation.

From the results, we find that ranking using latent groups information outperforms the baseline in almost all non-trivial cases. In the case of "Ubuntu" forum, the performance gain is less compared to other forums. We believe this is because in this technical support forum, the average user participation in threads is much less, thus making it hard to infer a reliable group distribution in a thread. In addition, the optimal number of user groups differs greatly between "Fitness" forum and "Wow Gaming" forum. We conjecture the reason behind this is that in the "Fitness" forum, users may be interested in a larger variety of topics and thus the user distribution in different topics is not very obvious. In contrast, people in the gaming forum are more specific to the topics they are interested in.

It is known that LDA tends to perform poorly when there are too few words/users. To have a general idea of how much user participation is "enough" for decent prediction, we show a graph (Figure 5) depicting the relationships among the number of users, the number of words, and the position of the positive instances in the ranked lists. In this graph, every dot is a positive thread instance in "Wow Gaming" forum. Red color shows that the positive thread is indeed getting higher ranks than others. We observe that threads with around 16 participants can already achieve a decent performance.

5.3 Hybrid System Performance

In this section, we evaluate the performance of the hybrid system output. Parameters used in each forum data set are the optimal parameters found in the previous sections. Here we show the effect of the tuning parameter λ (described in Section 4.3). Also, we compare three different scoring schemes used to generate the final ranked list. Performance of the hybrid system is shown in Table 3.

We can see that the combination of the two systems always outperforms any one model alone.

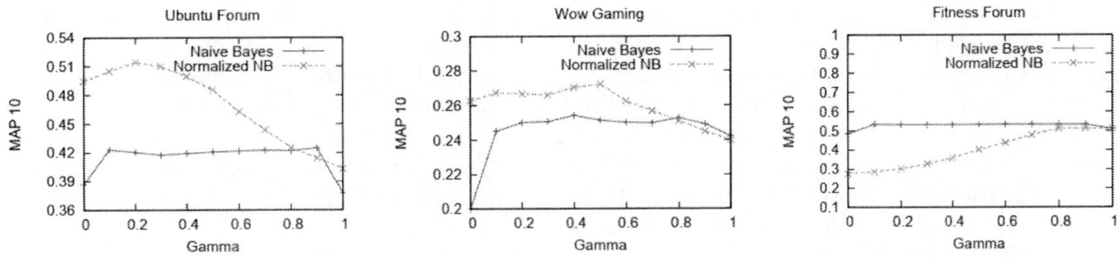

Figure 3: Content-based filtering results: MAP@10 vs. γ (contribution of topic-based features).

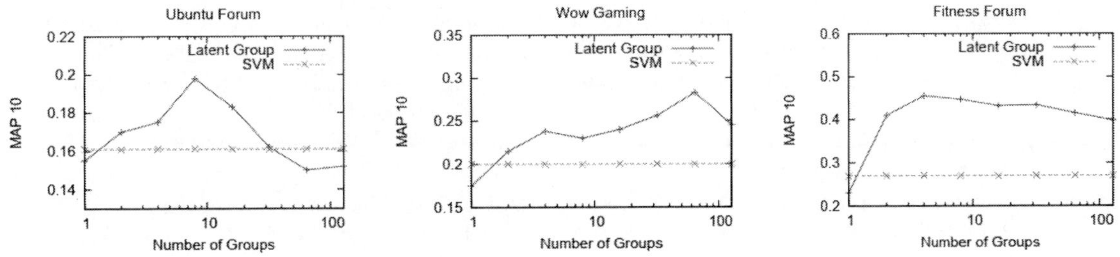

Figure 4: Collaborative filtering results: MAP@10 vs. user group number.

Forum	**Contribution Factor λ**		
	0.0	1.0	Optimal
Ubuntu	0.523	0.198	**0.534** ($\lambda = 0.9$)
Wow	0.278	0.283	**0.304** ($\lambda = 0.1$)
Fitness	0.545	0.457	**0.551** ($\lambda = 0.85$)

Table 3: Performance of the hybrid system with different λ values.

This is intuitive since the two models use different information sources. A MAP@10 score of 0.5 means that around half of the suggested results do have user participation. We think this is a good result considering that this is not a trivial task.

We also notice that based on the nature of different forums, the optimal λ value could be substantially different. For example, in "Wow gaming" forum where people participate in more threads, a higher λ value is observed which favors collaborative filtering score. In contrast, in "Ubuntu" forum, where people participate in far fewer threads, the content-based system is more reliable in thread prediction, hence a lower λ is used. This observation also shows that the hybrid system is more robust against differences among forums compared with single model systems.

6 Conclusion

In this paper, we proposed a new system that can intelligently recommend threads from online community according to a user's interest. The system uses both content-based filtering and collaborative-filtering techniques. In content-based filtering, we solve the problem of data sparsity in online content by smoothing using latent topic information. In collaborative filtering, we model users' participation in threads with latent groups under an LDA framework. The two systems compliment each other and their combination achieves better performance than individual ones. Our experiments across different forums demonstrate the robustness of our methods and the difference among forums. In the future work, we plan to explore how social information could help further refine a user's interest.

References

Gediminas Adomavicius and Alexander Tuzhilin. 2005. Toward the next generation of recommender systems: A survey of the state-of-the-art and possible extensions. *IEEE TRANSACTIONS ON KNOWLEDGE AND DATA ENGINEERING*, 17(6):734–749.

Marko Balabanovic and Yoav Shoham. 1997.

Fab: Content-based, collaborative recommendation. *Communications of the ACM*, 40:66–72.

Chumki Basu, Haym Hirsh, and William Cohen. 1998. Recommendation as classification: Using social and content-based information in recommendation. In *In Proceedings of the Fifteenth National Conference on Artificial Intelligence*, pages 714–720. AAAI Press.

Paul N. Bennett. 2000. Assessing the calibration of naive bayes' posterior estimates.

David Blei, Andrew Y. Ng, and Michael I. Jordan. 2001. Latent dirichlet allocation. *Journal of Machine Learning Research*, 3:2003.

John S. Breese, David Heckerman, and Carl Kadie. 1998. Empirical analysis of predictive algorithms for collaborative filtering. pages 43–52. Morgan Kaufmann.

Y H Chien and E I George, 1999. *A bayesian model for collaborative filtering*. Number 1.

Joaquin Delgado and Naohiro Ishii. 1999. Memory-based weighted-majority prediction for recommender systems.

Thomas L. Griffiths and Mark Steyvers. 2004. Finding scientific topics. *Proceedings of the National Academy of Sciences of the United States of America*, 101(Suppl 1):5228–5235, April.

Thomas Hofmann. 2003. Collaborative filtering via gaussian probabilistic latent semantic analysis. In *Proceedings of the 26th annual international ACM SIGIR conference on Research and development in informaion retrieval*, SIGIR '03, pages 259–266, New York, NY, USA. ACM.

Thomas Hofmann. 2004. Latent semantic models for collaborative filtering. *ACM Trans. Inf. Syst.*, 22(1):89–115.

Qing Li, Jia Wang, Yuanzhu Peter Chen, and Zhangxi Lin. 2010. User comments for news recommendation in forum-based social media. *Inf. Sci.*, 180:4929–4939, December.

Nick Littlestone. 1988. Learning quickly when irrelevant attributes abound: A new linear-threshold algorithm. In *Machine Learning*, pages 285–318.

Atsuyoshi Nakamura and Naoki Abe. 1998. Collaborative filtering using weighted majority prediction algorithms. In *Proceedings of the Fifteenth International Conference on Machine Learning*, ICML '98, pages 395–403, San Francisco, CA, USA. Morgan Kaufmann Publishers Inc.

Dmitry Pavlov, Ramnath Balasubramanyan, Byron Dom, Shyam Kapur, and Jignashu Parikh. 2004. Document preprocessing for naive bayes classification and clustering with mixture of multinomials. In *Proceedings of the tenth ACM SIGKDD international conference on Knowledge discovery and data mining*, KDD '04, pages 829–834, New York, NY, USA. ACM.

Michael Pazzani, Daniel Billsus, S. Michalski, and Janusz Wnek. 1997. Learning and revising user profiles: The identification of interesting web sites. In *Machine Learning*, pages 313–331.

Elaine Rich. 1979. User modeling via stereotypes. *Cognitive Science*, 3(4):329–354.

J. Rocchio, 1971. *Relevance Feedback in Information Retrieval*.

Gerard Salton and Christopher Buckley. 1988. Term-weighting approaches in automatic text retrieval. In *INFORMATION PROCESSING AND MANAGEMENT*, pages 513–523.

Badrul Sarwar, George Karypis, Joseph Konstan, and John Reidl. 2001. Item-based collaborative filtering recommendation algorithms. In *WWW '01: Proceedings of the 10th international conference on World Wide Web*, pages 285–295, New York, NY, USA. ACM.

Upendra Shardanand and Pattie Maes. 1995. Social information filtering: Algorithms for automating "word of mouth". In *CHI*, pages 210–217.

Lyle Ungar, Dean Foster, Ellen Andre, Star Wars, Fred Star Wars, Dean Star Wars, and Jason Hiver Whispers. 1998. Clustering methods for collaborative filtering. AAAI Press.

Hao Wu, Jiajun Bu, Chun Chen, Can Wang, Guang Qiu, Lijun Zhang, and Jianfeng Shen. 2010. Modeling dynamic multi-topic discussions in online forums. In *AAAI*.

Inferring Selectional Preferences from Part-Of-Speech N-grams

Hyeju Jang and Jack Mostow
Project LISTEN (www.cs.cmu.edu/~listen), School of Computer Science
Carnegie Mellon University
Pittsburgh, PA 15213, USA
hyejuj@cs.cmu.edu, mostow@cs.cmu.edu

Abstract

We present the PONG method to compute selectional preferences using part-of-speech (POS) N-grams. From a corpus labeled with grammatical dependencies, PONG learns the distribution of word relations for each POS N-gram. From the much larger but unlabeled Google N-grams corpus, PONG learns the distribution of POS N-grams for a given pair of words. We derive the probability that one word has a given grammatical relation to the other. PONG estimates this probability by combining both distributions, whether or not either word occurs in the labeled corpus. PONG achieves higher average precision on 16 relations than a state-of-the-art baseline in a pseudo-disambiguation task, but lower coverage and recall.

1 Introduction

Selectional preferences specify plausible fillers for the arguments of a predicate, e.g., *celebrate*. Can you celebrate a birthday? Sure. Can you celebrate a pencil? Arguably yes: *Today the Acme Pencil Factory celebrated its one-billionth pencil*. However, such a contrived example is unnatural because unlike *birthday*, *pencil* lacks a strong association with *celebrate*. How can we compute the degree to which *birthday* or *pencil* is a plausible and typical object of *celebrate*?

Formally, we are interested in computing the probability $\Pr(r \mid t, R)$, where (as Table 1 specifies), t is a target word such as *celebrate*, r is a word possibly related to it, such as *birthday* or *pencil*, and R is a possible relation between them, whether a semantic role such as the agent of an action, or a grammatical dependency such as the object of a verb. We call t the "target" because originally it referred to a vocabulary word targeted for instruction, and r its "relative."

Notation	Description
R	a relation between words
t	a target word
r, r'	possible relatives of t
g	a word N-gram
g_i and g_j	i^{th} and j^{th} words of g
p	the POS N-gram of g

Table 1: Notation used throughout this paper

Previous work on selectional preferences has used them primarily for natural language analytic tasks such as word sense disambiguation (Resnik, 1997), dependency parsing (Zhou et al., 2011), and semantic role labeling (Gildea and Jurafsky, 2002). However, selectional preferences can also apply to natural language generation tasks such as sentence generation and question generation. For generation tasks, choosing the right word to express a specified argument of a relation requires knowing its connotations – that is, its selectional preferences. Therefore, it is useful to know selectional preferences for many different relations. Such knowledge could have many uses. In education, they could help teach word connotations. In machine learning they could help computers learn languages. In machine translation, they could help generate more natural wording.

This paper introduces a method named PONG (for Part-Of-Speech N-Grams) to compute selectional preferences for many different relations by combining part-of-speech information and Google N-grams. PONG achieves higher precision on a pseudo-disambiguation task than the best previous model (Erk et al., 2010), but lower coverage.

The paper is organized as follows. Section 2 describes the relations for which we compute selectional preferences. Section 3 describes PONG. Section 4 evaluates PONG. Section 5 relates PONG to prior work. Section 6 concludes.

2 Relations Used

Selectional preferences characterize constraints on the arguments of predicates. Selectional preferences for semantic roles (such as agent and patient) are generally more informative than for grammatical dependencies (such as subject and object). For example, consider these semantically equivalent but grammatically distinct sentences:

Pat opened the door.

The door was opened by Pat.

In both sentences the agent of *opened*, namely *Pat*, must be capable of opening something – an informative constraint on *Pat*. In contrast, knowing that the grammatical subject of *opened* is *Pat* in the first sentence and *the door* in the second sentence tells us only that they are nouns.

Despite this limitation, selectional preferences for grammatical dependencies are still useful, for a number of reasons. First, in practice they approximate semantic role labels. For instance, typically the grammatical subject of *opened* is its agent. Second, grammatical dependencies can be extracted by parsers, which tend to be more accurate than current semantic role labelers. Third, the number of different grammatical dependencies is large enough to capture diverse relations, but not so large as to have sparse data for individual relations. Thus in this paper, we use grammatical dependencies as relations.

A parse tree determines the basic grammatical dependencies between the words in a sentence. For instance, in the parse of *Pat opened the door*, the verb *opened* has *Pat* as its subject and *door* as its object, and *door* has *the* as its determiner. Besides these basic dependencies, we use two additional types of dependencies.

Composing two basic dependencies yields a *collapsed dependency* (de Marneffe and Manning, 2008). For example, consider this sentence:

The airplane flies in the sky.

Here *sky* is the prepositional object of *in*, which is the head of a prepositional phrase attached to *flies*. Composing these two dependencies yields the collapsed dependency *prep_in* between *flies* and *sky*, which captures an important semantic relation between these two content words: *sky* is the location where *flies* occurs. Other function words yield different collapsed dependencies. For example, consider these two sentences:

The airplane flies over the ocean.

The airplane flies and lands.

Collapsed dependencies for the first sentence include *prep_over* between *flies* and *ocean*, which characterizes their relative vertical position, and *conj_and* between *flies* and *lands*, which links two actions that an airplane can perform. As these examples illustrate, collapsing dependencies involving prepositions and conjunctions can yield informative dependencies between content words.

Besides collapsed dependencies, PONG infers inverse dependencies. Inverse selectional preferences are selectional preferences of arguments for their predicates, such as a preference of a subject or object for its verb. They capture semantic regularities such as the set of verbs that an agent can perform, which tend to outnumber the possible agents for a verb (Erk et al., 2010).

3 Method

To compute selectional preferences, PONG combines information from a limited corpus labeled with the grammatical dependencies described in Section 2, and a much larger unlabeled corpus. The key idea is to abstract word sequences labeled with grammatical relations into POS N-grams, in order to learn a mapping from POS N-grams to those relations. For instance, PONG abstracts the parsed sentence *Pat opened the door* as NN VB DT NN, with the first and last NN as the subject and object of the VB. To estimate the distribution of POS N-grams containing particular target and relative words, PONG POS-tags Google N-grams (Franz and Brants, 2006).

Section 3.1 derives PONG's probabilistic model for combining information from labeled and unlabeled corpora. Section 3.2 and Section 3.3 describe how PONG estimates probabilities from each corpus. Section 3.4 discusses a sparseness problem revealed during probability estimation, and how we address it in PONG.

3.1 Probabilistic model

We quantify the selectional preference for a relative r to instantiate a relation R of a target t as the probability $\Pr(r \mid t, R)$, estimated as follows. By the definition of conditional probability:

$$\Pr(r \mid t,R) = \frac{\Pr(r,t,R)}{\Pr(t,R)}$$

We care only about the relative probability of different r for fixed t and R, so we rewrite it as:

$$\propto \Pr(r,t,R)$$

We use the chain rule:

$$= \Pr(R \mid r,t) \cdot \Pr(r \mid t) \cdot \Pr(t)$$

and notice that t is held constant:

$$\propto \Pr(R \mid r,t) \cdot \Pr(r \mid t)$$

We estimate the second factor as follows:

$$\Pr(r \mid t) = \frac{\Pr(t,r)}{\Pr(t)} = \frac{\text{freq}(t,r)}{\text{freq}(t)}$$

We calculate the denominator freq(t) as the number of N-grams in the Google N-gram corpus that contain t, and the numerator freq(t, r) as the number of N-grams containing both t and r.

To estimate the factor $\Pr(R \mid r, t)$ directly from a corpus of text labeled with grammatical relations, it would be trivial to count how often a word r bears relation R to target word t. However, the results would be limited to the words in the corpus, and many relation frequencies would be estimated sparsely or missing altogether; t or r might not even occur.

Instead, we abstract each word in the corpus as its part-of-speech (POS) label. Thus we abstract *The big boy ate meat* as DT JJ NN VB NN. We call this sequence of POS tags a POS N-gram. We use POS N-grams to predict word relations. For instance, we predict that in any word sequence with this POS N-gram, the JJ will modify (*amod*) the first NN, and the second NN will be the direct object (*dobj*) of the VB.

This prediction is not 100% reliable. For example, the initial 5-gram of *The big boy ate meat pie* has the same POS 5-gram as before. However, the *dobj* of its VB (*ate*) is not the second NN (*meat*), but the subsequent NN (*pie*). Thus POS N-grams predict word relations only in a probabilistic sense.

To transform $\Pr(R \mid r, t)$ into a form we can estimate, we first apply the definition of conditional probability:

$$\Pr(R \mid t,r) = \frac{\Pr(R,t,r)}{\Pr(t,r)}$$

To estimate the numerator $\Pr(R, t, r)$, we first marginalize over the POS N-gram p:

$$= \sum_p \frac{\Pr(R,t,r,p)}{\Pr(t,r)}$$

We expand the numerator using the chain rule:

$$= \sum_p \frac{\Pr(R \mid t,r,p) \cdot \Pr(p \mid t,r) \cdot \Pr(t,r)}{\Pr(t,r)}$$

Cancelling the common factor yields:

$$= \sum_p \Pr(R \mid p,t,r) \cdot \Pr(p \mid t,r)$$

We approximate the first term $\Pr(R \mid p, t, r)$ as $\Pr(R \mid p)$, based on the simplifying assumption that R is conditionally independent of t and r, given p. In other words, we assume that given a POS N-gram, the target and relative words t and r give no additional information about the probability of a relation. However, their respective positions i and j in the POS N-gram p matter, so we condition the probability on them:

$$\Pr(R \mid p,t,r) \approx \Pr(R \mid p,i,j)$$

Summing over their possible positions, we get

$$\Pr(R \mid r,t)$$

$$\approx \sum_p \sum_{i \neq j} \Pr(R \mid p,i,j) \cdot \Pr(p \mid t = g_i, r = g_j)$$

As Figure 1 shows, we estimate $\Pr(R \mid p, i, j)$ by abstracting the labeled corpus into POS N-grams. We estimate $\Pr(p \mid t = g_i, r = g_j)$ based on the frequency of partially lexicalized POS N-grams like DT JJ:*red* NN:*hat* VB NN among Google N-grams with t and r in the specified positions.

Sections 3.2 and 3.3 describe how we estimate $\Pr(R \mid p, i, j)$ and $\Pr(p \mid t = g_i, r = g_j)$, respectively. Note that PONG estimates relative rather than absolute probabilities. Therefore it cannot (and does not) compare them against a fixed threshold to make decisions about selectional preferences.

3.2 Mapping POS N-grams to relations

To estimate $\Pr(R \mid p, i, j)$, we use the Penn Treebank Wall Street Journal (WSJ) corpus, which is labeled with grammatical relations using the Stanford dependency parser (Klein and Manning, 2003).

To estimate the probability $\Pr(R \mid p, i, j)$ of a relation R between a target at position i and a relative at position j in a POS N-gram p, we compute what fraction of the word N-grams g with POS N-gram p have relation R between some target t and relative r at positions i and j:

$$\Pr(R \mid p, i, j) = \frac{\text{freq}(g \ s.t. \text{POS}(g) = p \wedge \text{relation}(g_i, g_j) = R)}{\text{freq}(g \ s.t. \text{POS}(g) = p \wedge \text{relation}(g_i, g_j))}$$

3.3 Estimating POS N-gram distributions

Given a target and relative, we need to estimate their distribution of POS N-grams and positions.

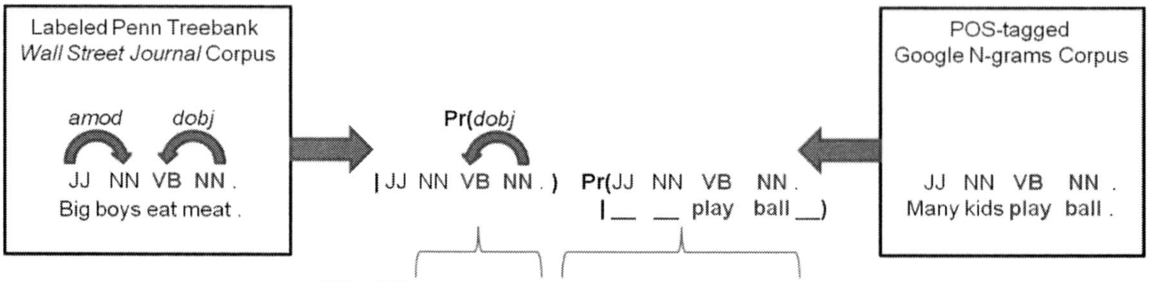

$$\Pr(R|r,t) = \sum_{p} \sum_{i \neq j} \Pr(R|p,i,j) \cdot \Pr(p|t = g_i, r = g_j)$$

Figure 1: Overview of PONG.
From the labeled corpus, PONG extracts abstract mappings from POS N-grams to relations.
From the unlabeled corpus, PONG estimates POS N-gram probability given a target and relative.

A labeled corpus is too sparse for this purpose, so we use the much larger unlabeled Google N-grams corpus (Franz and Brants, 2006).

The probability that an N-gram with target t at position i and relative r at position j will have the POS N-gram p is:

$$\Pr(p \mid t = g_i, r = g_j) = \frac{\text{freq}(g \ s.t. \text{POS}(g) = p, g_i = t, g_j = r))}{\text{freq}(g \ s.t. g_i = t \wedge g_j = r)}$$

To compute this ratio, we first use a well-indexed table to efficiently retrieve all N-grams with words t and r at the specified positions. We then obtain their POS N-grams from the Stanford POS tagger (Toutanova et al., 2003), and count how many of them have the POS N-gram p.

3.4 Reducing POS N-gram sparseness

We abstract word N-grams into POS N-grams to address the sparseness of the labeled corpus, but even the POS N-grams can be sparse. For n=5, the rarer ones occur too sparsely (if at all) in our labeled corpus to estimate their frequency.

To address this issue, we use a coarser POS tag set than the Penn Treebank POS tag set. As Table 2 shows, we merge tags for adjectives, nouns, adverbs, and verbs into four coarser tags.

Coarse	Original
ADJ	JJ, JJR, JJS
ADVERB	RB, RBR, RBS
NOUN	NN, NNS, NNP, NNPS
VERB	VB, VBD, VBG, VBN, VBP, VBZ

Table 2: Coarser POS tag set used in PONG

To gauge the impact of the coarser POS tags, we calculated $\Pr(r \mid t, R)$ for 76 test instances used in an earlier unpublished study by Liu Liu, a former Project LISTEN graduate student. Each instance consists of two randomly chosen words in the WSJ corpus labeled with a grammatical relation. Coarse POS tags increased coverage of this pilot set – that is, the fraction of instances for which PONG computes a probability – from 69% to 92%.

Using the universal tag set (Petrov et al., 2011) as an even coarser tag set is an interesting future direction, especially for other languages. Its smaller size (12 tags vs. our 23) should reduce data sparseness, but increase the risk of over-generalization.

4 Evaluation

To evaluate PONG, we use a standard pseudo-disambiguation task, detailed in Section 4.1. Section 4.2 describes our test set. Section 4.3 lists the metrics we evaluate on this test set. Section 4.4 describes the baselines we compare PONG against on these metrics, and Section 4.5 describes the relations we compare them on. Section 4.6 reports our results. Section 4.7 analyzes sources of error.

4.1 Evaluation task

The pseudo-disambiguation task (Gale et al., 1992; Schutze, 1992) is as follows: given a target word t, a relation R, a relative r, and a random distracter r', prefer either r or r', whichever is likelier to have relation R to word t.

This evaluation does not use a threshold: just prefer whichever word is likelier according to the model being evaluated. If the model assigns only one of the words a probability, prefer it, based on the assumption that the unknown probability of the other word is lower. If the model assigns the same probability to both words, or no probability to either word, do not prefer either word.

4.2 Test set

As a source of evaluation data, we used the British National Corpus (BNC). As a common test corpus for all the methods we evaluated, we selected one half of BNC by sorting filenames alphabetically and using the odd-numbered files. We used the other half of BNC as a training corpus for the baseline methods we compared PONG to.

A test set for the pseudo-disambiguation task task consists of tuples of the form (*R, t, r, r'*). To construct a test set, we adapted the process used by Rooth et al. (1999) and Erk et al. (2010).

First, we chose 100 (*R, t*) pairs for each relation *R* at random from the test corpus. Rooth et al. (1999) and Erk et al. (2010) chose such pairs from a training corpus to ensure that it contained the target *t*. In contrast, choosing pairs from an unseen test corpus includes target words whether or not they occur in the training corpus.

To obtain a sample stratified by frequency, rather than skewed heavily toward high-frequency pairs, Erk et al. (2010) drew (*R, t*) pairs from each of five frequency bands in the entire British National Corpus (BNC): 50-100 occurrences; 101-200; 201-500; 500-1000; and more than 1000. However, we use only half of BNC as our test corpus, so to obtain a comparable test set, we drew 20 (*R, t*) pairs from each of the corresponding frequency bands in that half: 26-50 occurrences; 51-100; 101-250; 251-500; and more than 500.

For each chosen (*R, t*) pair, we drew a separate (*R, t, r*) triple from each of six frequency bands: 1-25 occurrences; 26-50; 51-100; 101-250; 251-500; and more than 500. We necessarily omitted frequency bands that contained no such triples. We filtered out triples where *r* did not have the most frequent part of speech for the relation *R*. For example, this filter would exclude the triple (*dobj, celebrate, the*) because a direct object is most frequently a noun, but *the* is a determiner.

Then, like Erk et al. (2010), we paired the relative *r* in each (*R, t, r*) triple with a distracter *r'* with the same (most frequent) part of speech as the relative *r*, yielding the test tuple (*R, t, r, r'*). Rooth et al. (1999) restricted distracter candidates to words with between 30 and 3,000 occurrences in BNC; accordingly, we chose only distracters with between 15 and 1,500 occurrences in our test corpus. We selected *r'* from these candidates randomly, with probability proportional to their frequency in the test corpus. Like Rooth et al. (1999), we excluded as distracters any actual relatives, i.e. candidates *r'* where the test corpus contained the triple (*R, t, r'*). Table 3 shows the resulting number of (*R, t, r, r'*) test tuples for each relation.

Relation R	# tuples for R	# tuples for R^T
advmod	121	131
amod	162	128
conj_and	155	151
dobj	145	167
nn	173	158
nsubj	97	124
prep_of	144	153
xcomp	139	140

Table 3: Test set size for each relation

4.3 Metrics

We report four evaluation metrics: precision, coverage, recall, and F-score. Precision (called "accuracy" in some papers on selectional preferences) is the percentage of all covered tuples where the original relative *r* is preferred. Coverage is the percentage of tuples for which the model prefers *r* to *r'* or vice versa. Recall is the percentage of all tuples where the original relative is preferred, i.e., precision times coverage. F-score is the harmonic mean of precision and recall.

4.4 Baselines

We compare PONG to two baseline methods.

EPP is a state-of-the-art model for which Erk et al. (2010) reported better performance than both Resnik's (1996) WordNet model and Rooth's (1999) EM clustering model. EPP computes selectional preferences using distributional similarity, based on the assumption that relatives are likely to appear in the same contexts as relatives seen in the training corpus. EPP computes the similarity of a potential relative's vector space representation to relatives in the training corpus.

EPP has various options for its vector space representation, similarity measure, weighting scheme, generalization space, and whether to use PCA. In re-implementing EPP, we chose the options that performed best according to Erk et al. (2010), with one exception. To save work, we chose not to use PCA, which Erk et al. (2010) described as performing only slightly better in the dependency-based space.

Relation	Target	Relative	Description
advmod	verb	adverb	Adverbial modifier
amod	noun	adjective	Adjective modifier
conj_and	noun	noun	Conjunction with "*and*"
dobj	verb	noun	Direct object
nn	noun	noun	Noun compound modifier
nsubj	verb	noun	Nominal subject
prep_of	noun	noun	Prepositional modifier
xcomp	verb	verb	Open clausal complement

Table 4: Relations tested in the pseudo-disambiguation experiment.
Relation names and descriptions are from de Marneffe and Manning (2008) except for *prep_of*.
Target and relative POS are the most frequent POS pairs for the relations in our labeled WSJ corpus.

Relation	Precision (%)			Coverage (%)			Recall (%)			F-score (%)		
	PONG	EPP	DEP	PONG	EPP	DEP	PONG	EPP	DEP	PONG	EPP	DEP
advmod	78.7	-	98.6	72.1	-	69.2	56.7	-	68.3	65.9	-	80.7
advmod^T	89.0	71.0	97.4	69.5	100	59.5	61.8	71.0	58.0	73.0	71.0	72.7
amod	78.8	-	99.0	90.1	-	61.1	71.0	-	60.5	74.7	-	75.1
amod^T	84.1	74.0	97.3	83.6	99.2	57.0	70.3	73.4	55.5	76.6	73.7	70.6
conj_and	77.2	74.2	100	73.6	100	52.3	56.8	74.2	52.3	65.4	74.2	68.6
conj_and^T	80.5	70.2	97.3	74.8	100	49.7	60.3	70.2	48.3	68.9	70.2	64.6
dobj	87.2	80.0	97.7	80.7	100	60.0	70.3	80.0	58.6	77.9	80.0	73.3
dobj^T	89.6	80.2	98.1	92.2	100	64.1	82.6	80.2	62.9	86.0	80.2	76.6
nn	86.7	73.8	97.2	95.3	99.4	63.0	82.7	73.4	61.3	84.6	73.6	75.2
nn^T	83.8	79.7	99.0	93.7	100	60.8	78.5	79.7	60.1	81.0	79.7	74.8
nsubj	76.1	77.3	100	69.1	100	42.3	52.6	77.3	42.3	62.2	77.3	59.4
nsubj^T	78.5	66.9	95.0	86.3	100	48.4	67.7	66.9	46.0	72.7	66.9	62.0
prep_of	88.4	77.8	98.4	84.0	100	44.4	74.3	77.8	43.8	80.3	77.8	60.6
prep_of^T	79.2	76.5	97.4	81.7	100	50.3	64.7	76.5	49.0	71.2	76.5	65.2
xcomp	84.0	61.9	95.3	85.6	100	61.2	71.9	61.9	58.3	77.5	61.9	72.3
xcomp^T	86.4	78.6	98.9	89.3	100	63.6	77.1	78.6	62.9	81.5	78.6	76.9
average	**83.0**	**74.4**	**97.9**	**82.6**	**99.9**	**56.7**	**68.7**	**74.4**	**55.5**	**75.0**	**74.4**	**70.5**

Table 5: Coverage, Precision, Recall, and F-score for various relations; R^T is the inverse of relation R.
PONG uses POS N-grams, EPP uses distributional similarity, and DEP uses dependency parses.

To score a potential relative r_0, EPP uses this formula:

$$Selpref_{R,t}(r_0) = \sum_{r \in Seenargs(R,t)} \frac{wt_{R,t}(r)}{Z_{R,t}} \cdot sim(r_0, r)$$

Here $sim(r_0, r)$ is the nGCM similarity defined below between vector space representations of r_0 and a relative r seen in the training data:

$$sim_{nGCM}(a, a') = \exp\left(-\sqrt{\sum_{i=1}^{n}\left(\frac{a_{b_i}}{\|\vec{a}\|} - \frac{a'_{b_i}}{\|\vec{a'}\|}\right)^2}\right)$$

$$\text{where } \|\vec{a}\| = \sqrt{\sum_{i=1}^{n} a_{b_i}^2}$$

The weight function $wt_{r,t}(a)$ is analogous to inverse document frequency in Information Retrieval.

DEP, our second baseline method, runs the Stanford dependency parser to label the training corpus with grammatical relations, and uses their frequencies to predict selectional preferences. To do the pseudo-disambiguation task, DEP compares the frequencies of (R, t, r) and (R, t, r').

4.5 Relations tested

To test PONG, EPP, and DEP, we chose the most frequent eight relations between content words in the WSJ corpus, which occur over 10,000 times and are described in Table 4. We also tested their inverse relations. However, EPP does not compute selectional preferences for adjective and adverb as relatives. For this reason, we did not test EPP on *advmod* and *amod* relations with adverbs and adjectives as relatives.

4.6 Experimental results

Table 5 displays results for all 16 relations. To compute statistical significance conservatively in comparing methods, we used paired t-tests with N = 16 relations.

PONG's precision was significantly better than EPP ($p<0.001$) but worse than DEP ($p<0.0001$). Still, PONG's high precision validates its underlying assumption that POS N-grams strongly predict grammatical dependencies.

On coverage and recall, EPP beat PONG, which beat DEP ($p<0.0001$). PONG's F-score was higher, but not significantly, than EPP's ($p>0.5$) or DEP's ($p>0.02$).

4.7 Error analysis

In the pseudo-disambiguation task of choosing which of two words is related to a target, PONG makes errors of coverage (preferring neither word) and precision (preferring the wrong word).

Coverage errors, which occurred 17.4% of the time on average, arose only when PONG failed to estimate a probability for either word. PONG fails to score a potential relative r of a target t with a specified relation R if the labeled corpus has no POS N-grams that (a) map to R, (b) contain the POS of t and r, and (c) match Google word N-grams with t and r at those positions. Every relation has at least one POS N-gram that maps to it, so condition (a) never fails. PONG uses the most frequent POS of t and r, and we believe that condition (b) never fails. However, condition (c) can and does fail when t and r do not co-occur in any Google N-grams, at least that match a POS N-gram that can map to relation R. For example, *oversee* and *diet* do not co-occur in any Google N-grams, so PONG cannot score *diet* as a potential *dobj* of *oversee*.

Precision errors, which occur 17% of the time on average, arose when (a) PONG scored the distracter but failed to score the true relative, or (b) scored them both but preferred the distracter. Case (a) accounted for 44.62% of the errors on the covered test tuples.

One likely cause of errors in case (b) is over-generalization when PONG abstracts a word N-gram labeled with a relation by mapping its POS N-gram to that relation. In particular, the coarse POS tag set may discard too much information. Another likely cause of errors is probabilities estimated poorly due to sparse data. The probability of a relation for a POS N-gram rare in the training corpus is likely to be inaccurate. So is the probability of a POS N-gram for rare co-occurrences of a target and relative in Google word N-grams. Using a smaller tag set may reduce the sparse data problem but increase the risk of over-generalization.

5 Relation to Prior Work

In predicting selectional preferences, a key issue is generalization. Our DEP baseline simply counts co-occurrences of target and relative words in a corpus to predict selectional preferences, but only for words seen in the corpus. Prior work, summarized in
Table 6, has therefore tried to infer the similarity of unseen relatives to seen relatives. To illustrate, consider the problem of inducing that the direct objects of *celebrate* tend to be days or events.

Resnik (1996) combined WordNet with a labeled corpus to model the probability that relatives of a predicate belong to a particular conceptual class. This method could notice, for example, that the direct objects of *celebrate* tend to belong to the conceptual class *event*. Thus it could prefer *anniversary* or *occasion* as the object of *celebrate* even if unseen in its training corpus. However, this method depends strongly on the WordNet taxonomy.

Rather than use linguistic resources such as WordNet, Rooth et al. (1999) and Wald et al. (2008) induced semantically annotated subcategorization frames from unlabeled corpora. They modeled semantic classes as hidden variables, which they estimated using EM-based clustering. Ritter (2010) computed selectional preferences by using unsupervised topic models such as LinkLDA, which infers semantic classes of words automatically instead of requiring a pre-defined set of classes as input.

The contexts in which a linguistic unit occurs provide information about its meaning. Erk (2007) and Erk et al. (2010) modeled the contexts of a word as the distribution of words that co-occur with it. They calculated the semantic similarity of two words as the similarity of their context distributions according to various measures. Erk et al. (2010) reported the state-of-the-art method we used as our EPP baseline.

In contrast to prior work that explored various solutions to the generalization problem, we don't so much solve this problem as circumvent it. Instead of generalizing from a training corpus directly to unseen words, PONG abstracts a word N-gram to a POS N-gram and maps it to the relations that the word N-gram is labeled with.

Reference	Relation to target	Lexical resource	Primary corpus (labeled) & information used	Generalization corpus (unlabeled) & information used	Method
Resnik, 1996	Verb-object Verb-subject Adjective-noun Modifier-head Head-modifier	Senses in WordNet noun taxonomy	Target, relative, and relation in a parsed, partially sense-tagged corpus (Brown corpus)	none	Information theoretic model
Rooth et al., 1999	Verb-object Verb-subject	none	Target, relative, and relation in a parsed corpus (parsed BNC)	none	EM-based clustering
Ritter, 2010	Verb-subject Verb-object Subject-verb-object	none	Subject-verb-object tuples from 500 million web-pages	none	LDA model
Erk, 2007	Predicate and Semantic roles	none	Target, relative, and relation in a semantic role labeled corpus (FrameNet)	Words and their relations in a parsed corpus (BNC)	Similarity model based on word co-occurrence
Erk et al., 2010	SYN option: Verb-subject Verb-object, and their inverse relations SEM option: verb and semantic roles that have nouns as their headword in a primary corpus, and their inverse relations	none	Target, relative, and relation in SYN option: a parsed corpus (parsed BNC) SEM option: a semantic role labeled corpus (FrameNet)	Two options: WORDSPACE: an unlabeled corpus (BNC) DEPSPACE: Words and their subject and object relations in a parsed corpus (parsed BNC)	Similarity model using vector space representation of words
Zhou et al., 2011	Any (relations not distinguished)	none	Counts of words in Web or Google N-gram	none	PMI (Pointwise Mutual Information)
This paper	All grammatical dependencies in a parsed corpus, and their inverse relations	none	POS N-gram distribution for relations in parsed WSJ corpus	POS N-gram distribution for target and relative in Google N-gram	Combine both POS N-gram distributions

Table 6: Comparison with prior methods to compute selectional preferences

To compute selectional preferences, whether the words are in the training corpus or not, PONG applies these abstract mappings to word N-grams in the much larger Google N-grams corpus.

Some prior work on selectional preferences has used POS N-grams and a large unlabeled corpus. The most closely related work we found was by Gormley et al. (2011). They used patterns in POS N-grams to generate test data for their selectional preferences model, but not to infer preferences. Zhou et al. (2011) identified selectional preferences of one word for another by using Pointwise Mutual Information (PMI) (Fano, 1961) to check whether they co-occur more frequently in a large corpus than predicted by their unigram frequencies. However, their method did not distinguish among different relations.

6 Conclusion

This paper describes, derives, and evaluates PONG, a novel probabilistic model of selectional preferences. PONG uses a labeled corpus to map POS N-grams to grammatical relations. It combines this mapping with probabilities estimated from a much larger POS-tagged but unlabeled Google N-grams corpus.

We tested PONG on the eight most common relations in the WSJ corpus, and their inverses – more relations than evaluated in prior work. Compared to the state-of-the-art EPP baseline (Erk et al., 2010), PONG averaged higher precision but lower coverage and recall. Compared to the DEP baseline, PONG averaged lower precision but higher coverage and recall. All these differences were substantial ($p < 0.001$). Compared to both baselines, PONG's average F-score was higher, though not significantly.

Some directions for future work include: First, improve PONG by incorporating models of lexical similarity explored in prior work. Second, use the universal tag set to extend PONG to other languages, or to perform better in English. Third, in place of grammatical relations, use rich, diverse semantic roles, while avoiding sparsity. Finally, use selectional preferences to teach word connotations by using various relations to generate example sentences or useful questions.

Acknowledgments

The research reported here was supported by the Institute of Education Sciences, U.S. Department of Education, through Grant R305A080157. The opinions expressed are those of the authors and do not necessarily represent the views of the Institute or the U.S. Department of Education. We thank the helpful reviewers and Katrin Erk for her generous assistance.

References

de Marneffe, M.-C. and Manning, C.D. 2008. Stanford Typed Dependencies Manual. http://nlp.stanford.edu/software/dependencies_manual.pdf, Stanford University, Stanford, CA.

Erk, K. 2007. A Simple, Similarity-Based Model for Selectional Preferences. In Proceedings of the 45th Annual Meeting of the Association of Computational Linguistics, Prague, Czech Republic, June, 2007, 216-223.

Erk, K., Padó, S. and Padó, U. 2010. A Flexible, Corpus-Driven Model of Regular and Inverse Selectional Preferences. Computational Linguistics 36(4), 723-763.

Fano, R. 1961. Transmission O F Information: A Statistical Theory of Communications. MIT Press, Cambridge, MA.

Franz, A. and Brants, T. 2006. All Our N-Gram Are Belong to You.

Gale, W.A., Church, K.W. and Yarowsky, D. 1992. Work on Statistical Methods for Word Sense Disambiguation. In Proceedings of the AAAI Fall Symposium on Probabilistic Approaches to Natural Language, Cambridge, MA, October 23–25, 1992, 54-60.

Gildea, D. and Jurafsky, D. 2002. Automatic Labeling of Semantic Roles. Computational Linguistics 28(3), 245-288.

Gormley, M.R., Dredze, M., Durme, B.V. and Eisner, J. 2011. Shared Components Topic Models with Application to Selectional Preference, NIPS Workshop on Learning Semantics Sierra Nevada, Spain.

im Walde, S.S., Hying, C., Scheible, C. and Schmid, H. 2008. Combining Em Training and the Mdl Principle for an Automatic Verb Classification Incorporating Selectional Preferences. In Proceedings of the 46th Annual Meeting of the Association for Computational Linguistics, Columbus, OH, 2008, 496-504.

Klein, D. and Manning, C.D. 2003. Accurate Unlexicalized Parsing. In Proceedings of the 41st Annual Meeting of the Association for Computational Linguistics, Sapporo, Japan, July 7-12, 2003, E.W. HINRICHS and D. ROTH, Eds.

Petrov, S., Das, D. and McDonald, R.T. 2011. A Universal Part-of-Speech Tagset. ArXiv 1104.2086.

Resnik, P. 1996. Selectional Constraints: An Information-Theoretic Model and Its Computational Realization. Cognition 61, 127-159.

Resnik, P. 1997. Selectional Preference and Sense Disambiguation. In ACL SIGLEX Workshop on

Tagging Text with Lexical Semantics: Why, What, and How, Washington, DC, April 4-5, 1997, 52-57.

Ritter, A., Mausam and Etzioni, O. 2010. A Latent Dirichlet Allocation Method for Selectional Preferences. In Proceedings of the 48th Annual Meeting of the Association for Computational Linguistics, Uppsala, Sweden, 2010, 424-434.

Rooth, M., Riezler, S., Prescher, D., Carroll, G. and Beil, F. 1999. Inducing a Semantically Annotated Lexicon Via Em-Based Clustering. In Proceedings of the 37th Annual Meeting of the Association for Computational Linguistics on Computational Linguistics, College Park, MD, 1999, Association for Computational Linguistics, 104-111.

Schutze, H. 1992. Context Space. In Proceedings of the AAAI Fall Symposium on Intelligent Probabilistic Approaches to Natural Language, Cambridge, MA, 1992, 113-120.

Toutanova, K., Klein, D., Manning, C. and Singer, Y. 2003. Feature-Rich Part-of-Speech Tagging with a Cyclic Dependency Network. In Proceedings of the Human Language Technology Conference and Annual Meeting of the North American Chapter of the Association for Computational Linguistics (HLT-NAACL), Edmonton, Canada, 2003, 252–259.

Zhou, G., Zhao, J., Liu, K. and Cai, L. 2011. Exploiting Web-Derived Selectional Preference to Improve Statistical Dependency Parsing. In Proceedings of the 49th Annual Meeting of the Association for Computational Linguistics, Portland, OR, 2011, 1556–1565.

WebCAGe – A Web-Harvested Corpus Annotated with GermaNet Senses

Verena Henrich, Erhard Hinrichs, and Tatiana Vodolazova
University of Tübingen
Department of Linguistics
{firstname.lastname}@uni-tuebingen.de

Abstract

This paper describes an automatic method for creating a domain-independent sense-annotated corpus harvested from the web. As a proof of concept, this method has been applied to German, a language for which sense-annotated corpora are still in short supply. The sense inventory is taken from the German wordnet GermaNet. The web-harvesting relies on an existing mapping of GermaNet to the German version of the web-based dictionary Wiktionary. The data obtained by this method constitute WebCAGe (short for: *Web-Harvested Corpus Annotated with GermaNet Senses*), a resource which currently represents the largest sense-annotated corpus available for German. While the present paper focuses on one particular language, the method as such is language-independent.

1 Motivation

The availability of large sense-annotated corpora is a necessary prerequisite for any supervised and many semi-supervised approaches to word sense disambiguation (WSD). There has been steady progress in the development and in the performance of WSD algorithms for languages such as English for which hand-crafted sense-annotated corpora have been available (Agirre et al., 2007; Erk and Strapparava, 2012; Mihalcea et al., 2004), while WSD research for languages that lack these corpora has lagged behind considerably or has been impossible altogether.

Thus far, sense-annotated corpora have typically been constructed manually, making the creation of such resources expensive and the compilation of larger data sets difficult, if not completely infeasible. It is therefore timely and appropriate to explore alternatives to manual annotation and to investigate automatic means of creating sense-annotated corpora. Ideally, any automatic method should satisfy the following criteria:

(1) The method used should be language independent and should be applicable to as many languages as possible for which the necessary input resources are available.

(2) The quality of the automatically generated data should be extremely high so as to be usable as is or with minimal amount of manual post-correction.

(3) The resulting sense-annotated materials (i) should be non-trivial in size and should be dynamically expandable, (ii) should not be restricted to a narrow subject domain, but be as domain-independent as possible, and (iii) should be freely available for other researchers.

The method presented below satisfies all of the above criteria and relies on the following resources as input: (i) a sense inventory and (ii) a mapping between the sense inventory in question and a web-based resource such as Wiktionary[1] or

[1] http://www.wiktionary.org/

Wikipedia[2].

As a proof of concept, this automatic method has been applied to German, a language for which sense-annotated corpora are still in short supply and fail to satisfy most if not all of the criteria under (3) above. While the present paper focuses on one particular language, the method as such is language-independent. In the case of German, the sense inventory is taken from the German wordnet GermaNet[3] (Henrich and Hinrichs, 2010; Kunze and Lemnitzer, 2002). The web-harvesting relies on an existing mapping of GermaNet to the German version of the web-based dictionary Wiktionary. This mapping is described in Henrich et al. (2011). The resulting resource consists of a web-harvested corpus WebCAGe (short for: *Web-Harvested Corpus Annotated with GermaNet Senses*), which is freely available at: http://www.sfs.uni-tuebingen.de/en/webcage.shtml

The remainder of this paper is structured as follows: Section 2 provides a brief overview of the resources GermaNet and Wiktionary. Section 3 introduces the mapping of GermaNet to Wiktionary and how this mapping can be used to automatically harvest sense-annotated materials from the web. The algorithm for identifying the target words in the harvested texts is described in Section 4. In Section 5, the approach of automatically creating a web-harvested corpus annotated with GermaNet senses is evaluated and compared to existing sense-annotated corpora for German. Related work is discussed in Section 6, together with concluding remarks and an outlook on future work.

2 Resources

2.1 GermaNet

GermaNet (Henrich and Hinrichs, 2010; Kunze and Lemnitzer, 2002) is a lexical semantic network that is modeled after the Princeton WordNet for English (Fellbaum, 1998). It partitions the lexical space into a set of concepts that are interlinked by semantic relations. A semantic concept is represented as a *synset*, i.e., as a set of words whose individual members (referred to as *lexical units*) are taken to be (near) synonyms. Thus, a synset is a set-representation of the semantic relation of synonymy.

There are two types of semantic relations in GermaNet. *Conceptual relations* hold between two semantic concepts, i.e. synsets. They include relations such as hypernymy, part-whole relations, entailment, or causation. *Lexical relations* hold between two individual lexical units. Antonymy, a pair of opposites, is an example of a lexical relation.

GermaNet covers the three word categories of adjectives, nouns, and verbs, each of which is hierarchically structured in terms of the hypernymy relation of synsets. The development of GermaNet started in 1997, and is still in progress. GermaNet's version 6.0 (release of April 2011) contains 93407 lexical units, which are grouped into 69594 synsets.

2.2 Wiktionary

Wiktionary is a web-based dictionary that is available for many languages, including German. As is the case for its sister project Wikipedia, it is written collaboratively by volunteers and is freely available[4]. The dictionary provides information such as part-of-speech, hyphenation, possible translations, inflection, etc. for each word. It includes, among others, the same three word classes of adjectives, nouns, and verbs that are also available in GermaNet. Distinct word senses are distinguished by sense descriptions and accompanied with example sentences illustrating the sense in question.

Further, Wiktionary provides relations to other words, e.g., in the form of synonyms, antonyms, hypernyms, hyponyms, holonyms, and meronyms. In contrast to GermaNet, the relations are (mostly) not disambiguated.

For the present project, a dump of the German Wiktionary as of February 2, 2011 is uti-

[2] http://www.wikipedia.org/

[3] Using a wordnet as the gold standard for the sense inventory is fully in line with standard practice for English where the Princeton WordNet (Fellbaum, 1998) is typically taken as the gold standard.

[4] Wiktionary is available under the Creative Commons Attribution/Share-Alike license http://creativecommons.org/licenses/by-sa/3.0/deed.en

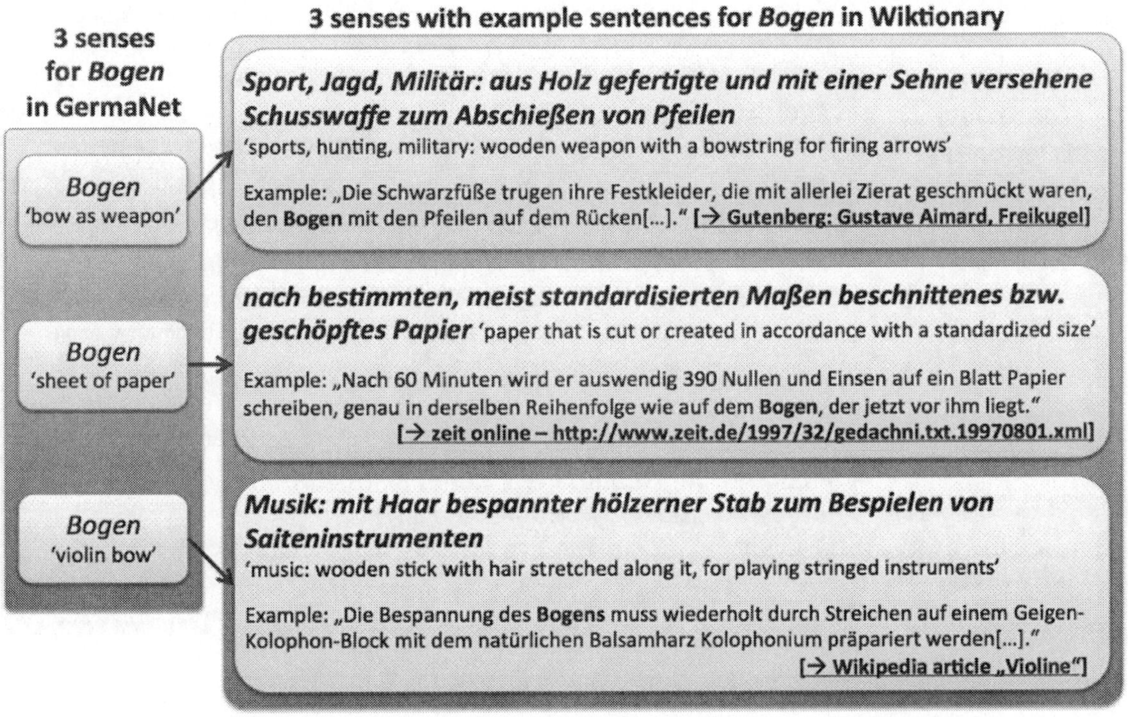

Figure 1: Sense mapping of GermaNet and Wiktionary using the example of *Bogen*.

lized, consisting of 46457 German words comprising 70339 word senses. The Wiktionary data was extracted by the freely available Java-based library JWKTL[5].

3 Creation of a Web-Harvested Corpus

The starting point for creating WebCAGe is an existing mapping of GermaNet senses with Wiktionary sense definitions as described in Henrich et al. (2011). This mapping is the result of a two-stage process: i) an automatic word overlap alignment algorithm in order to match GermaNet senses with Wiktionary sense descriptions, and ii) a manual post-correction step of the automatic alignment. Manual post-correction can be kept at a reasonable level of effort due to the high accuracy (93.8%) of the automatic alignment.

The original purpose of this mapping was to automatically add Wiktionary sense descriptions to GermaNet. However, the alignment of these two resources opens up a much wider range of possibilities for data mining community-driven resources such as Wikipedia and web-generated content more generally. It is precisely this potential that is fully exploited for the creation of the WebCAGe sense-annotated corpus.

Fig. 1 illustrates the existing GermaNet-Wiktionary mapping using the example word *Bogen*. The polysemous word *Bogen* has three distinct senses in GermaNet which directly correspond to three separate senses in Wiktionary[6]. Each Wiktionary sense entry contains a definition and one or more example sentences illustrating the sense in question. The examples in turn are often linked to external references, including sentences contained in the German Gutenberg text archive[7] (see link in the topmost Wiktionary sense entry in Fig. 1), Wikipedia articles (see link for the third Wiktionary sense entry in Fig. 1), and other textual sources (see the second sense entry in Fig. 1). It is precisely this collection of

[5]http://www.ukp.tu-darmstadt.de/software/jwktl

[6]Note that there are further senses in both resources not displayed here for reasons of space.

[7]http://gutenberg.spiegel.de/

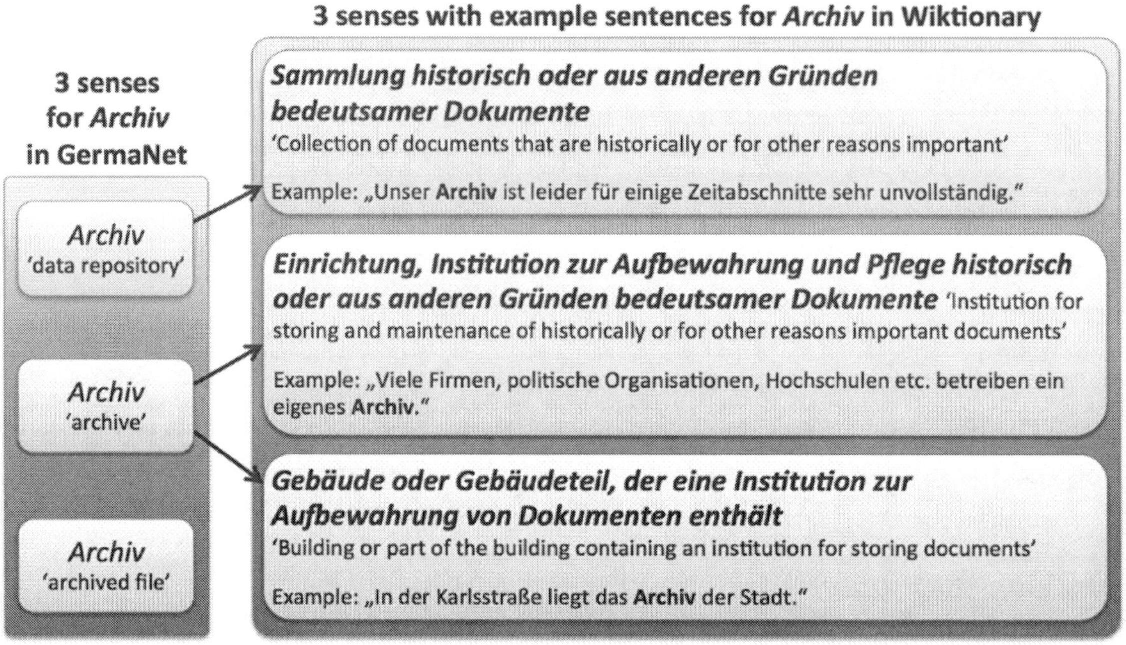

Figure 2: Sense mapping of GermaNet and Wiktionary using the example of *Archiv*.

heterogeneous material that can be harvested for the purpose of compiling a sense-annotated corpus. Since the target word (rendered in Fig. 1 in bold face) in the example sentences for a particular Wiktionary sense is linked to a GermaNet sense via the sense mapping of GermaNet with Wiktionary, the example sentences are automatically sense-annotated and can be included as part of WebCAGe.

Additional material for WebCAGe is harvested by following the links to Wikipedia, the Gutenberg archive, and other web-based materials. The external webpages and the Gutenberg texts are obtained from the web by a web-crawler that takes some URLs as input and outputs the texts of the corresponding web sites. The Wikipedia articles are obtained by the open-source Java Wikipedia Library JWPL [8]. Since the links to Wikipedia, the Gutenberg archive, and other web-based materials also belong to particular Wiktionary sense entries that in turn are mapped to GermaNet senses, the target words contained in these materials are automatically sense-annotated.

Notice that the target word often occurs more than once in a given text. In keeping with the widely used heuristic of "one sense per discourse", multiple occurrences of a target word in a given text are all assigned to the same GermaNet sense. An inspection of the annotated data shows that this heuristic has proven to be highly reliable in practice. It is correct in 99.96% of all target word occurrences in the Wiktionary example sentences, in 96.75% of all occurrences in the external webpages, and in 95.62% of the Wikipedia files.

WebCAGe is developed primarily for the purpose of the word sense disambiguation task. Therefore, only those target words that are genuinely ambiguous are included in this resource. Since WebCAGe uses GermaNet as its sense inventory, this means that each target word has at least two GermaNet senses, i.e., belongs to at least two distinct synsets.

The GermaNet-Wiktionary mapping is not always one-to-one. Sometimes one GermaNet sense is mapped to more than one sense in Wiktionary. Fig. 2 illustrates such a case. For the word *Archiv* each resource records three distinct senses. The first sense ('data repository')

[8]http://www.ukp.tu-darmstadt.de/software/jwpl/

in GermaNet corresponds to the first sense in Wiktionary, and the second sense in GermaNet ('archive') corresponds to both the second and third senses in Wiktionary. The third sense in GermaNet ('archived file') does not map onto any sense in Wiktionary at all. As a result, the word *Archiv* is included in the WebCAGe resource with precisely the sense mappings connected by the arrows shown in Fig. 2. The fact that the second GermaNet sense corresponds to two sense descriptions in Wiktionary simply means that the target words in the example are both annotated by the same sense. Furthermore, note that the word *Archiv* is still genuinely ambiguous since there is a second (one-to-one) mapping between the first senses recorded in GermaNet and Wiktionary, respectively. However, since the third GermaNet sense is not mapped onto any Wiktionary sense at all, WebCAGe will not contain any example sentences for this particular GermaNet sense.

The following section describes how the target words within these textual materials can be automatically identified.

4 Automatic Detection of Target Words

For highly inflected languages such as German, target word identification is more complex compared to languages with an impoverished inflectional morphology, such as English, and thus requires automatic lemmatization. Moreover, the target word in a text to be sense-annotated is not always a simplex word but can also appear as subpart of a complex word such as a compound. Since the constituent parts of a compound are not usually separated by blank spaces or hyphens, German compounding poses a particular challenge for target word identification. Another challenging case for automatic target word detection in German concerns particle verbs such as *ankündigen* 'announce'. Here, the difficulty arises when the verbal stem (e.g., *kündigen*) is separated from its particle (e.g., *an*) in German verb-initial and verb-second clause types.

As a preprocessing step for target word identification, the text is split into individual sentences, tokenized, and lemmatized. For this purpose, the sentence detector and the tokenizer of the suite of Apache OpenNLP tools[9] and the TreeTagger (Schmid, 1994) are used. Further, compounds are split by using BananaSplit[10]. Since the automatic lemmatization obtained by the tagger and the compound splitter are not 100% accurate, target word identification also utilizes the full set of inflected forms for a target word whenever such information is available. As it turns out, Wiktionary can often be used for this purpose as well since the German version of Wiktionary often contains the full set of word forms in tables[11] such as the one shown in Fig. 3 for the word *Bogen*.

Kasus	Singular	Plural 1	Plural 2
Nominativ	der Bogen	die Bogen	die Bögen
Genitiv	des Bogens	der Bogen	der Bögen
Dativ	dem Bogen	den Bogen	den Bögen
Akkusativ	den Bogen	die Bogen	die Bögen

Figure 3: Wiktionary inflection table for *Bogen*.

Fig. 4 shows an example of such a sense-annotated text for the target word *Bogen* 'violin bow'. The text is an excerpt from the Wikipedia article *Violine* 'violin', where the target word (rendered in bold face) appears many times. Only the second occurrence shown in the figure (marked with a 2 on the left) exactly matches the word *Bogen* as is. All other occurrences are either the plural form *Bögen* (4 and 7), the genitive form *Bogens* (8), part of a compound such as *Bogenstange* (3), or the plural form as part of a compound such as in *Fernambukbögen* and *Schülerbögen* (5 and 6). The first occurrence of the target word in Fig. 4 is also part of a compound. Here, the target word occurs in the singular as part of the adjectival compound *bogengestrichenen*.

For expository purposes, the data format shown in Fig. 4 is much simplified compared to the actual; XML-based format in WebCAGe. The infor-

[9] http://incubator.apache.org/opennlp/

[10] http://niels.drni.de/s9y/pages/bananasplit.html

[11] The inflection table cannot be extracted with the Java Wikipedia Library JWPL. It is rather extracted from the Wiktionary dump file.

```
  [...] Das Wort Geige stammt aus dem deutschen Sprachraum und
  umfasste im Mittelalter alle <tag lexUnit="19087" lemma="Bogen"
1 wcat="NN">bogen</tag>gestrichenen Saiteninstrumente. [...]

2 Der <tag lexUnit="19087" lemma="Bogen" wcat="NN">Bogen</tag>
  besteht häufig aus dem Rotholz Pernambuk (Fernambuk). Gutes
  Pernambuk ist gerade gewachsen und die Fasern verlaufen
  parallel, die <tag lexUnit="19087" lemma="Bogen"
3 wcat="NN">Bogen</tag>stange kann besonders dünn gearbeitet
  werden und weist eine ideale Elastizität auf. Das Holz eignet
  sich somit besonders für qualitativ hochwertige <tag
4 lexUnit="19087" lemma="Bogen" wcat="NN">Bögen</tag>. Da das
  Vorkommen der Holzart begrenzt ist, haben Fernambuk<tag
5 lexUnit="19087" lemma="Bogen" wcat="NN">bögen</tag> einen
  entsprechen hohen Preis. Einfachere Schüler<tag lexUnit="19087"
6 lemma="Bogen" wcat="NN">bögen</tag> sind meist aus Brasilholz
  gefertigt. Heute werden, auch von Berufsgeigern, zunehmend <tag
7 lexUnit="19087" lemma="Bogen" wcat="NN">Bögen</tag> aus
  Kohlefaser (Karbonfiber) verwendet.

  Am unteren Ende des <tag lexUnit="19087" lemma="Bogen"
8 wcat="NN">Bogens</tag> befindet sich der sogenannte Frosch aus
  Ebenholz, meist verziert mit einer runden Perlmutt-Einlage.
  [...]
                      Source: http://de.wikipedia.org/wiki/Violine
```

Figure 4: Excerpt from Wikipedia article *Violine* 'violin' tagged with target word *Bogen* 'violin bow'.

mation for each occurrence of a target word consists of the GermaNet sense, i.e., the lexical unit ID, the lemma of the target word, and the GermaNet word category information, i.e., *ADJ* for adjectives, *NN* for nouns, and *VB* for verbs.

5 Evaluation

In order to assess the effectiveness of the approach, we examine the overall size of WebCAGe and the relative size of the different text collections (see Table 1), compare WebCAGe to other sense-annotated corpora for German (see Table 2), and present a precision- and recall-based evaluation of the algorithm that is used for automatically identifying target words in the harvested texts (see Table 3).

Table 1 shows that Wiktionary (7644 tagged word tokens) and Wikipedia (1732) contribute by far the largest subsets of the total number of tagged word tokens (10750) compared with the external webpages (589) and the Gutenberg texts (785). These tokens belong to 2607 distinct polysemous words contained in GermaNet, among which there are 211 adjectives, 1499 nouns, and 897 verbs (see Table 2). On average, these words have 2.9 senses in GermaNet (2.4 for adjectives, 2.6 for nouns, and 3.6 for verbs).

Table 2 also shows that WebCAGe is considerably larger than the other two sense-annotated corpora available for German ((Broscheit et al., 2010) and (Raileanu et al., 2002)). It is important to keep in mind, though, that the other two resources were manually constructed, whereas WebCAGe is the result of an automatic harvesting method. Such an automatic method will only constitute a viable alternative to the labor-intensive manual method if the results are of sufficient quality so that the harvested data set can be used as is or can be further improved with a minimal amount of manual post-editing.

For the purpose of the present evaluation, we conducted a precision- and recall-based analysis for the text types of Wiktionary examples, external webpages, and Wikipedia articles sep-

Table 1: Current size of WebCAGe.

		Wiktionary examples	External webpages	Wikipedia articles	Gutenberg texts	All texts
Number of tagged word tokens	adjectives	575	31	79	28	713
	nouns	4103	446	1643	655	6847
	verbs	2966	112	10	102	3190
	all word classes	7644	589	1732	785	10750
Number of tagged sentences	adjectives	565	31	76	26	698
	nouns	3965	420	1404	624	6413
	verbs	2945	112	10	102	3169
	all word classes	7475	563	1490	752	10280
Total number of sentences	adjectives	623	1297	430	65030	67380
	nouns	4184	9630	6851	376159	396824
	verbs	3087	5285	263	146755	155390
	all word classes	7894	16212	7544	587944	619594

Table 2: Comparing WebCAGe to other sense-tagged corpora of German.

		WebCAGe	Broscheit et al., 2010	Raileanu et al., 2002
Sense tagged words	adjectives	211	6	0
	nouns	1499	18	25
	verbs	897	16	0
	all word classes	2607	40	25
Number of tagged word tokens		10750	approx. 800	2421
Domain independent		yes	yes	medical domain

arately for the three word classes of adjectives, nouns, and verbs. Table 3 shows that precision and recall for all three word classes that occur for Wiktionary examples, external webpages, and Wikipedia articles lies above 92%. The only sizeable deviations are the results for verbs that occur in the Gutenberg texts. Apart from this one exception, the results in Table 3 prove the viability of the proposed method for automatic harvesting of sense-annotated data. The average precision for all three word classes is of sufficient quality to be used as-is if approximately 2-5% noise in the annotated data is acceptable. In order to eliminate such noise, manual post-editing is required. However, such post-editing is within acceptable limits: it took an experienced research assistant a total of 25 hours to hand-correct all the occurrences of sense-annotated target words and to manually sense-tag any missing target words for the four text types.

6 Related Work and Future Directions

With relatively few exceptions to be discussed shortly, the construction of sense-annotated corpora has focussed on purely manual methods. This is true for SemCor, the WordNet Gloss Corpus, and for the training sets constructed for English as part of the SensEval and SemEval shared task competitions (Agirre et al., 2007; Erk and Strapparava, 2012; Mihalcea et al., 2004). Purely manual methods were also used for the German sense-annotated corpora constructed by Broscheit et al. (2010) and Raileanu et al. (2002) as well as for other languages including the Bulgarian and

Table 3: Evaluation of the algorithm of identifying the target words.

		Wiktionary examples	External webpages	Wikipedia articles	Gutenberg texts
Precision	adjectives	97.70%	95.83%	99.34%	100%
	nouns	98.17%	98.50%	95.87%	92.19%
	verbs	97.38%	92.26%	100%	69.87%
	all word classes	97.32%	96.19%	96.26%	87.43%
Recall	adjectives	97.70%	97.22%	98.08%	97.14%
	nouns	98.30%	96.03%	92.70.%	97.38%
	verbs	97.51%	99.60%	100%	89.20%
	all word classes	97.94%	97.32%	93.36%	95.42%

the Chinese sense-tagged corpora (Koeva et al., 2006; Wu et al., 2006). The only previous attempts of harvesting corpus data for the purpose of constructing a sense-annotated corpus are the semi-supervised method developed by Yarowsky (1995), the knowledge-based approach of Leacock et al. (1998), later also used by Agirre and Lopez de Lacalle (2004), and the automatic association of Web directories (from the Open Directory Project, ODP) to WordNet senses by Santamaría et al. (2003).

The latter study (Santamaría et al., 2003) is closest in spirit to the approach presented here. It also relies on an automatic mapping between wordnet senses and a second web resource. While our approach is based on automatic mappings between GermaNet and Wiktionary, their mapping algorithm maps WordNet senses to ODP subdirectories. Since these ODP subdirectories contain natural language descriptions of websites relevant to the subdirectory in question, this textual material can be used for harvesting sense-specific examples. The ODP project also covers German so that, in principle, this harvesting method could be applied to German in order to collect additional sense-tagged data for WebCAGe.

The approach of Yarowsky (1995) first collects all example sentences that contain a polysemous word from a very large corpus. In a second step, a small number of examples that are representative for each of the senses of the polysemous target word is selected from the large corpus from step 1. These representative examples are manually sense-annotated and then fed into a decision-list supervised WSD algorithm as a seed set for iteratively disambiguating the remaining examples collected in step 1. The selection and annotation of the representative examples in Yarowsky's approach is performed completely manually and is therefore limited to the amount of data that can reasonably be annotated by hand.

Leacock et al. (1998), Agirre and Lopez de Lacalle (2004), and Mihalcea and Moldovan (1999) propose a set of methods for automatic harvesting of web data for the purposes of creating sense-annotated corpora. By focusing on web-based data, their work resembles the research described in the present paper. However, the underlying harvesting methods differ. While our approach relies on a wordnet to Wiktionary mapping, their approaches all rely on the monosemous relative heuristic. Their heuristic works as follows: In order to harvest corpus examples for a polysemous word, the WordNet relations such as synonymy and hypernymy are inspected for the presence of unambiguous words, i.e., words that only appear in exactly one synset. The examples found for these monosemous relatives can then be sense-annotated with the particular sense of its ambiguous word relative. In order to increase coverage of the monosemous relatives approach, Mihalcea and Moldovan (1999) have developed a gloss-based extension, which relies on word overlap of the gloss and the WordNet sense in question for all those cases where a monosemous relative is not contained in the WordNet dataset.

The approaches of Leacock et al., Agirre and Lopez de Lacalle, and Mihalcea and Moldovan as well as Yarowsky's approach provide interesting directions for further enhancing the WebCAGe resource. It would be worthwhile to use the automatically harvested sense-annotated examples as the seed set for Yarowsky's iterative method for creating a large sense-annotated corpus. Another fruitful direction for further automatic expansion of WebCAGe is to use the heuristic of monosemous relatives used by Leacock et al., by Agirre and Lopez de Lacalle, and by Mihalcea and Moldovan. However, we have to leave these matters for future research.

In order to validate the language independence of our approach, we plan to apply our method to sense inventories for languages other than German. A precondition for such an experiment is an existing mapping between the sense inventory in question and a web-based resource such as Wiktionary or Wikipedia. With BabelNet, Navigli and Ponzetto (2010) have created a multilingual resource that allows the testing of our approach to languages other than German. As a first step in this direction, we applied our approach to English using the mapping between the Princeton WordNet and the English version of Wiktionary provided by Meyer and Gurevych (2011). The results of these experiments, which are reported in Henrich et al. (2012), confirm the general applicability of our approach.

To conclude: This paper describes an automatic method for creating a domain-independent sense-annotated corpus harvested from the web. The data obtained by this method for German have resulted in the WebCAGe resource which currently represents the largest sense-annotated corpus available for this language. The publication of this paper is accompanied by making WebCAGe freely available.

Acknowledgements

The research reported in this paper was jointly funded by the SFB 833 grant of the DFG and by the CLARIN-D grant of the BMBF. We would like to thank Christina Hoppermann, Marie Hinrichs as well as three anonymous EACL 2012 reviewers for their helpful comments on earlier versions of this paper. We are very grateful to Reinhild Barkey, Sarah Schulz, and Johannes Wahle for their help with the evaluation reported in Section 5. Special thanks go to Yana Panchenko and Yannick Versley for their support with the webcrawler and to Emanuel Dima and Klaus Suttner for helping us to obtain the Gutenberg and Wikipedia texts.

References

Agirre, E., Lopez de Lacalle, O. 2004. Publicly available topic signatures for all WordNet nominal senses. *Proceedings of the 4th International Conference on Languages Resources and Evaluations* (LREC'04), Lisbon, Portugal, pp. 1123–1126

Agirre, E., Marquez, L., Wicentowski, R. 2007. *Proceedings of the 4th International Workshop on Semantic Evaluations*. Assoc. for Computational Linguistics, Stroudsburg, PA, USA

Broscheit, S., Frank, A., Jehle, D., Ponzetto, S. P., Rehl, D., Summa, A., Suttner, K., Vola, S. 2010. Rapid bootstrapping of Word Sense Disambiguation resources for German. *Proceedings of the 10. Konferenz zur Verarbeitung Natürlicher Sprache*, Saarbrücken, Germany, pp. 19–27

Erk, K., Strapparava, C. 2010. *Proceedings of the 5th International Workshop on Semantic Evaluation*. Assoc. for Computational Linguistics, Stroudsburg, PA, USA

Fellbaum, C. (ed.). 1998. *WordNet An Electronic Lexical Database*. The MIT Press.

Henrich, V., Hinrichs, E. 2010. GernEdiT – The GermaNet Editing Tool. *Proceedings of the Seventh Conference on International Language Resources and Evaluation* (LREC'10), Valletta, Malta, pp. 2228–2235

Henrich, V., Hinrichs, E., Vodolazova, T. 2011. Semi-Automatic Extension of GermaNet with Sense Definitions from Wiktionary. *Proceedings of the 5th Language & Technology Conference: Human Language Technologies as a Challenge for Computer Science and Linguistics* (LTC'11), Poznan, Poland, pp. 126–130

Henrich, V., Hinrichs, E., Vodolazova, T. 2012. An Automatic Method for Creating a Sense-Annotated Corpus Harvested from the Web. Poster presented at *13th International Conference on Intelligent Text Processing and Computational Linguistics* (CICLing-2012), New Delhi, India, March 2012

Koeva, S., Leseva, S., Todorova, M. 2006. Bulgarian Sense Tagged Corpus. *Proceedings of the 5th SALTMIL Workshop on Minority Languages:*

Strategies for Developing Machine Translation for Minority Languages, Genoa, Italy, pp. 79–87

Kunze, C., Lemnitzer, L. 2002. GermaNet representation, visualization, application. *Proceedings of the 3rd International Language Resources and Evaluation* (LREC'02), Las Palmas, Canary Islands, pp. 1485–1491

Leacock, C., Chodorow, M., Miller, G. A. 1998. Using corpus statistics and wordnet relations for sense identification. *Computational Linguistics*, 24(1):147–165

Meyer, C. M., Gurevych, I. 2011. What Psycholinguists Know About Chemistry: Aligning Wiktionary and WordNet for Increased Domain Coverage. *Proceedings of the 5th International Joint Conference on Natural Language Processing* (IJCNLP), Chiang Mai, Thailand, pp. 883–892

Mihalcea, R., Moldovan, D. 1999. An Automatic Method for Generating Sense Tagged Corpora. *Proceedings of the American Association for Artificial Intelligence* (AAAI'99), Orlando, Florida, pp. 461–466

Mihalcea, R., Chklovski, T., Kilgarriff, A. 2004. *Proceedings of Senseval-3: Third International Workshop on the Evaluation of Systems for the Semantic Analysis of Text*, Barcelona, Spain

Navigli, R., Ponzetto, S. P. 2010. BabelNet: Building a Very Large Multilingual Semantic Network. *Proceedings of the 48th Annual Meeting of the Association for Computational Linguistics* (ACL'10), Uppsala, Sweden, pp. 216–225

Raileanu, D., Buitelaar, P., Vintar, S., Bay, J. 2002. Evaluation Corpora for Sense Disambiguation in the Medical Domain. *Proceedings of the 3rd International Language Resources and Evaluation* (LREC'02), Las Palmas, Canary Islands, pp. 609–612

Santamaría, C., Gonzalo, J., Verdejo, F. 2003. Automatic Association of Web Directories to Word Senses. *Computational Linguistics* 29 (3), MIT Press, PP. 485–502

Schmid, H. 1994. Probabilistic Part-of-Speech Tagging Using Decision Trees. *Proceedings of the International Conference on New Methods in Language Processing*, Manchester, UK

Wu, Y., Jin, P., Zhang, Y., Yu, S. 2006. A Chinese Corpus with Word Sense Annotation. *Proceedings of 21st International Conference on Computer Processing of Oriental Languages* (ICCPOL'06), Singapore, pp. 414–421

Yarowsky, D. 1995. Unsupervised word sense disambiguation rivaling supervised methods. *Proceedings of the 33rd Annual Meeting on Association for Computational Linguistics* (ACL'95), Association for Computational Linguistics, Stroudsburg, PA, USA, pp. 189–196

Learning to Behave by Reading

Regina Barzilay
Computer Science and Artificial Intelligence Laboratory
Massachusetts Institute of Technology
regina@csail.mit.edu

Abstract

In this talk, I will address the problem of grounding linguistic analysis in control applications, such as game playing and robot navigation. We assume access to natural language documents that describe the desired behavior of a control algorithm (e.g., game strategy guides). Our goal is to demonstrate that knowledge automatically extracted from such documents can dramatically improve performance of the target application. First, I will present a reinforcement learning algorithm for learning to map natural language instructions to executable actions. This technique has enabled automation of tasks that until now have required human participation — for example, automatically configuring software by consulting how-to guides. Next, I will present a Monte-Carlo search algorithm for game playing that incorporates information from game strategy guides. In this framework, the task of text interpretation is formulated as a probabilistic model that is trained based on feedback from Monte-Carlo search. When applied to the Civilization strategy game, a language-empowered player outperforms its traditional counterpart by a significant margin.

Lexical surprisal as a general predictor of reading time

Irene Fernandez Monsalve, Stefan L. Frank and **Gabriella Vigliocco**
Division of Psychology and Language Sciences
University College London
{ucjtife, s.frank, g.vigliocco}@ucl.ac.uk

Abstract

Probabilistic accounts of language processing can be psychologically tested by comparing word-reading times (RT) to the conditional word probabilities estimated by language models. Using surprisal as a linking function, a significant correlation between unlexicalized surprisal and RT has been reported (e.g., Demberg and Keller, 2008), but success using lexicalized models has been limited. In this study, phrase structure grammars and recurrent neural networks estimated both lexicalized and unlexicalized surprisal for words of independent sentences from narrative sources. These same sentences were used as stimuli in a self-paced reading experiment to obtain RTs. The results show that lexicalized surprisal according to both models is a significant predictor of RT, outperforming its unlexicalized counterparts.

1 Introduction

Context-sensitive, prediction-based processing has been proposed as a fundamental mechanism of cognition (Bar, 2007): Faced with the problem of responding in real-time to complex stimuli, the human brain would use basic information from the environment, in conjunction with previous experience, in order to extract meaning and anticipate the immediate future. Such a cognitive style is a well-established finding in low level sensory processing (e.g., Kveraga et al., 2007), but has also been proposed as a relevant mechanism in higher order processes, such as language. Indeed, there is ample evidence to show that human language comprehension is both incremental and predictive. For example, on-line detection of semantic or syntactic anomalies can be observed in the brain's EEG signal (Hagoort et al., 2004) and eye gaze is directed in anticipation at depictions of plausible sentence completions (Kamide et al., 2003). Moreover, probabilistic accounts of language processing have identified *unpredictability* as a major cause of processing difficulty in language comprehension. In such incremental processing, parsing would entail a pre-allocation of resources to expected interpretations, so that effort would be related to the suitability of such an allocation to the actually encountered stimulus (Levy, 2008).

Possible sentence interpretations can be constrained by both linguistic and extra-linguistic context, but while the latter is difficult to evaluate, the former can be easily modeled: The predictability of a word for the human parser can be expressed as the conditional probability of a word given the sentence so far, which can in turn be estimated by language models trained on text corpora. These probabilistic accounts of language processing difficulty can then be validated against empirical data, by taking reading time (RT) on a word as a measure of the effort involved in its processing.

Recently, several studies have followed this approach, using "surprisal" (see Section 1.1) as the linking function between effort and predictability. These can be computed for each word in a text, or alternatively for the words' parts of speech (POS). In the latter case, the obtained estimates can give an indication of the importance of syntactic structure in developing upcoming-word expectations, but ignore the rich lexical information that is doubtlessly employed by the human parser to constrain predictions. However, whereas such an *unlexicalized* (i.e., POS-based) surprisal has been shown to significantly predict RTs, success with *lexical* (i.e., word-based) surprisal has been limited. This can be attributed to data sparsity (larger training corpora might be needed to provide accurate lexical surprisal than for the unlexicalized counterpart), or to the noise introduced by participant's world knowledge, inaccessible to the models. The present study thus sets out to find such a lexical surprisal effect, trying to overcome possible limitations of previous research.

1.1 Surprisal theory

The concept of surprisal originated in the field of information theory, as a measure of the amount of information conveyed by a particular event. Improbable ('surprising') events carry more information than expected ones, so that surprisal is inversely related to probability, through a logarithmic function. In the context of sentence processing, if $w_1, ..., w_{t-1}$ denotes the sentence so far, then the cognitive effort required for processing the next word, w_t, is assumed to be proportional to its surprisal:

$$\begin{aligned} \text{effort}(t) &\propto \text{surprisal}(w_t) \\ &= -\log(P(w_t|w_1, ..., w_{t-1})) \end{aligned} \quad (1)$$

Different theoretical groundings for this relationship have been proposed (Hale, 2001; Levy 2008; Smith and Levy, 2008). Smith and Levy derive it by taking a scale free assumption: Any linguistic unit can be subdivided into smaller entities (e.g., a sentence is comprised of words, a word of phonemes), so that time to process the whole will equal the sum of processing times for each part. Since the probability of the whole can be expressed as the product of the probabilities of the subunits, the function relating probability and effort must be logarithmic. Levy (2008), on the other hand, grounds surprisal in its information-theoretical context, describing difficulty encountered in on-line sentence processing as a result of the need to update a probability distribution over possible parses, being directly proportional to the difference between the previous and updated distributions. By expressing the difference between these in terms of relative entropy, Levy shows that difficulty at each newly encountered word should be equal to its surprisal.

1.2 Empirical evidence for surprisal

The simplest statistical language models that can be used to estimate surprisal values are n-gram models or Markov chains, which condition the probability of a given word only on its $n-1$ preceding ones. Although Markov models theoretically limit the amount of prior information that is relevant for prediction of the next step, they are often used in linguistic context as an approximation to the full conditional probability. The effect of bigram probability (or forward transitional probability) has been repeatedly observed (e.g. McDonald and Shillcock, 2003), and Smith and Levy (2008) report an effect of lexical surprisal as estimated by a trigram model on RTs for the Dundee corpus (a collection of newspaper texts with eye-tracking data from ten participants; Kennedy and Pynte, 2005).

Phrase structure grammars (PSGs) have also been amply used as language models (Boston et al., 2008; Brouwer et al., 2010; Demberg and Keller, 2008; Hale, 2001; Levy, 2008). PSGs can combine statistical exposure effects with explicit syntactic rules, by annotating norms with their respective probabilities, which can be estimated from occurrence counts in text corpora. Information about hierarchical sentence structure can thus be included in the models. In this way, Brouwer et al. trained a probabilistic context-free grammar (PCFG) on 204,000 sentences extracted from Dutch newspapers to estimate lexical surprisal (using an Earley-Stolcke parser; Stolcke, 1995), showing that it could account for the noun phrase coordination bias previously described and explained by Frazier (1987) in terms of a minimal-attachment preference of the human parser. In contrast, Demberg and Keller used texts from a naturalistic source (the Dundee corpus) as the experimental stimuli, thus evaluating surprisal as a wide-coverage account of processing difficulty. They also employed a PSG, trained on a one-million-word language sample from the Wall Street Journal (part of the Penn Treebank II, Marcus et al., 1993). Using Roark's (2001) incremental parser, they found significant effects of unlexicalized surprisal on RTs (see also Boston et al. for a similar approach and results for German texts). However, they failed to find an effect for lexicalized surprisal, over and above forward transitional probability. Roark et al. (2009) also looked at the effects of *syntactic* and *lexical* surprisal, using RT data for short narrative texts. However, their estimates of these two surprisal values differ from those described above: In order to tease apart semantic and syntactic effects, they used Demberg and Keller's lexicalized surprisal as a total surprisal measure, which they decompose into syntactic and lexical components. Their results show significant effects of both syntactic and lexical surprisal, although the latter was found to hold only for closed class words. Lack of a wider effect was attributed to data sparsity: The models were trained on the relatively small Brown corpus (over one million words from 500 samples of American English text), so that surprisal estimates for the less frequent content words would not have been accurate enough.

Using the same training and experimental language samples as Demberg and Keller (2008), and only unlexicalized surprisal estimates, Frank (2009) and Frank and Bod (2011) focused on comparing different language models, including various *n*-gram models, PSGs and recurrent networks (RNN). The latter were found to be the better predictors of RTs, and PSGs could not explain any variance in RT over and above the RNNs, suggesting that human processing relies on linear rather than hierarchical representations.

Summing up, the only models taking into account actual words that have been consistently shown to simulate human behaviour with naturalistic text samples are bigram models.[1] A possible limitation in previous studies can be found in the stimuli employed. In reading real newspaper texts, prior knowledge of current affairs is likely to highly influence RTs, however, this source of variability cannot be accounted for by the models. In addition, whereas the models treat each sentence as an independent unit, in the text corpora employed they make up coherent texts, and are therefore clearly dependent. Thirdly, the stimuli used by Demberg and Keller (2008) comprise a very particular linguistic style: journalistic editorials, reducing the ability to generalize conclusions to language in general. Finally, failure to find lexical surprisal effects can also be attributed to the training texts. Larger corpora are likely to be needed for training language models on actual words than on POS (both the Brown corpus and the WSJ are relatively small), and in addition, the particular journalistic style of the WSJ might not be the best alternative for modeling human behaviour. Although similarity between the training and experimental data sets (both from newspaper sources) can improve the linguistic performance of the models, their ability to simulate human behaviour might be limited: Newspaper texts probably form just a small fraction of a person's linguistic experience. This study thus aims to tackle some of the identified limitations: Rather than cohesive texts, independent sentences, from a narrative style are used as experimental stimuli for which word-reading times are collected (as explained in Section 3). In addition, as discussed in the following section, language models are trained on a larger corpus, from a more representative language sample. Following Frank (2009) and Frank and Bod (2011), two contrasting types of models are employed: hierarchical PSGs and linear RNNs.

2 Models

2.1 Training data

The training texts were extracted from the written section of the British National Corpus (BNC), a collection of language samples from a variety of sources, designed to provide a comprehensive representation of current British English. A total of 702,412 sentences, containing only the 7,754 most frequent words (the open-class words used by Andrews et al., 2009, plus the 200 most frequent words in English) were selected, making up a 7.6-million-word training corpus. In addition to providing a larger amount of data than the WSJ, this training set thus provides a more representative language sample.

2.2 Experimental sentences

Three hundred and sixty-one sentences, all comprehensible out of context and containing only words included in the subset of the BNC used to train the models, were randomly selected from three freely accessible on-line novels[2] (for additional details, see Frank, 2012). The fictional narrative provides a good contrast to the pre-

[1]Although Smith and Levy (2008) report an effect of trigrams, they did not check if it exceeded that of simpler bigrams.

[2]Obtained from `www.free-online-novels.com`. Having not been published elsewhere, it is unlikely participants had read the novels previously.

viously examined newspaper editorials from the Dundee corpus, since participants did not need prior knowledge regarding the details of the stories, and a less specialised language and style were employed. In addition, the randomly selected sentences did not make up coherent texts (in contrast, Roark et al., 2009, employed short stories), so that they were independent from each other, both for the models and the readers.

2.3 Part-of-speech tagging

In order to produce POS-based surprisal estimates, versions of both the training and experimental texts with their words replaced by POS were developed: The BNC sentences were parsed by the Stanford Parser, version 1.6.7 (Klein and Manning, 2003), whilst the experimental texts were tagged by an automatic tagger (Tsuruoka and Tsujii, 2005), with posterior review and correction by hand following the Penn Treebank Project Guidelines (Santorini, 1991). By training language models and subsequently running them on the POS versions of the texts, unlexicalized surprisal values were estimated.

2.4 Phrase-structure grammars

The Treebank formed by the parsed BNC sentences served as training data for Roark's (2001) incremental parser. Following Frank and Bod (2011), a range of grammars was induced, differing in the features of the tree structure upon which rule probabilities were conditioned. In four grammars, probabilities depended on the left-hand side's ancestors, from one up to four levels up in the parse tree (these grammars will be denoted a_1 to a_4). In four other grammars (s_1 to s_4), the ancestors' left siblings were also taken into account. In addition, probabilities were conditioned on the current head node in all grammars. Subsequently, Roark's (2001) incremental parser parsed the experimental sentences under each of the eight grammars, obtaining eight surprisal values for each word. Since earlier research (Frank, 2009) showed that decreasing the parser's base beam width parameter improves performance, it was set to 10^{-18} (the default being 10^{-12}).

2.5 Recurrent neural network

The RNN (see Figure 1) was trained in three stages, each taking the selected (unparsed) BNC sentences as training data.

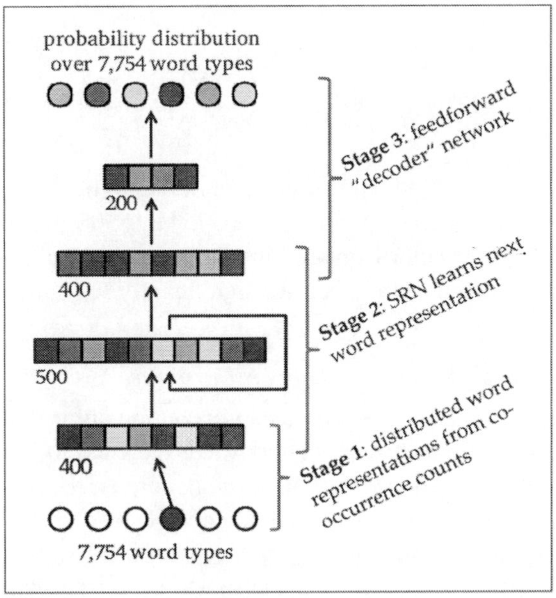

Figure 1: Architecture of neural network language model, and its three learning stages. Numbers indicate the number of units in each network layer.

Stage 1: Developing word representations

Neural network language models can benefit from using distributed word representations: Each word is assigned a vector in a continuous, high-dimensional space, such that words that are paradigmatically more similar are closer together (e.g., Bengio et al., 2003; Mnih and Hinton, 2007). Usually, these representations are learned together with the rest of the model, but here we used a more efficient approach in which word representations are learned in an unsupervised manner from simple co-occurrences in the training data. First, vectors of word co-occurrence frequencies were developed using Good-Turing (Gale and Sampson, 1995) smoothed frequency counts from the training corpus. Values in the vector corresponded to the smoothed frequencies with which each word directly preceded or followed the represented word. Thus, each word w was assigned a vector $(f_{w,1}, ..., f_{w,15508})$, such that $f_{w,v}$ is the number of times word v directly precedes (for $v \leq 7754$) or follows (for $v > 7754$) word w. Next, the frequency counts were transformed into Pointwise Mutual Information (PMI) values (see Equation 2), following Bullinaria and Levy's (2007) findings that PMI produced more psychologically accurate predictions than other measures:

$$\text{PMI}(w, v) = \log\left(\frac{f_{w,v}\sum_{i,j} f_{i,j}}{\sum_i f_{i,v}\sum_j f_{w,j}}\right) \quad (2)$$

Finally, the 400 columns with the highest variance were selected from the 7754×15508-matrix of row vectors, making them more computationally manageable, but not significantly less informative.

Stage 2: Learning temporal structure

Using the standard backpropagation algorithm, a simple recurrent network (SRN) learned to predict, at each point in the training corpus, the next word's vector given the sequence of word vectors corresponding to the sentence so far. The total corpus was presented five times, each time with the sentences in a different random order.

Stage 3: Decoding predicted word representations

The distributed output of the trained SRN served as training input to the feedforward "decoder" network, that learned to map the distributed representations back to localist ones. This network, too, used standard backpropagation. Its output units had softmax activation functions, so that the output vector constitutes a probability distribution over word types. These translate directly into surprisal values, which were collected over the experimental sentences at ten intervals over the course of Stage 3 training (after presenting 2K, 5K, 10K, 20K, 50K, 100K, 200K, and 350K sentences, and after presenting the full training corpus once and twice). These will be denoted by RNN-1 to RNN-10.

A much simpler RNN model suffices for obtaining unlexicalized surprisal. Here, we used the same models as described by Frank and Bod (2011), albeit trained on the POS tags of our BNC training corpus. These models employed so-called Echo State Networks (ESN; Jaeger and Haas, 2004), which are RNNs that do not develop internal representations because weights of input and recurrent connections remain fixed at random values (only the output connection weights are trained). Networks of six different sizes were used. Of each size, three networks were trained, using different random weights. The best and worst model of each size were discarded to reduce the effect of the random weights.

3 Experiment

3.1 Procedure

Text display followed a self-paced reading paradigm: Sentences were presented on a computer screen one word at a time, with onset of the next word being controlled by the subject through a key press. The time between word onset and subsequent key press was recorded as the RT (measured in milliseconds) on that word by that subject.[3] Words were presented centrally aligned in the screen, and punctuation marks appeared with the word that preceded them. A fixed-width font type (Courier New) was used, so that physical size of a word equalled number of characters. Order of presentation was randomized for each subject. The experiment was time-bounded to 40 minutes, and the number of sentences read by each participant varied between 120 and 349, with an average of 224. Yes-no comprehension questions followed 46% of the sentences.

3.2 Participants

A total of 117 first year psychology students took part in the experiment. Subjects unable to answer correctly to more than 20% of the questions and 47 participants who were non-native English speakers were excluded from the analysis, leaving a total of 54 subjects.

3.3 Design

The obtained RTs served as the dependent variable against which a mixed-effects multiple regression analysis with crossed random effects for subjects and items (Baayen et al., 2008) was performed. In order to control for low-level lexical factors that are known to influence RTs, such as word length or frequency, a baseline regression model taking them into account was built. Subsequently, the decrease in the model's deviance, after the inclusion of surprisal as a fixed factor to the baseline, was assessed using likelihood tests. The resulting χ^2 statistic indicates the extent to which each surprisal estimate accounts for RT, and can thus serve as a measure of the psychological accuracy of each model.

However, this kind of analysis assumes that RT for a word reflects processing of only that word,

[3]The collected RT data are available for download at www.stefanfrank.info/EACL2012.

but spill-over effects (in which processing difficulty at word w_t shows up in the RT on w_{t+1}) have been found in self-paced and natural reading (Just et al., 1982; Rayner, 1998; Rayner and Pollatsek, 1987). To evaluate these effects, the decrease in deviance after adding surprisal of the *previous* item to the baseline was also assessed.

The following control predictors were included in the baseline regression model:

Lexical factors:

- *Number of characters:* Both physical size and number of characters have been found to affect RTs for a word (Rayner and Pollatsek, 1987), but the fixed-width font used in the experiment assured number of characters also encoded physical word length.

- *Frequency and forward transitional probability:* The effects of these two factors have been repeatedly reported (e.g. Juhasz and Rayner, 2003; Rayner, 1998). Given the high correlations between surprisal and these two measures, their inclusion in the baseline assures that the results can be attributed to predictability in context, over and above frequency and bigram probability. Frequency was estimated from occurrence counts of each word in the full BNC corpus (written section). The same transformation (negative logarithm) was applied as for computing surprisal, thus obtaining "unconditional" and bigram surprisal values.

- *Previous word lexical factors:* Lexical factors for the previous word were included in the analysis to control for spill-over effects.

Temporal factors and autocorrelation:

RT data over naturalistic texts violate the regression assumption of independence of observations in several ways, and important word-by-word sequential correlations exist. In order to ensure validity of the statistical analysis, as well as providing a better model fit, the following factors were also included:

- *Sentence position:* Fatigue and practice effects can influence RTs. Sentence position in the experiment was included both as linear and quadratic factor, allowing for the modeling of initial speed-up due to practice, followed by a slowing down due to fatigue.

- *Word position:* Low-level effects of word order, not related to predictability itself, were modeled by including word position in the sentence, both as a linear and quadratic factor (some of the sentences were quite long, so that the effect of word position is unlikely to be linear).

- *Reading time for previous word:* As suggested by Baayen and Milin (2010), including RT on the previous word can control for several autocorrelation effects.

4 Results

Data were analysed using the free statistical software package R (R Development Core Team, 2009) and the lme4 library (Bates et al., 2011). Two analyses were performed for each language model, using surprisal for either current or previous word as the dependent variable. Unlikely reading times (lower than 50ms or over 3000ms) were removed from the analysis, as were clitics, words followed by punctuation, words following punctuation or clitics (since factors for previous word were included in the analysis), and sentence-initial words, leaving a total of 132,298 data points (between 1,335 and 3,829 per subject).

4.1 Baseline model

Theoretical considerations guided the selection of the initial predictors presented above, but an empirical approach led actual regression model building. Initial models with the original set of fixed effects, all two-way interactions, plus random intercepts for subjects and items were evaluated, and least significant factors were removed one at a time, until only significant predictors were left ($|t| > 2$). A different strategy was used to assess which by-subject and by item random slopes to include in the model. Given the large number of predictors, starting from the saturated model with all random slopes generated non-convergence problems and excessively long running times. By-subject and by-item random slopes for each fixed effect were therefore assessed individually, using likelihood tests. The final baseline model included by-subject random intercepts, by-subject random slopes for sentence position and word position, and by-item slopes for previous RT. All factors (random slopes and fixed effects) were centred and standardized to avoid

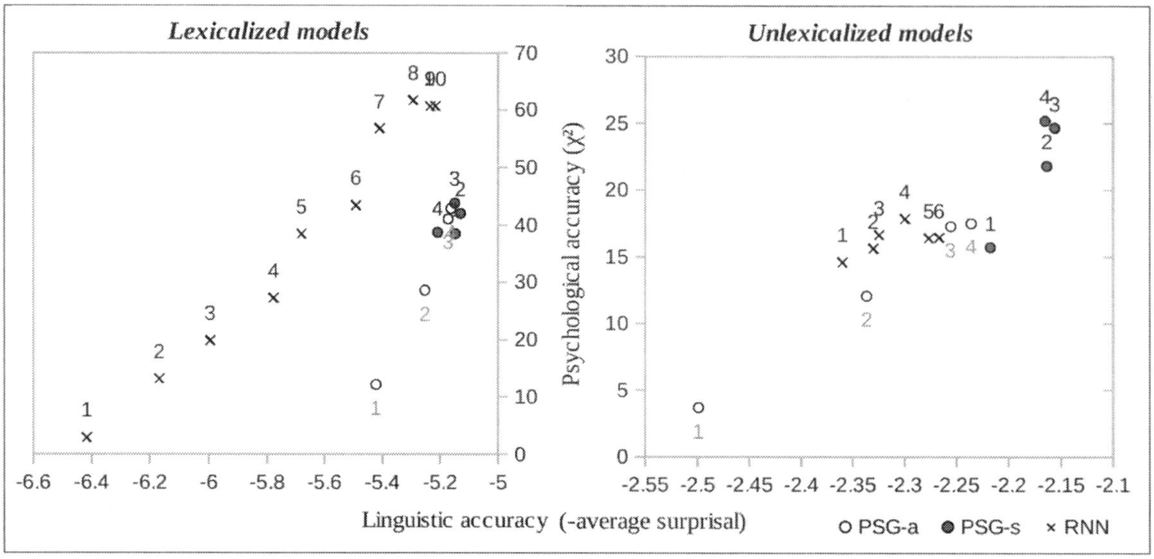

Figure 2: Psychological accuracy (combined effect of current and previous surprisal) against linguistic accuracy of the different models. Numbered labels denote the maximum number of levels up in the tree from which conditional information is used (PSG); point in training when estimates were collected (word-based RNN); or network size (POS-based RNN).

multicollinearity-related problems.

4.2 Surprisal effects

All model categories (PSGs and RNNs) produced lexicalized surprisal estimates that led to a significant ($p < 0.05$) decrease in deviance when included as a fixed factor in the baseline, with positive coefficients: Higher surprisal led to longer RTs. Significant effects were also found for their unlexicalized counterparts, albeit with considerably smaller χ^2-values.

Both for the lexicalized and unlexicalized versions, these effects persisted whether surprisal for the previous or current word was taken as the independent variable. However, the effect size was much larger for previous surprisal, indicating the presence of strong spill-over effects (e.g. lexicalized PSG-s_3: current surprisal: $\chi^2(1) = 7.29$, $p = 0.007$; previous surprisal: $\chi^2(1) = 36.73$, $p \ll 0.001$).

From hereon, only results for the combined effect of both (inclusion of previous and current surprisal as fixed factors in the baseline) are reported. Figure 2 shows the psychological accuracy of each model ($\chi^2(2)$ values) plotted against its linguistic accuracy (i.e., its quality as a language model, measured by the negative average surprisal on the experimental sentences: the higher this value, the "less surprised" the model is by the test corpus). For the lexicalized models, RNNs clearly outperform PSGs. Moreover, the RNN's accuracy increases as training progresses (the highest psychological accuracy is achieved at point 8, when 350K training sentences were presented). The PSGs taking into account sibling nodes are slightly better than their ancestor-only counterparts (the best psychological model is PSG-s_3). Contrary to the trend reported by Frank and Bod (2011), the unlexicalized PSGs and RNNs reach similar levels of psychological accuracy, with the PSG-s_4 achieving the highest χ^2-value.

Model comparison	$\chi^2(2)$	p-value
PSG over RNN	12.45	0.002
RNN over PSG	30.46	$\ll$0.001

Table 1: Model comparison between best performing word-based PSG and RNN.

Although RNNs outperform PSGs in the lexicalized estimates, comparisons between the best performing model (i.e. highest χ^2) in each category showed both were able to explain variance over and above each other (see Table 1). It is worth noting, however, that if comparisons are made amongst models including surprisal for current, but not previous word, the PSG is unable to explain a significant amount of variance over and above the RNN ($\chi^2(1) = 2.28; p = 0.13$).[4] Lexicalized models achieved greater psychological accuracy than their unlexicalized counterparts, but the latter could still explain a small amount of variance over and above the former (see Table 2).[5]

Model comparison	$\chi^2(2)$	p-value
Best models overall:		
POS- over word-based	10.40	0.006
word- over POS-based	47.02	$\ll$0.001
PSGs:		
POS- over word-based	6.89	0.032
word- over POS-based	25.50	$\ll$0.001
RNNs:		
POS- over word-based	5.80	0.055
word- over POS-based	49.74	$\ll$0.001

Table 2: Word- vs. POS-based models: comparisons between best models overall, and best models within each category.

4.3 Differences across word classes

In order to make sure that the lexicalized surprisal effects found were not limited to closed-class words (as Roark et al., 2009, report), a further model comparison was performed by adding by-POS random slopes of surprisal to the models containing the baseline plus surprisal. If particular syntactic categories were contributing to the overall effect of surprisal more than others, including such random slopes would lead to additional variance being explained. However, this was not the case: inclusion of by-POS random slopes of surprisal did not lead to a significant improvement in model fit (PSG: $\chi^2(1) = 0.86, p = 0.35$; RNN: $\chi^2(1) = 3.20, p = 0.07$).[6]

5 Discussion

The present study aimed to find further evidence for surprisal as a wide-coverage account of language processing difficulty, and indeed, the results show the ability of lexicalized surprisal to explain a significant amount of variance in RT data for naturalistic texts, over and above that accounted for by other low-level lexical factors, such as frequency, length, and forward transitional probability. Although previous studies had presented results supporting such a probabilistic language processing account, evidence for word-based surprisal was limited: Brouwer et al. (2010) only examined a specific psycholinguistic phenomenon, rather than a random language sample; Demberg and Keller (2008) reported effects that were only significant for POS but not word-based surprisal; and Smith and Levy (2008) found an effect of lexicalized surprisal (according to a trigram model), but did not assess whether simpler predictability estimates (i.e., by a bigram model) could have accounted for those effects.

Demberg and Keller's (2008) failure to find lexicalized surprisal effects can be attributed both to the language corpus used to train the language models, as well as to the experimental texts used. Both were sourced from newspaper texts: As training corpora these are unrepresentative of a person's linguistic experience, and as experimental texts they are heavily dependent on participant's world knowledge. Roark et al. (2009), in contrast, used a more representative, albeit relatively small, training corpus, as well as narrative-style stimuli, thus obtaining RTs less dependent on participant's prior knowledge. With such an experimental set-up, they were able to demonstrate the effects of lexical surprisal for RT of closed-class, but not open-class, words, which they attributed to their differential frequency and to training-data sparsity: The limited Brown corpus would have been enough to produce accurate estimates of surprisal for function words, but not for the less frequent content words. A larger training corpus, constituting a broad language sample, was used in our study, and the detected surprisal effects were shown to hold across syntactic category (modeling slopes for POS separately did not improve model fit). However, direct comparison with Roark et al.'s results is not possible: They employed alternative definitions of structural and lexical surprisal, which they derived by decomposing the total surprisal as obtained with a fully lexicalized PSG model.

In the current study, a similar approach to that taken by Demberg and Keller (2008) was used to

[4]Best models in this case were PSG-a_3 and RNN-7.

[5]Since best performing lexicalized and unlexicalized models belonged to different groups: RNN and PSG, respectively, Table 2 also shows comparisons within model type.

[6]Comparison was made on the basis of previous word surprisal (best models in this case were PSG-s_3 and RNN-9).

define structural (or unlexicalized), and lexicalized surprisal, but the results are strikingly different: Whereas Demberg and Keller report a significant effect for POS-based estimates, but not for word-based surprisal, our results show that lexicalized surprisal is a far better predictor of RTs than its unlexicalized counterpart. This is not surprising, given that while the unlexicalized models only have access to syntactic sources of information, the lexicalized models, like the human parser, can also take into account lexical co-occurrence trends. However, when a training corpus is not large enough to accurately capture the latter, it might still be able to model the former, given the higher frequency of occurrence of each possible item (POS vs. word) in the training data. Roark et al. (2009) also included in their analysis a POS-based surprisal estimate, which lost significance when the two components of the lexicalized surprisal were present, suggesting that such unlexicalized estimates can be interpreted only as a coarse version of the fully lexicalized surprisal, incorporating both syntactic and lexical sources of information at the same time. The results presented here do not replicate this finding: The best unlexicalized estimates were able to explain additional variance over and above the best word-based estimates. However, this comparison contrasted two different model types: a word-based RNN and a POS-based PSG, so that the observed effects could be attributed to the model representations (hierarchical vs. linear) rather than to the item of analysis (POS vs. words). Within-model comparisons showed that unlexicalized estimates were still able to account for additional variance, although only reaching significance at the 0.05 level for the PSGs.

Previous results reported by Frank (2009) and Frank and Bod (2011) regarding the higher psychological accuracy of RNNs and the inability of the PSGs to explain any additional variance in RT, were not replicated. Although for the word-based estimates RNNs outperform the PSGs, we found both to have independent effects. Furthermore, in the POS-based analysis, performance of PSGs and RNNs reaches similarly high levels of psychological accuracy, with the best-performing PSG producing slightly better results than the best-performing RNN. This discrepancy in the results could reflect contrasting reading styles in the two studies: natural reading of newspaper texts, or self-paced reading of independent, narrative sentences. The absence of global context, or the unnatural reading methodology employed in the current experiment, could have led to an increased reliance on hierarchical structure for sentence comprehension. The sources and structures relied upon by the human parser to elaborate upcoming-word expectations could therefore be task-dependent. On the other hand, our results show that the independent effects of word-based PSG estimates only become apparent when investigating the effect of surprisal of the previous word. That is, considering only the current word's surprisal, as in Frank and Bod's analysis, did not reveal a significant contribution of PSGs over and above RNNs. Thus, additional effects of PSG surprisal might only be apparent when spill-over effects are investigated by taking previous word surprisal as a predictor of RT.

6 Conclusion

The results here presented show that lexicalized surprisal can indeed model RT over naturalistic texts, thus providing a wide-coverage account of language processing difficulty. Failure of previous studies to find such an effect could be attributed to the size or nature of the training corpus, suggesting that larger and more general corpora are needed to model successfully both the structural and lexical regularities used by the human parser to generate predictions. Another crucial finding presented here is the importance of spill-over effects: Surprisal of a word had a much larger influence on RT of the following item than of the word itself. Previous studies where lexicalized surprisal was only analysed in relation to current RT could have missed a significant effect only manifested on the following item. Whether spill-over effects are as important for different RT collection paradigms (e.g., eye-tracking) remains to be tested.

Acknowledgments

The research presented here was funded by the European Union Seventh Framework Programme (FP7/2007-2013) under grant number 253803. The authors acknowledge the use of the UCL *Legion* High Performance Computing Facility, and associated support services, in the completion of this work.

References

Gerry T.M. Altmann and Yuki Kamide. 1999. Incremental interpretation at verbs: Restricting the domain of subsequent reference. *Cognition*, 73:247–264.

Mark Andrews, Gabriella Vigliocco, and David P. Vinson. 2009. Integrating experiential and distributional data to learn semantic representations. *Psychological Review*, 116:463–498.

R. Harald Baayen and Petar Milin. 2010. Analyzing reaction times. *International Journal of Psychological Research*, 3:12–28.

R. Harald Baayen, Doug J. Davidson, and Douglas M. Bates. 2008. Mixed-effects modeling with crossed random effects for subjects and items. *Journal of Memory and Language*, 59:390–412.

Moshe Bar. 2007. The proactive brain: using analogies and associations to generate predictions. *Trends in Cognitive Sciences*, 11:280–289.

Douglas Bates, Martin Maechler, and Ben Bolker, 2011. *lme4: Linear mixed-effects models using S4 classes.* Available from: http://CRAN.R-project.org/package=lme4 (R package version 0.999375-39).

Yoshua Bengio, Réjean Ducharme, Pascal Vincent, and Christian Jauvin. 2003. A neural probabilistic language model. *Journal of Machine Learning Research*, 3:1137–1155.

Marisa Ferrara Boston, John Hale, Reinhold Kliegl, Umesh Patil, and Shravan Vasishth. 2008. Parsing costs as predictors of reading difficulty: An evaluation using the potsdam sentence corpus. *Journal of Eye Movement Research,*, 2:1–12.

Harm Brouwer, Hartmut Fitz, and John C. J. Hoeks. 2010. Modeling the noun phrase versus sentence coordination ambiguity in Dutch: evidence from surprisal theory. In *Proceedings of the 2010 Workshop on Cognitive Modeling and Computational Linguistics*, pages 72–80, Stroudsburg, PA, USA.

John A. Bullinaria and Joseph P. Levy. 2007. Extracting semantic representations from word co-occurrence statistics: A computational study. *Behavior Research Methods*, 39:510–526.

Vera Demberg and Frank Keller. 2008. Data from eye-tracking corpora as evidence for theories of syntactic processing complexity. *Cognition*, 109:193–210.

Stefan L. Frank and Rens Bod. 2011. Insensitivity of the human sentence-processing system to hierarchical structure. *Psychological Science*, 22:829–834.

Stefan L. Frank. 2009. Surprisal-based comparison between a symbolic and a connectionist model of sentence processing. In *Proceedings of the 31st Annual Conference of the Cognitive Science Society*, pages 1139–1144, Austin, TX.

Stefan L. Frank. 2012. Uncertainty reduction as a measure of cognitive processing load in sentence comprehension. *Manuscript submitted for publication.*

Peter Hagoort, Lea Hald, Marcel Bastiaansen, and Karl Magnus Petersson. 2004. Integration of word meaning and world knowledge in language comprehension. *Science*, 304:438–441.

John Hale. 2001. A probabilistic earley parser as a psycholinguistic model. In *Proceedings of the second meeting of the North American Chapter of the Association for Computational Linguistics on Language technologies*, pages 1–8, Stroudsburg, PA.

Herbert Jaeger and Harald Haas. 2004. Harnessing nonlinearity: predicting chaotic systems and saving energy in wireless communication. *Science*, pages 78–80.

Barbara J. Juhasz and Keith Rayner. 2003. Investigating the effects of a set of intercorrelated variables on eye fixation durations in reading. *Journal of Experimental Psychology: Learning, Memory and Cognition*, 29:1312–1318.

Marcel A. Just, Patricia A. Carpenter, and Jacqueline D. Woolley. 1982. Paradigms and processes in reading comprehension. *Journal of Experimental Psychology: General*, 111:228–238.

Yuki Kamide, Christoph Scheepers, and Gerry T. M. Altmann. 2003. Integration of syntactic and semantic information in predictive processing: cross-linguistic evidence from German and English. *Journal of Psycholinguistic Research*, 32:37–55.

Alan Kennedy and Joël Pynte. 2005. Parafoveal-on foveal effects in normal reading. *Vision Research*, 45:153–168.

Dan Klein and Christopher D. Manning. 2003. Accurate unlexicalized parsing. In *Proceedings of the 41st Meeting of the Association for Computational Linguistics,*, pages 423–430.

Kestutis Kveraga, Avniel S. Ghuman, and Moshe Bar. 2007. Top-down predictions in the cognitive brain. *Brain and Cognition*, 65:145–168.

Roger Levy. 2008. Expectation-based syntactic comprehension. *Cognition*, 106:1126–1177.

Mitchell P. Marcus, Mary Ann Marcinkiewicz, and Beatrice Santorini. 1993. Building a large annotated corpus of English: the Penn Treebank. *Computational Linguistics*, 19:313–330.

Scott A. McDonald and Richard C. Shillcock. 2003. Low-level predictive inference in reading: the influence of transitional probabilities on eye movements. *Vision Research*, 43:1735–1751.

Andriy Mnih and Geoffrey Hinton. 2007. Three new graphical models for statistical language modelling. *Proceedings of the 25th International Conference of Machine Learning*, pages 641–648.

Keith Rayner and Alexander Pollatsek. 1987. Eye movements in reading: A tutorial review. In

M. Coltheart, editor, *Attention and performance XII: the psychology of reading.*, pages 327–362. Lawrence Erlbaum Associates, London, UK.

Keith Rayner. 1998. Eye movements in reading and information processing: 20 years of research. *Psychological Bulletin*, 124:372–422.

Brian Roark, Asaf Bachrach, Carlos Cardenas, and Christophe Pallier. 2009. Deriving lexical and syntactic expectation-based measures for psycholinguistic modeling via incremental top-down parsing. In *Proceedings of the 2009 Conference on Empirical Methods in Natural Language Processing: Volume 1 - Volume 1*, pages 324–333, Stroudsburg, PA.

Brian Roark. 2001. Probabilistic top-down parsing and language modeling. *Computational Linguistics*, 27:249–276.

Beatrice Santorini. 1991. Part-of-speech tagging guidelines for the Penn Treebank Project. Technical report, Philadelphia, PA.

Nathaniel J. Smith and Roger Levy. 2008. Optimal processing times in reading: a formal model and empirical investigation. In *Proceedings of the 30th Annual Conference of the Cognitive Science Society*, pages 595–600, Austin,TX.

Andreas Stolcke. 1995. An efficient probabilistic context-free parsing algorithm that computes prefix probabilities. *Computational linguistics*, 21:165–201.

Yoshimasa Tsuruoka and Jun'ichi Tsujii. 2005. Bidirectional inference with the easiest-first strategy for tagging sequence data. In *Proceedings of the conference on Human Language Technology and Empirical Methods in Natural Language Processing*, pages 467–474, Stroudsburg, PA.

Spectral Learning for Non-Deterministic Dependency Parsing

Franco M. Luque
Universidad Nacional de Córdoba
and CONICET
Córdoba X5000HUA, Argentina
francolq@famaf.unc.edu.ar

Ariadna Quattoni and **Borja Balle** and **Xavier Carreras**
Universitat Politècnica de Catalunya
Barcelona E-08034
{aquattoni,bballe,carreras}@lsi.upc.edu

Abstract

In this paper we study spectral learning methods for non-deterministic split head-automata grammars, a powerful hidden-state formalism for dependency parsing. We present a learning algorithm that, like other spectral methods, is efficient and non-susceptible to local minima. We show how this algorithm can be formulated as a technique for inducing hidden structure from distributions computed by forward-backward recursions. Furthermore, we also present an inside-outside algorithm for the parsing model that runs in cubic time, hence maintaining the standard parsing costs for context-free grammars.

1 Introduction

Dependency structures of natural language sentences exhibit a significant amount of non-local phenomena. Historically, there have been two main approaches to model non-locality: (1) increasing the order of the factors of a dependency model (e.g. with sibling and grandparent relations (Eisner, 2000; McDonald and Pereira, 2006; Carreras, 2007; Martins et al., 2009; Koo and Collins, 2010)), and (2) using hidden states to pass information across factors (Matsuzaki et al., 2005; Petrov et al., 2006; Musillo and Merlo, 2008).

Higher-order models have the advantage that they are relatively easy to train, because estimating the parameters of the model can be expressed as a convex optimization. However, they have two main drawbacks. (1) The number of parameters grows significantly with the size of the factors, leading to potential data-sparsity problems. A solution to address the data-sparsity problem is to explicitly tell the model what properties of higher-order factors need to be remembered. This can be achieved by means of feature engineering, but compressing such information into a state of bounded size will typically be labor intensive, and will not generalize across languages. (2) Increasing the size of the factors generally results in polynomial increases in the parsing cost.

In principle, hidden variable models could solve some of the problems of feature engineering in higher-order factorizations, since they could automatically induce the information in a derivation history that should be passed across factors. Potentially, they would require less feature engineering since they can learn from an annotated corpus an optimal way to compress derivations into hidden states. For example, one line of work has added hidden annotations to the non-terminals of a phrase-structure grammar (Matsuzaki et al., 2005; Petrov et al., 2006; Musillo and Merlo, 2008), resulting in compact grammars that obtain parsing accuracies comparable to lexicalized grammars. A second line of work has modeled hidden sequential structure, like in our case, but using PDFA (Infante-Lopez and de Rijke, 2004). Finally, a third line of work has induced hidden structure from the history of actions of a parser (Titov and Henderson, 2007).

However, the main drawback of the hidden variable approach to parsing is that, to the best of our knowledge, there has not been any convex formulation of the learning problem. As a result, training a hidden-variable model is both expensive and prone to local minima issues.

In this paper we present a learning algorithm for hidden-state split head-automata grammars (SHAG) (Eisner and Satta, 1999). In this formalism, head-modifier sequences are generated by a collection of finite-state automata. In our case, the underlying machines are probabilistic non-deterministic finite state automata (PNFA), which we parameterize using the *operator model* representation. This representation allows the use of simple spectral algorithms for estimating the model parameters from data (Hsu et al., 2009; Bailly, 2011; Balle et al., 2012). In all previous work, the algorithms used to induce hidden structure require running repeated inference on training data—e.g. Expectation-Maximization (Dempster et al., 1977), or split-merge algorithms. In contrast, spectral methods are simple and very efficient —parameter estimation is reduced to computing some data statistics, performing SVD, and inverting matrices.

The main contributions of this paper are:

- We present a spectral learning algorithm for inducing PNFA with applications to head-automata dependency grammars. Our formulation is based on thinking about the distribution generated by a PNFA in terms of the forward-backward recursions.
- Spectral learning algorithms in previous work only use statistics of prefixes of sequences. In contrast, our algorithm is able to learn from substring statistics.
- We derive an inside-outside algorithm for non-deterministic SHAG that runs in cubic time, keeping the costs of CFG parsing.
- In experiments we show that adding non-determinism improves the accuracy of several baselines. When we compare our algorithm to EM we observe a reduction of two orders of magnitude in training time.

The paper is organized as follows. Next section describes the necessary background on SHAG and operator models. Section 3 introduces Operator SHAG for parsing, and presents a spectral learning algorithm. Section 4 presents a parsing algorithm. Section 5 presents experiments and analysis of results, and section 6 concludes.

2 Preliminaries

2.1 Head-Automata Dependency Grammars

In this work we use split head-automata grammars (SHAG) (Eisner and Satta, 1999; Eisner, 2000), a context-free grammatical formalism whose derivations are projective dependency trees. We will use $x_{i:j} = x_i x_{i+1} \cdots x_j$ to denote a sequence of symbols x_t with $i \leq t \leq j$. A SHAG generates sentences $s_{0:N}$, where symbols $s_t \in \mathcal{X}$ with $1 \leq t \leq N$ are regular words and $s_0 = \star \notin \mathcal{X}$ is a special root symbol. Let $\bar{\mathcal{X}} = \mathcal{X} \cup \{\star\}$. A derivation y, i.e. a dependency tree, is a collection of *head-modifier* sequences $\langle h, d, x_{1:T} \rangle$, where $h \in \bar{\mathcal{X}}$ is a word, $d \in \{\text{LEFT}, \text{RIGHT}\}$ is a direction, and $x_{1:T}$ is a sequence of T words, where each $x_t \in \mathcal{X}$ is a *modifier* of h in direction d. We say that h is the *head* of each x_t. Modifier sequences $x_{1:T}$ are ordered head-outwards, i.e. among $x_{1:T}$, x_1 is the word closest to h in the derived sentence, and x_T is the furthest. A derivation y of a sentence $s_{0:N}$ consists of a LEFT and a RIGHT head-modifier sequence for each s_t. As special cases, the LEFT sequence of the root symbol is always empty, while the RIGHT one consists of a single word corresponding to the head of the sentence. We denote by $\mathcal{Y}$ the set of all valid derivations.

Assume a derivation y contains $\langle h, \text{LEFT}, x_{1:T} \rangle$ and $\langle h, \text{RIGHT}, x'_{1:T'} \rangle$. Let $\mathcal{L}(y, h)$ be the derived sentence *headed* by h, which can be expressed as $\mathcal{L}(y, x_T) \cdots \mathcal{L}(y, x_1)\ h\ \mathcal{L}(y, x'_1) \cdots \mathcal{L}(y, x'_{T'})$.[1] The language generated by a SHAG are the strings $\mathcal{L}(y, \star)$ for any $y \in \mathcal{Y}$.

In this paper we use probabilistic versions of SHAG where probabilities of head-modifier sequences in a derivation are independent of each other:

$$\mathbb{P}(y) = \prod_{\langle h,d,x_{1:T} \rangle \in y} \mathbb{P}(x_{1:T} | h, d) \quad . \qquad (1)$$

In the literature, standard *arc-factored* models further assume that

$$\mathbb{P}(x_{1:T} | h, d) = \prod_{t=1}^{T+1} \mathbb{P}(x_t | h, d, \sigma_t) \quad , \qquad (2)$$

where x_{T+1} is always a special STOP word, and σ_t is the state of a deterministic automaton generating $x_{1:T+1}$. For example, setting $\sigma_1 = \text{FIRST}$ and $\sigma_{t>1} = \text{REST}$ corresponds to first-order models, while setting $\sigma_1 = \text{NULL}$ and $\sigma_{t>1} = x_{t-1}$ corresponds to sibling models (Eisner, 2000; McDonald et al., 2005; McDonald and Pereira, 2006).

[1]Throughout the paper we assume we can distinguish the words in a derivation, irrespective of whether two words at different positions correspond to the same symbol.

2.2 Operator Models

An operator model $\mathbf{A}$ with n states is a tuple $\langle \alpha_1, \alpha_\infty^\top, \{A_a\}_{a \in \mathcal{X}} \rangle$, where $A_a \in \mathbb{R}^{n \times n}$ is an *operator* matrix and $\alpha_1, \alpha_\infty \in \mathbb{R}^n$ are vectors. $\mathbf{A}$ computes a function $f : \mathcal{X}^* \rightarrow \mathbb{R}$ as follows:

$$f(x_{1:T}) = \alpha_\infty^\top A_{x_T} \cdots A_{x_1} \alpha_1 \quad . \qquad (3)$$

One intuitive way of understanding operator models is to consider the case where f computes a probability distribution over strings. Such a distribution can be described in two equivalent ways: by making some independence assumptions and providing the corresponding parameters, or by explaining the process used to compute f. This is akin to describing the distribution defined by an HMM in terms of a factorization and its corresponding transition and emission parameters, or using the inductive equations of the forward algorithm. The operator model representation takes the latter approach.

Operator models have had numerous applications. For example, they can be used as an alternative parameterization of the function computed by an HMM (Hsu et al., 2009). Consider an HMM with n hidden states and initial-state probabilities $\pi \in \mathbb{R}^n$, transition probabilities $T \in \mathbb{R}^{n \times n}$, and observation probabilities $O_a \in \mathbb{R}^{n \times n}$ for each $a \in \mathcal{X}$, with the following meaning:

- $\pi(i)$ is the probability of starting at state i,
- $T(i, j)$ is the probability of transitioning from state j to state i,
- O_a is a diagonal matrix, such that $O_a(i, i)$ is the probability of generating symbol a from state i.

Given an HMM, an equivalent operator model can be defined by setting $\alpha_1 = \pi$, $A_a = TO_a$ and $\alpha_\infty = \vec{1}$. To see this, let us show that the forward algorithm computes the expression in equation (3). Let σ_t denote the state of the HMM at time t. Consider a state-distribution vector $\alpha_t \in \mathbb{R}^n$, where $\alpha_t(i) = \mathbb{P}(x_{1:t-1}, \sigma_t = i)$. Initially $\alpha_1 = \pi$. At each step in the chain of products (3), $\alpha_{t+1} = A_{x_t} \alpha_t$ updates the state distribution from positions t to $t + 1$ by applying the appropriate operator, i.e. by emitting symbol x_t and transitioning to the new state distribution. The probability of $x_{1:T}$ is given by $\sum_i \alpha_{T+1}(i)$. Hence, $A_a(i, j)$ is the probability of generating symbol a and moving to state i given that we are at state j.

HMM are only one example of distributions that can be parameterized by operator models. In general, operator models can parameterize any PNFA, where the parameters of the model correspond to probabilities of emitting a symbol from a state *and* moving to the next state.

The advantage of working with operator models is that, under certain mild assumptions on the operator parameters, there exist algorithms that can estimate the operators from observable statistics of the input sequences. These algorithms are extremely efficient and are not susceptible to local minima issues. See (Hsu et al., 2009) for theoretical proofs of the learnability of HMM under the operator model representation.

In the following, we write $x = x_{i:j} \in \mathcal{X}^*$ to denote sequences of symbols, and use $A_{x_{i:j}}$ as a shorthand for $A_{x_j} \cdots A_{x_i}$. Also, for convenience we assume $\mathcal{X} = \{1, \ldots, l\}$, so that we can index vectors and matrices by symbols in $\mathcal{X}$.

3 Learning Operator SHAG

We will define a SHAG using a collection of operator models to compute probabilities. Assume that for each possible head h in the vocabulary $\bar{\mathcal{X}}$ and each direction $d \in \{\text{LEFT}, \text{RIGHT}\}$ we have an operator model that computes probabilities of modifier sequences as follows:

$$\mathbb{P}(x_{1:T} | h, d) = (\alpha_\infty^{h,d})^\top A_{x_T}^{h,d} \cdots A_{x_1}^{h,d} \alpha_1^{h,d} \quad .$$

Then, this collection of operator models defines an *operator SHAG* that assigns a probability to each $y \in \mathcal{Y}$ according to (1). To learn the model parameters, namely $\langle \alpha_1^{h,d}, \alpha_\infty^{h,d}, \{A_a^{h,d}\}_{a \in \mathcal{X}} \rangle$ for $h \in \bar{\mathcal{X}}$ and $d \in \{\text{LEFT}, \text{RIGHT}\}$, we use spectral learning methods based on the works of Hsu et al. (2009), Bailly (2011) and Balle et al. (2012).

The main challenge of learning an operator model is to infer a hidden-state space from observable quantities, i.e. quantities that can be computed from the distribution of sequences that we observe. As it turns out, we cannot recover the actual hidden-state space used by the operators we wish to learn. The key insight of the spectral learning method is that we can recover a hidden-state space that corresponds to a projection of the original hidden space. Such projected space is equivalent to the original one in the sense that we can find operators in the projected space that parameterize the *same* probability distribution over sequences.

In the rest of this section we describe an algorithm for learning an operator model. We will assume a fixed head word and direction, and drop h and d from all terms. Hence, our goal is to learn the following distribution, parameterized by operators α_1, $\{A_a\}_{a \in \mathcal{X}}$, and α_∞:

$$\mathbb{P}(x_{1:T}) = \alpha_\infty^\top A_{x_T} \cdots A_{x_1} \alpha_1 \ . \quad (4)$$

Our algorithm shares many features with the previous spectral algorithms of Hsu et al. (2009) and Bailly (2011), though the derivation given here is based upon the general formulation of Balle et al. (2012). The main difference is that our algorithm is able to learn operator models from *substring* statistics, while algorithms in previous works were restricted to statistics on prefixes. In principle, our algorithm should extract much more information from a sample.

3.1 Preliminary Definitions

The spectral learning algorithm will use statistics estimated from samples of the target distribution. More specifically, consider the function that computes the expected number of occurrences of a substring x in a random string x' drawn from $\mathbb{P}$:

$$\begin{aligned} f(x) &= \mathbb{E}(x \sqsubseteq_\sharp x') \\ &= \sum_{x' \in \mathcal{X}^*} (x \sqsubseteq_\sharp x') \mathbb{P}(x') \\ &= \sum_{p,s \in \mathcal{X}^*} \mathbb{P}(pxs) \ , \end{aligned} \quad (5)$$

where $x \sqsubseteq_\sharp x'$ denotes the number of times x appears in x'. Here we assume that the true values of $f(x)$ for bigrams are known, though in practice the algorithm will work with empirical estimates of these.

The information about f known by the algorithm is organized in matrix form as follows. Let $P \in \mathbb{R}^{l \times l}$ be a matrix containing the value of $f(x)$ for all strings of length two, i.e. bigrams.[2]. That is, each entry in $P \in \mathbb{R}^{l \times l}$ contains the expected number of occurrences of a given bigram:

$$P(b, a) = \mathbb{E}(ab \sqsubseteq_\sharp x) \ . \quad (6)$$

[2]In fact, while we restrict ourselves to strings of length two, an analogous algorithm can be derived that considers longer strings to define P. See (Balle et al., 2012) for details.

Furthermore, for each $b \in \mathcal{X}$ let $P_b \in \mathbb{R}^{l \times l}$ denote the matrix whose entries are given by

$$P_b(c, a) = \mathbb{E}(abc \sqsubseteq_\sharp x) \ , \quad (7)$$

the expected number of occurrences of trigrams. Finally, we define vectors $p_1 \in \mathbb{R}^l$ and $p_\infty \in \mathbb{R}^l$ as follows: $p_1(a) = \sum_{s \in \mathcal{X}^*} \mathbb{P}(as)$, the probability that a string begins with a particular symbol; and $p_\infty(a) = \sum_{p \in \mathcal{X}^*} \mathbb{P}(pa)$, the probability that a string ends with a particular symbol.

Now we show a particularly useful way to express the quantities defined above in terms of the operators $\langle \alpha_1, \alpha_\infty^\top, \{A_a\}_{a \in \mathcal{X}} \rangle$ of $\mathbb{P}$. First, note that each entry of P can be written in this form:

$$\begin{aligned} P(b, a) &= \sum_{p,s \in \mathcal{X}^*} \mathbb{P}(pabs) \quad (8) \\ &= \sum_{p,s \in \mathcal{X}^*} \alpha_\infty^\top A_s A_b A_a A_p \alpha_1 \\ &= (\alpha_\infty^\top \sum_{s \in \mathcal{X}^*} A_s) A_b A_a (\sum_{p \in \mathcal{X}^*} A_p \alpha_1) \ . \end{aligned}$$

It is not hard to see that, since $\mathbb{P}$ is a probability distribution over $\mathcal{X}^*$, actually $\alpha_\infty^\top \sum_{s \in \mathcal{X}^*} A_s = \vec{1}^\top$. Furthermore, since $\sum_{p \in \mathcal{X}^*} A_p = \sum_{k \geq 0} (\sum_{a \in \mathcal{X}} A_a)^k = (I - \sum_{a \in \mathcal{X}} A_a)^{-1}$, we write $\tilde{\alpha}_1 = (I - \sum_{a \in \mathcal{X}} A_a)^{-1} \alpha_1$. From (8) it is natural to define a *forward* matrix $F \in \mathbb{R}^{n \times l}$ whose ath column contains the sum of all hidden-state vectors obtained after generating all prefixes ended in a:

$$F(:, a) = A_a \sum_{p \in \mathcal{X}^*} A_p \alpha_1 = A_a \tilde{\alpha}_1 \ . \quad (9)$$

Conversely, we also define a *backward* matrix $B \in \mathbb{R}^{l \times n}$ whose ath row contains the probability of generating a from any possible state:

$$B(a, :) = \alpha_\infty^\top \sum_{s \in \mathcal{X}^*} A_s A_a = \vec{1}^\top A_a \ . \quad (10)$$

By plugging the forward and backward matrices into (8) one obtains the factorization $P = BF$. With similar arguments it is easy to see that one also has $P_b = B A_b F$, $p_1 = B \alpha_1$, and $p_\infty^\top = \alpha_\infty^\top F$. Hence, if B and F were known, one could in principle invert these expressions in order to recover the operators of the model from empirical estimations computed from a sample. In the next section we show that in fact one does not need to know B and F to learn an operator model for $\mathbb{P}$, but rather that having a "good" factorization of P is enough.

3.2 Inducing a Hidden-State Space

We have shown that an operator model $\mathbf{A}$ computing $\mathbb{P}$ induces a factorization of the matrix P, namely $P = BF$. More generally, it turns out that when the rank of P equals the minimal number of states of an operator model that computes $\mathbb{P}$, then one can prove a duality relation between operators and factorizations of P. In particular, one can show that, for any rank factorization $P = QR$, the operators given by $\bar{\alpha}_1 = Q^+ p_1$, $\bar{\alpha}_\infty^\top = p_\infty^\top R^+$, and $\bar{A}_a = Q^+ P_a R^+$, yield an operator model for $\mathbb{P}$. A key fact in proving this result is that the function $\mathbb{P}$ is invariant to the basis chosen to represent operator matrices. See (Balle et al., 2012) for further details.

Thus, we can recover an operator model for $\mathbb{P}$ from any rank factorization of P, provided a rank assumption on P holds (which hereafter we assume to be the case). Since we only have access to an approximation of P, it seems reasonable to choose a factorization which is robust to estimation errors. A natural such choice is the thin SVD decomposition of P (i.e. using top n singular vectors), given by: $P = U(\Sigma V^\top) = U(U^\top P)$. Intuitively, we can think of U and $U^\top P$ as projected backward and forward matrices. Now that we have a factorization of P we can construct an operator model for $\mathbb{P}$ as follows: [3]

$$\bar{\alpha}_1 = U^\top p_1 \ , \tag{11}$$

$$\bar{\alpha}_\infty^\top = p_\infty^\top (U^\top P)^+ \ , \tag{12}$$

$$\bar{A}_a = U^\top P_a (U^\top P)^+ \ . \tag{13}$$

Algorithm 1 presents pseudo-code for an algorithm learning operators of a SHAG from training head-modifier sequences using this spectral method. Note that each operator model in the SHAG is learned separately. The running time of the algorithm is dominated by two computations. First, a pass over the training sequences to compute statistics over unigrams, bigrams and trigrams. Second, SVD and matrix operations for computing the operators, which run in time cubic in the number of symbols l. However, note that when dealing with sparse matrices many of these operations can be performed more efficiently.

[3] To see that equations (11-13) define a model for $\mathbb{P}$, one must first see that the matrix $M = F(\Sigma V^\top)^+$ is invertible with inverse $M^{-1} = U^\top B$. Using this and recalling that $p_1 = B\alpha_1$, $P_a = BA_aF$, $p_\infty^\top = \alpha_\infty^\top F$, one obtains that:

$$\begin{aligned}
\bar{\alpha}_1 &= U^\top B \alpha_1 = M^{-1}\alpha_1 \ , \\
\bar{\alpha}_\infty^\top &= \alpha_\infty^\top F (U^\top BF)^+ = \alpha_\infty^\top M \ , \\
\bar{A}_a &= U^\top B A_a F (U^\top BF)^+ = M^{-1} A_a M \ .
\end{aligned}$$

Finally:

$$\begin{aligned}
\mathbb{P}(x_{1:T}) &= \alpha_\infty^\top A_{x_T} \cdots A_{x_1} \alpha_1 \\
&= \alpha_\infty^\top M M^{-1} A_{x_T} M \cdots M^{-1} A_{x_1} M M^{-1} \alpha_1 \\
&= \bar{\alpha}_\infty^\top \bar{A}_{x_T} \cdots \bar{A}_{x_1} \bar{\alpha}_1
\end{aligned}$$

Algorithm 1 Learn Operator SHAG

inputs:

- An alphabet $\mathcal{X}$
- A training set TRAIN $= \{\langle h^i, d^i, x^i_{1:T}\rangle\}_{i=1}^M$
- The number of hidden states n

```
for each h ∈ X̄ and d ∈ {LEFT, RIGHT} do
    Compute an empirical estimate from TRAIN of
    statistics matrices p̂_1, p̂_∞, P̂, and {P̂_a}_{a∈X}
    Compute the SVD of P̂ and let Û be the matrix
    of top n left singular vectors of P̂
    Compute the observable operators for h and d:
        α̂_1^{h,d} = Û^T p̂_1
        (α̂_∞^{h,d})^T = p̂_∞^T (Û^T P̂)^+
        Â_a^{h,d} = Û^T P̂_a (Û^T P̂)^+   for each a ∈ X
end for
return Operators ⟨α̂_1^{h,d}, α̂_∞^{h,d}, Â_a^{h,d}⟩
    for each h ∈ X̄, d ∈ {LEFT, RIGHT}, a ∈ X
```

4 Parsing Algorithms

Given a sentence $s_{0:N}$ we would like to find its most likely derivation, $\hat{y} = \mathrm{argmax}_{y \in \mathcal{Y}(s_{0:N})} \mathbb{P}(y)$. This problem, known as MAP inference, is known to be intractable for hidden-state structure prediction models, as it involves finding the most likely tree structure while summing out over hidden states. We use a common approximation to MAP based on first computing posterior marginals of tree edges (i.e. dependencies) and then maximizing over the tree structure (see (Park and Darwiche, 2004) for complexity of general MAP inference and approximations). For parsing, this strategy is sometimes known as MBR decoding; previous work has shown that empirically it gives good performance (Goodman, 1996; Clark and Curran, 2004; Titov and Henderson, 2006; Petrov and Klein, 2007). In our case, we use the non-deterministic SHAG to compute posterior marginals of dependencies. We first explain the general strategy of MBR decoding, and then present an algorithm to compute marginals.

Let (s_i, s_j) denote a dependency between head word i and modifier word j. The posterior or *marginal probability* of a dependency (s_i, s_j) given a sentence $s_{0:N}$ is defined as

$$\mu_{i,j} = \mathbb{P}((s_i, s_j) \mid s_{0:N}) = \sum_{y \in \mathcal{Y}(s_{0:N}) \,:\, (s_i,s_j) \in y} \mathbb{P}(y) \ .$$

To compute marginals, the sum over derivations can be decomposed into a product of inside and outside quantities (Baker, 1979). Below we describe an inside-outside algorithm for our grammars. Given a sentence $s_{0:N}$ and marginal scores $\mu_{i,j}$, we compute the parse tree for $s_{0:N}$ as

$$\hat{y} = \underset{y \in \mathcal{Y}(s_{0:N})}{\operatorname{argmax}} \sum_{(s_i,s_j) \in y} \log \mu_{i,j} \qquad (14)$$

using the standard projective parsing algorithm for arc-factored models (Eisner, 2000). Overall we use a two-pass parsing process, first to compute marginals and then to compute the best tree.

4.1 An Inside-Outside Algorithm

In this section we sketch an algorithm to compute marginal probabilities of dependencies. Our algorithm is an adaptation of the parsing algorithm for SHAG by Eisner and Satta (1999) to the case of non-deterministic head-automata, and has a runtime cost of $O(n^2N^3)$, where n is the number of states of the model, and N is the length of the input sentence. Hence the algorithm maintains the standard cubic cost on the sentence length, while the quadratic cost on n is inherent to the computations defined by our model in Eq. (3). The main insight behind our extension is that, because the computations of our model involve state-distribution vectors, we need to extend the standard inside/outside quantities to be in the form of such state-distribution quantities.[4]

Throughout this section we assume a fixed sentence $s_{0:N}$. Let $\mathcal{Y}(x_{i:j})$ be the set of derivations that yield a subsequence $x_{i:j}$. For a derivation y, we use $\mathrm{root}(y)$ to indicate the root word of it, and use $(x_i, x_j) \in y$ to refer a dependency in y from head x_i to modifier x_j. Following Eisner and Satta (1999), we use decoding structures related to complete half-constituents (or "triangles", denoted C) and incomplete half-constituents (or "trapezoids", denoted I), each decorated with a direction (denoted L and R). We assume familiarity with their algorithm.

We define $\theta^{\mathrm{I,R}}_{i,j} \in \mathbb{R}^n$ as the inside score-vector of a right trapezoid dominated by dependency (s_i, s_j),

$$\theta^{\mathrm{I,R}}_{i,j} = \sum_{\substack{y \in \mathcal{Y}(s_{i:j}) \,:\, (s_i,s_j) \in y \ , \\ y = \{\langle s_i, \mathrm{R}, x_{1:t} \rangle\} \cup y' \ , \ x_t = s_j}} \mathbb{P}(y') \alpha^{s_i,\mathrm{R}}(x_{1:t}) \ . \qquad (15)$$

The term $\mathbb{P}(y')$ is the probability of head-modifier sequences in the range $s_{i:j}$ that do not involve s_i. The term $\alpha^{s_i,\mathrm{R}}(x_{1:t})$ is a *forward* state-distribution vector —the qth coordinate of the vector is the probability that s_i generates right modifiers $x_{1:t}$ and remains at state q. Similarly, we define $\phi^{\mathrm{I,R}}_{i,j} \in \mathbb{R}^n$ as the outside score-vector of a right trapezoid, as

$$\phi^{\mathrm{I,R}}_{i,j} = \sum_{\substack{y \in \mathcal{Y}(s_{0:i} s_{j:n}) \,:\, \mathrm{root}(y) = s_0, \\ y = \{\langle s_i, \mathrm{R}, x_{t:T} \rangle\} \cup y' \ , \ x_t = s_j}} \mathbb{P}(y') \beta^{s_i,\mathrm{R}}(x_{t+1:T}) \ , \qquad (16)$$

where $\beta^{s_i,\mathrm{R}}(x_{t+1:T}) \in \mathbb{R}^n$ is a *backward* state-distribution vector —the qth coordinate is the probability of being at state q of the right automaton of s_i and generating $x_{t+1:T}$. Analogous inside-outside expressions can be defined for the rest of structures (left/right triangles and trapezoids). With these quantities, we can compute marginals as

$$\mu_{i,j} = \begin{cases} (\phi^{\mathrm{I,R}}_{i,j})^\top \, \theta^{\mathrm{I,R}}_{i,j} \, Z^{-1} & \text{if } i < j \ , \\ (\phi^{\mathrm{I,L}}_{i,j})^\top \, \theta^{\mathrm{I,L}}_{i,j} \, Z^{-1} & \text{if } j < i \ , \end{cases} \qquad (17)$$

where $Z = \sum_{y \in \mathcal{Y}(s_{0:N})} \mathbb{P}(y) = (\alpha^{\star,\mathrm{R}}_{\infty})^\top \, \theta^{\mathrm{C,R}}_{0,N}$.

Finally, we sketch the equations for computing inside scores in $O(N^3)$ time. The outside equations can be derived analogously (see (Paskin, 2001)). For $0 \le i < j \le N$:

$$\theta^{\mathrm{C,R}}_{i,i} = \alpha^{s_i,\mathrm{R}}_1 \qquad (18)$$

$$\theta^{\mathrm{C,R}}_{i,j} = \sum_{k=i+1}^{j} \theta^{\mathrm{I,R}}_{i,k} \left((\alpha^{s_k,\mathrm{R}}_{\infty})^\top \, \theta^{\mathrm{C,R}}_{k,j} \right) \qquad (19)$$

$$\theta^{\mathrm{I,R}}_{i,j} = \sum_{k=i}^{j} A^{s_i,\mathrm{R}}_{s_j} \theta^{\mathrm{C,R}}_{i,k} \left((\alpha^{s_j,\mathrm{L}}_{\infty})^\top \, \theta^{\mathrm{C,L}}_{k+1,j} \right) \qquad (20)$$

[4]Technically, when working with the projected operators the state-distribution vectors will not be distributions in the formal sense. However, they correspond to a projection of a state distribution, for some projection that we do not recover from data (namely M^{-1} in footnote 3). This projection has no effect on the computations because it cancels out.

5 Experiments

The goal of our experiments is to show that incorporating hidden states in a SHAG using operator models can consistently improve parsing accuracy. A second goal is to compare the spectral learning algorithm to EM, a standard learning method that also induces hidden states.

The first set of experiments involve fully unlexicalized models, i.e. parsing part-of-speech tag sequences. While this setting falls behind the state-of-the-art, it is nonetheless valid to analyze empirically the effect of incorporating hidden states via operator models, which results in large improvements. In a second set of experiments, we combine the unlexicalized hidden-state models with simple lexicalized models. Finally, we present some analysis of the automaton learned by the spectral algorithm to see the information that is captured in the hidden state space.

5.1 Fully Unlexicalized Grammars

We trained fully unlexicalized dependency grammars from dependency treebanks, that is, $\mathcal{X}$ are PoS tags and we parse PoS tag sequences. In all cases, our modifier sequences include special START and STOP symbols at the boundaries. [5] [6] We compare the following SHAG models:

- DET: a baseline deterministic grammar with a single state.
- DET+F: a deterministic grammar with two states, one emitting the first modifier of a sequence, and another emitting the rest (see (Eisner and Smith, 2010) for a similar deterministic baseline).
- SPECTRAL: a non-deterministic grammar with n hidden states trained with the spectral algorithm. n is a parameter of the model.
- EM: a non-deterministic grammar with n states trained with EM. Here, we estimate operators $\langle \widehat{\alpha}_1, \widehat{\alpha}_\infty, \widehat{A}_a^{h,d} \rangle$ using forward-backward for the E step. To initialize, we mimicked an HMM initialization: (1) we set $\widehat{\alpha}_1$ and $\widehat{\alpha}_\infty$ randomly; (2) we created a random transition matrix $T \in \mathbb{R}^{n \times n}$; (3) we created a diagonal matrix $O_a^{h,d} \in \mathbb{R}^{n \times n}$, where $O_a^{h,d}(i,i)$ is the probability of generating symbol a from h and d (estimated from training); (4) we set $\widehat{A}_a^{h,d} = TO_a^{h,d}$.

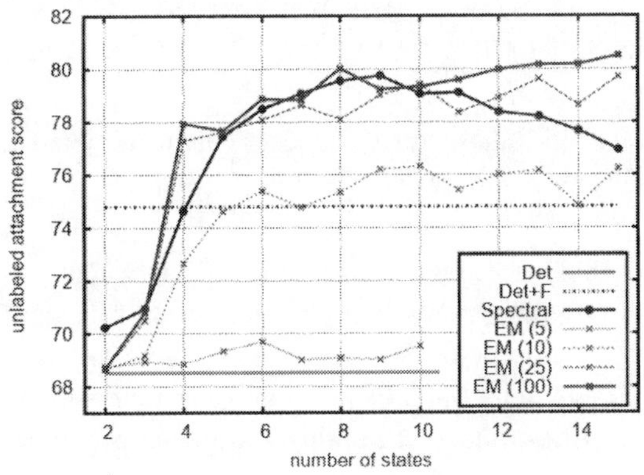

Figure 1: Accuracy curve on English development set for fully unlexicalized models.

We trained SHAG models using the standard WSJ sections of the English Penn Treebank (Marcus et al., 1994). Figure 1 shows the Unlabeled Attachment Score (UAS) curve on the development set, in terms of the number of hidden states for the spectral and EM models. We can see that DET+F largely outperforms DET[7], while the hidden-state models obtain much larger improvements. For the EM model, we show the accuracy curve after 5, 10, 25 and 100 iterations.[8]

In terms of peak accuracies, EM gives a slightly better result than the spectral method (80.51% for EM with 15 states versus 79.75% for the spectral method with 9 states). However, the spectral algorithm is much faster to train. With our Matlab implementation, it took about 30 seconds, while *each iteration* of EM took from 2 to 3 minutes, depending on the number of states. To give a concrete example, to reach an accuracy close to 80%, there is a factor of 150 between the training times of the spectral method and EM (where we compare the peak performance of the spectral method versus EM at 25 iterations with 13 states).

[5] Even though the operators α_1 and α_∞ of a PNFA account for start and stop probabilities, in preliminary experiments we found that having explicit START and STOP symbols results in more accurate models.

[6] Note that, for parsing, the operators for the START and STOP symbols can be packed into α_1 and α_∞ respectively. One just defines $\alpha_1' = A_{\text{START}}\,\alpha_1$ and $\alpha_\infty'^{\top} = \alpha_\infty^{\top}\,A_{\text{STOP}}$.

[7] For parsing with deterministic SHAG we employ MBR inference, even though Viterbi inference can be performed exactly. In experiments on development data DET improved from 62.65% using Viterbi to 68.52% using MBR, and DET+F improved from 72.72% to 74.80%.

[8] We ran EM 10 times under different initial conditions and selected the run that gave the best absolute accuracy after 100 iterations. We did not observe significant differences between the runs.

	DET	DET+F	SPECTRAL	EM
WSJ	69.45%	75.91%	80.44%	81.68%

Table 1: Unlabeled Attachment Score of fully unlexicalized models on the WSJ test set.

Table 1 shows results on WSJ test data, selecting the models that obtain peak performances in development. We observe the same behavior: hidden-states largely improve over deterministic baselines, and EM obtains a slight improvement over the spectral algorithm. Comparing to previous work on parsing WSJ PoS sequences, Eisner and Smith (2010) obtained an accuracy of 75.6% using a deterministic SHAG that uses information about dependency lengths. However, they used Viterbi inference, which we found to perform worse than MBR inference (see footnote 7).

5.2 Experiments with Lexicalized Grammars

We now turn to combining lexicalized deterministic grammars with the unlexicalized grammars obtained in the previous experiment using the spectral algorithm. The goal behind this experiment is to show that the information captured in hidden states is complimentary to head-modifier lexical preferences.

In this case $\mathcal{X}$ consists of lexical items, and we assume access to the PoS tag of each lexical item. We will denote as t_a and w_a the PoS tag and word of a symbol $a \in \bar{\mathcal{X}}$. We will estimate conditional distributions $\mathbb{P}(a \mid h, d, \sigma)$, where $a \in \mathcal{X}$ is a modifier, $h \in \bar{\mathcal{X}}$ is a head, d is a direction, and σ is a deterministic state. Following Collins (1999), we use three configurations of deterministic states:

- LEX: a single state.
- LEX+F: two distinct states for first modifier and rest of modifiers.
- LEX+FCP: four distinct states, encoding: first modifier, previous modifier was a coordination, previous modifier was punctuation, and previous modifier was some other word.

To estimate $\mathbb{P}$ we use a back-off strategy:

$$\mathbb{P}(a|h, d, \sigma) = \mathbb{P}_A(t_a|h, d, \sigma)\mathbb{P}_B(w_a|t_a, h, d, \delta)$$

To estimate $\mathbb{P}_A$ we use two back-off levels, the fine level conditions on $\{w_h, d, \sigma\}$ and the coarse level conditions on $\{t_h, d, \sigma\}$. For $\mathbb{P}_B$ we use three levels, which from fine to coarse are $\{t_a, w_h, d, \sigma\}$, $\{t_a, t_h, d, \sigma\}$ and $\{t_a\}$. We follow Collins (1999) to estimate $\mathbb{P}_A$ and $\mathbb{P}_B$ from a treebank using a back-off strategy.

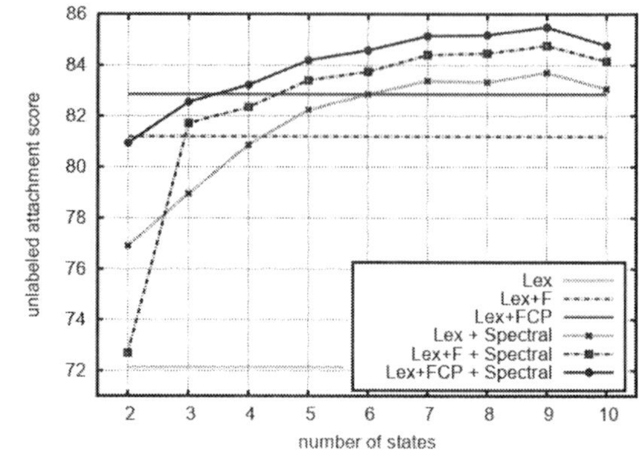

Figure 2: Accuracy curve on English development set for lexicalized models.

We use a simple approach to combine lexical models with the unlexical hidden-state models we obtained in the previous experiment. Namely, we use a log-linear model that computes scores for head-modifier sequences as

$$\begin{aligned} \mathrm{s}(\langle h, d, x_{1:T}\rangle) = \; & \log \mathbb{P}_{\mathrm{sp}}(x_{1:T}|h, d) \\ & + \log \mathbb{P}_{\mathrm{det}}(x_{1:T}|h, d) \quad , \end{aligned} \tag{21}$$

where $\mathbb{P}_{\mathrm{sp}}$ and $\mathbb{P}_{\mathrm{det}}$ are respectively spectral and deterministic probabilistic models. We tested combinations of each deterministic model with the spectral unlexicalized model using different number of states. Figure 2 shows the accuracies of single deterministic models, together with combinations using different number of states. In all cases, the combinations largely improve over the purely deterministic lexical counterparts, suggesting that the information encoded in hidden states is complementary to lexical preferences.

5.3 Results Analysis

We conclude the experiments by analyzing the state space learned by the spectral algorithm. Consider the space $\mathbb{R}^n$ where the forward-state vectors lie. Generating a modifier sequence corresponds to a path through the n-dimensional state space. We clustered sets of forward-state vectors in order to create a DFA that we can use to visualize the phenomena captured by the state space.

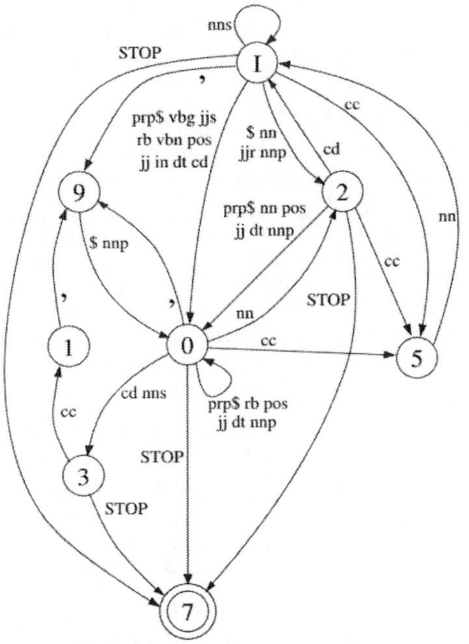

Figure 3: DFA approximation for the generation of NN left modifier sequences.

To build a DFA, we computed the forward vectors corresponding to frequent prefixes of modifier sequences of the development set. Then, we clustered these vectors using a Group Average Agglomerative algorithm using the cosine similarity measure (Manning et al., 2008). This similarity measure is appropriate because it compares the angle between vectors, and is not affected by their magnitude (the magnitude of forward vectors decreases with the number of modifiers generated). Each cluster i defines a state in the DFA, and we say that a sequence $x_{1:t}$ is in state i if its corresponding forward vector at time t is in cluster i. Then, transitions in the DFA are defined using a procedure that looks at how sequences traverse the states. If a sequence $x_{1:t}$ is at state i at time $t-1$, and goes to state j at time t, then we define a transition from state i to state j with label x_t. This procedure may require merging states to give a consistent DFA, because different sequences may define different transitions for the same states and modifiers. After doing a merge, new merges may be required, so the procedure must be repeated until a DFA is obtained.

For this analysis, we took the spectral model with 9 states, and built DFA from the non-deterministic automata corresponding to heads and directions where we saw largest improvements in accuracy with respect to the baselines.

A DFA for the automaton (NN, LEFT) is shown in Figure 3. The vectors were originally divided in ten clusters, but the DFA construction required two state mergings, leading to a eight state automaton. The state named I is the initial state. Clearly, we can see that there are special states for punctuation (state 9) and coordination (states 1 and 5). States 0 and 2 are harder to interpret. To understand them better, we computed an estimation of the probabilities of the transitions, by counting the number of times each of them is used. We found that our estimation of generating STOP from state 0 is 0.67, and from state 2 it is 0.15. Interestingly, state 2 can transition to state 0 generating prp$, POS or DT, that are usual endings of modifier sequences for nouns (recall that modifiers are generated head-outwards, so for a left automaton the final modifier is the left-most modifier in the sentence).

6 Conclusion

Our main contribution is a basic tool for inducing sequential hidden structure in dependency grammars. Most of the recent work in dependency parsing has explored explicit feature engineering. In part, this may be attributed to the high cost of using tools such as EM to induce representations. Our experiments have shown that adding hidden-structure improves parsing accuracy, and that our spectral algorithm is highly scalable.

Our methods may be used to enrich the representational power of more sophisticated dependency models. For example, future work should consider enhancing lexicalized dependency grammars with hidden states that summarize lexical dependencies. Another line for future research should extend the learning algorithm to be able to capture vertical hidden relations in the dependency tree, in addition to sequential relations.

Acknowledgements We are grateful to Gabriele Musillo and the anonymous reviewers for providing us with helpful comments. This work was supported by a Google Research Award and by the European Commission (PASCAL2 NoE FP7-216886, XLike STREP FP7-288342). Borja Balle was supported by an FPU fellowship (AP2008-02064) of the Spanish Ministry of Education. The Spanish Ministry of Science and Innovation supported Ariadna Quattoni (JCI-2009-04240) and Xavier Carreras (RYC-2008-02223 and "KNOW2" TIN2009-14715-C04-04).

References

Raphael Bailly. 2011. Quadratic weighted automata: Spectral algorithm and likelihood maximization. *JMLR Workshop and Conference Proceedings – ACML*.

James K. Baker. 1979. Trainable grammars for speech recognition. In D. H. Klatt and J. J. Wolf, editors, *Speech Communication Papers for the 97th Meeting of the Acoustical Society of America*, pages 547–550.

Borja Balle, Ariadna Quattoni, and Xavier Carreras. 2012. Local loss optimization in operator models: A new insight into spectral learning. Technical Report LSI-12-5-R, Departament de Llenguatges i Sistemes Informàtics (LSI), Universitat Politècnica de Catalunya (UPC).

Xavier Carreras. 2007. Experiments with a higher-order projective dependency parser. In *Proceedings of the CoNLL Shared Task Session of EMNLP-CoNLL 2007*, pages 957–961, Prague, Czech Republic, June. Association for Computational Linguistics.

Stephen Clark and James R. Curran. 2004. Parsing the wsj using ccg and log-linear models. In *Proceedings of the 42nd Meeting of the Association for Computational Linguistics (ACL'04), Main Volume*, pages 103–110, Barcelona, Spain, July.

Michael Collins. 1999. *Head-Driven Statistical Models for Natural Language Parsing*. Ph.D. thesis, University of Pennsylvania.

Arthur P. Dempster, Nan M. Laird, and Donald B. Rubin. 1977. Maximum likelihood from incomplete data via the em algorithm. *Journal of the royal statistical society, Series B*, 39(1):1–38.

Jason Eisner and Giorgio Satta. 1999. Efficient parsing for bilexical context-free grammars and head-automaton grammars. In *Proceedings of the 37th Annual Meeting of the Association for Computational Linguistics (ACL)*, pages 457–464, University of Maryland, June.

Jason Eisner and Noah A. Smith. 2010. Favor short dependencies: Parsing with soft and hard constraints on dependency length. In Harry Bunt, Paola Merlo, and Joakim Nivre, editors, *Trends in Parsing Technology: Dependency Parsing, Domain Adaptation, and Deep Parsing*, chapter 8, pages 121–150. Springer.

Jason Eisner. 2000. Bilexical grammars and their cubic-time parsing algorithms. In Harry Bunt and Anton Nijholt, editors, *Advances in Probabilistic and Other Parsing Technologies*, pages 29–62. Kluwer Academic Publishers, October.

Joshua Goodman. 1996. Parsing algorithms and metrics. In *Proceedings of the 34th Annual Meeting of the Association for Computational Linguistics*, pages 177–183, Santa Cruz, California, USA, June. Association for Computational Linguistics.

Daniel Hsu, Sham M. Kakade, and Tong Zhang. 2009. A spectral algorithm for learning hidden markov models. In *COLT 2009 - The 22nd Conference on Learning Theory*.

Gabriel Infante-Lopez and Maarten de Rijke. 2004. Alternative approaches for generating bodies of grammar rules. In *Proceedings of the 42nd Meeting of the Association for Computational Linguistics (ACL'04), Main Volume*, pages 454–461, Barcelona, Spain, July.

Terry Koo and Michael Collins. 2010. Efficient third-order dependency parsers. In *Proceedings of the 48th Annual Meeting of the Association for Computational Linguistics*, pages 1–11, Uppsala, Sweden, July. Association for Computational Linguistics.

Christopher D. Manning, Prabhakar Raghavan, and Hinrich Schütze. 2008. *Introduction to Information Retrieval*. Cambridge University Press, Cambridge, first edition, July.

Mitchell P. Marcus, Beatrice Santorini, and Mary A. Marcinkiewicz. 1994. Building a large annotated corpus of english: The penn treebank. *Computational Linguistics*, 19.

Andre Martins, Noah Smith, and Eric Xing. 2009. Concise integer linear programming formulations for dependency parsing. In *Proceedings of the Joint Conference of the 47th Annual Meeting of the ACL and the 4th International Joint Conference on Natural Language Processing of the AFNLP*, pages 342–350, Suntec, Singapore, August. Association for Computational Linguistics.

Takuya Matsuzaki, Yusuke Miyao, and Jun'ichi Tsujii. 2005. Probabilistic CFG with latent annotations. In *Proceedings of the 43rd Annual Meeting of the Association for Computational Linguistics (ACL'05)*, pages 75–82, Ann Arbor, Michigan, June. Association for Computational Linguistics.

Ryan McDonald and Fernando Pereira. 2006. Online learning of approximate dependency parsing algorithms. In *Proceedings of the 11th Conference of the European Chapter of the Association for Computational Linguistics*, pages 81–88.

Ryan McDonald, Fernando Pereira, Kiril Ribarov, and Jan Hajic. 2005. Non-projective dependency parsing using spanning tree algorithms. In *Proceedings of Human Language Technology Conference and Conference on Empirical Methods in Natural Language Processing*, pages 523–530, Vancouver, British Columbia, Canada, October. Association for Computational Linguistics.

Gabriele Antonio Musillo and Paola Merlo. 2008. Unlexicalised hidden variable models of split dependency grammars. In *Proceedings of ACL-08: HLT, Short Papers*, pages 213–216, Columbus, Ohio, June. Association for Computational Linguistics.

James D. Park and Adnan Darwiche. 2004. Complexity results and approximation strategies for map explanations. *Journal of Artificial Intelligence Research*, 21:101–133.

Mark Paskin. 2001. Cubic-time parsing and learning algorithms for grammatical bigram models. Technical Report UCB/CSD-01-1148, University of California, Berkeley.

Slav Petrov and Dan Klein. 2007. Improved inference for unlexicalized parsing. In *Human Language Technologies 2007: The Conference of the North American Chapter of the Association for Computational Linguistics; Proceedings of the Main Conference*, pages 404–411, Rochester, New York, April. Association for Computational Linguistics.

Slav Petrov, Leon Barrett, Romain Thibaux, and Dan Klein. 2006. Learning accurate, compact, and interpretable tree annotation. In *Proceedings of the 21st International Conference on Computational Linguistics and 44th Annual Meeting of the Association for Computational Linguistics*, pages 433–440, Sydney, Australia, July. Association for Computational Linguistics.

Ivan Titov and James Henderson. 2006. Loss minimization in parse reranking. In *Proceedings of the 2006 Conference on Empirical Methods in Natural Language Processing*, pages 560–567, Sydney, Australia, July. Association for Computational Linguistics.

Ivan Titov and James Henderson. 2007. A latent variable model for generative dependency parsing. In *Proceedings of the Tenth International Conference on Parsing Technologies*, pages 144–155, Prague, Czech Republic, June. Association for Computational Linguistics.

Combining Tree Structures, Flat Features and Patterns for Biomedical Relation Extraction

Md. Faisal Mahbub Chowdhury [†‡] **and Alberto Lavelli** [‡]
[‡] Fondazione Bruno Kessler (FBK-irst), Italy
[†] University of Trento, Italy
{chowdhury,lavelli}@fbk.eu

Abstract

Kernel based methods dominate the current trend for various relation extraction tasks including protein-protein interaction (PPI) extraction. PPI information is critical in understanding biological processes. Despite considerable efforts, previously reported PPI extraction results show that none of the approaches already known in the literature is consistently better than other approaches when evaluated on different benchmark PPI corpora. In this paper, we propose a novel hybrid kernel that combines (automatically collected) dependency patterns, trigger words, negative cues, walk features and regular expression patterns along with tree kernel and shallow linguistic kernel. The proposed kernel outperforms the exiting state-of-the-art approaches on the BioInfer corpus, the largest PPI benchmark corpus available. On the other four smaller benchmark corpora, it performs either better or almost as good as the existing approaches. Moreover, empirical results show that the proposed hybrid kernel attains considerably higher precision than the existing approaches, which indicates its capability of learning more accurate models. This also demonstrates that the different types of information that we use are able to complement each other for relation extraction.

1 Introduction

Kernel methods are considered the most effective techniques for various relation extraction (RE) tasks on both general (e.g. newspaper text) and specialized (e.g. biomedical text) domains. In particular, as the importance of syntactic structures for deriving the relationships between entities in text has been growing, several graph and tree kernels have been designed and experimented.

Early RE approaches more or less fall in one of the following categories: *(i)* exploitation of statistics about co-occurrences of entities, *(ii)* usage of patterns and rules, and *(iii)* usage of flat features to train machine learning (ML) classifiers. These approaches have been studied for a long period and have their own pros and cons. Exploitation of co-occurrence statistics results in high recall but low precision, while rule or pattern based approaches can increase precision but suffer from low recall. Flat feature based ML approaches employ various kinds of linguistic, syntactic or contextual information and integrate them into the feature space. They obtain relatively good results but are hindered by drawbacks of limited feature space and excessive feature engineering. Kernel based approaches have become an attractive alternative solution, as they can exploit huge amount of features without an explicit representation.

In this paper, we propose a new hybrid kernel for RE. We apply the kernel to Protein–protein interaction (PPI) extraction, the most widely researched topic in biomedical relation extraction. PPI[1] information is very critical in understanding biological processes. Considerable progress has been made for this task. Nevertheless, empirical results of previous studies show that none of the approaches already known in the literature is consistently better than other approaches when evaluated on different benchmark PPI corpora (see Table 4). This demands further study and innovation

[1]PPIs occur when two or more proteins bind together, and are integral to virtually all cellular processes, such as metabolism, signalling, regulation, and proliferation (Tikk et al., 2010).

of new approaches that are sensitive to the variations of complex linguistic constructions.

The proposed hybrid kernel is the composition of one tree kernel and two feature based kernels (one of them is already known in the literature and the other is proposed in this paper for the first time). The novelty of the newly proposed feature based kernel is that it envisages to accommodate the advantages of pattern based approaches. More precisely:

1. We propose a new feature based kernel (details in Section 4.1) by using syntactic dependency patterns, trigger words, negative cues, regular expression (henceforth, regex) patterns and walk features (i.e. e-walks and v-walks)[2].

2. The syntactic dependency patterns are automatically collected from a type of dependency subgraph (we call it *reduced graph*, more details in Section 4.1.1) during runtime.

3. We only use the regex patterns, trigger words and negative cues mentioned in the literature (Ono et al., 2001; Fundel et al., 2007; Bui et al., 2010). The objective is to verify whether we can exploit knowledge which is already known and used.

4. We propose a hybrid kernel by combining the proposed feature based kernel (outlined above) with the Shallow Linguistic (SL) kernel (Giuliano et al., 2006) and the Path-enclosed Tree (PET) kernel (Moschitti, 2004).

The aim of our work is to take advantage of different types of information (i.e., dependency patterns, regex patterns, trigger words, negative cues, syntactic dependencies among words and constituent parse trees) and their different representations (i.e. flat features, tree structures and graphs) which can complement each other to learn more accurate models.

[2]The syntactic dependencies of the words of a sentence create a dependency graph. A **v-walk** feature consists of $(word_i - dependency\_type_{i,i+1} - word_{i+1})$, and an **e-walk** feature is composed of $(dependency\_type_{i-1,i} - word_i - dependency\_type_{i,i+1})$. Note that, in a dependency graph, the words are nodes while the dependency types are edges.

The remainder of the paper is organized as follows. In Section 2, we briefly review previous work. Section 3 lists the datasets. Then, in Section 4, we define our proposed hybrid kernel and describe its individual component kernels. Section 5 outlines the experimental settings. Following that, empirical results are discussed in Section 6. Finally, we conclude with a summary of our study as well as suggestions for further improvement of our approach.

2 Related Work

In this section, we briefly discuss some of the recent work on PPI extraction. Several RE approaches have been reported to date for the PPI task, most of which are kernel based methods. Tikk et al. (2010) reported a benchmark evaluation of various kernels on PPI extraction. An interesting finding is that the Shallow Linguistic (SL) kernel (Giuliano et al., 2006) (to be discussed in Section 4.2), despite its simplicity, is on par with the best kernels in most of the evaluation settings.

Kim et al. (2010) proposed walk-weighted subsequence kernel using e-walks, partial matches, non-contiguous paths, and different weights for different sub-structures (which are used to capture structural similarities during kernel computation). Miwa et al. (2009a) proposed a hybrid kernel, which combines the all-paths graph (APG) kernel (Airola et al., 2008), the bag-of-words kernel, and the subset tree kernel (Moschitti, 2006) (applied on the shortest dependency paths between target protein pairs). They used multiple parser inputs. The system is regarded as the current state-of-the-art PPI extraction system because of its high results on different PPI corpora (see the results in Table 4).

As an extension of their work, they boosted system performance by training on multiple PPI corpora instead of on a single corpus and adopting a corpus weighting concept with support vector machine (SVM) which they call SVM-CW (Miwa et al., 2009b). Since most of their results are reported by training on the combination of multiple corpora, it is not possible to compare them directly with the results published in the other related works (that usually adopt 10-fold cross validation on a single PPI corpus). To be comparable with the vast majority of the existing work, we also report results using 10-fold cross validation

Corpus	Sentences	Positive pairs	Negative pairs
BioInfer	1,100	2,534	7,132
AIMed	1,955	1,000	4,834
IEPA	486	335	482
HPRD50	145	163	270
LLL	77	164	166

Table 1: Basic statistics of the 5 benchmark PPI corpora.

on single corpora.

Apart from the approaches described above, there also exist other studies that used kernels for PPI extraction (e.g. subsequence kernel (Bunescu and Mooney, 2006)).

A notable exception is the work published by Bui et al. (2010). They proposed an approach that consists of two phases. In the first phase, their system categorizes the data into different groups (i.e. subsets) based on various properties and patterns. Later they classify candidate PPI pairs inside each of the groups using SVM trained with features specific for the corresponding group.

3 Data

There are 5 benchmark corpora for the PPI task that are frequently used: HPRD50 (Fundel et al., 2007), IEPA (Ding et al., 2002), LLL (Nédellec, 2005), BioInfer (Pyysalo et al., 2007) and AIMed (Bunescu et al., 2005). These corpora adopt different PPI annotation formats. For a comparative evaluation Pyysalo et al. (2008) put all of them in a common format which has become the standard evaluation format for the PPI task. In our experiments, we use the versions of the corpora converted to such format.

Table 1 shows various statistics regarding the 5 (converted) corpora.

4 Proposed Hybrid Kernel

The hybrid kernel that we propose is as follows:

$$K_{Hybrid}\,(R_1,\, R_2) = K_{TPWF}\,(R_1,\, R_2) \\ + K_{SL}\,(R_1,\, R_2) + w * K_{PET}\,(R_1,\, R_2)$$

where K_{TPWF} stands for the new feature based kernel (henceforth, TPWF kernel) computed using flat features collected by exploiting patterns, trigger words, negative cues and walk features. K_{SL} and K_{PET} stand for the Shallow Linguistic (SL) kernel and the Path-enclosed Tree (PET) kernel respectively. w is a multiplicative constant used for the PET kernel. It allows the hybrid kernel to assign more (or less) weight to the information obtained using tree structures depending on the corpus. The proposed hybrid kernel is valid according to the closure properties of kernels.

Both the TPWF and SL kernels are linear kernels, while PET kernel is computed using Unlexicalized Partial Tree (uPT) kernel (Severyn and Moschitti, 2010). The following subsections explain each of the individual kernels in more detail.

4.1 Proposed TPWF Kernel

4.1.1 Reduced graph, trigger words, negative cues and dependency patterns

For each of the candidate entity pairs, we construct a type of subgraph from the dependency graph formed by the syntactic dependencies among the words of a sentence. We call it "`reduced graph`" and define it in the following way:

> A **reduced graph** is a subgraph of the dependency graph of a sentence which includes:
>
> - the two candidate entities and their governor nodes up to their least common governor (if exists).
> - dependent nodes (if exist) of all the nodes added in the previous step.
> - the immediate governor(s) (if exists) of the least common governor.

Figure 1 shows an example of a reduced graph. A reduced graph is an extension of the smallest common subgraph of the dependency graph that aims at overcoming its limitations. It is a known issue that the smallest common subgraph (or subtree) sometimes does not contain cue words. Previously, Chowdhury et al. (2011a) proposed a linguistically motivated extension of the minimal (i.e. smallest) common subtree (which includes the candidate entity pairs), known as Mildly Extended Dependency Tree (MEDT). However, the rules used for MEDT are too constrained. Our objective in constructing the reduced graph is *to include any potential modifier(s) or cue word(s)* that describes the relation between the given pair of entities. Sometimes such modifiers or cue words are not directly dependent (syntactically) on any

	BioInfer			AIMed			IEPA			HPRD50			LLL		
	P	R	F	P	R	F	P	R	F	P	R	F	P	R	F
Only walk features	51.8	71.2	60.0	48.7	63.2	55.0	61.0	75.2	67.4	60.2	65.0	62.5	64.6	87.8	74.4
Features: dep. patterns, trigger, neg. cues, walks	53.8	68.8	60.4	50.6	63.9	56.5	63.9	74.6	68.9	65.0	71.8	68.2	66.5	89.6	76.4
Features: dep. patterns, trigger, neg. cues, walks, regex patterns	53.5	68.6	60.1	52.5	62.9	57.2	63.8	74.6	68.8	65.1	69.9	67.5	67.4	88.4	76.5

Table 2: Results of the proposed TPWF feature based kernel on 5 benchmark PPI corpora before and after adding features collected using dependency patterns, regex patterns, trigger words and negative cues to the walk features. The TPWF kernel is a component of the new hybrid kernel.

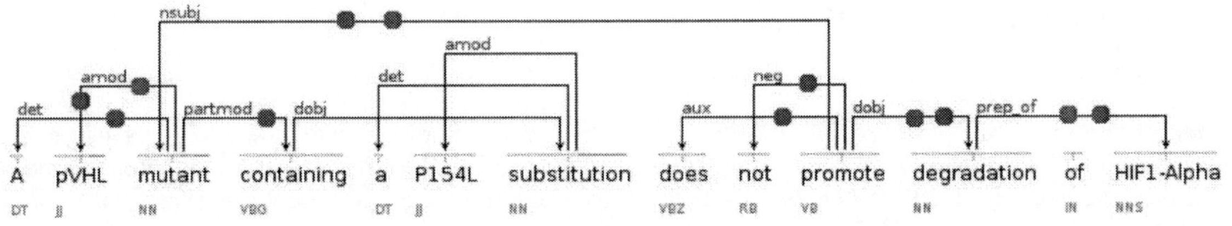

Figure 1: Dependency graph for the sentence "A pVHL mutant containing a P154L substitution does not promote degradation of HIF1-Alpha" generated by the Stanford parser. The edges with blue dots form the smallest common subgraph for the candidate entity pair **pVHL** and **HIF1-Alpha**, while the edges with red dots form the *reduced graph* for the pair.

of the entities (of the candidate pair). Rather they are dependent on some other word(s) which is dependent on one (or both) of the entities. The word "*not*" in Figure 1 is one such example. The reduced graph aims to preserve these cue words.

The following types of features are collected from the reduced graph of a candidate pair:

1. *HasTriggerWord*: whether the least common governor(s) of the target entity pairs inside the reduced graph matches any trigger word.
2. *Trigger-X*: whether the least common governor(s) of the target entity pairs inside the reduced graph matches the trigger word 'X'.
3. *HasNegWord*: whether the reduced graph contains any negative word.
4. *DepPattern-i*: whether the reduced graph contains all the syntactic dependencies of the *i*-th pattern of dependency pattern list.

The dependency pattern list is automatically constructed from the training data during the learning phase. Each pattern is a set of syntactic dependencies of the corresponding reduced graph of a (positive or negative) entity pair in the training data. For example, the dependency pattern for the reduced graph in Figure 1 is {*det, amod, partmod, nsubj, aux, neg, dobj, prep_of*}. The same dependency pattern might be constructed for multiple (positive or negative) entity pairs. However, if it is constructed for both positive and negative pairs, it has to be discarded from the pattern list.

The dependency patterns allow some kind of underspecification as they do not contain the lexical items (i.e. words) but contain the likely combination of syntactic dependencies that a given related pair of entities would pose inside their reduced graph.

The list of trigger words contains 144 words previously used by Bui et al. (2010) and Fundel et al. (2007). The list of negative cues contain 18 words, most of which are mentioned in Fundel et al. (2007).

4.1.2 Walk features

We extract *e-walk* and *v-walk* features from the Mildly Extended Dependency Tree (MEDT) (Chowdhury et al., 2011a) of each candidate pair. Reduced graphs sometimes include some unin-

	BioInfer			AIMed			IEPA			HPRD50			LLL		
Pos. / Neg.	2,534 / 7,132			1,000 / 4,834			335 / 482			163 / 270			164 / 166		
	P	**R**	**F**	**P**	**R**	**F**	**P**	**R**	**F**	**P**	**R**	**F**	**P**	**R**	**F**
Proposed TPWF kernel (without regex)	53.8	68.8	60.4	50.6	63.9	56.5	63.9	74.6	68.9	65.0	71.8	68.2	66.5	89.6	76.4
Proposed TPWF kernel (with regex)	53.5	68.6	60.1	52.5	62.9	57.2	63.8	74.6	68.8	65.1	69.9	67.5	67.4	88.4	76.5
SL kernel	60.8	65.8	63.2	56.2	64.4	60.0	73.3	71.9	72.6	62.0	65.0	63.5	74.9	85.4	79.8
PET kernel	72.8	74.9	73.9	44.8	72.8	55.5	70.7	77.9	74.2	65.0	73.0	68.8	72.1	89.6	79.9
Proposed hybrid kernel **(PET + SL + TPWF** (without regex))	80.0	71.4	75.5	64.2	58.2	61.1	81.1	69.3	74.7	72.9	59.5	65.5	70.4	95.7	81.1
Proposed hybrid kernel **(PET + SL + TPWF** (with regex))	80.1	72.0	75.9	64.4	58.3	61.2	79.3	69.6	74.1	71.9	61.4	66.2	70.6	95.1	81.0

Table 3: Results of the proposed hybrid kernel and its individual components. *Pos.* and *Neg.* refer to number positive and negative relations respectively. PET refers to the path-enclosed tree kernel, SL refers to the shallow linguistic kernel, and TPWF refers to the kernel computed using trigger, pattern, negative cue and walk features.

formative words which produce uninformative walk features. Hence, they are not suitable for walk feature generation. MEDT suits better for this purpose. The walk features extracted from MEDTs have the following properties:

- The directionality of the edges (or nodes) in an e-walk (or v-walk) is not considered. In other words, e.g., $pos(stimulatory) - amod - pos(effects)$ and $pos(effects) - amod - pos(stimulatory)$ are treated as the same feature.

- The v-walk features are of the form $(pos_i - dependency\_type_{i,i+1} - pos_{i+1})$. Here, pos_i is the POS tag of $word_i$, i is the governor node and $i + 1$ is the dependent node.

- The e-walk features are of the form $(dep.\_type_{i-1,i} - pos_i - dep.\_type_{i,i+1})$ and $(dep.\_type_{i-1,i} - lemma_i - dep.\_type_{i,i+1})$. Here, $lemma_i$ is the lemmatized form of $word_i$.

- Usually, the e-walk features are constructed using dependency types between $\{governor\_of\_X,\ node\_X\}$ and $\{node\_X,\ dependent\_of\_X\}$. However, we also extract e-walk features from the dependency types between any two dependents and their common governor (i.e. $\{node\_X,\ dependent\_1\_of\_X\}$ and $\{node\_X,\ dependent\_2\_of\_X\}$).

Apart from the above types of features, we also add features for lemmas of the immediate preceding and following words of the candidate entities. These feature names are augmented with *-1* or *+1* depending on whether the corresponding words are preceded or followed by a candidate entity.

4.1.3 Regular expression patterns

We use a set of 22 regex patterns as binary features. These patterns were previously used by Ono et al. (2001) and Bui et al. (2010). If there is a match for a pattern (e.g. "*Entity_1.*activates.*Entity_2*" where *Entity_1* and *Entity_2* form the candidate entity pair) in a given sentence, value *1* is added for the feature (i.e., pattern) inside the feature vector.

4.2 Shallow Linguistic (SL) Kernel

The Shallow Linguistic (SL) kernel was proposed by Giuliano et al. (2006). It is one of the best performing kernels applied on different biomedical RE tasks such as PPI and DDI (drug-drug interaction) extraction (Tikk et al., 2010; Segura-Bedmar et al., 2011; Chowdhury and Lavelli, 2011b; Chowdhury et al., 2011c). It is defined as follows:

$$K_{SL}(R_1, R_2) = K_{LC}(R_1, R_2) + K_{GC}(R_1, R_2)$$

	BioInfer			AIMed			IEPA			HPRD50			LLL		
Pos. / Neg.	2,534 / 7,132			1,000 / 4,834			335 / 482			163 / 270			164 / 166		
	P	**R**	**F**	**P**	**R**	**F**	**P**	**R**	**F**	**P**	**R**	**F**	**P**	**R**	**F**
SL kernel (Giuliano et al., 2006)	–	–	–	60.9	57.2	59.0	–	–	–	–	–	–	–	–	–
APG kernel (Airola et al., 2008)	56.7	67.2	61.3	52.9	61.8	56.4	69.6	82.7	<u>75.1</u>	64.3	65.8	63.4	72.5	87.2	76.8
Hybrid kernel and multiple parser input (Miwa et al., 2009a)	65.7	71.1	<u>68.1</u>	55.0	68.8	60.8	67.5	78.6	71.7	68.5	76.1	70.9	77.6	86.0	80.1
SVM-CW, multiple parser input and graph, walk and BOW features (Miwa et al., 2009b)	–	–	67.6	–	–	<u>64.2</u>	–	–	74.4	–	–	69.7	–	–	80.5
kBSPS kernel (Tikk et al., 2010)	49.9	61.8	55.1	50.1	41.4	44.6	58.8	89.7	70.5	62.2	87.1	<u>71.0</u>	69.3	93.2	78.1
Walk weighted subsequence kernel (Kim et al., 2010)	61.8	54.2	57.6	61.4	53.3	56.6	73.8	71.8	72.9	66.7	69.2	67.8	76.9	91.2	<u>82.4</u>
2 phase extraction (Bui et al., 2010)	61.7	57.5	60.0	55.3	68.5	61.2	–	–	–	–	–	–	–	–	–
Our proposed hybrid kernel (**PET + SL + TPWF** without regex)	80.0	71.4	**75.5**	64.2	58.2	**61.1**	81.1	69.3	**74.7**	72.9	59.5	**65.5**	70.4	95.7	**81.1**

Table 4: Comparison of the results on the 5 benchmark PPI corpora. *Pos.* and *Neg.* refer to number positive and negative relations respectively. The <u>underlined</u> numbers indicate the best results for the corresponding corpus reported by any of the existing state-of-the-art approaches. The results of Bui et al. (2010) on LLL, HPRD50, and IEPA are not reported since thy did not use all the positive and negative examples during cross validation. Miwa et al. (2009b) showed that better results can be obtained using multiple corpora for training. However, we consider only those results of their experiments where they used single training corpus as it is the standard evaluation approach adopted by all the other studies on PPI extraction for comparing results. All the results of the previous approaches reported in this table are directly quoted from their respective original papers.

where K_{SL}, K_{GC} and K_{LC} correspond to SL, global context (GC) and local context (LC) kernels respectively. The GC kernel exploits contextual information of the words occurring before, between and after the pair of entities (to be investigated for RE) in the corresponding sentence; while the LC kernel exploits contextual information surrounding individual entities.

4.3 Path-enclosed tree (PET) Kernel

The path-enclosed tree (PET) kernel[3] was first proposed by Moschitti (2004) for semantic role labeling. It was later successfully adapted by Zhang et al. (2005) and other works for relation extraction on general texts (such as newspaper domain). A PET is the smallest common subtree of a phrase structure tree that includes the two entities involved in a relation.

A tree kernel calculates the similarity between two input trees by counting the number of common sub-structures. Different techniques have been proposed to measure such similarity. We use the Unlexicalized Partial Tree (uPT) kernel (Severyn and Moschitti, 2010) for the computation of the PET kernel since a comparative evaluation by Chowdhury et al. (2011a) reported that uPT kernels achieve better results for PPI extraction than the other techniques used for tree kernel computation.

[3] Also known as shortest path-enclosed tree (SPT) kernel.

5 Experimental Settings

We have followed the same criteria commonly used for the PPI extraction tasks, i.e. abstract-wise 10-fold cross validation on individual corpus and one-answer-per-occurrence criterion. In fact, we have used exactly the same (abstract-wise) fold splitting of the 5 benchmark (converted) corpora used by Tikk et al. (2010) for benchmarking various kernel methods[4].

The Charniak-Johnson reranking parser (Charniak and Johnson, 2005), along with a self-trained biomedical parsing model (McClosky, 2010), has been used for tokenization, POS-tagging and parsing of the sentences. Before parsing the sentences, all the entities are blinded by assigning names as $EntityX$ where X is the entity index. In each example, the POS tags of the two candidate entities are changed to $EntityX$. The parse trees produced by the Charniak-Johnson reranking parser are then processed by the Stanford parser[5] (Klein and Manning, 2003) to obtain syntactic dependencies according to the Stanford Typed Dependency format.

The Stanford parser often skips some syntactic dependencies in output. We use the following two rules to add some of such dependencies:

- If there is a *"conj_and"* or *"conj_or"* dependency between two words *X* and *Y*, then *X* should be dependent on any word *Z* on which *Y* is dependent and vice versa.

- If there are two verbs *X* and *Y* such that inside the corresponding sentence they have only the word *"and"* or *"or"* between them, then any word *Z* dependent on *X* should be also dependent on *Y* and vice versa.

Our system exploits SVM-LIGHT-TK[6] (Moschitti, 2006; Joachims, 1999). We made minor changes in the toolkit to compute the proposed hybrid kernel. The ratio of negative and positive examples has been used as the value of the cost-ratio-factor parameter. We have done parameter tuning following the approach described by Hsu et al. (2003).

[4]Downloaded from http://informatik.hu-berlin.de/forschung /gebiete/wbi/ppi-benchmark .

[5]http://nlp.stanford.edu/software/lex-parser.shtml

[6]http://disi.unitn.it/moschitti/Tree-Kernel.htm

6 Results and Discussion

To measure the contribution of the features collected from the reduced graphs (using dependency patterns, trigger words and negative cues) and regex patterns, we have applied the new TPWF kernel on the 5 PPI corpora before and after using these features. Results shown in Table 2 clearly indicate that usage of these features improve the performance. The improvement of performance is primarily due to the usage of dependency patterns which resulted in higher precision for all the corpora.

We have tried to measure the contribution of the regex patterns. However, from the empirical results a clear trend does not emerge (see Table 2).

Table 3 shows a comparison among the results of the proposed hybrid kernel and its individual components. As we can see, the overall results of the hybrid kernel (with and without using regex pattern features) are better than those by any of its individual component kernels. Interestingly, precision achieved on the 4 benchmark corpora (other than the smallest corpus LLL) is much higher for the hybrid kernel than for the individual components. This strongly indicates that these different types of information (i.e. dependency patterns, regex patterns, triggers, negative cues, syntactic dependencies among words and constituent parse trees) and their different representations (i.e. flat features, tree structures and graphs) can complement each other to learn more accurate models.

Table 4 shows a comparison of the PPI extraction results of our proposed hybrid kernel with those of other state-of-the-art approaches. Since the contribution of regex patterns in the performance of the hybrid kernel was not relevant (as Tables 2 and 3 show), we used the results of proposed hybrid kernel without regex for the comparison. As we can see, the proposed kernel achieves *significantly higher results* on the BioInfer corpus, the largest benchmark PPI corpus (2,534 positive PPI pair annotations) available, than any of the existing approaches. Moreover, the results of the proposed hybrid kernel are on par with the state-of-the-art results on the other smaller corpora.

Furthermore, empirical results show that the proposed hybrid kernel attains *considerably higher precision* than the existing approaches.

Since a dependency pattern, by construction, contains all the syntactic dependencies inside the corresponding reduced graph, it may happen that some of the dependencies (e.g. *det* or determiner) are not informative for classifying the label of the corresponding class label (i.e., positive or negative relation) of the pattern. Their presence inside a pattern might make it unnecessarily rigid and less general. So, we tried to identify and discard such non informative dependencies by measuring probabilities of the dependencies with respect to the class label and then removing any of them which has probability lower than a threshold (we tried with different threshold values). But doing so decreased the performance. This suggests that the syntactic dependencies of a dependency pattern are not independent of each other even if some of them might have low probability (with respect to the class label) individually. We plan to further investigate whether there could be different criteria for identifying non informative dependencies. For the work reported in this paper, we used the dependency patterns as they are initially constructed.

We also did experiments to see whether collecting features for trigger words from the whole reduced graph would help. But that also decreased performance. This suggests that trigger words are more likely to appear in the least common governors.

7 Conclusion

In this paper, we have proposed a new hybrid kernel for RE that combines two vector based kernels and a tree kernel. The proposed kernel outperforms any of the exiting approaches by a wide margin on the BioInfer corpus, the largest PPI benchmark corpus available. On the other four smaller benchmark corpora, it performs either better or almost as good as the existing state-of-the art approaches.

We have also proposed a novel feature based kernel, called TPWF kernel, using (automatically collected) dependency patterns, trigger words, negative cues, walk features and regular expression patterns. The TPWF kernel is used as a component of the new hybrid kernel.

Empirical results show that the proposed hybrid kernel achieves considerably higher precision than the existing approaches, which indicates its capability of learning more accurate models. This also demonstrates that the different types of information that we use are able to complement each other for relation extraction.

We believe there are at least three ways to further improve the proposed approach. First of all, the 22 regular expression patterns (collected from Ono et al. (2001) and Bui et al. (2010)) are applied at the level of the sentences and this sometimes produces unwanted matches. For example, consider the sentence "$X\ activates\ Y\ and\ inhibits\ Z$" where *X*, *Y*, and *Z* are entities. The pattern "$Entity1. * activates. * Entity2$" matches both the *X–Y* and *X–Z* pairs in the sentence. But only the *X–Y* pair should be considered. So, the patterns should be constrained to reduce the number of unwanted matches. For example, they could be applied on smaller linguistic units than full sentences. Secondly, different techniques could be used to identify less-informative syntactic dependencies inside dependency patterns to make them more accurate and effective. Thirdly, usage of automatically collected paraphrases of regular expression patterns instead of the patterns directly could be also helpful. Weakly supervised collection of paraphrases for RE has been already investigated (e.g. Romano et al. (2006)) and, hence, can be tried for improving the TPWF kernel (which is a component of the proposed hybrid kernel).

Acknowledgments

This work was carried out in the context of the project "eOnco - Pervasive knowledge and data management in cancer care". The authors are grateful to Alessandro Moschitti for his help in the use of SVM-LIGHT-TK. We also thank the anonymous reviewers for helpful suggestions.

References

Antti Airola, Sampo Pyysalo, Jari Bjorne, Tapio Pahikkala, Filip Ginter, and Tapio Salakoski. 2008. All-paths graph kernel for protein-protein interaction extraction with evaluation of cross-corpus learning. *BMC Bioinformatics*, 9(Suppl 11):S2.

Quoc-Chinh Bui, Sophia Katrenko, and Peter M.A. Sloot. 2010. A hybrid approach to extract protein-protein interactions. *Bioinformatics*.

Razvan Bunescu and Raymond J. Mooney. 2006. Subsequence kernels for relation extraction. In *Proceedings of NIPS 2006*, pages 171–178.

Razvan Bunescu, Ruifang Ge, Rohit J. Kate, Edward M. Marcotte, Raymond J. Mooney, Arun Kumar Ramani, and Yuk Wah Wong. 2005. Comparative experiments on learning information extractors for proteins and their interactions. *Artificial Intelligence in Medicine*, 33(2):139–155.

Eugene Charniak and Mark Johnson. 2005. Coarse-to-fine n-best parsing and maxent discriminative reranking. In *Proceedings of ACL 2005*.

Md. Faisal Mahbub Chowdhury and Alberto Lavelli. 2011b. Drug-drug interaction extraction using composite kernels. In *Proceedings of DDIExtraction2011: First Challenge Task: Drug-Drug Interaction Extraction*, pages 27–33, Huelva, Spain, September.

Md. Faisal Mahbub Chowdhury, Alberto Lavelli, and Alessandro Moschitti. 2011a. A study on dependency tree kernels for automatic extraction of protein-protein interaction. In *Proceedings of BioNLP 2011 Workshop*, pages 124–133, Portland, Oregon, USA, June.

Md. Faisal Mahbub Chowdhury, Asma Ben Abacha, Alberto Lavelli, and Pierre Zweigenbaum. 2011c. Two dierent machine learning techniques for drug-drug interaction extraction. In *Proceedings of DDIExtraction2011: First Challenge Task: Drug-Drug Interaction Extraction*, pages 19–26, Huelva, Spain, September.

J. Ding, D. Berleant, D. Nettleton, and E. Wurtele. 2002. Mining MEDLINE: abstracts, sentences, or phrases? *Pacific Symposium on Biocomputing*, pages 326–337.

Katrin Fundel, Robert Küffner, and Ralf Zimmer. 2007. Relex–relation extraction using dependency parse trees. *Bioinformatics*, 23(3):365–371.

Claudio Giuliano, Alberto Lavelli, and Lorenza Romano. 2006. Exploiting shallow linguistic information for relation extraction from biomedical literature. In *Proceedings of EACL 2006*, pages 401–408.

CW Hsu, CC Chang, and CJ Lin, 2003. *A practical guide to support vector classification*. Department of Computer Science and Information Engineering, National Taiwan University, Taipei, Taiwan.

Thorsten Joachims. 1999. Making large-scale support vector machine learning practical. In *Advances in kernel methods: support vector learning*, pages 169–184. MIT Press, Cambridge, MA, USA.

Seonho Kim, Juntae Yoon, Jihoon Yang, and Seog Park. 2010. Walk-weighted subsequence kernels for protein-protein interaction extraction. *BMC Bioinformatics*, 11(1).

Dan Klein and Christopher D. Manning. 2003. Accurate unlexicalized parsing. In *Proceedings of ACL 2003*, pages 423–430, Sapporo, Japan.

David McClosky. 2010. *Any Domain Parsing: Automatic Domain Adaptation for Natural Language Parsing*. Ph.D. thesis, Department of Computer Science, Brown University.

Makoto Miwa, Rune Sætre, Yusuke Miyao, and Jun'ichi Tsujii. 2009a. Protein-protein interaction extraction by leveraging multiple kernels and parsers. *International Journal of Medical Informatics*, 78.

Makoto Miwa, Rune Sætre, Yusuke Miyao, and Jun'ichi Tsujii. 2009b. A rich feature vector for protein-protein interaction extraction from multiple corpora. In *Proceedings of EMNLP 2009*, pages 121–130, Singapore.

Alessandro Moschitti. 2004. A study on convolution kernels for shallow semantic parsing. In *Proceedings of ACL 2004*, Barcelona, Spain.

Alessandro Moschitti. 2006. Making Tree Kernels Practical for Natural Language Learning. In *Proceedings of EACL 2006*, Trento, Italy.

Claire Nédellec. 2005. Learning language in logic - genic interaction extraction challenge. *Proceedings of the ICML 2005 workshop: Learning Language in Logic (LLL05)*, pages 31–37.

Toshihide Ono, Haretsugu Hishigaki, Akira Tanigami, and Toshihisa Takagi. 2001. Automated extraction of information on protein–protein interactions from the biological literature. *Bioinformatics*, 17(2):155–161.

Sampo Pyysalo, Filip Ginter, Juho Heimonen, Jari Björne, Jorma Boberg, Jouni Jarvinen, and Tapio Salakoski. 2007. Bioinfer: a corpus for information extraction in the biomedical domain. *BMC Bioinformatics*, 8(1):50.

Sampo Pyysalo, Antti Airola, Juho Heimonen, Jari Björne, Filip Ginter, and Tapio Salakoski. 2008. Comparative analysis of five protein-protein interaction corpora. *BMC Bioinformatics*, 9(Suppl 3):S6.

Lorenza Romano, Milen Kouylekov, Idan Szpektor, Ido Dagan, and Alberto Lavelli. 2006. Investigating a generic paraphrase–based approach for relation extraction. In *Proceedings of EACL 2006*, pages 409–416.

Isabel Segura-Bedmar, Paloma Martínez, and Cesar de Pablo-Sánchez. 2011. Using a shallow linguistic kernel for drug-drug interaction extraction. *Journal of Biomedical Informatics*, In Press, Corrected Proof, Available online, 24 April.

Aliaksei Severyn and Alessandro Moschitti. 2010. Fast cutting plane training for structural kernels. In *Proceedings of ECML-PKDD 2010*.

Domonkos Tikk, Philippe Thomas, Peter Palaga, Jörg Hakenberg, and Ulf Leser. 2010. A Comprehensive Benchmark of Kernel Methods to Extract Protein-Protein Interactions from Literature. *PLoS Computational Biology*, 6(7), July.

Min Zhang, Jian Su, Danmei Wang, Guodong Zhou, and Chew Lim Tan. 2005. Discovering relations between named entities from a large raw corpus using tree similarity-based clustering. In *Natural Language Processing – IJCNLP 2005*, volume 3651 of *Lecture Notes in Computer Science*, pages 378–389. Springer Berlin / Heidelberg.

Coordination Structure Analysis using Dual Decomposition

Atsushi Hanamoto [1] Takuya Matsuzaki [1] Jun'ichi Tsujii [2]
1. Department of Computer Science, University of Tokyo, Japan
2. Web Search & Mining Group, Microsoft Research Asia, China
{hanamoto, matuzaki}@is.s.u-tokyo.ac.jp
jtsujii@microsoft.com

Abstract

Coordination disambiguation remains a difficult sub-problem in parsing despite the frequency and importance of coordination structures. We propose a method for disambiguating coordination structures. In this method, dual decomposition is used as a framework to take advantage of both HPSG parsing and coordinate structure analysis with alignment-based local features. We evaluate the performance of the proposed method on the Genia corpus and the Wall Street Journal portion of the Penn Treebank. Results show it increases the percentage of sentences in which coordination structures are detected correctly, compared with each of the two algorithms alone.

1 Introduction

Coordination structures often give syntactic ambiguity in natural language. Although a wrong analysis of a coordination structure often leads to a totally garbled parsing result, coordination disambiguation remains a difficult sub-problem in parsing, even for state-of-the-art parsers.

One approach to solve this problem is a grammatical approach. This approach, however, often fails in noun and adjective coordinations because there are many possible structures in these coordinations that are grammatically correct. For example, a noun sequence of the form "n_0 n_1 *and* n_2 n_3" has as many as five possible structures (Resnik, 1999). Therefore, a grammatical approach is not sufficient to disambiguate coordination structures. In fact, the Stanford parser (Klein and Manning, 2003) and Enju (Miyao and Tsujii, 2004) fail to disambiguate a sentence *I am a freshman advertising and marketing major*. Table 1 shows the output from them and the correct coordination structure.

The coordination structure above is obvious to humans because there is a symmetry of conjuncts (*-ing*) in the sentence. Coordination structures often have such structural and semantic symmetry of conjuncts. One approach is to capture local symmetry of conjuncts. However, this approach fails in VP and sentential coordinations, which can easily be detected by a grammatical approach. This is because conjuncts in these coordinations do not necessarily have local symmetry.

It is therefore natural to think that considering both the syntax and local symmetry of conjuncts would lead to a more accurate analysis. However, it is difficult to consider both of them in a dynamic programming algorithm, which has been often used for each of them, because it explodes the computational and implementational complexity. Thus, previous studies on coordination disambiguation often dealt only with a restricted form of coordination (e.g. noun phrases) or used a heuristic approach for simplicity.

In this paper, we present a statistical analysis model for coordination disambiguation that uses the dual decomposition as a framework. We consider both of the syntax, and structural and semantic symmetry of conjuncts so that it outperforms existing methods that consider only either of them. Moreover, it is still simple and requires only $O(n^4)$ time per iteration, where n is the number of words in a sentence. This is equal to that of coordination structure analysis with alignment-based local features. The overall system still has a quite simple structure because we need just slight modifications of existing models in this approach,

Stanford parser/Enju

I am a (freshman advertising) and (marketing major)

Correct coordination structure

I am a freshman ((advertising and marketing) major)

Table 1: Output from the Stanford parser, Enju and the correct coordination structure

so we can easily add other modules or features for future.

The structure of this paper is as follows. First, we describe three basic methods required in the technique we propose: 1) coordination structure analysis with alignment-based local features, 2) HPSG parsing, and 3) dual decomposition. Finally, we show experimental results that demonstrate the effectiveness of our approach. We compare three methods: coordination structure analysis with alignment-based local features, HPSG parsing, and the dual-decomposition-based approach that combines both.

2 Related Work

Many previous studies for coordination disambiguation have focused on a particular type of NP coordination (Hogan, 2007). Resnik (1999) disambiguated coordination structures by using semantic similarity of the conjuncts in a taxonomy. He dealt with two kinds of patterns, [n_0 n_1 and n_2 n_3] and [n_1 and n_2 n_3], where n_i are all nouns. He detected coordination structures based on similarity of form, meaning and conceptual association between n_1 and n_2 and between n_1 and n_3. Nakov and Hearst (2005) used the Web as a training set and applied it to a task that is similar to Resnik's.

In terms of integrating coordination disambiguation with an existing parsing model, our approach resembles the approach by Hogan (2007). She detected noun phrase coordinations by finding symmetry in conjunct structure and the dependency between the lexical heads of the conjuncts. They are used to rerank the n-best outputs of the Bikel parser (2004), whereas two models interact with each other in our method.

Shimbo and Hara (2007) proposed an alignment-based method for detecting and disambiguating non-nested coordination structures. They disambiguated coordination structures based on the edit distance between two conjuncts. Hara et al. (2009) extended the method, dealing with nested coordinations as well. We used their method as one of the two sub-models.

3 Background

3.1 Coordination structure analysis with alignment-based local features

Coordination structure analysis with alignment-based local features (Hara et al., 2009) is a hybrid approach to coordination disambiguation that combines a simple grammar to ensure consistent global structure of coordinations in a sentence, and features based on sequence alignment to capture local symmetry of conjuncts. In this section, we describe the method briefly.

A sentence is denoted by $\boldsymbol{x} = x_1 ... x_k$, where x_i is the i-th word of $\boldsymbol{x}$. A *coordination boundaries set* is denoted by $\boldsymbol{y} = y_1 ... y_k$, where

$$y_i = \begin{cases} (b_l, e_l, b_r, e_r) & \text{(if } x_i \text{ is a coordinating conjunction having left conjunct } x_{b_l} ... x_{e_l} \text{ and right conjunct } x_{b_r} ... x_{e_r}) \\ null & \text{(otherwise)} \end{cases}$$

In other words, y_i has a non-null value only when it is a coordinating conjunction. For example, a sentence *I bought books and stationary* has a coordination boundaries set $(null, null, null, (3, 3, 5, 5), null)$.

The score of a coordination boundaries set is defined as the sum of score of all coordinating conjunctions in the sentence.

$$\begin{aligned} score(\boldsymbol{x}, \boldsymbol{y}) &= \sum_{m=1}^{k} score(\boldsymbol{x}, y_m) \\ &= \sum_{m=1}^{k} \boldsymbol{w} \cdot \boldsymbol{f}(\boldsymbol{x}, y_m) \end{aligned} \quad (1)$$

where $\boldsymbol{f}(\boldsymbol{x}, y_m)$ is a real-valued feature vector of the coordination conjunct x_m. We used almost the same feature set as Hara et al. (2009): namely, the surface word, part-of-speech, suffix and prefix of the words, and their combinations. We used the averaged perceptron to tune the weight vector $\boldsymbol{w}$.

Hara et al. (2009) proposed to use a context-free grammar to find a properly nested coordination structure. That is, the scoring function Eq (1)

COORD	Coordination.
CJT	Conjunct.
N	Non-coordination.
CC	Coordinating conjunction like "and".
W	Any word.

Table 2: Non-terminals

Rules for coordinations:

$\mathsf{COORD}_{i,m} \rightarrow \mathsf{CJT}_{i,j}\mathsf{CC}_{j+1,k-1}\mathsf{CJT}_{k,m}$

Rules for conjuncts:

$\mathsf{CJT}_{i,j} \rightarrow (\mathsf{COORD}|\mathsf{N})_{i,j}$

Rules for non-coordinations:

$\mathsf{N}_{i,k} \rightarrow \mathsf{COORD}_{i,j}\mathsf{N}_{j+1,k}$

$\mathsf{N}_{i,j} \rightarrow \mathsf{W}_{i,i}(\mathsf{COORD}|\mathsf{N})_{i+1,j}$

$\mathsf{N}_{i,i} \rightarrow \mathsf{W}_{i,i}$

Rules for pre-terminals:

$\mathsf{CC}_{i,i} \rightarrow (and|or|but|,|;|+|+/-)_i$

$\mathsf{CC}_{i,i+1} \rightarrow (,|;)_i(and|or|but)_{i+1}$

$\mathsf{CC}_{i,i+2} \rightarrow (as)_i(well)_{i+1}(as)_{i+2}$

$\mathsf{W}_{i,i} \rightarrow *_i$

Table 3: Production rules

is only defined on the coordination structures that are licensed by the grammar. We only slightly extended their grammar for convering more variety of coordinating conjunctions.

Table 2 and Table 3 show the non-terminals and production rules used in the model. The only objective of the grammar is to ensure the consistency of two or more coordinations in a sentence, which means for any two coordinations they must be either non-overlapping or nested coordinations. We use a bottom-up chart parsing algorithm to output the coordination boundaries with the highest score. Note that these production rules don't need to be isomorphic to those of HPSG parsing and actually they aren't. This is because the two methods interact only through dual decomposition and the search spaces defined by the methods are considered separately.

This method requires $O(n^4)$ time, where n is the number of words. This is because there are $O(n^2)$ possible coordination structures in a sentence, and the method requires $O(n^2)$ time to get a feature vector of each coordination structure.

3.2 HPSG parsing

HPSG (Pollard and Sag, 1994) is one of the linguistic theories based on lexicalized grammar

Figure 1: subject-head schema (left) and head-complement schema (right); taken from Miyao et al. (2004).

formalism. In a lexicalized grammar, quite a small numbers of schemata are used to explain general grammatical constraints, compared with other theories. On the other hand, rich word-specific characteristics are embedded in lexical entries. Both of schemata and lexical entries are represented by typed feature structures, and constraints in parsing are checked by *unification* among them. Figure 1 shows examples of HPSG schema.

Figure 2 shows an HPSG parse tree of the sentence "*Spring has come.*" First, the lexical entries of "*has*" and "*come*" are joined by head-complement schema. Unification gives the HPSG sign of mother. After applying schemata to HPSG signs repeatedly, the HPSG sign of the whole sentence is output.

We use Enju for an English HPSG parser (Miyao et al., 2004). Figure 3 shows how a coordination structure is built in the Enju grammar. First, a coordinating conjunction and the right conjunct are joined by coord_right_schema. Afterwards, the parent and the left conjunct are joined by coord_left_schema.

The Enju parser is equipped with a disambiguation model trained by the maximum entropy method (Miyao and Tsujii, 2008). Since we do not need the probability of each parse tree, we treat the model just as a linear model that defines the score of a parse tree as the sum of feature weights. The features of the model are defined on local subtrees of a parse tree.

The Enju parser takes $O(n^3)$ time since it uses the CKY algorithm, and each cell in the CKY parse table has at most a constant number of edges because we use beam search algorithm. Thus, we can regard the parser as a decoder for a weighted CFG.

3.3 Dual decomposition

Dual decomposition is a classical method to solve complex optimization problems that can be de-

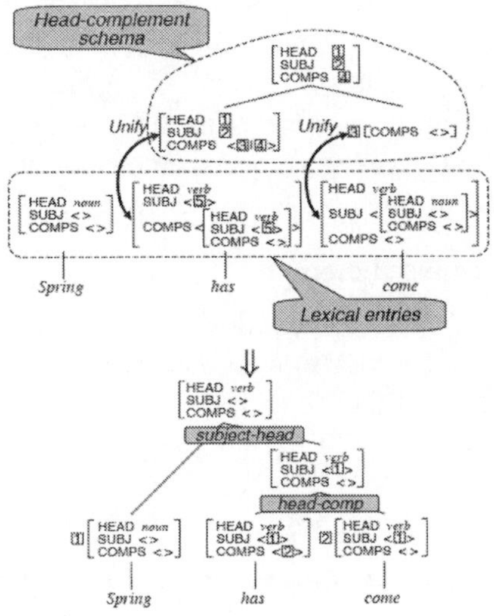

Figure 2: HPSG parsing; taken from Miyao et al. (2004).

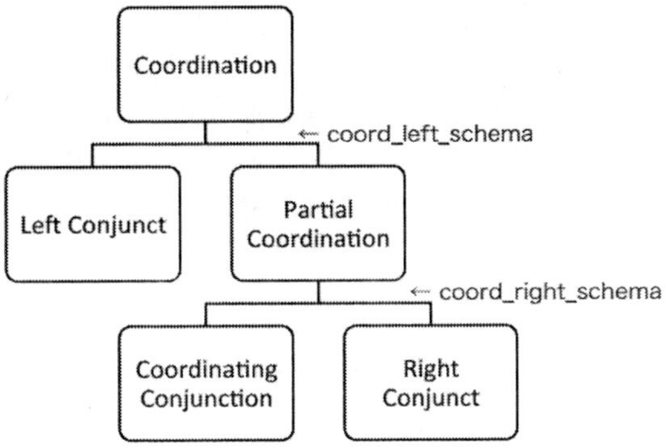

Figure 3: Construction of coordination in Enju

composed into efficiently solvable sub-problems. It is becoming popular in the NLP community and has been shown to work effectively on several NLP tasks (Rush et al., 2010).

We consider an optimization problem

$$\arg\max_{x}(f(x) + g(x)) \quad (2)$$

which is difficult to solve (e.g. NP-hard), while $\arg\max_x f(x)$ and $\arg\max_x g(x)$ are effectively solvable. In dual decomposition, we solve

$$\min_{u}\max_{x,y}(f(x) + g(y) + u(x - y))$$

instead of the original problem.

To find the minimum value, we can use a subgradient method (Rush et al., 2010). The subgradient method is given in Table 4. As the algorithm

$u^{(1)} \leftarrow 0$
for $k = 1$ to K **do**
  $x^{(k)} \leftarrow \arg\max_x(f(x) + u^{(k)}x)$
  $y^{(k)} \leftarrow \arg\max_y(g(y) - u^{(k)}y)$
  if $x = y$ **then**
    return $u^{(k)}$
  end if
  $u^{(k+1)} \leftarrow u^k - a_k(x^{(k)} - y^{(k)})$
end for
return $u^{(K)}$

Table 4: The subgradient method

shows, you can use existing algorithms and don't need to have an exact algorithm for the optimization problem, which are features of dual decomposition.

If $x^{(k)} = y^{(k)}$ occurs during the algorithm, then we simply take $x^{(k)}$ as the primal solution, which is the exact answer. If not, we simply take $x^{(K)}$, the answer of coordination structure analysis with alignment-based features, as an approximate answer to the primal solution. The answer does not always solve the original problem Eq (2), but previous works (e.g., (Rush et al., 2010)) has shown that it is effective in practice. We use it in this paper.

4 Proposed method

In this section, we describe how we apply dual decomposition to the two models.

4.1 Notation

We define some notations here. First we describe weighted CFG parsing, which is used for both coordination structure analysis with alignment-based features and HPSG parsing. We follows the formulation by Rush et al., (2010). We assume a context-free grammar in Chomsky normal form, with a set of non-terminals N. All rules of the grammar are either the form $A \rightarrow BC$ or $A \rightarrow w$ where $A, B, C \in N$ and $w \in V$. For rules of the form $A \rightarrow w$ we refer to A as the pre-terminal for w.

Given a sentence with n words, $w_1 w_2 ... w_n$, a parse tree is a set of rule productions of the form $\langle A \rightarrow BC, i, k, j\rangle$ where $A, B, C \in N$, and $1 \leq i \leq k \leq j \leq n$. Each rule production represents the use of CFG rule $A \rightarrow BC$ where non-terminal A spans words $w_i ... w_j$, non-terminal B

spans word $w_i...w_k$, and non-terminal C spans word $w_{k+1}...w_j$ if $k < j$, and the use of CFG rule $A \rightarrow w_i$ if $i = k = j$.

We now define the *index set* for the coordination structure analysis as

$$\mathcal{I}_{csa} = \{\langle A \rightarrow BC, i, k, j\rangle : A, B, C \in N, \\ 1 \leq i \leq k \leq j \leq n\}$$

Each parse tree is a vector $y = \{y_r : r \in \mathcal{I}_{csa}\}$, with $y_r = 1$ if rule r is in the parse tree, and $y_r = 0$ otherwise. Therefore, each parse tree is represented as a vector in $\{0, 1\}^m$, where $m = |\mathcal{I}_{csa}|$. We use $\mathcal{Y}$ to denote the set of all valid parse-tree vectors. The set $\mathcal{Y}$ is a subset of $\{0, 1\}^m$.

In addition, we assume a vector $\theta^{csa} = \{\theta_r^{csa} : r \in \mathcal{I}_{csa}\}$ that specifies a score for each rule production. Each θ_r^{csa} can take any real value. The optimal parse tree is $y^* = \arg\max_{y \in \mathcal{Y}} y \cdot \theta^{csa}$ where $y \cdot \theta^{csa} = \sum_r y_r \cdot \theta_r^{csa}$ is the inner product between y and θ^{csa}.

We use similar notation for HPSG parsing. We define $\mathcal{I}_{hpsg}$, $\mathcal{Z}$ and θ^{hpsg} as the index set for HPSG parsing, the set of all valid parse-tree vectors and the weight vector for HPSG parsing respectively.

We extend the index sets for both the coordination structure analysis with alignment-based features and HPSG parsing to make a constraint between the two sub-problems. For the coordination structure analysis with alignment-based features we define the extended index set to be $\mathcal{I}'_{csa} = \mathcal{I}_{csa} \bigcup \mathcal{I}_{uni}$ where

$$\mathcal{I}_{uni} = \{(a, b, c) : a, b, c \in \{1...n\}\}$$

Here each triple (a, b, c) represents that word w_c is recognized as the last word of the right conjunct and the scope of the left conjunct or the coordinating conjunction is $w_a...w_b$[1]. Thus each parse-tree vector y will have additional components $y_{a,b,c}$. Note that this representation is over-complete, since a parse tree is enough to determine unique coordination structures for a sentence: more explicitly, the value of $y_{a,b,c}$ is 1 if rule $\mathsf{COORD}_{a,c} \rightarrow \mathsf{CJT}_{a,b}\mathsf{CC}_{\_,\_}\mathsf{CJT}_{\_,c}$ or $\mathsf{COORD}_{\_,c} \rightarrow \mathsf{CJT}_{\_,\_}\mathsf{CC}_{a,b}\mathsf{CJT}_{\_,c}$ is in the parse tree; otherwise it is 0.

We apply the same extension to the HPSG index set, also giving an over-complete representation. We define $z_{a,b,c}$ analogously to $y_{a,b,c}$.

4.2 Proposed method

We now describe the dual decomposition approach for coordination disambiguation. First, we define the set $\mathcal{Q}$ as follows:

$$\mathcal{Q} = \{(y, z) : y \in \mathcal{Y}, z \in \mathcal{Z}, y_{a,b,c} = z_{a,b,c} \\ \text{for all } (a, b, c) \in \mathcal{I}_{uni}\}$$

Therefore, $\mathcal{Q}$ is the set of all (y, z) pairs that agree on their coordination structures. The coordination structure analysis with alignment-based features and HPSG parsing problem is then to solve

$$\max_{(y,z) \in \mathcal{Q}} (y \cdot \theta^{csa} + \gamma z \cdot \theta^{hpsg}) \quad (3)$$

where $\gamma > 0$ is a parameter dictating the relative weight of the two models and is chosen to optimize performance on the development test set.

This problem is equivalent to

$$\max_{z \in \mathcal{Z}} (g(z) \cdot \theta^{csa} + \gamma z \cdot \theta^{hpsg}) \quad (4)$$

where $g : \mathcal{Z} \rightarrow \mathcal{Y}$ is a function that maps a HPSG tree z to its set of coordination structures $z = g(y)$.

We solve this optimization problem by using dual decomposition. Figure 4 shows the resulting algorithm. The algorithm tries to optimize the combined objective by separately solving the sub-problems again and again. After each iteration, the algorithm updates the weights $u(a, b, c)$. These updates modify the objective functions for the two sub-problems, encouraging them to agree on the same coordination structures. If $y^{(k)} = z^{(k)}$ occurs during the iterations, then the algorithm simply returns $y^{(k)}$ as the exact answer. If not, the algorithm returns the answer of coordination analysis with alignment features as a heuristic answer.

It is needed to modify original sub-problems for calculating (1) and (2) in Table 4. We modified the sub-problems to regard the score of $u(a, b, c)$ as a bonus/penalty of the coordination. The modified coordination structure analysis with alignment features adds $u^{(k)}(i, j, m)$ and $u^{(k)}(j+1, l-$

[1]This definition is derived from the structure of a coordination in Enju (Figure 3). The triples show where the coordinating conjunction and right conjunct are in coord_right_schema, and the left conjunct and partial coordination are in coord_left_schema. Thus they alone enable not only the coordination structure analysis with alignment-based features but Enju to uniquely determine the structure of a coordination.

$u^{(1)}(a,b,c) \leftarrow 0$ for all $(a,b,c) \in \mathcal{I}_{uni}$
for $k = 1$ to K **do**
  $y^{(k)} \leftarrow \arg\max_{y \in \mathcal{Y}}(y \cdot \theta^{csa} - \sum_{(a,b,c) \in \mathcal{I}_{uni}} u^{(k)}(a,b,c) y_{a,b,c})$ ... (1)
  $z^{(k)} \leftarrow \arg\max_{z \in \mathcal{Z}}(z \cdot \theta^{hpsg} + \sum_{(a,b,c) \in \mathcal{I}_{uni}} u^{(k)}(a,b,c) z_{a,b,c})$ ... (2)
  if $y^{(k)}(a,b,c) = z^{(k)}(a,b,c)$ for all $(a,b,c) \in \mathcal{I}_{uni}$ **then**
    return $y^{(k)}$
  end if
  for all $(a,b,c) \in \mathcal{I}_{uni}$ **do**
    $u^{(k+1)}(a,b,c) \leftarrow u^{(k)}(a,b,c) - a_k(y^{(k)}(a,b,c) - z^{(k)}(a,b,c))$
  end for
end for
return $y^{(K)}$

Figure 4: Proposed algorithm

$1, m)$, as well as adding $\boldsymbol{w} \cdot \boldsymbol{f}(\boldsymbol{x}, (i,j,l,m))$ to the score of the subtree, when the rule production $\mathsf{COORD}_{i,m} \rightarrow \mathsf{CJT}_{i,j}\mathsf{CC}_{j+1,l-1}\mathsf{CJT}_{l,m}$ is applied.

The modified Enju adds $u^{(k)}(a,b,c)$ when coord_right_schema is applied, where word $w_a...w_b$ is recognized as a coordinating conjunction and the last word of the right conjunct is w_c, or coord_left_schema is applied, where word $w_a...w_b$ is recognized as the left conjunct and the last word of the right conjunct is w_c.

5 Experiments

5.1 Test/Training data

We trained the alignment-based coordination analysis model on both the Genia corpus (Kim et al., 2003) and the Wall Street Journal portion of the Penn Treebank (Marcus et al., 1993), and evaluated the performance of our method on (i) the Genia corpus and (ii) the Wall Street Journal portion of the Penn Treebank. More precisely, we used HPSG treebank converted from the Penn Treebank and Genia, and further extracted the training/test data for coordination structure analysis with alignment-based features using the annotation in the Treebank. Table 5 shows the corpus used in the experiments.

The Wall Street Journal portion of the Penn Treebank in the test set has 2317 sentences from WSJ articles, and there are 1356 coordinations in the sentences, while the Genia corpus in the test set has 1764 sentences from MEDLINE abstracts, and there are 1848 coordinations in the sentences. Coordinations are further subcategorized into phrase types such as a NP coordination or PP coordination. Table 6 shows the percentage of each phrase type in all coordianitons. It indicates the Wall Street Journal portion of the Penn Treebank has more VP coordinations and S coordianitons, while the Genia corpus has more NP coordianitons and ADJP coordiations.

COORD	WSJ	Genia
NP	63.7	66.3
VP	13.8	11.4
ADJP	6.8	9.6
S	11.4	6.0
PP	2.4	5.1
Others	1.9	1.5

Table 6: The percentage of each conjunct type (%) of each test set

5.2 Implementation of sub-problems

We used Enju (Miyao and Tsujii, 2004) for the implementation of HPSG parsing, which has a wide-coverage probabilistic HPSG grammar and an efficient parsing algorithm, while we reimplemented Hara et al., (2009)'s algorithm with slight modifications.

5.2.1 Step size

We used the following step size in our algorithm (Figure 4). First, we initialized a_0, which is chosen to optimize performance on the development set. Then we defined $a_k = a_0 \cdot 2^{-\eta_k}$, where η_k is the number of times that $L(u^{(k')}) > L(u^{(k'-1)})$ for $k' \leq k$.

	Task (i)	Task (ii)
Training	WSJ (sec. 2–21) + Genia (No. 1–1600)	WSJ (sec. 2–21)
Development	Genia (No. 1601–1800)	WSJ (sec. 22)
Test	Genia (No. 1801–1999)	WSJ (sec. 23)

Table 5: The corpus used in the experiments

	Proposed	Enju	CSA
Precision	**72.4**	66.3	65.3
Recall	**67.8**	65.5	60.5
F1	**70.0**	65.9	62.8

Table 7: Results of Task (i) on the test set. The precision, recall, and F1 (%) for the proposed method, Enju, and Coordination structure analysis with alignment-based features (CSA)

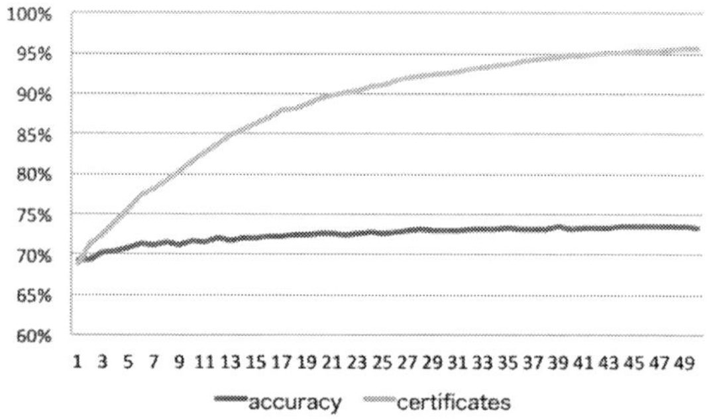

Figure 5: Performance of the approach as a function of K of Task (i) on the development set. accuracy (%): the percentage of sentences that are correctly parsed. certificates (%): the percentage of sentences for which a certificate of optimality is obtained.

5.3 Evaluation metric

We evaluated the performance of the tested methods by the accuracy of coordination-level bracketing (Shimbo and Hara, 2007); i.e., we count each of the coordination scopes as one output of the system, and the system output is regarded as correct if both of the beginning of the first output conjunct and the end of the last conjunct match annotations in the Treebank (Hara et al., 2009).

5.4 Experimental results of Task (i)

We ran the dual decomposition algorithm with a limit of $K = 50$ iterations. We found the two sub-problems return the same answer during the algorithm in over 95% of sentences.

We compare the accuracy of the dual decomposition approach to two baselines: Enju and coordination structure analysis with alignment-based features. Table 7 shows all three results. The dual decomposition method gives a statistically significant gain in precision and recall over the two methods[2].

Table 8 shows the recall of coordinations of each type. It indicates our re-implementation of CSA and Hara et al. (2009) have a roughly similar performance, although their experimental settings are different. It also shows the proposed method took advantage of Enju and CSA in NP coordination, while it is likely just to take the answer of Enju in VP and sentential coordinations. This means we might well use dual decomposition only on NP coordinations to have a better result.

Figure 5 shows performance of the approach as a function of K, the maximum number of iterations of dual decomposition. The graphs show that values of K much less than 50 produce almost identical performance to $K = 50$ (with $K = 50$, the accuracy of the method is 73.4%, with $K = 20$ it is 72.6%, and with $K = 1$ it is 69.3%). This means you can use smaller K in practical use for speed.

5.5 Experimental results of Task (ii)

We also ran the dual decomposition algorithm with a limit of $K = 50$ iterations on Task (ii). Table 9 and 10 show the results of task (ii). They show the proposed method outperformed the two methods statistically in precision and recall[3].

Figure 6 shows performance of the approach as a function of K, the maximum number of iterations of dual decomposition. The convergence speed for WSJ was faster than that for Genia. This is because a sentence of WSJ often have a simpler coordination structure, compared with that of Genia.

[2] $p < 0.01$ (by chi-square test)

[3] $p < 0.01$ (by chi-square test)

COORD	#	Proposed	Enju	CSA		#	Hara et al. (2009)
Overall	1848	**67.7**	63.3	61.9		3598	61.5
NP	1213	**67.5**	61.4	64.1		2317	64.2
VP	208	**79.8**	78.8	66.3		456	54.2
ADJP	193	58.5	**59.1**	54.4		312	80.4
S	111	51.4	**52.3**	34.2		188	22.9
PP	110	**64.5**	59.1	57.3		167	59.9
Others	13	**78.3**	73.9	65.2		140	49.3

Table 8: The number of coordinations of each type (#), and the recall (%) for the proposed method, Enju, coordination structure analysis with alignment-based features (CSA) , and Hara et al. (2009) of Task (i) on the development set. Note that Hara et al. (2009) uses a different test set and different annotation rules, although its test data is also taken from the Genia corpus. Thus we cannot compare them directly.

	Proposed	Enju	CSA
Precision	**76.3**	70.7	66.0
Recall	**70.6**	69.0	60.1
F1	**73.3**	69.9	62.9

Table 9: Results of Task (ii) on the test set. The precision, recall, and F1 (%) for the proposed method, Enju, and Coordination structure analysis with alignment-based features (CSA)

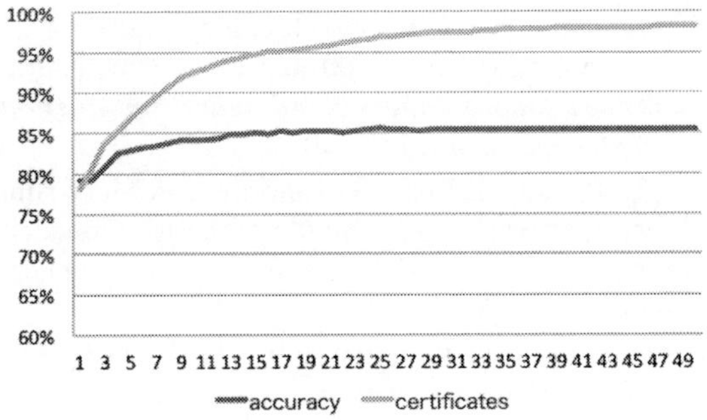

Figure 6: Performance of the approach as a function of K of Task (ii) on the development set. accuracy (%): the percentage of sentences that are correctly parsed. certificates (%): the percentage of sentences for which a certificate of optimality is provided.

COORD	#	Proposed	Enju	CSA
Overall	1017	**71.6**	68.1	60.7
NP	573	**76.1**	71.0	67.7
VP	187	62.0	**62.6**	47.6
ADJP	73	**82.2**	75.3	79.5
S	141	**64.5**	62.4	42.6
PP	19	**52.6**	47.4	47.4
Others	24	62.5	**70.8**	54.2

Table 10: The number of coordinations of each type (#), and the recall (%) for the proposed method, Enju, and coordination structure analysis with alignment-based features (CSA) of Task (ii) on the development set.

6 Conclusion and Future Work

In this paper, we presented an efficient method for detecting and disambiguating coordinate structures. Our basic idea was to consider both grammar and symmetries of conjuncts by using dual decomposition. Experiments on the Genia corpus and the Wall Street Journal portion of the Penn Treebank showed that we could obtain statistically significant improvement in accuracy when using dual decomposition.

We would need a further study in the following points of view: First, we should evaluate our method with corpus in different domains. Because characteristics of coordination structures differs from corpus to corpus, experiments on other corpus would lead to a different result. Second, we would want to add some features to coordination structure analysis with alignment-based local features such as ontology. Finally, we can add other methods (e.g. dependency parsing) as sub-problems to our method by using the extension of dual decomposition, which can deal with more than two sub-problems.

Acknowledgments

The second author is partially supported by KAKENHI Grant-in-Aid for Scientific Research C 21500131 and Microsoft CORE project 7.

References

Kazuo Hara, Masashi Shimbo, Hideharu Okuma, and Yuji Matsumoto. 2009. Coordinate structure analysis with global structural constraints and alignment-based local features. In *Proceedings of the 47th Annual Meeting of the ACL and the 4th IJCNLP of the AFNLP*, pages 967–975, Aug.

Deirdre Hogan. 2007. Coordinate noun phrase disambiguation in a generative parsing model. In *Proceedings of the 45th Annual Meeting of the Association of Computational Linguistics (ACL 2007)*, pages 680–687.

Jun-Dong Kim, Tomoko Ohta, and Jun'ich Tsujii. 2003. Genia corpus - a semantically annotated corpus for bio-textmining. *Bioinformatics*, 19.

Dan Klein and Christopher D. Manning. 2003. Fast exact inference with a factored model for natural language parsing. *Advances in Neural Information Processing Systems*, 15:3–10.

Mitchell P. Marcus, Beatrice Santorini, and Mary Ann Marcinkiewicz. 1993. Building a large annotated corpus of english: The penn treebank. *Computational Linguistics*, 19:313–330.

Yusuke Miyao and Jun'ich Tsujii. 2004. Deep linguistic analysis for the accurate identification of predicate-argument relations. In *Proceeding of COLING 2004*, pages 1392–1397.

Yusuke Miyao and Jun'ich Tsujii. 2008. Feature forest models for probabilistic hpsg parsing. *MIT Press*, 1(34):35–80.

Yusuke Miyao, Takashi Ninomiya, and Jun'ichi Tsujii. 2004. Corpus-oriented grammar development for acquiring a head-driven phrase structure grammar from the penn treebank. In *Proceedings of the First International Joint Conference on Natural Language Processing (IJCNLP 2004)*.

Preslav Nakov and Marti Hearst. 2005. Using the web as an implicit training set: Application to structural ambiguity resolution. In *Proceedings of the Human Language Technology Conference and Conference on Empirical Methods in Natural Language (HLT-EMNLP 2005)*, pages 835–842.

Carl Pollard and Ivan A. Sag. 1994. Head-driven phrase structure grammar. *University of Chicago Press*.

Philip Resnik. 1999. Semantic similarity in a takonomy. *Journal of Artificial Intelligence Research*, 11:95–130.

Alexander M. Rush, David Sontag, Michael Collins, and Tommi Jaakkola. 2010. On dual decomposition and linear programming relaxations for natural language processing. In *Proceeding of the conference on Empirical Methods in Natural Language Processing*.

Masashi Shimbo and Kazuo Hara. 2007. A discriminative learning model for coordinate conjunctions. In *Proceedings of the 2007 Joint Conference on Empirical Methods in Natural Language Processing and Computational Natural Language Learning*, pages 610–619, Jun.

Cutting the Long Tail: Hybrid Language Models for Translation Style Adaptation

Arianna Bisazza and **Marcello Federico**
Fondazione Bruno Kessler
Trento, Italy
{bisazza, federico}@fbk.eu

Abstract

In this paper, we address statistical machine translation of public conference talks. Modeling the style of this genre can be very challenging given the shortage of available in-domain training data. We investigate the use of a hybrid LM, where infrequent words are mapped into classes. Hybrid LMs are used to complement word-based LMs with statistics about the language style of the talks. Extensive experiments comparing different settings of the hybrid LM are reported on publicly available benchmarks based on TED talks, from Arabic to English and from English to French. The proposed models show to better exploit in-domain data than conventional word-based LMs for the target language modeling component of a phrase-based statistical machine translation system.

1 Introduction

The translation of TED conference talks[1] is an emerging task in the statistical machine translation (SMT) community (Federico et al., 2011). The variety of topics covered by the speeches, as well as their specific language style, make this a very challenging problem.

Fixed expressions, colloquial terms, figures of speech and other phenomena recurrent in the talks should be properly modeled to produce translations that are not only fluent but that also employ the right register. In this paper, we propose a language modeling technique that leverages in-domain training data for style adaptation.

Hybrid class-based LMs are trained on text where only infrequent words are mapped to Part-of-Speech (POS) classes. In this way, topic-specific words are discarded and the model focuses on generic words that we assume more useful to characterize the language style. The factorization of similar expressions made possible by this mixed text representation yields a better n-gram coverage, but with a much higher discriminative power than POS-level LMs.

Hybrid LM also differs from POS-level LM in that it uses a word-to-class mapping to determine POS tags. Consequently, it doesn't require the decoding overload of factored models nor the tagging of all parallel data used to build phrase tables. A hybrid LM trained on in-domain data can thus be easily added to an existing baseline system trained on large amounts of background data.

The proposed models are used in addition to standard word-based LMs, in the framework of log-linear phrase-based SMT.

The remainder of this paper is organized as follows. After discussing the language style adaptation problem, we will give an overview of relevant work. In the following sections we will describe in detail hybrid LM and its possible variants. Finally, we will present an empirical analysis of the proposed technique, including intrinsic evaluation and SMT experiments.

2 Background

Our working scenario is the translation of TED talks transcripts as proposed by the IWSLT Evaluation Campaign[2]. This genre covers a variety of topics ranging from business to psychology. The available training material – both parallel and

[1] http://www.ted.com/talks

[2] http://www.iwslt2011.org

Beginning of Sentence: [s]

	TED		NEWS
1st	[s] Thank you . [/s]	1st	[s] (AP) -
2	[s] Thank you very much	2	[s] WASHINGTON (...
3	[s] I 'm going to	3	[s] NEW YORK (AP
4	[s] And I said ,	4	[s] (CNN) –
5	[s] I don 't know	5	[s] NEW YORK (R...
6	[s] He said , “	6	[s] He said : “
7	[s] I said , “	7	[s] ” I don 't
8	[s] And of course ,	8	[s] It was last updated
9	[s] And one of the	9	[s] At the same time
10	[s] And I want to	...	
11	[s] And that 's what	69	[s] I don 't know
12	[s] We 're going to	612	[s] I 'm going to
13	[s] And I think that	2434	[s] ” I said ,
14	[s] And you can see	7034	[s] He said , “
15	[s] And this is a	8199	[s] And I said ,
16	[s] And this is the	8233	[s] Thank you very much
17	[s] And he said ,	...	
18	[s] So this is a	∅	*[s] Thank you . [/s]*

End of Sentence: [/s]

	TED		NEWS
1st	[s] Thank you . [/s]	1st	” he said . [/s]
2	you very much . [/s]	2	” she said . [/s]
3	in the world . [/s]	3	, he said . [/s]
4	and so on . [/s]	4	” he said . [/s]
5	, you know . [/s]	5	in a statement . [/s]
6	of the world . [/s]	6	the United States . [/s]
7	around the world . [/s]	7	to this report . [/s]
8	. Thank you . [/s]	8	” he added . [/s]
9	the United States . [/s]	9	, police said . [/s]
10	all the time . [/s]	10	, officials said . [/s]
11	to do it . [/s]	...	
12	and so forth . [/s]	13	in the world . [/s]
13	don 't know . [/s]	17	around the world . [/s]
14	to do that . [/s]	46	of the world . [/s]
15	in the future . [/s]	129	all the time . [/s]
16	the same time . [/s]	157	and so on . [/s]
17	, you know ? [/s]	1652	, you know . [/s]
18	to do this . [/s]	5509	you very much . [/s]

Table 1: Common sentence-initial and sentence-final 5-grams, as ranked by frequency, in the TED and NEWS corpora. Numbers denote the frequency rank.

monolingual – consists of a rather small collection of TED talks plus a variety of large out-of-domain corpora, such as news stories and UN proceedings.

Given the diversity of topics, the in-domain data alone cannot ensure sufficient coverage to an SMT system. The addition of background data can certainly improve the n-gram coverage and thus the fluency of our translations, but it may also move our system towards an unsuitable language style, such as that of written news.

In our study, we focus on the subproblem of target language modeling and consider two English text collections, namely the in-domain TED and the out-of-domain NEWS[3], summarized in Table 2. Because of its larger size – two orders of magnitude – the NEWS corpus can provide a better LM coverage than the TED on the test data. This is reflected both on perplexity and on the average length of the context (or history $\overline{h}$) actually used by these two LMs to score the test's reference translations. Note that the latter measure is bounded at the LM order minus one, and is inversely proportional to the number of back-offs performed by the model. Hence, we use this value to estimate how well an n-gram LM fits the test data. Indeed, despite the genre mismatch, the perplexity of a NEWS 5-gram LM on the TED-2010 test reference translations is 104 versus 112 for the in-domain LM, and the average history size is 2.5 versus 1.7 words.

[3]http://www.statmt.org/wmt11/translation-task.html

LM Data	$\lvert S \rvert$	$\lvert W \rvert$	$\lvert V \rvert$	PP	$\overline{h_{5g}}$
TED-En	124K	2.4M	51K	112	1.7
NEWS-En	30.7M	782M	2.2M	104	2.5

Table 2: Training data and coverage statistics of two 5-gram LMs used for the TED task: number of sentences and tokens, vocabulary size; perplexity and average word history.

TED		NEWS	
1st	,	1st	the
...		...	
9	I	40	I
12	you	64	you
90	actually	965	actually
268	stuff	2479	guy
370	guy	2861	stuff
436	amazing	4706	amazing

Table 3: Excerpts from TED and NEWS training vocabularies, as ranked by frequency. Numbers denote the frequency rank.

Yet we observe that the style of public speeches is much better represented in the in-domain corpus than in the out-of-domain one. For instance, let us consider the vocabulary distribution[4] of the

[4]Hesitations and filler words, typical of spoken language, are not covered in our study because they are generally not reported in the TED talk transcripts.

two corpora (Table 3). The very first forms, as ranked by frequency, are quite similar in the two corpora. However, there are important exceptions: the pronouns *I* and *you* are among the top 20 frequent forms in the TED, while in the NEWS they are ranked only 40th and 64th respectively. Other interesting cases are the words *actually*, *stuff*, *guy* and *amazing*, all ranked about 10 times higher in the TED than in the NEWS corpus.

We can also analyze the most typical ways to start and end a sentence in the two text collections. As shown in Table 1, the frequency ranking of sentence-initial and sentence-final 5-grams in the in-domain corpus is notably different from the out-of-domain one. TED's most frequent sentence-initial 5-gram "*[s] Thank you . [/s]* " is not at all attested in the NEWS corpus. As for the 4th most common sentence start "*[s] And I said ,*" is only ranked 8199th in the NEWS, and so on. Notably, the top ranked NEWS 5-grams include names of cities (*Washington*, *New York*) and of news agency (*AP*, *Reuters*). As regards sentence endings, we observe similar contrasts: for instance, the word sequence "*and so on . [/s]* " is ranked 4th in the TED and 157th in the NEWS while "*, you know . [/s]* " is 5th in the TED and only 1652th in the NEWS.

These figures confirm that the talks have a specific language style, remarkably different from that of the written news genre. In summary, talks are characterized by a massive use of first and second persons, by shorter sentences, and by more colloquial lexical and syntactic constructions.

3 Related Work

The brittleness of n-gram LMs in case of mismatch between training and task data is a well known issue (Rosenfeld, 2000). So called *domain adaptation* methods (Bellegarda, 2004) can improve the situation, once a limited amount of task specific data become available. Ideally, domain-adaptive LMs aim to improve model robustness under changing conditions, involving possible variations in vocabulary, syntax, content, and style. Most of the known LM adaption techniques (Bellegarda, 2004), however, address all these variations in a holistic way. A possible reason for this is that LM adaptation methods were originally developed under the automatic speech recognition framework, which typically assumes the presence of one single LM. The progressive adoption of the log-linear modeling framework in many NLP tasks has recently introduced the use of multiple LM components (features), which permit to naturally factor out and integrate different aspects of language into one model. In SMT, the factored model (Koehn and Hoang, 2007), for instance, permits to better tailor the LM to the task syntax, by complementing word-based n-grams with a part-of-speech (POS) LM , that can be estimated even on a limited amount of task-specific data. Besides many works addressing holistic LM domain adaptation for SMT, e.g. Foster and Kuhn (2007), recently methods were also proposed to explicitly adapt the LM to the discourse topic of a talk (Ruiz and Federico, 2011). Our work makes another step in this direction by investigating hybrid LMs that try to explicitly represent the speaking style of the talk genre. As a difference from standard class-based LMs (Brown et al., 1992) or the more recent local LMs (Monz, 2011), which are used to predict sequences of classes or word-class pairs, our hybrid LM is devised to predict sequences of classes interleaved by words. While we do not claim any technical novelty in the model itself, to our knowledge a deep investigation of hybrid LMs for the sake of style adaptation is definitely new. Finally, the term *hybrid LM* was inspired by Yazgan and Saraçlar (2004), which called with this name a LM predicting sequences of words and sub-words units, devised to let a speech recognizer detect out-of-vocabulary-words.

4 Hybrid Language Model

Hybrid LMs are n-gram models trained on a mixed text representation where each word is either mapped to a class or left as is. This choice is made according to a measure of word commonness and is univocal for each word type.

The rationale is to discard topic-specific words, while preserving those words that best characterize the language style (note that word frequency is computed on the in-domain corpus only). Mapping non-frequent terms to classes naturally leads to a shorter tail in the frequency distribution, as visualized by Figure 1. A model trained on such data has a better n-gram coverage of the test set and may take advantage of a larger context when scoring translation hypotheses.

As classes, we use deterministically assigned POS tags, obtained by first tagging the data with

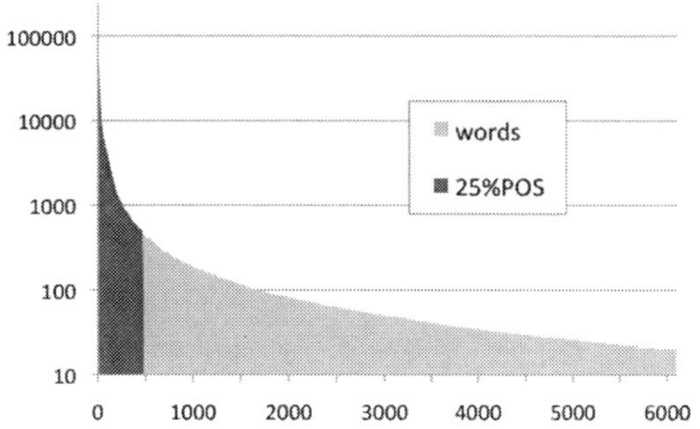

Figure 1: Type frequency distribution in the English TED corpus before and after POS-mapping of words with less than 500 occurrences (25% of tokens). The rank in the frequency list (x-axis) is plotted against the respective frequency in logarithmic scale. Types with less than 20 occurrences are omitted from the graph.

Tree Tagger (Schmid, 1994) and then choosing the most likely tag for each word type. In this way, we avoid the overload of searching for the best tagging decisions at run-time at the cost of a slightly higher imprecision (see Section 5.1). The hybridly mapped data is used to train a high-order n-gram LM that is plugged into an SMT decoder as an additional feature on target word sequences. During the translation process, words are mapped to their class just before querying the hybrid LM, therefore translation models can be trained on plain un-tagged data.

As exemplified in Table 4, hybrid LMs can draw useful statistics on the context of common words even from a small corpus such as the TED. To have an idea of data sparseness, consider that in the unprocessed TED corpus the most frequent 5-gram containing the common word *guy* occurs only 3 times. After the mapping of words with frequency <500, the highest 5-gram frequency grows to 17, the second one to 9, and so on.

guy	598
a guy VBN NP NP	17
guy VBN NP NP ,	9
guy , NP NP ,	8
a guy called NP NP	8
this guy , NP NP	6
guy VBN NP NP .	6
by a guy VBN NP	5
a JJ guy . [/s]	5
I was VBG this guy	4
guy VBN NP . [/s]	4

actually	3978
[s] This is actually a	20
[s] It 's actually a	17
, you can actually VB	13
is actually a JJ NN	13
This is actually a NN	12
[s] And this is actually	12
[s] And that 's actually	10
, but it 's actually	10
NN , it 's actually	9
we're actually going to	8

Table 4: Most common hybrid 5-grams containing the words *guy* and *actually*, along with absolute frequency.

4.1 Word commonness criteria

The most intuitive way to measure word commonness is by absolute term frequency (F). We will use this criterion in most of our experiments. A finer solution would be to also consider the commonness of a word across different talks. At this end, we propose to use the *fdf* statistics, that is the product of relative term *f*requency and *d*ocument *f*requency[5]:

$$fdf_w = \frac{c(w)}{\sum_{w'} c(w')} \times \frac{c(d_w)}{c(d)}$$

where d_w are the documents (talks) containing at least one occurrence of the word w.

If available, real talk boundaries can be used to define the documents. Alternatively, we can simply split the corpus into chunks of fixed size. In this work we use this approximation.

Another issue is how to set the threshold. Independently from the chosen commonness measure, we can reason in terms of the ratio of tokens that are mapped to POS classes (W_P). For instance, in our experiments with English, we can set the threshold to F=500 and observe that W_P corresponds to 25% of the tokens (and 99% of the types). In the same corpus, a similar ratio is obtained with *fdf*=0.012.

In our study, we consider three ratios W_P=\{.25, .50, .75\} that correspond to different levels of language modeling: from a domain-generic word-level LM to a lexically anchored POS-level LM.

4.2 Handling morphology

Token frequency-based measures may not be suitable for languages other than English. When translating into French, for instance, we have to deal with a much richer morphology.

As a solution we can use lemmas, univocally assigned to word types in the same manner as POS tags. Lemmas can be employed in two ways: only for word selection, as a frequency measure, or also for word representation, as a mapping for common words. In the former, we preserve inflected variants that may be useful to model the language style, but we also risk to see n-gram coverage decrease due to the presence of rare types. In the latter, only canonical forms and POS tags

[5]This differs from the *tf-idf* widely used in information retrieval, which is used to measure the *relevance* of a term in a *document*. Instead, we measure *commonness* of a term in the *whole corpus*.

appear in the processed text, thus introducing a further level of abstraction from the original text.

Here follows a TED sentence in its original version (first line) and after three different hybrid mappings – namely W_P=.25, W_P=.25 with lemma forms, and W_P=.50:

Now you laugh, but that quote has kind of a sting to it, right.
Now you **VB** , but that **NN** has kind of a **NN** to it, right.
Now you **VB** , but that **NN** have kind of a **NN** to it, right.
RB you **VB** , **CC** that **NN** **VBZ** **NN** of a **NN** to it, **RB** .

Hybrid 10g LM	$\|V\|$	POS-Err	$\overline{h_{10g}}$
all words	51299	0.0%	1.7
all lemmas	38486	0.0%	1.9
.25 POS/words	475	1.9%	2.7
.50 POS/words	93	4.1%	3.5
.75 POS/words	50	5.7%	4.1
allPOS	43	6.6%	4.4
.25 POS/lemmas	302	1.8%	2.8
.25 POS/words(fdf)	301	1.9%	2.7

Table 5: Comparison of LMs obtained from different hybrid mappings of the English TED corpus: vocabulary size, POS error rate, and average word history on IWSLT–tst2010's reference translations.

5 Evaluation

In this section we perform an intrinsic evaluation of the proposed LM technique, then we measure its impact on translation quality when integrated into a state-of-the-art phrase-based SMT system.

5.1 Intrinsic evaluation

We analyze here a set of hybrid LMs trained on the English TED corpus by varying the ratio of POS-mapped words and the word representation technique (word vs lemma). All models were trained with the IRSTLM toolkit (Federico et al., 2008), using a very high n-gram order (10) and Witten-Bell smoothing.

First, we estimate an upper bound of the POS tagging errors introduced by deterministic tagging. At this end, the hybridly mapped data is compared with the actual output of Tree Tagger on the TED training corpus (see Table 5). Naturally, the impact of tagging errors correlates with the ratio of POS-mapped tokens, as no error is counted on non-mapped tokens. For instance, we note that the POS error rate is only 1.9% in our primary setting, W_P=.25 and word representation, whereas on a fully POS-mapped text it is 6.6%. Note that the English tag set used by Tree Tagger includes 43 classes.

Now we focus on the main goal of hybrid text representation, namely increasing the coverage of the in-domain LM on the test data. Here too, we measure coverage by the average length of word history $\overline{h}$ used to score the test reference translations (see Section 2). We do not provide perplexity figures, since these are not directly comparable across models with different vocabularies. As shown by Table 5, n-gram coverage increases with the ratio of POS-mapped tokens, ranging from 1.7 on an all-words LM to 4.4 on an all-POS LM. Of course, the more words are mapped, the less discriminative our model will be. Thus, choosing the best hybrid mapping means finding the best trade-off between coverage and informativeness.

We also applied hybrid LM to the French language, again using Tree Tagger to create the POS mapping. The tag set in this case comprises 34 classes and the POS error rate with W_P=.25 is 1.2% (compare with 1.9% in English). As previously discussed, morphology has a notable effect on the modeling of French. In fact, the vocabulary reduction obtained by mapping all the words to their most probable lemma is -45% (57959 to 31908 types in the TED corpus), while in English it is only -25%.

5.2 SMT baseline

Our SMT experiments address the translation of TED talks from Arabic to English and from English to French. The training and test datasets were provided by the organizers of the IWSLT11 evaluation, and are summarized in Table 6. Marked in bold are the corpora used for hybrid LM training. Dev and test sets have a single reference translation.

For both language pairs, we set up competitive phrase-based systems[6] using the Moses toolkit (Koehn et al., 2007). The decoder features a statistical log-linear model including a phrase translation model and a phrase reordering model (Tillmann, 2004; Koehn et al., 2005), two word-based language models, distortion, word and phrase penalties. The translation and reordering models are obtained by combining models independently trained on the available paral-

[6]The SMT systems used in this paper are thoroughly described in (Ruiz et al., 2011).

Corpus		$\|S\|$	$\|W\|$	$\bar{\ell}$
AR-EN	TED	90K	1.7M	18.9
	UN	7.9M	220M	27.8
EN	**TED**	**124K**	**2.4M**	**19.5**
	NEWS	30.7M	782M	25.4
AR test	dev2010	934	19K	20.0
	tst2010	1664	30K	18.1
EN-FR	TED	105K	2.0M	19.5
	UN	11M	291M	26.5
	NEWS	111K	3.1M	27.6
FR	**TED**	**107K**	**2.2M**	**20.6**
	NEWS	11.6M	291M	25.2
EN test	dev2010	934	20K	21.5
	tst2010	1664	32K	19.1

Table 6: IWSLT11 training and test data statistics: number of sentences $|S|$, number of tokens $|W|$ and average sentence length $\bar{\ell}$. Token numbers are computed on the target language, except for the test sets.

lel corpora: namely TED and NEWS for Arabic-English; TED, NEWS and UN for English-French. To this end we applied the fill-up method (Nakov, 2008; Bisazza et al., 2011) in which out-of-domain phrase tables are merged with the in-domain table by adding only new phrase pairs. Out-of-domain phrases are marked with a binary feature whose weight is tuned together with the SMT system weights.

For each target language, two standard 5-gram LMs are trained separately on the monolingual TED and NEWS datasets, and log-linearly combined at decoding time. In the Arabic-English task, we use a hierarchical reordering model (Galley and Manning, 2008; Hardmeier et al., 2011), while in the English-French task we use a default word-based bidirectional model. The distortion limit is set to the default value of 6. Note that the use of large n-gram LMs and of lexicalized reordering models was shown to wipe out the improvement achievable by POS-level LM (Kirchhoff and Yang, 2005; Birch et al., 2007).

Concerning data preprocessing we apply standard tokenization to the English and French text, while for Arabic we use an in-house tokenizer that removes diacritics and normalizes special characters and digits. Arabic text is then segmented with AMIRA (Diab et al., 2004) according to the ATB scheme[7]. The Arabic-English system uses cased translation models, while the English-French system uses lowercased models and a standard recasing post-process.

Feature weights are tuned on dev2010 by means of a minimum error training procedure (MERT) (Och, 2003). Following suggestions by Clark et al. (2011) and Cettolo et al. (2011) on controlling optimizer instability, we run MERT four times on the same configuration and use the average of the resulting weights to evaluate translation performance.

5.3 Hybrid LM integration

As previously stated, hybrid LMs are trained only on in-domain data and are added to the log-linear decoder as an additional target LM. To this end, we use the class-based LM implementation provided in Moses and IRSTLM, which applies the word-to-class mapping to translation hypotheses before LM querying[8]. The order of the additional LM is set to 10 in the Arabic-English evaluation and 7 in the English-French, as these appeared to be the best settings in preliminary tests.

Translation quality is measured by BLEU (Papineni et al., 2002), METEOR (Banerjee and Lavie, 2005) and TER (Snover et al., 2006)[9]. To test whether differences among systems are statistically significant we use approximate randomization as done in (Riezler and Maxwell, 2005)[10].

Model variants. The effect on MT quality of various hybrid LM variants is shown in Table 7. Note that allPOS and allLemmas refer to deterministically assigned POS tags and lemmas, respectively. Concerning the ratio of POS-mapped tokens, the best performing values are W_P=.25 in Arabic-English and W_P=.50 in English-French. These hybrid mappings outperform all the uniform representations (words, lemmas and POS) with statistically significant BLEU and METEOR improvements.

The *fdf* experiment involves the use of document frequency for the selection of common words. Its performance is very close to that of hy-

[7]The Arabic Treebank tokenization scheme isolates conjunctions *w+* and *f+*, prepositions *l+*, *k+*, *b+*, future marker *s+*, pronominal suffixes, but not the article *Al+*.

[8]Detailed instructions on how to build and use hybrid LMs can be found at http://hlt.fbk.eu/people/bisazza.

[9]We use case-sensitive BLEU and TER, but case-*insensitive* METEOR to enable the use of paraphrase tables distributed with the tool (version 1.3).

[10]Translation scores and significance tests were computed with the *Multeval* toolkit (Clark et al., 2011): https://github.com/jhclark/multeval.

(a) Arabic to English, IWSLT–tst2010

Added InDomain 10gLM	BLEU↑	MET ↑	TER ↓
.00 POS/words (all words)†	26.1	30.5	55.4
.00 POS/lemmas (all lem.)	26.0	30.5	55.4
1.0 POS/words (all POS)†	25.9	30.6	55.3
.25 POS/words†	26.5	30.6	54.7
.50 POS/words	26.5	30.6	54.9
.75 POS/words	26.3	30.7	55.0
.25 POS/words(fdf)	26.5	30.7	54.7
.25 POS/lemmaF	26.4	30.6	54.8
.25 POS/lemmas	26.5	30.8	54.6

(b) English to French, IWSLT–tst2010

Added InDomain 7gLM	BLEU↑	MET ↑	TER ↓
.00 POS/words (all words)	31.1	52.5	49.9
.00 POS/lemmas (all lem.)†	31.2	52.6	49.7
1.0 POS/words (all POS)†	31.4	52.8	49.8
.25 POS/lemmas†	31.5	52.9	49.7
.50 POS/lemmas	31.9	53.3	49.5
.75 POS/lemmas	31.7	53.2	49.6
.50 POS/lemmas(fdf)	31.9	53.3	49.5
.50 POS/lemmaF	31.6	53.0	49.6
.50 POS/words	31.7	53.1	49.5

Table 7: Comparison of various hybrid LM variants. Translation quality is measured with BLEU, METEOR and TER (all in percentage form). The settings used for weight tuning are marked with †. Best models according to all metrics are highlighted in bold.

brid LMs simply based on term frequency; only METEOR gains 0.1 points in Arabic-English. A possible reason for this is that document frequency was computed on fixed-size text chunks rather than on real document boundaries (see Section 4.1). The *lemmaF* experiment refers to the use of canonical forms for frequency measuring: this technique does not seem to help in either language pair. Finally, we compare the use of lemmas versus surface forms to represent common words. As expected, lemmas appear to be helpful for French language modeling. Interestingly this is also the case for English, even if by a small margin (+0.2 METEOR, -0.1 TER).

Summing up, hybrid mapping appears as a winning strategy compared to uniform mapping. Although differences among LM variants are small, the best model in Arabic-English is .25-POS/lemmas, which can be thought of as a domain-generic lemma-level LM. In English-French, instead, the highest scores are achieved by .50-POS/lemmas or .50-POS/lemmas(fdf), that is POS-level LM with few frequently occurring lexical anchors (vocabulary size 59). An interpretation of this result is that, for French, modeling the syntax is more helpful than modeling the style. We also suspect that the French TED corpus is more irregular and diverse with respect to the style, than its English counterpart. In fact, while the English corpus include transcripts of talks given by English speakers, the French one is mostly a collection of (human) translations. Typical features of the speech style may have been lost in this process.

Comparison with baseline. In Table 8 the best performing hybrid LM is compared against the baseline that only includes the standard LMs described in Section 5.2. To complete our evaluation, we also report the effect of an in-domain LM trained on 50 word classes induced from the corpus by maximum-likelihood based clustering (Och, 1999).

In the two language pairs, both types of LM result in consistent improvements over the baseline. However, the gains achieved by the hybrid approach are larger and all statistically significant. The hybrid approach is significantly better than the unsupervised one by TER in Arabic-English and by BLEU and METEOR in English-French (these siginificances are not reported in

(a) Arabic to English, IWSLT–tst2010

Added InDomain 10g LM	BLEU↑	MET ↑	TER ↓
none (baseline)	26.0	30.4	55.6
unsup. classes	26.4°	30.8•	55.1°
hybrid	26.5•(+.5)	30.8•(+.4)	54.6•(-1.0)

(b) English to French, IWSLT–tst2010

Added InDomain 7g LM	BLEU↑	MET ↑	TER ↓
none (baseline)	31.2	52.7	49.8
unsup. classes	31.5	52.9	49.6
hybrid	31.9•(+.7)	53.3•(+.6)	49.5°(-.3)

Table 8: Final MT results: baseline *vs* unsupervised word classes-based LM and best hybrid LM. Statistically significant improvements over the baseline are marked with • at the $p < .01$ and ° at the $p < .05$ level.

the table for clarity). The proposed method appears to better leverage the available in-domain data, achieving improvements according to all metrics: +0.5/+0.4/-1.0 BLEU/METEOR/TER in Arabic-English and +0.7/-0.6/-0.3 in English-French, without requiring any bitext annotation or decoder modification.

Talk-level analysis. To conclude the study, we analyze the effect of our best hybrid LM on Arabic-English translation quality, at the single talk level. The test used in the experiments (tst2010) consists of 11 transcripts with an average length of 151$\pm$73 sentences. For each talk, we compare the baseline BLEU score with that obtained by adding a .25-POS/lemmas hybrid LM. Results are presented in Figure 2. The dark and light columns denote baseline and hybrid-LM BLEU scores, respectively, and refer to the left y-axis. Additional data points, plotted on the right y-axis in reverse order, represent talk-level perplexities (PP) of a standard 5-gram LM trained on TED ($\circ$) and those of the .25-POS/lemmas 10-gram hybrid LM ($\triangle$), computed on reference translations.

What emerges first is a dramatic variation of performance among the speeches, with baseline BLEU scores ranging from 33.95 on talk "00" to only 12.42 on talk "02". The latter talk appears as a corner case also according to perplexities (397 by word LM and 111 by hybrid LM). Notably, the perplexities of the two LMs correlate well with each other, but the hybrid's PP is much more stable across talks: its standard deviation is only 14 points, while that of the word-based PP is 79. The BLEU improvement given by hybrid LM, however modest, is consistent across the talks, with only two outliers: a drop of -0.2 on talk "00", and a drop of -0.7 on talk "02". The largest gain (+1.1) is observed on talk "10", from 16.8 to 17.9 BLEU.

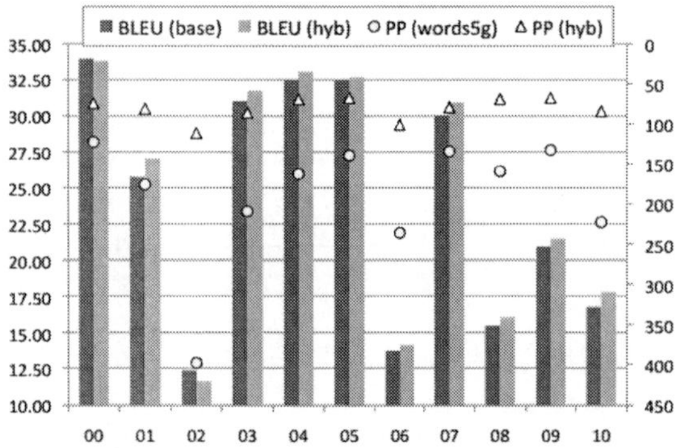

Figure 2: Talk-level evaluation on Arabic-English (IWSLT-tst2010). Left y-axis: BLEU impact of a .25-POS/lemma hybrid LM. Right y-axis: perplexities by word LM and by hybrid LM.

6 Conclusions

We have proposed a language modeling technique that leverages the in-domain data for SMT style adaptation. Trained to predict mixed sequences of POS classes and frequent words, hybrid LMs are devised to capture typical lexical and syntactic constructions that characterize the style of speech transcripts.

Compared to standard language models, hybrid LMs generalize better to the test data and partially compensate for the disproportion between in-domain and out-of-domain training data. At the same time, hybrid LMs show more discriminative power than merely POS-level LMs. The integration of hybrid LMs into a competitive phrase-based SMT system is straightforward and leads to consistent improvements on the TED task, according to three different translation quality metrics.

Target language modeling is only one aspect of the statistical translation problem. Now that the usability of the proposed method has been assessed for language modeling, future work will address the extension of the idea to the modeling of phrase translation and reordering.

Acknowledgments

This work was supported by the T4ME network of excellence (IST-249119), funded by the DG INFSO of the European Commission through the 7th Framework Programme. We thank the anonymous reviewers for their valuable suggestions.

References

Satanjeev Banerjee and Alon Lavie. 2005. METEOR: An automatic metric for MT evaluation with improved correlation with human judgments. In *Proceedings of the ACL Workshop on Intrinsic and Extrinsic Evaluation Measures for Machine Translation and/or Summarization*, pages 65–72, Ann Arbor, Michigan, June. Association for Computational Linguistics.

Jerome R. Bellegarda. 2004. Statistical language model adaptation: review and perspectives. *Speech Communication*, 42(1):93 – 108.

Alexandra Birch, Miles Osborne, and Philipp Koehn. 2007. CCG supertags in factored statistical machine translation. In *Proceedings of the Second Workshop on Statistical Machine Translation*, pages 9–16, Prague, Czech Republic, June. Association for Computational Linguistics.

Arianna Bisazza, Nick Ruiz, and Marcello Federico. 2011. Fill-up versus Interpolation Methods for Phrase-based SMT Adaptation. In *International Workshop on Spoken Language Translation (IWSLT)*, San Francisco, CA.

P. F. Brown, V. J. Della Pietra, P. V. deSouza, J. C. Lai, and R. L. Mercer. 1992. Class-based n-gram models of natural language. *Computational Linguistics*, 18(4):467–479.

Mauro Cettolo, Nicola Bertoldi, and Marcello Federico. 2011. Methods for smoothing the optimizer instability in SMT. In *MT Summit XIII: the Thirteenth Machine Translation Summit*, pages 32–39, Xiamen, China.

Jonathan Clark, Chris Dyer, Alon Lavie, and Noah Smith. 2011. Better hypothesis testing for statistical machine translation: Controlling for optimizer instability. In *Proceedings of the Association for Computational Lingustics*, ACL 2011, Portland, Oregon, USA. Association for Computational Linguistics. available at http://www.cs.cmu.edu/ jhclark/pubs/significance.pdf.

Mona Diab, Kadri Hacioglu, and Daniel Jurafsky. 2004. Automatic Tagging of Arabic Text: From Raw Text to Base Phrase Chunks. In Daniel Marcu Susan Dumais and Salim Roukos, editors, *HLT-NAACL 2004: Short Papers*, pages 149–152, Boston, Massachusetts, USA, May 2 - May 7. Association for Computational Linguistics.

Marcello Federico, Nicola Bertoldi, and Mauro Cettolo. 2008. IRSTLM: an Open Source Toolkit for Handling Large Scale Language Models. In *Proceedings of Interspeech*, pages 1618–1621, Melbourne, Australia.

Marcello Federico, Luisa Bentivogli, Michael Paul, and Sebastian Stüker. 2011. Overview of the IWSLT 2011 Evaluation Campaign. In *International Workshop on Spoken Language Translation (IWSLT)*, San Francisco, CA.

George Foster and Roland Kuhn. 2007. Mixture-model adaptation for SMT. In *Proceedings of the Second Workshop on Statistical Machine Translation*, pages 128–135, Prague, Czech Republic, June. Association for Computational Linguistics.

Michel Galley and Christopher D. Manning. 2008. A simple and effective hierarchical phrase reordering model. In *EMNLP '08: Proceedings of the Conference on Empirical Methods in Natural Language Processing*, pages 848–856, Morristown, NJ, USA. Association for Computational Linguistics.

Christian Hardmeier, Jörg Tiedemann, Markus Saers, Marcello Federico, and Mathur Prashant. 2011. The Uppsala-FBK systems at WMT 2011. In *Proceedings of the Sixth Workshop on Statistical Machine Translation*, pages 372–378, Edinburgh, Scotland, July. Association for Computational Linguistics.

Katrin Kirchhoff and Mei Yang. 2005. Improved language modeling for statistical machine translation. In *Proceedings of the ACL Workshop on Building and Using Parallel Texts*, pages 125–128, Ann Arbor, Michigan, June. Association for Computational Linguistics.

Philipp Koehn and Hieu Hoang. 2007. Factored translation models. In *Proceedings of the 2007 Joint Conference on Empirical Methods in Natural Language Processing and Computational Natural Language Learning (EMNLP-CoNLL)*, pages 868–876, Prague, Czech Republic, June. Association for Computational Linguistics.

Philipp Koehn, Amittai Axelrod, Alexandra Birch Mayne, Chris Callison-Burch, Miles Osborne, and David Talbot. 2005. Edinburgh system description for the 2005 IWSLT speech translation evaluation. In *Proc. of the International Workshop on Spoken Language Translation*, October.

P. Koehn, H. Hoang, A. Birch, C. Callison-Burch, M. Federico, N. Bertoldi, B. Cowan, W. Shen, C. Moran, R. Zens, C. Dyer, O. Bojar, A. Constantin, and E. Herbst. 2007. Moses: Open Source Toolkit for Statistical Machine Translation. In *Proceedings of the 45th Annual Meeting of the Association for Computational Linguistics Companion Volume Proceedings of the Demo and Poster Sessions*, pages 177–180, Prague, Czech Republic.

Christof Monz. 2011. Statistical Machine Translation with Local Language Models. In *Proceedings of the 2011 Conference on Empirical Methods in Natural Language Processing*, pages 869–879, Edinburgh, Scotland, UK., July. Association for Computational Linguistics.

Preslav Nakov. 2008. Improving English-Spanish Statistical Machine Translation: Experiments in Domain Adaptation, Sentence Paraphrasing, Tokenization, and Recasing. . In *Workshop on Statistical Machine Translation, Association for Computational Linguistics*.

Franz Josef Och. 1999. An efficient method for determining bilingual word classes. In *Proceedings of the 9th Conference of the European Chapter of the Association for Computational Linguistics (EACL)*, pages 71–76.

Franz Josef Och. 2003. Minimum Error Rate Training in Statistical Machine Translation. In Erhard Hinrichs and Dan Roth, editors, *Proceedings of the*

41st Annual Meeting of the Association for Computational Linguistics, pages 160–167.

Kishore Papineni, Salim Roukos, Todd Ward, and Wei-Jing Zhu. 2002. BLEU: a method for automatic evaluation of machine translation. In *Proceedings of the 40th Annual Meeting of the Association of Computational Linguistics (ACL)*, pages 311–318, Philadelphia, PA.

Stefan Riezler and John T. Maxwell. 2005. On some pitfalls in automatic evaluation and significance testing for MT. In *Proceedings of the ACL Workshop on Intrinsic and Extrinsic Evaluation Measures for Machine Translation and/or Summarization*, pages 57–64, Ann Arbor, Michigan, June. Association for Computational Linguistics.

R. Rosenfeld. 2000. Two decades of statistical language modeling: where do we go from here? *Proceedings of the IEEE*, 88(8):1270 –1278.

Nick Ruiz and Marcello Federico. 2011. Topic adaptation for lecture translation through bilingual latent semantic models. In *Proceedings of the Sixth Workshop on Statistical Machine Translation*, pages 294–302, Edinburgh, Scotland, July. Association for Computational Linguistics.

Nick Ruiz, Arianna Bisazza, Fabio Brugnara, Daniele Falavigna, Diego Giuliani, Suhel Jaber, Roberto Gretter, and Marcello Federico. 2011. FBK @ IWSLT 2011. In *International Workshop on Spoken Language Translation (IWSLT)*, San Francisco, CA.

Helmut Schmid. 1994. Probabilistic part-of-speech tagging using decision trees. In *Proceedings of International Conference on New Methods in Language Processing*.

Matthew Snover, Bonnie Dorr, Rich Schwartz, Linnea Micciulla, and John Makhoul. 2006. A study of translation edit rate with targeted human annotation. In *5th Conference of the Association for Machine Translation in the Americas (AMTA)*, Boston, Massachusetts, August.

Christoph Tillmann. 2004. A Unigram Orientation Model for Statistical Machine Translation. In *Proceedings of the Joint Conference on Human Language Technologies and the Annual Meeting of the North American Chapter of the Association of Computational Linguistics (HLT-NAACL)*.

A. Yazgan and M. Saraçlar. 2004. Hybrid language models for out of vocabulary word detection in large vocabulary conversational speech recognition. In *Proceedings of ICASSP*, volume 1, pages I – 745–8 vol.1, may.

Detecting Highly Confident Word Translations from Comparable Corpora without Any Prior Knowledge

Ivan Vulić and Marie-Francine Moens
Department of Computer Science
KU Leuven
Celestijnenlaan 200A
Leuven, Belgium
{ivan.vulic,marie-francine.moens}@cs.kuleuven.be

Abstract

In this paper, we extend the work on using latent cross-language topic models for identifying word translations across comparable corpora. We present a novel precision-oriented algorithm that relies on per-topic word distributions obtained by the *bilingual LDA* (BiLDA) latent topic model. The algorithm aims at harvesting only the most probable word translations across languages in a greedy fashion, without any prior knowledge about the language pair, relying on a symmetrization process and the one-to-one constraint. We report our results for Italian-English and Dutch-English language pairs that outperform the current state-of-the-art results by a significant margin. In addition, we show how to use the algorithm for the construction of high-quality initial seed lexicons of translations.

1 Introduction

Bilingual lexicons serve as an invaluable resource of knowledge in various natural language processing tasks, such as dictionary-based cross-language information retrieval (Carbonell et al., 1997; Levow et al., 2005) and statistical machine translation (SMT) (Och and Ney, 2003). In order to construct high quality bilingual lexicons for different domains, one usually needs to possess parallel corpora or build such lexicons by hand. Compiling such lexicons manually is often an expensive and time-consuming task, whereas the methods for mining the lexicons from parallel corpora are not applicable for language pairs and domains where such corpora is unavailable or missing. Therefore the focus of researchers turned to comparable corpora, which consist of documents with partially overlapping content, usually available in abundance. Thus, it is much easier to build a high-volume comparable corpus. A representative example of such a comparable text collection is Wikipedia, where one may observe articles discussing the similar topic, but strongly varying in style, length and vocabulary, while still sharing a certain amount of main concepts (or topics).

Over the years, several approaches for mining translations from non-parallel corpora have emerged (Rapp, 1995; Fung and Yee, 1998; Rapp, 1999; Diab and Finch, 2000; Déjean et al., 2002; Chiao and Zweigenbaum, 2002; Gaussier et al., 2004; Fung and Cheung, 2004; Morin et al., 2007; Haghighi et al., 2008; Shezaf and Rappoport, 2010; Laroche and Langlais, 2010), all sharing the same Firthian assumption, often called the *distributionial hypothesis* (Harris, 1954), which states that words with a similar meaning are likely to appear in similar contexts across languages. All these methods have examined different representations of word contexts and different methods for matching words across languages, but they all have in common a need for a seed lexicon of translations to efficiently bridge the gap between languages. That seed lexicon is usually crawled from the Web or obtained from parallel corpora. Recently, Li et al. (2011) have proposed an approach that improves precision of the existing methods for bilingual lexicon extraction, based on improving the comparability of the corpus under consideration, prior to extracting actual bilingual lexicons. Other methods such as (Koehn and Knight, 2002) try to design a bootstrapping algorithm based on an initial seed lexicon of translations and various lexical evidences. However, the quality of their initial seed lexicon is disputable, since the construction of their lexicon is language-pair biased and cannot be completely employed on distant languages. It solely relies on unsatisfactory language-pair independent cross-language clues such as words shared across languages.

Recent work from Vulić et al.(2011) utilized the distributional hypothesis in a different direction. It attempts to abrogate the need of a seed lexicon as a prerequisite for bilingual lexicon extraction. They train a cross-language topic model on document-aligned comparable corpora and introduce different methods for identifying word translations across languages, underpinned by per-topic word distributions from the trained topic model. Due to the fact that they deal with comparable Wikipedia data, their translation model contains a lot of noise, and some words are poorly translated simply because there are not enough occurrences in the corpus. The goal of this work is to design an algorithm which will learn to harvest only the most probable translations from the per-word topic distributions. The translations learned by the algorithm then might serve as a highly accurate, precision-based initial seed lexicon, which can then be used as a tool for translating source word vectors into the target language. The key advantage of such a lexicon lies in the fact that there is no language-pair dependent prior knowledge involved in its construction (e.g., orthographic features). Hence, it is completely applicable to any language pair for which there exist sufficient comparable data for training of the topic model.

Since comparable corpora often construct a very noisy environment, it is of the utmost importance for a precision-oriented algorithm to learn when to stop the process of matching words, and which candidate pairs are surely not translations of each other. The method described in this paper follows this intuition: while extracting a bilingual lexicon, we try to rematch words, keeping only the most confident candidate pairs and disregarding all the others. After that step, the most confident candidate pairs might be used with some of the existing context-based techniques to find translations for the words discarded in the previous step. The algorithm is based on: (1) the assumption of symmetry, and (2) the one-to-one constraint. The idea of symmetrization has been borrowed from the symmetrization heuristics introduced for word alignments in SMT (Och and Ney, 2003), where the intersection heuristics is employed for a precision-oriented algorithm. In our setting, it basically means that we keep a translation pair (w_i^S, w_j^T) if and only if, after the symmetrization process, the top translation candidate for the source word w_i^S is the target word w_i^T and vice versa. The one-to-one constraint aims at matching the most confident candidates during the early stages of the algorithm, and then excluding them from further search. The utility of the constraint for parallel corpora has already been evaluated by Melamed (2000).

The remainder of the paper is structured as follows. Section 2 gives a brief overview of the methods, relying on per-topic word distributions, which serve as the tool for computing cross-language similarity between words. In Section 3, we motivate the main assumptions of the algorithm and describe the full algorithm. Section 4 justifies the underlying assumptions of the algorithm by providing comparisons with a current-state-of-the-art system for Italian-English and Dutch-English language pairs. It also contains another set of experiments which investigates the potential of the algorithm in building a language-pair unbiased seed lexicon, and compares the lexicon with other seed lexicons. Finally, Section 5 lists conclusion and possible paths of future work.

2 Calculating Initial Cross-Language Word Similarity

This section gives a quick overview of the **Cue** method, the **TI** method, and their combination, described by Vulić et al.(2011), which proved to be the most efficient and accurate for identifying potential word translations once the cross-language BiLDA topic model is trained and the associated per-topic distributions are obtained for both source and target corpora. The BiLDA model we use is a natural extension of the standard LDA model and, along with the definition of per-topic word distributions, has been presented in (Ni et al., 2009; De Smet and Moens, 2009; Mimno et al., 2009). BiLDA takes advantage of the document alignment by using a single variable that contains the topic distribution θ. This variable is language-independent, because it is shared by each of the paired bilingual comparable documents. Topics for each document are sampled from θ, from which the words are then sampled in conjugation with the vocabulary distribution ϕ

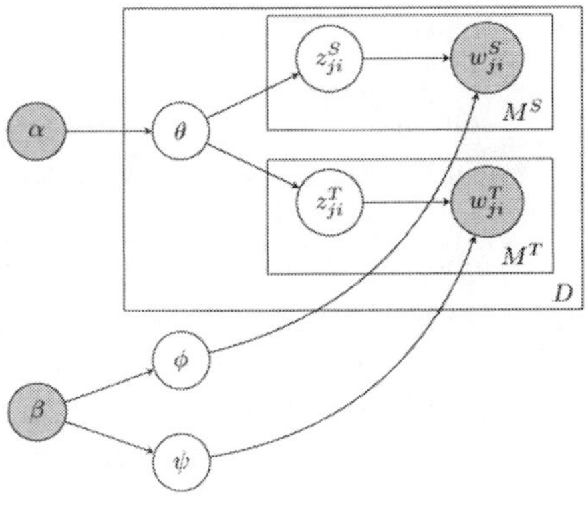

Figure 1: The bilingual LDA (BiLDA) model

(for language S) and ψ (for language T).

2.1 Cue Method

A straightforward approach to express similarity between words tries to emphasize the associative relation in a natural way - modeling the probability $P(w_2^T|w_1^S)$, i.e. the probability that a target word w_2^T will be generated as a response to a cue source word w_1^S, where the link between the words is established via the shared topic space: $P(w_2^T|w_1^S) = \sum_{k=1}^{K} P(w_2^T|z_k)P(z_k|w_1^S)$, where K denotes the number of cross-language topics.

2.2 TI Method

This approach constructs word vectors over a shared space of cross-language topics, where values within vectors are the *TF-ITF* scores (term frequency - inverse topic frequency), computed in a completely analogical manner as the *TF-IDF* scores for the original word-document space (Manning and Schütze, 1999). *Term frequency*, given a source word w_i^S and a topic z_k, measures the importance of the word w_i^S within the particular topic z_k, while *inverse topical frequency (ITF)* of the word w_i^S measures the general importance of the source word w_i^S across all topics. The final *TF-ITF* score for the source word w_i^S and the topic z_k is given by $TF-ITF_{i,k} = TF_{i,k} \cdot ITF_i$.

The *TF-ITF* scores for target words associated with target topics are calculated in an analogical manner and the standard cosine similarity is then used to find the most similar target word vectors for a given source word vector.

2.3 Combining the Methods

Topic models have the ability to build clusters of words which might not always co-occur together in the same textual units and therefore add extra information of potential relatedness. These two methods for automatic bilingual lexicon extraction interpret and exploit underlying per-topic word distributions in different ways, so combining the two should lead to even better results. The two methods are linearly combined, with the overall score given by:

$$Sim_{TI+Cue}(w_1^S, w_2^T) = \lambda Sim_{TI}(w_1^S, w_2^T) + (1-\lambda)Sim_{Cue}(w_1^S, w_2^T) \quad (1)$$

Both methods posses several desirable properties. According to Griffiths et al. (2007), the conditioning for the **Cue** method automatically compromises between word frequency and semantic relatedness since higher frequency words tend to have higher probability across all topics, but the distribution over topics $P(z_k|w_1^S)$ ensures that semantically related topics dominate the sum. The similar phenomenon is captured by the **TI** method by the usage of *TF*, which rewards high frequency words, and *ITF*, which assigns a higher importance for words semantically more related to a specific topic. These properties are incorporated in the combination of the methods. As the final result, the combined method provides, for each source word, a ranked list of target words with associated scores that measure the strength of cross-language similarity. The higher the score, the more confident a translation pair is. We will use this observation in the next section during the algorithm construction.

The lexicon constructed by solely applying the combination of these methods without any additional assumptions will serve as a baseline in the results section.

3 Constructing the Algorithm

This section explains the underlying assumptions of the algorithm: the **assumption of symmetry** and the **one-to-one assumption**. Finally, it provides the complete outline of the algorithm.

3.1 Assumption of Symmetry

First, we start with the intuition that the **assumption of symmetry** strengthens the confidence of a translation pair. In other words, if the most probable translation candidate for a source word w_1^S is a target word w_2^T and, vice versa, the most probable translation candidate of the target word w_2^T

is the source word w_1^S, and their *TI+Cue* scores are above a certain threshold, we can claim that the words w_1^S and w_2^T are a translation pair. The definition of the symmetric relation can also be relaxed. Instead of observing only one top candidate from the lists, we can observe top N candidates from both sides and include them in the search space, and then re-rank the potential candidates taking into account their associated *TI+Cue* scores and their respective positions in the list. We will call N the **search space depth**. Here is the outline of the re-ranking method if the search space consists of the top N candidates on both sides:

1. Given is a source word w_s^S, for which we actually want to find the most probable translation candidate. Initialize an empty list $Final_s = \{\}$ in which target language candidates with their recalculated associated scores will be stored.
2. Obtain *TI+Cue* scores for all target words. Keep only N best scoring target candidates: $\{w_{s,1}^T, \ldots, w_{s,N}^T\}$ along with their respective scores.
3. For each target candidate from $\{w_{s,1}^T, \ldots, w_{s,N}^T\}$ acquire *TI+Cue* scores over the entire source vocabulary. Keep only N best scoring source language candidates. Each word $w_{s,i}^T \in \{w_{s,1}^T, \ldots, w_{s,N}^T\}$ now has a list of N source language candidates associated with it: $\{w_{i,1}^S, w_{i,2}^S \ldots, w_{i,N}^S\}$.
4. For each target candidate word $w_{s,i}^T \in \{w_{s,1}^T, \ldots, w_{s,N}^T\}$, do as follows:
   (a) If one of the words from the associated list is the given source word w_s^S, remember: (1) the position m, denoting how high in the list the word w_s^S was found, and (2) the associated *TI+Cue* score $Sim_{TI+Cue}(w_{s,i}^T, w_{i,m}^S = w_s^S)$. Calculate:
   (i) $G_{1,i} = Sim_{TI+Cue}(w_s^S, w_{s,i}^T)/i$
   (ii) $G_{2,i} = Sim_{TI+Cue}(w_{s,i}^T, w_{i,m}^S)/m$
   Following that, calculate GM_i, the geometric mean of the values $G_{1,i}$ and $G_{2,i}$[1]: $GM_i = \sqrt{G_{1,i} \cdot G_{2,i}}$. Add a tuple $(w_{s,i}^T, GM_i)$ to the list $Final_s$.
   (b) If we have reached the end of the list for the target candidate word $w_{s,i}^T$ without finding the given source word w_s^S, and $i < N$, continue with the next word $w_{s,i+1}^T$. Do not add any tuple to $Final_s$ in this step.
5. If the list $Final_s$ is not empty, sort the tuples in the list in descending order according to their GM_i scores. The first element of the sorted list contains a word $w_{s,high}^T$, the final translation candidate of the source word w_s^S. If the list $Final_s$ is not empty, the final result of this process will be the cross-language word translation pair $(w_s^S, w_{s,high}^T)$.

[1] Scores $G_{1,i}$ and $G_{2,i}$ are structured in such a way to balance between positions in the ranked lists and the *TI+Cue* scores, since they reward candidate words which have high *TI+Cue* scores associated with them, and penalize words if they are found lower in the list of potential candidates.

We will call this symmetrization process the **symmetrizing re-ranking**. It attempts at pushing the correct cross-language synonym to the top of the candidates list, taking into account both the strength of similarities defined through the *TI+Cue* scores in both directions, and positions in ranked lists. A blatant example depicting how this process helps boost precision is presented in Figure 2. We can also design a thresholded variant of this procedure by imposing an extra constraint. When calculating target language candidates for the source word w_s^S in Step 2, we proceed further only if the first target candidate scores above a certain threshold P and, additionally, in Step 3, we keep lists of N source language candidates for only those target words for which the first source language candidate in their respective list scored above the same threshold P. We will call this procedure the **thresholded symmetrizing re-ranking**, and this version will be employed in the final algorithm.

3.2 One-to-one Assumption

Melamed (2000) has already established that most source words in parallel corpora tend to translate to only one target word. That tendency is modeled by the **one-to-one assumption**, which constrains each source word to have at most one translation on the target side. Melamed's paper reports that this bias leads to a significant positive impact on precision and recall of bilingual lexicon extraction from parallel corpora. This assumption should also be reasonable for many types of comparable corpora such as Wikipedia or news corpora, which are topically aligned or cover similar themes. We

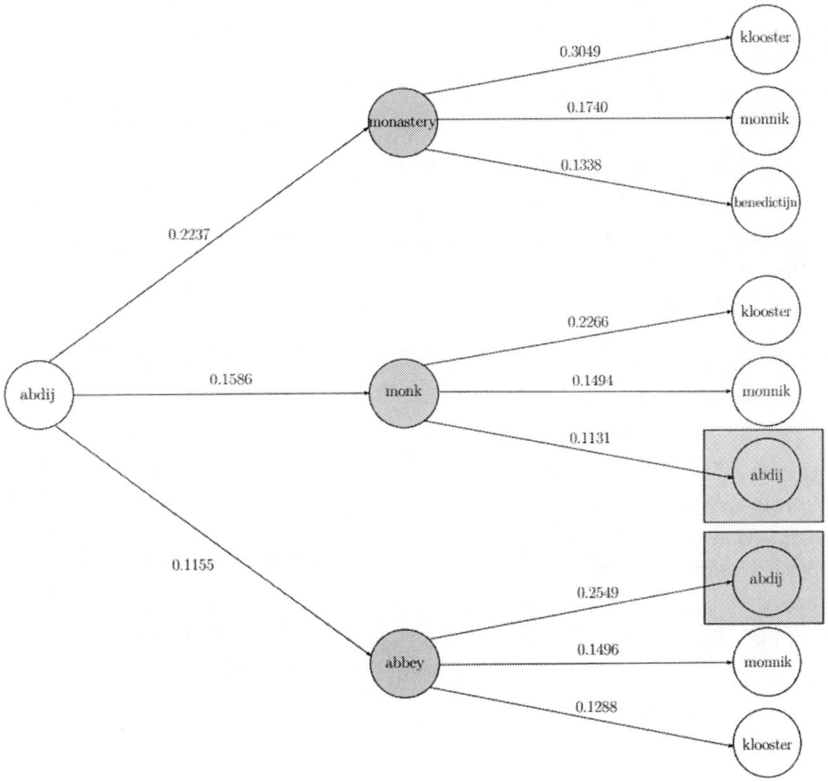

Figure 2: An example where the assumption of symmetry and the one-to-one assumption clearly help boost precision. If we keep top $N_c = 3$ candidates from both sides, the algorithm is able to detect that the correct Dutch-English translation pair is *(abdij, abbey)*. The *TI+Cue* method without any assumptions would result with an indirect association *(abdij, monastery)*. If only the one-to-one assumption was present, the algorithm would greedily learn the correct direct association *(monastery, klooster)*, remove those words from their respective vocabularies and then again result with another indirect association *(abdij, monk)*. By additionally employing the assumption of symmetry with the re-ranking method from Subsection 3.1, the algorithm correctly learns the translation pair *(abdij, abbey)*. Correct translation pairs *(klooster, monastery)* and *(monnik, monk)* are also obtained. Again here, the pair *(monnik, monk)* would not be obtained without the one-to-one assumption.

will prove that the assumption leads to better precision scores even for bilingual lexicon extraction from such comparable data. The intuition behind introducing this constraint is fairly simple. Without the assumption, the similarity scores between source and target words are calculated independently of each other. We will illustrate the problem arising from the independence assumption with an example.

Suppose we have an Italian word *arcipelago*, and we would like to detect its correct English translation (*archipelago*). However, after the *TI+Cue* method is employed, and even after the symmetrizing re-ranking process from the previous step is used, we still acquire a wrong translation candidate pair *(arcipelago, island)*. Why is that so? The word (*arcipelago*) (or its translation) and the acquired translation (*island*) are semantically very close, and therefore have similar distributions over cross-language topics, but *island* is a much more frequent term. The *TI+Cue* method concludes that two words are potential translations whenever their distributions over cross-language topics are much more similar than expected by chance. Moreover, it gives a preference to more frequent candidates, so it will eventually end up learning an **indirect association**[2] between words *arcipelago* and *island*. The one-to-one assumption should mitigate the problem of such indirect associations if we design our algorithm in such a way that it learns the most confident **direct associations**[2] first:

[2]A direct association, as defined in (Melamed, 2000), is an association between two words (in this setting found by the *TI+Cue* method) where the two words are indeed mutual translations. Otherwise, it is an indirect association.

1. Learn the correct direct association pair *(isola, island)*.
2. Remove the words *isola* and *island* from their respective vocabularies.
3. Since *island* is not in the vocabulary, the indirect association between *arcipelago* and *island* is not present any more. The algorithm learns the correct direct association *(arcipelago, archipelago)*.

3.3 The Algorithm

3.3.1 One-Vocabulary-Pass

First, we will provide a version of the algorithm with a fixed threshold P which completes only one pass through the source vocabulary. Let V^S denote a given source vocabulary, and let V^T denote a given target vocabulary. We need to define several parameters of the algorithm. Let N_0 be the initial maximum search space depth for the thresholded symmetrizing re-ranking procedure. In Figure 2, the current depth N_c is 3, while the maximum depth might be set to a value higher than 3. The algorithm with the fixed threshold P proceeds as follows:

1. Initialize the maximum search space depth $N_M = N_0$. Initialize an empty lexicon L.
2. For each source word $w_s^S \in V^S$ do:
   (a) Set the current search space depth $N_c = 1$.[3]
   (b) Perform the thresholded symmetrizing re-ranking procedure with the current search space set to N_c and the threshold P. If a translation pair $(w_s^S, w_{s,high}^T)$ is found, go to the Sub-step 2(d).
   (c) If a translation pair is not found, and $N_c < N_M$, increment the current search space $N_c = N_c + 1$ and return to the previous Sub-step 2(b). If a translation pair is not found and $N_c = N_M$, return to Step 2 and proceed with the next word.
   (d) For the found translation pair $(w_s^S, w_{s,high}^T)$, remove words w_s^S and $w_{s,high}^T$ from their respective vocabularies: $V^S = V^S - \{w_s^S\}$ and $V^T = V^T - \{w_{s,high}^T\}$ to satisfy the one-to-one constraint. Add the pair $(w_s^S, w_{s,high}^T)$ to the lexicon L.

[3]The intuition here is simple – we are trying to detect a direct association as high as possible in the list. In other words, if the first translation candidate for the source word *isola* is the target word *island*, and, vice versa, the first translation candidate for the target word *island* is *isola*, we do not need to expand our search depth, because these two words are the most likely translations.

We will name this procedure the **one-vocabulary-pass** and employ it later in an iterative algorithm with a varying threshold and a varying maximum search space depth.

3.3.2 The Final Algorithm

Let us now define P_0 as the initial threshold, let P_f be the threshold at which we stop decreasing the value for threshold and start expanding our maximum search space depth for the thresholded symmetrizing re-ranking, and let dec_p be a value for which we decrease the current threshold in each step. Finally, let N_f be the limit for the maximum search space depth, and N_M denote the current maximum search space depth. The final algorithm is given by:

1. Initialize the maximum search space depth $N_M = N_0$ and the starting threshold $P = P_0$. Initialize an empty lexicon L_{final}.
2. Check the stopping criterion: If $N_M > N_f$, go to Step 5, otherwise continue with Step 3.
3. Perform the *one-vocabulary-pass* with the current values of P and N_M. Whenever a translation pair is found, it is added to the lexicon L_{final}. Additionally, we can also save the threshold and the depth at which that pair was found.
4. Decrease P: $P = P - dec_p$, and check if $P < P_f$. If still not $P < P_f$, go to Step 3 and perform the *one-vocabulary-pass* again. Otherwise, if $P < P_f$ and there are still unmatched words in the source vocabulary, reset P: $P = P_0$, increment N_M: $N_M = N_M + 1$ and go to Step 2.
5. Return L_{final} as the final output of the algorithm.

The parameters of the algorithm model its behavior. Typically, we would like to set P_0 to a high value, and N_0 to a low value, which makes our constraints strict and narrows our search space, and consequently, extracts less translation pairs in the first steps of the algorithm, but the set of those translation pairs should be highly accurate. Once it is not possible to extract any more pairs with such strict constraints, the algorithm relaxes them by lowering the threshold and expanding the search space by incrementing the maximum search space depth. The algorithm may leave some of the source words unmatched, which is also dependent on the parameters of the algorithm, but, due to the one-to-one assumption, that scenario also occurs whenever a target vocabulary contains more words than a source vocabulary.

The number of operations of the algorithm also depends on the parameters, but it mostly depends on the sizes of the given vocabularies. The complexity is $O(|V^S||V^T|)$, but the algorithm is computationally feasible even for large vocabularies.

4 Results and Discussion

4.1 Training Collections

The data used for training of the models is collected from various sources and varies strongly in theme, style, length and its comparableness. In order to reduce data sparsity, we keep only lemmatized non-proper noun forms.

For Italian-English language pair, we use $18,898$ Wikipedia article pairs to train BiLDA, covering different themes with different scopes and subtopics being addressed. Document alignment is established via interlingual links from the Wikipedia metadata. Our vocabularies consist of $7,160$ Italian nouns and $9,116$ English nouns.

For Dutch-English language pair, we use $7,602$ Wikipedia article pairs, and $6,206$ Europarl document pairs, and combine them for training.[4] Our final vocabularies consist of $15,284$ Dutch nouns and $12,715$ English nouns.

Unlike, for instance, Wikipedia articles, where document alignment is established via interlingual links, in some cases it is necessary to perform document alignment as the initial step. Since our work focuses on Wikipedia data, we will not get into detail with algorithms for document alignment. An IR-based method for document alignment is given in (Utiyama and Isahara, 2003; Munteanu and Marcu, 2005), and a feature-based method can be found in (Vu et al., 2009).

4.2 Experimental Setup

All our experiments rely on BiLDA training with comparable data. Corpora and software for BiLDA training are obtained from Vulić et al. (2011). We train the BiLDA model with 2000 topics using Gibbs sampling, since that number of topics displays the best performance in their paper. The linear interpolation parameter for the combined *TI+Cue* method is set to $\lambda = 0.1$.

The parameters of the algorithm, adjusted on a set of 500 randomly sampled Italian words, are set to the following values in all experiments, except where noted different: $P_0 = 0.20$, $P_f = 0.00$, $dec_p = 0.01$, $N_0 = 3$, and $N_f = 10$.

The initial ground truth for our source vocabularies has been constructed by the freely available *Google Translate* tool. The final ground truth for our test sets has been established after we have manually revised the list of pairs obtained by *Google Translate*, deleting incorrect entries and adding additional correct entries. All translation candidates are evaluated against this benchmark lexicon.

4.3 Experiment I: Do Our Assumptions Help Lexicon Extraction?

With this set of experiments, we wanted to test whether both the assumption of symmetry and the one-to-one assumption are useful in improving precision of the initial *TI+Cue* lexicon extraction method. We compare three different lexicon extraction algorithms: (1) the basic *TI+Cue* extraction algorithm (**LALG-BASIC**) which serves as the baseline algorithm[5], (2) the algorithm from Section 3, but without the one-to-one assumption (**LALG-SYM**), meaning that if we find a translation pair, we still keep words from the translation pair in their respective vocabularies, and (3) the complete algorithm from Section 3 (**LALG-ALL**). In order to evaluate these lexicon extraction algorithms for both Italian-English and Dutch-English, we have constructed a test set of 650 Italian nouns, and a test set of 1000 Dutch nouns of high and medium frequency. Precision scores for both language pairs and for all lexicon extraction algorithms are provided in Table 1.

Based on these results, it is clearly visible that both assumptions our algorithm makes are valid

[4] In case of Europarl, we use only the evidence of document alignment during the training and do not benefit from the parallelness of the sentences in the corpus.

[5] We have also tested whether LALG-BASIC outperforms a method modeling direct co-occurrence, that uses cosine to detect similarity between word vectors consisting of TF-IDF scores in the shared document space (Cimiano et al., 2009). Precision using that method is significantly lower, e.g. 0.5538 vs. 0.6708 of LALG-BASIC for Italian-English.

LEX Algorithm	Italian-English	Dutch-English
LALG-BASIC	0.6708	0.6560
LALG-SYM	0.6862	0.6780
LALG-ALL	**0.7215**	**0.7170**

Table 1: Precision scores on our test sets for the 3 different lexicon extraction algorithms.

and contribute to better overall scores. Therefore in all further experiments we will use the *LALG-ALL* extraction algorithm.

4.4 Experiment II: How Does Thresholding Affect Precision?

The next set of experiments aims at exploring how precision scores change while we gradually decrease threshold values. The main goal of these experiments is to detect when to stop with the extraction of translation candidates in order to preserve a lexicon of only highly accurate translations. We have fixed the maximum search space depth $N_0 = N_f = 3$. We used the same test sets from Experiment I. Figure 3 displays the change of precision in relation to different threshold values, where we start harvesting translations from the threshold $P_0 = 0.2$ down to $P_f = 0.0$. Since our goal is to extract as many correct translation pairs as possible, but without decreasing the precision scores, we have also examined what impact this gradual decrease of threshold also has on the number of extracted translations. We have opted for the F_β measure (van Rijsbergen, 1979):

$$F_\beta = (1 + \beta^2)\frac{Precision \cdot Recall}{\beta^2 \cdot Precision + Recall} \quad (2)$$

Since our task is precision-oriented, we have set $\beta = 0.5$. $F_{0.5}$ measure values precision as twice as important as recall. The $F_{0.5}$ scores are also provided in Figure 3.

4.5 Experiment III: Building a Seed Lexicon

Finally, we wanted to test how many accurate translation pairs our best scoring LALG-ALL algorithm is able to acquire from the entire source vocabulary, with very high precision still remaining paramount. The obtained highly-precise seed lexicon then might be employed for an additional bootstrapping procedure similar to (Koehn and Knight, 2002; Fung and Cheung, 2004) or simply for translating context vectors as in (Gaussier et al., 2004).

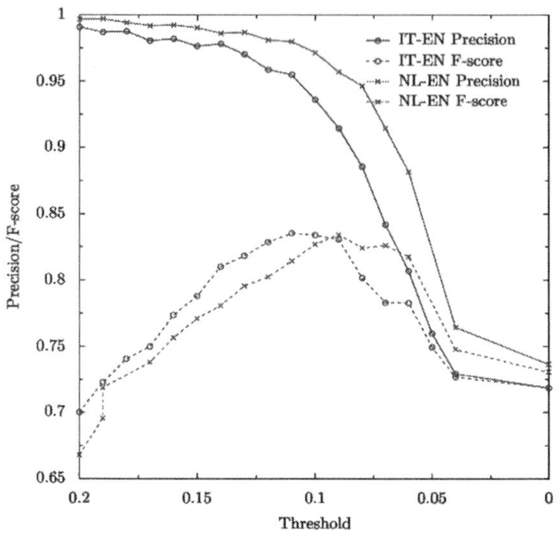

Figure 3: Precision and $F_{0.5}$ scores in relation to threshold values. We can observe that the algorithm retrieves only highly accurate translations for both language pairs while the threshold goes down from value 0.2 to 0.1, while precision starts to drop significantly after the threshold of 0.1. $F_{0.5}$ scores also reach their peaks within that threshold region.

If we do not know anything about a given language pair, we can only use words shared across languages as lexical clues for the construction of a seed lexicon. It often leads to a low precision lexicon, since many false friends are detected.

For Italian-English, we have found 431 nouns shared between the two languages, of which 350 were correct translations, leading to a precision of 0.8121. As an illustration, if we take the first 431 translation pairs retrieved by LALG-ALL, there are 427 correct translation pairs, leading to a precision of 0.9907. Some pairs do not share any orthographic similarities: *(uccello, bird)*, *(tastiera, keyboard)*, *(salute, health)*, *(terremoto, earthquake)* etc.

Following Koehn and Knight (2002), we have also employed simple transformation rules for the adoption of words from one language to another. The rules specific to the Italian-English translation process that have been employed are: (R1) if an Italian noun ends in $-ione$, but not in $-zione$, strip the final *e* to obtain the corresponding English noun. Otherwise, strip the suffix $-zione$, and append $-tion$; (R2) if a noun ends in $-ia$, but not in $-zia$ or $-fia$, replace the suffix $-ia$ with $-y$. If a noun ends in $-zia$, replace the suffix with $-cy$ and if a noun ends in $-fia$, replace

Lexicon	Italian-English # Correct	Italian-English Precision	Italian-English $F_{0.5}$	Dutch-English # Correct	Dutch-English Precision	Dutch-English $F_{0.5}$
LEX-1	350	0.8121	0.1876	898	0.8618	0.2308
LEX-2	766	0.8938	0.3473	**1376**	0.9011	**0.3216**
LEX-LALG	**782**	**0.8958**	**0.3524**	1106	**0.9559**	0.2778
LEX-1+LEX-LALG	1070	0.8785	0.4290	1860	0.9082	0.3961
LEX-R+LEX-LALG	1141	**0.9239**	0.4548	1507	**0.9642**	0.3500
LEX-2+LEX-LALG	**1429**	0.8926	**0.5102**	**2261**	0.9217	**0.4505**

Table 2: A comparison of different lexicons. For lexicons employing our LALG-ALL algorithm, only translation candidates that scored above the threshold $P = 0.11$ have been kept.

it with $-phy$. Similar rules have been introduced for Dutch-English: the suffix $-tie$ is replaced by $-tion$, $-sie$ by $-sion$, and $-teit$ by $-ty$.

Finally, we have compared the results of the following constructed lexicons:

- A lexicon containing only words shared across languages (**LEX-1**).
- A lexicon containing shared words and translation pairs found by applying the language-specific transformation rules (**LEX-2**).
- A lexicon containing only translation pairs obtained by the LALG-ALL algorithm that score above a certain threshold P (**LEX-LALG**).
- A combination of the lexicons LEX-1 and LEX-LALG (**LEX-1+LEX-LALG**). Non-matching duplicates are resolved by taking the translation pair from LEX-LALG as the correct one. Note that this lexicon is completely language-pair independent.
- A lexicon combining only translation pairs found by applying the language-specific transformation rules and LEX-LALG (**LEX-R+LEX-LALG**).
- A combination of the lexicons LEX-2 and LEX-LALG, where non-matching duplicates are resolved by taking the translation pair from LEX-LALG if it is present in LEX-1, and from LEX-2 otherwise (**LEX-2+LEX-LALG**).

According to the results from Table 2, we can conclude that adding translation pairs extracted by our LALG-ALL algorithm has a major positive impact on both precision and coverage. Obtaining results for two different language pairs proves that the approach is generic and applicable to any other language pairs. The previous approach relying on work from Koehn and Knight (2002) has been outperformed in terms of precision and coverage. Additionally, we have shown that adding simple translation rules for languages sharing same roots might lead to even better scores (LEX-2+LEX-LALG). However, it is not always possible to rely on such knowledge, and the usefulness of the designed LALG-ALL algorithm really comes to the fore when the algorithm is applied on distant language pairs which do not share many words and cognates, and word translation rules cannot be easily established. In such cases, without any prior knowledge about the languages involved in a translation process, one is left with the linguistically unbiased LEX-1+LEX-LALG lexicon, which also displays a promising performance.

5 Conclusions and Future Work

We have designed an algorithm that focuses on acquiring and keeping only highly confident translation candidates from multilingual comparable corpora. By employing the algorithm we have improved precision scores of the methods relying on per-topic word distributions from a cross-language topic model. We have shown that the algorithm is able to produce a highly reliable bilingual seed lexicon even when all other lexical clues are absent, thus making our algorithm suitable even for unrelated language pairs. In future work, we plan to further improve the algorithm and use it as a source of translational evidence for different alignment tasks in the setting of non-parallel corpora.

Acknowledgments

The research has been carried out in the framework of the TermWise Knowledge Platform (IOF-KP/09/001) funded by the Industrial Research Fund K.U. Leuven, Belgium.

References

Jaime G. Carbonell, Jaime G. Yang, Robert E. Frederking, Ralf D. Brown, Yibing Geng, Danny Lee, Yiming Frederking, Robert E, Ralf D. Geng, and Yiming Yang. 1997. Translingual information retrieval: A comparative evaluation. In *Proceedings of the 15th International Joint Conference on Artificial Intelligence*, pages 708–714.

Yun-Chuang Chiao and Pierre Zweigenbaum. 2002. Looking for candidate translational equivalents in specialized, comparable corpora. In *Proceedings of the 19th International Conference on Computational Linguistics*, pages 1–5.

Philipp Cimiano, Antje Schultz, Sergej Sizov, Philipp Sorg, and Steffen Staab. 2009. Explicit versus latent concept models for cross-language information retrieval. In *Proceedings of the 21st International Joint Conference on Artifical Intelligence*, pages 1513–1518.

Wim De Smet and Marie-Francine Moens. 2009. Cross-language linking of news stories on the Web using interlingual topic modeling. In *Proceedings of the CIKM 2009 Workshop on Social Web Search and Mining*, pages 57–64.

Hervé Déjean, Éric Gaussier, and Fatia Sadat. 2002. An approach based on multilingual thesauri and model combination for bilingual lexicon extraction. In *Proceedings of the 19th International Conference on Computational Linguistics*, pages 1–7.

Mona T. Diab and Steve Finch. 2000. A statistical translation model using comparable corpora. In *Proceedings of the 6th Triennial Conference on Recherche d'Information Assistée par Ordinateur (RIAO)*, pages 1500–1508.

Pascale Fung and Percy Cheung. 2004. Mining very-non-parallel corpora: Parallel sentence and lexicon extraction via bootstrapping and EM. In *Proceedings of the Conference on Empirical Methods in Natural Language Processing*, pages 57–63.

Pascale Fung and Lo Yuen Yee. 1998. An IR approach for translating new words from nonparallel, comparable texts. In *Proceedings of the 17th International Conference on Computational Linguistics*, pages 414–420.

Eric Gaussier, Jean-Michel Renders, Irina Matveeva, Cyril Goutte, and Hervé Déjean. 2004. A geometric view on bilingual lexicon extraction from comparable corpora. In *Proceedings of the 42nd Annual Meeting of the Association for Computational Linguistics*, pages 526–533.

Thomas L. Griffiths, Mark Steyvers, and Joshua B. Tenenbaum. 2007. Topics in semantic representation. *Psychological Review*, 114(2):211–244.

Aria Haghighi, Percy Liang, Taylor Berg-Kirkpatrick, and Dan Klein. 2008. Learning bilingual lexicons from monolingual corpora. In *Proceedings of the 46th Annual Meeting of the Association for Computational Linguistics*, pages 771–779.

Zellig S. Harris. 1954. Distributional structure. *Word 10*, (23):146–162.

Philipp Koehn and Kevin Knight. 2002. Learning a translation lexicon from monolingual corpora. In *Proceedings of the ACL-02 Workshop on Unsupervised Lexical Acquisition*, pages 9–16.

Audrey Laroche and Philippe Langlais. 2010. Revisiting context-based projection methods for term-translation spotting in comparable corpora. In *Proceedings of the 23rd International Conference on Computational Linguistics*, pages 617–625.

Gina-Anne Levow, Douglas W. Oard, and Philip Resnik. 2005. Dictionary-based techniques for cross-language information retrieval. *Information Processing and Management*, 41:523–547.

Bo Li, Eric Gaussier, and Akiko Aizawa. 2011. Clustering comparable corpora for bilingual lexicon extraction. In *Proceedings of the 49th Annual Meeting of the Association for Computational Linguistics: Human Language Technologies*, pages 473–478.

Christopher D. Manning and Hinrich Schütze. 1999. *Foundations of Statistical Natural Language Processing*. MIT Press, Cambridge, MA, USA.

I. Dan Melamed. 2000. Models of translational equivalence among words. *Computational Linguistics*, 26:221–249.

David Mimno, Hanna M. Wallach, Jason Naradowsky, David A. Smith, and Andrew McCallum. 2009. Polylingual topic models. In *Proceedings of the 2009 Conference on Empirical Methods in Natural Language Processing*, pages 880–889.

Emmanuel Morin, Béatrice Daille, Koichi Takeuchi, and Kyo Kageura. 2007. Bilingual terminology mining - using brain, not brawn comparable corpora. In *Proceedings of the 45th Annual Meeting of the Association for Computational Linguistics*, pages 664–671.

Dragos Stefan Munteanu and Daniel Marcu. 2005. Improving machine translation performance by exploiting non-parallel corpora. *Computational Linguistics*, 31:477–504.

Xiaochuan Ni, Jian-Tao Sun, Jian Hu, and Zheng Chen. 2009. Mining multilingual topics from Wikipedia. In *Proceedings of the 18th International World Wide Web Conference*, pages 1155–1156.

Franz Josef Och and Hermann Ney. 2003. A systematic comparison of various statistical alignment models. *Computational Linguistics*, 29(1):19–51.

Reinhard Rapp. 1995. Identifying word translations in non-parallel texts. In *Proceedings of the 33rd Annual Meeting of the Association for Computational Linguistics*, pages 320–322.

Reinhard Rapp. 1999. Automatic identification of word translations from unrelated English and German corpora. In *Proceedings of the 37th Annual*

Meeting of the Association for Computational Linguistics, pages 519–526.

Daphna Shezaf and Ari Rappoport. 2010. Bilingual lexicon generation using non-aligned signatures. In *Proceedings of the 48th Annual Meeting of the Association for Computational Linguistics*, pages 98–107.

Masao Utiyama and Hitoshi Isahara. 2003. Reliable measures for aligning Japanese-English news articles and sentences. In *Proceedings of the 41st Annual Meeting of the Association for Computational Linguistics*, pages 72–79.

C. J. van Rijsbergen. 1979. *Information Retrieval*. Butterworth.

Thuy Vu, Ai Ti Aw, and Min Zhang. 2009. Feature-based method for document alignment in comparable news corpora. In *Proceedings of the 12th Conference of the European Chapter of the Association for Computational Linguistics*, pages 843–851.

Ivan Vulić, Wim De Smet, and Marie-Francine Moens. 2011. Identifying word translations from comparable corpora using latent topic models. In *Proceedings of the 49th Annual Meeting of the Association for Computational Linguistics: Human Language Technologies*, pages 479–484.

Efficient Parsing with Linear Context-Free Rewriting Systems

Andreas van Cranenburgh
Huygens ING & ILLC, University of Amsterdam
Royal Netherlands Academy of Arts and Sciences
Postbus 90754, 2509 LT The Hague, the Netherlands
andreas.van.cranenburgh@huygens.knaw.nl

Abstract

Previous work on treebank parsing with discontinuous constituents using Linear Context-Free Rewriting systems (LCFRS) has been limited to sentences of up to 30 words, for reasons of computational complexity. There have been some results on binarizing an LCFRS in a manner that minimizes parsing complexity, but the present work shows that parsing long sentences with such an optimally binarized grammar remains infeasible. Instead, we introduce a technique which removes this length restriction, while maintaining a respectable accuracy. The resulting parser has been applied to a discontinuous treebank with favorable results.

1 Introduction

Discontinuity in constituent structures (cf. figure 1 & 2) is important for a variety of reasons. For one, it allows a tight correspondence between syntax and semantics by letting constituent structure express argument structure (Skut et al., 1997). Other reasons are phenomena such as extraposition and word-order freedom, which arguably require discontinuous annotations to be treated systematically in phrase-structures (McCawley, 1982; Levy, 2005). Empirical investigations demonstrate that discontinuity is present in non-negligible amounts: around 30% of sentences contain discontinuity in two German treebanks (Maier and Søgaard, 2008; Maier and Lichte, 2009). Recent work on treebank parsing with discontinuous constituents (Kallmeyer and Maier, 2010; Maier, 2010; Evang and Kallmeyer, 2011; van Cranenburgh et al., 2011) shows that it is feasible to directly parse discontinuous constituency annotations, as given in the German Negra (Skut et al., 1997) and Tiger (Brants et al., 2002) corpora, or those that can be extracted from traces such as in the Penn treebank (Marcus et al., 1993) annotation. However, the computational complexity is such that until now, the length of sentences needed to be restricted. In the case of Kallmeyer and Maier (2010) and Evang and Kallmeyer (2011) the limit was 25 words. Maier (2010) and van Cranenburgh et al. (2011) manage to parse up to 30 words with heuristics and optimizations, but no further. Algorithms have been suggested to binarize the grammars in such a way as to minimize parsing complexity, but the current paper shows that these techniques are not sufficient to parse longer sentences. Instead, this work presents a novel form of coarse-to-fine parsing which does alleviate this limitation.

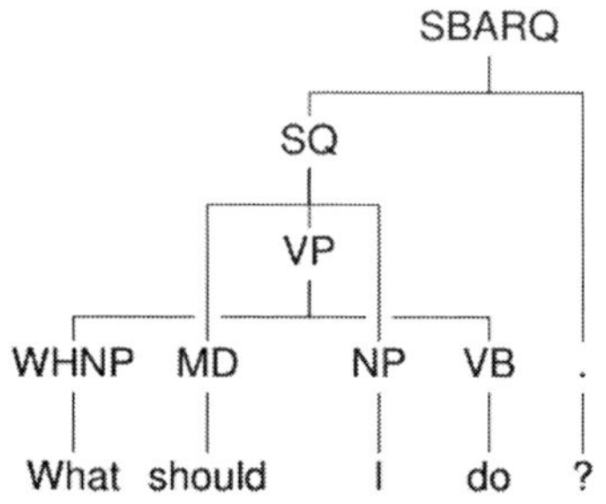

Figure 1: A tree with WH-movement from the Penn treebank, in which traces have been converted to discontinuity. Taken from Evang and Kallmeyer (2011).

The rest of this paper is structured as follows. First, we introduce linear context-free rewriting systems (LCFRS). Next, we discuss and evaluate binarization strategies for LCFRS. Third, we present a technique for approximating an LCFRS by a PCFG in a coarse-to-fine framework. Lastly, we evaluate this technique on a large corpus without the usual length restrictions.

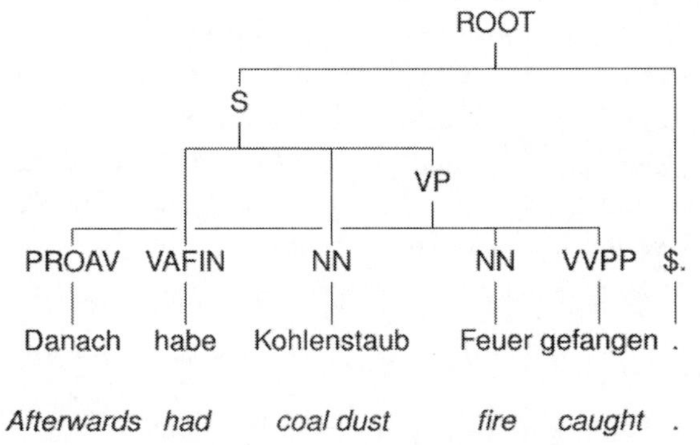

Figure 2: A discontinuous tree from the Negra corpus. Translation: *After that coal dust had caught fire.*

$$\mathrm{ROOT}(ab) \rightarrow \mathrm{S}(a)\ \$.(b)$$
$$\mathrm{S}(abcd) \rightarrow \mathrm{VAFIN}(b)\ \mathrm{NN}(c)\ \mathrm{VP}_2(a,d)$$
$$\mathrm{VP}_2(a,bc) \rightarrow \mathrm{PROAV}(a)\ \mathrm{NN}(b)\ \mathrm{VVPP}(c)$$
$$\mathrm{PROAV}(\mathrm{Danach}) \rightarrow \epsilon$$
$$\mathrm{VAFIN}(\mathrm{habe}) \rightarrow \epsilon$$
$$\mathrm{NN}(\mathrm{Kohlenstaub}) \rightarrow \epsilon$$
$$\mathrm{NN}(\mathrm{Feuer}) \rightarrow \epsilon$$
$$\mathrm{VVPP}(\mathrm{gefangen}) \rightarrow \epsilon$$
$$\$.(.) \rightarrow \epsilon$$

Figure 3: The productions that can be read off from the tree in figure 2. Note that lexical productions rewrite to ϵ, because they do not rewrite to any non-terminals.

2 Linear Context-Free Rewriting Systems

Linear Context-Free Rewriting Systems (LCFRS; Vijay-Shanker et al., 1987; Weir, 1988) subsume a wide variety of mildly context-sensitive formalisms, such as Tree-Adjoining Grammar (TAG), Combinatory Categorial Grammar (CCG), Minimalist Grammar, Multiple Context-Free Grammar (MCFG) and synchronous CFG (Vijay-Shanker and Weir, 1994; Kallmeyer, 2010). Furthermore, they can be used to parse dependency structures (Kuhlmann and Satta, 2009). Since LCFRS subsumes various synchronous grammars, they are also important for machine translation. This makes it possible to use LCFRS as a syntactic backbone with which various formalisms can be parsed by compiling grammars into an LCFRS, similar to the TuLiPa system (Kallmeyer et al., 2008). As all mildly context-sensitive formalisms, LCFRS are parsable in polynomial time, where the degree depends on the productions of the grammar. Intuitively, LCFRS can be seen as a generalization of context-free grammars to rewriting other objects than just continuous strings: productions are context-free, but instead of strings they can rewrite tuples, trees or graphs.

We focus on the use of LCFRS for parsing with discontinuous constituents. This follows up on recent work on parsing the discontinuous annotations in German corpora with LCFRS (Maier, 2010; van Cranenburgh et al., 2011) and work on parsing the Wall Street journal corpus in which traces have been converted to discontinuous constituents (Evang and Kallmeyer, 2011). In the case of parsing with discontinuous constituents a non-terminal may cover a tuple of discontinuous strings instead of a single, contiguous sequence of terminals. The number of components in such a tuple is called the *fan-out* of a rule, which is equal to the number of gaps plus one; the fan-out of the grammar is the maximum fan-out of its production. A context-free grammar is a LCFRS with a fan-out of 1. For convenience we will will use the rule notation of simple RCG (Boullier, 1998), which is a syntactic variant of LCFRS, with an arguably more transparent notation.

A LCFRS is a tuple $G = \langle N, T, V, P, S \rangle$. N is a finite set of non-terminals; a function *dim* : $N \rightarrow \mathbb{N}$ specifies the unique fan-out for every non-terminal symbol. T and V are disjoint finite sets of terminals and variables. S is the distinguished start symbol with $dim(S) = 1$. P is a finite set of rewrite rules (productions) of the form:

$$A(\alpha_1, \ldots \alpha_{dim(A)}) \rightarrow B_1(X_1^1, \ldots, X_{dim(B_1)}^1) \ldots B_m(X_1^m, \ldots, X_{dim(B_m)}^m)$$

for $m \geq 0$, where $A, B_1, \ldots, B_m \in N$, each $X_j^i \in V$ for $1 \leq i \leq m$, $1 \leq j \leq dim(A_j)$ and $\alpha_i \in (T \cup V)^*$ for $1 \leq i \leq dim(A_i)$.

Productions must be *linear*: if a variable occurs in a rule, it occurs exactly once on the left hand side (LHS), and exactly once on the right hand side (RHS). A rule is *ordered* if for any two variables X_1 and X_2 occurring in a non-terminal on the RHS, X_1 precedes X_2 on the LHS iff X_1 precedes X_2 on the RHS.

Every production has a fan-out determined by the fan-out of the non-terminal symbol on the left-hand side. Apart from the fan-out productions also have a rank: the number of non-terminals on the right-hand side. These two variables determine the time complexity of parsing with a grammar. A production can be *instantiated* when its variables can be bound to non-overlapping spans such that for each component α_i of the LHS, the concatenation of its terminals and bound variables forms a contiguous span in the input, while the endpoints of each span are non-contiguous.

As in the case of a PCFG, we can read off LCFRS productions from a treebank (Maier and Søgaard, 2008), and the relative frequencies of productions form a maximum likelihood estimate, for a probabilistic LCFRS (PLCFRS), i.e., a (discontinuous) treebank grammar. As an example, figure 3 shows the productions extracted from the tree in figure 2.

3 Binarization

A probabilistic LCFRS can be parsed using a CKY-like tabular parsing algorithm (cf. Kallmeyer and Maier, 2010; van Cranenburgh et al., 2011), but this requires a binarized grammar.[1] Any LCFRS can be binarized. Crescenzi et al. (2011) state "while CFGs can always be reduced to rank two (Chomsky Normal Form), this is not the case for LCFRS with any fan-out greater than one." However, this assertion is made under the assumption of a fixed fan-out. If this assumption is relaxed then it is easy to binarize either deterministically or, as will be investigated in this work, optimally with a dynamic programming approach. Binarizing an LCFRS may increase its fan-out, which results in an increase in asymptotic complexity. Consider the following production:

$$X(pqrs) \to A(p,r)\ B(q)\ C(s) \qquad (1)$$

Henceforth, we assume that non-terminals on the right-hand side are ordered by the order of their first variable on the left-hand side. There are two ways to binarize this production. The first is from left to right:

$$X(ps) \to X_{AB}(p)\ C(s) \qquad (2)$$

$$X_{AB}(pqr) \to A(p,r)\ B(q) \qquad (3)$$

This binarization maintains the fan-out of 1. The second way is from right to left:

$$X(pqrs) \to A(p,r)\ X_{BC}(q,s) \qquad (4)$$

$$X_{BC}(q,s) \to B(q)\ C(s) \qquad (5)$$

[1]Other algorithms exist which support n-ary productions, but these are less suitable for statistical treebank parsing.

This binarization introduces a production with a fan-out of 2, which could have been avoided. After binarization, an LCFRS can be parsed in $\mathcal{O}(|G| \cdot |w|^p)$ time, where $|G|$ is the size of the grammar, $|w|$ is the length of the sentence. The degree p of the polynomial is the maximum parsing complexity of a rule, defined as:

$$\text{parsing complexity} := \varphi + \varphi_1 + \varphi_2 \qquad (6)$$

where φ is the fan-out of the left-hand side and φ_1 and φ_2 are the fan-outs of the right-hand side of the rule in question (Gildea, 2010). As Gildea (2010) shows, there is no one to one correspondence between fan-out and parsing complexity: it is possible that parsing complexity can be reduced by increasing the fan-out of a production. In other words, there can be a production which can be binarized with a parsing complexity that is minimal while its fan-out is sub-optimal. Therefore we focus on parsing complexity rather than fan-out in this work, since parsing complexity determines the actual time complexity of parsing with a grammar. There has been some work investigating whether the increase in complexity can be minimized effectively (Gómez-Rodríguez et al., 2009; Gildea, 2010; Crescenzi et al., 2011).

More radically, it has been suggested that the power of LCFRS should be limited to well-nested structures, which gives an asymptotic improvement in parsing time (Gómez-Rodríguez et al., 2010). However, there is linguistic evidence that not all language use can be described in well-nested structures (Chen-Main and Joshi, 2010). Therefore we will use the full power of LCFRS in this work—parsing complexity is determined by the treebank, not by a priori constraints.

3.1 Further binarization strategies

Apart from optimizing for parsing complexity, for linguistic reasons it can also be useful to parse the head of a constituent first, yielding so-called head-driven binarizations (Collins, 1999). Additionally, such a head-driven binarization can be 'Markovized'–i.e., the resulting production can be constrained to apply to a limited amount of horizontal context as opposed to the full context in the original constituent (e.g., Klein and Manning, 2003), which can have a beneficial effect on accuracy. In the notation of Klein and Manning (2003) there are two Markovization parameters: h and v. The first parameter describes the amount of

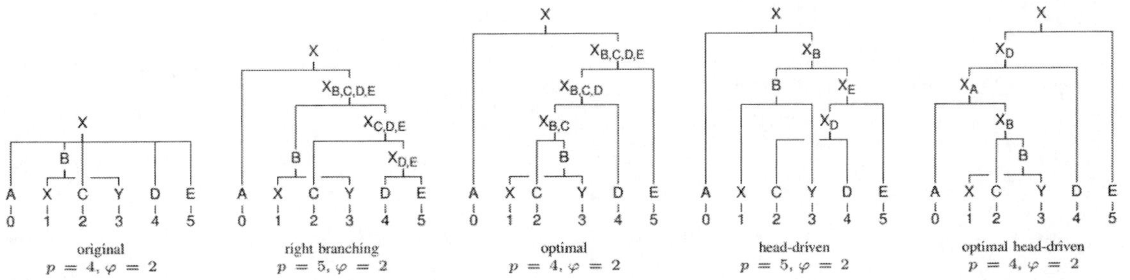

Figure 4: The four binarization strategies. C is the head node. Underneath each tree is the maximum parsing complexity and fan-out among its productions.

horizontal context for the artificial labels of a binarized production. In a normal form binarization, this parameter equals infinity, because the binarized production should only apply in the exact same context as the context in which it originally belongs, as otherwise the set of strings accepted by the grammar would be affected. An artificial label will have the form $X_{A,B,C}$ for a binarized production of a constituent X that has covered children A, B, and C of X. The other extreme, $h = 1$, enables generalizations by stringing parts of binarized constituents together, as long as they share one non-terminal. In the previous example, the label would become just X_A, i.e., the presence of B and C would no longer be required, which enables switching to any binarized production that has covered A as the last node. Limiting the amount of horizontal context on which a production is conditioned is important when the treebank contains many unique constituents which can only be parsed by stringing together different binarized productions; in other words, it is a way of dealing with the data sparseness about n-ary productions in the treebank.

The second parameter describes parent annotation, which will not be investigated in this work; the default value is $v = 1$ which implies only including the immediate parent of the constituent that is being binarized; including grandparents is a way of weakening independence assumptions.

Crescenzi et al. (2011) also remark that an *optimal* head-driven binarization allows for Markovization. However, it is questionable whether such a binarization is worthy of the name Markovization, as the non-terminals are not introduced deterministically from left to right, but in an arbitrary fashion dictated by concerns of parsing complexity; as such there is not a Markov process based on a meaningful (e.g., temporal) ordering and there is no probabilistic interpretation of Markovization in such a setting.

To summarize, we have at least four binarization strategies (cf. figure 4 for an illustration):

1. **right branching:** A right-to-left binarization. No regard for optimality or statistical tweaks.
2. **optimal:** A binarization which minimizes parsing complexity, introduced in Gildea (2010). Binarizing with this strategy is exponential in the resulting optimal fan-out (Gildea, 2010).
3. **head-driven:** Head-outward binarization with horizontal Markovization. No regard for optimality.
4. **optimal head-driven:** Head-outward binarization with horizontal Markovization. Minimizes parsing complexity. Introduced in and proven to be NP-hard by Crescenzi et al. (2011).

3.2 Finding optimal binarizations

An issue with the minimal binarizations is that the algorithm for finding them has a high computational complexity, and has not been evaluated empirically on treebank data.[2] Empirical investigation is interesting for two reasons. First of all, the high computational complexity may not be relevant with constant factors of constituents, which can reasonably be expected to be relatively small. Second, it is important to establish whether an asymptotic improvement is actually obtained through optimal binarizations, and whether this translates to an improvement in practice.

Gildea (2010) presents a general algorithm to binarize an LCFRS while minimizing a given scoring function. We will use this algorithm with two different scoring functions.

[2]Gildea (2010) evaluates on a dependency bank, but does not report whether any improvement is obtained over a naive binarization.

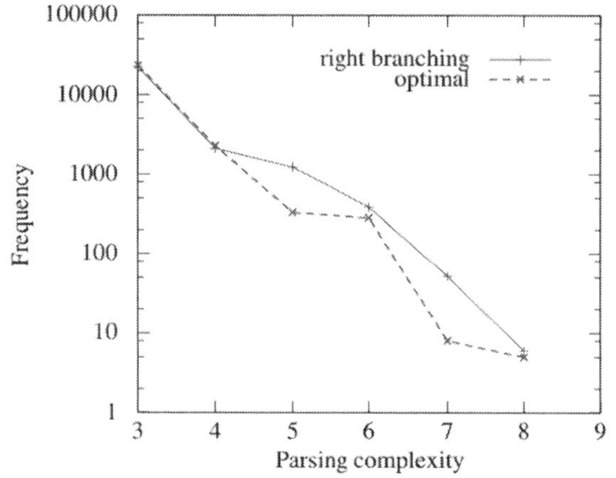

Figure 5: The distribution of parsing complexity among productions in binarized grammars read off from NEGRA-25. The y-axis has a logarithmic scale.

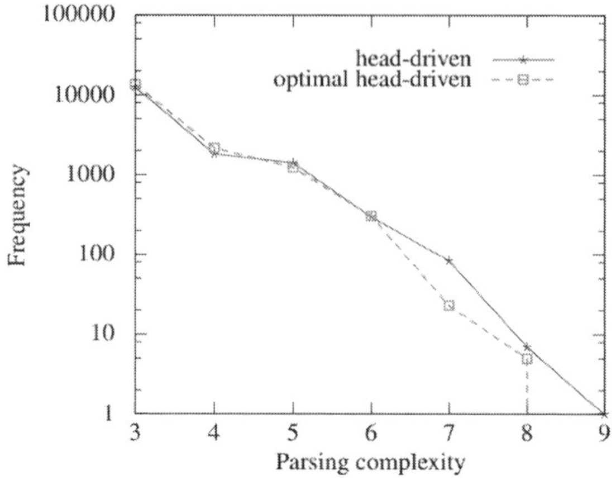

Figure 6: The distribution of parsing complexity among productions in Markovized, head-driven grammars read off from NEGRA-25. The y-axis has a logarithmic scale.

The first directly optimizes parsing complexity. Given a (partially) binarized constituent c, the function returns a tuple of scores, for which a linear order is defined by comparing elements starting from the most significant (left-most) element. The tuples contain the parsing complexity p, and the fan-out φ to break ties in parsing complexity; if there are still ties after considering the fan-out, the sum of the parsing complexities of the subtrees of c is considered, which will give preference to a binarization where the worst case complexity occurs once instead of twice. The formula is then:

$$opt(c) = \langle p, \varphi, s \rangle$$

The second function is the similar except that only head-driven strategies are accepted. A head-driven strategy is a binarization in which the head is introduced first, after which the rest of the children are introduced one at a time.

$$opt\text{-}hd(c) = \begin{cases} \langle p, \varphi, s \rangle & \text{if } c \text{ is head-driven} \\ \langle \infty, \infty, \infty \rangle & \text{otherwise} \end{cases}$$

Given a (partial) binarization c, the score should reflect the maximum complexity and fan-out in that binarization, to optimize for the worst case, as well as the sum, to optimize the average case. This aspect appears to be glossed over by Gildea (2010). Considering only the score of the last production in a binarization produces suboptimal binarizations.

3.3 Experiments

As data we use version 2 of the Negra (Skut et al., 1997) treebank, with the common training, development and test splits (Dubey and Keller, 2003). Following common practice, punctuation, which is left out of the phrase-structure in Negra, is reattached to the nearest constituent.

In the course of experiments it was discovered that the heuristic method for punctuation attachment used in previous work (e.g., Maier, 2010; van Cranenburgh et al., 2011), as implemented in `rparse`,[3] introduces additional discontinuity. We applied a slightly different heuristic: punctuation is attached to the highest constituent that contains a neighbor to its right. The result is that punctuation can be introduced into the phrase-structure without any additional discontinuity, and thus without artificially inflating the fan-out and complexity of grammars read off from the treebank. This new heuristic provides a significant improvement: instead of a fan-out of 9 and a parsing complexity of 19, we obtain values of 4 and 9 respectively.

The parser is presented with the gold part-of-speech tags from the corpus. For reasons of efficiency we restrict sentences to 25 words (including punctuation) in this experiment: NEGRA-25. A grammar was read off from the training part of NEGRA-25, and sentences of up to 25 words in the development set were parsed using the resulting PLCFRS, using the different binarization schemes. First with a right-branching, right-to-left binarization, and second with the minimal binarization according to parsing complexity and fan-

[3] Available from `http://www.wolfgang-maier.net/rparse/downloads`. Retrieved March 25th, 2011

	right branching	optimal	head-driven	optimal head-driven
Markovization	v=1, h=∞	v=1, h=∞	v=1, h=2	v=1, h=2
fan-out	4	4	4	4
complexity	8	8	9	8
labels	12861	12388	4576	3187
clauses	62072	62097	53050	52966
time to binarize	1.83 s	46.37 s	2.74 s	28.9 s
time to parse	246.34 s	193.94 s	2860.26 s	716.58 s
coverage	96.08 %	96.08 %	98.99 %	98.73 %
F_1 score	66.83 %	66.75 %	72.37 %	71.79 %

Table 1: The effect of binarization strategies on parsing efficiency, with sentences from the development section of NEGRA-25.

out. The last two binarizations are head-driven and Markovized—the first straightforwardly from left-to-right, the latter optimized for minimal parsing complexity. With Markovization we are forced to add a level of parent annotation to tame the increase in productivity caused by $h = 1$.

The distribution of parsing complexity (measured with eq. 6) in the grammars with different binarization strategies is shown in figure 5 and 6. Although the optimal binarizations do seem to have some effect on the distribution of parsing complexities, it remains to be seen whether this can be cashed out as a performance improvement in practice. To this end, we also parse using the binarized grammars.

In this work we binarize and parse with `disco-dop` introduced in van Cranenburgh et al. (2011).[4] In this experiment we report scores of the (exact) Viterbi derivations of a treebank PLCFRS; cf. table 1 for the results. Times represent CPU time (single core); accuracy is given with a generalization of PARSEVAL to discontinuous structures, described in Maier (2010).

Instead of using Maier's implementation of discontinuous F_1 scores in `rparse`, we employ a variant that ignores (a) punctuation, and (b) the root node of each tree. This makes our evaluation incomparable to previous results on discontinuous parsing, but brings it in line with common practice on the Wall street journal benchmark. Note that this change yields scores about 2 or 3 percentage points lower than those of `rparse`.

Despite the fact that obtaining optimal binarizations is exponential (Gildea, 2010) and NP-hard (Crescenzi et al., 2011), they can be computed relatively quickly on this data set.[5] Importantly, in the first case there is no improvement on fan-out or parsing complexity, while in the head-driven case there is a minimal improvement because of a single production with parsing complexity 15 without optimal binarization. On the other hand, the optimal binarizations might still have a significant effect on the average case complexity, rather than the worst-case complexities. Indeed, in both cases parsing with the optimal grammar is faster; in the first case, however, when the time for binarization is considered as well, this advantage mostly disappears.

The difference in F_1 scores might relate to the efficacy of Markovization in the binarizations. It should be noted that it makes little theoretical sense to 'Markovize' a binarization when it is not a left-to-right or right-to-left binarization, because with an optimal binarization the non-terminals of a constituent are introduced in an arbitrary order.

More importantly, in our experiments, these techniques of optimal binarizations did not scale to longer sentences. While it is possible to obtain an optimal binarization of the unrestricted Negra corpus, parsing long sentences with the resulting grammar remains infeasible. Therefore we need to look at other techniques for parsing longer sentences. We will stick with the straightforward

[4] All code is available from: `http://github.com/andreasvc/disco-dop`.

[5] The implementation exploits two important optimizations. The first is the use of bit vectors to keep track of which non-terminals are covered by a partial binarization. The second is to skip constituents without discontinuity, which are equivalent to CFG productions.

head-driven, head-outward binarization strategy, despite this being a computationally sub-optimal binarization.

One technique for efficient parsing of LCFRS is the use of context-summary estimates (Kallmeyer and Maier, 2010), as part of a best-first parsing algorithm. This allowed Maier (2010) to parse sentences of up to 30 words. However, the calculation of these estimates is not feasible for longer sentences and large grammars (van Cranenburgh et al., 2011).

Another strategy is to perform an online approximation of the sentence to be parsed, after which parsing with the LCFRS can be pruned effectively. This is the strategy that will be explored in the current work.

4 Context-free grammar approximation for coarse-to-fine parsing

Coarse-to-fine parsing (Charniak et al., 2006) is a technique to speed up parsing by exploiting the information that can be gained from parsing with simpler, coarser grammars—e.g., a grammar with a smaller set of labels on which the original grammar can be projected. Constituents that do not contribute to a full parse tree with a coarse grammar can be ruled out for finer grammars as well, which greatly reduces the number of edges that need to be explored. However, by changing just the labels only the grammar constant is affected. With discontinuous treebank parsing the asymptotic complexity of the grammar also plays a major role. Therefore we suggest to parse not just with a coarser grammar, but with a coarser grammar formalism, following a suggestion in van Cranenburgh et al. (2011).

This idea is inspired by the work of Barthélemy et al. (2001), who apply it in a non-probabilistic setting where the coarse grammar acts as a guide to the non-deterministic choices of the fine grammar. Within the coarse-to-fine approach the technique becomes a matter of pruning with some probabilistic threshold. Instead of using the coarse grammar only as a guide to solve non-deterministic choices, we apply it as a pruning step which also discards the most suboptimal parses. The basic idea is to extract a grammar that defines a superset of the language we want to parse, but with a fan-out of 1. More concretely, a context-free grammar can be read off from discontinuous trees that have been transformed to context-free trees by the procedure introduced in Boyd (2007). Each discontinuous node is split into a set of new nodes, one for each component; for example a node NP_2 will be split into two nodes labeled NP*1 and NP*2 (like Barthélemy et al., we mark components with an index to reduce overgeneration). Because Boyd's transformation is reversible, chart items from this grammar can be converted back to discontinuous chart items, and can guide parsing of an LCFRS. This guiding takes the form of a white list. After parsing with the coarse grammar, the resulting chart is pruned by removing all items that fail to meet a certain criterion. In our case this is whether a chart item is part of one of the k-best derivations—we use $k = 50$ in all experiments (as in van Cranenburgh et al., 2011). This has similar effects as removing items below a threshold of marginalized posterior probability; however, the latter strategy requires computation of outside probabilities from a parse forest, which is more involved with an LCFRS than with a PCFG. When parsing with the fine grammar, whenever a new item is derived, the white list is consulted to see whether this item is allowed to be used in further derivations; otherwise it is immediately discarded. This coarse-to-fine approach will be referred to as CFG-CTF, and the transformed, coarse grammar will be referred to as a split-PCFG.

Splitting discontinuous nodes for the coarse grammar introduces new nodes, so obviously we need to binarize after this transformation. On the other hand, the coarse-to-fine approach requires a mapping between the grammars, so after reversing the transformation of splitting nodes, the resulting discontinuous trees must be binarized (and optionally Markovized) in the same manner as those on which the fine grammar is based.

To resolve this tension we elect to binarize twice. The first time is before splitting discontinuous nodes, and this is where we introduce Markovization. This same binarization will be used for the fine grammar as well, which ensures the models make the same kind of generalizations. The second binarization is after splitting nodes, this time with a binary normal form (2NF; all productions are either unary, binary, or lexical).

Parsing with this grammar proceeds as follows. After obtaining an exhaustive chart from the coarse stage, the chart is pruned so as to only contain items occurring in the k-best derivations. When parsing in the fine stage, each new item is

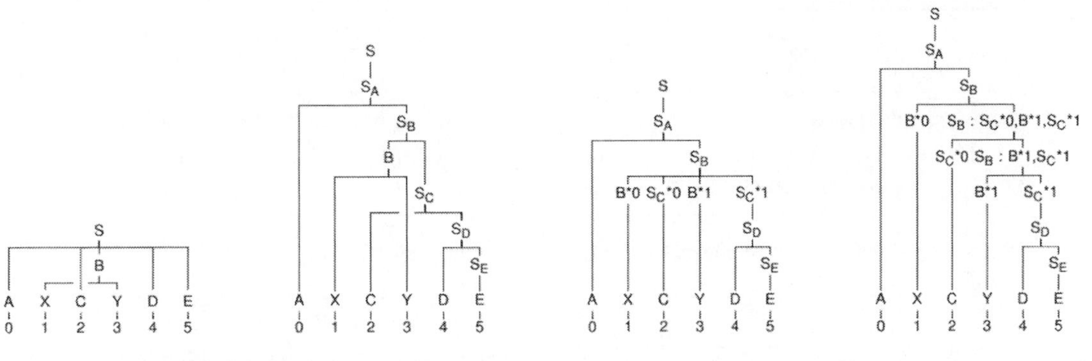

Figure 7: Transformations for a context-free coarse grammar. From left to right: the original constituent, Markovized with $v = 1$, $h = 1$, discontinuities resolved, normal form (second binarization).

model	train	dev	test	rules	labels	fan-out	complexity
Split-PCFG	17988	975	968	57969	2026	1	3
PLCFRS	17988	975	968	55778	947	4	9
Disco-DOP	17988	975	968	2657799	702246	4	9

Table 2: Some statistics on the coarse and fine grammars read off from NEGRA-40.

looked up in this pruned coarse chart, with multiple lookups if the item is discontinuous (one for each component).

To summarize, the transformation happens in four steps (cf. figure 7 for an illustration):

1. **Treebank tree:** Original (discontinuous) tree
2. **Binarization:** Binarize discontinuous tree, optionally with Markovization
3. **Resolve discontinuity:** Split discontinuous nodes into components, marked with indices
4. **2NF:** A binary normal form is applied; all productions are either unary, binary, or lexical.

5 Evaluation

We evaluate on Negra with the same setup as in section 3.3. We report discontinuous F_1 scores as well as exact match scores. For previous results on discontinuous parsing with Negra, see table 3. For results with the CFG-CTF method see table 4.

We first establish the viability of the CFG-CTF method on NEGRA-25, with a head-driven $v = 1$, $h = 2$ binarization, and reporting again the scores of the exact Viterbi derivations from a treebank PLCFRS versus a PCFG using our transformations. Figure 8 compares the parsing times of LCFRS with and without the new CFG-CTF method. The graph shows a steep incline for parsing with LCFRS directly, which makes it infeasible to parse longer sentences, while the CFG-CTF method is faster for

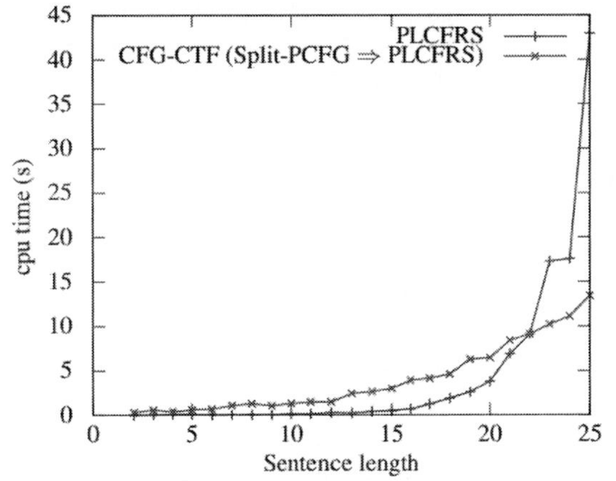

Figure 8: Efficiency of parsing PLCFRS with and without coarse-to-fine. The latter includes time for both coarse & fine grammar. Datapoints represent the average time to parse sentences of that length; each length is made up of 20–40 sentences.

sentences of length > 22 despite its overhead of parsing twice.

The second experiment demonstrates the CFG-CTF technique on longer sentences. We restrict the length of sentences in the training, development and test corpora to 40 words: NEGRA-40. As a first step we apply the CFG-CTF technique to parse with a PLCFRS as the fine grammar, pruning away all items not occurring in the 10,000 best derivations

	words	PARSEVAL (F_1)	Exact match
DPSG: Plaehn (2004)	≤ 15	73.16	39.0
PLCFRS: Maier (2010)	≤ 30	71.52	31.65
Disco-DOP: van Cranenburgh et al. (2011)	≤ 30	73.98	34.80

Table 3: Previous work on discontinuous parsing of Negra.

	words	PARSEVAL (F_1)	Exact match
PLCFRS, dev set	≤ 25	72.37	36.58
Split-PCFG, dev set	≤ 25	70.74	33.80
Split-PCFG, dev set	≤ 40	66.81	27.59
CFG-CTF, PLCFRS, dev set	≤ 40	67.26	27.90
CFG-CTF, Disco-DOP, dev set	≤ 40	74.27	34.26
CFG-CTF, Disco-DOP, test set	≤ 40	72.33	33.16
CFG-CTF, Disco-DOP, dev set	∞	73.32	33.40
CFG-CTF, Disco-DOP, test set	∞	71.08	32.10

Table 4: Results on NEGRA-25 and NEGRA-40 with the CFG-CTF method. NB: As explained in section 3.3, these F_1 scores are incomparable to the results in table 3; for comparison, the F_1 score for Disco-DOP on the dev set ≤ 40 is 77.13 % using that evaluation scheme.

from the PCFG chart. The result shows that the PLCFRS gives a slight improvement over the split--pcfg, which accords with the observation that the latter makes stronger independence assumptions in the case of discontinuity.

In the next experiments we turn to an all-fragments grammar encoded in a PLCFRS using Goodman's (2003) reduction, to realize a (discontinuous) Data-Oriented Parsing (DOP; Scha, 1990) model—which goes by the name of Disco-DOP (van Cranenburgh et al., 2011). This provides an effective yet conceptually simple method to weaken the independence assumptions of treebank grammars. Table 2 gives statistics on the grammars, including the parsing complexities. The fine grammar has a parsing complexity of 9, which means that parsing with this grammar has complexity $\mathcal{O}(|w|^9)$. We use the same parameters as van Cranenburgh et al. (2011), except that unlike van Cranenburgh et al., we can use $v = 1$, $h = 1$ Markovization, in order to obtain a higher coverage. The DOP grammar is added as a third stage in the coarse-to-fine pipeline. This gave slightly better results than substituting the the DOP grammar for the PLCFRS stage. Parsing with NEGRA-40 took about 11 hours and 4 GB of memory. The same model from NEGRA-40 can also be used to parse the full development set, without length restrictions, establishing that the CFG-CTF method effectively eliminates any limitation of length for parsing with LCFRS.

6 Conclusion

Our results show that optimal binarizations are clearly not the answer to parsing LCFRS efficiently, as they do not significantly reduce parsing complexity in our experiments. While they provide some efficiency gains, they do not help with the main problem of longer sentences.

We have presented a new technique for large-scale parsing with LCFRS, which makes it possible to parse sentences of any length, with favorable accuracies. The availability of this technique may lead to a wider acceptance of LCFRS as a syntactic backbone in computational linguistics.

Acknowledgments

I am grateful to Willem Zuidema, Remko Scha, Rens Bod, and three anonymous reviewers for comments.

References

François Barthélemy, Pierre Boullier, Philippe Deschamp, and Éric de la Clergerie. 2001. Guided parsing of range concatenation languages. In *Proc. of ACL*, pages 42–49.

Pierre Boullier. 1998. Proposal for a natural language processing syntactic backbone. Technical Report RR-3342, INRIA-Rocquencourt, Le Chesnay, France. URL http://www.inria.fr/RRRT/RR-3342.html.

Adriane Boyd. 2007. Discontinuity revisited: An improved conversion to context-free representations. In *Proceedings of the Linguistic Annotation Workshop*, pages 41–44.

Sabine Brants, Stefanie Dipper, Silvia Hansen, Wolfgang Lezius, and George Smith. 2002. The Tiger treebank. In *Proceedings of the workshop on treebanks and linguistic theories*, pages 24–41.

Eugene Charniak, Mark Johnson, M. Elsner, J. Austerweil, D. Ellis, I. Haxton, C. Hill, R. Shrivaths, J. Moore, M. Pozar, et al. 2006. Multilevel coarse-to-fine PCFG parsing. In *Proceedings of NAACL-HLT*, pages 168–175.

Joan Chen-Main and Aravind K. Joshi. 2010. Unavoidable ill-nestedness in natural language and the adequacy of tree local-mctag induced dependency structures. In *Proceedings of TAG+*. URL http://www.research.att.com/~srini/TAG+10/papers/chenmainjoshi.pdf.

Michael Collins. 1999. *Head-driven statistical models for natural language parsing*. Ph.D. thesis, University of Pennsylvania.

Pierluigi Crescenzi, Daniel Gildea, Aandrea Marino, Gianluca Rossi, and Giorgio Satta. 2011. Optimal head-driven parsing complexity for linear context-free rewriting systems. In *Proc. of ACL*.

Amit Dubey and Frank Keller. 2003. Parsing german with sister-head dependencies. In *Proc. of ACL*, pages 96–103.

Kilian Evang and Laura Kallmeyer. 2011. PLCFRS parsing of English discontinuous constituents. In *Proceedings of IWPT*, pages 104–116.

Daniel Gildea. 2010. Optimal parsing strategies for linear context-free rewriting systems. In *Proceedings of NAACL HLT 2010.*, pages 769–776.

Carlos Gómez-Rodríguez, Marco Kuhlmann, and Giorgio Satta. 2010. Efficient parsing of well-nested linear context-free rewriting systems. In *Proceedings of NAACL HLT 2010.*, pages 276–284.

Carlos Gómez-Rodríguez, Marco Kuhlmann, Giorgio Satta, and David Weir. 2009. Optimal reduction of rule length in linear context-free rewriting systems. In *Proceedings of NAACL HLT 2009*, pages 539–547.

Joshua Goodman. 2003. Efficient parsing of DOP with PCFG-reductions. In Rens Bod, Remko Scha, and Khalil Sima'an, editors, *Data-Oriented Parsing*. The University of Chicago Press.

Laura Kallmeyer. 2010. *Parsing Beyond Context-Free Grammars*. Cognitive Technologies. Springer Berlin Heidelberg.

Laura Kallmeyer, Timm Lichte, Wolfgang Maier, Yannick Parmentier, Johannes Dellert, and Kilian Evang. 2008. Tulipa: Towards a multi-formalism parsing environment for grammar engineering. In *Proceedings of the Workshop on Grammar Engineering Across Frameworks*, pages 1–8.

Laura Kallmeyer and Wolfgang Maier. 2010. Data-driven parsing with probabilistic linear context-free rewriting systems. In *Proceedings of the 23rd International Conference on Computational Linguistics*, pages 537–545.

Dan Klein and Christopher D. Manning. 2003. Accurate unlexicalized parsing. In *Proc. of ACL*, volume 1, pages 423–430.

Marco Kuhlmann and Giorgio Satta. 2009. Treebank grammar techniques for non-projective dependency parsing. In *Proceedings of EACL*, pages 478–486.

Roger Levy. 2005. *Probabilistic models of word order and syntactic discontinuity*. Ph.D. thesis, Stanford University.

Wolfgang Maier. 2010. Direct parsing of discontinuous constituents in German. In *Proceedings of the SPMRL workshop at NAACL HLT 2010*, pages 58–66.

Wolfgang Maier and Timm Lichte. 2009. Characterizing discontinuity in constituent treebanks.

In *Proceedings of Formal Grammar 2009*, pages 167–182. Springer.

Wolfgang Maier and Anders Søgaard. 2008. Treebanks and mild context-sensitivity. In *Proceedings of Formal Grammar 2008*, page 61.

Mitchell P. Marcus, Mary Ann Marcinkiewicz, and Beatrice Santorini. 1993. Building a large annotated corpus of english: The penn treebank. *Computational linguistics*, 19(2):313–330.

James D. McCawley. 1982. Parentheticals and discontinuous constituent structure. *Linguistic Inquiry*, 13(1):91–106.

Oliver Plaehn. 2004. Computing the most probable parse for a discontinuous phrase structure grammar. In Harry Bunt, John Carroll, and Giorgio Satta, editors, *New developments in parsing technology*, pages 91–106. Kluwer Academic Publishers, Norwell, MA, USA.

Remko Scha. 1990. Language theory and language technology; competence and performance. In Q.A.M. de Kort and G.L.J. Leerdam, editors, *Computertoepassingen in de Neerlandistiek*, pages 7–22. LVVN, Almere, the Netherlands. Original title: *Taaltheorie en taaltechnologie; competence en performance*. Translation available at `http://iaaa.nl/rs/LeerdamE.html`.

Stuart M. Shieber. 1985. Evidence against the context-freeness of natural language. *Linguistics and Philosophy*, 8:333–343.

Wojciech Skut, Brigitte Krenn, Thorten Brants, and Hans Uszkoreit. 1997. An annotation scheme for free word order languages. In *Proceedings of ANLP*, pages 88–95.

Andreas van Cranenburgh, Remko Scha, and Federico Sangati. 2011. Discontinuous data-oriented parsing: A mildly context-sensitive all-fragments grammar. In *Proceedings of SPMRL*, pages 34–44.

K. Vijay-Shanker and David J. Weir. 1994. The equivalence of four extensions of context-free grammars. *Theory of Computing Systems*, 27(6):511–546.

K. Vijay-Shanker, David J. Weir, and Aravind K. Joshi. 1987. Characterizing structural descriptions produced by various grammatical formalisms. In *Proc. of ACL*, pages 104–111.

David J. Weir. 1988. *Characterizing mildly context-sensitive grammar formalisms*. Ph.D. thesis, University of Pennsylvania. URL `http://repository.upenn.edu/dissertations/AAI8908403/`.

Evaluating language understanding accuracy with respect to objective outcomes in a dialogue system

Myroslava O. Dzikovska and **Peter Bell** and **Amy Isard** and **Johanna D. Moore**
Institute for Language, Cognition and Computation
School of Informatics, University of Edinburgh, United Kingdom
{m.dzikovska,peter.bell,amy.isard,j.moore}@ed.ac.uk

Abstract

It is not always clear how the differences in intrinsic evaluation metrics for a parser or classifier will affect the performance of the system that uses it. We investigate the relationship between the intrinsic evaluation scores of an interpretation component in a tutorial dialogue system and the learning outcomes in an experiment with human users. Following the PARADISE methodology, we use multiple linear regression to build predictive models of learning gain, an important objective outcome metric in tutorial dialogue. We show that standard intrinsic metrics such as F-score alone do not predict the outcomes well. However, we can build predictive performance functions that account for up to 50% of the variance in learning gain by combining features based on standard evaluation scores and on the confusion matrix entries. We argue that building such predictive models can help us better evaluate performance of NLP components that cannot be distinguished based on F-score alone, and illustrate our approach by comparing the current interpretation component in the system to a new classifier trained on the evaluation data.

1 Introduction

Much of the work in natural language processing relies on intrinsic evaluation: computing standard evaluation metrics such as precision, recall and F-score on the same data set to compare the performance of different approaches to the same NLP problem. However, once a component, such as a parser, is included in a larger system, it is not always clear that improvements in intrinsic evaluation scores will translate into improved overall system performance. Therefore, extrinsic or task-based evaluation can be used to complement intrinsic evaluations. For example, NLP components such as parsers and co-reference resolution algorithms could be compared in terms of how much they contribute to the performance of a textual entailment (RTE) system (Sammons et al., 2010; Yuret et al., 2010); parser performance could be evaluated by how well it contributes to an information retrieval task (Miyao et al., 2008).

However, task-based evaluation can be difficult and expensive for interactive applications. Specifically, task-based evaluation for dialogue systems typically involves collecting data from a number of people interacting with the system, which is time-consuming and labor-intensive. Thus, it is desirable to develop an off-line evaluation procedure that relates intrinsic evaluation metrics to predicted interaction outcomes, reducing the need to conduct experiments with human participants.

This problem can be addressed via the use of the PARADISE evaluation methodology for spoken dialogue systems (Walker et al., 2000). In a PARADISE study, after an initial data collection with users, a performance function is created to predict an outcome metric (e.g., user satisfaction) which can normally only be measured through user surveys. Typically, a multiple linear regression is used to fit a predictive model of the desired metric based on the values of interaction parameters that can be derived from system logs without additional user studies (e.g., dialogue length, word error rate, number of misunderstandings).

PARADISE models have been used extensively in task-oriented spoken dialogue systems to establish which components of the system most need improvement, with user satisfaction as the outcome metric (Möller et al., 2007; Möller et al., 2008; Walker et al., 2000; Larsen, 2003). In tutorial dialogue, PARADISE studies investigated which manually annotated features predict learning outcomes, to justify new features needed in the system (Forbes-Riley et al., 2007; Rotaru and Litman, 2006; Forbes-Riley and Litman, 2006).

We adapt the PARADISE methodology to evaluating individual NLP components, linking commonly used intrinsic evaluation scores with extrinsic outcome metrics. We describe an evaluation of an interpretation component of a tutorial dialogue system, with student learning gain as the target outcome measure. We first describe the evaluation setup, which uses standard classification accuracy metrics for system evaluation (Section 2). We discuss the results of the intrinsic system evaluation in Section 3. We then show that standard evaluation metrics do not serve as good predictors of system performance for the system we evaluated. However, adding confusion matrix features improves the predictive model (Section 4). We argue that in practical applications such predictive metrics should be used alongside standard metrics for component evaluations, to better predict how different components will perform in the context of a specific task. We demonstrate how this technique can help differentiate the output quality between a majority class baseline, the system's output, and the output of a new classifier we trained on our data (Section 5). Finally, we discuss some limitations and possible extensions to this approach (Section 6).

2 Evaluation Procedure

2.1 Data Collection

We collected transcripts of students interacting with BEETLE II (Dzikovska et al., 2010b), a tutorial dialogue system for teaching conceptual knowledge in the basic electricity and electronics domain. The system is a learning environment with a self-contained curriculum targeted at students with no knowledge of high school physics. When interacting with the system, students spend 3-5 hours going through pre-prepared reading material, building and observing circuits in a simulator, and talking with a dialogue-based computer tutor via a text-based chat interface.

During the interaction, students can be asked two types of questions. Factual questions require them to name a set of objects or a simple property, e.g., "Which components in circuit 1 are in a closed path?" or "Are bulbs A and B wired in series or in parallel". Explanation and definition questions require longer answers that consist of 1-2 sentences, e.g., "Why was bulb A on when switch Z was open?" (expected answer "Because it was still in a closed path with the battery") or "What is voltage?" (expected answer "Voltage is the difference in states between two terminals"). We focus on the performance of the system on these long-answer questions, since reacting to them appropriately requires processing more complex input than factual questions.

We collected a corpus of 35 dialogues from paid undergraduate volunteers interacting with the system as part of a formative system evaluation. Each student completed a multiple-choice test assessing their knowledge of the material before and after the session. In addition, system logs contained information about how each student's utterance was interpreted. The resulting data set contains 3426 student answers grouped into 35 subsets, paired with test results. The answers were then manually annotated to create a gold standard evaluation corpus.

2.2 BEETLE II Interpretation Output

The interpretation component of BEETLE II uses a syntactic parser and a set of hand-authored rules to extract the domain-specific semantic representations of student utterances from the text. The student answer is first classified with respect to its domain-specific speech act, as follows:

- Answer: a contentful expression to which the system responds with a tutoring action, either accepting it as correct or remediating the problems as discussed in (Dzikovska et al., 2010a).
- Help request: any expression indicating that the student does not know the answer and without domain content.
- Social: any expression such as "sorry" which appears to relate to social interaction and has no recognizable domain content.
- Uninterpretable: the system could not arrive at any interpretation of the utterance. It will respond by identifying the likely source of error, if possible (e.g., a word it does not understand) and asking the student to rephrase their utterance (Dzikovska et al., 2009).

If the student utterance was determined to be an answer, it is further diagnosed for correctness as discussed in (Dzikovska et al., 2010b), using a domain reasoner together with semantic representations of expected correct answers supplied by human tutors. The resulting diagnosis contains the following information:

- Consistency: whether the student statement correctly describes the facts mentioned in the question and the simulation environment: e.g., student saying "Switch X is closed" is labeled inconsistent if the question stipulated that this switch is open.
- Diagnosis: an analysis of how well the student's explanation matches the expected answer. It consists of 4 parts
  - Matched: parts of the student utterance that matched the expected answer
  - Contradictory: parts of the student utterance that contradict the expected answer
  - Extra: parts of the student utterance that do not appear in the expected answer
  - Not-mentioned: parts of the expected answer missing from the student utterance.

The speech act and the diagnosis are passed to the tutorial planner which makes decisions about feedback. They constitute the output of the interpretation component, and its quality is likely to affect the learning outcomes, therefore we need an effective way to evaluate it. In future work, performance of individual pipeline components could also be evaluated in a similar fashion.

2.3 Data Annotation

The general idea of breaking down the student answer into correct, incorrect and missing parts is common in tutorial dialogue systems (Nielsen et al., 2008; Dzikovska et al., 2010b; Jordan et al., 2006). However, representation details are highly system specific, and difficult and time-consuming to annotate. Therefore we implemented a simplified annotation scheme which classifies whole answers as correct, partially correct but incomplete, or contradictory, without explicitly identifying the correct and incorrect parts. This makes it easier to create the gold standard and still retains useful information, because tutoring systems often choose the tutoring strategy based on the general answer class (correct, incomplete, or contradictory). In addition, this allows us to cast the problem in terms of classifier evaluation, and to use standard classifier evaluation metrics. If more detailed annotations were available, this approach could easily be extended, as discussed in Section 6.

We employed a hierarchical annotation scheme shown in Figure 1, which is a simplification of the DeMAND coding scheme (Campbell et al., 2009). Student utterances were first annotated as either related to domain content, or not containing any domain content, but expressing the student's metacognitive state or attitudes. Utterances expressing domain content were then coded with respect to their correctness, as being fully correct, partially correct but incomplete, containing some errors (rather than just omissions) or irrelevant[1]. The "irrelevant" category was used for utterances which were correct in general but which did not directly answer the question. Inter-annotator agreement for this annotation scheme on the corpus was $\kappa = 0.69$.

The speech acts and diagnoses logged by the system can be automatically mapped into our annotation labels. Help requests and social acts are assigned the "non-content" label; answers are assigned a label based on which diagnosis fields were filled: "contradictory" for those answers labeled as either inconsistent, or containing something in the contradictory field; "incomplete" if there is something not mentioned, but something matched as well, and "irrelevant" if nothing matched (i.e., the entire expected answer is in not-mentioned). Finally, uninterpretable utterances are treated as unclassified, analogous to a situation where a statistical classifier does not output a label for an input because the classification probability is below its confidence threshold.

This mapping was then compared against the manually annotated labels to compute the intrinsic evaluation scores for the BEETLE II interpreter described in Section 3.

3 Intrinsic Evaluation Results

The interpretation component of BEETLE II was developed based on the transcripts of 8 sessions

[1]Several different subcategories of non-content utterances, and of contradictory utterances, were recorded. However, they resulting classes were too small and so were collapsed into a single category for purposes of this study.

Category	Subcategory	Description
Non-content		Metacognitive and social expressions without domain content, e.g., "I don't know", "I need help", "you are stupid"
Content		The utterance includes domain content.
	correct	The student answer is fully correct
	pc_incomplete	The student said something correct, but incomplete, with some parts of the expected answer missing
	contradictory	The student's answer contains something incorrect or contradicting the expected answer, rather than just an omission
	irrelevant	The student's statement is correct in general, but it does not answer the question.

Figure 1: Annotation scheme used in creating the gold standard

Label	Count	Frequency
correct	1438	0.43
pc_incomplete	796	0.24
contradictory	808	0.24
irrelevant	105	0.03
non_content	232	0.07

Table 1: Distribution of annotated labels in the evaluation corpus

of students interacting with earlier versions of the system. These sessions were completed prior to the beginning of the experiment during which our evaluation corpus was collected, and are not included in the corpus. Thus, the corpus constitutes unseen testing data for the BEETLE II interpreter.

Table 1 shows the distribution of codes in the annotated data. The distribution is unbalanced, and therefore in our evaluation results we use two different ways to average over per-class evaluation scores. Macro-average combines per-class scores disregarding the class sizes; micro-average weighs the per-class scores by class size. The overall classification accuracy (defined as the number of correctly classified instances out of all instances) is mathematically equivalent to micro-averaged recall; however, macro-averaging better reflects performance on small classes, and is commonly used for unbalanced classification problems (see, e.g., (Lewis, 1991)).

The detailed evaluation results are presented in Table 2. We will focus on two metrics: the overall classification accuracy (listed as "micro-averaged recall" as discussed above), and the macro-averaged F score.

The majority class baseline is to assign "correct" to every instance. Its overall accuracy is 43%, the same as BEETLE II. However, this is obviously not a good choice for a tutoring system, since students who make mistakes will never get tutoring feedback. This is reflected in a much lower value of the F score (0.12 macroaverage F score for baseline vs. 0.44 for BEETLE II). Note also that there is a large difference in the micro- and macro- averaged scores. It is not immediately clear which of these metrics is the most important, and how they relate to actual system performance. We discuss machine learning models to help answer this question in the next section.

4 Linking Evaluation Measures to Outcome Measures

Although the intrinsic evaluation shows that the BEETLE II interpreter performs better than the baseline on the F score, ultimately system developers are not interested in improving interpretation for its own sake: they want to know whether the time spent on improvements, and the complications in system design which may accompany them, are worth the effort. Specifically, do such changes translate into improvement in overall system performance?

To answer this question without running expensive user studies we can build a model which predicts likely outcomes based on the data observed so far, and then use the model's predictions as an additional evaluation metric. We chose a multiple linear regression model for this task, linking the classification scores with learning gain as measured during the data collection. This approach follows the general PARADISE approach (Walker et al., 2000), but while PARADISE is typically used to determine which system components need

Label	baseline			BEETLE II		
	prec.	recall	F1	prec.	recall	F1
correct	0.43	1.00	0.60	0.93	0.52	0.67
pc_incomplete	0.00	0.00	0.00	0.42	0.53	0.47
contradictory	0.00	0.00	0.00	0.57	0.22	0.31
irrelevant	0.00	0.00	0.00	0.17	0.15	0.16
non-content	0.00	0.00	0.00	0.91	0.41	0.57
macroaverage	0.09	0.20	0.12	0.60	0.37	0.44
microaverage	0.18	0.43	0.25	0.70	0.43	0.51

Table 2: Intrinsic Evaluation Results for the BEETLE II and a majority class baseline

the most improvement, we focus on finding a better performance metric for a single component (interpretation), using standard evaluation scores as features.

Recall from Section 2.1 that each participant in our data collection was given a pre-test and a post-test, measuring their knowledge of course material. The test score was equal to the proportion of correctly answered questions. The normalized learning gain, $\frac{post-pre}{1-pre}$ is a metric typically used to assess system quality in intelligent tutoring, and this is the metric we are trying to model.

Thus, the training data for our model consists of 35 instances, each corresponding to a single dialogue and the learning gain associated with it. We can compute intrinsic evaluation scores for each dialogue, in order to build a model that predicts that student's learning gain based on these scores. If the model's predictions are sufficiently reliable, we can also use them for predicting the learning gain that a student could achieve when interacting with a new version of the interpretation component for the system, not yet tested with users. We can then use the predicted score to compare different implementations and choose the one with the highest predicted learning gain.

4.1 Features

Table 4 lists the feature sets we used. We tried two basic types of features. First, we used the evaluation scores reported in the previous section as features. Second, we hypothesized that some errors that the system makes are likely to be worse than others from a tutoring perspective. For example, if the student gives a contradictory answer, accepting it as correct may lead to student misconceptions; on the other hand, calling an irrelevant answer "partially correct but incomplete" may be less of a problem. Therefore, we computed separate confusion matrices for each student. We normalized each confusion matrix cell by the total number of incorrect classifications for that student. We then added features based on confusion frequencies to our feature set.[2]

Ideally, we should add 20 different features to our model, corresponding to every possible confusion. However, we are facing a sparse data problem, illustrated by the overall confusion matrix for the corpus in Table 3. For example, we only observed 25 instances where a contradictory utterance was miscategorized as correct (compared to 200 "contradictory–pc_incomplete" confusions), and so for many students this misclassification was never observed, and predictions based on this feature are not likely to be reliable. Therefore, we limited our features to those misclassifications that occurred at least twice for each student (i.e., at least 70 times in the entire corpus). The list of resulting features is shown in the "conf" row of Table 4. Since only a small number of features was included, this limits the applicability of the model we derived from this data set to the systems which make similar types of confusions. However, it is still interesting to investigate whether confusion probabilities provide additional information compared to standard evaluation metrics. We discuss how better coverage could be obtained in Section 6.

4.2 Regression Models

Table 5 shows the regression models we obtained using different feature sets. All models were obtained using stepwise linear regression, using the Akaike information criterion (AIC) for variable

[2]We also experimented with using % unclassified as an additional feature, since % of rejections is known to be a problem for spoken dialogue systems. However, it did not improve the models, and we do not report it here for brevity.

	Actual				
Predicted	contradictory	correct	irrelevant	non-content	pc_incomplete
contradictory	175	86	3	0	43
correct	25	752	1	4	26
irrelevant	31	12	16	4	29
non-content	1	3	2	95	3
pc_incomplete	200	317	40	28	419

Table 3: Confusion matrix for BEETLE II. System predicted values are in rows; actual values in columns.

selection implemented in the R stepwise regression library. As measures of model quality, we report R^2, the percentage of variance accounted for by the models (a typical measure of fit in regression modeling), and mean squared error (MSE). These were estimated using leave-one-out cross-validation, since our data set is small.

We used feature ablation to evaluate the contribution of different features. First, we investigated models using precision, recall or F-score alone. As can be seen from the table, precision is not predictive of learning gain, while F-score and recall perform similarly to one another, with $R^2 = 0.12$. In comparison, the model using only confusion frequencies has substantially higher estimated R^2 and a lower MSE.[3] In addition, out of the 3 confusion features, only one is selected as predictive. This supports our hypothesis that different types of errors may have different importance within a practical system.

The confusion frequency feature chosen by the stepwise model ("predicted-pc_incomplete-actual-contradictory") has a reasonable theoretical justification. Previous research shows that students who give more correct or partially correct answers, either in human-human or human-computer dialogue, exhibit higher learning gains, and this has been established for different systems and tutoring domains (Litman et al., 2009). Consequently, % of contradictory answers is negatively predictive of learning gain. It is reasonable to suppose, as predicted by our model, that systems that do not identify such answers well, and therefore do not remediate them correctly, will do worse in terms of learning outcomes.

Based on this initial finding, we investigated the models that combined either F scores or the full set of intrinsic evaluation scores with confusion frequencies. Note that if the full set of metrics (precision, recall, F score) is used, the model derives a more complex formula which covers about 33% of the variance. Our best models, however, combine the averaged scores with confusion frequencies, resulting in a higher R^2 and a lower MSE (22% relative decrease between the "scores.f" and "conf+scores.f" models in the table). This shows that these features have complementary information, and that combining them in an application-specific way may help to predict how the components will behave in practice.

5 Using prediction models in evaluation

The models from Table 5 can be used to compare different possible implementations of the interpretation component, under the assumption that the component with a higher predicted learning gain score is more appropriate to use in an ITS. To show how our predictive models can be used in making implementation decisions, we compare three possible choices for an interpretation component: the original BEETLE II interpreter, the baseline classifier described earlier, and a new decision tree classifier trained on our data.

We built a decision tree classifier using the Weka implementation of C4.5 pruned decision trees, with default parameters. As features, we used lexical similarity scores computed by the `Text::Similarity` package[4]. We computed 8 features: the similarity between student answer and either the expected answer text or the question text, using 4 different scores: raw number of overlapping words, F1 score, lesk score and cosine score. Its intrinsic evaluation scores are shown in Table 6, estimated using 10-fold cross-validation.

We can compare BEETLE II and baseline classifier using the "scores.all" model. The predicted

[3]The decrease in MSE is not statistically significant, possibly because of the small data set. However, since we observe the same pattern of results across our models, it is still useful to examine.

[4]http://search.cpan.org/dist/Text-Similarity/

Name	Variables
scores.fm	fmeasure.microaverage, fmeasure.macroaverage, fmeasure.correct, fmeasure.contradictory, fmeasure.pc_incomplete,fmeasure.non-content, fmeasure.irrelevant
scores.precision	precision.microaverage, precision.macroaverage, precision.correct, precision.contradictory, precision.pc_incomplete,precision.non-content, precision.irrelevant
scores.recall	recall.microaverage, recall.macroaverage, recall.correct, recall.contradictory, recall.pc_incomplete,recall.non-content, recall.irrelevant
scores.all	scores.fm + scores.precision + scores.recall
conf	Freq.predicted.contradictory.actual.correct, Freq.predicted.pc_incomplete.actual.correct, Freq.predicted.pc_incomplete.actual.contradictory

Table 4: Feature sets for regression models

Variables	Cross-validation R^2	Cross-validation MSE	Formula
scores.f	0.12 (0.02)	0.0232 (0.0302)	$0.32 + 0.56 * fmeasure.microaverage$
scores.precision	0.00 (0.00)	0.0242 (0.0370)	0.61
scores.recall	0.12 (0.02)	0.0232 (0.0310)	$0.37 + 0.56 * recall.microaverage$
conf	0.25 (0.03)	0.0197 (0.0262)	$0.74 - 0.56 * Freq.predicted.pc\_incomplete.actual.contradictory$
scores.all	0.33 (0.03)	0.0218 (0.0264)	$0.63 + 4.20 * fmeasure.microaverage - 1.30 * precision.microaverage - 2.79 * recall.microaverage - 0.07 * recall.non - content$
conf+scores.f	0.36 (0.03)	0.0179 (0.0281)	$0.52 - 0.66 * Freq.predicted.pc\_incomplete.actual.contradictory + 0.42 * fmeasure.correct - 0.07 * fmeasure.non - content$
full (conf+scores.all)	0.49 (0.02)	0.0189 (0.0248)	$0.88 - 0.68 * Freq.predicted.pc\_incomplete.actual.contradictory - 0.06 * precision.non\_domain + 0.28 * recall.correct - 0.79 * precision.microaverage + 0.65 * fmeasure.microaverage$

Table 5: Regression models for learning gain. R^2 and MSE estimated with leave-one-out cross-validation. Standard deviation in parentheses.

score for BEETLE II is 0.66. The predicted score for the baseline is 0.28. We cannot use the models based on confusion scores ("conf", "conf+scores.f" or "full") for evaluating the baseline, because the confusions it makes are always to predict that the answer is correct when the actual label is "incomplete" or "contradictory". Such situations were too rare in our training data, and therefore were not included in the models (as discussed in Section 4.1). Additional data will need to be collected before this model can reasonably predict baseline behavior.

Compared to our new classifier, BEETLE II has lower overall accuracy (0.43 vs. 0.53), but performs micro- and macro- averaged scores. BEETLE II precision is higher than that of the classifier. This is not unexpected given how the system was designed: since misunderstandings caused dialogue breakdown in pilot tests, the interpreter was built to prefer rejecting utterances as uninterpretable rather than assigning them to an incorrect class, leading to high precision but lower recall.

However, we can use all our predictive models to evaluate the classifier. We checked the the confusion matrix (not shown here due to space limitations), and saw that the classifier made some of the same types of confusions that BEETLE II interpreter made. On the "scores.all" model, the predicted learning gain score for the classifier is 0.63, also very close to BEETLE II. But with the "conf+scores.all" model, the predicted score is 0.89, compared to 0.59 for BEETLE II, indicating that we should prefer the newly built classifier.

Looking at individual class performance, the classifier performs better than the BEETLE II interpreter on identifying "correct" and "contradictory" answers, but does not do as well for partially correct but incomplete, and for irrelevant answers. Using our predictive performance metric highlights the differences between the classifiers and effectively helps determine which confusion types are the most important.

One limitation of this prediction, however, is that the original system's output is considerably more complex: the BEETLE II interpreter explicitly identifies correct, incorrect and missing parts of the student answer which are then used by the system to formulate adaptive feedback. This is an important feature of the system because it allows for implementation of strategies such as acknowledging and restating correct parts of the answer. However, we could still use a classifier to "double-check" the interpreter's output. If the predictions made by the original interpreter and the classifier differ, and in particular when the classifier assigns the "contradictory" label to an answer, BEETLE II may choose to use a generic strategy for contradictory utterances, e.g. telling the student that their answer is incorrect without specifying the exact problem, or asking them to re-read portions of the material.

Label	prec.	recall	F1
correct	0.66	0.76	0.71
pc_incomplete	0.38	0.34	0.36
contradictory	0.40	0.35	0.37
irrelevant	0.07	0.04	0.05
non-content	0.62	0.76	0.68
macroaverage	0.43	0.45	0.43
microaverage	0.51	0.53	0.52

Table 6: Intrinsic evaluation scores for our newly built classifier.

6 Discussion and Future Work

In this paper, we proposed an approach for cost-sensitive evaluation of language interpretation within practical applications. Our approach is based on the PARADISE methodology for dialogue system evaluation (Walker et al., 2000). We followed the typical pattern of a PARADISE study, but instead of relying on a variety of features that characterize the interaction, we used scores that reflect only the performance of the interpretation component. For BEETLE II we could build regression models that account for nearly 50% variance in the desired outcomes, on par with models reported in earlier PARADISE studies (Möller et al., 2007; Möller et al., 2008; Walker et al., 2000; Larsen, 2003). More importantly, we demonstrated that combining averaged scores with features based on confusion frequencies improves prediction quality and allows us to see differences between systems which are not obvious from the scores alone.

Previous work on task-based evaluation of NLP components used RTE or information extraction as target tasks (Sammons et al., 2010; Yuret et al., 2010; Miyao et al., 2008), based on standard corpora. We specifically targeted applications which involve human-computer interaction, where running task-based evaluations is particularly expensive, and building a predictive model of system performance can simplify system development.

Our evaluation data limited the set of features that we could use in our models. For most confusion features, there were not enough instances in the data to build a model that would reliably predict learning gain for those cases. One way to solve this problem would be to conduct a user study in which the system simulates random errors appearing some of the time. This could provide the data needed for more accurate models.

The general pattern we observed in our data is that a model based on F-scores alone predicts only a small proportion of the variance. If a full set of metrics (including F-score, precision and recall) is used, linear regression derives a more complex equation, with different weights for precision and recall. Instead of the linear model, we may consider using a model based on F_β score, $F_\beta = (1 + \beta^2)\frac{PR}{\beta^2 P + R}$, and fitting it to the data to derive the β weight rather than using the standard F_1 score. We plan to investigate this in the future.

Our method would apply to a wide range of systems. It can be used straightforwardly with many current spoken dialogue systems which rely on classifiers to support language understanding in domains such as call routing and technical support (Gupta et al., 2006; Acomb et al., 2007). We applied it to a system that outputs more complex logical forms, but we showed that we could simplify its output to a set of labels which still allowed us to make informed decisions. Similar simplifications could be derived for other systems based on domain-specific dialogue acts typically used in dialogue management. For slot-based systems, it may be useful to consider concept accuracy for recognizing individual slot values. Finally, for tutoring systems it is possible to annotate the answers on a more fine-grained level. Nielsen et al. (2008) proposed an annotation scheme based on the output of a dependency parser, and trained a classifier to identify individual dependencies as "expressed", "contradicted" or "unaddressed". Their system could be evaluated using the same approach.

The specific formulas we derived are not likely to be highly generalizable. It is a well-known limitation of PARADISE evaluations that models built based on one system often do not perform well when applied to different systems (Möller et al., 2008). But using them to compare implementation variants during the system development, without re-running user evaluations, can provide important information, as we illustrated with an example of evaluating a new classifier we built for our interpretation task. Moreover, the confusion frequency feature that our models picked is consistent with earlier results from a different tutoring domain (see Section 4.2). Thus, these models could provide a starting point when making system development choices, which can then be confirmed by user evaluations in new domains.

The models we built do not fully account for the variance in the training data. This is expected, since interpretation performance is not the only factor influencing the objective outcome: other factors, such choosing the the appropriate tutoring strategy, are also important. Similar models could be built for other system components to account for their contribution to the variance. Finally, we could consider using different learning algorithms. Möller et al. (2008) examined decision trees and neural networks in addition to multiple linear regression for predicting user satisfaction in spoken dialogue. They found that neural networks had the best prediction performance for their task. We plan to explore other learning algorithms for this task as part of our future work.

7 Conclusion

In this paper, we described an evaluation of an interpretation component of a tutorial dialogue system using predictive models that link intrinsic evaluation scores with learning outcomes. We showed that adding features based on confusion frequencies for individual classes significantly improves the prediction. This approach can be used to compare different implementations of language interpretation components, and to decide which option to use, based on the predicted improvement in a task-specific target outcome metric trained on previous evaluation data.

Acknowledgments

We thank Natalie Steinhauser, Gwendolyn Campbell, Charlie Scott, Simon Caine, Leanne Taylor, Katherine Harrison and Jonathan Kilgour for help with data collection and preparation; and Christopher Brew for helpful comments and discussion. This work has been supported in part by the US ONR award N000141010085.

References

Kate Acomb, Jonathan Bloom, Krishna Dayanidhi, Phillip Hunter, Peter Krogh, Esther Levin, and Roberto Pieraccini. 2007. Technical support dialog systems: Issues, problems, and solutions. In *Proceedings of the Workshop on Bridging the Gap: Academic and Industrial Research in Dialog Technologies*, pages 25–31, Rochester, NY, April.

Gwendolyn C. Campbell, Natalie B. Steinhauser, Myroslava O. Dzikovska, Johanna D. Moore, Charles B. Callaway, and Elaine Farrow. 2009. The DeMAND coding scheme: A "common language" for representing and analyzing student discourse. In *Proceedings of 14th International Conference on Artificial Intelligence in Education (AIED), poster session*, Brighton, UK, July.

Myroslava O. Dzikovska, Charles B. Callaway, Elaine Farrow, Johanna D. Moore, Natalie B. Steinhauser, and Gwendolyn E. Campbell. 2009. Dealing with interpretation errors in tutorial dialogue. In *Proceedings of the SIGDIAL 2009 Conference*, pages 38–45, London, UK, September.

Myroslava Dzikovska, Diana Bental, Johanna D. Moore, Natalie B. Steinhauser, Gwendolyn E. Campbell, Elaine Farrow, and Charles B. Callaway. 2010a. Intelligent tutoring with natural language support in the Beetle II system. In *Sustaining TEL: From Innovation to Learning and Practice - 5th European Conference on Technology Enhanced Learning, (EC-TEL 2010)*, Barcelona, Spain, October.

Myroslava O. Dzikovska, Johanna D. Moore, Natalie Steinhauser, Gwendolyn Campbell, Elaine Farrow, and Charles B. Callaway. 2010b. Beetle II: a system for tutoring and computational linguistics experimentation. In *Proceedings of the 48th Annual Meeting of the Association for Computational Linguistics (ACL-2010) demo session*, Uppsala, Sweden, July.

Kate Forbes-Riley and Diane J. Litman. 2006. Modelling user satisfaction and student learning in a spoken dialogue tutoring system with generic, tutoring, and user affect parameters. In *Proceedings of the Human Language Technology Conference of the North American Chapter of the Association of Computational Linguistics (HLT-NAACL '06)*, pages 264–271, Stroudsburg, PA, USA.

Kate Forbes-Riley, Diane Litman, Amruta Purandare, Mihai Rotaru, and Joel Tetreault. 2007. Comparing linguistic features for modeling learning in computer tutoring. In *Proceedings of the 2007 conference on Artificial Intelligence in Education: Building Technology Rich Learning Contexts That Work*, pages 270–277, Amsterdam, The Netherlands. IOS Press.

Narendra K. Gupta, Gökhan Tür, Dilek Hakkani-Tür, Srinivas Bangalore, Giuseppe Riccardi, and Mazin Gilbert. 2006. The AT&T spoken language understanding system. *IEEE Transactions on Audio, Speech & Language Processing*, 14(1):213–222.

Pamela W. Jordan, Maxim Makatchev, and Umarani Pappuswamy. 2006. Understanding complex natural language explanations in tutorial applications. In *Proceedings of the Third Workshop on Scalable Natural Language Understanding*, ScaNaLU '06, pages 17–24.

Lars Bo Larsen. 2003. Issues in the evaluation of spoken dialogue systems using objective and subjective measures. In *Proceedings of the 2003 IEEE Workshop on Automatic Speech Recognition and Understanding*, pages 209–214.

David D. Lewis. 1991. Evaluating text categorization. In *Proceedings of the workshop on Speech and Natural Language*, HLT '91, pages 312–318, Stroudsburg, PA, USA.

Diane Litman, Johanna Moore, Myroslava Dzikovska, and Elaine Farrow. 2009. Using natural language processing to analyze tutorial dialogue corpora across domains and modalities. In *Proceedings of 14th International Conference on Artificial Intelligence in Education (AIED)*, Brighton, UK, July.

Yusuke Miyao, Rune Sætre, Kenji Sagae, Takuya Matsuzaki, and Jun'ichi Tsujii. 2008. Task-oriented evaluation of syntactic parsers and their representations. In *Proceedings of ACL-08: HLT*, pages 46–54, Columbus, Ohio, June.

Sebastian Möller, Paula Smeele, Heleen Boland, and Jan Krebber. 2007. Evaluating spoken dialogue systems according to de-facto standards: A case study. *Computer Speech & Language*, 21(1):26 – 53.

Sebastian Möller, Klaus-Peter Engelbrecht, and Robert Schleicher. 2008. Predicting the quality and usability of spoken dialogue services. *Speech Communication*, pages 730–744.

Rodney D. Nielsen, Wayne Ward, and James H. Martin. 2008. Learning to assess low-level conceptual understanding. In *Proceedings 21st International FLAIRS Conference*, Coconut Grove, Florida, May.

Mihai Rotaru and Diane J. Litman. 2006. Exploiting discourse structure for spoken dialogue performance analysis. In *Proceedings of the 2006 Conference on Empirical Methods in Natural Language Processing*, EMNLP '06, pages 85–93, Stroudsburg, PA, USA.

Mark Sammons, V.G.Vinod Vydiswaran, and Dan Roth. 2010. "Ask not what textual entailment can do for you...". In *Proceedings of the 48th Annual Meeting of the Association for Computational Linguistics*, pages 1199–1208, Uppsala, Sweden, July.

Marilyn A. Walker, Candace A. Kamm, and Diane J. Litman. 2000. Towards Developing General Models of Usability with PARADISE. *Natural Language Engineering*, 6(3).

Deniz Yuret, Aydin Han, and Zehra Turgut. 2010. SemEval-2010 task 12: Parser evaluation using textual entailments. In *Proceedings of the 5th International Workshop on Semantic Evaluation*, pages 51–56, Uppsala, Sweden, July.

Experimenting with Distant Supervision for Emotion Classification

Matthew Purver* and **Stuart Battersby**†
*Interaction Media and Communication Group †Chatterbox Analytics
School of Electronic Engineering and Computer Science
Queen Mary University of London
Mile End Road, London E1 4NS, UK
m.purver@qmul.ac.uk stuart@cbanalytics.co.uk

Abstract

We describe a set of experiments using automatically labelled data to train supervised classifiers for multi-class emotion detection in Twitter messages with no manual intervention. By cross-validating between models trained on different labellings for the same six basic emotion classes, and testing on manually labelled data, we conclude that the method is suitable for some emotions (happiness, sadness and anger) but less able to distinguish others; and that different labelling conventions are more suitable for some emotions than others.

1 Introduction

We present a set of experiments into classifying Twitter messages into the six basic emotion classes of (Ekman, 1972). The motivation behind this work is twofold: firstly, to investigate the possibility of detecting emotions of multiple classes (rather than purely positive or negative sentiment) in such short texts; and secondly, to investigate the use of *distant supervision* to quickly bootstrap large datasets and classifiers without the need for manual annotation.

Text classification according to *emotion* and *sentiment* is a well-established research area. In this and other areas of text analysis and classification, recent years have seen a rise in use of data from online sources and social media, as these provide very large, often freely available datasets (see e.g. (Eisenstein et al., 2010; Go et al., 2009; Pak and Paroubek, 2010) amongst many others). However, one of the challenges this poses is that of data annotation: given very large amounts of data, often consisting of very short texts, written in unconventional style and without accompanying metadata, audio/video signals or access to the author for disambiguation, how can we easily produce a gold-standard labelling for training and/or for evaluation and test? One possible solution that is becoming popular is crowd-sourcing the labelling task, as the easy access to very large numbers of annotators provided by tools such as Amazon's Mechanical Turk can help with the problem of dataset size; however, this has its own attendant problems of annotator reliability (see e.g. (Hsueh et al., 2009)), and cannot directly help with the inherent problem of ambiguity – using many annotators does not guarantee that they can understand or correctly assign the author's intended interpretation or emotional state.

In this paper, we investigate a different approach via *distant supervision* (see e.g. (Mintz et al., 2009)). By using conventional markers of emotional content within the texts themselves as a surrogate for explicit labels, we can quickly retrieve large subsets of (noisily) labelled data. This approach has the advantage of giving us direct access to the authors' own intended interpretation or emotional state, without relying on third-party annotators. Of course, the labels themselves may be noisy: ambiguous, vague or not having a direct correspondence with the desired classification. We therefore experiment with multiple such conventions with apparently similar meanings – here, emoticons (following (Read, 2005)) and Twitter hashtags – allowing us to examine the similarity of classifiers trained on independent labels but intended to detect the same underlying class. We also investigate the precision and correspondence of particular labels with the desired emotion classes by testing on a small set of manually labelled data.

We show that the success of this approach depends on both the conventional markers chosen and the emotion classes themselves. Some emotions are both reliably marked by different conventions and distinguishable from other emotions; this seems particularly true for *happiness*, *sadness* and *anger*, indicating that this approach can provide not only the basic distinction required for sentiment analysis but some more finer-grained information. Others are either less distinguishable from short text messages, or less reliably marked.

2 Related Work

2.1 Emotion and Sentiment Classification

Much research in this area has concentrated on the related tasks of *subjectivity* classification (distinguishing objective from subjective texts – see e.g. (Wiebe and Riloff, 2005)); and *sentiment* classification (classifying subjective texts into those that convey positive, negative and neutral sentiment – see e.g. (Pang and Lee, 2008)). We are interested in *emotion* detection: classifying subjective texts according to a finer-grained classification of the emotions they convey, and thus providing richer and more informative data for social media analysis than simple positive/negative sentiment. In this study we confine ourselves to the six basic emotions identified by Ekman (1972) as being common across cultures; other finer-grained classifications are of course available.

2.1.1 Emotion Classification

The task of emotion classification is by nature a multi-class problem, and classification experiments have therefore achieved lower accuracies than seen in the binary problems of sentiment and subjectivity classification. Danisman and Alpkocak (2008) used vector space models for the same six-way emotion classification we examine here, and achieved F-measures around 32%; Seol et al. (2008) used neural networks for an 8-way classification (hope, love, thank, neutral, happy, sad, fear, anger) and achieved per-class accuracies of 45% to 65%. Chuang and Wu (2004) used supervised classifiers (SVMs) and manually defined keyword features over a seven-way classification consisting of the same six-class taxonomy plus a *neutral* category, and achieved an average accuracy of 65.5%, varying from 56% for *disgust* to 74% for *anger*. However, they achieved significant improvements using acoustic features available in their speech data, improving accuracies up to a maximum of 81.5%.

2.2 Conventions

As we are using text data, such intonational and prosodic cues are unavailable, as are the other rich sources of emotional cues we obtain from gesture, posture and facial expression in face-to-face communication. However, the prevalence of online text-based communication has led to the emergence of textual conventions understood by the users to perform some of the same functions as these acoustic and non-verbal cues. The most familiar of these is the use of emoticons, either Western-style (e.g. :), :-(etc.) or Eastern-style (e.g. (^_^), (>_<) etc.). Other conventions have emerged more recently for particular interfaces or domains; in Twitter data, one common convention is the use of *hashtags* to add or emphasise emotional content – see (1).

(1) a. Best day in ages! #Happy :)

b. Gets so #angry when tutors don't email back... Do you job idiots!

Linguistic and social research into the use of such conventions suggests that their function is generally to emphasise or strengthen the emotion or sentiment conveyed by a message, rather than to add emotional content which would not otherwise be present. Walther and D'Addario (2001) found that the contribution of emoticons towards the sentiment of a message was outweighed by the verbal content, although negative ones tended to shift interpretation towards the negative. Ip (2002) experimented with emoticons in instant messaging, with the results suggesting that emoticons do not add positivity or negativity but rather increase valence (making positive messages more positive and vice versa). Similarly Derks et al. (2008a; 2008b) found that emoticons are used in strengthening the intensity of a verbal message (although they serve other functions such as expressing humour), and hypothesized that they serve similar functions to actual nonverbal behavior; Provine et al. (2007) also found that emoticons are used to "punctuate" messages rather than replace lexical content, appearing in similar grammatical locations to verbal laughter and preserving phrase structure.

2.3 Distant Supervision

These findings suggest, of course, that emoticons and related conventional markers are likely to be useful features for sentiment and emotion classification. They also suggest, though, that they might be used as surrogates for manual emotion class labels: if their function is often to complement the verbal content available in messages, they should give us a way to automatically label messages according to emotional class, while leaving us with messages with enough verbal content to achieve reasonable classification.

This approach has been exploited in several ways in recent work; Tanaka et al. (2005) used Japanese-style emoticons as classification labels, and Go et al. (2009) and Pak and Paroubek (2010) used Western-style emoticons to label and classify Twitter messages according to positive and negative sentiment, using traditional supervised classification methods. The highest accuracies appear to have been achieved by Go et al. (2009), who used various combinations of features (unigrams, bigrams, part-of-speech tags) and classifiers (Naïve Bayes, maximum entropy, and SVMs), achieving their best accuracy of 83.0% with unigram and bigram features and a maximum entropy; using only unigrams with a SVM classifier achieved only slightly lower accuracy at 82.2%. Ansari (2010) then provides an initial investigation into applying the same methods to six-way emotion classification, treating each emotion independently as a binary classification problem and showing that accuracy varied with emotion class as well as with dataset size. The highest accuracies achieved were up to 81%, but these were on very small datasets (e.g. 81.0% accuracy on *fear*, but with only around 200 positive and negative data instances).

We view this approach as having several advantages; apart from the ease of data collection it allows by avoiding manual annotation, it gives us access to the author's own intended interpetations, as the markers are of course added by the authors themselves at time of writing. In some cases such as the examples of (1) above, the emotion conveyed may be clear to a third-party annotator; but in others it may not be clear at all without the marker – see (2):

(2) a. Still trying to recover from seeing the #bluewaffle on my TL #disgusted #sick

b. Leftover ToeJams with Kettle Salt and Vinegar chips. #stress #sadness #comfort #letsturnthisfrownupsidedown

3 Methodology

We used a collection of Twitter messages, all marked with emoticons or hashtags corresponding to one of Ekman (1972)'s six emotion classes. For emoticons, we used Ansari (2010)'s taxonomy, taken from the Yahoo messenger classification. For hashtags, we used emotion names themselves together with the main related adjective – both are used commonly on Twitter in slightly different ways as shown in (3); note that emotion names are often used as marked verbs as well as nouns. Details of the classes and markers are given in Table 1.

(3) a. Gets so #angry when tutors don't email back... Do you job idiots!

b. I'm going to say it, Paranormal Activity 2 scared me and I didn't sleep well last night because of it. #fear #demons

c. Girls that sleep w guys without even fully getting to know them #disgust me

Messages with multiple conventions (see (4)) were collected and used in the experiments, ensuring that the marker being used as a label in a particular experiment was not available as a feature in that experiment. Messages with no markers were not collected. While this prevents us from experimenting with the classification of neutral or objective messages, it would require manual annotation to distinguish these from emotion-carrying messages which are not marked. We assume that any implementation of the techniques we investigate here would be able to use a preliminary stage of subjectivity and/or sentiment detection to identify these messages, and leave this aside here.

(4) a. just because people are celebs they dont reply to your tweets! NOT FAIR #Angry :(I wish They would reply! #Please

Data was collected from Twitter's Streaming API service.[1] This provides a 1-2% random sample of all tweets with no constraints on language

[1] See `http://dev.twitter.com/docs/streaming-api`.

Table 1: Conventional markers used for emotion classes.

<table>
<tr><td>happy</td><td>:-) :) ;-) :D :P 8) 8-| <@o</td></tr>
<tr><td>sad</td><td>:-(:(;-(:-< :'(</td></tr>
<tr><td>anger</td><td>:-@ :@</td></tr>
<tr><td>fear</td><td>:| :-o :-O</td></tr>
<tr><td>surprise</td><td>:s :S</td></tr>
<tr><td>disgust</td><td>:$ +o(</td></tr>
<tr><td>happy</td><td>#happy #happiness</td></tr>
<tr><td>sad</td><td>#sad #sadness</td></tr>
<tr><td>anger</td><td>#angry #anger</td></tr>
<tr><td>fear</td><td>#scared #fear</td></tr>
<tr><td>surprise</td><td>#surprised #surprise</td></tr>
<tr><td>disgust</td><td>#disgusted #disgust</td></tr>
</table>

or location. These are collected in near real time and stored in a local database. An English language selection filter was applied; scripts collecting each conventional marker set were alternated throughout different times of day and days of the week to avoid any bias associated with e.g. weekends or mornings. The numbers of messages collected varied with the popularity of the markers themselves: for emoticons, we obtained a maximum of 837,849 (for happy) and a minimum of 10,539 for anger; for hashtags, a maximum of 10,219 for happy and a minimum of 536 for disgust.[2]

Classification in all experiments was using support vector machines (SVMs) (Vapnik, 1995) via the LIBSVM implementation of Chang and Lin (2001) with a linear kernel and unigram features. Unigram features included all words and hashtags (other than those used as labels in relevant experiments) after removal of URLs and Twitter usernames. Some improvement in performance might be available using more advanced features (e.g. n-grams), other classification methods (e.g. maximum entropy, as lexical features are unlikely to be independent) and/or feature weightings (e.g. the variant of TFIDF used for sentiment classification by Martineau (2009)). Here, our interest is more in the difference between the emotion and convention marker classes - we leave investigation of absolute performance for future work.

[2]One possible way to increase dataset sizes for the rarer markers might be to include synonyms in the hashtag names used; however, people's use and understanding of hashtags is not straightforwardly predictable from lexical form. Instead, we intend to run a longer-term data gathering exercise.

4 Experiments

Throughout, the markers (emoticons and/or hashtags) used as labels in any experiment were removed before feature extraction in that experiment – labels were not used as features.

4.1 Experiment 1: Emotion detection

To simulate the task of detecting emotion classes from a general stream of messages, we first built for each convention type C and each emotion class E a dataset D_E^C of size N containing (a) as positive instances, $N/2$ messages containing markers of the emotion class E and no other markers of type C, and (b) as negative instances, $N/2$ messages containing markers of type C of *any other* emotion class. For example, the positive instance set for emoticon-marked anger was based on those tweets which contained :-@ or :@, but none of the emoticons from the happy, sad, surprise, disgust or fear classes; any hashtags were allowed, including those associated with emotion classes. The negative instance set contained a representative sample of the same number of instances, with each having at least one of the happy, sad, surprise, disgust or fear emoticons but not containing :-@ or :@.

This of course excludes messages with no emotional markers; for this to act as an approximation of the general task therefore requires a assumption that unmarked messages reflect the same distribution over emotion classes as marked messages. For emotion-carrying but unmarked messages, this does seem intuitively likely, but requires investigation. For neutral objective messages it is clearly false, but as stated above we assume a preliminary stage of subjectivity detection in any practical application.

Performance was evaluated using 10-fold cross-validation. Results are shown as the **bold** figures in Table 2; despite the small dataset sizes in some cases, a χ^2 test shows all to be significantly different from chance. The best-performing classes show accuracies very similar to those achieved by Go et al. (2009) for their binary positive/negative classification, as might be expected; for emoticon markers, the best classes are happy, sad and anger; interestingly the best classes for hashtag markers are not the same

Table 2: Experiment 1: Within-class results. Same-convention (**bold**) figures are accuracies over 10-fold cross-validation; cross-convention (*italic*) figures are accuracies over full sets.

		Train	
Convention	Test	emoticon	hashtag
emoticon	happy	**79.8%**	*63.5%*
emoticon	sad	**79.9%**	*65.5%*
emoticon	anger	**80.1%**	*62.9%*
emoticon	fear	**76.2%**	*58.5%*
emoticon	surprise	**77.4%**	*48.2%*
emoticon	disgust	**75.2%**	*54.6%*
hashtag	happy	*67.7%*	**82.5%**
hashtag	sad	*67.1%*	**74.6%**
hashtag	anger	*62.8%*	**74.7%**
hashtag	fear	*60.6%*	**77.2%**
hashtag	surprise	*51.9%*	**67.4%**
hashtag	disgust	*64.6%*	**78.3%**

– `happy` performs best, but `disgust` and `fear` outperform `sad` and `anger`, and `surprise` performs particularly badly. For `sad`, one reason may be a dual meaning of the tag `#sad` (one emotional and one expressing ridicule); for `anger` one possibility is the popularity on Twitter of the game "Angry Birds"; for `surprise`, the data seems split between two rather distinct usages, ones expressing the author's emotion, but one expressing an intended effect on the audience (see (5)). However, deeper analysis is needed to establish the exact causes.

(5) a. broke 100 followers. #surprised im glad that the HOFF is one of them.

b. Who's excited for the Big Game? We know we are AND we have a #surprise for you!

To investigate whether the different convention types actually convey similar properties (and hence are used to mark similar messages) we then compared these accuracies to those obtained by training classifiers on the dataset for a different convention: in other words, for each emotion class E, train a classifier on dataset D_E^{C1} and test on D_E^{C2}. As the training and testing sets are different, we now test on the entire dataset rather than using cross-validation. Results are shown as the *italic* figures in Table 2; a χ^2 test shows all to be significantly different from the bold same-convention results. Accuracies are lower overall, but the highest figures (between 63% and 68%) are achieved for `happy`, `sad` and `anger`; here perhaps we can have some confidence that not only are the markers acting as predictable labels themselves, but also seem to be labelling the same thing (and therefore perhaps are actually labelling the emotion we are hoping to label).

4.2 Experiment 2: Emotion discrimination

To investigate whether these independent classifiers can be used in multi-class classification (distinguishing emotion classes from each other rather than just distinguishing one class from a general "other" set), we next cross-tested the classifiers between emotion classes: training models on one emotion and testing on the others – for each convention type C and each emotion class $E1$, train a classifier on dataset D_{E1}^C and test on D_{E2}^C, D_{E3}^C etc. The datasets in Experiment 1 had an uneven balance of emotion classes (including a high proportion of `happy` instances) which could bias results; for this experiment, therefore, we created datasets with an even balance of emotions among the negative instances. For each convention type C and each emotion class $E1$, we built a dataset D_{E1}^C of size N containing (a) as positive instances, $N/2$ messages containing markers of the emotion class $E1$ and no other markers of type C, and (b) as negative instances, $N/2$ messages consisting of $N/10$ messages containing only markers of class $E2$, $N/10$ messages containing only markers of class $E3$ etc. Results were then generated as in Experiment 1.

Within-class results are shown in Table 3 and are similar to those obtained in Experiment 1; again, differences between bold/italic results are statistically significant. Cross-class results are shown in Table 4. The `happy` class was well distinguished from other emotion classes for both convention types (i.e. cross-class classification accuracy is low compared to the within-class figures in italics and parentheses). The `sad` class also seems well distinguished when using hashtags as labels, although less so when using emoticons. However, other emotion classes show a surprisingly high cross-class performance in many cases – in other words, they are producing disappointingly similar classifiers.

This poor discrimination for negative emotion classes may be due to ambiguity or vagueness in the label, similarity of the verbal content associ-

Table 4: Experiment 2: Cross-class results. Same-class figures from 10-fold cross-validation are shown in *(italics)* for comparison; all other figures are accuracies over full sets.

		Train					
Convention	Test	happy	sad	anger	fear	surprise	disgust
emoticon	happy	*(78.1%)*	17.3%	39.6%	26.7%	28.3%	42.8%
emoticon	sad	16.5%	*(78.9%)*	59.1%	71.9%	69.9%	55.5%
emoticon	anger	29.8%	67.0%	*(79.7%)*	74.2%	76.4%	67.5%
emoticon	fear	27.0%	69.9%	64.4%	*(75.3%)*	74.0%	61.2%
emoticon	surprise	25.4%	69.9%	67.7%	76.3%	*(78.1%)*	66.4%
emoticon	disgust	42.2%	54.4%	61.1%	64.2%	64.1%	*(73.9%)*
hashtag	happy	*(81.1%)*	10.7%	45.3%	47.8%	52.7%	43.4%
hashtag	sad	13.8%	*(77.9%)*	47.7%	49.7%	46.5%	54.2%
hashtag	anger	44.6%	45.2%	*(74.3%)*	72.0%	63.0%	62.9%
hashtag	fear	45.0%	50.4%	68.6%	*(74.7%)*	63.9%	60.7%
hashtag	surprise	51.5%	45.7%	67.4%	70.7%	*(70.2%)*	64.2%
hashtag	disgust	40.4%	53.5%	74.7%	71.8%	70.8%	*(74.2%)*

Table 3: Experiment 2: Within-class results. Same-convention (**bold**) figures are accuracies over 10-fold cross-validation; cross-convention (*italic*) figures are accuracies over full sets.

		Train	
Convention	Test	emoticon	hashtag
emoticon	happy	**78.1%**	*61.2%*
emoticon	sad	**78.9%**	*60.2%*
emoticon	anger	**79.7%**	*63.7%*
emoticon	fear	**75.3%**	*55.9%*
emoticon	surprise	**78.1%**	*53.1%*
emoticon	disgust	**73.9%**	*51.5%*
hashtag	happy	*68.7%*	**81.1%**
hashtag	sad	*65.4%*	**77.9%**
hashtag	anger	*63.9%*	**74.3%**
hashtag	fear	*58.9%*	**74.7%**
hashtag	surprise	*51.8%*	**70.2%**
hashtag	disgust	*55.4%*	**74.2%**

ated with the emotions, or of genuine frequent co-presence of the emotions. Given the close lexical specification of emotions in hashtag labels, the latter reasons seem more likely; however, with emoticon labels, we suspect that the emoticons themselves are often used in ambiguous or vague ways.

As one way of investigating this directly, we tested classifiers across labelling conventions as well as across emotion classes, to determine whether the (lack of) cross-class discrimination holds across convention marker types. In the case of ambiguity or vagueness of emoticons, we would expect emoticon-trained models to fail to discriminate hashtag-labelled test sets, but hashtag-trained models to discriminate emoticon-labelled test sets well; if on the other hand the cause lies in the overlap of verbal content or the emotions themselves, the effect should be similar in either direction. This experiment also helps determine in more detail whether the labels used label similar underlying properties.

Table 5 shows the results. For the three classes `happy`, `sad` and perhaps `anger`, models trained using emoticon labels do a reasonable job of distinguishing classes in hashtag-labelled data, and vice versa. However, for the other classes, discrimination is worse. Emoticon-trained models appear to give (undesirably) higher performance across emotion classes in hashtag-labelled data (for the problematic non-`happy` classes). Hashtag-trained models perform around the random 50% level on emoticon-labelled data for those classes, even when tested on nominally the same emotion as they are trained on. For both label types, then, the lower within-class and higher cross-class performance with these negative classes (`fear`, `surprise`, `disgust`) suggests that these emotion classes are genuinely hard to tell apart (they are all negative emotions, and may use similar words), or are simply often expressed simultaneously. The higher performance of emoticon-trained classifiers compared to hashtag-trained classifiers, though, also suggests vagueness or ambiguity in emoticons: data labelled with emoticons nominally thought to be

Table 5: Experiment 2: Cross-class, cross-convention results (train on hashtags, test on emoticons and vice versa). All figures are accuracies over full sets. Accuracies over 60% are shown in **bold**.

		Train					
Convention	Test	happy	sad	anger	fear	surprise	disgust
emoticon	happy	**61.2%**	40.4%	44.1%	47.4%	52.0%	45.9%
emoticon	sad	38.3%	**60.2%**	55.1%	51.5%	47.1%	53.9%
emoticon	anger	47.0%	48.0%	**63.7%**	56.2%	50.9%	56.6%
emoticon	fear	39.8%	57.7%	57.1%	55.9%	50.8%	56.1%
emoticon	surprise	43.7%	55.2%	59.2%	58.4%	53.1%	54.0%
emoticon	disgust	51.5%	48.0%	53.5%	55.1%	53.1%	51.5%
hashtag	happy	**68.7%**	32.5%	43.6%	32.1%	35.4%	50.4%
hashtag	sad	33.8%	**65.4%**	53.2%	**65.0%**	**61.8%**	48.8%
hashtag	anger	43.9%	55.5%	**63.9%**	59.6%	**60.4%**	53.0%
hashtag	fear	44.3%	54.6%	56.1%	58.9%	**61.5%**	54.3%
hashtag	surprise	54.2%	45.3%	49.8%	49.9%	51.8%	52.3%
hashtag	disgust	41.5%	57.6%	**61.6%**	**62.2%**	59.3%	55.4%

associated with `surprise` produces classifiers which perform well on data labelled with many other hashtag classes, suggesting that those emotions were present in the training data. Conversely, the more specific hashtag labels produce classifiers which perform poorly on data labelled with emoticons and which thus contains a range of actual emotions.

4.3 Experiment 3: Manual labelling

To confirm whether either (or both) set of automatic (distant) labels do in fact label the underlying emotion class intended, we used human annotators via Amazon's Mechanical Turk to label a set of 1,000 instances. These instances were all labelled with emoticons (we did not use hashtag-labelled data: as hashtags are so lexically close to the names of the emotion classes being labelled, their presence may influence labellers unduly)[3] and were evenly distributed across the 6 classes, in so far as indicated by the emoticons. Labellers were asked to choose the primary emotion class (from the fixed set of six) associated with the message; they were also allowed to specify if any other classes were also present. Each data instance was labelled by three different annotators.

Agreement between labellers was poor overall. The three annotators unanimously agreed in only 47% of cases overall; although two of three agreed in 83% of cases. Agreement was worst for the three classes already seen to be problematic: `surprise`, `fear` and `disgust`. To create our dataset for this experiment, we therefore took only instances which were given the same primary label by all labellers – i.e. only those examples which we could take as reliably and unambiguously labelled. This gave an unbalanced dataset, with numbers varying from 266 instances for `happy` to only 12 instances for each of `surprise` and `fear`. Classifiers were trained using the datasets from Experiment 2. Performance is shown in Table 6; given the imbalance between class numbers in the test dataset, evaluation is given as recall, precision and F-score for the class in question rather than a simple accuracy figure (which is biased by the high proportion of `happy` examples).

Table 6: Experiment 3: Results on manual labels.

Train	Class	Precision	Recall	F-score
emoticon	happy	79.4%	75.6%	**77.5%**
emoticon	sad	43.5%	73.2%	**54.5%**
emoticon	anger	62.2%	37.3%	**46.7%**
emoticon	fear	6.8%	63.6%	12.3%
emoticon	surprise	15.0%	90.0%	25.7%
emoticon	disgust	8.3%	25.0%	12.5%
hashtag	happy	78.9%	51.9%	**62.6%**
hashtag	sad	47.9%	81.7%	**60.4%**
hashtag	anger	58.2%	76.0%	**65.9%**
hashtag	fear	10.1%	81.8%	18.0%
hashtag	surprise	5.9%	60.0%	10.7%
hashtag	disgust	6.7%	66.7%	11.8%

[3]Although, of course, one may argue that they do the same for their intended audience of readers – in which case, such an effect is legitimate.

Again, results for `happy` are good, and correspond fairly closely to the levels of accuracy reported by Go et al. (2009) and others for the binary positive/negative sentiment detection task. Emoticons give significantly better performance than hashtags here. Results for `sad` and `anger` are reasonable, and provide a baseline for further experiments with more advanced features and classification methods once more manually annotated data is available for these classes. In contrast, hashtags give much better performance with these classes than the (perhaps vague or ambiguous) emoticons.

The remaining emotion classes, however, show poor performance for both labelling conventions. The observed low precision and high recall can be adjusted using classifier parameters, but F-scores are not improved. Note that Experiment 1 shows that both emoticon and hashtag labels are to some extent predictable, even for these classes; however, Experiment 2 shows that they may not be reliably different to each other, and Experiment 3 tells us that they do not appear to coincide well with human annotator judgements of emotions. More reliable labels may therefore be required; although we do note that the low reliability of the human annotations for these classes, and the correspondingly small amount of annotated data used in this evaluation, means we hesitate to draw strong conclusions about `fear`, `surprise` and `disgust`. An approach which considers multiple classes to be associated with individual messages may also be beneficial: using majority-decision labels rather than unanimous labels improves F-scores for `surprise` to 23-35% by including many examples also labelled as `happy` (although this gives no improvements for other classes).

5 Survey

To further detemine whether emoticons used as emotion class labels are ambiguous or vague in meaning, we set up a web survey to examine whether people could reliably classify these emoticons.

5.1 Method

Our survey asked people to match up which of the six emotion classes (selected from a drop-down menu) best matched each emoticon. Each drop-down menu included a 'Not Sure' option. To avoid any effect of ordering, the order of the emoticon list and each drop-down menu was randomised every time the survey page was loaded. The survey was distributed via Twitter, Facebook and academic mailing lists. Respondents were not given the opportunity to give their own definitions or to provide finer-grained classifications, as we wanted to establish purely whether they would reliably associate labels with the six emotions in our taxonomy.

5.2 Results

The survey was completed by 492 individuals; full results are shown in Table 7. It demonstrated agreement with the predefined emoticons for `sad` and most of the emoticons for `happy` (people were unsure what 8-| and <@o meant). For all the emoticons listed as `anger`, `surprise` and `disgust`, the survey showed that people are reliably *un*sure as to what these mean. For the emoticon `:-o` there was a direct contrast between the defined meaning and the survey meaning; the definition of this emoticon following Ansari (2010) was `fear`, but the survey reliably assigned this to `surprise`.

Given the small scale of the survey, we hesitate to draw strong conclusions about the emoticon meanings themselves (in fact, recent conversations with schoolchildren – see below – have indicated very different interpretations from these adult survey respondents). However, we do conclude that for most emotions outside `happy` and `sad`, emoticons may indeed be an unreliable label; as hashtags also appear more reliable in the classification experiments, we expect these to be a more promising approach for fine-grained emotion discrimination in future.

6 Conclusions

The approach shows reasonable performance at individual emotion label prediction, for both emoticons and hashtags. For some emotions (happiness, sadness and anger), performance across label conventions (training on one, and testing on the other) is encouraging; for these classes, performance on those manually labelled examples where annotators agree is also reasonable. This gives us confidence not only that the approach produces reliable classifiers which can predict the labels, but that these classifiers are actually detecting the desired underlying emotional classes,

Table 7: Survey results showing the defined emotion, the most popular emotion from the survey, the percentage of votes this emotion received, and the χ^2 significance test for the distribution of votes. These are indexed by emoticon.

<table>
<tr><th>Emoticon</th><th>Defined Emotion</th><th>Survey Emotion</th><th>% of votes</th><th>Significance of votes distribution</th></tr>
<tr><td>:-)</td><td>Happy</td><td>Happy</td><td>94.9</td><td>$\chi^2 = 3051.7$ ($p < 0.001$)</td></tr>
<tr><td>:)</td><td>Happy</td><td>Happy</td><td>95.5</td><td>$\chi^2 = 3098.2$ ($p < 0.001$)</td></tr>
<tr><td>;-)</td><td>Happy</td><td>Happy</td><td>87.4</td><td>$\chi^2 = 2541$ ($p < 0.001$)</td></tr>
<tr><td>:D</td><td>Happy</td><td>Happy</td><td>85.7</td><td>$\chi^2 = 2427.2$ ($p < 0.001$)</td></tr>
<tr><td>:P</td><td>Happy</td><td>Happy</td><td>59.1</td><td>$\chi^2 = 1225.4$ ($p < 0.001$)</td></tr>
<tr><td>8)</td><td>Happy</td><td>Happy</td><td>61.9</td><td>$\chi^2 = 1297.4$ ($p < 0.001$)</td></tr>
<tr><td>8-|</td><td>Happy</td><td>Not Sure</td><td>52.2</td><td>$\chi^2 = 748.6$ ($p < 0.001$)</td></tr>
<tr><td><@o</td><td>Happy</td><td>Not Sure</td><td>84.6</td><td>$\chi^2 = 2335.1$ ($p < 0.001$)</td></tr>
<tr><td>:-(</td><td>Sad</td><td>Sad</td><td>91.3</td><td>$\chi^2 = 2784.2$ ($p < 0.001$)</td></tr>
<tr><td>:(</td><td>Sad</td><td>Sad</td><td>89.0</td><td>$\chi^2 = 2632.1$ ($p < 0.001$)</td></tr>
<tr><td>;-(</td><td>Sad</td><td>Sad</td><td>67.9</td><td>$\chi^2 = 1504.9$ ($p < 0.001$)</td></tr>
<tr><td>:-<</td><td>Sad</td><td>Sad</td><td>56.1</td><td>$\chi^2 = 972.59$ ($p < 0.001$)</td></tr>
<tr><td>:'(</td><td>Sad</td><td>Sad</td><td>80.7</td><td>$\chi^2 = 2116$ ($p < 0.001$)</td></tr>
<tr><td>:-@</td><td>Anger</td><td>Not Sure</td><td>47.8</td><td>$\chi^2 = 642.47$ ($p < 0.001$)</td></tr>
<tr><td>:@</td><td>Anger</td><td>Not Sure</td><td>50.4</td><td>$\chi^2 = 691.6$ ($p < 0.001$)</td></tr>
<tr><td>:s</td><td>Surprise</td><td>Not Sure</td><td>52.2</td><td>$\chi^2 = 757.7$ ($p < 0.001$)</td></tr>
<tr><td>:$</td><td>Disgust</td><td>Not Sure</td><td>62.8</td><td>$\chi^2 = 1136$ ($p < 0.001$)</td></tr>
<tr><td>+o(</td><td>Disgust</td><td>Not Sure</td><td>64.2</td><td>$\chi^2 = 1298.1$ ($p < 0.001$)</td></tr>
<tr><td>:|</td><td>Fear</td><td>Not Sure</td><td>55.1</td><td>$\chi^2 = 803.41$ ($p < 0.001$)</td></tr>
<tr><td>:-o</td><td>Fear</td><td>Surprise</td><td>89.2</td><td>$\chi^2 = 2647.8$ ($p < 0.001$)</td></tr>
</table>

without requiring manual annotation. We therefore plan to pursue this approach with a view to improving performance by investigating training with combined mixed-convention datasets, and cross-training between classifiers trained on separate conventions.

However, this cross-convention performance is much better for some emotions (happiness, sadness and anger) than others (fear, surprise and disgust). Indications are that the poor performance on these latter emotion classes is to a large degree an effect of ambiguity or vagueness of the emoticon and hashtag conventions we have used as labels here; we therefore intend to investigate other conventions with more specific and/or less ambiguous meanings, and the combination of multiple conventions to provide more accurately/specifically labelled data. Another possibility might be to investigate approaches to analyse emoticons semantically on the basis of their shape, or use features of such an analysis – see (Ptaszynski et al., 2010; Radulovic and Milikic, 2009) for some interesting recent work in this direction.

Acknowledgements

The authors are supported in part by the Engineering and Physical Sciences Research Council (grants EP/J010383/1 and EP/J501360/1) and the Technology Strategy Board (R&D grant 700081). We thank the reviewers for their comments.

References

Saad Ansari. 2010. Automatic emotion tone detection in twitter. Master's thesis, Queen Mary University of London.

Chih-Chung Chang and Chih-Jen Lin, 2001. *LIBSVM: a library for Support Vector Machines*. Software available at `http://www.csie.ntu.edu.tw/~cjlin/libsvm`.

Ze-Jing Chuang and Chung-Hsien Wu. 2004. Multi-modal emotion recognition from speech and text. *Computational Linguistics and Chinese Language Processing*, 9(2):45–62, August.

Taner Danisman and Adil Alpkocak. 2008. Feeler: Emotion classification of text using vector space model. In *AISB 2008 Convention, Communication, Interaction and Social Intelligence*, volume 2, pages 53–59, Aberdeen.

Daantje Derks, Arjan Bos, and Jasper von Grumbkow. 2008a. Emoticons and online message interpretation. *Social Science Computer Review*, 26(3):379–388.

Daantje Derks, Arjan Bos, and Jasper von Grumbkow. 2008b. Emoticons in computer-mediated communication: Social motives and social context. *CyberPsychology & Behavior*, 11(1):99–101, February.

Jacob Eisenstein, Brendan O'Connor, Noah A. Smith, and Eric P. Xing. 2010. A latent variable model for geographic lexical variation. In *Proceedings of the 2010 Conference on Empirical Methods in Natural Language Processing*, pages 1277–1287, Cambridge, MA, October. Association for Computational Linguistics.

Paul Ekman. 1972. Universals and cultural differences in facial expressions of emotion. In J. Cole, editor, *Nebraska Symposium on Motivation 1971*, volume 19. University of Nebraska Press.

Alec Go, Richa Bhayani, and Lei Huang. 2009. Twitter sentiment classification using distant supervision. Master's thesis, Stanford University.

Pei-Yun Hsueh, Prem Melville, and Vikas Sindhwani. 2009. Data quality from crowdsourcing: A study of annotation selection criteria. In *Proceedings of the NAACL HLT 2009 Workshop on Active Learning for Natural Language Processing*, pages 27–35, Boulder, Colorado, June. Association for Computational Linguistics.

Amy Ip. 2002. The impact of emoticons on affect interpretation in instant messaging. Carnegie Mellon University.

Justin Martineau. 2009. Delta TFIDF: An improved feature space for sentiment analysis. *Artificial Intelligence*, 29:258–261.

Mike Mintz, Steven Bills, Rion Snow, and Dan Jurafsky. 2009. Distant supervision for relation extraction without labeled data. In *Proceedings of ACL-IJCNLP 2009*.

Alexander Pak and Patrick Paroubek. 2010. Twitter as a corpus for sentiment analysis and opinion mining. In *Proceedings of the 7th conference on International Language Resources and Evaluation*.

Bo Pang and Lillian Lee. 2008. Opinion mining and sentiment analysis. *Foundations and Trends in Information Retrieval*, 2(1–2):1–135.

Robert Provine, Robert Spencer, and Darcy Mandell. 2007. Emotional expression online: Emoticons punctuate website text messages. *Journal of Language and Social Psychology*, 26(3):299–307.

M. Ptaszynski, J. Maciejewski, P. Dybala, R. Rzepka, and K Araki. 2010. CAO: A fully automatic emoticon analysis system based on theory of kinesics. In *Proceedings of The 24th AAAI Conference on Artificial Intelligence (AAAI-10)*, pages 1026–1032, Atlanta, GA.

F. Radulovic and N. Milikic. 2009. Smiley ontology. In *Proceedings of The 1st International Workshop On Social Networks Interoperability*.

Jonathon Read. 2005. Using emoticons to reduce dependency in machine learning techniques for sentiment classification. In *Proceedings of the 43rd Meeting of the Association for Computational Linguistics*. Association for Computational Linguistics.

Young-Soo Seol, Dong-Joo Kim, and Han-Woo Kim. 2008. Emotion recognition from text using knowledge based ANN. In *Proceedings of ITC-CSCC*.

Y. Tanaka, H. Takamura, and M. Okumura. 2005. Extraction and classification of facemarks with kernel methods. In *Proceedings of IUI*.

Vladimir N. Vapnik. 1995. *The Nature of Statistical Learning Theory*. Springer.

Joseph Walther and Kyle D'Addario. 2001. The impacts of emoticons on message interpretation in computer-mediated communication. *Social Science Computer Review*, 19(3):324–347.

J. Wiebe and E. Riloff. 2005. Creating subjective and objective sentence classifiers from unannotated texts . In *Proceedings of the 6th International Conference on Computational Linguistics and Intelligent Text Processing (CICLing-05)*, volume 3406 of *Springer LNCS*. Springer-Verlag.

Feature-Rich Part-of-speech Tagging for Morphologically Complex Languages: Application to Bulgarian

Georgi Georgiev and Valentin Zhikov
Ontotext AD
135 Tsarigradsko Sh., Sofia, Bulgaria
{georgi.georgiev,valentin.zhikov}@ontotext.com

Petya Osenova and Kiril Simov
IICT, Bulgarian Academy of Sciences
25A Acad. G. Bonchev, Sofia, Bulgaria
{petya,kivs}@bultreebank.org

Preslav Nakov
Qatar Computing Research Institute, Qatar Foundation
Tornado Tower, floor 10, P.O. Box 5825, Doha, Qatar
pnakov@qf.org.qa

Abstract

We present experiments with part-of-speech tagging for Bulgarian, a Slavic language with rich inflectional and derivational morphology. Unlike most previous work, which has used a small number of grammatical categories, we work with 680 morpho-syntactic tags. We combine a large morphological lexicon with prior linguistic knowledge and guided learning from a POS-annotated corpus, achieving accuracy of 97.98%, which is a significant improvement over the state-of-the-art for Bulgarian.

1 Introduction

Part-of-speech (POS) tagging is the task of assigning each of the words in a given piece of text a contextually suitable grammatical category. This is not trivial since words can play different syntactic roles in different contexts, e.g., *can* is a noun in "*I opened a can of coke.*" but a verb in "*I can write.*" Traditionally, linguists have classified English words into the following eight basic POS categories: noun, pronoun, adjective, verb, adverb, preposition, conjunction, and interjection; this list is often extended a bit, e.g., with determiners, particles, participles, etc., but the number of categories considered is rarely more than 15.

Computational linguistics works with a larger inventory of POS tags, e.g., the Penn Treebank (Marcus et al., 1993) uses 48 tags: 36 for part-of-speech, and 12 for punctuation and currency symbols. This increase in the number of tags is partially due to finer granularity, e.g., there are special tags for determiners, particles, modal verbs, cardinal numbers, foreign words, existential *there*, etc., but also to the desire to encode morphological information as part of the tags.

For example, there are six tags for verbs in the Penn Treebank: VB (verb, base form; e.g., *sing*), VBD (verb, past tense; e.g., *sang*), VBG (verb, gerund or present participle; e.g., *singing*), VBN (verb, past participle; e.g., *sung*) VBP (verb, non-3rd person singular present; e.g., *sing*), and VBZ (verb, 3rd person singular present; e.g., *sings*); these tags are morpho-syntactic in nature. Other corpora have used even larger tagsets, e.g., the Brown corpus (Kučera and Francis, 1967) and the Lancaster-Oslo/Bergen (LOB) corpus (Johansson et al., 1986) use 87 and 135 tags, respectively.

POS tagging poses major challenges for morphologically complex languages, whose tagsets encode a lot of additional morpho-syntactic features (for most of the basic POS categories), e.g., gender, number, person, etc. For example, the BulTreeBank (Simov et al., 2004) for Bulgarian uses 680 tags, while the Prague Dependency Treebank (Hajič, 1998) for Czech has over 1,400 tags.

Below we present experiments with POS tagging for Bulgarian, which is an inflectional language with rich morphology. Unlike most previous work, which has used a reduced set of POS tags, we use all 680 tags in the BulTreeBank. We combine prior linguistic knowledge and statistical learning, achieving accuracy comparable to that reported for state-of-the-art systems for English.

The remainder of the paper is organized as follows: Section 2 provides an overview of related work, Section 3 describes Bulgarian morphology, Section 4 introduces our approach, Section 5 describes the datasets, Section 6 presents our experiments in detail, Section 7 discusses the results, Section 8 offers application-specific error analysis, and Section 9 concludes and points to some promising directions for future work.

2 Related Work

Most research on part-of-speech tagging has focused on English, and has relied on the Penn Treebank (Marcus et al., 1993) and its tagset for training and evaluation. The task is typically addressed as a sequential tagging problem; one notable exception is the work of Brill (1995), who proposed non-sequential transformation-based learning.

A number of different sequential learning frameworks have been tried, yielding 96-97% accuracy: Lafferty et al. (2001) experimented with conditional random fields (CRFs) (95.7% accuracy), Ratnaparkhi (1996) used a maximum entropy sequence classifier (96.6% accuracy), Brants (2000) employed a hidden Markov model (96.6% accuracy), Collins (2002) adopted an averaged perception discriminative sequence model (97.1% accuracy). All these models fix the order of inference from left to right.

Toutanova et al. (2003) introduced a cyclic dependency network (97.2% accuracy), where the search is bi-directional. Shen et al. (2007) have further shown that better results (97.3% accuracy) can be obtained using guided learning, a framework for bidirectional sequence classification, which integrates token classification and inference order selection into a single learning task and uses a perceptron-like (Collins and Roark, 2004) passive-aggressive classifier to make the easiest decisions first. Recently, Tsuruoka et al. (2011), proposed a simple perceptron-based classifier applied from left to right but augmented with a lookahead mechanism that searches the space of future actions, yielding 97.3% accuracy.

For morphologically complex languages, the problem of POS tagging typically includes morphological disambiguation, which yields a much larger number of tags. For example, for Arabic, Habash and Rambow (2005) used support vector machines (SVM), achieving 97.6% accuracy with 139 tags from the Arabic Treebank (Maamouri et al., 2003). For Czech, Hajič et al. (2001) combined a hidden Markov model (HMM) with linguistic rules, which yielded 95.2% accuracy using an inventory of over 1,400 tags from the Prague Dependency Treebank (Hajič, 1998). For Icelandic, Dredze and Wallenberg (2008) reported 92.1% accuracy with 639 tags developed for the Icelandic frequency lexicon (Pind et al., 1991), they used guided learning and tag decomposition: First, a coarse POS class is assigned (e.g., noun, verb, adjective), then, additional fine-grained morphological features like case, number and gender are added, and finally, the proposed tags are further reconsidered using non-local features. Similarly, Smith et al. (2005) decomposed the complex tags into factors, where models for predicting part-of-speech, gender, number, case, and lemma are estimated separately, and then composed into a single CRF model; this yielded competitive results for Arabic, Korean, and Czech.

Most previous work on Bulgarian POS tagging has started with large tagsets, which were then reduced. For example, Dojchinova and Mihov (2004) mapped their initial tagset of 946 tags to just 40, which allowed them to achieve 95.5% accuracy using the transformation-based learning of Brill (1995), and 98.4% accuracy using manually crafted linguistic rules. Similarly, Georgiev et al. (2009), who used maximum entropy and the BulTreeBank (Simov et al., 2004), grouped its 680 fine-grained POS tags into 95 coarse-grained ones, and thus improved their accuracy from 90.34% to 94.4%. Simov and Osenova (2001) used a recurrent neural network to predict (a) 160 morpho-syntactic tags (92.9% accuracy) and (b) 15 POS tags (95.2% accuracy).

Some researchers did not reduce the tagset: Savkov et al. (2011) used 680 tags (94.7% accuracy), and Tanev and Mitkov (2002) used 303 tags and the BULMORPH morphological analyzer (Krushkov, 1997), achieving P=R=95%.

3 Bulgarian Morphology

Bulgarian is an Indo-European language from the Slavic language group, written with the Cyrillic alphabet and spoken by about 9-12 million people. It is also a member of the Balkan Sprachbund and thus differs from most other Slavic languages: it has no case declensions, uses a suffixed definite article (which has a short and a long form for singular masculine), and lacks verb infinitive forms. It further uses special evidential verb forms to express unwitnessed, retold, and doubtful activities.

Bulgarian is an inflective language with very rich morphology. For example, Bulgarian verbs have 52 synthetic wordforms on average, while pronouns have altogether more than ten grammatical features (not necessarily shared by all pronouns), including case, gender, person, number, definiteness, etc.

This rich morphology inevitably leads to ambiguity proliferation; our analysis of BulTreeBank shows four major types of ambiguity:

1. Between the wordforms of the same lexeme, i.e., in the paradigm. For example, дивана, an inflected form of диван ('sofa', masculine), can mean (a) 'the sofa' (definite, singular, short definite article) or (b) a count form, e.g., as in два дивана ('two sofas').

2. Between two or more lexemes, i.e., conversion. For example, като can be (a) a subordinator meaning 'as, when', or (b) a preposition meaning 'like, such as'.

3. Between a lexeme and an inflected wordform of another lexeme, i.e., across-paradigms. For example, политика can mean (a) 'the politician' (masculine, singular, definite, short definite article) or (b) 'politics' (feminine, singular, indefinite).

4. Between the wordforms of two or more lexemes, i.e., across-paradigms and quasi-conversion. For example, върви can mean (a) 'walks' (verb, 2nd or 3rd person, present tense) or (b) 'strings, laces' (feminine, plural, indefinite).

Some morpho-syntactic ambiguities in Bulgarian are occasional, but many are systematic, e.g., neuter singular adjectives have the same forms as adverbs. Overall, most ambiguities are local, and thus arguably resolvable using n-grams, e.g., compare хубаво дете ('beautiful child'), where хубаво is a neuter adjective, and "Пея хубаво." ('I sing beautifully.'), where it is an adverb of manner. Other ambiguities, however, are non-local and may require discourse-level analysis, e.g., "Видях го." can mean 'I saw him.', where го is a masculine pronoun, or 'I saw it.', where it is a neuter pronoun. Finally, there are ambiguities that are very hard or even impossible[1] to resolve, e.g., "Детето влезе весело." can mean both 'The child came in happy.' (весело is an adjective) and 'The child came in happily.' (it is an adverb); however, the latter is much more likely.

[1]The problem also exists for English, e.g., the annotators of the Penn Treebank were allowed to use tag combinations for inherently ambiguous cases: JJ|NN (adjective or noun as prenominal modifier), JJ|VBG (adjective or gerund/present participle), JJ|VBN (adjective or past participle), NN|VBG (noun or gerund), and RB|RP (adverb or particle).

In many cases, strong domain preferences exist about how various systematic ambiguities should be resolved. We made a study for the newswire domain, analyzing a corpus of 546,029 words, and we found that ambiguity type 2 (lexeme-lexeme) prevailed for functional parts-of-speech, while the other types were more frequent for inflecting parts-of-speech. Below we show the most frequent types of morpho-syntactic ambiguities and their frequency in our corpus:

- на: preposition ('of') vs. emphatic particle, with a ratio of 28,554 to 38;
- да: auxiliary particle ('to') vs. affirmative particle, with a ratio of 12,035 to 543;
- е: 3rd person present auxiliary verb ('to be') vs. particle ('well') vs. interjection ('wow'), with a ratio of 9,136 to 21 to 5;
- singular masculine noun with a short definite article vs. count form of a masculine noun, with a ratio of 6,437 to 1,592;
- adverb vs. neuter singular adjective, with a ratio of 3,858 to 1,753.

Overall, the following factors should be taken into account when modeling Bulgarian morphosyntax: (1) locality vs. non-locality of grammatical features, (2) interdependence of grammatical features, and (3) domain-specific preferences.

4 Method

We used the guided learning framework described in (Shen et al., 2007), which has yielded state-of-the-art results for English and has been successfully applied to other morphologically complex languages such as Icelandic (Dredze and Wallenberg, 2008); we found it quite suitable for Bulgarian as well. We used the feature set defined in (Shen et al., 2007), which includes the following:

1. The feature set of Ratnaparkhi (1996), including prefix, suffix and lexical, as well as some bigram and trigram context features;

2. Feature templates as in (Ratnaparkhi, 1996), which have been shown helpful in bidirectional search;

3. More bigram and trigram features and bi-lexical features as in (Shen et al., 2007).

Note that we allowed prefixes and suffixes of length up to 9, as in (Toutanova et al., 2003) and (Tsuruoka and Tsujii, 2005).

We further extended the set of features with the tags proposed for the current word token by a morphological lexicon, which maps words to possible tags; it is exhaustive, i.e., the correct tag is always among the suggested ones for each token.

We also used 70 linguistically-motivated, high-precision rules in order to further reduce the number of possible tags suggested by the lexicon. The rules are similar to those proposed by Hinrichs and Trushkina (2004) for German; we implemented them as constraints in the CLaRK system (Simov et al., 2003).

Here is an example of a rule: If a wordform is ambiguous between a masculine count noun (Ncmt) and a singular short definite masculine noun (Ncmsh), the Ncmt tag should be chosen if the previous token is a numeral or a number.

The 70 rules were developed by linguists based on observations over the training dataset only. They target primarily the most frequent cases of ambiguity, and to a lesser extent some infrequent but very problematic cases. Some rules operate over classes of words, while other refer to particular wordforms. The rules were designed to be 100% accurate on our training dataset; our experiments show that they are also 100% accurate on the test and on the development dataset.

Note that some of the rules are dependent on others, and thus the order of their cascaded application is important. For example, the wordform я is ambiguous between an accusative feminine singular short form of a personal pronoun ('her') and an interjection ('wow'). To handle this properly, the rule for interjection, which targets sentence initial positions, followed by a comma, needs to be executed first. The rule for personal pronouns is only applied afterwards.

Word	Tags
Той	**Ppe-os3m**
обаче	*Cc*; **Dd**
няма	Afsi; Vnitf-o3s; Vnitf-r3s; Vpitf-o2s; Vpitf-o3s; **Vpitf-r3s**
възможност	**Ncfsi**
да	*Ta*;**Tx**
следи	*Ncfpi*; *Vpitf-o2s*; *Vpitf-o3s*; **Vpitf-r3s**; *Vpitz–2s*
. . .	. . .

Table 1: **Sample fragment showing the possible tags suggested by the lexicon.** The tags that are further filtered by the rules are in italic; the correct tag is bold.

The rules are quite efficient at reducing the POS ambiguity. On the test dataset, before the rule application, 34.2% of the tokens (excluding punctuation) had more than one tag in our morphological lexicon. This number is reduced to 18.5% after the cascaded application of the 70 linguistic rules. Table 1 illustrates the effect of the rules on a small sentence fragment. In this example, the rules have left only one tag (the correct one) for three of the ambiguous words. Since the rules in essence decrease the average number of tags per token, we calculated that the lexicon suggests 1.6 tags per token on average, and after the application of the rules this number decreases to 1.44 per token.

5 Datasets

5.1 BulTreeBank

We used the latest version of the BulTreeBank (Simov and Osenova, 2004), which contains 20,556 sentences and 321,542 word tokens (four times less than the English Penn Treebank), annotated using a total of 680 unique morpho-syntactic tags. See (Simov et al., 2004) for a detailed description of the BulTreeBank tagset.

We split the data into training/development/test as shown in Table 2. Note that only 552 of all 680 tag types were used in the training dataset, and the development and the test datasets combined contain a total of 128 new tag types that were not seen in the training dataset. Moreover, 32% of the word types in the development dataset and 31% of those in the testing dataset do not occur in the training dataset. Thus, data sparseness is an issue at two levels: word-level and tag-level.

Dataset	Sentences	Tokens	Types	Tags
Train	16,532	253,526	38,659	552
Dev	2,007	32,995	9,635	425
Test	2,017	35,021	9,627	435

Table 2: **Statistics about our datasets.**

5.2 Morphological Lexicon

In order to alleviate the data sparseness issues, we further used a large morphological lexicon for Bulgarian, which is an extended version of the dictionary described in (Popov et al., 1998) and (Popov et al., 2003). It contains over 1.5M inflected wordforms (for 110K lemmata and 40K proper names), each mapped to a set of possible morpho-syntactic tags.

6 Experiments and Evaluation

State-of-the-art POS taggers for English typically build a lexicon containing all tags a word type has taken in the training dataset; this lexicon is then used to limit the set of possible tags that an input token can be assigned, i.e., it imposes a hard constraint on the possibilities explored by the POS tagger. For example, if *can* has only been tagged as a verb and as a noun in the training dataset, it will be only assigned those two tags at test time; other tags such as adjective, adverb and pronoun will not be considered. Out-of-vocabulary words, i.e., those that were not seen in the training dataset, are constrained as well, e.g., to a small set of frequent open-class tags.

In our experiments, we used a morphological lexicon that is much larger than what could be built from the training corpus only: building a lexicon from the training corpus only is of limited utility since one can hardly expect to see in the training corpus all 52 synthetic forms a verb can possibly have. Moreover, we did not use the tags listed in the lexicon as hard constraints (except in one of our baselines); instead, we experimented with a different, non-restrictive approach: we used the lexicon's predictions as features or soft constraints, i.e., as suggestions only, thus allowing each token to take any possible tag. Note that for both known and out-of-vocabulary words we used all 680 tags rather than the 552 tags observed in the training dataset; we could afford to explore this huge search space thanks to the efficiency of the guided learning framework. Allowing all 680 tags on training helped the model by exposing it to a larger set of negative examples.

We combined these lexicon features with standard features extracted from the training corpus. We further experimented with the 70 contextual linguistic rules, using them (a) as soft and (b) as hard constraints. Finally, we set four baselines: three that do not use the lexicon and one that does.

#	Baselines	Accuracy (%) (token-level)
1	MFT + unknowns are wrong	78.10
2	MFT + unknowns are Ncmsi	78.52
3	MFT + guesser for unknowns	79.49
4	MFT + lexicon tag-classes	94.40

Table 3: **Most-frequent-tag (MFT) baselines.**

6.1 Baselines

First, we experimented with the most-frequent-tag baseline, which is standard for POS tagging. This baseline ignores context altogether and assigns each word type the POS tag it was most frequently seen with in the training dataset; ties are broken randomly. We coped with word types not seen in the training dataset using three simple strategies: (a) we considered them all wrong, (b) we assigned them Ncmsi, which is the most frequent open-class tag in the training dataset, or (c) we used a very simple guesser, which assigned Ncfsi, Ncnsi, Ncfsi, and Ncmsf, if the target word ended by -а, -о, -и, and -ът, respectively, otherwise, it assigned Ncmsi. The results are shown in lines 1-3 of Table 3: we can see that the token-level accuracy ranges in 78-80% for (a)-(c), which is relatively high, given that we use a large inventory of 680 morpho-syntactic tags.

We further tried a baseline that uses the above-described morphological lexicon, in addition to the training dataset. We first built two frequency lists, containing respectively (1) the most frequent tag in the training dataset for each word type, as before, and (2) the most frequent tag in the training dataset for each class of tags that can be assigned to some word type, according to the lexicon. For example, the most frequent tag for политика is Ncfsi, and the most frequent tag for the tag-class {Ncmt;Ncmsi} is Ncmt.

Given a target word type, this new baseline first tries to assign it the most frequent tag from the first list. If this is not possible, which happens (i) in case of ties or (ii) when the word type was not seen on training, it extracts the tag-class from the lexicon and consults the second list. If there is a single most frequent tag in the corpus for this tag-class, it is assigned; otherwise a random tag from this tag-class is selected.

Line 4 of Table 3 shows that this latter baseline achieves a very high accuracy of 94.40%. Note, however, that this is over-optimistic: the lexicon contains a tag-class for each word type in our testing dataset, i.e., while there can be word types not seen in the training dataset, there are no word types that are not listed in the lexicon. Thus, this high accuracy is probably due to a large extent to the scale and quality of our morphological lexicon, and it might not be as strong with smaller lexicons; we plan to investigate this in future work.

6.2 Lexicon Tags as Soft Constraints

We experimented with three types of features:

1. Word-related features only;

2. Word-related features + the tags suggested by the lexicon;

3. Word-related features + the tags suggested by the lexicon but then further filtered using the 70 contextual linguistic rules.

Table 4 shows the sentence-level and the token-level accuracy on the test dataset for the three kinds of features: shown on lines 1, 3 and 4, respectively. We can see that using the tags proposed by the lexicon as features (lines 3 and 4) has a major positive impact, yielding up to 49% error reduction at the token-level and up to 37% at the sentence-level, as compared to using word-related features alone (line 1).

Interestingly, filtering the tags proposed by the lexicon using the 70 contextual linguistic rules yields a minor decrease in accuracy both at the word token-level and at the sentence-level (compare line 4 to line 2). This is surprising since the linguistic rules are extremely reliable: they were designed to be 100% accurate on the training dataset, and we found them experimentally to be 100% correct on the development and on the testing dataset as well.

One possible explanation is that by limiting the set of available tags for a given token at training time, we prevent the model from observing some potentially useful negative examples. We tested this hypothesis by using the unfiltered lexicon predictions at training time but then making use of the filtered ones at testing time; the results are shown on line 5. We can observe a small increase in accuracy compared to line 4: from 97.80% to 97.84% at the token-level, and from 70.30% to 70.40% at the sentence-level. Although these differences are tiny, they suggest that having more negative examples at training is helpful.

We can conclude that using the lexicon as a source of soft constraints has a major positive impact, e.g., because it provides access to important external knowledge that is complementary to what can be learned from the training corpus alone; the improvements when using linguistic rules as soft constraints are more limited.

6.3 Linguistic Rules as Hard Constraints

Next, we experimented with using the suggestions of the linguistic rules as hard constraints. Table 4 shows that this is a very good idea. Comparing line 1 to line 2, which do not use the morphological lexicon, we can see very significant improvements: from 95.72% to 97.20% at the token-level and from 52.95% to 64.50% at the sentence-level. The improvements are smaller but still consistent when the morphological lexicon is used: comparing lines 3 and 4 to lines 6 and 7, respectively, we see an improvement from 97.83% to 97.91% and from 97.80% to 97.93% at the token-level, and about 1% absolute at the sentence-level.

6.4 Increasing the Beam Size

Finally, we increased the beam size of guided learning from 1 to 3 as in (Shen et al., 2007). Comparing line 7 to line 8 in Table 4, we can see that this yields further token-level improvement: from 97.93% to 97.98%.

7 Discussion

Table 5 compares our results to previously reported evaluation results for Bulgarian. The first four lines show the token-level accuracy for standard POS tagging tools trained and evaluated on the BulTreeBank:[2] TreeTagger (Schmid, 1994), which uses decision trees, TnT (Brants, 2000), which uses a hidden Markov model, SVMtool (Giménez and Màrquez, 2004), which is based on support vector machines, and ACOPOST (Schröder, 2002), implementing the memory-based model of Daelemans et al. (1996). The following lines report the token-level accuracy reported in previous work, as compared to our own experiments using guided learning.

We can see that we outperform by a very large margin (92.53% vs. 97.98%, which represents 73% error reduction) the systems from the first four lines, which are directly comparable to our experiments: they are trained and evaluated on the BulTreeBank using the full inventory of 680 tags.

We further achieved statistically significant improvement ($p < 0.0001$; Pearson's chi-squared test (Plackett, 1983)) over the best pervious result on 680 tags: from 94.65% to 97.98%, which represents 62.24% error reduction at the token-level.

[2] We used the pre-trained TreeTagger; for the rest, we report the accuracy given on the Webpage of the BulTreeBank: www.bultreebank.org/taggers/taggers.html

#	Lexicon (*source of*)	Linguistic Rules (applied to filter): (a) *the lexicon features*	(b) *the output tags*	Beam size	Accuracy (%) Sentence-level	Token-level
1	–	–	–	1	52.95	95.72
2	–	–	yes	1	64.50	97.20
3	features	–	–	1	70.40	97.83
4	features	yes	–	1	70.30	97.80
5	features	yes, *for test only*	–	1	70.40	97.84
6	features	–	yes	1	71.34	97.91
7	features	yes	yes	1	71.69	97.93
8	features	yes	yes	3	71.94	97.98

Table 4: **Evaluation results on the test dataset.** Line 1 shows the evaluation results when using features derived from the text corpus only; these features are used by all systems in the table. Line 2 further uses the contextual linguistic rules to limit the set of possible POS tags that can be predicted. Note that these rules (1) consult the lexicon, and (2) always predict a single POS tag. Line 3 uses the POS tags listed in the lexicon as features, i.e., as soft suggestions only. Line 4 is like line 3, but the list of feature-tags proposed by the lexicon is filtered by the contextual linguistic rules. Line 5 is like line 4, but the linguistic rules filtering is only applied at test time; it is not done on training. Lines 6 and 7 are similar to lines 3 and 4, respectively, but here the linguistic rules are further applied to limit the set of possible POS tags that can be predicted, i.e., the rules are used as hard constraints. Finally, line 8 is like line 7, but here the beam size is increased to 3.

Overall, we improved over almost all previously published results. Our accuracy is second only to the manual rules approach of Dojchinova and Mihov (2004). Note, however, that they used 40 tags only, i.e., their inventory is 17 times smaller than ours. Moreover, they have optimized their tagset specifically to achieve very high POS tagging accuracy by choosing not to attempt to resolve some inherently hard systematic ambiguities, e.g., they do not try to choose between second and third person past singular verbs, whose inflected forms are identical in Bulgarian and hard to distinguish when the subject is not present (Bulgarian is a pro-drop language).

In order to compare our results more closely to the smaller tagsets in Table 5, we evaluated our best model with respect to (a) the first letter of the tag only (which is part-of-speech only, no morphological information; 13 tags), e.g., Ncmsf becomes N, and (b) the first two letters of the tag (POS + limited morphological information; 49 tags), e.g., Ncmsf becomes Nc. This yielded 99.30% accuracy for (a) and 98.85% for (b). The latter improves over (Dojchinova and Mihov, 2004), while using a bit larger number of tags.

Our best token-level accuracy of 97.98% is comparable and even slightly better than the state-of-the-art results for English: 97.33% when using Penn Treebank data only (Shen et al., 2007), and 97.50% for Penn Treebank plus some additional unlabeled data (Søgaard, 2011). Of course, our results are only indirectly comparable to English.

Still, our performance is impressive because (1) our model is trained on 253,526 tokens only while the standard training sections 0-18 of the Penn Treebank contain a total of 912,344 tokens, i.e., almost four times more, and (2) we predict 680 rather than just 48 tags as for the Penn Treebank, which is 14 times more.

Note, however, that (1) we used a large external morphological lexicon for Bulgarian, which yielded about 50% error reduction (without it, our accuracy was 95.72% only), and (2) our train/dev/test sentences are generally shorter, and thus arguably simpler for a POS tagger to analyze: we have 17.4 words per test sentence in the BulTreeBank vs. 23.7 in the Penn Treebank.

Our results also compare favorably to the state-of-the-art results for other morphologically complex languages that use large tagsets, e.g., 95.2% for Czech with 1,400+ tags (Hajič et al., 2001), 92.1% for Icelandic with 639 tags (Dredze and Wallenberg, 2008), 97.6% for Arabic with 139 tags (Habash and Rambow, 2005).

8 Error Analysis

In this section, we present error analysis with respect to the impact of the POS tagger's performance on other processing steps in a natural language processing pipeline, such as lemmatization and syntactic dependency parsing.

First, we explore the most frequently confused pairs of tags for our best-performing POS tagging system; these are shown in Table 6.

Tool/Authors	Method	# Tags	Accuracy (token-level, %)
*TreeTagger	Decision Trees	680	89.21
*ACOPOST	Memory-based Learning	680	89.91
*SVMtool	Support Vector Machines	680	92.22
*TnT	Hidden Markov Model	680	92.53
(Georgiev et al., 2009)	Maximum Entropy	680	90.34
(Simov and Osenova, 2001)	Recurrent Neural Network	160	92.87
(Georgiev et al., 2009)	Maximum Entropy	95	94.43
(Savkov et al., 2011)	SVM + Lexicon + Rules	680	94.65
(Tanev and Mitkov, 2002)	Manual Rules	303	95.00(=P=R)
(Simov and Osenova, 2001)	Recurrent Neural Network	15	95.17
(Dojchinova and Mihov, 2004)	Transformation-based Learning	40	95.50
(Dojchinova and Mihov, 2004)	Manual Rules + Lexicon	40	98.40
	Guided Learning	680	95.72
	Guided Learning + Lexicon	680	97.83
This work	Guided Learning + Lexicon + Rules	680	97.98
	Guided Learning + Lexicon + Rules	*49*	*98.85*
	Guided Learning + Lexicon + Rules	*13*	*99.30*

Table 5: **Comparison to previous work for Bulgarian.** The first four lines report evaluation results for various standard POS tagging tools, which were retrained and evaluated on the BulTreeBank. The following lines report token-level accuracy for previously published work, as compared to our own experiments using guided learning.

We can see that most of the wrong tags share the same part-of-speech (indicated by the initial uppercase letter), such as V for verb, N for noun, etc. This means that most errors refer to the morphosyntactic features. For example, personal or impersonal verb; definite or indefinite feminine noun; singular or plural masculine adjective, etc. At the same time, there are also cases, where the error has to do with the part-of-speech label itself. For example, between an adjective and an adverb, or between a numeral and an indefinite pronoun.

We want to use the above tagger to develop (1) a rule-based lemmatizer, using the morphological lexicon, e.g., as in (Plisson et al., 2004), and (2) a dependency parser like MaltParser (Nivre et al., 2007), trained on the dependency part of the BulTreeBank. We thus study the potential impact of wrong tags on the performance of these tools.

The lemmatizer relies on the lexicon and uses string transformation functions defined via two operations – *remove* and *concatenate*:

`if` tag = Tag `then`
{remove OldEnd; concatenate NewEnd}

where Tag is the tag of the wordform, OldEnd is the string that has to be removed from the end of the wordform, and NewEnd is the string that has to be concatenated to the beginning of the wordform in order to produce the lemma.

Here is an example of such a rule:

`if` tag = Vpitf-o1s `then`
{remove ох; concatenate а}

The application of the above rule to the past simple verb form четох ('I read') would remove ох, and then concatenate а. The result would be the correct lemma чета ('to read').

Such rules are generated for each wordform in the morphological lexicon; the above functional representation allows for compact representation in a finite state automaton. Similar rules are applied to the unknown words, where the lemmatizer tries to guess the correct lemma.

Obviously, the applicability of each rule crucially depends on the output of the POS tagger. If the tagger suggests the correct tag, then the wordform would be lemmatized correctly. Note that, in some cases of wrongly assigned POS tags in a given context, we might still get the correct lemma. This is possible in the majority of the erroneous cases in which the part-of-speech has been assigned correctly, but the wrong grammatical alternative has been selected. In such cases, the error does not influence lemmatization.

In order to calculate the proportion of such cases, we divided each tag into two parts: (a) grammatical features that are common for all wordforms of a given lemma, and (b) features that are specific to the wordform.

Freq.	Gold Tag	Proposed Tag
43	Ansi	Dm
23	Vpitf-r3s	Vnitf-r3s
16	Npmsh	Npmsi
14	Vpiif-r3s	Vniif-r3s
13	Npfsd	Npfsi
12	Dm	Ansi
12	Vpitcam-smi	Vpitcao-smi
12	Vpptf-r3p	Vpitf-r3p
11	Vpptf-r3s	Vpptf-o3s
10	Mcmsi	Pfe-os-mi
10	Ppetas3n	Ppetas3m
10	Ppetds3f	Psot–3–f
9	Npnsi	Npnsd
9	Vpptf-o3s	Vpptf-r3s
8	Dm	A-pi
8	Ppxts	Ppxtd
7	Mcfsi	Pfe-os-fi
7	Npfsi	Npfsd
7	Ppetas3m	Ppetas3n
7	Vnitf-r3s	Vpitf-r3s
7	Vpitcam-p-i	Vpitcao-p-i

Table 6: **Most frequently confused pairs of tags.**

The part-of-speech features are always determined by the lemma. For example, Bulgarian verbs have the lemma features *aspect* and *transitivity*. If they are correct, then the lemma is predicted also correctly, regardless of whether correct or wrong on the grammatical features. For example, if the verb participle form (aorist or imperfect) has its correct aspect and transitivity, then it is lemmatized also correctly, regardless of whether the imperfect or aorist features were guessed correctly; similarly, for other error types. We evaluated these cases for the 711 errors in our experiment, and we found that 206 of them (about 29%) were non-problematic for lemmatization.

For the MaltParser, we encode most of the grammatical features of the wordforms as specific features for the parser. Hence, it is much harder to evaluate the problematic cases due to the tagger. Still, we were able to make an estimation of some cases. Our strategy was to ignore the grammatical features that do not always contribute to the syntactic behavior of the wordforms. Such grammatical features for the verbs are *aspect* and *tense*. Thus, proposing perfective instead of imperfective for a verb or present instead of past tense would not cause problems for the MaltParser. Among our 711 errors, 190 cases (or about 27%) were not problematic for parsing.

Finally, we should note that there are two special classes of tokens for which it is generally hard to predict some of the grammatical features: (1) abbreviations and (2) numerals written with digits. In sentences, they participate in agreement relations only if they are pronounced as whole phrases; unfortunately, it is very hard for the tagger to guess such relations since it does not have at its disposal enough features, such as the inflection of the numeral form, that might help detect and use the agreement pattern.

9 Conclusion and Future Work

We have presented experiments with part-of-speech tagging for Bulgarian, a Slavic language with rich inflectional and derivational morphology. Unlike most previous work for this language, which has limited the number of possible tags, we used a very rich tagset of 680 morpho-syntactic tags as defined in the BulTreeBank. By combining a large morphological lexicon with prior linguistic knowledge and guided learning from a POS-annotated corpus, we achieved accuracy of 97.98%, which is a significant improvement over the state-of-the-art for Bulgarian. Our token-level accuracy is also comparable to the best results reported for English.

In future work, we want to experiment with a richer set of features, e.g., derived from unlabeled data (Søgaard, 2011) or from the Web (Umansky-Pesin et al., 2010; Bansal and Klein, 2011). We further plan to explore ways to decompose the complex Bulgarian morpho-syntactic tags, e.g., as proposed in (Simov and Osenova, 2001) and (Smith et al., 2005). Modeling long-distance syntactic dependencies (Dredze and Wallenberg, 2008) is another promising direction; we believe this can be implemented efficiently using posterior regularization (Graca et al., 2009) or expectation constraints (Bellare et al., 2009).

Acknowledgments

We would like to thank the anonymous reviewers for their useful comments, which have helped us improve the paper.

The research presented above has been partially supported by the EU FP7 project 231720 EuroMatrixPlus, and by the SmartBook project, funded by the Bulgarian National Science Fund under grant D002-111/15.12.2008.

References

Mohit Bansal and Dan Klein. 2011. Web-scale features for full-scale parsing. In *Proceedings of the 49th Annual Meeting of the Association for Computational Linguistics: Human Language Technologies*, ACL-HLT '10, pages 693–702, Portland, Oregon, USA.

Kedar Bellare, Gregory Druck, and Andrew McCallum. 2009. Alternating projections for learning with expectation constraints. In *Proceedings of the 25th Conference on Uncertainty in Artificial Intelligence*, UAI '09, pages 43–50, Montreal, Quebec, Canada.

Thorsten Brants. 2000. TnT – a statistical part-of-speech tagger. In *Proceedings of the Sixth Applied Natural Language Processing*, ANLP '00, pages 224–231, Seattle, Washington, USA.

Eric Brill. 1995. Transformation-based error-driven learning and natural language processing: a case study in part-of-speech tagging. *Comput. Linguist.*, 21:543–565.

Michael Collins and Brian Roark. 2004. Incremental parsing with the perceptron algorithm. In *Proceedings of the 42nd Meeting of the Association for Computational Linguistics, Main Volume*, ACL '04, pages 111–118, Barcelona, Spain.

Michael Collins. 2002. Discriminative training methods for hidden Markov models: theory and experiments with perceptron algorithms. In *Proceedings of the Conference on Empirical Methods in Natural Language Processing*, EMNLP '02, pages 1–8, Philadelphia, PA, USA.

Walter Daelemans, Jakub Zavrel, Peter Berck, and Steven Gillis. 1996. MBT: A memory-based part of speech tagger generator. In Eva Ejerhed and Ido Dagan, editors, *Fourth Workshop on Very Large Corpora*, pages 14–27, Copenhagen, Denmark.

Veselka Dojchinova and Stoyan Mihov. 2004. High performance part-of-speech tagging of Bulgarian. In Christoph Bussler and Dieter Fensel, editors, *AIMSA*, volume 3192 of *Lecture Notes in Computer Science*, pages 246–255. Springer.

Mark Dredze and Joel Wallenberg. 2008. Icelandic data driven part of speech tagging. In *Proceedings of the 44th Annual Meeting of the Association of Computational Linguistics: Short Papers*, ACL '08, pages 33–36, Columbus, Ohio, USA.

Georgi Georgiev, Preslav Nakov, Petya Osenova, and Kiril Simov. 2009. Cross-lingual adaptation as a baseline: adapting maximum entropy models to Bulgarian. In *Proceedings of the RANLP'09 Workshop on Adaptation of Language Resources and Technology to New Domains*, AdaptLRTtoND '09, pages 35–38, Borovets, Bulgaria.

Jesús Giménez and Lluís Màrquez. 2004. SVMTool: A general POS tagger generator based on support vector machines. In *Proceedings of the 4th International Conference on Language Resources and Evaluation*, LREC '04, Lisbon, Portugal.

Joao Graca, Kuzman Ganchev, Ben Taskar, and Fernando Pereira. 2009. Posterior vs parameter sparsity in latent variable models. In Yoshua Bengio, Dale Schuurmans, John D. Lafferty, Christopher K. I. Williams, and Aron Culotta, editors, *Advances in Neural Information Processing Systems 22*, NIPS '09, pages 664–672. Curran Associates, Inc., Vancouver, British Columbia, Canada.

Nizar Habash and Owen Rambow. 2005. Arabic tokenization, part-of-speech tagging and morphological disambiguation in one fell swoop. In *Proceedings of the 43rd Annual Meeting of the Association for Computational Linguistics*, ACL '05, pages 573–580, Ann Arbor, Michigan.

Jan Hajič, Pavel Krbec, Pavel Květoň, Karel Oliva, and Vladimír Petkevič. 2001. Serial combination of rules and statistics: A case study in Czech tagging. In *Proceedings of the 39th Annual Meeting of the Association for Computational Linguistics*, ACL '01, pages 268–275, Toulouse, France.

Jan Hajič. 1998. Building a Syntactically Annotated Corpus: The Prague Dependency Treebank. In Eva Hajičová, editor, *Issues of Valency and Meaning. Studies in Honor of Jarmila Panevová*, pages 12–19. Prague Karolinum, Charles University Press.

Erhard W. Hinrichs and Julia S. Trushkina. 2004. Forging agreement: Morphological disambiguation of noun phrases. *Research on Language & Computation*, 2:621–648.

Stig Johansson, Eric Atwell, Roger Garside, and Geoffrey Leech, 1986. *The Tagged LOB Corpus: Users' manual*. ICAME, The Norwegian Computing Centre for the Humanities, Bergen University, Norway.

Hristo Krushkov. 1997. *Modelling and building machine dictionaries and morphological processors (in Bulgarian)*. Ph.D. thesis, University of Plovdiv, Faculty of Mathematics and Informatics, Plovdiv, Bulgaria.

Henry Kučera and Winthrop Nelson Francis. 1967. *Computational analysis of present-day American English*. Brown University Press, Providence, RI.

John D. Lafferty, Andrew McCallum, and Fernando C. N. Pereira. 2001. Conditional random fields: Probabilistic models for segmenting and labeling sequence data. In *Proceedings of the 18th International Conference on Machine Learning*, ICML '01, pages 282–289, San Francisco, CA, USA.

Mohamed Maamouri, Ann Bies, Hubert Jin, and Tim Buckwalter. 2003. Arabic Treebank: Part 1 v 2.0. LDC2003T06.

Mitchell P. Marcus, Mary Ann Marcinkiewicz, and Beatrice Santorini. 1993. Building a large annotated corpus of English: the Penn Treebank. *Comput. Linguist.*, 19:313–330.

Joakim Nivre, Johan Hall, Jens Nilsson, Atanas Chanev, Gülsen Eryigit, Sandra Kübler, Svetoslav Marinov, and Erwin Marsi. 2007. MaltParser: A language-independent system for data-driven dependency parsing. *Natural Language Engineering*, 13(2):95–135.

Jörgen Pind, Fridrik Magnússon, and Stefán Briem. 1991. The Icelandic frequency dictionary. Technical report, The Institute of Lexicography, University of Iceland, Reykjavik, Iceland.

Robin L. Plackett. 1983. Karl Pearson and the Chi-Squared Test. *International Statistical Review / Revue Internationale de Statistique*, 51(1):59–72.

Joël Plisson, Nada Lavrač, and Dunja Mladenić. 2004. A rule based approach to word lemmatization. In *Proceedings of the 7th International Multiconference: Information Society*, IS '2004, pages 83–86, Ljubljana, Slovenia.

Dimitar Popov, Kiril Simov, and Svetlomira Vidinska. 1998. *Dictionary of Writing, Pronunciation and Punctuation of Bulgarian Language (in Bulgarian)*. Atlantis KL, Sofia, Bulgaria.

Dimityr Popov, Kiril Simov, Svetlomira Vidinska, and Petya Osenova. 2003. *Spelling Dictionary of Bulgarian*. Nauka i izkustvo, Sofia, Bulgaria.

Adwait Ratnaparkhi. 1996. A maximum entropy model for part-of-speech tagging. In Eva Ejerhed and Ido Dagan, editors, *Fourth Workshop on Very Large Corpora*, pages 133–142, Copenhagen, Denmark.

Aleksandar Savkov, Laska Laskova, Petya Osenova, Kiril Simov, and Stanislava Kancheva. 2011. A web-based morphological tagger for Bulgarian. In Daniela Majchráková and Radovan Garabík, editors, *Slovko 2011. Sixth International Conference. Natural Language Processing, Multilinguality*, pages 126–137, Modra/Bratislava, Slovakia.

Helmut Schmid. 1994. Probabilistic part-of-speech tagging using decision trees. In *International Conference on New Methods in Language Processing*, pages 44–49, Manchester, UK.

Ingo Schröder. 2002. A case study in part-of-speech-tagging using the ICOPOST toolkit. Technical Report FBI-HH-M-314/02, Department of Computer Science, University of Hamburg.

Libin Shen, Giorgio Satta, and Aravind Joshi. 2007. Guided learning for bidirectional sequence classification. In *Proceedings of the 45th Annual Meeting of the Association of Computational Linguistics*, ACL '07, pages 760–767, Prague, Czech Republic.

Kiril Simov and Petya Osenova. 2001. A hybrid system for morphosyntactic disambiguation in Bulgarian. In *Proceedings of the EuroConference on Recent Advances in Natural Language Processing*, RANLP '01, pages 5–7, Tzigov chark, Bulgaria.

Kiril Simov and Petya Osenova. 2004. BTB-TR04: BulTreeBank morphosyntactic annotation of Bulgarian texts. Technical Report BTB-TR04, Bulgarian Academy of Sciences.

Kiril Ivanov Simov, Alexander Simov, Milen Kouylekov, Krasimira Ivanova, Ilko Grigorov, and Hristo Ganev. 2003. Development of corpora within the CLaRK system: The BulTreeBank project experience. In *Proceedings of the 10th conference of the European chapter of the Association for Computational Linguistics*, EACL '03, pages 243–246, Budapest, Hungary.

Kiril Simov, Petya Osenova, and Milena Slavcheva. 2004. BTB-TR03: BulTreeBank morphosyntactic tagset. Technical Report BTB-TR03, Bulgarian Academy of Sciences.

Noah A. Smith, David A. Smith, and Roy W. Tromble. 2005. Context-based morphological disambiguation with random fields. In *Proceedings of Human Language Technology Conference and Conference on Empirical Methods in Natural Language Processing*, pages 475–482, Vancouver, British Columbia, Canada.

Anders Søgaard. 2011. Semi-supervised condensed nearest neighbor for part-of-speech tagging. In *Proceedings of the 49th Annual Meeting of the Association for Computational Linguistics*, ACL-HLT '10, pages 48–52, Portland, Oregon, USA.

Hristo Tanev and Ruslan Mitkov. 2002. Shallow language processing architecture for Bulgarian. In *Proceedings of the 19th International Conference on Computational Linguistics*, COLING '02, pages 1–7, Taipei, Taiwan.

Kristina Toutanova, Dan Klein, Christopher D. Manning, and Yoram Singer. 2003. Feature-rich part-of-speech tagging with a cyclic dependency network. In *Proceedings of the Conference of the North American Chapter of the Association for Computational Linguistics*, NAACL '03, pages 173–180, Edmonton, Canada.

Yoshimasa Tsuruoka and Jun'ichi Tsujii. 2005. Bidirectional inference with the easiest-first strategy for tagging sequence data. In *Proceedings of the Conference on Human Language Technology and Empirical Methods in Natural Language Processing*, HLT-EMNLP '05, pages 467–474, Vancouver, British Columbia, Canada.

Yoshimasa Tsuruoka, Yusuke Miyao, and Jun'ichi Kazama. 2011. Learning with lookahead: Can history-based models rival globally optimized models? In *Proceedings of the 49th Annual Meeting of the Association for Computational Linguistics: Human Language Technologies*, ACL-HLT '10, pages 238–246, Portland, Oregon, USA.

Shulamit Umansky-Pesin, Roi Reichart, and Ari Rappoport. 2010. A multi-domain web-based algorithm for POS tagging of unknown words. In *Proceedings of the 23rd International Conference on Computational Linguistics: Posters*, COLING '10, pages 1274–1282, Beijing, China.

Instance-Driven Attachment of Semantic Annotations over Conceptual Hierarchies

Janara Christensen*
University of Washington
Seattle, Washington 98195
janara@cs.washington.edu

Marius Paşca
Google Inc.
Mountain View, California 94043
mars@google.com

Abstract

Whether automatically extracted or human generated, open-domain factual knowledge is often available in the form of semantic annotations (e.g., *composed-by*) that take one or more specific instances (e.g., *rhapsody in blue, george gershwin*) as their arguments. This paper introduces a method for converting flat sets of instance-level annotations into hierarchically organized, concept-level annotations, which capture not only the broad semantics of the desired arguments (e.g., 'People' rather than 'Locations'), but also the correct level of generality (e.g., 'Composers' rather than 'People', or 'Jazz Composers'). The method refrains from encoding features specific to a particular domain or annotation, to ensure immediate applicability to new, previously unseen annotations. Over a gold standard of semantic annotations and concepts that best capture their arguments, the method substantially outperforms three baselines, on average, computing concepts that are less than one step in the hierarchy away from the corresponding gold standard concepts.

1 Introduction

Background: Knowledge about the world can be thought of as semantic assertions or annotations, at two levels of granularity: instance level (e.g., *rhapsody in blue*, *tristan und isolde*, *george gershwin*, *richard wagner*) and concept level (e.g., 'Musical Compositions', 'Works of Art', 'Composers'). Instance-level annotations correspond to factual knowledge that can be found in repositories extracted automatically from text (Banko et al., 2007; Wu and Weld, 2010) or manually created within encyclopedic resources (Remy, 2002). Such facts could state, for instance, that *rhapsody in blue* was *composed-by george gershwin*, or that *tristan und isolde* was *composed-by richard wagner*. In comparison, concept-level annotations more concisely and effectively capture the underlying semantics of the annotations by identifying the concepts corresponding to the arguments, e.g., 'Musical Compositions' are *composed-by* 'Composers'.

The frequent occurrence of instances, relative to more abstract concepts, in Web documents and popular Web search queries (Barr et al., 2008; Li, 2010), is both an asset and a liability from the point of view of knowledge acquisition. On one hand, it makes instance-level annotations relatively easy to find, either from manually created resources (Remy, 2002; Bollacker et al., 2008), or extracted automatically from text (Banko et al., 2007). On the other hand, it makes concept-level annotations more difficult to acquire directly. While *"Rhapsody in Blue was composed by George Gershwin [..]"* may occur in some form within Web documents, the more abstract *"Musical compositions are composed by musicians [..]"* is unlikely to occur. A more practical approach to collecting concept-level annotations is to indirectly derive them from already plentiful instance-level annotations, effectively distilling factual knowledge into more abstract, concise and generalizable knowledge.

Contributions: This paper introduces a method for converting flat sets of specific, instance-level annotations into hierarchically organized, concept-level annotations. As illustrated in Figure 1, the resulting annotations must capture not just the broad semantics of the desired arguments (e.g., 'People' rather than 'Locations' or 'Prod-

*Contributions made during an internship at Google.

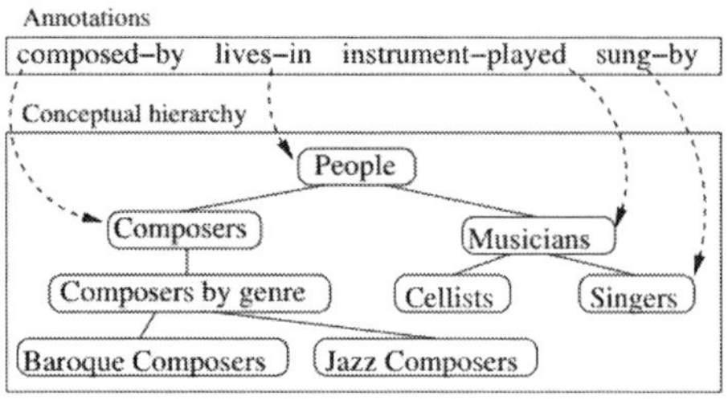

Figure 1: **Hierarchical Semantic Annotations**: The attachment of semantic annotations (e.g., *composed-by*) into a conceptual hierarchy, a portion of which is shown in the diagram, requires the identification of the correct concept at the correct level of generality (e.g., 'Composers' rather than 'Jazz Composers' or 'People', for the right argument of *composed-by*).

ucts', as the right argument of the annotation *composed-by*), but actually identify the concepts at the correct level of generality/specificity (e.g., 'Composers' rather than 'Artists' or 'Jazz Composers') in the underlying conceptual hierarchy.

To ensure portability to new, previously unseen annotations, the proposed method avoids encoding features specific to a particular domain or annotation. In particular, the use of annotations' labels (*composed-by*) as lexical features might be tempting, but would anchor the annotation model to that particular annotation. Instead, the method relies only on features that generalize across annotations. Over a gold standard of semantic annotations and concepts that best capture their arguments, the method substantially outperforms three baseline methods. On average, the method computes concepts that are less than one step in the hierarchy away from the corresponding gold standard concepts of the various annotations.

2 Hierarchical Semantic Annotations

2.1 Task Description

Data Sources: The computation of hierarchical semantic annotations relies on the following data sources:

- a target annotation r (e.g., *acted-in*) that takes M arguments;
- N annotations I=$\{<i_{1j}, \ldots, i_{Mj}>\}_{j=1}^{N}$ of r at instance level, e.g., {<*leonardo dicaprio, inception*>, <*milla jovovich, fifth element*>} (in this example, M=2);
- mappings $\{i \rightarrow c\}$ from instances to concepts to which they belong, e.g., *milla jovovich* → 'American Actors', *milla jovovich* → 'People from Kiev', *milla jovovich* → 'Models';
- mappings $\{c_s \rightarrow c_g\}$ from more specific concepts to more general concepts, as encoded in a hierarchy H, e.g., 'American Actors'→'Actors', 'People from Kiev'→'People from Ukraine', 'Actors'→'Entertainers'.

Thus, the main inputs are the conceptual hierarchy H, and the instance-level annotations I. The hierarchy contains instance-to-concept mappings, as well as specific-to-general concept mappings. Via transitivity, instances (*milla jovovich*) and concepts ('American Actors') may be immediate children of more general concepts ('Actors'), or transitive descendants of more general concepts ('Entertainers'). The hierarchy is not required to be a tree; in particular, a concept may have multiple parent concepts. The instance-level annotations may be created collaboratively by human contributors, or extracted automatically from Web documents or some other data source.

Goal: Given the data sources, the goal is to determine to which concept c in the hierarchy H the arguments of the target concept-level annotation r should be attached. While the left argument of *acted-in* could attach to 'American Actors', 'People from Kiev', 'Entertainers' or 'People', it is best attached to the concept 'Actors'. The goal is to select the concept c that most appropriately generalizes across the instances. Over the set I of instance-level annotations, selecting a method for this goal can be thought of as a minimization problem. The metric to be minimized is the sum of the distances between each predicted concept c and the correct concept c_{gold}, where the distance is the number of edges between c and c_{gold} in H.

Intuitions and Challenges: Given instances such as *milla jovovich* that instantiate an argument of an annotation like *acted-in*, the conceptual hierarchy can be used to propagate the annotation upwards, from instances to their concepts, then in turn further upwards to more general concepts. The best concept would be one of the many candidate concepts reached during propagation. Intuitively, when compared to other candidate concepts, a higher proportion of the descendant instances of the best concept should instantiate (or match) the annotation. At the same time, relative to other candidate concepts, the best concept should have more descendant instances.

While the intuitions seem clear, their inclusion in a working method faces a series of practical challenges. First, the data sources may be noisy. One form of noise is missing or erroneous

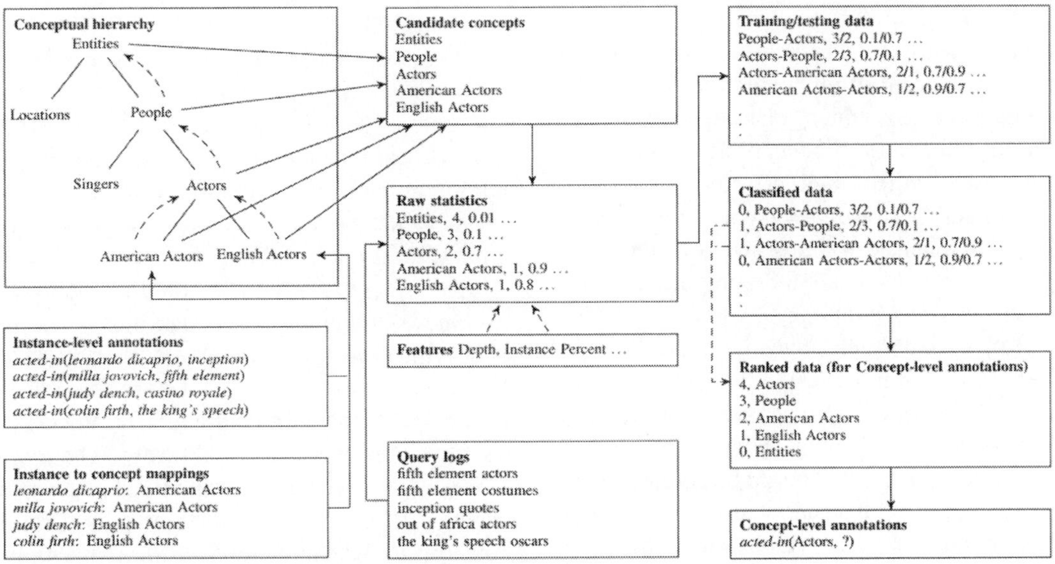

Figure 2: **Method Overview**: Inferring concept-level annotations from instance-level annotations.

instance-level annotations, which may artificially skew the distribution of matching instances towards a less than optimal region in the hierarchy. If the input annotations for *acted-in* are available almost exhaustively for all descendant instances of 'American Actors', and are available for only a few of the descendant instances of 'Belgian Actors', 'Italian Actors' etc., then the distribution over the hierarchy may incorrectly suggest that the left argument of *acted-in* is 'American Actors' rather than the more general 'Actors'. In another example, if virtually all instances that instantiate the left argument of the annotation *won-award* are mapped to the concept 'Award Winning Actors', then it would be difficult to distinguish 'Award Winning Actors' from the more general 'Actors' or 'People', as best concept to be computed for the annotation. Another type of noise is missing or erroneous edges in the hierarchy, which could artificially direct propagation towards irrelevant regions of the hierarchy, or prevent propagation from even reaching relevant regions of the hierarchy. For example, if the hierarchy incorrectly maps 'Actors' to 'Entertainment', then 'Entertainment' and its ancestor concepts incorrectly become candidate concepts during propagation for the left argument of *acted-in*. Conversely, if missing edges caused 'Actors' to not have any children in the hierarchy, then 'Actors' would not even be reached and considered as a candidate concept during propagation.

Second, to apply evidence collected from some annotations to a new annotation, the evidence must generalize across annotations. However, collected evidence or statistics may vary widely across annotations. Observing that 90% of all descendant instances of the concept 'Actors' match an annotation *acted-in* constitutes strong evidence that 'Actors' is a good concept for *acted-in*. In contrast, observing that only 0.09% of all descendant instances of the concept 'Football Teams' match *won-super-bowl* should not be as strong negative evidence as the percentage suggests.

2.2 Inferring Concept-Level Annotations

Determining Candidate Concepts: As illustrated in the left part of Figure 2, the first step towards inferring concept-level from instance-level annotations is to propagate the instances that instantiate a particular argument of the annotation, upwards in the hierarchy. Starting from the left arguments of the annotation *acted-in*, namely *leonardo dicaprio*, *milla jovovich* etc., the propagation reaches their parent concepts 'American Actors', 'English Actors', then their parent and ancestor concepts 'Actors', 'People', 'Entities' etc. The concepts reached during upward propagation become candidate concepts. In subsequent steps, the candidates are modeled, scored and ranked such that ideally the best concept is ranked at the top.

Ranking Candidate Concepts: The identification of a ranking function is cast as a semi-supervised learning problem. Given the correct (gold) concept of an annotation, it would be tempting to employ binary classification directly, by marking the correct concept as a positive example, and all other candidate concepts as negative examples. Unfortunately, this would produce a highly imbalanced training set, with thousands of negative examples and, more importantly, with only one positive example. Another disadvantage of using binary classification directly is that it is difficult to capture the preference for concepts closer in the hierarchy to the correct concept, over concepts many edges away. Finally, the absolute values of the features that might be employed may be comparable within an annotation, but incomparable across annotations, which reduces the portability of the resulting model to new annotations.

To address the above issues, the ranking function proposed does not construct training examples from raw features collected for each individual candidate concept. Instead, it constructs training examples from pairwise comparisons of a candidate concept with another candidate concept. Concretely, a pairwise comparison is labeled as a positive example if the first concept is closer to the correct concept than the second, or as negative otherwise. The pairwise formulation has three immediate advantages. First, it accomodates the preference for concepts closer to the gold concept. Second, the pairwise formulation produces a larger, more balanced training set. Third, decisions of whether the first concept being compared is more relevant than the second are more likely to generalize across annotations, than absolute decisions of whether (and how much) a particular concept is relevant for a given annotation.

Compiling Ranking Features: The features are grouped into four categories: (A) annotation co-occurrence features, (B) concept features, (C) argument co-occurrence features, and (D) combination features, as described below.

(A) *Annotation Co-occurrence Features*: The annotation co-occurrence features emphasize how well an annotation applies to a concept. These features include (1) MATCHED INSTANCES the number of descendant instances of the concept that appear with the annotation, (2) INSTANCE PERCENT the percentage of matched instances in the concept, (3) MORE THAN THREE MATCHING INSTANCES and (4) MORE THAN TEN MATCHING INSTANCES, which indicate when the matching descendant instances might be noise.

Also in this category are features that relay information about the candidate concept's children concepts. These features include (1) MATCHED CHILDREN the number of child concepts containing at least one matching instance, (2) CHILDREN PERCENT the percentage of child concepts with at least one matching instance, (3) AVG INSTANCE PERCENT CHILDREN the average percentage of matching descendant instances of the child concepts, and (4) INSTANCE PERCENT TO INSTANCE PERCENT CHILDREN the ratio between INSTANCE PERCENT and AVERAGE INSTANCE PERCENT OF CHILDREN. The last feature is meant to capture dramatic changes in percentages when moving in the hierarchy from child concepts to the candidate concept in question.

(B) *Concept Features*: Concept features approximate the generality of the concepts: (1) NUM INSTANCES the number of descendant instances of the concept, (2) NUM CHILDREN the number of child concepts, and (3) DEPTH the distance to the concept's farthest descendant.

(C) *Argument Co-occurrence Features*: The argument co-occurrence features model the likelihood that an annotation applies to a concept by looking at co-occurrences with another argument of the same annotation. Intuitively, if a concept representing one argument has a high co-occurrence with an instance that is some other argument, a relationship more likely exists between members of the concept and the instance. For example, given *acted-in*, 'Actors' is likely to have a higher co-occurrence with *casablanca* than 'People' is. These features are generated from a set of Web queries. Therefore, the collected values are likely to be affected by different noise than that present in the original dataset. For every concept and instance pair from the arguments of a given annotation, they feature the number of times each of the tokens in the concept appears in the same query with each of the tokens in the instance, normalizing to the respective number of tokens. The procedure generates, for each candidate concept, an average co-occurrence score (AVG CO-OCCURRENCE) and a total co-occurrence score (TOTAL CO-OCCURRENCE) over all instances the concept is paired with.

(D) *Combination Features*: The last group of features are combinations of the above features: (1) DEPTH, INSTANCE PERCENT which is DEPTH multiplied by INSTANCE PERCENT, and

Concept	Distance ToCorrect	Match Inst	Total Inst	Match Child	Total Child	AvgInst PercOfChild	Depth	Avg Cooccur	Total Cooccur
People	4	36512	879423	22	29	4%	14	0.67	33506
Actors	0	29101	54420	6	10	32%	6	2.08	99971
English Actors	2	3091	5922	3	4	37%	3	2.75	28378

Labeled Concept Pair		Annotation Co-occurrence Features					Concept Features			Arg Co-occurrence Features		Combination Features	
Concept Pair	Label	Match Inst	Inst Perc	Match Child	Child Perc	AvgInst PercChild	Num Inst	Num Child	Depth	Avg Cooccur	Total Cooccur	Depth InstPerc	DepthInst PercChild
People-Actors	0	1.25	0.08	3.67	1.26	0.13	1.25	3.67	2.33	0.32	0.34	0.18	0.66
Actors-People	1	0.8	12.88	0.27	0.79	7.65	0.8	0.27	0.43	3.11	2.98	5.52	1.51
Actors-English Actors	1	9.41	1.02	2.0	0.8	0.87	9.41	2.0	2.0	0.76	3.52	2.05	4.1
English Actors-Actors	0	0.11	0.98	0.5	1.25	1.15	0.11	0.5	0.5	1.32	0.28	0.49	0.24
English Actors-People	1	0.08	12.57	0.14	0.99	8.82	0.08	0.14	0.21	4.12	0.85	2.69	0.37
People-English Actors	0	11.81	0.08	7.33	1.01	0.11	11.81	7.33	4.67	0.24	1.18	0.37	2.72

Table 1: **Training/Testing Examples**: The top table shows examples of raw statistics gathered for three candidate concepts for the left argument of the annotation *acted-in*. The second table shows the training/testing examples generated from these concepts and statistics. Each example represents a pair of concepts which is labeled positive if the first concept is closer to the correct concept than the second concept. Features shown here are the ratio between a statistic for the first concept and a statistic for the second (e.g. DEPTH for Actors-English Actors is 2 as 'Actors' has depth of 6 and 'English Actors' has depth of 3). Some features omitted due to space constraints.

(2) DEPTH, INSTANCE PERCENT, CHILDREN, which is the DEPTH multipled by the INSTANCE PERCENT multiplied by MATCHED CHILDREN. Both these features seek to balance the perceived relevance of an annotation to a candidate concept, with the generality of the candidate concept.

Generating Learning Examples: For a given annotation, the ranking features described so far are computed for each candidate concept (e.g., 'Movie Actors', 'Models', 'Actors'). However, the actual training and testing examples are generated for pairs of candidate concepts (e.g., <'Film Actors', 'Models'>, <'Film Actors', 'Actors'>, <'Models, 'Actors'>). A training example represents a comparison between two candidate concepts, and specifies which of the two is more relevant. To create training and testing examples, the values of the features of the first concept in the pair are respectively combined with the values of the features of the second concept in the pair to produce values corresponding to the entire pair.

Following classification of testing examples, concepts are ranked according to the number of other concepts which they are classified as more relevant than. Table 1 shows examples of training/testing data.

3 Experimental Setting

3.1 Data Sources

Conceptual Hierarchy: The experiments compute concept-level annotations relative to a conceptual hierarchy derived automatically from the Wikipedia (Remy, 2002) category network, as described in (Ponzetto and Navigli, 2009). The hierarchy filters out edges (e.g., from 'British Film Actors' to 'Cinema of the United Kingdom') from the Wikipedia category network that do not correspond to IsA relations. A concept in the hierarchy is a Wikipedia category (e.g., 'English Film Actors') that has zero or more Wikipedia categories as child concepts, and zero or more Wikipedia categories (e.g., 'English People by Occupation', 'British Film Actors') as parent concepts. Each concept in the hierarchy has zero or more instances, which are the Wikipedia articles listed (in Wikipedia) under the respective categories (e.g., *colin firth* is an instance of 'English Actors').

Instance-Level Annotations: The experiments exploit a set of binary instance-level annotations (e.g., *acted-in*, *composed*) among Wikipedia instances, as available in Freebase (Bollacker et al., 2008). The annotation is a Freebase property (e.g., */music/composition/composer*). Internally, the left and right arguments are Freebase topic identifiers mapped to their corresponding Wikipedia articles (e.g., */m/03f4k* mapped to the Wikipedia article on *george gershwin*). In this paper, the derived annotations and instances are displayed in a shorter, more readable form for conciseness and clarity. As features do not use the label of the annotation, labels are never used in the experiments and evaluation.

Web Search Queries: The argument co-occurrence features described above are computed over a set of around 100 million anonymized Web search queries from 2010.

3.2 Experimental Runs

The experimental runs exploit ranking features described in the previous section, employing:

• one of three learning algorithms: naive Bayes (NAIVEBAYES), maximum entropy (MAXENT), or perceptron (PERCEPTRON) (Mitchell, 1997), chosen for their scalability to larger datasets via distributed implementations.

• one of three ways of combining the values of features collected for individual candidate concepts into values of features for pairs of candidate concepts: the raw ratio of the values of the respective features of the two concepts (0 when the denominator is 0); the ratio scaled to the interval [0, 1]; or a binary value indicating which of the values is larger.

For completeness, the experiments include three additional, baseline runs. Each baseline computes scores for all candidate concepts based on the respective metric; then candidate concepts are ranked in decreasing order of their scores. The baselines metrics are:

• INSTPERCENT ranks candidate concepts by the percentage of matched instances that are descendants of the concept. It emphasizes concepts which are "proven" to belong to the annotation;

• ENTROPY ranks candidate concepts by the entropy (Shannon, 1948) of the proportion of matched descendant instances of the concept;

• AVGDEPTH ranks candidate concepts by their distances to half of the maximum hierarchy height, emphasizing a balance of generality and specificity.

3.3 Evaluation Procedure

Gold Standard of Concept-Level Annotations: A random, weighted sample of 200 annotation labels (e.g., corresponding to *composed-by*, *play-instrument*) is selected, out of the set of labels of all instance-level annotations collected from Freebase. During sampling, the weights are the counts of distinct instance-level annotations (e.g., <*rhapsody in blue*, *george gershwin*>) available for the label. The arguments of the annotation labels are then manually annotated with a gold concept, which is the category from the Wikipedia hierarchy that best captures their semantics. The manual annotation is carried out independently by two human judges, who then verify each other's work and discard inconsistencies. For example, the gold concept of the left argument of *composed-by* is annotated to be the Wikipedia category 'Musical Compositions'. In the process, some annotation labels are discarded, when (a) it is not clear what concept captures an argument (e.g., for the right argument of *function-of-building*), or (b) more than 5000 candidate concepts are available via propagation for one of the arguments, which would cause too many training or testing examples to be generated via concept pairs, and slow down the experiments. The retained 139 annotation labels, whose arguments have been labeled with their respective gold concepts, form the gold standard for the experiments. More precisely, an entry in the resulting gold standard consists of an annotation label, one of its arguments being considered (left or right), and a gold concept that best captures that argument. The set of annotation labels from the gold standard is quite diverse and covers many domains of potential interest, e.g., *has-company*('Industries', 'Companies'), *written-by*('Films', 'Screenwriters'), *member-of*('Politicians','Political Parties'), or *part-of-movement*('Artists', 'Art Movements').

Evaluation Metric: Following previous work on selectional preferences (Kozareva and Hovy, 2010; Ritter et al., 2010), each entry in the gold standard, (i.e., each argument for a given annotation) is evaluated separately. Experimental runs compute a ranked list of candidate concepts for each entry in the gold standard. In theory, a computed candidate concept is better if it is closer semantically to the gold concept. In practice, the accuracy of a ranked list of candidate concepts, relative to the gold concept of the annotation label, is measured by two scoring metrics that correspond to the mean reciprocal rank score (MRR) (Voorhees and Tice, 2000) and a modification of it (DRR) (Paşca and Alfonseca, 2009):

$$MRR = \frac{1}{N}\sum_{i=1}^{N}\max_{rank}\frac{1}{rank_i}$$

N is the number of annotations and $rank_i$ is the rank of the gold concept in the returned list for MRR. An annotation a_i receives no credit for MRR if the gold concept does not appear in the corresponding ranked list.

$$DRR = \frac{1}{N}\sum_{i=1}^{N}\max_{rank}\frac{1}{rank_i \times (1 + Len)}$$

For DRR, $rank_i$ is the rank of a candidate concept in the returned list and Len is the length of

Annotation (Number of Candidate Concepts)	Examples of Instances	Top Ranked Concepts
Composers *compose* Musical Compositions (3038)	aaron copland; black sabbath	Music by Nationality; Composers; Classical Composers
Musical Compositions *composed-by* Composers (1734)	we are the champions; yorckscher marsch	Musical Compositions; Compositions by Composer; Classical Music
Foods *contain* Nutrients (1112)	acca sellowiana; lasagna	Foods; Edible Plants; Food Ingredients
Organizations *has-boardmember* People (3401)	conocophillips; spence school	Companies by Stock Exchange; Companies Listed on the NYSE; Companies
Educational Organizations *has-graduate* Alumni (4072)	air force institute of technology; deering high school	Education by Country; Schools by Country; Universities and Colleges by Country
Television Actors *guest-role* Fictional Characters (4823)	melanie griffith; patti laBelle	Television Actors by Nationality; Actors; American Actors
Musical Groups *has-member* Musicians (2287)	steroid maximus; u2	Musical Groups; Musical Groups by Genre; Musical Groups by Nationality
Record Labels *represent* Musician (920)	columbia records; vandit	Record Labels; Record Labels by Country; Record Labels by Genre
Awards *awarded-to* People (458)	academy award for best original song; erasmus prize	Film Awards; Awards; Grammy Awards
Foods *contain* **Nutrients** (177)	lycopene; glutamic acid	Carboxylic Acids ; Acids; Essential Nutrients
Architects *design* **Buildings and Structures** (4811)	20 times square; berkeley building	Buildings and Structures; Buildings and Structures by Architect; Houses by Country
People *died-from* **Causes of Death** (577)	malaria; skiing	Diseases; Infectious Diseases; Causes of Death
Art Directors *direct* **Films** (1265)	batman begins; the lion king	Films; Films by Director; Film
Episodes *guest-star* **Television Actors** (1067)	amy poehler; david caruso	Television Actors by Nationality; Actors; American Actors
Television Network *has-tv-show* **Television Series** (2492)	george of the jungle; great expectations	Television Series by Network; Television Series; Television Series by Genre
Musicians *play* **Musical Instruments** (423)	accordion; tubular bell	Musical Instruments; Musical Instruments by Nationality; Percussion Instruments
Politicians *member-of* **Political Parties** (938)	independent moralizing front; national coalition party	Political Parties; Political Parties by Country; Political Parties by Ideology

Table 2: **Concepts Computed for Gold-Standard Annotations**: Examples of entries from the gold standard and counts of candidate concepts (Wikipedia categories) reached from upward propagation of instances (Wikipedia instances). The target gold concept is shown in bold. Also shown are examples of Wikipedia instances, and the top concepts computed by the best-performing learning algorithm for the respective gold concepts.

the minimum path in the hierarchy between the concept and the gold concept. Len is minimum (0) if the candidate concept is the same as the gold standard concept. A given annotation a_i receives no credit for DRR if no path is found between the returned concepts and the gold concept.

As an illustration, for a single annotation, the right argument of *composed-by*, the ranked list of concepts returned by an experimental may be ['Symphonies by Anton Bruckner', 'Symphonies by Joseph Haydn', 'Symphonies by Gustav Mahler', 'Musical Compositions', ..], with the gold concept being 'Musical Compositions'. The length of the path between 'Symphonies by Anton Bruckner' etc. and 'Musical Compositions' is 2 (via 'Symphonies'). Therefore, the MRR score would be 0.25 (given by the fourth element of the ranked list), whereas the DRR score would be 0.33 (given by the first element of the ranked list).

MRR and DRR are computed in five-fold cross validation. Concretely, the gold standard is split into five folds such that the sets of annotation labels in each fold are disjoint. Thus, none of the annotation labels in testing appears in training. This restriction makes the evaluation more rigurous and conservative as it actually assesses the extent the models learned are applicable to new, previously unseen annotation labels. If this restriction were relaxed, the baselines would preform equivalently as they do not depend on the training data, but the learned methods would likely do better.

4 Evaluation Results

4.1 Quantitative Results

Conceptual Hierarchy: The conceptual hierarchy contains 108,810 Wikipedia categories, and its maximum depth, measured as the distance from a concept to its farthest descendant, is 16.

Candidate Concepts: On average, for the gold standard, the method propagates a given annotation from instances to 1,525 candidate concepts, from which the single best concept must be determined. The left part of Table 2 illustrates the number of candidate concepts reached during propagation for a sample of annotations.

Experimental Run	Accuracy			
	N=1		N=20	
	MRR	DRR	MRR	DRR
→ With raw-ratio features:				
NAIVEBAYES	0.021	0.180	0.054	0.222
MAXENT	0.029	0.168	0.045	0.208
PERCEPTRON	0.029	0.176	0.045	0.216
→ With scaled-ratio features:				
NAIVEBAYES	0.050	0.170	0.112	0.243
MAXENT	**0.245**	**0.456**	**0.430**	**0.513**
PERCEPTRON	0.245	0.391	0.367	0.461
→ With binary features:				
NAIVEBAYES	0.115	0.297	0.224	0.361
MAXENT	0.165	0.390	0.293	0.441
PERCEPTRON	0.180	0.332	0.330	0.429
→ For baselines:				
INSTPERCENT	0.029	0.173	0.045	0.224
ENTROPY	0.000	0.110	0.007	0.136
AVGDEPTH	0.007	0.018	0.028	0.045

Table 3: **Precision Results**: Accuracy of ranked lists of concepts (Wikipedia categories) computed by various runs, as an average over the gold standard of concept-level annotations, considering the top N candidate concepts computed for each gold standard entry.

4.2 Qualitative Results

Precision: Table 3 compares the precision of the ranked lists of candidate concepts produced by the experimental runs. The MRR and DRR scores in the table consider either at most 20 of the concepts in the ranked list computed by a given experimental run, or only the first, top ranked computed concept. Note that, in the latter case, the MRR and DRR scores are equivalent to precision@1 scores.

Several conclusions can be drawn from the results. First, as expected by definition of the scoring metrics, DRR scores are higher than the stricter MRR scores, as they give partial credit to concepts that, while not identical to the gold concepts, are still close approximations. This is particularly noticeable for the runs MAXENT and PERCEPTRON with raw-ratio features (4.6 and 4.8 times higher respectively). Second, among the baselines, INSTPERCENT is the most accurate, with the computed concepts identifying the gold concept strictly at rank 22 on average (for an MRR score 0.045), and loosely at an average of 4 steps away from the gold concept (for a DRR score of 0.224). Third, the accuracy of the learning algorithms varies with how the pairwise feature values are combined. Overall, raw-ratio feature values perform the worst, and scaled-ratio the best, with binary in-between. Fourth, the scores of the best experimental run, MAXENT with scaled-ratio features, are 0.430 (MRR) and 0.513 (DRR) over the top 20 computed concepts, and 0.245 (MRR) and 0.456 (DRR) when considering only the first concept. These scores correspond to the ranked list being less than one step away in the hierarchy. The very first computed concept exactly matches the gold concept in about one in four cases, and is slightly more than one step away from it. In comparison, the very first concept computed by the best baseline matches the gold concept in about one in 35 cases (0.029 MRR), and is about 6 steps away (0.173 DRR). The accuracies of the various learning algorithms (not shown) were also measured and correlated roughly with the MRR and DRR scores.

Discussion: The baseline runs INSTPERCENT and ENTROPY produce categories that are far too specific. For the gold annotation *composed-by*('Composers', 'Musical Compositions'), INSTPERCENT produces 'Scottish Flautists' for the left argument and 'Operas by Ernest Reyer' for the right. AVGDEPTH does not suffer from over-specification, but often produces concepts that have been reached via propagation, yet are not close to the gold concept. For *composed-by*, AVGDEPTH produces 'Film' for the left argument and 'History by Region' for the right.

4.3 Error Analysis

The right part of Table 2 provides a more detailed view into the best performing experimental run, showing actual ranked lists of concepts produced for a sample of the gold standard entries by MAXENT with scaled-ratio. A separate analysis of the results indicates that the most common cause of errors is noise in the conceptual hierarchy, in the form of *unbalanced instance-level annotations* and *missing hierarchy edges*. Unbalanced annotations are annotations where certain subtrees of the hierarchy are artificially more populated than other subtrees. For the left argument of the annotation *has-profession*, 0.05% of 'New York Politicians' are matched but 70% of 'Bushrangers' are matched. Such imbalances may be inherent to how annotations are added to Freebase: different human contributors may add new annotations to particular portions of Freebase, but miss other relevant portions.

The results are also affected by missing edges in the hierarchy. Of the more than 100K concepts in the hierarchy, 3479 are roots of subhierarchies that are mutually disconnected. Examples are 'People by Region', 'Shades of Red', and

'Members of the Parliament of Northern Ireland', all of which should have parents in the hierarchy. If a few edges are missing in a particular region of the hierarchy, the method can recover, but if so many edges are missing that a gold concept has very few descendants, then propagation can be substantially affected. In the worst case, the gold concept becomes disconnected, and thus will be missing from the set of candidate concepts compiled during propagation. For example, for the annotation *team-color*('Sports Clubs', 'Colors'), the only descendant concept of 'Colors' in the hierarchy is 'Horse Coat Colors', meaning that the gold concept 'Colors' is not reached during propagation from instances upwards in the hierarchy.

5 Related Work

Similar to the task of attaching a semantic annotation to the concept in a hierarchy that has the best level of generality is the task of finding selectional preferences for relations. Most relevant to this paper is work that seeks to find the appropriate concept in a hierarchy for an argument of a specific relation (Ribas, 1995; McCarthy, 1997; Li and Abe, 1998). Li and Abe (1998) address this problem by attempting to identify the best tree cut in a hierarchy for an argument of a given verb. They use the minimum description length principle to select a set of concepts from a hierarchy to represent the selectional preferences. This work makes several limiting assumptions including that the hierarchy is a tree, and every instance belongs to just one concept. Clark and Weir (2002) investigate the task of generalizing a single relation-concept pair. A relation is propagated up a hierarchy until a chi-square test determines the difference between the probability of the child and parent concepts to be significant where the probabilities are relation-concept frequencies. This method has no direct translation to the task discussed here; it is unclear how to choose the correct concept if instances generalize to different concepts.

In other research on selectional preferences, Pantel et al. (2007), Kozareva and Hovy (2010) and Ritter et al. (2010) focus on generating admissible arguments for relations, and Erk (2007) and Bergsma et al. (2008) investigate classifying a relation-instance pair as plausible or not.

Important to this paper is the Wikipedia category network (Remy, 2002) and work on refining it. Ponzetto and Navigli (2009) disambiguate Wikipedia categories by using WordNet synsets and use this semantic information to construct a taxonomy. The resulting taxonomy is the conceptual hierarchy used in the evaluation.

Another related area of work is the discovery of relations between concepts. Nastase and Strube (2008) use Wikipedia category names and category structure to generate a set of relations between concepts. Yan et al. (2009) discover relations between Wikipedia concepts via deep linguistic information and Web frequency information. Mohamed et al. (2011) generate candidate relations by coclustering text contexts for every pair of concepts in a hierarchy. In a sense, this area of research is complementary to that discussed in this paper. These methods induce new relations, and the proposed method can be used to find appropriate levels of generalization for the arguments of any given relation.

6 Conclusions

This paper introduces a method to convert flat sets of instance-level annotations to hierarchically organized, concept-level annotations. The method determines the appropriate concept for a given semantic annotation in three stages. First, it propagates annotations upwards in the hierarchy, forming a set of candidate concepts. Second, it classifies each candidate concept as more or less appropriate than each other candidate concept within an annotation. Third, it ranks candidate concepts by the number of other concepts relative to which it is classified as more appropriate. Because the features are comparisons between concepts within a single semantic annotation, rather than considerations of individual concepts, the method is able to generalize across annotations, and can thus be applied to new, previously unseen annotations. Experiments demonstrate that, on average, the method is able to identify the concept of a given annotation's argument within one hierarchy edge of the gold concept.

The proposed method can take advantage of existing work on open-domain information extraction. The output of such work is usually instance-level annotations, although often at surface level (non-disambiguated arguments) rather than semantic level (disambiguated arguments). After argument disambiguation (e.g., (Dredze et al., 2010)), the annotations can be used as input to determining concept-level annotations. Thus, the method has the potential to generalize any existing database of instance-level annotations to concept-level annotations.

References

Michele Banko, Michael Cafarella, Stephen Soderland, Matt Broadhead, and Oren Etzioni. 2007. Open information extraction from the Web. In *Proceedings of the 20th International Joint Conference on Artificial Intelligence (IJCAI-07)*, pages 2670–2676, Hyderabad, India.

Cory Barr, Rosie Jones, and Moira Regelson. 2008. The linguistic structure of English Web-search queries. In *Proceedings of the 2008 Conference on Empirical Methods in Natural Language Processing (EMNLP-08)*, pages 1021–1030, Honolulu, Hawaii.

Shane Bergsma, Dekang Lin, and Randy Goebel. 2008. Discriminative learning of selectional preference from unlabeled text. In *Proceedings of the 2008 Conference on Empirical Methods in Natural Language Processing (EMNLP-08)*, pages 59–68, Honolulu, Hawaii.

Kurt Bollacker, Colin Evans, Praveen Paritosh, Tim Sturge, and Jamie Taylor. 2008. Freebase: A collaboratively created graph database for structuring human knowledge. In *Proceedings of the 2008 International Conference on Management of Data (SIGMOD-08)*, pages 1247–1250, Vancouver, Canada.

Stephen Clark and David Weir. 2002. Class-based probability estimation using a semantic hierarchy. *Computational Linguistics*, 28(2):187–206.

Mark Dredze, Paul McNamee, Delip Rao, Adam Gerber, and Tim Finin. 2010. Entity disambiguation for knowledge base population. In *Proceedings of the 23rd International Conference on Computational Linguistics (COLING-10)*, pages 277–285, Beijing, China.

Katrin Erk. 2007. A simple, similarity-based model for selectional preferences. In *Proceedings of the 45th Annual Meeting of the Association for Computational Linguistics (ACL-07)*, pages 216–223, Prague, Czech Republic.

Zornitsa Kozareva and Eduard Hovy. 2010. Learning arguments and supertypes of semantic relations using recursive patterns. In *Proceedings of the 48th Annual Meeting of the Association for Computational Linguistics (ACL-10)*, pages 1482–1491, Uppsala, Sweden.

Hang Li and Naoki Abe. 1998. Generalizing case frames using a thesaurus and the mdl principle. In *Proceedings of the ECAI-2000 Workshop on Ontology Learning*, pages 217–244, Berlin, Germany.

Xiao Li. 2010. Understanding the semantic structure of noun phrase queries. In *Proceedings of the 48th Annual Meeting of the Association for Computational Linguistics (ACL-10)*, pages 1337–1345, Uppsala, Sweden.

Diana McCarthy. 1997. Word sense disambiguation for acquisition of selectional preferences. In *Proceedings of the ACL/EACL Workshop on Automatic Information Extraction and Building of Lexical Semantic Resources for NLP Applications*, pages 52–60, Madrid, Spain.

Tom Mitchell. 1997. *Machine Learing*. McGraw Hill.

Thahir Mohamed, Estevam Hruschka, and Tom Mitchell. 2011. Discovering relations between noun categories. In *Proceedings of the 2011 Conference on Empirical Methods in Natural Language Processing (EMNLP-11)*, pages 1447–1455, Edinburgh, United Kingdom.

Vivi Nastase and Michael Strube. 2008. Decoding Wikipedia categories for knowledge acquisition. In *Proceedings of the 23rd National Conference on Artificial Intelligence (AAAI-08)*, pages 1219–1224, Chicago, Illinois.

M. Paşca and E. Alfonseca. 2009. Web-derived resources for Web Information Retrieval: From conceptual hierarchies to attribute hierarchies. In *Proceedings of the 32nd International Conference on Research and Development in Information Retrieval (SIGIR-09)*, pages 596–603, Boston, Massachusetts.

Patrick Pantel, Rahul Bhagat, Timothy Chklovski, and Eduard Hovy. 2007. ISP: Learning inferential selectional preferences. In *Proceedings of the Annual Meeting of the North American Chapter of the Association for Computational Linguistics (NAACL-07)*, pages 564–571, Rochester, New York.

Simone Paolo Ponzetto and Roberto Navigli. 2009. Large-scale taxonomy mapping for restructuring and integrating Wikipedia. In *Proceedings of the 21st International Joint Conference on Artifical Intelligence (IJCAI-09)*, pages 2083–2088, Barcelona, Spain.

Melanie Remy. 2002. Wikipedia: The free encyclopedia. *Online Information Review*, 26(6):434.

Francesc Ribas. 1995. On learning more appropriate selectional restrictions. In *Proceedings of the 7th Conference of the European Chapter of the Association for Computational Linguistics (EACL-97)*, pages 112–118, Madrid, Spain.

Alan Ritter, Mausam, and Oren Etzioni. 2010. A latent dirichlet allocation method for selectional preferences. In *Proceedings of the 48th Annual Meeting of the Association for Computational Linguistics (ACL-10)*, pages 424–434, Uppsala, Sweden.

Claude Shannon. 1948. A mathematical theory of communication. *Bell System Technical Journal*, 27:379–423,623–656.

Ellen Voorhees and Dawn Tice. 2000. Building a question-answering test collection. In *Proceedings of the 23rd International Conference on Research and Development in Information Retrieval (SIGIR-00)*, pages 200–207, Athens, Greece.

Fei Wu and Daniel S. Weld. 2010. Open information extraction using wikipedia. In *Proceedings of the 48th Annual Meeting of the Association for Computational Linguistics (ACL-10)*, pages 118–127, Uppsala, Sweden.

Yulan Yan, Naoaki Okazaki, Yutaka Matsuo, Zhenglu Yang, and Mitsuru Ishizuka. 2009. Unsupervised relation extraction by mining Wikipedia texts using information from the Web. In *Proceedings of the Joint Conference of the 47th Annual Meeting of the ACL and the 4th International Joint Conference on Natural Language Processing of the AFNLP (ACL-IJCNLP-09)*, pages 1021–1029, Suntec, Singapore.

Joint Satisfaction of Syntactic and Pragmatic Constraints Improves Incremental Spoken Language Understanding

Andreas Peldszus
University of Potsdam
Department for Linguistics
peldszus@uni-potsdam.de

Okko Buß
University of Potsdam
Department for Linguistics
okko@ling.uni-potsdam.de

Timo Baumann
University of Hamburg
Department for Informatics
baumann@informatik.uni-hamburg.de

David Schlangen
University of Bielefeld
Department for Linguistics
david.schlangen@uni-bielefeld.de

Abstract

We present a model of semantic processing of spoken language that (a) is robust against ill-formed input, such as can be expected from automatic speech recognisers, (b) respects both syntactic and pragmatic constraints in the computation of most likely interpretations, (c) uses a principled, expressive semantic representation formalism (RMRS) with a well-defined model theory, and (d) works continuously (producing meaning representations on a word-by-word basis, rather than only for full utterances) and incrementally (computing only the additional contribution by the new word, rather than re-computing for the whole utterance-so-far).

We show that the joint satisfaction of syntactic and pragmatic constraints improves the performance of the NLU component (around 10 % absolute, over a syntax-only baseline).

1 Introduction

Incremental processing for spoken dialogue systems (i. e., the processing of user input even while it still may be extended) has received renewed attention recently (Aist et al., 2007; Baumann et al., 2009; Buß and Schlangen, 2010; Skantze and Hjalmarsson, 2010; DeVault et al., 2011; Purver et al., 2011). Most of the practical work, however, has so far focussed on realising the potential for generating more responsive system behaviour through making available processing results earlier (e. g. (Skantze and Schlangen, 2009)), but has otherwise followed a typical pipeline architecture where processing results are passed only in one direction towards the next module.

In this paper, we investigate whether the other potential advantage of incremental processing—providing "higher-level"-feedback to lower-level modules, in order to improve subsequent processing of the lower-level module—can be realised as well. Specifically, we experimented with giving a syntactic parser feedback about whether semantic readings of nominal phrases it is in the process of constructing have a denotation in the given context or not. Based on the assumption that speakers do plan their referring expressions so that they can successfully refer, we use this information to re-rank derivations; this in turn has an influence on how the derivations are expanded, given continued input. As we show in our experiments, for a corpus of realistic dialogue utterances collected in a Wizard-of-Oz setting, this strategy led to an absolute improvement in computing the intended denotation of around 10 % over a baseline (even more using a more permissive metric), both for manually transcribed test data as well as for the output of automatic speech recognition.

The remainder of this paper is structured as follows: We discuss related work in the next section, and then describe in general terms our model and its components. In Section 4 we then describe the data resources we used for the experiments and the actual implementation of the model, the baselines for comparison, and the results of our experiments. We close with a discussion and an outlook on future work.

2 Related Work

The idea of using real-world reference to inform syntactic structure building has been previously explored by a number of authors. Stoness et al. (2004, 2005) describe a proof-of-concept implementation of a "continuous understanding" module that uses reference information in guiding a bottom-up chart-parser, which is evaluated on a single dialogue transcript. In contrast, our model uses a probabilistic top-down parser with beam search (following Roark (2001)) and is evaluated on a large number of real-world utterances as processed by an automatic speech recogniser. Similarly, DeVault and Stone (2003) describe a system that implements interaction between a parser and higher-level modules (in this case, even more principled, trying to prove presuppositions), which however is also only tested on a small, constructed data-set.

Schuler (2003) and Schuler et al. (2009) present a model where information about reference is used directly within the speech recogniser, and hence informs not only syntactic processing but also word recognition. To this end, the processing is folded into the decoding step of the ASR, and is realised as a hierarchical HMM. While technically interesting, this approach is by design non-modular and restricted in its syntactic expressivity.

The work presented here also has connections to work in psycholinguistics. Padó et al. (2009) present a model that combines syntactic and semantic models into one plausibility judgement that is computed incrementally. However, that work is evaluated for its ability to predict reading time data and not for its accuracy in computing meaning.

3 The Model

3.1 Overview

Described abstractly, the model computes the probability of a syntactic derivation (and its accompanying logical form) as a combination of a syntactic probability (as in a typical PCFG) and a semantic or pragmatic plausibility.[1] The pragmatic plausibility here comes from the presupposition that the speaker intended her utterance to successfully refer, i. e. to have a denotation in the current situation (a unique one, in the case of definite reference). Hence, readings that do have a denotation are preferred over those that do not.

The components of our model are described in the following sections: first the parser which computes the syntactic probability in an incremental, top-down manner; the semantic construction algorithm which associates (underspecified) logical forms to derivations; the reference resolution component that computes the pragmatic plausibility; and the combination that incorporates the feedback from this pragmatic signal.

3.2 Parser

Roark (2001) introduces a strategy for incremental probabilistic top-down parsing and shows that it can compete with high-coverage bottom-up parsers. One of the reasons he gives for choosing a top-down approach is that it enables fully left-connected derivations, where at every processing step new increments directly find their place in the existing structure. This monotonically enriched structure can then serve as a context for incremental language understanding, as the author claims, although this part is not further developed by Roark (2001). He discusses a battery of different techniques for refining his results, mostly based on grammar transformations and on conditioning functions that manipulate a derivation probability on the basis of local linguistic and lexical information.

We implemented a basic version of his parser without considering additional conditioning or lexicalizations. However, we applied left-factorization to parts of the grammar to delay certain structural decisions as long as possible. The search-space is reduced by using beam search. To match the next token, the parser tries to expand the existing derivations. These derivations are stored in a priorized queue, which means that the most probable derivation will always be served first. Derivations resulting from rule expansions are kept in the current queue, derivations resulting from a successful lexical match are pushed in a new queue. The parser proceeds with the next most probable derivation until the current queue is empty or until a threshhold is reached at which remaining analyses are pruned. This threshhold is determined dynamically: If the probability of the current derivation is lower than the product of the best derivation's probability on the new queue, the number of derivations in the new queue, and a base beam factor (an initial parameter for the size of the search beam), then all further old deriva-

[1]Note that, as described below, in the actual implementation the weights given to particular derivations are not real probabilities anymore, as derivations fall out of the beam and normalisation is not performed after re-weighting.

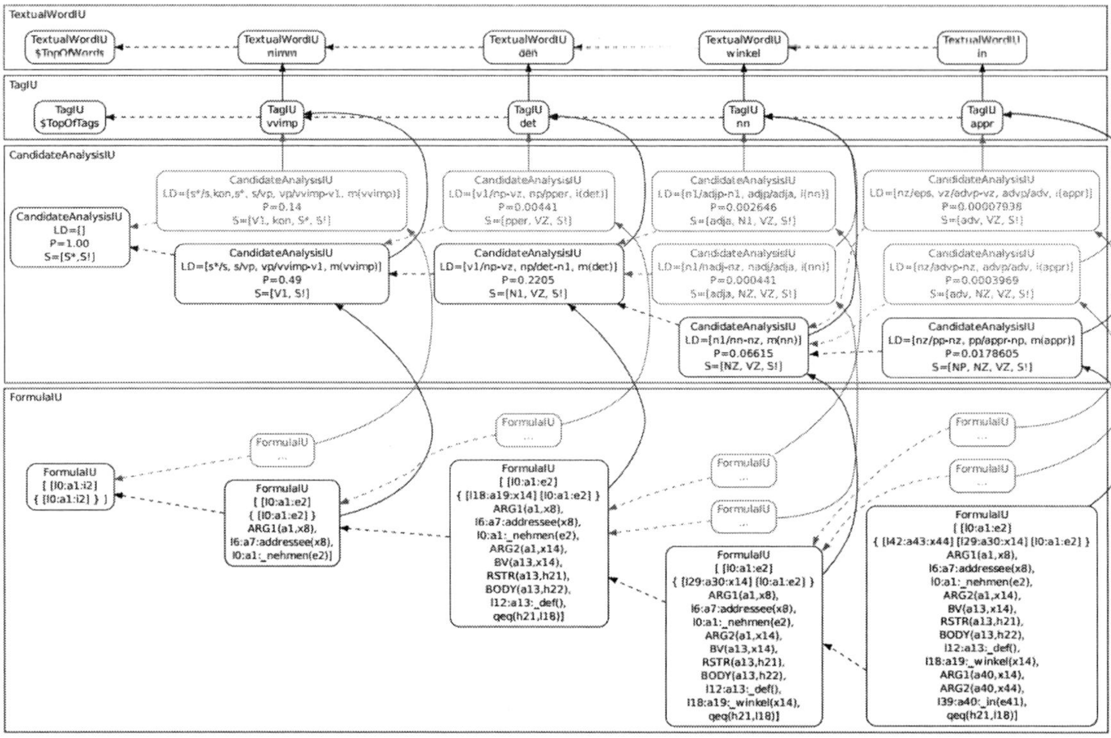

Figure 1: An example network of incremental units, including the levels of words, POS-tags, syntactic derivations and logical forms. See section 3 for a more detailed description.

tions are pruned. Due to probabilistic weighing and the left factorization of the rules, left recursion poses no direct threat in such an approach.

Additionally, we implemented three robust lexical operations: *insertions* consume the current token without matching it to the top stack item; *deletions* can "consume" a requested but actually non-existent token; *repairs* adjust unknown tokens to the requested token. These robust operations have strong penalties on the probability to make sure they will survive in the derivation only in critical situations. Additionally, only a single one of them is allowed to occur between the recognition of two adjacent input tokens.

Figure 1 illustrates this process for the first few words of the example sentence "nimm den winkel in der dritten reihe" (*take the bracket in the third row*), using the *incremental unit* (IU) model to represent increments and how they are linked; see (Schlangen and Skantze, 2009).[2] Here, syntactic derivations ("CandidateAnalysisIUs") are represented by three features: a list of the last parser actions of the derivation (LD), with rule expansions or (robust) lexical matches; the derivation probability (P); and the remaining stack (S), where S* is the grammar's start symbol and S! an explicit end-of-input marker. (To keep the Figure small, we artificially reduced the beam size and cut off alternatives paths, shown in grey.)

3.3 Semantic Construction Using RMRS

As a novel feature, we use for the representation of meaning increments (that is, the contributions of new words and syntactic constructions) as well as for the resulting logical forms the formalism *Robust Minimal Recursion Semantics* (Copestake, 2006). This is a representation formalism that was originally constructed for semantic underspecification (of scope and other phenomena) and then adapted to serve the purposes of semantics repre-

[2]Very briefly: rounded boxes in the Figures represent IUs, and dashed arrows link an IU to its predecessor on the same level, where the levels correspond to processing stages. The Figure shows the levels of input words, POS-tags, syntactic derivations and logical forms. Multiple IUs sharing the same predecessor can be regarded as alternatives. Solid arrows indicate which information from a previous level an IU is grounded in (based on); here, every semantic IU is grounded in a syntactic IU, every syntactic IU in a POS-tag-IU, and so on.

sentations in heterogeneous situations where information from deep and shallow parsers must be combined. In RMRS, meaning representations of a first order logic are underspecified in two ways: First, the scope relationships can be underspecified by splitting the formula into a list of *elementary predications* (EP) which receive a label ℓ and are explicitly related by stating scope constraints to hold between them (e.g. *qeq*-constraints). This way, all scope readings can be compactly represented. Second, RMRS allows underspecification of the predicate-argument-structure of EPs. Arguments are bound to a predicate by anchor variables a, expressed in the form of an *argument relation* ARGREL(a,x). This way, predicates can be introduced without fixed arity and arguments can be introduced without knowing which predicates they are arguments of. We will make use of this second form of underspecification and enrich lexical predicates with arguments incrementally.

Combining two RMRS structures involves at least joining their list of EPs and ARGRELs and of scope constraints. Additionally, equations between the variables can connect two structures, which is an essential requirement for semantic construction. A semantic algebra for the combination of RMRSs in a non-lexicalist setting is defined in (Copestake, 2007). Unsaturated semantic increments have open slots that need to be filled by what is called the *hook* of another structure. Hook and slot are triples $[\ell{:}a{:}x]$ consisting of a label, an anchor and an index variable. Every variable of the hook is equated with the corresponding one in the slot. This way the semantic representation can grow monotonically at each combinatory step by simply adding predicates, constraints and equations.

Our approach differs from (Copestake, 2007) only in the organisation of the slots: In an incremental setting, a proper semantic representation is desired for every single state of growth of the syntactic tree. Typically, RMRS composition assumes that the order of semantic combination is parallel to a bottom-up traversal of the syntactic tree. Yet, this would require *for every incremental step* first to calculate an adequate underspecified semantic representation for the projected nodes on the lower right border of the tree and then to proceed with the combination not only of the new semantic increments but of the complete tree. For our purposes, it is more elegant to proceed with semantic combination in synchronisation with the syntactic expansion of the tree, i.e. in a top-down left-to-right fashion. This way, no underspecification of projected nodes and no re-interpretation of already existing parts of the tree is required. This, however, requires adjustments to the slot structure of RMRS. Left-recursive rules can introduce multiple slots of the same sort before they are filled, which is not allowed in the classic (R)MRS semantic algebra, where only one named slot of each sort can be open at a time. We thus organize the slots as a stack of unnamed slots, where multiple slots of the same sort can be stored, but only the one on top can be accessed. We then define a basic combination operation equivalent to forward function composition (as in standard lambda calculus, or in CCG (Steedman, 2000)) and combine substructures in a principled way across multiple syntactic rules without the need to represent slot names.

Each lexical items receives a generic representation derived from its lemma and the basic semantic type (individual, event, or underspecified denotations), determined by its POS tag. This makes the grammar independent of knowledge about what later (semantic) components will actually be able to process ("understand").[3] Parallel to the production of syntactic derivations, as the tree is expanded top-down left-to-right, semantic macros are activated for each syntactic rule, composing the contribution of the new increment. This allows for a monotonic semantics construction process that proceeds in lockstep with the syntactic analysis.

Figure 1 (in the "FormulaIU" box) illustrates the results of this process for our example derivation. Again, alternatives paths have been cut to keep the size of the illustration small. Notice that, apart from the end-of-input marker, the stack of semantic slots (in curly brackets) is always synchronized with the parser's stack.

3.4 Computing Noun Phrase Denotations

Formally, the task of this module is, given a model $\mathcal{M}$ of the current context, to compute the set of all variable assignments such that $\mathcal{M}$ satisfies ϕ: $\mathcal{G} = \{g \mid \mathcal{M} \models^g \phi\}$. If $|\mathcal{G}| > 1$, we say that ϕ refers ambiguously; if $|\mathcal{G}| = 1$, it refers uniquely;

[3]This feature is not used in the work presented here, but it could be used for enabling the system to learn the meaning of unknown words.

and if $|\mathcal{G}| = 0$, it fails to refer. This process does not work directly on RMRS formulae, but on extracted and unscoped first-order representations of their nominal content.

3.5 Parse Pruning Using Reference Information

After all possible syntactic hypotheses at an increment have been derived by the parser and the corresponding semantic representations have been constructed, reference resolution information can be used to re-rank the derivations. If pragmatic feedback is enabled, the probability of every reprentation that does not resolve in the current context is degraded by a constant factor (we used 0.001 in our experiments described below, determined by experimentation). The degradation thus changes the derivation order in the parsing queue for the next input item and increases the chances of degraded derivations to be pruned in the following parsing step.

4 Experiments and Results

4.1 Data

We use data from the Pentomino puzzle piece domain (which has been used before for example by (Fernández and Schlangen, 2007; Schlangen et al., 2009)), collected in a Wizard-of-Oz study. In this specific setting, users gave instructions to the system (the wizard) in order to manipulate (select, rotate, mirror, delete) puzzle pieces on an upper board and to put them onto a lower board, reaching a pre-specified goal state. Figure 2 shows an example configuration. Each participant took part in several rounds in which the distinguishing characteristics for puzzle pieces (color, shape, proposed name, position on the board) varied widely. In total, 20 participants played 284 games.

We extracted the semantics of an utterance from the wizard's response action. In some cases, such a mapping was not possible to do (e. g. because the wizard did not perform a next action, mimicking a non-understanding by the system), or potentially unreliable (if the wizard performed several actions at or around the end of the utterance). We discarded utterances without a clear semantics alignment, leaving 1687 semantically annotated user utterances. The wizard of course was able to use her model of the previous discourse for resolving references, including anaphoric ones; as

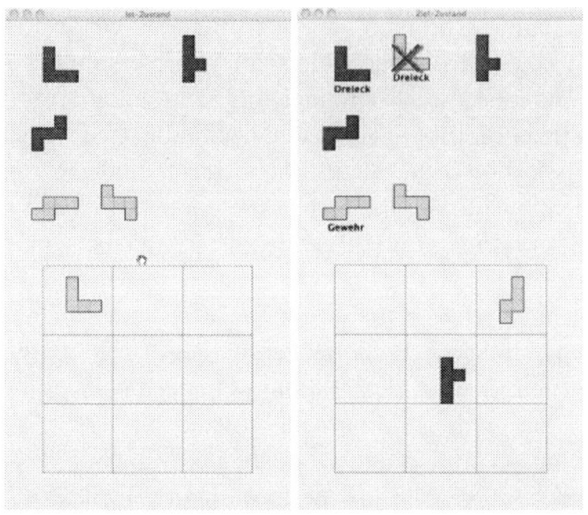

Figure 2: The game board used in the study, as presented to the player: (a) the current state of the game on the left, (b) the goal state to be reached on the right.

our study does not focus on these, we have disregarded another 661 utterances in which pieces are referred to by pronouns, leaving us with 1026 utterances for evaluation. These utterances contained on average 5.2 words (median 5 words; std dev 2 words).

In order to test the robustness of our method, we generated speech recognition output using an acoustic model trained for spontaneous (German) speech. We used leave-one-out language model training, i. e. we trained a language model for every utterance to be recognized which was based on all the other utterances in the corpus. Unfortunately, the audio recordings of the first recording day were too quiet for successful recognition (with a deletion rate of 14 %). We thus decided to limit the analysis for speech recognition output to the remaining 633 utterances from the other recording days. On this part of the corpus word error rate (WER) was at 18 %.

The subset of the full corpus that we used for evaluation, with the utterances selected according to the criteria described above, nevertheless still only consists of natural, spontaneous utterances (with all the syntactic complexity that brings) that are representative for interactions in this type of domain.

4.2 Grammar and Resolution Model

The grammar used in our experiments was hand-constructed, inspired by a cursory inspection of the corpus and aiming to reach good coverage

Words	Predicates	Status
nimm	nimm(e)	-1
nimm den	nimm(e,x) def(x)	0
nimm den Winkel	nimm(e,x) def(x) winkel(x)	0
nimm den Winkel in	nimm(e,x) def(x) winkel(x) in(x,y)	0
nimm den Winkel in der	nimm(e,x) def(x) winkel(x) in(x,y) def(y)	0
nimm den Winkel in der dritten	nimm(e,x) def(x) winkel(x) in(x,y) def(y) third(y)	1
nimm den Winkel in der dritten Reihe	nimm(e,x) def(x) winkel(x) in(x,y) def(y) third(y) row(y)	1

Table 1: Example of logical forms (flattened into first-order base-language formulae) and reference resolution results for incrementally parsing and resolving 'nimm den winkel in der dritten reihe'

for a core fragment. We created 30 rules, whose weights were also set by hand (as discussed below, this is an obvious area for future improvement), sparingly and according to standard intuitions. When parsing, the first step is the assignment of a POS tag to each word. This is done by a simple lookup tagger that stores the most frequent tag for each word (as determined on a small subset of our corpus).[4]

The situation model used in reference resolution is automatically derived from the internal representation of the current game state. (This was recorded in an XML-format for each utterance in our corpus.) Variable assignments were then derived from the relevant *nominal* predicate structures,[5] consisting of extracted simple predications, e. g. *red*(x) and *cross*(x) for the NP in a phrase such as "take the red cross". For each unique predicate argument X in these EP structures (such as as x above), the set of domain objects that satisfied all predicates of which X was an argument were determined. For example for the phrase above, X mapped to all elements that were *red* and *cross*es.

Finally, the size of these sets was determined: no elements, one element, or multiple elements, as described above. Emptiness of at least one set denoted that no resolution was possible (for instance, if no red crosses were available, x's set was empty), uniqueness of all sets denoted that an exact resolution was possible while multiple elements in at least some sets denoted ambiguity. This status was then leveraged for parse pruning, as per Section 3.5.

A more complex example using the scene depicted in Figure 2 and the sentence "nimm den winkel in der dritten reihe" (*take the bracket in the third row*) is shown in Table 1. The first column shows the incremental word hypothesis string, the second the set of predicates derived from the most recent RMRS representation and the third the resolution status (-1 for no resolution, 0 for some resolution and 1 for a unique resolution).

[4]A more sophisticated approach has recently been proposed by Beuck et al. (2011); this could be used in our setup.

[5]The domain model did not allow making a plausibility judgement based on verbal resolution.

4.3 Baselines and Evaluation Metric

4.3.1 Variants / Baselines

To be able to accurately quantify and assess the effect of our reference-feedback strategy, we implemented different variants / baselines. These all differ in how, at each step, the reading is determined that is evaluated against the gold standard, and are described in the following:

In the **Just Syntax (JS)** variant, we simply take single-best derivation, as determined by syntax alone and evaluate this.

The **External Filtering (EF)** variant adds information from reference resolution, but keeps it separate from the parsing process. Here, we look at the 5 highest ranking derivations (as determined by syntax alone), and go through them beginning at the highest ranked, picking the first derivation where reference resolution can be performed uniquely; this reading is then put up for evaluation. If there is no such reading, the highest ranking one will be put forward for evaluation (as in JS).

Syntax/Pragmatics Interaction (SPI) is the variant described in the previous section. Here, all active derivations are sent to the reference resolution module, and are re-weighted as described above; after this has been done, the highest-ranking reading is evaluated.

Finally, the **Combined Interaction and Filtering (CIF)** variant combines the previous two strategies, by using reference-feedback in computing the ranking for the derivations, and then again using reference-information to identify the most promising reading within the set of 5 highest ranking ones.

4.3.2 Metric

When a reading has been identified according to one of these methods, a score s is computed as follows: $s = 1$, if the correct referent (according to the gold standard) is computed as the denotation for this reading; $s = 0$ if no unique referent can be computed, but the correct one is part of the set of possible referents; $s = -1$ if no referent can be computed at all, or the correct one is not part of the set of those that are computed.

As this is done incrementally for each word (adding the new word to the parser chart), for an utterance of length m we get a sequence of m such numbers. (In our experiments we treat the "end of utterance" signal as a pseudo-word, since knowing that an utterance has concluded allows the parser to close off derivations and remove those that are still requiring elements. Hence, we in fact have sequences of $m+1$ numbers.) A combined score for the whole utterance is computed according to the following formula:

$$su = \sum_{n=1}^{m} (s_n * n/m)$$

(where s_n is the score at position n). The factor n/m causes "later" decisions to count more towards the final score, reflecting the idea that it is more to be expected (and less harmful) to be wrong early on in the utterance, whereas the longer the utterance goes on, the more pressing it becomes to get a correct result (and the more damaging if mistakes are made).[6]

Note that this score is not normalised by utterance length m; the maximally achievable score being $(m + 1)/2$. This has the additional effect of increasing the weight of long utterances when averaging over the score of all utterances; we see this as desirable, as the analysis task becomes harder the longer the utterance is.

We use success in resolving reference to evaluate the performance of our parsing and semantic construction component, where more traditionally, metrics like parse bracketing accuracy might be used. But as we are building this module for an interactive system, ultimately, accuracy in recovering meaning is what we are interested in, and so we see this not just as a proxy, but actually as a more valuable metric. Moreover, this metric can be applied at each incremental step, which is not clear how to do with more traditional metrics.

4.4 Experiments

Our parser, semantic construction and reference resolution modules are implemented within the InproTK toolkit for incremental spoken dialogue systems development (Schlangen et al., 2010). In this toolkit, incremental hypotheses are modified as more information becomes available over time. Our modules support all such modifications (i. e. also allow to revert their states and output if word input is revoked).

As explained in Section 4.1, we used offline recognition results in our evaluation. However, the results would be identical if we were to use the incremental speech recognition output of InproTK directly.

The system performs several times faster than real-time on a standard workstation computer. We thus consider it ready to improve practical end-to-end incremental systems which perform within-turn actions such as those outlined in (Buß and Schlangen, 2010).

The parser was run with a base-beam factor of 0.01; this parameter may need to be adjusted if a larger grammar was used.

4.5 Results

Table 2 shows an overview of the experiment results. The table lists, separately for the manual transcriptions and the ASR transcripts, first the number of times that the final reading did not resolve at all, or to a wrong entitiy; did not uniquely resolve, but included the correct entity in its denotiation; or did uniquely resolve to the correct entity (-1, 0, and 1, respectively). The next lines show "strict accuracy" (proportion of "1" among all results) at the end of utterance, and "relaxed accuracy" (which allows ambiguity, i.e., is the set $\{0, 1\}$). *incr.scr* is the incremental score as described above, which includes in the evaluation the development of references and not just the final state. (And in that sense, is the most appropriate metric here, as it captures the incremental behaviour.) This score is shown both as absolute

[6]This metric compresses into a single number some of the concerns of the incremental metrics developed in (Baumann et al., 2011), which can express more fine-grainedly the temporal development of hypotheses.

		JS	EF	SPI	CIF
transcript	−1	563	518	364	363
	0	197	198	267	268
	1	264	308	392	392
	str.acc.	25.7 %	30.0 %	38.2 %	38.2 %
	rel.acc.	44.9 %	49.3 %	64.2 %	64.3 %
	incr.scr	−1568	−1248	−536	−504
	avg.incr.scr	−1.52	−1.22	−0.52	−0.49
recognition	−1	362	348	254	255
	0	122	121	173	173
	1	143	158	196	195
	str.acc.	22.6 %	25.0 %	31.0 %	30.8 %
	rel.acc.	41.2 %	44.1 %	58.3 %	58.1 %
	incr.scr	−1906	−1730	−1105	−1076
	avg.incr.scr	−1.86	−1.69	−1.01	−1.05

Table 2: Results of the Experiments. See text for explanation of metrics.

number as well as averaged for each utterance.

As these results show, the strategy of providing the parser with feedback about the real-world utility of constructed phrases (in the form of reference decisions) improves the parser, in the sense that it helps the parser to successfully retrieve the intended meaning more often compared to an approach that only uses syntactic information (**JS**) or that uses pragmatic information only outside of the main programme: 38.2 % strict or 64.2 % relaxed for **SPI** over 25.7 % / 44.9 % for **JS**, an absolute improvement of 12.5 % for strict or even more, 19.3 %, for the relaxed metric; the incremental metric shows that this advantage holds not only at the final word, but also consistently within the utterance, the average incremental score for an utterance being −0.49 for **SPI** and −1.52 for **JS**. The improvement is somewhat smaller against the variant that uses some reference information, but does not integrate this into the parsing process (**EF**), but it is still consistently present. Adding such n-best-list processing to the output of the parser+reference-combination (as variant **CIF** does) finally does not further improve the performance noticeably. When processing partially defective material (the output of the speech recogniser), the difference between the variants is maintained, showing a clear advantage of **SPI**, although performance of all variants is degraded somewhat.

Clearly, accuracy is rather low for the baseline condition (**JS**); this is due to the large number of non-standard constructions in our spontaneous material (e.g., utterances like "löschen, unten" (*delete, bottom*) which we did not try to cover with syntactic rules, and which may not even contain NPs. The **SPI** condition can promote derivations resulting from robust rules (here, *deletion*) which then can refer. In general though state-of-the art grammar engineering may narrow the gap between **JS** and **SPI** – this remains to be tested – but we see as an advantage of our approach that it can improve over the (easy-to-engineer) set of core grammar rules.

5 Conclusions

We have described a model of semantic processing of natural, spontaneous speech that strives to jointly satisfy syntactic and pragmatic constraints (the latter being approximated by the assumption that referring expressions are intended to indeed successfully refer in the given context). The model is robust, accepting also input of the kind that can be expected from automatic speech recognisers, and incremental, that is, can be fed input on a word-by-word basis, computing at each increment only exactly the contribution of the new word. Lastly, as another novel contribution, the model makes use of a principled formalism for semantic representation, RMRS (Copestake, 2006).

While the results show that our approach of combining syntactic and pragmatic information can work in a real-world setting on realistic data—previous work in this direction has so far only been at the proof-of-concept stage—there is much room for improvement. First, we are now exploring ways of bootstrapping a grammar and derivation weights from hand-corrected parses. Secondly, we are looking at making the variable assignment / model checking function probabilistic, assigning probabilities (degree of strength of belief) to candidate resolutions (as for example the model of Schlangen et al. (2009) does). Another next step—which will be very easy to take, given the modular nature of the implementation framework that we have used—will be to integrate this component into an interactive end-to-end system, and testing other domains in the process.

Acknowledgements We thank the anonymous reviewers for their helpful comments. The work reported here was supported by a DFG grant in the Emmy Noether programme to the last author and a stipend from DFG-CRC (SFB) 632 to the first author.

References

Gregory Aist, James Allen, Ellen Campana, Carlos Gomez Gallo, Scott Stoness, Mary Swift, and Michael K. Tanenhaus. 2007. Incremental understanding in human-computer dialogue and experimental evidence for advantages over nonincremental methods. In *Proceedings of Decalog 2007, the 11th International Workshop on the Semantics and Pragmatics of Dialogue*, Trento, Italy.

Timo Baumann, Michaela Atterer, and David Schlangen. 2009. Assessing and improving the performance of speech recognition for incremental systems. In *Proceedings of the North American Chapter of the Association for Computational Linguistics - Human Language Technologies (NAACL HLT) 2009 Conference*, Boulder, Colorado, USA, May.

Timo Baumann, Okko Buß, and David Schlangen. 2011. Evaluation and optimization of incremental processors. *Dialogue and Discourse*, 2(1):113–141.

Niels Beuck, Arne Köhn, and Wolfgang Menzel. 2011. Decision strategies for incremental pos tagging. In *Proceedings of the 18th Nordic Conference of Computational Linguistics, NODALIDA-2011*, Riga, Latvia.

Okko Buß and David Schlangen. 2010. Modelling sub-utterance phenomena in spoken dialogue systems. In *Proceedings of the 14th International Workshop on the Semantics and Pragmatics of Dialogue (Pozdial 2010)*, pages 33–41, Poznan, Poland, June.

Ann Copestake. 2006. Robust minimal recursion semantics. Technical report, Cambridge Computer Lab. Unpublished draft.

Ann Copestake. 2007. Semantic composition with (robust) minimal recursion semantics. In *Proceedings of the Workshop on Deep Linguistic Processing*, DeepLP '07, pages 73–80, Stroudsburg, PA, USA. Association for Computational Linguistics.

David DeVault and Matthew Stone. 2003. Domain inference in incremental interpretation. In *Proceedings of ICOS 4: Workshop on Inference in Computational Semantics*, Nancy, France, September. INRIA Lorraine.

David DeVault, Kenji Sagae, and David Traum. 2011. Incremental Interpretation and Prediction of Utterance Meaning for Interactive Dialogue. *Dialogue and Discourse*, 2(1):143–170.

Raquel Fernández and David Schlangen. 2007. Referring under restricted interactivity conditions. In Simon Keizer, Harry Bunt, and Tim Paek, editors, *Proceedings of the 8th SIGdial Workshop on Discourse and Dialogue*, pages 136–139, Antwerp, Belgium, September.

Ulrike Padó, Matthew W Crocker, and Frank Keller. 2009. A probabilistic model of semantic plausibility in sentence processing. *Cognitive Science*, 33(5):794–838.

Matthew Purver, Arash Eshghi, and Julian Hough. 2011. Incremental semantic construction in a dialogue system. In J. Bos and S. Pulman, editors, *Proceedings of the 9th International Conference on Computational Semantics (IWCS)*, pages 365–369, Oxford, UK, January.

Brian Roark. 2001. *Robust Probabilistic Predictive Syntactic Processing: Motivations, Models, and Applications*. Ph.D. thesis, Department of Cognitive and Linguistic Sciences, Brown University.

David Schlangen and Gabriel Skantze. 2009. A general, abstract model of incremental dialogue processing. In *EACL '09: Proceedings of the 12th Conference of the European Chapter of the Association for Computational Linguistics*, pages 710–718. Association for Computational Linguistics, mar.

David Schlangen, Timo Baumann, and Michaela Atterer. 2009. Incremental reference resolution: The task, metrics for evaluation, and a bayesian filtering model that is sensitive to disfluencies. In *Proceedings of SIGdial 2009, the 10th Annual SIGDIAL Meeting on Discourse and Dialogue*, London, UK, September.

David Schlangen, Timo Baumann, Hendrik Buschmeier, Okko Buß, Stefan Kopp, Gabriel Skantze, and Ramin Yaghoubzadeh. 2010. Middleware for Incremental Processing in Conversational Agents. In *Proceedings of SigDial 2010*, Tokyo, Japan, September.

William Schuler, Stephen Wu, and Lane Schwartz. 2009. A framework for fast incremental interpretation during speech decoding. *Computational Linguistics*, 35(3).

William Schuler. 2003. Using model-theoretic semantic interpretation to guide statistical parsing and word recognition in a spoken language interface. In *Proceedings of the 41st Meeting of the Association for Computational Linguistics (ACL 2003)*, Sapporo, Japan. Association for Computational Linguistics.

Gabriel Skantze and Anna Hjalmarsson. 2010. Towards incremental speech generation in dialogue systems. In *Proceedings of the SIGdial 2010 Conference*, pages 1–8, Tokyo, Japan, September.

Gabriel Skantze and David Schlangen. 2009. Incremental dialogue processing in a micro-domain. In *Proceedings of the 12th Conference of the European Chapter of the Association for Computational Linguistics (EACL 2009)*, pages 745–753, Athens, Greece, March.

Mark Steedman. 2000. *The Syntactic Process*. MIT Press, Cambridge, Massachusetts.

Scott C. Stoness, Joel Tetreault, and James Allen. 2004. Incremental parsing with reference interaction. In *Proceedings of the Workshop on Incremental Parsing at the ACL 2004*, pages 18–25, Barcelona, Spain, July.

Scott C. Stoness, James Allen, Greg Aist, and Mary Swift. 2005. Using real-world reference to improve spoken language understanding. In *AAAI Workshop on Spoken Language Understanding*, pages 38–45.

Learning How to Conjugate the Romanian Verb. Rules for Regular and Partially Irregular Verbs

Liviu P. Dinu
Faculty of Mathematics
and Computer Science
University of Bucharest
ldinu@fmi.unibuc.ro

Vlad Niculae
Faculty of Mathematics
and Computer Science
University of Bucharest
vlad@vene.ro

Octavia-Maria Şulea
Faculty of Foreign Languages
and Literatures
Faculty of Mathematics
and Computer Science
University of Bucharest
mary.octavia@gmail.com

Abstract

In this paper we extend our work described in (Dinu et al., 2011) by adding more conjugational rules to the labelling system introduced there, in an attempt to capture the entire dataset of Romanian verbs extracted from (Barbu, 2007), and we employ machine learning techniques to predict a verb's correct label (which says what conjugational pattern it follows) when only the infinitive form is given.

1 Introduction

Using only a restricted group of verbs, in (Dinu et al., 2011) we validated the hypothesis that patterns can be identified in the conjugation of the Romanian (partially irregular) verb and that these patterns can be learnt automatically so that, given the infinitive of a verb, its correct conjugation for the indicative present tense can be produced. In this paper, we extend our investigation to the whole dataset described in (Barbu, 2008) and attempt to capture, beside the general ending patterns during conjugation, as much of the phonological alternations occuring in the stem of verbs (apophony) from the dataset as we can.

Traditionally, Romanian has received a Latin-inspired classification of verbs into 4 (or sometimes 5) conjugational classes based on the ending of their infinitival form alone (Costanzo, 2011). However, this infinitive-based classification has proved itself inadequate due to its inability to account for the behavior of partially irregular verbs (whose stems have a smaller number of allomorphs than the completely irregular) during their conjugation.

There have been, thus, numerous attempts throughout the history of Romanian Linguistics to give other conjugational classifications based on the way the verb actually conjugates. Lombard (1955), looking at a corpus of 667 verbs, combined the traditional 4 classes with the way in which the biggest two subgroups conjugate (one using the suffix "ez", the other "esc") and arrived at 6 classes. Ciompec (Ciompec et. al., 1985 in Costanzo, 2011) proposed 10 conjugational classes, while Felix (1964) proposed 12, both of them looking at the inflection of the verbs and number of allomorphs of the stem. Romalo (1968, p. 5-203) produced a list of 38 verb types, which she eventually reduced to 10.

For the purpose of machine translation, Moisil (1960) proposed 5 regrouped classes of verbs, with numerous subgroups, and introduced the method of letters with variable values, while Papastergiou et al. (2007) have recently developed a classification from a (second) language acquisition point of view, dividing the 1st and 4th traditional classes into 3 and respectively 5 subclasses, each with a different conjugational pattern, and offering rules for alternations in the stem.

Of the more extensive classifications, Barbu (2007) distinguished 41 conjugational classes for all tenses and 30 for the indicative present alone, covering a whole corpus of more that 7000 contemporary Romanian verbs, a corpus which was also used in the present paper. However, her classes were developed on the basis of the suffixes each verb receives during conjugation, and the classification system did not take into account the alternations occuring in the stem of irregular and partially irregular verbs. The system of rules presented below took into account both the endings pattern and the type of stem alternation for each verb.

In what follows we describe our method for labeling the dataset and finding a model able to predict the labels.

2 Approach

The problem which we are aiming to solve is to determine how to conjugate a verb, given its infinitive form. The traditional infinitive-based classification taught in school does not take one all the way to solving this problem. Many conjugational patterns exist within each of these four classes.

2.1 Labeling the dataset

Following our own observations, the alternations identified in (Papastergiou et al., 2007) and the classes of suffix patterns given in (Barbu, 2007), we developed a number of conjugational rules which were narrowed down to the 30 most productive in relation to the dataset. Each of these 30 rules (or patterns) contains 6 regular expressions through which the rule models how a (different) type of Romanian verb conjugates in the indicative present. They each consist of 6 regular expressions because there are three persons (first, second, and third) times two numbers (singular and plural).

Rule 10, for example, models, as stated in the list that follows, how verbs of the type "a cânta" (to sing) conjugate in the indicative present, by having the first regular expression model the first person singular form "(eu) cânt" (in regular expression format: ^(.+)$), the second, model the second person singular form "(tu) cânţi" (^(.+)ţi$), the third, model the third person singular form "(ei) cântă" (^(.+)ă$), and so forth. Thus, rule 10 catches the alternation t→ţ for the 2nd person singular, while modelling a particular type of verb class with a particular set of suffixes. Note that the dot accepts any letter in the Romanian alphabet and that, for each of the six forms, the value of the capturing groups (those between brackets) remains constant, in this case *cân*. These groups correspond to all parts of the stem that remain unchanged and ensure that, given the infinitive and the regular expressions, one can work backwards and produce the correct conjugation.

For a clearer understanding of one such rule, Table 1 shows an example of how the verb "a tresălta" is modeled by rule 14.

Person	Regexp	Example
1st singular	^(.+)a(.+)t$	tresalt
2nd singular	^(.+)a(.+)ţi$	tresalţi
3rd singular	^(.+)a(.+)tă$	tresaltă
1st plural	^(.+)ă(.+)tăm$	tresăltăm
2nd plural	^(.+)ă(.+)taţi$	tresăltaţi
3rd plural	^(.+)a(.+)tă$	tresaltă

Table 1: Rule 14 modelling "a tresălta"

Below, we list all the rules used, with the stem alternations they capture and an example of a verb that they model. Note that, when we say (no) alternation, we mean (no) alternation in the stem. So the difference between rules 1, 20, 22, and the sort lies in the suffix that is added to the stem for each verb form. They may share some suffixes, but not all and/or not for the same person and number.

1. no alternation; "a spera" (to hope);
2. alternation: ă→e for the 2nd person singular; "a număra" (to count);
3. no alternation; "a intra" (to enter), stem ends in "tr", "pl", "bl" or "fl" which determines the addition of "u" at the end of the 1st person singular form;
4. alternation: it lacks t→ţ for the 2nd person singular, which otherwise normally occurs; "a mişca" (to move), stem ends in "şca";
5. no alternation; "a tăia" (to cut), ends in "ia" and has a vowel before;
6. no alternation; "a speria" (to scare), ends in "ia" and has a consonant before;
7. no alternation; "a dansa" (to dance), conjugated with the suffix "ez";
8. no alternation; "a copia" (to copy), conjugated with a modified "ez" due to the stem ending in "ia";
9. altenation c→ch(e) or g→gh(e); "a parca" (to park), conjugated with "ez", ending in "ca" or "ga";
10. alternation: t→ţ for the 2nd person singular; "a cânta" (to sing);
11. alternation: s→ş which replaces the usual t→ţ for the 2nd person singular; "a exista" (to exist);

12. alternation: a→ea for the 3rd person singular and plural, t→ţ for the 2nd person singular; "a deştepta" (to awake/arouse);

13. alternation: e→ea for the 3rd person singular and plural, t→ţ for the 2nd person singular; "a deşerta" (to empty);

14. alternation: ă→a for all the forms except the 1st and 2nd person plural; "a tresălta" (to start, to take fright);

15. alternation: ă→a in the 3rd person singular and plural, ă→e in the 2nd person singular; "a desfăta" (to delight);

16. alternation: ă→a for all the forms except for the 1st and 2nd person plural; "a părea" (to seem);

17. alternation: d→z for the 2nd person singular due to palatalization, along with ă→e; "a vedea" (to see), stem ends in "d";

18. alternation: ă→a for all forms except the 1st and 2nd person plural, d→z for the 2nd person singular due to palatalization; "a cădea" (to fall);

19. no alternation; "a veghea" (to watch over), conjugates with another type of "ez" ending pattern;

20. no alternations; "a merge" (to walk), receives the typical ending pattern for the third conjugational class;

21. alternation: t→ţ for the 2nd person singular; "a promite" (to promise);

22. no alternation; "a scrie" (to write);

23. alternations: şt→sc for the 1st person singular and 3rd person plural; "a naşte" (to give birth), ends in "şte";

24. alternation: "n" is deleted from the stem in the 2nd person singular; "a pune" (to put), ends in "ne";

25. alternation: d→z in the 2nd person singular due to palatalization; "a crede" (to believe), stem ends in "d";

26. no alternation; "a sui" (to climb), ends in "ui", "ăi", or "âi";

27. no alternation; "a citi" (to read), conjugates with the suffix "esc" ;

28. this type preserves the "i" from the infinitive; "a locui" (to reside), ends in "ăi", "oi", or ui" and conjugates with "esc";

29. alternation: o→oa in the 3rd person singular and plural; end in "î", "a omorî" (to kill);

30. no alternation; "a hotărî" (to decide), ends in "î" and conjugates with "ăsc", a variant of "esc"

2.2 Classifiers and features

Each infinitive in the dataset received a label corresponding to the first rule that correctly produces a conjugation for it. This was implemented in order to reduce the ambiguity of the data, which was due to some verbs having alternate conjugation patterns. The unlabeled verbs were thrown out, while the labeled ones were used to train and evaluate a classifier.

The context sensitive nature of the alternations leads to the idea that n-gram character windows are useful. In the preprocessing step, the list of infinitives is transformed to a sparse matrix whose lines correspond to samples, and whose features are the occurence or the frequency of a specific n-gram. This feature extraction step has three free parameters: the maximum n-gram length, the optional binarization of the features (taking only binary occurences instead of counts), and the optional appending of a terminator character. The terminator character allows the classifier to identify and assign a different weight to the n-grams that overlap with the suffix of the string.

For example, consider the English infinitive *to walk*. We will assume the following illustrative values for the parameters: n-gram size of 3 and appending the terminator character. Firstly, a terminator is appended to the end, yielding the string *walk$*. Subsequently, the string is broken into 1, 2 and 3-grams: *w*, *a*, *l*, *k*, *$*, *wa*, *al*, *lk*, *k$*, *wal*, *alk*, *lk$*. Next, this list is turned into a vector using a standard process. We have first built a dictionary of all the n-grams from the whole dataset. These, in order, encode the features. The verb *(to) walk* is therefore encoded as a row vector with ones in the columns corresponding to the features *w*, *a*, etc. and zeros in the rest. In this particular case, there is no difference between binary and count

rule no.	verbs	rule no.	verbs
1	547	16	13
2	8	17	6
3	18	18	4
4	5	19	14
5	8	20	124
6	16	21	25
7	3330	22	15
8	273	23	7
9	89	24	41
10	4	25	51
11	5	26	185
12	4	27	1554
13	106	28	486
14	13	29	5
15	5	30	27

Table 2: Number of verbs captured by each of our rules

features because all of the n-grams of this short verb occur only once. But for a verb such as *(to) tantalize*, the feature corresponding to the 2-gram *ta* would get a value of 2 in a count reprezentation, but only a value of 1 in a binary one.

The system was put together using the scikit-learn machine learning library for Python (Pedregosa et al., 2011), which provides a fast, scalable implementation of linear support vector machines based on *liblinear* (Fan et al., 2008), along with n-gram extraction and grid search functionality.

3 Results

Tabel 2 shows how well the rules fitted the dataset. Out of 7,295 verbs in the dataset, 349 were uncaptured by our rules. As expected, the rule capturing the most verbs (3,330) is the one modelling those from the 1st conjugational class (whose infinitives end in "a") which conjugate with the "ez" suffix and are regular, namely rule 7, created for verbs like "a dansa". The second largest class, also as expected, is the one belonging to verbs from the 4th conjugational group (whose infinitives end in "i"), which are regular, meaning no alternation in the stem, and conjugate with the "esc" suffix. This class is modeled by rule number 27.

The support vector classifier was evaluated using a 10-fold cross-validation. The multi-class problem is treated using the one-versus-all scheme. The parameters chosen by grid search are a maximum n-gram length of 5, with appended terminator and with non-binarized (count) features. The estimated correct classification rate is 90.64%, with a weighted averaged precision of 80.90%, recall of 90.64% and F_1 score of 89.89%. Appending the artificial terminator character '$' consistently improves accuracy by around 0.7%. Because each word was represented as a bag of character n-grams instead of a continuous string, and because, by its nature, a SVM yields sparse solutions, combined with the evaluation using cross-validation, we can safely say that the model does not overfit and indeed learns useful decision boundaries.

4 Conclusions and Future Works

Our results show that the labelling system based on the verb conjugation model we developed can be learned with reasonable accuracy. In the future, we plan to develop a multiple tiered labelling system that will allow for general alternations, such as the ones occuring as a result of palatalization, to be defined only once for all verbs that have them, taking cues from the idea of letters with multiple values. This, we feel, will highly improve the acuracy of the classifier.

5 Acknowledgements

The authors would like to thank the anonymous reviewers for their helpful comments. All authors contributed equally to this work. The research of Liviu P. Dinu was supported by the CNCS, IDEI - PCE project 311/2011, "The Structure and Interpretation of the Romanian Nominal Phrase in Discourse Representation Theory: the Determiners."

References

Ana-Maria Barbu. *Conjugarea verbelor românești. Dicționar: 7500 de verbe românești grupate pe clase de conjugare.* Bucharest: Coresi, 2007. 4th edition, revised. (In Romanian.) (263 pp.).

Ana-Maria Barbu. Romanian lexical databases: Inflected and syllabic forms dictionaries. In *Sixth International Language Resources and Evaluation (LREC'08)*, 2008.

Angelo Roth Costanzo. *Romance Conjugational Classes: Learning from the Peripheries.* PhD thesis, Ohio State University, 2011.

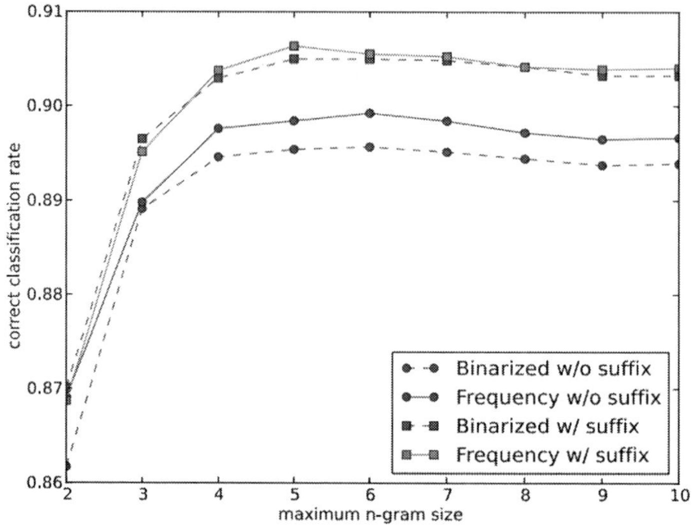

Figure 1: 10-fold cross validation scores for various combination of parameters. Only the values corresponding to the best C regularization parameters are shown.

Liviu P. Dinu, Emil Ionescu, Vlad Niculae, and Octavia-Maria Şulea. Can alternations be learned? a machine learning approach to verb alternations. In *Recent Advances in Natural Language Processing 2011*, September 2011.

Rong-En Fan, Kai-Wei Chang, Cho-Jui Hsieh, Xiang-Rui Wang, and Chih-Jen Lin. Liblinear: A library for large linear classification. *Journal of Machine Learning Research*, 9:1871–1874, June 2008. ISSN 1532-4435.

Jiři Felix. *Classification des verbes roumains*, volume VII. Philosophica Pragensia, 1964.

Alf Lombard. *Le verbe roumain. Etude morphologique*, volume 1. Lund, C. W. K. Gleerup, 1955.

Grigore C. Moisil. Probleme puse de traducerea automată. conjugarea verbelor în limba română. *Studii si cercetări lingvistice*, XI(1): 7–29, 1960.

I. Papastergiou, N. Papastergiou, and L. Mandeki. Verbul românesc - reguli pentru înlesnirea însuşirii indicativului prezent. In *Romanian National Symposium "Directions in Romanian Philological Research", 7th Edition*, May 2007.

F. Pedregosa, G. Varoquaux, A. Gramfort, V. Michel, B. Thirion, O. Grisel, M. Blondel, P. Prettenhofer, R. Weiss, V. Dubourg, J. Vanderplas, A. Passos, D. Cournapeau, M. Brucher, M. Perrot, and E. Duchesnay. Scikit-learn: Machine learning in Python. *Journal of Machine Learning Research*, 12:2825–2830, Oct 2011.

Valeria Guţu Romalo. *Morfologie Structurală a limbii române*. Editura Academiei Republicii Socialiste România, 1968.

Measuring Contextual Fitness Using Error Contexts Extracted from the Wikipedia Revision History

Torsten Zesch
Ubiquitous Knowledge Processing Lab (UKP-DIPF)
German Institute for Educational Research and Educational Information, Frankfurt
Ubiquitous Knowledge Processing Lab (UKP-TUDA)
Department of Computer Science, Technische Universität Darmstadt
http://www.ukp.tu-darmstadt.de

Abstract

We evaluate measures of contextual fitness on the task of detecting real-word spelling errors. For that purpose, we extract naturally occurring errors and their contexts from the Wikipedia revision history. We show that such natural errors are better suited for evaluation than the previously used artificially created errors. In particular, the precision of statistical methods has been largely over-estimated, while the precision of knowledge-based approaches has been under-estimated. Additionally, we show that knowledge-based approaches can be improved by using semantic relatedness measures that make use of knowledge beyond classical taxonomic relations. Finally, we show that statistical and knowledge-based methods can be combined for increased performance.

1 Introduction

Measuring the contextual fitness of a term in its context is a key component in different NLP applications like speech recognition (Inkpen and Désilets, 2005), optical character recognition (Wick et al., 2007), co-reference resolution (Bean and Riloff, 2004), or malapropism detection (Bolshakov and Gelbukh, 2003). The main idea is always to test what fits better into the current context: the actual term or a possible replacement that is phonetically, structurally, or semantically similar. We are going to focus on malapropism detection as it allows evaluating measures of contextual fitness in a more direct way than evaluating in a complex application which always entails influence from other components, e.g. the quality of the optical character recognition module (Walker et al., 2010).

A malapropism or real-word spelling error occurs when a word is replaced with another correctly spelled word which does not suit the context, e.g. "People with lots of *honey* usually live in big houses.", where 'money' was replaced with 'honey'. Besides typing mistakes, a major source of such errors is the failed attempt of automatic spelling correctors to correct a misspelled word (Hirst and Budanitsky, 2005). A real-word spelling error is hard to detect, as the erroneous word is not misspelled and fits syntactically into the sentence. Thus, measures of contextual fitness are required to detect words that do not fit their contexts.

Existing measures of contextual fitness can be categorized into knowledge-based (Hirst and Budanitsky, 2005) and statistical methods (Mays et al., 1991; Wilcox-OHearn et al., 2008). Both test the lexical cohesion of a word with its context. For that purpose, knowledge-based approaches employ the structural knowledge encoded in lexical-semantic networks like WordNet (Fellbaum, 1998), while statistical approaches rely on co-occurrence counts collected from large corpora, e.g. the Google Web1T corpus (Brants and Franz, 2006).

So far, evaluation of contextual fitness measures relied on artificial datasets (Mays et al., 1991; Hirst and Budanitsky, 2005) which are created by taking a sentence that is known to be correct, and replacing a word with a similar word from the vocabulary. This has a couple of disadvantages: (i) the replacement might be a synonym of the original word and perfectly valid in the given context, (ii) the generated error might be very unlikely to be made by a human, and (iii) inserting artificial errors often leads to unnatural sentences that are quite easy to correct, e.g. if the word class has changed. However, even if the word class is unchanged, the original word and its replacement might still be variants of the same lemma, e.g. a noun in singular and plural, or a verb in present and past form. This usually leads to a sentence where the error can be easily detected using syntactical or statistical methods, but is almost impossible to detect for knowledge-based measures of contextual fitness, as the meaning of the word stays more or less unchanged. To estimate the impact of this issue, we randomly sampled 1,000 artificially created real-word spelling errors[1] and found 387 singular/plural pairs and 57 pairs which were in another direct relation (e.g. adjective/adverb). This means that almost half of the artificially created errors are not suited for an evaluation targeted at finding optimal measures of contextual fitness, as they over-estimate the performance of statistical measures while underestimating the potential of semantic measures. In order to investigate this issue, we present a framework for mining naturally occurring errors and their contexts from the Wikipedia revision history. We use the resulting English and German datasets to evaluate statistical and knowledge-based measures.

We make the full experimental framework publicly available[2] which will allow reproducing our experiments as well as conducting follow-up experiments. The framework contains (i) methods to extract natural errors from Wikipedia, (ii) reference implementations of the knowledge-based and the statistical methods, and (iii) the evaluation datasets described in this paper.

2 Mining Errors from Wikipedia

Measures of contextual fitness have previously been evaluated using artificially created datasets, as there are very few sources of sentences with naturally occurring errors and their corrections. Recently, the revision history of Wikipedia has been introduced as a valuable knowledge source for NLP (Nelken and Yamangil, 2008; Yatskar et al., 2010). It is also a possible source of natural errors, as it is likely that Wikipedia editors make real-word spelling errors at some point, which are then corrected in subsequent revisions of the same article. The challenge lies in discriminating real-word spelling errors from all sorts of other changes, including non-word spelling errors, reformulations, or the correction of wrong facts. For that purpose, we apply a set of precision-oriented heuristics narrowing down the number of possible error candidates. Such an approach is feasible, as the high number of revisions in Wikipedia allows to be extremely selective.

2.1 Accessing the Revision Data

We access the Wikipedia revision data using the freely available Wikipedia Revision Toolkit (Ferschke et al., 2011) together with the JWPL Wikipedia API (Zesch et al., 2008a).[3] The API outputs plain text converted from Wiki-Markup, but the text still contains a small portion of left-over markup and other artifacts. Thus, we perform additional cleaning steps removing (i) tokens with more than 30 characters (often URLs), (ii) sentences with less than 5 or more than 200 tokens, and (iii) sentences containing a high fraction of special characters like ':' usually indicating Wikipedia-specific artifacts like lists of language links. The remaining sentences are part-of-speech tagged and lemmatized using TreeTagger (Schmid, 2004). Using these cleaned and annotated articles, we form pairs of adjacent article revisions (r_i and r_{i+1}).

2.2 Sentence Alignment

Fully aligning all sentences of the adjacent revisions is a quite costly operation, as sentences can be split, joined, replaced, or moved in the article. However, we are only looking for sentence pairs which are almost identical except for the real-word spelling error and its correction. Thus, we form all sentence pairs and then apply an aggressive but cheap filter that rules out all sentences which (i) are equal, or (ii) whose lengths differ more than a small number of characters. For the resulting much smaller subset of sentence pairs, we compute the Jaro distance (Jaro, 1995) between each pair. If the distance exceeds a certain threshold t_{sim} (0.05 in this case), we do not further consider the pair. The small amount of remaining sentence pairs is passed to the sentence pair filter for in-depth inspection.

[1] The same artificial data as described in Section 3.2.

[2] http://code.google.com/p/dkpro-spelling-asl/

[3] http://code.google.com/p/jwpl/

2.3 Sentence Pair Filtering

The sentence pair filter further reduces the number of remaining sentence pairs by applying a set of heuristics including *surface level* and *semantic level* filters. Surface level filters include:

Replaced Token Sentences need to consist of identical tokens, except for one replaced token.

No Numbers The replaced token may not be a number.

UPPER CASE The replaced token may not be in upper case.

Case Change The change should not only involve case changes, e.g. changing 'english' into 'English'.

Edit Distance The edit distance between the replaced token and its correction need to be below a certain threshold.

After applying the surface level filters, the remaining sentence pairs are well-formed and contain exactly one changed token at the same position in the sentence. However, the change does not need to characterize a real-word spelling error, but could also be a normal spelling error or a semantically motivated change. Thus, we apply a set of semantic filters:

Vocabulary The replaced token needs to occur in the vocabulary. We found that even quite comprehensive word lists discarded too many valid errors as Wikipedia contains articles from a very wide range of domains. Thus, we use a frequency filter based on the Google Web1T n-gram counts (Brants and Franz, 2006). We filter all sentences where the replaced token has a very low unigram count. We experimented with different values and found 25,000 for English and 10,000 for German to yield good results.

Same Lemma The original token and the replaced token may not have the same lemma, e.g. 'car' and 'cars' would not pass this filter.

Stopwords The replaced token should not be in a short list of stopwords (mostly function words).

Named Entity The replaced token should not be part of a named entity. For this purpose, we applied the Stanford NER (Finkel et al., 2005).

Normal Spelling Error We apply the Jazzy spelling detector[4] and rule out all cases in which it is able to detect the error.

Semantic Relation If the original token and the replaced token are in a close lexical-semantic relations, the change is likely to be semantically motivated, e.g. if "house" was replaced with "hut". Thus, we do not consider cases, where we detect a direct semantic relation between the original and the replaced term. For this purpose, we use WordNet (Fellbaum, 1998) for English and GermaNet (Lemnitzer and Kunze, 2002) for German.

[4] http://jazzy.sourceforge.net/

3 Resulting Datasets

3.1 Natural Error Datasets

Using our framework for mining real-word spelling errors in context, we extracted an English dataset[5], and a German dataset[6]. Although the output generally was of high quality, manual post-processing was necessary[7], as (i) for some pairs the available context did not provide enough information to decide which form was correct, and (ii) a problem that might be specific to Wikipedia – vandalism. The revisions are full of cases where words are replaced with similar sounding but greasy alternatives. A relatively mild example is "In romantic comedies, there is a love story about a man and a woman who fall in love, along with silly or funny comedy *farts*.", where 'parts' was replaced with 'farts' only to be changed back shortly afterwards by a Wikipedia vandalism hunter. We removed all cases that resulted from obvious vandalism. For further experiments, a small list of offensive terms could be added to the stopword list to facilitate this process.

A connected problem is correct words that get falsely corrected by Wikipedia editors (without the malicious intend from the previous examples, but with similar consequences). For example, the initially correct sentence "Dung beetles roll it into a ball, sometimes being up to 50 times their own weight." was 'corrected' by exchanging *weight* with *wait*. We manually removed such obvious mistakes, but are still left with some borderline cases. In the sentence "By the 1780s the *goals* of England were so full that convicts were often chained up in rotting old ships." the obvious error

[5] Using a revision dump from April 5, 2011.

[6] Using a revision dump from August 13, 2010.

[7] The most efficient and precise way of finding real-word spelling errors would of course be to apply measures of contextual fitness. However, the resulting dataset would then only contain errors that are detectable by the measures we want to evaluate – a clearly unacceptable bias. Thus, a certain amount of manual validation is inevitable.

'goal' was changed by some Wikipedia editor to 'jail'. However, actually it should have been the old English form for jail 'gaol' which can be deduced when looking at the full context and later versions of the article. We decided to not remove these rare cases, because 'jail' is a valid correction in this context.

After manual inspection, we are left with 466 English and 200 German errors. Given that we restricted our experiment to 5 million English and German revisions, much larger datasets can be extracted if the whole revision history is taken into account. Our snapshot of the English Wikipedia contains $305 \cdot 10^6$ revisions. Even if not all of them correspond to article revisions, it is safe to assume that more than 10,000 real-word spelling errors can be extracted from this version of Wikipedia.

Using the same amount of source revisions, we found significantly more English than German errors. This might be due to (i) English having more short nouns or verbs than German that are more likely to be confused with each other, and (ii) the English Wikipedia being known to attract a larger amount of non-native editors which might lead to higher rates of real-word spelling errors. However, this issue needs to be further investigated e.g. based on comparable corpora build on the basis of different language editions of Wikipedia. Further refining the identification of real-word errors in Wikipedia would allow evaluating how frequent such errors actually occur, and how long it takes the Wikipedia editors to detect them. If errors persist over a long time, using measures of contextual fitness for detection would be even more important.

Another interesting observation is that the average edit distance is around 1.4 for both datasets. This means that a substantial proportion of errors involve more than one edit operation. Given that many measures of contextual fitness allow at most one edit, many naturally occurring errors will not be detected. However, allowing a larger edit distance enormously increases the search space resulting in increased run-time and possibly decreased detection precision due to more false positives.

3.2 Artificial Error Datasets

In contrast to the quite challenging process of mining naturally occurring errors, creating artificial errors is relatively straightforward. From a corpus that is known to be free of spelling errors, sentences are randomly sampled. For each sentence, a random word is selected and all strings with edit distance smaller than a given threshold (2 in our case) are generated. If one of those generated strings is a known word from the vocabulary, it is picked as the artificial error.

Previous work on evaluating real-word spelling correction (Hirst and Budanitsky, 2005; Wilcox-OHearn et al., 2008; Islam and Inkpen, 2009) used a dataset sampled from the Wall Street Journal corpus which is not freely available. Thus, we created a comparable English dataset of 1,000 artificial errors based on the easily available Brown corpus (Francis W. Nelson and Kuçera, 1964).[8] Additionally, we created a German dataset with 1,000 artificial errors based on the TIGER corpus.[9]

4 Measuring Contextual Fitness

There are two main approaches for measuring the contextual fitness of a word in its context: the statistical (Mays et al., 1991) and the knowledge-based approach (Hirst and Budanitsky, 2005).

4.1 Statistical Approach

Mays et al. (1991) introduced an approach based on the noisy-channel model. The model assumes that the correct sentence s is transmitted through a noisy channel adding 'noise' which results in a word w being replaced by an error e leading the wrong sentence s' which we observe. The probability of the correct word w given that we observe the error e can be computed as $P(w|e) = P(w) \cdot P(e|w)$. The channel model $P(e|w)$ describes how likely the typist is to make an error. This is modeled by the parameter α.[10] The remaining probability mass $(1 - \alpha)$ is distributed equally among all words in the vocabulary within an edit distance of 1 ($edits(w)$):

$$P(e|w) = \begin{cases} \alpha & \text{if } e = w \\ (1-\alpha)/|edits(w)| & \text{if } e \neq w \end{cases}$$

The source model $P(w)$ is estimated using a trigram language model, i.e. the probability of the

[8] http://www.archive.org/details/BrownCorpus (CC-by-na).

[9] http://www.ims.uni-stuttgart.de/projekte/TIGER/ The corpus contains 50,000 sentences of German newspaper text, and is freely available under a non-commercial license.

[10] We optimize α on a held-out development set of errors.

intended word w_i is computed as the conditional probability $P(w_i|w_{i-1}w_{i-2})$. Hence, the probability of the correct sentence $s = w_1 \dots w_n$ can be estimated as

$$P(s) = \prod_{i=1}^{n+2} P(w_i|w_{i-1}w_{i-2})$$

The set of candidate sentences S_c contains all versions of the observed sentence s' derived by replacing one word with a word from $edits(w)$, while all other words in the sentence remain unchanged. The correct sentence s is those sentence from S_c that maximizes $P(s|s') = \arg\max_{s \in S_c} P(s) \cdot P(s'|s)$.

4.2 Knowledge Based Approach

Hirst and Budanitsky (2005) introduced a knowledge-based approach that detects real-word spelling errors by checking the semantic relations of a target word with its context. For this purpose, they apply WordNet as the source of lexical-semantic knowledge.

The algorithm flags all words as error candidates and then applies filters to remove those words from further consideration that are unlikely to be errors. First, the algorithm removes all closed-class word candidates as well as candidates which cannot be found in the vocabulary. Candidates are then tested for having lexical cohesion with their context, by (i) checking whether the same surface form or lemma appears again in the context, or (ii) a semantically related concept is found in the context. In both cases, the candidate is removed from the list of candidates. For each remaining possible real-word spelling error, edits are generated by inserting, deleting, or replacing characters up to a certain edit distance (usually 1). Each edit is then tested for lexical cohesion with the context. If at least one of it fits into the context, the candidate is selected as a real-word error.

Hirst and Budanitsky (2005) use two additional filters: First, they remove candidates that are "common non-topical words". It is unclear how the list of such words was compiled. Their list of examples contains words like 'find' or 'world' which we consider to be perfectly valid candidates. Second, they also applied a filter using a list of known multi-words, as the probability for words to accidentally form multi-words is low.

Dataset	P	R	F
Artificial-English	.77	.50	.60
Natural-English	.54	.26	.35
Artificial-German	.90	.49	.63
Natural-German	.77	.20	.32

Table 1: Performance of the statistical approach using a trigram model based on Google Web1T.

It is unclear which list was used. We could use multi-words from WordNet, but coverage would be rather limited. We decided not to use both filters in order to better assess the influence of the underlying semantic relatedness measure on the overall performance.

The knowledge based approach uses semantic relatedness measures to determine the cohesion between a candidate and its context. In the experiments by Budanitsky and Hirst (2006), the measure by (Jiang and Conrath, 1997) yields the best results. However, a wide range of other measures have been proposed, cf. (Zesch and Gurevych, 2010). Some measures using a wider definition of semantic relatedness (Gabrilovich and Markovitch, 2007; Zesch et al., 2008b) instead of only using taxonomic relations in a knowledge source.

As semantic relatedness measures usually return a numeric value, we need to determine a threshold θ in order to come up with a binary related/unrelated decision. Budanitsky and Hirst (2006) used a characteristic gap in the standard evaluation dataset by Rubenstein and Goodenough (1965) that separates unrelated from related word pairs. We do not follow this approach, but optimize the threshold on a held-out development set of real-word spelling errors.

5 Results & Discussion

In this section, we report on the results obtained in our evaluation of contextual fitness measures using artificial and natural errors in English and German.

5.1 Statistical Approach

Table 1 summarizes the results obtained by the statistical approach using a trigram model based on the Google Web1T data (Brants and Franz, 2006). On the English artificial errors, we observe a quite high F-measure of .60 that drops to

Dataset	N-gram model	Size	P	R	F
Art-En	Google Web	$7 \cdot 10^{11}$	.77	.50	.60
		$7 \cdot 10^{10}$	.78	.48	.59
		$7 \cdot 10^{9}$	.76	.42	.54
	Wikipedia	$2 \cdot 10^{9}$	.72	.37	.49
Nat-En	Google Web	$7 \cdot 10^{11}$	.54	.26	.35
		$7 \cdot 10^{10}$	.51	.23	.31
		$7 \cdot 10^{9}$	.46	.19	.27
	Wikipedia	$2 \cdot 10^{9}$	.49	.19	.27
Art-De	Google Web	$8 \cdot 10^{10}$	.90	.49	.63
		$8 \cdot 10^{9}$	.90	.47	.61
		$8 \cdot 10^{8}$	.88	.36	.51
	Wikipedia	$7 \cdot 10^{8}$	.90	.37	.52
Nat-De	Google Web	$8 \cdot 10^{10}$	.77	.20	.32
		$8 \cdot 10^{9}$	.68	.14	.23
		$8 \cdot 10^{8}$	.65	.10	.17
	Wikipedia	$7 \cdot 10^{8}$	.70	.13	.22

Table 2: Influence of the n-gram model on the performance of the statistical approach.

.35 when switching to the naturally occurring errors which we extracted from Wikipedia. On the German dataset, we observe almost the same performance drop (from .63 to .32).

These observations correspond to our earlier analysis where we showed that the artificial data contains many cases that are quite easy to correct using a statistical model, e.g. where a plural form of a noun is replaced with its singular form (or vice versa) as in "I bought a car." vs. "I bought a cars.". The naturally occurring errors often contain much harder contexts, as shown in the following example: "Through the open window they heard sounds below in the street: cartwheels, a tired horse's plodding step, vices." where 'vices' should be corrected to 'voices'. While the lemma 'voice' is clearly semantically related to other words in the context like 'hear' or 'sound', the position at the end of the sentence is especially difficult for the trigram-based statistical approach. The only trigram that connects the error to the context is ('step', ',', *vices/voices*) which will probably yield a low frequency count even for very large trigram models. Higher order n-gram models would help, but suffer from the usual data-sparseness problems.

Influence of the N-gram Model For building the trigram model, we used the Google Web1T data, which has some known quality issues and is not targeted towards the Wikipedia articles from which we sampled the natural errors. Thus, we also tested a trigram model based on Wikipedia. However, it is much smaller than the Web model, which leads us to additionally testing smaller Web models. Table 2 summarizes the results.

We observe that "more data is better data" still holds, as the largest Web model always outperforms the Wikipedia model in terms of recall. If we reduce the size of the Web model to the same order of magnitude as the Wikipedia model, the performance of the two models is comparable. We would have expected to see better results for the Wikipedia model in this setting, but its higher quality does not lead to a significant difference.

Even if statistical approaches quite reliably detect real-word spelling errors, the size of the required n-gram models remains a serious obstacle for use in real-world applications. The English Web1T trigram model is about 25GB, which currently is not suited for being applied in settings with limited storage capacities e.g. for intelligent input assistance in mobile devices. As we have seen above, using smaller models will decrease recall to a point where hardly any error will be detected anymore. Thus, we will now have a look on knowledge-based approaches which are less demanding in terms of the required resources.

Dataset	P	R	F
Artificial-English	.26	.15	.19
Natural-English	.29	.18	.23
Artificial-German	.47	.16	.24
Natural-German	.40	.13	.19

Table 3: Performance of the knowledge-based approach using the JiangConrath semantic relatedness measure.

5.2 Knowledge-based Approach

Table 3 shows the results for the knowledge-based measure. In contrast to the statistical approach, the results on the artificial errors are not higher than on the natural errors, but almost equal for German and even lower for English; another piece of evidence supporting our view that the properties of artificial datasets over-estimate the performance of statistical measures.

Influence of the Relatedness Measure As was pointed out before, Budanitsky and Hirst (2006)

Dataset	Measure	θ	P	R	F
Art-En	JiangConrath	0.5	.26	.15	.19
	Lin	0.5	.22	.17	.19
	Lesk	0.5	.19	.16	.17
	ESA-Wikipedia	0.05	**.43**	.13	.20
	ESA-Wiktionary	0.05	.35	**.20**	**.25**
	ESA-Wordnet	0.05	.33	.15	.21
Nat-En	JiangConrath	0.5	.29	.18	.23
	Lin	0.5	.26	**.21**	.23
	Lesk	0.5	.19	.19	.19
	ESA-Wikipedia	0.05	**.48**	.14	.22
	ESA-Wiktionary	0.05	.39	**.21**	**.27**
	ESA-Wordnet	0.05	.36	.15	.21

Table 4: Performance of knowledge-based approach using different relatedness measures.

show that the measure by Jiang and Conrath (1997) yields the best results in their experiments on malapropism detection. In addition, we test another path-based measure by Lin (1998), the gloss-based measure by Lesk (1986), and the ESA measure (Gabrilovich and Markovitch, 2007) based on concept vectors from Wikipedia, Wiktionary, and WordNet. Table 4 summarizes the results. In contrast to the findings of Budanitsky and Hirst (2006), JiangConrath is not the best path-based measure, as Lin provides equal or better performance. Even more importantly, other (non path-based) measures yield better performance than both path-based measures. Especially ESA based on Wiktionary provides a good overall performance, while ESA based on Wikipedia provides excellent precision. The advantage of ESA over the other measure types can be explained with its ability to incorporate semantic relationships beyond classical taxonomic relations (as used by path-based measures).

5.3 Combining the Approaches

The statistical and the knowledge-based approach use quite different methods to assess the contextual fitness of a word in its context. This makes it worthwhile trying to combine both approaches. We ran the statistical method (using the full Wikipedia trigram model) and the knowledge-based method (using the ESA-Wiktionary relatedness measure) in parallel and then combined the resulting detections using two strategies: (i) we merge the detections of both approaches in order to obtain higher recall ('Union'), and (ii) we only count an error as detected if both methods agree on a detection ('Intersection'). When comparing the combined results in Table 5 with the best precision or recall obtained by a single measure ('Best-Single'), we observe that precision can be significantly improved using the 'Union' strategy, while recall is only moderately improved using the 'Intersect' strategy. This means that (i) a large subset of errors is detected by both approaches that due to their different sources of knowledge mutually reinforce the detection leading to increased precision, and (ii) a small but otherwise undetectable subset of errors requires considering detections made by one approach only.

Dataset	Comb.-Strategy	P	R	F
Artificial-English	Best-Single	.77	.50	.60
	Union	.52	**.55**	.54
	Intersection	**.91**	.15	.25
Natural-English	Best-Single	.54	.26	.35
	Union	.40	**.36**	.38
	Intersection	**.82**	.11	.19

Table 5: Results obtained by a combination of the best statistical and knowledge-based configuration. 'Best-Single' is the best precision or recall obtained by a single measure. 'Union' merges the detections of both approaches. 'Intersection' only detects an error if both methods agree on a detection.

6 Related Work

To our knowledge, we are the first to create a dataset of naturally occurring errors based on the revision history of Wikipedia. Max and Wisniewski (2010) used similar techniques to create a dataset of errors from the French Wikipedia. However, they target a wider class of errors including non-word spelling errors, and their class of real-word errors conflates malapropisms as well as other types of changes like reformulations. Thus, their dataset cannot be easily used for our purposes and is only available in French, while our framework allows creating datasets for all major languages with minimal manual effort.

Another possible source of real-word spelling errors are learner corpora (Granger, 2002), e.g. the Cambridge Learner Corpus (Nicholls, 1999). However, annotation of errors is difficult and costly (Rozovskaya and Roth, 2010), only a small fraction of observed errors will be real-word spelling errors, and learners are likely to make different mistakes than proficient language users.

Islam and Inkpen (2009) presented another statistical approach using the Google Web1T data (Brants and Franz, 2006) to create the n-gram model. It slightly outperformed the approach by Mays et al. (1991) when evaluated on a corpus of artificial errors based on the WSJ corpus. However, the results are not directly comparable, as Mays et al. (1991) used a much smaller n-gram model and our results in Section 5.1 show that the size of the n-gram model has a large influence on the results. Eventually, we decided to use the Mays et al. (1991) approach in our study, as it is easier to adapt and augment.

In a re-evaluation of the statistical model by Mays et al. (1991), Wilcox-OHearn et al. (2008) found that it outperformed the knowledge-based method by Hirst and Budanitsky (2005) when evaluated on a corpus of artificial errors based on the WSJ corpus. This is consistent with our findings on the artificial errors based on the Brown corpus, but - as we have seen in the previous section - evaluation on the naturally occurring errors shows a different picture. They also tried to improve the model by permitting multiple corrections and using fixed-length context windows instead of sentences, but obtained discouraging results.

All previously discussed methods are unsupervised in a way that they do not rely on any training data with annotated errors. However, real-word spelling correction has also been tackled by supervised approaches (Golding and Schabes, 1996; Jones and Martin, 1997; Carlson et al., 2001). Those methods rely on predefined *confusion-sets*, i.e. sets of words that are often confounded e.g. {peace, piece} or {weather, whether}. For each set, the methods learn a model of the context in which one or the other alternative is more probable. This yields very high precision, but only for the limited number of previously defined confusion sets. Our framework for extracting natural errors could be used to increase the number of known confusion sets.

7 Conclusions and Future Work

In this paper, we evaluated two main approaches for measuring the contextual fitness of terms: the statistical approach by Mays et al. (1991) and the knowledge-based approach by Hirst and Budanitsky (2005) on the task of detecting real-word spelling errors. For that purpose, we extracted a dataset with naturally occurring errors and their contexts from the Wikipedia revision history. We show that evaluating measures of contextual fitness on this dataset provides a more realistic picture of task performance. In particular, using artificial datasets over-estimates the performance of the statistical approach, while it underestimates the performance of the knowledge-based approach.

We show that n-gram models targeted towards the domain from which the errors are sampled do not improve the performance of the statistical approach if larger n-gram models are available. We further show that the performance of the knowledge-based approach can be improved by using semantic relatedness measures that incorporate knowledge beyond the taxonomic relations in a classical lexical-semantic resource like WordNet. Finally, by combining both approaches, significant increases in precision or recall can be achieved.

In future work, we want to evaluate a wider range of contextual fitness measures, and learn how to combine them using more sophisticated combination strategies. Both - the statistical as well as the knowledge-based approach - will benefit from a better model of the typist, as not all edit operations are equally likely (Kernighan et al., 1990). On the side of the error extraction, we are going to further improve the extraction process by incorporating more knowledge about the revisions. For example, vandalism is often reverted very quickly, which can be detected when looking at the full set of revisions of an article.

We hope that making the experimental framework publicly available will foster future research in this field, as our results on the natural errors show that the problem is still quite challenging.

Acknowledgments

This work has been supported by the Volkswagen Foundation as part of the Lichtenberg-Professorship Program under grant No. I/82806. We Andreas Kellner and Tristan Miller for checking the datasets, and the anonymous reviewers for their helpful feedback.

References

David Bean and Ellen Riloff. 2004. Unsupervised learning of contextual role knowledge for coreference resolution. In *Proc. of HLT/NAACL*, pages 297–304.

Igor A. Bolshakov and Alexander Gelbukh. 2003. On Detection of Malapropisms by Multistage Collocation Testing. In *Proceedings of NLDB-2003, 8th International Workshop on Applications of Natural Language to Information Systems*, number Cic.

Thorsten Brants and Alex Franz. 2006. Web 1T 5-gram Version 1.

Alexander Budanitsky and Graeme Hirst. 2006. Evaluating wordnet-based measures of lexical semantic relatedness. *Computational Linguistics*, 32(1):13–47.

Andrew J Carlson, Jeffrey Rosen, and Dan Roth. 2001. Scaling Up Context-Sensitive Text Correction. In *Proceedings of IAAI*.

C Fellbaum. 1998. *WordNet An Electronic Lexical Database*. MIT Press, Cambridge, MA.

Oliver Ferschke, Torsten Zesch, and Iryna Gurevych. 2011. Wikipedia Revision Toolkit: Efficiently Accessing Wikipedia's Edit History. In *Proceedings of the 49th Annual Meeting of the Association for Computational Linguistics: Human Language Technologies. System Demonstrations*, pages 97–102, Portland, OR, USA.

Jenny Rose Finkel, Trond Grenager, and Christopher Manning. 2005. Incorporating non-local information into information extraction systems by Gibbs sampling. In *Proceedings of the 43rd Annual Meeting on Association for Computational Linguistics - ACL '05*, pages 363–370, Morristown, NJ, USA. Association for Computational Linguistics.

Francis W. Nelson and Henry Kuçera. 1964. Manual of information to accompany a standard corpus of present-day edited American English, for use with digital computers.

Evgeniy Gabrilovich and Shaul Markovitch. 2007. Computing Semantic Relatedness using Wikipedia-based Explicit Semantic Analysis. In *Proceedings of the 20th International Joint Conference on Artificial Intelligence*, pages 1606–1611.

Andrew R. Golding and Yves Schabes. 1996. Combining Trigram-based and feature-based methods for context-sensitive spelling correction. In *Proceedings of the 34th annual meeting on Association for Computational Linguistics -*, pages 71–78, Morristown, NJ, USA. Association for Computational Linguistics.

Sylviane Granger, 2002. *A birds-eye view of learner corpus research*, pages 3–33. John Benjamins Publishing Company.

Graeme Hirst and Alexander Budanitsky. 2005. Correcting real-word spelling errors by restoring lexical cohesion. *Natural Language Engineering*, 11(1):87–111, March.

Diana Inkpen and Alain Désilets. 2005. Semantic similarity for detecting recognition errors in automatic speech transcripts. In *Proceedings of the conference on Human Language Technology and Empirical Methods in Natural Language Processing - HLT '05*, number October, pages 49–56, Morristown, NJ, USA. Association for Computational Linguistics.

Aminul Islam and Diana Inkpen. 2009. Real-word spelling correction using Google Web IT 3-grams. In *Proceedings of the 2009 Conference on Empirical Methods in Natural Language Processing Volume 3 - EMNLP '09*, Morristown, NJ, USA. Association for Computational Linguistics.

M A Jaro. 1995. Probabilistic linkage of large public health data file. *Statistics in Medicine*, 14:491–498.

Jay J Jiang and David W Conrath. 1997. Semantic Similarity Based on Corpus Statistics and Lexical Taxonomy. In *Proceedings of the 10th International Conference on Research in Computational Linguistics*, Taipei, Taiwan.

Michael P Jones and James H Martin. 1997. Contextual spelling correction using latent semantic analysis. In *Proceedings of the fifth conference on Applied natural language processing -*, pages 166–173, Morristown, NJ, USA. Association for Computational Linguistics.

Mark D Kernighan, Kenneth W Church, and William A Gale. 1990. A Spelling Correction Program Based on a Noisy Channel Model. In *Proceedings of the 13th International Conference on Computational Linguistics*, pages 205–210, Helsinki, Finland.

Lothar Lemnitzer and Claudia Kunze. 2002. GermaNet - Representation, Visualization, Application. In *Proceedings of the 3rd International Conference on Language Resources and Evaluation (LREC)*, pages 1485–1491.

M Lesk. 1986. Automatic sense disambiguation using machine readable dictionaries: how to tell a pine cone from an ice cream cone. *Proceedings of the 5th annual international conference*, pages 24–26.

Dekang Lin. 1998. An Information-Theoretic Definition of Similarity. In *Proceedings of International Conference on Machine Learning*, pages 296–304, Madison, Wisconsin.

Aurelien Max and Guillaume Wisniewski. 2010. Mining Naturally-occurring Corrections and Paraphrases from Wikipedias Revision History. In *Proceedings of the Seventh conference on International Language Resources and Evaluation (LREC'10)*, pages 3143–3148.

Eric Mays, Fred. J Damerau, and Robert L Mercer. 1991. Context based spelling correction. *Information Processing & Management*, 27(5):517–522.

Rani Nelken and Elif Yamangil. 2008. Mining Wikipedia's Article Revision History for Training Computational Linguistics Algorithms. In *Proceedings of the AAAI Workshop on Wikipedia and Artificial Intelligence: An Evolving Synergy (WikiAI)*, WikiAI08.

Diane Nicholls. 1999. The Cambridge Learner Corpus - Error Coding and Analysis for Lexicography and ELT. In *Summer Workshop on Learner Corpora*, Tokyo, Japan.

Alla Rozovskaya and Dan Roth. 2010. Annotating ESL Errors: Challenges and Rewards. In *The 5th Workshop on Innovative Use of NLP for Building Educational Applications (NAACL-HLT)*.

H Rubenstein and J B Goodenough. 1965. Contextual Correlates of Synonymy. *Communications of the ACM*, 8(10):627–633.

Helmut Schmid. 2004. Efficient Parsing of Highly Ambiguous Context-Free Grammars with Bit Vectors. In *Proceedings of the 20th International Conference on Computational Linguistics (COLING 2004)*, Geneva, Switzerland.

Daniel D. Walker, William B. Lund, and Eric K. Ringger. 2010. Evaluating Models of Latent Document Semantics in the Presence of OCR Errors. *Proceedings of the 2010 Conference on Empirical Methods in Natural Language Processing*, (October):240–250.

M. Wick, M. Ross, and E. Learned-Miller. 2007. Context-sensitive error correction: Using topic models to improve OCR. In *Ninth International Conference on Document Analysis and Recognition (ICDAR 2007) Vol 2*, pages 1168–1172. Ieee, September.

Amber Wilcox-OHearn, Graeme Hirst, and Alexander Budanitsky. 2008. Real-word spelling correction with trigrams: A reconsideration of the Mays, Damerau, and Mercer model. In *Proceedings of the 9th international conference on Computational linguistics and intelligent text processing (CICLing)*.

Mark Yatskar, Bo Pang, Cristian Danescu-Niculescu-Mizil, and Lillian Lee. 2010. For the sake of simplicity: unsupervised extraction of lexical simplifications from Wikipedia. In *Human Language Technologies: The 2010 Annual Conference of the North American Chapter of the Association for Computational Linguistics*, HLT '10, pages 365–368.

Torsten Zesch and Iryna Gurevych. 2010. Wisdom of Crowds versus Wisdom of Linguists - Measuring the Semantic Relatedness of Words. *Journal of Natural Language Engineering*, 16(1):25–59.

Torsten Zesch, Christof Müller, and Iryna Gurevych. 2008a. Extracting Lexical Semantic Knowledge from Wikipedia and Wiktionary. In *Proceedings of the Conference on Language Resources and Evaluation (LREC)*.

Torsten Zesch, Christof Müller, and Iryna Gurevych. 2008b. Using wiktionary for computing semantic relatedness. In *Proceedings of the 23rd AAAI Conference on Artificial Intelligence*, pages 861–867, Chicago, IL, USA, Jul.

Perplexity Minimization for Translation Model Domain Adaptation in Statistical Machine Translation

Rico Sennrich
Institute of Computational Linguistics
University of Zurich
Binzmühlestr. 14
CH-8050 Zürich
sennrich@cl.uzh.ch

Abstract

We investigate the problem of domain adaptation for parallel data in Statistical Machine Translation (SMT). While techniques for domain adaptation of monolingual data can be borrowed for parallel data, we explore conceptual differences between translation model and language model domain adaptation and their effect on performance, such as the fact that translation models typically consist of several features that have different characteristics and can be optimized separately. We also explore adapting multiple (4–10) data sets with no *a priori* distinction between in-domain and out-of-domain data except for an in-domain development set.

1 Introduction

The increasing availability of parallel corpora from various sources, welcome as it may be, leads to new challenges when building a statistical machine translation system for a specific domain. The task of determining which parallel texts should be included for training, and which ones hurt translation performance, is tedious when performed through trial-and-error. Alternatively, methods for a weighted combination exist, but there is conflicting evidence as to which approach works best, and the issue of determining weights is not adequately resolved.

The picture looks better in language modelling, where model interpolation through perplexity minimization has become a widespread method of domain adaptation. We investigate the applicability of this method for translation models, and discuss possible applications.

We move the focus away from a binary combination of in-domain and out-of-domain data. If we can scale up the number of models whose contributions we weight, this reduces the need for *a priori* knowledge about the fitness[1] of each potential training text, and opens new research opportunities, for instance experiments with clustered training data.

2 Domain Adaptation for Translation Models

To motivate efforts in domain adaptation, let us review why additional training data can improve, but also decrease translation quality.

Adding more training data to a translation system is easy to motivate through the data sparseness problem. Koehn and Knight (2001) show that translation quality correlates strongly with how often a word occurs in the training corpus. Rare words or phrases pose a problem in several stages of MT modelling, from word alignment to the computation of translation probabilities through Maximum Likelihood Estimation. Unknown words are typically copied verbatim to the target text, which may be a good strategy for named entities, but is often wrong otherwise. In general, more data allows for a better word alignment, a better estimation of translation probabilities, and for the consideration of more context (in phrase-based or syntactic SMT).

A second effect of additional data is not necessarily positive. Translations are inherently ambiguous, and a strong source of ambiguity is the

[1] We borrow this term from early evolutionary biology to emphasize that the question in domain adaptation is not how "good" or "bad" the data is, but how well-adapted it is to the task at hand.

domain of a text. The German word "Wort" (engl. *word*) is typically translated as *floor* in Europarl, a corpus of Parliamentary Proceedings (Koehn, 2005), owing to the high frequency of phrases such as *you have the floor*, which is translated into German as *Sie haben das Wort*. This translation is highly idiomatic and unlikely to occur in other contexts. Still, adding Europarl as out-of-domain training data shifts the probability distribution of $p(t|\text{"Wort"})$ in favour of $p(\text{"floor"}|\text{"Wort"})$, and may thus lead to improper translations.

We will refer to the two problems as the data sparseness problem and the ambiguity problem. Adding out-of-domain data typically mitigates the data sparseness problem, but exacerbates the ambiguity problem. The net gain (or loss) of adding more data changes from case to case. Because there are (to our knowledge) no tools that predict this net effect, it is a matter of empirical investigation (or, in less suave terms, trial-and-error), to determine which corpora to use.[2]

From this understanding of the reasons for and against out-of-domain data, we formulate the following hypotheses:

1. A weighted combination can control the contribution of the out-of-domain corpus on the probability distribution, and thus limit the ambiguity problem.

2. A weighted combination eliminates the need for data selection, offering a robust baseline for domain-specific machine translation.

We will discuss three mixture modelling techniques for translation models. Our aim is to adapt all four features of the standard Moses SMT translation model: the phrase translation probabilities $p(\bar{t}|\bar{s})$ and $p(\bar{s}|\bar{t})$, and the lexical weights $lex(\bar{t}|\bar{s})$ and $lex(\bar{s}|\bar{t})$.[3]

2.1 Linear Interpolation

A well-established approach in language modelling is the linear interpolation of several models, i.e. computing the weighted average of the individual model probabilities. It is defined as follows:

$$p(x|y;\lambda) = \sum_{i=1}^{n} \lambda_i p_i(x|y) \tag{1}$$

with λ_i being the interpolation weight of each model i, and with $(\sum_i \lambda_i) = 1$.

For SMT, linear interpolation of translation models has been used in numerous systems. The approaches diverge in how they set the interpolation weights. Some authors use uniform weights (Cohn and Lapata, 2007), others empirically test different interpolation coefficients (Finch and Sumita, 2008; Yasuda et al., 2008; Nakov and Ng, 2009; Axelrod et al., 2011), others apply monolingual metrics to set the weights for TM interpolation (Foster and Kuhn, 2007; Koehn et al., 2010).

There are reasons against all these approaches. Uniform weights are easy to implement, but give little control. Empirically, it has been shown that they often do not perform optimally (Finch and Sumita, 2008; Yasuda et al., 2008). An optimization of BLEU scores on a development set is promising, but slow and impractical. There is no easy way to integrate linear interpolation into log-linear SMT frameworks and perform optimization through MERT. Monolingual optimization objectives such as language model perplexity have the advantage of being well-known and readily available, but their relation to the ambiguity problem is indirect at best.

Linear interpolation is seemingly well-defined in equation 1. Still, there are a few implementation details worth pointing out. If we directly interpolate each feature in the translation model, and define the feature values of non-occurring phrase pairs as 0, this disregards the meaning of each feature. If we estimate $p(x|y)$ via MLE as in equation 2, and $c(y) = 0$, then $p(x|y)$ is strictly speaking undefined. Alternatively to a naive algorithm, which treats unknown phrase pairs as having a probability of 0, which results in a deficient probability distribution, we propose and implement the following algorithm. For each value pair (x, y) for which we compute $p(x|y)$, we replace λ_i with 0 for all models i with $p(y) = 0$, then renormalize the weight vector λ to 1. We do this for $p(\bar{t}|\bar{s})$ and $lex(\bar{t}|\bar{s})$, but not for $p(\bar{s}|\bar{t})$ and $lex(\bar{s}|\bar{t})$, the reasoning being the con-

[2] A frustrating side-effect is that these findings rarely generalize. For instance, we were unable to reproduce the finding by Ceauşu et al. (2011) that patent translation systems are highly domain-sensitive and suffer from the inclusion of parallel training data from other patent subdomains.

[3] We can ignore the fifth feature, the phrase penalty, which is a constant.

sequences for perplexity minimization (see section 2.4). Namely, we do not want to penalize a small in-domain model for having a high out-of-vocabulary rate on the source side, but we do want to penalize models that know the source phrase, but not its correct translation. A second modification pertains to the lexical weights $lex(\bar{s}|\bar{t})$ and $lex(\bar{t}|\bar{s})$, which form no true probability distribution, but are derived from the individual word translation probabilities of a phrase pair (see (Koehn et al., 2003)). We propose to not interpolate the features directly, but the word translation probabilities which are the basis of the lexical weight computation. The reason for this is that word pairs are less sparse than phrase pairs, so that we can even compute lexical weights for phrase pairs which are unknown in a model.[4]

2.2 Weighted Counts

Weighting of different corpora can also be implemented through a modified Maximum Likelihood Estimation. The traditional equation for MLE is:

$$p(x|y) = \frac{c(x,y)}{c(y)} = \frac{c(x,y)}{\sum_{x'} c(x',y)} \quad (2)$$

where c denotes the count of an observation, and p the model probability. If we generalize the formula to compute a probability from n corpora, and assign a weight λ_i to each, we get[5]:

$$p(x|y;\lambda) = \frac{\sum_{i=1}^{n} \lambda_i c_i(x,y)}{\sum_{i=1}^{n} \sum_{x'} \lambda_i c_i(x',y)} \quad (3)$$

The main difference to linear interpolation is that this equation takes into account how well-evidenced a phrase pair is. This includes the distinction between lack of evidence and negative evidence, which is missing in a naive implementation of linear interpolation.

Translation models trained with weighted counts have been discussed before, and have been shown to outperform uniform ones in some settings. However, researchers who demonstrated this fact did so with arbitrary weights (e.g. (Koehn, 2002)), or by empirically testing different weights (e.g. (Nakov and Ng, 2009)). We do not know of any research on automatically determining weights for this method, or which is not limited to two corpora.

[4]For instance if the word pairs (the,der) and (man,Mann) are known, but the phrase pair (the man, der Mann) is not.

[5]Unlike equation 1, equation 3 does not require that $(\sum_i \lambda_i) = 1$.

2.3 Alternative Paths

A third method is using multiple translation models as alternative decoding paths (Birch et al., 2007), an idea which Koehn and Schroeder (2007) first used for domain adaptation. This approach has the attractive theoretical property that adding new models is guaranteed to lead to equal or better performance, given the right weights. At best, a model is beneficial with appropriate weights. At worst, we can set the feature weights so that the decoding paths of one model are never picked for the final translation. In practice, each translation model adds 5 features and thus 5 more dimensions to the weight space, which leads to longer search, search errors, and/or overfitting. The expectation is that, at least with MERT, using alternative decoding paths does not scale well to a high number of models.

A suboptimal choice of weights is not the only weakness of alternative paths, however. Let us assume that all models have the same weights. Note that, if a phrase pair occurs in several models, combining models through alternative paths means that the decoder selects the path with the highest probability, whereas with linear interpolation, the probability of the phrase pair would be the (weighted) average of all models. Selecting the highest-scoring phrase pair favours statistical outliers and hence is the less robust decision, prone to data noise and data sparseness.

2.4 Perplexity Minimization

In language modelling, perplexity is frequently used as a quality measure for language models (Chen and Goodman, 1998). Among other applications, language model perplexity has been used for domain adaptation (Foster and Kuhn, 2007). For translation models, perplexity is most closely associated with EM word alignment (Brown et al., 1993) and has been used to evaluate different alignment algorithms (Al-Onaizan et al., 1999).

We investigate translation model perplexity minimization as a method to set model weights in mixture modelling. For the purpose of optimization, the cross-entropy $H(p)$, the perplexity $2^{H(p)}$, and other derived measures are equivalent. The cross-entropy $H(p)$ is defined as:[6]

[6]See (Chen and Goodman, 1998) for a short discussion of the equation. In short, a lower cross-entropy indicates that the model is better able to predict the development set.

$$H(p) = -\sum_{x,y} \tilde{p}(x,y) \log_2 p(x|y) \quad (4)$$

The phrase pairs (x, y) whose probability we measure, and their empirical probability $\tilde{p}$ need to be extracted from a development set, whereas p is the model probability. To obtain the phrase pairs, we process the development set with the same word alignment and phrase extraction tools that we use for training, i.e. GIZA++ and heuristics for phrase extraction (Och and Ney, 2003). The objective function is the minimization of the cross-entropy, with the weight vector λ as argument:

$$\hat{\lambda} = \arg\min_{\lambda} -\sum_{x,y} \tilde{p}(x,y) \log_2 p(x|y;\lambda) \quad (5)$$

We can fill in equations 1 or 3 for $p(x|y;\lambda)$. The optimization itself is convex and can be done with off-the-shelf software.[7] We use L-BFGS with numerically approximated gradients (Byrd et al., 1995).

Perplexity minimization has the advantage that it is well-defined for both weighted counts and linear interpolation, and can be quickly computed. Other than in language modelling, where $p(x|y)$ is the probability of a word given a n-gram history, conditional probabilities in translation models express the probability of a target phrase given a source phrase (or vice versa), which connects the perplexity to the ambiguity problem. The higher the probability of "correct" phrase pairs, the lower the perplexity, and the more likely the model is to successfully resolve the ambiguity. The question is in how far perplexity minimization coincides with empirically good mixture weights.[8] This depends, among others, on the other model components in the SMT framework, for instance the language model. We will not evaluate perplexity minimization against empirically optimized mixture weights, but apply it in situations where the latter is infeasible, e.g. because of the number of models.

[7] A quick demonstration of convexity: equation 1 is affine; equation 3 linear-fractional. Both are convex in the domain $\mathbb{R}_{>0}$. Consequently, equation 4 is also convex because it is the weighted sum of convex functions.

[8] There are tasks for which perplexity is known to be unreliable, e.g. for comparing models with different vocabularies. However, such confounding factors do not affect the optimization algorithm, which works with a fixed set of phrase pairs, and merely varies λ.

Our main technical contributions are as follows: Additionally to perplexity optimization for linear interpolation, which was first applied by Foster et al. (2010), we propose perplexity optimization for weighted counts (equation 3), and a modified implementation of linear interpolation. Also, we independently perform perplexity minimization for all four features of the standard SMT translation model: the phrase translation probabilities $p(\bar{t}|\bar{s})$ and $p(\bar{s}|\bar{t})$, and the lexical weights $lex(\bar{t}|\bar{s})$ and $lex(\bar{s}|\bar{t})$.

3 Other Domain Adaptation Techniques

So far, we discussed mixture modelling for translation models, which is only a subset of domain adaptation techniques in SMT.

Mixture-modelling for language models is well established (Foster and Kuhn, 2007). Language model adaptation serves the same purpose as translation model adaptation, i.e. skewing the probability distribution in favour of in-domain translations. This means that LM adaptation may have similar effects as TM adaptation, and that the two are to some extent redundant. Foster and Kuhn (2007) find that "both TM and LM adaptation are effective", but that "combined LM and TM adaptation is not better than LM adaptation on its own".

A second strand of research in domain adaptation is data selection, i.e. choosing a subset of the training data that is considered more relevant for the task at hand. This has been done for language models using techniques from information retrieval (Zhao et al., 2004), or perplexity (Lin et al., 1997; Moore and Lewis, 2010). Data selection has also been proposed for translation models (Axelrod et al., 2011). Note that for translation models, data selection offers an unattractive trade-off between the data sparseness and the ambiguity problem, and that the optimal amount of data to select is hard to determine.

Our discussion of mixture-modelling is relatively coarse-grained, with 2-10 models being combined. Matsoukas et al. (2009) propose an approach where each sentence is weighted according to a classifier, and Foster et al. (2010) extend this approach by weighting individual phrase pairs. These more fine-grained methods need not be seen as alternatives to coarse-grained ones. Foster et al. (2010) combine the two, applying linear interpolation to combine the instance-weighted out-of-domain model with an in-domain model.

4 Evaluation

Apart from measuring the performance of the approaches introduced in section 2, we want to investigate the following open research questions.

1. Does an implementation of linear interpolation that is more closely tailored to translation modelling outperform a naive implementation?

2. How do the approaches perform outside a binary setting, i.e. when we do not work with one in-domain and one out-of-domain model, but with a higher number of models?

3. Can we apply perplexity minimization to other translation model features such as the lexical weights, and if yes, does a separate optimization of each translation model feature improve performance?

4.1 Data and Methods

In terms of tools and techniques used, we mostly adhere to the work flow described for the WMT 2011 baseline system[9]. The main tools are Moses (Koehn et al., 2007), SRILM (Stolcke, 2002), and GIZA++ (Och and Ney, 2003), with settings as described in the WMT 2011 guide. We report two translation measures: BLEU (Papineni et al., 2002) and METEOR 1.3 (Denkowski and Lavie, 2011). All results are lowercased and tokenized, measured with five independent runs of MERT (Och and Ney, 2003) and MultEval (Clark et al., 2011) for resampling and significance testing.

We compare three baselines and four translation model mixture techniques. The three baselines are a purely in-domain model, a purely out-of-domain model, and a model trained on the concatenation of the two, which corresponds to equation 3 with uniform weights. Additionally, we evaluate perplexity optimization with weighted counts and the two implementations of linear interpolation contrasted in section 2.1. The two linear interpolations that are contrasted are a naive one, i.e. a direct, unnormalized interpolation of all translation model features, and a modified one that normalizes λ for each phrase pair $(\bar{s}, \bar{t})$ for $p(\bar{t}|\bar{s})$ and recomputes the lexical weights based on interpolated word translation probabilites. The fourth weighted combination is using alternative decoding paths with weights set through MERT. The four weighted combinations are evaluated twice: once applied to the original four or ten parallel data sets, once in a binary setting in which all out-of-domain data sets are first concatenated.

Data set	sentences	words (fr)
Alpine (in-domain)	220k	4 700k
Europarl	1 500k	44 000k
JRC Acquis	1 100k	24 000k
OpenSubtitles v2	2 300k	18 000k
Total train	5 200k	91 000k
Dev	1424	33 000
Test	991	21 000

Table 1: Parallel data sets for German – French translation task.

Data set	sentences	words
Alpine (in-domain)	650k	13 000k
News-commentary	150k	4 000k
Europarl	2 000k	60 000k
News	25 000k	610 000k
Total	28 000k	690 000k

Table 2: Monolingual French data sets for German – French translation task.

Since we want to concentrate on translation model domain adaptation, we keep other model components, namely word alignment and the lexical reordering model, constant throughout the experiments. We contrast two language models. An unadapted, out-of-domain language model trained on data sets provided for the WMT 2011 translation task, and an adapted language model which is the linear interpolation of all data sets, optimized for minimal perplexity on the in-domain development set.

While unadapted language models are becoming more rare in domain adaptation research, they allow us to contrast different TM mixtures without the effect on performance being (partially) hidden by language model adaptation with the same effect.

The first data set is a DE–FR translation scenario in the domain of mountaineering. The in-domain corpus is a collection of Alpine Club pub-

[9] http://www.statmt.org/wmt11/baseline.html

lications (Volk et al., 2010). As parallel out-of-domain dataset, we use Europarl, a collection of parliamentary proceedings (Koehn, 2005), JRC-Acquis, a collection of legislative texts (Steinberger et al., 2006), and OpenSubtitles v2, a parallel corpus extracted from film subtitles[10] (Tiedemann, 2009). For language modelling, we use in-domain data and data from the 2011 Workshop on Statistical Machine Translation. The respective sizes of the data sets are listed in tables 1 and 2.

As the second data set, we use the Haitian Creole – English data from the WMT 2011 featured translation task. It consists of emergency SMS sent in the wake of the 2010 Haiti earthquake. Originally, Microsoft Research and CMU operated under severe time constraints to build a translation system for this language pair. This limits the ability to empirically verify how much each data set contributes to translation quality, and increases the importance of automated and quick domain adaptation methods.

Note that both data sets have a relatively high ratio of in-domain to out-of-domain parallel training data (1:20 for DE–EN and 1:5 for HT–EN) Previous research has been performed with ratios of 1:100 (Foster et al., 2010) or 1:400 (Axelrod et al., 2011). Since domain adaptation becomes more important when the ratio of IN to OUT is low, and since such low ratios are also realistic[11], we also include results for which the amount of in-domain parallel data has been restricted to 10% of the available data set.

We used the same development set for language/translation model adaptation and setting the global model weights with MERT. While it is theoretically possible that MERT will give too high weights to models that are optimized on the same development set, we found no empirical evidence for this in experiments with separate development sets.

4.2 Results

The results are shown in tables 5 and 6. In the DE–FR translation task, results vary between 13.5 and 18.9 BLEU points; in the HT–EN task, between 24.3 and 33.8. Unsurprisingly, an adapted LM performs better than an out-of-domain one, and using all available in-domain parallel data is better than using only part of it. The same is not true for out-of-domain data, which highlights the problem discussed in the introduction. For the DE–FR task, adding 86 million words of out-of-domain parallel data to the 5 million in-domain data set does not lead to consistent performance gains. We observe a decrease of 0.3 BLEU points with an out-of-domain LM, and an increase of 0.4 BLEU points with an adapted LM. The out-of-domain training data has a larger positive effect if less in-domain data is available, with a gain of 1.4 BLEU points. The results in the HT–EN translation task (table 6) paint a similar picture. An interesting side note is that even tiny amounts of in-domain parallel data can have strong effects on performance. A training set of 1600 emergency SMS (38 000 tokens) yields a comparable performance to an out-of-domain data set of 1.5 million tokens.

As to the domain adaptation experiments, weights optimized through perplexity minimization are significantly better in the majority of cases, and never significantly worse, than uniform

Data set	units	words (en)
SMS (in-domain)	16 500	380 000
Medical	1 600	10 000
Newswire	13 500	330 000
Glossary	35 700	90 000
Wikipedia	8 500	110 000
Wikipedia NE	10 500	34 000
Bible	30 000	920 000
Haitisurf dict	3 700	4000
Krengle dict	1 600	2 600
Krengle	650	4 200
Total train	120 000	1 900 000
Dev	900	22 000
Test	1274	25 000

Table 3: Parallel data sets for Haiti Creole – English translation task.

Data set	sentences	words
SMS (in-domain)	16k	380k
News	113 000k	2 650 000k

Table 4: Monolingual English data sets for Haiti Creole – English translation task.

[10] http://www.opensubtitles.org

[11] We predict that the availability of parallel data will steadily increase, most data being out-of-domain for any given task.

System	out-of-domain LM full IN TM		adapted LM full IN TM		adapted LM small IN TM	
	BLEU	METEOR	BLEU	METEOR	BLEU	METEOR
in-domain	16.8	35.9	17.9	37.0	15.7	33.5
out-of-domain	13.5	31.3	14.8	32.3	14.8	32.3
counts (concatenation)	16.5	35.7	18.3	37.3	17.1	35.4
binary in/out						
weighted counts	17.4	36.6	18.7	37.9	17.6	36.2
linear interpolation (naive)	17.4	36.7	18.8	37.9	17.6	36.1
linear interpolation (modified)	17.2	36.5	18.9	38.0	17.6	36.2
alternative paths	17.2	36.5	18.6	37.8	17.4	36.0
4 models						
weighted counts	17.3	36.6	18.8	37.8	17.4	36.0
linear interpolation (naive)	17.1	36.5	18.5	37.7	17.3	35.9
linear interpolation (modified)	17.2	36.5	18.7	37.9	17.3	36.0
alternative paths	17.0	36.2	18.3	37.4	16.3	35.1

Table 5: Domain adaptation results DE–FR. Domain: Alpine texts. Full IN TM: Using the full in-domain parallel corpus; small IN TM: using 10% of available in-domain parallel data.

weights.[12] However, the difference is smaller for the experiments with an adapted language model than for those with an out-of-domain one, which confirms that the benefit of language model adaptation and translation model adaptation are not fully cumulative. Performance-wise, there seems to be no clear winner between weighted counts and the two alternative implementations of linear interpolation. We can still argue for weighted counts on theoretical grounds. A weighted MLE (equation 3) returns a true probability distribution, whereas a naive implementation of linear interpolation results in a deficient model. Consequently, probabilities are typically lower in the naively interpolated model, which results in higher (worse) perplexities. While the deficiency did not affect MERT or decoding negatively, it might become problematic in other applications, for instance if we want to use an interpolated model as a component in a second perplexity-based combination of models.[13]

When moving from a binary setting with one in-domain and one out-of-domain translation model (trained on all available out-of-domain data) to 4–10 translation models, we observe a serious performance degradation for alternative paths, while performance of the perplexity optimization methods does not change significantly. This is positive for perplexity optimization because it demonstrates that it requires less *a priori* information, and opens up new research possibilities, i.e. experiments with different clusterings of parallel data. The performance degradation for alternative paths is partially due to optimization problems in MERT, but also due to a higher susceptibility to statistical outliers, as discussed in section 2.3.[14]

A pessimistic interpretation of the results would point out that performance gains compared to the best baseline system are modest or even inexistent in some settings. However, we want to stress two important points. First, we often do not know *a priori* whether adding an out-of-domain data set boosts or weakens translation performance. An automatic weighting of data sets reduces the need for trial-and-error experimentation and is worthwhile even if a performance increase is not guaranteed. Second, the potential impact of a weighted combination depends on the translation scenario and the available data sets. Generally, we expect non-uniform weighting to have a bigger impact when the models that are combined are more dissimilar (in terms of fitness for the task), and if the ratio of in-domain to out-of-domain data is low. Conversely, there are situa-

[12]This also applies to linear interpolation with uniform weights, which is not shown in the tables.

[13]Specifically, a deficient model would be dispreferred by the perplexity minimization algorithm.

[14]We empirically verified this weakness in a synthetic experiment with a randomly split training corpus and identical weights for each path.

System	out-of-domain LM		adapted LM			
	full IN TM		full IN TM		small IN TM	
	BLEU	METEOR	BLEU	METEOR	BLEU	METEOR
in-domain	30.4	30.7	33.4	31.7	29.7	28.6
out-of-domain	24.3	28.0	28.9	30.2	28.9	30.2
counts (concatenation)	30.3	31.2	33.6	32.4	31.3	31.3
binary in/out						
weighted counts	31.0	31.6	33.8	32.4	31.5	31.3
linear interpolation (naive)	30.8	31.4	33.7	32.4	31.9	31.3
linear interpolation (modified)	30.8	31.5	33.7	32.4	31.7	31.2
alternative paths	30.8	31.3	33.2	32.4	29.8	30.7
10 models						
weighted counts	31.0	31.5	33.5	32.3	31.8	31.5
linear interpolation (naive)	30.9	31.4	33.8	32.4	31.9	31.3
linear interpolation (modified)	31.0	31.6	33.8	32.5	32.1	31.5
alternative paths	25.9	29.2	24.3	29.1	29.8	30.9

Table 6: Domain adaptation results HT–EN. Domain: emergency SMS. Full IN TM: Using the full in-domain parallel corpus; small IN TM: using 10% of available in-domain parallel data.

tions where we actually expect a simple concatenation to be optimal, e.g. when the data sets have very similar probability distributions.

4.2.1 Individually Optimizing Each TM Feature

It is hard to empirically show how translation model perplexity optimization compares to using monolingual perplexity measures for the purpose of weighting translation models, as e.g. done by (Foster and Kuhn, 2007; Koehn et al., 2010). One problem is that there are many different possible configurations for the latter. We can use source side or target side language models, operate with different vocabularies, smoothing techniques, and n-gram orders.

One of the theoretical considerations that favour measuring perplexity on the translation model rather than using monolingual measures is that we can optimize each translation model feature separately. In the default Moses translation model, the four features are $p(\bar{s}|\bar{t})$, $lex(\bar{s}|\bar{t})$, $p(\bar{t}|\bar{s})$ and $lex(\bar{t}|\bar{s})$.

We empirically test different optimization schemes as follows. We optimize perplexity on each feature independently, obtaining 4 weight vectors. We then compute one model with one weight vector per feature (namely the feature that the vector was optimized on), and four models that use one of the weight vectors for all features. A further model uses a weight vector that is the

weights	perplexity 1	2	3	4	BLEU
weighted counts					
uniform	5.12	7.68	4.84	13.67	30.3
separate	**4.68**	**6.62**	**4.24**	**8.57**	**31.0**
1	**4.68**	6.84	4.50	10.86	30.3
2	4.78	**6.62**	4.48	10.54	30.3
3	4.86	7.31	**4.24**	9.15	30.8
4	5.33	7.87	4.52	**8.57**	30.9
average	4.72	6.71	4.38	9.95	30.4
linear interpolation (modified)					
uniform	19.89	82.78	4.80	10.78	30.6
separate	**5.45**	**8.56**	**4.28**	**8.85**	**31.0**
1	**5.45**	8.79	4.40	8.89	30.8
2	5.71	**8.56**	4.54	8.91	30.9
3	6.46	11.88	**4.28**	9.07	31.0
4	6.12	10.86	4.47	**8.85**	30.9
average	5.73	9.72	4.34	8.89	30.9
LM	6.01	9.83	4.56	8.96	30.8

Table 7: Contrast between a separate optimization of each feature and applying the weight vector optimized on one feature to the whole model. HT–EN with out-of-domain LM.

average of the other four. For linear interpolation, we also include a model whose weights have been optimized through language model perplexity optimization, with a 3-gram language model (modified Knesey-Ney smoothing) trained on the target side of each parallel data set.

Table 7 shows the results. In terms of BLEU score, a separate optimization of each feature is a winner in our experiment in that no other scheme is better, with 8 of the 11 alternative weighting schemes (excluding uniform weights) being significantly worse than a separate optimization. The differences in BLEU score are small, however, since the alternative weighting schemes are generally felicitious in that they yield both a lower perplexity and better BLEU scores than uniform weighting. While our general expectation is that lower perplexities correlate with higher translation performance, this relation is complicated by several facts. Since the interpolated models are deficient (i.e. their probabilities do not sum to 1), perplexities for weighted counts and our implementation of linear interpolation cannot be compard. Also, note that not all features are equally important for decoding. Their weights in the log-linear model are set through MERT and vary between optimization runs.

5 Conclusion

This paper contributes to SMT domain adaptation research in several ways. We expand on work by (Foster et al., 2010) in establishing translation model perplexity minimization as a robust baseline for a weighted combination of translation models.[15] We demonstrate perplexity optimization for weighted counts, which are a natural extension of unadapted MLE training, but are of little prominence in domain adaptation research. We also show that we can separately optimize the four variable features in the Moses translation model through perplexity optimization.

We break with prior domain adaptation research in that we do not rely on a binary clustering of in-domain and out-of-domain training data. We demonstrate that perplexity minimization scales well to a higher number of translation models. This is not only useful for domain adaptation, but for various tasks that profit from mixture modelling. We envision that a weighted combination could be useful to deal with noisy datasets, or applied after a clustering of training data.

[15]The source code is available in the Moses repository `http://github.com/moses-smt/mosesdecoder`

Acknowledgements

This research was funded by the Swiss National Science Foundation under grant 105215_126999.

References

Yaser Al-Onaizan, Jan Curin, Michael Jahr, Kevin Knight, John Lafferty, Dan Melamed, Franz-Josef Och, David Purdy, Noah A. Smith, and David Yarowsky. 1999. Statistical machine translation. Technical report, Final Report, JHU Summer Workshop.

Amittai Axelrod, Xiaodong He, and Jianfeng Gao. 2011. Domain adaptation via pseudo in-domain data selection. In *Proceedings of the EMNLP 2011 Workshop on Statistical Machine Translation*.

Alexandra Birch, Miles Osborne, and Philipp Koehn. 2007. CCG supertags in factored statistical machine translation. In *Proceedings of the Second Workshop on Statistical Machine Translation*, pages 9–16, Prague, Czech Republic, June. Association for Computational Linguistics.

Peter F. Brown, Vincent J. Della Pietra, Stephen A. Della Pietra, and Robert L. Mercer. 1993. The Mathematics of Statistical Machine Translation: Parameter Estimation. *Computational Linguistics*, 19(2):263–311.

Richard H. Byrd, Peihuang Lu, Jorge Nocedal, and Ciyou Zhu. 1995. A limited memory algorithm for bound constrained optimization. *SIAM J. Sci. Comput.*, 16:1190–1208, September.

Alexandru Ceauşu, John Tinsley, Jian Zhang, and Andy Way. 2011. Experiments on domain adaptation for patent machine translation in the PLuTO project. In *Proceedings of the 15th conference of the European Association for Machine Translation*, Leuven, Belgium.

Stanley F. Chen and Joshua Goodman. 1998. An empirical study of smoothing techniques for language modeling. *Computer Speech & Language*, 13:359–393.

Jonathan H. Clark, Chris Dyer, Alon Lavie, and Noah A. Smith. 2011. Better hypothesis testing for statistical machine translation: Controlling for optimizer instability. In *Proceedings of the 49th Annual Meeting of the Association for Computational Linguistics: Human Language Technologies*, pages 176–181, Portland, Oregon, USA, June. Association for Computational Linguistics.

Trevor Cohn and Mirella Lapata. 2007. Machine Translation by Triangulation: Making Effective Use of Multi-Parallel Corpora. In *Proceedings of the*

45th Annual Meeting of the Association of Computational Linguistics, pages 728–735, Prague, Czech Republic, June. Association for Computational Linguistics.

Michael Denkowski and Alon Lavie. 2011. Meteor 1.3: Automatic Metric for Reliable Optimization and Evaluation of Machine Translation Systems. In *Proceedings of the EMNLP 2011 Workshop on Statistical Machine Translation*.

Andrew Finch and Eiichiro Sumita. 2008. Dynamic model interpolation for statistical machine translation. In *Proceedings of the Third Workshop on Statistical Machine Translation*, StatMT '08, pages 208–215, Stroudsburg, PA, USA. Association for Computational Linguistics.

George Foster and Roland Kuhn. 2007. Mixture-model adaptation for smt. In *Proceedings of the Second Workshop on Statistical Machine Translation*, StatMT '07, pages 128–135, Stroudsburg, PA, USA. Association for Computational Linguistics.

George Foster, Cyril Goutte, and Roland Kuhn. 2010. Discriminative instance weighting for domain adaptation in statistical machine translation. In *Proceedings of the 2010 Conference on Empirical Methods in Natural Language Processing*, pages 451–459, Stroudsburg, PA, USA. Association for Computational Linguistics.

Philipp Koehn and Kevin Knight. 2001. Knowledge sources for word-level translation models. In Lillian Lee and Donna Harman, editors, *Proceedings of the 2001 Conference on Empirical Methods in Natural Language Processing*, pages 27–35.

Philipp Koehn and Josh Schroeder. 2007. Experiments in domain adaptation for statistical machine translation. In *Proceedings of the Second Workshop on Statistical Machine Translation*, StatMT '07, pages 224–227, Stroudsburg, PA, USA. Association for Computational Linguistics.

Philipp Koehn, Franz Josef Och, and Daniel Marcu. 2003. Statistical phrase-based translation. In *NAACL '03: Proceedings of the 2003 Conference of the North American Chapter of the Association for Computational Linguistics on Human Language Technology*, pages 48–54, Morristown, NJ, USA. Association for Computational Linguistics.

Philipp Koehn, Hieu Hoang, Alexandra Birch, Chris Callison-Burch, Marcello Federico, Nicola Bertoldi, Brooke Cowan, Wade Shen, Christine Moran, Richard Zens, Chris Dyer, Ondřej Bojar, Alexandra Constantin, and Evan Herbst. 2007. Moses: Open Source Toolkit for Statistical Machine Translation. In *ACL 2007, Proceedings of the 45th Annual Meeting of the Association for Computational Linguistics Companion Volume Proceedings of the Demo and Poster Sessions*, pages 177–180, Prague, Czech Republic, June. Association for Computational Linguistics.

Philipp Koehn, Barry Haddow, Philip Williams, and Hieu Hoang. 2010. More linguistic annotation for statistical machine translation. In *Proceedings of the Joint Fifth Workshop on Statistical Machine Translation and MetricsMATR*, pages 115–120, Uppsala, Sweden, July. Association for Computational Linguistics.

Philipp Koehn. 2002. Europarl: A Multilingual Corpus for Evaluation of Machine Translation.

Philipp Koehn. 2005. Europarl: A parallel corpus for statistical machine translation. In *Machine Translation Summit X*, pages 79–86, Phuket, Thailand.

Sung-Chien Lin, Chi-Lung Tsai, Lee-Feng Chien, Keh-Jiann Chen, and Lin-Shan Lee. 1997. Chinese language model adaptation based on document classification and multiple domain-specific language models. In George Kokkinakis, Nikos Fakotakis, and Evangelos Dermatas, editors, *EUROSPEECH*. ISCA.

Spyros Matsoukas, Antti-Veikko I. Rosti, and Bing Zhang. 2009. Discriminative corpus weight estimation for machine translation. In *Proceedings of the 2009 Conference on Empirical Methods in Natural Language Processing: Volume 2 - Volume 2*, pages 708–717, Stroudsburg, PA, USA. Association for Computational Linguistics.

Robert C. Moore and William Lewis. 2010. Intelligent selection of language model training data. In *Proceedings of the ACL 2010 Conference Short Papers*, ACLShort '10, pages 220–224, Stroudsburg, PA, USA. Association for Computational Linguistics.

Preslav Nakov and Hwee Tou Ng. 2009. Improved statistical machine translation for resource-poor languages using related resource-rich languages. In *Proceedings of the 2009 Conference on Empirical Methods in Natural Language Processing: Volume 3 - Volume 3*, EMNLP '09, pages 1358–1367, Stroudsburg, PA, USA. Association for Computational Linguistics.

Franz Josef Och and Hermann Ney. 2003. A systematic comparison of various statistical alignment models. *Computational Linguistics*, 29(1):19–51.

Kishore Papineni, Salim Roukos, Todd Ward, and Wei-Jing Zhu. 2002. Bleu: A method for automatic evaluation of machine translation. In *ACL '02: Proceedings of the 40th Annual Meeting on Association for Computational Linguistics*, pages 311–318, Morristown, NJ, USA. Association for Computational Linguistics.

Ralf Steinberger, Bruno Pouliquen, Anna Widiger, Camelia Ignat, Tomaz Erjavec, Dan Tufis, and Daniel Varga. 2006. The JRC-Acquis: A multilingual aligned parallel corpus with 20+ languages. In *Proceedings of the 5th International Conference on Language Resources and Evaluation (LREC'2006)*.

A. Stolcke. 2002. SRILM – An Extensible Language Modeling Toolkit. In *Seventh International Conference on Spoken Language Processing*, pages 901–904, Denver, CO, USA.

Jörg Tiedemann. 2009. News from opus - a collection of multilingual parallel corpora with tools and interfaces. In N. Nicolov, K. Bontcheva, G. Angelova, and R. Mitkov, editors, *Recent Advances in Natural Language Processing*, volume V, pages 237–248. John Benjamins, Amsterdam/Philadelphia, Borovets, Bulgaria.

Martin Volk, Noah Bubenhofer, Adrian Althaus, Maya Bangerter, Lenz Furrer, and Beni Ruef. 2010. Challenges in building a multilingual alpine heritage corpus. In *Proceedings of the Seventh conference on International Language Resources and Evaluation (LREC'10)*, Valletta, Malta. European Language Resources Association (ELRA).

Keiji Yasuda, Ruiqiang Zhang, Hirofumi Yamamoto, and Eiichiro Sumita. 2008. Method of selecting training data to build a compact and efficient translation model. In *Proceedings of the 3rd International Joint Conference on Natural Language Processing (IJCNLP)*.

Bing Zhao, Matthias Eck, and Stephan Vogel. 2004. Language model adaptation for statistical machine translation with structured query models. In *Proceedings of the 20th international conference on Computational Linguistics*, COLING '04, Stroudsburg, PA, USA. Association for Computational Linguistics.

Subcat-LMF: Fleshing out a standardized format for subcategorization frame interoperability

Judith Eckle-Kohler[‡] and **Iryna Gurevych**[†‡]
† Ubiquitous Knowledge Processing Lab (UKP-DIPF)
German Institute for Educational Research and Educational Information
‡ Ubiquitous Knowledge Processing Lab (UKP-TUDA)
Department of Computer Science
Technische Universität Darmstadt
http://www.ukp.tu-darmstadt.de

Abstract

This paper describes Subcat-LMF, an ISO-LMF compliant lexicon representation format featuring a uniform representation of subcategorization frames (SCFs) for the two languages English and German. Subcat-LMF is able to represent SCFs at a very fine-grained level. We utilized Subcat-LMF to standardize lexicons with large-scale SCF information: the English VerbNet and two German lexicons, i.e., a subset of IMSlex and GermaNet verbs. To evaluate our LMF-model, we performed a cross-lingual comparison of SCF coverage and overlap for the standardized versions of the English and German lexicons. The Subcat-LMF DTD, the conversion tools and the standardized versions of VerbNet and IMSlex subset are publicly available.[1]

1 Introduction

Computational lexicons providing accurate *lexical-syntactic* information, such as subcategorization frames (SCFs) are vital for many NLP applications involving parsing and word sense disambiguation. In parsing, SCFs have been successfully used to improve the output of statistical parsers (Klenner (2007), Deoskar (2008), Sigogne et al. (2011)) which is particularly significant in high-precision domain-independent parsing. In word sense disambiguation, SCFs have been identified as important features for verb sense disambiguation (Brown et al., 2011), which is due to the correlation of verb senses and SCFs (Andrew et al., 2004).

SCFs specify syntactic arguments of verbs and other predicate-like lexemes, e.g. the verb *say* takes two arguments that can be realized, for instance, as noun phrase and *that*-clause as in *He says that the window is open.*

Although a number of freely available, large-scale and accurate SCF lexicons exist, e.g. COMLEX (Grishman et al., 1994), VerbNet (Kipper et al., 2008) for English, availability and limitations in size and coverage remain an inherent issue. This applies even more to languages other than English.

One particular approach to address this issue is the combination and integration of existing manually built SCF lexicons. Lexicon integration has widely been adopted for increasing the coverage of lexicons regarding *lexical-semantic information types*, such as semantic roles, selectional restrictions, and word senses (e.g., Shi and Mihalcea (2005), the Semlink project[2], Navigli and Ponzetto (2010), Niemann and Gurevych (2011), Meyer and Gurevych (2011)).

Currently, SCFs are represented idiosyncratically in existing SCF lexicons. However, integration of SCFs requires a common, interoperable representation format. Monolingual SCF integration based on a common representation format has already been addressed by King and Crouch (2005) and just recently by Necsulescu et al. (2011) and Padró et al. (2011). However, neither King and Crouch (2005) nor Necsulescu et al. (2011) or Padró et al. (2011) make use of existing standards in order to create a uniform SCF representation for lexicon merging. The definition of an interoperable representation format according to an existing standard, such as the ISO standard Lexical Markup Framework (LMF, ISO 24613:2008, see Francopoulo et al. (2006)), is the

[1] http://www.ukp.tu-darmstadt.de/data/uby

[2] http://verbs.colorado.edu/semlink/

prerequisite for re-using this format in different contexts, thus contributing to the standardization and interoperability of language resources.

While LMF models exist that cover the representation of SCFs (see Quochi et al. (2008), Buitelaar et al. (2009)), their suitability for representing SCFs at a large scale remains unclear: neither of these LMF-models has been used for standardizing lexicons with a large number of SCFs, such as VerbNet. Furthermore, the question of their applicability to different languages has not been investigated yet, a situation that is complicated by the fact that SCFs are highly language-specific.

The goal of this paper is to address these gaps for the two languages English and German by presenting a uniform LMF representation of SCFs for English and German which is utilized for the standardization of large-scale English and German SCF lexicons. The contributions of this paper are threefold: (1) We present the LMF model Subcat-LMF, an LMF-compliant lexicon representation format featuring a uniform and very fine-grained representation of SCFs for English and German. Subcat-LMF is a subset of Uby-LMF (Eckle-Kohler et al., 2012), the LMF model of the large integrated lexical resource Uby (Gurevych et al., 2012). (2) We convert lexicons with large-scale SCF information to Subcat-LMF: the English VerbNet and two German lexicons, i.e., GermaNet (Kunze and Lemnitzer, 2002) and a subset of IMSlex[3] (Eckle-Kohler, 1999). (3) We perform a comparison of these three lexicons regarding SCF coverage and SCF overlap, based on the standardized representation.

The remainder of this paper is structured as follows: Section 2 gives a detailed description of Subcat-LMF and section 3 demonstrates its usefulness for representing and cross-lingually comparing large-scale English and German lexicons. Section 4 provides a discussion including related work and section 5 concludes.

2 Subcat-LMF

2.1 ISO-LMF: a meta-model

LMF defines a *meta-model* of lexical resources, covering NLP lexicons and Machine Readable Dictionaries. This meta-model is based on the Unified Modeling Language (UML) and specifies a core package and a number of extensions for modeling different types of lexicons, including subcategorization lexicons.

The development of an LMF-compliant lexicon model requires two steps: in the first step, the structure of the lexicon model has to be defined by choosing a combination of the LMF core package and zero to many extensions (i.e. UML packages). While the LMF core package models a lexicon in terms of lexical entries, each of which is defined as the pairing of one to many forms and zero to many senses, the LMF extensions provide UML classes for different types of lexicon organization, e.g., covering the synset-based organization of WordNet and the class-based organization of VerbNet. The first step results in a set of UML classes that are associated according to the UML diagrams given in ISO LMF.

In the second step, these UML classes may be enriched by attributes. While neither attributes nor their values are given by the standard, the standard states that both are to be linked to Data Categories (DCs) defined in a Data Category Registry (DCR) such as ISOCat.[4] DCs that are not available in ISOCat may be defined and submitted for standardization. The second step results in a so-called Data Category Selection (DCS).

DCs specify the linguistic vocabulary used in an LMF model. Consider as an example the linguistic term *direct object* that often occurs in SCFs of verbs taking an accusative NP as argument. In ISOCat, there are two different specifications of this term, one explicitly referring to the capability of becoming the clause subject in passivization[5], the other not mentioning passivization at all.[6] Consequently, the use of a DCR plays a major role regarding the *semantic interoperability* of lexicons (Ide and Pustejovsky, 2010). Different resources that share a common definition of their linguistic vocabulary are said to be *semantically interoperable*.

2.2 Fleshing out ISO-LMF

Approach: We started our development of Subcat-LMF with a thorough inspection of large-scale English and German resources providing SCFs for verbs, nouns, and adjectives. For

[3] http://www.ims.uni-stuttgart.de/projekte/IMSLex/

[4] http://www.isocat.org/, the implementation of the ISO 12620 DCR (Broeder et al., 2010).

[5] http://www.isocat.org/datcat/DC-1274

[6] http://www.isocat.org/datcat/DC-2263

English, our analysis included VerbNet[7] and FrameNet syntactically annotated example sentences from Ruppenhofer et al. (2010). For German, we inspected GermaNet, SALSA annotation guidelines (Burchardt et al., 2006) and IMSlex documentation (Eckle-Kohler, 1999). In addition, the EAGLES synopsis on morphosyntactic phenomena[8] (Calzolari and Monachini, 1996), as well as the EAGLES recommendations on subcategorization[9] have been used to identify DCs relevant for SCFs.

We specified Subcat-LMF by a DTD yielding an XML serialization of ISO-LMF. Thus, existing lexicons can be standardized, i.e. converted into Subcat-LMF format, based on the DTD.[10]

Lexicon structure: Next, we defined the lexicon structure of Subcat-LMF. In addition to the core package, Subcat-LMF primarily makes use of the LMF Syntax and Semantics extension. Figure 1 shows the most important classes of Subcat-LMF including `SynsemCorrespondence` where the linking of syntactic and semantic arguments is encoded. It might by worth noting that both synsets from GermaNet and verb classes from VerbNet can be represented in Subcat-LMF by using the `Synset` and `SubcategorizationFrameSet` class.

Diverging linguistic properties of SCFs in English and German: For verbs (and also for predicate-like nouns and adjectives), SCFs specify the syntactic and morphosyntactic properties of their arguments that have to be present in concrete realizations of these arguments within a sentence. While some properties of syntactic arguments in English and German correspond (both English and German are Germanic languages and hence closely related), there are other properties, mainly morphosyntactic ones that diverge. By way of examples, we illustrate some of these divergences in the following (we contrast English examples with their German equivalents):

- overt case marking in German:
  He helps him. vs. *Er hilft ihm.* (dative)
- specific verb form in verb phrase arguments:
  He suggested cleaning the house. (ing-form)
  vs.
  Er schlug vor, das Haus zu putzen. (to-infinitive)
- morphosyntactic marking of verb phrase arguments in the main clause: *He managed to win.* (no marking) vs.
  Er hat es geschafft zu gewinnen. (obligatory *es*)
- morphosyntactic marking of clausal arguments in the main clause: *That depends on who did it.* (preposition) vs.
  Das hängt davon ab, wer es getan hat. (pronominal adverb)

Uniform Data Categories for English and German: Thus, the main challenge in developing Subcat-LMF has been the specification of DCs (attributes and attribute values) *in such a way*, that a uniform specification of SCFs in the two languages English and German can be achieved. The specification of DCs for Subcat-LMF involved fleshing out ISO-LMF, because it is a meta-standard in the sense that it provides only few linguistic terms, i.e. DCs, and these DCs are not linked to any DCR: in the Syntax Extension, the standard only provides 7 class names, see Figure 1), complemented by 17 example attributes given in an informative, non-binding Annex F. These are by far not sufficient to represent the fine-grained SCFs available in such large-scale lexicons as VerbNet.

In contrast, the Syntax part of Subcat-LMF comprises 58 DCs that are properly linked to ISOCat DCs; a number of DCs were missing in ISOCat, so we entered them ourselves.[11] The majority of the attributes in Subcat-LMF are attached to the `SyntacticArgument` class. The corresponding DCs can be divided into two main groups:

Cross-lingually valid DCs for the specification of grammatical functions (e.g. `subject`, `prepositionalComplement`) and syntactic categories (e.g. `nounPhrase`, `prepositionalPhrase`), see Table 1.

Partly language-specific morphosyntactic DCs that further specify the syntactic arguments (e.g. attribute `case`, attribute `verbForm` and

[7] SCFs in VerbNet also cover SCFs in VALEX, a lexicon automatically extracted from corpora.

[8] http://www.ilc.cnr.it/EAGLES96/morphsyn/

[9] http://www.ilc.cnr.it/EAGLES96/synlex/

[10] Available at http://www.ukp.tu-darmstadt.de/data/uby

[11] The Subcat-LMF DCS is publicly available on the ISOCat website.

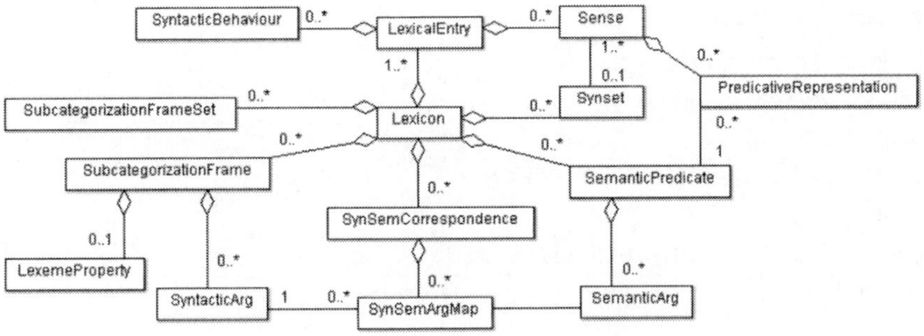

Figure 1: Selected classes of Subcat-LMF.

Values of `grammaticalFunction`	Example
subject	*They arrived in time.*
subjectComplement	*He becomes a teacher.*
directObject	*He saw a rainbow.*
objectComplement	*They elected him governor.*
complement	*He told him a story.*
prepositionalComplement	*It depends on several factors.*
adverbialComplement	*They moved far away.*
Values of `syntacticCategory`	**Example**
nounPhrase	*The train stopped.*
reflexive	*He drank himself sick.*
expletive	*It is raining.*
prepositionalPhrase	*It depends on several factors.*
adverbPhrase	*They moved far away.*
adjectivePhrase	*The light turned red.*
verbPhrase	*She tried to exercise.*
declarativeClause	*He says he agrees.*
subordinateClause	*He believes that it works.*

Table 1: Cross-lingually valid (English-German) attributes and values of the `SyntacticArgument` class.

values `toInfinitive`, `bareInfinitive`, `ingForm`, `participle`), see Table 2.

In the class `LexemeProperty`, we introduced an attribute `syntacticProperty` to encode control and raising properties of verbs taking infinitival verb phrase arguments.[12]

In Subcat-LMF, syntactic arguments can be specified by a selection of appropriate attribute-value pairs. While all syntactic arguments are uniformly specified by a grammatical function and a syntactic category, the use of the morphosyntactic attributes depends on the particular type of syntactic argument. Different phrase types are specified by different subsets of morphosyntactic attributes, see Table 2. The following examples illustrate some of these attributes:

- `number`: the number of a noun phrase argument can be lexically governed by the verb as in *These types of fish mix well together.*
- `verbForm`: the verb form of a clausal complement can be required to be a bare infinitive as in *They demanded that he be there.*
- `tense`: not only the verb form, but also the tense of a verb phrase complement can be lexically governed, e.g., to be a participle in the past tense as in *They had it removed.*

[12]Control or raising specify the co-reference between the implicit subject of the infinitival argument and syntactic arguments in the main clause, either the subject (subject control or raising) or direct object (object control or raising).

Morphosyntactic attributes and values	NP	PP	VP	C
case: nominative, genitive, dative, accusative	x	x		
determiner: possessive, indefinite	x		x	
number: singular, plural	x			
verbForm: toInfinitive, bareInfinitive, ingForm(!), Participle			x	x
tense: present, past			x	
complementizer: thatType, whType, yesNoType				x
prepositionType: external ontological type, e.g. locative		x	x	x
preposition: (string) (!)		x	x	x
lexeme: (string) (!)	x			x

Table 2: Morphosyntactic attributes of `SyntacticArgument` and phrase types for which the attributes are appropriate (NP: noun phrase, PP: prepositional phrase, VP: verb phrase, C: clause). Language-specific attributes are marked by (!).

3 Utilizing Subcat-LMF

3.1 Standardizing large-scale lexicons

Lexicon Data: We converted VerbNet (VN) and two German lexicons, i.e., GermaNet (GN) and a subset of IMSlex (ILS) to Subcat-LMF format. ILS has been developed independently from GN and the lexicon data were published in Eckle-Kohler (1999).

VN is organized in verb classes based on Levin-style syntactic alternations (Levin, 1993): verbs with common SCFs and syntactic alternation behavior that also share common semantic roles are grouped into classes. VN (version 3.1) lists 568 frames that are encoded as phrase structure rules (XML element `SYNTAX`), specifying phrase types and semantic roles of the arguments, as well as selectional, syntactic and morphosyntactic restrictions on the arguments. Additionally, a descriptive specification of each frame is given (XML element `DESCRIPTION`). The verb *learn*, for instance, has the following VN frame:

```
DESCRIPTION (primary):  NP V NP
SYNTAX: Agent V Topic
```

We extracted both the descriptive specifications and the phrase structure rules, using the API available for VN[13], resulting in 682 unique VN frames.[14]

GN provides detailed SCFs for verbs, in contrast to the Princeton WordNet: GN version 6.0 from April 2011 accessed by the GN API[15] lists 202 frames. GN SCFs are represented as a dot-separated sequence of letter pairs. Each letter pair specifies a syntactic argument: the first letter encodes the grammatical function and the second letter the syntactic category.[16] For instance, the following shows the GN code for transitive verbs: `NN.AN`.

ILS is represented in delimiter-separated values format and contains 784 verbs in total. Of these 784 verbs, 740 of them are also present in GN, and 44 are listed in ILS only. Although ILS contains only verbs that take clausal arguments and verb phrase arguments, a total number of 220 SCFs is present in ILS, also including SCFs without clausal and verb phrase arguments. ILS lists for each verb lemma a number of SCFs, thus specifying coarse-grained verb senses given by a lemma-SCF pair.[17] The SCFs are represented as parenthesized lists. For instance, the ILS SCF for transitive verbs is: `(subj(NPnom),obj(NPacc))`.

Automatic Conversion: We implemented Java tools for the conversion of VN, GN and ILS to Subcat-LMF. These tools convert the source lexicons based on a manual mapping of lexicon units and terms (e.g., VN verb class, GN synset) to Subcat-LMF. For the majority of SCFs, this mapping is defined on argument level. Lexical data is extracted from the source lexicons by using the native APIs (VN, GN) and additional Perl scripts.

[13] http://verbs.colorado.edu/verb-index/inspector/

[14] The VN API was used with the view options wrexyzsq for verb frame pairs and ctuqw for verb class information.

[15] GermaNet Java API 2.0.2

[16] See http://www.sfs.uni-tuebingen.de/GermaNet/-verb_frames.shtml

[17] In addition, ILS provides a semantic class label for each verb; however, these semantic labels are attached at lemma level, i.e. they need to be disambiguated.

	# LexicalEntry	# Sense	# Subcat.Frame	# SemanticPred.
LMF-VN orig. VN	3962 (3962 verbs)	31891 (31891 groups of verb, frame, sem.pred.)	284 (568 frames)	617 (572 sem. Pred.)
LMF-GN orig. GN	8626 (8626 verbs)	12981 (12981 verb-synset pairs)	147 (202 GN frames)	84 (no sem. Pred.)
LMF-ILS orig. ILS	784 (784 verbs)	3675 (3675 verb-frame pairs)	217 (220 SCFs)	10 (no sem. Pred.)

Table 3: Evaluation of the automatic conversion. Numbers of Subcat-LMF instances in the converted lexicons compared to numbers of corresponding units in original lexicons.

Evaluation of Automatic Conversion: Table 3 shows the mapping of the major source lexicon units (such as verb-synset pairs) to Subcat-LMF and lists the corresponding numbers of units.

For VN, groups of VN verb, frame and semantic predicate have been mapped to LMF senses. VN classes have been mapped to `SubcategorizationFrameSet`. Thus, the original VN-sense, a pairing of verb lemma and class, can be recovered by grouping LMF senses that share the same verb class. There is a significant difference between the original VN frames and their Subcat-LMF representation: the semantic information present in VN frames (semantic roles and selectional restrictions) is mapped to semantic arguments in Subcat-LMF, i.e. the mapping splits VN frames into a purely syntactic and a purely semantic part. Consequently, the number of unique SCFs in the Subcat-LMF version of VN is much smaller than the number of frames in the original VN. The conversion tool creates for each sense (specifying a unique verb, frame, semantic predicate combination) a `SynSemCorrespondence`.
On the other hand, the Subcat-LMF version of VN contains more semantic predicates than VN. This is due to selectional restrictions for semantic arguments that are specified in Subcat-LMF within semantic predicates, in contrast to VN.

For GN, verb-synset pairs (i.e., GN lexical units), have been mapped to LMF senses. Few GN frame codes also specify semantic role information, e.g. manner, location. These were mapped to the semantics part of Subcat-LMF resulting in 84 semantic predicates that encode the semantic role information in their semantic arguments.

ILS specifies similar semantic role information as GN; these few cases were mapped in the same way as for GN. Therefore, the LMF version of ILS, too, specifies less SCFs, but additional semantic predicates not present in the original.

Discussion: Grammatical functions of arguments are specified distinctly in the three lexicons. While both GN and ILS specify grammatical functions, they are not explicitly encoded in VN. They have to be inferred on the basis of the phrase structure rules given in the `SYNTAX` element. We assigned `subject` to the noun phrase which directly precedes the verb and `directObject` to the noun phrase directly following the verb *and* having the semantic role Patient. The semantic role information has to be considered at this point, because not all noun phrase arguments are able to become the subject in a corresponding passive sentence. An example is the verb *learn* which has the VN frame `NP(Agent) V NP(Topic)`; here, the Topic-NP is not able to become the subject of a corresponding passive sentence. We assigned the grammatical function `complement` to all other phrase types.

Argument order constraints in SCFs are represented in LMF by a list implementation of syntactic arguments. Most SCFs from VN require the subject to be the first argument, reflecting the basic word order in English sentences. VN lists one exception to this rule for the verb *appear*, illustrated by the example *On the horizon appears a ship.*

Argument optionality in VN is expressed at the semantic level and at the syntactic level in parallel: it is explicitly specified at the semantic level and implicitly specified at the syntactic level. At the syntactic level, two SCF versions exist in VN, one with the optional argument, the other without it. In addition, the semantic predicate attached to these SCFs marks optional (semantic) arguments by a ?-sign. GN, on the other hand, expresses argument optionality at the level of syntactic arguments, i.e., within the frame code. In Subcat-LMF, optionality is represented at the syntactic level by an (optional) attribute `optional` for syntactic arguments, thus reflecting the explicit representation used in GN and the implicit representation present in VN.[18]

GN frames specify syntactic alternations of argument realizations, e.g. adverbial complements that can alternatively be realized as adverb phrase, prepositional phrase or noun phrase. We encoded this generalization in Subcat-LMF by introducing attribute values for these aggregated syntactic categories.

3.2 Cross-lingual comparison of lexicons

Lexicons that are standardized according to Subcat-LMF can be quantitatively compared regarding SCFs. For two lexicons, such a comparison gives answers to questions, such as: how many SCFs are present in both lexicons (overlapping SCFs), how many SCFs are only listed in one of the lexicons (complementary SCFs). Answers to these questions are important, for instance, for assessing the potential gain in SCF coverage that can be achieved by lexicon merging.

In order to validate our claim that Subcat-LMF yields a cross-lingually uniform SCF representation, we contrast the monolingual comparison of GN and ILS with the cross-lingual comparison of VN, GN and VN and ILS. Assuming that our claim is valid, the cross-lingual comparisons can be expected to yield similar results regarding overlapping and complementary SCFs as the monolingual comparison.

Comparison: The comparison of SCFs from two lexicons that are in Subcat-LMF format can be performed on the basis of the uniform DCs. As Subcat-LMF is implemented in XML, we compared string representations of SCFs. SCFs from VN, GN and ILS were converted to strings by concatenating attribute values of syntactic arguments and `lexemeProperty`. We created string representations of different granularities: First, fine-grained, language-specific string SCFs have been generated by concatenating all attribute values apart from the attribute `optional` which is specific to GN (resulting in a considerably smaller number of SCFs in GN). Second, fine-grained, but cross-lingual string SCFs were considered; these omit the attributes `case`, `lexeme`, `preposition` and the attribute value `ingForm`. Finally, coarse-grained cross-lingual string SCFs were compared. These only contain the values of the attributes `syntactic category`, `complementizer` and `verbForm` (without the attribute value `ingForm`). For instance, a coarse cross-lingual string SCF for transitive verbs is `nounPhrasenounPhrase`.

Table 4 lists the results of our quantitative comparison. For each lexicon pair, the number of overlapping SCFs and the numbers of complementary SCFs are given. Regarding VN and the German lexicons, the overlap at the language-specific level is (close to) zero, which is due to the specification of case, e.g. dative, for German arguments. However, the numbers for cross-lingual SCFs clearly validate our claim: the numbers of overlapping SCFs for the German lexicon pair and for the two German-English pairs are comparable, ranging from 12 to 18 for the fine-grained SCFs and from 20 to 21 for the coarse SCFs.

Based on the sets of cross-lingually overlapping SCFs, we made an estimation on how many high frequent verbs actually have SCFs that are in the cross-lingual SCF overlap of an English-German lexicon pair. For this, we used the lemma frequency lists of the English and German WaCky corpora (Baroni et al., 2009) and extracted verbs from VN, GN and ILS that are on 100 top ranked positions of these lists, starting from rank 100.[19] Table 5 shows the results for the cross-lingual SCF overlap between VN – GN and between VN – ILS. While only around 40% of the high frequent verbs have an SCF in the fine-grained SCF overlap, more than 70% are in the coarse overlap between VN – GN, and even more than 80% in the coarse overlap between VN – ILS.

Analysis of results: The small numbers of overlapping *cross-lingual* SCFs (relative to the total number of SCFs), at both levels of granularity, indicate that the three lexicons each encode substantially different lexical-syntactic properties of

[18]As a consequence, all semantic arguments specified in the Subcat-LMF version of VN have a corresponding syntactic argument.

[19]Since the WaCky frequency lists do not contain POS information, our lists of extracted verbs contain some noise, which we tolerated, because we aimed at an approximate estimate.

	language-specific (fine-grained)	cross-lingual (fine-grained)	cross-lingual (coarse)
GN vs. ILS	72 GN 21 both, 196 ILS	61 GN, 23 both, 69 ILS	40 GN, 24 both, 23 ILS
VN vs. GN	284 VN, 0 both, 93 GN	96 VN, **15** both, 69 GN	29 VN, **24** both, 40 GN
VN vs. ILS	283 VN, 1 both, 216 ILS	93 VN, **18** both, 74 ILS	31 VN, **22** both, 25 ILS

Table 4: Comparison of lexicon pairs regarding SCF overlap and complementary SCFs.

VN-GN overlap fine-grained (15 SCFs)	VN-GN overlap coarse (24 SCFs)	VN-ILS overlap fine-grained (18 SCFs)	VN-ILS overlap coarse (22 SCFs)
43% VN verbs	85% VN verbs	41% VN verbs	84% VN verbs
41% GN verbs	71% GN verbs	43% ILS verbs	87% ILS verbs

Table 5: Percentage of 100 high frequent verbs from VN, GN, ILS with a SCF in the cross-lingual SCF overlap (fine-grained vs. coarse) between VN – GN and VN – ILS.

verbs. This can at least partly be explained by the historic development of these lexicons in different contexts, e.g., Levin's work on verb classes (VN), Lexical Functional Grammar (ILS), as well as their use for different purposes and applications.

Another reason of the small SCF overlap is the comparison of strings derived from the XML format. A more sophisticated representation format, notably one that provides semantic typing and type hierarchies, e.g., OWL, could be employed to define hierarchies of grammatical functions (e.g. direct object would be a sub-type of complement) and other attributes. These would presumably support the identification of further overlapping SCFs.

During a subsequent qualitative analysis of the overlapping and complementary SCFs, we collected some enlightening background information. Overlapping SCFs in the cross-lingual comparison (both fine-grained and coarse) include prominent SCFs corresponding to transitive and intransitive verbs, as well as verbs with that-clause and verbs with to-infinitive.

GN and ILS are highly complementary regarding SCFs: for instance, while many SCFs with adverbial arguments are unique in GN, only ILS provides a fine-grained specification of prepositional complements including the preposition, as well as the case the preposition requires.[20] VN, too, contains a large number of SCFs with a detailed specification of possible prepositions, partly specified as language-independent preposition types. A large number of complementary SCFs in VN vs. GN and GN vs. ILS are due to a diverging linguistic analysis of extraposed subject clauses with an *es* (*it*) in the main clause (e.g., *It annoys him that the train is late.*). In GN, such clauses are not specified as subject, whereas in VN and ILS they are.

Regarding VN and ILS, only VN lists subject control for verbs, while both VN and ILS list object control and subject raising. GN, on the other hand, does not specify control or raising at all.

4 Discussion

4.1 Previous Work

Merging SCFs: Previous work on merging SCF lexicons has only been performed in a monolingual setting and lacks the use of standards. King and Crouch (2005) describe the process of unifying several large-scale verb lexicons for English, including VN and WordNet. They perform a conversion of these lexicons into a uniform, but non-standard representation format, resulting in a lexicon which is integrated at the level of verb senses, SCFs and lexical-semantics. Thus, the result of their work is not applicable to cross-lingual settings.

Necsulescu et al. (2011) and Padró et al. (2011) report on approaches to automatic merging of two Spanish SCF lexicons. As these lexicons lack sense information apart from the SCFs, their merging approach only works on a very coarse-grained sense level given by lemma-SCF pairs. The fully automatic merging approach described

[20] In German, prepositions govern the case of their noun phrase.

in (Padró et al., 2011) assumes that one of the lexicons to be integrated is already represented in the target representation format, i.e. given two lexicons, they map one lexicon to the format of the other. Moreover, their approach requires a significant overlap of SCFs and verbs in any two lexicons to be merged. The authors state that it is presently unclear, how much overlap is required to obtain sufficiently precise merging results.

Standardizing SCFs: Much previous work on standardizing NLP lexicons in LMF has focused on WordNet-like resources. Soria et al. (2009) describe WordNet-LMF, an LMF model for representing wordnets which has been used in the KYOTO project.[21] Later, WordNet-LMF has been adapted by Henrich and Hinrichs (2010) to GermaNet and by Toral et al. (2010) to the Italian WordNet. WordNet-LMF does not provide the possibility to represent subcategorization at all. The adaption of WordNet-LMF to GN (Henrich and Hinrichs, 2010) allows SCFs to be respresented as string values. However, this extension is not sufficient, because it provides no means to model the syntax-semantics interface, which specifies correspondences between syntactic and semantic arguments of verbs and other predicates. Quochi et al. (2008) report on an LMF model that covers the syntax-semantics mapping just mentioned; it has been used for standardizing an Italian domain-specific lexicon. Buitelaar et al. (2009) describe LexInfo, an LMF-model that is used for lexicalizing ontologies. LexInfo is implemented in OWL and specifies a linking of syntactic and semantic arguments. For SCFs and arguments, a type hierarchy is defined. In their paper, Buitelaar et al. (2009) show only few SCFs and do not indicate what kinds of SCFs can be represented with LexInfo in principle. On the LexInfo website[22], the current LexInfo version 2.0 can be viewed, but no further documentation is given. We inspected LexInfo version 2.0 and found that it specifies a large number of fine-grained SCFs. However, LexInfo has not been evaluated so far on large-scale SCF lexicons, such as VerbNet.

4.2 Subcat-LMF

Subcat-LMF enables the uniform representation of fine-grained SCFs across the two languages English and German. By mapping large-scale SCF lexicons to Subcat-LMF, we have demonstrated its usability for uniformly representing a wide range of SCFs and other lexical-syntactic information types in English and German.

As our cross-lingual comparison of lexicons has revealed many complementary SCFs in VN, GN and ILS, mono- and cross-lingual alignments of these lexicons at sense level would lead to a major increase in SCF coverage. Moreover, the cross-lingually uniform representation of SCFs can be exploited for an additional alignment of the lexicons at the level of SCF arguments. Such a fine-grained alignment of SCFs can be used, for instance, to project VN semantic roles to GN, thus yielding a German resource for semantic role labeling (see Gildea and Jurafsky (2002), Swier and Stevenson (2005)).

Subcat-LMF could be used for standardizing further English and German lexicons. The automatic conversion of lexicons to Subcat-LMF requires the manual definition of a mapping, at least for syntactic arguments. Furthermore, the automatic merging approach by Padró et al. (2011) could be tested for English: given our standardized version of VN, other English SCF lexicons could be merged fully automatically with the Subcat-LMF version of VN.

5 Conclusion

Subcat-LMF contributes to fostering the standardization of language resources and their interoperability at the lexical-syntactic level across English and German. The Subcat-LMF DTD including links to ISOCat, all conversion tools, and the standardized versions of VN and ILS[23] are publicly available at http://www.ukp.tu-darmstadt.de/data/uby.

Acknowledgments

This work has been supported by the Volkswagen Foundation as part of the Lichtenberg-Professorship Program under grant No. I/82806. We thank the anonymous reviewers for their valuable comments. We also thank Dr. Jungi Kim and Christian M. Meyer for their contributions to this paper, and Yevgen Chebotar and Zijad Maksuti for their contributions to the conversion software.

[21] http://www.kyoto-project.eu/

[22] See http://lexinfo.net/

[23] The converted version of GN can not be made available due to licensing.

References

Galen Andrew, Trond Grenager, and Christopher D. Manning. 2004. Verb sense and subcategorization: using joint inference to improve performance on complementary tasks. In *Proceedings of the 2004 Conference on Empirical Methods in Natural Language Processing (EMNLP)*, pages 150–157, Barcelona, Spain.

Marco Baroni, Silvia Bernardini, Adriano Ferraresi, and Eros Zanchetta. 2009. The WaCky wide web: a collection of very large linguistically processed web-crawled corpora. *Language Resources and Evaluation*, 43(3):209–226.

Daan Broeder, Marc Kemps-Snijders, Dieter Van Uytvanck, Menzo Windhouwer, Peter Withers, Peter Wittenburg, and Claus Zinn. 2010. A Data Category Registry- and Component-based Metadata Framework. In *Proceedings of the Seventh International Conference on Language Resources and Evaluation (LREC)*, pages 43–47, Valletta, Malta.

Susan Windisch Brown, Dmitriy Dligach, and Martha Palmer. 2011. VerbNet Class Assignment as a WSD Task. In *Proceedings of the 9th International Conference on Computational Semantics (IWCS)*, pages 85–94, Oxford, UK.

Paul Buitelaar, Philipp Cimiano, Peter Haase, and Michael Sintek. 2009. Towards Linguistically Grounded Ontologies. In Lora Aroyo, Paolo Traverso, Fabio Ciravegna, Philipp Cimiano, Tom Heath, Eero Hyvönen, Riichiro Mizoguchi, Eyal Oren, Marta Sabou, and Elena Simperl, editors, *The Semantic Web: Research and Applications*, pages 111–125, Berlin Heidelberg. Springer-Verlag.

Aljoscha Burchardt, Katrin Erk, Anette Frank, Andrea Kowalski, Sebastian Padó, and Manfred Pinkal. 2006. The SALSA Corpus: a German Corpus Resource for Lexical Semantics. In *Proceedings of the Fifth International Conference on Language Resources and Evaluation (LREC)*, pages 969–974, Genoa, Italy.

Nicoletta Calzolari and Monica Monachini. 1996. EAGLES Proposal for Morphosyntactic Standards: in view of a ready-to-use package. In G. Perissinotto, editor, *Research in Humanities Computing*, volume 5, pages 48–64. Oxford University Press, Oxford, UK.

Tejaswini Deoskar. 2008. Re-estimation of lexical parameters for treebank PCFGs. In *Proceedings of the 22nd International Conference on Computational Linguistics (COLING)*, pages 193–200, Manchester, United Kingdom.

Judith Eckle-Kohler, Iryna Gurevych, Silvana Hartmann, Michael Matuschek, and Christian M. Meyer. 2012. UBY-LMF – A Uniform Format for Standardizing Heterogeneous Lexical-Semantic Resources in ISO-LMF. In *Proceedings of the 8th International Conference on Language Resources and Evaluation (LREC 2012)*, page (to appear), Istanbul, Turkey.

Judith Eckle-Kohler. 1999. *Linguistisches Wissen zur automatischen Lexikon-Akquisition aus deutschen Textcorpora*. Logos-Verlag, Berlin, Germany. PhDThesis.

Gil Francopoulo, Nuria Bel, Monte George, Nicoletta Calzolari, Monica Monachini, Mandy Pet, and Claudia Soria. 2006. Lexical Markup Framework (LMF). In *Proceedings of the Fifth International Conference on Language Resources and Evaluation (LREC)*, pages 233–236, Genoa, Italy.

Daniel Gildea and Daniel Jurafsky. 2002. Automatic labeling of semantic roles. *Computational Linguistics*, 28:245–288, September.

Ralph Grishman, Catherine Macleod, and Adam Meyers. 1994. Comlex Syntax: Building a Computational Lexicon. In *Proceedings of the 15th International Conference on Computational Linguistics (COLING)*, pages 268–272, Kyoto, Japan.

Iryna Gurevych, Judith Eckle-Kohler, Silvana Hartmann, Michael Matuschek, Christian M. Meyer, and Christian Wirth. 2012. Uby - A Large-Scale Unified Lexical-Semantic Resource. In *Proceedings of the 13th Conference of the European Chapter of the Association for Computational Linguistics (EACL 2012)*, page (to appear), Avignon, France.

Verena Henrich and Erhard Hinrichs. 2010. Standardizing wordnets in the ISO standard LMF: Wordnet-LMF for GermaNet. In *Proceedings of the 23rd International Conference on Computational Linguistics (COLING)*, pages 456–464, Beijing, China.

Nancy Ide and James Pustejovsky. 2010. What Does Interoperability Mean, anyway? Toward an Operational Definition of Interoperability. In *Proceedings of the Second International Conference on Global Interoperability for Language Resources*, Hong Kong.

Tracy Holloway King and Dick Crouch. 2005. Unifying lexical resources. In *Proceedings of the Interdisciplinary Workshop on the Identification and Representation of Verb Features and Verb Classes*, Saarbruecken, Germany.

Karin Kipper, Anna Korhonen, Neville Ryant, and Martha Palmer. 2008. A Large-scale Classification of English Verbs. *Language Resources and Evaluation*, 42:21–40.

Manfred Klenner. 2007. Shallow dependency labeling. In *Proceedings of the 45th Annual Meeting of the Association for Computational Linguistics (ACL), Companion Volume Proceedings of the Demo and Poster Sessions*, pages 201–204, Prague, Czech Republic.

Claudia Kunze and Lothar Lemnitzer. 2002. GermaNet — representation, visualization, application. In *Proceedings of the Third International Conference on Language Resources and Evaluation*

(LREC), pages 1485–1491, Las Palmas, Canary Islands, Spain.

Beth Levin. 1993. *English Verb Classes and Alternations*. The University of Chicago Press, Chicago, USA.

Christian M. Meyer and Iryna Gurevych. 2011. What Psycholinguists Know About Chemistry: Aligning Wiktionary and WordNet for Increased Domain Coverage. In *Proceedings of the 5th International Joint Conference on Natural Language Processing (IJCNLP)*, pages 883–892, Chiang Mai, Thailand.

Roberto Navigli and Simone Paolo Ponzetto. 2010. BabelNet: Building a very large multilingual semantic network. In *Proceedings of the 48th Annual Meeting of the Association for Computational Linguistics (ACL)*, pages 216–225, Uppsala, Sweden.

Silvia Necsulescu, Núria Bel, Munsta Padró, Montserrat Marimon, and Eva Revilla. 2011. Towards the Automatic Merging of Language Resources. In *Proceedings of the 2011 ESSLI Workshop on Lexical Resources (WoLeR 2011)*, Ljubljana, Slovenia.

Elisabeth Niemann and Iryna Gurevych. 2011. The People's Web meets Linguistic Knowledge: Automatic Sense Alignment of Wikipedia and WordNet. In *Proceedings of the 9th International Conference on Computational Semantics (IWCS)*, pages 205–214, Oxford, UK.

Muntsa Padró, Núria Bel, and Silvia Necsulescu. 2011. Towards the Automatic Merging of Lexical Resources: Automatic Mapping. In *Proceedings of the International Conference on Recent Advances in Natural Language Processing*, pages 296–301, Hissar, Bulgaria.

Valeria Quochi, Monica Monachini, Riccardo Del Gratta, and Nicoletta Calzolari. 2008. A lexicon for biology and bioinformatics: the bootstrep experience. In *Proceedings of the Sixth International Conference on Language Resources and Evaluation (LREC'08)*, pages 2285–2292, Marrakech, Morocco, may.

Josef Ruppenhofer, Michael Ellsworth, Miriam R. L. Petruck, Christopher R. Johnson, and Jan Scheffczyk. 2010. FrameNet II: Extended Theory and Practice, September.

Lei Shi and Rada Mihalcea. 2005. Putting pieces together: Combining FrameNet, VerbNet and WordNet for robust semantic parsing. In *Proceedings of the Sixth International Conference on Intelligent Text Processing and Computational Linguistics (CICLing)*, pages 100–111, Mexico City, Mexico.

Anthony Sigogne, Matthieu Constant, and Éric Laporte. 2011. Integration of data from a syntactic lexicon into generative and discriminative probabilistic parsers. In *Proceedings of the International Conference on Recent Advances in Natural Language Processing*, pages 363–370, Hissar, Bulgaria.

Claudia Soria, Monica Monachini, and Piek Vossen. 2009. Wordnet-LMF: fleshing out a standardized format for Wordnet interoperability. In *Proceedings of the 2009 International Workshop on Intercultural Collaboration*, pages 139–146, Palo Alto, California, USA.

Robert S. Swier and Suzanne Stevenson. 2005. Exploiting a verb lexicon in automatic semantic role labelling. In *Proceedings of the conference on Human Language Technology and Empirical Methods in Natural Language Processing (HLT'05)*, pages 883–890, Vancouver, British Columbia, Canada.

Antonio Toral, Stefania Bracale, Monica Monachini, and Claudia Soria. 2010. Rejuvenating the Italian WordNet: upgrading, standarising, extending. In *Proceedings of the 5th Global WordNet Conference*, Bombay, India.

The effect of domain and text type on text prediction quality

Suzan Verberne, Antal van den Bosch, Helmer Strik, Lou Boves
Centre for Language Studies
Radboud University Nijmegen
s.verberne@let.ru.nl

Abstract

Text prediction is the task of suggesting text while the user is typing. Its main aim is to reduce the number of keystrokes that are needed to type a text. In this paper, we address the influence of text type and domain differences on text prediction quality.

By training and testing our text prediction algorithm on four different text types (Wikipedia, Twitter, transcriptions of conversational speech and FAQ) with equal corpus sizes, we found that there is a clear effect of text type on text prediction quality: training and testing on the same text type gave percentages of saved keystrokes between 27 and 34%; training on a different text type caused the scores to drop to percentages between 16 and 28%.

In our case study, we compared a number of training corpora for a specific data set for which training data is sparse: questions about neurological issues. We found that both text type and topic domain play a role in text prediction quality. The best performing training corpus was a set of medical pages from Wikipedia. The second-best result was obtained by leave-one-out experiments on the test questions, even though this training corpus was much smaller (2,672 words) than the other corpora (1.5 Million words).

1 Introduction

Text prediction is the task of suggesting text while the user is typing. Its main aim is to reduce the number of keystrokes that are needed to type a text, thereby saving time. Text prediction algorithms have been implemented for mobile devices, office software (Open Office Writer), search engines (Google query completion), and in special-needs software for writers who have difficulties typing (Garay-Vitoria and Abascal, 2006). In most applications, the scope of the prediction is the completion of the current word; hence the often-used term 'word completion'.

The most basic method for word completion is checking after each typed character whether the prefix typed since the last whitespace is unique according to a lexicon. If it is, the algorithm suggests to complete the prefix with the lexicon entry. The algorithm may also suggest to complete a prefix even before the word's uniqueness point is reached, using statistical information on the previous context. Moreover, it has been shown that significantly better prediction results can be obtained if not only the prefix of the current word is included as previous context, but also previous words (Fazly and Hirst, 2003) or characters (Van den Bosch and Bogers, 2008).

In the current paper, we follow up on this work by addressing the influence of text type and domain differences on text prediction quality. Brief messages on mobile devices (such as text messages, Twitter and Facebook updates) are of a different style and lexicon than documents typed in office software (Westman and Freund, 2010). In addition, the topic domain of the text also influences its content. These differences may cause an algorithm trained on one text type or domain to perform poorly on another.

The questions that we aim to answer in this paper are (1) "What is the effect of text type differences on the quality of a text prediction algorithm?" and (2) "What is the best choice of training data if domain- and text type-specific data is sparse?". To answer these questions, we perform three experiments:

1. A series of within-text type experiments on four different types of Dutch text: Wikipedia articles, Twitter data, transcriptions of con-

versational speech and web pages of Frequently Asked Questions (FAQ).

2. A series of across-text type experiments in which we train and test on different text types;
3. A case study using texts from a specific domain and text type: questions about neurological issues. Training data for this combination of language (Dutch), text type (FAQ) and domain (medical/neurological) is sparse. Therefore, we search for the type of training data that gives the best prediction results for this corpus. We compare the following training corpora:
   - The corpora that we compared in the text type experiments: Wikipedia, Twitter, Speech and FAQ, 1.5 Million words per corpus.
   - A 1.5 Million words training corpus that is of the same domain as the target data: medical pages from Wikipedia;
   - The 359 questions from the neuro-QA data themselves, evaluated in a leave-one-out setting (359 times training on 358 questions and evaluating on the remaining questions).

The prospective application of the third series of experiments is the development of a text prediction algorithm in an online care platform: an online community for patients seeking information about their illness. In this specific case the target group is patients with language disabilities due to neurological disorders.

The remainder of this paper is organized as follows: In Section 2 we give a brief overview of text prediction methods discussed in the literature. In Section 3 we present our approach to text prediction. Sections 4 and 5 describe the experiments that we carried out and the results we obtained. We phrase our conclusions in Section 6.

2 Text prediction methods

Text prediction methods have been developed for several different purposes. The older algorithms were built as communicative devices for people with disabilities, such as motor and speech impairments. More recently, text prediction is developed for writing with reduced keyboards, specifically for writing (composing messages) on mobile devices (Garay-Vitoria and Abascal, 2006).

All modern methods share the general idea that previous context (which we will call the 'buffer') can be used to predict the next block of characters (the 'predictive unit'). If the user gets correct suggestions for continuation of the text then the number of keystrokes needed to type the text is reduced. The unit to be predicted by a text prediction algorithm can be anything ranging from a single character (which actually does not save any keystrokes) to multiple words. Single words are the most widely used as prediction units because they are recognizable at a low cognitive load for the user, and word prediction gives good results in terms of keystroke savings (Garay-Vitoria and Abascal, 2006).

There is some variation among methods in the size and type of buffer used. Most methods use character n-grams as buffer, because they are powerful and can be implemented independently of the target language (Carlberger, 1997). In many algorithms the buffer is cleared at the start of each new word (making the buffer never larger than the length of the current word). In the paper by (Van den Bosch and Bogers, 2008), two extensions to the basic prefix-model are compared. They found that an algorithm that uses the previous n characters as buffer, crossing word borders without clearing the buffer, performs better than both a prefix character model and an algorithm that includes the full previous word as feature. In addition to using the previously typed characters and/or words in the buffer, word characteristics such as frequency and recency could also be taken into account (Garay-Vitoria and Abascal, 2006).

Possible evaluation measures for text prediction are the proportion of words that are correctly predicted, the percentage of keystrokes that could maximally be saved (if the user would always make the correct decision), and the time saved by the use of the algorithm (Garay-Vitoria and Abascal, 2006). The performance that can be obtained by text prediction algorithms depends on the language they are evaluated on. Lower results are obtained for higher-inflected languages such as German than for low-inflected languages such as English (Matiasek et al., 2002). In their overview of text prediction systems, (Garay-Vitoria and Abascal, 2006) report performance scores ranging from 29% to 56% of keystrokes saved.

An important factor that is known to influence the quality of text prediction systems, is training set size (Lesher et al., 1999; Van den Bosch, 2011). The paper by (Van den Bosch, 2011) shows log-linear learning curves for word prediction (a constant improvement each time the training corpus size is doubled), when the training set size is increased incrementally from 10^2 to $3*10^7$ words.

3 Our approach to text prediction

We implement a text prediction algorithm for Dutch, which is a productive compounding language like German, but has a somewhat simpler inflectional system. We do not focus on the effect of training set size, but on the effect of text type and topic domain differences.

Our approach to text prediction is largely inspired by (Van den Bosch and Bogers, 2008). We experiment with two different buffer types that are based on character n-grams:

- 'Prefix of current word' contains all characters of only the word currently keyed in, where the buffer shifts by one character position with every new character.
- 'Buffer15' buffer also includes any other characters keyed in belonging to previously keyed-in words.

Modeling character history beyond the current word can naturally be done with a buffer model in which the buffer shifts by one position per character, while a typical left-aligned prefix model (that never shifts and fixes letters to their positional feature) would not be able to do this.

In the buffer, all characters from the text are kept, including whitespace and punctuation. The predictive unit is one token (word or punctuation symbol). In both the buffer and the prediction label, any capitalization is kept. At each point in the typing process, our algorithm gives one suggestion: the word that is the most likely continuation of the current buffer.

We save the training data as a classification data set: each character in the buffer fills a feature slot and the word that is to be predicted is the classification label. Figures 1 and 2 give examples of each of the buffer types Prefix and Buffer15 that we created for the text fragment "*tot een niveau*" in the context "stelselmatig bij elke verkiezing tot een niveau van' '(*structurally with each election to a level of*). We use the implementation of the IGTree decision tree algorithm in TiMBL (Daelemans et al., 1997) to train our models.

3.1 Evaluation

We evaluate our algorithms on corpus data. This means that we have to make assumptions about user behaviour. We assume that the user confirms a suggested word as soon as it is suggested correctly, not typing any additional characters before confirming. We evaluate our text prediction algorithms in terms of the percentage of keystrokes saved K:

$$K = \frac{\sum_{i=0}^{n}(F_i) - \sum_{i=0}^{n}(W_i)}{\sum_{i=0}^{n}(F_i)} * 100 \qquad (1)$$

in which n is the number of words in the test set, W_i is the number of keystrokes that have been typed before the word i is correctly suggested and F_i is the number of keystrokes that would be needed to type the complete word i. For example, our algorithm correctly predicts the word *niveau* after the context `i n g _ t o t _ e e n _ n i v` in the test set. Assuming that the user confirms the word *niveau* at this point, three keystrokes were needed for the prefix *niv*. So, $W_i = 3$ and $F_i = 6$. The number of keystrokes needed for whitespace and punctuation are unchanged: these have to be typed anyway, independently of the support by a text prediction algorithm.

4 Text type experiments

In this section, we describe the first and second series of experiments. The case study on questions from the neurological domain is described in Section 5.

4.1 Data

In the text type experiments, we evaluate our text prediction algorithm on four different types of Dutch text: Wikipedia, Twitter data, transcriptions of conversational speech, and web pages of Frequently Asked Questions (FAQ). The Wikipedia corpus that we use is part of the Lassy corpus (Van Noord, 2009); we obtained a version from the summer of 2010.[1] The Twitter data are collected continuously and automatically filtered for language by Erik Tjong Kim Sang (Tjong Kim Sang, 2011). We used the tweets from all users that posted at least 19 tweets (excluding retweets) during one day in June 2011. This is a set of 1 Million Twitter messages from 30,000

[1] http://www.let.rug.nl/vannoord/trees/Treebank/Machine/NLWIKI20100826/COMPACT/

_	_	_	_	_	_	_	_	_	_	_	_	_	_	t	tot
_	_	_	_	_	_	_	_	_	_	_	_	_	t	o	tot
_	_	_	_	_	_	_	_	_	_	_	_	t	o	t	tot
_	_	_	_	_	_	_	_	_	_	_	_	_	_	e	een
_	_	_	_	_	_	_	_	_	_	_	_	_	e	e	een
_	_	_	_	_	_	_	_	_	_	_	_	e	e	n	een
_	_	_	_	_	_	_	_	_	_	_	_	_	_	n	niveau
_	_	_	_	_	_	_	_	_	_	_	_	_	n	i	niveau
_	_	_	_	_	_	_	_	_	_	_	_	n	i	v	niveau
_	_	_	_	_	_	_	_	_	_	_	n	i	v	e	niveau
_	_	_	_	_	_	_	_	_	_	n	i	v	e	a	niveau
_	_	_	_	_	_	_	_	_	n	i	v	e	a	u	niveau

Figure 1: Example of buffer type 'Prefix' for the text fragment "(elke verkiezing) tot een niveau". Underscores represent whitespaces.

l	k	e	_	v	e	r	k	i	e	z	i	n	g	_	tot
k	e	_	v	e	r	k	i	e	z	i	n	g	_	t	tot
e	_	v	e	r	k	i	e	z	i	n	g	_	t	o	tot
_	v	e	r	k	i	e	z	i	n	g	_	t	o	t	tot
v	e	r	k	i	e	z	i	n	g	_	t	o	t	_	een
e	r	k	i	e	z	i	n	g	_	t	o	t	_	e	een
r	k	i	e	z	i	n	g	_	t	o	t	_	e	e	een
k	i	e	z	i	n	g	_	t	o	t	_	e	e	n	een
i	e	z	i	n	g	_	t	o	t	_	e	e	n	_	niveau
e	z	i	n	g	_	t	o	t	_	e	e	n	_	n	niveau
z	i	n	g	_	t	o	t	_	e	e	n	_	n	i	niveau
i	n	g	_	t	o	t	_	e	e	n	_	n	i	v	niveau
n	g	_	t	o	t	_	e	e	n	_	n	i	v	e	niveau
g	_	t	o	t	_	e	e	n	_	n	i	v	e	a	niveau
_	t	o	t	_	e	e	n	_	n	i	v	e	a	u	niveau

Figure 2: Example of buffer type 'Buffer15' for the text fragment "(elke verkiezing) tot een niveau". Underscores represent whitespaces.

different users. The transcriptions of conversational speech are from the Spoken Dutch Corpus (CGN) (Oostdijk, 2000); for our experiments, we only use the category 'spontaneous speech'. We obtained the FAQ data by downloading the first 1,000 pages that Google returns for the query 'faq' with the language restriction Dutch. After cleaning the pages from HTML and other coding, the resulting corpus contained approximately 1.7 Million words of questions and answers.

4.2 Within-text type experiments

For each of the four text types, we compare the buffer types 'Prefix' and 'Buffer15'. In each experiment, we use 1.5 Million words from the corpus to train the algorithm and 100,000 words to test it. The results are in Table 1.

4.3 Across-text type experiments

We investigate the importance of text type differences for text prediction with a series of experiments in which we train and test our algorithm on texts of different text types. We keep the size of the train and test sets the same: 1.5 Million words and 100,000 words respectively. The results are in Table 2.

4.4 Discussion of the results

Table 1 shows that for all text types, the buffer of 15 characters that crosses word borders gives better results than the prefix of the current word only. We get a relative improvement of 35% (for FAQ) to 62% (for Speech) of Buffer15 compared to Prefix-only.

Table 2 shows that text type differences have an influence on text prediction quality: all across-text type experiments lead to lower results than the within-text type experiments. From the results in Table 2, we can deduce that of the four text types, speech and Twitter language resemble each other more than they resemble the other two, and Wikipedia and FAQ resemble each other more. Twitter and Wikipedia data are the least similar: training on Wikipedia data makes the text prediction score for Twitter data drop from 29.2 to 16.5%.[2]

[2]Note that the results are not symmetric. For example,

Table 1: Results from the within-text type experiments in terms of percentages of saved keystrokes. *Prefix* means: 'use the previous characters of the current word as features'. *Buffer 15* means 'use a buffer of the previous 15 characters as features'.

	Prefix	Buffer15
Wikipedia	22.2%	30.5%
Twitter	21.3%	29.2%
Speech	20.7%	33.4%
FAQ	20.2%	27.2%

Table 2: Results from the across-text type experiments in terms of percentages of saved keystrokes, using the best-scoring configuration from the within-text type experiments: a buffer of 15 characters

Trained on	Tested on Wikipedia	Tested on Twitter	Tested on Speech	Tested on FAQ
Wikipedia	30.5%	16.5%	22.3%	24.9%
Twitter	17.9%	29.2%	27.9%	20.7%
Speech	19.7%	22.5%	33.4%	21.0%
FAQ	22.6%	18.2%	22.9%	27.2%

5 Case study: questions about neurological issues

Online care platforms aim to bring together patients and experts. Through this medium, patients can find information about their illness, and get in contact with fellow-sufferers. Patients who suffer from neurological damage may have communicative disabilities because their speaking and writing skills are impaired. For these patients, existing online care platforms are often not easily accessible. Aphasia, for example, hampers the exchange of information because the patient has problems with word finding.

In the project 'Communicatie en revalidatie DigiPoli' (ComPoli), language and speech technologies are implemented in the infrastructure of an existing online care platform in order to facilitate communication for patients suffering from neurological damage. Part of the online care platform is a list of frequently asked questions about neurological diseases with answers. A user can browse through the questions using a chat-by-click interface (Geuze et al., 2008). Besides reading the listed questions and answers, the user has the option to submit a question that is not yet included in the list. The newly submitted questions are sent to an expert who answers them and adds both question and answer to the chat-by-click database. In typing the question to be submitted, the user will be supported by a text prediction application.

The aim of this section is to find the best training corpus for newly formulated questions in the neurological domain. We realize that questions formulated by users of a web interface are different from questions formulated by experts for the purpose of a FAQ-list. Therefore, we plan to gather real user data once we have a first version of the user interface running online. For developing the text prediction algorithm that is behind the initial version of the application, we aim to find the best training corpus using the questions from the chat-by-click data as training set.

5.1 Data

The chat-by-click data set on neurological issues consists of 639 questions with corresponding answers. A small sample of the data (translated to English) is shown in Table 3. In order to create the test data for our experiments, we removed duplicate questions from the chat-by-click data, leaving a set of 359 questions.[3]

In the previous sections, we used corpora of 100,000 words as test collections and we calculated the percentage of saved keystrokes over the

training on Wikipedia, testing on Twitter gives a different result from training on Twitter, testing on Wikipedia. This is due to the size and domain of the vocabularies in both data sets and the richness of the contexts (in order for the algorithm to predict a word, it has to have seen it in the train set). If the test set has a larger vocabulary than the train set, a lower proportion of words can be predicted than when it is the other way around.

[3]Some questions and answers are repeated several times in the chat-by-click data because they are located at different places in the chat-by-click hierarchy.

Table 3: A sample of the neuro-QA data, translated to English.

question_0_505	Can (P)LS be cured?
answer_0_505	Unfortunately, a real cure is not possible. However, things can be done to combat the effects of the diseases, mainly relieving symptoms such as stiffness and spasticity. The phisical therapist and rehabilitation specialist can play a major role in symptom relief. Moreover, there are medications that can reduce spasticity.
question_0_508	How is (P)LS diagnosed?
answer_0_508	The diagnosis PLS is difficult to establish, especially because the symptoms strongly resemble HSP symptoms (Strumpell's disease). Apart from blood and muscle research, several neurological examinations will be carried out.

Table 4: Results for the neuro-QA questions only in terms of percentages of saved keystrokes, using different training sets. The text prediction configuration used in all settings is Buffer15. The test samples are 359 questions with an average length of 7.5 words. The percentages of saved keystrokes are means over the 359 questions.

Training corpus	# words	Mean % of saved keystrokes in neuro-QA questions (stdev)	OOV-rate
Twitter	1.5 Million	13.3% (12.5)	28.5%
Speech	1.5 Million	14.1% (13.2)	26.6%
Wikipedia	1.5 Million	16.1% (13.1)	19.4%
FAQ	1.5 Million	19.4% (15.6)	20.0%
Medical Wikipedia	1.5 Million	28.1% (16.5)	7.0%
Neuro-QA questions (leave-one-out)	2,672	26.5% (19.9)	17.8%

complete test corpus. In the reality of our case study however, users will type only brief fragments of text: the length of the question they want to submit. This means that there is potentially a large deviation in the effectiveness of the text prediction algorithm per user, depending on the content of the small text they are typing. Therefore, we decided to evaluate our training corpora separately on each of the 359 unique questions, so that we can report both mean and standard deviation of the text prediction scores on small (realistically sized) samples. The average number of words per question is 7.5; the total size of the neuro-QA corpus is 2,672 words.

5.2 Experiments

We aim to find the training set that gives the best text prediction result for the neuro-QA questions. We compare the following training corpora:

- The corpora that we compared in the text type experiments: Wikipedia, Twitter, Speech and FAQ, 1.5 Million words per corpus.
- A 1.5 Million words training corpus that is of the same topic domain as the target data: Wikipedia articles from the medical domain;
- The 359 questions from the neuro-QA data themselves, evaluated in a leave-one-out setting (359 times training on 358 questions and evaluating on the remaining questions).

In order to create the 'medical Wikipedia' corpus, we consulted the category structure of the Wikipedia corpus. The Wikipedia category 'Geneeskunde' (*Medicine*) contains 69,898 pages and in the deeper nodes of the hierarchy we see many non-medical pages, such as trappist beers (ordered under beer, booze, alcohol, Psychoactive drug, drug, and then medicine). If we remove all pages that are more than five levels under the 'Geneeskunde' category root, 21,071 pages are left, which contain fairly over the 1.5 Million words that we need. We used the first 1.5 Million words of the corpus in our experiments.

The text prediction results for the different corpora are in Table 4. For each corpus, the out-of-vocabulary rate is given: the percentage of words in the Neuro-QA questions that do not occur in the corpus.[4]

5.3 Discussion of the results

We measured the statistical significance of the mean differences between all text prediction scores using a Wilcoxon Signed Rank test on paired results for the 359 questions. We found that

[4]The OOV-rate for the Neuro-QA corpus itself is the average of the OOV-rate of each leave-one-out experiment: the proportion of words that only occur in one question.

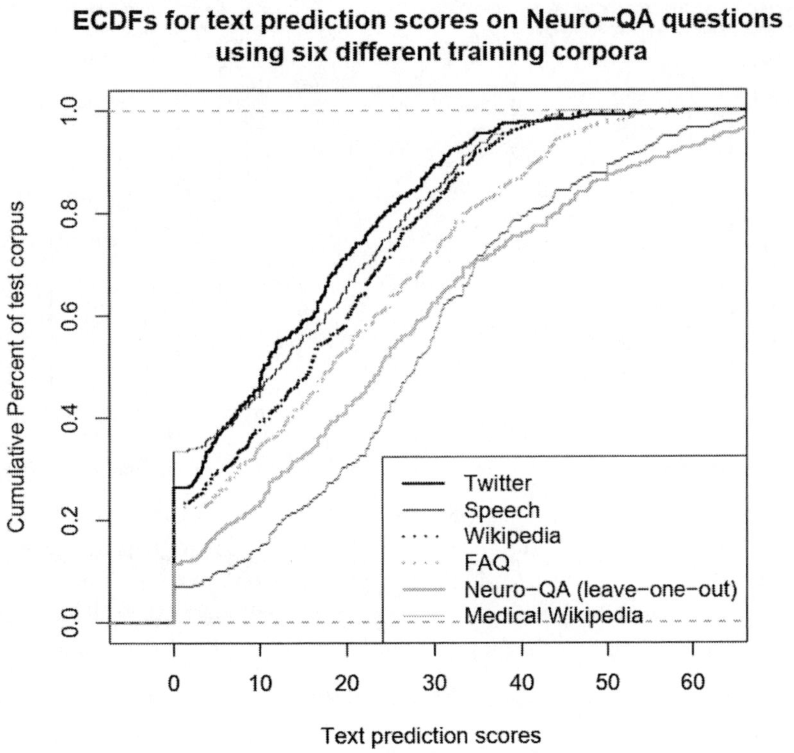

Figure 3: Empirical CDFs for text prediction scores on Neuro-QA data. Note that the curves that are at the bottom-right side represent the better-performing settings.

the difference between the Twitter and Speech corpora on the task is not significant ($P = 0.18$). The difference between Neuro-QA and Medical Wikipedia is significant with $P = 0.02$; all other differences are significant with $P < 0.01$.

The Medical Wikipedia corpus and the leave-one-out experiments on the Neuro-QA data give better text prediction scores than the other corpora. The Medical Wikipedia even scores slightly better than the Neuro-QA data itself. Twitter and Speech are the least-suited training corpora for the Neuro-QA questions, and FAQ data gives a bit better results than a general Wikipedia corpus.

These results suggest that both text type and topic domain play a role in text prediction quality, but the high scores for the Medical Wikipedia corpus shows that topic domain is even more important than text type.[5] The column 'OOV-rate' shows that this is probably due to the high coverage of terms in the Neuro-QA data by the Medical Wikipedia corpus.

Table 4 also shows that the standard deviation among the 359 samples is relatively large. For some questions, we 0% of the keystrokes are saved, while for other, scores of over 80% are obtained (by the Neuro-QA and Medical Wikipedia training corpora). We further analyzed the differences between the training sets by plotting the Empirical Cumulative Distribution Function (ECDF) for each experiment. An ECDF shows the development of text prediction scores (shown on the X-axis) by walking through the test set in 359 steps (shown on the Y-axis).

The ECDFs for our training corpora are in Figure 3. Note that the curves that are at the bottom-right side represent the better-performing settings (they get to a higher maximum after having seen a smaller portion of the samples). From Figure 3, it is again clear that the Neuro-QA and Medical Wikipedia corpora outperform the other training corpora, and that of the other four, FAQ is the best-performing corpus. Figure 3 also shows a large difference in the sizes of the starting percentiles: The proportion of samples with a text prediction

[5]We should note here that we did not control for domain differences between the four different text types. They are intended to be 'general domain' but Wikipedia articles will naturally be of different topics than conversational speech.

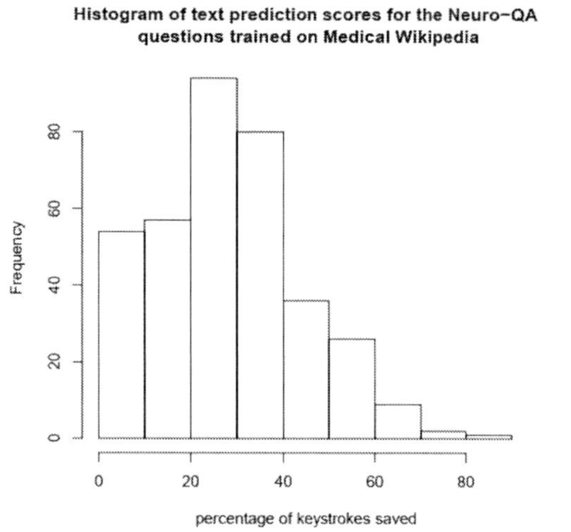

Figure 4: Histogram of text prediction scores for the Neuro-QA questions trained on Medical Wikipedia. Each bin represents 36 questions.

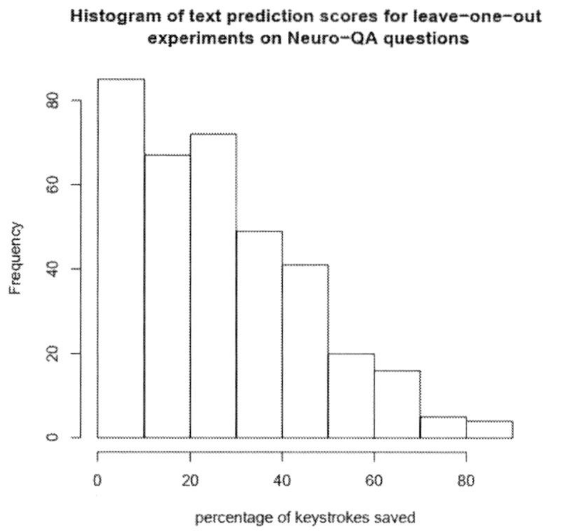

Figure 5: Histogram of text prediction scores for leave-one-out experiments on Neuro-QA questions. Each bin represents 36 questions.

score of 0% is less than 10% for the Medical Wikipedia up to more than 30% for Speech.

We inspected the questions that get a text prediction score of 0%. We see many medical terms in these questions, and many of the utterances are not even questions, but multi-word terms representing topical headers in the chat-by-click data. Seven samples get a zero-score in the output of all six training corpora, e.g.:

- glycogenose III.
- potassium-aggrevated myotonias.

26 samples get a zero-score in the output of all training corpora except for Medical Wikipedia and Neuro-QA itself. These are mainly short headings with domain-specific terms such as:

- idiopatische neuralgische amyotrofie.
- Markesbery-Griggs distale myopathie.
- oculopharyngeale spierdystrofie.

Interestingly, the ECDFs show that the Medical Wikipedia and Neuro-QA corpora cross at around percentile 70 (around the point of 40% saved keystrokes). This indicates that although the means of the two result samples are close to each other, the distribution the scores for the individual questions is different. The histograms of both distributions (Figures 4 and 5) confirm this: the algorithm trained on the Medical Wikipedia corpus leads a larger number of samples with scores around the mean, while the leave-one-out experiments lead to a larger number of samples with low prediction scores and a larger number of samples with high prediction scores. This is also reflected by the higher standard deviation for Neuro-QA than for Medical Wikipedia.

Since both the leave-one-out training on the Neuro-QA questions and the Medical Wikipedia led to good results but behave differently for different portions of the test data, we also evaluated a combination of both corpora on our test set: We created training corpora consisting of the Medical Wikipedia corpus, complemented by 90% of the Neuro-QA questions, testing on the remaining 10% of the Neuro-QA questions. This led to mean percentage of saved keystrokes of 28.6%, not significantly higher than just the Medical Wikipedia corpus.

6 Conclusions

In Section 1, we asked two questions: (1) "What is the effect of text type differences on the quality of a text prediction algorithm?" and (2) "What is the best choice of training data if domain- and text type-specific data is sparse?"

By training and testing our text prediction algorithm on four different text types (Wikipedia, Twitter, transcriptions of conversational speech and FAQ) with equal corpus sizes, we found that there is a clear effect of text type on text prediction quality: training and testing on the same text type gave percentages of saved keystrokes between 27 and 34%; training on a different text type caused the scores to drop to percentages between 16 and 28%.

In our case study, we compared a number of training corpora for a specific data set for which training data is sparse: questions about neurological issues. We found significant differences between the text prediction scores obtained with the six training corpora: the Twitter and Speech corpora were the least suited, followed by the Wikipedia and FAQ corpus. The highest scores were obtained by training the algorithm on the medical pages from Wikipedia, immediately followed by leave-one-out experiments on the 359 neurological questions. The large differences between the lexical coverage of the medical domain played a central role in the scores for the different training corpora.

Because we obtained good results by both the Medical Wikipedia corpus and the neuro-QA questions themselves, we opted for a combination of both data types as training corpus in the initial version of the online text prediction application. Currently, a demonstration version of the application is running for ComPoli-users. We hope to collect questions from these users to re-train our algorithm with more representative examples.

Acknowledgments

This work is part of the research programme 'Communicatie en revalidatie digiPoli' (ComPoli[6]), which is funded by ZonMW, the Netherlands organisation for health research and development.

References

J. Carlberger. 1997. Design and Implementation of a Probabilistic Word Prediciton Program. Master thesis, Royal Institute of Technology (KTH), Sweden.

W. Daelemans, A. Van Den Bosch, and T. Weijters. 1997. IGTree: Using trees for compression and classification in lazy learning algorithms. *Artificial Intelligence Review*, 11(1):407–423.

A. Fazly and G. Hirst. 2003. Testing the efficacy of part-of-speech information in word completion. In *Proceedings of the 2003 EACL Workshop on Language Modeling for Text Entry Methods*, pages 9–16.

[6]http://lands.let.ru.nl/~strik/research/ComPoli/

N. Garay-Vitoria and J. Abascal. 2006. Text prediction systems: a survey. *Universal Access in the Information Society*, 4(3):188–203.

J. Geuze, P. Desain, and J. Ringelberg. 2008. Rephrase: chat-by-click: a fundamental new mode of human communication over the internet. In *CHI'08 extended abstracts on Human factors in computing systems*, pages 3345–3350. ACM.

G.W. Lesher, B.J. Moulton, D.J. Higginbotham, et al. 1999. Effects of ngram order and training text size on word prediction. In *Proceedings of the RESNA '99 Annual Conference*, pages 52–54.

Johannes Matiasek, Marco Baroni, and Harald Trost. 2002. FASTY - A Multi-lingual Approach to Text Prediction. In Klaus Miesenberger, Joachim Klaus, and Wolfgang Zagler, editors, *Computers Helping People with Special Needs*, volume 2398 of *Lecture Notes in Computer Science*, pages 165–176. Springer Berlin / Heidelberg.

N. Oostdijk. 2000. The spoken Dutch corpus: overview and first evaluation. In *Proceedings of LREC-2000, Athens*, volume 2, pages 887–894.

Erik Tjong Kim Sang. 2011. Het gebruik van Twitter voor Taalkundig Onderzoek. In *TABU: Bulletin voor Taalwetenschap*, volume 39, pages 62–72. In Dutch.

A. Van den Bosch and T. Bogers. 2008. Efficient context-sensitive word completion for mobile devices. In *Proceedings of the 10th international conference on Human computer interaction with mobile devices and services*, pages 465–470. ACM.

A. Van den Bosch. 2011. Effects of context and recency in scaled word completion. *Computational Linguistics in the Netherlands Journal*, 1:79–94, 12/2011.

G. Van Noord. 2009. Huge parsed corpora in LASSY. In *Proceedings of The 7th International Workshop on Treebanks and Linguistic Theories (TLT7)*.

S. Westman and L. Freund. 2010. Information Interaction in 140 Characters or Less: Genres on Twitter. In *Proceedings of the third symposium on Information Interaction in Context (IIiX)*, pages 323–328. ACM.

The Impact of Spelling Errors on Patent Search

Benno Stein and **Dennis Hoppe** and **Tim Gollub**

Bauhaus-Universität Weimar
99421 Weimar, Germany
`<first name>.<last name>@uni-weimar.de`

Abstract

The search in patent databases is a risky business compared to the search in other domains. A single document that is relevant but overlooked during a patent search can turn into an expensive proposition. While recent research engages in specialized models and algorithms to improve the effectiveness of patent retrieval, we bring another aspect into focus: the detection and exploitation of patent inconsistencies. In particular, we analyze spelling errors in the assignee field of patents granted by the United States Patent & Trademark Office. We introduce technology in order to improve retrieval effectiveness despite the presence of typographical ambiguities. In this regard, we (1) quantify spelling errors in terms of edit distance and phonological dissimilarity and (2) render error detection as a learning problem that combines word dissimilarities with patent meta-features. For the task of finding all patents of a company, our approach improves recall from 96.7% (when using a state-of-the-art patent search engine) to 99.5%, while precision is compromised by only 3.7%.

1 Introduction

Patent search forms the heart of most retrieval tasks in the intellectual property domain—cf. Table 1, which provides an overview of various user groups along with their typical (•) and related (∘) tasks. The due diligence task, for example, is concerned with legal issues that arise while investigating another company. Part of an investigation is a patent portfolio comparison between one or more competitors (Lupu et al., 2011). Within all tasks recall is preferred over precision, a fact which distinguishes patent search from general web search. This retrieval constraint has produced a variety of sophisticated approaches tailored to the patent domain: citation analysis (Magdy and Jones, 2010), the learning of section-specific retrieval models (Lopez and Romary, 2010), and automated query generation (Xue and Croft, 2009). Each approach improves retrieval performance, but what keeps them from attaining maximum effectiveness in terms of recall are the inconsistencies found in patents: incomplete citation sets, incorrectly assigned classification codes, and, not least, spelling errors.

Our paper deals with spelling errors in an obligatory and important field of each patent, namely, the patent assignee name. Bibliographic fields are widely used among professional patent searchers in order to constrain keyword-based search sessions (Joho et al., 2010). The assignee name is particularly helpful for patentability searches and portfolio analyses since it determines the company holding the patent. Patent experts address these search tasks by formulating queries containing the company name in question, in the hope of finding all patents owned by that company. A formal and more precise description of this relevant search task is as follows: Given a query q which specifies a company, and a set D of patents, determine the set $D_q \subset D$ comprised of all patents held by the respective company.

For this purpose, all assignee names in the patents in D should be analyzed. Let A denote the set of all assignee names in D, and let $a \sim q$ denote the fact that an assignee name $a \in A$ refers to company q. Then in the portfolio search task, all patents filed under a are relevant. The retrieval of D_q can thus be rendered as a query expansion

Table 1: User groups and patent-search-related retrieval tasks in the patent domain (Hunt et al., 2007).

		User group					
		Analyst	Attorney	Manager	Inventor	Investor	Researcher
Patent search task	Patentability	●	○		●		○
	State of the art					○	●
	Infringement		●				
	Opposition		●			●	
	Due diligence		●	●			
	Portfolio	●	○	●		●	

task, where q is expanded by the disjunction of assignee names A_q with $A_q = \{a \in A \mid a \sim q\}$.

While the trivial expansion of q by the entire set A ensures maximum recall but entails an unacceptable precision, the expansion of q by the empty set yields a reasonable baseline. The latter approach is implemented in patent search engines such as PatBase[1] or FreePatentsOnline,[2] which return all patents where the company name q occurs as a substring of the assignee name a. This baseline is simple but reasonable; due to trademark law, a company name q must be a unique identifier (i.e. a key), and an assignee name a that contains q can be considered as relevant. It should be noted in this regard that $|q| < |a|$ holds for most elements in A_q, since the assignee names often contain company suffixes such as "Ltd" or "Inc".

Our hypothesis is that due to misspelled assignee names a substantial fraction of relevant patents cannot be found by the baseline approach. In this regard, the types of spelling errors in assignee names given in Table 2 should be considered.

Table 2: Types of spelling errors with increasing problem complexity according to Stein and Curatolo (2006). The first row refers to lexical errors, whereas the last two rows refer to phonological errors. For each type, an example is given, where a misspelled company name is followed by the correctly spelled variant.

Spelling error type	**Example**
Permutations or dropped letters	Whirpool Corporation → Whirlpool Corporation
Misremembering spelling details	Whetherford International → Weatherford International
Spelling out the pronunciation	Emulecks Corporation → Emulex Corporation

In order to raise the recall for portfolio search without significantly impairing precision, an approach more sophisticated than the standard retrieval approach, which is the expansion of q by the empty set, is needed. Such an approach must strive for an expansion of q by a subset of A_q, whereby this subset should be as large as possible.

1.1 Contributions

The paper provides a new solution to the problem outlined. This solution employs machine learning on orthographic features, as well as on patent meta features, to reliably detect spelling errors. It consists of two steps: (1) the computation of A_q^+, the set of assignee names that are in a certain edit distance neighborhood to q; and (2) the filtering of A_q^+, yielding the set A_q^*, which contains those assignee names from A_q^+ that are classified as misspellings of q. The power of our approach can be seen from Table 3, which also shows a key result of our research; a retrieval system that exploits our classifier will miss only 0.5% of the relevant patents, while retrieval precision is compromised by only 3.7%.

Another contribution relates to a new, manually-labeled corpus comprising spelling errors in the assignee field of patents (cf. Section 3). In this regard, we consider the over 2 million patents granted by the USPTO between 2001 and 2010. Last, we analyze indications of deliberately inserted spelling errors (cf. Section 4).

Table 3: Mean average Precision, Recall, and F-Measure ($\beta = 2$) for different expansion sets for q in a portfolio search task, which is conducted on our test corpus (cf. Section 3).

Expansion set for q		**Precision**	**Recall**	F_2
$\emptyset$	(baseline)	**0.993**	0.967	0.968
A_q^*	(machine learning)	0.956	**0.995**	0.980
A	(trivial)	0.001	1.0	0.005
A_q^+	(edit distance)	0.274	1.0	0.672

[1]www.patbase.com

[2]www.freepatentsonline.com

1.2 Causes for Inconsistencies in Patents

We identify the following six factors for inconsistencies in the bibliographic fields of patents, in particular for assignee names: (1) Misspellings are introduced due to the lack of knowledge, the lack of attention, and due to spelling disabilities. Intellevate Inc. (2006) reports that 98% of a sample of patents taken from the USPTO database contain errors, most which are spelling errors. (2) Spelling errors are only removed by the USPTO upon request (U.S. Patent & Trademark Office, 2010). (3) Spelling variations of inventor names are permitted by the USPTO. The Manual of Patent Examining Procedure (MPEP) states in paragraph 605.04(b) that "if the applicant's full name is 'John Paul Doe,' either 'John P. Doe' or 'J. Paul Doe' is acceptable." Thus, it is valid to introduce many different variations: with and without initials, with and without a middle name, or with and without suffixes. This convention applies to assignee names, too. (4) Companies often have branches in different countries, where each branch has its own company suffix, e.g., "Limited" (United States), "GmbH" (Germany), or "Kabushiki Kaisha" (Japan). Moreover, the usage of punctuation varies along company suffix abbreviations: "L.L.C." in contrast to "LLC", for example. (5) Indexing errors emerge from OCR processing patent applications, because similar looking letters such as "e" versus "c" or "l" versus "I" are likely to be misinterpreted. (6) With the advent of electronic patent application filing, the number of patent reexamination steps was reduced. As a consequence, the chance of undetected spelling errors increases (Adams, 2010).

All of the mentioned factors add to a highly inconsistent USPTO corpus.

2 Related Work

Information within a corpus can only be retrieved effectively if the data is both accurate and unique (Müller and Freytag, 2003). In order to yield data that is accurate and unique, approaches to data cleansing can be utilized to identify and remove inconsistencies. Müller and Freytag (2003) classify inconsistencies, where duplicates of entities in a corpus are part of a semantic anomaly. These duplicates exist in a database if two or more different tuples refer to the same entity. With respect to the bibliographic fields of patents, the assignee names "Howlett-Packard" and "Hewett-Packard" are distinct but refer to the same company. These kinds of near-duplicates impede the identification of duplicates (Naumann and Herschel, 2010).

Near-duplicate Detection The problem of identifying near-duplicates is also known as record linkage, or name matching; it is subject of active research (Elmagarmid et al., 2007). With respect to text documents, slightly modified passages in these documents can be identified using fingerprints (Potthast and Stein, 2008). On the other hand, for data fields which contain natural language such as the assignee name field, string similarity metrics (Cohen et al., 2003) as well as spelling correction technology are exploited (Damerau, 1964; Monge and Elkan, 1997). String similarity metrics compute a numeric value to capture the similarity of two strings. Spelling correction algorithms, by contrast, capture the likelihood for a given word being a misspelling of another word. In our analysis, the similarity metric *SoftTfIdf* is applied, which performs best in name matching tasks (Cohen et al., 2003), as well as the complete range of spelling correction algorithms shown in Figure 1: Soundex, which relies on similarity hashing (Knuth, 1997), the Levenshtein distance, which gives the minimum number of edits needed to transform a word into another word (Levenshtein, 1966), and SmartSpell, a phonetic production approach that computes the likelihood of a misspelling (Stein and Curatolo, 2006). In order to combine the strength of multiple metrics within a near-duplicate detection task, several authors resort to machine learning (Bilenko and Mooney, 2002; Cohen et al., 2003). Christen (2006) concludes that it is important to exploit all kinds of knowledge about the type of data in question, and that inconsistencies are domain-specific. Hence, an effective near-duplicate detection approach should employ domain-specific heuristics and algorithms (Müller and Freytag, 2003). Following this argumentation, we augment various word similarity assessments with patent-specific meta-features.

Patent Search Commercial patent search engines, such as PatBase and FreePatentsOnline, handle near-duplicates in assignee names as follows. For queries which contain a company name followed by a wildcard operator, PatBase suggests

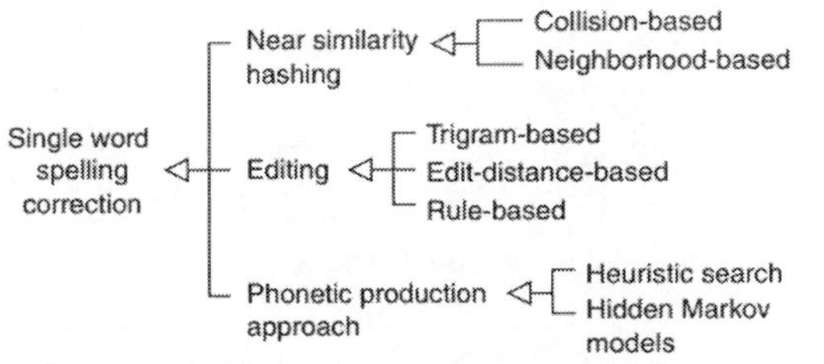

Figure 1: Classification of spelling correction methods according to Stein and Curatolo (2006).

a set of additional companies (near-duplicates), which can be considered alongside the company name in question. These suggestions are solely retrieved based on a trailing wildcard query. Each additional company name can then be marked individually by a user to expand the original query. In case the entire set of suggestions is considered, this strategy conforms to the expansion of a query by the empty set, which equals a reasonable baseline approach. This query expansion strategy, however, has the following drawbacks: (1) The strategy captures only inconsistencies that succeed the given company name in the original query. Thus, near-duplicates which contain spelling errors in the company name itself are not found. Even if PatBase would support left trailing wildcards, then only the full combination of wildcard expressions would cover all possible cases of misspellings. (2) Given an acronym of a company such as IBM, it is infeasible to expand the abbreviation to "International Business Machines" without considering domain knowledge.

Query Expansion Methods for Patent Search To date, various studies have investigated query expansion techniques in the patent domain that focus on prior-art search and invalidity search (Magdy and Jones, 2011). Since we are dealing with queries that comprise only a company name, existing methods cannot be applied. Instead, the near-duplicate task in question is more related to a text reuse detection task discussed by Hagen and Stein (2011); given a document, passages which also appear identical or slightly modified in other documents, have to be retrieved by using standard keyword-based search engines. Their approach is guided by the user-over-ranking hypothesis introduced by Stein and Hagen (2011). It states that "the best retrieval performance can be achieved with queries returning about as many results as can be considered at user site." If we make use of their terminology, then we can distinguish the query expansion sets (cf. Table 3) into two categories: (1) The trivial as well as the edit distance expansion sets are *underspecific*, i.e., users cannot cope with the large amount of irrelevant patents returned; the precision is close to zero. (2) The baseline approach, by contrast, is *overspecific*; it returns too few documents, i.e., the achieved recall is not optimal. As a consequence, these query expansion sets are not suitable for portfolio search. Our approach, on the other hand, excels in both precision and recall.

Query Spelling Correction Queries which are submitted to standard web search engines differ from queries which are posed to patent search engines with respect to both length and language diversity. Hence, research in the field of web search is concerned with suggesting reasonable alternatives to misspelled queries rather than correcting single words (Li et al., 2011). Since standard spelling correction dictionaries (e.g. ASpell) are not able to capture the rich language used in web queries, large-scale knowledge sources such as Wikipedia (Li et al., 2011), query logs (Chen et al., 2007), and large n-gram corpora (Brants et al., 2007) are employed. It should be noted that the set of correctly written assignee names is unknown for the USPTO patent corpus.

Moreover, spelling errors are modeled on the basis of language models (Li et al., 2011). Okuno (2011) proposes a generative model to encounter spelling errors, where the original query is expanded based on alternatives produced by a small edit distance to the original query. This strategy correlates to the trivial query expansion set (cf. Section 1). Unlike using a small edit distance, we allow a reasonable high edit distance to maximize the recall.

Trademark Search The trademark search is about identifying registered trademarks which are similar to a new trademark application. Similarities between trademarks are assessed based on figurative and verbal criteria. In the former case, the focus is on image-based retrieval techniques. Trademarks are considered verbally similar for a variety of reasons, such as pronunciation, spelling, and conceptual closeness, e.g., swapping letters or using numbers for words. The verbal similarity of trademarks, on the other hand, can be determined by using techniques comparable to near-duplicate detection: phonological parsing, fuzzy search, and edit distance computation (Fall and Giraud-Carrier, 2005).

3 Detection of Spelling Errors

This section presents our machine learning approach to expand a company query q; the classifier c delivers the set $A_q^* = \{a \in A \mid c(q,a) = 1\}$, an approximation of the ideal set of relevant assignee names A_q. As a classification technology a support vector machine with linear kernel is used, which receives each pair (q, a) as a six-dimensional feature vector. For training and test purposes we identified misspellings for 100 different company names. A detailed description of the constructed test corpus and a report on the classifiers performance is given in the remainder of this section.

3.1 Feature Set

The feature set comprises six features, three of them being orthographic similarity metrics, which are computed for every pair (q, a). Each metric compares a given company name q with the first $|q|$ words of the assignee name a:

1. *SoftTfIdf.* The SoftTfIdf metric is considered, since the metric is suitable for the comparison of names (Cohen et al., 2003). The metric incorporates the Jaro-Winkler metric (Winkler, 1999) with a distance threshold of 0.9. The frequency values for the similarity computation are trained on A.
2. *Soundex.* The Soundex spelling correction algorithm captures phonetic errors. Since the algorithm computes hash values for both q and a, the feature is 1 if these hash values are equal, 0 otherwise.
3. *Levenshtein distance.* The Levenshtein distance for (q, a) is normalized by the character length of q.

To obtain further evidence for a misspelling in an assignee name, meta information about the patents in D, to which the assignee name refers to, is exploited. In this regard, the following three features are derived:

1. *Assignee Name Frequency.* The number of patents filed under an assignee name a: $F_{\mathit{Freq}}(a) = \mathit{Freq}(a, D)$. We assume that the probability of a misspelling to occur multiple times is low, and thus an assignee name with a misspelled company name has a low frequency.
2. *IPC Overlap.* The IPC codes of a patent specify the technological areas it applies to. We assume that patents filed under the same company name are likely to share the same set of IPC codes, regardless whether the company name is misspelled or not. Hence, if we determine the IPC codes of patents which contain q in the assignee name, $\mathit{IPC}(q)$, and the IPC codes of patents filed under assignee name a, $\mathit{IPC}(a)$, then the intersection size of the two sets serves as an indicator for a misspelled company name in a:

$$F_{IPC}(q,a) = \frac{\mathit{IPC}(q) \cap \mathit{IPC}(a)}{\mathit{IPC}(q) \cup \mathit{IPC}(a)}$$

3. *Company Suffix Match.* The suffix match relies on the company suffixes $\mathit{Suffixes}(q)$ that occur in the assignee names of A containing q. Similar to the IPC overlap feature, we argue that if the company suffix of a exists in the set $\mathit{Suffixes}(q)$, a misspelling in a is likely: $F_{\mathit{Suffixes}}(q,a) = 1$ iff $\mathit{Suffixes}(a) \in \mathit{Suffixes}(q)$.

3.2 Webis Patent Retrieval Assignee Corpus

A key contribution of our work is a new corpus called Webis Patent Retrieval Assignee Corpus 2012 (Webis-PRA-12). We compiled the corpus in order to assess the impact of misspelled companies on patent retrieval and the effectiveness of our classifier to detect them.[3] The corpus is built on the basis of 2 132 825 patents D granted by the USPTO between 2001 and 2010; the patent corpus is provided publicly by the USPTO in XML format. Each patent contains bibliographic fields as well as textual information such as the abstract and the claims section. Since we are interested in the assignee name a associated with each patent $d \in D$, we parse each patent and extract the assignee name. This yields the set A of 202 846 different assignee names. Each assignee name refers to a set of patents, which size varies from 1 to 37 202 (the number of patents filed under "International Business Machines Corporation"). It should be noted that for a portfolio

[3]The Webis-PRA-12 corpus is freely available via `www.webis.de/research/corpora`

Table 4: Statistics of spelling errors for the 100 companies in the Webis-PRA-12 corpus. Considered are the number of words and the number of letters in the company names, as well as the number of different company suffixes that are used together with a company name (denoted as variants of q)

	Total	Num. of words in q			Num. of letters in q			Num. of variants of q		
		1	2	3-4	2-10	11-15	16-35	1-5	6-15	16-96
Number of companies in Q	100	36	53	11	30	35	35	45	32	23
Avg. num. of misspellings in A	3.79	2.13	3.75	9.36	1.16	2.94	6.88	0.91	3.81	9.39

search task the number of patents which refer to an assignee name matters for the computation of precision and recall. If we, however, isolate the task of detecting misspelled company names, then it is also reasonable to weight each assignee name equally and independently from the number of patents it refers to. Both scenarios are addressed in the experiments.

Given A, the corpus construction task is to map each assignee name $a \in A$ to the company name q it refers to. This gives for each company name q the set of relevant assignee names A_q. For our corpus, we do not construct A_q for all company names but take a selection of 100 company names from the 2011 Fortune 500 ranking as our set of company names Q. Since the Fortune 500 ranking contains only large companies, the test corpus may appear to be biased towards these companies. However, rather than the company size the structural properties of a company name are determinative; our sample includes short, medium, and long company names, as well as company names with few, medium, and many different company suffixes. Table 4 shows the distribution of company names in Q along these criteria in the first row.

For each company name $q \in Q$, we apply a semi-automated procedure to derive the set of relevant assignee names A_q. In a first step, all assignee names in A which do not refer to the company name q are filtered automatically. From a preliminary evaluation we concluded that the Levenshtein distance $d(q, a)$ with a relative threshold of $|q|/2$ is a reasonable choice for this filtering step. The resulting sets $A_q^+ = \{a \in A \mid d(q, a) \leq |q|/2)$ contain, in total over Q, 14 189 assignee names. These assignee names are annotated by human assessors within a second step to derive the final set A_q for each $q \in Q$. Altogether we identify 1 538 assignee names that refer to the 100 companies in Q. With respect to our classification task, the assignee names in each A_q are positive examples; the remaining assignee names $A_q^+ \setminus A_q$ form the set of negative examples (12 651 in total).

During the manual assessment, names of assignees which include the correct company name q were distinguished from misspelled ones. The latter holds true for 379 of the 1 538 assignee names. These names are not retrievable by the baseline system, and thus form the main target for our classifier. The second row of Table 4 reports on the distribution of the 379 misspelled assignee names. As expectable, the longer the company name, the more spelling errors occur. Companies which file patents under many different assignee names are likelier to have patents with misspellings in the company name.

3.3 Classifier Performance

For the evaluation with the Webis-PRA-12 corpus, we train a support vector machine,[4] which considers the six outlined features, and compare it to the other expansion techniques. For the training phase, we use 2/3 of the positive examples to form a balanced training set of 1 025 positive and 1 025 negative examples. After 10-fold cross validation, the achieved classification accuracy is 95.97%.

For a comparison of the expansion techniques on the test set, which contains the examples not considered in the training phase, two tasks are distinguished: finding near duplicates in assignee names (cf. Table 5, Columns 3–5), and finding all patents of a company (cf. Table 5, Columns 6–8). The latter refers to the actual task of portfolio search. It can be observed that the performance improvements on both tasks are pretty similar. The baseline expansion $\emptyset$ yields a recall of 0.83 in the first task. The difference of 0.17 to a perfect recall can be addressed by considering query expansion techniques. If the trivial expansion A is applied to the task the maximum recall can be achieved, which, however,

[4]We use the implementation of the WEKA toolkit with default parameters.

Table 5: The search results (macro-averaged) for two retrieval tasks and various expansion techniques. Besides Precision and Recall, the F-Measure with $\beta = 2$ is stated.

Misspelling detection	Task: assignee names			Task: patents		
	P	R	F_2	P	R	F_2
Baseline ($\emptyset$)	**.975**	.829	.838	**.993**	.967	.968
Trivial (A)	.000	**1.0**	.001	.001	**1.0**	.005
Edit distance (A_q^+)	.274	**1.0**	.499	.412	**1.0**	.672
SVM (Levenshtein)	.752	.981	.853	.851	.991	.911
SVM (SoftTfIdf)	.702	.980	.796	.826	.993	.886
SVM (Soundex)	.433	.931	.624	.629	.984	.759
SVM (orthographic features)	.856	.975	.922	.942	.990	.967
SVM (A_q^*, all features)	.884	.975	**.938**	.956	.995	**.980**

is bought with precision close to zero. Using the edit distance expansion A_q^+ yields a precision of 0.274 while keeping the recall at maximum. Finally, the machine learning expansion A_q^* leads to a dramatic improvement (cf. Table 5, bottom lines), whereas the exploitation of patent meta-features significantly outperforms the exclusive use of orthography-related features; the increase in recall which is achieved by A_q^* is statistically significant (matched pair t-test) for both tasks (assignee names task: $t = -7.6856$, $df = 99$, $p = 0.00$; patents task: $t = -2.1113$, $df = 99$, $p = 0.037$). Note that when being applied as a single feature none of the spelling metrics (Levenshtein, SoftTfIdf, Soundex) is able to achieve a recall close to 1 without significantly impairing the precision.

4 Distribution of Spelling Errors

Encouraged by the promising retrieval results achieved on the Webis-PRA-12 corpus, we extend the analysis of spelling errors in patents to the entire USPTO corpus of granted patents between 2001 and 2010. The analysis focuses on the following two research questions:

1. *Are spelling errors an increasing issue in patents?* According to Adams (2010), the amount of spelling errors should have been increased in the last years due to the electronic patent filing process (cf. Section 1.2). We address this hypothesis by analyzing the distribution of spelling errors in company names that occur in patents granted between 2001 and 2010.

2. *Are misspellings introduced deliberately in patents?* We address this question by analyzing the patents with respect to the eight technological areas based on the International Patent Classification scheme IPC: A (Human necessities), B (Performing operations; transporting), C (Chemistry; metallurgy), D (Textiles; paper), E (Fixed constructions), F (Mechanical engineering; lighting; heating; weapons; blasting), G (Physics), and H (Electricity). If spelling errors are introduced accidentally, then we expect them to be uniformly distributed across all areas. A biased distribution, on the other hand, indicates that errors might be inserted deliberately.

In the following, we compile a second corpus on the basis of the entire set A of assignee names. In order to yield a uniform distribution of the companies across years, technological areas and countries, a set of 120 assignee names is extracted for each dimension. After the removal of duplicates, we revised these assignee names manually in order to check (and correct) their spelling. Finally, trailing business suffixes are removed, which results in a set of 3 110 company names. For each company name q, we generate the set A_q^* as described in Section 3.

The results of our analysis are shown in Table 6. Table 6(a) refers to the first research question and shows that the amount of misspellings in companies decreased over the years from 6.67% in 2001 to 4.74% in 2010 (cf. Row 3). These results let us reject the hypothesis of Adams (2010). Nevertheless, the analysis provides evidence that spelling errors are still an issue. For example, the company identified with most spelling errors are "Koninklijke Philips Electronics" with 45 misspellings in 2008, and "Centre National de la Recherche Scientifique" with 28 misspellings in 2009. The results are consistent with our findings with re-

Table 6: Distribution of spelling errors for 3 110 company identifiers in the USPTO patents. The mean of spelling errors per company identifier and the standard deviation σ refer to companies with misspellings. The last row in each table shows the number of patents that are additionally found if the original query q is expanded by A_q^*.

(a) Distribution of spelling errors between the years 2001 and 2010.

	Year									
Measure	2001	2002	2003	2004	2005	2006	2007	2008	2009	2010
Number of companies	1 028	1 066	1 115	1 151	1 219	1 261	1 274	1 210	1 224	1 268
Number of companies with misspellings	67	63	53	65	65	60	65	64	53	60
Companies with misspellings (%)	6.52	5.91	4.75	5.65	5.33	4.76	5.1	5.29	4.33	4.73
Mean	2.78	2.35	2.23	2.28	2.18	2.48	2.23	3.0	2.64	2.8
Standard deviation σ	4.62	3.3	3.63	3.13	2.8	3.55	2.87	6.37	4.71	4.6
Maximum misspellings per company	24	12	16	12	10	18	12	45	28	22
Additional number of patents	7.1	7.21	7.43	7.68	7.91	8.48	7.83	8.84	8.92	8.92

(b) Distribution of spelling errors based on the IPC scheme.

	IPC code							
Measure	A	B	C	D	E	F	G	H
Number of companies	954	1 231	811	277	412	771	1 232	949
Number of companies with misspellings	59	70	51	7	10	33	83	63
Companies with misspellings (%)	6.18	5.69	6.29	2.53	2.43	4.28	6.74	6.64
Mean	3.0	2.49	3.57	1.86	2.8	1.88	3.29	4.05
Standard deviation σ	5.28	3.65	7.03	1.99	4.22	2.31	5.72	7.13
Maximum misspellings per company	32	14	40	3	12	6	24	35
Additional number of patents	9.25	9.67	11.12	4.71	4.6	4.79	8.92	12.84

spect to the Fortune 500 sample (cf. Table 4), where company names that are longer and presumably more difficult to write contain more spelling errors.

In contrast to the uniform distribution of misspellings over the years, the situation with regard to the technological areas is different (cf. Table 6(b)). Most companies are associated with the IPC sections G and B, which both refer to technical domains (cf. Table 6(b), Row 1). The percentage of misspellings in these sections increased compared to the spelling errors grouped by year. A significant difference can be seen for the sections D and E. Here, the number of assigned companies drops below 450 and the percentage of misspellings decreases significantly from about 6% to 2.5%. These findings might support the hypothesis that spelling errors are inserted deliberately in technical domains.

5 Conclusions

While researchers in the patent domain concentrate on retrieval models and algorithms to improve the search performance, the original aspect of our paper is that it points to a different (and orthogonal) research avenue: the analysis of patent inconsistencies. With the analysis of spelling errors in assignee names we made a first yet considerable contribution in this respect; searches with assignee constraints become a more sensible operation. We showed how a special treatment of spelling errors can significantly raise the effectiveness of patent search. The identification of this untapped potential, but also the utilization of machine learning to combine patent features with typography, form our main contributions.

Our current research broadens the application of a patent spelling analysis. In order to identify errors that are introduced deliberately we investigate different types of misspellings (edit distance versus phonological). Finally, we consider the analysis of acquisition histories of companies as promising research direction: since acquired companies often own granted patents, these patents should be considered while searching for the company in question in order to further increase the recall.

Acknowledgements

This work is supported in part by the German Science Foundation under grants STE1019/2-1 and FU205/22-1.

References

Stephen Adams. 2010. The Text, the Full Text and nothing but the Text: Part 1 – Standards for creating Textual Information in Patent Documents and General Search Implications. *World Patent Information*, 32(1):22–29, March.

Mikhail Bilenko and Raymond J. Mooney. 2002. Learning to Combine Trained Distance Metrics for Duplicate Detection in Databases. Technical Report AI 02-296, Artificial Intelligence Laboratory, University of Austin, Texas, USA, Austin, TX, February.

Thorsten Brants, Ashok C. Popat, Peng Xu, Franz J. Och, and Jeffrey Dean. 2007. Large Language Models in Machine Translation. In *EMNLP-CoNLL '07: Proceedings of the 2007 Joint Conference on Empirical Methods in Natural Language Processing and Computational Natural Language Learning*, pages 858–867. ACL, June.

Qing Chen, Mu Li, and Ming Zhou. 2007. Improving Query Spelling Correction Using Web Search Results. In *EMNLP-CoNLL '07: Proceedings of the 2007 Joint Conference on Empirical Methods in Natural Language Processing and Computational Natural Language Learning*, pages 181–189. ACL, June.

Peter Christen. 2006. A Comparison of Personal Name Matching: Techniques and Practical Issues. In *ICDM '06: Workshops Proceedings of the sixth IEEE International Conference on Data Mining*, pages 290–294. IEEE Computer Society, December.

William W. Cohen, Pradeep Ravikumar, and Stephen E. Fienberg. 2003. A Comparison of String Distance Metrics for Name-Matching Tasks. In Subbarao Kambhampati and Craig A. Knoblock, editors, *IIWeb '03: Proceedings of the IJCAI workshop on Information Integration on the Web*, pages 73–78, August.

Fred J. Damerau. 1964. A Technique for Computer Detection and Correction of Spelling Errors. *Communications of the ACM*, 7(3):171–176.

Ahmed K. Elmagarmid, Panagiotis G. Ipeirotis, and Vassilios S. Verykios. 2007. Duplicate Record Detection: A Survey. *IEEE Trans. Knowl. Data Eng.*, 19(1):1–16.

Caspas J. Fall and Christophe Giraud-Carrier. 2005. Searching Trademark Databases for Verbal Similarities. *World Patent Information*, 27(2):135–143.

Matthias Hagen and Benno Stein. 2011. Candidate Document Retrieval for Web-Scale Text Reuse Detection. In *18th International Symposium on String Processing and Information Retrieval (SPIRE 11)*, volume 7024 of *Lecture Notes in Computer Science*, pages 356–367. Springer.

David Hunt, Long Nguyen, and Matthew Rodgers, editors. 2007. *Patent Searching: Tools & Techniques*. Wiley.

Intellevate Inc. 2006. Patent Quality, a blog entry. http://www.patenthawk.com/blog/2006/01/patent_quality.html, January.

Hideo Joho, Leif A. Azzopardi, and Wim Vanderbauwhede. 2010. A Survey of Patent Users: An Analysis of Tasks, Behavior, Search Functionality and System Requirements. In *IIix '10: Proceeding of the third symposium on Information Interaction in Context*, pages 13–24, New York, NY, USA. ACM.

Donald E. Knuth. 1997. *The Art of Computer Programming, Volume I: Fundamental Algorithms, 3rd Edition*. Addison-Wesley.

Vladimir I. Levenshtein. 1966. Binary codes capable of correcting deletions, insertions and reversals. *Soviet Physics Doklady*, 10(8):707–710. Original in *Doklady Akademii Nauk SSSR* 163(4): 845-848.

Yanen Li, Huizhong Duan, and ChengXiang Zhai. 2011. CloudSpeller: Spelling Correction for Search Queries by Using a Unified Hidden Markov Model with Web-scale Resources. In *Spelling Alteration for Web Search Workshop*, pages 10–14, July.

Patrice Lopez and Laurent Romary. 2010. Experiments with Citation Mining and Key-Term Extraction for Prior Art Search. In Martin Braschler, Donna Harman, and Emanuele Pianta, editors, *CLEF 2010 LABs and Workshops, Notebook Papers*, September.

Mihai Lupu, Katja Mayer, John Tait, and Anthony J. Trippe, editors. 2011. *Current Challenges in Patent Information Retrieval*, volume 29 of *The Information Retrieval Series*. Springer.

Walid Magdy and Gareth J. F. Jones. 2010. Applying the KISS Principle for the CLEF-IP 2010 Prior Art Candidate Patent Search Task. In Martin Braschler, Donna Harman, and Emanuele Pianta, editors, *CLEF 2010 LABs and Workshops, Notebook Papers*, September.

Walid Magdy and Gareth J.F. Jones. 2011. A Study on Query Expansion Methods for Patent Retrieval. In *PAIR '11: Proceedings of the 4th workshop on Patent information retrieval*, AAAI Workshop on Plan, Activity, and Intent Recognition, pages 19–24, New York, NY, USA. ACM.

Alvaro E. Monge and Charles Elkan. 1997. An Efficient Domain-Independent Algorithm for Detecting Approximately Duplicate Database Records. In *DMKD '09: Proceedings of the 2nd workshop on Research Issues on Data Mining and Knowledge Discovery*, pages 23–29, New York, NY, USA. ACM.

Heiko Müller and Johann-C. Freytag. 2003. Problems, Methods and Challenges in Comprehensive Data Cleansing. Technical Report HUB-IB-164, Humboldt-Universität zu Berlin, Institut für Informatik, Germany.

Felix Naumann and Melanie Herschel. 2010. *An Introduction to Duplicate Detection*. Synthesis Lectures on Data Management. Morgan & Claypool Publishers.

Yoh Okuno. 2011. Spell Generation based on Edit Distance. In *Spelling Alteration for Web Search Workshop*, pages 25–26, July.

Martin Potthast and Benno Stein. 2008. New Issues in Near-duplicate Detection. In Christine Preisach, Hans Burkhardt, Lars Schmidt-Thieme, and Reinhold Decker, editors, *Data Analysis, Machine Learning and Applications. Selected papers from the 31th Annual Conference of the German Classification Society (GfKl 07)*, Studies in Classification, Data Analysis, and Knowledge Organization, pages 601–609, Berlin Heidelberg New York. Springer.

Benno Stein and Daniel Curatolo. 2006. Phonetic Spelling and Heuristic Search. In Gerhard Brewka, Silvia Coradeschi, Anna Perini, and Paolo Traverso, editors, *17th European Conference on Artificial Intelligence (ECAI 06)*, pages 829–830, Amsterdam, Berlin, August. IOS Press.

Benno Stein and Matthias Hagen. 2011. Introducing the User-over-Ranking Hypothesis. In *Advances in Information Retrieval. 33rd European Conference on IR Resarch (ECIR 11)*, volume 6611 of *Lecture Notes in Computer Science*, pages 503–509, Berlin Heidelberg New York, April. Springer.

U.S. Patent & Trademark Office. 2010. Manual of Patent Examining Procedure (MPEP), Eighth Edition, July.

William W. Winkler. 1999. The State of Record Linkage and Current Research Problems. Technical report, Statistical Research Division, U.S. Bureau of the Census.

Xiaobing Xue and Bruce W. Croft. 2009. Automatic Query Generation for Patent Search. In *CIKM '09: Proceeding of the eighteenth ACM conference on Information and Knowledge Management*, pages 2037–2040, New York, NY, USA. ACM.

UBY – A Large-Scale Unified Lexical-Semantic Resource Based on LMF

Iryna Gurevych[†‡], Judith Eckle-Kohler[‡], Silvana Hartmann[‡], Michael Matuschek[‡], Christian M. Meyer[‡] and Christian Wirth[‡]
† Ubiquitous Knowledge Processing Lab (UKP-DIPF)
German Institute for Educational Research and Educational Information
‡ Ubiquitous Knowledge Processing Lab (UKP-TUDA)
Department of Computer Science
Technische Universität Darmstadt
http://www.ukp.tu-darmstadt.de

Abstract

We present UBY, a large-scale lexical-semantic resource combining a wide range of information from expert-constructed and collaboratively constructed resources for English and German. It currently contains nine resources in two languages: English WordNet, Wiktionary, Wikipedia, FrameNet and VerbNet, German Wikipedia, Wiktionary and GermaNet, and multilingual OmegaWiki modeled according to the LMF standard. For FrameNet, VerbNet and all collaboratively constructed resources, this is done for the first time. Our LMF model captures lexical information at a fine-grained level by employing a large number of Data Categories from ISOCat and is designed to be directly extensible by new languages and resources. All resources in UBY can be accessed with an easy to use publicly available API.

1 Introduction

Lexical-semantic resources (LSRs) are the foundation of many NLP tasks such as word sense disambiguation, semantic role labeling, question answering and information extraction. They are needed on a large scale in different languages. The growing demand for resources is met neither by the largest single expert-constructed resources (ECRs), such as WordNet and FrameNet, whose coverage is limited, nor by collaboratively constructed resources (CCRs), such as Wikipedia and Wiktionary, which encode lexical-semantic knowledge in a less systematic form than ECRs, because they are lacking expert supervision.

Previously, there have been several independent efforts of combining existing LSRs to enhance their coverage w.r.t. their breadth and depth, i.e. (i) the number of lexical items, and (ii) the types of lexical-semantic information contained (Shi and Mihalcea, 2005; Johansson and Nugues, 2007; Navigli and Ponzetto, 2010b; Meyer and Gurevych, 2011). As these efforts often targeted particular applications, they focused on aligning selected, specialized information types. To our knowledge, no single work focused on modeling a wide range of ECRs and CCRs in multiple languages and a large variety of information types in a standardized format. Frequently, the presented model is not easily scalable to accommodate an open set of LSRs in multiple languages and the information mined automatically from corpora. The previous work also lacked the aspects of lexicon format standardization and API access. We believe that easy access to information in LSRs is crucial in terms of their acceptance and broad applicability in NLP.

In this paper, we propose a solution to this. We define a standardized format for modeling LSRs. This is a prerequisite for resource interoperability and the smooth integration of resources. We employ the ISO standard Lexical Markup Framework (LMF: ISO 24613:2008), a metamodel for LSRs (Francopoulo et al., 2006), and Data Categories (DCs) selected from ISOCat.[1] One of the main challenges of our work is to develop a model that is standard-compliant, yet able to express the information contained in diverse LSRs, and that in the long term supports the integration of the various resources.

The main contributions of this paper can be

[1] http://www.isocat.org/

summarized as follows: (1) We present an LMF-based model for large-scale multilingual LSRs called UBY-LMF. We model the lexical-semantic information down to a fine-grained level of information (e.g. syntactic frames) and employ standardized definitions of linguistic information types from ISOCat. (2) We present UBY, a large-scale LSR implementing the UBY-LMF model. UBY currently contains nine resources in two languages: English WordNet (WN, Fellbaum (1998), Wiktionary[2] (WKT-en), Wikipedia[3] (WP-en), FrameNet (FN, Baker et al. (1998)), and VerbNet (VN, Kipper et al. (2008)); German Wiktionary (WKT-de), Wikipedia (WP-de), and GermaNet (GN, Kunze and Lemnitzer (2002)), and the English and German entries of OmegaWiki[4] (OW), referred to as OW-en and OW-de. OW, a novel CCR, is inherently multilingual – its basic structure are multilingual synsets, which are a valuable addition to our multilingual UBY. Essential to UBY are the nine pairwise sense alignments between resources, which we provide to enable resource interoperability on the sense level, e.g. by providing access to the often complementary information for a sense in different resources. (3) We present a Java-API which offers unified access to the information contained in UBY.

We will make the UBY-LMF model, the resource UBY and the API freely available to the research community.[5] This will make it easy for the NLP community to utilize UBY in a variety of tasks in the future.

2 Related Work

The work presented in this paper concerns standardization of LSRs, large-scale integration thereof at the representational level, and the unified access to lexical-semantic information in the integrated resources.

Standardization of resources. Previous work includes models for representing lexical information relative to ontologies (Buitelaar et al., 2009; McCrae et al., 2011), and standardized single wordnets (English, German and Italian wordnets) in the ISO standard LMF (Soria et al., 2009; Henrich and Hinrichs, 2010; Toral et al., 2010).

McCrae et al. (2011) propose LEMON, a conceptual model for lexicalizing ontologies as an extension of the LexInfo model (Buitelaar et al., 2009). LEMON provides an LMF-implementation in the Web Ontology Language (OWL), which is similar to UBY-LMF, as it also uses DCs from ISOCat, but diverges further from the standard (e.g. by removing structural elements such as the predicative representation class). While we focus on modeling lexical-semantic information comprehensively and at a fine-grained level, the goal of LEMON is to support the linking between ontologies and lexicons. This goal entails a task-targeted application: domain-specific lexicons are extracted from ontology specifications and merged with existing LSRs on demand. As a consequence, there is no available large-scale instance of the LEMON model.

Soria et al. (2009) define WordNet-LMF, an LMF model for representing wordnets used in the KYOTO project, and Henrich and Hinrichs (2010) do this for GN, the German wordnet. These models are similar, but they still present different implementations of the LMF meta-model, which hampers interoperability between the resources. We build upon this work, but extend it significantly: UBY goes beyond modeling a single ECR and represents a large number of both ECRs and CCRs with very heterogeneous content in the same format. Also, UBY-LMF features deeper modeling of lexical-semantic information. Henrich and Hinrichs (2010), for instance, do not explicitly model the argument structure of subcategorization frames, since each frame is represented as a string. In UBY-LMF, we represent them at a fine-grained level necessary for the transparent modeling of the syntax-semantics interface.

Large-scale integration of resources. Most previous research efforts on the integration of resources targeted at world knowledge rather than lexical-semantic knowledge. Well known examples are YAGO (Suchanek et al., 2007), or DBPedia (Bizer et al., 2009).

Atserias et al. (2004) present the Meaning Multilingual Central Repository (MCR). MCR integrates five local wordnets based on the Interlingual Index of EuroWordNet (Vossen, 1998). The overall goal of the work is to improve word sense disambiguation. This work is similar to ours, as it

[2] http://www.wiktionary.org/
[3] http://www.wikipedia.org/
[4] http://www.omegawiki.org/
[5] http://www.ukp.tu-darmstadt.de/data/uby

aims at a large-scale multilingual resource and includes several resources. It is however restricted to a single type of resource (wordnets) and features a single type of lexical information (semantic relations) specified upon synsets. Similarly, de Melo and Weikum (2009) create a multilingual wordnet by integrating wordnets, bilingual dictionaries and information from parallel corpora. None of these resources integrate lexical-semantic information, such as syntactic subcategorization or semantic roles.

McFate and Forbus (2011) present NULEX, a syntactic lexicon automatically compiled from WN, WKT-en and VN. As their goal is to create an open-license resource to enhance syntactic parsing, they enrich verbs and nouns in WN with inflection information from WKT-en and syntactic frames from VN. Thus, they only use a small part of the lexical information present in WKT-en.

Padró et al. (2011) present their work on lexicon merging within the Panacea Project. One goal of Panacea is to create a lexical resource development platform that supports large-scale lexical acquisition and can be used to combine existing lexicons with automatically acquired ones. To this end, Padró et al. (2011) explore the automatic integration of subcategorization lexicons. Their current work only covers Spanish, and though they mention the LMF standard as a potential data model, they do not make use of it.

Shi and Mihalcea (2005) integrate FN, VN and WN, and Palmer (2009) presents a combination of Propbank, VN and FN in a resource called SEMLINK in order to enhance semantic role labeling. Similar to our work, multiple resources are integrated, but their work is restricted to a single language and does not cover CCRs, whose popularity and importance has grown tremendously over the past years. In fact, with the exception of NULEX, CCRs have only been considered in the sense alignment of individual resource pairs (Navigli and Ponzetto, 2010a; Meyer and Gurevych, 2011).

API access for resources. An important factor to the success of a large, integrated resource is a single public API, which facilitates the access to the information contained in the resource. The most important LSRs so far can be accessed using various APIs, for instance the Java WordNet API,[6] or the Java-based Wikipedia API.[7]

With a stronger focus of the NLP community on sharing data and reproducing experimental results these tools are becoming important as never before. Therefore, a major design objective of UBY is a single API. This is similar in spirit to the motivation of Pradhan et al. (2007), who present integrated access to corpus annotations as a main goal of their work on standardizing and integrating corpus annotations in the OntoNotes project.

To summarize, related work focuses either on the standardization of single resources (or a single type of resource), which leads to several slightly different formats constrained to these resources, or on the integration of several resources in an idiosyncratic format. CCRs have not been considered at all in previous work on resource standardization, and the level of detail of the modeling is insufficient to fully accommodate different types of lexical-semantic information. API access is rarely provided. This makes it hard for the community to exploit their results on a large scale. Thus, it diminishes the impact that these projects might achieve upon NLP beyond their original specific purpose, if their results were represented in a unified resource and could easily be accessed by the community through a single public API.

3 UBY – Data model

LMF defines a metamodel of LSRs in the Unified Modeling Language (UML). It provides a number of UML packages and classes for modeling many different types of resources, e.g. wordnets and multilingual lexicons. The design of a standard-compliant lexicon model in LMF involves two steps: in the first step, the structure of the lexicon model has to be defined by choosing a combination of the LMF core package and zero to many extensions (i.e. UML packages). In the second step, these UML classes are enriched by attributes. To contribute to semantic interoperability, it is essential for the lexicon model that the attributes and their values refer to Data Categories (DCs) taken from a reference repository. DCs are standardized specifications of the terms that are used for attributes and their values, or in other words, the linguistic vocabulary occurring

[6] http://sourceforge.net/projects/jwordnet/

[7] http://code.google.com/p/jwpl/

in a lexicon model. Consider, for instance, the term *lexeme* that is defined differently in WN and FN: in FN, a lexeme refers to a word form, not including the sense aspect. In WN, on the contrary, a lexeme is an abstract pairing of meaning and form. According to LMF, the DCs are to be selected from ISOCat, the implementation of the ISO 12620 Data Category Registry (DCR, Broeder et al. (2010)), resulting in a Data Category Selection (DCS).

Design of UBY-LMF. We have designed UBY-LMF[8] as a model of the union of various heterogeneous resources, namely WN, GN, FN, and VN on the one hand and CCRs on the other hand.

Two design principles guided our development of UBY-LMF: first, to preserve the information available in the original resources and to uniformly represent it in UBY-LMF. Second, to be able to extend UBY in the future by further languages, resources, and types of linguistic information, in particular, alignments between different LSRs.

Wordnets, FN and VN are largely complementary regarding the information types they provide, see, e.g. Baker and Fellbaum (2009). Accordingly, they use different organizational units to represent this information. Wordnets, such as WN and GN, primarily contain information on lexical-semantic relations, such as synonymy, and use synsets (groups of lexemes that are synonymous) as organizational units. FN focuses on groups of lexemes that evoke the same prototypical situation (so-called *semantic frames*, Fillmore (1982)) involving semantic roles (so-called *frame elements*). VN, a large-scale verb lexicon, is organized in Levin-style verb classes (Levin, 1993) (groups of verbs that share the same syntactic alternations and semantic roles) and provides rich subcategorization frames including semantic roles and a specification of semantic predicates.

UBY-LMF employs several direct subclasses of `Lexicon` in order to account for the various organization types found in the different LSRs considered. While the `LexicalEntry` class reflects the traditional headword-based lexicon organization, `Synset` represents synsets from wordnets, `SemanticPredicate` models FN semantic frames, and `SubcategorizationFrameSet` corresponds to VN alternation classes. `SubcategorizationFrame` is composed of syntactic arguments, while `SemanticPredicate` is composed of semantic arguments. The linking between syntactic and semantic arguments is represented by the `SynSemCorrespondence` class.

The `SenseAxis` class is very important in UBY-LMF, as it connects the different source LSRs. Its role is twofold: first, it links the corresponding word senses from different languages, e.g. English and German. Second, it represents monolingual sense alignments, i.e. sense alignments between different lexicons in the *same* language. The latter is a novel interpretation of `SenseAxis` introduced by UBY-LMF.

The organization of lexical-semantic knowledge found in WP, WKT, and OW can be modeled with the classes in UBY-LMF as well. WP primarily provides encyclopedic information on nouns. It mainly consists of article pages which are modeled as `Senses` in UBY-LMF.

WKT is in many ways similar to traditional dictionaries, because it enumerates senses under a given headword on an entry page. Thus, WKT entry pages can be represented by `LexicalEntries` and WKT senses by `Senses`.

OW is different from WKT and WP, as it is organized in multilingual synsets. To model OW in UBY-LMF, we split the synsets per language and included them as monolingual `Synsets` in the corresponding `Lexicon` (e.g., OW-en or OW-de). The original multilingual information is preserved by adding a `SenseAxis` between corresponding synsets in OW-en and OW-de.

The LMF standard itself contains only few linguistic terms and does neither specify attributes nor their values. Therefore, an important task in developing UBY-LMF has been the specification of attributes and their values along with the proper attachment of attributes to LMF classes. In particular, this task involved selecting DCs from ISOCat and, if necessary, adding new DCs to ISOCat.

Extensions in UBY-LMF. Although UBY-LMF is largely compliant with LMF, the task of building a homogeneous lexicon model for many highly heterogeneous LSRs led us to extend LMF in several ways: we added two new classes and several new relationships between classes.

First, we were facing a huge variety of lexical-semantic labels for many different dimensions of

[8] See www.ukp.tu-darmstadt.de/data/uby

semantic classification. Examples of such dimensions include ontological type (e.g. selectional restrictions in VN and FN), domain (e.g. Biology in WN), style and register (e.g. labels in WKT, OW), or sentiment (e.g. sentiment of lexical units in FN). Since we aim at an extensible LMF-model, capable of representing further dimensions of semantic classification, we did not squeeze the information on semantic classes present in the considered LSRs into existing LMF classes. Instead, we addressed this issue by introducing a more general class, `SemanticLabel`, which is an optional subclass of `Sense`, `SemanticPredicate`, and `SemanticArgument`. This new class has three attributes, encoding the name of the label, its type (e.g. ontological, register, sentiment), and a numeric quantification (e.g. sentiment strength).

Second, we attached the subclass `Frequency` to most of the classes in UBY-LMF, in order to encode frequency information. This is of particular importance when using the resource in machine learning applications. This extension of the standard has already been made in WordNet-LMF (Soria et al., 2009). Currently, the `Frequency` class is used to keep corpus frequencies for lexical units in FN, but we plan to use it for enriching many other classes with frequency information in future work, such as `Senses` or `SubcategorizationFrames`.

Third, the representation of FN in LMF required adding two new relationships between LMF classes: we added a relationship between `SemanticArgument` and `Definition`, in order to represent the definitions available for frame elements in FN. In addition, we added a relationship between the `Context` class and the `MonoLingualExternalRef`, to represent the links to annotated corpus sentences in FN.

Finally, WKT turned out to be hard to tackle, because it contains a special kind of ambiguity in the semantic relations and translation links listed for senses: the targets of both relations and translation links are ambiguous, as they refer to lemmas (word forms), rather than to senses (Meyer and Gurevych, 2010). These ambiguous relation targets could not directly be represented in LMF, since sense and translation relations are defined between senses. To resolve this, we added a relationship between `SenseRelation` and `FormRepresentation`, in order to encode the ambiguous WKT relation target as a word form. Disambiguating the WKT relation targets to infer the target sense is left to future work.

A related issue occurred, when we mapped WN to LMF. WN encodes morphologically related forms as sense relations. UBY-LMF represents these related forms not only as sense relations (as in WordNet-LMF), but also at the morphological level using the `RelatedForm` class from the LMF Morphology extension. In LMF, however, the `RelatedForm` class for morphologically related lexemes is not associated with the corresponding sense in any way. Discarding the WN information on the senses involved in a particular morphological relation would lead to information loss in some cases. Consider as an example the WN verb *buy* (purchase) which is derivationally related to the noun *buy*, while on the other hand *buy* (accept as true, e.g. *I can't buy this story*) is not derivationally related to the noun *buy*. We addressed this issue by adding a sense attribute to the `RelatedForm` class. Thus, in extension of LMF, UBY-LMF allows sense relations to refer to a form relation target and morphological relations to refer to a sense relation target.

Data Categories in UBY-LMF. We encountered large differences in the availability of DCs in ISOCat for the morpho-syntactic, lexical-syntactic, and lexical-semantic parts of UBY-LMF. Many DCs were missing in ISOCat and we had to enter them ourselves. While this was feasible at the morpho-syntactic and lexical-syntactic level, due to a large body of standardization results available, it was much harder at the lexical-semantic level where standardization is still ongoing. At the lexical-semantic level, UBY-LMF currently allows string values for a number of attribute values, e.g. for semantic roles. We can easily integrate the results of the ongoing standardization efforts into UBY-LMF in the future.

4 UBY – Population with information

4.1 Representing LSRs in UBY-LMF

UBY-LMF is represented by a DTD (as suggested by the standard) which can be used to automatically convert any given resource into the corresponding XML format.[9] This conversion requires a detailed analysis of the resource to be converted, followed by the definition of a mapping of the

[9] Therefore, UBY-LMF can be considered as a serialization of LMF.

concepts and terms used in the original resource to the UBY-LMF model. There are two major tasks involved in the development of an automatic conversion routine: first, the basic organizational unit in the source LSR has to be identified and mapped, e.g. synset in WN or semantic frame in FN, and second, it has to be determined, how a (LMF) sense is defined in the source LSR.

A notable aspect of converting resources into UBY-LMF is the harmonization of linguistic terminology used in the LSRs. For instance, a WN *Word* and a GN *Lexical Unit* are mapped to `Sense` in UBY-LMF.

We developed reusable conversion routines for the future import of updated versions of the source LSRs into UBY, provided the structure of the source LSR remains stable. These conversion routines extract lexical data from the source LSRs by calling their native APIs (rather than processing the underlying XML data). Thus, all lexical information which can be accessed via the APIs is converted into UBY-LMF.

Converting the LSRs introduced in the previous section yielded an instantiation of UBY-LMF named UBY. The `LexicalResource` instance UBY currently comprises 10 `Lexicon` instances, one each for OW-de and OW-en, and one lexicon each for the remaining eight LSRs.

4.2 Adding Sense Alignments

Besides the uniform and standardized representation of the single LSRs, one major asset of UBY is the semantic interoperability of resources at the sense level. In the following, we (i) describe how we converted already existing sense alignments of resources into LMF, and (ii) present a framework to infer alignments automatically for any pair of resources.

Existing Alignments. Previous work on sense alignment yielded several alignments, such as WN–WP-en (Niemann and Gurevych, 2011), WN–WKT-en (Meyer and Gurevych, 2011) and VN–FN (Palmer, 2009).

We converted these alignments into UBY-LMF by creating a `SenseAxis` instance for each pair of aligned senses. This involved mapping the sense IDs from the proprietary alignment files to the corresponding sense IDs in UBY.

In addition, we integrated the sense alignments already present in OW and WP. Some OW entries provide links to the corresponding WP page. Also, the German and English language editions of WP and OW are connected by inter-language links between articles (`Senses` in UBY). We can expect that these links have high quality, as they were entered manually by users and are subject to community control. Therefore, we straightforwardly imported them into UBY.

Alignment Framework. Automatically creating new alignments is difficult because of word ambiguities, different granularities of senses, or language specific conceptualizations (Navigli, 2006). To support this task for a large number of resources across languages, we have designed a flexible alignment framework based on the state-of-the-art method of Niemann and Gurevych (2011). The framework is generic in order to allow alignments between different kinds of entities as found in different resources, e.g. WN synsets, FN frames or WP articles. The only requirement is that the individual entities are distinguishable by a unique identifier in each resource.

The alignment consists of the following steps: First, we extract the alignment candidates for a given resource pair, e.g. WN sense candidates for a WKT-en entry. Second, we create a gold standard by manually annotating a subset of candidate pairs as "valid" or "non-valid". Then, we extract the sense representations (e.g. lemmatized bag-of-words based on glosses) to compute the similarity of word senses (e.g. by cosine similarity). The gold standard with corresponding similarity values is fed into Weka (Hall et al., 2009) to train a machine learning classifier, and in the final step this classifier is used to automatically classify the candidate sense pairs as (non-)valid alignment. Our framework also allows us to train on a combination of different similarity measures.

Using our framework, we were able to reproduce the results reported by Niemann and Gurevych (2011) and Meyer and Gurevych (2011) based on the publicly available evaluation datasets[10] and the configuration details reported in the corresponding papers.

Cross-Lingual Alignment. In order to align word senses across languages, we extended the monolingual sense alignment described above to the cross-lingual setting. Our approach utilizes

[10]http://www.ukp.tu-darmstadt.de/data/sense-alignment/

Moses,[11] trained on the Europarl corpus. The lemma of one of the two senses to be aligned as well as its representations (e.g. the gloss) is translated into the language of the other resource, yielding a monolingual setting. E.g., the WN synset {*vessel, watercraft*} with its gloss *'a craft designed for water transportation'* is translated into {*Schiff, Wasserfahrzeug*} and *'Ein Fahrzeug für Wassertransport'*, and then the candidate extraction and all downstream steps can take place in German. An inherent problem with this approach is that incorrect translations also lead to invalid alignment candidates. However, these are most probably filtered out by the machine learning classifier as the calculated similarity between the sense representations (e.g. glosses) should be low if the candidates do not match.

We evaluated our approach by creating a cross-lingual alignment between WN and OW-de, i.e. the concepts in OW with a German lexicalization.[12] To our knowledge, this is the first study on aligning OW with another LSR. OW is especially interesting for this task due to its multilingual concepts, as described by Matuschek and Gurevych (2011). The created gold standard could, for instance, be re-used to evaluate alignments for other languages in OW.

To compute the similarity of word senses, we followed the approach by Niemann and Gurevych (2011) while covering both translation directions. We used the cosine similarity for comparing the German OW glosses with the German translations of WN glosses and cosine and personalized page rank (PPR) similarity for comparison of the German OW glosses translated into English with the original English WN glosses. Note that PPR similarity is not available for German as it is based on WN. Thereby, we filtered out the OW concepts without a German gloss which left us with 11,806 unique candidate pairs. We randomly selected 500 WN synsets for analysis yielding 703 candidate pairs. These were manually annotated as being (non-)alignments. For the subsequent machine learning task we used a simple threshold-based classifier and ten-fold cross validation.

Table 1 summarizes the results of different system configurations. We observe that translation into English works significantly better than into German. Also, the more elaborate similarity measure PPR yields better results than cosine similarity, while the best result is achieved by a combination of both. Niemann and Gurevych (2011) make a similar observation for the monolingual setting. Our F-measure of 0.717 in the best configuration lies between the results of Meyer and Gurevych (2011) (0.66) and Niemann and Gurevych (2011) (0.78), and thus verifies the validity of the machine translation approach. Therefore, the best alignment was subsequently integrated into UBY.

Translation direction	Similarity measure	P	R	F_1
EN > DE	Cosine (Cos)	0.666	0.575	0.594
DE > EN	Cos	0.674	0.658	0.665
DE > EN	PPR	0.721	**0.712**	0.716
DE > EN	PPR + Cos	**0.723**	**0.712**	**0.717**

Table 1: Cross-lingual alignment results

5 Evaluating UBY

We performed an intrinsic evaluation of UBY by computing a number of resource statistics. Our evaluation covers two aspects: first, it addresses the question if our automatic conversion routines work correctly. Second, it provides indicators for assessing UBY in terms of the gain in coverage compared to the single LSRs.

Correctness of conversion. Since we aim to preserve the maximal amount of information from the original LSRs, we should be able to replace any of the original LSRs and APIs by UBY and the UBY-API without losing information. As the conversion is largely performed automatically, systematic errors and information loss could be introduced by a faulty conversion routine. In order to detect such errors and to prove the correctness of the automatic conversion and the resulting representation, we have compared the original resource statistics of the classes and information types in the source LSRs to the corresponding classes in their UBY counterparts. For instance, the number of lexical relations in WordNet has been compared to the number of `SenseRelations` in the UBY WordNet lexicon.[13]

[11] http://www.statmt.org/moses/

[12] OmegaWiki consists of interlinked language-independent concepts to which lexicalizations in several languages are attached.

[13] For detailed analysis results see the UBY website.

Lexicon	Lexical Entry	Sense	Sense Relation
FN	9,704	11,942	–
GN	83,091	93,407	329,213
OW-de	30,967	34,691	60,054
OW-en	51,715	57,921	85,952
WP-de	790,430	838,428	571,286
WP-en	2,712,117	2,921,455	3,364,083
WKT-de	85,575	72,752	434,358
WKT-en	335,749	421,848	716,595
WN	156,584	206,978	8,559
VN	3,962	31,891	–
UBY	**4,259,894**	**4,691,313**	**5,300,941**

Table 2: UBY resource statistics (selected classes).

Lexicon pair	Languages	SenseAxis
WN–WP-en	EN–EN	50,351
WN–WKT-en	EN–EN	99,662
WN–VN	EN–EN	40,716
FN–VN	EN–EN	17,529
WP-en–OW-en	EN–EN	3,960
WP-de–OW-de	DE–DE	1,097
WN–OW-de	EN–DE	23,024
WP-en–WP-de	EN–DE	463,311
OW-en–OW-de	EN–DE	58,785
UBY	**All**	**758,435**

Table 3: UBY alignment statistics.

Gain in coverage. UBY offers an increased coverage compared to the single LSRs as reflected in the resource statistics. Tables 2 and 3 show the statistics on central classes in UBY. As UBY is organized in several Lexicons, the number of UBY lexical entries is the sum of the lexical entries in all 10 Lexicons. Thus, UBY contains more than 4.2 million lexical entries, 4.6 million senses, 5.3 million semantic relations between senses and more than 750,000 alignments. These statistics represent the total numbers of lexical entries, senses and sense relations in UBY without filtering of identical (i.e. corresponding) lexical entries, senses and relations. Listing the number of unique senses would require a full alignment between all integrated resources, which is currently not available.

We can, however, show that UBY contains over 3.08 million unique lemma-POS combinations for English and over 860,000 for German, over 3.94 million in total, see Table 4. Therefore, we assessed the coverage on lemma level. Table 4 also shows the number of lemmas with entries in one or more than one lexicon, additionally split by POS and language. Lemmas occurring only once in UBY increase the coverage at lemma level. For lemmas with parallel entries in several UBY lexicons, new information becomes available in the form of additional sense definitions and complementary information types attached to lemmas.

Finally, the increase in coverage at sense level can be estimated for senses that are aligned across at least two UBY-lexicons. We gain access to all available, partly complementary information types attached to these aligned senses, e.g. semantic relations, subcategorization frames, encyclopedic or multilingual information. The number of pairwise sense alignments provided by UBY is given in Table 3. In addition, we computed how many senses simultaneously take part in at least two pairwise sense alignments. For English, this applies to 31,786 senses, for which information from 3 UBY lexicons is available.

EN Lexicons	noun	verb	adjective
5	1	699	-
4	1,630	1,888	430
3	8,439	1,948	2,271
2	53,856	4,727	12,290
1	2,900,652	50,209	41,731
Σ (unique EN)	3,080,771		
DE Lexicons	noun	verb	adjective
4	1,546	-	-
3	10,374	372	342
2	26,813	3,174	2,643
1	803,770	6,108	7,737
Σ (unique DE)	862,879		

Table 4: Number of lemmas (split by POS and language) with entries in i UBY lexicons, $i = 1, \ldots, 5$.

6 Using UBY

UBY API. For convenient access to UBY, we implemented a Java-API which is built around the Hibernate[14] framework. Hibernate allows to easily store the XML data which results from converting resources into Uby-LMF into a corresponding SQL database.

Our main design principle was to keep the access to the resource as simple as possible, despite the rich and complex structure of UBY. Another

[14]http://www.hibernate.org/

important design aspect was to ensure that the functionality of the individual, resource-specific APIs or user interfaces is mirrored in the UBY API. This enables porting legacy applications to our new resource. To facilitate the transition to UBY, we plan to provide reference tables which list the corresponding UBY-API operations for the most important operations in the WN API, some of which are shown in Table 5.

WN function	UBY function
Dictionary	**UBY**
getIndexWord(pos, lemma)	getLexicalEntries(pos, lemma)
IndexWord	**LexicalEntry**
getLemma()	getLemmaForm()
Synset	**Synset**
getGloss()	getDefinitionText()
getWords()	getSenses()
Pointer	**SynsetRelation**
getType()	getRelName()
Word	**Sense**
getPointers()	getSenseRelations()

Table 5: Some equivalent operations in WN API and UBY API.

While it is possible to limit access to single resources by a parameter and thus mimic the behavior of the legacy APIs (e.g. only retrieve Synsets and their relations from WN), the true power of UBY API becomes visible when no such constraints are applied. In this case, all imported resources are queried to get one combined result, while retaining the source of the respective information. On top of this, the information about existing sense alignments across resources can be accessed via `SenseAxis` relations, so that the returned combined result covers not only the lexical, but also the sense level.

Community issues. One of the most important reasons for UBY is creating an easy-to-use powerful LSR to advance NLP research and development. Therefore, community building around the resource is one of our major concerns. To this end, we will offer free downloads of the lexical data and software presented in this paper under open licenses, namely: The UBY-LMF DTD, mappings and conversion tools for existing resources and sense alignments, the Java API, and, as far as licensing allows,[15] already converted resources. If resources cannot be made available for download, the conversion tools will still allow users with access to these resources to import them into UBY easily. In this way, it will be possible for users to build their "custom UBY" containing selected resources. As the underlying resources are subject to continuous change, updates of the corresponding components will be made available on a regular basis.

7 Conclusions

We presented UBY, a large-scale, standardized LSR containing nine widely used resources in two languages: English WN, WKT-en, WP-en, FN and VN, German WP-de, WKT-de, and GN, and OW in English and German. As all resources are modeled in UBY-LMF, UBY enables structural interoperability across resources and languages down to a fine-grained level of information. For FN, VN and all of the CCRs in English and German, this is done for the first time. Besides, by integrating sense alignments we also enable the lexical-semantic interoperability of resources. We presented a unified framework for aligning any LSRs pairwise and reported on experiments which align OW-de and WN. We will release the UBY-LMF model, the resource and the UBY-API at the time of publication.[16] Due to the added value and the large scale of UBY, as well as its ease of use, we believe UBY will boost the performance of NLP making use of lexical-semantic knowledge.

Acknowledgments

This work has been supported by the Emmy Noether Program of the German Research Foundation (DFG) under grant No. GU 798/3-1 and by the Volkswagen Foundation as part of the Lichtenberg-Professorship Program under grant No. I/82806. We thank Richard Eckart de Castilho, Yevgen Chebotar, Zijad Maksuti and Tri Duc Nghiem for their contributions to this project.

References

Jordi Atserias, Luís Villarejo, German Rigau, Eneko Agirre, John Carroll, Bernardo Magnini, and Piek

[15] Only GermaNet is subject to a restricted license and cannot be redistributed in UBY format.

[16] http://www.ukp.tu-darmstadt.de/data/uby

Vossen. 2004. The Meaning Multilingual Central Repository. In *Proceedings of the second international WordNet Conference (GWC 2004)*, pages 23–30, Brno, Czech Republic.

Collin F. Baker and Christiane Fellbaum. 2009. WordNet and FrameNet as complementary resources for annotation. In *Proceedings of the Third Linguistic Annotation Workshop*, ACL-IJCNLP '09, pages 125–129, Suntec, Singapore.

Collin F. Baker, Charles J. Fillmore, and John B. Lowe. 1998. The Berkeley FrameNet project. In *Proceedings of the 36th Annual Meeting of the Association for Computational Linguistics and 17th International Conference on Computational Linguistics (COLING-ACL'98*, pages 86–90, Montreal, Canada.

Christian Bizer, Jens Lehmann, Georgi Kobilarov, Sören Auer, Christian Becker, Richard Cyganiak, and Sebastian Hellmann. 2009. DBpedia A Crystallization Point for the Web of Data. *Journal of Web Semantics: Science, Services and Agents on the World Wide Web*, (7):154–165.

Daan Broeder, Marc Kemps-Snijders, Dieter Van Uytvanck, Menzo Windhouwer, Peter Withers, Peter Wittenburg, and Claus Zinn. 2010. A Data Category Registry- and Component-based Metadata Framework. In *Proceedings of the 7th International Conference on Language Resources and Evaluation (LREC)*, pages 43–47, Valletta, Malta.

Paul Buitelaar, Philipp Cimiano, Peter Haase, and Michael Sintek. 2009. Towards Linguistically Grounded Ontologies. In Lora Aroyo, Paolo Traverso, Fabio Ciravegna, Philipp Cimiano, Tom Heath, Eero Hyvönen, Riichiro Mizoguchi, Eyal Oren, Marta Sabou, and Elena Simperl, editors, *The Semantic Web: Research and Applications*, pages 111–125, Berlin/Heidelberg, Germany. Springer.

Gerard de Melo and Gerhard Weikum. 2009. Towards a universal wordnet by learning from combined evidence. In *Proceedings of the 18th ACM conference on Information and knowledge management (CIKM '09)*, CIKM '09, pages 513–522, New York, NY, USA. ACM.

Christiane Fellbaum. 1998. *WordNet: An Electronic Lexical Database*. MIT Press, Cambridge, MA, USA.

Charles J. Fillmore. 1982. Frame Semantics. In The Linguistic Society of Korea, editor, *Linguistics in the Morning Calm*, pages 111–137. Hanshin Publishing Company, Seoul, Korea.

Gil Francopoulo, Nuria Bel, Monte George, Nicoletta Calzolari, Monica Monachini, Mandy Pet, and Claudia Soria. 2006. Lexical Markup Framework (LMF). In *Proceedings of the 5th International Conference on Language Resources and Evaluation (LREC)*, pages 233–236, Genoa, Italy.

Mark Hall, Eibe Frank, Geoffrey Holmes, Bernhard Pfahringer, Peter Reutemann, and Ian H. Witten. 2009. The WEKA Data Mining Software: An Update. *ACM SIGKDD Explorations Newsletter*, 11(1):10–18.

Verena Henrich and Erhard Hinrichs. 2010. Standardizing wordnets in the ISO standard LMF: Wordnet-LMF for GermaNet. In *Proceedings of the 23rd International Conference on Computational Linguistics (COLING)*, pages 456–464, Beijing, China.

Richard Johansson and Pierre Nugues. 2007. Using WordNet to extend FrameNet coverage. In *Proceedings of the Workshop on Building Frame-semantic Resources for Scandinavian and Baltic Languages, at NODALIDA*, pages 27–30, Tartu, Estonia.

Karin Kipper, Anna Korhonen, Neville Ryant, and Martha Palmer. 2008. A Large-scale Classification of English Verbs. *Language Resources and Evaluation*, 42:21–40.

Claudia Kunze and Lothar Lemnitzer. 2002. GermaNet – representation, visualization, application. In *Proceedings of the Third International Conference on Language Resources and Evaluation (LREC)*, pages 1485–1491, Las Palmas, Canary Islands, Spain.

Beth Levin. 1993. *English Verb Classes and Alternations*. The University of Chicago Press, Chicago, IL, USA.

Michael Matuschek and Iryna Gurevych. 2011. Where the journey is headed: Collaboratively constructed multilingual Wiki-based resources. In SFB 538: Mehrsprachigkeit, editor, *Hamburger Arbeiten zur Mehrsprachigkeit*, Hamburg, Germany.

John McCrae, Dennis Spohr, and Philipp Cimiano. 2011. Linking Lexical Resources and Ontologies on the Semantic Web with Lemon. In *The Semantic Web: Research and Applications*, volume 6643 of *Lecture Notes in Computer Science*, pages 245–259. Springer, Berlin/Heidelberg, Germany.

Clifton J. McFate and Kenneth D. Forbus. 2011. NULEX: an open-license broad coverage lexicon. In *Proceedings of the 49th Annual Meeting of the Association for Computational Linguistics: Human Language Technologies: short papers - Volume 2*, HLT '11, pages 363–367, Portland, OR, USA.

Christian M. Meyer and Iryna Gurevych. 2010. Worth its Weight in Gold or Yet Another Resource — A Comparative Study of Wiktionary, OpenThesaurus and GermaNet. In Alexander Gelbukh, editor, *Computational Linguistics and Intelligent Text Processing: 11th International Conference*, volume 6008 of *Lecture Notes in Computer Science*, pages 38–49. Berlin/Heidelberg: Springer, Iaşi, Romania.

Christian M. Meyer and Iryna Gurevych. 2011. What Psycholinguists Know About Chemistry: Aligning Wiktionary and WordNet for Increased Domain

Coverage. In *Proceedings of the 5th International Joint Conference on Natural Language Processing (IJCNLP)*, pages 883–892, Chiang Mai, Thailand.

Roberto Navigli and Simone Paolo Ponzetto. 2010a. BabelNet: Building a Very Large Multilingual Semantic Network. In *Proceedings of the 48th Annual Meeting of the Association for Computational Linguistics*, pages 216–225, Uppsala, Sweden, July.

Roberto Navigli and Simone Paolo Ponzetto. 2010b. Knowledge-rich Word Sense Disambiguation Rivaling Supervised Systems. In *Proceedings of the 48th Annual Meeting of the Association for Computational Linguistics*, pages 1522–1531, Uppsala, Sweden.

Roberto Navigli. 2006. Meaningful Clustering of Senses Helps Boost Word Sense Disambiguation Performance. In *Proceedings of the 21st International Conference on Computational Linguistics and the 44th Annual Meeting of the Association for Computational Linguistics (COLING-ACL)*, pages 105–112, Sydney, Australia.

Elisabeth Niemann and Iryna Gurevych. 2011. The People's Web meets Linguistic Knowledge: Automatic Sense Alignment of Wikipedia and WordNet. In *Proceedings of the 9th International Conference on Computational Semantics (IWCS)*, pages 205–214, Oxford, UK.

Muntsa Padró, Núria Bel, and Silvia Necsulescu. 2011. Towards the Automatic Merging of Lexical Resources: Automatic Mapping. In *Proceedings of the International Conference on Recent Advances in Natural Language Processing (RANLP)*, pages 296–301, Hissar, Bulgaria.

Martha Palmer. 2009. Semlink: Linking PropBank, VerbNet and FrameNet. In *Proceedings of the Generative Lexicon Conference (GenLex-09)*, pages 9–15, Pisa, Italy.

Sameer S. Pradhan, Eduard Hovy, Mitch Marcus, Martha Palmer, Lance Ramshaw, and Ralph Weischedel. 2007. OntoNotes: A Unified Relational Semantic Representation. In *Proceedings of the International Conference on Semantic Computing*, pages 517–526, Washington, DC, USA.

Lei Shi and Rada Mihalcea. 2005. Putting Pieces Together: Combining FrameNet, VerbNet and WordNet for Robust Semantic Parsing. In *Proceedings of the Sixth International Conference on Intelligent Text Processing and Computational Linguistics (CICLing)*, pages 100–111, Mexico City, Mexico.

Claudia Soria, Monica Monachini, and Piek Vossen. 2009. Wordnet-LMF: fleshing out a standardized format for Wordnet interoperability. In *Proceedings of the 2009 International Workshop on Intercultural Collaboration*, pages 139–146, Palo Alto, CA, USA.

Fabian M. Suchanek, Gjergji Kasneci, and Gerhard Weikum. 2007. Yago: A Core of Semantic Knowledge. In *Proceedings of the 16th International Conference on World Wide Web*, pages 697–706, Banff, Canada.

Antonio Toral, Stefania Bracale, Monica Monachini, and Claudia Soria. 2010. Rejuvenating the Italian WordNet: Upgrading, Standarising, Extending. In *Proceedings of the 5th Global WordNet Conference (GWC)*, Bombay, India.

Piek Vossen, editor. 1998. *EuroWordNet: A Multilingual Database with Lexical Semantic Networks*. Kluwer Academic Publishers, Dordrecht, Netherlands.

Word Sense Induction for Novel Sense Detection

Jey Han Lau,[♠♡] **Paul Cook,**[♡] **Diana McCarthy,**[♣]
David Newman,[◇] and **Timothy Baldwin**[♠♡]
♠ NICTA Victoria Research Laboratory
♡ Dept of Computer Science and Software Engineering, University of Melbourne
◇ Dept of Computer Science, University of California Irvine
♣ Lexical Computing
jhlau@csse.unimelb.edu.au, paulcook@unimelb.edu.au,
diana@dianamccarthy.co.uk, newman@uci.edu, tb@ldwin.net

Abstract

We apply topic modelling to automatically induce *word senses* of a target word, and demonstrate that our word sense induction method can be used to automatically detect words with emergent novel senses, as well as token occurrences of those senses. We start by exploring the utility of standard topic models for word sense induction (WSI), with a pre-determined number of topics (=senses). We next demonstrate that a non-parametric formulation that learns an appropriate number of senses per word actually performs better at the WSI task. We go on to establish state-of-the-art results over two WSI datasets, and apply the proposed model to a novel sense detection task.

1 Introduction

Word sense induction (WSI) is the task of automatically inducing the different senses of a given word, generally in the form of an unsupervised learning task with senses represented as clusters of token instances. It contrasts with word sense disambiguation (WSD), where a fixed sense inventory is assumed to exist, and token instances of a given word are disambiguated relative to the sense inventory. While WSI is intuitively appealing as a task, there have been no real examples of WSI being successfully deployed in end-user applications, other than work by Schutze (1998) and Navigli and Crisafulli (2010) in an information retrieval context. A key contribution of this paper is the successful application of WSI to the lexicographical task of novel sense detection, i.e. identifying words which have taken on new senses over time.

One of the key challenges in WSI is learning the appropriate sense granularity for a given word, i.e. the number of senses that best captures the token occurrences of that word. Building on the work of Brody and Lapata (2009) and others, we approach WSI via topic modelling — using Latent Dirichlet Allocation (LDA: Blei et al. (2003)) and derivative approaches — and use the topic model to determine the appropriate sense granularity. Topic modelling is an unsupervised approach to jointly learn topics — in the form of multinomial probability distributions over words — and per-document topic assignments — in the form of multinomial probability distributions over topics. LDA is appealing for WSI as it both assigns senses to words (in the form of topic allocation), and outputs a representation of each sense as a weighted list of words. LDA offers a solution to the question of sense granularity determination via non-parametric formulations, such as a Hierarchical Dirichlet Process (HDP: Teh et al. (2006), Yao and Durme (2011)).

Our contributions in this paper are as follows. We first establish the effectiveness of HDP for WSI over both the SemEval-2007 and SemEval-2010 WSI datasets (Agirre and Soroa, 2007; Manandhar et al., 2010), and show that the non-parametric formulation is superior to a standard LDA formulation with oracle determination of sense granularity for a given word. We next demonstrate that our interpretation of HDP-based WSI is superior to other topic model-based approaches to WSI, and indeed, better than the best-published results for both SemEval datasets. Finally, we apply our method to the novel sense detection task based on a dataset developed in this research, and achieve highly encouraging results.

2 Methodology

In topic modelling, documents are assumed to exhibit multiple topics, with each document having its own distribution over topics. Words are generated in each document by first sampling a topic from the document's topic distribution, then sampling a word from that topic. In this work we use the topic models's probabilistic assignment of topics to words for the WSI task.

2.1 Data Representation and Pre-processing

In the context of WSI, topics form our sense representation, and words in a sentence are generated conditioned on a particular sense of the target word. The "document" in the WSI case is a single sentence or a short document fragment containing the target word, as we would not expect to be able to generate a full document from the sense of a single target word.[1] In the case of the SemEval datasets, we use the word contexts provided in the dataset, while in our novel sense detection experiments, we use a context window of three sentences, one sentence to either side of the token occurrence of the target word.

As our baseline representation, we use a bag of words, where word frequency is kept but not word order. All words are lemmatised, and stopwords and low frequency terms are removed.

We also experiment with the addition of positional context word information, as commonly used in WSI. That is, we introduce an additional word feature for each of the three words to the left and right of the target word.

Padó and Lapata (2007) demonstrated the importance of syntactic dependency relations in the construction of semantic space models, e.g. for WSD. Based on these findings, we include dependency relations as additional features in our topic models,[2] but just for dependency relations that involve the target word.

2.2 Topic Modelling

Topic models learn a probability distribution over topics for each document, by simply aggregating the distributions over topics for each word in the document. In WSI terms, we take this distribution over topics for each target word ("instance" in WSI parlance) as our distribution over senses for that word.

In our initial experiments, we use LDA topic modelling, which requires us to set T, the number of topics to be learned by the model. The LDA generative process is: (1) draw a latent topic z from a document-specific topic distribution $P(t = z|d)$ then; (2) draw a word w from the chosen topic $P(w|t = z)$. Thus, the probability of producing a single copy of word w given a document d is given by:

$$P(w|d) = \sum_{z=1}^{T} P(w|t = z)P(t = z|d).$$

In standard LDA, the user needs to specify the number of topics T. In non-parametric variants of LDA, the model dynamically learns the number of topics as part of the topic modelling. The particular implementation of non-parametric topic model we experiment with is Hierarchical Dirichlet Process (HDP: Teh et al. (2006)),[3] where, for each document, a distribution of mixture components $P(t|d)$ is sampled from a base distribution G_0 as follows: (1) choose a base distribution $G_0 \sim DP(\gamma, H)$; (2) for each document d, generate distribution $P(t|d) \sim DP(\alpha_0, G_0)$; (3) draw a latent topic z from the document's mixture component distribution $P(t|d)$, in the same manner as for LDA; and (4) draw a word w from the chosen topic $P(w|t = z)$.[4]

For both LDA and HDP, we individually topic model each target word, and determine the sense assignment z for a given instance by aggregating over the topic assignments for each word in the instance and selecting the sense with the highest aggregated probability, $\arg\max_z P(t = z|d)$.

3 SemEval Experiments

To facilitate comparison of our proposed method for WSI with previous approaches, we use the dataset from the SemEval-2007 and SemEval-2010 word sense induction tasks (Agirre and

[1] Notwithstanding the one sense per discourse heuristic (Gale et al., 1992).

[2] We use the Stanford Parser to do part of speech tagging and to extract the dependency relations (Klein and Manning, 2003; De Marneffe et al., 2006).

[3] We use the C++ implementation of HDP (`http://www.cs.princeton.edu/~blei/topicmodeling.html`) in our experiments.

[4] The two HDP parameters γ and α_0 control the variability of senses in the documents. In particular, γ controls the degree of sharing of topics across documents — a high γ value leads to more topics, as topics for different documents are more dissimilar. α_0, on the other hand, controls the degree of mixing of topics within a document — a high α_0 generates fewer topics, as topics are less homogeneous within a document.

Soroa, 2007; Manandhar et al., 2010). We first experiment with the SemEval-2010 dataset, as it includes explicit training and test data for each target word and utilises a more robust evaluation methodology. We then return to experiment with the SemEval-2007 dataset, for comparison purposes with other published results for topic modelling approaches to WSI.

3.1 SemEval-2010

3.1.1 Dataset and Methodology

Our primary WSI evaluation is based on the dataset provided by the SemEval-2010 WSI shared task (Manandhar et al., 2010). The dataset contains 100 target words: 50 nouns and 50 verbs. For each target word, a fixed set of training and test instances are supplied, typically 1 to 3 sentences in length, each containing the target word.

The default approach to evaluation for the SemEval-2010 WSI task is in the form of WSD over the test data, based on the senses that have been automatically induced from the training data. Because the induced senses will likely vary in number and nature between systems, the WSD evaluation has to incorporate a sense alignment step, which it performs by splitting the test instances into two sets: a mapping set and an evaluation set. The optimal mapping from induced senses to gold-standard senses is learned from the mapping set, and the resulting sense alignment is used to map the predictions of the WSI system to pre-defined senses for the evaluation set. The particular split we use to calculate WSD effectiveness in this paper is 80%/20% (mapping/test), averaged across 5 random splits.[5]

The SemEval-2010 training data consists of approximately 163K training instances for the 100 target words, all taken from the web. The test data is approximately 9K instances taken from a variety of news sources. Following the standard approach used by the participating systems in the SemEval-2010 task, we induce senses only from the training instances, and use the learned model to assign senses to the test instances.

[5]A 60%/40% split is also provided as part of the task setup, but the results are almost identical to those for the 80%/20% split, and so are omitted from this paper. The original task also made use of V-measure and Paired F-score to evaluate the induced word sense clusters, but have degenerate behaviour in correlating strongly with the number of senses induced by the method (Manandhar et al., 2010), and are hence omitted from this paper.

In our original experiments with LDA, we set the number of topics (T) for each target word to the number of senses represented in the test data for that word (varying T for each target word). This is based on the unreasonable assumption that we will have access to gold-standard information on sense granularity for each target word, and is done to establish an upper bound score for LDA. We then relax the assumption, and use a fixed T setting for each of sets of nouns ($T = 7$) and verbs ($T = 3$), based on the average number of senses from the test data in each case. Finally, we introduce positional context features for LDA, once again using the fixed T values for nouns and verbs.

We next apply HDP to the WSI task, using positional features, but learning the number of senses automatically for each target word via the model. Finally, we experiment with adding dependency features to the model.

To summarise, we provide results for the following models:

1. **LDA+Variable** T: LDA with variable T for each target word based on the number of gold-standard senses.
2. **LDA+Fixed** T: LDA with fixed T for each of nouns and verbs.
3. **LDA+Fixed** T**+Position**: LDA with fixed T and extra positional word features.
4. **HDP+Position**: HDP (which automatically learns T), with extra positional word features.
5. **HDP+Position+Dependency**: HDP with both positional word and dependency features.

We compare our models with two baselines from the SemEval-2010 task: (1) Baseline Random — randomly assign each test instance to one of four senses; (2) Baseline MFS — most frequent sense baseline, assigning all test instances to one sense; and also a benchmark system (**UoY**), in the form of the University of York system (Korkontzelos and Manandhar, 2010), which achieved the best overall WSD results in the original SemEval-2010 task.

3.2 SemEval-2010 Results

The results of our experiments over the SemEval-2010 dataset are summarised in Table 1.

System	WSD (80%/20%)		
	All	Verbs	Nouns
Baselines			
Baseline Random	0.57	0.66	0.51
Baseline MFS	0.59	0.67	0.53
LDA			
Variable T	0.64	0.69	0.60
Fixed T	0.63	0.68	0.59
Fixed T +Position	0.63	0.68	0.60
HDP			
+Position	0.68	0.72	0.65
+Position+Dependency	0.68	0.72	0.65
Benchmark			
UoY	0.62	0.67	0.59

Table 1: WSD F-score over the SemEval-2010 dataset

Looking first at the results for LDA, we see that the first LDA approach (variable T) is very competitive, outperforming the benchmark system. In this approach, however, we assume perfect knowledge of the number of gold senses of each target word, meaning that the method isn't truly unsupervised. When we fixed T for each of the nouns and verbs, we see a small drop in F-score, but encouragingly the method still performs above the benchmark. Adding positional word features improves the results very slightly for nouns.

When we relax the assumption on the number of word senses in moving to HDP, we observe a marked improvement in F-score over LDA. This is highly encouraging and somewhat surprising, as in hiding information about sense granularity from the model, we have actually *improved* our results. We return to discuss this effect below. For the final feature, we add dependency features to the HDP model (in addition to retaining the positional word features), but see no movement in the results.[6] While the dependency features didn't reduce F-score, their utility is questionable as the generation of the features from the Stanford parser is computationally expensive.

To better understand these results, we present the top-10 terms for each of the senses induced for the word *cheat* in Table 2. These senses are learnt using HDP with both positional word features (e.g. *husband_#-1*, indicating the lemma *husband* to the immediate left of the target word) and dependency features (e.g. *cheat#prep_on#wife*). The first observation to make is that senses 7, 8 and 9 are "junk" senses, in that the top-10 terms do not convey a coherent sense. These topics are an artifact of HDP: they are learnt at a much later stage of the iterative process of Gibbs sampling and are often smaller than other topics (i.e. have more zero-probability terms). We notice that they are assigned as topics to instances very rarely (although they are certainly used to assign topics to non-target *words* in the instances), and as such, they do not present a real issue when assigning the sense to an instance, as they are likely to be overshadowed by the dominant senses.[7] This conclusion is born out when we experimented with manually filtering out these topics when assigning instance to senses: there was no perceptible change in the results, reinforcing our suggestion that these topics do not impact on target word sense assignment.

Comparing the results for HDP back to those for LDA, HDP tends to learn almost double the number of senses per target word as are in the gold-standard (and hence are used for the "Variable T" version of LDA). Far from hurting our WSD F-score, however, the extra topics are dominated by junk topics, and boost WSD F-score for the "genuine" topics. Based on this insight, we ran LDA once again with variable T (and positional and dependency features), but this time setting T to the value learned by HDP, to give LDA the facility to use junk topics. This resulted in an F-score of 0.66 across all word classes (verbs = 0.71, nouns = 0.62), demonstrating that, surprisingly, even for the same T setting, HDP achieves superior results to LDA. I.e., not only does HDP learn T automatically, but the topic model learned for a given T is superior to that for LDA.

Looking at the other senses discovered for *cheat*, we notice that the model has induced a myriad of senses: the relationship sense of cheat (senses 1, 3 and 4, e.g. *husband cheats*); the exam usage of cheat (sense 2); the competition/game usage of cheat (sense 5); and cheating in the political domain (sense 6). Although the senses are possibly "split" a little more than desirable (e.g. senses 1, 3 and 4 arguably describe the same sense), the overall quality of the produced senses

[6] An identical result was observed for LDA.

[7] In the WSD evaluation, the alignment of induced senses to the gold senses is learnt automatically based on the mapping instances. E.g. if all instances that are assigned sense a have gold sense x, then sense a is mapped to gold sense x. Therefore, if the proportion of junk senses in the mapping instances is low, their influence on WSD results will be negligible.

Sense Num	Top-10 Terms
1	cheat think want ... love feel tell guy cheat#nsubj#include find
2	cheat student cheating test game school cheat#aux#to teacher exam study
3	husband wife cheat wife_#1 tiger husband_#-1 cheat#prep_on#wife ... woman cheat#nsubj#husband
4	cheat woman relationship cheating partner reason cheat#nsubj#man woman_#-1 cheat#aux#to spouse
5	cheat game play player cheating poker cheat#aux#to card cheated money
6	cheat exchange china chinese foreign cheat_#-2 cheat_#2 china_#-1 cheat#aux#to team
7	tina bette kirk walk accuse mon pok symkyn nick star
8	fat jones ashley pen body taste weight expectation parent able
9	euro goal luck fair france irish single 2000 cheat#prep_at#point complain

Table 2: The top-10 terms for each of the senses induced for the verb *cheat* by the HDP model (with positional word and dependency features)

is encouraging. Also, we observe a spin-off benefit of topic modelling approaches to WSI: the high-ranking words in each topic can be used to gist the sense, and anecdotally confirm the impact of the different feature types (i.e. the positional word and dependency features).

3.3 Comparison with other Topic Modelling Approaches to WSI

The idea of applying topic modelling to WSI is not entirely new. Brody and Lapata (2009) proposed an LDA-based model which assigns different weights to different feature sets (e.g. unigram tokens vs. dependency relations), using a "layered" feature representation. They carry out extensive parameter optimisation of both the (fixed) number of senses, number of layers, and size of the context window.

Separately, Yao and Durme (2011) proposed the use of non-parametric topic models in WSI. The authors preprocess the instances slightly differently, opting to remove the target word from each instance and stem the tokens. They also tuned the hyperparameters of the topic model to optimise the WSI effectiveness over the evaluation set, and didn't use positional or dependency features.

Both of these papers were evaluated over only the SemEval-2007 WSI dataset (Agirre and Soroa, 2007), so we similarly apply our HDP method to this dataset for direct comparability. In the remainder of this section, we refer to Brody and Lapata (2009) as BL, and Yao and Durme (2011) as YVD.

The SemEval-2007 dataset consists of roughly 27K instances, for 65 target verbs and 35 target nouns. BL report on results only over the noun instances, so we similarly restrict our attention to the nouns in this paper. Training data was not provided as part of the original dataset, so we follow the approach of BL and YVD in constructing our own training dataset for each target word from instances extracted from the British National Corpus (BNC: Burnard (2000)).[8] Both BL and YVD separately report slightly higher in-domain results from training on WSJ data (the SemEval-2007 data was taken from the WSJ). For the purposes of model comparison under identical training settings, however, it is appropriate to report on results for only the BNC.

System	F-Score
BL	0.855
YVD	0.857
SemEval Best (I2R)	0.868
Our method (default parameters)	0.842
Our method (tuned parameters)	0.869

Table 3: F-score for the SemEval-2007 WSI task, for our HDP method with default and tuned parameter settings, as compared to competitor topic modelling and other approaches to WSI

We experiment with both our original method (with both positional word and dependency features, and default parameter settings for HDP) without any parameter tuning, and the same method with the tuned parameter settings of YVD, for direct comparability. We present the results in Table 3, including the results for the best-performing system in the original SemEval-2007 task (I2R: Niu et al. (2007)).

The results are enlightening: with default parameter settings, our methodology is slightly below the results of the other three models. Bear

[8] In creating the training dataset, each instance is made up of the sentence the target word occurs in, as we as one sentence to either side of that sentence, i.e. 3 sentences in total per instance.

in mind, however, that the two topic modelling-based approaches were tuned extensively to the dataset. When we use the tuned hyperparameter settings of YVD, our results rise around 2.5% to surpass both topic modelling approaches, and marginally outperform the I2R system from the original task. Recall that both BL and YVD report higher results again using in-domain training data, so we would expect to see further gains again over the I2R system in following this path.

Overall, these results agree with our findings over the SemEval-2010 dataset (Section 3.2), underlining the viability of topic modelling to automated word sense induction.

3.4 Discussion

As part of our preprocessing, we remove all stopwords (other than for the positional word and dependency features), as described in Section 2.1. We separately experimented with not removing stopwords, based on the intuition that prepositions such as *to* and *on* can be informative in determining word sense based on local context. The results were markedly worse, however. We also tried appending part of speech information to each word lemma, but the resulting data sparseness meant that results dropped marginally.

When determining the sense for an instance, we aggregate the sense assignments for each word in the instance (not just the target word). An alternate strategy is to use only the target word topic assignment, but again, the results for this strategy were inferior to the aggregate method.

In the SemEval-2007 experiments (Section 3.3), we found that YVD's hyperparameter settings yielded better results than the default settings. We experimented with parameter tuning over the SemEval-2010 dataset (including YVD's optimal setting on the 2007 dataset), but found that the default setting achieved the best overall results: although the WSD F-score improved a little for nouns, it worsened for verbs. This observation is not unexpected: as the hyperparameters were optimised for nouns in their experiments, the settings might not be appropriate for verbs. This also suggests that their results may be due in part to overfitting the SemEval-2007 data.

4 Identifying Novel Senses

Having established the effectiveness of our approach at WSI, we next turn to an application of WSI, in identifying words which have taken on novel senses over time, based on analysis of diachronic data. Our topic modelling approach is particularly attractive for this task as, not only does it jointly perform type-level WSI, and token-level WSD based on the induced senses (in assigning topics to each instance), but it is possible to gist the induced senses via the contents of the topic (typically using the topic words with highest marginal probability).

The meanings of words can change over time; in particular, words can take on new senses. Contemporary examples of new word-senses include the meanings of *swag* and *tweet* as used below:

1. *We all know Frankie is adorable, but does he have swag?* [*swag* = 'style']
2. *The alleged victim gave a description of the man on Twitter and tweeted that she thought she could identify him.* [*tweet* = 'send a message on Twitter']

These senses of *swag* and *tweet* are not included in many dictionaries or computational lexicons — e.g., neither of these senses is listed in Wordnet 3.0 (Fellbaum, 1998) — yet appear to be in regular usage, particularly in text related to pop culture and online media.

The manual identification of such new word-senses is a challenge in lexicography over and above identifying new words themselves, and is essential to keeping dictionaries up-to-date. Moreover, lexicons that better reflect contemporary usage could benefit NLP applications that use sense inventories.

The challenge of identifying changes in word sense has only recently been considered in computational linguistics. For example, Sagi et al. (2009), Cook and Stevenson (2010), and Gulordava and Baroni (2011) propose type-based models of semantic change. Such models do not account for polysemy, and appear best-suited to identifying changes in predominant sense. Bamman and Crane (2011) use a parallel Latin–English corpus to induce word senses and build a WSD system, which they then apply to study diachronic variation in word senses. Crucially, in this token-based approach there is a clear connection between word senses and tokens, making it possible to identify usages of a specific sense.

Based on the findings in Section 3.2, here we apply the HDP method for WSI to the task of identifying new word-senses. In contrast to Bamman and Crane (2011) our token-based approach does not require parallel text to induce senses.

4.1 Method

Given two corpora — a reference corpus which we take to represent standard usage, and a second corpus of newer texts — we identify senses that are novel to the second corpus compared to the reference corpus. For a given word w, we pool all usages of w in the reference corpus and second corpus, and run the HDP WSI method on this super-corpus to induce the senses of w. We then tag all usages of w in both corpora with their single most-likely automatically-induced sense.

Intuitively, if a word w is used in some sense s in the second corpus, and w is never used in that sense in the reference corpus, then w has acquired a new sense, namely s. We capture this intuition into a novelty score ("Nov") that indicates whether a given word w has a new sense in the second corpus, s, compared to the reference corpus, r, as below:

$$\text{Nov}(w) = \max\left(\left\{\frac{p_s(t_i) - p_r(t_i)}{p_r(t_i)} : t_i \in T\right\}\right) \tag{1}$$

where $p_s(t_i)$ and $p_r(t_i)$ are the probability of sense t_i in the second corpus and reference corpus, respectively, calculated using smoothed maximum likelihood estimates, and T is the set of senses induced for w. Novelty is high if there is some sense t that has much higher relative frequency in s than r and that is also relatively infrequent in r.

4.2 Data

Because we are interested in the identification of novel word-senses for applications such as lexicon maintenance, we focus on relatively newly-coined word-senses. In particular, we take the written portion of the BNC — consisting primarily of British English text from the late 20th century — as our reference corpus, and a similarly-sized random sample of documents from the ukWaC (Ferraresi et al., 2008) — a Web corpus built from the `.uk` domain in 2007 which includes a wide range of text types — as our second corpus. Text genres are represented to different extents in these corpora with, for example, text types related to the Internet being much more common in the ukWaC. Such differences are a noted challenge for approaches to identifying lexical semantic differences between corpora (Peirsman et al., 2010), but are difficult to avoid given the corpora that are available. We use TreeTagger (Schmid, 1994) to tokenise and lemmatise both corpora.

Evaluating approaches to identifying semantic change is a challenge, particularly due to the lack of appropriate evaluation resources; indeed, most previous approaches have used very small datasets (Sagi et al., 2009; Cook and Stevenson, 2010; Bamman and Crane, 2011). Because this is a preliminary attempt at applying WSI techniques to identifying new word-senses, our evaluation will also be based on a rather small dataset.

We require a set of words that are known to have acquired a new sense between the late 20th and early 21st centuries. The Concise Oxford English Dictionary aims to document contemporary usage, and has been published in numerous editions including Thompson (1995, COD95) and Soanes and Stevenson (2008, COD08). Although some of the entries have been substantially revised between editions, many have not, enabling us to easily identify new senses amongst the entries in COD08 relative to COD95. A manual linear search through the entries in these dictionaries would be very time consuming, but by exploiting the observation that new words often correspond to concepts that are culturally salient (Ayto, 2006), we can quickly identify some candidates for words that have taken on a new sense.

Between the time periods of our two corpora, computers and the Internet have become much more mainstream in society. We therefore extracted all entries from COD08 containing the word *computing* (which is often used as a topic label in this dictionary) that have a token frequency of at least 1000 in the BNC. We then read the entries for these 87 lexical items in COD95 and COD08 and identified those which have a clear computing sense in COD08 that was not present in COD95. In total we found 22 such items. This process, along with all the annotation in this section, is carried out by a native English-speaking author of this paper.

To ensure that the words identified from the dictionaries do in fact have a new sense in the ukWaC sample compared to the BNC, we examine the usage of these words in the corpora. We extract a random sample of 100 usages of each lemma from the BNC and ukWaC sample and annotate these usages as to whether they correspond to the novel sense or not. This binary distinction is easier than fine-grained sense annotation, and since we do not use these annotations for formal evaluation — only for selecting items for our dataset — we do not carry out an inter-annotator agreement study here. We eliminate any lemma for which we find evidence of the novel sense in the BNC, or for which we do not find evidence of the novel sense in the ukWaC sample.[9] We further check word sketches (Kilgarriff and Tugwell, 2002)[10] for each of these lemmas in the BNC and ukWaC for collocates that likely correspond to the novel sense; we exclude any lemma for which we find evidence of the novel sense in the BNC, or fail to find evidence of the novel sense in the ukWaC sample. At the end of this process we have identified the following 5 lemmas that have the indicated novel senses in the ukWaC compared to the BNC: *domain* (n) "Internet domain"; *export* (v) "export data"; *mirror* (n) "mirror website"; *poster* (n) "one who posts online"; and *worm* (n) "malicious program". For each of the 5 lemmas with novel senses, a second annotator — also a native English-speaking author of this paper — annotated the sample of 100 usages from the ukWaC. The observed agreement and unweighted Kappa between the two annotators is 97.2% and 0.92, respectively, indicating that this is indeed a relatively easy annotation task. The annotators discussed the small number of disagreements to reach consensus.

For our dataset we also require items that have *not* acquired a novel sense in the ukWaC sample. For each of the above 5 lemmas we identified a distractor lemma of the same part-of-speech that has a similar frequency in the BNC, and that has not undergone sense change between COD95 and COD08. The 5 distractors are: *cinema* (n); *guess* (v); *symptom* (n); *founder* (n); and *racism* (n).

4.3 Results

We compute novelty ("Nov", Equation 1) for all 10 items in our dataset, based on the output of the topic modelling. The results are shown in column "Novelty" in Table 4. The lemmas with a novel sense have higher novelty scores than the distractors according to a one-sided Wilcoxon rank sum test ($p < .05$).

Lemma	Novelty	Freq. ratio	Novel sense freq.
domain (n)	116.2	2.60	41
worm (n)	68.4	1.04	30
mirror (n)	38.4	0.53	10
guess (v)	16.5	0.93	–
export (v)	13.8	0.88	28
founder (n)	11.0	1.20	–
cinema (n)	9.7	1.30	–
poster (n)	7.9	1.83	4
racism (n)	2.4	0.98	–
symptom (n)	2.1	1.16	–

Table 4: Novelty score ("Nov"), ratio of frequency in the ukWaC sample and BNC, and frequency of the novel sense in the manually-annotated 100 instances from the ukWaC sample (where applicable), for all lemmas in our dataset. Lemmas shown in boldface have a novel sense in the ukWaC sample compared to the BNC.

When a lemma takes on a new sense, it might also increase in frequency. We therefore also consider a baseline in which we rank the lemmas by the ratio of their frequency in the second and reference corpora. These results are shown in column "Freq. ratio" in Table 4. The difference between the frequency ratios for the lemmas with a novel sense, and the distractors, is not significant ($p > .05$).

Examining the frequency of the novel senses — shown in column "Novel sense freq." in Table 4 — we see that the lowest-ranked lemma with a novel sense, *poster*, is also the lemma with the least-frequent novel sense. This result is unsurprising as our novelty score will be higher for higher-frequency novel senses. The identification of infrequent novel senses remains a challenge.

The top-ranked topic words for the sense corresponding to the maximum in Equation 1 for the highest-ranked distractor, *guess*, are the following: @card@, *post*, ..., *n't*, *comment*, *think*, *subject*, *forum*, *view*, *guess*. This sense seems to correspond to usages of *guess* in the context of online forums, which are better represented in the ukWaC sample than the BNC. Because of the challenges posed by such differences between corpora (discussed in Section 4.2) we are unsurprised to see such an error, but this could be addressed in the future by building comparable cor-

[9] We use the IMS Open Corpus Workbench (`http://cwb.sourceforge.net/`) to extract the usages of our target lemmas from the corpora. This extraction process fails in some cases, and so we also eliminate such items from our dataset.

[10] `http://www.sketchengine.co.uk/`

Lemma	Topic Selection Methodology Nov			Oracle (single topic)			Oracle (multiple topics)		
	Precision	Recall	F-score	Precision	Recall	F-score	Precision	Recall	F-score
domain (n)	1.00	0.29	0.45	1.00	0.56	0.72	0.97	0.88	0.92
export (v)	0.93	0.96	0.95	0.93	0.96	0.95	0.90	1.00	0.95
mirror (n)	0.67	1.00	0.80	0.67	1.00	0.80	0.67	1.00	0.80
poster (n)	0.00	0.00	0.00	0.44	1.00	0.62	0.44	1.00	0.62
worm (n)	0.93	0.90	0.92	0.93	0.90	0.92	0.86	1.00	0.92

Table 5: Results for identifying the gold-standard novel senses based on the three topic selection methodologies of: (1) Nov; (2) oracle selection of a single topic; and (3) oracle selection of multiple topics.

pora for use in this application.

Having demonstrated that our method for identifying novel senses can distinguish lemmas that have a novel sense in one corpus compared to another from those that do not, we now consider whether this method can also automatically identify the *usages* of the induced novel sense.

For each lemma with a gold-standard novel sense, we define the automatically-induced novel sense to be the single sense corresponding to the maximum in Equation 1. We then compute the precision, recall, and F-score of this novel sense with respect to the gold-standard novel sense, based on the 100 annotated tokens for each of the 5 lemmas with a novel sense. The results are shown in the first three numeric columns of Table 5.

In the case of *export* and *worm* the results are remarkably good, with precision and recall both over 0.90. For *domain*, the low recall is a result of the majority of usages of the gold-standard novel sense ("Internet domain") being split across two induced senses — the top-two highest ranked induced senses according to Equation 1. The poor performance for *poster* is unsurprising due to the very low frequency of this lemma's gold-standard novel sense.

These results are based on our novelty ranking method ("Nov"), and the assumption that the novel sense will be represented in a single topic. To evaluate the theoretical upper-bound for a topic-ranking method which uses our HDP-based WSI method and selects a single topic to capture the novel sense, we next evaluate an optimal topic selection approach. In the middle three numeric columns of Table 5, we present results for an experimental setup in which the single best induced sense — in terms of F-score — is selected as the novel sense by an oracle. We see big improvements in F-score for *domain* and *poster*. This encouraging result suggests refining the sense selection heuristic could theoretically improve our method for identifying novel senses, and that the topic modelling approach proposed in this paper has considerable promise for automatic novel sense detection. Of particular note is the result for *poster*: although the gold-standard novel sense of *poster* is rare, all of its usages are grouped into a single topic.

Finally, we consider whether an oracle which can select the best subset of induced senses — in terms of F-score — as the novel sense could offer further improvements. In this case — results shown in the final three columns of Table 5 — we again see an increase in F-score to 0.92 for *domain*. For this lemma the gold-standard novel sense usages were split across multiple induced topics, and so we are unsurprised to find that a method which is able to select multiple topics as the novel sense performs well. Based on these findings, in future work we plan to consider alternative formulations of novelty.

5 Conclusion

We propose the application of topic modelling to the task of word sense induction (WSI), starting with a simple LDA-based methodology with a fixed number of senses, and culminating in a nonparametric method based on a Hierarchical Dirichlet Process (HDP), which automatically learns the number of senses for a given target word. Our HDP-based method outperforms all methods over the SemEval-2010 WSI dataset, and is also superior to other topic modelling-based approaches to WSI based on the SemEval-2007 dataset. We applied the proposed WSI model to the task of identifying words which have taken on new senses, including identifying the token occurrences of the new word sense. Over a small dataset developed in this research, we achieved highly encouraging results.

References

Eneko Agirre and Aitor Soroa. 2007. SemEval-2007 Task 02: Evaluating word sense induction and discrimination systems. In *Proceedings of the Fourth International Workshop on Semantic Evaluations (SemEval-2007)*, pages 7–12, Prague, Czech Republic.

John Ayto. 2006. *Movers and Shakers: A Chronology of Words that Shaped our Age*. Oxford University Press, Oxford.

David Bamman and Gregory Crane. 2011. Measuring historical word sense variation. In *Proceedings of the 2011 Joint International Conference on Digital Libraries (JCDL 2011)*, pages 1–10, Ottawa, Canada.

D. Blei, A. Ng, and M. Jordan. 2003. Latent dirichlet allocation. *Journal of Machine Learning Research*, 3:993–1022.

S. Brody and M. Lapata. 2009. Bayesian word sense induction. pages 103–111, Athens, Greece.

Lou Burnard. 2000. *The British National Corpus Users Reference Guide*. Oxford University Computing Services.

Paul Cook and Suzanne Stevenson. 2010. Automatically identifying changes in the semantic orientation of words. In *Proceedings of the Seventh International Conference on Language Resources and Evaluation (LREC 2010)*, pages 28–34, Valletta, Malta.

Marie-Catherine De Marneffe, Bill Maccartney, and Christopher D. Manning. 2006. Generating typed dependency parses from phrase structure parses. Genoa, Italy.

Christiane Fellbaum, editor. 1998. *WordNet: An Electronic Lexical Database*. MIT Press, Cambridge, MA.

Adriano Ferraresi, Eros Zanchetta, Marco Baroni, and Silvia Bernardini. 2008. Introducing and evaluating ukwac, a very large web-derived corpus of english. In *Proceedings of the 4th Web as Corpus Workshop: Can we beat Google*, pages 47–54, Marrakech, Morocco.

William A. Gale, Kenneth W. Church, and David Yarowsky. 1992. One sense per discourse. pages 233–237.

Kristina Gulordava and Marco Baroni. 2011. A distributional similarity approach to the detection of semantic change in the Google Books Ngram corpus. In *Proceedings of the GEMS 2011 Workshop on GEometrical Models of Natural Language Semantics*, pages 67–71, Edinburgh, Scotland.

Adam Kilgarriff and David Tugwell. 2002. Sketching words. In Marie-Hélène Corréard, editor, *Lexicography and Natural Language Processing: A Festschrift in Honour of B. T. S. Atkins*, pages 125–137. Euralex, Grenoble, France.

Dan Klein and Christopher D. Manning. 2003. Fast exact inference with a factored model for natural language parsing. In *Advances in Neural Information Processing Systems 15 (NIPS 2002)*, pages 3–10, Whistler, Canada.

Ioannis Korkontzelos and Suresh Manandhar. 2010. Uoy: Graphs of unambiguous vertices for word sense induction and disambiguation. In *Proceedings of the 5th International Workshop on Semantic Evaluation*, pages 355–358, Uppsala, Sweden.

Suresh Manandhar, Ioannis Klapaftis, Dmitriy Dligach, and Sameer Pradhan. 2010. SemEval-2010 Task 14: Word sense induction & disambiguation. In *Proceedings of the 5th International Workshop on Semantic Evaluation*, pages 63–68, Uppsala, Sweden.

Roberto Navigli and Giuseppe Crisafulli. 2010. Inducing word senses to improve web search result clustering. In *Proceedings of the 2010 Conference on Empirical Methods in Natural Language Processing*, pages 116–126, Cambridge, USA.

Zheng-Yu Niu, Dong-Hong Ji, and Chew-Lim Tan. 2007. I2R: Three systems for word sense discrimination, chinese word sense disambiguation, and english word sense disambiguation. In *Proceedings of the Fourth International Workshop on Semantic Evaluations (SemEval-2007)*, pages 177–182, Prague, Czech Republic.

Sebastian Padó and Mirella Lapata. 2007. Dependency-based construction of semantic space models. *Comput. Linguist.*, 33:161–199.

Yves Peirsman, Dirk Geeraerts, and Dirk Speelman. 2010. The automatic identification of lexical variation between language varieties. *Natural Language Engineering*, 16(4):469–491.

Eyal Sagi, Stefan Kaufmann, and Brady Clark. 2009. Semantic density analysis: Comparing word meaning across time and space. In *Proceedings of the EACL 2009 Workshop on GEMS: GEometrical Models of Natural Language Semantics*, pages 104–111, Athens, Greece.

Helmut Schmid. 1994. Probabilistic part-of-speech tagging using decision trees. In *Proceedings of the International Conference on New Methods in Language Processing*, pages 44–49, Manchester, UK.

Hinrich Schutze. 1998. Automatic word sense discrimination. *Computational Linguistics*, 24(1):97–123.

Catherine Soanes and Angus Stevenson, editors. 2008. *The Concise Oxford English Dictionary*. Oxford University Press, eleventh (revised) edition. Oxford Reference Online.

Y. W. Teh, M. I. Jordan, M. J. Beal, and D. M. Blei. 2006. Hierarchical Dirichlet processes. *Journal of the American Statistical Association*, 101:1566–1581.

Della Thompson, editor. 1995. *The Concise Oxford Dictionary of Current English*. Oxford University Press, Oxford, ninth edition.

Xuchen Yao and Benjamin Van Durme. 2011. Non-parametric bayesian word sense induction. In *Proceedings of TextGraphs-6: Graph-based Methods for Natural Language Processing*, pages 10–14, Portland, Oregon.

Learning Language from Perceptual Context

Raymond Mooney
University of Texas at Austin
mooney@cs.utexas.edu

Abstract

Machine learning has become the dominant approach to building natural-language processing systems. However, current approaches generally require a great deal of laboriously constructed human-annotated training data. Ideally, a computer would be able to acquire language like a child by being exposed to linguistic input in the context of a relevant but ambiguous perceptual environment. As a step in this direction, we have developed systems that learn to sportscast simulated robot soccer games and to follow navigation instructions in virtual environments by simply observing sample human linguistic behavior in context. This work builds on our earlier work on supervised learning of semantic parsers that map natural language into a formal meaning representation. In order to apply such methods to learning from observation, we have developed methods that estimate the meaning of sentences given just their ambiguous perceptual context.

Learning for Microblogs with Distant Supervision: Political Forecasting with Twitter

Micol Marchetti-Bowick
Microsoft Corporation
475 Brannan Street
San Francisco, CA 94122
micolmb@microsoft.com

Nathanael Chambers
Department of Computer Science
United States Naval Academy
Annapolis, MD 21409
nchamber@usna.edu

Abstract

Microblogging websites such as Twitter offer a wealth of insight into a population's current mood. Automated approaches to identify general sentiment toward a particular topic often perform two steps: *Topic Identification* and *Sentiment Analysis*. Topic Identification first identifies tweets that are relevant to a desired topic (e.g., a politician or event), and Sentiment Analysis extracts each tweet's attitude toward the topic. Many techniques for Topic Identification simply involve selecting tweets using a keyword search. Here, we present an approach that instead uses distant supervision to train a classifier on the tweets returned by the search. We show that distant supervision leads to improved performance in the Topic Identification task as well in the downstream Sentiment Analysis stage. We then use a system that incorporates distant supervision into both stages to analyze the sentiment toward President Obama expressed in a dataset of tweets. Our results better correlate with Gallup's Presidential Job Approval polls than previous work. Finally, we discover a surprising baseline that outperforms previous work without a Topic Identification stage.

1 Introduction

Social networks and blogs contain a wealth of data about how the general public views products, campaigns, events, and people. Automated algorithms can use this data to provide instant feedback on what people are saying about a topic. Two challenges in building such algorithms are (1) identifying topic-relevant posts, and (2) identifying the attitude of each post toward the topic. This paper studies distant supervision (Mintz et al., 2009) as a solution to both challenges. We apply our approach to the problem of predicting Presidential Job Approval polls from Twitter data, and we present results that improve on previous work in this area. We also present a novel baseline that performs remarkably well without using topic identification.

Topic identification is the task of identifying text that discusses a topic of interest. Most previous work on microblogs uses simple keyword searches to find topic-relevant tweets on the assumption that short tweets do not need more sophisticated processing. For instance, searches for the name "Obama" have been assumed to return a representative set of tweets about the U.S. President (O'Connor et al., 2010). One of the main contributions of this paper is to show that keyword search can lead to noisy results, and that the same keywords can instead be used in a distantly supervised framework to yield improved performance.

Distant supervision uses noisy signals in text as positive labels to train classifiers. For instance, the token "Obama" can be used to identify a series of tweets that discuss U.S. President Barack Obama. Although searching for token matches can return false positives, using the resulting tweets as positive training examples provides supervision from a distance. This paper experiments with several diverse sets of keywords to train distantly supervised classifiers for topic identification. We evaluate each classifier on a hand-labeled dataset of political and apolitical tweets, and demonstrate an improvement in F1 score over simple keyword search (.39 to .90 in the best case). We also make available the first labeled dataset for topic identification in politics to encourage future work.

Sentiment analysis encompasses a broad field of research, but most microblog work focuses on two moods: positive and negative sentiment.

Algorithms to identify these moods range from matching words in a sentiment lexicon to training classifiers with a hand-labeled corpus. Since labeling corpora is expensive, recent work on Twitter uses emoticons (i.e., ASCII smiley faces such as *:-(* and *:-)*) as noisy labels in tweets for distant supervision (Pak and Paroubek, 2010; Davidov et al., 2010; Kouloumpis et al., 2011). This paper presents new analysis of the downstream effects of topic identification on sentiment classifiers and their application to political forecasting.

Interest in measuring the political mood of a country has recently grown (O'Connor et al., 2010; Tumasjan et al., 2010; Gonzalez-Bailon et al., 2010; Carvalho et al., 2011; Tan et al., 2011). Here we compare our sentiment results to Presidential Job Approval polls and show that the sentiment scores produced by our system are positively correlated with both the *Approval* and *Disapproval* job ratings.

In this paper we present a method for coupling two distantly supervised algorithms for topic identification and sentiment classification on Twitter. In Section 4, we describe our approach to topic identification and present a new annotated corpus of political tweets for future study. In Section 5, we apply distant supervision to sentiment analysis. Finally, Section 6 discusses our system's performance on modeling Presidential Job Approval ratings from Twitter data.

2 Previous Work

The past several years have seen sentiment analysis grow into a diverse research area. The idea of sentiment applied to microblogging domains is relatively new, but there are numerous recent publications on the subject. Since this paper focuses on the microblog setting, we concentrate on these contributions here.

The most straightforward approach to sentiment analysis is using a sentiment *lexicon* to label tweets based on how many sentiment words appear. This approach tends to be used by applications that measure the general mood of a population. O'Connor et al. (2010) use a ratio of positive and negative word counts on Twitter, Kramer (2010) counts lexicon words on Facebook, and Thelwall (2011) uses the publicly available SentiStrength algorithm to make weighted counts of keywords based on predefined polarity strengths.

In contrast to lexicons, many approaches instead focus on ways to train supervised classifiers. However, labeled data is expensive to create, and examples of Twitter classifiers trained on hand-labeled data are few (Jiang et al., 2011). Instead, distant supervision has grown in popularity. These algorithms use emoticons to serve as semantic indicators for sentiment. For instance, a sad face (e.g., *:-(*) serves as a noisy label for a negative mood. Read (2005) was the first to suggest emoticons for UseNet data, followed by Go et al. (Go et al., 2009) on Twitter, and many others since (Bifet and Frank, 2010; Pak and Paroubek, 2010; Davidov et al., 2010; Kouloumpis et al., 2011). Hashtags (e.g., *#cool* and *#happy*) have also been used as noisy sentiment labels (Davidov et al., 2010; Kouloumpis et al., 2011). Finally, multiple models can be blended into a single classifier (Barbosa and Feng, 2010). Here, we adopt the emoticon algorithm for sentiment analysis, and evaluate it on a specific domain (politics).

Topic identification in Twitter has received much less attention than sentiment analysis. The majority of approaches simply select a single keyword (e.g., "Obama") to represent their topic (e.g., "US President") and retrieve all tweets that contain the word (O'Connor et al., 2010; Tumasjan et al., 2010; Tan et al., 2011). The underlying assumption is that the keyword is precise, and due to the vast number of tweets, the search will return a large enough dataset to measure sentiment toward that topic. In this work, we instead use a distantly supervised system similar in spirit to those recently applied to sentiment analysis.

Finally, we evaluate the approaches presented in this paper on the domain of politics. Tumasjan et al. (2010) showed that the results of a recent German election could be predicted through frequency counts with remarkable accuracy. Most similar to this paper is that of O'Connor et al. (2010), in which tweets relating to President Obama are retrieved with a keyword search and a sentiment lexicon is used to measure overall approval. This extracted approval ratio is then compared to Gallup's Presidential Job Approval polling data. We directly compare their results with various distantly supervised approaches.

3 Datasets

The experiments in this paper use seven months of tweets from Twitter (www.twitter.com) collected between June 1, 2009 and December 31, 2009. The corpus contains over 476 million tweets labeled with usernames and timestamps, collected through Twitter's 'spritzer' API without keyword filtering. Tweets are aligned with polling data in Section 6 using their timestamps.

The full system is evaluated against the publicly available daily Presidential Job Approval polling data from Gallup[1]. Every day, Gallup asks 1,500 adults in the United States about whether they approve or disapprove of "the job President Obama is doing as president." The results are compiled into two trend lines for *Approval* and *Disapproval* ratings, as shown in Figure 1. We compare our positive and negative sentiment scores against these two trends.

4 Topic Identification

This section addresses the task of **Topic Identification** in the context of microblogs. While the general field of topic identification is broad, its use on microblogs has been somewhat limited. Previous work on the political domain simply uses keywords to identify topic-specific tweets (e.g., O'Connor et al. (2010) use "Obama" to find presidential tweets). This section shows that *distant supervision* can use the same keywords to build a classifier that is much more robust to noise than approaches that use pure keyword search.

4.1 Distant Supervision

Distant supervision uses noisy signals to identify positive examples of a topic in the face of unlabeled data. As described in Section 2, recent sentiment analysis work has applied distant supervision using emoticons as the signals. The approach extracts tweets with ASCII smiley faces (e.g., *:)* and *;)*) and builds classifiers trained on these positive examples. We apply distant supervision to topic identification and evaluate its effectiveness on this subtask.

As with sentiment analysis, we need to collect positive and negative examples of tweets about the target topic. Instead of emoticons, we extract positive tweets containing one or more predefined keywords. Negative tweets are randomly chosen from the corpus. Examples of positive and negative tweets that can be used to train a classifier based on the keyword "Obama" are given here:

[1] http://gallup.com/poll/113980/gallup-daily-obama-job-approval.aspx

ID	Type	Keywords
PC-1	Obama	*obama*
PC-2	General	*republican, democrat, senate, congress, government*
PC-3	Topic	*health care, economy, tax cuts, tea party, bailout, sotomayor*
PC-4	Politician	*obama, biden, mccain, reed, pelosi, clinton, palin*
PC-5	Ideology	*liberal, conservative, progressive, socialist, capitalist*

Table 1: The keywords used to select positive training sets for each political classifier (a subset of all PC-3 and PC-5 keywords are shown to conserve space).

> **positive:** *LOL, obama made a bears reference in green bay. uh oh.*
>
> **negative:** *New blog up! It regards the new iPhone 3G S: <URL>*

We then use these automatically extracted datasets to train a multinomial Naive Bayes classifier. Before feature collection, the text is normalized as follows: (a) all links to photos (twitpics) are replaced with a single generic token, (b) all non-twitpic URLs are replaced with a token, (c) all user references (e.g., *@MyFriendBob*) are collapsed, (d) all numbers are collapsed to INT, (e) tokens containing the same letter twice or more in a row are condensed to a two-letter string (e.g. the word *ahhhhh* becomes *ahh*), (f) lowercase the text and insert spaces between words and punctuation. The text of each tweet is then tokenized, and the tokens are used to collect unigram and bigram features. All features that occur fewer than 10 times in the training corpus are ignored.

Finally, after training a classifier on this dataset, every tweet in the corpus is classified as either positive (i.e., relevant to the topic) or negative (i.e., irrelevant). The positive tweets are then sent to the second sentiment analysis stage.

4.2 Keyword Selection

Keywords are the input to our proposed distantly supervised system, and of course, the input to previous work that relies on keyword search. We evaluate classifiers based on different keywords to measure the effects of keyword selection.

O'Connor et al. (2010) used the keywords "Obama" and "McCain", and Tumasjan et al. (2010) simply extracted tweets containing Germany's political party names. Both approaches extracted matching tweets, considered them rele-

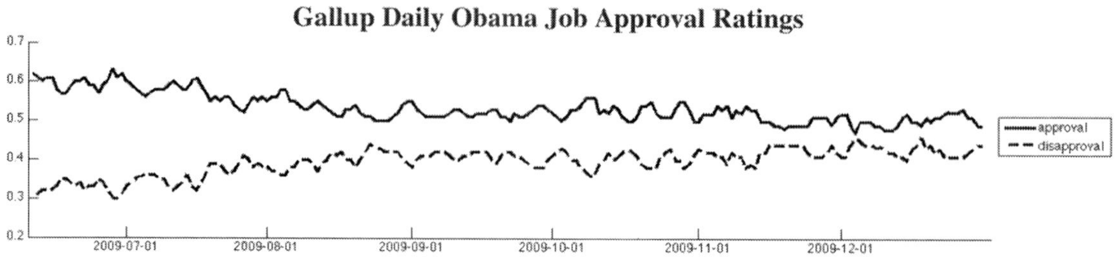

Figure 1: Gallup presidential job Approval and Disapproval ratings measured between June and Dec 2009.

vant (correctly, in many cases), and applied sentiment analysis. However, different keywords may result in very different extractions. We instead attempted to build a generic "political" topic classifier. To do this, we experimented with the five different sets of keywords shown in Table 1. For each set, we extracted all tweets matching one or more keywords, and created a balanced positive/negative training set by then selecting negative examples randomly from non-matching tweets. A couple examples of ideology (PC-5) extractions are shown here:

> *You often hear of deontologist libertarians and utilitarian* ***liberals*** *but are there any Aristotelian socialists?*
>
> *<url> - Then, slather on a* ***liberal*** *amount of plaster, sand down smooth, and paint however you want. I hope this helps!*

The second tweet is an example of the noisy nature of keyword extraction. Most extractions are accurate, but different keywords retrieve very different sets of tweets. Examples for the political topics (PC-3) are shown here:

> *RT @PoliticalMath: hope the president's* ***health care*** *predictions <url> are better than his stimulus predictions <url>*
>
> *@adamjschmidt You mean we could have chosen* ***health care*** *for every man woman and child in America or the Iraq war?*

Each keyword set builds a classifier using the approach described in Section 4.1.

4.3 Labeled Datasets

In order to evaluate distant supervision against keyword search, we created two new labeled datasets of political and apolitical tweets.

The **Political Dataset** is an amalgamation of all four keyword extractions (PC-1 is a subset of PC-4) listed in Table 1. It consists of 2,000 tweets randomly chosen from the keyword searches of PC-2, PC-3, PC-4, and PC-5 with 500 tweets from each. This combined dataset enables an evaluation of how well each classifier can identify tweets from other classifiers. The **General Dataset** contains 2,000 random tweets from the entire corpus. This dataset allows us to evaluate how well classifiers identify political tweets in the wild.

This paper's authors initially annotated the same 200 tweets in the General Dataset to compute inter-annotator agreement. The Kappa was 0.66, which is typically considered *good* agreement. Most disagreements occurred over tweets about money and the economy. We then split the remaining portions of the two datasets between the two annotators. The Political Dataset contains 1,691 political and 309 apolitical tweets, and the General Dataset contains 28 political tweets and 1,978 apolitical tweets. These two datasets of 2000 tweets each are publicly available for future evaluation and comparison to this work[2].

4.4 Experiments

Our first experiment addresses the question of keyword variance. We measure performance on the Political Dataset, a combination of all of our proposed political keywords. Each keyword set contributed to 25% of the dataset, so the evaluation measures the extent to which a classifier identifies other keyword tweets. We classified the 2000 tweets with the five *distantly supervised* classifiers and the one "Obama" *keyword* extractor from O'Connor et al. (2010).

Results are shown on the left side of Figure 2. Precision and recall calculate correct identification of the political label. The five distantly supervised approaches perform similarly, and show remarkable robustness despite their different training sets. In contrast, the keyword extractor only

[2] http://www.usna.edu/cs/nchamber/data/twitter

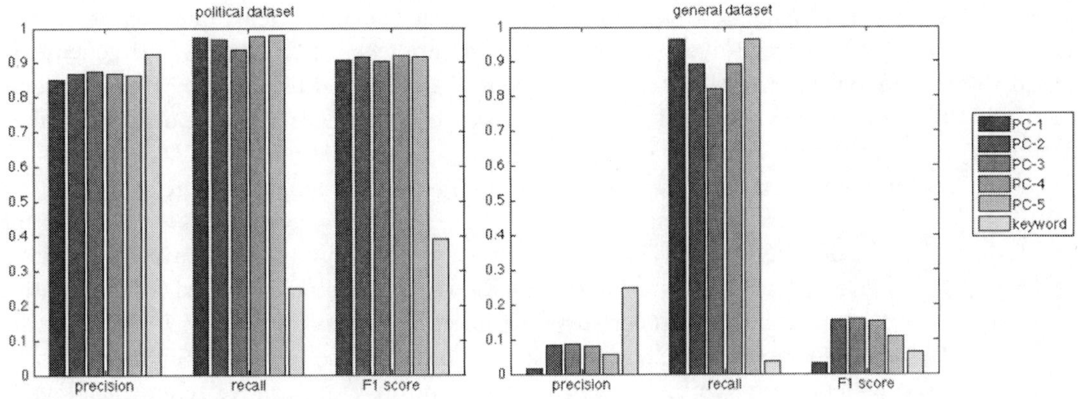

Figure 2: Five distantly supervised classifiers and the Obama keyword classifier. Left panel: the Political Dataset of political tweets. Right panel: the General Dataset representative of Twitter as a whole.

captures about a quarter of the political tweets. PC-1 is the distantly supervised analog to the Obama keyword extractor, and we see that distant supervision increases its F1 score dramatically from 0.39 to 0.90.

The second evaluation addresses the question of classifier performance on Twitter as a whole, not just on a political dataset. We evaluate on the General Dataset just as on the Political Dataset. Results are shown on the right side of Figure 2. Most tweets posted to Twitter are not about politics, so the apolitical label dominates this more representative dataset. Again, the five distant supervision classifiers have similar results. The Obama keyword search has the highest precision, but drastically sacrifices recall. Four of the five classifiers outperform keyword search in F1 score.

4.5 Discussion

The Political Dataset results show that distant supervision adds robustness to a keyword search. The distantly supervised "Obama" classifier (PC-1) improved the basic "Obama" keyword search by 0.51 absolute F1 points. Furthermore, distant supervision doesn't require additional human input, but simply adds a trained classifier. Two example tweets that an Obama keyword search misses but that its distantly supervised analog captures are shown here:

> *Why does Congress get to opt out of the Obummercare and we can't. A company gets fined if they don't comply. Kiss freedom goodbye.*

> *I agree with the lady from california, I am sixty six years old and for the first time in my life I am ashamed of our government.*

These results also illustrate that distant supervision allows for flexibility in construction of the classifier. Different keywords show little change in classifier performance.

The General Dataset experiment evaluates classifier performance in the wild. The keyword approach again scores below those trained on noisy labels. It classifies most tweets as apolitical and thus achieves very low recall for tweets that are actually about politics. On the other hand, distant supervision creates classifiers that over-extract political tweets. This is a result of using balanced datasets in training; such effects can be mitigated by changing the training balance. Even so, four of the five distantly trained classifiers score higher than the raw keyword approach. The only underperformer was PC-1, which suggests that when building a classifier for a relatively broad topic like politics, a variety of keywords is important.

The next section takes the output from our classifiers (i.e., our topic-relevant tweets) and evaluates a fully automated sentiment analysis algorithm against real-world polling data.

5 Targeted Sentiment Analysis

The previous section evaluated algorithms that extract topic-relevant tweets. We now evaluate methods to distill the overall sentiment that they express. This section compares two common approaches to sentiment analysis.

We first replicated the technique used in O'Connor et al. (2010), in which a lexicon of positive and negative sentiment words called OpinionFinder (Wilson and Hoffmann, 2005) is used to evaluate the sentiment of each tweet (others have used similar lexicons (Kramer, 2010; Thelwall et al., 2010)). We evaluate our full distantly supervised approach to theirs. We also experimented with SentiStrength, a lexicon-based program built to identify sentiment in online comments of the social media website, MySpace. Though MySpace is close in genre to Twitter, we did not observe a performance gain. All reported results thus use OpinionFinder to facilitate a more accurate comparison with previous work.

Second, we built a distantly supervised system using tweets containing emoticons as done in previous work (Read, 2005; Go et al., 2009; Bifet and Frank, 2010; Pak and Paroubek, 2010; Davidov et al., 2010; Kouloumpis et al., 2011). Although distant supervision has previously been shown to outperform sentiment lexicons, these evaluations do not consider the extra topic identification step.

5.1 Sentiment Lexicon

The OpinionFinder lexicon is a list of 2,304 positive and 4,151 negative sentiment terms (Wilson and Hoffmann, 2005). We ignore neutral words in the lexicon and we do not differentiate between *weak* and *strong* sentiment words. A tweet is labeled positive if it contains any positive terms, and negative if it contains any negative terms. A tweet can be marked as both positive and negative, and if a tweet contains words in neither category, it is marked neutral. This procedure is the same as used by O'Connor et al. (2010). The sentiment scores S_{pos} and S_{neg} for a given set of N tweets are calculated as follows:

$$S_{pos} = \frac{\sum_x 1\{x_{label} = positive\}}{N} \tag{1}$$

$$S_{pos} = \frac{\sum_x 1\{x_{label} = negative\}}{N} \tag{2}$$

where $1\{x_{label} = positive\}$ is 1 if the tweet x is labeled positive, and N is the number of tweets in the corpus. For the sake of comparison, we also calculate a **sentiment ratio** as done in O'Connor et al. (2010):

$$S_{ratio} = \frac{\sum_x 1\{x_{label} = positive\}}{\sum_x 1\{x_{label} = negative\}} \tag{3}$$

5.2 Distant Supervision

To build a trained classifier, we automatically generated a positive training set by searching for tweets that contain at least one positive emoticon and no negative emoticons. We generated a negative training set using an analogous process. The emoticon symbols used for positive sentiment were *:) =) :-) :] =] :-] :} :o) :D =D :-D :P =P :-P C:*. Negative emoticons were *:(=(:-(:[=[:-[:{ :-c :c} D: D= :S :/ =/ :-/ :'(:_(*. Using this data, we train a multinomial Naive Bayes classifier using the same method used for the political classifiers described in Section 4.1. This classifier is then used to label topic-specific tweets as expressing positive or negative sentiment. Finally, the three overall sentiment scores S_{pos}, S_{neg}, and S_{ratio} are calculated from the results.

6 Predicting Approval Polls

This section uses the two-stage Targeted Sentiment Analysis system described above in a real-world setting. We analyze the sentiment of Twitter users toward U.S. President Barack Obama. This allows us to both evaluate distant supervision against previous work on the topic, and demonstrate a practical application of the approach.

6.1 Experiment Setup

The following experiments combine both topic identification and sentiment analysis. The previous sections described six topic identification approaches, and two sentiment analysis approaches. We evaluate all combinations of these systems, and compare their final sentiment scores for each day in the nearly seven-month period over which our dataset spans.

Gallup's Daily Job Approval reports two numbers: Approval and Disapproval. We calculate individual sentiment scores S_{pos} and S_{neg} for each day, and compare the two sets of trends using Pearson's correlation coefficient. O'Connor et al. do not explicitly evaluate these two, but instead use the ratio S_{ratio}. We also calculate this daily ratio from Gallup for comparison purposes by dividing the Approval by the Disapproval.

6.2 Results and Discussion

The first set of results uses the lexicon-based classifier for sentiment analysis and compares the different topic identification approaches. The first table in Table 2 reports Pearson's correlation coefficient with Gallup's Approval and Disapproval ratings. Regardless of the Topic classifier, all

Sentiment Lexicon

Topic Classifier	Approval	Disapproval
keyword	-0.22	0.42
PC-1	-0.65	0.71
PC-2	-0.61	0.71
PC-3	-0.51	0.65
PC-4	-0.49	0.60
PC-5	-0.65	0.74

Distantly Supervised Sentiment

Topic Classifier	Approval	Disapproval
keyword	0.27	0.38
PC-1	**0.71**	**0.73**
PC-2	0.33	0.46
PC-3	0.05	0.31
PC-4	0.08	0.26
PC-5	0.54	0.62

Table 2: Correlation between Gallup polling data and the extracted sentiment with a lexicon (trends shown in Figure 3) and distant supervision (Figure 4).

Sentiment Lexicon

keyword	PC-1	PC-2	PC-3	PC-4	PC-5
.22	.63	.46	.33	.27	.61

Distantly Supervised Sentiment

keyword	PC-1	PC-2	PC-3	PC-4	PC-5
.40	.64	.46	.30	.28	.60

Table 3: Correlation between Gallup Approval / Disapproval ratio and extracted sentiment ratio scores.

systems inversely correlate with Presidential Approval. However, they correlate well with Disapproval. Figure 3 graphically shows the trend lines for the keyword and the distantly supervised system PC-1. The visualization illustrates how the keyword-based approach is highly influenced by day-by-day changes, whereas PC-1 displays a much smoother trend.

The second set of results uses distant supervision for sentiment analysis and again varies the topic identification approach. The second table in Table 2 gives the correlation numbers and Figure 4 shows the keyword and PC-1 trend lines.The results are widely better than when a lexicon is used for sentiment analysis. Approval is no longer inversely correlated, and two of the distantly supervised systems strongly correlate (PC-1, PC-5).

The best performing system (PC-1) used distant supervision for both topic identification and sentiment analysis. Pearson's correlation coefficient for this approach is 0.71 with Approval and 0.73 with Disapproval.

Finally, we compute the ratio S_{ratio} between the positive and negative sentiment scores (Equation 3) to compare to O'Connor et al. (2010). Table 3 shows the results. The distantly supervised topic identification algorithms show little change between a sentiment lexicon or a classifier. However, O'Connor et al.'s keyword approach improves when used with a distantly supervised sentiment classifier (.22 to .40). Merging Approval and Disapproval into one ratio appears to mask the sentiment lexicon's poor correlation with Approval. The ratio may not be an ideal evaluation metric for this reason. Real-world interest in Presidential Approval ratings desire separate Approval and Disapproval scores, as Gallup reports. Our results (Table 2) show that distant supervision avoids a negative correlation with Approval, but the ratio hides this important advantage.

One reason the ratio may mask the negative Approval correlation is because tweets are often classified as both positive and negative by a lexicon (Section 5.1). This could explain the behavior seen in Figure 3 in which both the positive and negative sentiment scores rise over time. However, further experimentation did not rectify this pattern. We revised S_{pos} and S_{neg} to make binary decisions for a lexicon: a tweet is labeled positive if it strictly contains more positive words than negative (and vice versa). Correlation showed little change. Approval was still negatively correlated, Disapproval positive (although less so in both), and the ratio scores actually dropped further. The sentiment ratio continued to hide the poor Approval performance by a lexicon.

6.3 New Baseline: Topic-Neutral Sentiment

Distant supervision for sentiment analysis outperforms that with a sentiment lexicon (Table 2). Distant supervision for topic identification further improves the results (PC-1 v. keyword). The best system uses distant supervision in both stages (PC-1 with distantly supervised sentiment), outperforming the purely keyword-based algorithm of O'Connor et al. (2010). However, the question of how important topic identification is has not yet been addressed here or in the literature.

Both O'Connor et al. (2010) and Tumasjan et al. (2010) created joint systems with two topic identification and sentiment analysis stages. But

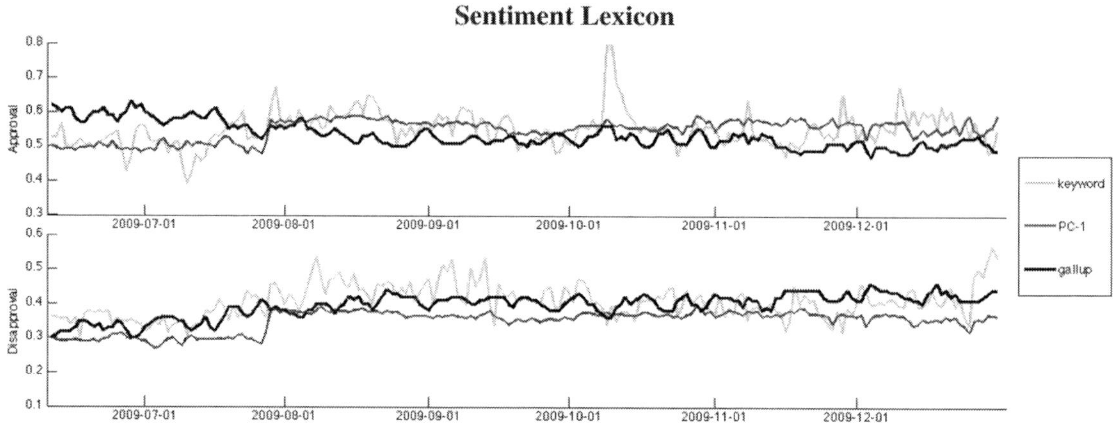

Figure 3: Presidential job approval and disapproval calculated using two different topic identification techniques, and using a sentiment lexicon for sentiment analysis. Gallup polling results are shown in black.

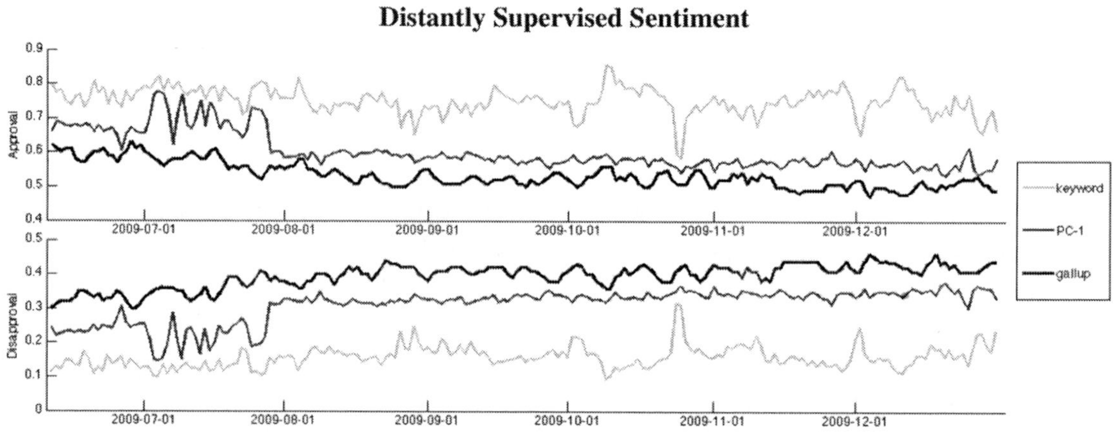

Figure 4: Presidential job approval sentiment scores calculated using two different topic identification techniques, and using the emoticon classifier for sentiment analysis. Gallup polling results are shown in black.

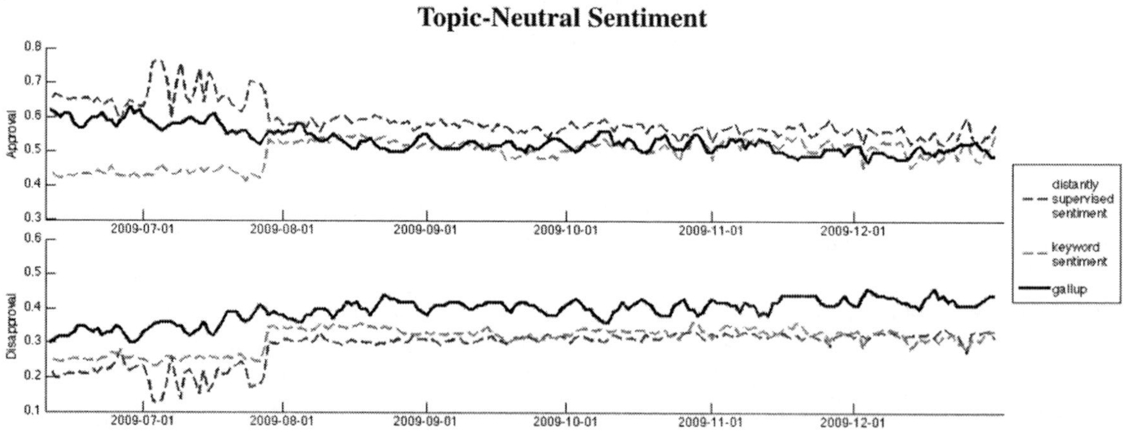

Figure 5: Presidential job approval sentiment scores calculated using the entire twitter corpus, with two different techniques for sentiment analysis. Gallup polling results are shown in black for comparison.

Topic-Neutral Sentiment

Algorithm	Approval	Disapproval
Distant Sup.	**0.69**	**0.74**
Keyword Lexicon	-0.63	0.69

Table 4: Pearson's correlation coefficient of Sentiment Analysis without Topic Identification.

what if the topic identification step were removed and sentiment analysis instead run on the entire Twitter corpus? To answer this question, we ran the distantly supervised emoticon classifier to classify *all* tweets in the 7 months of Twitter data. For each day, we computed the positive and negative sentiment scores as above. The evaluation is identical, except for the removal of topic identification. Correlation results are shown in Table 4.

This baseline parallels the results seen when topic identification is used: the sentiment lexicon is again inversely correlated with Approval, and distant supervision outperforms the lexicon approach in both ratings. This is not surprising given previous distantly supervised work on sentiment analysis (Go et al., 2009; Davidov et al., 2010; Kouloumpis et al., 2011). However, our distant supervision also performs as well as the best performing *topic-specific* system. The best performing topic classifier, PC-1, correlated with Approval with r=0.71 (0.69 here) and Disapproval with r=0.73 (0.74 here). Computing overall sentiment on Twitter performs as well as political-specific sentiment. This unintuitive result suggests a new baseline that all topic-based systems should compute.

7 Discussion

This paper introduces a new methodology for gleaning topic-specific sentiment information. We highlight four main contributions here.

First, this work is one of the first to evaluate distant supervision for topic identification. All five political classifiers outperformed the lexicon-driven keyword equivalent that has been widely used in the past. Our model achieved .90 F1 compared to the keyword .39 F1 on our political tweet dataset. On twitter as a whole, distant supervision increased F1 by over 100%. The results also suggest that performance is relatively insensitive to the specific choice of seed keywords that are used to select the training set for the political classifier.

Second, the sentiment analysis experiments build upon what has recently been shown in the literature: distant supervision with emoticons is a valuable methodology. We also expand upon prior work by discovering drastic performance differences between positive and negative lexicon words. The OpinionFinder lexicon failed to correlate (inversely) with Gallup's Approval polls, whereas a distantly trained classifier correlated strongly with both Approval and Disapproval (Pearson's .71 and .73). We only tested OpinionFinder and SentiStrength, so it is possible that another lexicon might perform better. However, our results suggest that lexicons vary in their quality across sentiment, and distant supervision may provide more robustness.

Third, our results outperform previous work on Presidential Job Approval prediction (O'Connor et al., 2010). We presented two novel approaches to the domain: a coupled distantly supervised system, and a topic-neutral baseline, both of which outperform previous results. In fact, the baseline surprisingly matches or outperforms the more sophisticated approaches that use topic identification. The baseline correlates .69 with Approval and .74 with Disapproval. This suggests a new baseline that should be used in all topic-specific sentiment applications.

Fourth, we described and made available two new annotated datasets of political tweets to facilitate future work in this area.

Finally, Twitter users are not a representative sample of the U.S. population, yet the high correlation between political sentiment on Twitter and Gallup ratings makes these results all the more intriguing for polling methodologies. Our specific 7-month period of time differs from previous work, and thus we hesitate to draw strong conclusions from our comparisons or to extend implications to non-political domains. Future work should further investigate distant supervision as a tool to assist topic detection in microblogs.

Acknowledgments

We thank Jure Leskovec for the Twitter data, Brendan O'Connor for open and frank correspondence, and the reviewers for helpful suggestions.

References

Luciano Barbosa and Junlan Feng. 2010. Robust sentiment detection on twitter from biased and noisy data. In *Proceedings of the 23rd International Conference on Computational Linguistics (COLING 2010)*.

Albert Bifet and Eibe Frank. 2010. Sentiment knowledge discovery in twitter streaming data. In *Lecture Notes in Computer Science*, volume 6332, pages 1–15.

Paula Carvalho, Luis Sarmento, Jorge Teixeira, and Mario J. Silva. 2011. Liars and saviors in a sentiment annotated corpus of comments to political debates. In *Proceedings of the Association for Computational Linguistics (ACL-2011)*, pages 564–568.

Dmitry Davidov, Oren Tsur, and Ari Rappoport. 2010. Enhanced sentiment learning using twitter hashtags and smileys. In *Proceedings of the 23rd International Conference on Computational Linguistics (COLING 2010)*.

Alec Go, Richa Bhayani, and Lei Huang. 2009. Twitter sentiment classification using distant supervision. Technical report.

Sandra Gonzalez-Bailon, Rafael E. Banchs, and Andreas Kaltenbrunner. 2010. Emotional reactions and the pulse of public opinion: Measuring the impact of political events on the sentiment of online discussions. Technical report.

Long Jiang, Mo Yu, Ming Zhou, Xiaohua Liu, and Tiejun Zhao. 2011. Target-dependent twitter sentiment classification. In *Proceedings of the Association for Computational Linguistics (ACL-2011)*.

Efthymios Kouloumpis, Theresa Wilson, and Johanna Moore. 2011. Twitter sentiment analysis: The good the bad and the omg! In *Proceedings of the Fifth International AAAI Conference on Weblogs and Social Media*.

Adam D. I. Kramer. 2010. An unobtrusive behavioral model of 'gross national happiness'. In *Proceedings of the 28th International Conference on Human Factors in Computing Systems (CHI 2010)*.

Mike Mintz, Steven Bills, Rion Snow, and Dan Jurafsky. 2009. Distant supervision for relation extraction without labeled data. In *Proceedings of the Joint Conference of the 47th Annual Meeting of the ACL and the 4th International Joint Conference on Natural Language Processing of the AFNLP*, ACL '09, pages 1003–1011.

Brendan O'Connor, Ramnath Balasubramanyan, Bryan R. Routledge, and Noah A. Smith. 2010. From tweets to polls: Linking text sentiment to public opinion time series. In *Proceedings of the AAAI Conference on Weblogs and Social Media*.

Alexander Pak and Patrick Paroubek. 2010. Twitter as a corpus for sentiment analysis and opinion mining. In *Proceedings of the Seventh International Conference On Language Resources and Evaluation (LREC)*.

Jonathon Read. 2005. Using emoticons to reduce dependency in machine learning techniques for sentiment classification. In *Proceedings of the ACL Student Research Workshop (ACL-2005)*.

Chenhao Tan, Lillian Lee, Jie Tang, Long Jiang, Ming Zhou, and Ping Li. 2011. User-level sentiment analysis incorporating social networks. In *Proceedings of the 17th ACM SIGKDD Conference on Knowledge Discovery and Data Mining*.

Mike Thelwall, Kevan Buckley, Georgios Paltoglou, Di Cai, and Arvid Kappas. 2010. Sentiment strength detection in short informal text. *Journal of the American Society for Information Science and Technology*, 61(12):2544–2558.

Mike Thelwall, Kevan Buckley, and Georgios Paltoglou. 2011. Sentiment in twitter events. *Journal of the American Society for Information Science and Technology*, 62(2):406–418.

Andranik Tumasjan, Timm O. Sprenger, Philipp G. Sandner, and Isabell M. Welpe. 2010. Election forecasts with twitter: How 140 characters reflect the political landscape. *Social Science Computer Review*.

J.; Wilson, T.; Wiebe and P. Hoffmann. 2005. Recognizing contextual polarity in phrase-level sentiment analysis. In *Proceedings of the Conference on Human Language Technology and Empirical Methods in Natural Language Processing*.

Learning from evolving data streams: online triage of bug reports

Grzegorz Chrupala
Spoken Language Systems
Saarland University
gchrupala@lsv.uni-saarland.de

Abstract

Open issue trackers are a type of social media that has received relatively little attention from the text-mining community. We investigate the problems inherent in learning to triage bug reports from time-varying data. We demonstrate that concept drift is an important consideration. We show the effectiveness of online learning algorithms by evaluating them on several bug report datasets collected from open issue trackers associated with large open-source projects. We make this collection of data publicly available.

1 Introduction

There has been relatively little research to date on applying machine learning and Natural Language Processing techniques to automate software project workflows. In this paper we address the problem of bug report triage.

1.1 Issue tracking

Large software projects typically track defect reports, feature requests and other issue reports using an issue tracker system. Open source projects tend to use trackers which are open to both developers and users. If the product has many users its tracker can receive an overwhelming number of issue reports: Mozilla was receiving almost 300 reports per day in 2006 (Anvik et al. 2006). Someone has to monitor those reports and **triage** them, that is decide which component they affect and which developer or team of developers should be responsible for analyzing them and fixing the reported defects. An automated agent assisting the staff responsible for such triage has the potential to substantially reduce the time and cost of this task.

1.2 Issue trackers as social media

In a large software project with a loose, not strictly hierarchical organization, standards and practices are not exclusively imposed top-down but also tend to spontaneously arise in a bottom-up fashion, arrived at through interaction of individual developers, testers and users. The individuals involved may negotiate practices explicitly, but may also imitate and influence each other via implicitly acquired reputation and status. This process has a strong emergent component: an informal taxonomy may arise and evolve in an issue tracker via the use of free-form tags or labels. Developers, testers and users can attach tags to their issue reports in order to informally classify them. The issue tracking software may give users feedback by informing them which tags were frequently used in the past, or suggest tags based on the content of the report or other information. Through this collaborative, feedback driven process involving both human and machine participants, an evolving consensus on the label inventory and semantics typically arises, without much top-down control (Halpin et al. 2007).

This kind of emergent taxonomy is known as a **folksonomy** or **collaborative tagging** and is very common in the context of social web applications. Large software projects, especially those with open policies and little hierarchical structures, tend to exhibit many of the same emergent social properties as the more prototypical social applications. While this is a useful phenomenon, it presents a special challenge from the machine-learning point of view.

1.3 Concept drift

Many standard supervised approaches in machine-learning assume a stationary distribution from which training examples are independently drawn. The set of training examples is processed as a *batch*, and the resulting learned decision function (such as a classifier) is then used on test items, which are assumed to be drawn from the same stationary distribution.

If we need an automated agent which uses human labels to learn to tag objects the batch learning approach is inadequate. Examples arrive one-by-one in a stream, not as a batch. Even more importantly, both the output (label) distribution and the input distribution from which the examples come are emphatically **not** stationary. As a software project progresses and matures, the type of issues reported is going to change. As project members and users come and go, the vocabulary they use to describe the issues will vary. As the consensus tag folksonomy emerges, the label and training example distribution will evolve. This phenomenon is sometimes referred to as **concept drift** (Widmer and Kubat 1996, Tsymbal 2004).

Early research on learning to triage tended to either not notice the problem (Čubranić and Murphy 2004), or acknowledge but not address it (Anvik et al. 2006): the evaluation these authors used assigned bug reports randomly to training and evaluation sets, discarding the temporal sequencing of the data stream.

Bhattacharya and Neamtiu (2010) explicitly address the issue of online training and evaluation. In their setup, the system predicts the output for an item based only on items preceding it in time. However, their approach to incremental learning is simplistic: they use a batch classifier, but retrain it from scratch after receiving each training example. A fully retrained batch classifier will adapt only slowly to changing data stream, as more recent example have no more influence on the decision function that less recent ones.

Tamrawi et al. (2011) propose an incremental approach to bug triage: the classes are ranked according to a fuzzy set membership function, which is based on incrementally updated feature/class co-occurrence counts. The model is efficient in online classification, but also adapts only slowly.

1.4 Online learning

This paucity of research on online learning from issue tracker streams is rather surprising, given that truly incremental learners have been well-known for many years. In fact one of the first learning algorithms proposed was Rosenblatt's perceptron, a simple mistake-driven discriminative classification algorithm (Rosenblatt 1958). In the current paper we address this situation and show that by using simple, standard online learning methods we can improve on batch or pseudo-online learning. We also show that when using a sophisticated state-of-the-art stochastic gradient descent technique the performance gains can be quite large.

1.5 Contributions

Our main contributions are the following: Firstly, we explicitly show that concept-drift is pervasive and serious in real bug report streams. We then address this problem by leveraging state-of-the-art online learning techniques which automatically track the evolving data stream and incrementally update the model after each data item. We also adopt the continuous evaluation paradigm, where the learner predicts the output for each example before using it to update the model. Secondly, we address the important issue of reproducibility in research in bug triage automation by making available the data sets which we collected and used, in both their raw and preprocessed forms.

2 Open issue-tracker data

Open source software repositories and their associated issue trackers are a naturally occurring source of large amounts of (partially) labeled data. There seems to be growing interest in exploiting this rich resource as evidenced by existing publications as well as the appearance of a dedicated workshop (Working Conference on Mining Software Repositories).

In spite of the fact that the data is publicly available in open repositories, it is not possible to directly compare the results of the research conducted on bug triage so far: authors use non-trivial project-specific filtering, re-labeling and pre-processing heuristics; these steps are usually not specified in enough detail that they could be easily reproduced.

Field	Meaning
Identifier	Issue ID
Title	Short description of issue
Description	Content of issue report, which may include steps to reproduce, error messages, stack traces etc.
Author	ID of report submitter
CCS	List of IDs of people CC'd on the issue report
Labels	List of tags associated with issue
Status	Label describing the current status of the issue (e.g. Invalid, Fixed, Won't Fix)
Assigned To	ID of person who has been assigned to deal with the issue
Published	Date on which issue report was submitted

Table 1: Issue report record

To help remedy this situation we decided to collect data from several open issue trackers, use the minimal amount of simple preprocessing and filter heuristics to get useful input data, and publicly share both the raw and preprocessed data.

We designed a simple record type which acts as a common denominator for several tracker formats. Thus we can use a common representation for issue reports from various trackers. The fields in our record are shown in Table 1.

Below we describe the issue trackers used and the datasets we build from them. As discussed above (and in more detail in Section 4.1), we use progressive validation rather than a split into training and test set. However, in order to avoid developing on the test data, we split each data stream into two substreams, by assigning odd-numbered examples to the test stream and the even-numbered ones to the development stream. We can use the development stream for exploratory data analysis and feature and parameter tuning, and then use progressive validation to evaluate on entirely unseen test data. Below we specify the size and number of unique labels in the development sets; the test sets are very similar in size.

Chromium Chromium is the open source-project behind Google's Chrome browser (`http://code.google.com/p/chromium/`). We retrieved all the bugs from the issue tracker, of which 66,704 have one of the closed statuses. We generated two data sets from the Chromium issues:

- Chromium SUBCOMPONENT. Chromium uses special tags to help triage the bug reports. Tags prefixed with `Area-` specify which subcomponent of the project the bug should be routed to. In some cases more than one `Area-` tag is present. Since this affects less than 1% of reports, for simplicity we treat these as single, compound labels. The development set contains 31,953 items, and 75 unique output labels.
- Chromium ASSIGNED. In this dataset the output is the value of the `assignedTo` field. We discarded issues where the field was left empty, as well as the ones which contained the placeholder value `all-bugs-test.chromium.org`. The development set contains 16,154 items and 591 unique output labels.

Android Android is a mobile operating system project (`http://code.google.com/p/android/`). We retrieved all the bugs reports, of which 6,341 had a closed status. We generated two datasets:

- Android SUBCOMPONENT. The reports which are labeled with tags prefixed with `Component-`. The development set contains 888 items and 12 unique output labels.
- Android ASSIGNED. The output label is the value of the `assignedTo` field. We discarded issues with the field left empty. The development set contains 718 items and 72 unique output labels.

Firefox Firefox is the well-known web-browser project (`https://bugzilla.mozilla.org`).

We obtained a total of 81,987 issues with a closed status.

- Firefox ASSIGNED. We discarded issues where the field was left empty, as well as the ones which contained a placeholder value (`nobody`). The development set contains 12,733 items and 503 unique output labels.

Launchpad Launchpad is an issue tracker run by Canonical Ltd for mostly Ubuntu-related projects (`https://bugs.launchpad.`

net/). We obtained a total of 99,380 issues with a closed status.

- Launchpad ASSIGNED. We discarded issues where the field was left empty. The development set contains 18,634 items and 1,970 unique output labels.

3 Analysis of concept drift

In the introduction we have hypothesized that in issue tracker streams concept drift would be an especially acute problem. In this section we show how class distributions evolve over time in the data we collected.

A time-varying distribution is difficult to summarize with a single number, but it is easy to appreciate in a graph. Figures 1 and 2 show concept drift for several of our data streams. The horizontal axis indexes the position in the data stream. The vertical axis shows the class proportions at each position, averaged over a window containing 7% of all the examples in the stream, i.e. in each thin vertical bar the proportion of colors used corresponds to the smoothed class distribution at a particular position in the stream.

Consider the plot for Chromium SUBCOMPONENT. We can see that a bit before the middle point in the stream class proportions change quite dramatically: The orange BROWSERUI and violet MISC almost disappears, while blue INTERNALS, pink UI and dark red UNDEFINED take over. This likely corresponds to an overhaul in the label inventory and/or recommended best practice for triage in this project. There are also more gradual and smaller scale changes throughout the data stream.

The Android SUBCOMPONENT stream contains much less data so the plot is less smooth, but there are clear transitions in this image also. We see that light blue GOOGLE all but disappears after about two thirds point and the proportion of violet TOOLS and light-green DALVIK dramatically increases.

In Figure 2 we see the evolution of class proportions in the ASSIGNED datasets. Each plot's idiosyncratic shape illustrates that there is wide variation in the amount and nature of concept drift in different software project issue trackers.

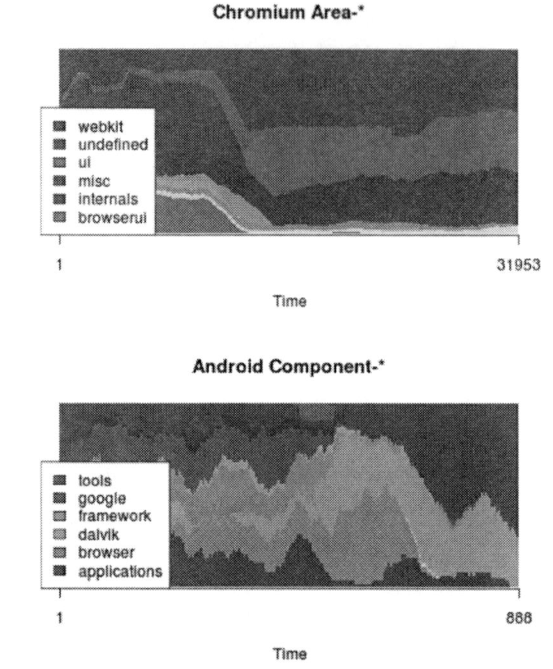

Figure 1: SUBCOMPONENT class distribution change over time

4 Experimental results

In an online setting it is important to use an evaluation regime which closely mimics the continuous use of the system in a real-life situation.

4.1 Progressive validation

When learning from data streams the standard evaluation methodology where data is split into a separate training and test set is not applicable. An evaluation regime know as progressive validation has been used to accurately measure the generalization performance of online algorithms (Blum et al. 1999). Under progressive evaluation, an input example from a temporally ordered sequence is sent to the learner, which returns the prediction. The error incurred on this example is recorded, and the true output is only then sent to the learner which may update its model based on it. The final error is the mean of the per-example errors. Thus even though there is no separate test set, the prediction for each input is generated based on a model trained on examples which do not include it.

In previous work on bug report triage, Bhattacharya and Neamtiu (2010) and Tamrawi et al. (2011) used an evaluation scheme (close to) pro-

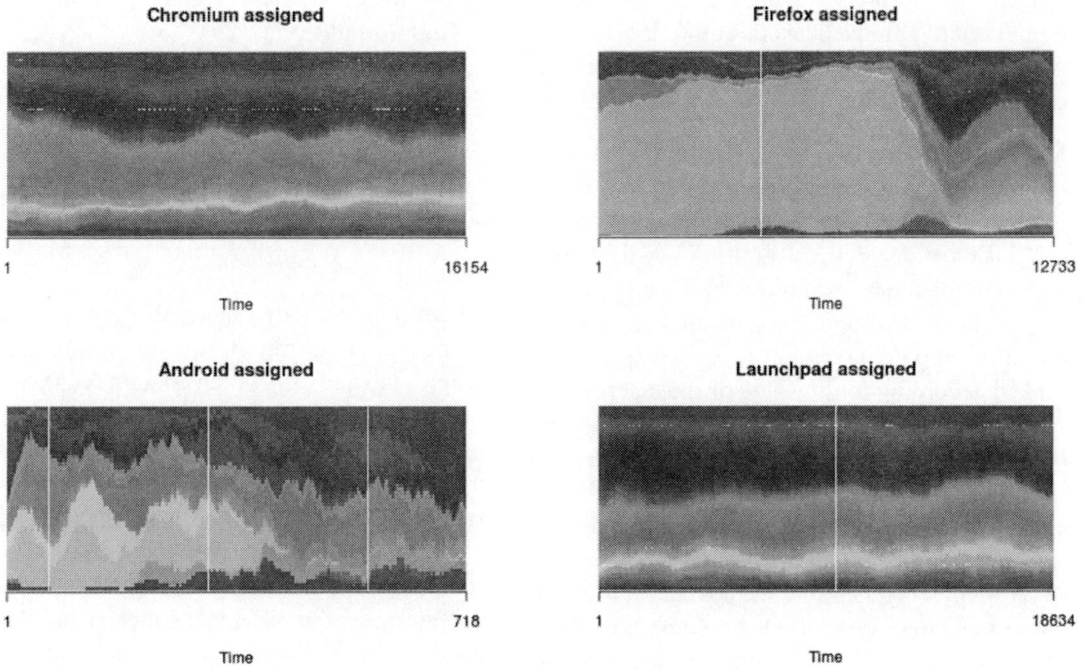

Figure 2: ASSIGNED class distribution change over time

gressive validation. They omit the initial $\frac{1}{11}^{\text{th}}$ of the examples from the mean.

4.2 Mean reciprocal rank

A bug report triaging agent is most likely to be used in a semi-automatic workflow, where a human triager is presented with a ranked list of possible outputs (component labels or developer IDs). As such it is important to evaluate not only accuracy of the top ranking suggesting, but rather the quality of the whole ranked list.

Previous research (Bhattacharya and Neamtiu 2010, Tamrawi et al. 2011) made an attempt at approximating this criterion by reporting scores which indicate whether the true output is present in the top n elements of the ranking, for several values of n. Here we suggest borrowing the mean reciprocal rank (MRR) metric from the information retrieval domain (Voorhees 2000). It is defined as the mean of the reciprocals of the rank at which the true output is found:

$$\text{MRR} = \frac{1}{N} \sum_{i=1}^{N} \text{rank}(i)^{-1}$$

where $\text{rank}(i)$ indicates the rank of the ith true output. MRR has the advantage of providing a single number which summarizes the quality of whole rankings for all the examples. MRR is also a special case of Mean Average Precision when there is only one true output per item.

4.3 Input representation

Since in this paper we focus on the issues related to concept drift and online learning, we kept the feature set relatively simple. We preprocess the text in the issue report title and description fields by removing HTML markup, tokenizing, lowercasing and removing most punctuation. We then extracted the following feature types:

- Title unigram and bigram counts
- Description unigram and bigram counts
- Author ID (binary indicator feature)
- Year, month and day of submission (binary indicator features)

4.4 Models

We tested a simple online baseline, a pseudo-online algorithm which uses a batch model and repeatedly retrains it, an online model used in previous research on bug triage and two generic online learning algorithms.

Window Frequency Baseline This baseline does not use any input features. It outputs the ranked list of labels for the current item based on the relative frequencies of output labels in the window of k previous items. We tested windows of size 100 and 1000 and report the better result.

SVM Minibatch This model uses the multiclass linear Support Vector Machine model (Crammer and Singer 2002) as implemented in SVM Light (Joachims 1999). SVM is known as a state-of-the-art batch model in classification in general and in text categorization in particular. The output classes for an input example are ranked according to the value of the discriminant values returned by the SVM classifier. In order to adapt the model to an online setting we retrain it every n examples on the window of k previous examples. The parameters n and k can have large influence on the prediction, but it is not clear how to set them when learning from streams. Here we chose the values (100,1000) based on how feasible the run time was and on the performance during exploratory experiments on Chromium SUBCOMPONENT. Interestingly, keeping the window parameter relatively small helps performance: a window of 1,000 works better than a window of 5,000.

Perceptron We implemented a single-pass online multiclass Perceptron with a constant learning rate. It maintains a weight vector for each output seen so far: the prediction function ranks outputs according to the inner product of the current example with the corresponding weight vector. The update function takes the true output and the predicted output. If they are not equal, the current input is subtracted from the weight vector corresponding to the predicted output and added to the weight vector corresponding to the true output (see Algorithm 1). We hash each feature to an integer value and use it as the feature's index in the weight vectors in order to bound memory usage in an online setting (Weinberger et al. 2009). The Perceptron is a simple but strong baseline for online learning.

Bugzie This is the model described in Tamrawi et al. (2011). The output classes are ranked according to the fuzzy set membership function defined as follows:

$$\mu(y, X) = 1 - \prod_{x \in X} \left(1 - \frac{n(y,x)}{n(y) + n(x) - n(y,x)}\right)$$

Algorithm 1 Multiclass online perceptron

function PREDICT($Y, \mathbf{W}, \mathbf{x}$)
  return $\{(y, \mathbf{W}_y^T \mathbf{x}) \mid y \in Y\}$

procedure UPDATE($\mathbf{W}, \mathbf{x}, \hat{y}, y$)
  if $\hat{y} \neq y$ **then**
    $\mathbf{W}_{\hat{y}} \leftarrow \mathbf{W}_{\hat{y}} - \mathbf{x}$
    $\mathbf{W}_y \leftarrow \mathbf{W}_y + \mathbf{x}$

where y is the output label, X the set of features in the input issue report, $n(y,x)$ the number of examples labeled as y which contain feature x, $n(y)$ number of examples labeled y and $n(x)$ number of examples containing feature x. The counts are updated online. Tamrawi et al. (2011) also use two so called caches: the label cache keeps the $j\%$ most recent labels and the term cache the k most significant features for each label. Since in Tamrawi et al. (2011)'s experiments the label cache did not affect the results significantly, here we always set j to 100%. We select the optimal k parameter from $\{100, 1000, 5000\}$ based on the development set.

Regression with Stochastic Gradient Descent This model performs online multiclass learning by means of a reduction to regression. The regressor is a linear model trained using Stochastic Gradient Descent (Zhang 2004). SGD updates the current parameter vector $\mathbf{w}^{(t)}$ based on the gradient of the loss incurred by the regressor on the current example $(\mathbf{x}^{(t)}, y^{(t)})$:

$$\mathbf{w}^{(t+1)} = \mathbf{w}^{(t)} - \eta(t)\nabla L(y^{(t)}, \mathbf{w}^{(t)T}\mathbf{x}^{(t)})$$

The parameter $\eta(t)$ is the learning rate at time t, and L is the loss function. We use the squared loss:

$$L(y, \hat{y}) = (y - \hat{y})^2$$

We reduce multiclass learning to regression using a one-vs-all-type scheme, by effectively transforming an example $(\mathbf{x}, y) \in X \times Y$ into $|Y|$ $(\mathbf{x}', y') \in X' \times \{0, 1\}$ examples, where Y is the set of labels seen so far. The transform T is defined as follows:

$$T(\mathbf{x}, y) = \{(\mathbf{x}', I(y = y')) \mid y' \in Y, x'_{h(i,y')} = x_i\}$$

where $h(i, y')$ composes the index i with the label y' (by hashing).

For a new input $\mathbf{x}$ the ranking of the outputs $y \in Y$ is obtained according to the value of the prediction of the base regressor on the binary example corresponding to each class label.

As our basic regression learner we use the efficient implementation of regression via SGD, Vowpal Wabbit (VW) (Langford et al. 2011). VW implements setting adaptive individual learning rates for each feature as proposed by Duchi et al. (2010), McMahan and Streeter (2010).

This is appropriate when there are many sparse features, and is especially useful in learning from text from fast evolving data. The features such as unigram and bigram counts that we rely on are notoriously sparse, and this is exacerbated by the change over time in bug report streams.

4.5 Results

Figures 3 and 4 show the progressive validation results on all the development data streams. The horizontal lines indicate the mean MRR scores for the whole stream. The curves show a moving average of MRR in a window comprised of 7% of the total number of items. In most of the plots it is evident how the prediction performance depends on the concept drift illustrated in the plots in Section 3: for example on Chromium SUBCOMPONENT the performance of all the models drops a bit before the midpoint in the stream while the learners adapt to the change in label distribution that is happening at this time. This is especially pronounced for Bugzie, since it is not able to learn from mistakes and adapt rapidly, but simply accumulates counts.

For five out of the six datasets, Regression SGD gives the best overall performance. On Launchpad ASSIGNED, Bugzie scores higher – we investigate this anomaly below.

Another observation is that the window-based frequency baseline can be quite hard to beat: In three out of the six cases, the minibatch SVM model is no better than the baseline. Bugzie sometimes performs quite well, but for Chromium SUBCOMPONENT and Firefox ASSIGNED it scores below the baseline.

Regarding the quality of the different datasets, an interesting indicator is the relative error reduction by the best model over the baseline (see Table 2). It is especially hard to extract meaningful information about the labeling from the inputs on the Firefox ASSIGNED dataset. One possible cause of this can be that the assignment labeling practices in this project are not consistent: this impression seems to be born out by informal inspection.

Dataset		RER
Chromium	SUB	0.36
Android	SUB	0.38
Chromium	AS	0.21
Android	AS	0.19
Firefox	AS	0.16
Launchpad	AS	0.49

Table 2: Best model's error relative to baseline on the development set

Task	Model	MRR	Acc
Chromium	Window	0.5747	0.3467
	SVM	0.5766	0.4535
	Perceptron	0.5793	0.4393
	Bugzie	0.4971	0.2638
	Regression	**0.7271**	**0.5672**
Android	Window	0.5209	0.3080
	SVM	0.5459	0.4255
	Perceptron	0.5892	0.4390
	Bugzie	0.6281	0.4614
	Regression	**0.7012**	**0.5610**

Table 3: SUBCOMPONENT evaluation results on test set.

On the other hand as the scores in Table 2 indicate, Chromium SUBCOMPONENT, Android SUBCOMPOMENT and Launchpad ASSIGNED contain enough high-quality signal for the best model to substantially outperform the label frequency baseline.

On Launchpad ASSIGNED Regression SGD performs worse than Bugzie. The concept drift plot for these data suggests one reason: there is very little change in class distribution over time as compared to the other datasets. In fact, even though the issue reports in Launchpad range from year 2005 to 2011, the more recent ones are heavily overrepresented: 84% of the items in the development data are from 2011. Thus fast adaptation is less important in this case and Bugzie is able to perform well.

On the other hand, the reason for the less than stellar score achieved with Regression SGD is due to another special feature of this dataset: it has by far the largest number of labels, almost 2,000. This degrades the performance for the one-vs-all scheme we use with SGD Regression. Preliminary investigation indicates that the problem is mostly caused by our application of the "hash-

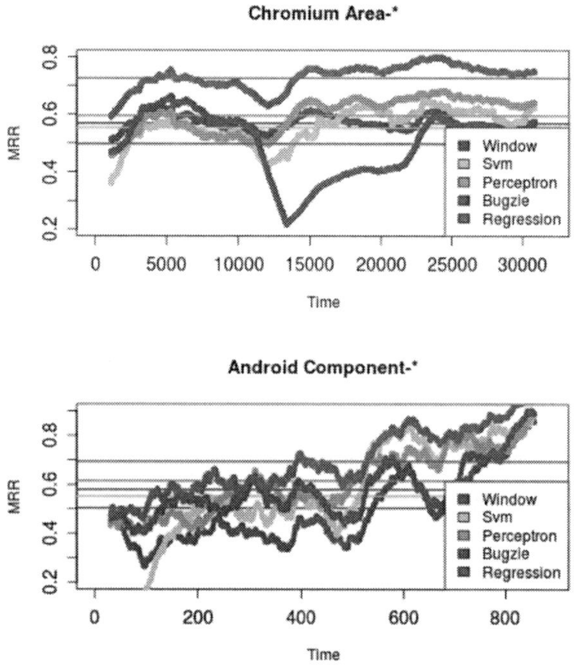

Figure 3: SUBCOMPONENT evaluation results on the development set

Task	Model	MRR	Acc
Chromium	Window	0.0999	0.0472
	SVM	0.0908	0.0550
	Perceptron	0.1817	0.1128
	Bugzie	0.2063	0.0960
	Regression	**0.3074**	**0.2157**
Android	Window	0.3198	0.1684
	SVM	0.2541	0.1684
	Perceptron	0.3225	0.2057
	Bugzie	0.3690	0.2086
	Regression	**0.4446**	**0.2951**
Firefox	Window	0.5695	0.4426
	SVM	0.4604	0.4166
	Perceptron	0.5191	0.4306
	Bugzie	0.5402	0.4100
	Regression	**0.6367**	**0.5245**
Launchpad	Window	0.0725	0.0337
	SVM	0.1006	0.0704
	Perceptron	0.3323	0.2607
	Bugzie	**0.5271**	**0.4339**
	Regression	0.4702	0.3879

Table 4: ASSIGNED evaluation results on test set

ing trick" to feature-label pairs (see section 4.4), which leads to excessive collisions with very large label sets. Our current implementation can use at most 29 bit-sized hashes which is insufficient for datasets like Launchpad ASSIGNED. We are currently removing this limitation and we expect it will lead to substantial gains on massively multiclass problems.

In Tables 3 and 4 we present the overall MRR results on the test data streams. The picture is similar to the development data discussed above.

5 Discussion and related work

Our results show that by choosing the appropriate learner for the scenario of learning from data streams, we can achieve much better results than by attempting to twist batch algorithm to fit the online learning setting. Even a simple and well-know algorithm such as Perceptron can be effective, but by using recent advances in research on SGD algorithms we can obtain substantial improvements on the best previously used approach. Below we review the research on bug report triage most relevant to our work.

Čubranić and Murphy (2004) seems to be the first attempt to automate bug triage. The authors cast bug triage as a text classification task and use the data representation (bag of words) and learning algorithm (Naive Bayes) typical for text classification at the time. They collect over 15,000 bug reports from the Eclipse project. The maximum accuracy they report is 30% which was achieved by using 90% of the data for training.

In Anvik et al. (2006) the authors experiment with three learning algorithms: Naive Bayes, SVM and Decision Tree: SVM performs best in their experiments. They evaluate using precision and recall rather than accuracy. They report results on the Eclipse and Firefox projects, with precision 57% and 64% respectively, but very low recall (7% and 2%).

Matter et al. (2009) adopt a different approach to bug triage. In addition to the project's issue tracker data, they use also the source-code version control data. They build an *expertise model* for each developer which is a word count vector of the source code changes committed. They also build a word count vector for each bug report, and use the cosine between the report and the expertise model to rank developers. Using this approach (with a heuristic term weighting scheme) they report 33.6% accuracy on Eclipse.

Bhattacharya and Neamtiu (2010) acknowledge the evolving nature of bug report streams and attempt to apply incremental learning methods to bug triage. They use a two-step approach:

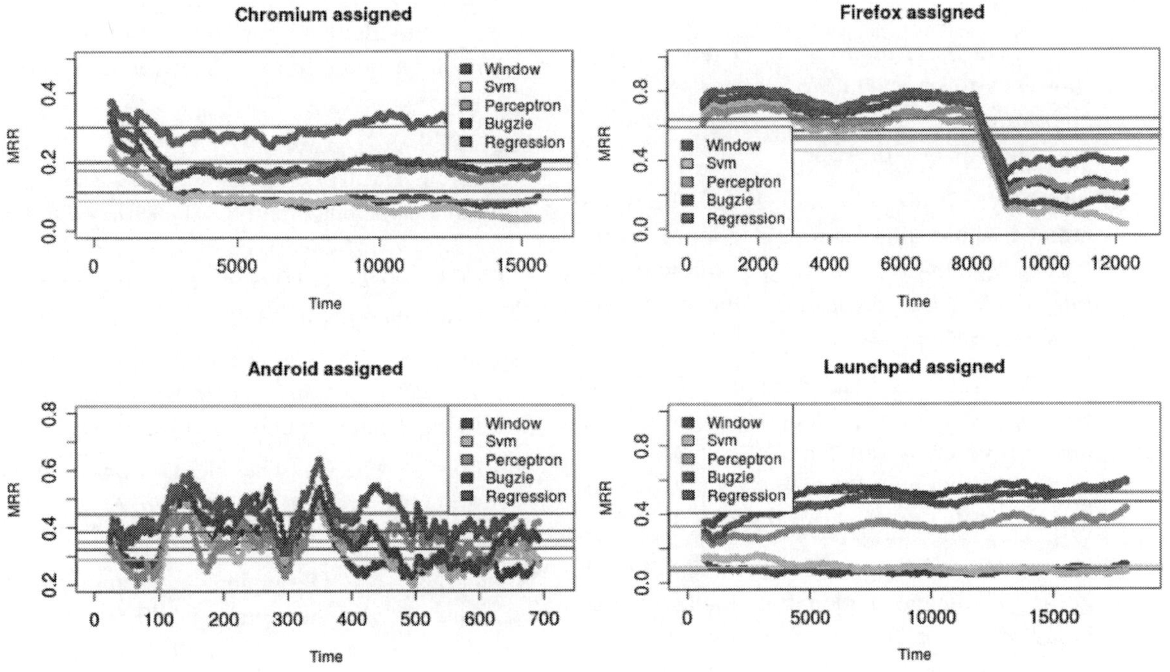

Figure 4: ASSIGNED evaluation results on the development set

first they predict the most likely developer to assign to a bug using a classifier. In a second step they rank candidate developers according to how likely they were to take over a bug from the developer predicted in the first step. Their approach to incremental learning simply involves fully retraining a batch classifier after each item in the data stream. They test their approach on fixed bugs in Mozilla and Eclipse, reporting accuracies of 27.5% and 38.2% respectively.

Tamrawi et al. (2011) propose the Bugzie model where developers are ranked according to the fuzzy set membership function as defined in section 4.4. They also use the label (developer) cache and term cache to speed up processing and make the model adapt better to the evolving data stream. They evaluate Bugzie and compare its performance to the models used in Bhattacharya and Neamtiu (2010) on seven issue trackers: Bugzie has superior performance on all of them ranging from 29.9% to 45.7% for top-1 output. They do not use separate validation sets for system development and parameter tuning.

In comparison to Bhattacharya and Neamtiu (2010) and Tamrawi et al. (2011), here we focus much more on the analysis of concept drift in data streams and on the evaluation of learning under its constraints. We also show that for evolving issue tracker data, in a large majority of cases SGD Regression handily outperforms Bugzie.

6 Conclusion

We demonstrate that concept drift is a real, pervasive issue for learning from issue tracker streams. We show how to adapt to it by leveraging recent research in online learning algorithms. We also make our dataset collection publicly available to enable direct comparisons between different bug triage systems.[1]

We have identified a good learning framework for mining bug reports: in future we would like to explore smarter ways of extracting useful signals from the data by using more linguistically informed preprocessing and higher-level features such as word classes.

Acknowledgments

This work was carried out in the context of the Software-Cluster project EMERGENT and was partially funded by BMBF under grant number 01IC10S01O.

[1] Available from http://goo.gl/ZquBe

References

Anvik, J., Hiew, L., and Murphy, G. (2006). Who should fix this bug? In *Proceedings of the 28th international conference on Software engineering*, pages 361–370. ACM.

Bhattacharya, P. and Neamtiu, I. (2010). Fine-grained incremental learning and multi-feature tossing graphs to improve bug triaging. In *International Conference on Software Maintenance (ICSM)*, pages 1–10. IEEE.

Blum, A., Kalai, A., and Langford, J. (1999). Beating the hold-out: Bounds for k-fold and progressive cross-validation. In *Proceedings of the twelfth annual conference on Computational learning theory*, pages 203–208. ACM.

Crammer, K. and Singer, Y. (2002). On the algorithmic implementation of multiclass kernel-based vector machines. *The Journal of Machine Learning Research*, 2:265–292.

Duchi, J., Hazan, E., and Singer, Y. (2010). Adaptive subgradient methods for online learning and stochastic optimization. *Journal of Machine Learning Research.*

Halpin, H., Robu, V., and Shepherd, H. (2007). The complex dynamics of collaborative tagging. In *Proceedings of the 16th international conference on World Wide Web*, pages 211–220. ACM.

Joachims, T. (1999). Making large-scale svm learning practical. In Schölkopf, B., Burges, C., and Smola, A., editors, *Advances in Kernel Methods-Support Vector Learning*. MIT-Press.

Langford, J., Hsu, D., Karampatziakis, N., Chapelle, O., Mineiro, P., Hoffman, M., Hofman, J., Lamkhede, S., Chopra, S., Faigon, A., Li, L., Rios, G., and Strehl, A. (2011). Vowpal wabbit. `https://github.com/JohnLangford/vowpal_wabbit/wiki`.

Matter, D., Kuhn, A., and Nierstrasz, O. (2009). Assigning bug reports using a vocabulary-based expertise model of developers. In *Sixth IEEE Working Conference on Mining Software Repositories*.

McMahan, H. and Streeter, M. (2010). Adaptive bound optimization for online convex optimization. *Arxiv preprint arXiv:1002.4908.*

Rosenblatt, F. (1958). The perceptron: A probabilistic model for information storage and organization in the brain. *Psychological review*, 65(6):386.

Tamrawi, A., Nguyen, T., Al-Kofahi, J., and Nguyen, T. (2011). Fuzzy set and cache-based approach for bug triaging. In *Proceedings of the 19th ACM SIGSOFT symposium and the 13th European conference on Foundations of software engineering*, pages 365–375. ACM.

Tsymbal, A. (2004). The problem of concept drift: definitions and related work. *Computer Science Department, Trinity College Dublin.*

Voorhees, E. (2000). The TREC-8 question answering track report. *NIST Special Publication*, pages 77–82.

Weinberger, K., Dasgupta, A., Langford, J., Smola, A., and Attenberg, J. (2009). Feature hashing for large scale multitask learning. In *Proceedings of the 26th Annual International Conference on Machine Learning*, pages 1113–1120. ACM.

Widmer, G. and Kubat, M. (1996). Learning in the presence of concept drift and hidden contexts. *Machine learning*, 23(1):69–101.

Zhang, T. (2004). Solving large scale linear prediction problems using stochastic gradient descent algorithms. In *Proceedings of the twenty-first international conference on Machine learning*, page 116. ACM.

Čubranić, D. and Murphy, G. C. (2004). Automatic bug triage using text categorization. In *In SEKE 2004: Proceedings of the Sixteenth International Conference on Software Engineering & Knowledge Engineering*, pages 92–97. KSI Press.

Towards a model of formal and informal address in English

Manaal Faruqui
Computer Science and Engineering
Indian Institute of Technology
Kharagpur, India
manaalfar@gmail.com

Sebastian Padó
Institute of Computational Linguistics
Heidelberg University
Heidelberg, Germany
pado@cl.uni-heidelberg.de

Abstract

Informal and formal ("T/V") address in dialogue is not distinguished overtly in modern English, e.g. by pronoun choice like in many other languages such as French ("tu"/"vous"). Our study investigates the status of the T/V distinction in English literary texts. Our main findings are: (a) human raters can label monolingual English utterances as T or V fairly well, given sufficient context; (b), a bilingual corpus can be exploited to induce a supervised classifier for T/V without human annotation. It assigns T/V at sentence level with up to 68% accuracy, relying mainly on lexical features; (c), there is a marked asymmetry between lexical features for formal speech (which are conventionalized and therefore general) and informal speech (which are text-specific).

1 Introduction

In many Indo-European languages, there are two pronouns corresponding to the English *you*. This distinction is generally referred to as the *T/V dichotomy*, from the Latin pronouns *tu* (informal, T) and *vos* (formal, V) (Brown and Gilman, 1960). The V form (such as *Sie* in German and *Vous* in French) can express neutrality or polite distance and is used to address social superiors. The T form (German *du*, French *tu*) is employed towards friends or addressees of lower social standing, and implies solidarity or lack of formality.

English used to have a T/V distinction until the 18th century, using *you* as V pronoun and *thou* for T. However, in contemporary English, *you* has taken over both uses, and the T/V distinction is not marked anymore. In NLP, this makes generation in English and translation into English easy. Conversely, many NLP tasks suffer from the lack of information about formality, e.g. the extraction of social relationships or, notably, machine translation from English into languages with a T/V distinction which involves a pronoun choice.

In this paper, we investigate the possibility to recover the T/V distinction for (monolingual) sentences of 19th and 20th-century English such as:

(1) Can I help **you**, Sir? (V)
(2) **You** are my best friend! (T)

After describing the creation of an English corpus of T/V labels via annotation projection (Section 3), we present an annotation study (Section 4) which establishes that taggers can indeed assign T/V labels to monolingual English utterances in context fairly reliably. Section 5 investigates how T/V is expressed in English texts by experimenting with different types of features, including words, semantic classes, and expressions based on Politeness Theory. We find word features to be most reliable, obtaining an accuracy of close to 70%.

2 Related Work

There is a large body of work on the T/V distinction in (socio-)linguistics and translation studies, covering in particular the conditions governing T/V usage in different languages (Kretzenbacher et al., 2006; Schüpbach et al., 2006) and the difficulties in translation (Ardila, 2003; Künzli, 2010). However, many observations from this literature are difficult to operationalize. Brown and Levinson (1987) propose a general theory of politeness which makes many detailed predictions. They assume that the pragmatic goal of being polite gives rise to general communication strategies, such as avoiding to lose face (cf. Section 5.2).

In computational linguistics, it is a common observation that for almost every language pair, there are distinctions that are expressed overtly

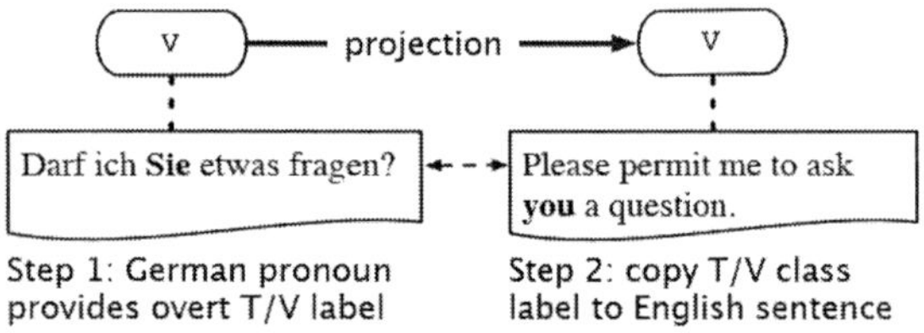

Figure 1: T/V label induction for English sentences in a parallel corpus with annotation projection

in one language, but remain covert in the other. Examples include morphology (Fraser, 2009) and tense (Schiehlen, 1998). A technique that is often applied in such cases is *annotation projection*, the use of parallel corpora to copy information from a language where it is overtly realized to one where it is not (Yarowsky and Ngai, 2001; Hwa et al., 2005; Bentivogli and Pianta, 2005).

The phenomenon of formal and informal address has been considered in the contexts of translation into (Hobbs and Kameyama, 1990; Kanayama, 2003) and generation in Japanese (Bateman, 1988). Li and Yarowsky (2008) learn pairs of formal and informal constructions in Chinese with a paraphrase mining strategy. Other relevant recent studies consider the extraction of social networks from corpora (Elson et al., 2010). A related study is (Bramsen et al., 2011) which considers another sociolinguistic distinction, classifying utterances as "upspeak" and "downspeak" based on the social relationship between speaker and addressee.

This paper extends a previous pilot study (Faruqui and Padó, 2011). It presents more annotation, investigates a larger and better motivated feature set, and discusses the findings in detail.

3 A Parallel Corpus of Literary Texts

This section discusses the construction of T/V gold standard labels for English sentences. We obtain these labels from a parallel English–German corpus using the technique of annotation projection (Yarowsky and Ngai, 2001) sketched in Figure 1: We first identify the T/V status of German pronouns, then copy this T/V information onto the corresponding English sentence.

3.1 Data Selection and Preparation

Annotation projection requires a parallel corpus. We found commonly used parallel corpora like EUROPARL (Koehn, 2005) or the JRC Acquis corpus (Steinberger et al., 2006) to be unsuitable for our study since they either contain almost no direct address at all or, if they do, just formal address (V). Fortunately, for many literary texts from the 19th and early 20th century, copyright has expired, and they are freely available in several languages.

We identified 110 stories and novels among the texts provided by Project Gutenberg (English) and Project Gutenberg-DE (German)[1] that were available in both languages, with a total of 0.5M sentences per language. Examples are Dickens' *David Copperfield* or Tolstoy's *Anna Karenina*. We excluded plays and poems, as well as 19th-century adventure novels by Sir Walter Scott and James F. Cooper which use anachronistic English for stylistic reasons, including words that previously (until the 16th century) indicated T ("thee", "didst").

We cleaned the English and German novels manually by deleting the tables of contents, prologues, epilogues, as well as chapter numbers and titles occurring at the beginning of each chapter to obtain properly parallel texts. The files were then formatted to contain one sentence per line using the sentence splitter and tokenizer provided with EUROPARL (Koehn, 2005). Blank lines were inserted to preserve paragraph boundaries. All novels were lemmatized and POS-tagged using TreeTagger (Schmid, 1994).[2] Finally, they were sentence-aligned using Gargantuan (Braune and Fraser, 2010), an aligner that supports one-to-many alignments, and word-aligned in both directions using Giza++ (Och and Ney, 2003).

3.2 T/V Gold Labels for English Utterances

As Figure 1 shows, the automatic construction of T/V labels for English involves two steps.

Step 1: Labeling German Pronouns as T/V. German has three relevant personal pronouns for the T/V distinction: *du* (T), *sie* (V), and *ihr* (T/V). However, various ambiguities makes their interpretation non-straightforward.

The pronoun *ihr* can both be used for plural T address or for a somewhat archaic singular or plural V address. In principle, these usages should be distinguished by capitalization (V pronouns are generally capitalized in German), but many T instances in our corpora informal use are nevertheless capitalized. Additional, *ihr* can be the

[1] http://www.gutenberg.org, http://gutenberg.spiegel.de/

[2] It must be expected that the tagger degrades on this dataset; however we did not quantify this effect.

dative form of the 3rd person feminine pronoun *sie* (*she/her*). These instances are neutral with respect to T/V but were misanalysed by TreeTagger as instances of the T/V lemma *ihr*. Since TreeTagger does not provide person information, and we did not want to use a full parser, we decided to omit *ihr/Ihr* from consideration.[3]

Of the two remaining pronouns (*du* and *sie*), *du* expresses (singular) T. A minor problem is presented by novels set in France, where *du* is used as an nobiliary particle. These instances can be recognised reliably since the names before and after *du* are generally unknown to the German tagger. Thus we do not interpret *du* as T if the word preceding or succeeding it has "unknown" as its lemma.

The V pronoun, *sie*, doubles as the pronoun for third person (*she/they*) when not capitalized. We therefore interpret only capitalized instances of *Sie* as V. Furthermore, we ignore utterance-initial positions, where all words are capitalized. This is defined as tokens directly after a sentence boundary (POS `$.`) or after a bracket (POS `$(`).

These rules concentrate on precision rather than recall. They leave many instances of German second person pronouns unlabeled; however, this is not a problem since we do not currently aim at obtaining complete coverage on the English side of our parallel corpus. From the 0.5M German sentences, about 14% of the sentences were labeled as T or V (37K for V and 28K for T). In a random sample of roughly 300 German sentences which we analysed, we did not find any errors. This puts the precision of our heuristics at above 99%.

Step 2: Annotation Projection. We now copy the information over onto the English side. We originally intended to transfer T/V labels between German and English word-aligned pronouns. However, we pronouns are not necessarily translated into pronouns; additionally, we found word alignment accuracy for pronouns to be far from perfect, due to the variability in function word translation. For these reason, we decided to look at T/V labels at the level of complete sentences, ignoring word alignment. This is generally unproblematic – address is almost always consistent within sentences: of the 65K German sentences with T or V labels, only 269 ($< 0.5\%$) contain both T and V. Our projection on the English side results in 25K V and 18K T sentences[4], of which 255 (0.6%) are labeled as both T and V. We exclude these sentences.

Comparison	No context	In context
A1 vs. A2	75% (.49)	79% (.58)
A1 vs. GS	60% (.20)	70% (.40)
A2 vs. GS	65% (.30)	76% (.52)
(A1 ∩ A2) vs. GS	67% (.34)	79% (.58)

Table 1: Manual annotation for T/V on a 200-sentence sample. Comparison among human annotators (A1 and A2) and to projected gold standard (GS). All cells show raw agreement and Cohen's κ (in parentheses).

Note that this strategy relies on the *direct correspondence assumption* (Hwa et al., 2005), that is, it assumes that the T/V status of an utterance is not changed in translation. We believe that this is a reasonable assumption, given that T/V is determined by the social relation between interlocutors; but see Section 4 for discussion.

3.3 Data Splitting

Finally, we divided our English data into training, development and test sets with 74 novels (26K sentences), 19 novels (9K sentences) and 13 novels (8K sentences), respectively. The corpus is available for download at `http://www.nlpado.de/~sebastian/data.shtml`.

4 Human Annotation of T/V for English

This section investigates how well the T/V distinction can be made in English by human raters, and on the basis of what information. Two annotators with near native-speaker competence in English were asked to label 200 random sentences from the training set as T or V. Sentences were first presented in isolation ("no context"). Subsequently, they were presented with three sentences pre- and post-context each ("in context").

Table 1 shows the results of the annotation study. The first line compares the annotations of the two annotators against each other (inter-annotator agreement). The next two lines compare the taggers' annotations against the gold standard labels projected from German (GS). The last line compares the annotator-assigned labels to the GS for the instances on which the annotators agree. For all cases, we report raw accuracy and Cohen's κ (1960), i.e. chance-corrected agreement.

[3]Instances of *ihr* as possessive pronoun occurred as well, but could be filtered out on the basis of the POS tag.

[4]Our sentence aligner supports one-to-many alignments and often aligns single German to multiple English sentences.

We first observe that the T/V distinction is considerably more difficult to make for individual sentences (no context) than when the discourse is available. In context, inter-annotator agreement increases from 75% to 79%, and agreement with the gold standard rises by 10%. It is notable that the two annotators agree worse with one another than with the gold standard (see below for discussion). On those instances where they agree, Cohen's κ reaches 0.58 in context, which is interpreted as approaching good agreement (Fleiss, 1981). Although far from perfect, this inter-annotator agreement is comparable to results for the annotation of fine-grained word sense or sentiment (Navigli, 2009; Bermingham and Smeaton, 2009).

An analysis of disagreements showed that many sentences can be uttered in both T and V contexts and cannot be labeled without context:

(3) "And perhaps sometime **you** may see her."

This case (gold label: V) is disambiguated by the previous sentence which indicates a hierarchical social relation between speaker and addressee:

(4) "And she is a sort of relation of **your lordship's**," said Dawson. ...

Still, even a three-sentence window is often not sufficient, since the surrounding sentences may be just as uninformative. In these cases, more global information about the situation is necessary. Even with perfect information, however, judgments can sometimes deviate, as there are considerable "grey areas" in T/V usage (Kretzenbacher et al., 2006).

In addition, social rules like T/V usage vary in time and between countries (Schüpbach et al., 2006). This helps to explain why annotators agree better with one another than with the gold standard: 21st century annotators tend to be unfamiliar with 19th century T/V usage. Consider this example from a book written in second person perspective:

(5) Finally, **you** acquaint Caroline with the fatal result: she begins by consoling **you**. "One hundred thousand francs lost! We shall have to practice the strictest economy", **you** imprudently add.[5]

Here, the author and translator use V to refer to the reader, while today's usage would almost certainly be T, as presumed by both annotators. Conversations between lovers or family members form another example, where T is modern usage, but the novels tend to use V:

(6) [...] she covered her face with the other to conceal her tears. "Corinne!", said Oswald, "Dear Corinne! My absence has then rendered **you** unhappy!"[6]

In sum, our annotation study establishes that the T/V distinction, although not realized by different pronouns in English, can be recovered manually from text, provided that discourse context is available. A substantial part of the errors is due to social changes in T/V usage.

5 Monolingual T/V Modeling

The second part of the paper explores the automatic prediction of the T/V distinction for English sentences. Given the ability to create an English training corpus with T/V labels with the annotation projection methods described in Section 3.2, we can phrase T/V prediction for English as a standard supervised learning task. Our experiments have a twin motivation: (a), on the NLP side, we are mainly interested in obtaining a robust classifier to assign the labels T and V to English sentences; (b), on the sociolinguistic side, we are interested in investigating through which features the categories T and V are expressed in English.

5.1 Classification Framework

We phrase T/V labeling as a binary classification task at the sentence level, performing the classification with L2-regularized logistic regression using the LibLINEAR library (Fan et al., 2008). Logistic regression defines the probability that a binary response variable y takes some value as a logit-transformed linear combination of the features f_i, each of which is assigned a coefficient β_i.

$$p(y=1) = \frac{1}{1+e^{-z}} \text{ with } z = \sum_i \beta_i f_i \quad (7)$$

Regularization incorporates the size of the coefficient vector β into the objective function, subtracting it from the likelihood of the data given the model. This allows the user to trade faithfulness to the data against generalization.[7]

[5] H. de Balzac: Petty Troubles of Married Life

[6] A.L.G. de Staël: Corinne

[7] We use LIBLINEAR's default parameters and set the cost (regularization) parameter to 0.01.

$\frac{p(C\|V)}{p(C\|T)}$	Words
4.59	Mister, sir, Monsieur, sirrah, ...
2.36	Mlle., Mr., M., Herr, Dr., ...
1.60	Gentlemen, patients, rascals, ...

Table 2: 3 of the 400 clustering-based semantic classes (classes most indicative for V)

5.2 Feature Types

We experiment with three features types that are candidates to express the T/V English distinction.

Word Features. The intuition to use word features draws on the parallel between T/V and information retrieval tasks like document classification: some words are presumably correlated with formal address (like titles), while others should indicate informal address (like first names). In a preliminary experiment, we noticed that in the absence of further constraints, many of the most indicative features are names of persons from particular novels which are systematically addressed formally (like Phileas Fogg from J. Vernes' *Around the world in eighty days*) or informally (like Mowgli, Baloo, and Bagheera from R. Kipling's *Jungle Book*). These features clearly do not generalize to new books. We therefore added a constraint to remove all features which did not occur in at least three novels. To reduce the number of word features to a reasonable order of magnitude, we also performed a χ^2-based feature selection (Manning et al., 2008) on the training set. Preliminary experiments established that selecting the top 800 word features yielded a model with good generalization.

Semantic Class Features. Our second feature type is semantic class features. These can be seen as another strategy to counteract the sparseness at the level of word features. We cluster words into 400 semantic classes on the basis of distributional and morphological similarity features which are extracted from an unlabeled English collection of Gutenberg novels comprising more than 100M tokens, using the approach by Clark (2003). These features measure how similar tokens are to one another in terms of their occurrences in the document and are useful in Named Entity Recognition (Finkel and Manning, 2009). As features in the T/V classification of a given sentence, we simply count for each class the number of tokens in this class present in the current sentence. For illustration, Table 2 shows the three classes most indicative for V, ranked by the ratio of probabilities for T and V, estimated on the training set.

Politeness Theory Features. The third feature type is based on the Politeness Theory (Brown and Levinson, 1987). Brown and Levinson's prediction is that politeness levels will be detectable in concrete utterances in a number of ways, e.g. a higher use of conjunctive or hedges in polite speech. Formal address (i.e., V as opposed to T) is one such expression. Politeness Theory therefore predicts that other politeness indicators should correlate with the T/V classification. This holds in particular for English, where pronoun choice is unavailable to indicate politeness.

We constructed 16 features on the basis of Politeness Theory predictions, that is, classes of expressions indicating either formality or informality. From a computational perspective, the problem with Politeness Theory predictions is that they are only described qualitatively and by example, without detailed lists. For each feature, we manually identified around 10 words or multi-word relevant expressions. Table 3 shows these 16 features with their intended classes and some example expressions. Similar to the semantic class features, the value of each politeness feature is the sum of the frequencies of its members in a sentence.

5.3 Context: Size and Type

As our annotation study in Section 4 found, context is crucial for human annotators, and this presumably carries over to automatic methods human annotators: if the features for a sentence are computed just on that sentence, we will face extremely sparse data. We experiment with symmetrical window contexts, varying the size between $n = 0$ (just the target sentence) and $n = 10$ (target sentence plus 10 preceding and 10 succeeding sentences).

This kind of simple "sentence context" makes an important oversimplification, however. It lumps together material from different speech turns as well as from "narrative" sentences, which may generate misleading features. For example, narrative sentences may refer to protagonists by their full names including titles (strong features for V) even when these protagonists are in T-style conversations:

(8) "You are the love of my life", said Sir Phileas Fogg.[8] (T)

[8] J. Verne: Around the world in 80 days

Class	Example expressions	Class	Example expressions
Inclusion (T)	let's, shall we	Exclamations (T)	hey, yeah
Subjunctive I (T)	can, will	Subjunctive II (V)	could, would
Proximity (T)	this, here	Distance (V)	that, there
Negated question (V)	didn't I, hasn't it	Indirect question (V)	would there, is there
Indefinites (V)	someone, something	Apologizing (V)	bother, pardon
Polite adverbs (V)	marvellous, superb	Optimism (V)	I hope, would you
Why + modal (V)	why would(n't)	Impersonals (V)	necessary, have to
Polite markers (V)	please, sorry	Hedges (V)	in fact, I guess

Table 3: 16 Politeness theory-based features with intended classes and example expressions

Example (8) also demonstrates that narrative material and direct speech may even be mixed within individual sentences.

For these reasons, we introduce an alternative concept of context, namely *direct speech context*, whose purpose is to exclude narrative material. We compute direct speech context in two steps: (a), segmentation of sentences into chunks that are either completely narrative or speech, and (b), labeling of chunks with a classifier that distinguishes these two classes. The segmentation step (a) takes place with a regular expression that subdivides sentences on every occurrence of quotes (" , " , ' , ', etc.). As training data for the classification step (b), we manually tagged 1000 chunks from our training data as either B-DS (begin direct speech), I-DS (inside direct speech) and O (outside direct speech, i.e. narrative material).[9] We used this dataset to train the CRF-based sequence tagger Mallet (McCallum, 2002) using all tokens, including punctuation, as features.[10] This tagger is used to classify all chunks in our dataset, resulting in output like the following example:

(9)	(B-DS)	"I am going to see his Ghost!
	(I-DS)	It will be his Ghost not him!"
	(O)	Mr. Lorry quietly chafed the hands that held his arm.[11]

Direct speech chunks belonging to the same sentence are subsequently recombined.

We define the direct speech context of size n for a given sentence as the n preceding and following direct speech chunks that are labeled B-DS or I-DS while skipping any chunks labeled O. Note that this definition of direct speech context still lumps together utterances by different speakers and can therefore yield misleading features in the case of asymmetric conversational situations, in addition to possible direct speech misclassifications.

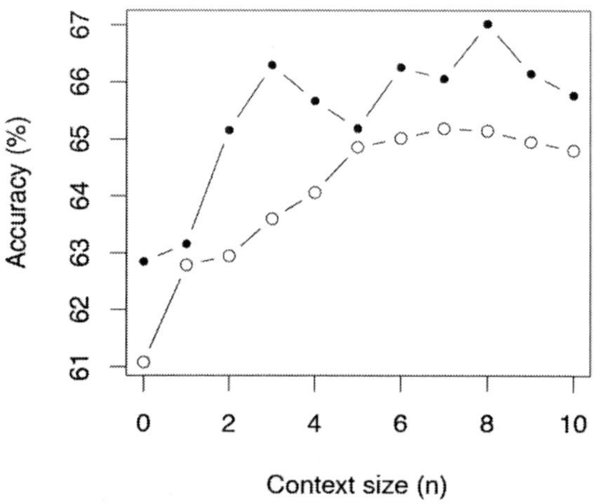

Figure 2: Accuracy vs. number of sentences in context (empty circles: sentence context; solid circles: direct speech context)

6 Experimental Evaluation

6.1 Evaluation on the Development Set

We first perform model selection on the development set and then validate our results on the test set (cf. Section 3.3).

Influence of Context. Figure 2 shows the influence of size and type of context, using only words as features. Without context, we obtain a performance of 61.1% (sentence context) and of 62.9% (direct speech context). These numbers beat the random baseline (50.0%) and the frequency baseline (59.1%). The addition of more context further improves performance substantially for both context types. The ideal context size is fairly large, namely 7 sentences and 8 direct speech chunks, re-

[9] The labels are chosen after IOB notation conventions (Ramshaw and Marcus, 1995).

[10] We also experimented with rule-based chunk labeling based on quotes, but found the use of quotes too inconsistent.

[11] C. Dickens: A tale of two cities.

Model	Accuracy
Random Baseline	50.0
Frequency Baseline	59.1
Words	**67.0****
SemClass	57.5
PoliteClass	59.6
Words + SemClass	66.6**
Words + PoliteClass	66.4**
Words + PoliteClass + SemClass	66.2**
Raw human IAA (no context)	75.0
Raw human IAA (in context)	79.0

Table 4: T/V classification accuracy on the development set (direct speech context, size 8). **: Significant difference to frequency baseline (p<0.01)

spectively. This indicates that sparseness is indeed a major challenge, and context can become large before the effects mentioned in Section 5.3 counteract the positive effect of more data. Direct speech context outperforms sentence context throughout, with a maximum accuracy of 67.0% as compared to 65.2%, even though it shows higher variation, which we attribute to the less stable nature of the direct speech chunks and their automatically created labels. From now on, we adopt a direct speech context of size 8 unless specified differently.

Influence of Features. Table 4 shows the results for different feature types. The best model (word features only) is highly significantly better than the frequency baseline (which it beats by 8%) as determined by a bootstrap resampling test (Noreen, 1989). It gains 17% over the random baseline, but is still more than 10% below inter-annotator agreement in context, which is often seen as an upper bound for automatic models.

Disappointingly, the comparison of the feature groups yields a null result: We are not able to improve over the results for just word features with either the semantic class or the politeness features. Neither feature type outperforms the frequency baseline significantly (p>0.05). Combinations of the different feature types also do worse than just words. The differences between the best model (just words) and the combination models are all not significant (p>0.05). These negative results warrant further analysis. It follows in Section 6.3.

6.2 Results on the Test Set

Table 5 shows the results of evaluating models with the best feature set and with different context sizes on the test set, in order to verify that we did

Model	Accuracy	Δ to dev set
Frequency baseline	59.3	+ 0.2
Words (no context)	62.5	- 0.4
Words (context size 6)	67.3	+ 1.0
Words (context size 8)	**67.5**	+ 0.5
Words (context size 10)	66.8	+ 1.0

Table 5: T/V classification accuracy on the test set and differences to dev set results (direct speech context)

not overfit on the development set when picking the best model. The tendencies correspond well to the development set: the frequency baseline is almost identical, as are the results for the different models. The differences to the development set are all equal to or smaller than 1% accuracy, and the best result at 67.5% is 0.5% better than on the development set. This is a reassuring result, as our model appears to generalize well to unseen data.

6.3 Analysis by Feature Types

The results from Section 6.1 motivate further analysis of the individual feature types.

Analysis of Word Features. Word features are by far the most effective features. Table 6 lists the top twenty words indicating T and V (ranked by the ratio of probabilities for the two classes on the training set). The list still includes some proper names like *Vrazumihin* or *Louis-Gaston* (even though all features have to occur in at least three novels), but they are relatively infrequent. The most prominent indicators for the formal class V are titles (*monsieur*, *(ma)'am*) and instances of formulaic language (*Permit (me)*, *Excuse (me)*). There are also some terms which are not straightforward indicators of formal address (*angelic*, *stubbornness*), but are associated with a high register.

There is a notable asymmetry between T and V. The word features for T are considerably more difficult to interpret. We find some forms of earlier period English (*thee, hast, thou, wilt*) that result from occasional archaic passages in the novels as well first names (*Louis-Gaston, Justine*). Nevertheless, most features are not straightforward to connect to specifically informal speech.

Analysis of Semantic Class Features. We ranked the semantic classes we obtained by distributional clustering in a similar manner to the word features. Table 2 shows the top three classes indicative for V. Almost all others of the 400 clusters do not have a strong formal/informal association

Top 20 words for V		Top 20 words for T	
Word w	$\frac{P(w\|V)}{P(w\|T)}$	Word w	$\frac{P(w\|T)}{P(w\|V)}$
Excuse	36.5	thee	94.3
Permit	35.0	amenable	94.3
'ai	29.2	stuttering	94.3
'am	29.2	guardian	94.3
stubbornness	29.2	hast	92.0
flights	29.2	Louis-Gaston	92.0
monsieur	28.6	lease-making	92.0
Vrazumihin	28.6	melancholic	92.0
mademoiselle	26.5	ferry-boat	92.0
angelic	26.5	Justine	92.0
Allow	24.5	Thou	66.0
madame	21.2	responsibility	63.8
delicacies	21.2	thou	63.8
entrapped	21.2	Iddibal	63.8
lack-a-day	21.2	twenty-fifth	63.8
ma	21.0	Chic	63.8
duke	18.0	allegiance	63.8
policeman	18.0	Jouy	63.8
free-will	18.0	wilt	47.0
Canon	18.0	shall	47.0

Table 6: Most indicative word features for T or V

but mix formal, informal, and neutral vocabulary. This tendency is already apparent in class 3: *Gentlemen* is clearly formal, while *rascals* is informal. *patients* can belong to either class. Even in class 1, we find *Sirrah*, a contemptuous term used in addressing a man or boy with a low formality score ($p(w|V)/p(w|T) = 0.22$). From cluster 4 onward, none of the clusters is strongly associated with either V or T ($p(c|V)/p(c|T) \approx 1$).

Our interpretation of these observations is that in contrast to text categorization, there is no clear-cut topical or domain difference between T and V: both categories co-occur with words from almost any domain. In consequence, semantic classes do not, in general, represent strong unambiguous indicators. Similar to the word features, the situation is worse for T than for V: there still are reasonably strong features for V, the "marked" case, but it is more difficult to find indicators for T.

Analysis of politeness features. A major reason for the ineffectiveness of the Politeness Theory-based features seems to be their low frequency: in the best model, with a direct speech context of size 8, only an average of 7 politeness features was active for any given sentence. However, frequency was not the only problem – the politeness features were generally unable to discriminate well between T and V. For all features, the values of $p(f|V)/p(f|T)$ are between 0.9 and 1.3, that is, the features were only weakly indicative of one of the classes. Furthermore, not all features turned out to be indicative of the class we designed them for. The best indicator for V was the Indefinites feature (*somehow, someone* cf. Table 3), as expected. In contrast, the best indicator for T was the Negation question feature which was supposedly an indicator for V (*didn't I, haven't we*).

A majority of politeness features (13 of the 16) had $p(f|V)/p(f|T)$ values above 1, that is, were indicative for the class V. Thus for this feature type, like for the others, it appears to be more difficult to identify T than to identify V. This negative result can be attributed at least in part to our method of hand-crafting lists of expressions for these features. The inadvertent inclusion of overly general terms V might be responsible for the features' inability to discriminate well, while we have presumably missed specific terms which has hurt coverage. This situation may in the future be remedied with the semi-automatic acquisition of instantiations of politeness features.

6.4 Analysis of Individual Novels

One possible hypothesis regarding the difficulty of finding indicators for the class T is that indicators for T tend to be more novel-specific than indicators for V, since formal language is more conventionalized (Brown and Levinson, 1987). If this were the case, then our strategy of building well-generalizing models by combining text from different novels would naturally result in models that have problems with picking up T features.

To investigate this hypothesis, we trained models with the best parameters as before (8-sentence direct speech context, words as features). However, this time we trained novel-specific models, splitting each novel into 50% training data and 50% testing data. We required novels to contain more than 200 labeled sentences. This ruled out most short stories, leaving us with 7 novels in the test set. The results are shown in Table 7 and show a clear improvement. The accuracy is 13% higher than in our main experiment (67% vs. 80%), even though the models were trained on considerably less data. Six of the seven novels perform above the 67.5% result from the main experiment.

The top-ranked features for T and V show a much higher percentage of names for both T and V than in the main experiment. This is to be ex-

Novel	Accuracy
H. Beecher-Stove: Uncle Tom's Cabin	90.0
J. Spyri: Cornelli	88.3
E. Zola: Lourdes	83.9
H. de Balzac: Cousin Pons	82.3
C. Dickens: The Pickwick Papers	77.7
C. Dickens: Nicholas Nickleby	74.8
F. Hodgson Burnett: Little Lord	61.6
All (micro average)	80.0

Table 7: T/V prediction models for individual novels (50% of each novel for training and 50% testing)

pected, since this experiment does not restrict itself to features that occurred in at least three novels. The price we pay for this is worse generalization to other novels. There is also still a T/V asymmetry: more top features are shared among the V lists of individual novels and with the main experiment V list than on the T side. Like in the main experiment (cf. Section 6.3), V features indicate titles and other features of elevated speech, while T features mostly refer to novel-specific protagonists and events. In sum, these results provide evidence for a difference in status of T and V.

7 Discussion and Conclusions

In this paper, we have studied the distinction between formal and information (T/V) address, which is not expressed overtly through pronoun choice or morphosyntactic marking in modern English. Our hypothesis was that the T/V distinction can be recovered in English nevertheless. Our manual annotation study has shown that annotators can in fact tag monolingual English sentences as T or V with reasonable accuracy, but only if they have sufficient context. We exploited the overt information from German pronouns to induce T/V labels for English and used this labeled corpus to train a monolingual T/V classifier for English. We experimented with features based on words, semantic classes, and Politeness Theory predictions.

With regard to our NLP goal of building a T/V classifier, we conclude that T/V classification is a phenomenon that can be modelled on the basis of corpus features. A major factor in classification performance is the inclusion of a wide context to counteract sparse data, and more sophisticated context definitions improve results. We currently achieve top accuracies of 67%-68%, which still leave room for improvement. We next plan to couple our T/V classifier with a machine translation system for a task-based evaluation on the translation of direct address into German and other languages with different T/V pronouns.

Considering our sociolinguistic goal of determining the ways in which English realizes the T/V distinction, we first obtained a negative result: only word features perform well, while semantic classes and politeness features do hardly better than a frequency baseline. Notably, there are no clear "topical" divisions between T and V, like for example in text categorization: almost all words are very weakly correlated with either class, and semantically similar words can co-occur with different classes. Consequently, distributionally determined semantic classes are not helpful for the distinction. Politeness features are difficult to operationalize with sufficiently high precision and recall.

An interesting result is the asymmetry between the linguistic features for V and T at the lexical level. V language appears to be more conventionalized; the models therefore identified formulaic expressions and titles as indicators for V. On the other hand, very few such generic features exist for the class T; consequently, the classifier has a hard time learning good discriminating and yet generic features. Those features that are indicative of T, such as first names, are highly novel-specific and were deliberately excluded from the main experiment. When we switched to individual novels, the models picked up such features, and accuracy increased – at the cost of lower generalizability between novels. A more technical solution to this problem would be the training of a single-class classifier for V, treating T as the "default" class (Tax and Duin, 1999).

Finally, an error analysis showed that many errors arise from sentences that are too short or unspecific to determine T or V reliably. This points to the fact that T/V should not be modelled as a sentence-level classification task in the first place: T/V is not a choice made for each sentence, but one that is determined once for each pair of interlocutors and rarely changed. In future work, we will attempt to learn social networks from novels (Elson et al., 2010), which should provide constraints on all instances of communication between a speaker and an addressee. However, the big – and unsolved, as far as we know – challenge is to automatically assign turns to interlocutors, given the varied and often inconsistent presentation of direct speech turns in novels.

References

John Ardila. 2003. (Non-Deictic, Socio-Expressive) T-/V-Pronoun Distinction in Spanish/English Formal Locutionary Acts. *Forum for Modern Language Studies*, 39(1):74–86.

John A. Bateman. 1988. Aspects of clause politeness in Japanese: An extended inquiry semantics treatment. In *Proceedings of ACL*, pages 147–154, Buffalo, New York.

Luisa Bentivogli and Emanuele Pianta. 2005. Exploiting parallel texts in the creation of multilingual semantically annotated resources: the MultiSemCor Corpus. *Journal of Natural Language Engineering*, 11(3):247–261.

Adam Bermingham and Alan F. Smeaton. 2009. A study of inter-annotator agreement for opinion retrieval. In *Proceedings of ACM SIGIR*, pages 784–785.

Philip Bramsen, Martha Escobar-Molano, Ami Patel, and Rafael Alonso. 2011. Extracting social power relationships from natural language. In *Proceedings of ACL/HLT*, pages 773–782, Portland, OR.

Fabienne Braune and Alexander Fraser. 2010. Improved unsupervised sentence alignment for symmetrical and asymmetrical parallel corpora. In *Coling 2010: Posters*, pages 81–89, Beijing, China.

Roger Brown and Albert Gilman. 1960. The pronouns of power and solidarity. In Thomas A. Sebeok, editor, *Style in Language*, pages 253–277. MIT Press, Cambridge, MA.

Penelope Brown and Stephen C. Levinson. 1987. *Politeness: Some Universals in Language Usage*. Number 4 in Studies in Interactional Sociolinguistics. Cambridge University Press.

Alexander Clark. 2003. Combining distributional and morphological information for part of speech induction. In *Proceedings of EACL*, pages 59–66, Budapest, Hungary.

J. Cohen. 1960. A Coefficient of Agreement for Nominal Scales. *Educational and Psychological Measurement*, 20(1):37–46.

David Elson, Nicholas Dames, and Kathleen McKeown. 2010. Extracting social networks from literary fiction. In *Proceedings of ACL*, pages 138–147, Uppsala, Sweden.

Rong-En Fan, Kai-Wei Chang, Cho-Jui Hsieh, Xiang-Rui Wang, and Chih-Jen Lin. 2008. LIBLINEAR: A library for large linear classification. *Journal of Machine Learning Research*, 9:1871–1874.

Manaal Faruqui and Sebastian Padó. 2011. "I Thou Thee, Thou Traitor": Predicting formal vs. informal address in English literature. In *Proceedings of ACL/HLT 2011*, pages 467–472, Portland, OR.

Jenny Rose Finkel and Christopher D. Manning. 2009. Nested named entity recognition. In *Proceedings of EMNLP*, pages 141–150, Singapore.

Joseph L. Fleiss. 1981. *Statistical methods for rates and proportions*. John Wiley, New York, 2nd edition.

Alexander Fraser. 2009. Experiments in morphosyntactic processing for translating to and from German. In *Proceedings of the EACL MT workshop*, pages 115–119, Athens, Greece.

Jerry Hobbs and Megumi Kameyama. 1990. Translation by abduction. In *Proceedings of COLING*, pages 155–161, Helsinki, Finland.

Rebecca Hwa, Philipp Resnik, Amy Weinberg, Clara Cabezas, and Okan Kolak. 2005. Bootstrapping parsers via syntactic projection across parallel texts. *Journal of Natural Language Engineering*, 11(3):311–325.

Hiroshi Kanayama. 2003. Paraphrasing rules for automatic evaluation of translation into Japanese. In *Proceedings of the Second International Workshop on Paraphrasing*, pages 88–93, Sapporo, Japan.

Philipp Koehn. 2005. Europarl: A Parallel Corpus for Statistical Machine Translation. In *Proceedings of the 10th Machine Translation Summit*, pages 79–86, Phuket, Thailand.

Heinz L. Kretzenbacher, Michael Clyne, and Doris Schüpbach. 2006. Pronominal Address in German: Rules, Anarchy and Embarrassment Potential. *Australian Review of Applied Linguistics*, 39(2):17.1–17.18.

Alexander Künzli. 2010. Address pronouns as a problem in French-Swedish translation and translation revision. *Babel*, 55(4):364–380.

Zhifei Li and David Yarowsky. 2008. Mining and modeling relations between formal and informal Chinese phrases from web corpora. In *Proceedings of EMNLP*, pages 1031–1040, Honolulu, Hawaii.

Christopher D. Manning, Prabhakar Raghavan, and Hinrich Schütze. 2008. *Introduction to Information Retrieval*. Cambridge University Press, Cambridge, UK, 1st edition.

Andrew Kachites McCallum. 2002. Mallet: A machine learning for language toolkit. http://mallet.cs.umass.edu.

Roberto Navigli. 2009. Word Sense Disambiguation: a survey. *ACM Computing Surveys*, 41(2):1–69.

Eric W. Noreen. 1989. *Computer-intensive Methods for Testing Hypotheses: An Introduction*. John Wiley and Sons Inc.

Franz Josef Och and Hermann Ney. 2003. A Systematic Comparison of Various Statistical Alignment Models. *Computational Linguistics*, 29(1):19–51.

Lance Ramshaw and Mitch Marcus. 1995. Text chunking using transformation-based learning. In *Proceeding of the 3rd ACL Workshop on Very Large Corpora*, Cambridge, MA.

Michael Schiehlen. 1998. Learning tense translation from bilingual corpora. In *Proceedings of ACL/COLING*, pages 1183–1187, Montreal, Canada.

Helmut Schmid. 1994. Probabilistic Part-of-Speech Tagging Using Decision Trees. In *Proceedings of the International Conference on New Methods in Language Processing*, pages 44–49, Manchester, UK.

Doris Schüpbach, John Hajek, Jane Warren, Michael Clyne, Heinz Kretzenbacher, and Catrin Norrby. 2006. A cross-linguistic comparison of address pronoun use in four European languages: Intralingual and interlingual dimensions. In *Proceedings of the Annual Meeting of the Australian Linguistic Society*, Brisbane, Australia.

Ralf Steinberger, Bruno Pouliquen, Anna Widiger, Camelia Ignat, Tomaž Erjavec, and Dan Tufis. 2006. The JRC-Acquis: A multilingual aligned parallel corpus with 20+ languages. In *Proceedings of LREC*, pages 2142–2147, Genoa, Italy.

David M. J. Tax and Robert P. W. Duin. 1999. Support vector domain description. *Pattern Recognition Letters*, 20:1191–1199.

David Yarowsky and Grace Ngai. 2001. Inducing multilingual POS taggers and NP bracketers via robust projection across aligned corpora. In *Proceedings of NAACL*, pages 200–207, Pittsburgh, PA.

Character-based Kernels for Novelistic Plot Structure

Micha Elsner
Institute for Language, Cognition and Computation (ILCC)
School of Informatics
University of Edinburgh
melsner0@gmail.com

Abstract

Better representations of plot structure could greatly improve computational methods for summarizing and generating stories. Current representations lack abstraction, focusing too closely on events. We present a kernel for comparing novelistic plots at a higher level, in terms of the cast of characters they depict and the social relationships between them. Our kernel compares the characters of different novels to one another by measuring their frequency of occurrence over time and the descriptive and emotional language associated with them. Given a corpus of 19th-century novels as training data, our method can accurately distinguish held-out novels in their original form from artificially disordered or reversed surrogates, demonstrating its ability to robustly represent important aspects of plot structure.

1 Introduction

Every culture has stories, and storytelling is one of the key functions of human language. Yet while we have robust, flexible models for the structure of informative documents (for instance (Chen et al., 2009; Abu Jbara and Radev, 2011)), current approaches have difficulty representing the narrative structure of fictional stories. This causes problems for any task requiring us to model fiction, including summarization and generation of stories; Kazantseva and Szpakowicz (2010) show that state-of-the-art summarizers perform extremely poorly on short fictional texts[1]. A major problem with applying models for informative text to fiction is that the most important structure underlying the narrative—its *plot*—occurs at a high level of abstraction, while the actual narration is of a series of lower-level events.

A short synopsis of Jane Austen's novel *Pride and Prejudice*, for example, is that Elizabeth Bennet first thinks Mr. Darcy is arrogant, but later grows to love him. But this is not stated straightforwardly in the text; the reader must infer it from the behavior of the characters as they participate in various everyday scenes.

In this paper, we present the plot kernel, a coarse-grained, but robust representation of novelistic plot structure. The kernel evaluates the similarity between two novels in terms of the characters and their relationships, constructing functional analogies between them. These are intended to correspond to the labelings produced by human literary critics when they write, for example, that Elizabeth Bennet and Emma Woodhouse are protagonists of their respective novels. By focusing on which characters and relationships are important, rather than specifically how they interact, our system can abstract away from events and focus on more easily-captured notions of what makes a good story.

The ability to find correspondences between characters is key to eventually summarizing or even generating interesting stories. Once we can effectively model the kinds of people a romance or an adventure story is usually about, and what kind of relationships should exist between them, we can begin trying to analyze new texts by comparison with familiar ones. In this work, we evaluate our system on the comparatively easy task

[1] Apart from Kazantseva, we know of one other attempt to apply a modern summarizer to fiction, by the artist Jason Huff, using Microsoft Word 2008's extractive summary feature: http://jason-huff.com/projects/autosummarize. Although this cannot be treated as a scientific experiment, the results are unusably bad; they consist mostly of short exclamations containing the names of major characters.

of recognizing acceptable novels (section 6), but recognition is usually a good first step toward generation—a recognition model can always be used as part of a generate-and-rank pipeline, and potentially its underlying representation can be used in more sophisticated ways. We show a detailed analysis of the character correspondences discovered by our system, and discuss their potential relevance to summarization, in section 9.

2 Related work

Some recent work on story understanding has focused on directly modeling the series of events that occur in the narrative. McIntyre and Lapata (2010) create a story generation system that draws on earlier work on narrative schemas (Chambers and Jurafsky, 2009). Their system ensures that generated stories contain plausible event-to-event transitions and are coherent. Since it focuses only on events, however, it cannot enforce a global notion of what the characters want or how they relate to one another.

Our own work draws on representations that explicitly model emotions rather than events. Alm and Sproat (2005) were the first to describe stories in terms of an emotional trajectory. They annotate emotional states in 22 Grimms' fairy tales and discover an increase in emotion (mostly positive) toward the ends of stories. They later use this corpus to construct a reasonably accurate classifier for emotional states of sentences (Alm et al., 2005). Volkova et al. (2010) extend the human annotation approach using a larger number of emotion categories and applying them to freely-defined chunks instead of sentences. The largest-scale emotional analysis is performed by Mohammad (2011), using crowd-sourcing to construct a large emotional lexicon with which he analyzes adult texts such as plays and novels. In this work, we adopt the concept of emotional trajectory, but apply it to particular characters rather than works as a whole.

In focusing on characters, we follow Elson et al. (2010), who analyze narratives by examining their social network relationships. They use an automatic method based on quoted speech to find social links between characters in 19th century novels. Their work, designed for computational literary criticism, does not extract any temporal or emotional structure.

A few projects attempt to represent story structure in terms of both characters and their emotional states. However, they operate at a very detailed level and so can be applied only to short texts. Scheherazade (Elson and McKeown, 2010) allows human annotators to mark character goals and emotional states in a narrative, and indicate the causal links between them. AESOP (Goyal et al., 2010) attempts to learn a similar structure automatically. AESOP's accuracy, however, is relatively poor even on short fables, indicating that this fine-grained approach is unlikely to be scalable to novel-length texts; our system relies on a much coarser analysis.

Kazantseva and Szpakowicz (2010) summarize short stories, although unlike the other projects we discuss here, they explicitly try to avoid giving away plot details—their goal is to create "spoiler-free" summaries focusing on characters, settings and themes, in order to attract potential readers. They do find it useful to detect character mentions, and also use features based on verb aspect to automatically exclude plot events while retaining descriptive passages. They compare their genre-specific system with a few state-of-the-art methods for summarizing news, and find it outperforms them substantially.

We evaluate our system by comparing real novels to artificially produced surrogates, a procedure previously used to evaluate models of discourse coherence (Karamanis et al., 2004; Barzilay and Lapata, 2005) and models of syntax (Post, 2011). As in these settings, we anticipate that performance on this kind of task will be correlated with performance in applied settings, so we use it as an easier preliminary test of our capabilities.

3 Dataset

We focus on the 19th century novel, partly following Elson et al. (2010) and partly because these texts are freely available via Project Gutenberg. Our main dataset is composed of romances (which we loosely define as novels focusing on a courtship or love affair). We select 41 texts, taking 11 as a development set and the remaining 30 as a test set; a complete list is given in Appendix A. We focus on the novels used in Elson et al. (2010), but in some cases add additional romances by an already-included author. We also selected 10 of the least romantic works as an out-of-domain set; experiments on these are in section 8.

4 Preprocessing

In order to compare two texts, we must first extract the characters in each and some features of their relationships with one another. Our first step is to split the text into chapters, and each chapter into paragraphs; if the text contains a running dialogue where each line begins with a quotation mark, we append it to the previous paragraph. We segment each paragraph with MXTerminator (Reynar and Ratnaparkhi, 1997) and parse it with the self-trained Charniak parser (McClosky et al., 2006). Next, we extract a list of characters, compute dependency tree-based unigram features for each character, and record character frequencies and relationships over time.

4.1 Identifying characters

We create a list of possible character references for each work by extracting all strings of proper nouns (as detected by the parser), then discarding those which occur less than 5 times. Grouping these into a useful character list is a problem of cross-document coreference.

Although cross-document coreference has been extensively studied (Bhattacharya and Getoor, 2005) and modern systems can achieve quite high accuracy on the TAC-KBP task, where the list of available entities is given in advance (Dredze et al., 2010), novelistic text poses a significant challenge for the methods normally used. The typical 19th-century novel contains many related characters, often named after one another. There are complicated social conventions determining which titles are used for whom—for instance, the eldest unmarried daughter of a family can be called "Miss Bennet", while her younger sister must be "Miss Elizabeth Bennet". And characters often use nicknames, such as "Lizzie".

Our system uses the multi-stage clustering approach outlined in Bhattacharya and Getoor (2005), but with some features specific to 19th century European names. To begin, we merge all identical mentions which contain more than two words (leaving bare first or last names unmerged). Next, we heuristically assign each mention a gender (masculine, feminine or neuter) using a list of gendered titles, then a list of male and female first names[2]. We then merge mentions where each is longer than one word, the genders do not clash, and the first and last names are consistent (Charniak, 2001). We then merge single-word mentions with matching multiword mentions if they appear in the same paragraph, or if not, with the multiword mention that occurs in the most paragraphs. When this process ends, we have resolved each mention in the novel to some specific character. As in previous work, we discard very infrequent characters and their mentions.

[2]The most frequent names from the 1990 US census.

reply left-of-[name]	17
right-of-[name] feel	14
right-of-[name] look	10
right-of-[name] mind	7
right-of-[name] make	7

Table 1: Top five stemmed unigram dependency features for "Miss Elizabeth Bennet", protagonist of *Pride and Prejudice*, and their frequencies.

For the reasons stated, this method is error-prone. Our intuition is that the simpler method described in Elson et al. (2010), which merges each mention to the most recent possible coreferent, must be even more so. However, due to the expense of annotation, we make no attempt to compare these methods directly.

4.2 Unigram character features

Once we have obtained the character list, we use the dependency relationships extracted from our parse trees to compute features for each character. Similar feature sets are used in previous work in word classification, such as (Lin and Pantel, 2001). A few example features are shown in Table 1.

To find the features, we take each mention in the corpus and count up all the words outside the mention which depend on the mention head, except proper nouns and stop words. We also count the mention's own head word, and mark whether it appears to the right or the left (in general, this word is a verb and the direction reflects the mention's role as subject or object). We lemmatize all feature words with the WordNet (Miller et al., 1990) stemmer. The resulting distribution over words is our set of unigram features for the character. (We do not prune rare features, although they have proportionally little influence on our measurement of similarity.)

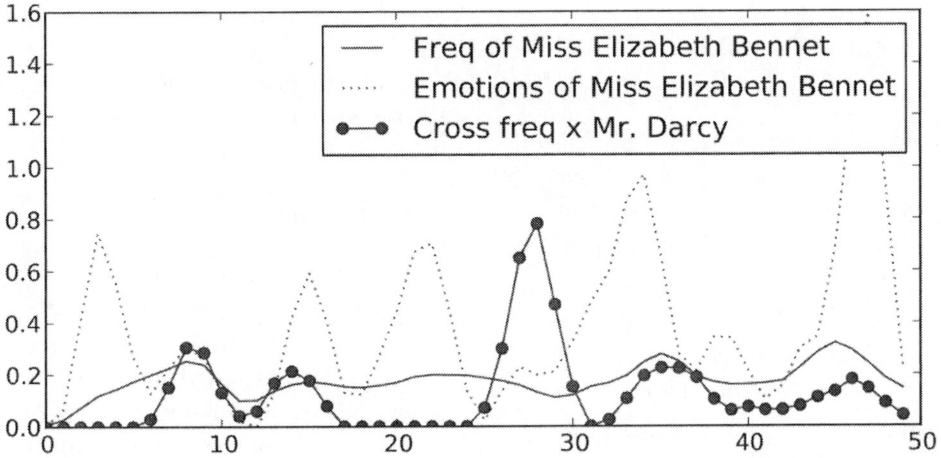

Figure 1: Normalized frequency and emotions associated with "Miss Elizabeth Bennet", protagonist of *Pride and Prejudice*, and frequency of paragraphs about her and "Mr. Darcy", smoothed and projected onto 50 basis points.

4.3 Temporal relationships

We record two time-varying features for each character, each taking one value per chapter. The first is the character's frequency as a proportion of all character mentions in the chapter. The second is the frequency with which the character is associated with emotional language—their emotional trajectory (Alm et al., 2005). We use the strong subjectivity cues from the lexicon of Wilson et al. (2005) as a measurement of emotion. If, in a particular paragraph, only one character is mentioned, we count all emotional words in that paragraph and add them to the character's total. To render the numbers comparable across works, each paragraph subtotal is normalized by the amount of emotional language in the novel as a whole. Then the chapter score is the average over paragraphs.

For pairwise character relationships, we count the number of paragraphs in which only two characters are mentioned, and treat this number (as a proportion of the total) as a measurement of the strength of the relationship between that pair[3]. Elson et al. (2010) show that their method of finding conversations between characters is more precise in showing whether a relationship exists, but the co-occurrence technique is simpler, and we care mostly about the strength of key relationships rather than the existence of infrequent ones.

Finally, we perform some smoothing, by taking a weighted moving average of each feature value with a window of the three values on either side. Then, in order to make it easy to compare books with different numbers of chapters, we linearly interpolate each series of points into a curve and project it onto a fixed basis of 50 evenly spaced points. An example of the final output is shown in Figure 1.

5 Kernels

Our plot kernel $k(x, y)$ measures the similarity between two novels x and y in terms of the features computed above. It takes the form of a convolution kernel (Haussler, 1999) where the "parts" of each novel are its characters $u \in x$, $v \in y$ and c is a kernel over characters:

$$k(x, y) = \sum_{u \in x} \sum_{v \in y} c(u, v) \quad (1)$$

We begin by constructing a first-order kernel over characters, $c_1(u, v)$, which is defined in terms of a kernel d over the unigram features and a kernel e over the single-character temporal features. We represent the unigram feature counts as distributions $p_u(w)$ and $p_v(w)$, and compute their similarity as the amount of shared mass, times a small penalty of .1 for mismatched genders:

[3] We tried also counting emotional language in these paragraphs, but this did not seem to help in development experiments.

$$d(p_u, p_v) = \exp(-\alpha(1 - \textstyle\sum_w min(p_u(w), p_v(w)))) \times .1\, \mathbb{I}\{gen_u = gen_v\}$$

We compute similarity between a pair of time-varying curves (which are projected onto 50 evenly spaced points) using standard cosine distance, which approximates the normalized integral of their product.

$$e(u, v) = \left(\frac{u \bullet v}{\sqrt{\|u\|\|v\|}}\right)^{\beta} \quad (2)$$

The weights α and β are parameters of the system, which scale d and e so that they are comparable to one another, and also determine how fast the similarity scales up as the feature sets grow closer; we set them to 5 and 10 respectively.

We sum together the similarities of the character frequency and emotion curves to measure overall temporal similarity between the characters. Thus our first-order character kernel c_1 is:

$$c_1(u, v) = d(p_u, p_v)(e(u_{freq}, v_{freq}) + e(u_{emo}, v_{emo}))$$

We use c_1 and equation 1 to construct a first-order plot kernel (which we call k_1), and also as an ingredient in a second-order character kernel c_2 which takes into account the curve of pairwise frequencies $\widehat{u, u'}$ between two characters u and u' in the same novel.

$$c_2(u, v) = c_1(u, v) \sum_{u' \in x} \sum_{v' \in y} e(\widehat{u, u'}, \widehat{v, v'}) c_1(u', v')$$

In other words, u is similar to v if, for some relationships of u with other characters u', there are similar characters v' who serves the same role for v. We use c_2 and equation 1 to construct our full plot kernel k_2.

5.1 Sentiment-only baseline

In addition to our plot kernel systems, we implement a simple baseline intended to test the effectiveness of tracking the emotional trajectory of the novel without using character identities. We give our baseline access to the same subjectivity lexicon used for our temporal features. We compute the number of emotional words used in each chapter (regardless of which characters they co-occur with), smoothed and normalized as described in subsection 4.3. This produces a single time-varying curve for each novel, representing the average emotional intensity of each chapter. We use our curve kernel e (equation 2) to measure similarity between novels.

6 Experiments

We evaluate our kernels on their ability to distinguish between real novels from our dataset and artificial surrogate novels of three types. First, we alter the **order** of a real novel by permuting its chapters before computing features. We construct one uniformally-random permutation for each test novel. Second, we change the identities of the **characters** by reassigning the temporal features for the different characters uniformally at random while leaving the unigram features unaltered. (For example, we might assign the frequency, emotion and relationship curves for "Mr. Collins" to "Miss Elizabeth Bennet" instead.) Again, we produce one test instance of this type for each test novel. Third, we experiment with a more difficult ordering task by taking the chapters in **reverse**.

In each case, we use our kernel to perform a ranking task, deciding whether $k(x, y) > k(x, y_{perm})$. Since this is a binary forced-choice classification, a random baseline would score 50%. We evaluate performance in the case where we are given only a single training document x, and for a whole training set X, in which case we combine the decisions using a weighted nearest neighbor (WNN) strategy:

$$\sum_{x \in X} k(x, y) > \sum_{x \in X} k(x, y_{perm})$$

In each case, we perform the experiment in a leave-one-out fashion; we include the 11 development documents in X, but not in the test set. Thus there are 1200 single-document comparisons and 30 with WNN. The results of our three systems (the baseline, the first-order kernel k_1 and the second-order kernel k_2) are shown in Table 2. (The sentiment-only baseline has no character-specific features, and so cannot perform the **character** task.)

Using the full dataset and second-order kernel k_2, our system's performance on these tasks is quite good; we are correct 90% of the time for **order** and **character** examples, and 67% for the

	order	character	reverse
sentiment only	46.2	-	51.5
single doc k_1	59.5	63.7	50.7
single doc k_2	61.8	67.7	51.6
WNN sentiment	50	-	53
WNN k_1	77	90	63
WNN k_2	90	90	67

Table 2: Accuracy of kernels ranking 30 real novels against artificial surrogates (chance accuracy 50%).

more difficult **reverse** cases. Results of this quality rely heavily on the WNN strategy, which trusts close neighbors more than distant ones.

In the single training point setup, the system is much less accurate. In this setting, the system is forced to make decisions for all pairs of texts independently, including pairs it considers very dissimilar because it has failed to find any useful correspondences. Performance for these pairs is close to chance, dragging down overall scores (52% for **reverse**) even if the system performs well on pairs where it finds good correspondences, enabling a higher WNN score (67%).

The **reverse** case is significantly harder than **order**. This is because randomly permuting a novel actually breaks up the temporal continuity of the text—for instance, a minor character who appeared in three adjacent chapters might now appear in three separate places. Reversing the text does not cause this kind of disruption, so correctly detecting a reversal requires the system to represent patterns with a distinct temporal orientation, for instance an intensification in the main character's emotions, or in the number of paragraphs focusing on pairwise relationships, toward the end of the text.

The baseline system is ineffective at detecting either ordering or reversals[4]. The first-order kernel k_1 is as good as k_2 in detecting character permutations, but less effective on reorderings and reversals. As we will show in section 9, k_1 places more emphasis on correspondences between minor characters and between places, while k_2 is more sensitive to protagonists and their relationships, which carry the richest temporal information.

7 Significance testing

In addition to using our kernel as a classifier, we can directly test its ability to distinguish real from altered novels via a non-parametric two-sample significance test, the Maximum Mean Discrepancy (MMD) test (Gretton et al., 2007). Given samples from a pair of distributions p and q and a kernel k, this test determines whether the null hypothesis that p and q are identically distributed in the kernel's feature space can be rejected. The advantage of this test is that, since it takes all pairwise comparisons (except self-comparisons) within and across the classes into account, it uses more information than our classification experiments, and can therefore be more sensitive.

As in Gretton et al. (2007), we find an unbiased estimate of the test statistic MMD^2 for sample sets $x \sim p$, $y \sim q$, each with m samples, by pairing the two as $z = (x_i, y_i)$ and computing:

$$MMD^2(x,y) = \frac{1}{(m)(m-1)} \sum_{i \neq j}^{m} h(z_i, z_j)$$

$$h(z_i,z_j) = k(x_i,x_j)+k(y_i,y_j)-k(x_i,y_j)-k(x_j,y_i)$$

Intuitively, MMD^2 approaches 0 if the kernel cannot distinguish x from y and is positive otherwise. The null distribution is computed by the bootstrap method; we create null-distributed samples by randomly swapping x_i and y_i in elements of z and computing the test statistic. We use 10000 test permutations. Using both k_1 and k_2, we can reject the null hypothesis that the distribution of novels is equal to **order** or **characters** with $p < .001$; for reversals, we cannot reject the null hypothesis.

8 Out-of-domain data

In our main experiments, we tested our kernel only on romances; here we investigate its ability to generalize across genres. We take as our training set X the same romances as above, but as our test set Y a disjoint set of novels focusing mainly on crime, children and the supernatural.

Our results (Table 3) are not appreciably different from those of the in-domain experiments (Table 2) considering the small size of the dataset. This shows our system to be robust, but shallow;

[4]The baseline detects reversals as well as the plot kernels given only a single point of comparison, but these results do not transfer to the WNN strategy. This suggests that unlike the plot kernels, the baseline is no more accurate for documents it considers similar than for those it judges are distant.

	order	character	reverse
sentiment only	33.0	-	53.4
single doc k_1	59.5	61.7	52.7
single doc k_2	63.7	62.0	57.3
WNN sentiment	20	-	70
WNN k_1	80	90	80
WNN k_2	100	80	70

Table 3: Accuracy of kernels ranking 10 non-romance novels against artificial surrogates, with 41 romances used for comparison.

the patterns it can represent generalize acceptably across domains, but this suggests it is describing broad concepts like "main character" rather than genre-specific ones like "female romantic lead".

9 Character-level analysis

To gain some insight into exactly what kinds of similarities the system picks up on when comparing two works, we sorted the characters detected by our system into categories and measured their contribution to the kernel's overall scores. We selected four Jane Austen works from the development set[5] and hand-categorized each character detected by our system. (We performed the categorization based on the most common full name mention in each cluster. This name is usually a good identifier for all the mentions in the cluster, but if our coreference system has made an error, it may not be.)

Our categorization for characters is intended to capture the stereotypical plot dynamics of literary romance, sorting the characters according to their gender and a simple notion of their plot function. The genders are **female**, **male**, **plural** ("the Crawfords") or **not a character** ("London"). The functional classes are **protagonist** (used for the female viewpoint character and her eventual husband), **marriageable** (single men and women who are seeking to marry within the story) and **other** (older characters, children, and characters married before the story begins).

We evaluate the pairwise kernel similarities among our four works, and add up the proportional contribution made by character pairs of each type to the eventual score. (For instance, the similarity between "Elizabeth Bennet" and "Emma Woodhouse", both labeled "female protagonist", contributes 26% of the kernel similarity between the works in which they appear.) We plot these as Hinton-style diagrams in Figure 2. The size of each black rectangle indicates the magnitude of the contribution. (Since kernel functions are symmetric, we show only the lower diagonal.)

Under the kernel for unigram features, d (top), the most common character types—non-characters (almost always places) and non-marriageable women—contribute most to the kernel scores; this is especially true for places, since they often occur with similar descriptive terms. The diagram also shows the effect of the kernel's penalty for gender mismatches, since females pair more strongly with females and males with males. Character roles have relatively little impact.

The first-order kernel c_1 (middle), which takes into account frequency and emotion as well as unigrams, is much better than d at distinguishing places from real characters, and assigns somewhat more weight to protagonists.

Finally, c_2 (bottom), which takes into account second-order relationships, places much more emphasis on female protagonists and much less on places. This is presumably because the female protagonists of Jane Austen's novels are the viewpoint characters, and the novels focus on their relationships, while characters do not tend to have strong relationships with places. An increased tendency to match male marriageable characters with marriageable females, and "other" males with "other" females, suggests that c_2 relies more on character function and less on unigrams than c_1 when finding correspondences between characters.

As we concluded in the previous section, the frequent confusion between categories suggests that the analogies we construct are relatively non-specific. We might hope to create role-based summary of novels by finding their nearest neighbors and then propagating the character categories (for example, "___ is the protagonist of this novel. She lives at ___. She eventually marries ___, her other suitors are ___ and her older guardian is ___.") but the present system is probably not adequate for the purpose. We expect that detecting a fine-grained set of emotions will help to separate character functions more clearly.

[5] *Pride and Prejudice*, *Emma*, *Mansfield Park* and *Persuasion*.

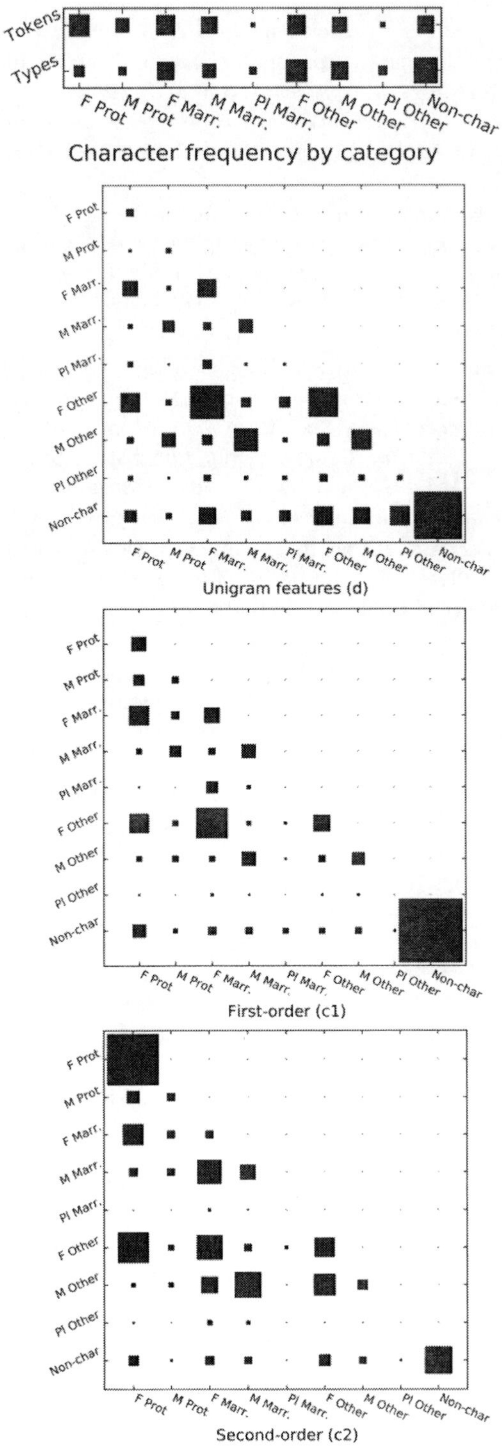

Figure 2: Affinity diagrams showing character types contributing to the kernel similarity between four works by Jane Austen.

10 Conclusions

This work presents a method for describing novelistic plots at an abstract level. It has three main contributions: the description of a plot in terms of analogies between characters, the use of emotional and frequency trajectories for individual characters rather than whole works, and evaluation using artificially disordered surrogate novels. In future work, we hope to sharpen the analogies we construct so that they are useful for summarization, perhaps by finding an external standard by which we can make the notion of "analogous" characters precise. We would also like to investigate what gains are possible with a finer-grained emotional vocabulary.

Acknowledgements

Thanks to Sharon Goldwater, Mirella Lapata, Victoria Adams and the ProbModels group for their comments on preliminary versions of this work, Kira Mourão for suggesting graph kernels, and three reviewers for their comments.

References

Amjad Abu Jbara and Dragomir Radev. 2011. Coherent citation-based summarization of scientific papers. In *Proceedings of ACL 2011*, Portland, Oregon.

Cecilia Ovesdotter Alm and Richard Sproat. 2005. Emotional sequencing and development in fairy tales. In *ACII*, pages 668–674.

Cecilia Ovesdotter Alm, Dan Roth, and Richard Sproat. 2005. Emotions from text: Machine learning for text-based emotion prediction. In *Proceedings of Human Language Technology Conference and Conference on Empirical Methods in Natural Language Processing*, pages 579–586, Vancouver, British Columbia, Canada, October. Association for Computational Linguistics.

Regina Barzilay and Mirella Lapata. 2005. Modeling local coherence: an entity-based approach. In *Proceedings of the 43rd Annual Meeting of the Association for Computational Linguistics (ACL'05)*.

Indrajit Bhattacharya and Lise Getoor. 2005. Relational clustering for multi-type entity resolution. In *Proceedings of the 4th international workshop on Multi-relational mining*, MRDM '05, pages 3–12, New York, NY, USA. ACM.

Nathanael Chambers and Dan Jurafsky. 2009. Unsupervised learning of narrative schemas and their participants. In *Proceedings of the Joint Conference of the 47th Annual Meeting of the ACL and the*

4th International Joint Conference on Natural Language Processing of the AFNLP, pages 602–610, Suntec, Singapore, August. Association for Computational Linguistics.

Eugene Charniak. 2001. Unsupervised learning of name structure from coreference data. In *Second Meeting of the North American Chapter of the Association for Computational Linguistics (NACL-01)*.

Harr Chen, S.R.K. Branavan, Regina Barzilay, and David R. Karger. 2009. Global models of document structure using latent permutations. In *Proceedings of Human Language Technologies: The 2009 Annual Conference of the North American Chapter of the Association for Computational Linguistics*, pages 371–379, Boulder, Colorado, June. Association for Computational Linguistics.

Mark Dredze, Paul McNamee, Delip Rao, Adam Gerber, and Tim Finin. 2010. Entity disambiguation for knowledge base population. In *Proceedings of the 23rd International Conference on Computational Linguistics (Coling 2010)*, pages 277–285, Beijing, China, August. Coling 2010 Organizing Committee.

David K. Elson and Kathleen R. McKeown. 2010. Building a bank of semantically encoded narratives. In Nicoletta Calzolari (Conference Chair), Khalid Choukri, Bente Maegaard, Joseph Mariani, Jan Odijk, Stelios Piperidis, Mike Rosner, and Daniel Tapias, editors, *Proceedings of the Seventh conference on International Language Resources and Evaluation (LREC'10)*, Valletta, Malta, May. European Language Resources Association (ELRA).

David Elson, Nicholas Dames, and Kathleen McKeown. 2010. Extracting social networks from literary fiction. In *Proceedings of the 48th Annual Meeting of the Association for Computational Linguistics*, pages 138–147, Uppsala, Sweden, July. Association for Computational Linguistics.

Amit Goyal, Ellen Riloff, and Hal Daume III. 2010. Automatically producing plot unit representations for narrative text. In *Proceedings of the 2010 Conference on Empirical Methods in Natural Language Processing*, pages 77–86, Cambridge, MA, October. Association for Computational Linguistics.

Arthur Gretton, Karsten M. Borgwardt, Malte Rasch, Bernhard Schlkopf, and Alexander J. Smola. 2007. A kernel method for the two-sample-problem. In B. Schölkopf, J. Platt, and T. Hoffman, editors, *Advances in Neural Information Processing Systems 19*, pages 513–520. MIT Press, Cambridge, MA.

David Haussler. 1999. Convolution kernels on discrete structures. Technical Report UCSC-CRL-99-10, Computer Science Department, UC Santa Cruz.

Nikiforos Karamanis, Massimo Poesio, Chris Mellish, and Jon Oberlander. 2004. Evaluating centering-based metrics of coherence. In *ACL*, pages 391–398.

Anna Kazantseva and Stan Szpakowicz. 2010. Summarizing short stories. *Computational Linguistics*, pages 71–109.

Dekang Lin and Patrick Pantel. 2001. Induction of semantic classes from natural language text. In *Proceedings of the seventh ACM SIGKDD international conference on Knowledge discovery and data mining*, KDD '01, pages 317–322, New York, NY, USA. ACM.

David McClosky, Eugene Charniak, and Mark Johnson. 2006. Effective self-training for parsing. In *Proceedings of the Human Language Technology Conference of the NAACL, Main Conference*, pages 152–159.

Neil McIntyre and Mirella Lapata. 2010. Plot induction and evolutionary search for story generation. In *Proceedings of the 48th Annual Meeting of the Association for Computational Linguistics*, pages 1562–1572, Uppsala, Sweden, July. Association for Computational Linguistics.

G. Miller, A.R. Beckwith, C. Fellbaum, D. Gross, and K. Miller. 1990. Introduction to WordNet: an on-line lexical database. *International Journal of Lexicography*, 3(4).

Saif Mohammad. 2011. From once upon a time to happily ever after: Tracking emotions in novels and fairy tales. In *Proceedings of the 5th ACL-HLT Workshop on Language Technology for Cultural Heritage, Social Sciences, and Humanities*, pages 105–114, Portland, OR, USA, June. Association for Computational Linguistics.

Matt Post. 2011. Judging grammaticality with tree substitution grammar derivations. In *Proceedings of the 49th Annual Meeting of the Association for Computational Linguistics: Human Language Technologies*, pages 217–222, Portland, Oregon, USA, June. Association for Computational Linguistics.

Jeffrey C. Reynar and Adwait Ratnaparkhi. 1997. A maximum entropy approach to identifying sentence boundaries. In *Proceedings of the Fifth Conference on Applied Natural Language Processing*, pages 16–19, Washington D.C.

Ekaterina P. Volkova, Betty Mohler, Detmar Meurers, Dale Gerdemann, and Heinrich H. Bülthoff. 2010. Emotional perception of fairy tales: Achieving agreement in emotion annotation of text. In *Proceedings of the NAACL HLT 2010 Workshop on Computational Approaches to Analysis and Generation of Emotion in Text*, pages 98–106, Los Angeles, CA, June. Association for Computational Linguistics.

Theresa Wilson, Janyce Wiebe, and Paul Hoffmann. 2005. Recognizing contextual polarity in phrase-level sentiment analysis. In *Proceedings of Human Language Technology Conference and Conference on Empirical Methods in Natural Language*

Processing, pages 347–354, Vancouver, British Columbia, Canada, October. Association for Computational Linguistics.

A List of texts

Dev set (11 works)			
Austen	*Emma, Mansfield Park, Northanger Abbey, Persuasion, Pride and Prejudice, Sense and Sensibility*	Brontë, Emily	*Wuthering Heights*
Burney	*Cecilia* (1782)	Hardy	*Tess of the D'Urbervilles*
James	*The Ambassadors*	Scott	*Ivanhoe*
Test set (30 works)			
Braddon	*Aurora Floyd*	Brontë, Anne	*The Tenant of Wildfell Hall*
Brontë, Charlotte	*Jane Eyre, Villette*	Bulwer-Lytton	*Zanoni*
Disraeli	*Coningsby, Tancred*	Edgeworth	*The Absentee, Belinda, Helen*
Eliot	*Adam Bede, Daniel Deronda, Middlemarch*	Gaskell	*Mary Barton, North and South*
Gissing	*In the Year of Jubilee, New Grub Street*	Hardy	*Far From the Madding Crowd, Jude the Obscure, Return of the Native, Under the Greenwood Tree*
James	*The Wings of the Dove*	Meredith	*The Egoist, The Ordeal of Richard Feverel*
Scott	*The Bride of Lammermoor*	Thackeray	*History of Henry Esmond, History of Pendennis, Vanity Fair*
Trollope	*Doctor Thorne*		
Out-of-domain set (10 works)			
Ainsworth	*The Lancashire Witches*	Bulwer-Lytton	*Paul Clifford*
Dickens	*Oliver Twist, The Pickwick Papers*	Collins	*The Moonstone*
Conan-Doyle	*A Study in Scarlet, The Sign of the Four*	Hughes	*Tom Brown's Schooldays*
Stevenson	*Treasure Island*	Stoker	*Dracula*

Table 4: 19th century novels used in our study.

Smart Paradigms and the Predictability and Complexity of Inflectional Morphology

Grégoire Détrez and Aarne Ranta
Department of Computer Science and Engineering
Chalmers University of Technology and University of Gothenburg

Abstract

Morphological lexica are often implemented on top of morphological paradigms, corresponding to different ways of building the full inflection table of a word. Computationally precise lexica may use hundreds of paradigms, and it can be hard for a lexicographer to choose among them. To automate this task, this paper introduces the notion of a **smart paradigm**. It is a meta-paradigm, which inspects the base form and tries to infer which low-level paradigm applies. If the result is uncertain, more forms are given for discrimination. The number of forms needed in average is a measure of **predictability** of an inflection system. The overall **complexity** of the system also has to take into account the code size of the paradigms definition itself. This paper evaluates the smart paradigms implemented in the open-source GF Resource Grammar Library. Predictability and complexity are estimated for four different languages: English, French, Swedish, and Finnish. The main result is that predictability does not decrease when the complexity of morphology grows, which means that smart paradigms provide an efficient tool for the manual construction and/or automatically bootstrapping of lexica.

1 Introduction

Paradigms are a cornerstone of grammars in the European tradition. A classical Latin grammar has five paradigms for nouns ("declensions") and four for verbs ("conjugations"). The modern reference on French verbs, *Bescherelle* (Bescherelle, 1997), has 88 paradigms for verbs. Swedish grammars traditionally have, like Latin, five paradigms for nouns and four for verbs, but a modern computational account (Hellberg, 1978), aiming for more precision, has 235 paradigms for Swedish.

Mathematically, a paradigm is a function that produces inflection tables. Its argument is a word string (either a **dictionary form** or a **stem**), and its value is an n-tuple of strings (the word forms):

$$P : \text{String} \rightarrow \text{String}^n$$

We assume that the exponent n is determined by the language and the part of speech. For instance, English verbs might have $n = 5$ (for *sing, sings, sang, sung, singing*), whereas for French verbs in *Bescherelle*, $n = 51$. We assume the tuples to be ordered, so that for instance the French second person singular present subjunctive is always found at position 17. In this way, word-paradigm pairs can be easily converted to morphogical lexica and to transducers that map form descriptions to surface forms and back. A properly designed set of paradigms permits a compact representation of a lexicon and a user-friendly way to extend it.

Different paradigm systems may have different numbers of paradigms. There are two reasons for this. One is that traditional paradigms often in fact require more arguments than one:

$$P : \text{String}^m \rightarrow \text{String}^n$$

Here $m \leq n$ and the set of arguments is a subset of the set of values. Thus the so-called fourth verb conjugation in Swedish actually needs three forms to work properly, for instance *sitta, satt, suttit* for the equivalent of *sit, sat, sat* in English. In Hellberg (1978), as in the French *Bescherelle*, each paradigm is defined to take exactly one argument, and hence each vowel alternation pattern must be a different paradigm.

The other factor that affects the number of paradigms is the nature of the string operations allowed in the function P. In Hellberg (1978), noun paradigms only permit the concatenation of suffixes to a stem. Thus the paradigms are identified with suffix sets. For instance, the inflection patterns *bil–bilar* ("car–cars") and *nyckel–nycklar* ("key–keys") are traditionally both treated as instances of the second declension, with the plural ending *ar* and the contraction of the unstressed *e* in the case of *nyckel*. But in Hellberg, the word *nyckel* has *nyck* as its "technical stem", to which the paradigm numbered 231 adds the singular ending *el* and the plural ending *lar*.

The notion of paradigm used in this paper allows multiple arguments and powerful string operations. In this way, we will be able to reduce the number of paradigms drastically: in fact, each lexical category (noun, adjective, verb), will have just *one* paradigm but with a variable number of arguments. Paradigms that follow this design will be called **smart paradigms** and are introduced in Section 2. Section 3 defines the notions of **predictability** and **complexity** of smart paradigm systems. Section 4 estimates these figures for four different languages of increasing richness in morphology: English, Swedish, French, and Finnish. We also evaluate the smart paradigms as a data compression method. Section 5 explores some uses of smart paradigms in lexicon building. Section 6 compares smart paradigms with related techniques such as morphology guessers and extraction tools. Section 7 concludes.

2 Smart paradigms

In this paper, we will assume a notion of paradigm that allows multiple arguments and arbitrary computable string operations. As argued in (Kaplan and Kay, 1994) and amply demonstrated in (Beesley and Karttunen, 2003), no generality is lost if the string operators are restricted to ones computable by finite-state transducers. Thus the examples of paradigms that we will show (only informally), can be converted to matching and replacements with regular expressions.

For example, a majority of French verbs can be defined by the following paradigm, which analyzes a variable-size suffix of the infinitive form and dispatches to the *Bescherelle* paradigms (identified by a number and an example verb):

$$\text{mkV} : \text{String} \rightarrow \text{String}^{51}$$

$$\text{mkV}(s) =$$

- conj19finir(s), if s ends *ir*
- conj53rendre(s), if s ends *re*
- conj14assiéger(s), if s ends *éger*
- conj11jeter(s), if s ends *eler* or *eter*
- conj10céder(s), if s ends *éder*
- conj07placer(s), if s ends *cer*
- conj08manger(s), if s ends *ger*
- conj16payer(s), if s ends *yer*
- conj06parler(s), if s ends *er*

Notice that the cases must be applied in the given order; for instance, the last case applies only to those verbs ending with *er* that are not matched by the earlier cases.

Also notice that the above paradigm is just like the more traditional ones, in the sense that we cannot be sure if it really applies to a given verb. For instance, the verb *partir* ends with *ir* and would hence receive the same inflection as *finir*; however, its real conjugation is number 26 in *Bescherelle*. That mkV uses 19 rather than number 26 has a good reason: a vast majority of *ir* verbs is inflected in this conjugation, and it is also the productive one, to which new *ir* verbs are added.

Even though there is no mathematical difference between the mkV paradigm and the traditional paradigms like those in *Bescherelle*, there is a reason to call mkV a **smart paradigm**. This name implies two things. First, a smart paradigm implements some "artificial intelligence" to pick the underlying "stupid" paradigm. Second, a smart paradigm uses heuristics (informed guessing) if string matching doesn't decide the matter; the guess is informed by statistics of the distributions of different inflection classes.

One could thus say that smart paradigms are "second-order" or "meta-paradigms", compared to more traditional ones. They implement a lot of linguistic knowledge and intelligence, and thereby enable tasks such as lexicon building to be performed with less expertise than before. For instance, instead of "07" for *foncer* and "06" for *marcher*, the lexicographer can simply write "mkV" for all verbs instead of choosing from 88 numbers.

In fact, just "V", indicating that the word is a verb, will be enough, since the name of the paradigm depends only on the part of speech. This follows the model of many dictionaries and methods of language teaching, where **characteristic forms** are used instead of paradigm identifiers. For instance, another variant of mkV could use as its second argument the first person plural present indicative to decide whether an *ir* verb is in conjugation 19 or in 26:

$$\text{mkV} : \text{String}^2 \rightarrow \text{String}^{51}$$

$$\text{mkV}(s, t) =$$

- conj26partir(s), if for some x, $s = x{+}ir$ and $t = x{+}ons$
- conj19finir(s), if s ends with *ir*
- (all the other cases that can be recognized by this extra form)
- mkV(s) otherwise (fall-back to the one-argument paradigm)

In this way, a series of smart paradigms is built for each part of speech, with more and more arguments. The trick is to investigate which new forms have the best discriminating power. For ease of use, the paradigms should be displayed to the user in an easy to understand format, e.g. as a table specifying the possible argument lists:

verb	*parler*
verb	*parler, parlons*
verb	*parler, parlons, parlera, parla, parlé*
noun	*chien*
noun	*chien*, masculine
noun	*chien, chiens*, masculine

Notice that, for French nouns, the gender is listed as one of the pieces of information needed for lexicon building. In many cases, it can be inferred from the dictionary form just like the inflection; for instance, that most nouns ending *e* are feminine. A gender argument in the smart noun paradigm makes it possible to override this default behaviour.

2.1 Paradigms in GF

Smart paradigms as used in this paper have been implemented in the GF programming language (Grammatical Framework, (Ranta, 2011)). GF is a functional programming lnguage enriched with regular expressions. For instance, the following function implements a part of the one-argument French verb paradigm shown above. It uses a case expression to pattern match with the argument s; the pattern _ matches anything, while + divides a string to two pieces, and | expresses alternation. The functions `conj19finir` etc. are defined elsewhere in the library. Function application is expressed without parentheses, by the juxtaposition of the function and the argument.

```
mkV : Str -> V
mkV s = case s of {
  _ + "ir" -> conj19finir s ;
  _ + ("eler"|"eter")
          -> conj11jeter s ;
  _ + "er" -> conj06parler s ;
  }
```

The GF Resource Grammar Library[1] has comprehensive smart paradigms for 18 languages: Amharic, Catalan, Danish, Dutch, English, Finnish, French, German, Hindi, Italian, Nepalese, Norwegian, Romanian, Russian, Spanish, Swedish, Turkish, and Urdu. A few other languages have complete sets of "traditional" inflection paradigms but no smart paradigms.

Six languages in the library have comprehensive morphological dictionaries: Bulgarian (53k lemmas), English (42k), Finnish (42k), French (92k), Swedish (43k), and Turkish (23k). They have been extracted from other high-quality resources via conversions to GF using the paradigm systems. In Section 4, four of them will be used for estimating the strength of the smart paradigms, that is, the predictability of each language.

3 Cost, predictability, and complexity

Given a language $\mathcal{L}$, a lexical category C, and a set P of smart paradigms for C, the **predictability** of the morphology of C in $\mathcal{L}$ by P depends inversely on the average number of arguments needed to generate the correct inflection table for a word. The lower the number, the more predictable the system.

Predictability can be estimated from a lexicon that contains such a set of tables. Formally, a smart paradigm is a family P_m of functions

$$P_m : \text{String}^m \rightarrow \text{String}^n$$

where m ranges over some set of integers from 1 to n, but need not contain all those integers. A **lexicon** L is a finite set of inflection tables,

$$L = \{w_i : \text{String}^n \mid i = 1, \ldots, M_L\}$$

[1] Source code and documentation in http://www.grammaticalframework.org/lib.

As the n is fixed, this is a lexicon specialized to one part of speech. A **word** is an element of the lexicon, that is, an inflection table of size n.

An **application** of a smart paradigm P_m to a word $w \in L$ is an inflection table resulting from applying P_m to the appropriate subset $\sigma_m(w)$ of the inflection table w,

$$P_m[w] = P_m(\sigma_m(w)) : \text{String}^n$$

Thus we assume that all arguments are existing word forms (rather than e.g. stems), or features such as the gender.

An application is **correct** if

$$P_m[w] = w$$

The **cost of a word** w is the minimum number of arguments needed to make the application correct:

$$cost(w) = \underset{m}{\text{argmin}}(P_m[w] = w)$$

For practical applications, it is useful to require P_m to be **monotonic**, in the sense that increasing m preserves correctness.

The **cost of a lexicon** L is the average cost for its words,

$$\text{cost}(L) = \frac{\sum_{i=1}^{M_L} \text{cost}(w_i)}{M_L}$$

where M_L is the number of words in the lexicon, as defined above.

The **predictability** of a lexicon could be defined as a quantity inversely dependent on its cost. For instance, an information-theoretic measure could be defined

$$\text{predict}(L) = \frac{1}{1 + \log \text{cost}(L)}$$

with the intuition that each added argument corresponds to a choice in a decision tree. However, we will not use this measure in this paper, but just the concrete cost.

The **complexity of a paradigm system** is defined as the size of its code in a given coding system, following the idea of Kolmogorov complexity (Solomonoff, 1964). The notion assumes a coding system, which we fix to be GF source code. As the results are relative to the coding system, they are only usable for comparing definitions in the same system. However, using GF source code size rather than e.g. a finite automaton size gives in our view a better approximation of the "cognitive load" of the paradigm system, its "learnability". As a functional programming language, GF permits abstractions comparable to those available for human language learners, who don't need to learn the repetitive details of a finite automaton.

We define the **code complexity** as the size of the abstract syntax tree of the source code. This size is given as the number of nodes in the syntax tree; for instance,

- $\text{size}(f(x_1, \ldots, x_n)) = 1 + \sum_{i=1}^{n} \text{size}(x_i)$
- $\text{size}(s) = 1$, for a string literal s

Using the abstract syntax size makes it possible to ignore programmer-specific variation such as identifier size. Measurements of the GF Resource Grammar Library show that code size measured in this way is in average 20% of the size of source files in bytes. Thus a source file of 1 kB has the code complexity around 200 on the average.

Notice that code complexity is defined in a way that makes it into a straightforward generalization of the cost of a word as expressed in terms of paradigm applications in GF source code. The source code complexity of a paradigm application is

$$\text{size}(P_m[w]) = 1 + m$$

Thus the complexity for a word w is its cost plus one; the addition of one comes from the application node for the function P_m and corresponds to knowing the part of speech of the word.

4 Experimental results

We conducted experiments in four languages (English, Swedish, French and Finnish[2]), presented here in order of morphological richness. We used trusted full form lexica (i.e. lexica giving the complete inflection table of every word) to compute the predictability, as defined above, in terms of the smart paradigms in GF Resource Grammar Library.

We used a simple algorithm for computing the cost c of a lexicon L with a set P_m of smart paradigms:

[2]This choice correspond to the set of language for which both comprehensive smart paradigms and morphological dictionaries were present in GF with the exception of Turkish, which was left out because of time constraints.

- set $c := 0$
- for each word w_i in L,
  - for each m in growing order for which P_m is defined:
    if $P_m[w] = w$, then $c := c + m$, else try with next m
- return c

The average cost is c divided by the size of L.

The procedure presupposes that it is always possible to get the correct inflection table. For this to be true, the smart paradigms must have a "worst case scenario" version that is able to generate all forms. In practice, this was not always the case but we checked that the number of problematic words is so small that it wouldn't be statistically significant. A typical problem word was the equivalent of the verb *be* in each language.

Another source of deviation is that a lexicon may have inflection tables with size deviating from the number n that normally defines a lexical category. Some words may be "defective", i.e. lack some forms (e.g. the singular form in "plurale tantum" words), whereas some words may have several variants for a given form (e.g. *learned* and *learnt* in English). We made no effort to predict defective words, but just ignored them. With variant forms, we treated a prediction as correct if it matched any of the variants.

The above algorithm can also be used for helping to select the optimal sets of characteristic forms; we used it in this way to select the first form of Swedish verbs and the second form of Finnish nouns.

The results are collected in Table 1. The sections below give more details of the experiment in each language.

4.1 English

As gold standard, we used the electronic version of the Oxford Advanced Learner's Dictionary of Current English[3] which contains about 40,000 root forms (about 70,000 word forms).

Nouns. We considered English nouns as having only two forms (singular and plural), excluding the genitive forms which can be considered to be clitics and are completely predictable. About one third of the nouns of the lexicon were not included in the experiment because one of the form was missing. The vast majority of the remaining 15,000 nouns are very regular, with predictable deviations such as *kiss - kisses* and *fly - flies* which can be easily predicted by the smart paradigm. With the average cost of 1.05, this was the most predictable lexicon in our experiment.

Verbs. Verbs are the most interesting category in English because they present the richest morphology. Indeed, as shown by Table 1, the cost for English verbs, 1.21, is similar to what we got for morphologically richer languages.

4.2 Swedish

As gold standard, we used the SALDO lexicon (Borin et al., 2008).

Nouns. The noun inflection tables had 8 forms (singular/plural indefinite/definite nominative/genitive) plus a gender (uter/neuter). Swedish nouns are intrinsically very unpredictable, and there are many examples of homonyms falling under different paradigms (e.g. *val - val* "choice" vs. *val -valar* "whale"). The cost 1.70 is the highest of all the lexica considered. Of course, there may be room for improving the smart paradigm.

Verbs. The verbs had 20 forms, which included past participles. We ran two experiments, by choosing either the infinitive or the present indicative as the base form. In traditional Swedish grammar, the base form of the verb is considered to be the infinitive, e.g. *spela, leka* ("play" in two different senses). But this form doesn't distinguish between the "first" and the "second conjugation". However, the present indicative, here *spelar, leker*, does. Using it gives a predictive power 1.13 as opposed to 1.22 with the infinitive. Some modern dictionaries such as Lexin[4] therefore use the present indicative as the base form.

4.3 French

For French, we used the Morphalou morphological lexicon (Romary et al., 2004). As stated in the documentation[5] the current version of the lexicon (version 2.0) is not complete, and in particular, many entries are missing some or all inflected forms. So for those experiments we only

[3] available in electronic form at `http://www.eecs.qmul.ac.uk/~mpurver/software.html`

[4] `http://lexin.nada.kth.se/lexin/`

[5] `http://www.cnrtl.fr/lexiques/morphalou/LMF-Morphalou.php#body_3.4.11`, accessed 2011-11-04

Table 1: Lexicon size and average cost for the nouns (N) and verbs (V) in four languages, with the percentage of words correctly inferred from one and two forma (i.e. $m = 1$ and $m \leq 2$, respectively).

Lexicon	Forms	Entries	Cost	$m = 1$	$m \leq 2$
Eng N	2	15,029	1.05	95%	100%
Eng V	5	5,692	1.21	84%	95%
Swe N	9	59,225	1.70	46%	92%
Swe V	20	4,789	1.13	97%	97%
Fre N	3	42,390	1.25	76%	99%
Fre V	51	6,851	1.27	92%	94%
Fin N	34	25,365	1.26	87%	97%
Fin V	102	10,355	1.09	96%	99%

included entries where all the necessary forms were presents.

Nouns: Nouns in French have two forms (singular and plural) and an intrinsic gender (masculine or feminine), which we also considered to be a part of the inflection table. Most of the unpredictability comes from the impossibility to guess the gender.

Verbs: The paradigms generate all of the simple (as opposed to compound) tenses given in traditional grammars such as the *Bescherelle*. Also the participles are generated. The auxiliary verb of compound tenses would be impossible to guess from morphological clues, and was left out of consideration.

4.4 Finnish

The Finnish gold standard was the KOTUS lexicon (Kotimaisten Kielten Tutkimuskeskus, 2006). It has around 90,000 entries tagged with part of speech, 50 noun paradigms, and 30 verb paradigms. Some of these paradigms are rather abstract and powerful; for instance, grade alternation would multiply many of the paradigms by a factor of 10 to 20, if it was treated in a concatenative way. For instance, singular nominative-genitive pairs show alternations such as *talo–talon* ("house"), *katto–katon* ("roof"), *kanto–kannon* ("stub"), *rako–raon* ("crack"), and *sato–sadon* ("harvest"). All of these are treated with one and the same paradigm, which makes the KOTUS system relatively abstract.

The total number of forms of Finnish nouns and verbs is a question of definition. Koskenniemi (Koskenniemi, 1983) reports 2000 for nouns and 12,000 for verbs, but most of these forms result by adding particles and possessive suffixes in an agglutinative way. The traditional number and case count for nouns gives 26, whereas for verbs the count is between 100 and 200, depending on how participles are counted. Notice that the definition of predictability used in this paper doesn't depend on the number of forms produced (i.e. not on n but only on m); therefore we can simply ignore this question. However, the question is interesting if we think about paradigms as a data compression method (Section 4.5).

Nouns. Compound nouns are a problem for morphology prediction in Finnish, because inflection is sensitive to the vowel harmony and number of syllables, which depend on where the compound boundary goes. While many compounds are marked in KOTUS, we had to remove some compounds with unmarked boundaries. Another peculiarity was that adjectives were included in nouns; this is no problem since the inflection patterns are the same, if comparison forms are ignored. The figure 1.26 is better than the one reported in (Ranta, 2008), which is 1.42; the reason is mainly that the current set of paradigms has a better coverage of three-syllable nouns.

Verbs. Even though more numerous in forms than nouns, Finnish verbs are highly predictable (1.09).

4.5 Complexity and data compression

The cost of a lexicon has an effect on learnability. For instance, even though Finnish words have ten or a hundred times more forms than English forms, these forms can be derived from roughly the same number of characteristic forms as in English. But this is of course just a part of the truth: it might still be that the paradigm system itself is much more complex in some languages than oth-

Table 2: Paradigm complexities for nouns and verbs in the four languages, computed as the syntax tree size of GF code.

language	noun	verb	total
English	403	837	991
Swedish	918	1039	1884
French	351	2193	2541
Finnish	4772	3343	6885

ers.

Following the definitions of Section 3, we have counted the the complexity of the smart paradigm definitions for nouns and verbs in the different languages in the GF Resource Grammar Library. Notice that the total complexity of the system is lower than the sum of the parts, because many definitions (such as morphophonological transformations) are reused in different parts of speech. The results are in Table 2.

These figures suggest that Finnish indeed has a more complex morphology than French, and English is the simplest. Of course, the paradigms were not implemented with such comparisons in mind, and it may happen that some of the differences come from different coding styles involved in the collaboratively built library. Measuring code syntax trees rather than source code text neutralizes some of this variation (Section 3).

Finally, we can estimate the power of smart paradigms as a data compression function. In a sense, a paradigm is a function designed for the very purpose of compressing a lexicon, and one can expect better compression than with generic tools such as bzip2. Table 3 shows the compression rates for the same full-form lexica as used in the predictability experiment (Table 1). The sizes are in kilobytes, where the code size for paradigms is calculated as the number of constructors multiplied by 5 (Section 3). The source lexicon size is a simple character count, similar to the full-form lexicon.

Unexpectedly, the compression rate of the paradigms improves as the number of forms in the full-form lexicon increases (see Table 1 for these numbers). For English and French nouns, bzip2 is actually better. But of course, unlike the paradigms, it also gives a global compression over all entries in the lexicon. Combining the two methods by applying bzip2 to the source code gives, for the Finnish verb lexicon, a file of 60 kB, which implies a joint compression rate of 227.

That the compression rates for the code can be higher than the numbers of forms in the full-form lexicon is explained by the fact that the generated forms are longer than the base forms. For instance, the full-form entry of the Finnish verb *uida* ("swim") is 850 bytes, which means that the average form size is twice the size of the basic form.

5 Smart paradigms in lexicon building

Building a high-quality lexicon needs a lot of manual work. Traditionally, when one is not writing all the forms by hand (which would be almost impossible in languages with rich morphology), sets of paradigms are used that require the lexicographer to specify the base form of the word and an identifier for the paradigm to use. This has several usability problems: one has to remember all the paradigm identifiers and choose correctly from them.

Smart paradigm can make this task easier, even accessible to non-specialist, because of their ability to guess the most probable paradigm from a single base form. As shown by Table 1, this is more often correct than not, except for Swedish nouns. If this information is not enough, only a few more forms are needed, requiring only practical knowledge of the language. Usually (92% to 100% in Table 1), adding a second form ($m = 2$) is enough to cover all words. Then the best practice for lexicon writing might be always to give these two forms instead of just one.

Smart paradigms can also be used for an automatic bootstrapping of a list of base forms into a full form lexicon. As again shown by the last column of Table 1, one form alone can provide an excellent first approximation in most cases. What is more, it is often the case that uncaught words belong to a limited set of "irregular" words, such as the irregular verbs in many languages. All new words can then be safely inferred from the base form by using smart paradigms.

6 Related work

Smart paradigms were used for a study of Finnish morphology in (Ranta, 2008). The present paper can be seen as a generalization of that experiment to more languages and with the notion of code

Table 3: Comparison between using bzip2 and paradigms+lexicon source as a compression method. Sizes in kB.

Lexicon	Fullform	bzip2	fullform/bzip2	Source	fullform/source
Eng N	264	99	2.7	135	2.0
Eng V	245	78	3.2	57	4.4
Swe N	6,243	1,380	4.5	1,207	5.3
Swe V	840	174	4.8	58	15
Fre N	952	277	3.4	450	2.2
Fre V	3,888	811	4.8	98	40
Fin N	11,295	2,165	5.2	343	34
Fin V	13,609	2,297	5.9	123	114

complexity. Also the paradigms for Finnish are improved here (cf. Section 4.4 above).

Even though smart paradigm-like descriptions are common in language text books, there is to our knowledge no computational equivalent to the smart paradigms of GF. Finite state morphology systems often have a function called a **guesser**, which, given a word form, tries to guess either the paradigm this form belongs to or the dictionary form (or both). A typical guesser differs from a smart paradigms in that it does not make it possible to correct the result by giving more forms. Examples of guessers include (Chanod and Tapanainen, 1995) for French, (Hlaváčová, 2001) for Czech, and (Nakov et al., 2003) for German.

Another related domain is the unsupervised learning of morphology where machine learning is used to automatically build a language morphology from corpora (Goldsmith, 2006). The main difference is that with the smart paradigms, the paradigms and the guess heuristics are implemented manually and with a high certainty; in unsupervised learning of morphology the paradigms are induced from the input forms with much lower certainty. Of particular interest are (Chan, 2006) and (Dreyer and Eisner, 2011), dealing with the automatic extraction of paradigms from text and investigate how good these can become. The main contrast is, again, that our work deals with handwritten paradigms that are correct by design, and we try to see how much information we can drop before losing correctness.

Once given, a set of paradigms can be used in automated lexicon extraction from raw data, as in (Forsberg et al., 2006) and (Clément et al., 2004), by a method that tries to collect a sufficient number of forms to determine that a word belongs to a certain paradigm. Smart paradigms can then give the method to actually construct the full inflection tables from the characteristic forms.

7 Conclusion

We have introduced the notion of smart paradigms, which implement the linguistic knowledge involved in inferring the inflection of words. We have used the paradigms to estimate the predictability of nouns and verbs in English, Swedish, French, and Finnish. The main result is that, with the paradigms used, less than two forms in average is always enough. In half of the languages and categories, one form is enough to predict more than 90% of forms correctly. This gives a promise for both manual lexicon building and automatic bootstrapping of lexicon from word lists.

To estimate the overall complexity of inflection systems, we have also measured the size of the source code for the paradigm systems. Unsurprisingly, Finnish is around seven times as complex as English, and around three times as complex as Swedish and French. But this cost is amortized when big lexica are built.

Finally, we looked at smart paradigms as a data compression method. With simple morphologies, such as English nouns, bzip2 gave a better compression of the lexicon than the source code using paradigms. But with Finnish verbs, the compression rate was almost 20 times higher with paradigms than with bzip2.

The general conclusion is that smart paradigms are a good investment when building morphological lexica, as they ease the task of both human lexicographers and automatic bootstrapping methods. They also suggest a method to assess the complexity and learnability of languages, related to Kolmogorov complexity. The results in the current paper are just preliminary in this respect, since they might still tell more about particular implementations of paradigms than about the languages themselves.

Acknowledgements

We are grateful to the anonymous referees for valuable remarks and questions. The research leading to these results has received funding from the European Union's Seventh Framework Programme (FP7/2007-2013) under grant agreement no FP7-ICT-247914 (the MOLTO project).

References

[Beesley and Karttunen2003] Kenneth R. Beesley and Lauri Karttunen. 2003. *Finite State Morphology*. CSLI Publications.

[Bescherelle1997] Bescherelle. 1997. *La conjugaison pour tous*. Hatier.

[Borin et al.2008] Lars Borin, Markus Forsberg, and Lennart Lönngren. 2008. Saldo 1.0 (svenskt associationslexikon version 2). *Språkbanken*, 05.

[Chan2006] Erwin Chan. 2006. Learning probabilistic paradigms for morphology in a latent class model. In *Proceedings of the Eighth Meeting of the ACL Special Interest Group on Computational Phonology and Morphology*, SIGPHON '06, pages 69–78, Stroudsburg, PA, USA. Association for Computational Linguistics.

[Chanod and Tapanainen1995] Jean-Pierre Chanod and Pasi Tapanainen. 1995. Creating a tagset, lexicon and guesser for a french tagger. *CoRR*, cmp-lg/9503004.

[Clément et al.2004] Lionel Clément, Benoît Sagot, and Bernard Lang. 2004. Morphology based automatic acquisition of large-coverage lexica. In *Proceedings of LREC-04, Lisboa, Portugal*, pages 1841–1844.

[Dreyer and Eisner2011] Markus Dreyer and Jason Eisner. 2011. Discovering morphological paradigms from plain text using a dirichlet process mixture model. In *Proceedings of the Conference on Empirical Methods in Natural Language Processing*, EMNLP '11, pages 616–627, Stroudsburg, PA, USA. Association for Computational Linguistics.

[Forsberg et al.2006] Markus Forsberg, Harald Hammarström, and Aarne Ranta. 2006. Morphological Lexicon Extraction from Raw Text Data. In T. Salakoski, editor, *FinTAL 2006*, volume 4139 of *LNCS/LNAI*.

[Goldsmith2006] John Goldsmith. 2006. An Algorithm for the Unsupervised Learning of Morphology. *Nat. Lang. Eng.*, 12(4):353–371.

[Hellberg1978] Staffan Hellberg. 1978. *The Morphology of Present-Day Swedish*. Almqvist & Wiksell.

[Hlaváčová2001] Jaroslava Hlaváčová. 2001. Morphological guesser of czech words. In Václav Matoušek, Pavel Mautner, Roman Moucek, and Karel Taušer, editors, *Text, Speech and Dialogue*, volume 2166 of *Lecture Notes in Computer Science*, pages 70–75. Springer Berlin / Heidelberg.

[Kaplan and Kay1994] R. Kaplan and M. Kay. 1994. Regular Models of Phonological Rule Systems. *Computational Linguistics*, 20:331–380.

[Koskenniemi1983] Kimmo Koskenniemi. 1983. *Two-Level Morphology: A General Computational Model for Word-Form Recognition and Production*. Ph.D. thesis, University of Helsinki.

[Kotimaisten Kielten Tutkimuskeskus2006] Kotimaisten Kielten Tutkimuskeskus. 2006. KOTUS Wordlist. `http://kaino.kotus.fi/sanat/nykysuomi`.

[Nakov et al.2003] Preslav Nakov, Yury Bonev, and et al. 2003. Guessing morphological classes of unknown german nouns.

[Ranta2008] Aarne Ranta. 2008. How predictable is Finnish morphology? an experiment on lexicon construction. In J. Nivre and M. Dahllöf and B. Megyesi, editor, *Resourceful Language Technology: Festschrift in Honor of Anna Sågvall Hein*, pages 130–148. University of Uppsala. `http://publications.uu.se/abstract.xsql?dbid=8933`.

[Ranta2011] Aarne Ranta. 2011. *Grammatical Framework: Programming with Multilingual Grammars*. CSLI Publications, Stanford. ISBN-10: 1-57586-626-9 (Paper), 1-57586-627-7 (Cloth).

[Romary et al.2004] Laurent Romary, Susanne Salmon-Alt, and Gil Francopoulo. 2004. Standards going concrete: from LMF to Morphalou. In *The 20th International Conference on Computational Linguistics - COLING 2004*, Genève/Switzerland. coling.

[Solomonoff1964] Ray J. Solomonoff. 1964. A formal theory of inductive inference: Parts 1 and 2. *Information and Control*, 7:1–22 and 224–254.

Probabilistic Hierarchical Clustering of Morphological Paradigms

Burcu Can
Department of Computer Science
University of York
Heslington, York, YO10 5GH, UK
burcucan@gmail.com

Suresh Manandhar
Department of Computer Science
University of York
Heslington, York, YO10 5GH, UK
suresh@cs.york.ac.uk

Abstract

We propose a novel method for learning morphological paradigms that are structured within a hierarchy. The hierarchical structuring of paradigms groups morphologically similar words close to each other in a tree structure. This allows detecting morphological similarities easily leading to improved morphological segmentation. Our evaluation using (Kurimo et al., 2011a; Kurimo et al., 2011b) dataset shows that our method performs competitively when compared with current state-of-art systems.

1 Introduction

Unsupervised morphological segmentation of a text involves learning rules for segmenting words into their *morphemes*. Morphemes are the smallest meaning bearing units of words. The learning process is fully unsupervised, using only raw text as input to the learning system. For example, the word *respectively* is split into morphemes *respect*, *ive* and *ly*. Many fields, such as machine translation, information retrieval, speech recognition etc., require morphological segmentation since new words are always created and storing all the word forms will require a massive dictionary. The task is even more complex, when morphologically complicated languages (i.e. agglutinative languages) are considered. The sparsity problem is more severe for more morphologically complex languages. Applying morphological segmentation mitigates data sparsity by tackling the issue with out-of-vocabulary (OOV) words.

In this paper, we propose a paradigmatic approach. A morphological *paradigm* is a pair (StemList, SuffixList) such that each concatenation of Stem+Suffix (where Stem $\in$ StemList and Suffix $\in$ SuffixList) is a valid word form. The learning of morphological paradigms is not novel as there has already been existing work in this area such as Goldsmith (2001), Snover et al. (2002), Monson et al. (2009), Can and Manandhar (2009) and Dreyer and Eisner (2011). However, none of these existing approaches address learning of the hierarchical structure of paradigms.

Hierarchical organisation of words help capture morphological similarities between words in a compact structure by factoring these similarities through stems, suffixes or prefixes. Our inference algorithm simultaneously infers latent variables (i.e. the morphemes) along with their hierarchical organisation. Most hierarchical clustering algorithms are single-pass, where once the hierarchical structure is built, the structure does not change further.

The paper is structured as follows: section 2 gives the related work, section 3 describes the probabilistic hierarchical clustering scheme, section 4 explains the morphological segmentation model by embedding it into the clustering scheme and describes the inference algorithm along with how the morphological segmentation is performed, section 5 presents the experiment settings along with the evaluation scores, and finally section 6 presents a discussion with a comparison with other systems that participated in Morpho Challenge 2009 and 2010 .

2 Related Work

We propose a Bayesian approach for learning of paradigms in a hierarchy. If we ignore the hierarchical aspect of our learning algorithm, then our

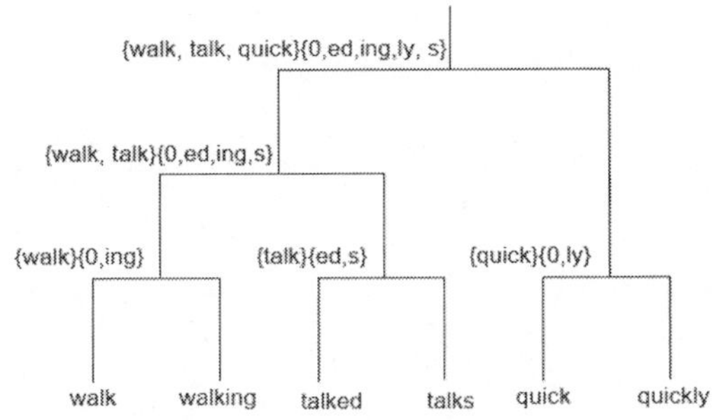

Figure 1: A sample tree structure.

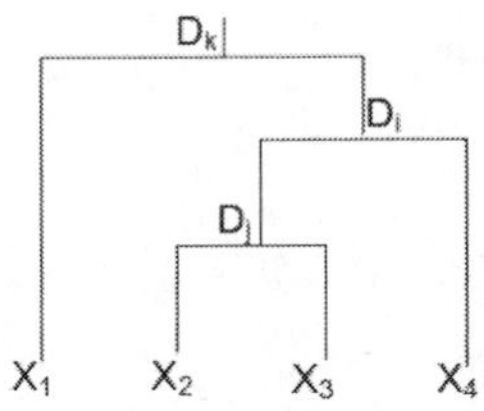

Figure 2: A segment of a tree with with internal nodes D_i, D_j, D_k having data points $\{x_1, x_2, x_3, x_4\}$. The subtree below the internal node D_i is called T_i, the subtree below the internal node D_j is T_j, and the subtree below the internal node D_k is T_k.

method is similar to the Dirichlet Process (DP) based model of Goldwater et al. (2006). From this perspective, our method can be understood as adding a hierarchical structure learning layer on top of the DP based learning method proposed in Goldwater et al. (2006). Dreyer and Eisner (2011) propose an infinite Diriclet mixture model for capturing paradigms. However, they do not address learning of hierarchy.

The method proposed in Chan (2006) also learns within a hierarchical structure where Latent Dirichlet Allocation (LDA) is used to find stem-suffix matrices. However, their work is supervised, as true morphological analyses of words are provided to the system. In contrast, our proposed method is fully unsupervised.

3 Probabilistic Hierarchical Model

The hierarchical clustering proposed in this work is different from existing hierarchical clustering algorithms in two aspects:

- It is not single-pass as the hierarchical structure changes.
- It is probabilistic and is not dependent on a distance metric.

3.1 Mathematical Definition

In this paper, a hierarchical structure is a binary tree in which each internal node represents a cluster.

Let a data set be $\mathbf{D} = \{x_1, x_2, \ldots, x_n\}$ and T be the entire tree, where each data point x_i is located at one of the leaf nodes (see Figure 2). Here, D_k denotes the data points in the branch T_k. Each node defines a probabilistic model for words that the cluster acquires. The probabilistic model can be denoted as $p(x_i|\theta)$ where θ denotes the parameters of the probabilistic model.

The marginal probability of data in any node can be calculated as:

$$p(D_k) = \int p(D_k|\boldsymbol{\theta})p(\boldsymbol{\theta}|\boldsymbol{\beta})d\boldsymbol{\theta} \qquad (1)$$

The likelihood of data under any subtree is defined as follows:

$$p(D_k|T_k) = p(D_k)p(D_l|T_l)p(D_r|T_r) \qquad (2)$$

where the probability is defined in terms of left T_l and right T_r subtrees. Equation 2 provides a recursive decomposition of the likelihood in terms of the likelihood of the left and the right subtrees until the leaf nodes are reached. We use the marginal probability (Equation 1) as prior information since the marginal probability bears the probability of having the data from the left and right subtrees within a single cluster.

4 Morphological Segmentation

In our model, data points are words to be clustered and each cluster represents a paradigm. In the hierarchical structure, words will be organised in such a way that morphologically similar words will be located close to each other to be grouped in the same paradigms. Morphological similarity refers to at least one common morpheme between words. However, we do not make a distinction between morpheme types. Instead, we assume that each word is organised as a stem+suffix combination.

4.1 Model Definition

Let a dataset $\boldsymbol{D}$ consist of words to be analysed, where each word w_i has a latent variable which is the split point that analyses the word into its stem s_i and suffix m_i:

$$\boldsymbol{D} = \{w_1 = s_1 + m_1, \ldots, w_n = s_n + m_n\}$$

The marginal likelihood of words in the node k is defined such that:

$$\begin{aligned} p(D_k) &= p(S_k)p(M_k) \\ &= p(s_1, s_2, \ldots, s_n)p(m_1, m_2, \ldots, m_n) \end{aligned}$$

The words in each cluster represents a paradigm that consists of stems and suffixes. The hierarchical model puts words sharing the same stems or suffixes close to each other in the tree. Each word is part of all the paradigms on the path from the leaf node having that word to the root. The word can share either its stem or suffix with other words in the same paradigm. Hence, a considerable number of words can be generated through this approach that may not be seen in the corpus.

We postulate that stems and suffixes are generated independently from each other. Thus, the probability of a word becomes:

$$p(w = s + m) = p(s)p(m) \tag{3}$$

We define two Dirichlet processes to generate stems and suffixes independently:

$$\begin{aligned} G_s|\beta_s, P_s &\sim DP(\beta_s, P_s) \\ G_m|\beta_m, P_m &\sim DP(\beta_m, P_m) \\ s|G_s &\sim G_s \\ m|G_m &\sim G_m \end{aligned}$$

where $DP(\beta_s, P_s)$ denotes a Dirichlet process that generates stems. Here, β_s is the concentration parameter, which determines the number of stem types generated by the Dirichlet process. The smaller the value of the concentration parameter, the less likely to generate new stem types the process is. In contrast, the larger the value of concentration parameter, the more likely it is to generate new stem types, yielding a more uniform distribution over stem types. If $\beta_s < 1$, sparse stems are supported, it yields a more skewed distribution. To support a small number of stem types in each cluster, we chose $\beta_s < 1$.

Here, P_s is the base distribution. We use the base distribution as a prior probability distribution for morpheme lengths. We model morpheme lengths implicitly through the morpheme letters:

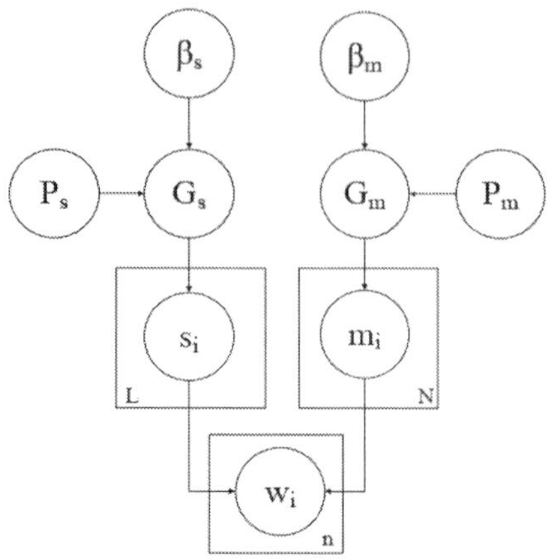

Figure 3: The plate diagram of the model, representing the generation of a word w_i from the stem s_i and the suffix m_i that are generated from Dirichlet processes. In the representation, solid-boxes denote that the process is repeated with the number given on the corner of each box.

$$P_s(s_i) = \prod_{c_i \in s_i} p(c_i) \tag{4}$$

where c_i denotes the letters, which are distributed uniformly. Modelling morpheme letters is a way of modelling the morpheme length since shorter morphemes are favoured in order to have fewer factors in Equation 4 (Creutz and Lagus, 2005b).

The Dirichlet process, $DP(\beta_m, P_m)$, is defined for suffixes analogously. The graphical representation of the entire model is given in Figure 3.

Once the probability distributions $\mathbf{G} = \{G_s, G_m\}$ are drawn from both Dirichlet processes, words can be generated by drawing a stem from G_s and a suffix from G_m. However, we do not attempt to estimate the probability distributions $\mathbf{G}$; instead, $\mathbf{G}$ is integrated out. The joint probability of stems is calculated by integrating out G_s:

$$\begin{aligned} &p(s_1, s_2, \ldots, s_M) \\ &\quad = \int p(G_s) \prod_{i=1}^{L} p(s_i|G_s) dG_s \end{aligned} \tag{5}$$

where L denotes the number of stem tokens. The joint probability distribution of stems can be tackled as a Chinese restaurant process. The Chinese restaurant process introduces dependencies between stems. Hence, the joint probability of stems $S = \{s_1, \dots, s_L\}$ becomes:

$$\begin{aligned} & p(s_1, s_2, \dots, s_L) \\ & = p(s_1)p(s_2|s_1)\dots p(s_M|s_1,\dots,s_{M-1}) \\ & = \frac{\Gamma(\beta_s)}{\Gamma(L+\beta_s)}\beta_s^{K-1}\prod_{i=1}^{K}P_s(s_i)\prod_{i=1}^{K}(n_{s_i}-1)! \end{aligned} \tag{6}$$

where K denotes the number of stem types. In the equation, the second and the third factor correspond to the case where novel stems are generated for the first time; the last factor corresponds to the case in which stems that have already been generated for n_{s_i} times previously are being generated again. The first factor consists of all denominators from both cases.

The integration process is applied for probability distributions G_m for suffixes analogously. Hence, the joint probability of suffixes $M = \{m_1, \dots, m_N\}$ becomes:

$$\begin{aligned} & p(m_1, m_2, \dots, m_N) \\ & = p(m_1)p(m_2|m_1)\dots p(m_N|m_1,\dots,m_{N-1}) \\ & = \frac{\Gamma(\alpha)}{\Gamma(N+\alpha)}\alpha^{T}\prod_{i=1}^{T}P_m(m_i)\prod_{i=1}^{T}(n_{m_i}-1)! \end{aligned} \tag{7}$$

where T denotes the number of suffix types and n_{m_i} is the number of stem types m_i which have been already generated.

Following the joint probability distribution of stems, the conditional probability of a stem given previously generated stems can be derived as:

$$p(s_i|S^{-s_i}, \beta_s, P_s) = \begin{cases} \frac{n_{s_i}^{S^{-s_i}}}{L-1+\beta_s} & \text{if } s_i \in S^{-s_i} \\ \frac{\beta_s * P_s(s_i)}{L-1+\beta_s} & \text{otherwise} \end{cases} \tag{8}$$

where $n_{s_i}^{S^{-s_i}}$ denotes the number of stem instances s_i that have been previously generated, where S^{-s_i} denotes the stem set excluding the new instance of the stem s_i.

The conditional probability of a suffix given the other suffixes that have been previously generated is defined similarly:

$$p(m_i|M^{-m_i}, \beta_m, P_m) = \begin{cases} \frac{n_{m_i}^{M^{-m_i}}}{N-1+\beta_m} & \text{if } m_i \in M^{-m_i} \\ \frac{\beta_m * P_m(m_i)}{N-1+\beta_m} & \text{otherwise} \end{cases} \tag{9}$$

where $n_{m^i}^{M_k^{-i}}$ is the number of instances m_i that have been generated previously where M^{-m^i} is the set of suffixes, excluding the new instance of the suffix m_i.

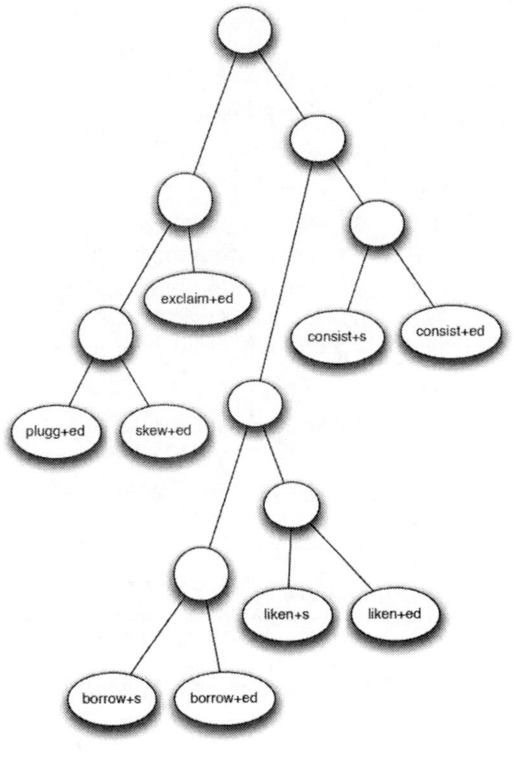

Figure 4: A portion of a sample tree.

A portion of a tree is given in Figure 4. As can be seen on the figure, all words are located at leaf nodes. Therefore, the root node of this subtree consists of words {plugg+ed, skew+ed, exclaim+ed, borrow+s, borrow+ed, liken+s, liken+ed, consist+s, consist+ed}.

4.2 Inference

The initial tree is constructed by randomly choosing a word from the corpus and adding this into a randomly chosen position in the tree. When constructing the initial tree, latent variables are also assigned randomly, i.e. each word is split at a random position (see Algorithm 1).

We use Metropolis Hastings algorithm (Hastings, 1970), an instance of Markov Chain Monte Carlo (MCMC) algorithms, to infer the optimal hierarchical structure along with the morphological segmentation of words (given in Algorithm 2). During each iteration i, a leaf node $D_i = \{w_i = s_i + m_i\}$ is drawn from the current tree structure. The drawn leaf node is removed from the tree. Next, a node D_k is drawn uniformly from the tree

Algorithm 1 Creating initial tree.

input: data $D = \{w_1 = s_1 + m_1, \ldots, w_n = s_n + m_n\}$,
initialise: $root \leftarrow D_1$ where $D_1 = \{w_1 = s_1 + m_1\}$
initialise: $c \leftarrow n - 1$
while $c >= 1$ **do**
    Draw a word w_j from the corpus.
    Split the word randomly such that $w_j = s_j + m_j$
    Create a new node D_j where $D_j = \{w_j = s_j + m_j\}$
    Choose a sibling node D_k for D_j
    Merge $D_{new} \leftarrow D_j \uplus D_k$
    Remove w_j from the corpus
    $c \leftarrow c - 1$
end while
output: Initial tree

to make it a sibling node to D_i. In addition to a sibling node, a split point $w_i = s_i^{'} + m_i^{'}$ is drawn uniformly. Next, the node $D_i = \{w_i = s_i^{'} + m_i^{'}\}$ is inserted as a sibling node to D_k. After updating all probabilities along the path to the root, the new tree structure is either accepted or rejected by applying the Metropolis-Hastings update rule. The likelihood of data under the given tree structure is used as the sampling probability.

We use a simulated annealing schedule to update P_{Acc}:

$$P_{Acc} = \left(\frac{p_{next}(D|T)}{p_{cur}(D|T)}\right)^{\frac{1}{\gamma}} \quad (10)$$

where γ denotes the current temperature, $p_{next}(D|T)$ denotes the marginal likelihood of the data under the new tree structure, and $p_{cur}(D|T)$ denotes the marginal likelihood of data under the latest accepted tree structure. If $(p_{next}(D|T) > p_{cur}(D|T))$ then the update is accepted (see line 9, Algorithm 2), otherwise, the tree structure is still accepted with a probability of p_{Acc} (see line 14, Algorithm 2). In our experiments (see section 5) we set γ to 2. The system temperature is reduced in each iteration of the Metropolis Hastings algorithm:

$$\gamma \leftarrow \gamma - \eta \quad (11)$$

Most tree structures are accepted in the earlier stages of the algorithm, however, as the temperature decreases only tree structures that lead lead to a considerable improvement in the marginal probability $p(D|T)$ are accepted.

Algorithm 2 Inference algorithm

1: **input:** data $D = \{w_1 = s_1 + m_1, \ldots, w_n = s_n + m_n\}$, initial tree T, initial temperature of the system γ, the target temperature of the system κ, temperature decrement η
2: **initialise:** $i \leftarrow 1$, $w \leftarrow w_i = s_i + m_i$, $p_{cur}(D|T) \leftarrow p(D|T)$
3: **while** $\gamma > \kappa$ **do**
4:     Remove the leaf node D_i that has the word $w_i = s_i + m_i$
5:     Draw a split point for the word such that $w_i = s_i^{'} + m_i^{'}$
6:     Draw a sibling node D_j
7:     $D_m \leftarrow D_i \uplus D_j$
8:     Update $p_{next}(D|T)$
9:     **if** $p_{next}(D|T) >= p_{cur}(D|T)$ **then**
10:         Accept the new tree structure
11:         $p_{cur}(D|T) \leftarrow p_{next}(D|T)$
12:     **else**
13:         $random \sim Normal(0, 1)$
14:         **if** $random < \left(\frac{p_{next}(D|T)}{p_{cur}(D|T)}\right)^{\frac{1}{\gamma}}$ **then**
15:             Accept the new tree structure
16:             $p_{cur}(D|T) \leftarrow p_{next}(D|T)$
17:         **else**
18:             Reject the new tree structure
19:             Re-insert the node D_i at its previous position with the previous split point
20:         **end if**
21:     **end if**
22:     $w \leftarrow w_{i+1} = s_{i+1} + m_{i+1}$
23:     $\gamma \leftarrow \gamma - \eta$
24: **end while**
25: **output:** A tree structure where each node corresponds to a paradigm.

An illustration of sampling a new tree structure is given in Figure 5 and 6. Figure 5 shows that D_0 will be removed from the tree in order to sample a new position on the tree, along with a new split point of the word. Once the leaf node is removed from the tree, the parent node is removed from the tree, as the parent node D_5 will consist of only one child. Figure 6 shows that D_8 is sampled to be the sibling node of D_0. Subsequently, the two nodes are merged within a new cluster that

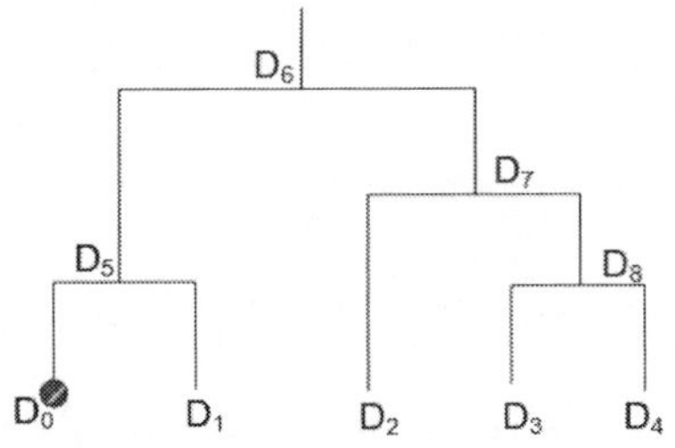

Figure 5: D_0 will be removed from the tree.

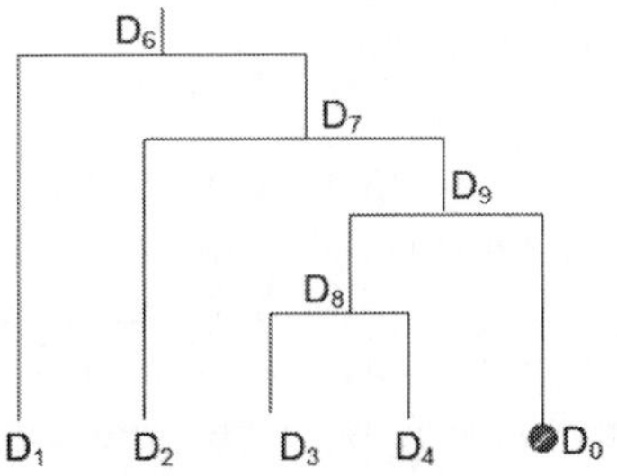

Figure 6: D_8 is sampled to be the sibling of D_0.

introduces a new node D_9.

4.3 Morphological Segmentation

Once the optimal tree structure is inferred, along with the morphological segmentation of words, any novel word can be analysed. For the segmentation of novel words, the root node is used as it contains all stems and suffixes which are already extracted from the training data. Morphological segmentation is performed in two ways: segmentation at a single point and segmentation at multiple points.

4.3.1 Single Split Point

In order to find single split point for the morphological segmentation of a word, the split point yielding the maximum probability given inferred stems and suffixes is chosen to be the final analysis of the word:

$$\arg\max_{j} p(w_i = s_j + m_j | D_{root}, \beta_m, P_m, \beta_s, P_s) \tag{12}$$

where D_{root} refers to the root of the entire tree.

Here, the probability of a segmentation of a given word given D_{root} is calculated as given below:

$$p(w_i = s_j + m_j | D_{root}, \beta_m, P_m, \beta_s, P_s) = p(s_j | S_{root}, \beta_s, P_s)\, p(m_j | M_{root}, \beta_m, P_m) \tag{13}$$

where S_{root} denotes all the stems in D_{root} and M_{root} denotes all the suffixes in D_{root}. Here $p(s_j | S_{root}, \beta_s, P_s)$ is calculated as given below:

$$p(s_i | S_{root}, \beta_s, P_s) = \begin{cases} \frac{n_{s_i}^{S_{root}}}{L+\beta_s} & \text{if } s_i \in S_{root} \\ \frac{\beta_s * P_s(s_i)}{L+\beta_s} & \text{otherwise} \end{cases} \tag{14}$$

Similarly, $p(m_j | M_{root}, \beta_m, P_m)$ is calculated as:

$$p(m_i | M_{root}, \beta_m, P_m) = \begin{cases} \frac{n_{m_i}^{M_{root}}}{N+\beta_m} & \text{if } m_i \in M_{root} \\ \frac{\beta_m * P_m(m_i)}{N+\beta_m} & \text{otherwise} \end{cases} \tag{15}$$

4.3.2 Multiple Split Points

In order to discover words with multiple split points, we propose a hierarchical segmentation where each segment is split further. The rules for generating multiple split points is given by the following context free grammar:

$$w \leftarrow s_1\, m_1 | s_2\, m_2 \tag{16}$$
$$s_1 \leftarrow s\, m | s\, s \tag{17}$$
$$s_2 \leftarrow s \tag{18}$$
$$m_1 \leftarrow m\, m \tag{19}$$
$$m_2 \leftarrow s\, m | m\, m \tag{20}$$

Here, s is a pre-terminal node that generates all the stems from the root node. And similarly, m is a pre-terminal node that generates all the suffixes from the root node. First, using Equation 16, the word (e.g. housekeeper) is split into $s_1\ m_1$ (e.g. housekeep+er) or $s_2\ m_2$ (house+keeper). The first segment is regarded as a stem, and the second segment is either a stem or a suffix, considering the probability of having a compound word. Equation 12 is used to decide whether the second segment is a stem or a suffix. At the second segmentation level, each segment is split once more. If the first production rule is followed in the first segmentation level, the first segment s_1 can be analysed as $s\ m$ (e.g. housekeep+∅) or $s\ s$

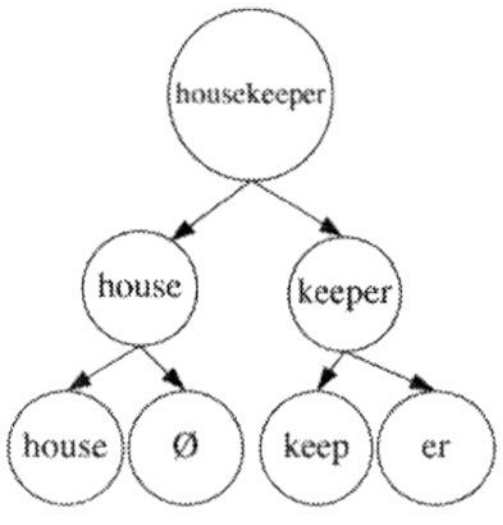

Figure 7: An example that depicts how the word *housekeeper* can be analysed further to find more split points.

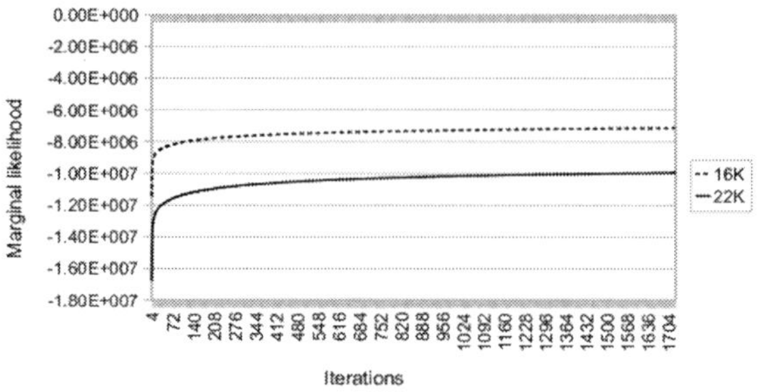

Figure 8: Marginal likelihood convergence for datasets of size 16K and 22K words.

(e.g. house+keep) (Equation 17). The decision to choose which production rule to apply is made using:

$$s_1 \leftarrow \begin{cases} s\ s \ \text{ if } p(s|S, \beta_s, P_s) > p(m|M, \beta_m, P_m) \\ s\ m \ \text{ otherwise} \end{cases} \tag{21}$$

where S and M denote all the stems and suffixes in the root node.

Following the same production rule, the second segment m_1 can only be analysed as $m\ m$ (er+∅). We postulate that words cannot have more than two stems and suffixes always follow stems. We do not allow any prefixes, circumfixes, or infixes. Therefore, the first production rule can output two different analyses: $s\ m\ m\ m$ and $s\ s\ m\ m$ (e.g. housekeep+er and house+keep+er).

On the other hand, if the word is analysed as $s_2\ m_2$ (e.g. house+keeper), then s_2 cannot be analysed further. (e.g. house). The second segment m_2 can be analysed further, such that $s\ m$ (stem+suffix) (e.g. keep+er, keeper+∅) or $m\ m$ (suffix+suffix). The decision to choose which production rule to apply is made as follows:

$$m_2 \leftarrow \begin{cases} s\ m \ \text{ if } p(s|S, \beta_s, P_s) > p(m|M, \beta_m, P_m) \\ m\ m \ \text{ otherwise} \end{cases} \tag{22}$$

Thus, the second production rule yields two different analyses: $s\ s\ m$ and $s\ m\ m$ (e.g. house+keep+er or house+keeper).

5 Experiments & Results

Two sets of experiments were performed for the evaluation of the model. In the first set of experiments, each word is split at single point giving a single stem and a single suffix. In the second set of experiments, potentially multiple split points are generated, by splitting each stem and suffix once more, if it is possible to do so.

Morpho Challenge (Kurimo et al., 2011b) provides a well established evaluation framework that additionally allows comparing our model in a range of languages. In both sets of experiments, the Morpho Challenge 2010 dataset is used (Kurimo et al., 2011b). Experiments are performed for English, where the dataset consists of 878,034 words. Although the dataset provides word frequencies, we have not used any frequency information. However, for training our model, we only chose words with frequency greater than 200.

In our experiments, we used dataset sizes of 10K, 16K, 22K words. However, for final evaluation, we trained our models on 22K words. We were unable to complete the experiments with larger training datasets due to memory limitations. We plan to report this in future work. Once the tree is learned by the inference algorithm, the final tree is used for the segmentation of the entire dataset. Several experiments are performed for each setting where the setting varies with the tree size and the model parameters. Model parameters are the concentration parameters $\beta = \{\beta_s, \beta_m\}$ of the Dirichlet processes. The concentration parameters, which are set for the experiments, are $0.1, 0.2, 0.02, 0.001, 0.002$.

In all experiments, the initial temperature of the system is assigned as $\gamma = 2$ and it is reduced to the temperature $\gamma = 0.01$ with decrements $\eta = 0.0001$. Figure 8 shows how the log likelihoods of trees of size 16K and 22K converge in time (where the time axis refers to sampling iterations).

Since different training sets will lead to different tree structures, each experiment is repeated three times keeping the experiment setting the same.

Data Size	P(%)	R(%)	F(%)	β_s, β_m
10K	81.48	33.03	47.01	0.1, 0.1
16K	86.48	35.13	50.02	0.002, 0.002
22K	89.04	36.01	51.28	0.002, 0.002

Table 1: Highest evaluation scores of single split point experiments obtained from the trees with 10K, 16K, and 22K words.

Data Size	P(%)	R(%)	F(%)	β_s, β_m
10K	62.45	57.62	59.98	0.1, 0.1
16K	67.80	57.72	62.36	0.002, 0.002
22K	68.71	62.56	62.56	0.001 0.001

Table 2: Evaluation scores of multiple split point experiments obtained from the trees with 10K, 16K, and 22K words.

5.1 Experiments with Single Split Points

In the first set of experiments, words are split into a single stem and suffix. During the segmentation, Equation 12 is used to determine the split position of each word. Evaluation scores are given in Table 1. The highest F-measure obtained is 51.28% with the dataset of 22K words. The scores are noticeably higher with the largest training set.

5.2 Experiments with Multiple Split Points

The evaluation scores of experiments with multiple split points are given in Table 2. The highest F-measure obtained is 62.56% with the dataset with 22K words. As for single split points, the scores are noticeably higher with the largest training set.

For both, single and multiple segmentation, the same inferred tree has been used.

5.3 Comparison with Other Systems

For all our evaluation experiments using Morpho Challenge 2010 (English and Turkish) and Morpho Challenge 2009 (English), we used 22k words for training. For each evaluation, we randomly chose 22k words for training and ran our MCMC inference procedure to learn our model. We generated 3 different models by choosing 3 different randomly generated training sets each consisting of 22k words. The results are the best results over these 3 models. We are reporting the best results out of the 3 models due to the small (22k word) datasets used. Use of larger datasets would have resulted in less variation and better results.

System	P(%)	R(%)	F(%)
Allomorf[1]	68.98	56.82	62.31
Morf. Base.[2]	74.93	49.81	59.84
PM-Union[3]	55.68	62.33	58.82
Lignos[4]	83.49	45.00	58.48
Prob. Clustering (multiple)	57.08	57.58	**57.33**
PM-mimic[3]	53.13	59.01	55.91
MorphoNet[5]	65.08	47.82	55.13
Rali-cof[6]	68.32	46.45	55.30
CanMan[7]	58.52	44.82	50.76

[1] Virpioja et al. (2009)
[2] Creutz and Lagus (2002)
[3] Monson et al. (2009)
[4] Lignos et al. (2009)
[5] Bernhard (2009)
[6] Lavallée and Langlais (2009)
[7] Can and Manandhar (2009)

Table 3: Comparison with other unsupervised systems that participated in Morpho Challenge 2009 for English.

We compare our system with the other participant systems in Morpho Challenge 2010. Results are given in Table 6 (Virpioja et al., 2011). Since the model is evaluated using the official (hidden) Morpho Challenge 2010 evaluation dataset where we submit our system for evaluation to the organisers, the scores are different from the ones that we presented Table 1 and Table 2.

We also demonstrate experiments with Morpho Challenge 2009 English dataset. The dataset consists of $384,904$ words. Our results and the results of other participant systems in Morpho Challenge 2009 are given in Table 3 (Kurimo et al., 2009). It should be noted that we only present the top systems that participated in Morpho Challenge 2009. If all the systems are considered, our system comes 5th out of 16 systems.

The problem of morphologically rich languages is not our priority within this research. Nevertheless, we provide evaluation scores on Turkish. The Turkish dataset consists of 617,298 words. We chose words with frequency greater than 50 for Turkish since the Turkish dataset is not large enough. The results for Turkish are given in Table 4. Our system comes 3rd out of 7 systems.

6 Discussion

The model can easily capture common suffixes such as *-less, -s, -ed, -ment*, etc. Some sample tree nodes obtained from trees are given in Table 6.

System	P(%)	R(%)	F(%)
Morf. CatMAP	79.38	31.88	45.49
Aggressive Comp.	55.51	34.36	42.45
Prob. Clustering (multiple)	72.36	25.81	**38.04**
Iterative Comp.	68.69	21.44	32.68
Nicolas	79.02	19.78	31.64
Morf. Base.	89.68	17.78	29.67
Base Inference	72.81	16.11	26.38

Table 4: Comparison with other unsupervised systems that participated in Morpho Challenge 2010 for Turkish.

regard+less, base+less, shame+less, bound+less, harm+less, regard+ed, relent+less
solve+d, high+-priced, lower+s, lower+-level, high+-level, lower+-income, histor+ians
pre+mise, pre+face, pre+sumed, pre+, pre+gnant
base+ment, ail+ment, over+looked, predica+ment, deploy+ment, compart+ment, embodi+ment
anti+-fraud, anti+-war, anti+-tank, anti+-nuclear, anti+-terrorism, switzer+, anti+gua, switzer+land
sharp+ened, strength+s, tight+ened, strength+ened, black+ened
inspir+e, inspir+ing, inspir+ed, inspir+es, earn+ing, ponder+ing
downgrade+s, crash+ed, crash+ing, lack+ing, blind+ing, blind+, crash+, compris+ing, compris+es, stifl+ing, compris+ed, lack+s, assist+ing, blind+ed, blind+er,

Table 5: Sample tree nodes obtained from various trees.

As seen from the table, morphologically similar words are grouped together. Morphological similarity refers to at least one common morpheme between words. For example, the words *high-priced* and *lower-level* are grouped in the same node through the word *high-level* which shares the same stem with *high-priced* and the same ending with *lower-level*.

As seen from the sample nodes, prefixes can also be identified, for example *anti+fraud, anti+war, anti+tank, anti+nuclear*. This illustrates the flexibility in the model by capturing the similarities through either stems, suffixes or prefixes. However, as mentioned above, the model does not consider any discrimination between different types of morphological forms during training. As the prefix *pre-* appears at the beginning of words, it is identified as a stem. However, identifying *pre-* as a stem does not yield a change in the morphological analysis of the word.

System	P(%)	R(%)	F(%)
Base Inference[1]	80.77	53.76	64.55
Iterative Comp.[1]	80.27	52.76	63.67
Aggressive Comp.[1]	71.45	52.31	60.40
Nicolas[2]	67.83	53.43	59.78
Prob. Clustering (multiple)	57.08	57.58	**57.33**
Morf. Baseline[3]	81.39	41.70	55.14
Prob. Clustering (single)	70.76	36.51	**48.17**
Morf. CatMAP[4]	86.84	30.03	44.63

[1] Lignos (2010)
[2] Nicolas et al. (2010)
[3] Creutz and Lagus (2002)
[4] Creutz and Lagus (2005a)

Table 6: Comparison of our model with other unsupervised systems that participated in Morpho Challenge 2010 for English.

Sometimes similarities may not yield a valid analysis of words. For example, the prefix *pre-* leads the words *pre+mise, pre+sumed, pre+gnant* to be analysed wrongly, whereas *pre-* is a valid prefix for the word *pre+face*. Another nice feature about the model is that compounds are easily captured through common stems: e.g. *doubt+fire, bon+fire, gun+fire, clear+cut*.

7 Conclusion & Future Work

In this paper, we present a novel probabilistic model for unsupervised morphology learning. The model adopts a hierarchical structure in which words are organised in a tree so that morphologically similar words are located close to each other.

In hierarchical clustering, tree-cutting would be a very useful thing to do but it is not addressed in the current paper. We used just the root node as a morpheme lexicon to apply segmentation. Clearly, adding tree cutting would improve the accuracy of the segmentation and will help us identify paradigms with higher accuracy. However, the segmentation accuracy obtained without using tree cutting provides a very useful indicator to show whether this approach is promising. And experimental results show that this is indeed the case.

In the current model, we did not use any syntactic information, only words. POS tags can be utilised to group words which are both morphologically and syntactically similar.

References

Delphine Bernhard. 2009. Morphonet: Exploring the use of community structure for unsupervised morpheme analysis. In *Working Notes for the CLEF 2009 Workshop*, September.

Burcu Can and Suresh Manandhar. 2009. Clustering morphological paradigms using syntactic categories. In *Working Notes for the CLEF 2009 Workshop*, September.

Erwin Chan. 2006. Learning probabilistic paradigms for morphology in a latent class model. In *Proceedings of the Eighth Meeting of the ACL Special Interest Group on Computational Phonology and Morphology*, SIGPHON '06, pages 69–78, Stroudsburg, PA, USA. Association for Computational Linguistics.

Mathias Creutz and Krista Lagus. 2002. Unsupervised discovery of morphemes. In *Proceedings of the ACL-02 workshop on Morphological and phonological learning - Volume 6*, MPL '02, pages 21–30, Stroudsburg, PA, USA. Association for Computational Linguistics.

Mathias Creutz and Krista Lagus. 2005a. Inducing the morphological lexicon of a natural language from unannotated text. In *In Proceedings of the International and Interdisciplinary Conference on Adaptive Knowledge Representation and Reasoning (AKRR 2005*, pages 106–113.

Mathias Creutz and Krista Lagus. 2005b. Unsupervised morpheme segmentation and morphology induction from text corpora using morfessor 1.0. *Technical Report A81*.

Markus Dreyer and Jason Eisner. 2011. Discovering morphological paradigms from plain text using a dirichlet process mixture model. In *Proceedings of the 2011 Conference on Empirical Methods in Natural Language Processing*, pages 616–627, Edinburgh, Scotland, UK., July. Association for Computational Linguistics.

John Goldsmith. 2001. Unsupervised learning of the morphology of a natural language. *Computational Linguistics*, 27(2):153–198.

Sharon Goldwater, Thomas L. Griffiths, and Mark Johnson. 2006. Interpolating between types and tokens by estimating power-law generators. In *In Advances in Neural Information Processing Systems 18*, page 18.

W. K. Hastings. 1970. Monte carlo sampling methods using markov chains and their applications. *Biometrika*, 57:97–109.

Mikko Kurimo, Sami Virpioja, Ville T. Turunen, Graeme W. Blackwood, and William Byrne. 2009. Overview and results of morpho challenge 2009. In *Proceedings of the 10th cross-language evaluation forum conference on Multilingual information access evaluation: text retrieval experiments*, CLEF'09, pages 578–597, Berlin, Heidelberg. Springer-Verlag.

Mikko Kurimo, Krista Lagus, Sami Virpioja, and Ville Turunen. 2011a. Morpho challenge 2009. `http://research.ics.tkk.fi/events/morphochallenge2009/`, June.

Mikko Kurimo, Krista Lagus, Sami Virpioja, and Ville Turunen. 2011b. Morpho challenge 2010. `http://research.ics.tkk.fi/events/morphochallenge2010/`, June.

Jean François Lavallée and Philippe Langlais. 2009. Morphological acquisition by formal analogy. In *Working Notes for the CLEF 2009 Workshop*, September.

Constantine Lignos, Erwin Chan, Mitchell P. Marcus, and Charles Yang. 2009. A rule-based unsupervised morphology learning framework. In *Working Notes for the CLEF 2009 Workshop*, September.

Constantine Lignos. 2010. Learning from unseen data. In Mikko Kurimo, Sami Virpioja, Ville Turunen, and Krista Lagus, editors, *Proceedings of the Morpho Challenge 2010 Workshop*, pages 35–38, Aalto University, Espoo, Finland.

Christian Monson, Kristy Hollingshead, and Brian Roark. 2009. Probabilistic paramor. In *Proceedings of the 10th cross-language evaluation forum conference on Multilingual information access evaluation: text retrieval experiments*, CLEF'09, September.

Lionel Nicolas, Jacques Farré, and Miguel A. Molinero. 2010. Unsupervised learning of concatenative morphology based on frequency-related form occurrence. In Mikko Kurimo, Sami Virpioja, Ville Turunen, and Krista Lagus, editors, *Proceedings of the Morpho Challenge 2010 Workshop*, pages 39–43, Aalto University, Espoo, Finland.

Matthew G. Snover, Gaja E. Jarosz, and Michael R. Brent. 2002. Unsupervised learning of morphology using a novel directed search algorithm: Taking the first step. In *Proceedings of the ACL-02 Workshop on Morphological and Phonological Learning*, pages 11–20, Morristown, NJ, USA. ACL.

Sami Virpioja, Oskar Kohonen, and Krista Lagus. 2009. Unsupervised morpheme discovery with allomorfessor. In *Working Notes for the CLEF 2009 Workshop*. September.

Sami Virpioja, Ville T. Turunen, Sebastian Spiegler, Oskar Kohonen, and Mikko Kurimo. 2011. Empirical comparison of evaluation methods for unsupervised learning of morphology. In *Traitement Automatique des Langues*.

Modeling Inflection and Word-Formation in SMT

Alexander Fraser* **Marion Weller*** **Aoife Cahill**† **Fabienne Cap***

*Institut für Maschinelle Sprachverarbeitung
Universität Stuttgart
D–70174 Stuttgart, Germany
{fraser,wellermn,cap}@ims.uni-stuttgart.de

†Educational Testing Service
Princeton, NJ 08541
USA
acahill@ets.org

Abstract

The current state-of-the-art in statistical machine translation (SMT) suffers from issues of sparsity and inadequate modeling power when translating into morphologically rich languages. We model both inflection and word-formation for the task of translating into German. We translate from English words to an underspecified German representation and then use linear-chain CRFs to predict the fully specified German representation. We show that improved modeling of inflection and word-formation leads to improved SMT.

1 Introduction

Phrase-based statistical machine translation (SMT) suffers from problems of data sparsity with respect to inflection and word-formation which are particularly strong when translating to a morphologically rich target language, such as German. We address the problem of inflection by first translating to a stem-based representation, and then using a second process to inflect these stems. We study several models for doing this, including: strongly lexicalized models, unlexicalized models using linguistic features, and models combining the strengths of both of these approaches. We address the problem of word-formation for compounds in German, by translating from English into German word parts, and then determining whether to merge these parts to form compounds.

We make the following new contributions: (i) we introduce the first SMT system combining inflection prediction with synthesis of portmanteaus and compounds. (ii) For inflection, we compare the mostly unlexicalized prediction of linguistic features (with a subsequent surface form generation step) versus the direct prediction of surface forms, and show that both approaches have complementary strengths. (iii) We combine the advantages of the prediction of linguistic features with the prediction of surface forms. We implement this in a CRF framework which improves on a standard phrase-based SMT baseline. (iv) We develop separate (but related) procedures for inflection prediction and dealing with word-formation (compounds and portmanteaus), in contrast with most previous work which usually either approaches both problems as inflectional problems, or approaches both problems as word-formation problems.

We evaluate on the end-to-end SMT task of translating from English to German of the 2009 ACL workshop on SMT. We achieve BLEU score increases on both the test set and the blind test set.

2 Overview of the translation process for inflection prediction

The work we describe is focused on generalizing phrase-based statistical machine translation to better model German NPs and PPs. We particularly want to ensure that we can generate novel German NPs, where what we mean by novel is that the (inflected) realization is not present in the parallel German training data used to build the SMT system, and hence cannot be produced by our baseline (a standard phrase-based SMT system). We first present our system for dealing with the difficult problem of inflection in German, including the inflection-dependent phenomenon of portmanteaus. Later, after performing an extensive analysis of this system, we will extend it to model compounds, a highly productive phenomenon in German (see Section 8).

The key linguistic knowledge sources that we use are morphological analysis and generation of German based on SMOR, a morphological analyzer/generator of German (Schmid et al., 2004) and the BitPar parser, which is a state-of-the-art parser of German (Schmid, 2004).

2.1 Issues of inflection prediction

In order to ensure coherent German NPs, we model linguistic features of each word in an NP. We model *case*, *gender*, and *number* agreement and whether or not the word is in the scope of a determiner (such as a definite article), which we label *in-weak-context* (this linguistic feature is necessary to determine the *type of inflection* of adjectives and other words: *strong, weak, mixed*). This is a diverse group of features. The *number* of a German noun can often be determined given only the English source word. The *gender* of a German noun is innate and often difficult to determine given only the English source word. *Case* is a function of the slot in the subcategorization frame of the verb (or preposition). There is agreement in all of these features in an NP. For instance the *number* of an article or adjective is determined by the head noun, while the *type of inflection* of an adjective is determined by the choice of article.

We can have a large number of surface forms. For instance, English *blue* can be translated as German *blau*, *blaue*, *blauer*, *blaues*, *blauen*. We predict which form is correct given the context. Our system can generate forms not seen in the training data. We follow a two-step process: in step-1 we translate to *blau* (the stem), in step-2 we predict features and generate the inflected form.[1]

2.2 Procedure

We begin building an SMT system by parsing the German training data with BitPar. We then extract morphological features from the parse. Next, we lookup the surface forms in the SMOR morphological analyzer. We use the morphological features in the parse to disambiguate the set of possible SMOR analyses. Finally, we output the "stems" of the German text, with the addition of markup taken from the parse (discussed in Section 2.3).

[1]E.g., *case*=nominative, *gender*=masculine, *number*=singular, *in-weak-context*=true; inflected: *blaue*.

We then build a standard Moses system translating from English to German stems. We obtain a sequence of stems and POS[2] from this system, and then predict the correct inflection using a sequence model. Finally we generate surface forms.

2.3 German Stem Markup

The translation process consists of two major steps. The first step is translation of English words to German stems, which are enriched with some inflectional markup. The second step is the full inflection of these stems (plus markup) to obtain the final sequence of inflected words. The purpose of the additional German inflectional markup is to strongly improve prediction of inflection in the second step through the addition of markup to the stems in the first step.

In general, all features to be predicted are stripped from the stemmed representation because they are subject to agreement restrictions of a noun or prepositional phrase (such as *case* of nouns or all features of adjectives). However, we need to keep all morphological features that are not dependent on, and thus not predictable from, the (German) context. They will serve as known input for the inflection prediction model. We now describe this markup in detail.

Nouns are marked with *gender* and *number*: we consider the *gender* of a noun as part of its stem, whereas *number* is a feature which we can obtain from English nouns.

Personal pronouns have number and gender annotation, and are additionally marked with *nominative* and *not-nominative*, because English pronouns are marked for this (except for *you*).

Prepositions are marked with the *case* their object takes: this moves some of the difficulty in predicting *case* from the inflection prediction step to the stem translation step. Since the choice of case in a PP is often determined by the PP's meaning (and there are often different meanings possible given different case choices), it seems reasonable to make this decision during stem translation.

Verbs are represented using their inflected surface form. Having access to inflected verb forms has a positive influence on case prediction in the second

[2]We use an additional target factor to obtain the coarse POS for each stem, applying a 7-gram POS model. Koehn and Hoang (2007) showed that the use of a POS factor only results in negligible BLEU improvements, but we need access to the POS in our inflection prediction models.

input	decoder output	inflected	merged
in	in<APPR><Dat>	in	**im**
	die<+ART><Def>	dem	
contrast	Gegensatz<+NN><Masc><Sg>	Gegensatz	Gegensatz
to	zu<APPR><Dat>	zu	**zur**
the	die<+ART><Def>	der	
animated	lebhaft<+ADJ><Pos>	lebhaften	lebhaften
debate	Debatte<+NN><Fem><Sg>	Debatte	Debatte

Table 1: Re-merging of prepositions and articles after inflection to form portmanteaus, *in dem* means *in the*.

step through subject-verb agreement.

Articles are reduced to their stems (the stem itself makes clear the definite or indefinite distinction, but lemmatizing involves removing markings of *case*, *gender* and *number* features).

Other words are also represented by their stems (except for words not covered by SMOR, where surface forms are used instead).

3 Portmanteaus

Portmanteaus are a word-formation phenomenon dependent on inflection. As we have discussed, standard phrase-based systems have problems with picking a definite article with the correct case, gender and number (typically due to sparsity in the language model, e.g., a noun which was never before seen in dative case will often not receive the correct article). In German, portmanteaus increase this sparsity further, as they are compounds of prepositions and articles which must agree with a noun.

We adopt the linguistically strict definition of the term portmanteau: the merging of two function words.[3] We treat this phenomena by splitting the component parts during training and re-merging during generation. Specifically for German, this requires splitting the words which have German POS tag APPRART into an APPR (preposition) and an ART (article). Merging is restricted, the article must be *definite*, *singular*[4] and the preposition can only take *accusative* or *dative* case. Some prepositions allow for merging with an article only for certain noun genders, for example the preposition in_{Dative} is only merged with the following article if the following noun is of masculine or neuter gender. The definite article must be inflected before making a decision about whether to merge a preposition and the article into a portmanteau. See Table 1 for examples.

[3] Some examples are: *zum* (to the) = *zu* (to) + *dem* (the) [German], *du* (from the) = *de* (from) + *le* (the) [French] or *al* (to the) = *a* (to) + *el* (the) [Spanish].

[4] This is the reason for which the preposition + article in Table 2 remain unmerged.

4 Models for Inflection Prediction

We present 5 procedures for inflectional prediction using supervised sequence models. The first two procedures use simple N-gram models over fully inflected surface forms.

1. Surface with no features is presented with an underspecified input (a sequence of stems), and returns the most likely inflected sequence.

2. Surface with case, number, gender is a hybrid system giving the surface model access to linguistic features. In this system prepositions have additionally been labeled with the case they mark (in both the underspecified input and the fully specified output the sequence model is built on) and gender and number markup is also available.

The rest of the procedures predict morphological features (which are input to a morphological generator) rather than surface words. We have developed a two-stage process for predicting fully inflected surface forms. The first stage takes a stem and predicts morphological features for that stem, based on the surrounding context. The aim of the first stage is to take a stem and predict four morphological features: *case*, *gender*, *number* and *type of inflection*. We experiment with a number of models for doing this. The second stage takes the stems marked with morphological features (predicted in the first stage) and uses a morphological generator to generate the full surface form. For the second stage, a modified version of SMOR (Schmid et al., 2004) is used, which, given a stem annotated with morphological features, generates exactly one surface form.

We now introduce our first linguistic feature prediction systems, which we call joint sequence models (JSMs). These are standard language models, where the "word" tokens are not represented as surface forms, but instead using POS and features. In testing, we supply the input as a sequence in underspecified form, where some of the features are specified in the stem markup (for instance, POS=Noun, *gender*=masculine, *number*=plural), and then use Viterbi search to find the most probable fully specified form (for instance, POS=Noun, *gender*=masculine, *number*=plural,

output decoder	input prediction	output prediction	inflected forms	gloss
haben<VAFIN>	haben-V	haben-V	haben	*have*
Zugang<+NN><Masc><Sg>	NN-Sg-Masc	NN-Masc.Acc.Sg.in-weak-context=false	Zugang	*access*
zu<APPR><Dat>	APPR-zu-Dat	APPR-zu-Dat	zu	*to*
die<+ART><Def>	ART-in-weak-context=true	ART-Neut.Dat.Pl.in-weak-context=true	den	*the*
betreffend<+ADJ><Pos>	ADJA	ADJA-Neut.Dat.Pl.in-weak-context=true	betreffenden	*respective*
Land<+NN><Neut><Pl>	NN-Pl-Neut	NN-Neut.Dat.Pl.in-weak-context=true	Ländern	*countries*

Table 2: Overview: inflection prediction steps using a single joint sequence model. All words except verbs and prepositions are replaced by their POS tags in the input. Verbs are inflected in the input ("haben", meaning "have" as in "they have", in the example). Prepositions are lexicalized ("zu" in the example) and indicate which *case* value they mark ("Dat", i.e., Dative in the example).

case=nominative, *in-weak-context*=true).[5]

3. Single joint sequence model on features. We illustrate the different stages of the inflection prediction when using a joint sequence model. The stemmed input sequence (cf. Section 2.3) contains several features that will be part of the input to the inflection prediction. With the exception of verbs and prepositions, the representation for feature prediction is based on POS-tags.

As *gender* and *number* are given by the heads of noun phrases and prepositional phrases, and the expected *type of inflection* is set by articles, the model has sufficient information to compute values for these features and there is no need to know the actual words. In contrast, the prediction of *case* is more difficult as it largely depends on the content of the sentence (e.g. which phrase is object, which phrase is subject). Assuming that verbs and prepositions indicate subcategorization frames, the model is provided crucial information for the prediction of case by keeping verbs (recall that verbs are produced by the stem translation system in their inflected form) and prepositions (the prepositions also have case markup) instead of replacing them with their tags.

After having predicted a single label with values for all features, an inflected word form for the stem and the features is generated. The prediction steps are illustrated in Table 2.

4. Using four joint sequence models (one for each linguistic feature). Here the four linguistic feature values are predicted separately. The assumption that the different linguistic features can be predicted independently of one another is a reasonable linguistic assumption to make given the additional German markup that we use. By splitting the inflection prediction problem into 4 component parts, we end up with 4 simpler models which are less sensitive to data sparseness.

Each linguistic feature is modeled independently (by a JSM) and has a different input representation based on the previously described markup. The input consists of a sequence of coarse POS tags, and for those stems that are marked up with the relevant feature, this feature value. Finally, we combine the predicted features together to produce the same final output as the single joint sequence model, and then generate each surface form using SMOR.

5. Using four CRFs (one for each linguistic feature). The sequence models already presented are limited to the n-gram feature space, and those that predict linguistic features are not strongly lexicalized. Toutanova et al. (2008) uses an MEMM which allows the integration of a wide variety of feature functions. We also wanted to experiment with additional feature functions, and so we train 4 separate linear chain CRF[6] models on our data (one for each linguistic feature we want to predict). We chose CRFs over MEMMs to avoid the label bias problem (Lafferty et al., 2001).

The CRF feature functions, for each German word w_i, are in Table 3. The common feature functions are used in all models, while each of the 4 separate models (one for each linguistic feature) includes the context of only that linguistic feature. We use $L1$ regularization to eliminate irrelevant feature functions, the regularization parameter is optimized on held out data.

[5] Joint sequence models are a particularly simple HMM. Unlike the HMMs used for POS-tagging, an HMM as used here only has a single emission possibility for each state, with probability 1. The states in the HMM are the fully specified representation. The emissions of the HMM are the stems+markup (the underspecified representation).

[6] We use the Wapiti Toolkit (Lavergne et al., 2010) on 4 x 12-Core Opteron 6176 2.3 GHz with 256GB RAM to train our CRF models. Training a single CRF model on our data was not tractable, so we use one for each linguistic feature.

Common	$\text{lemma}_{w_{i-5}\cdots w_{i+5}}$, $\text{tag}_{w_{i-7}\cdots w_{i+7}}$
Case	$\text{case}_{w_{i-5}\cdots w_{i+5}}$
Gender	$\text{gender}_{w_{i-5}\cdots w_{i+5}}$
Number	$\text{number}_{w_{i-5}\cdots w_{i+5}}$
in-weak-context	$\text{in-weak-context}_{w_{i-5}\cdots w_{i+5}}$

Table 3: Feature functions used in CRF models (feature functions are binary indicators of the pattern).

5 Experimental Setup

To evaluate our end-to-end system, we perform the well-studied task of news translation, using the Moses SMT package. We use the English/German data released for the 2009 ACL Workshop on Machine Translation shared task on translation.[7] There are 82,740 parallel sentences from news-commentary09.de-en and 1,418,115 parallel sentences from europarl-v4.de-en. The monolingual data contains 9.8 M sentences.[8]

To build the baseline, the data was tokenized using the Moses tokenizer and lowercased. We use GIZA++ to generate alignments, by running 5 iterations of Model 1, 5 iterations of the HMM Model, and 4 iterations of Model 4. We symmetrize using the "grow-diag-final-and" heuristic. Our Moses systems use default settings. The LM uses the monolingual data and is trained as a five-gram[9] using the SRILM-Toolkit (Stolcke, 2002). We run MERT separately for each system. The recaser used is the same for all systems. It is the standard recaser supplied with Moses, trained on all German training data. The dev set is wmt-2009-a and the test set is wmt-2009-b, and we report end-to-end case sensitive BLEU scores against the unmodified reference SGML file. The blind test set used is wmt-2009-blind (all lines).

In developing our inflection prediction systems (and making such decisions as n-gram order used), we worked on the so-called "clean data" task, predicting the inflection on stemmed reference sentences (rather than MT output). We used the 2000 sentence dev-2006 corpus for this task.

Our contrastive systems consist of two steps, the first is a translation step using a similar Moses system (except that the German side is stemmed, with the markup indicated in Section 2.3), and the second is inflection prediction as described previously in the paper. To derive the stem+markup representation we first parse the German training data and then produce the stemmed representation. We then build a system for translating from English words to German stems (the stem+markup representation), on the same data (so the German side of the parallel data, and the German language modeling uses the stem+markup representation). Likewise, MERT is performed using references which are in the stem+markup representation.

To train the inflection prediction systems, we use the monolingual data. The basic surface form model is trained on lowercased surface forms, the hybrid surface form model with features is trained on lowercased surface forms annotated with markup. The linguistic feature prediction systems are trained on the monolingual data processed as described previously (see Table 2).

Our JSMs are trained using the SRILM Toolkit. We use the SRILM disambig tool for predicting inflection, which takes a "map" that specifies the set of fully specified representations that each underspecified stem can map to. For surface form models, it specifies the mapping from stems to lowercased surface forms (or surface forms with markup for the hybrid surface model).

6 Results for Inflection Prediction

We build two different kinds of translation system, the baseline and the stem translation system (where MERT is used to train the system to produce a stem+markup sequence which agrees with the stemmed reference of the dev set). In this section we present the end-to-end translation results for the different inflection prediction models defined in Section 4, see Table 4.

If we translate from English into a stemmed German representation and then apply a unigram stem-to-surface-form model to predict the surface form, we achieve a BLEU score of 9.97 (line 2). This is only presented for comparison.

The baseline[10] is 14.16, line 1. We compare this with a 5-gram sequence model[11] that predicts

[7]http://www.statmt.org/wmt09/translation-task.html

[8]However, we reduced the monolingual data (only) by retaining only one copy of each unique line, which resulted in 7.55 M sentences.

[9]Add-1 smoothing for unigrams and Kneser-Ney smoothing for higher order n-grams, pruning defaults.

[10]This is a better case-sensitive score than the baselines on wmt-2009-b in experiments by top-performers Edinburgh and Karlsruhe at the shared task. We use Moses with default settings.

[11]Note that we use a different set, the "clean data" set, to determine the choice of n-gram order, see Section 7. We use

surface forms without access to morphological features, resulting in a BLEU score of 14.26. Introducing morphological features (*case* on prepositions, *number* and *gender* on nouns) increases the BLEU score to 14.58, which is in the same range as the single JSM system predicting all linguistic features at once.

This result shows that the mostly unlexicalized single JSM can produce competitive results with direct surface form prediction, despite not having access to a model of inflected forms, which is the desired final output. This strongly suggests that the prediction of morphological features can be used to achieve additional generalization over direct surface form prediction. When comparing the simple direct surface form prediction (line 3) with the hybrid system enriched with *number*, *gender* and *case* (line 4), it becomes evident that feature markup can also aid surface form prediction.

Since the single JSM has no access to lexical information, we used a language model to score different feature predictions: for each sentence of the development set, the 100 best feature predictions were inflected and scored with a language model. We then optimized weights for the two scores LM (language model on surface forms) and FP (feature prediction, the score assigned by the JSM). This method disprefers feature predictions with a top FP-score if the inflected sentence obtains a bad LM score and likewise disfavors low-ranked feature prediction with a high LM score. The prediction of *case* is the most difficult given no lexical information, thus scoring different prediction possibilities on inflected words is helpful. An example is when the *case* of a noun phrase leads to an inflected phrase which never occurs in the (inflected) language model (e.g., *case*=genitive vs. *case*=other). Applying this method to the single JSM leads to a negligible improvement (14.53 vs. 14.56). Using the n-best output of the stem translation system did not lead to any improvement.

The comparison between different feature prediction models is also illustrative. Performance decreases somewhat when using individual joint sequence models (one for each linguistic feature) compared to one single model (14.29, line 6).

The framework using the individual CRFs for

a 5-gram for surface forms and a 4-gram for JSMs, and the same smoothing (Kneser-Ney, add-1 for unigrams, default pruning).

1	baseline	14.16
2	unigram surface (no features)	9.97
3	surface (no features)	14.26
4	surface (with case, number, gender features)	14.58
5	1 JSM morphological features	14.53
6	4 JSMs morphological features	14.29
7	4 CRFs morphological features, lexical information	14.72

Table 4: BLEU scores (detokenized, case sensitive) on the development test set wmt-2009-b

each linguistic feature performs best (14.72, line 7). The CRF framework combines the advantages of surface form prediction and linguistic feature prediction by using feature functions that effectively cover the feature function spaces used by both forms of prediction. The performance of the CRF models results in a statistically significant improvement[12] ($p < 0.05$) over the baseline. We also tried CRFs with bilingual features (projected from English parses via the alignment output by Moses), but obtained only a small improvement of 0.03, probably because the required information is transferred in our stem markup (also a poor improvement beyond monolingual features is consistent with previous work, see Section 8.3). Details are omitted due to space.

We further validated our results by translating the blind test set from wmt-2009, which we have never looked at in any way. Here we also had a statistically significant difference between the baseline and the CRF-based prediction, the scores were 13.68 and 14.18.

7 Analysis of Inflection-based System

Stem Markup. The first step of translating from English to German stems (with the markup we previously discussed) is substantially easier than translating directly to inflected German (we see BLEU scores on stems+markup that are over 2.0 BLEU higher than the BLEU scores on inflected forms when running MERT). The addition of case to prepositions only lowered the BLEU score reached by MERT by about 0.2, but is very helpful for prediction of the case feature.

Inflection Prediction Task. Clean data task results[13] are given in Table 5. The 4 CRFs outperform the 4 JSMs by more than 2%.

[12]We used Kevin Gimpel's implementation of pairwise bootstrap resampling with 1000 samples.

[13]26,061 of 55,057 tokens in our test set are ambiguous. We report % surface form matches for ambiguous tokens.

Model	Accuracy
unigram surface (no features)	55.98
surface (no features)	86.65
surface (with case, number, gender features)	91.24
1 JSM morphological features	92.45
4 JSMs morphological features	92.01
4 CRFs morphological features, lexical information	94.29

Table 5: Comparing predicting surface forms directly with predicting morphological features.

training data	1 model	4 models
7.3 M sentences	92.41	91.88
1.5 M sentences	92.45	92.01
100000 sentences	90.20	90.64
1000 sentences	83.72	86.94

Table 6: Accuracy for different training data sizes of the single and the four separate joint sequence models.

As we mentioned in Section 4, there is a sparsity issue at small training data sizes for the single joint sequence model. This is shown in Table 6. At the largest training data sizes, modeling all 4 features together results in the best predictions of inflection. However using 4 separate models is worth this minimal decrease in performance, since it facilitates experimentation with the CRF framework for which the training of a single model is not currently tractable.

Overall, the inflection prediction works well for *gender*, *number* and *type of inflection*, which are local features to the NP that normally agree with the explicit markup output by the stem translation system (for example, the *gender* of a common noun, which is marked in the stem markup, is usually successfully propagated to the rest of the NP). Prediction of *case* does not always work well, and could maybe be improved through hierarchical labeled-syntax stem translation.

Portmanteaus. An example of where the system is improved because of the new handling of portmanteaus can be seen in the dative phrase *im internationalen Rampenlicht* (in the international spotlight), which does not occur in the parallel data. The accusative phrase *in das internationale Rampenlicht* does occur, however in this case there is no portmanteau, but a one-to-one mapping between *in the* and *in das*. For a given context, only one of accusative or dative case is valid, and a strongly disfluent sentence results from the incorrect choice. In our system, these two cases are handled in the same way (*def-article international Rampenlicht*). This allows us to generalize from the accusative example with no portmanteau and take advantage of longer phrase pairs, even when translating to something that will be inflected as dative and should be realized as a portmanteau. The baseline does not have this capability. It should be noted that the portmanteau merging method described in Section 3 remerges all occurrences of APPR and ART that can technically form a portmanteau. There are a few cases where merging, despite being grammatical, does not lead to a good result. Such exceptions require semantic interpretation and are difficult to capture with a fixed set of rules.

8 Adding Compounds to the System

Compounds are highly productive in German and lead to data sparsity. We split the German compounds in the training data, so that our stem translation system can now work with the individual words in the compounds. After we have translated to a split/stemmed representation, we determine whether to merge words together to form a compound. Then we merge them to create stems in the same representation as before and we perform inflection and portmanteau merging exactly as previously discussed.

8.1 Details of Splitting Process

We prepare the training data by splitting compounds in two steps, following the technique of Fritzinger and Fraser (2010). First, possible split points are extracted using SMOR, and second, the best split points are selected using the geometric mean of word part frequencies.

compound	word parts	gloss
Inflationsrate	Inflation Rate	inflation rate
auszubrechen	aus zu brechen	out to break (to break out)

Training data is then stemmed as described in Section 2.3. The formerly modifying words of the compound (in our example the words to the left of the rightmost word) do not have a stem markup assigned, except for two cases: i) they are nouns themselves or ii) they are particles separated from a verb. In these cases, former modifiers are represented identically to their individual occurring counterparts, which helps generalization.

8.2 Model for Compound Merging

After translation, compound parts have to be resynthesized into compounds before inflection. Two decisions have to be taken: i) where to merge and ii) how to merge. Following the work of Stymne and Cancedda (2011), we implement a linear-chain CRF merging system using the following features: stemmed (separated) surface form, part-of-speech[14] and frequencies from the training corpus for bigrams/merging of *word* and *word+1*, *word* as true prefix, *word+1* as true suffix, plus frequency comparisons of these. The CRF is trained on the split monolingual data. It only proposes merging decisions, merging itself uses a list extracted from the monolingual data (Popovic et al., 2006).

8.3 Experiments

We evaluated the end-to-end inflection system with the addition of compounds.[15] As in the inflection experiments described in Section 5, we use a 5-gram surface LM and a 7-gram POS LM, but for this experiment, they are trained on stemmed, split data. The POS LM helps compound parts and heads appear in correct order. The results are in Table 7. The BLEU score of the CRF on test is 14.04, which is low. However the system produces 19 compound types which are in the reference but not in the parallel data, and therefore not accessible to other systems. We also observe many more compounds in general. The 100-best inflection rescoring technique previously discussed reached 14.07 on the test set. Blind test results with CRF prediction are much better, 14.08, which is a statistically significant improvement over the baseline (13.68) and approaches the result we obtained without compounds (14.18). Correctly generated compounds are single words which usually carry the same information as multiple words in English, and are hence likely underweighted by BLEU. We again see many interesting generalizations. For instance, take the case of translating English *miniature cameras* to the German compound *Miniaturkameras*. *miniature camera* or *miniature cameras* does not occur in the training data, and so there is no appropriate phrase pair in any system (baseline, inflection, or inflection&compound-splitting). However, our system with compound splitting has learned from split composita that English *miniature* can be translated as German *Miniatur-* and gets the correct output.

[14]Compound modifiers get assigned a special tag based on the POS of their former heads, e.g., *Inflation* in the example is marked as a non-head of a noun.

[15]We found it most effective to merge word parts during MERT (so MERT uses the same stem references as before).

1	1 JSM morphological features	13.94
2	4 CRFs morphological features, lexical information	14.04

Table 7: Results with Compounds on the test set

9 Related Work

There has been a large amount of work on translating from a morphologically rich language to English, we omit a literature review here due to space considerations. Our work is in the opposite direction, which primarily involves problems of generation, rather than problems of analysis.

The idea of translating to stems and then inflecting is not novel. We adapted the work of Toutanova et al. (2008), which is effective but limited by the conflation of two separate issues: word formation and inflection.

Given a stem such as *brother*, Toutanova et. al's system might generate the "stem and inflection" corresponding to *and his brother*. Viewing *and* and *his* as inflection is problematic since a mapping from the English phrase *and his brother* to the Arabic stem for *brother* is required. The situation is worse if there are English words (e.g., adjectives) separating *his* and *brother*. This required mapping is a significant problem for generalization. We view this issue as a different sort of problem entirely, one of word-formation (rather than inflection). We apply a "split in preprocessing and resynthesize in postprocessing" approach to these phenomena, combined with inflection prediction that is similar to that of Toutanova et. al. The only work that we are aware of which deals with both issues is the work of de Gispert and Mariño (2008), which deals with verbal morphology and attached pronouns. There has been other work on solving inflection. Koehn and Hoang (2007) introduced factored SMT. We use more complex context features. Fraser (2009) tried to solve the inflection prediction problem by simply building an SMT system for translating from stems to inflected forms. Bojar and Kos (2010) improved on this by marking prepositions with the case they mark (one of the most important markups in our system). Both efforts were ineffective on large data sets. Williams and Koehn (2011) used unification in an SMT system to model some of the agreement phenomena that we model. Our CRF framework allows us to use more complex context features.

We have directly addressed the question as to whether inflection should be predicted using surface forms as the target of the prediction, or whether linguistic features should be predicted, along with the use of a subsequent generation step. The direct prediction of surface forms is limited to those forms observed in the training data, which is a significant limitation. However, it is reasonable to expect that the use of features (and morphological generation) could also be problematic as this requires the use of morphologically-aware syntactic parsers to annotate the training data with such features, and additionally depends on the coverage of morphological analysis and generation. Despite this, our research clearly shows that the feature-based approach is superior for English-to-German SMT. This is a striking result considering state-of-the-art performance of German parsing is poor compared with the best performance on English parsing. As parsing performance improves, the performance of linguistic-feature-based approaches will increase.

Virpioja et al. (2007), Badr et al. (2008), Luong et al. (2010), Clifton and Sarkar (2011), and others are primarily concerned with using morpheme segmentation in SMT, which is a useful approach for dealing with issues of word-formation. However, this does not deal directly with linguistic features marked by inflection. In German these linguistic features are marked very irregularly and there is widespread syncretism, making it difficult to split off morphemes specifying these features. So it is questionable as to whether morpheme segmentation techniques are sufficient to solve the inflectional problem we are addressing.

Much previous work looks at the impact of using source side information (i.e., feature functions on the aligned English), such as those of Avramidis and Koehn (2008), Yeniterzi and Oflazer (2010) and others. Toutanova et. al.'s work showed that it is most important to model target side coherence and our stem markup also allows us to access source side information. Using additional source side information beyond the markup did not produce a gain in performance.

For compound splitting, we follow Fritzinger and Fraser (2010), using linguistic knowledge encoded in a rule-based morphological analyser and then selecting the best analysis based on the geometric mean of word part frequencies. Other approaches use less deep linguistic resources (e.g., POS-tags Stymne (2008)) or are (almost) knowledge-free (e.g., Koehn and Knight (2003)). Compound merging is less well studied. Popovic et al. (2006) used a simple, list-based merging approach, merging all consecutive words included in a merging list. This approach resulted in too many compounds. We follow Stymne and Cancedda (2011), for compound merging. We trained a CRF using (nearly all) of the features they used and found their approach to be effective (when combined with inflection and portmanteau merging) on one of our two test sets.

10 Conclusion

We have shown that both the prediction of surface forms and the prediction of linguistic features are of interest for improving SMT. We have obtained the advantages of both in our CRF framework, and also integrated handling of compounds, and an inflection-dependent word formation phenomenon, portmanteaus. We validated our work on a well-studied large corpora translation task.

Acknowledgments

The authors wish to thank the anonymous reviewers for their comments. Aoife Cahill was partly supported by Deutsche Forschungsgemeinschaft grant SFB 732. Alexander Fraser, Marion Weller and Fabienne Cap were funded by Deutsche Forschungsgemeinschaft grant Models of Morphosyntax for Statistical Machine Translation. The research leading to these results has received funding from the European Community's Seventh Framework Programme (FP7/2007-2013) under grant agreement Nr. 248005. This work was supported in part by the IST Programme of the European Community, under the PASCAL2 Network of Excellence, IST-2007-216886. This publication only reflects the authors' views. We thank Thomas Lavergne and Helmut Schmid.

References

Eleftherios Avramidis and Philipp Koehn. 2008. Enriching Morphologically Poor Languages for Statistical Machine Translation. In *Proceedings of ACL-*

08: HLT, pages 763–770, Columbus, Ohio, June. Association for Computational Linguistics.

Ibrahim Badr, Rabih Zbib, and James Glass. 2008. Segmentation for English-to-Arabic statistical machine translation. In *Proceedings of ACL-08: HLT, Short Papers*, pages 153–156, Columbus, Ohio, June. Association for Computational Linguistics.

Ondřej Bojar and Kamil Kos. 2010. 2010 Failures in English-Czech Phrase-Based MT. In *Proceedings of the Joint Fifth Workshop on Statistical Machine Translation and MetricsMATR*, pages 60–66, Uppsala, Sweden, July. Association for Computational Linguistics.

Ann Clifton and Anoop Sarkar. 2011. Combining morpheme-based machine translation with post-processing morpheme prediction. In *Proceedings of the 49th Annual Meeting of the Association for Computational Linguistics: Human Language Technologies*, pages 32–42, Portland, Oregon, USA, June. Association for Computational Linguistics.

Adrià de Gispert and José B. Mariño. 2008. On the impact of morphology in English to Spanish statistical MT. *Speech Communication*, 50(11-12):1034–1046.

Alexander Fraser. 2009. Experiments in Morphosyntactic Processing for Translating to and from German. In *Proceedings of the Fourth Workshop on Statistical Machine Translation*, pages 115–119, Athens, Greece, March. Association for Computational Linguistics.

Fabienne Fritzinger and Alexander Fraser. 2010. How to Avoid Burning Ducks: Combining Linguistic Analysis and Corpus Statistics for German Compound Processing. In *Proceedings of the Fifth Workshop on Statistical Machine Translation*, pages 224–234. Association for Computational Linguistics.

Philipp Koehn and Hieu Hoang. 2007. Factored Translation Models. In *Proceedings of the 2007 Joint Conference on Empirical Methods in Natural Language Processing and Computational Natural Language Learning (EMNLP-CoNLL)*, pages 868–876, Prague, Czech Republic, June. Association for Computational Linguistics.

Philipp Koehn and Kevin Knight. 2003. Empirical methods for compound splitting. In *EACL '03: Proceedings of the 10th conference of the European chapter of the Association for Computational Linguistics*, pages 187–193, Morristown, NJ, USA. Association for Computational Linguistics.

John Lafferty, Andrew McCallum, and Fernando Pereira. 2001. Conditional random fields: Probabilistic models for segmenting and labeling sequence data. In *Proceedings of the International Conference on Machine Learning*, pages 282–289. Morgan Kaufmann, San Francisco, CA.

Thomas Lavergne, Olivier Cappé, and François Yvon. 2010. Practical very large scale CRFs. In *Proceedings the 48th Annual Meeting of the Association for Computational Linguistics (ACL)*, pages 504–513. Association for Computational Linguistics, July.

Minh-Thang Luong, Preslav Nakov, and Min-Yen Kan. 2010. A Hybrid Morpheme-Word Representation for Machine Translation of Morphologically Rich Languages. In *Proceedings of the 2010 Conference on Empirical Methods in Natural Language Processing*, pages 148–157, Cambridge, MA, October. Association for Computational Linguistics.

Maja Popovic, Daniel Stein, and Hermann Ney. 2006. Statistical Machine Translation of German Compound Words. In *Proceedings of FINTAL-06*, pages 616–624, Turku, Finland. Springer Verlag, LNCS.

Helmut Schmid, Arne Fitschen, and Ulrich Heid. 2004. SMOR: A German Computational Morphology Covering Derivation, Composition, and Inflection. In *4th International Conference on Language Resources and Evaluation*.

Helmut Schmid. 2004. Efficient Parsing of Highly Ambiguous Context-Free Grammars with Bit Vectors. In *Proceedings of Coling 2004*, pages 162–168, Geneva, Switzerland, Aug 23–Aug 27. COLING.

Andreas Stolcke. 2002. SRILM - An Extensible Language Modeling Toolkit. In *International Conference on Spoken Language Processing*.

Sara Stymne and Nicola Cancedda. 2011. Productive Generation of Compound Words in Statistical Machine Translation. In *Proceedings of the Sixth Workshop on Statistical Machine Translation*, pages 250–260, Edinburgh, Scotland UK, July. Association for Computational Linguistics.

Sara Stymne. 2008. German Compounds in Factored Statistical Machine Translation. In *Proceedings of GOTAL-08*, pages 464–475, Gothenburg, Sweden. Springer Verlag, LNCS/LNAI.

Kristina Toutanova, Hisami Suzuki, and Achim Ruopp. 2008. Applying Morphology Generation Models to Machine Translation. In *Proceedings of ACL-08: HLT*, pages 514–522, Columbus, Ohio, June. Association for Computational Linguistics.

Sami Virpioja, Jaakko J. Väyrynen, Mathias Creutz, and Markus Sadeniemi. 2007. Morphology-aware statistical machine translation based on morphs induced in an unsupervised manner. In *PROC. OF MT SUMMIT XI*, pages 491–498.

Philip Williams and Philipp Koehn. 2011. Agreement constraints for statistical machine translation into German. In *Proceedings of the Sixth Workshop on Statistical Machine Translation*, pages 217–226, Edinburgh, Scotland, July. Association for Computational Linguistics.

Reyyan Yeniterzi and Kemal Oflazer. 2010. Syntax-to-Morphology Mapping in Factored Phrase-Based

Statistical Machine Translation from English to Turkish. In *Proceedings of the 48th Annual Meeting of the Association for Computational Linguistics*, pages 454–464, Uppsala, Sweden, July. Association for Computational Linguistics.

Identifying Broken Plurals, Irregular Gender, and Rationality in Arabic Text

Sarah Alkuhlani and **Nizar Habash**
Center for Computational Learning Systems
Columbia University
{sma2149,nh2142}@columbia.edu

Abstract

Arabic morphology is complex, partly because of its richness, and partly because of common irregular word forms, such as broken plurals (which resemble singular nouns), and nouns with irregular gender (feminine nouns that look masculine and vice versa). In addition, Arabic morpho-syntactic agreement interacts with the lexical semantic feature of rationality, which has no morphological realization. In this paper, we present a series of experiments on the automatic prediction of the latent linguistic features of functional gender and number, and rationality in Arabic. We compare two techniques, using simple maximum likelihood (MLE) with back-off and a support vector machine based sequence tagger (Yamcha). We study a number of orthographic, morphological and syntactic learning features. Our results show that the MLE technique is preferred for words seen in the training data, while the Yamcha technique is optimal for unseen words, which are our real target. Furthermore, we show that for unseen words, morphological features help beyond orthographic features and that syntactic features help even more. A combination of the two techniques improves overall performance even further.

1 Introduction

Arabic morphology is complex, partly because of its richness, and partly because of its complex morpho-syntactic agreement rules which depend on functional features not necessarily expressed in word forms. Particularly challenging are broken plurals (which resemble singular nouns), nouns with irregular gender (masculine nouns that look feminine and feminine nouns that look masculine), and the semantic feature of rationality, which has no morphological realization (Smrž, 2007b; Alkuhlani and Habash, 2011). These features heavily participate in Arabic morpho-syntactic agreement. Alkuhlani and Habash (2011) show that without proper modeling, Arabic agreement cannot be accounted for in about a third of all noun-adjective pairs and a quarter of verb-subject pairs. They also report that over half of all plurals in Arabic are irregular, 8% of nominals have irregular gender and almost half of all proper nouns and 5% of all nouns are rational.

In this paper, we present results on the task of automatic identification of functional gender, number and rationality of Arabic words in context. We consider two supervised learning techniques: a simple maximum-likelihood model with back-off (MLE) and a support-vector-machine-based sequence tagger, Yamcha (Kudo and Matsumoto, 2003). We consider a large number of orthographic, morphological and syntactic learning features. Our results show that the MLE technique is preferred for words seen in the training data, while the Yamcha technique is optimal for unseen words, which are our real target. Furthermore, we show that for unseen words, morphological features help beyond orthographic features and that syntactic features help even more. A combination of the two techniques improves overall performance even further.

This paper is structured as follows: Sections 2 and 3 present relevant linguistic facts and related work, respectively. Section 4 presents the data collection we use and the metrics we target. Section 5 discusses our approach. And Section 6 presents our results.

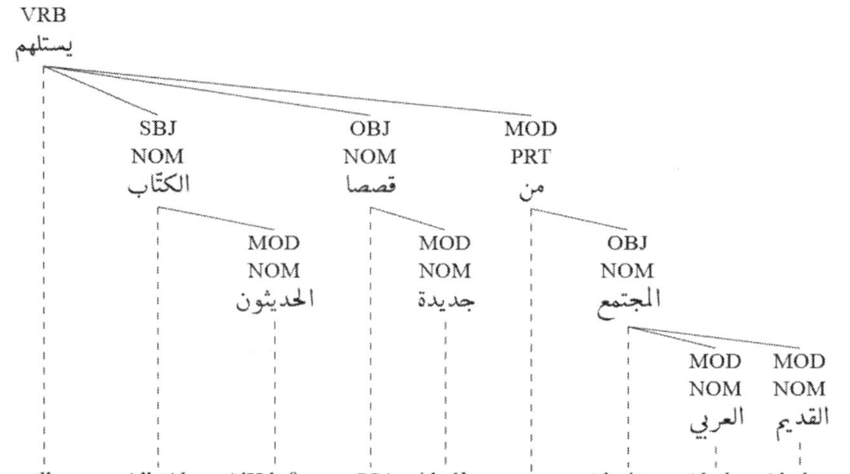

Word	ystlhm	AlktAb	AlHdyθwn	qSSA	jdydħ	mn	Almjtmς	Alςrby	Alqdym
Form	MS	MS	MP	MS	FS	NaNa	MS	MS	MS
Func	MSN	MPR	MPN	FPI	FSN	NaNaNa	MSI	MSN	MSN
Gloss	be-inspired	the-writers	the-modern	stories	new	from	culture	Arab	ancient
English	'Modern writers are inspired by ancient Arab culture to write new stories .'								

Figure 1: An example Arabic sentence showing its dependency representation together with the form-based and functional gender and number features and rationality. The dependency tree is in the CATiB treebank representation (Habash and Roth, 2009). The shown POS tags are VRB "verb", NOM "nominal (noun/adjective)", and PRT "particle". The relations are SBJ "subject", OBJ "object" and MOD "modifier". The form-based features are only for gender and number.

2 Linguistic Facts

Arabic has a rich and complex morphology. In addition to being both templatic (root/pattern) and concatenative (stems/affixes/clitics), Arabic's optional diacritics add to the degree of word ambiguity. We focus on two problems of Arabic morphology: the discrepancy between morphological form and function; and the complexity of morpho-syntactic agreement rules.

2.1 Form and Function

Arabic nominals (*i.e. nouns, proper nouns and adjectives*) and verbs inflect for gender: masculine (M) and feminine (F), and for number: singular (S), dual (D) and plural (P). These features are regularly expressed using a set of suffixes that uniquely convey gender and number combinations: $+\phi$ (MS), ة+ $+\hbar$[1] (FS), ون+ *+wn* (MP), and ات+ *+At* (FP). For example, the adjective ماهر *mAhr* 'clever' has the following forms among others: ماهر *mAhr* (MS), ماهرة *mAhrħ* (FS), ماهرون *mAhrwn* (MP), and ماهرات *mAhrAt* (FP). For a sizable minority of words, these features are expressed templatically, i.e., through pattern change, coupled with some singular suffix. A typical example of this phenomenon is the class of *broken plurals*, which accounts for over half of all plurals (Alkuhlani and Habash, 2011). In such cases, the form of the morphology (singular suffix) is inconsistent with the word's functional number (plural). For example, the word كاتب *kAtb* (MS) 'writer' has the broken plural: كتّاب *ktAb* ($\frac{MS}{MP}$).[2] See the second word in the example in Figure 1, which is the word كتّاب *ktAb* 'writers' prefixed with the definite article *Al+*. In addition to broken plurals, Arabic has words with irregular gender, e.g., the feminine singular adjective 'red' حمراء *HmrA'* ($\frac{MS}{FS}$), and the nouns خليفة *xlyfħ* ($\frac{FS}{MS}$) 'caliph' and حامل *HAml* ($\frac{MS}{FS}$) 'pregnant'. Verbs and nominal duals do not display this discrepancy.

2.2 Morpho-syntactic Agreement

Arabic gender and number features participate in morpho-syntactic agreement within specific con-

[1] Arabic transliteration is presented in the Habash-Soudi-Buckwalter (HSB) scheme (Habash et al., 2007): (in alphabetical order) *AbtθjHxdðrzsšSDTĎςγfqklmnhwy* and the additional symbols: ' ء, Â أ, Ǎ إ, Ā آ, ŵ ؤ, ŷ ئ, ħ ة, ý ى.

[2] This nomenclature denotes ($\frac{Form}{Function}$).

structions such as nouns with their adjectives and verbs with their subjects. Arabic agreement rules are more complex than the simple matching rules found in languages such as Spanish (Holes, 2004; Habash, 2010). For instance, Arabic adjectives agree with the nouns they modify in gender and number except for plural irrational (non-human) nouns, which always take feminine singular adjectives. Rationality ('humanness' 'عاقل/غير عاقل') is a morpho-lexical feature that is narrower than animacy. English expresses it mainly in pronouns (*he/she* vs. *it*) and relativizers (*men who...* vs. *cars/cows which...*). We follow the convention by Alkuhlani and Habash (2011) who specify rationality as part of the functional features of the word. The values of this feature are: rational (R), irrational (I), and not-specified (N). N is assigned to verbs, adjectives, numbers and quantifiers.[3] For example, in Figure 1, the plural rational noun الكتّاب *AlktAb* ($\frac{MS}{MPR}$) 'writers' takes the plural adjective الحديثون *AlHdyθwn* ($\frac{MP}{MPN}$) 'modern'; while the plural irrational word قصصا *qSSA* 'stories' ($\frac{MS}{FPI}$) takes the feminine singular adjective جديدة *jdydħ* ($\frac{FS}{FSN}$).

3 Related Work

Much work has been done on Arabic morphological analysis, morphological disambiguation and part-of-speech (POS) tagging (Al-Sughaiyer and Al-Kharashi, 2004; Soudi et al., 2007; Habash, 2010). The bulk of this work does not address form-function discrepancy or morpho-syntactic agreement issues. This includes the most commonly used resources and tools for Arabic NLP: the Buckwalter Arabic Morphological Analyzer (BAMA) (Buckwalter, 2004) which is used in the Penn Arabic Tree Bank (PATB) (Maamouri et al., 2004), and the various POS tagging and morphological disambiguation tools trained using them (Diab et al., 2004; Habash and Rambow, 2005). There are some important exceptions (Goweder et al., 2004; Habash, 2004; Smrž, 2007b; Elghamry et al., 2008; Abbès et al., 2004; Attia, 2008; Altantawy et al., 2010; Alkuhlani and Habash, 2011).

In terms of resources, Smrž (2007b)'s work contrasting illusory (form) features and functional features inspired our distinction of morphological form and function. However, unlike him, we do not distinguish between sub-functional (logical and formal) features. His ElixirFM analyzer (Smrž, 2007a) extends BAMA by including functional number and *some* functional gender information, but not rationality. This analyzer was used as part of the annotation of the Prague Arabic Dependency Treebank (PADT) (Smrž and Hajič, 2006). More recently, Alkuhlani and Habash (2011) built on the work of Smrž (2007b) and extended beyond it to fully annotate functional gender, number and rationality in the PATB part 3. We use their resource to train and evaluate our system.

In terms of techniques, Goweder et al. (2004) investigated several approaches using root and pattern morphology for identifying broken plurals in undiacritized Arabic text. Their effort resulted in an improved stemming system for Arabic information retrieval that collapses singulars and plurals. They report results on identifying broken plurals out of context. Similar to them, we undertake the task of identifying broken plurals; however, we also target the templatic gender and rationality features, and we do this in-context. Elghamry et al. (2008) presented an automatic cue-based algorithm that uses bilingual and monolingual cues to build a web-extracted lexicon enriched with gender, number and rationality features. Their automatic technique achieves an F-score of 89.7% against a gold standard set. Unlike them, we use a manually annotated corpus to train and test the prediction of gender, number and rationality features.

Our approach to identifying these features explores a large set of orthographic, morphological and syntactic learning features. This is very much following several previous efforts in Arabic NLP in which different tagsets and morphological features have been studied for a variety of purposes, e.g., base phrase chunking (Diab, 2007) and dependency parsing (Marton et al., 2010). In this paper we use the parser of Marton et al. (2010) as our source of syntactic learning features. We follow their splits for training, development and testing.

[3] We previously defined the rationality value N as *not-applicable* when we only considered nominals (Alkuhlani and Habash, 2011). In this work, we rename the rationality value N as *not-specified* without changing its meaning. We use the value Na (*not-applicable*) for parts-of-speech that do not have a meaningful value for any feature, e.g., prepositions have gender, number and rationality values of Na.

4 Problem Definition

Our goal is to predict the functional gender, number and rationality features for all words.

4.1 Corpus and Experimental Settings

We use the corpus of Alkuhlani and Habash (2011), which is based on the PATB. The corpus contains around 16.6K sentences and over 400K tokens. We use the train/development/test splits of Marton et al. (2010). We train on a quarter of the training set and classify words in sequence. We only use a portion of the training data to increase the percentage of words unseen in training. We also compare to using all of the training data in Section 6.7.

Our data is gold tokenized; however, all of the features we use are predicted using MADA (Habash and Rambow, 2005) following the work of Marton et al. (2010). Words whose tags are unknown in the training set are excluded from the evaluation, but not training. In terms of ambiguity, the percentage of word types with ambiguous gender, number and rationality in the train set is 1.35%, 0.79%, and 4.8% respectively. These percentages are consistent with how we perform on these features, with number being the easiest and rationality the hardest.

4.2 Metrics

We report all results in terms of token accuracy. Evaluation is done for the following sets: all words, seen words, and unseen words. A word is considered seen if it is in the training data regardless of whether it appears with the same lemma and POS tag or not. Defining seen words this way makes the decision on whether a word is seen or unseen unaffected by lemma and/or POS prediction errors in the development and test sets. Using our definition of seen words, 34.3% of words types (and 10.2% of word tokens) in the development set have not been seen in quarter of the training set.

We train single classifiers for G (gender), N (number), R (rationality), GN and GNR, and evaluate them. We also combine the tags of the single classifiers into larger tags (G+N, GN+R and G+N+R).

5 Approach

Our approach involves using two techniques: MLE with back-off and Yamcha. For each technique, we explore the effects of different learning features and try to come up with the best technique and feature set for each target feature.

5.1 Learning Features

We investigate the contribution of different learning features in predicting functional gender, number and rationality features. The learning features are explored in the following order:

Orthographic Features These features are organized in two sets: W1 is the unnormalized form of the word, and W2 includes W1 plus letter n-grams. The n-grams used are the first letter, first two letters, last letter, and last two letters of the word form. We tried using the Alif/Ya normalized forms of the words (Habash, 2010), but these behaved consistently worse than the unnormalized forms.

Morphological Features We explore the following morphological features inspired by the work of Marton et al. (2010):

- POS tags. We experiment with different POS tag sets: CATiB-6 (6 tags) (Habash et al., 2009), CATiB-EX (44 tags), Kulick (34 tags) (Kulick et al., 2006), Buckwalter (BW) (Buckwalter, 2004), which is the tag used in the PATB (430 tags), and a reduced form of BW tag that ignores case and mood (BW-) (217 tags). These tags differ in their granularity and range from very specific tags (Buckwalter) to more general tags (CATiB).
- Lemma. We use the diacritized lemma (Lemma), and the normalized and undiacritized form of the lemma, the LMM (LMM).
- Form-based features. Form-based features (F) are extracted from the word form and do not necessarily reflect functional features. These features are form-based gender, form-based number, person and the definite article.

Syntactic Features We use the following syntactic features (SYN) derived from the CATiB dependency version of the PATB (Habash and Roth, 2009): parent, dependency relation, order of appearance (the word comes before or after its parent), the distance between the word and its parent, and the parent's orthographic and morphological features.

For all of these features, we train on gold values, but only experiment with predicted values in the development and test sets. For predicting morphological features, we use the MADA system (Habash and Rambow, 2005). The MADA system corrects for suboptimal orthographic choices and effectively produces a consistent and unnormalized orthography. For the syntactic features, we use Marton et al. (2010)'s system.

5.2 Techniques

We describe below the two techniques we explored.

MLE with Back-off We implemented an MLE system with multiple back-off modes using our set of linguistic features. The order of the back-off is from specific to general. We start with an MLE system that uses only the word form, and backs off to the most common feature value across all words (excluding unknown and Na values). This simple MLE system is used as a baseline.

As we add more features to the MLE system, it tries to match all these features to predict the value for a given word. If such a combination of features is not seen in the training set, the system backs off to a more general combination of features. For example, if an MLE system is using the features W2+LMM+BW, the system tries to match this combination. If it is not seen in training, the system backs off to the following set: LMM+BW, and tries to return the most common value for this POS tag and lemma combination. If again it fails to find a match, it backs off to BW, and returns the most common value for that particular POS tag. If no word is seen with this POS tag, the system returns the most common value across all words.

Yamcha Sequence Tagger We use Yamcha (Kudo and Matsumoto, 2003), a support-vector-machine-based sequence tagger. We perform different experiments with the different sets of features presented above. After that, we apply a consistency filter that ensures that every word-lemma-pos combination always gets the same value for gender, number and rationality features. Yamcha in its default settings tags words using a window of two words before and two words after the word being tagged. This gives Yamcha an advantage over the MLE system which tags each word independently.

Single vs Joint Classification In this paper, we only discuss systems trained for a single classifier (for gender, for number and for rationality). In experiments we have done, we found that training single classifiers and combining their outcomes almost always outperforms a single joint classifier for the three target features. In other words, combining the results of G and N (G+N) outperforms the results of the single classifier GN. The same is also true for G+N+R, which outperforms GNR and GN+R. Therefore, we only present the results for the single classifiers G, N, R and their combination G+N+R.

6 Results

We perform a series of experiments increasing in feature complexity. We greedily select which features to pass on to the next level of experiments. In cases of ties, we pass the top two performers to the next step. We discuss each of these experiments next for both the MLE and Yamcha techniques. Statistical significance is measured using the McNemar test of statistical significance (McNemar, 1947).

6.1 Experiment Set I: Orthographic Features

The first set of experiments uses the orthographic features. See Table 1. The MLE system with the word only feature (W1) is effectively our baseline. It does surprisingly well for seen cases. In fact it is the highest performer across all experiments in this paper for seen cases. For unseen cases, it produces a miserable and expected low score of 21.0% accuracy. The addition of the n-gram features (W2) improves statistically significantly over W1 for unseen cases, but it is indistinguishable for seen cases. The Yamcha system shows the same difference in results between W1 and W2.

Across the two sets of features, the MLE system consistently outperforms Yamcha in the case of seen words, while Yamcha does better for unseen words. This can be explained by the fact that the MLE system matches only on the word form and if the word is unseen, it backs off to the most common value across all words. Moreover, Yamcha uses some limited context information that allows it to generalize for unseen words.

Among the target features, number is the easiest to predict, while rationality is the hardest.

	MLE								Yamcha							
	G		N		R		G+N+R		G		N		R		G+N+R	
Features	seen	unseen	seen	unseen	seen	unseen	seen	unseen	seen	unseen	seen	unseen	seen	unseen	seen	unseen
W1	**99.2**	61.6	**99.3**	69.2	**97.4**	44.7	**97.0**	21.0	95.9	67.8	96.7	72.0	94.5	67.4	90.2	35.2
W2	**99.2**	**81.7**	**99.3**	**81.6**	**97.4**	**63.4**	**97.0**	**49.1**	**97.1**	**86.6**	**97.7**	**87.1**	**95.6**	**82.0**	**92.8**	**65.5**

Table 1: Experiment Set I: Baselines and simple orthographic features. W1 is the word only. W2 is the word with additional 1-gram and 2-gram prefix and suffix features. All numbers are accuracy percentages.

	MLE								Yamcha							
	G		N		R		G+N+R		G		N		R		G+N+R	
Features	seen	unseen	seen	unseen	seen	unseen	seen	unseen	seen	unseen	seen	unseen	seen	unseen	seen	unseen
W2+F	99.2	86.9	99.3	88.9	97.4	63.4	96.9	51.9	97.7	89.8	98.1	91.7	96.0	83.5	93.8	72.0
W2+Lemma	97.4	68.3	97.6	71.5	95.6	**70.3**	95.2	**33.8**	97.4	**86.8**	97.7	86.4	96.1	82.2	93.3	65.4
W2+LMM	**99.1**	**68.8**	**99.3**	**71.7**	**97.2**	67.6	**96.8**	33.2	**97.5**	86.7	**97.9**	**86.6**	96.1	**82.6**	**93.5**	**65.7**
W2+CATIB	**99.1**	85.0	**99.3**	83.8	**97.4**	70.0	**97.1**	56.2	**97.5**	87.9	**98.0**	88.6	96.0	83.5	93.6	69.7
W2+CATIB-EX	**99.1**	85.7	**99.3**	84.3	**97.4**	70.4	**97.1**	56.7	**97.5**	88.0	97.9	88.1	96.0	83.6	93.6	69.9
W2+Kulick	99.0	86.7	99.1	85.6	97.1	78.7	96.7	65.5	97.3	88.8	97.9	89.4	95.8	83.5	93.3	70.9
W2+BW-	99.0	**88.8**	99.0	**88.8**	97.0	**80.7**	96.6	**68.5**	**97.5**	**89.7**	**98.0**	**91.2**	96.0	85.2	**93.7**	**73.2**
W2+BW	98.6	87.9	98.5	**88.8**	96.8	80.3	95.9	67.8	**97.5**	89.5	97.9	89.5	**96.1**	**85.7**	**93.7**	72.8

Table 2: Experiment Set II.a: Morphological features: (i) form-based gender and number, (ii) lemma and LMM (undiacritized lemma) and (iii) a variety of POS tag sets. For each subset, the best performers are bolded.

6.2 Experiment Set II: Morphological Features

Individual Morphological Features In this set of experiments, we use our best system from the previous set, W2, and add individual morphological features to it. We organize these features in three sub-groups: (i) form-based features (F), (ii) lemma and LMM, and (iii) the five POS tag sets. See Table 2.

The F, Lemma and LMM improve over the baseline in terms of unseen words for both MLE and Yamcha techniques. However, for seen words, these systems do worse than or equal to the baseline when the MLE technique is used. The MLE system in these cases tries to match the word and its morphological features as a single unit and if such a combination is not seen, it backs off to the morphological feature which is more general. Since we are using predicted data, prediction errors could be the reason behind this decrease in accuracy for seen words. Among these systems, W2+F is the best for both Yamcha and MLE except for rationality which is expected since there are no form-based features for rationality. In this set of experiments, Yamcha consistently outperforms MLE when it comes to unseen words, but for seen words, MLE does better almost always. LMM overall does better than Lemma. This is reasonable given that LMM is easier to predict; although LMM is more ambiguous.

As for the POS tag sets, looking at the MLE results, CATIB-EX is the best performer for seen words, and BW- is the best for unseen. CATIB-6 is a general POS tag set and since the MLE technique is very strict in its matching process (an exact match or no match), using a general key to match on adds a lot of ambiguity. With Yamcha, BW and BW- are the best among all POS. Yamcha is still doing consistently better in terms of unseen words. The best two systems from both Yamcha and MLE are used as the basic systems for the next subset of experiments where we combine the morphological features.

Combined Morphological Features Until this point, all experiments using the two techniques are similar. In this subset, MLE explores the effect of using the CATIB-EX and BW- with other morphological features. And Yamcha explores the effect of using BW- and BW with other morphological features. See Table 3. Again, Yamcha is still doing consistently better in terms of unseen words, but when it comes to seen words, MLE performs better. For seen words, our best results come from MLE using CATIB-EX and LMM. For unseen words, our best results come from Yamcha with the BW- tag and the form-based features

MLE									Yamcha								
Features:	G		N		R		G+N+R		Features:	G		N		R		G+N+R	
W2	seen	unseen	seen	unseen	seen	unseen	seen	unseen	W2	seen	unseen	seen	unseen	seen	unseen	seen	unseen
+CATIB-EX	**99.1**	85.7	**99.3**	84.3	**97.4**	70.4	**97.0**	56.7	**+BW**	97.5	89.5	97.9	89.5	96.1	85.7	93.7	72.8
+F	98.7	88.6	99.1	89.4	94.9	70.4	94.3	59.7	+F	97.8	90.6	98.2	92.4	96.3	85.3	94.2	75.4
+LMM	**99.1**	78.9	**99.3**	80.4	97.3	69.6	96.9	44.7	+LMM	97.6	88.9	98.1	88.9	96.5	85.7	94.1	72.3
+LMM+F	98.7	89.9	99.0	89.7	94.8	69.6	94.2	58.1	+LMM+F	**98.1**	90.4	**98.4**	**92.5**	**96.7**	**85.8**	**94.8**	**75.9**
+BW-	99.0	88.8	99.0	88.8	97.0	80.7	96.6	68.5	**+BW-**	97.5	89.7	98.0	91.2	96.0	85.2	93.7	73.2
+F	99.0	88.8	99.1	**89.9**	97.0	80.7	96.6	69.6	+F	97.7	**90.7**	98.2	**92.5**	96.1	85.6	94.0	75.3
+LMM	98.9	**90.0**	99.0	88.0	97.0	**83.6**	96.6	69.8	+LMM	97.7	89.6	98.1	90.4	96.2	85.1	94.0	72.5
+LMM+F	98.9	**90.0**	99.0	89.1	97.0	**83.6**	96.6	**70.8**	+LMM+F	98.0	90.3	98.2	92.4	96.5	85.7	94.5	75.1

Table 3: Experiment Set II.b: Combining different morphological features.

	Yamcha							
	G		N		R		G+N+R	
Features:	seen	unseen	seen	unseen	seen	unseen	seen	unseen
W2 +BW +F+SYN	97.3	90.6	97.8	92.5	96.1	86.1	93.5	76.0
W2 +BW +LMM+SYN	97.4	89.1	97.5	88.3	96.2	86.0	93.4	71.7
W2 +BW +LMM+F+SYN	**97.5**	**90.8**	**98.0**	92.5	**96.4**	**86.2**	**93.8**	**76.2**
W2 +BW- +F+SYN	97.4	90.7	97.9	**92.7**	96.1	85.2	93.5	75.0
W2 +BW- +LMM+SYN	97.4	89.5	97.7	89.8	96.1	85.7	93.4	72.1
W2 +BW- +LMM+F+SYN	97.4	**90.8**	97.9	**92.7**	96.2	85.3	93.6	75.2

Table 4: Experiment Set III: Syntactic features.

for both gender and number. For rationality, the best features to use with Yamcha are BW, LMM and form-based features. The lemma seems to actually hurt when predicting gender and number. This can be explained by the fact that gender and number features are often properties of the word form and not of the lemma. This is different for rationality, which is a property of the lemma and therefore, we expect the lemma to help.

The fact that the predicted BW set helps is not consistent with previous work by Marton et al. (2010). In that effort, BW helps parsing only in the gold condition. BW prediction accuracy is low because it includes case endings. We postulate that perhaps in our task, which is far more limited than general parsing, errors in case prediction may not matter too much. The more complex tag set may actually help establish good local agreement sequences (even if incorrect casewise), which is relevant to the target features.

6.3 Experiment Set III: Syntactic Features

This set of experiments adds syntactic features to the experiments in set II. We add syntax to the systems that uses Yamcha only since it is not obvious how to add syntactic information to the MLE system. Syntax improves the prediction accuracy for unseen words but not for seen words. In Yamcha, we can argue that the +/-2 word window allows some form of shallow syntax modeling, which is why Yamcha is doing better from the start. But the longer distance features are helping even more, perhaps because they capture agreement relations. The overall best system for unseen words is W2+BW+LMM+F+SYN, except for number, where W2+BW-+F+SYN is slightly better. In terms of G+N+R scores, W2+BW+LMM+F+SYN is statistically significantly better than all other systems in this set for seen and unseen words, except for unseen words with W2+BW+F+SYN. W2+BW+LMM+F+SYN is also statistically significantly better than its non-syntactic variant for both seen and unseen words. The prediction accuracy for seen words is still not as good as the MLE systems.

6.4 System Combination

The simple MLE W1 system, which happens to be the baseline, is the best predictor for seen words, and the more advanced Yamcha system using syntactic features is the best predictor for unseen words. Next, we create a new system that takes advantage of the two systems. We use the simple MLE W1 system for seen words, and Yamcha with syntax for unseen words. For unseen words, since each target feature has its own set of best learning features, we also build a combination system that uses the best systems for gender, number and rationality and combine their output into a single system for unseen words. For gender and rationality, we use W2+BW+LMM+F+SYN, and for number, we use W2+BW-+F+SYN. As expected the combination system outperforms the basic systems. For comparison: The MLE W1 system gets an (all, seen, unseen) scores of (89.3, 97.0, 21.0) for G+N+R, while the best single Yamcha syntactic system gets (92.0, 93.8, 76.2); the combination on the other hand gets (**94.9**, **97.0**, **76.2**). The overall (all) improvement over the MLE baseline or the best Yamcha translates into 52% error reduction or 36% error reduction, respectively.

6.5 Error Analysis

We conducted an analysis of the errors in the output of the combination system as well as the two systems that contributed to it.

In the combination system, out of the total error in G+N+R (5.1%), 53% of the cases are for seen words (3.0% of all seen) and 47% for unseen words (23.8% of all unseen). Overall, rationality errors are the biggest contributor to G+N+R error at 73% relative, followed by gender (33% relative) and number (26% relative). Among error cases of seen words, rationality errors soar to 87% relative, almost four times the corresponding gender and number errors (27% and 22%, respectively). However, among error cases of unseen words, rationality errors are 57% relative, while gender and number corresponding errors are (39% and 31%, respectively). As expected, rationality is much harder to tag than gender and number due to its higher word-form ambiguity and dependence on context.

We classified the type of errors in the MLE system for seen words, which we use in the combination system. We found that 86% of the G+N+R errors involve an ambiguity in the training data where the correct answer was present but not chosen. This is an expected limitation of the MLE approach. In the rest of the cases, the correct answer was not actually present in the training data. The proportion of ambiguity errors is almost identical for gender, number and rationality. However rationality overall is the biggest cause of error, simply due to its higher degree of ambiguity.

	All	seen	unseen
MLE W1	88.5	96.8	21.2
Yamcha BW+LMM+F	91.4	94.1	70.4
Yamcha BW+LMM+F+SYN	91.0	93.3	72.2
Combination	**94.1**	**96.8**	**72.4**

Table 5: Results on blind test. Scores for All/Seen/Unseen are shown for the G+N+R condition. We compare the MLE word baseline, with the best Yamcha system with and without syntactic features and the combined system.

Since the Yamcha system uses MADA features, we investigated the effect of the correctness of MADA features on the system prediction accuracy. The overall MADA accuracy in identifying the lemma and the Buckwalter tag *together* – a very harsh measure – is 77.0% (79.3% for seen and 56.8% for unseen). Our error analysis shows that when MADA is correct, the prediction accuracy for G+N+R is 95.6%, 96.5% and 84.4% for all, seen and unseen, respectively. However, this accuracy goes down to 79.2%, 82.5% and 65.5% for all, seen and unseen, respectively, when MADA is wrong. This suggests that the Yamcha system suffers when MADA makes wrong choices and improving MADA would lead to improvement in the system's performance.

6.6 Blind Test

Finally, we apply our baseline, best combination model and best single Yamcha syntactic model (with and without syntax) to the blind test set. The results are in Table 5. The results in the blind test are consistent with the development set. The MLE baseline is best on seen words, Yamcha is best on unseen words, syntactic features help in handling unseen words, and overall combination improves over all specific systems.

6.7 Additional Training Data

After experimenting on quarter of the train set to optimize for various settings, we train our combination system on the full train set and achieve (96.0, 96.8, 74.9) for G+N+R (all, seen, unseen) on the development set and (96.5, 96.8, 65.6) on the blind test set. As expected, the overall (all) scores are higher simply due to the additional training data. The results on seen and unseen words, which are redefined against the larger training set, are not higher than results for the quarter training data. Of course, these numbers should not be compared directly. The number of unseen word tokens in the full train set is 3.7% compared to 10.2% in quarter of the train set.

6.8 Comparison with MADA

We compare our results with the form-based features from the state-of-the-art morphological analyzer MADA (Habash and Rambow, 2005). We use the form-based gender and number features produced by MADA after we filter MADA choices by tokenization. Since MADA does not give a rationality value, we assign the value I (irrational) to nouns and proper nouns and the value N (not-specified) to verbs and adjectives. Everything else receives Na (not-applicable). The POS tags are determined by MADA.

On the development set, MADA achieves (72.6, 73.1, 58.6) for G+N+R (all, seen, unseen), where the seen/unseen distinction is based on the full training set in the previous section and is provided for comparison reasons only. The results for the test set are (71.4, 72.2, 53.7). These results are consistent with our expectation that MADA will do badly on this task since it is not designed for it (Alkuhlani and Habash, 2011). We should remind the reader that MADA-derived features are used as machine learning features in this paper, where they actually help. In the future, we plan to integrate this task inside of MADA.

6.9 Extrinsic Evaluation

We use the predicted gender, number and rationality features that we get from training on the full train set in a dependency syntactic parsing experiment. The parsing feature set we use is the best performing feature set described in (Marton et al., 2011), which used an earlier unpublished version of our MLE model. The parser we use is the Easy-First Parser (Goldberg and Elhadad, 2010). More details on this parsing experiment is in Marton et al. (2012).

The functional gender and number features increase the labeled attachment score by 0.4% absolute over a comparable model that uses the form-based gender and number features. Rationality on the other hand does not help much. One possible reason for this is the lower quality of the predicted rationality feature compared to the other features. Another possible reason is that the rationality feature is not utilized optimally in the parser.

7 Conclusions and Future Work

We presented a series of experiments for automatic prediction of the latent features of functional gender and number, and rationality in Arabic. We compared two techniques, a simple MLE with back-off and an SVM-based sequence tagger, Yamcha, using a number of orthographic, morphological and syntactic features. Our conclusions are that for words seen in training, the MLE model does best; for unseen word, Yamcha does best; and most interestingly, we found that syntactic features help the prediction for unseen words.

In the future, we plan to explore training on predicted features instead of gold features to minimize the effect of tagger errors. Furthermore, we plan to use our tools to collect vocabulary not covered by commonly used morphological analyzers and try to assign them correct functional features. Finally, we would like to use our predictions for gender, number and rationality as learning features for relevant NLP applications such as sentiment analysis, phrase-based chunking and named entity recognition.

Acknowledgments

We would like to thank Yuval Marton for help with the parsing experiments. The first author was funded by a scholarship from the Saudi Arabian Ministry of Higher Education. The rest of the work was funded under DARPA projects number HR0011-08-C-0004 and HR0011-08-C-0110.

References

Ramzi Abbès, Joseph Dichy, and Mohamed Hassoun. 2004. The Architecture of a Standard Arabic Lexical Database. Some Figures, Ratios and Categories from the DIINAR.1 Source Program. In Ali Farghaly and Karine Megerdoomian, editors, *COLING 2004 Computational Approaches to Arabic Script-based Languages*, pages 15–22, Geneva, Switzerland, August 28th. COLING.

Imad Al-Sughaiyer and Ibrahim Al-Kharashi. 2004. Arabic Morphological Analysis Techniques: A Comprehensive Survey. *Journal of the American Society for Information Science and Technology*, 55(3):189–213.

Sarah Alkuhlani and Nizar Habash. 2011. A Corpus for Modeling Morpho-Syntactic Agreement in Arabic: Gender, Number and Rationality. In *Proceedings of the 49th Annual Meeting of the Association for Computational Linguistics (ACL'11)*, Portland, Oregon, USA.

Mohamed Altantawy, Nizar Habash, Owen Rambow, and Ibrahim Saleh. 2010. Morphological Analysis and Generation of Arabic Nouns: A Morphemic Functional Approach. In *Proceedings of the seventh International Conference on Language Resources and Evaluation (LREC)*, Valletta, Malta.

Mohammed Attia. 2008. *Handling Arabic Morphological and Syntactic Ambiguity within the LFG Framework with a View to Machine Translation.* Ph.D. thesis, The University of Manchester, Manchester, UK.

Tim Buckwalter. 2004. Buckwalter arabic morphological analyzer version 2.0. LDC catalog number LDC2004L02, ISBN 1-58563-324-0.

Mona Diab, Kadri Hacioglu, and Daniel Jurafsky. 2004. Automatic Tagging of Arabic Text: From Raw Text to Base Phrase Chunks. In *Proceedings of the 5th Meeting of the North American Chapter of the Association for Computational Linguistics/Human Language Technologies Conference (HLT-NAACL04)*, pages 149–152, Boston, MA.

Mona Diab. 2007. Towards an Optimal POS tag set for Modern Standard Arabic Processing. In *Proceedings of Recent Advances in Natural Language Processing (RANLP)*, Borovets, Bulgaria.

Khaled Elghamry, Rania Al-Sabbagh, and Nagwa El-Zeiny. 2008. Cue-based bootstrapping of Arabic semantic features. In *JADT 2008: 9es Journées internationales d'Analyse statistique des Données Textuelles*.

Yoav Goldberg and Michael Elhadad. 2010. An efficient algorithm for easy-first non-directional dependency parsing. In *Human Language Technologies: The 2010 Annual Conference of the North American Chapter of he Association for Computational Linguistics*, pages 742–750, Los Angeles, California, June. Association for Computational Linguistics.

Abduelbaset Goweder, Massimo Poesio, Anne De Roeck, and Jeff Reynolds. 2004. Identifying Broken Plurals in Unvowelised Arabic Text. In Dekang Lin and Dekai Wu, editors, *Proceedings of EMNLP 2004*, pages 246–253, Barcelona, Spain, July.

Nizar Habash and Owen Rambow. 2005. Arabic Tokenization, Part-of-Speech Tagging and Morphological Disambiguation in One Fell Swoop. In *Proceedings of the 43rd Annual Meeting of the Association for Computational Linguistics (ACL'05)*, pages 573–580, Ann Arbor, Michigan.

Nizar Habash and Ryan Roth. 2009. CATiB: The Columbia Arabic Treebank. In *Proceedings of the ACL-IJCNLP 2009 Conference Short Papers*, pages 221–224, Suntec, Singapore.

Nizar Habash, Abdelhadi Soudi, and Tim Buckwalter. 2007. On Arabic Transliteration. In A. van den Bosch and A. Soudi, editors, *Arabic Computational Morphology: Knowledge-based and Empirical Methods*. Springer.

Nizar Habash, Reem Faraj, and Ryan Roth. 2009. Syntactic Annotation in the Columbia Arabic Treebank. In *Proceedings of MEDAR International Conference on Arabic Language Resources and Tools*, Cairo, Egypt.

Nizar Habash. 2004. Large Scale Lexeme Based Arabic Morphological Generation. In *Proceedings of Traitement Automatique des Langues Naturelles (TALN-04)*, pages 271–276. Fez, Morocco.

Nizar Habash. 2010. *Introduction to Arabic Natural Language Processing*. Morgan & Claypool Publishers.

Clive Holes. 2004. *Modern Arabic: Structures, Functions, and Varieties*. Georgetown Classics in Arabic Language and Linguistics. Georgetown University Press.

Taku Kudo and Yuji Matsumoto. 2003. Fast Methods for Kernel-Based Text Analysis. In *Proceedings of the 41st Annual Meeting of the Association for Computational Linguistics (ACL'03)*, pages 24–31, Sapporo, Japan, July.

Seth Kulick, Ryan Gabbard, and Mitch Marcus. 2006. Parsing the Arabic Treebank: Analysis and Improvements. In *Proceedings of the Treebanks and Linguistic Theories Conference*, pages 31–42, Prague, Czech Republic.

Mohamed Maamouri, Ann Bies, Tim Buckwalter, and Wigdan Mekki. 2004. The Penn Arabic Treebank: Building a Large-Scale Annotated Arabic Corpus. In *NEMLAR Conference on Arabic Language Resources and Tools*, pages 102–109, Cairo, Egypt.

Yuval Marton, Nizar Habash, and Owen Rambow. 2010. Improving Arabic Dependency Parsing with Lexical and Inflectional Morphological Features. In *Proceedings of the NAACL HLT 2010 First Workshop on Statistical Parsing of Morphologically-Rich Languages*, pages 13–21, Los Angeles, CA, USA, June.

Yuval Marton, Nizar Habash, and Owen Rambow. 2011. Improving Arabic Dependency Parsing with Form-based and Functional Morphological Features. In *Proceedings of the 49th Annual Meeting of the Association for Computational Linguistics (ACL'11)*, Portland, Oregon, USA.

Yuval Marton, Nizar Habash, and Owen Rabmow. 2012. Dependency Parsing of Modern Standard Arabic with Lexical and Inflectional Features. Manuscript submitted for publication.

Quinn McNemar. 1947. Note on the sampling error of the difference between correlated proportions or percentages. *Psychometrika*, 12(2):153–157.

Otakar Smrž and Jan Hajič. 2006. The Other Arabic Treebank: Prague Dependencies and Functions. In Ali Farghaly, editor, *Arabic Computational Linguistics: Current Implementations*. CSLI Publications.

Otakar Smrž. 2007a. ElixirFM – implementation of functional arabic morphology. In *ACL 2007 Proceedings of the Workshop on Computational Approaches to Semitic Languages: Common Issues and Resources*, pages 1–8, Prague, Czech Republic. ACL.

Otakar Smrž. 2007b. *Functional Arabic Morphology. Formal System and Implementation*. Ph.D. thesis, Charles University in Prague, Prague, Czech Republic.

Abdelhadi Soudi, Antal van den Bosch, and Günter Neumann, editors. 2007. *Arabic Computational Morphology. Knowledge-based and Empirical Methods*, volume 38 of *Text, Speech and Language Technology*. Springer, August.

Framework of Semantic Role Assignment based on Extended Lexical Conceptual Structure: Comparison with VerbNet and FrameNet

Yuichiroh Matsubayashi[†] **Yusuke Miyao**[†] **Akiko Aizawa**[†]

[†], National Institute of Informatics, Japan

{y-matsu,yusuke,aizawa}@nii.ac.jp

Abstract

Widely accepted resources for semantic parsing, such as PropBank and FrameNet, are not perfect as a semantic role labeling framework. Their semantic roles are not strictly defined; therefore, their meanings and semantic characteristics are unclear. In addition, it is presupposed that a single semantic role is assigned to each syntactic argument. This is not necessarily true when we consider internal structures of verb semantics. We propose a new framework for semantic role annotation which solves these problems by extending the theory of lexical conceptual structure (LCS). By comparing our framework with that of existing resources, including VerbNet and FrameNet, we demonstrate that our extended LCS framework can give a formal definition of semantic role labels, and that multiple roles of arguments can be represented strictly and naturally.

1 Introduction

Recent developments of large semantic resources have accelerated empirical research on semantic processing (Màrquez et al., 2008). Specifically, corpora with semantic role annotations, such as PropBank (Kingsbury and Palmer, 2002) and FrameNet (Ruppenhofer et al., 2006), are indispensable resources for semantic role labeling. However, there are two topics we have to carefully take into consideration regarding role assignment frameworks: (1) clarity of semantic role meanings and (2) the constraint that a single semantic role is assigned to each syntactic argument.

While these resources are undoubtedly invaluable for empirical research on semantic processing, current usage of semantic labels for SRL systems is questionable from a theoretical viewpoint. For example, most of the works on SRL have used PropBank's numerical role labels (Arg0 to Arg5). However, the meanings of these numbers depend on each verb in principle and PropBank does not expect semantic consistency, namely on Arg2 to Arg5. Moreover, Yi et al. (2007) explicitly showed that Arg2 to Arg5 are semantically inconsistent. The reason why such labels have been used in SRL systems is that verb-specific roles generally have a small number of instances and are not suitable for learning. However, it is necessary to avoid using inconsistent labels since those labels confuse machine learners and can be a cause of low accuracy in automatic processing. In addition, clarity of the definition of roles are particularly important for users to rationally know how to use each role in their applications. For this reasons, well-organized and generalized labels grounded in linguistic characteristics are needed in practice. Semantic roles of FrameNet and VerbNet (Kipper et al., 2000) are used more consistently to some extent, but the definition of the roles is not given in a formal manner and their semantic characteristics are unclear.

Sentence	[John]	threw	[a ball]	[from the window] .
Affection	Agent		Patient	
Movement	Source		Theme	Source/Path
PropBank	Arg0		Arg1	Arg2
VerbNet	Agent		Theme	Source
FrameNet	Agent		Theme	Source

Table 1: Examples of single role assignments with existing resources.

Another somewhat related problem of existing annotation frameworks is that it is presupposed that a single semantic role is assigned to each syntactic argument.[1] In fact, one syntactic argument can play multiple roles in the event (or events) expressed by a verb. For example, Table 1 shows a sentence containing the verb "throw" and semantic roles assigned to its arguments in each framework. The table shows that each framework assigns a single role, such as Arg0 and Agent, to each syntactic argument. However, we can acquire information from this sentence that John is an agent of the throwing event (the "Affection" row), as well as a source of the movement event of the ball (the "Movement" row). Existing frameworks of assigning single roles simply ignore such information that verbs inherently have in their semantics. We believe that giving a clear definition of multiple argument roles would be beneficial not only as a theoretical framework but also for practical applications that require detailed meanings derived from secondary roles.

This issue is also related to fragmentation and the unclear definition of semantic roles in these frameworks. As we exemplify in this paper, multiple semantic characteristics are conflated in a single role label in these resources due to the manner of single-role assignment. This means that semantic roles of existing resources are not monolithic and inherently not mutually independent, but they share some semantic characteristics.

The aim of this paper is more on theoretical discussion for role-labeling frameworks rather than introducing a new resource. We developed a framework of verb lexical semantics, which is an extension of the lexical conceptual structure (LCS) theory, and compare it with other existing frameworks which are used in VerbNet and FrameNet, as an annotation scheme of SRL. LCS is a decomposition-based approach to verb semantics and describes a meaning by composing a set of primitive predicates. The advantage of this approach is that primitive predicates and their compositions are formally defined. As a result, we can give a strict definition of semantic roles by grounding them to lexical semantic structures of verbs. In fact, we define semantic roles as argument slots in primitive predicates. With this approach, we demonstrate that some sort of semantic characteristics that VerbNet and FrameNet informally/implicitly describe in their roles can be given formal definitions and that multiple argument roles can be represented strictly and naturally by extending the LCS theory.

In the first half of this paper, we define our extended LCS framework and describe how it gives a formal definition of roles and solves the problem of multiple roles. In the latter half, we discuss the analysis of the empirical data we collected for 60 Japanese verbs and also discuss theoretical relationships with the frameworks of existing resources. We discuss in detail the relationships between our role labels and VerbNet's thematic roles. We also describe the relationship between our framework and FrameNet, with regards to the definitions of the relationships between semantic frames.

2 Related works

There have been several attempts in linguistics to assign multiple semantic properties to one argument. Gruber (1965) demonstrated the dispensability of the constraint that an argument takes only one semantic role, with some concrete examples. Rozwadowska (1988) suggested an approach of feature decomposition for semantic roles using her three features of *change*, *cause*, and *sentient*, and defined typical thematic roles by combining these features. This approach made it possible for us to classify semantic properties across thematic roles. However, Levin and Rappaport Hovav (2005) argued that the number of combinations using defined features is usually larger than the actual number of possible combinations; therefore, feature decomposition approaches should predict possible feature combinations.

Culicover and Wilkins (1984) divided their roles into two groups, action and perceptional roles, and explained that dual assignment of roles always involves one role from each set. Jackendoff (1990) proposed an LCS framework for representing the meaning of a verb by using several primitive predicates. Jackendoff also stated that an LCS represents two *tiers* in its structure, *action tier* and *thematic tier*, which are similar to Culicover and Wilkins's two sets. Essentially, these two approaches distinguished roles related to action and change, and successfully restricted com-

[1] To be precise, FrameNet permits multiple-role assignment, while it does not perform this systematically as we show in Table 1. It mostly defines a single role label for a corresponding syntactic argument, that plays multiple roles in several sub-events in a verb.

$$\left[\text{cause(affect(}i,j\text{), go(}j,\ \begin{bmatrix}\text{from(locate(in(}i\text{)))}\\ \text{fromward(locate(at(}k\text{)))}\\ \text{toward(locate(at(}l\text{)))}\end{bmatrix}\text{))}\right]$$

Figure 1: LCS of the verb *throw*.

binations of roles by taking a role from each set.

Dorr (1997) created an LCS-based lexical resource as an interlingual representation for machine translation. This framework was also used for text generation (Habash et al., 2003). However, the problem of multiple-role assignment was not completely solved on the resource. As a comparison of different semantic structures, Dorr (2001) and Hajičová and Kučerová (2002) analyzed the connection between LCS and PropBank roles, and showed that the mapping between LCS and PropBank roles was many to many correspondence and roles can map only by comparing a whole argument structure of a verb. Habash and Dorr (2001) tried to map LCS structures into thematic roles by using their thematic hierarchy.

3 Multiple role expression using lexical conceptual structure

Lexical conceptual structure is an approach to describe a generalized structure of an event or state represented by a verb. A meaning of a verb is represented as a structure composed of several primitive predicates. For example, the LCS structure for the verb "throw" is shown in Figure 1 and includes the predicates *cause, affect, go, from, fromward, toward, locate, in,* and *at*. The arguments of primitive predicates are filled by core arguments of the verb. This type of decomposition approach enables us to represent a case that one syntactic argument fills multiple slots in the structure. In Figure 1, the argument i appears twice in the structure: as the first argument of *affect* and the argument in *from*.

The primitives are designed to represent a full or partial *action-change-state* chain, which consists of a state, a change in or maintaining of a state, or an action that changes/maintains a state. Table 2 shows primitives that play important roles to represent that chain. Some primitives embed other primitives as their arguments and the semantics of the entire structure of an LCS structure is calculated according to the definition of each primitive. For instance, the LCS structure in Figure 1 represents the action changing the state of j. The inner structure of the second argument of *go* represents the path of the change.

Predicates	Semantic Functions
state(x, y)	First argument is in state specified by second argument.
cause(x, y)	Action in first argument causes change specified in second argument.
act(x)	First argument affects itself.
affect(x, y)	First argument affects second argument.
react(x, y)	First argument affects itself, due to the effect from second argument.
go(x, y)	First argument changes according to the path described in the second argument.
from(x)	Starting point of certain change event.
fromward(x)	Direction of starting point.
via(x)	Pass point of certain change event.
toward(x)	Direction of end point.
to(x)	End point of certain change event.
along(x)	Linear-shaped path of change event.

Table 2: Major primitive predicates and their semantic functions.

The overall definition of our extended LCS framework is shown in Figure 2.[2] Basically, our definition is based on Jackendoff's LCS framework (1990), but performed some simplifications and added extensions. The modification is performed in order to increase strictness and generality of representation and also a coverage for various verbs appearing in a corpus. The main differences between the two LCS frameworks are as follows. In our extended LCS framework, (i) the possible combinations of *cause, act, affect, react*, and *go* are clearly restricted, (ii) multiple actions or changes in an event can be described by introducing a *combination* function (*comb* for short), (iii) *GO, STAY* and *INCH* in Jackendoff's theory are incorporated into one function *go*, and (iv) most of the *change-of-state* events are represented as a metaphor using a spatial transition.

The idea of a *comb* function comes from a natural extension of Jackendoff's *EXCH* function. In our case, *comb* is not limited to describing a counter-transfer of the main event but can describe subordinate events occurring in relation to the main event.[3] We can also describe multiple

[2]Here we omitted the attributes taken by each predicate, in order to simplify the explanation. We also omitted an explanation for lower level primitives, such as STATE and PLACE groups, which are not necessarily important for the topic of this paper.

[3]In our extended LCS theory, we can describe multiple

$$\text{LCS} = \begin{bmatrix} \text{EVENT+} \\ \text{comb}\begin{bmatrix}\text{EVENT}\end{bmatrix}* \end{bmatrix} \qquad \text{STATE} = \begin{Bmatrix} \text{be} \\ \text{locate(PLACE)} \\ \text{orient(PLACE)} \\ \text{extent(PLACE)} \\ \text{connect(arg)} \end{Bmatrix}$$

$$\text{EVENT} = \begin{bmatrix} \begin{Bmatrix} \text{state(arg, STATE)} \\ \text{go(arg, PATH)} \\ \text{cause(act(arg1), go(arg1, PATH))} \\ \text{cause(affect(arg1, arg2), go(arg2, PATH))} \\ \text{cause(react(arg1, arg2), go(arg1, PATH))} \end{Bmatrix} \\ \text{manner(constant)?} \\ \text{mean(constant)?} \\ \text{instrument(constant)?} \\ \text{purpose(EVENT)*} \end{bmatrix}$$

$$\text{PLACE} = \begin{Bmatrix} \text{in(arg)} \\ \text{on(arg)} \\ \text{cover(arg)} \\ \text{fit(arg)} \\ \text{inscribed(arg)} \\ \text{beside(arg)} \\ \text{around(arg)} \\ \text{near(arg)} \\ \text{inside(arg)} \\ \text{at(arg)} \end{Bmatrix} \qquad \text{PATH=} \begin{bmatrix} \text{from(STATE)?} \\ \text{fromward(STATE)?} \\ \text{via(STATE)?} \\ \text{toward(STATE)?} \\ \text{to(STATE)?} \\ \text{along(arg)?} \end{bmatrix}$$

Figure 2: Description system of our LCS. Operators $+, *, ?$ follow the basic regular expression syntax. $\{\}$ represents a choice of the elements.

main events if the agent does more than two actions simultaneously and all the actions are the focus (e.g., John exchanges A with B). This extension is simple, but essential for creating LCS structures of predicates appearing in actual data. In our development of 60 Japanese predicates (verb and verbal noun) frequently appearing in Kyoto University Text Corpus (KTC) (Kurohashi and Nagao, 1997) , 37.6% of the frames included multiple events. By using the *comb* function, we can express complicated events with predicate decomposition and prevent missing (multiple) roles.

A key point for associating LCS framework with the existing frameworks of semantic roles is that each primitive predicate of LCS represents a fundamental function in semantics. The functions of the arguments of the primitive predicates can be explained using generalized semantic roles such as typical thematic roles. In order to simply represent the semantic functions of the arguments in the LCS primitives or make it easier to compare our extended LCS framework with other SRL frameworks, we define a semantic role set that corresponds to the semantic functions of the primitive predicates in the LCS structure (Table 3). We employed role names similarly to typical thematic roles in order to easily compare the role sets, but the definition is different. Also, due to the increase of the generality of LCS representation, we obtained clearer definition to explain a correspondence between LCS primitives and typical thematic roles than the Jackendoff's predicates. Note that the core semantic information of a verb represented by a LCS framework is embodied directly in its LCS structure and the information decreases if the structure is mapped to the semantic roles. The mapping is just for contrasting thematic roles. Each role is given an obvious meaning and designed to fit to the upper-level primitives of the LCS structure, which are the arguments of EVENT and PATH functions. In Table 4, we can see that these roles correspond almost one-to-one to the primitive arguments. One special role is *Protagonist*, which does not match an argument of a specific primitive. The *Protagonist* is assigned to the first argument in the main formula to distinguish that formula from the sub formulae. There are 13 defined roles, and

Role	Description
Protagonist	Entity which is viewpoint of verb.
Theme	Entity in which its state or change of state is mentioned.
State	Current state of certain entity.
Actor	Entity which performs action that changes/maintains its state.
Effector	Entity which performs action that changes/maintains a state of another entity.
Patient	Entity which is changed/maintained its state by another entity.
Stimulus	Entity which is cause of the action.
Source	Starting point of certain change event.
Source_dir	Direction of starting point.
Middle	Pass point of certain change event.
Goal	End point of certain change event.
Goal_dir	Direction of end point.
Route	Linear-shaped path of certain change event.

Table 3: Semantic role list for proposing extended LCS framework.

events in the semantic structure of a verb. However, generally, a verb focuses on one of those events and this makes a semantic variation among verbs such as buy, sell, and pay as well as difference of syntactic behavior of the arguments. Therefore, focused event should be distinguished from the others as lexical information. We expressed focused events as main formulae (formulae that are not surrounded by a *comb* function).

Predicate	1st arg	2nd arg
state	Theme	State
act	Actor	–
affect	Effector	Patient
react	Actor	Stimulus
go	Theme	PATH
from	Source	–
fromward	Source_dir	–
via	Middle	–
toward	Goal_dir	–
to	Goal	–
along	Route	–

Table 4: Correspondence between semantic roles and arguments of LCS primitives

Role	Single	Multiple	Grow (%)
Theme	21	108	414
State	1	1	0
Actor	12	13	8.3
Effector	73	92	26
Patient	77	79	2.5
Stimulus	0	0	0
Source	11	44	300
Source_dir	4	4	0
Middle	1	8	700
Goal	42	81	93
Goal_dir	2	3	50
Route	2	2	0
w/o Theme	225	327	45
Total	246	435	77

Table 5: Number of appearances of each role

this number is comparatively smaller than that in VerbNet. The discussion with regard to this number is described in the next section.

Essentially, the semantic functions of the arguments in LCS primitives are similar to those of traditional, or basic, thematic roles. However, there are two important differences. Our extended LCS framework principally guarantees that the primitive predicates do not contain any information concerning (i) selectional preference and (ii) complex structural relation of arguments. Primitives are designed to purely represent a function in an *action-change-state* chain, thus the information of selectional preference is annotated to a different layer; specifically, it is directly annotated to core arguments (e.g., we can annotate i with selPref(animate $\vee$ organization) in Figure 1). Also, the semantic function is already decomposed and the structural relation among the arguments is represented as a structure of primitives in LCS representation. Therefore, each argument slot of the primitive predicates does not include complicated meanings and represents a primitive semantic property which is highly functional. These characteristics are necessary to ensure clarity of the semantic role meanings. We believe that even though there surely exists a certain type of complex semantic role, it is reasonable to represent that role based on decomposed properties.

In order to show an instance of our extended LCS theory, we constructed a dictionary of LCS structures for 60 Japanese verbs (including event nouns) using our extended LCS framework. The 60 verbs were the most frequent verbs in KTC after excluding 100 most frequent ones.[4] We created the dictionary looking at the instances of the target verbs in KTC. To increase the coverage of senses and case frames, we also consulted the online Japanese dictionary *Digital Daijisen*[5] and Kyoto university case frames (Kawahara and Kurohashi, 2006) which is a compilation of case frames automatically acquired from a huge web corpus. There were 97 constructed frames in the dictionary.

Then we analyzed how many roles are additionally assigned by permitting multiple role assignment (see Table 5). The numbers of assigned roles for single role are calculated by counting roles that appear first for each target argument in the structure. Table 5 shows that the total number of assigned roles is 1.77 times larger than single-role assignment. The main reason is an increase in *Theme*. For single-role assignment, *Theme*, in our sense, in action verbs is always duplicated with *Actor*/*Patient*. On the other hand, LCS strictly divides a function for action and change; therefore the duplicated *Theme* is correctly annotated. Moreover, we obtained a 45% increase even when we did not count duplicated *Theme*. Most of increase are a result from the increase in *Source* and *Goal*. For example, *Effectors* of transmission verbs are also annotated with a *Source*, and *Effectors* of movement verbs are sometimes annotated with *Source* or *Goal*.

[4]We omitted top 100 verbs since these most frequent ones contain a phonogram form (Hiragana form) of a certain verb written with Kanji characters, and that phonogram form generally has a huge ambiguity because many different verbs have same pronunciation in Japanese.

[5]Available at http://dictionary.goo.ne.jp/jn/.

Resource	Frame-independent	# of roles
LCS	yes	13
VerbNet (v3.1)	yes	30
FrameNet (r1.4)	no	8884

Table 6: Number of roles in each resource.

4 Comparison with other resources

4.1 Number of semantic roles

The number of roles is related to the number of semantic properties represented in a framework and to the generality of that property. Table 6 lists the number of semantic roles defined in our extended LCS framework, VerbNet and FrameNet.

There are two ways to define semantic roles. One is *frame specific*, where the definition of each role depends on a specific lexical entry and such a role is never used in the other frames. The other is *frame independent*, which is to construct roles whose semantic function is generalized across all verbs. The number of roles in FrameNet is comparatively large because it defines roles in a frame-specific way. FrameNet respects individual meanings of arguments rather than generality of roles.

Compared with VerbNet, the number of roles defined in our extended LCS framework is less than half. However, this fact does not mean that the representation ability of our framework is lower than VerbNet. We manually checked and listed a corresponding representation in our extended LCS framework for each thematic role in VerbNet in Table 6. This table does not provide a perfect or complete mapping between the roles in these two frameworks because the mappings are not based on annotated data. However, we can roughly say that the VerbNet roles combine three types of information, a function of the argument in the action-change-state chain, selectional preference, and structural information of arguments, which are in different layers in LCS representation. VerbNet has many roles whose functions in the action-change-state chain are duplicated. For example, *Destination, Recipient,* and *Beneficiary* have the same property *end-state* (*Goal* in LCS) of a changing event. The difference between such roles comes from a specific sub-type of a changing event (possession), selectional preference, and structural information among the arguments. By distinguishing such roles, VerbNet roles may take into account specific syntactic behaviors of certain semantic roles. Packing such complex information to semantic roles is useful for analyzing argument realization. However, from the viewpoint of semantic representation, the clarity for semantic properties provided using a predicate decomposition approach is beneficial. The 13 roles for the LCS approach is sufficient for obtaining a function in the *action-change-state* chain. In our LCS framework, selectional preference can be assigned to arguments in an individual verb or verb class level instead of role labels themselves to maintain generality of semantic functions. In addition, our extended LCS framework can easily separate complex structural information from role labels because LCS directly represents a structure among the arguments. We can calculate the information from the LCS structure instead of coding it into role labels. As a result, our extended LCS framework maintains generality of roles and the number of roles is smaller than other frameworks.

4.2 Clarity of role meanings

We showed that an approach of predicate decomposition used in LCS theory clarified role meanings assigned to syntactic arguments. Moreover, LCS achieves high generality of roles by separating selectional preference or structural information from role labels. The complex meaning of one syntactic argument is represented by multiple appearances of the argument in an LCS structure. For example, we show an LCS structure and a frame in VerbNet with regard to the verb "buy" in Figure 3. The LCS structure consists of four formulae. The first one is the main formula and the others are sub-formulae that represent co-occurring actions. The semantic-role-like representation of the structure is given in Table 4: $i = \{\text{Protagonist, Effector, Source, Goal}\}$, $j = \{\text{Patient, Theme}\}$, $k = \{\text{Effector, Source, Goal}\}$, and $l = \{\text{Patient, Theme}\}$. Selectional preference is annotated to each argument as i: selPref(animate $\vee$ organization), j: selPref(any), k: selPref(animate $\vee$ organization), and l: selPref(valuable_entity). If we want to represent the information, such as "*Source* of what?", then we can extend the notation as *Source(j)* to refer to a changing object.

On the other hand, VerbNet combines multiple types of information into a single role as mentioned above. Also, the meaning of some

VerbNet role (# of uses)	Representation in LCS
Actor (9), Actor1 (9), Actor2 (9)	Actor or Effector in symmetric formulas in the structure
Agent (212)	(Actor ∨ Effector) ∧ Protagonist
Asset (6)	Theme ∧ Source of the change is (locate(in()) ∧ Protagonist) ∧ selPref(valuable entity)
Beneficiary (9)	(peripheral role ∨ (Goal ∧ locate(in()))) ∧ selPref(animate ∨ organization) ∧ ¬(Actor ∨ Effector) ∧ a transferred entity is something beneficial
Cause (21)	((Effector ∧ selPref(¬animate ∧ ¬organization)) ∨ Stimulus ∨ peripheral role)
Destination (32)	Goal
Experiencer (24)	Actor of react()
Instrument (25)	((Effector ∧ selPref(¬animate ∧ ¬organization)) ∨ peripheral role)
Location (45)	(Theme ∨ PATH roles ∨ peripheral role) ∧ selPref(location)
Material (6)	Theme ∨ Source of a change ∧ The Goal of the change is locate(fit()) ∧ the Goal fullfills selPref(physical_object)
Patient (59), Patient 1(11)	Patient ∨ Theme
Patient2 (11)	(Source ∨ Goal) ∧ connect()
Predicate (23)	Theme ∨ (Goal ∧ locate(fit())) ∨ peripheral role
Product (7)	Theme ∨ (Goal ∧ locate(fit()) ∧ selPref(physical_object))
Proposition (11)	Theme
Recipient (33)	Goal ∧ locate(in()) ∧ selPref(animate ∨ organization)
Source (34)	Source
Theme (162)	Theme
Theme1 (13), Theme2 (13)	Both of the two is Theme ∨ Theme1 is Theme and Theme2 is State
Topic (18)	Theme ∧ selPref(knowledge ∨ infromation)

Table 7: Relationship of roles between VerbNet and our LCS framework. VerbNet roles that appears more than five times in frame definition are analyzed. Each relationship shown here is only a partial and consistent part of the complete correspondence table. Note that complete table of mapping highly depends on each lexical entry (or verb class). Here, locate(in()) generally means possession or recognizing.

roles depends more on selectional preference or the structure of the arguments than a primitive function in the *action-change-state* chain. Such VerbNet roles are used for several different functions depending on verbs and their alternations, and it is therefore difficult to capture decomposed properties from the role label without having specific lexical knowledge. Moreover, some semantic functions, such as Mary is a *Goal* of the money in Figure 3, are completely discarded from the representation at the level of role labels.

There is another representation related to the argument meanings in VerbNet. This representation is a type of predicate decomposition using its original set of predicates, which are referred to as *semantic predicates*. For example, the verb "buy" in Figure 3 has the predicates *has_possession*, *transfer* and *cost* for composing the meaning of its event structure. The thematic roles are fillers of the predicates' arguments, thus the semantic predicates may implicitly provide additional functions to the roles and possibly represent multiple roles. Unfortunately, we cannot discover what each argument of the semantic predicates exactly means since the definition of each predicate is not

Example: "John bought a book from Mary for $10."

VerbNet: Agent V Theme {from} Source {for} Asset.
has_possession(start(E), Source, Theme),
has_possession(end(E), Agent, Theme),
transfer(during(E), Theme), cost(E, Asset)

LCS:

[cause(aff(*i*:John, *j*:a book), go(*j*, [to(loc(in(*i*)))]))
comb [cause(aff(*i*,*l*:$10), go(*l*, [from(loc(in(*i*))) / to(loc(at(*k*:Mary)))]))]
comb [cause(aff(*k*,*j*), go(*j*, [from(loc(in(*k*))) / to(loc(at(*i*)))]))]
comb [cause(aff(*k*,*l*), go(*l*, [to(loc(in(*k*)))]))]]

Figure 3: Comparison between the semantic predicate representation and the LCS structure of the verb *buy*.

publicly available. A requirement for obtaining implicit semantic functions from these semantic predicates is clearly defining how the roles (or functions) are calculated from these complex relations of semantic predicates.

FrameNet does not use semantic roles generalized among all verbs or does not represent seman-

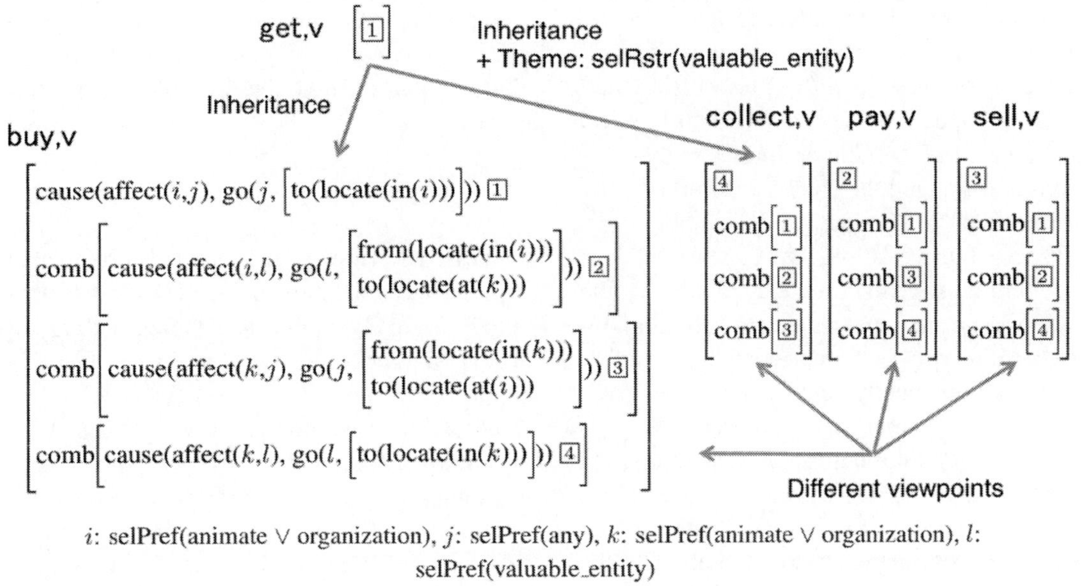

Figure 4: LCS of the verbs *get*, *buy*, *sell*, *pay*, and *collect* and their relationships calculated from the structures.

tic properties of roles using a predicate decomposition approach, but defines specific roles for each conceptual event/state to represent a specific background of the roles in the event/state. However, at the same time, FrameNet defines several types of parent-child relations between most of the frames and between their roles; therefore, we may say FrameNet implicitly describes a sort of decomposed property using roles in highly general or abstract frames and represents the inheritance of these semantic properties. One advantage of this approach is that the inheritance of a meaning between roles is controlled through the relations, which are carefully maintained by human efforts, and is not restricted by the representation ability of the decomposition system. On the other hand, the only way to represent generalized properties of a certain semantic role is enumerating all inherited roles by tracing ancestors. Also, a semantic relation between arguments in a certain frame, which is given by LCS structure and semantic predicates of VerbNet, is only defined by a natural language description for each frame in FrameNet. From a CL point of view, we consider that, at least, a certain level of formalization of semantic relation of arguments is important for utilize this information for application. LCS approach, or an approach using a well-defined predicate decomposition, can explicitly describe semantic properties and relationships between arguments in a lexical structure. The primitive properties can be clearly defined, even though the representation ability is restricted under the generality of roles.

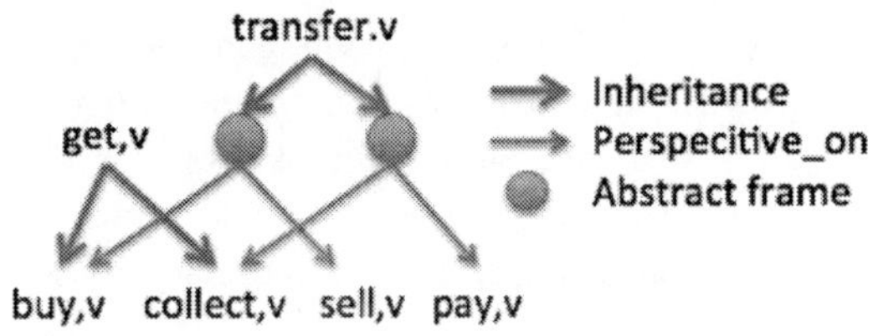

Figure 5: The frame relations among the verbs *get*, *buy*, *sell*, *pay*, and *collect* in FrameNet.

In addition, the frame-to-frame relations in FrameNet may be a useful resource for some application tasks such as paraphrasing and entailment. We argue that some types of relationships between frames are automatically calculated using the LCS approach. For example, one of the relations is based on an inclusion relation of two LCS structures. Figure 4 shows automatically calculated relations surrounding the verb "buy". Note that we chose a sense related to a commercial transaction, which means a exchange of a goods and money, for each word in order to compare the resulted relation graph with that of FrameNet. We call relations among "buy", "sell", "pay" and "collect" as *different viewpoints* since they contain exactly the same formulae, and the only difference is the main formula. The relation between "buy" and "get" is defined as *inheritance*; a part of the child structure exactly equals the parent structure. Interestingly, the relations surrounding the "buy" are similar to those in FrameNet (see Figure 5). We cannot describe all types of the relations we considered due to space limitations. However, the point is that these relationships are represented as rewriting rules between the two LCS representations and thus they are automatically calculated. Moreover, the grounds for relations maintain clarity based on concrete structural relations. A semantic relation construction of frames based on structural relationships is another possible application of LCS approaches that connects traditional LCS theories with resources representing a lexical network such as FrameNet.

4.3 Consistency on semantic structures

Constructing a LCS dictionary is generally a difficult work since LCS has a high flexibility for describing structures and different people tend to write different structures for a single verb. We maintained consistency of the dictionary by taking into account a similarity of the structures between the verbs that are in paraphrasing or entailment relations. This idea was inspired by automatic calculation of semantic relations of lexicon as we mentioned above. We created a LCS structure for each lexical entry as we can calculate semantic relations between related verbs and maintained high-level consistency among the verbs.

Using our extended LCS theory, we successfully created 97 frames for 60 predicates without any extra modification. From this result, we believe that our extended theory is stable to some extent. On the other hand, we found that an extra extension of the LCS theory is needed for some verbs to explain the different syntactic behaviors of one verb. For example, a condition for a certain syntactic behavior of a verb related to reciprocal alteration (see class 2.5 of Levin (Levin, 1993)) such as つながる (connect) and 統一 (integrate) cannot be explained without considering the number of entities in some arguments. Also, some verbs need to define an order of the internal events. For example, the Japanese verb 往復する (shuttle) means that going is a first action and coming back is a second action. These are not the problems that are directly related to a semantic role annotation on that we focus in this paper, but we plan to solve these problems with further extensions.

5 Conclusion

We discussed the two problems in current labeling approaches for argument-structure analysis: the problems in clarity of role meanings and multiple-role assignment. By focusing on the fact that an approach of predicate decomposition is suitable for solving these problems, we proposed a new framework for semantic role assignment by extending Jackendoff's LCS framework. The statistics of our LCS dictionary for 60 Japanese verbs showed that 37.6% of the created frames included multiple events and the number of assigned roles for one syntactic argument increased 77% from that in single-role assignment.

Compared to the other resources such as VerbNet and FrameNet, the role definitions in our extended LCS framework are clearer since the primitive predicates limit the meaning of each role to a function in the *action-change-state* chain. We also showed that LCS can separate three types of information, the functions represented by primitives, the selectional preference and structural relation of arguments, which are conflated in role labels in existing resources. As a potential of LCS, we demonstrated that several types of frame relations, which are similar to those in FrameNet, are automatically calculated using the structural relations between LCSs. We still must perform a thorough investigation for enumerating relations which can be represented in terms of rewriting rules for LCS structures. However, automatic construction of a consistent relation graph of semantic frames may be possible based on lexical structures.

We believe that this kind of decomposed analysis will accelerate both fundamental and application research on argument-structure analysis. As a future work, we plan to expand the dictionary and construct a corpus based on our LCS dictionary.

Acknowledgment

This work was partially supported by JSPS Grant-in-Aid for Scientific Research #22800078.

References

P.W. Culicover and W.K. Wilkins. 1984. *Locality in linguistic theory*. Academic Press.

Bonnie J. Dorr. 1997. Large-scale dictionary construction for foreign language tutoring and interlingual machine translation. *Machine Translation*, 12(4):271–322.

Bonnie J. Dorr. 2001. Lcs database. http://www.umiacs.umd.edu/~bonnie/LCS_Database_Documentation.html.

Jeffrey S Gruber. 1965. *Studies in lexical relations*. Ph.D. thesis, MIT.

N. Habash and B. Dorr. 2001. Large scale language independent generation using thematic hierarchies. In *Proceedings of MT summit VIII*.

N. Habash, B. Dorr, and D. Traum. 2003. Hybrid natural language generation from lexical conceptual structures. *Machine Translation*, 18(2):81–128.

Eva Hajičová and Ivona Kučerová. 2002. Argument/valency structure in propbank, lcs database and prague dependency treebank: A comparative pilot study. In *Proceedings of the Third International Conference on Language Resources and Evaluation (LREC 2002)*, pages 846–851.

Ray Jackendoff. 1990. *Semantic Structures*. The MIT Press.

D. Kawahara and S. Kurohashi. 2006. Case frame compilation from the web using high-performance computing. In *Proceedings of LREC-2006*, pages 1344–1347.

Paul Kingsbury and Martha Palmer. 2002. From Treebank to PropBank. In *Proceedings of LREC-2002*, pages 1989–1993.

Karin Kipper, Hoa Trang Dang, and Martha Palmer. 2000. Class-based construction of a verb lexicon. In *Proceedings of the National Conference on Artificial Intelligence*, pages 691–696. Menlo Park, CA; Cambridge, MA; London; AAAI Press; MIT Press; 1999.

Sadao Kurohashi and Makoto Nagao. 1997. Kyoto university text corpus project. *Proceedings of the Annual Conference of JSAI*, 11:58–61.

Beth Levin and Malka Rappaport Hovav. 2005. *Argument realization*. Cambridge University Press.

Beth Levin. 1993. *English verb classes and alternations: A preliminary investigation*. University of Chicago Press.

Lluís Màrquez, Xavier Carreras, Kenneth C. Litkowski, and Suzanne Stevenson. 2008. Semantic role labeling: an introduction to the special issue. *Computational linguistics*, 34(2):145–159.

B. Rozwadowska. 1988. Thematic restrictions on derived nominals. In W Wlikins, editor, *Syntax and Semantics*, volume 21, pages 147–165. Academic Press.

J. Ruppenhofer, M. Ellsworth, M.R.L. Petruck, C.R. Johnson, and J. Scheffczyk. 2006. FrameNet II: Extended Theory and Practice. *Berkeley FrameNet Release*, 1.

Szu-ting Yi, Edward Loper, and Martha Palmer. 2007. Can semantic roles generalize across genres? In *Proceedings of HLT-NAACL 2007*, pages 548–555.

Unsupervised Detection of Downward-Entailing Operators By Maximizing Classification Certainty

Jackie CK Cheung and Gerald Penn
Department of Computer Science
University of Toronto
Toronto, ON, M5S 3G4, Canada
{jcheung,gpenn}@cs.toronto.edu

Abstract

We propose an unsupervised, iterative method for detecting downward-entailing operators (DEOs), which are important for deducing entailment relations between sentences. Like the distillation algorithm of Danescu-Niculescu-Mizil et al. (2009), the initialization of our method depends on the correlation between DEOs and negative polarity items (NPIs). However, our method trusts the initialization more and aggressively separates likely DEOs from spurious distractors and other words, unlike distillation, which we show to be equivalent to one iteration of EM prior re-estimation. Our method is also amenable to a bootstrapping method that co-learns DEOs and NPIs, and achieves the best results in identifying DEOs in two corpora.

1 Introduction

Reasoning about text has been a long-standing challenge in NLP, and there has been considerable debate both on what constitutes inference and what techniques should be used to support inference. One task involving inference that has recently received much attention is that of recognizing textual entailment (RTE), in which the goal is to determine whether a hypothesis sentence can be entailed from a piece of source text (Bentivogli et al., 2010, for example).

An important consideration in RTE is whether a sentence or context produces an entailment relation for events that are a superset or subset of the original sentence (MacCartney and Manning, 2008). By default, contexts are upward-entailing, allowing reasoning from a set of events to a superset of events as seen in (1). In the scope of a *downward-entailing operator* (DEO), however, this entailment relation is reversed, such as in the scope of the classical DEO *not* (2). There are also operators which are neither upward- nor downward entailing, such as the expression *exactly three* (3).

(1) *She sang in French.* $\Rightarrow$ *She sang.* (upward-entailing)

(2) *She did not sing in French.* $\Leftarrow$ *She did not sing.* (downward-entailing)

(3) *Exactly three students sang.* $\not\Leftrightarrow$ *Exactly three students sang in French.* (neither upward- nor downward-entailing)

Danescu-Niculescu-Mizil et al. (2009) (henceforth DLD09) proposed the first computational methods for detecting DEOs from a corpus. They proposed two unsupervised algorithms which rely on the correlation between DEOs and *negative polarity items* (NPIs), which by the definition of Ladusaw (1980) must appear in the context of DEOs. An example of an NPI is *yet*, as in the sentence *This project is not complete yet*. The first baseline method proposed by DLD09 simply calculates a ratio of the relative frequencies of a word in NPI contexts versus in a general corpus, and the second is a *distillation* method which appears to refine the baseline ratios using a task-specific heuristic. Danescu-Niculescu-Mizil and Lee (2010) (henceforth DL10) extend this approach to Romanian, where a comprehensive list of NPIs is not available, by proposing a bootstrapping approach to co-learn DEOs and NPIs.

DLD09 are to be commended for having identified a crucial component of inference that nevertheless lends itself to a classification-based approach, as we will show. However, as noted by DL10, the performance of the distillation method is mixed across languages and in the semi-supervised bootstrapping setting, and there is no mathematical grounding of the heuristic to explain why it works and whether the approach can be refined or extended. This paper supplies the missing mathematical basis for distillation and shows that, while its intentions are fundamentally sound, the formulation of distillation neglects an important requirement that the method not be easily distracted by other word co-occurrences in NPI contexts. We call our alternative *certainty*, which uses an unusual posterior classification confidence score (based on the max function) to favour single, definite assignments of DEO-hood within every NPI context. DLD09 actually speculated on the use of max as an alternative, but within the context of an EM-like optimization procedure that throws away its initial parameter settings too willingly. Certainty iteratively and directly boosts the scores of the currently best-ranked DEO candidates relative to the alternatives in a Naïve Bayes model, which thus pays more respect to the initial weights, constructively building on top of what the model already knows. This method proves to perform better on two corpora than distillation, and is more amenable to the co-learning of NPIs and DEOs. In fact, the best results are obtained by co-learning the NPIs and DEOs in conjunction with our method.

2 Related work

There is a large body of literature in linguistic theory on downward entailment and polarity items[1], of which we will only mention the most relevant work here. The connection between downward-entailing contexts and negative polarity items was noticed by Ladusaw (1980), who stated the hypothesis that NPIs must be grammatically licensed by a DEO. However, DEOs are not the sole licensors of NPIs, as NPIs can also be found in the scope of questions, certain numeric expressions (i.e., non-monotone quantifiers), comparatives, and conditionals, among others. Giannakidou (2002) proposes that the property shared by these constructions and downward entailment is *non-veridicality*. If F is a propositional operator for proposition p, then an operator is non-veridical if $Fp \not\Rightarrow p$. Positive operators such as past tense adverbials are veridical (4), whereas questions, negation and other DEOs are non-veridical (5, 6).

(4) *She sang yesterday.* $\Rightarrow$ *She sang.*

(5) *She denied singing.* $\not\Rightarrow$ *She sang.*

(6) *Did she sing?* $\not\Rightarrow$ *She sang.*

While Ladusaw's hypothesis is thus accepted to be insufficient from a linguistic perspective, it is nevertheless a useful starting point for computational methods for detecting NPIs and DEOs, and has inspired successful techniques to detect DEOs, like the work by DLD09, DL10, and also this work. In addition to this hypothesis, we further assume that there should only be one plausible DEO candidate per NPI context. While there are counterexamples, this assumption is in practice very robust, and is a useful constraint for our learning algorithm. An analogy can be drawn to the one sense per discourse assumption in word sense disambiguation (Gale et al., 1992).

The related—and as we will argue, more difficult—problem of detecting NPIs has also been studied, and in fact predates the work on DEO detection. Hoeksema (1997) performed the first corpus-based study of NPIs, predominantly for Dutch, and there has also been work on detecting NPIs in German which assumes linguistic knowledge of licensing contexts for NPIs (Lichte and Soehn, 2007). Richter et al. (2010) make this assumption as well as use syntactic structure to extract NPIs that are multi-word expressions. Parse information is an especially important consideration in freer-word-order languages like German where a MWE may not appear as a contiguous string. In this paper, we explicitly do not assume detailed linguistic knowledge about licensing contexts for NPIs and do not assume that a parser is available, since neither of these are guaranteed when extending this technique to resource-poor languages.

3 Distillation as EM Prior Re-estimation

Let us first review the baseline and distillation methods proposed by DLD09, then show that distillation is equivalent to one iteration of EM prior

[1] See van der Wouden (1997) for a comprehensive reference.

re-estimation in a Naïve Bayes generative probabilistic model up to constant rescaling. The baseline method assigns a score to each word-type based on the ratio of its relative frequency within NPI contexts to its relative frequency within a general corpus. Suppose we are given a corpus $\mathcal{C}$ with extracted NPI contexts $\mathcal{N}$ and they contain $tokens(\mathcal{C})$ and $tokens(\mathcal{N})$ tokens respectively. Let y be a candidate DEO, $count^{\mathcal{C}}(y)$ be the unigram frequency of y in a corpus, and $count^{\mathcal{N}}(y)$ be the unigram frequency of y in $\mathcal{N}$. Then, we define $S(y)$ to be the ratio between the relative frequencies of y within NPI contexts and in the entire corpus[2]:

$$S(y) = \frac{count^{\mathcal{N}}(y)/tokens(\mathcal{N})}{count^{\mathcal{C}}(y)/tokens(\mathcal{C})}. \tag{7}$$

The scores are then used as a ranking to determine word-types that are likely to be DEOs. This method approximately captures Ladusaw's hypothesis by highly ranking words that appear in NPI contexts more often than would be expected by chance. However, the problem with this approach is that DEOs are not the only words that co-occur with NPIs. In particular, there exist many *piggybackers*, which, as defined by DLD09, collocate with DEOs due to semantic relatedness or chance, and would thus incorrectly receive a high $S(y)$ score.

Examples of piggybackers found by DLD09 include the proper noun *Milken*, and the adverb *vigorously*, which collocate with DEOs like *deny* in the corpus they used. DLD09's solution to the piggybacker problem is a method that they term *distillation*. Let $\mathcal{N}_y$ be the NPI contexts that contain word y; i.e., $\mathcal{N}_y = \{c \in \mathcal{N} | c \ni y\}$. In distillation, each word-type is given a distilled score according to the following equation:

$$S_d(y) = \frac{1}{|\mathcal{N}_y|} \sum_{p \in \mathcal{N}_y} \frac{S(y)}{\sum_{y' \in p} S(y')}. \tag{8}$$

where p indexes the set of NPI contexts which contain y[3], and the denominator is the number of NPI contexts which contain y.

DLD09 find that distillation seems to improve the performance of DEO detection in BLLIP. Later work by DL10, however, shows that distillation does not seem to improve performance over the baseline method in Romanian, and the authors also note that distillation does not improve performance in their experiments on co-learning NPIs and DEOs via bootstrapping.

A better mathematical grounding of the distillation method's apparent heuristic in terms of existing probabilistic models sheds light on the mixed performance of distillation across languages and experimental settings. In particular, it turns out that the distillation method of DLD09 is equivalent to one iteration of EM prior re-estimation in a Naïve Bayes model. Given a lexicon $\mathcal{L}$ of L words, let each NPI context be one sample generated by the model. One sample consists of a latent categorical (i.e., a multinomial with one trial) variable Y whose values range over $\mathcal{L}$, corresponding to the DEO that licenses the context, and observed Bernoulli variables $\vec{X} = X_{i=1\ldots L}$ which indicate whether a word appears in the NPI context (Figure 1). This method does not attempt to model the order of the observed words, nor the number of times each word appears. Formally, a Naïve Bayes model is given by the following expression:

$$P(\vec{X}, Y) = \prod_{i=1}^{L} P(X_i|Y)P(Y). \tag{9}$$

The probability of a DEO given a particular NPI context is

$$P(Y|\vec{X}) \propto \prod_{i=1}^{L} P(X_i|Y)P(Y). \tag{10}$$

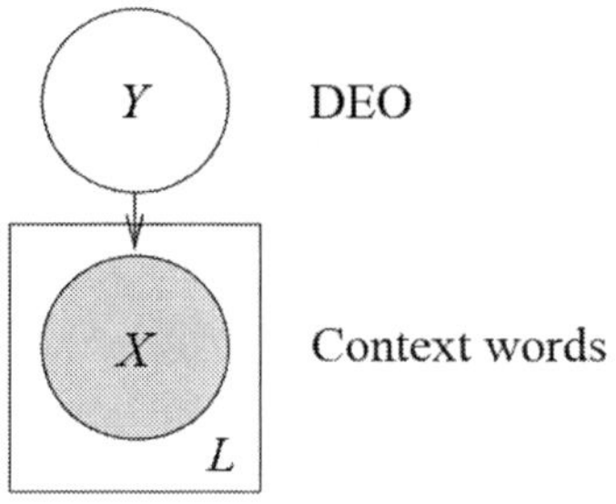

Figure 1: Naïve Bayes formulation of DEO detection.

[2] DLD09 actually use the number of NPI contexts containing y rather than $count^{\mathcal{N}}(y)$, but we find that using the raw count works better in our experiments.

[3] In DLD09, the corresponding equation does not indicate that p should be the contexts that include y, but it is clear from the surrounding text that our version is the intended meaning. If all the NPI contexts were included in the summation, $S_d(y)$ would reduce to inverse relative frequency.

The probability of a set of observed NPI contexts $\mathcal{N}$ is the product of the probabilities for each sample:

$$P(\mathcal{N}) = \prod_{\vec{X} \in \mathcal{N}} P(\vec{X}) \quad (11)$$

$$P(\vec{X}) = \sum_{y \in \mathcal{L}} P(\vec{X}, y). \quad (12)$$

We first instantiate the baseline method of DLD09 by initializing the parameters to the model, $P(X_i = 1|y)$ and $P(Y = y)$, such that $P(Y = y)$ is proportional to $S(y)$. Recall that this initialization utilizes domain knowledge about the correlation between NPIs and DEOs, inspired by Ladusaw's hypothesis:

$$P(Y = y) = S(y) / \sum_{y'} S(y') \quad (13)$$

$$P(X_i = 1|y) = \begin{cases} 1 & \text{if } X_i \text{ corresponds to } y \\ 0.5 & \text{otherwise.} \end{cases} \quad (14)$$

This initialization of $P(X_i = 1|y)$ ensures that the the value of y corresponds to one of the words in the NPI context, and the initialization of $P(Y)$ is simply a normalization of $S(y)$.

Since we are working in an unsupervised setting, there are no labels for Y available. A common and reasonable assumption about learning the parameter settings in this case is to find the parameters that maximize the likelihood of the observed training data; i.e., the NPI contexts:

$$\hat{\theta} = \underset{\theta}{\operatorname{argmax}}\ P(\mathcal{N}; \theta). \quad (15)$$

The EM algorithm is a well-known iterative algorithm for performing this optimization. Assuming that the prior $P(Y = y)$ is a categorical distribution, the M-step estimate of these parameters after one iteration through the corpus is as follows:

$$P^{t+1}(Y = y) = \sum_{\vec{X} \in \mathcal{N}} \frac{P^t(y|\vec{X})}{\sum_{y'} P^t(y'|\vec{X})} \quad (16)$$

We do not re-estimate $P(X_i = 1|y)$ because their role is simply to ensure that the DEO responsible for an NPI context exists in the context. Estimating these parameters would exacerbate the problems with EM for this task which we will discuss shortly.

$P(Y)$ gives a prior probability that a certain word-type y is a DEO in an NPI context, without normalizing for the frequency of y in NPI contexts. Since we are interested in estimating the context-independent probability that y is a DEO, we must calculate the probability that a word is a DEO given that it appears in an NPI context. Let X_y be the observed variable corresponding to y. Then, the expression we are interested in is $P(y|X_y = 1)$. We now show that $P(y|X_y = 1) = P(y)/P(X_y = 1)$, and that this expression is equivalent to (8).

$$P(y|X_y = 1) = \frac{P(y, X_y = 1)}{P(X_y = 1)} \quad (17)$$

Recall that $P(y, X_y = 0) = 0$ because of the assumption that a DEO appears in the NPI context that it generates. Thus,

$$P(y, X_y = 1) = P(y, X_y = 1) + P(y, X_y = 0) = P(y) \quad (18)$$

One iteration of EM to calculate this probability is equivalent to the distillation method of DLD09. In particular, the numerator of (17), which we just showed to be equal to the estimate of $P(Y)$ given by (16), is exactly the sum of the responsibilities for a particular y, and is proportional to the summation in (8) modulo normalization, because $P(\vec{X}|y)$ is constant for all y in the context. The denominator $P(X_y = 1)$ is simply the proportion of contexts containing y, which is proportional to $|\mathcal{N}_y|$. Since both the numerator and denominator are equivalent up to a constant factor, an identical ranking is produced by distillation and EM prior re-estimation.

Unfortunately, the EM algorithm does not provide good results on this task. In fact, as more iterations of EM are run, the performance drops drastically, even though the corpus likelihood is increasing. The reason is that unsupervised EM learning is not constrained or biased towards learning a good set of DEOs. Rather, a higher data likelihood can be achieved simply by assigning high prior probabilities to frequent word-types.

This can be seen qualitatively by considering the top-ranking DEOs after several iterations of EM/distillation (Figure 2). The top-ranking words are simply function words or other words common in the corpus, which have nothing to do with downward entailment. In effect,

1 iteration	*2 iterations*	*3 iterations*
denies	the	the
denied	to	to
unaware	denied	that
longest	than	than
hardly	that	and
lacking	if	has
deny	has	if
nobody	denies	of
opposes	and	denied
highest	but	denies

Figure 2: Top 10 DEOs after iterations of EM on BLLIP.

EM/distillation overrides the initialization based on Ladusaw's hypothesis and finds another solution with a higher data likelihood. We will also provide a quantitative analysis of the effects of EM/distillation in Section 5.

4 Alternative to EM: Maximizing the Posterior Classification Certainty

We have seen that in trying to solve the piggybacker problem, EM/distillation too readily abandons the initialization based on Ladusaw's hypothesis, leading to an incorrect solution. Instead of optimizing the data likelihood, what we need is a measure of the number of plausible DEO candidates there are in an NPI context, and a method that refines the scores towards having only one such plausible candidate per context. To this end, we define the *classification certainty* to be the product of the maximum posterior classification probabilities over the DEO candidates. For a set of hidden variables $y^{\mathcal{N}}$ for NPI contexts $\mathcal{N}$, this is the expression:

$$Certainty(y^{\mathcal{N}}|\mathcal{N}) = \prod_{\vec{X} \in \mathcal{N}} \max_{y} P(y|\vec{X}). \quad (19)$$

To increase this certainty score, we propose a novel iterative heuristic method for refining the baseline initializations of $P(Y)$. Unlike EM/distillation, our method biases learning towards trusting the initialization, but refines the scores towards having only one plausible DEO per context in the training corpus. This is accomplished by treating the problem as a DEO classification problem, and then maximizing an objective ratio that favours one DEO per context. Our method is not guaranteed to increase classification certainty between iterations, but we will show that it does increase certainty very quickly in practice.

The key observation that allows us to resolve the tension between trusting the initialization and enforcing one DEO per NPI context is that the distributions of words that co-occur with DEOs and piggybackers are different, and that this difference follows from Ladusaw's hypothesis. In particular, while DEOs may appear with or without piggybackers in NPI contexts, piggybackers do not appear without DEOs in NPI contexts, because Ladusaw's hypothesis stipulates that a DEO is required to license the NPI in the first place. Thus, the presence of a high-scoring DEO candidate among otherwise low-scoring words is strong evidence that the high-scoring word is not a piggybacker and its high score from the initialization is deserved. Conversely, a DEO candidate which always appears in the presence of other strong DEO candidates is likely a piggybacker whose initial high score should be discounted.

We now describe our heuristic method that is based on this intuition. For clarity, we use scores rather than probabilities in the following explanation, though it is equally applicable to either. As in EM/distillation, the method is initialized with the baseline $S(y)$ scores. One iteration of the method proceeds as follows. Let the score of the strongest DEO candidate in an NPI context p be:

$$M(p) = \max_{y \in p} S_h^t(y), \quad (20)$$

where $S_h^t(y)$ is the score of candidate y at the tth iteration according to this heuristic method.

Then, for each word-type y in each context p, we compare the current score of y to the scores of the other words in p. If y is currently the strongest DEO candidate in p, then we give y credit equal to the proportional change to $M(p)$ if y were removed (Context p without y is denoted $p \setminus y$). A large change means that y is the only plausible DEO candidate in p, while a small change means that there are other plausible DEO candidates. If y is not currently the strongest DEO candidate, it receives no credit:

$$cred(p, y) = \begin{cases} \frac{M(p) - M(p \setminus y)}{M(p)} & \text{if } S_h^t(y) = M(p) \\ 0 & \text{otherwise.} \end{cases} \quad (21)$$

NPI contexts

$$A\ B\ C, B\ C, B\ C, D\ C$$

Original scores

$$S(A) = 5, S(B) = 4, S(C) = 1, S(D) = 2$$

Updated scores

$$S_h(A) = 5 \times (5 - 4)/5 = 1$$
$$S_h(B) = 4 \times (0 + 2 \times (4 - 1)/4)/3 = 2$$
$$S_h(C) = 1 \times (0 + 0 + 0) = 0$$
$$S_h(D) = 2 \times (2 - 1)/2 = 1$$

Figure 3: Example of one iteration of the certainty-based heuristic on four NPI contexts with four words in the lexicon.

Then, the average credit received by each y is a measure of how much we should trust the current score for y. The updated score for each DEO candidate is the original score multiplied by this average:

$$S_h^{t+1}(y) = \frac{S_h^t(y)}{|\mathcal{N}_y|} \times \sum_{p \in \mathcal{N}_y} cred(p, y). \quad (22)$$

The probability $P^{t+1}(Y = y)$ is then simply $S_h^{t+1}(y)$ normalized:

$$P^{t+1}(Y = y) = \frac{S_h^{t+1}(y)}{\sum_{y' \in \mathcal{L}} S_h^{t+1}(y')}. \quad (23)$$

We iteratively reduce the scores in this fashion to get better estimates of the relative suitability of word-types as DEOs.

An example of this method and how it solves the piggybacker problem is given in Figure 3. In this example, we would like to learn that B and D are DEOs, A is a piggybacker, and C is a frequent word-type, such as a stop word. Using the original scores, piggybacker A would appear to be the most likely word to be a DEO. However, by noticing that it never occurs on its own with words that are unlikely to be DEOs (in the example, word C), our heuristic penalizes A more than B, and ranks B higher after one iteration. EM prior re-estimation would not correctly solve this example, as it would converge on a solution where C receives all of the probability mass because it appears in all of the contexts, even though it is unlikely to be a DEO according to the initialization.

5 Experiments

We evaluate the performance of these methods on the BLLIP corpus (~30M words) and the AFP portion of the Gigaword corpus (~338M words). Following DLD09, we define an NPI context to be all the words to the left of an NPI, up to the closest comma or semi-colon, and removed NPI contexts which contain the most common DEOs like *not*. We further removed all empty NPI contexts or those which only contain other punctuation. After this filtering, there were 26696 NPI contexts in BLLIP and 211041 NPI contexts in AFP, using the same list of 26 NPIs defined by DLD09.

We first define an automatic measure of performance that is common in information retrieval. We use average precision to quantify how well a system separates DEOs from non-DEOs. Given a list of known DEOs, G, and non-DEOs, the average precision of a ranked list of items, X, is defined by the following equation:

$$AP(X) = \frac{\sum_{k=1}^{n} P(X_{1\ldots k}) \times \mathbf{1}(x_k \in G)}{|G|}, \quad (24)$$

where $P(X_{1\ldots k})$ is the precision of the first k items and $\mathbf{1}(x_k \in G)$ is an indicator function which is 1 if x is in the gold standard list of DEOs and 0 otherwise.

DLD09 simply evaluated the top 150 output DEO candidates by their systems, and qualitatively judged the precision of the top-k candidates at various values of k up to 150. Average precision can be seen as a generalization of this evaluation procedure that is sensitive to the ranking of DEOs and non-DEOs. For development purposes, we use the list of 150 annotations by DLD09. Of these, 90 were DEOs, 30 were not, and 30 were classified as "other" (they were either difficult to classify, or were other types of non-veridical operators like comparatives or conditionals). We discarded the 30 "other" items and ignored all items not in the remaining 120 items when evaluating a ranked list of DEO candidates. We call this measure AP_{120}.

In addition, we annotated DEO candidates from the top-150 rankings produced by our certainty-

absolve, abstain, banish, bereft, boycott, caution, clear, coy, delay, denial, desist, devoid, disavow, discount, dispel, disqualify, downplay, exempt, exonerate, foil, forbid, forego, impossible, inconceivable, irrespective, limit, mitigate, nip, noone, omit, outweigh, precondition, pre-empt, prerequisite, refute, remove[5], repel, repulse, scarcely, scotch, scuttle, seldom, sensitive, shy, sidestep, snuff, thwart, waive, zero-tolerance

Figure 4: Lemmata of DEOs identified in this work not found by DLD09.

based heuristic on BLLIP and also by the distillation and heuristic methods on AFP, in order to better evaluate the final output of the methods. This produced an additional 68 DEOs (narrowly defined) (Figure 4), 58 non-DEOs, and 31 "other" items[4]. Adding the DEOs and non-DEOs we found to the 120 items from above, we have an expanded list of 246 items to rank, and a corresponding average precision which we call AP_{246}.

We employ the frequency cut-offs used by DLD09 for sparsity reasons. A word-type must appear at least 10 times in an NPI context and 150 times in the corpus overall to be considered. We treat BLLIP as a development corpus and use AP_{120} on AFP to determine the number of iterations to run our heuristic (5 iterations for BLLIP and 13 iterations for AFP). We run EM/distillation for one iteration in development and testing, because more iterations hurt performance, as explained in Section 3.

We first report the AP_{120} results of our experiments on the BLLIP corpus (Table 1 second column). Our method outperforms both EM/distillation and the baseline method. These results are replicated on the final test set from AFP using the full set of annotations AP_{246} (Table 1 third column). Note that the scores are lower when using all the annotations because there are more non-DEOs relative to DEOs in this list, making the ranking task more challenging.

A better understanding of the algorithms can

Method	BLLIP AP_{120}	AFP AP_{246}
Baseline	.879	.734
Distillation	.946	.785
This work	**.955**	**.809**

Table 1: Average precision results on the BLLIP and AFP corpora.

be obtained by examining the data likelihood and the classification certainty at each iteration of the algorithms (Figure 5). Whereas EM/distillation maximizes the former expression, the certainty-based heuristic method actually decreases data likelihood for the first couple of iterations before increasing it again. In terms of classification certainty, EM/distillation converges to a lower classification certainty score compared to our heuristic method. Thus, our method better captures the assumption of one DEO per NPI context.

6 Bootstrapping to Co-Learn NPIs and DEOs

The above experiments show that the heuristic method outperforms the EM/distillation method given a list of NPIs. We would like to extend this result to novel domains, corpora, and languages. DLD09 and DL10 proposed the following bootstrapping algorithm for co-learning NPIs and DEOs given a much smaller list of NPIs as a seed set.

1. Begin with a small set of seed NPIs
2. Iterate:
   (a) Use the current list of NPIs to learn a list of DEOs
   (b) Use the current list of DEOs to learn a list of NPIs

Interestingly, DL10 report that while this method works in Romanian data, it does not work in the English BLLIP corpus. They speculate that the reason might be due to the nature of the English DEO *any*, which can occur in all classes of DE contexts according to an analysis by Haspelmath (1997). Further, they find that in Romanian, distillation does not perform better than the baseline method during Step (2a). While this linguistic explanation may certainly be a factor, we raise

[4]The complete list will be made publicly available.

[5]We disagree with DLD09 that *remove* is not downward-entailing; e.g., *The detergent removed stains from his clothing.* ⇒ *The detergent removed stains from his shirts.*

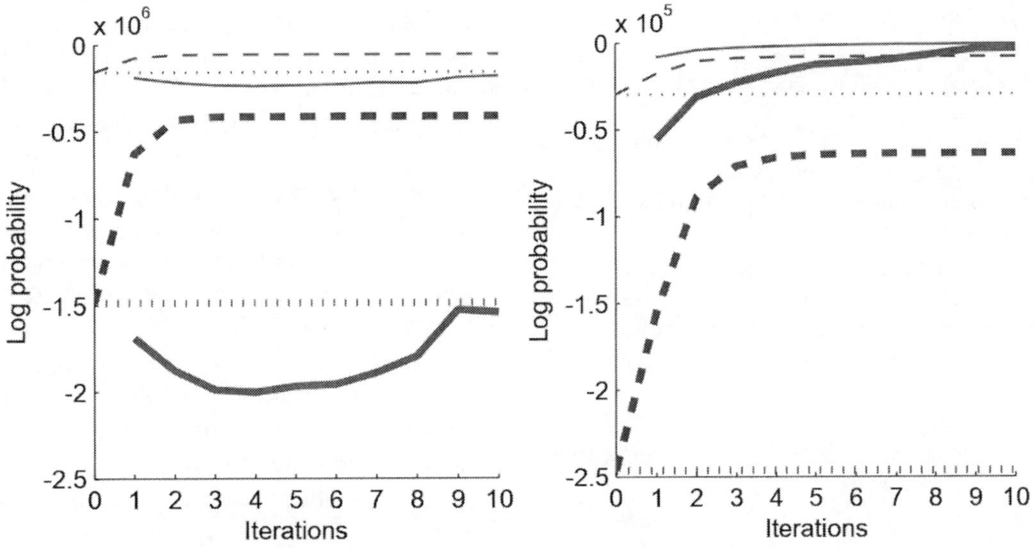

(a) Data log likelihood.

(b) Log classification certainty probabilities.

Figure 5: Log likelihood and classification certainty probabilities of NPI contexts in two corpora. Thinner lines near the top are for BLLIP; thicker lines for AFP. Blue dotted: baseline; red dashed: distillation; green solid: our certainty-based heuristic method. $P(\vec{X}|y)$ probabilities are not included since they would only result in a constant offset in the log domain.

a second possibility that the distillation algorithm itself may be responsible for these results. As evidence, we show that the heuristic algorithm is able to work in English with just the single seed NPI *any*, and in fact the bootstrapping approach in conjunction with our heuristic even outperforms the above approaches when using a static list of NPIs.

In particular, we use the methods described in the previous sections for Step (2a), and the following ratio to rank NPI candidates in Step (2b), corresponding to the baseline method to detect DEOs in reverse:

$$T(x) = \frac{count^{\mathcal{D}}(x)/tokens(\mathcal{D})}{count^{\mathcal{C}}(x)/tokens(\mathcal{C})}. \qquad (25)$$

Here, $count^{\mathcal{D}}(x)$ refers to the number of occurrences of NPI candidate x in DEO contexts $\mathcal{D}$, defined to be the words to the right of a DEO operator up to a comma or semi-colon. We do not use the EM/distillation or heuristic methods in Step (2b). Learning NPIs from DEOs is a much harder problem than learning DEOs from NPIs. Because DEOs (and other non-veridical operators) license NPIs, the majority of occurrences of NPIs will be in the context of a DEO, modulo ambiguity of DEOs such as the free-choice *any* and other spurious correlations such as piggybackers as discussed earlier. In the other direction, it is not the case that DEOs always or nearly always appear in the context of an NPI. Rather, the most common collocations of DEOs are the selectional preferences of the DEO, such as common arguments to verbal DEOs, prepositions that are part of the subcategorization of the DEO, and words that together with the surface form of the DEO comprise an idiomatic expression or multi-word expression. Further, NPIs are more likely to be composed of multiple words, while many DEOs are single words, possibly with PP subcategorization requirements which can be filled in post hoc. Because of these issues, we cannot trust the initialization to learn NPIs nearly as much as with DEOs, and cannot use the distillation or certainty methods for this step. Rather, the hope is that learning a noisy list of "pseudo-NPIs", which often occur in negative contexts but may not actually be NPIs, can still improve the performance of DEO detection.

There are a number of parameters to the method which we tuned to the BLLIP corpus using AP_{120}. At the end of Step (2a), we use the current top 25 DEOs plus 5 per iteration as the DEO list for the next step. To the initial seed NPI of

Method	BLLIP AP_{120}	AFP AP_{246}
Baseline	.889 (+.010)	.739 (−.005)
Distillation	.930 (−.016)	.804 (+.019)
This work	**.962** (+.007)	**.821** (+.012)

Table 2: Average precision results with bootstrapping on the BLLIP and AFP corpora. Absolute gain in average precision compared to using a fixed list of NPIs given in brackets.

anymore, anything, anytime, avail, bother, bothered, budge, budged, countenance, faze, fazed, inkling, iota, jibe, mince, nor, whatsoever, whit

Figure 6: Probable NPIs found by bootstrapping using the certainty-based heuristic method.

any, we add the top 5 ranking NPI candidates at the end of Step (2b) in each subsequent iteration. We ran the bootstrapping algorithm for 11 iterations for all three algorithms. The final evaluation was done on AFP using AP_{246}.

The results show that bootstrapping can indeed improve performance, even in English (Table 2). Using bootstrapping to co-learn NPIs and DEOs actually results in better performance than specifying a static list of NPIs. The certainty-based heuristic in particular achieves gains with bootstrapping in both corpora, in contrast to the baseline and distillation methods. Another factor that we found to be important is to add a sufficient number of NPIs to the NPI list each iteration, as adding too few NPIs results in only a small change in the NPI contexts available for DEO detection. DL10 only added one NPI per iteration, which may explain why they did not find any improvement with bootstrapping in English. It also appears that learning the pseudo-NPIs does not hurt performance in detecting DEO, and further, that a number of true NPIs are learned by our method (Figure 6).

7 Conclusion

We have proposed a novel unsupervised method for discovering downward-entailing operators from raw text based on their co-occurrence with negative polarity items. Unlike the distillation method of DLD09, which we show to be an instance of EM prior re-estimation, our method directly addresses the issue of piggybackers which spuriously correlate with NPIs but are not downward-entailing. This is achieved by maximizing the posterior classification certainty of the corpus in a way that respects the initialization, rather than maximizing the data likelihood as in EM/distillation. Our method outperforms distillation and a baseline method on two corpora as well as in a bootstrapping setting where NPIs and DEOs are jointly learned. It achieves the best performance in the bootstrapping setting, rather than when using a fixed list of NPIs. The performance of our algorithm suggests that it is suitable for other corpora and languages.

Interesting future research directions include detecting DEOs of more than one word as well as distinguishing the particular word sense and subcategorization that is downward-entailing. Another problem that should be addressed is the scope of the downward entailment, generalizing work being done in detecting the scope of negation (Councill et al., 2010, for example).

Acknowledgments

We would like to thank Cristian Danescu-Niculescu-Mizil for his help with replicating his results on the BLLIP corpus. This project was supported by the Natural Sciences and Engineering Research Council of Canada.

References

Luisa Bentivogli, Peter Clark, Ido Dagan, Hoa T. Dang, and Danilo Giampiccolo. 2010. The sixth pascal recognizing textual entailment challenge. In *The Text Analysis Conference (TAC 2010)*.

Isaac G. Councill, Ryan McDonald, and Leonid Velikovich. 2010. What's great and what's not: Learning to classify the scope of negation for improved sentiment analysis. In *Proceedings of the Workshop on Negation and Speculation in Natural Language Processing*, pages 51–59. Association for Computational Linguistics.

Cristian Danescu-Niculescu-Mizil and Lillian Lee. 2010. Don't 'have a clue'?: Unsupervised co-learning of downward-entailing operators. In *Proceedings of the ACL 2010 Conference Short Papers*, pages 247–252. Association for Computational Linguistics.

Cristian Danescu-Niculescu-Mizil, Lillian Lee, and Richard Ducott. 2009. Without a 'doubt'?: Unsupervised discovery of downward-entailing operators. In *Proceedings of Human Language Technologies: The 2009 Annual Conference of the North American Chapter of the Association for Computational Linguistics*.

William A. Gale, Kenneth W. Church, and David Yarowsky. 1992. One sense per discourse. In *Proceedings of the Workshop on Speech and Natural Language*, pages 233–237. Association for Computational Linguistics.

Anastasia Giannakidou. 2002. Licensing and sensitivity in polarity items: from downward entailment to nonveridicality. *CLS*, 38:29–53.

Martin Haspelmath. 1997. *Indefinite pronouns*. Oxford University Press.

Jack Hoeksema. 1997. Corpus study of negative polarity items. *IV-V Jornades de corpus linguistics 1996–1997*.

William A. Ladusaw. 1980. On the notion 'affective' in the analysis of negative-polarity items. *Journal of Linguistic Research*, 1(2):1–16.

Timm Lichte and Jan-Philipp Soehn. 2007. The retrieval and classification of negative polarity items using statistical profiles. *Roots: Linguistics in Search of Its Evidential Base*, pages 249–266.

Bill MacCartney and Christopher D. Manning. 2008. Modeling semantic containment and exclusion in natural language inference. In *Proceedings of the 22nd International Conference on Computational Linguistics*.

Frank Richter, Fabienne Fritzinger, and Marion Weller. 2010. Who can see the forest for the trees? extracting multiword negative polarity items from dependency-parsed text. *Journal for Language Technology and Computational Linguistics*, 25:83–110.

Ton van der Wouden. 1997. *Negative Contexts: Collocation, Polarity and Multiple Negation*. Routledge.

Elliphant: Improved Automatic Detection of Zero Subjects and Impersonal Constructions in Spanish

Luz Rello*
NLP and Web Research Groups
Univ. Pompeu Fabra
Barcelona, Spain

Ricardo Baeza-Yates
Yahoo! Research
Barcelona, Spain

Ruslan Mitkov
Research Group in
Computational Linguistics
Univ. of Wolverhampton, UK

Abstract

In pro-drop languages, the detection of explicit subjects, zero subjects and non-referential impersonal constructions is crucial for anaphora and co-reference resolution. While the identification of explicit and zero subjects has attracted the attention of researchers in the past, the automatic identification of impersonal constructions in Spanish has not been addressed yet and this work is the first such study. In this paper we present a corpus to underpin research on the automatic detection of these linguistic phenomena in Spanish and a novel machine learning-based methodology for their computational treatment. This study also provides an analysis of the features, discusses performance across two different genres and offers error analysis. The evaluation results show that our system performs better in detecting explicit subjects than alternative systems.

1 Introduction

Subject ellipsis is the omission of the subject in a sentence. We consider not only missing referential subject (zero subject) as manifestation of ellipsis, but also non-referential impersonal constructions.

Various natural language processing (NLP) tasks benefit from the identification of elliptical subjects, primarily anaphora resolution (Mitkov, 2002) and co-reference resolution (Ng and Cardie, 2002). The difficulty in detecting missing subjects and non-referential pronouns has been acknowledged since the first studies on the computational treatment of anaphora (Hobbs, 1977; Hirst, 1981). However, this task is of crucial importance when processing pro-drop languages since subject ellipsis is a pervasive phenomenon in these languages (Chomsky, 1981). For instance, in our Spanish corpus, 29% of the subjects are elided.

Our method is based on classification of all expressions in subject position, including the recognition of Spanish non-referential impersonal constructions which, to the best of our knowledge, has not yet been addressed. The necessity of identifying such kind of elliptical constructions has been specifically highlighted in work about Spanish zero pronouns (Ferrández and Peral, 2000) and co-reference resolution (Recasens and Hovy, 2009).

The main contributions of this study are:

- A public annotated corpus in Spanish to compare different strategies for detecting explicit subjects, zero subjects and impersonal constructions.
- The first ML based approach to this problem in Spanish and a thorough analysis regarding features, learnability, genre and errors.
- The best performing algorithms to automatically detect explicit subjects and impersonal constructions in Spanish.

The remainder of the paper is organized as follows. Section 2 describes the classes of Spanish subjects, while Section 3 provides a literature review. Section 4 describes the creation and the annotation of the corpus and in Section 5 the machine learning (ML) method is presented. The analysis of the features, the learning curves, the

* This work was partially funded by a 'La Caixa' grant for master students.

genre impact and the error analysis are all detailed in Section 6. Finally, in Section 7, conclusions are drawn and plans for future work are discussed. This work is an extension of the first author master's thesis (Rello, 2010) and a preliminary version of the algorithm was presented in Rello et al. (2010).

2 Classes of Spanish Subjects

Literature related to ellipsis in NLP (Ferrández and Peral, 2000; Rello and Illisei, 2009a; Mitkov, 2010) and linguistic theory (Bosque, 1989; Brucart, 1999; Real Academia Española, 2009) has served as a basis for establishing the classes of this work.

Explicit subjects are phonetically realized and their syntactic position can be pre-verbal or post-verbal. In the case of post-verbal subjects (a), the syntactic position is restricted by some conditions (Real Academia Española, 2009).

(a) Carecerán de validez *las disposiciones que contradigan otra de rango superior.*[1]
The dispositions which contradict higher range ones will not be valid.

Zero subjects (b) appear as the result of a nominal ellipsis. That is, a lexical element –the elliptic subject–, which is needed for the interpretation of the meaning and the structure of the sentence, is elided; therefore, it can be retrieved from its context. The elision of the subject can affect the entire noun phrase and not just the noun head when a definite article occurs (Brucart, 1999).

(b) Ø Fue refrendada por el pueblo español.
(It) was countersigned by the people of Spain.

The class of *impersonal constructions* is formed by impersonal clauses (c) and reflexive impersonal clauses with particle *se* (d) (Real Academia Española, 2009).

(c) No hay matrimonio sin consentimiento.
(There is) no marriage without consent.

(d) Se estará a lo que establece el apartado siguiente.
(It) will be what is established in the next section.

[1]All the examples provided are taken from our corpus. In the examples, explicit subjects are presented in *italics*. Zero subjects are presented by the symbol Ø and in the English translations the subjects which are elided in Spanish are marked with parentheses. Impersonal constructions are not explicitly indicated.

3 Related Work

Identification of non-referential pronouns, although a crucial step in co-reference and anaphora resolution systems (Mitkov, 2010),[2] has been applied only to the pleonastic *it* in English (Evans, 2001; Boyd et al., 2005; Bergsma et al., 2008) and expletive pronouns in French (Danlos, 2005). Machine learning methods are known to perform better than rule-based techniques for identifying non-referential expressions (Boyd et al., 2005). However, there is some debate as to which approach may be optimal in anaphora resolution systems (Mitkov and Hallett, 2007).

Both English and French texts use an explicit word, with some grammatical information (a third person pronoun), which is non-referential (Mitkov, 2010). By contrast, in Spanish, non-referential expressions are not realized by expletive or pleonastic pronouns but rather by a certain kind of ellipsis. For this reason, it is easy to mistake them for zero pronouns, which are, in fact, referential.

Previous work on detecting Spanish subject ellipsis focused on distinguishing verbs with explicit subjects and verbs with zero subjects (zero pronouns), using rule-based methods (Ferrández and Peral, 2000; Rello and Illisei, 2009b). The Ferrández and Peral algorithm (2000) outperforms the (Rello and Illisei, 2009b) approach with 57% accuracy in identifying zero subjects. In (Ferrández and Peral, 2000), the implementation of a zero subject identification and resolution module forms part of an anaphora resolution system.

ML based studies on the identification of explicit non-referential constructions in English present accuracies of 71% (Evans, 2001), 87.5% (Bergsma et al., 2008) and 88% (Boyd et al., 2005), while 97.5% is achieved for French (Danlos, 2005). However, in these languages, non-referential constructions are explicit and not omitted which makes this task more challenging for Spanish.

4 Corpus

We created and annotated a corpus composed of legal texts (law) and health texts (psychiatric

[2]In zero anaphora resolution, the identification of zero anaphors first requires that they be distinguished from non-referential impersonal constructions (Mitkov, 2010).

papers) originally written in peninsular Spanish. The corpus is named after its annotated content "Explicit Subjects, Zero Subjects and Impersonal Constructions" (ESZIC_es Corpus).

To the best of our knowledge, the existing corpora annotated with elliptical subjects belong to other genres. *The Blue Book* (handbook) and *Lexesp* (journalistic texts) used in (Ferrández and Peral, 2000) contain zero subjects but not impersonal constructions. On the other hand, the Spanish AnCora corpus based on journalistic texts includes zero pronouns and impersonal constructions (Recasens and Martí, 2010) while the Z-corpus (Rello and Illisei, 2009b) comprises legal, instructional and encyclopedic texts but has no annotated impersonal constructions.

The ESZIC corpus contains a total of 6,827 verbs including 1,793 zero subjects. Except for AnCora-ES, with 10,791 elliptic pronouns, our corpus is larger than the ones used in previous approaches: about 1,830 verbs including zero and explicit subjects in (Ferrández and Peral, 2000) (the exact number is not mentioned in the paper) and 1,202 zero subjects in (Rello and Illisei, 2009b).

The corpus was parsed by Connexor's Machinese Syntax (Connexor Oy, 2006), which returns lexical and morphological information as well as the dependency relations between words by employing a functional dependency grammar (Tapanainen and Järvinen, 1997).

To annotate our corpus we created an annotation tool that extracts the finite clauses and the annotators assign to each example one of the defined annotation tags. Two volunteer graduate students of linguistics annotated the verbs after one training session. The annotations of a third volunteer with the same profile were used to compute the inter-annotator agreement. During the annotation phase, we evaluated the adequacy and clarity of the annotation guidelines and established a typology of the rising borderline cases, which is included in the annotation guidelines.

Table 1 shows the linguistic and formal criteria used to identify the chosen categories that served as the basis for the corpus annotation. For each tag, in addition to the two criteria that are crucial for identifying subject ellipsis ([$\pm$ elliptic] and [$\pm$ referential]) a combination of syntactic, semantic and discourse knowledge is also encoded during the annotation. The linguistic motivation for each of the three categories is shown against the thirteen annotation tags to which they belong (Table 1).

Afterwards, each of the tags are grouped in one of the three main classes.

- Explicit subjects: [- elliptic, + referential].
- Zero subjects: [+ elliptic, + referential].
- Impersonal constructions: [+ elliptic, - referential].

Of these annotated verbs, 71% have an explicit subject, 26% have a zero subject and 3% belong to an impersonal construction (see Table 2).

Number of instances	Legal	Health	All
Explicit subjects	2,739	2,116	4,855
Zero subjects	619	1,174	1,793
Impersonals	71	108	179
Total	3,429	3,398	6,827

Table 2: Instances per class in ESZIC Corpus.

To measure inter-annotator reliability we use Fleiss' Kappa statistical measure (Fleiss, 1971). We extracted 10% of the instances of each of the texts of the corpus covering the two genres.

Fleiss' Kappa	Legal	Health	All
Two Annotators	0.934	0.870	0.902
Three Annotators	0.925	0.857	0.891

Table 3: Inter-annotator Agreement.

In Table 3 we present the Fleiss kappa inter-annotator agreement for two and three annotators. These results suggest that the annotation is reliable since it is common practice among researchers in computational linguistics to consider 0.8 as a minimum value of acceptance (Artstein and Poesio, 2008).

5 Machine Learning Approach

We opted for an ML approach given that our previous rule-based methodology improved only 0.02 over the 0.55 F-measure of a simple baseline (Rello and Illisei, 2009b). Besides, ML based methods for the identification of explicit non-referential constructions in English appear to perform better than than rule-based ones (Boyd et al., 2005).

Linguistic information		Phonetic realization		Syntactic category	Verbal diathesis	Semantic interpr.	Discourse
Annotation Categories	**Annotation Tags**	Elliptic noun phrase	Ell. noun phrase head	Nominal subject	Active	Active participant	Referential subject
Explicit subject	Explicit subject	–	–	+	+	+	+
	Reflex passive subject	–	–	+	+	–	+
	Passive subject	–	–	+	–	–	+
Zero subject	Omitted subject	+	–	+	+	+	+
	Omitted subject head	–	+	+	+	+	+
	Non-nominal subject	–	–	–	+	+	+
	Reflex passive omitted subject	+	–	+	+	–	+
	Reflex pass. omitted subject head	–	+	+	+	–	+
	Reflex pass. non-nominal subject	–	–	–	+	–	+
	Passive omitted subject	+	–	+	–	–	+
	Pass. non-nominal subject	–	–	–	–	–	+
Impersonal construction	Reflex imp. clause (with *se*)	–	–	n/a	–	n/a	–
	Imp. construction (without *se*)	–	–	n/a	+	n/a	–

Table 1: ESZIC Corpus Annotation Tags.

5.1 Features

We built the training data from the annotated corpus and defined fourteen features. The linguistically motivated features are inspired by previous ML approaches in Chinese (Zhao and Ng, 2007) and English (Evans, 2001). The values for the features (see Table 4) were derived from information provided both by Connexor's Machinese Syntax parser and a set of lists.

We can describe each of the features as broadly belonging to one of ten classes, as follows:

1 PARSER: the presence or absence of a subject in the clause, as identified by the parser. We are not aware of a formal evaluation of Connexor's accuracy. It presents an accuracy of 74.9% evaluated against our corpus and we used it as a simple baseline.

2 CLAUSE: the clause types considered are: main clauses, relative clauses starting with a complex conjunction, clauses starting with a simple conjunction, and clauses introduced using punctuation marks (commas, semicolons, etc). We implemented a method to identify these different types of clauses, as the parser does not explicitly mark the boundaries of clauses within sentences. The method took into account the existence of a finite verb, its dependencies, the existence of conjunctions and punctuation marks.

3 LEMMA: lexical information extracted from the parser, the lemma of the finite verb.

4-5 NUMBER, PERSON: morphological information of the verb, its grammatical number and its person.

6 AGREE: feature which encodes the tense, mood, person, and number of the verb in the clause, and its agreement in person, number,

Feature	Definition	Value
1 PARSER	Parsed subject	True, False
2 CLAUSE	Clause type	Main, Rel, Imp, Prop, Punct
3 LEMMA	Verb lemma	Parser's lemma tag
4 NUMBER	Verb morphological number	SG, PL
5 PERSON	Verb morphological person	P1, P2, P3
6 AGREE	Agreement in person, number, tense and mood	FTFF, TTTT, FFFF, TFTF, TTFF, FTFT, FTTF, TFTT, FFFT, TTTF, FFTF, TFFT, FFTT, FTTT, TFFF, TTFT
7 NHPREV	Previous noun phrases	Number of noun phrases previous to the verb
8 NHTOT	Total noun phrases	Number of noun phrases in the clause
9 INF	Infinitive	Number of infinitives in the clause
10 SE	Spanish particle *se*	True, False
11 A	Spanish preposition *a*	True, False
12 POS_{pre}	Four parts of the speech previous to the verb	292 different values combining the parser's POS tags
14 POS_{pos}	Four parts of the speech following the verb	280 different values combining the parser's POS tags
14 $VERB_{type}$	Type of verb: copulative, impersonal pronominal, transitive and intransitive	CIPX, XIXX, XXXT, XXPX, XXXI, CIXX, XXPT, XIPX, XIPT, XXXX, XIXI, CXPI, XXPI, XIPI, CXPX

Table 4: Features, definitions and values.

tense, and mood with the preceding verb in the sentence and also with the main verb of the sentence.[3]

7-9 NHPREV, NHTOT, INF: the candidates for the subject of the clause are represented by the number of noun phrases in the clause that precede the verb, the total number of noun phrases in the clause, and the number of infinitive verbs in the clause.

10 SE: a binary feature encoding the presence or absence of the Spanish particle *se* when it occurs immediately before or after the verb or with a maximum of one token lying between the verb and itself. Particle *se* occurs in passive reflex clauses with zero subjects and in some impersonal constructions.

11 A: a binary feature encoding the presence or absence of the Spanish preposition *a* in the clause. Since the distinction between passive reflex clauses with zero subjects and impersonal constructions sometimes relies on the appearance of preposition *a* (to, for, etc.). For instance, example (e) is a passive reflex clause containing a zero subject while example (s) is an impersonal construction.

(e) Se admiten los alumnos que reúnan los requisitos.
Ø (They) accept the students who fulfill the requirements.

(f) Se admite a los alumnos que reúnan los requisitos.
(It) is accepted for the students who fulfill the requirements.

12-3 POS_{pre}, POS_{pos}: the part of the speech (POS) of eight tokens, that is, the 4-grams preceding and the 4-grams following the instance.

14 $VERB_{type}$: the verb is classified as copulative, pronominal, transitive, or with an impersonal use.[4] Verbs belonging to more than one class are also accommodated with different feature values for each of the possible combinations of verb type.

5.2 Evaluation

To determine the most accurate algorithm for our classification task, two comparisons of learning algorithms implemented in WEKA (Witten and Frank, 2005) were carried out. Firstly, the classification was performed using 20% of the training instances. Secondly, the seven highest performing classifiers were compared using 100% of the

[3] In Spanish, when a finite verb appears in a subordinate clause, its tense and mood can assist in recognition of these features in the verb of the main clause and help to enforce some restrictions required by this verb, especially when both verbs share the same referent as subject.

[4] We used four lists provided by Molino de Ideas s.a. containing 11,060 different verb lemmas belonging to the Royal Spanish Academy Dictionary (Real Academia Española, 2001).

Class	P	R	F	Acc.
Explicit subj.	90.1%	92.3%	91.2%	87.3%
Zero subj.	77.2%	74.0%	75.5%	87.4%
Impersonals	85.6%	63.1%	72.7%	98.8%

Table 5: K* performance (87.6% accuracy for ten-fold cross validation).

training data and ten-fold cross-validation. The corpus was partitioned into training and tested using ten-fold cross-validation for randomly ordered instances in both cases. The lazy learning classifier K* (Cleary and Trigg, 1995), using a blending parameter of 40%, was the best performing one, with an accuracy of 87.6% for ten-fold cross-validation. K* differs from other instance-based learners in that it computes the distance between two instances using a method motivated by information theory, where a maximum entropy-based distance function is used (Cleary and Trigg, 1995). Table 5 shows the results for each class using ten-fold cross-validation. In contrast to previous work, the K* algorithm (Cleary and Trigg, 1995) was found to provide the most accurate classification in the current study. Other approaches have employed various classification algorithms, including JRip in WEKA (Müller, 2006), with precision of 74% and recall of 60%, and K-nearest neighbors in TiMBL: both in (Evans, 2001) with precision of 73% and recall of 69%, and in (Boyd et al., 2005) with precision of 82% and recall of 71%.

Since there is no previous ML approach for this task in Spanish, our baselines for the explicit subjects and the zero subjects are the parser output and the previous rule-based work with the highest performance (Ferrández and Peral, 2000). For the impersonal constructions the baseline is a simple greedy algorithm that classifies as an impersonal construction every verb whose lemma is categorized as a verb with impersonal use according to the RAE dictionary (Real Academia Española, 2001).

Our method outperforms the Connexor parser which identifies the explicit subjects but makes no distinction between zero subjects and impersonal constructions. Connexor yields 74.9% overall accuracy and 80.2% and 65.6% F-measure for explicit and elliptic subjects, respectively.

To compare with Ferrández and Peral (Ferrández and Peral, 2000) we do consider it without impersonal constructions. We achieve a precision of 87% for explicit subjects compared to 80%, and a precision of 87% for zero subjects compared to their 98%. The overall accuracy is the same for both techniques, 87.5%, but our results are more balanced. Nevertheless, the approaches and corpora used in both studies are different, and hence it is not possible to do a fair comparison. For example, their corpus has 46% of zero subjects while ours has only 26%.

Algorithm	Explicit subjects	Zero subjects	Impersonals
RAE	–	–	70.4%
Connexor	71.7%	83.0%	
Ferr./Peral	79.7%	**98.4%**	–
Elliphant	**87.3%**	87.4%	**98.8%**

Table 6: Summary of accuracy comparison with previous work.

For impersonal constructions our method outperforms the RAE baseline (precision 6.5%, recall 77.7%, F-measure 12.0% and accuracy 70.4%). Table 6 summarizes the comparison. The low performance of the RAE baseline is due to the fact that verbs with impersonal use are often ambiguous. For these cases, we first tagged them as ambiguous and then, we defined additional criteria after analyzing then manually. The resulting annotated criteria are stated in Table 1.

6 Analysis

Through these analyses we aim to extract the most effective features and the information that would complement the output of an standard parser to achieve this task. We also examine the learning process of the algorithm to find out how many instances are needed to train it efficiently and determine how much Elliphant is genre dependent. The analyses indicate that our approach is robust: it performs nearly as well with just six features, has a steep learning curve, and seems to generalize well to other text collections.

6.1 Best Features

We carried out three different experiments to evaluate the most effective group of features, and the features themselves considering the individual predictive ability of each one along with their degree of redundancy.

Based on the following three feature selection

methods we can state that there is a complex and balanced interaction between the features.

6.1.1 Grouping Features

In the first experiment we considered the 11 groups of relevant ordered features from the training data, which were selected using each WEKA attribute selection algorithm and performed the classifications over the complete training data, using only the different groups features selected.

The most effective group of six features (NHPREV, PARSER, NHTOT, POS_{pos}, PERSON, LEMMA) was the one selected by WEKA's SymmetricalUncertAttribute technique, which gives an accuracy of 83.5%. The most frequently selected features by all methods are PARSER, POS_{pos}, and NHTOT, and they alone get an accuracy of 83.6% together. As expected, the two pairs of features that perform best (both 74.8% accuracy) are PARSER with either POS_{pos} or NHTOT. Based on how frequent each feature is selected by WEKA's attribute selection algorithms, we can rank the features as following: (1) PARSER, (2) NHTOT, (3) POS_{pos}, (4) NHPREV and (5) LEMMA.

6.1.2 "Complex" vs. "Simple" Features

Second, a set of experiments was conducted in which features were selected on the basis of the degree of computational effort needed to generate them. We propose two sets of features. One group corresponds to "simple" features, whose values can be obtained by trivial exploitation of the tags produced in the parser's output (PARSER, LEMMA, PERSON, POS_{pos}, POS_{pre}). The second group of features, "complex" features (CLAUSE, AGREE, NHPREV, NHTOT, VERB_{type}) have values that required the implementation of more sophisticated modules to identify the boundaries of syntactic constituents such as clauses and noun phrases. The accuracy obtained when the classifier exclusively exploits "complex" features is 82.6% while for "simple" features is 79.9%. No impersonal constructions are identified when only "complex" features are used.

6.1.3 One-left-out Feature

In the third experiment, to estimate the weight of each feature, classifications were made in which each feature was omitted from the training instances that were presented to the classifier. Omission of all but one of the "simple" features led to a reduction in accuracy, justifying their inclusion in the training instances. Nevertheless, the majority of features present low informativeness except for feature A which does not make any meaningful contribution to the classification. The feature PARSER presents the greatest difference in performance (86.3% total accuracy); however, this is no big loss, considering it is the main feature. Hence, as most features do not bring a significant loss in accuracy, the features need to be combined to improve the performance.

6.2 Learning Analysis

The learning curve of Figure 1 (left) presents the increase of the performance obtained by Elliphant using the training data randomly ordered. The performance reaches its plateau using 90% of the training instances. Using different ordering of the training set we obtain the same result.

Figure 1 (right) presents the precision for each class and overall in relation to the number of training instances for each one of them. Recall grows similarly to precision. Under all conditions, subjects are classified with a high precision since the information given by the parser (collected in the features) achieves an accuracy of 74.9% for the identification of explicit subjects.

The impersonal construction class has the fastest learning curve. When utilizing a training set of only 163 instances (90% of the training data), it reaches a precision of 63.2%. The unstable behaviour for impersonal constructions can be attributed to not having enough training data for that class, since impersonals are not frequent in Spanish. On the other hand, the zero subject class is learned more gradually.

The learning curve for the explicit subject class is almost flat due to the great variety of subjects occurring in the training data. In addition, reaching a precision of 92.0% for explicit subjects using just 20% of the training data is far more expensive in terms of the number of training instances (978) as seen in Figure 1 (right). Actually, with just 20% of the training data we can already achieve a precision of 85.9%.

This demonstrates that Elliphant does not need very large sets of expensive training data and is able to reach adequate levels of performance when exploiting far fewer training instances. In fact, we see that we only need a modest set of

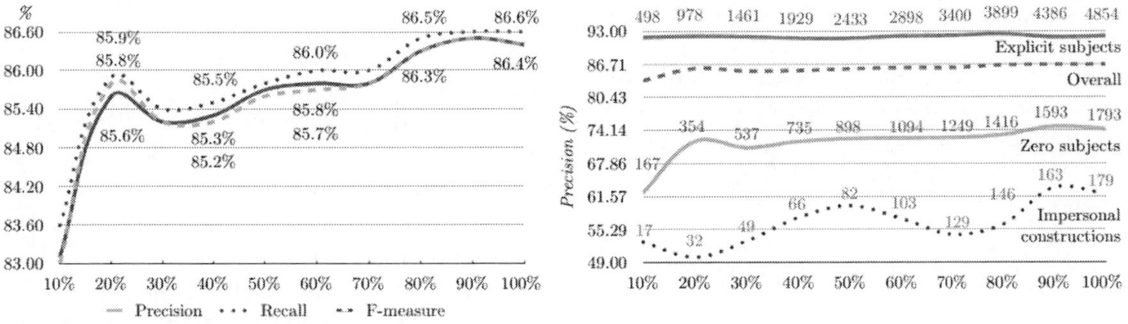

Figure 1: Learning curve for precision, recall and F-measure (left) and with respect to the number of instances of each class (right) for a given percentage of training data.

annotated instances (fewer than 1,500) to achieve good results.

6.3 Impact of Genre

To examine the influence of the different text genres on this method, we divided our training data into two subgroups belonging to different genres (legal and health) and analyze the differences.

A comparative evaluation using ten-fold cross-validation over the two subgroups shows that Elliphant is more successful when classifying instances of explicit subjects in legal texts (89.8% accuracy) than health texts (85.4% accuracy). This may be explained by the greater uniformity of the sentences in the legal genre compared to ones from the health genre, as well as the fact that there are a larger number of explicit subjects in the legal training data (2,739 compared with 2,116 in the health texts). Further, texts from the health genre present the additional complication of specialized named entities and acronyms, which are used quite frequently. Similarly, better performance in the detection of zero subjects and impersonal sentences in the health texts may be due to their more frequent occurrence and hence greater learnability.

Training/Testing	Legal	Health	All
Legal	90.0%	86.8%	89.3%
Health	86.8%	85.9%	88.7%
All	92.5%	93.7%	87.6%

Table 7: Accuracy of cross-genre training and testing evaluation (ten-fold evaluation).

We have also studied the effect of training the classifier on data derived from one genre and testing on instances derived from a different genre. Table 7 shows that instances from legal texts are more homogeneous, as the classifier obtains higher accuracy when testing and training only on legal instances (90.0%). In addition, legal texts are also more informative, because when both legal and health genres are combined as training data, only instances from the health genre show a significant increased accuracy (93.7%). These results reveal that the health texts are the most heterogeneous ones. In fact, we also found subsets of the legal documents where our method achieves an accuracy of 94.6%, implying more homogeneous texts.

6.4 Error Analysis

Since the features of the system are linguistically motivated, we performed a linguistic analysis of the erroneously classified instances to find out which patterns are more difficult to classify and which type of information would improve the method (Rello et al., 2011).

We extract the erroneously classified instances of our training data and classify the errors. According to the distribution of the errors per class (Table 8) we take into account the following four classes of errors for the analysis: (a) impersonal constructions classified as zero subjects, (b) impersonal constructions classified as explicit subjects, (c) zero subjects classified as explicit subjects, and (d) explicit subjects classified as zero subjects. The diagonal numbers are the true predicted cases. The classification of impersonal constructions is less balanced than the ones for explicit subjects and zero subjects. Most of the wrongly identified instances are classified as explicit subject, given that this class is the largest one. On the other hand, 25% of the zero subjects are classified as explicit subject, while only 8% of the explicit subjects are identified as zero subjects.

Class	Zero subjects	Explicit subjects	Impers.
Zero subj.	1327	453 **(c)**	13
Explicit subj.	368 **(d)**	4481	6
Impersonals	25 **(a)**	41 **(b)**	113

Table 8: Confusion Matrix (ten-fold validation).

For the analysis we first performed an exploration of the feature values which allows us to generate smaller samples of the groups of errors for the further linguistic analyses. Then, we explore the linguistic characteristics of the instances by examining the clause in which the instance appears in our corpus. A great variety of different patterns are found. We mention only the linguistic characteristics in the errors which at least double the corpus general trends.

In all groups (a-d) there is a tendency of using the following elements: post-verbal prepositions, auxiliary verbs, future verbal tenses, subjunctive verbal mode, negation, punctuation marks appearing before the verb and the preceding noun phrases, concessive and adverbial subordinate clauses. In groups (a) and (b) the lemma of the verb may play a relevant role, for instance verb *haber ('there is/are')* appears in the errors seven times more than in the training while verb *tratar ('to be about', 'to deal with')* appears 12 times more. Finally, in groups (c) and (d) we notice the frequent occurrence of idioms which include verbs with impersonal uses, such as *es decir ('that is to say')* and words which can be subject on their own *i.e. ambos ('both')* or *todo ('all')*.

7 Conclusions and Future Work

In this study we learn which is the most accurate approach for identifying explicit subjects and impersonal constructions in Spanish and which are the linguistic characteristics and features that help to perform this task. The corpus created is freely available online.[5] Our method complements previous work on Spanish anaphora resolution by addressing the identification of non-referential constructions. It outperforms current approaches in explicit subject detection and impersonal constructions, doing better than the parser for every class.

A possible future avenue to explore could be to combine our approach with Ferrández and Peral (Ferrández and Peral, 2000) by employing both algorithms in sequence: first Ferrández and Peral's algorithm to detect all zero subjects and then ours to identify explicit subjects and impersonals. Assuming that the same accuracy could be maintained, on our data set the combined performance could potentially be in the range of 95%.

Future research goals are the extrinsic evaluation of our system by integrating our system in NLP tasks and its adaptation to other Romance pro-drop languages. Finally, we believe that our ML approach could be improved as it is the first attempt of this kind.

Acknowledgements

We thank Richard Evans, Julio Gonzalo and the anonymous reviewers for their wise comments.

References

R. Artstein and M. Poesio. 2008. Inter-coder agreement for computational linguistics. *Computational Linguistics*, 34(4):555–596.

S. Bergsma, D. Lin, and R. Goebel. 2008. Distributional identification of non-referential pronouns. In *Proceedings of the 46th Annual Meeting of the Association for Computational Linguistics: Human Language Technologies (ACL/HLT-08)*, pages 10–18.

I. Bosque. 1989. Clases de sujetos tácitos. In Julio Borrego Nieto, editor, *Philologica: homenaje a Antonio Llorente*, volume 2, pages 91–112. Servicio de Publicaciones, Universidad Pontificia de Salamanca, Salamanca.

A. Boyd, W. Gegg-Harrison, and D. Byron. 2005. Identifying non-referential *it*: a machine learning approach incorporating linguistically motivated patterns. In *Proceedings of the ACL Workshop on Feature Engineering for Machine Learning in Natural Language Processing. 43rd Annual Meeting of the Association for Computational Linguistics (ACL-05)*, pages 40–47.

J. M. Brucart. 1999. La elipsis. In I. Bosque and V. Demonte, editors, *Gramática descriptiva de la lengua española*, volume 2, pages 2787–2863. Espasa-Calpe, Madrid.

N. Chomsky. 1981. *Lectures on Government and Binding*. Mouton de Gruyter, Berlin, New York.

J.G. Cleary and L.E. Trigg. 1995. K*: an instance-based learner using an entropic distance measure. In *Proceedings of the 12th International Conference on Machine Learning (ICML-95)*, pages 108–114.

[5]ESZIC_es Corpus is available at: `http://luzrello.com/Projects.html`.

Connexor Oy, 2006. *Machinese language model.*

L. Danlos. 2005. Automatic recognition of French expletive pronoun occurrences. In Robert Dale, Kam-Fai Wong, Jiang Su, and Oi Yee Kwong, editors, *Natural language processing. Proceedings of the 2nd International Joint Conference on Natural Language Processing (IJCNLP-05)*, pages 73–78, Berlin, Heidelberg, New York. Springer. Lecture Notes in Computer Science, Vol. 3651.

R. Evans. 2001. Applying machine learning: toward an automatic classification of *it*. *Literary and Linguistic Computing*, 16(1):45–57.

A. Ferrández and J. Peral. 2000. A computational approach to zero-pronouns in Spanish. In *Proceedings of the 38th Annual Meeting of the Association for Computational Linguistics (ACL-2000)*, pages 166–172.

J. L. Fleiss. 1971. Measuring nominal scale agreement among many raters. *Psychological Bulletin*, 76(5):378–382.

G. Hirst. 1981. *Anaphora in natural language understanding: a survey.* Springer-Verlag.

J. Hobbs. 1977. Resolving pronoun references. *Lingua*, 44:311–338.

R. Mitkov and C. Hallett. 2007. Comparing pronoun resolution algorithms. *Computational Intelligence*, 23(2):262–297.

R. Mitkov. 2002. *Anaphora resolution.* Longman, London.

R. Mitkov. 2010. Discourse processing. In Alexander Clark, Chris Fox, and Shalom Lappin, editors, *The handbook of computational linguistics and natural language processing*, pages 599–629. Wiley Blackwell, Oxford.

C. Müller. 2006. Automatic detection of nonreferential *it* in spoken multi-party dialog. In *Proceedings of the 11th Conference of the European Chapter of the Association for Computational Linguistics (EACL-06)*, pages 49–56.

V. Ng and C. Cardie. 2002. Identifying anaphoric and non-anaphoric noun phrases to improve coreference resolution. In *Proceedings of the 19th International Conference on Computational Linguistics (COLING-02)*, pages 1–7.

Real Academia Española. 2001. *Diccionario de la lengua española.* Espasa-Calpe, Madrid, 22 edition.

Real Academia Española. 2009. *Nueva gramática de la lengua española.* Espasa-Calpe, Madrid.

M. Recasens and E. Hovy. 2009. A deeper look into features for coreference resolution. In Lalitha Devi Sobha, António Branco, and Ruslan Mitkov, editors, *Anaphora Processing and Applications. Proceedings of the 7th Discourse Anaphora and Anaphor Resolution Colloquium (DAARC-09)*, pages 29–42. Springer, Berlin, Heidelberg, New York. Lecture Notes in Computer Science, Vol. 5847.

M. Recasens and M.A. Martí. 2010. Ancora-co: Coreferentially annotated corpora for Spanish and Catalan. *Language resources and evaluation*, 44(4):315–345.

L. Rello and I. Illisei. 2009a. A comparative study of Spanish zero pronoun distribution. In *Proceedings of the International Symposium on Data and Sense Mining, Machine Translation and Controlled Languages, and their application to emergencies and safety critical domains (ISMTCL-09)*, pages 209–214. Presses Universitaires de Franche-Comté, Besançon.

L. Rello and I. Illisei. 2009b. A rule-based approach to the identification of Spanish zero pronouns. In *Student Research Workshop. International Conference on Recent Advances in Natural Language Processing (RANLP-09)*, pages 209–214.

L. Rello, P. Suárez, and R. Mitkov. 2010. A machine learning method for identifying non-referential impersonal sentences and zero pronouns in Spanish. *Procesamiento del Lenguaje Natural*, 45:281–287.

L. Rello, G. Ferraro, and A. Burga. 2011. Error analysis for the improvement of subject ellipsis detection. *Procesamiento de Lenguaje Natural*, 47:223–230.

L. Rello. 2010. Elliphant: A machine learning method for identifying subject ellipsis and impersonal constructions in Spanish. Master's thesis, Erasmus Mundus, University of Wolverhampton & Universitat Autònoma de Barcelona.

P. Tapanainen and T. Järvinen. 1997. A non-projective dependency parser. In *Proceedings of the 5th Conference on Applied Natural Language Processing (ANLP-97)*, pages 64–71.

I. H. Witten and E. Frank. 2005. *Data mining: practical machine learning tools and techniques.* Morgan Kaufmann, London, 2 edition.

S. Zhao and H.T. Ng. 2007. Identification and resolution of Chinese zero pronouns: a machine learning approach. In *Proceedings of the 2007 Joint Conference on Empirical Methods in Natural Language Processing and Computational Natural Language Learning (EMNLP/CNLL-07)*, pages 541–550.

Validation of sub-sentential paraphrases acquired from parallel monolingual corpora

Houda Bouamor **Aurélien Max** **Anne Vilnat**

LIMSI-CNRS & Univ. Paris Sud
Orsay, France
firstname.lastname@limsi.fr

Abstract

The task of paraphrase acquisition from related sentences can be tackled by a variety of techniques making use of various types of knowledge. In this work, we make the hypothesis that their performance can be increased if candidate paraphrases can be validated using information that characterizes paraphrases independently of the set of techniques that proposed them. We implement this as a bi-class classification problem (i.e. *paraphrase* vs. *not paraphrase*), allowing any paraphrase acquisition technique to be easily integrated into the combination system. We report experiments on two languages, English and French, with 5 individual techniques on parallel monolingual parallel corpora obtained *via* multiple translation, and a large set of classification features including surface to contextual similarity measures. Relative improvements in F-measure close to 18% are obtained on both languages over the best performing techniques.

1 Introduction

The fact that natural language allows messages to be conveyed in a great variety of ways constitutes an important difficulty for NLP, with applications in both text analysis and generation. The term *paraphrase* is now commonly used in the NLP litterature to refer to textual units of equivalent meaning at the phrasal level (including single words). For instance, the phrases *six months* and *half a year* form a paraphrase pair applicable in many different contexts, as they would appropriately denote the same concept. Although one can envisage to manually build high-coverage lists of synonyms, enumerating meaning equivalences at the level of phrases is too daunting a task for humans. Because this type of knowledge can however greatly benefit many NLP applications, automatic acquisition of such paraphrases has attracted a lot of attention (Androutsopoulos and Malakasiotis, 2010; Madnani and Dorr, 2010), and significant research efforts have been devoted to this objective (Callison-Burch, 2007; Bhagat, 2009; Madnani, 2010).

Central to acquiring paraphrases is the need of assessing the quality of the candidate paraphrases produced by a given technique. Most works to date have resorted to human evaluation of paraphrases on the levels of *grammaticality* and *meaning equivalence*. Human evaluation is however often criticized as being both costly and non reproducible, and the situation is even more complicated by the inherent complexity of the task that can produce low inter-judge agreement. Task-based evaluation involving the use of paraphrasing into some application thus seem an acceptable solution, provided the evaluation methodologies for the given task are deemed acceptable. This, in turn, puts the emphasis on observing the impact of paraphrasing on the targeted application and is rarely accompanied by a study of the intrinsic limitations of the paraphrase acquisition technique used.

The present work is concerned with the task of sub-sentential paraphrase acquisition from pairs of related sentences. A large variety of techniques have been proposed that can be applied to this task. They typically make use of different kinds of automatically or manually acquired knowledge. We make the hypothesis that their performance can be increased if candidate paraphrases can be validated using information that characterize paraphrases in complement to the set of techniques that proposed them. We propose to implement this as a bi-class classification problem (i.e. *paraphrase* vs. *not paraphrase*), allowing any paraphrase acquisition technique to be easily integrated into the combination system. In this article, we report experiments on two languages, English and French, with 5 individual techniques based on *a*) statistical word alignment models, *b*) translational equivalence, *c*) handcoded rules of term variation, *d*) syntactic similarity, and *e*) edit distance on word sequences. We used parallel monolingual parallel corpora obtained *via* multiple translation from a single language as our sources of related sentences, and a large set of features including surface to contextual similarity measures. Relative improvements in F-measure close to 18% are obtained on both languages over the best performing techniques.

The remainder of this article is organized as follows. We first briefly review previous work on sub-sentential paraphrase acquisition in section 2. We then describe our experimental setting in section 3 and the individual techniques that we have studied in section 4. Section 5 is devoted to our approach for validating paraphrases proposed by individual techniques. Finally, section 6 concludes the article and presents some of our future work in the area of paraphrase acquisition.

2 Related work

The hypothesis that if two words or, by extension, two phrases, occur in similar contexts then they may be interchangeable has been extensively tested. The *distributional hypothesis*, attributed to Zellig Harris, was for example applied to syntactic dependency paths in the work of Lin and Pantel (2001). Their results take the form of equivalence patterns with two arguments such as {*X asks for Y, X requests Y, X's request for Y, X wants Y, Y is requested by X*, ...}.

Using comparable corpora, where the same information probably exists under various linguistic forms, increases the likelihood of finding very close contexts for sub-sentential units. Barzilay and Lee (2003) proposed a multi-sequence alignment algorithm that takes structurally similar sentences and builds a compact lattice representation that encodes local variations. The work by Bhagat and Ravichandran (2008) describes an application of a similar technique on a very large scale.

The hypothesis that two words or phrases are interchangeable if they share a common translation into one or more other languages has also been extensively studied in works on sub-sentential paraphrase acquisition. Bannard and Callison-Burch (2005) described a pivoting approach that can exploit bilingual parallel corpora in several languages. The same technique has been applied to the acquisition of local paraphrasing patterns in Zhao et al. (2008). The work of Callison-Burch (2008) has shown how the monolingual context of a sentence to paraphrase can be used to improve the quality of the acquired paraphrases.

Another approach consists in modelling local paraphrasing identification rules. The work of Jacquemin (1999) on the identification of term variants, which exploits rewriting morphosyntactic rules and descriptions of morphological and semantic lexical families, can be extended to extract the various forms corresponding to input patterns from large monolingual corpora.

When parallel monolingual corpora aligned at the sentence level are available (e.g. multiple translations into the same language), the task of sub-sentential paraphrase acquisition can be cast as one of word alignment between two aligned sentences (Cohn et al., 2008). Barzilay and McKeown (2001) applied the distributionality hypothesis on such parallel sentences, and Pang *et al.* (2003) proposed an algorithm to align sentences by recursive fusion of their common syntactic constituants.

Finally, they has been a recent interest in automatic evaluation of paraphrases (Callison-Burch et al., 2008; Liu et al., 2010; Chen and Dolan, 2011; Metzler et al., 2011).

3 Experimental setting

We used the main aspects of the methodology described by Cohn et al. (2008) for constructing evaluation corpora and assessing the performance of techniques on the task of sub-sentential paraphrase acquisition. Pairs of related sentences are hand-aligned to define a set of reference *atomic* paraphrase pairs at the level of words or phrases, denoted as $\mathcal{R}_{\text{atom}}$[1].

[1]Note that in this study we do not distinguish between "Sure" and "Possible" alignments, and when reusing anno-

	single language translation	multiple language translation	video descriptions	multiply-translated subtitles	news headlines
# tokens	4,476	4,630	1,452	2,721	1,908
# unique tokens	656	795	357	830	716
% aligned tokens (excluding identities)	60.58	48.80	23.82	29.76	14.46
lexical overlap (tokens)	77.21	61.03	59.50	32.51	39.63
lexical overlap (lemmas content words)	83.77	71.04	64.83	39.54	45.31
translation edit rate (TER)	0.32	0.55	0.76	0.68	0.62
penalized n-gram prec. (BLEU)	0.33	0.15	0.13	0.14	0.39

Table 1: Various indicators of sentence pair comparability for different corpus types. Statistics are reported for French on sets of 100 sentence pairs.

We conducted a small-scale study to assess different types of corpora of related sentences:

1. **single language translation** Corpora obtained by several independent human translation of the same sentences (e.g. (Barzilay and McKeown, 2001)).

2. **multiple language translation** Same as above, but where a sentence is translated from 4 different languages into the same language (Bouamor et al., 2010).

3. **video descriptions** Descriptions of short YouTube videos obtained *via* Mechanical Turk (Chen and Dolan, 2011).

4. **multiply-translated subtitles** Aligned multiple translations of contributed movie subtitles (Tiedemann, 2007).

5. **comparable news headlines** News headlines collected from Google News clusters (e.g. (Dolan et al., 2004)).

We collected 100 sentence pairs of each type in French, for which various comparability measures are reported on Table 1. In particular, the "**% aligned tokens**" row indicates the proportion of tokens from the sentence pairs that could be manually aligned by a native-speaker annotator.[2] Obviously, the more common tokens two sentences from a pair contain, the fewer sub-sentential paraphrases may be extracted from that pair. However, high lexical overlap increases the probability that two sentences be indeed paraphrases, and in turn the probability that some of their phrases be paraphrases. Furthermore, the presence of common token may serve as useful clues to guide paraphrase extraction.

For our experiments, we chose to use parallel monolingual corpora obtained by single language translation, the most direct resource type for acquiring sub-sentential paraphrase pairs. This allows us to define acceptable references for the task and resort to the most consensual evaluation technique for paraphrase acquisition to date. Using such corpora, we expect to be able to extract *precise* paraphrases (see Table 1), which will be natural candidates for further validation, which will be addressed in section 5.3.

Figure 1 illustrates a reference alignment obtained on a pair of English sentential paraphrases and the list of atomic paraphrase pairs that can be extracted from it, against which acquisition techniques will be evaluated. Note that we do not consider pairs of identical units during evaluation, so we filter them out from the list of reference paraphrase pairs.

The example in Figure 1 shows different cases that point to the inherent complexity of this task, even for human annotators: it could be argued, for instance, that a correct atomic paraphrase pair should be *reached* ↔ *amounted to* rather than *reached* ↔ *amounted*. Also, aligning independently *260* ↔ *0.26* and *million* ↔ *billion* is assuredly an error, while the pair *260 million* ↔ *0.26 billion* would have been appropriate. A case of alignment that seems non trivial can be observed in the provided example (*during the entire year* ↔ *annual*). The abovementioned reasons will explain in part the difficulties in reaching high performance values using such gold standards.

Reference *composite* paraphrase pairs (denoted as $\mathcal{R}$), obtained by joining adjacent atomic paraphrase pairs from $\mathcal{R}_{\text{atom}}$ up to 6 tokens[3], will

tated corpora using them we considered all alignments as being correct.

[2] The same annotator hand-aligned the 5*100=500 paraphrase pairs using the YAWAT (Germann, 2008) manual alignment tool.

[3] We used standard biphrase extraction heuristics (Koehn

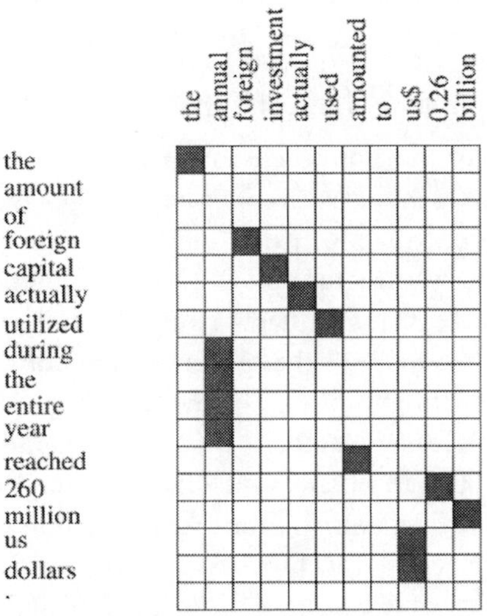

capital ↔ investment
utilized ↔ used
during the entire year ↔ annual
reached ↔ amounted
260 ↔ 0.26
million ↔ billion
us dollars ↔ us$

Figure 1: Reference alignments for a pair of English sentential paraphrases from the annotation corpus of Cohn et al. (2008) (note that possible and sure alignments are not distinguished here) and the list of atomic paraphrase pairs extracted from these alignments.

also be considered when measuring performance. Evaluated techniques have to output atomic candidate paraphrase pairs (denoted as $\mathcal{H}_{\text{atom}}$) from which composite paraphrase pairs (denoted as $\mathcal{H}$) are computed. The usual measures of *precision* (P), *recall* (R) and *F-measure* (F_1) can then be defined in the following way (Cohn et al., 2008):

$$P = \frac{|\mathcal{H}_{\text{atom}} \cap \mathcal{R}|}{|\mathcal{H}_{\text{atom}}|} \quad R = \frac{|\mathcal{H} \cap \mathcal{R}_{\text{atom}}|}{|\mathcal{R}_{\text{atom}}|} \quad F_1 = \frac{2pr}{p+r}$$

We conducted experiments using two different corpora in English and French. In each case, a held-out development corpus of 150 sentential paraphrase pairs was used for development and tuning, and all techniques were evaluated on the same test set consisting of 375 sentential paraphrase pairs. For English, we used the MTC corpus described in (Cohn et al., 2008), consisting of multiply-translated Chinese sentences into English, and used as our gold standard both the alignments marked as "Sure" and "Possible". For French, we used the CESTA corpus of news articles[4] obtained by translating into French from English.

We used the YAWAT (Germann, 2008) manual alignment tool. Inter-annotator agreement values (averaging with each annotation set as the gold standard) are 66.1 for English and 64.6 for French, which we interpret as acceptable values. Manual inspection of the two corpora reveals that the French corpus tends to contain more literal translations, possibly due to the original languages of the sentences, which are closer to the target language than Chinese is to English.

4 Individual techniques for paraphrase acquisition

As discussed in section 2, the acquisition of sub-sentential paraphrases is a challenging task that has previously attracted a lot of work. In this work, we consider the scenario where sentential paraphrases are available and words and phrases from one sentence can be aligned to words and phrases from the other sentence to form atomic paraphrase pairs. We now describe several techniques that perform the task of sub-sentential unit alignment. We have selected and implemented five techniques which we believe are representative of the type of knowledge that these techniques use, and have reused existing tools, initially developed for other tasks, when possible.

4.1 Statistical learning of word alignments (Giza)

The GIZA++ tool (Och and Ney, 2004) computes statistical word alignment models of increasing complexity from parallel corpora. While originally developed in the bilingual context of Statistical Machine Translation, nothing prevents building such models on monolingual corpora. However, in order to build reliable models, it is necessary to use enough training material including minimal redundancy of words. To this end, we provided GIZA++ with all possible sentence pairs from our mutiply-translated corpus to improve the quality of its word alignments (note that

et al., 2007) : all words from a phrase must be aligned to at least one word from the other and not to words outside, but unaligned words at phrase boundaries are not used.

[4] http://www.elda.org/article125.html

we used symmetrized alignments from the alignments in both directions). This constitutes a significant advantage for this technique that techniques working on each sentence pair independently do not have.

4.2 Translational equivalence (Pivot)

Translational equivalence can be exploited to determine that two phrases may be paraphrases. Bannard and Callison-Burch (2005) defined a paraphrasing probability between two phrases based on their translation probability through all possible *pivot* phrases as:

$$P_{para}(p_1, p_2) = \sum_{piv} P_t(piv|p_1) P_t(p_2|piv)$$

where P_t denotes translation probabilies. We used the Europarl corpus[5] of parliamentary debates in English and French, consisting of approximately 1.7 million parallel sentences : this allowed us to use the same resource to build paraphrases for English, using French as the pivot language, and for French, using English as the pivot language. The GIZA++ tool was used for word alignment and the MOSES Statistical Machine Translation toolkit (Koehn et al., 2007) was used to compute phrase translation probabilities from these word alignments. For each sentential paraphrase pair, we applied the following algorithm: for each phrase, we build the entire set of paraphrases using the previous definition. We then extract its best paraphrase as the one exactly appearing in the other sentence with maximum paraphrase probability, using a minimal threshold value of 10^{-4}.

4.3 Linguistic knowledge on term variation (Fastr)

The FASTR tool (Jacquemin, 1999) was designed to spot term/phrase variants in large corpora. Variants are described through metarules expressing how the morphosyntactic structure of a term variant can be derived from a given term by means of regular expressions on word morphosyntactic categories. Paradigmatic variation can also be expressed by expressing constraints between words, imposing that they be of the same morphological or semantic family. Both constraints rely on preexisting repertoires available for English and French. To compute candidate paraphrase pairs using FASTR, we first consider all phrases from the first sentence and search for variants in the other sentence, then do the reverse process and finally take the intersection of the two sets.

4.4 Syntactic similarity (Synt)

The algorithm introduced by Pang et al. (2003) takes two sentences as input and merges them by top-down syntactic fusion guided by compatible syntactic substructure. A lexical blocking mechanism prevents constituents from fusionning when there is evidence of the presence of a word in another constituent of one of the sentence. We use the Berkeley Probabilistic parser (Klein and Manning, 2003) to obtain syntactic trees for English and its adapted version for French (Candito et al., 2010). Because this process is highly sensitive to syntactic parse errors, we use in our implementation k-best parses and retain the most compact fusion from any pair of candidate parses.

4.5 Edit rate on word sequences (TER$_p$)

TER$_p$ (Translation Edit Rate Plus) (Snover et al., 2010) is a score designed for the evaluation of Machine Translation output. Its typical use takes a system hypothesis to compute an optimal set of word edits that can transform it into some existing reference translation. Edit types include exact word matching, word insertion and deletion, block movement of contiguous words (computed as an approximation), as well as optionally variants substitution through stemming, synonym or paraphrase matching.[6] Each edit type is parameterized by at least one weight which can be optimized using e.g. hill climbing. TER$_p$ being a tunable metric, our experiments will include tuning TER$_p$ systems towards either precision ($\rightarrow P$), recall ($\rightarrow R$), or F-measure ($\rightarrow F_1$).[7]

4.6 Evaluation of individual techniques

Results for the 5 individual techniques are given on the left part of Table 2. It is first apparent that all techniques but TER$_p$ fared better on the French corpus than on the English corpus. This can certainly be explained by the fact that the former results from more literal translations (from

[5]http://statmt.org/europarl

[6]Note that for these experiments we did not use the stemming module, the interface to WordNet for synonym matching and the provided paraphrase table for English, due to the fact that these resources were available for English only.

[7]*Hill climbing* was used for all tunings as done by Snover et al. (2010), and we used one iteration starting with uniform weights and 100 random restarts.

	Individual techniques							Combinations	
	GIZA	PIVOT	FASTR	SYNT	TER_p $\rightarrow P$	TER_p $\rightarrow R$	TER_p $\rightarrow F_1$	union	validation
	English								
P	31.01	31.78	37.38	**52.17**	50.00	29.15	33.37	21.44	50.51
R	38.30	18.50	6.71	2.53	5.83	45.19	**45.37**	**60.87**	41.19
F_1	34.27	23.39	11.38	4.83	10.44	35.44	**38.46**	31.71	**45.37**
	French								
P	28.99	29.53	52.48	**62.50**	31.35	30.26	31.43	17.58	40.77
R	**45.98**	26.66	8.59	8.65	44.22	44.60	44.10	**63.36**	45.85
F_1	35.56	28.02	14.77	15.20	**36.69**	36.05	**36.70**	27.53	**43.16**

Table 2: Results on the test set on English and French for the 5 individual paraphrase acquisition techniques (left part) and for the 2 combination techniques (right part).

English to French, compared with from Chinese to English), which should be consequently easier to word-align. This is for example clearly shown by the results of the statistical aligner GIZA, which obtains a 7.68 advantage on recall for French over English.

The two linguistically-aware techniques, FASTR and SYNT, have a very strong precision on the more parallel French corpus, but fail to achieve an acceptable recall on their own. This is not surprising : FASTR metarules are focussed on term variant extraction, and SYNT requires two syntactic trees to be highly comparable to extract sub-sentential paraphrases. When these constrained conditions are met, these two techniques appear to perform quite well in terms of precision.

GIZA and TER_p perform roughly in the same range on French, with acceptable precision and recall, TER_p performing overall better, with e.g. a 1.14 advantage on F-measure on French and 4.19 on English. The fact that TER_p performs comparatively better on English than on French[8], with a 1.76 advantage on F-measure, is not contradictory: the implemented edit distance makes it possible to align reasonably distant words and phrases independently from syntax, and to find alignments for close remaining words, so the differences of performance between the two languages are not necessarily expected to be comparable with the results of a statistical alignment technique. English being a poorly-inflected language, alignment clues between two sentential paraphrases are expected to be more numerous than for highly-inflected French.

PIVOT is on par with GIZA as regards precision, but obtains a comparatively much lower recall (differences of 19.32 and 19.80 on recall on French and English respectively). This may first be due in part to the paraphrasing score threshold used for PIVOT, but most certainly to the use of a bilingual corpus from the domain of parliamentary debates to extract paraphrases when our test sets are from the news domain: we may be observing differences inherent to the domain, and possibly facing the issue of numerous "out-of-vocabulary" phrases, in particular for named entities which frequently occur in the news domain.

Importantly, we can note that we obtain at best a recall of 45.98 on French (GIZA) and of 45.37 on English (TER_p). This may come as a disappointment but, given the broad set of techniques evaluated, this should rather underline the inherent complexity of the task. Also, recall that the metrics used do not consider identity paraphrases (e.g. *at the same time* $\leftrightarrow$ *at the same time*), as well as the fact that gold standard alignment is a very difficult process as shown by interjudge agreement values and our example from section 3. This, again, confirms that the task that is addressed is indeed a difficult one, and provides further justification for initially focussing on *parallel* monolingual corpora, albeit scarce, for conducting fine-grained studies on sub-sentential paraphrasing.

Lastly, we can also note that precision is not very high, with (at best, using $TER_{p \rightarrow P}$) average values for all techniques of 40.97 and 40.46 on French and English, respectively. Several facts may provide explanations for this observation. First, it should be noted that none of those techniques, except SYNT, was originally developed

[8]Recall that all specific linguistic modules for English only from TER_p had been disabled, so the better performance on English cannot be explained by a difference in terms of resources used.

for the task of sub-sentential paraphrase acquisition from monolingual parallel corpora. This results in definitions that are at best closely related to this task.[9] Designing new techniques was not one of the objectives of our study, so we have reused existing techniques, originally developed with different aims (bilingual parallel corpora word alignment (GIZA), term variant recognition (FASTR), Machine Translation evaluation (TER_p)). Also, techniques such as GIZA and TER_p attempt to align as many words as possible in a sentence pair, when gold standard alignments sometimes contain gaps.[10] Finally, the metrics used will count as false small variations of gold standard paraphrases (e.g. missing function word): the acceptability or not of such candidates could be either evaluated in a scenario where such "acceptable" variants would be taken into account, and could be considered in the context of some actual use of the acquired paraphrases in some application. Nonetheless, on average the techniques in our study produce more candidates that are not in the gold standard: this will be an important fact to keep in mind when tackling the task of combining their outputs. In particular, we will investigate the use of features indicating the combination of techniques that predicted a given paraphrase pair, aiming to capture consensus information.

5 Paraphrase validation

5.1 Technique complementarity

Before considering combining and validating the outputs of individual techniques, it is informative to look at some notion of "complementarity" between techniques, in terms of how many correct paraphrases a technique would add to a combined set. The following formula was used to account for the complementarity between the set of candidates from some technique i, t_i, and the set for some technique j, t_j:

$$C(t_i, t_j) = \text{recall}(t_i \cup t_j) - \max(\text{recall}(t_i), \text{recall}(t_j))$$

[9]Recall, however, that our best performing technique on F-measure, TER_p, was optimized to our task using a held out development set.

[10]It is arguable whether such cases should happen in sentence pairs obtained by translating the same original sentence into the same language, but this clearly depends on the interpretation of the expected level of annotation by the annotators.

Results on the test set for the two languages are given in Table 3. A number of pairs of techniques have strong complementarity values, the strongest one being for GIZA and TER_p for both languages. According to these figures, PIVOT identify paraphrases which are slightly more similar to those of TER_p than those of GIZA. Interestingly, FASTR and SYNT exhibit a strong complementarity, where in French, for instance, they only have a very small proportion of paraphrases in common. Considering the set of all other techniques, GIZA provides the more new paraphrases on French and TER_p on English.

	GIZA	PIVOT	FASTR	SYNT	$\text{TER}_{p\rightarrow R}$	*all others*
			English			
GIZA	-	4.65	2.83	0.59	**10.31**	8.31
PIVOT	**4.65**	-	2.30	1.88	3.12	3.72
FASTR	**2.83**	2.30	-	2.42	1.71	0.53
SYNT	0.59	1.88	**2.42**	-	0.59	0.00
$\text{TER}_{p\rightarrow R}$	**10.31**	3.12	1.71	0.59	-	12.20
			French			
GIZA	-	9.79	3.64	2.20	**10.73**	8.91
PIVOT	**9.79**	-	2.26	5.22	7.84	3.39
FASTR	3.64	2.26	-	**7.28**	3.01	0.19
SYNT	2.20	5.22	**7.28**	-	1.76	0.44
$\text{TER}_{p\rightarrow R}$	**10.73**	7.84	3.01	1.76	-	5.65

Table 3: Values of *complementarity* on the test set for both languages, where the following formula was used for the set of technique outputs $T = \{t_1, t_2, ..., t_n\}$: $C(t_i, t_j) = \text{recall}(t_i \cup t_j) - \max(\text{recall}(t_i), \text{recall}(t_j))$. Complementarity values are computed between all pairs of individual techniques, and each individual technique and the set of all other techniques. Values in bold indicate highest values for the technique of each row.

5.2 Naive combination by union

We first implemented a naive combination obtained by taking the union of all techniques. Results are given in the first column of the right part of Table 2. The first result is quite encouraging: in both languages, more than 6 paraphrases from the gold standard out of 10 are found by at least one of the techniques, which, given our previous discussion, constitutes a good result and provide a clear justification for combining different techniques for improving performance on this task. Precision is mechanically lowered to account for roughly 1 correct paraphrase over 5 candidates for both languages. F-measure values are much lower than those of TER_p and GIZA, showing that the union of all techniques is only interesting for recall-oriented paraphrase acquisition. In the next section, we will show how the results of the union can be validated using machine learning to improve these figures.

5.3 Paraphrase validation via automatic classification

A natural improvement to the naive combination of paraphrase candidates from all techniques can consist in validating candidate paraphrases by using several models that may be good indicators of their paraphrasing status. We can therefore cast our problem as one of biclass classification (i.e. "paraphrase" vs. "not paraphrase").

We have used a maximum entropy classifier[11] with the following features, aiming at capturing information on the paraphrase status of a candidate pair:

Morphosyntactic equivalence (POS) It may be the case that some sequences of part-of-speech can be rewritten as different sequences, e.g. as a result of verb nominalization. We therefore use features to indicate the sequences of part-of-speech for a pair of candidate paraphrases. We used the preterminal symbols of the syntactic trees of the parser used for SYNT.

Character-based distance (CAR) Morphological variants often have close word forms, and more generally close word forms in sentential paraphase pairs may indicate related words. We used features for discretized values of the edit distance between the two phrases of a candidate paraphrase pair as measured by the Levenshtein distance.

Stem similarity (STEM) Inflectional morphology, which is quite productive in languages such as French, can increase vocabulary size significantly, while in sentential paraphrases common stems may indicate related words. We used a binary feature indicating whether the stemmed phrases of a candidate paraphrase pair match.[12]

Token set identity (BOW) Syntactic rearrangements may involve the same sets of words in various orders. We used discretized features indicating the proportion of common tokens in the set of tokens for the two phrases of a candidate paraphrase pair.

Context similarity (CTXT) It can be derived from the distributionality hypothesis that the more two phrases will be seen in similar contexts, the more they are likely to be paraphrases. We used discretized features indicating how similar the contexts of occurrences of two paraphrases are. For this, we used the full set of bilingual English-French data available for the translation task of the Workshop on Statistical Machine Translation[13], totalling roughly 30 million parallel sentences: this again ensures that the same resources are used for experiments in the two languages. We collect all occurrences for the phrases in a pair, and build a vector of content words cooccurring within a distance of 10 words from each phrase. We finally compute the cosine between the vectors of the two phrases of a candidate paraphrase pair.

Relative position in a sentence (REL) Depending on the language in which parallel sentences are analyzed, it may be the case that subsentential paraphrases occur at close locations in their respective sentence. We used a discretized feature indicating the relative position of the two phrases in their original sentence.

Identity check (COOC) We used a binary feature indicating whether one of the two phrases from a candidate pair, or the two, occurred at some other location in the other sentence.

Phrase length ratio (LEN) We used a discretized feature indicating phrase length ratio.

Source techniques (SRC) Finally, as our setting validates paraphrase candidates produced by a set of techniques, we used features indicating which combination of techniques predicted a paraphrase candidate. This can allow learning that paraphrases in the intersection of the predicted sets for some techniques may produce good results.

We used a held out training set consisting of 150 sentential paraphrase pairs from the same corpora as our previous developement and test sets for both languages. Positive examples were taken from the candidate paraphrase pairs from any of

[11] We used the implementation available at: http://homepages.inf.ed.ac.uk/lzhang10/maxent_toolkit.html

[12] We use the implementations of the Snowball stemmer from English and French available from: http://snowball.tartarus.org

[13] http://www.statmt.org/wmt11/translation-task.html

the 5 techniques in our study which belong to the gold standard, and we used a corresponding number of negative examples (randomly selected) from candidate pairs not in the gold standard. The right part of Table 2 provides the results for our validation experiments of the union set for all previous techniques.

We obtain our best results for this study using the output of our validation classifier over the set of all candidate paraphrase pairs. On French, it yields an improvement in F-measure (43.16) of +6.46 over the best individual technique (TER_p) and of +15.63 over the naive union from all individual techniques. On English, the improvement in F-measure (45.37) is for the same conditions of respectively +6.91 (over TER_p) and +13.66. We unfortunately observe an important decrease in recall over the naive union, of respectively -17.54 and -19.68 for French and English. Increasing our amount of training data to better represent the full range of paraphrase types may certainly overcome this in part. This would indeed be sensible, as better covering the variety of paraphrase types as a one-time effort would help all subsequent validations. Figure 2 shows how performance varies on French with number of training examples for various feature configurations. However, some paraphrase types will require integration of more complex knowledge, as is the case, for instance, for paraphrase pairs involving some anaphora and its antecedent (e.g. *China* $\leftrightarrow$ *it*).

While these results, which are very comparable for the two languages studied, are already satisfying given the complexity of our task, further inspection of false positives and negatives may help us to develop additional models that will help us obtain a better classification performance.

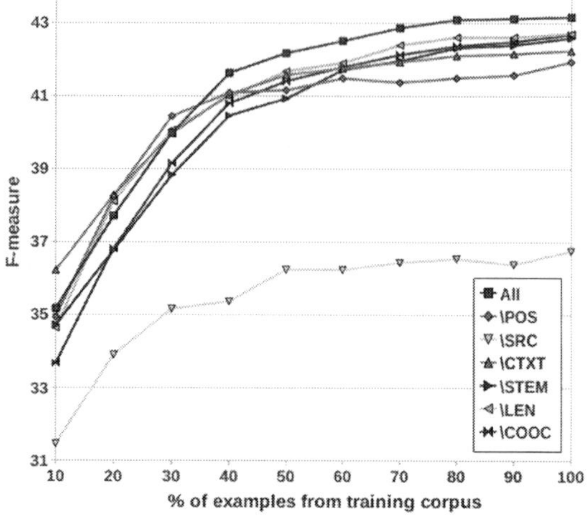

Figure 2: Learning curves obtained on French by removing features individually.

6 Conclusions and future work

In this article, we have addressed the task of combining the results of sub-sentential paraphrase acquition from parallel monolingual corpora using a large variety of techniques. We have provided justifications for using highly parallel corpora consisting of multiply translated sentences from a single language. All our experiments were conducted on both English and French using comparable resources, so although the results cannot be directly compared they give some acceptable comparison points. The best recall of any individual technique is around 45 for both language, and F-measure in the range 36-38, indicating that the task under study is a very challenging one. Our validation strategy based on bi-class classification using a broad set of features applicable to all candidate paraphrase pairs allowed us to obtain a 18% relative improvement in F-measure over the best individual technique for both languages.

Our future work include performing a deeper error analysis of our current results, to better comprehend what characteristics of paraphrase still defy current validation. Also, we want to investigate adding new individual techniques to provide so far unseen candidates. Another possible approach would be to submit all pairs of sub-sentential paraphrase pairs from a sentence pair to our validation process, which would obviously require some optimization and devising sensible heuristics to limit time complexity. We also intend to collect larger corpora for all other corpus types appearing in Table 1 and conducting anew our acquisition and validation tasks.

Acknowledgements

The authors would like to thank the reviewers for their comments and suggestions, as well as Guillaume Wisniewski for helpful discussions. This work was partly funded by ANR project Edylex (ANR-09-CORD-008).

References

Ion Androutsopoulos and Prodromos Malakasiotis. 2010. A Survey of Paraphrasing and Textual Entailment Methods. *Journal of Artificial Intelligence Research*, 38:135–187.

Colin Bannard and Chris Callison-Burch. 2005. Paraphrasing with Bilingual Parallel Corpora. In *Proceedings of ACL*, Ann Arbor, USA.

Regina Barzilay and Lillian Lee. 2003. Learning to paraphrase: an unsupervised approach using multiple-sequence alignment. In *Proceedings of NAACL-HLT*, Edmonton, Canada.

Regina Barzilay and Kathleen R. McKeown. 2001. Extracting paraphrases from a parallel corpus. In *Proceedings of ACL*, Toulouse, France.

Rahul Bhagat and Deepak Ravichandran. 2008. Large scale acquisition of paraphrases for learning surface patterns. In *Proceedings of ACL-HLT*, Columbus, USA.

Rahul Bhagat. 2009. *Learning Paraphrases from Text*. Ph.D. thesis, University of Southern California.

Houda Bouamor, Aurélien Max, and Anne Vilnat. 2010. Comparison of Paraphrase Acquisition Techniques on Sentential Paraphrases. In *Proceedings of IceTAL*, Rejkavik, Iceland.

Chris Callison-Burch, Trevor Cohn, and Mirella Lapata. 2008. Parametric: An automatic evaluation metric for paraphrasing. In *Proceedings of COLING*, Manchester, UK.

Chris Callison-Burch. 2007. *Paraphrasing and Translation*. Ph.D. thesis, University of Edinburgh.

Chris Callison-Burch. 2008. Syntactic Constraints on Paraphrases Extracted from Parallel Corpora. In *Proceedings of EMNLP*, Hawai, USA.

Marie Candito, Benoît Crabbé, and Pascal Denis. 2010. Statistical French dependency parsing: treebank conversion and first results. In *Proceedings of LREC*, Valletta, Malta.

David Chen and William Dolan. 2011. Collecting highly parallel data for paraphrase evaluation. In *Proceedings of ACL*, Portland, USA.

Trevor Cohn, Chris Callison-Burch, and Mirella Lapata. 2008. Constructing corpora for the development and evaluation of paraphrase systems. *Computational Linguistics*, 34(4).

Bill Dolan, Chris Quirk, and Chris Brockett. 2004. Unsupervised construction of large paraphrase corpora: Exploiting massively parallel news sources. In *Proceedings of COLING*, Geneva, Switzerland.

Ulrich Germann. 2008. Yawat : Yet Another Word Alignment Tool. In *Proceedings of the ACL-HLT, demo session*, Columbus, USA.

Christian Jacquemin. 1999. Syntagmatic and paradigmatic representations of term variation. In *Proceedings of ACL*, College Park, USA.

Dan Klein and Christopher D. Manning. 2003. Accurate unlexicalized parsing. In *Proceedings of ACL*, Sapporo, Japan.

Philipp Koehn, Hieu Hoang, Alexandra Birch, Chris Callison-Burch, Marcello Federico, Nicola Bertoldi, Brooke Cowan, Wade Shen, Christine Moran, Richard Zens, Chris Dyer, Ondrej Bojar, Alexandra Constantin, and Evan Herbst. 2007. Moses: Open Source Toolkit for Statistical Machine Translation. In *Proceedings of ACL, demo session*, Prague, Czech Republic.

Dekang Lin and Patrick Pantel. 2001. Discovery of inference rules for question answering. *Natural Language Engineering*, 7(4):343–360.

Chang Liu, Daniel Dahlmeier, and Hwee Tou Ng. 2010. PEM: A paraphrase evaluation metric exploiting parallel texts. In *Proceedings of EMNLP*, Cambridge, USA.

Nitin Madnani and Bonnie J. Dorr. 2010. Generating Phrasal and Sentential Paraphrases: A Survey of Data-Driven Methods . *Computational Linguistics*, 36(3).

Nitin Madnani. 2010. *The Circle of Meaning: From Translation to Paraphrasing and Back*. Ph.D. thesis, University of Maryland College Park.

Donald Metzler, Eduard Hovy, and Chunliang Zhang. 2011. An empirical evaluation of data-driven paraphrase generation techniques. In *Proceedings of ACL-HLT*, Portland, USA.

Franz Josef Och and Herman Ney. 2004. The alignment template approach to statistical machine translation. *Computational Linguistics*, 30(4).

Bo Pang, Kevin Knight, and Daniel Marcu. 2003. Syntax-based alignement of multiple translations: Extracting paraphrases and generating new sentences. In *Proceedings of NAACL-HLT*, Edmonton, Canada.

Matthew Snover, Nitin Madnani, Bonnie J. Dorr, and Richard Schwartz. 2010. TER-Plus: paraphrase, semantic, and alignment enhancements to Translation Edit Rate. *Machine Translation*, 23(2-3).

Jörg Tiedemann. 2007. Building a Multilingual Parallel Subtitle Corpus. In *Proceedings of the Conference on Computational Linguistics in the Netherlands*, Leuven, Belgium.

Shiqi Zhao, Haifeng Wang, Ting Liu, and Sheng Li. 2008. Pivot Approach for Extracting Paraphrase Patterns from Bilingual Corpora. In *Proceedings of ACL-HLT*, Columbus, USA.

Determining the placement of German verbs in English–to–German SMT

Anita Gojun **Alexander Fraser**
Institute for Natural Language Processing
University of Stuttgart, Germany
{gojunaa, fraser}@ims.uni-stuttgart.de

Abstract

When translating English to German, existing reordering models often cannot model the long-range reorderings needed to generate German translations with verbs in the correct position. We reorder English as a preprocessing step for English-to-German SMT. We use a sequence of hand-crafted reordering rules applied to English parse trees. The reordering rules place English verbal elements in the positions within the clause they will have in the German translation. This is a difficult problem, as German verbal elements can appear in different positions within a clause (in contrast with English verbal elements, whose positions do not vary as much). We obtain a significant improvement in translation performance.

1 Introduction

Phrase-based SMT (PSMT) systems translate word sequences (phrases) from a source language into a target language, performing reordering of target phrases in order to generate a fluent target language output. The reordering models, such as, for example, the models implemented in Moses (Koehn et al., 2007), are often limited to a certain reordering range since reordering beyond this distance cannot be performed accurately. This results in problems of fluency for language pairs with large differences in constituent order, such as English and German. When translating from English to German, verbs in the German output are often incorrectly left near their position in English, creating problems of fluency. Verbs are also often omitted since the distortion model cannot move verbs to positions which are licensed by the German language model, making the translations difficult to understand.

A common approach for handling the long-range reordering problem within PSMT is performing syntax-based or part-of-speech-based (POS-based) reordering of the input as a preprocessing step before translation (e.g., Collins et al. (2005), Gupta et al. (2007), Habash (2007), Xu et al. (2009), Niehues and Kolss (2009), Katz-Brown et al. (2011), Genzel (2010)).

We reorder English to improve the translation to German. The verb reordering process is implemented using deterministic reordering rules on English parse trees. The sequence of reorderings is derived from the clause type and the composition of a given verbal complex (a (possibly discontiguous) sequence of verbal elements in a single clause). Only one rule can be applied in a given context and for each word to be reordered, there is a unique reordered position. We train a standard PSMT system on the reordered English training and tuning data and use it to translate the reordered English test set into German.

This paper is structured as follows: in section 2, we outline related work. In section 3, English and German verb positioning is described. The reordering rules are given in section 4. In section 5, we show the relevance of the reordering, present the experiments and present an extensive error analysis. We discuss some problems observed in section 7 and conclude in section 8.

2 Related work

There have been a number of attempts to handle the long-range reordering problem within PSMT. Many of them are based on the reordering of a source language sentence as a preprocessing step before translation. Our approach is related to the work of Collins et al. (2005). They reordered German sentences as a preprocessing step for German-to-English SMT. Hand-crafted reordering rules are applied on German parse trees in order to move the German verbs into the positions corresponding to the positions of the English verbs. Subsequently, the reordered German sentences are translated into English leading to better translation performance when compared with the translation of the original German sentences.

We apply this method on the opposite translation direction, thus having English as a source language and German as a target language. However, we cannot simply invert the reordering rules which are applied on German as a source language in order to reorder the English input. While the reordering of German implies movement of the German verbs into a single position, when reordering English, we need to split the English verbal complexes and, where required, move their parts into different positions. Therefore, we need to identify exactly which parts of a verbal complex must be moved and their possible positions in a German sentence.

Reordering rules can also be extracted automatically. For example, Niehues and Kolss (2009) automatically extracted discontiguous reordering rules (allowing gaps between POS tags which can include an arbitrary number of words) from a word-aligned parallel corpus with POS tagged source side. Since many different rules can be applied on a given sentence, a number of reordered sentence alternatives are created which are encoded as a word lattice (Dyer et al., 2008). They dealt with the translation directions German-to-English and English-to-German, but translation improvement was obtained only for the German-to-English direction. This may be due to missing information about clause boundaries since English verbs often have to be moved to the clause end. Our reordering has access to this kind of knowledge since we are working with a full syntactic parser of English.

Genzel (2010) proposed a language-independent method for learning reordering rules where the rules are extracted from parsed source language sentences. For each node, all possible reorderings (permutations) of a limited number of the child nodes are considered. The candidate reordering rules are applied on the dev set which is then translated and evaluated. Only those rule sequences are extracted which maximize the translation performance of the reordered dev set.

For the extraction of reordering rules, Genzel (2010) uses shallow constituent parse trees which are obtained from dependency parse trees. The trees are annotated using both Penn Treebank POS tags and using Stanford dependency types. However, the constraints on possible reorderings are too restrictive in order to model all word movements required for English-to-German translation. In particular, the reordering rules involve only the permutation of direct child nodes and do not allow changing of child-parent relationships (deleting of a child or attaching a node to a new father node). In our implementation, a verb can be moved to any position in a parse tree (according to the reordering rules): the reordering can be a simple permutation of child nodes, or attachment of these nodes to a new father node (cf. movement of *bought* and *read* in figure 1[1]).

Thus, in contrast to Genzel (2010), our approach does not have any constraints with respect to the position of nodes marking a verb within the tree. Only the syntactic structure of the sentence restricts the distance of the linguistically motivated verb movements.

3 Verb positions in English and German

3.1 Syntax of German sentences

Since in this work, we concentrate on verbs, we use the notion *verbal complex* for a sequence consisting of verbs, verbal particles and negation.

The verb positions in the German sentences depend on clause type and the tense as shown in table 1. Verbs can be placed in 1st, 2nd or clause-final position. Additionally, if a composed tense is given, the parts of a verbal complex can be interrupted by the *middle field* (MF) which contains arbitrary sentence constituents, e.g., subjects and objects (noun phrases), adjuncts (prepositional phrases), adverbs, etc. We assume that the German sentences are SVO (analogously to English); topicalization is beyond the scope of our work.

In this work, we consider two possible positions of the negation in German: (1) directly in

[1] The verb movements shown in figure 1 will be explained in detail in section 4.

	1st	2nd	MF	clause-final
decl	subject	**finV**	any	∅
	subject	**finV**	any	**mainV**
int/perif	**finV**	subject	any	∅
	finV	subject	any	**mainV**
sub/inf	relCon	subject	any	**finV**
	relCon	subject	any	**VC**

Table 1: Position of the German subjects and verbs in declarative clauses (*decl*), interrogative clauses and clauses with a peripheral clause (*int/perif*), subordinate/infinitival (*sub/inf*) clauses. *mainV* = main verb, *finV* = finite verb, *VC* = verbal complex, *any* = arbitrary words, *relCon* = relative pronoun or conjunction. We consider extraponed consituents in *perif*, as well as optional interrogatives in *int* to be in position 0.

front of the main verb, and (2) directly after the finite verb. The two negation positions are illustrated in the following examples:

(1) Ich behaupte, dass ich es **nicht** gesagt habe.
I claim that I it not say did.

(2) Ich denke **nicht**, dass er das gesagt hat.
I think not that he that said has.

It should, however, be noted that in German, the negative particle *nicht* can have several positions in a sentence depending on the context (verb arguments, emphasis). Thus, more analysis is ideally needed (e.g., discourse, etc.).

3.2 Comparison of verb positions

English and German verbal complexes differ both in their construction and their position. The German verbal complex can be discontiguous, i.e., its parts can be placed in different positions which implies that a (large) number of other words can be placed between the verbs (situated in the MF). In English, the verbal complex can only be interrupted by adverbials and subjects (in interrogative clauses). Furthermore, in German, the finite verb can sometimes be the last element of the verbal complex, while in English, the finite verb is always the first verb in the verbal complex.

In terms of positions, the verbs in English and German can differ significantly. As previously noted, the German verbal complex can be discontiguous, simultaneously occupying 1st/2nd and clause-final position (cf. rows *decl* and *int/perif* in table 1), which is not the case in English. While in English, the verbal complex is placed in the 2nd position in declarative, or in the 1st position in interrogative clauses, in German, the entire verbal complex can additionally be placed at the clause end in subordinate or infinitival clauses (cf. row *sub/inf* in table 1).

Because of these differences, for nearly all types of English clauses, reordering is needed in order to place the English verbs in the positions which correspond to the correct verb positions in German. Only English declarative clauses with simple present and simple past tense have the same verb position as their German counterparts. We give statistics on clause types and their relevance for the verb reordering in section 5.1.

4 Reordering of the English input

The reordering is carried out on English parse trees. We first enrich the parse trees with clause type labels, as described below. Then, for each node marking a clause (*S* nodes), the corresponding sequence of reordering rules is carried out. The appropriate reordering is derived from the clause type label and the composition of the given verbal complex. The reordering rules are deterministic. Only one rule can be applied in a given context and for each verb to be reordered, there is a unique reordered position.

The reordering procedure is the same for the training and the testing data. It is carried out on English parse trees resulting in modified parse trees which are read out in order to generate the reordered English sentences. These are input for training a PSMT system or input to the decoder. The processing steps are shown in figure 1.

For the development of the reordering rules, we used a small sample of the training data. In particular, by observing the English parse trees extracted randomly from the training data, we developed a set of rules which transform the original trees in such a way that the English verbs are moved to the positions which correspond to the placement of verbs in German.

4.1 Labeling clauses with their type

As shown in section 3.1, the verb positions in German depend on the clause type. Since we use English parse trees produced by the generative parser of Charniak and Johnson (2005) which do not have any function labels, we implemented a simple rule-based clause type labeling script which

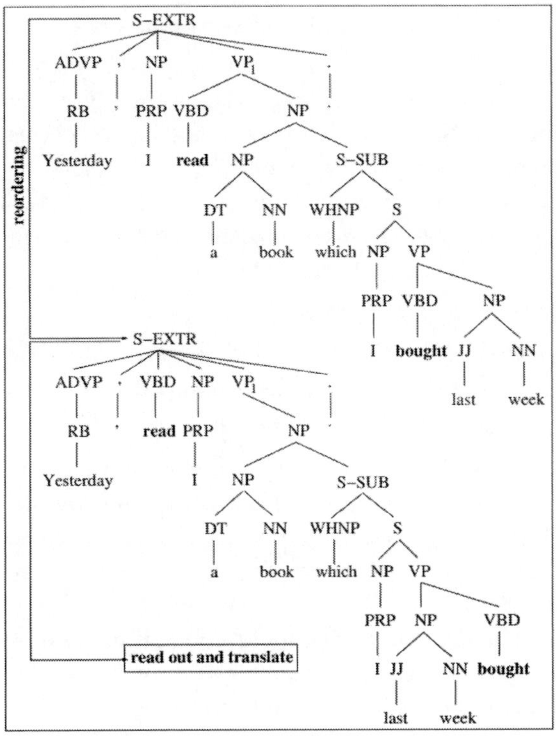

Figure 1: Processing steps: Clause type labeling annotates the given original tree with clause type labels (in figure, *S-EXTR* and *S-SUB*). Subsequently, the reordering is performed (cf. movement of the verbs *read* and *bought*). The reordered sentence is finally read out and given to the decoder.

enriches every clause starting node with the corresponding clause type label. The label depends on the context (father, child nodes) of a given clause node. If, for example, the first child node of a given *S* node is *WH** (wh-word) or *IN* (subordinating conjunction), then the clause type label is *SUB* (subordinate clause, cf. figure 1).

We defined five clause type labels which indicate main clauses (*MAIN*), main clauses with a peripheral clause in the prefield (*EXTR*), subordinate (*SUB*), infinitival (*XCOMP*) and interrogative clauses (*INT*).

4.2 Clause boundary identification

The German verbs are often placed at the clause end (cf. rows *decl*, *int/perif* and *sub/inf* in table 1), making it necessary to move their English counterparts into the corresponding positions within an English tree. For this reason, we identify the clause ends (the right boundaries). The search for the clause end is implemented as a breadth-first search for the next *S* node or sentence end. The starting node is the node which marks the verbal phrase in which the verbs are enclosed. When the next node marking a clause is identified, the search stops and returns the position in front of the identified clause marking node.

When, for example, searching for the clause boundary of *S-EXTR* in figure 1, we search recursively for the first clause marking node within VP_1, which is *S-SUB*. The position in front of *S-SUB* is marked as clause-final position of *S-EXTR*.

4.3 Basic verb reordering rules

The reordering procedure takes into account the following word categories: verbs, verb particles, the infinitival particle *to* and the negative particle *not*, as well as its abbreviated form *'t*. The reordering rules are based on POS labels in the parse tree.

The reordering procedure is a sequence of applications of the reordering rules. For each element of an English verbal complex, its properties are derived (tense, main verb/auxiliary, finiteness). The reordering is then carried out corresponding to the clause type and verbal properties of a verb to be processed.

In the following, the reordering rules are presented. Examples of reordered sentences are given in table 2, and are discussed further here.

Main clause (S-MAIN)

(i) simple tense: no reordering required (cf. $appears_{finV}$ in input 1);

(ii) composed tense: the main verb is moved to the clause end. If a negative particle exists, it is moved in front of the reordered main verb, while the optional verb particle is moved after the reordered main verb (cf. $[has]_{finV}$ $[been\ developing]_{mainV}$ in input 2).

Main clause with peripheral clause (S-EXTR)

(i) simple tense: the finite verb is moved together with an optional particle to the 1st position (i.e. in front of the subject);

(ii) composed tense: the main verb, as well as optional negative and verb particles are moved to the clause end. The finite verb is moved in the 1st position, i.e. in front of the subject (cf. $have_{finV}$ $[gone\ up]_{mainV}$ in input 3).

Subordinate clause (S-SUB)

(i) simple tense: the finite verb is moved to the clause end (cf. *boasts*$_{finV}$ in input 3);

(ii) composed tense: the main verb, as well as optional negative and verb particles are moved to the clause end, the finite verb is placed after the reordered main verb (cf. *have*$_{finV}$ *[been executed]*$_{mainV}$ in input 5).

Infinitival clause (S-XCOMP)
The entire English verbal complex is moved from the 2nd position to the clause-final position (cf. *[to discuss]*$_{VC}$ in input 4).

Interrogative clause (S-INT)

(i) simple tense: no reordering required;

(ii) composed tense: the main verb, as well as optional negative and verb particles are moved to the clause end (cf. *[did]*$_{finV}$ *know*$_{mainV}$ in input 5).

4.4 Reordering rules for other phenomena

4.4.1 Multiple auxiliaries in English

Some English tenses require a sequence of auxiliaries, not all of which have a German counterpart. In the reordering process, non-finite auxiliaries are considered to be a part of the main verb complex and are moved together with the main verb (cf. movement of *has*$_{finV}$ *[been developing]*$_{mainV}$ in input 2).

4.4.2 Simple vs. composed tenses

In English, there are some tenses composed of an auxiliary and a main verb which correspond to a German tense composed of only one verb, e.g., *am reading* ⇔ *lese* and *does John read?* ⇔ *liest John?* Splitting such English verbal complexes and only moving the main verbs would lead to constructions which do not exist in German. Therefore, in the reordering process, the English verbal complex in present continuous, as well as interrogative phrases composed of *do* and a main verb, are not split. They are handled as *one* main verb complex and reordered as a single unit using the rules for main verbs (e.g. *[because I am reading a book]*$_{SUB}$ ⇒ *because I a book am reading* ⇔ *weil ich ein Buch lese*.[2]

4.4.3 Flexible position of German verbs

We stated that the English verbs are never moved outside the subclause they were originally in. In German there are, however, some constructions (infinitival and relative clauses), in which the main verb can be placed *after* a subsequent clause. Consider two German translations of the English sentence *He has promised to come*:

(3a) Er hat [zu kommen]$_S$ versprochen.
he has to come promised.

(3b) Er hat versprochen, [zu kommen]$_S$.
he has promised, to come.

In (3a), the German main verb *versprochen* is placed after the infinitival clause *zu kommen* (*to come*), while in (3b), the same verb is placed in front of it. Both alternatives are grammatically correct.

If a German verb should come after an embedded clause as in example (3a) or precede it (cf. example (3b)), depends not only on syntactic but also on stylistic factors. Regarding the verb reordering problem, we would therefore have to examine the given sentence in order to derive the *correct* (or *more probable*) new verb position which is beyond the scope of this work. Therefore, we allow only for reorderings which do not cross clause boundaries as shown in example (3b).

5 Experiments

In order to evaluate the translation of the reordered English sentences, we built two SMT systems with Moses (Koehn et al., 2007). As training data, we used the Europarl corpus which consists of 1,204,062 English/German sentence pairs. The baseline system was trained on the original English training data while the contrastive system was trained on the reordered English training data. In both systems, the same original German sentences were used. We used WMT 2009 dev and test sets to tune and test the systems. The baseline system was tuned and tested on the original data while for the contrastive system, we used the reordered English side of the dev and test sets. The German 5-gram language model used in both systems was trained on the WMT 2009 German language modeling data, a large German newspaper corpus consisting of 10,193,376 sentences.

[2]We only consider present continuous and verbs in combination with *do* for this kind of reordering. There are also other tenses which could (or should) be treated in the same way (cf. *has been developing* on input 2, table 2). We do not do this to keep the reordering rules simple and general.

Input 1	The programme **appears to be** successful for published data **shows** that MRSA **is** on the decline in the UK.
Reordered	The programme **appears** successful **to be** for published data **shows** that MRSA on the decline in the UK **is**.
Input 2	The real estate market in Bulgaria **has been developing** at an unbelievable rate - all of Europe **has** its eyes on this heretofore rarely heard-of Balkan nation.
Reordered	The real estate market in Bulgaria **has** at an unbelievable rate **been developing** - all of Europe **has** its eyes on this heretofore rarely heard-of Balkan nation.
Input 3	While Bulgaria **boasts** the European Union's lowest real estate prices, they **have** still **gone up** by 21 percent in the past five years.
Reordered	While Bulgaria the European Union's lowest real estate prices **boasts**, **have** they still by 21 percent in the past five years **gone up**.
Input 4	Professionals and politicians from 192 countries **are slated to discuss** the Bali Roadmap that **focuses** on efforts **to cut** greenhouse gas emissions after 2012, when the Kyoto Protocol **expires**.
Reordered	Professionals and politicians from 192 countries **are slated** the Bali Roadmap **to discuss** that on efforts **focuses** greenhouse gas emissions after 2012 **to cut**, when the Kyoto Protocol **expires**.
Input 5	**Did** you **know** that in that same country, since 1976, 34 mentally-retarded offenders **have been executed**?
Reordered	**Did** you **know** that in that same country, since 1976, 34 mentally-retarded offenders **been executed have**?

Table 2: Examples of reordered English sentences

5.1 Applied rules

In order to see how many English clauses are relevant for reordering, we derived statistics about clause types and the number of reordering rules applied on the training data.

In table 3, the number of the English clauses with all considered clause type/tense combination are shown. The bold numbers indicate combinations which are relevant to the reordering. Overall, 62% of all EN clauses from our training data (2,706,117 clauses) are relevant for the verb reordering. Note that there is an additional category *rest* which indicates incorrect clause type/tense combinations and might thus not be correctly reordered. These are mostly due to parsing and/or tagging errors.

The performance of the systems was measured by BLEU (Papineni et al., 2002). The evaluation results are shown in table 4. The contrastive system outperforms the baseline. Its BLEU score is 13.63 which is a gain of 0.61 BLEU points over the baseline. This is a statistically significant improvement at $p<0.05$ (computed with Gimpel's implementation of the pairwise bootstrap resampling method (Koehn, 2004)).

Manual examination of the translations produced by both systems confirms the result of the automatic evaluation. Many translations produced by the contrastive system now have verbs in the correct positions. If we compare the generated translations for input sentence 1 in table 5, we see that the contrastive system generates a translation in which all verbs are placed correctly. In the baseline translation, only the translation of the finite verb *was*, namely *war*, is placed correctly, while the translation of the main verb (*diagnosed* → *festgestellt*) should be placed at the clause end as in the translation produced by our system.

tense	MAIN	EXTR	SUB	INT	XCOMP
simple	675,095	**170,806**	**449,631**	8,739	-
composed	**343,178**	**116,729**	**277,733**	**8,817**	**314,573**
rest	98,464	5,158	90,139	306	146,746

Table 3: Counts of English clause types and used tenses. Bold numbers indicate clause type/tense combinations where reordering is required.

	Baseline	**Reordered**
BLEU	13.02	13.63

Table 4: Scores of baseline and contrastive systems

5.2 Evaluation

Often, the English verbal complex is translated only partially by the baseline system. For example, the English verbal complexes in sentence 2 in table 5 *will climb* and *will drop* are only partially translated (*will climb* → *wird (will)*, *will drop* → *fallen (fall)*). Moreover, the generated verbs are placed incorrectly. In our translation, all verbs are translated and placed correctly.

Another problem which was often observed in the baseline is the omission of the verbs in the German translations. The baseline translation of the example sentence 3 in table 5 illustrates such a case. There is no translation of the English infinitival verbal complex *to have*. In the translation generated by the contrastive system, the verbal complex does get translated (*zu haben*) and is also placed correctly. We think this is because the reordering model is not able to identify the position for the verb which is licensed by the language model, causing a hypothesis with no verb to be scored higher than the hypotheses with incorrectly placed verbs.

6 Error analysis

6.1 Erroneous reordering in our system

In some cases, the reordering of the English parse trees fails. Most erroneous reorderings are due to a number of different parsing and tagging errors.

Coordinated verbs are also problematic due to their complexity. Their composition can vary, and thus it would require a large number of different reordering rules to fully capture this. In our reordering script, the movement of complex structures such as verbal phrases consisting of a sequence of child nodes is not implemented (only nodes with one child, namely the verb, verbal particle or negative particle are moved).

6.2 Splitting of the English verbal complex

Since in many cases, the German verbal complex is discontiguous, we need to split the English verbal complex and move its parts into different positions. This ensures the correct placement of German verbs. However, this does not ensure that the German verb forms are correct because of highly ambiguous English verbs. In some cases, we can lose contextual information which would be useful for disambiguating ambiguous verbs and generating the appropriate German verb forms.

6.2.1 Subject–verb agreement

Let us consider the English clause in (4a) and its reordered version in (4b):

(4a) ... because they **have said** it to me yesterday.
(4b) ... because they it to me yesterday **said have**.

In (4b), the English verbs *said have* are separated from the subject *they*. The English *said have* can be translated in several ways into German. Without any information about the subject (the distance between the verbs and the subject can be very large), it is relatively likely that an erroneous German translation is generated.

On the other hand, in the baseline SMT system, the subject *they* is likely to be a part of a translation phrase with the correct German equivalent (*they have said* $\rightarrow$ *sie haben gesagt*). *They* is then used as a disambiguating context which is missing in the reordered sentence (but the order is wrong).

6.2.2 Verb dependency

A similar problem occurs in a verbal complex:

(5a) They **have said** it to me yesterday.
(5b) They **have** it to me yesterday **said**.

In sentence (5a), the English consecutive verbs *have said* are a sequence consisting of a finite auxiliary *have* and the past participle *said*. They should be translated into the corresponding German verbal complex *haben gesagt*. But, if the verbs are split, we will probably get translations which are completely independent. Even if the German auxiliary is correctly inflected, it is hard to predict how *said* is going to be translated. If the distance between the auxiliary *habe* and the hypothesized translation of *said* is large, the language model will not be able to help select the correct translation. Here, the baseline SMT system again has an advantage as the verbs are consecutive. It is likely they will be found in the training data and extracted with the correct German phrase (but the German order is again incorrect).

6.3 Collocations

Collocations (verb–object pairs) are another case which can lead to a problem:

(6a) I think that the discussion **would take place** later this evening.
(6b) I think that the discussion **place** later this evening **take would**.

The English collocation in (6a) consisting of the verb *take* and the object *place* corresponds to the German verb *stattfinden*. Without this specific object, the verb *take* is likely to be translated literally. In the reordered sentence, the verbal complex *take would* is indeed separated from the object *place* which would probably lead to the literal translation of both parts of the mentioned collocation. So, as already described in the preceding paragraphs, an important source of contextual information is lost which could ensure the correct translation of the given phrase.

This problem is not specific to English–to–German. For instance, the same problem occurs when translating German into English. If, for ex-

Input 1	An MRSA - an antibiotic resistant staphylococcus - infection **was** recently **diagnosed** in the traumatology ward of János hospital.
Reordered input	An MRSA - an antibiotic resistant staphylococcus - infection **was** recently in the traumatology ward of János hospital **diagnosed**.
Baseline translation	Ein MRSA - ein Antibiotikum resistenter Staphylococcus - **war** vor kurzem in der **festgestellt** A MRSA - an antibiotic resistant Staphylococcus - was before recent in the diagnosed traumatology Ward von János Krankenhaus. traumatology ward of János hospital.
Reordered translation	Ein MRSA - ein Antibiotikum resistenter Staphylococcus - Infektion **wurde** vor kurzem in den A MRSA - an antibiotic resistant Staphylococcus - infection was before recent in the traumatology Station der János Krankenhaus **diagnostiziert**. traumatology ward of János hospital diagnosed.

Input 2	The ECB **predicts** that 2008 inflation **will climb** to 2.5 percent from the earlier 2.1, but **will drop** back to 1.9 percent in 2009.
Reordered input	The ECB **predicts** that 2008 inflation to 2.5 percent from the earlier 2.1 **will climb**, but back to 1.9 percent in 2009 **will drop**.
Baseline translation	Die EZB **sagt**, dass 2008 die Inflationsrate **wird** auf 2,5 Prozent aus der früheren 2,1, sondern The ECB says, that 2008 the inflation rate will to 2.5 percent from the earlier 2.1, but **fallen** zurück auf 1,9 Prozent im Jahr 2009. fall back to 1.9 percent in the year 2009.
Reordered translation	Die EZB **prophezeit**, dass 2008 die Inflation zu 2,5 Prozent aus der früheren 2,1 **ansteigen** The ECB predicts, that 2008 the inflation rate to 2.5 percent from the earlier 2.1 climb **wird**, aber auf 1,9 Prozent in 2009 **sinken wird**. will, but to 1.9 percent in 2009 fall will.

Input 3	Labour Minister Mónika Lamperth **appears not to have** a sensitive side.
R. input	Labour Minister Mónika Lamperth **appears** a sensitive side **not to have** .
Baseline translation	Arbeitsminister Mónika Lamperth **scheint nicht** eine sensible Seite. Labour Minister Mónika Lamperth appears not a sensitive side.
Reordered translation	Arbeitsminister Mónika Lamperth **scheint** eine sensible Seite **nicht zu haben**. Labour Minister Mónika Lamperth appears a sensitive side not to have.

Table 5: Example translations, the baseline has problems with verbal elements, reordered is correct

ample, the object *Kauf (buying)* of the collocation *nehmen + in Kauf (accept)* is separated from the verb *nehmen (take)*, they are very likely to be translated literally (rather than as the idiom meaning "to accept"), thus leading to an erroneous English translation.

6.4 Error statistics

We manually checked 100 randomly chosen English sentences to see how often the problems described in the previous sections occur. From a total of 276 clauses, 29 were not reordered correctly. 20 errors were caused by incorrect parsing and/or POS tags, while the remaining 9 are mostly due to different kinds of coordination. Table 6 shows correctly reordered clauses which might pose a problem for translation (see sections 6.2–6.3). Although the positions of the verbs in the translations are now correct, the distance between subjects and verbs, or between verbs in a single VP might lead to the generation of erroneously inflected verbs. The separate generation of German verbal morphology is an interesting area of future work, see (de Gispert and Mariño, 2008). We also found 2 problematic collocations but note that this only gives a rough idea of the problem, further study is needed.

6.5 POS-based disambiguation of the English verbs

With respect to the problems described in 6.2.1 and 6.2.2, we carried out an experiment in which

	total	d $\geq$ 5 tokens
subject–verb	40	19
verb dependency	32	14
collocations	8	2

Table 6: *total* is the number of clauses found for the respective phenomenon. *$d \geq 5$ tokens* is the number of clauses where the distance between relevant tokens is at least 5, which is problematic.

	Baseline + POS	Reordered + POS
BLEU	13.11	13.68

Table 7: BLEU scores of the baseline and the contrastive SMT system using verbal POS tags

we used POS tags in order to disambiguate the English verbs. For example, the English verb *said* corresponds to the German participle *gesagt*, as well as to the finite verb in simple past, e.g. *sagte*. We attached the POS tags to the English verbs in order to simulate a disambiguating suffix of a verb (e.g. *said* ⇒ *said_VBN, said_VBD*). The idea behind this was to extract the correct verbal translation phrases and score them with appropriate translation probabilities (e.g. *p(said_VBN, gesagt)* > *p(said_VBN, sagte)*.

We built and tested two PSMT systems using the data enriched with verbal POS tags. The first system is trained and tested on the original English sentences, while the contrastive one was trained and tested on the reordered English sentences. Evaluation results are shown in table 7.

The baseline obtains a gain of 0.09 and the contrastive system of 0.05 BLEU points over the corresponding PSMT system without POS tags. Although there are verbs which are now generated correctly, the overall translation improvement lies under our expectation. We will directly model the inflection of German verbs in future work.

7 Discussion and future work

We implemented reordering rules for English verbal complexes because their placement differs significantly from German placement. The implementation required dealing with three important problems: (i) definition of the clause boundaries, (ii) identification of the new verb positions and (iii) correct splitting of the verbal complexes.

We showed some phenomena for which a stochastic reordering would be more appropriate. For example, since in German, the auxiliary and the main verb of a verbal complex can occupy different positions in a clause, we had to define the English counterparts of the two components of the German verbal complex. We defined non-finite English verbal elements as a part of the main verb complex which are then moved together with the main verb. This rigid definition could be relaxed by considering multiple different splittings and movements of the English verbs.

Furthermore, the reordering rules are applied on a clause not allowing for movements across the clause boundaries. However, we also showed that in some cases, the main verbs may be moved after the succeeding subclause. Stochastic rules could allow for both placements or carry out the more probable reordering given a specific context. We will address these issues in future work.

Unfortunately, some important contextual information is lost when splitting and moving English verbs. When English verbs are highly ambiguous, erroneous German verbs can be generated. The experiment described in section 6.5 shows that more effort should be made in order to overcome this problem. The incorporation of separate morphological generation of inflected German verbs would improve translation.

8 Conclusion

We presented a method for reordering English as a preprocessing step for English–to–German SMT. To our knowledge, this is one of the first papers which reports on experiments regarding the reordering problem for English–to–German SMT. We showed that the reordering rules specified in this work lead to improved translation quality. We observed that verbs are placed correctly more often than in the baseline, and that verbs which were omitted in the baseline are now often generated. We carried out a thorough analysis of the rules applied and discussed problems which are related to highly ambiguous English verbs. Finally we presented ideas for future work.

Acknowledgments

This work was funded by Deutsche Forschungsgemeinschaft grant Models of Morphosyntax for Statistical Machine Translation.

References

Eugene Charniak and Mark Johnson. 2005. Coarse-to-fine n-best parsing and MaxEnt discriminative reranking. In *ACL*.

Michael Collins, Philipp Koehn, and Ivona Kučerová. 2005. Clause restructuring for statistical machine translation. In *ACL*.

Adrià de Gispert and José B. Mariño. 2008. On the impact of morphology in English to Spanish statistical MT. *Speech Communication*, 50(11-12).

Chris Dyer, Smaranda Muresan, and Philip Resnik. 2008. Generalizing word lattice translation. In *ACL-HLT*.

Dmitriy Genzel. 2010. Automatically learning source-side reordering rules for large scale machine translation. In *COLING*.

Deepa Gupta, Mauro Cettolo, and Marcello Federico. 2007. POS-based reordering models for statistical machine translation. In *Proceedings of the Machine Translation Summit (MT-Summit)*.

Nizar Habash. 2007. Syntactic preprocessing for statistical machine translation. In *Proceedings of the Machine Translation Summit (MT-Summit)*.

Jason Katz-Brown, Slav Petrov, Ryan McDonald, Franz Och, David Talbot, Hiroshi Ichikawa, Masakazu Seno, and Hideto Kazawa. 2011. Training a parser for machine translation reordering. In *EMNLP*.

Philipp Koehn, Hieu Hoang, Alexandra Birch, Chris Callison-Burch, Marcello Federico, Nicola Bertoldi, Brooke Cowan, Wade Shen, Christine Moran, Richard Zens, Chris Dyer, Ondrej Bojar, Alexandra Constantin, and Evan Herbst. 2007. Moses: Open source toolkit for statistical machine translation. In *ACL, Demonstration Program*.

Philipp Koehn. 2004. Statistical significance tests for machine translation evaluation. In *EMNLP*.

Jan Niehues and Muntsin Kolss. 2009. A POS-based model for long-range reorderings in SMT. In *EACL Workshop on Statistical Machine Translation*.

Kishore Papineni, Salim Roukos, Todd Ward, and Wei-Jing Zhu. 2002. BLEU: a method for automatic evaluation of machine translation. In *ACL*.

Peng Xu, Jaecho Kang, Michael Ringgaard, and Franz Och. 2009. Using a dependency parser to improve SMT for subject-object-verb languages. In *NAACL*.

Syntax-Based Word Ordering Incorporating a Large-Scale Language Model

Yue Zhang
University of Cambridge
Computer Laboratory
yz360@cam.ac.uk

Graeme Blackwood
University of Cambridge
Engineering Department
gwb24@eng.cam.ac.uk

Stephen Clark
University of Cambridge
Computer Laboratory
sc609@cam.ac.uk

Abstract

A fundamental problem in text generation is word ordering. Word ordering is a computationally difficult problem, which can be constrained to some extent for particular applications, for example by using synchronous grammars for statistical machine translation. There have been some recent attempts at the unconstrained problem of generating a sentence from a multi-set of input words (Wan et al., 2009; Zhang and Clark, 2011). By using CCG and learning guided search, Zhang and Clark reported the highest scores on this task. One limitation of their system is the absence of an N-gram language model, which has been used by text generation systems to improve fluency. We take the Zhang and Clark system as the baseline, and incorporate an N-gram model by applying online large-margin training. Our system significantly improved on the baseline by 3.7 BLEU points.

1 Introduction

One fundamental problem in text generation is word ordering, which can be abstractly formulated as finding a grammatical order for a multiset of words. The word ordering problem can also include word choice, where only a subset of the input words are used to produce the output.

Word ordering is a difficult problem. Finding the best permutation for a set of words according to a bigram language model, for example, is NP-hard, which can be proved by linear reduction from the traveling salesman problem. In practice, exploring the whole search space of permutations is often prevented by adding constraints. In phrase-based machine translation (Koehn et al., 2003; Koehn et al., 2007), a distortion limit is used to constrain the position of output phrases. In syntax-based machine translation systems such as Wu (1997) and Chiang (2007), synchronous grammars limit the search space so that polynomial time inference is feasible. In fluency improvement (Blackwood et al., 2010), parts of translation hypotheses identified as having high local confidence are held fixed, so that word ordering elsewhere is strictly local.

Some recent work attempts to address the fundamental word ordering task directly, using syntactic models and heuristic search. Wan et al. (2009) uses a dependency grammar to solve word ordering, and Zhang and Clark (2011) uses CCG (Steedman, 2000) for word ordering and word choice. The use of syntax models makes their search problems harder than word permutation using an N-gram language model only. Both methods apply heuristic search. Zhang and Clark developed a bottom-up best-first algorithm to build output syntax trees from input words, where search is guided by learning for both efficiency and accuracy. The framework is flexible in allowing a large range of constraints to be added for particular tasks.

We extend the work of Zhang and Clark (2011) (Z&C) in two ways. First, we apply online large-margin training to guide search. Compared to the perceptron algorithm on "constituent level features" by Z&C, our training algorithm is theoretically more elegant (see Section 3) and converges more smoothly empirically (see Section 5). Using online large-margin training not only improves the output quality, but also allows the incorporation of an N-gram language-model into the system. N-gram models have been used as a standard component in statistical machine translation, but have not been applied to the syntactic model of Z&C. Intuitively, an N-gram model can improve local fluency when added to a syntax model. Our experiments show that a four-gram model trained using the English GigaWord corpus gave improvements when added to the syntax-based baseline system.

The contributions of this paper are as follows. First, we improve on the performance of the Z&C system for the challenging task of the general word ordering problem. Second, we develop a novel method for incorporating a large-scale language model into a syntax-based generation system. Finally, we analyse large-margin training in the context of learning-guided best-first search, offering a novel solution to this computationally hard problem.

2 The statistical model and decoding algorithm

We take Z&C as our baseline system. Given a multi-set of input words, the baseline system builds a CCG derivation by choosing and ordering words from the input set. The scoring model is trained using CCGBank (Hockenmaier and Steedman, 2007), and best-first decoding is applied. We apply the same decoding framework in this paper, but apply an improved training process, and incorporate an N-gram language model into the syntax model. In this section, we describe and discuss the baseline statistical model and decoding framework, motivating our extensions.

2.1 Combinatory Categorial Grammar

CCG, and parsing with CCG, has been described elsewhere (Clark and Curran, 2007; Hockenmaier and Steedman, 2002); here we provide only a short description.

CCG (Steedman, 2000) is a lexicalized grammar formalism, which associates each word in a sentence with a lexical category. There is a small number of basic lexical categories, such as noun (N), noun phrase (NP), and prepositional phrase (PP). Complex lexical categories are formed recursively from basic categories and slashes, which indicate the directions of arguments. The CCG grammar used by our system is read off the derivations in CCGbank, following Hockenmaier and Steedman (2002), meaning that the CCG combinatory rules are encoded as rule instances, together with a number of additional rules which deal with punctuation and type-changing. Given a sentence, its CCG derivation can be produced by first assigning a lexical category to each word, and then recursively applying CCG rules bottom-up.

2.2 The decoding algorithm

In the decoding algorithm, a hypothesis is an *edge*, which corresponds to a sub-tree in a CCG derivation. Edges are built bottom-up, starting from leaf edges, which are generated by assigning all possible lexical categories to each input word. Each leaf edge corresponds to an input word with a particular lexical category. Two existing edges can be combined if there exists a CCG rule which combines their category labels, and if they do not contain the same input word more times than its total count in the input. The resulting edge is assigned a category label according to the combinatory rule, and covers the concatenated surface strings of the two sub-edges in their order or combination. New edges can also be generated by applying unary rules to a single existing edge. Starting from the leaf edges, the bottom-up process is repeated until a goal edge is found, and its surface string is taken as the output.

This derivation-building process is reminiscent of a bottom-up CCG parser in the edge combination mechanism. However, it is fundamentally different from a bottom-up parser. Since, for the generation problem, the order of two edges in their combination is flexible, the search problem is much harder than that of a parser. With no input order specified, no efficient dynamic-programming algorithm is available, and less contextual information is available for disambiguation due to the lack of an input string.

In order to combat the large search space, best-first search is applied, where candidate hypotheses are ordered by their scores, and kept in an agenda, and a limited number of accepted hypotheses are recorded in a chart. Here the chart is essentially a set of beams, each of which contains the highest scored edges covering a particular number of words. Initially, all leaf edges are generated and scored, before they are put onto the agenda. During each step in the decoding process, the top edge from the agenda is expanded. If it is a goal edge, it is returned as the output, and the

Algorithm 1 The decoding algorithm.

```
a ← INITAGENDA( )
c ← INITCHART( )
while not TIMEOUT( ) do
    new ← []
    e ← POPBEST(a)
    if GOALTEST(e) then
        return e
    end if
    for e' ∈ UNARY(e, grammar) do
        APPEND(new, e)
    end for
    for ẽ ∈ c do
        if CANCOMBINE(e, ẽ) then
            e' ← BINARY(e, ẽ, grammar)
            APPEND(new, e')
        end if
        if CANCOMBINE(ẽ, e) then
            e' ← BINARY(ẽ, e, grammar)
            APPEND(new, e')
        end if
    end for
    for e' ∈ new do
        ADD(a, e')
    end for
    ADD(c, e)
end while
```

decoding finishes. Otherwise it is extended with unary rules, and combined with existing edges in the chart using binary rules to produce new edges. The resulting edges are scored and put onto the agenda, while the original edge is put onto the chart. The process repeats until a goal edge is found, or a timeout limit is reached. In the latter case, a default output is produced using existing edges in the chart.

Pseudocode for the decoder is shown as Algorithm 1. Again it is reminiscent of a best-first parser (Caraballo and Charniak, 1998) in the use of an agenda and a chart, but is fundamentally different due to the fact that there is no input order.

2.3 Statistical model and feature templates

The baseline system uses a linear model to score hypotheses. For an edge e, its score is defined as:

$$f(e) = \Phi(e) \cdot \theta,$$

where $\Phi(e)$ represents the feature vector of e and θ is the parameter vector of the model.

During decoding, feature vectors are computed incrementally. When an edge is constructed, its score is computed from the scores of its sub-edges and the incrementally added structure:

$$\begin{aligned} f(e) &= \Phi(e) \cdot \theta \\ &= \Big(\big(\sum_{e_s \in e} \Phi(e_s)\big) + \phi(e)\Big) \cdot \theta \\ &= \big(\sum_{e_s \in e} \Phi(e_s) \cdot \theta\big) + \phi(e) \cdot \theta \\ &= \big(\sum_{e_s \in e} f(e_s)\big) + \phi(e) \cdot \theta \end{aligned}$$

In the equation, $e_s \in e$ represents a sub-edge of e. Leaf edges do not have any sub-edges. Unary-branching edges have one sub-edge, and binary-branching edges have two sub-edges. The feature vector $\phi(e)$ represents the incremental structure when e is constructed over its sub-edges. It is called the "constituent-level feature vector" by Z&C. For leaf edges, $\phi(e)$ includes information about the lexical category label; for unary-branching edges, $\phi(e)$ includes information from the unary rule; for binary-branching edges, $\phi(e)$ includes information from the binary rule, and additionally the token, POS and lexical category bigrams and trigrams that result from the surface string concatenation of its sub-edges. The score $f(e)$ is therefore the sum of $f(e_s)$ (for all $e_s \in e$) plus $\phi(e) \cdot \theta$. The feature templates we use are the same as those in the baseline system.

An important aspect of the scoring model is that edges with different sizes are compared with each other during decoding. Edges with different sizes can have different numbers of features, which can make the training of a discriminative model more difficult. For example, a leaf edge with one word can be compared with an edge over the entire input. One way of reducing the effect of the size difference is to include the size of the edge as part of feature definitions, which can improve the comparability of edges of different sizes by reducing the number of features they have in common. Such features are applied by Z&C, and we make use of them here. Even with such features, the question of whether edges with different sizes are linearly separable is an empirical one.

3 Training

The efficiency of the decoding algorithm is dependent on the statistical model, since the best-first search is *guided* to a solution by the model, and a good model will lead to a solution being found more quickly. In the ideal situation for the best-first decoding algorithm, the model is perfect and the score of any gold-standard edge is higher than the score of any non-gold-standard edge. As a result, the top edge on the agenda is always a gold-standard edge, and therefore all edges on the chart are gold-standard before the gold-standard goal edge is found. In this oracle procedure, the minimum number of edges is expanded, and the output is correct. The best-first decoder is perfect in not only accuracy, but also speed. In practice this ideal situation is rarely met, but it determines the goal of the training algorithm: to produce the perfect model and hence decoder.

If we take gold-standard edges as positive examples, and non-gold-standard edges as negative examples, the goal of the training problem can be viewed as finding a large separating margin between the scores of positive and negative examples. However, it is infeasible to generate the full space of negative examples, which is factorial in the size of input. Like Z&C, we apply online learning, and generate negative examples based on the decoding algorithm.

Our training algorithm is shown as Algorithm 2. The algorithm is based on the decoder, where an agenda is used as a priority queue of edges to be expanded, and a set of accepted edges is kept in a chart. Similar to the decoding algorithm, the agenda is intialized using all possible leaf edges. During each step, the top of the agenda e is popped. If it is a gold-standard edge, it is expanded in exactly the same way as the decoder, with the newly generated edges being put onto the agenda, and e being inserted into the chart. If e is not a gold-standard edge, we take it as a negative example e_-, and take the lowest scored gold-standard edge on the agenda e_+ as a positive example, in order to make an udpate to the model parameter vector θ. Our parameter update algorithm is different from the baseline perceptron algorithm, as will be discussed later. After updating the parameters, the scores of agenda edges above and including e_-, together with all chart edges, are updated, and e_- is discarded before the start of the next processing step. By not putting any non-gold-standard edges onto the chart, the training speed is much faster; on the other hand a wide range of negative examples is pruned. We leave for further work possible alternative methods to generate more negative examples during training.

Algorithm 2 The training algorithm.

```
a ← INITAGENDA( )
c ← INITCHART( )
while not TIMEOUT( ) do
    new ← []
    e ← POPBEST(a)
    if GOLDSTANDARD(e) and GOALTEST(e)
then return e
    end if
    if not GOLDSTANDARD(e) then
        e_- ← e
        e_+ ← MINGOLD(a)
        UPDATEPARAMETERS(e_+, e_-)
        RECOMPUTESCORES(a, c)
        continue
    end if
    for e' ∈ UNARY(e, grammar) do
        APPEND(new, e)
    end for
    for ẽ ∈ c do
        if CANCOMBINE(e, ẽ) then
            e' ← BINARY(e, ẽ, grammar)
            APPEND(new, e')
        end if
        if CANCOMBINE(ẽ, e) then
            e' ← BINARY(ẽ, e, grammar)
            APPEND(new, e')
        end if
    end for
    for e' ∈ new do
        ADD(a, e')
    end for
    ADD(c, e)
end while
```

Another way of viewing the training process is that it pushes gold-standard edges towards the top of the agenda, and crucially pushes them above non-gold-standard edges. This is the view described by Z&C. Given a positive example e_+ and a negative example e_-, they use the perceptron algorithm to penalize the score for $\phi(e_-)$ and reward the score of $\phi(e_+)$, but do not update parameters for the sub-edges of e_+ and e_-. An argument for not penalizing the sub-edge scores for e_- is that the sub-edges must be gold-standard edges (since the training process is constructed so that only gold-standard edges are expanded). From the perspective of correctness, it is unnecessary to find a margin between the sub-edges of e_+ and those of e_-, since both are gold-standard edges.

However, since the score of an edge not only represents its correctness, but also affects its priority on the agenda, promoting the sub-edge of e_+ can lead to "easier" edges being constructed before "harder" ones (i.e. those that are less likely to be correct), and therefore improve the output accuracy. This perspective has been observed by other works of learning-guided-search (Shen et al., 2007; Shen and Joshi, 2008; Goldberg and Elhadad, 2010). Intuitively, the score difference between easy gold-standard and harder gold-standard edges should not be as great as the difference between gold-standard and non-gold-standard edges. The perceptron update cannot provide such control of separation, because the amount of update is fixed to 1.

As described earlier, we treat parameter update as finding a separation between correct and incorrect edges, in which the global feature vectors Φ, rather than ϕ, are considered. Given a positive example e_+ and a negative example e_-, we make a minimum update so that the score of e_+ is higher than that of e_- with some margin:

$$\theta \leftarrow \arg\min_{\theta'} \parallel \theta' - \theta_0 \parallel, \text{s.t.} \Phi(e_+)\theta' - \Phi(e_-)\theta' \geq 1$$

where θ_0 and θ denote the parameter vectors before and after the udpate, respectively. The update is similar to the update of online large-margin learning algorithms such as 1-best MIRA (Crammer et al., 2006), and has a closed-form solution:

$$\theta \leftarrow \theta_0 + \frac{f(e_-) - f(e_+) + 1}{\parallel \Phi(e_+) - \Phi(e_-) \parallel^2}(\Phi(e_+) - \Phi(e_-))$$

In this update, the global feature vectors $\Phi(e_+)$ and $\Phi(e_-)$ are used. Unlike Z&C, the scores of sub-edges of e_+ and e_- are also udpated, so that the sub-edges of e_- are less prioritized than those of e_+. We show empirically that this training algorithm significantly outperforms the perceptron training of the baseline system in Section 5. An advantage of our new training algorithm is that it enables the accommodation of a separately trained N-gram model into the system.

4 Incorporating an N-gram language model

Since the seminal work of the IBM models (Brown et al., 1993), N-gram language models have been used as a standard component in statistical machine translation systems to control output fluency. For the syntax-based generation system, the incorporation of an N-gram language model can potentially improve the local fluency of output sequences. In addition, the N-gram language model can be trained separately using a large amount of data, while the syntax-based model requires manual annotation for training.

The standard method for the combination of a syntax model and an N-gram model is linear interpolation. We incorporate fourgram, trigram and bigram scores into our syntax model, so that the score of an edge e becomes:

$$\begin{aligned} F(e) &= f(e) + g(e) \\ &= f(e) + \alpha \cdot g_{four}(e) + \beta \cdot g_{tri}(e) + \gamma \cdot g_{bi}(e), \end{aligned}$$

where f is the syntax model score, and g is the N-gram model score. g consists of three components, g_{four}, g_{tri} and g_{bi}, representing the log-probabilities of fourgrams, trigrams and bigrams from the language model, respectively. α, β and γ are the corresponding weights.

During decoding, $F(e)$ is computed incrementally. Again, denoting the sub-edges of e as e_s,

$$\begin{aligned} F(e) &= f(e) + g(e) \\ &= \Big(\sum_{e_s \in e} F(e_s)\Big) + \phi(e)\theta + g_\delta(e) \end{aligned}$$

Here $g_\delta(e) = \alpha \cdot g_{\delta four}(e) + \beta \cdot g_{\delta tri}(e) + \gamma \cdot g_{\delta bi}(e)$ is the sum of log-probabilities of the new N-grams resulting from the construction of e. For leaf edges and unary-branching edges, no new N-grams result from their construction (i.e. $g_\delta = 0$). For a binary-branching edge, new N-grams result from the surface-string concatenation of its sub-edges. The sum of log-probabilities of the new fourgrams, trigrams and bigrams contribute to g_δ with weights α, β and γ, respectively.

For training, there are at least three methods to tune α, β, γ and θ. One simple method is to train the syntax model θ independently, and select α, β, and γ empirically from a range of candidate values according to development tests. We call this method test-time interpolation. An alternative is to select α, β and γ first, initializing the vector θ as all zeroes, and then run the training algorithm for θ taking into account the N-gram language model. In this process, g is considered when finding a separation between positive and negative examples; the training algorithm finds a value of θ that best suits the precomputed α, β and γ values, together with the N-gram language model. We call this method g-precomputed interpolation. Yet another method is to initialize α, β, γ and θ as all zeroes, and run the training algorithm taking into account the N-gram language model. We call this method g-free interpolation.

The incorporation of an N-gram language model into the syntax-based generation system is weakly analogous to N-gram model insertion for syntax-based statistical machine translation systems, both of which apply a score from the N-gram model component in a derivation-building process. As discussed earlier, polynomial-time decoding is typically feasible for syntax-based machine translation systems without an N-gram language model, due to constraints from the grammar. In these cases, incorporation of N-gram language models can significantly increase the complexity of a dynamic-programming decoder (Bar-Hillel et al., 1961). Efficient search has been achieved using chart pruning (Chiang, 2007) and iterative numerical approaches to constrained optimization (Rush and Collins, 2011). In contrast, the incorporation of an N-gram language model into our decoder is more straightforward, and does not add to its asymptotic complexity, due to the heuristic nature of the decoder.

5 Experiments

We use sections 2–21 of CCGBank to train our syntax model, section 00 for development and section 23 for the final test. Derivations from CCGBank are transformed into inputs by turning their surface strings into multi-sets of words. Following Z&C, we treat base noun phrases (i.e. NPs that do not recursively contain other NPs) as atomic units for the input. Output sequences are compared with the original sentences to evaluate their quality. We follow previous work and use the BLEU metric (Papineni et al., 2002) to compare outputs with references.

Z&C use two methods to construct leaf edges. The first is to assign lexical categories according to a dictionary. There are 26.8 lexical categories for each word on average using this method, corresponding to 26.8 leaf edges. The other method is to use a pre-processing step — a CCG supertagger (Clark and Curran, 2007) — to prune candidate lexical categories according to the gold-standard sequence, assuming that for some problems the ambiguities can be reduced (e.g. when the input is already partly correctly ordered). Z&C use different probability cutoff levels (the β parameter in the supertagger) to control the pruning. Here we focus mainly on the dictionary method, which leaves lexical category disambiguation entirely to the generation system. For comparison, we also perform experiments with lexical category pruning. We chose $\beta = 0.0001$, which leaves 5.4 leaf edges per word on average.

CCGBank	Sentences	Tokens
training	39,604	929,552
development	1,913	45,422
GigaWord v4	**Sentences**	**Tokens**
AFP	30,363,052	684,910,697
XIN	15,982,098	340,666,976

Table 1: Number of sentences and tokens by language model source.

We used the SRILM Toolkit (Stolcke, 2002) to build a true-case 4-gram language model estimated over the CCGBank training and development data and a large additional collection of fluent sentences in the Agence France-Presse (AFP) and Xinhua News Agency (XIN) subsets of the English GigaWord Fourth Edition (Parker et al., 2009), a total of over 1 billion tokens. The GigaWord data was first pre-processed to replicate the CCGBank tokenization. The total number of sentences and tokens in each LM component is shown in Table 1. The language model vocabulary consists of the 46,574 words that occur in the concatenation of the CCGBank training, development, and test sets. The LM probabilities are estimated using modified Kneser-Ney smoothing (Kneser and Ney, 1995) with interpolation of lower n-gram orders.

5.1 Development experiments

A set of development test results without lexical category pruning (i.e. using the full dictionary) is shown in Table 2. We train the baseline system and our systems under various settings for 10 iterations, and measure the output BLEU scores after each iteration. The timeout value for each sentence is set to 5 seconds. The highest score (max BLEU) and averaged score (avg. BLEU) of each system over the 10 training iterations are shown in the table.

Method	max BLEU	avg. BLEU
baseline	38.47	37.36
margin	41.20	39.70
margin +LM (g-precomputed)	41.50	40.84
margin +LM ($\alpha = 0,\ \beta = 0,\ \gamma = 0$)	40.83	—
margin +LM ($\alpha = 0.08,\ \beta = 0.016,\ \gamma = 0.004$)	38.99	—
margin +LM ($\alpha = 0.4,\ \beta = 0.08,\ \gamma = 0.02$)	36.17	—
margin +LM ($\alpha = 0.8,\ \beta = 0.16,\ \gamma = 0.04$)	34.74	—

Table 2: Development experiments without lexical category pruning.

The first three rows represent the baseline system, our largin-margin training system (margin), and our system with the N-gram model incorporated using g-precomputed interpolation. For interpolation we manually chose $\alpha = 0.8, \beta = 0.16$ and $\gamma = 0.04$, respectively. These values could be optimized by development experiments with alternative configurations, which may lead to further improvements. Our system with large-margin training gives higher BLEU scores than the baseline system consistently over all iterations. The N-gram model led to further improvements.

The last four rows in the table show results of our system with the N-gram model added using test-time interpolation. The syntax model is trained with the optimal number of iterations, and different α, β, and γ values are used to integrate the language model. Compared with the system using no N-gram model (margin), test-time interpolation did not improve the accuracies.

The row with $\alpha, \beta, \gamma = 0$ represents our system with the N-gram model loaded, and the scores g_{four}, g_{tri} and g_{bi} computed for each N-gram during decoding, but the scores of edges are computed without using N-gram probabilities. The scoring model is the same as the syntax model (margin), but the results are lower than the row "margin", because computing N-gram probabilities made the system slower, exploring less hypotheses under the same timeout setting.[1]

The comparison between g-precomputed interpolation and test-time interpolation shows that the system gives better scores when the syntax model takes into consideration the N-gram model during training. One question that arises is whether g-free interpolation will outperform g-precomputed interpolation. g-free interpolation offers the freedom of α, β and γ during training, and can potentially reach a better combination of the parameter values. However, the training algorithm failed to converge with g-free interpolation. One possible explanation is that real-valued features from the language model made our large-margin training harder. Another possible reason is that our training process with heavy pruning does not accommodate this complex model.

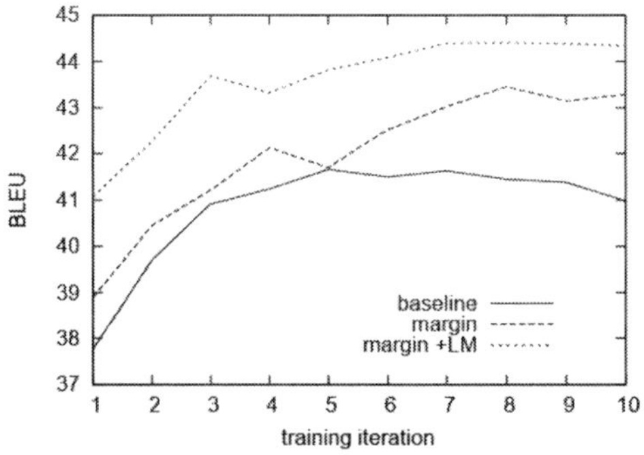

Figure 1: Development experiments with lexical category pruning ($\beta = 0.0001$).

Figure 1 shows a set of development experiments with lexical category pruning (with the supertagger parameter $\beta = 0.0001$). The scores of the three different systems are calculated by varying the number of training iterations. The large-margin training system (margin) gave consistently better scores than the baseline system, and adding a language model (margin +LM) improves the scores further.

Table 3 shows some manually chosen examples for which our system gave significant improvements over the baseline. For most other sentences the improvements are not as obvious. For each

[1]More decoding time could be given to the slower N-gram system, but we use 5 seconds as the timeout setting for all the experiments, giving the methods with the N-gram language model a slight disadvantage, as shown by the two rows "margin" and "margin +LM ($\alpha, \beta, \gamma = 0$).

baseline	margin	margin +LM
as a nonexecutive director Pierre Vinken , 61 years old , will join the board . 29 Nov.	61 years old , the board will join as a nonexecutive director Nov. 29 , Pierre Vinken .	as a nonexecutive director Pierre Vinken , 61 years old , will join the board Nov. 29 .
Lorillard nor smokers were aware of the Kent cigarettes of any research on the workers who studied the researchers	of any research who studied Neither the workers were aware of smokers on the Kent cigarettes nor the researchers	Neither Lorillard nor any research on the workers who studied the Kent cigarettes were aware of smokers of the researchers .
you But 35 years ago have to recognize that these events took place .	recognize But you took place that these events have to 35 years ago .	But you have to recognize that these events took place 35 years ago .
investors to pour cash into money funds continue in Despite yields recent declines	Despite investors , yields continue to pour into money funds recent declines in cash .	Despite investors , recent declines in yields continue to pour cash into money funds .
yielding The top money funds are currently well over 9 % .	The top money funds currently are yielding well over 9 % .	The top money funds are yielding well over 9 % currently .
where A buffet breakfast , held in the museum was food and drinks to . everyday visitors banned	everyday visitors are banned to where A buffet breakfast was held , food and drinks in the museum .	A buffet breakfast , everyday visitors are banned to where food and drinks was held in the museum .
A Commonwealth Edison spokesman said an administrative nightmare would be tracking down the past 3 12 years that the two million customers have . whose changed	tracking A Commonwealth Edison spokesman said that the two million customers whose addresses have changed down during the past 3 12 years would be an administrative nightmare .	an administrative nightmare whose addresses would be tracking down A Commonwealth Edison spokesman said that the two million customers have changed during the past 3 12 years .
The $ 2.5 billion Byron 1 plant , Ill. , was completed . near Rockford in 1985	The $ 2.5 billion Byron 1 plant was near completed in Rockford , Ill. , 1985 .	The $ 2.5 billion Byron 1 plant near Rockford , Ill. , was completed in 1985 .
will (During its centennial year , The Wall Street Journal report events of the past century that stand as milestones of American business history .)	as The Wall Street Journal (During its centennial year , milestones stand of American business history that will report events of the past century .)	During its centennial year events will report , The Wall Street Journal that stand as milestones of American business history (of the past century) .

Table 3: Some chosen examples with significant improvements (supertagger parameter $\beta = 0.0001$).

method, the examples are chosen from the development output with lexical category pruning, after the optimal number of training iterations, with the timeout set to 5s. We also tried manually selecting examples without lexical category pruning, but the improvements were not as obvious, partly because the overall fluency was lower for all the three systems.

Table 4 shows a set of examples chosen randomly from the development test outputs of our system with the N-gram model. The optimal number of training iterations is used, and a timeout of 1 minute is used in addition to the 5s timeout for comparison. With more time to decode each input, the system gave a BLEU score of 44.61, higher than 41.50 with the 5s timout.

While some of the outputs we examined are reasonably fluent, most are to some extent fragmentary.[2] In general, the system outputs are still far below human fluency. Some samples are syntactically grammatical, but are semantically anomalous. For example, person names are often confused with company names, verbs often take unrelated subjects and objects. The problem is much more severe for long sentences, which have more ambiguities. For specific tasks, extra information (such as the source text for machine translation) can be available to reduce ambiguities.

6 Final results

The final results of our system without lexical category pruning are shown in Table 5. Row "W09 CLE" and "W09 AB" show the results of the maximum spanning tree and assignment-based algorithms of Wan et al. (2009); rows "margin" and "margin +LM" show the results of our large-margin training system and our system with the N-gram model. All these results are directly comparable since we do not use any lexical category pruning for this set of results. For each of our systems, we fix the number of training iterations according to development test scores. Consistent with the development experiments, our sys-

[2]Part of the reason for some fragmentary outputs is the default output mechanism: partial derivations from the chart are greedily put together when timeout occurs before a goal hypothesis is found.

timeout = 5s	timeout = 1m
drooled the cars and drivers , like Fortune 500 executives . over the race	After schoolboys drooled over the cars and drivers , the race like Fortune 500 executives .
One big reason : thin margins .	One big reason : thin margins .
You or accountants look around ... and at an eye blinks . professional ballplayers	blinks nobody You or accountants look around ... and at an eye . professional ballplayers
most disturbing And of it , are educators , not students , for the wrongdoing is who .	And blamed for the wrongdoing , educators , not students who are disturbing , much of it is most .
defeat coaching aids the purpose of which is , He and other critics say can to . standardized tests learning progress	gauge coaching aids learning progress can and other critics say the purpose of which is to defeat , standardized tests .
The federal government of government debt because Congress has lifted the ceiling on U.S. savings bonds suspended sales	The federal government suspended sales of government debt because Congress has n't lifted the ceiling on U.S. savings bonds .

Table 4: Some examples chosen at random from development test outputs without lexical category pruning.

System	BLEU
W09 CLE	26.8
W09 AB	33.7
Z&C11	40.1
margin	42.5
margin +LM	43.8

Table 5: Test results without lexical category pruning.

System	BLEU
Z&C11	43.2
margin	44.7
margin +LM	46.1

Table 6: Test results with lexical category pruning (supertagger parameter $\beta = 0.0001$).

tem outperforms the baseline methods. The acuracies are significantly higher when the N-gram model is incorporated.

Table 6 compares our system with Z&C using lexical category pruning ($\beta = 0.0001$) and a 5s timeout for fair comparison. The results are similar to Table 5: our large-margin training systems outperforms the baseline by 1.5 BLEU points, and adding the N-gram model gave a further 1.4 point improvement. The scores could be significantly increased by using a larger timeout, as shown in our earlier development experiments.

7 Related Work

There is a recent line of research on text-to-text generation, which studies the linearization of dependency structures (Barzilay and McKeown, 2005; Filippova and Strube, 2007; Filippova and Strube, 2009; Bohnet et al., 2010; Guo et al., 2011). Unlike our system, and Wan et al. (2009), input dependencies provide additional information to these systems. Although the search space can be constrained by the assumption of projectivity, permutation of modifiers of the same head word makes exact inference for tree linearization intractable. The above systems typically apply approximate inference, such as beam-search. While syntax-based features are commonly used by these systems for linearization, Filippova and Strube (2009) apply a trigram model to control local fluency within constituents. A dependency-based N-gram model has also been shown effective for the linearization task (Guo et al., 2011).

The best-first inference and timeout mechanism of our system is similar to that of White (2004), a surface realizer from logical forms using CCG.

8 Conclusion

We studied the problem of word-ordering using a syntactic model and allowing permutation. We took the model of Zhang and Clark (2011) as the baseline, and extended it with online large-margin training and an N-gram language model. These extentions led to improvements in the BLEU evaluation. Analyzing the generated sentences suggests that, while highly fluent outputs can be produced for short sentences ($\leq$ 10 words), the system fluency in general is still way below human standard. Future work remains to apply the system as a component for specific text generation tasks, for example machine translation.

Acknowledgements

Yue Zhang and Stephen Clark are supported by the European Union Seventh Framework Programme (FP7-ICT-2009-4) under grant agreement no. 247762.

References

Yehoshua Bar-Hillel, M. Perles, and E. Shamir. 1961. On formal properties of simple phrase structure grammars. *Zeitschrift für Phonetik, Sprachwissenschaft und Kommunikationsforschung*, 14:143–172. Reprinted in Y. Bar-Hillel. (1964). *Language and Information: Selected Essays on their Theory and Application*, Addison-Wesley 1964, 116–150.

Regina Barzilay and Kathleen McKeown. 2005. Sentence fusion for multidocument news summarization. *Computational Linguistics*, 31(3):297–328.

Graeme Blackwood, Adrià de Gispert, and William Byrne. 2010. Fluency constraints for minimum Bayes-risk decoding of statistical machine translation lattices. In *Proceedings of the 23rd International Conference on Computational Linguistics (Coling 2010)*, pages 71–79, Beijing, China, August. Coling 2010 Organizing Committee.

Bernd Bohnet, Leo Wanner, Simon Mill, and Alicia Burga. 2010. Broad coverage multilingual deep sentence generation with a stochastic multi-level realizer. In *Proceedings of the 23rd International Conference on Computational Linguistics (Coling 2010)*, pages 98–106, Beijing, China, August. Coling 2010 Organizing Committee.

Peter F. Brown, Stephen Della Pietra, Vincent J. Della Pietra, and Robert L. Mercer. 1993. The mathematics of statistical machine translation: Parameter estimation. *Computational Linguistics*, 19(2):263–311.

Sharon A. Caraballo and Eugene Charniak. 1998. New figures of merit for best-first probabilistic chart parsing. *Comput. Linguist.*, 24:275–298, June.

David Chiang. 2007. Hierarchical Phrase-based Translation. *Computational Linguistics*, 33(2):201–228.

Stephen Clark and James R. Curran. 2007. Wide-coverage efficient statistical parsing with CCG and log-linear models. *Computational Linguistics*, 33(4):493–552.

Koby Crammer, Ofer Dekel, Joseph Keshet, Shai Shalev-Shwartz, and Yoram Singer. 2006. Online passive-aggressive algorithms. *Journal of Machine Learning Research*, 7:551–585.

Katja Filippova and Michael Strube. 2007. Generating constituent order in german clauses. In *Proceedings of the 45th Annual Meeting of the Association of Computational Linguistics*, pages 320–327, Prague, Czech Republic, June. Association for Computational Linguistics.

Katja Filippova and Michael Strube. 2009. Tree linearization in english: Improving language model based approaches. In *Proceedings of Human Language Technologies: The 2009 Annual Conference of the North American Chapter of the Association for Computational Linguistics, Companion Volume: Short Papers*, pages 225–228, Boulder, Colorado, June. Association for Computational Linguistics.

Yoav Goldberg and Michael Elhadad. 2010. An efficient algorithm for easy-first non-directional dependency parsing. In *Human Language Technologies: The 2010 Annual Conference of the North American Chapter of the Association for Computational Linguistics*, pages 742–750, Los Angeles, California, June. Association for Computational Linguistics.

Yuqing Guo, Deirdre Hogan, and Josef van Genabith. 2011. Dcu at generation challenges 2011 surface realisation track. In *Proceedings of the Generation Challenges Session at the 13th European Workshop on Natural Language Generation*, pages 227–229, Nancy, France, September. Association for Computational Linguistics.

Julia Hockenmaier and Mark Steedman. 2002. Generative models for statistical parsing with Combinatory Categorial Grammar. In *Proceedings of the 40th Meeting of the ACL*, pages 335–342, Philadelphia, PA.

Julia Hockenmaier and Mark Steedman. 2007. CCGbank: A corpus of CCG derivations and dependency structures extracted from the Penn Treebank. *Computational Linguistics*, 33(3):355–396.

R. Kneser and H. Ney. 1995. Improved backing-off for m-gram language modeling. In *International Conference on Acoustics, Speech, and Signal Processing, 1995. ICASSP-95*, volume 1, pages 181–184.

Philip Koehn, Franz Och, and Daniel Marcu. 2003. Statistical phrase-based translation. In *Proceedings of NAACL/HLT*, Edmonton, Canada, May.

Philipp Koehn, Hieu Hoang, Alexandra Birch, Chris Callison-Burch, Marcello Federico, Nicola Bertoldi, Brooke Cowan, Wade Shen, Christine Moran, Richard Zens, Chris Dyer, Ondrej Bojar, Alexandra Constantin, and Evan Herbst. 2007. Moses: Open source toolkit for statistical machine translation. In *Proceedings of the 45th Annual Meeting of the Association for Computational Linguistics Companion Volume Proceedings of the Demo and Poster Sessions*, pages 177–180, Prague, Czech Republic, June. Association for Computational Linguistics.

Kishore Papineni, Salim Roukos, Todd Ward, and Wei-Jing Zhu. 2002. Bleu: a method for automatic evaluation of machine translation. In *Proceedings of 40th Annual Meeting of the Association for Computational Linguistics*, pages 311–318, Philadelphia, Pennsylvania, USA, July. Association for Computational Linguistics.

Robert Parker, David Graff, Junbo Kong, Ke Chen, and Kazuaki Maeda. 2009. English Gigaword Fourth Edition, Linguistic Data Consortium.

Alexander M. Rush and Michael Collins. 2011. Exact decoding of syntactic translation models through lagrangian relaxation. In *Proceedings of the 49th Annual Meeting of the Association for Computational Linguistics: Human Language Technologies*, pages 72–82, Portland, Oregon, USA, June. Association for Computational Linguistics.

Libin Shen and Aravind Joshi. 2008. LTAG dependency parsing with bidirectional incremental construction. In *Proceedings of the 2008 Conference on Empirical Methods in Natural Language Processing*, pages 495–504, Honolulu, Hawaii, October. Association for Computational Linguistics.

Libin Shen, Giorgio Satta, and Aravind Joshi. 2007. Guided learning for bidirectional sequence classification. In *Proceedings of ACL*, pages 760–767, Prague, Czech Republic, June.

Mark Steedman. 2000. *The Syntactic Process*. The MIT Press, Cambridge, Mass.

Andreas Stolcke. 2002. SRILM - an extensible language modeling toolkit. In *Proceedings of the International Conference on Spoken Language Processing*, pages 901–904.

Stephen Wan, Mark Dras, Robert Dale, and Cécile Paris. 2009. Improving grammaticality in statistical sentence generation: Introducing a dependency spanning tree algorithm with an argument satisfaction model. In *Proceedings of the 12th Conference of the European Chapter of the ACL (EACL 2009)*, pages 852–860, Athens, Greece, March. Association for Computational Linguistics.

Michael White. 2004. Reining in CCG chart realization. In *Proc. INLG-04*, pages 182–191.

Dekai Wu. 1997. Stochastic inversion transduction grammars and bilingual parsing of parallel corpora. *Computational Linguistics*, 23(3).

Yue Zhang and Stephen Clark. 2011. Syntax-based grammaticality improvement using CCG and guided search. In *Proceedings of the 2011 Conference on Empirical Methods in Natural Language Processing*, pages 1147–1157, Edinburgh, Scotland, UK., July. Association for Computational Linguistics.

Midge: Generating Image Descriptions From Computer Vision Detections

Margaret Mitchell[†] **Jesse Dodge**[‡‡] **Amit Goyal**[††] **Kota Yamaguchi**[§] **Karl Stratos**[‖]
Xufeng Han[§] **Alyssa Mensch**[**] **Alex Berg**[§] **Tamara Berg**[§] **Hal Daumé III**[††]

[†]U. of Aberdeen and Oregon Health and Science University, m.mitchell@abdn.ac.uk
[§]Stony Brook University, {aberg,tlberg,xufhan,kyamagu}@cs.stonybrook.edu
[††]U. of Maryland, {hal,amit}@umiacs.umd.edu
[‖]Columbia University, stratos@cs.columbia.edu
[‡‡]U. of Washington, dodgejesse@gmail.com, [**]MIT, acmensch@mit.edu

Abstract

This paper introduces a novel generation system that composes humanlike descriptions of images from computer vision detections. By leveraging syntactically informed word co-occurrence statistics, the generator filters and constrains the noisy detections output from a vision system to generate syntactic trees that detail what the computer vision system sees. Results show that the generation system outperforms state-of-the-art systems, automatically generating some of the most natural image descriptions to date.

1 Introduction

It is becoming a real possibility for intelligent systems to talk about the visual world. New ways of mapping computer vision to generated language have emerged in the past few years, with a focus on pairing detections in an image to words (Farhadi et al., 2010; Li et al., 2011; Kulkarni et al., 2011; Yang et al., 2011). The goal in connecting vision to language has varied: systems have started producing language that is descriptive and poetic (Li et al., 2011), summaries that add content where the computer vision system does not (Yang et al., 2011), and captions copied directly from other images that are globally (Farhadi et al., 2010) and locally similar (Ordonez et al., 2011).

A commonality between all of these approaches is that they aim to produce natural-sounding descriptions from computer vision detections. This commonality is our starting point: We aim to design a system capable of producing natural-sounding descriptions from computer vision detections *that are flexible enough* to become more descriptive and poetic, or include likely information from a language model, or to be short and simple, but as true to the image as possible.

The bus by the road with a clear blue sky

Figure 1: Example image with generated description.

Rather than using a fixed template capable of generating one kind of utterance, our approach therefore lies in generating syntactic trees. We use a tree-generating process (Section 4.3) similar to a Tree Substitution Grammar, but preserving some of the idiosyncrasies of the Penn Treebank syntax (Marcus et al., 1995) on which most statistical parsers are developed. This allows us to automatically parse and train on an unlimited amount of text, creating data-driven models that flesh out descriptions around detected objects in a principled way, based on what is both likely and syntactically well-formed.

An example generated description is given in Figure 1, and example vision output/natural language generation (NLG) input is given in Figure 2. The system ("Midge") generates descriptions in present-tense, declarative phrases, as a naïve viewer without prior knowledge of the photograph's content.[1]

Midge is built using the following approach: An image processed by computer vision algorithms can be characterized as a triple $<A_i$, B_i, $C_i>$, where:

[1]Midge is available to try online at: http://recognition.cs.stonybrook.edu:8080/~mitchema/midge/.

stuff:	*sky*	.999	
	id:	1	
	atts:	clear:0.432, grey:0.853,	blue:0.945 white:0.501 ...
	b. box:	(1,1 440,141)	
stuff:	*road*	.908	
	id:	2	
	atts:	wooden:0.722	clear:0.020 ...
	b. box:	(1,236 188,94)	
object:	*bus*	.307	
	id:	3	
	atts:	black:0.872,	red:0.244 ...
	b. box:	(38,38 366,293)	
preps:	id 1, id 2: by	id 1, id 3: by	id 2, id 3: below

Figure 2: Example computer vision output and natural language generation input. Values correspond to scores from the vision detections.

- A_i is the set of object/stuff detections with bounding boxes and associated "attribute" detections within those bounding boxes.
- B_i is the set of action or pose detections associated to each $a_i \in A_i$.
- C_i is the set of spatial relationships that hold between the bounding boxes of each pair $a_i, a_j \in A_i$.

Similarly, a description of an image can be characterized as a triple $<A_d, B_d, C_d>$ where:

- A_d is the set of nouns in the description with associated modifiers.
- B_d is the set of verbs associated to each $a_d \in A_d$.
- C_d is the set of prepositions that hold between each pair of $a_d, a_e \in A_d$.

With this representation, mapping $<A_i, B_i, C_i>$ to $<A_d, B_d, C_d>$ is trivial. The problem then becomes: (1) How to filter out detections that are wrong; (2) how to order the objects so that they are mentioned in a natural way; (3) how to connect these ordered objects within a syntactically/semantically well-formed tree; and (4) how to add further descriptive information from language modeling alone, if required.

Our solution lies in using A_i and A_d as description anchors. In computer vision, object detections form the basis of action/pose, attribute, and spatial relationship detections; therefore, in our approach to language generation, nouns for the object detections are used as the basis for the description. Likelihood estimates of syntactic structure and word co-occurrence are conditioned on object nouns, and this enables each noun head in a description to select for the kinds of structures it tends to appear in (syntactic constraints) and the other words it tends to occur with (semantic constraints). This is a data-driven way to generate likely adjectives, prepositions, determiners, etc., taking the intersection of what the vision system predicts and how the object noun tends to be described.

2 Background

Our approach to describing images starts with a system from Kulkarni et al. (2011) that composes novel captions for images in the PASCAL sentence data set,[2] introduced in Rashtchian et al. (2010). This provides multiple object detections based on Felzenszwalb's mixtures of multiscale deformable parts models (Felzenszwalb et al., 2008), and stuff detections (roughly, mass nouns, things like sky and grass) based on linear SVMs for low level region features.

Appearance characteristics are predicted using trained detectors for colors, shapes, textures, and materials, an idea originally introduced in Farhadi et al. (2009). Local texture, Histograms of Oriented Gradients (HOG) (Dalal and Triggs, 2005), edge, and color descriptors inside the bounding box of a recognized object are binned into histograms for a vision system to learn to recognize when an object is rectangular, wooden, metal, etc. Finally, simple preposition functions are used to compute the spatial relations between objects based on their bounding boxes.

The original Kulkarni et al. (2011) system generates descriptions with a template, filling in slots by combining computer vision outputs with text based statistics in a conditional random field to predict the most likely image labeling. Template-based generation is also used in the recent Yang et al. (2011) system, which fills in likely verbs and prepositions by dependency parsing the human-written UIUC Pascal-VOC dataset (Farhadi et al., 2010) and selecting the dependent/head relation with the highest log likelihood ratio.

Template-based generation is useful for automatically generating consistent sentences, however, if the goal is to vary or add to the text produced, it may be suboptimal (cf. Reiter and Dale (1997)). Work that does not use template-based generation includes Yao et al. (2010), who generate syntactic trees, similar to the approach in this

[2]http://vision.cs.uiuc.edu/pascal-sentences/

Kulkarni et al.: This is a picture of three persons, one bottle and one diningtable. The first rusty person is beside the second person. The rusty bottle is near the first rusty person, and within the colorful diningtable. The second person is by the third rusty person. The colorful diningtable is near the first rusty person, and near the second person, and near the third rusty person.	**Kulkarni et al.:** This is a picture of two pottedplants, one dog and one person. The black dog is by the black person, and near the second feathered pottedplant.
Yang et al.: Three people are showing the bottle on the street	**Yang et al.:** The person is sitting in the chair in the room
Midge: people with a bottle at the table	**Midge:** a person in black with a black dog by potted plants

Figure 3: Descriptions generated by Midge, Kulkarni et al. (2011) and Yang et al. (2011) on the same images. Midge uses the Kulkarni et al. (2011) front-end, and so outputs are directly comparable.

paper. However, their system is not automatic, requiring extensive hand-coded semantic and syntactic details. Another approach is provided in Li et al. (2011), who use image detections to select and combine web-scale n-grams (Brants and Franz, 2006). This automatically generates descriptions that are either poetic or strange (e.g., "tree snowing black train").

A different line of work transfers captions of similar images directly to a query image. Farhadi et al. (2010) use <object,action,scene> triples predicted from the visual characteristics of the image to find potential captions. Ordonez et al. (2011) use global image matching with local reordering from a much larger set of captioned photographs. These transfer-based approaches result in natural captions (they are written by humans) that may not actually be true of the image.

This work learns and builds from these approaches. Following Kulkarni et al. and Li et al., the system uses large-scale text corpora to estimate likely words around object detections. Following Yang et al., the system can hallucinate likely words using word co-occurrence statistics alone. And following Yao et al., the system aims

black, blue, brown, colorful, golden, gray, green, orange, pink, red, silver, white, yellow, bare, clear, cute, dirty, feathered, flying, furry, pine, plastic, rectangular, rusty, shiny, spotted, striped, wooden

Table 1: Modifiers used to extract training corpus.

for naturally varied but well-formed text, generating syntactic trees rather than filling in a template.

In addition to these tasks, Midge automatically decides what the subject and objects of the description will be, leverages the collected word co-occurrence statistics to filter possible incorrect detections, and offers the flexibility to be as descriptive or as terse as possible, specified by the user at run-time. The end result is a fully automatic vision-to-language system that is beginning to generate syntactically and semantically well-formed descriptions with naturalistic variation. Example descriptions are given in Figures 4 and 5, and descriptions from other recent systems are given in Figure 3.

The results are promising, but it is important to note that Midge is a first-pass system through the steps necessary to connect vision to language at a deep syntactic/semantic level. As such, it uses basic solutions at each stage of the process, which may be improved: Midge serves as an illustration of the types of issues that should be handled to automatically generate syntactic trees from vision detections, and offers some possible solutions. It is evaluated against the Kulkarni et al. system, the Yang et al. system, and human-written descriptions on the same set of images in Section 5, and is found to significantly outperform the automatic systems.

3 Learning from Descriptive Text

To train our system on how people describe images, we use 700,000 (Flickr, 2011) images with associated descriptions from the dataset in Ordonez et al. (2011). This is separate from our evaluation image set, consisting of 840 PASCAL images. The Flickr data is messier than datasets created specifically for vision training, but provides the largest corpus of natural descriptions of images to date.

We normalize the text by removing emoticons and mark-up language, and parse each caption using the Berkeley parser (Petrov, 2010). Once parsed, we can extract syntactic information for individual (word, tag) pairs.

a cow with green grass | sheep with a gray sky by the road | people with boats | a brown cow | people at a wooden table

Figure 4: Example generated outputs.

Awkward Prepositions | **Incorrect Detections**

a person *on* the dog | boats *under* the sky | a black bicycle *at* a green potted plant | *the sky* | a *yellow* bus with people | cows by black *sheep* by the road

Figure 5: Example generated outputs: Not quite right

We compute the probabilities for different prenominal modifiers (*shiny*, *clear*, *glowing*, ...) and determiners (*a/an*, *the*, `None`, ...) given a head noun in a noun phrase (NP), as well as the probabilities for each head noun in larger constructions, listed in Section 4.3. Probabilities are conditioned only on open-class words, specifically, nouns and verbs. This means that a closed-class word (such as a preposition) is never used to generate an open-class word.

In addition to co-occurrence statistics, the parsed Flickr data adds to our understanding of the basic characteristics of visually descriptive text. Using WordNet (Miller, 1995) to automatically determine whether a head noun is a physical object or not, we find that 92% of the sentences have no more than 3 physical objects. This informs generation by placing a cap on how many objects are mentioned in each descriptive sentence: When more than 3 objects are detected, the system splits the description over several sentences. We also find that many of the descriptions are not sentences as well (tagged as S, 58% of the data), but quite commonly noun phrases (tagged as NP, 28% of the data), and expect that the number of noun phrases that form descriptions will be much higher with domain adaptation. This also informs generation, and the system is capable of generating both sentences (contains a main verb) and noun phrases (no main verb) in the final image description. We use the term 'sentence' in the rest of this paper to refer to both kinds of complex phrases.

4 Generation

Following Penn Treebank parsing guidelines (Marcus et al., 1995), the relationship between two head nouns in a sentence can usually be characterized among the following:

1. prepositional (a boy *on* the table)
2. verbal (a boy *cleans* the table)
3. verb with preposition (a boy *sits on* the table)
4. verb with particle (a boy *cleans up* the table)
5. verb with S or SBAR complement (a boy sees *that* the table is clean)

The generation system focuses on the first three kinds of relationships, which capture a wide range of utterances. The process of generation is approached as a problem of generating a semantically and syntactically well-formed tree based on object nouns. These serve as head noun anchors in a lexicalized syntactic derivation process that we call *tree growth*.

Vision detections are associated to a {tag word} pair, and the model fleshes out the tree details around head noun anchors by utilizing syntactic dependencies between words learned from the Flickr data discussed in Section 3. The analogy of growing a tree is quite appropriate here, where nouns are bundles of constraints akin to seeds, giving rise to the rest of the tree based on the lexicalized subtrees in which the nouns are likely to occur. An example generated tree structure is shown in Figure 6, with noun anchors in bold.

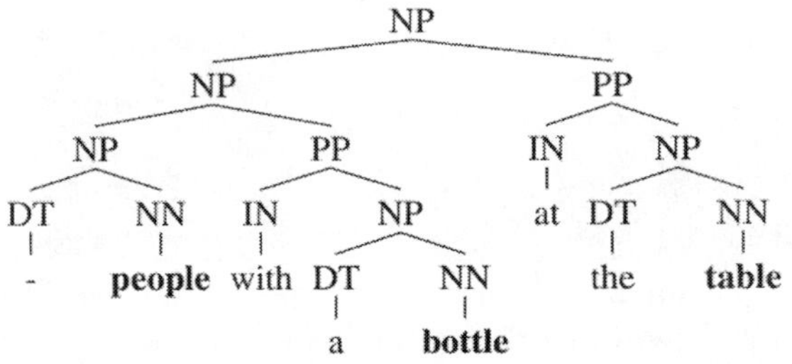

Figure 6: Tree generated from tree growth process.

Midge was developed using detections run on Flickr images, incorporating action/pose detections for verbs as well as object detections for nouns. In testing, we generate descriptions for the PASCAL images, which have been used in earlier work on the vision-to-language connection (Kulkarni et al., 2011; Yang et al., 2011), and allows us to compare systems directly. Action and pose detection for this data set still does not work well, and so the system does not receive these detections from the vision front-end. However, the system can still generate verbs when action and pose detectors have been run, and this framework allows the system to "hallucinate" likely verbal constructions between objects if specified at runtime. A similar approach was taken in Yang et al. (2011). Some examples are given in Figure 7.

We follow a three-tiered generation process (Reiter and Dale, 2000), utilizing *content determination* to first cluster and order the object nouns, create their local subtrees, and filter incorrect detections; *microplanning* to construct full syntactic trees around the noun clusters, and *surface realization* to order selected modifiers, realize them as postnominal or prenominal, and select final outputs. The system follows an overgenerate-and-select approach (Langkilde and Knight, 1998), which allows different final trees to be selected with different settings.

4.1 Knowledge Base

Midge uses a knowledge base that stores models for different tasks during generation. These models are primarily data-driven, but we also include a hand-built component to handle a small set of rules. The data-driven component provides the syntactically informed word co-occurrence statistics learned from the Flickr data, a model for ordering the selected nouns in a sentence, and a model to change computer vision attributes to attribute:value pairs. Below, we discuss the three main data-driven models within the generation pipeline. The hand-built component contains plural forms of singular nouns, the list of possible spatial relations shown in Table 3, and a mapping between attribute values and modifier surface forms (e.g., a *green* detection for *person* is to be realized as the postnominal modifier *in green*).

Unordered		Ordered
bottle, table, person	→	*person, bottle, table*
road, sky, cow	→	*cow, road, sky*

Figure 8: Example nominal orderings.

4.2 Content Determination

4.2.1 Step 1: Group the Nouns

An initial set of object detections must first be split into clusters that give rise to different sentences. If more than 3 objects are detected in the image, the system begins splitting these into different noun groups. In future work, we aim to compare principled approaches to this task, e.g., using mutual information to cluster similar nouns together. The current system randomizes which nouns appear in the same group.

4.2.2 Step 2: Order the Nouns

Each group of nouns are then ordered to determine when they are mentioned in a sentence. Because the system generates declarative sentences, this automatically determines the subject and objects. This is a novel contribution for a general problem in NLG, and initial evaluation (Section 5) suggests it works reasonably well.

To build the nominal ordering model, we use WordNet to associate all head nouns in the Flickr data to all of their hypernyms. A description is represented as an ordered set $[a_1...a_n]$ where each a_p is a noun with position p in the set of head nouns in the sentence. For the position p_i of each hypernym h_a in each sentence with n head nouns, we estimate $\text{p}(p_i|n, h_a)$.

During generation, the system greedily maximizes $\text{p}(p_i|n, h_a)$ until all nouns have been ordered. Example orderings are shown in Figure 8. This model automatically places animate objects near the beginning of a sentence, which follows psycholinguistic work in object naming (Branigan et al., 2007).

4.2.3 Step 3: Filter Incorrect Attributes

For the system to be able to extend coverage as new computer vision attribute detections become available, we develop a method to automatically

A person sitting on a sofa | Cows grazing | Airplanes flying | A person walking a dog

Figure 7: Hallucinating: Creating likely actions. Straightforward to do, but can often be wrong.

COLOR	purple blue green red white ...
MATERIAL	plastic wooden silver ...
SURFACE	furry fluffy hard soft ...
QUALITY	shiny rust dirty broken ...

Table 2: Example attribute classes and values.

group adjectives into broader attribute classes,[3] and the generation system uses these classes when deciding how to describe objects. To group adjectives, we use a bootstrapping technique (Kozareva et al., 2008) that learns which adjectives tend to co-occur, and groups these together to form an attribute class. Co-occurrence is computed using cosine (distributional) similarity between adjectives, considering adjacent nouns as context (i.e., JJ NN constructions). Contexts (nouns) for adjectives are weighted using Pointwise Mutual Information and only the top 1000 nouns are selected for every adjective. Some of the learned attribute classes are given in Table 2.

In the Flickr corpus, we find that each attribute (COLOR, SIZE, etc.), rarely has more than a single value in the final description, with the most common (COLOR) co-occurring less than 2% of the time. Midge enforces this idea to select the most likely word v for each attribute from the detections. In a noun phrase headed by an object noun, NP{NN noun}, the prenominal adjective (JJ v) for each attribute is selected using maximum likelihood.

4.2.4 Step 4: Group Plurals

How to generate natural-sounding spatial relations and modifiers for a set of objects, as opposed to a single object, is still an open problem (Funakoshi et al., 2004; Gatt, 2006). In this work, we use a simple method to group all same-type objects together, associate them to the plural form listed in the KB, discard the modifiers, and return spatial relations based on the first recognized member of the group.

4.2.5 Step 5: Gather Local Subtrees Around Object Nouns

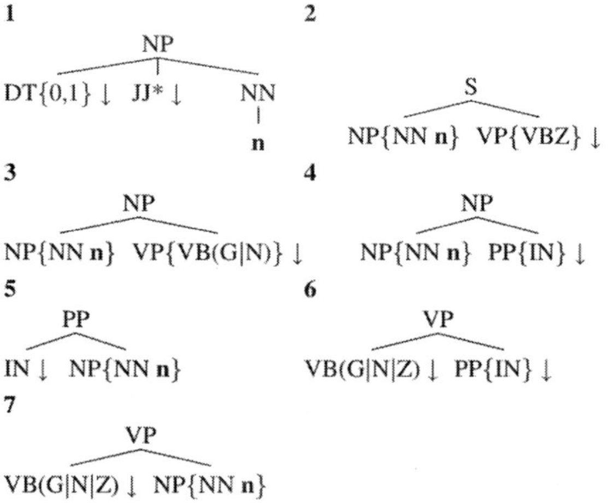

Figure 9: Initial subtree frames for generation, present-tense declarative phrases. ↓ marks a substitution site, * marks ≥ 0 sister nodes of this type permitted, {0,1} marks that this node can be included of excluded. **Input:** set of ordered nouns, **Output:** trees preserving nominal ordering.

Possible actions/poses and spatial relationships between objects nouns, represented by verbs and prepositions, are selected using the subtree frames listed in Figure 9. Each head noun selects for its likely local subtrees, some of which are not fully formed until the Microplanning stage. As an example of how this process works, see Figure 10, which illustrates the combination of Trees 4 and 5. For simplicity, we do not include the selection of further subtrees. The subject noun *duck* selects for prepositional phrases headed by different prepositions, and the object noun *grass* selects for prepositions that head the prepositional phrase in which it is embedded. Full PP subtrees are created during Microplanning by taking the intersection of both.

The leftmost noun in the sequence is given a rightward directionality constraint, placing it as the subject of the sentence, and so it will only se-

[3] What in computer vision are called *attributes* are called *values* in NLG. A value like *red* belongs to a COLOR attribute, and we use this distinction in the system.

a over b	a above b	b below a	b beneath a	a by b	b by a	a on b	b under a
	b underneath a	a upon b	a over b				
a by b	a against b	b against a	b around a	a around b	a at b	b at a	a beside b
	b beside a	a by b	b by a	a near b	b near a	b with a	a with b
a in b	a in b	b outside a	a within b	a by b	b by a		

Table 3: Possible prepositions from bounding boxes.

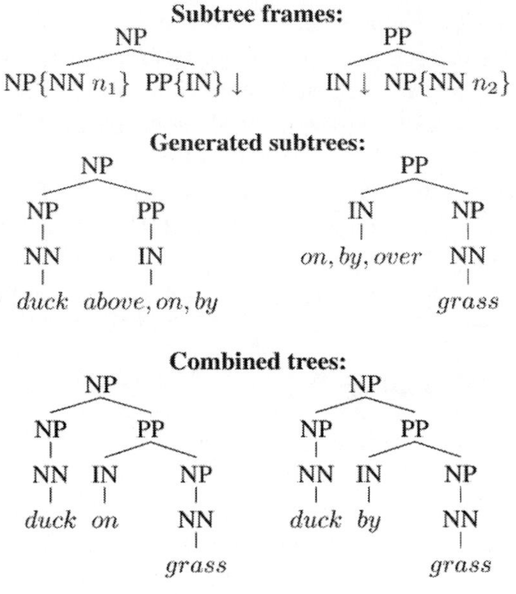

Figure 10: Example derivation.

lect for trees that expand to the right. The rightmost noun is given a leftward directionality constraint, placing it as an object, and so it will only select for trees that expand to its left. The noun in the middle, if there is one, selects for all its local subtrees, combining first with a noun to its right or to its left. We now walk through the derivation process for each of the listed subtree frames. Because we are following an overgenerate-and-select approach, all combinations above a probability threshold α and an observation cutoff γ are created.

Tree 1:
Collect all NP $\rightarrow$ (DT *det*) (JJ *adj*)* (NN *noun*) and NP $\rightarrow$ (JJ *adj*)* (NN *noun*) subtrees, where:

- p((JJ *adj*)|(NN *noun*)) $> \alpha$ for each *adj*
- p((DT *det*)|JJ, (NN *noun*)) $> \alpha$, and the probability of a determiner for the head noun is higher than the probability of no determiner.

Any number of adjectives (including none) may be generated, and we include the presence or absence of an adjective when calculating which determiner to include.

The reasoning behind the generation of these subtrees is to automatically learn whether to treat a given noun as a mass or count noun (not taking a determiner or taking a determiner, respectively) or as a given or new noun (phrases like *a sky* sound unnatural because *sky* is given knowledge, requiring the definite article *the*). The selection of determiner is not independent of the selection of adjective; *a sky* may sound unnatural, but *a blue sky* is fine. These trees take the dependency between determiner and adjective into account.

Trees 2 and 3:
Collect beginnings of VP subtrees headed by (VBZ *verb*), (VBG *verb*), and (VBN *verb*), notated here as VP{VBX *verb*}, where:

- p(VP{VBX *verb*}|NP{NN *noun*}=SUBJ) $> \alpha$

Tree 4:
Collect beginnings of PP subtrees headed by (IN *prep*), where:

- p(PP{IN *prep*}|NP{NN *noun*}=SUBJ) $> \alpha$

Tree 5:
Collect PP subtrees headed by (IN *prep*) with NP complements (OBJ) headed by (NN *noun*), where:

- p(PP{IN *prep*}|NP{NN *noun*}=OBJ) $> \alpha$

Tree 6:
Collect VP subtrees headed by (VBX *verb*) with embedded PP complements, where:

- p(PP{IN *prep*}|VP{VBX *verb*}=SUBJ) $> \alpha$

Tree 7:
Collect VP subtrees headed by (VBX *verb*) with embedded NP objects, where:

- p(VP{VBX *verb*}|NP{NN *noun*}=OBJ) $> \alpha$

4.3 Microplanning

4.3.1 Step 6: Create Full Trees

In Microplanning, full trees are created by taking the intersection of the subtrees created in Content Determination. Because the nouns are ordered, it is straightforward to combine the subtrees surrounding a noun in position 1 with subtrees surrounding a noun in position 2. Two

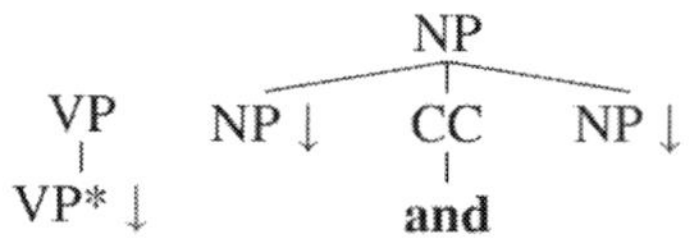

Figure 11: Auxiliary trees for generation.

further trees are necessary to allow the subtrees gathered to combine within the Penn Treebank syntax. These are given in Figure 11. If two nouns in a proposed sentence cannot be combined with prepositions or verbs, we backoff to combine them using (CC and).

Stepping through this process, all nouns will have a set of subtrees selected by Tree 1. Prepositional relationships between nouns are created by substituting Tree 1 subtrees into the NP nodes of Trees 4 and 5, as shown in Figure 10. Verbal relationships between nouns are created by substituting Tree 1 subtrees into Trees 2, 3, and 7. Verb with preposition relationships are created between nouns by substituting the VBX node in Tree 6 with the corresponding node in Trees 2 and 3 to grow the tree to the right, and the PP node in Tree 6 with the corresponding node in Tree 5 to grow the tree to the left. Generation of a full tree stops when all nouns in a group are dominated by the same node, either an S or NP.

4.4 Surface Realization

In the surface realization stage, the system selects a single tree from the generated set of possible trees and removes mark-up to produce a final string. This is also the stage where punctuation may be added. Different strings may be generated depending on different specifications from the user, as discussed at the beginning of Section 4 and shown in the online demo. To evaluate the system against other systems, we specify that the system should (1) not hallucinate likely verbs; and (2) return the longest string possible.

4.4.1 Step 7: Get Final Tree, Clear Mark-Up

We explored two methods for selecting a final string. In one method, a trigram language model built using the Europarl (Koehn, 2005) data with start/end symbols returns the highest-scoring description (normalizing for length). In the second method, we limit the generation system to select the most likely closed-class words (determiners, prepositions) while building the subtrees, overgenerating all possible adjective combinations. The final string is then the one with the most words. We find that the second method produces descriptions that seem more natural and varied than the n-gram ranking method for our development set, and so use the longest string method in evaluation.

4.4.2 Step 8: Prenominal Modifier Ordering

To order sets of selected adjectives, we use the top-scoring prenominal modifier ordering model discussed in Mitchell et al. (2011). This is an n-gram model constructed over noun phrases that were extracted from an automatically parsed version of the New York Times portion of the Gigaword corpus (Graff and Cieri, 2003). With this in place, *blue clear* sky becomes *clear blue* sky, *wooden brown* table becomes *brown wooden* table, etc.

5 Evaluation

Each set of sentences is generated with α (likelihood cutoff) set to .01 and γ (observation count cutoff) set to 3. We compare the system against human-written descriptions and two state-of-the-art vision-to-language systems, the Kulkarni et al. (2011) and Yang et al. (2011) systems.

Human judgments were collected using Amazon's Mechanical Turk (Amazon, 2011). We follow recommended practices for evaluating an NLG system (Reiter and Belz, 2009) and for running a study on Mechanical Turk (Callison-Burch and Dredze, 2010), using a balanced design with each subject rating 3 descriptions from each system. Subjects rated their level of agreement on a 5-point Likert scale including a neutral middle position, and since quality ratings are ordinal (points are not necessarily equidistant), we evaluate responses using a non-parametric test. Participants that took less than 3 minutes to answer all 60 questions and did not include a humanlike rating for at least 1 of the 3 human-written descriptions were removed and replaced. It is important to note that this evaluation compares full generation systems; many factors are at play in each system that may also influence participants' perception, e.g., sentence length (Napoles et al., 2011) and punctuation decisions.

The systems are evaluated on a set of 840 images evaluated in the original Kulkarni et al. (2011) system. Participants were asked to judge the statements given in Figure 12, from Strongly Disagree to Strongly Agree.

	Grammaticality	Main Aspects	Correctness	Order	Humanlikeness
Human	4 (3.77, 1.19)	4 (4.09, 0.97)	4 (3.81, 1.11)	4 (3.88, 1.05)	4 (3.88, 0.96)
Midge	3 (2.95, 1.42)	3 (2.86, 1.35)	3 (2.95, 1.34)	3 (2.92, 1.25)	3 (3.16, 1.17)
Kulkarni et al. 2011	3 (2.83, 1.37)	3 (2.84, 1.33)	3 (2.76, 1.34)	3 (2.78, 1.23)	3 (3.13, 1.23)
Yang et al. 2011	3 (2.95, 1.49)	2 (2.31, 1.30)	2 (2.46, 1.36)	2 (2.53, 1.26)	3 (2.97, 1.23)

Table 4: Median scores for systems, mean and standard deviation in parentheses. Distance between points on the rating scale cannot be assumed to be equidistant, and so we analyze results using a non-parametric test.

GRAMMATICALITY:
This description is **grammatically correct**.
MAIN ASPECTS:
This description **describes the main aspects** of this image.
CORRECTNESS:
This description **does not include extraneous** or incorrect information.
ORDER:
The objects described are mentioned in **a reasonable order**.
HUMANLIKENESS:
It sounds like a **person wrote** this description.

Figure 12: Mechanical Turk prompts.

We report the scores for the systems in Table 4. Results are analyzed using the non-parametric Wilcoxon Signed-Rank test, which uses median values to compare the different systems. Midge outperforms all recent automatic approaches on CORRECTNESS and ORDER, and Yang et al. additionally on HUMANLIKENESS and MAIN ASPECTS. Differences between Midge and Kulkarni et al. are significant at $p < .01$; Midge and Yang et al. at $p < .001$. For all metrics, human-written descriptions still outperform automatic approaches ($p < .001$).

These findings are striking, particularly because Midge uses the same input as the Kulkarni et al. system. Using syntactically informed word co-occurrence statistics from a large corpus of descriptive text improves over state-of-the-art, allowing syntactic trees to be generated that capture the variation of natural language.

6 Discussion

Midge automatically generates language that is as good as or better than template-based systems, tying vision to language at a syntactic/semantic level to produce natural language descriptions. Results are promising, but, there is more work to be done: Evaluators can still tell a difference between human-written descriptions and automatically generated descriptions.

Improvements to the generated language are possible at both the vision side and the language side. On the computer vision side, incorrect objects are often detected and salient objects are often missed. Midge does not yet screen out unlikely objects or add likely objects, and so provides no filter for this. On the language side, likelihood is estimated directly, and the system primarily uses simple maximum likelihood estimations to combine subtrees. The descriptive corpus that informs the system is not parsed with a domain-adapted parser; with this in place, the syntactic constructions that Midge learns will better reflect the constructions that people use.

In future work, we hope to address these issues as well as advance the syntactic derivation process, providing an adjunction operation (for example, to add likely adjectives or adverbs based on language alone). We would also like to incorporate meta-data – even when no vision detection fires for an image, the system may be able to generate descriptions of the time and place where an image was taken based on the image file alone.

7 Conclusion

We have introduced a generation system that uses a new approach to generating language, tying a syntactic model to computer vision detections. Midge generates a well-formed description of an image by filtering attribute detections that are unlikely and placing objects into an ordered syntactic structure. Humans judge Midge's output to be the most natural descriptions of images generated thus far. The methods described here are promising for generating natural language descriptions of the visual world, and we hope to expand and refine the system to capture further linguistic phenomena.

8 Acknowledgements

Thanks to the Johns Hopkins CLSP summer workshop 2011 for making this system possible, and to reviewers for helpful comments. This work is supported in part by Michael Collins and by NSF Faculty Early Career Development (CAREER) Award #1054133.

References

Amazon. 2011. Amazon mechanical turk: Artificial artificial intelligence.

Holly P. Branigan, Martin J. Pickering, and Mikihiro Tanaka. 2007. Contributions of animacy to grammatical function assignment and word order during production. *Lingua*, 118(2):172–189.

Thorsten Brants and Alex Franz. 2006. Web 1T 5-gram version 1.

Chris Callison-Burch and Mark Dredze. 2010. Creating speech and language data with Amazon's Mechanical Turk. *NAACL 2010 Workshop on Creating Speech and Language Data with Amazon's Mechanical Turk*.

Navneet Dalal and Bill Triggs. 2005. Histograms of oriented gradients for human detections. *Proceedings of CVPR 2005*.

Ali Farhadi, Ian Endres, Derek Hoiem, and David Forsyth. 2009. Describing objects by their attributes. *Proceedings of CVPR 2009*.

Ali Farhadi, Mohsen Hejrati, Mohammad Amin Sadeghi, Peter Young, Cyrus Rashtchian, Julia Hockenmaier, and David Forsyth. 2010. Every picture tells a story: generating sentences for images. *Proceedings of ECCV 2010*.

Pedro Felzenszwalb, David McAllester, and Deva Ramaman. 2008. A discriminatively trained, multiscale, deformable part model. *Proceedings of CVPR 2008*.

Flickr. 2011. http://www.flickr.com. Accessed 1.Sep.11.

Kotaro Funakoshi, Satoru Watanabe, Naoko Kuriyama, and Takenobu Tokunaga. 2004. Generating referring expressions using perceptual groups. *Proceedings of the 3rd INLG*.

Albert Gatt. 2006. Generating collective spatial references. *Proceedings of the 28th CogSci*.

David Graff and Christopher Cieri. 2003. *English Gigaword*. Linguistic Data Consortium, Philadelphia, PA. LDC Catalog No. LDC2003T05.

Philipp Koehn. 2005. Europarl: A parallel corpus for statistical machine translation. *MT Summit*. http://www.statmt.org/europarl/.

Zornitsa Kozareva, Ellen Riloff, and Eduard Hovy. 2008. Semantic class learning from the web with hyponym pattern linkage graphs. *Proceedings of ACL-08: HLT*.

Girish Kulkarni, Visruth Premraj, Sagnik Dhar, Siming Li, Yejin Choi, Alexander C. Berg, and Tamara Berg. 2011. Baby talk: Understanding and generating image descriptions. *Proceedings of the 24th CVPR*.

Irene Langkilde and Kevin Knight. 1998. Generation that exploits corpus-based statistical knowledge. *Proceedings of the 36th ACL*.

Siming Li, Girish Kulkarni, Tamara L. Berg, Alexander C. Berg, and Yejin Choi. 2011. Composing simple image descriptions using web-scale n-grams. *Proceedings of CoNLL 2011*.

Mitchell Marcus, Ann Bies, Constance Cooper, Mark Ferguson, and Alyson Littman. 1995. Treebank II bracketing guide.

George A. Miller. 1995. WordNet: A lexical database for english. *Communications of the ACM*, 38(11):39–41.

Margaret Mitchell, Aaron Dunlop, and Brian Roark. 2011. Semi-supervised modeling for prenominal modifier ordering. *Proceedings of the 49th ACL:HLT*.

Courtney Napoles, Benjamin Van Durme, and Chris Callison-Burch. 2011. Evaluating sentence compression: Pitfalls and suggested remedies. *ACL-HLT Workshop on Monolingual Text-To-Text Generation*.

Vicente Ordonez, Girish Kulkarni, and Tamara L Berg. 2011. Im2text: Describing images using 1 million captioned photographs. *Proceedings of NIPS 2011*.

Slav Petrov. 2010. Berkeley parser. GNU General Public License v.2.

Cyrus Rashtchian, Peter Young, Micah Hodosh, and Julia Hockenmaier. 2010. Collecting image annotations using amazon's mechanical turk. *Proceedings of the NAACL HLT 2010 Workshop on Creating Speech and Language Data with Amazon's Mechanical Turk*.

Ehud Reiter and Anja Belz. 2009. An investigation into the validity of some metrics for automatically evaluating natural language generation systems. *Computational Linguistics*, 35(4):529–558.

Ehud Reiter and Robert Dale. 1997. Building applied natural language generation systems. *Journal of Natural Language Engineering*, pages 57–87.

Ehud Reiter and Robert Dale. 2000. *Building Natural Language Generation Systems*. Cambridge University Press.

Yezhou Yang, Ching Lik Teo, Hal Daumé III, and Yiannis Aloimonos. 2011. Corpus-guided sentence generation of natural images. *Proceedings of EMNLP 2011*.

Benjamin Z. Yao, Xiong Yang, Liang Lin, Mun Wai Lee, and Song-Chun Zhu. 2010. I2T: Image parsing to text description. *Proceedings of IEEE 2010*, 98(8):1485–1508.

Generation of landmark-based navigation instructions from open-source data

Markus Dräger
Dept. of Computational Linguistics
Saarland University
mdraeger@coli.uni-saarland.de

Alexander Koller
Dept. of Linguistics
University of Potsdam
koller@ling.uni-potsdam.de

Abstract

We present a system for the real-time generation of car navigation instructions with landmarks. Our system relies exclusively on freely available map data from OpenStreetMap, organizes its output to fit into the available time until the next driving maneuver, and reacts in real time to driving errors. We show that female users spend significantly less time looking away from the road when using our system compared to a baseline system.

1 Introduction

Systems that generate route instructions are becoming an increasingly interesting application area for natural language generation (NLG) systems. Car navigation systems are ubiquitous already, and with the increased availability of powerful mobile devices, the wide-spread use of pedestrian navigation systems is on the horizon. One area in which NLG systems could improve existing navigation systems is in the use of *landmarks*, which would enable them to generate instructions such as "turn right after the church" instead of "after 300 meters". It has been shown in human-human studies that landmark-based route instructions are easier to understand (Lovelace et al., 1999) than distance-based ones and reduce driver distraction in in-car settings (Burnett, 2000), which is crucial for improved traffic safety (Stutts et al., 2001). From an NLG perspective, navigation systems are an obvious application area for situated generation, for which there has recently been increasing interest (see e.g. (Lessmann et al., 2006; Koller et al., 2010; Striegnitz and Majda, 2009)).

Current commercial navigation systems use only trivial NLG technology, and in particular are limited to distance-based route instructions. Even in academic research, there has been remarkably little work on NLG for landmark-based navigation systems. Some of these systems rely on map resources that have been hand-crafted for a particular city (Malaka et al., 2004), or on a combination of multiple complex resources (Raubal and Winter, 2002), which effectively limits their coverage. Others, such as Dale et al. (2003), focus on non-interactive one-shot instruction discourses. However, commercially successful car navigation systems continuously monitor whether the driver is following the instructions and provide modified instructions in real time when necessary. That is, two key problems in designing NLG systems for car navigation instructions are the availability of suitable map resources and the ability of the NLG system to generate instructions and react to driving errors in real time.

In this paper, we explore solutions to both of these points. We present the Virtual Co-Pilot, a system which generates route instructions for car navigation using landmarks that are extracted from the open-source OpenStreetMap resource.[1] The system computes a route plan and splits it into episodes that end in driving maneuvers. It then selects landmarks that describe the locations of these driving maneuvers, and aggregates instructions such that they can be presented (via a TTS system) in the time available within the episode. The system monitors the user's position and computes new, corrective instructions when the user leaves the intended path. We evaluate our system using a driving simulator, and compare it to a baseline that is designed to replicate a typical commercial navigation system. The Virtual Co-Pilot performs comparably to the baseline

[1] http://www.openstreetmap.org/

on the number of driving errors and on user satisfaction, and outperforms it significantly on the time female users spend looking away from the road. To our knowledge, this is the first time that the generation of landmarks has been shown to significantly improve the instructions of a wide-coverage navigation system.

Plan of the paper. We start by reviewing earlier literature on landmarks, route instructions, and the use of NLG for route instructions in Section 2. We then present the way in which we extract information on potential landmarks from OpenStreetMap in Section 3. Section 4 shows how we generate route instructions, and Section 5 presents the evaluation. Section 6 concludes.

2 Related Work

What makes an object in the environment a good landmark has been the topic of research in various disciplines, including cognitive science, computer science, and urban planning. Lynch (1960) defines landmarks as physical entities that serve as external points of reference that stand out from their surroundings. Kaplan (1976) specified a landmark as "a known place for which the individual has a well-formed representation". Although there are different definitions of landmarks, a common theme is that objects are considered landmarks if they have some kind of cognitive salience (both in terms of visual distinctiveness and frequeny of interaction).

The usefulness of landmarks in route instructions has been shown in a number of different human-human studies. Experimental results from Lovelace et al. (1999) show that people not only use landmarks intuitively when giving directions, but they also perceive instructions that are given to them to be of higher quality when those instructions contain landmark information. Similar findings have also been reported by Michon and Denis (2001) and Tom and Denis (2003).

Regarding car navigation systems specifically, Burnett (2000) reports on a road-based user study which compared a landmark-based navigation system to a conventional car navigation system. Here the provision of landmark information in route directions led to a decrease of navigational errors. Furthermore, glances at the navigation display were shorter and fewer, which indicates less driver distraction in this particular experimental condition. Minimizing driver distraction is a crucial goal of improved navigation systems, as driver inattention of various kinds is a leading cause of traffic accidents (25% of all police-reported car crashes in the US in 2000, according to Stutts et al. (2001)). Another road-based study conducted by May and Ross (2006) yielded similar results.

One recurring finding in studies on landmarks in navigation is that some user groups are able to benefit more from their inclusion than others. This is particularly the case for female users. While men tend to outperform women in wayfinding tasks, completing them faster and with fewer navigation errors (c.f. Allen (2000)), women are likely to show improved wayfinding performance when landmark information is given (e.g. Saucier et al. (2002)).

Despite all of this evidence from human-human studies, there has been remarkably little research on implemented navigation systems that use landmarks. Commercial systems make virtually no use of landmark information when giving directions, relying on metric representations instead (e.g. "Turn right in one hundred meters"). In academic research, there have only been a handful of relevant systems. A notable example is the DEEP MAP system, which was created in the SmartKom project as a mobile tourist information system for the city of Heidelberg (Malaka and Zipf, 2000; Malaka et al., 2004). DEEP MAP uses landmarks as waypoints for the planning of touristic routes for car drivers and pedestrians, while also making use of landmark information in the generation of route directions. Raubal and Winter (2002) combine data from digital city maps, facade images, cultural heritage information, and other sources to compute landmark descriptions that could be used in a pedestrian navigation system for the city of Vienna.

The key to the richness of these systems is a set of extensive, manually curated geographic and landmark databases. However, creation and maintenance of such databases is expensive, which makes it impractical to use these systems outside of the limited environments for which they were created. There have been a number of suggestions for automatically acquiring landmark data from existing electronic databases, for instance cadastral data (Elias, 2003) and airborne laser scans (Brenner and Elias, 2003). But the raw data for these approaches is still hard to obtain; information about landmarks is mostly limited to geometric data and does not specify the semantic type of a landmark (such as "church"); and updating the landmark database frequently when the real world changes (e.g., a shop closes down) remains an open issue.

The closest system in the literature to the research we present here is the CORAL system (Dale et al., 2003). CORAL generates a text of driving instructions with landmarks out of the output of a commercial web-based route planner. Unlike CORAL, our system relies purely on open-source map data. Also, our system generates driving instructions in real time (as opposed to a single discourse before the user starts driving) and reacts in real time to driving errors. Finally, we evaluate our system thoroughly for driving errors, user satisfaction, and driver distraction on an actual driving task, and find a significant improvement over the baseline.

3 OpenStreetMap

A system that generates landmark-based route directions requires two kinds of data. First, it must plan routes between points in space, and therefore needs data on the road network, i.e. the road segments that make up streets along with their connections. Second, the system needs information about the landmarks that are present in the environment. This includes geographic information such as position, but also semantic information such as the landmark type.

We have argued above that the availability of such data has been a major bottleneck in the development of landmark-based navigation systems. In the Virtual Co-Pilot system, which we present below, we solve this problem by using data from OpenStreetMap, an on-line map resource that provides both types of information mentioned above, in a unified data structure. The OpenStreetMap project is to maps what Wikipedia is to encyclopedias: It is a map of the entire world which can be edited by anyone wishing to participate. New map data is usually added by volunteers who measure streets using GPS devices and annotate them via a Web interface. The decentralized nature of the data entry process means that when the world changes, the map will be updated quickly. Existing map data can be viewed as a zoomable map on the OpenStreetMap website, or it can be downloaded in an XML format for offline use.

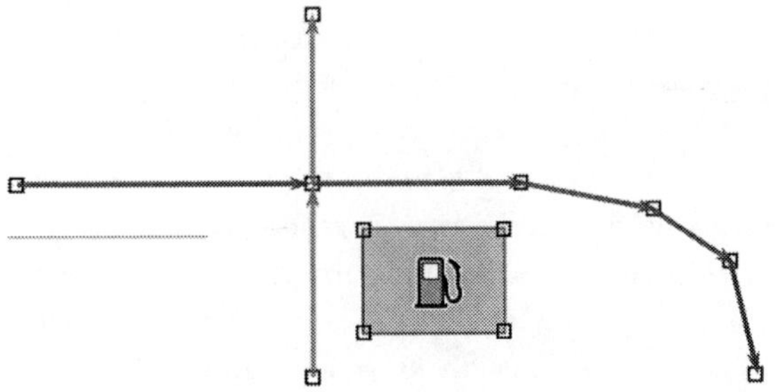

Figure 1: A graphical representation of some nodes and ways in OpenStreetMap.

	Landmark Type
Street Furniture	stop sign traffic lights pedestrian crossing
Visual Landmarks	church certain video stores certain supermarkets gas station pubs and bars

Figure 2: Landmarks used by the Virtual Co-Pilot.

Geographical data in OpenStreetMap is represented in terms of *nodes* and *ways*. Nodes represent points in space, defined by their latitude and longitude. Ways consist of sequences of edges between adjacent nodes; we call the individual edges *segments* below. They are used to represent streets (with curved streets consisting of multiple straight segments approximating their shape), but also a variety of other real-world entities: buildings, rivers, trees, etc. Nodes and ways can both be enriched with further information by attaching *tags*. Tags encode a wide range of additional information using a predefined type ontology. Among other things, they specify the types of buildings (church, cafe, supermarket, etc.); where a shop or restaurant has a name, it too is specified in a tag. Fig. 1 is a graphical representation of some OpenStreetMap data, consisting of nodes and ways for two streets (with two and five segments) and a building which has been tagged as a gas station.

For the Virtual Co-Pilot system, we have chosen a set of concrete landmark types that we consider useful (Fig. 2). We operationalize the criteria for good landmarks sketched in Section 2 by requiring that a landmark should be easily *visible*, and that it should be *generic* in that it is applicable not just for one particular city, but for any place for which OpenStreetMap data is available.

We end up with two classes of landmark types: *street furniture* and *visual landmarks*. Street furniture is a generic term for objects that are installed on streets. In this subset, we include *stop signs*, *traffic lights*, and *pedestrian crossings*. Our assumption is that these objects inherently possess a high salience, since they already require particular attention from the driver. "Visual landmarks" encompass roadside buildings that are not directly connected to the road infrastructure, but draw the driver's attention due to visual salience. Churches are an obvious member of this group; in addition, we include gas stations, pubs, and bars, as well as certain supermarket and video store chains (selected for wide distribution over different cities and recognizable, colorful signs).

Given a certain location at which the Virtual Co-Pilot is to be used, we automatically extract suitable landmarks along with their types and locations from OpenStreetMap. We also gather the road network information that is required for route planning, and collect informations on streets, such as their names, from the tags. We then transform this information into a *directed street graph*. The nodes of this graph are the OpenStreetMap nodes that are part of streets; two adjacent nodes are connected by a single directed edge for segments of one-way streets and a directed edge in each direction for ordinary street segments. Each edge is weighted with the Euclidean distance between the two nodes.

4 Generation of route directions

We will now describe how the Virtual Co-Pilot generates route directions from OpenStreetMap data. The system generates three types of messages (see Fig. 3). First, at every *decision point*, i.e. at the intersection where a driving maneuver such as turning left or right is required, the user is told to turn immediately in the given direction ("now turn right"). Second, if the driver has followed an instruction correctly, we generate a *confirmation message* after the driver has made the turn, letting them know they are still on the right track. Finally, we generate *preview messages* on the street leading up to the decision point. These preview messages describe the location of the next driving maneuver.

Of the three types, preview messages are the most interesting. Our system avoids the generation of metric distance indicators, as in "turn left in 100 meters". Instead, it tries to find landmarks that describe the position of the decision point: "Prepare to turn left after the church." When no landmark is available, the system tries to use street intersections as secondary landmarks, as in "Turn right at the next/second/third intersection." Metric distances are only used when both of these strategies fail.

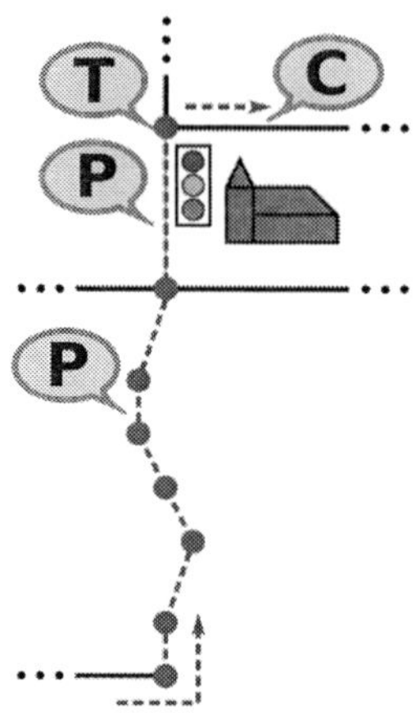

Figure 3: Schematic representation of an episode (dashed red line), with sample trigger positions of preview, turn instruction, and confirmation messages.

In-car NLG takes place in a heavily real-time setting, in which an utterance becomes uninterpretable or even misleading if it is given too late. This problem is exacerbated for NLG of speech because simply speaking the utterance takes time as well. One consequence that our system addresses is the problem of planning preview messages in such a way that they can be spoken before the decision point without overlapping each other. We handle this problem in the sentence planner, which may aggregate utterances to fit into the available time. A second problem is that the user's reactions to the generated utterances are unpredictable; if the driver takes a wrong turn, the system must generate updated instructions in real time.

Below, we describe the individual components of the system. We mostly follow a standard NLG pipeline (Reiter and Dale, 2000), with a focus on the sentence planner and an extension to interactive real-time NLG.

Segment123
From: Node1
To: Node2
On: "Main Street"

Segment124
From: Node2
To: Node3
On: "Main Street"

Segment125
From: Node3
To: Node4
On: "Park Street"

Segment126
From: Node4
To: Node5
On: "Park Street"

Figure 4: A simple example of a route plan consisting of four street segments.

4.1 Content determination and text planning

The first step in our system is to obtain a plan for reaching the destination. To this end, we compute a shortest path on the directed street graph described in Section 3. The result is an ordered list of street segments that need to be traversed in the given order to successfully reach the destination; see Fig. 4 for an example.

To be suitable as the input for an NLG system, this flat list of OpenStreetMap nodes needs to be subdivided into smaller message chunks. In turn-by-turn navigation, the general delimiter between such chunks are the driving maneuvers that the driver must execute at each decision point. We call each span between two decision points an *episode*. Episodes are not explicitly represented in the original route plan: although every segment has a street name associated with it, the name of a street sometimes changes as we go along, and because chains of segments are used to model curved streets in OpenStreetMap, even segments that are joined at an angle may be parts of the same street. Thus, in Fig. 4 it is not apparent which segment traversals require any navigational maneuvers.

We identify episode boundaries with the following heuristic. We first assume that episode boundaries occur when the street name changes from one segment to the next. However, staying on the road may involve a driving maneuver (and therefore a decision point) as well, e.g. when the road makes a sharp turn where a minor street forks off. To handle this case, we introduce decision points at nodes with multiple adjacent segments if the angle between the incoming and outgoing segment of the street exceeds a certain threshold. Conversely, our heuristic will sometimes end an episode where no driving maneuver is necessary, e.g. when an ongoing street changes its name. This is unproblematic in practice; the system will simply generate an instruction to keep driving straight ahead. Fig. 3 shows a graphical representation of an episode, with the street segments belonging to it drawn as red dashed lines.

4.2 Aggregation

Because we generate spoken instructions that are given to the user while they are driving, the timing of the instructions becomes a crucial issue, especially because a driver moves faster than the user of a pedestrian navigation system. It is undesirable for a second instruction to interrupt an earlier one. On the other hand, the second instruction cannot be delayed because this might make the user miss a turn or interpret the instruction incorrectly.

We must therefore control at which points instructions are given and make sure that they do not overlap. We do this by always presenting preview messages at *trigger positions* at certain fixed distances from the decision point. The sentence planner calculates where these trigger positions are located for each episode. In this way, we create time frames during which there is enough time for instructions to be presented.

However, some episodes are too short to accommodate the three trigger positions for the confirmation message and the two preview messages. In such episodes, we aggregate different messages. We remove the trigger positions for the two preview messages from the episode, and instead add the first preview message to the turn instruction message of the previous episode. This allows our system to generate instructions like "Now turn right, and then turn left after the church."

4.3 Generation of landmark descriptions

The Virtual Co-Pilot computes referring expressions to decision points by selecting appropriate landmarks. To this end, it first looks up landmark candidates within a given range of the decision point from the database created in Section 3. This yields an initial list of landmark candidates.

Some of these landmark candidates may be unsuitable for the given situation because of lack of *uniqueness*. If there are several visual landmarks of the same type along the course of an episode, all of these landmark candidates are removed. For episodes which contain multiple street furniture landmarks of the same type, the first three in each episode are retained; a referring expression for the decision point might then be "at the second traffic light". If the decision point is no more than three intersections away, we also add a landmark description of the form "at the third intersection". Furthermore, a landmark must be visible from the last segment of the current episode; we only retain a candidate if it is either adjacent to a segment of the current episode or if it is close to the end point of the very last segment of the episode. Among the landmarks that are left over, the system prefers visual landmarks over street furniture, and street furniture over intersections. If no landmark candidates are left over, the system falls back to metric distances.

Second, the Virtual Co-Pilot determines the spatial relationship between the landmark and the decision point so that an appropriate preposition can be used in the referring expression. If the decision point occurs before the landmark along the course of the episode, we use the preposition "in front of", otherwise, we use "after". Intersections are always used with "at" and metric distances with "in".

Finally, the system decides how to refer to the landmark objects themselves. Although it has access to the names of all objects from the OpenStreetMap data, the user may not know these names. We therefore refer to churches, gas stations, and any street furniture simply as "the church", "the gas station", etc. For supermarkets and bars, we assume that these buildings are more saliently referred to by their names, which are used in everyday language, and therefore use the names to refer to them.

The result of the sentence planning stage is a list of semantic representations, specifying the individual instructions that are to be uttered in each episode; an example is shown in Fig. 5. For each type of instruction, we then use a sentence template to generate linguistic surface forms by inserting the information contained in those plans into the slots provided by the templates (e.g. "Turn *direction preposition landmark*").

Preview message p_1:
Trigger position: Node3 $-$ 50m
Turn direction: right
Landmark: church
Preposition: after

Preview message $p_2 = p_1$, except:
Trigger position: Node3 $-$ 100m

Turn instruction t_1:
Trigger position: Node3
Turn direction: right

Confirmation message c_1:
Trigger position: Node3 $+$ 50m

Figure 5: Semantic representations of the different types of instructions in one episode.

4.4 Interactive generation

As a final point, the NLG process of a car navigation system takes place in an *interactive* setting: as the system generates and utters instructions, the user may either follow them correctly, or they may miss a turn or turn incorrectly because they misunderstood the instruction or were forced to disregard it by the traffic situation. The system must be able to detect such problems, recover from them, and generate new instructions in real time.

Our system receives a continuous stream of information about the position and direction of the user. It performs *execution monitoring* to check whether the user is still following the intended route. If a trigger position is reached, we present the instruction that we have generated for this position. If the user has left the route, the system reacts by planning a new route starting from the user's current position and generating a new set of instructions. We check whether the user is following the intended route in the following way. The system keeps track of the current episode of the route plan, and monitors the distance of the car to the final node of the episode. While the user is following the route correctly, the distance between the car and the final node should decrease or at least stay the same between two measurements. To accommodate for occasional deviations from the middle of the road, we allow five subsequent measurements to increase the distance; the sixth increase of the distance triggers a recomputation of the route plan and a freshly generated instruction. On the other hand, when the distance of the car to the final node falls below a certain threshold, we assume that the end of the episode has been reached, and activate the next episode. By monitoring whether the user is now approaching the final node of this new episode, we can in particular detect wrong turns at intersections.

Because each instruction carries the risk that it may not be followed correctly, there is a question as to whether it is worth planning out all remaining instructions for the complete route plan. After all, if the user does not follow the first instruction, the computation of all remaining instructions was a waste of time. We decided to compute all future instructions anyway because the aggregation procedure described above requires them. In practice, the NLG process is so efficient that all instructions can be done in real time, but this decision would have to be revisited for a slower system.

5 Evaluation

We will now report on an experiment in which we evaluated the performance of the Virtual Co-Pilot.

5.1 Experimental Method

5.1.1 Subjects

In total, 12 participants were recruited through printed ads and mailing lists. All of them were university students aged between 21 and 27 years. Our experiment was balanced for gender, hence we recruited 6 male and 6 female participants. All participants were compensated for their effort.

5.1.2 Design

The driving simulator used in the experiment replicates a real-world city center using a 3D model that contains buildings and streets as they can be perceived in reality. The street layout 3D model used by the driving simulator is based on OpenStreetMap data, and buildings were added to the virtual environment based on cadastral data. To increase the perceived realism of the model, some buildings were manually enhanced with photographic images of their real-world counterparts (see Fig. 7).

Figure 6 shows the set-up of the evaluation experiment. The virtual driving simulator environment (main picture in Fig. 7) was presented to the participants on a 20" computer screen (A). In addition, graphical navigation instructions (shown in the lower right of Fig. 7) were displayed on

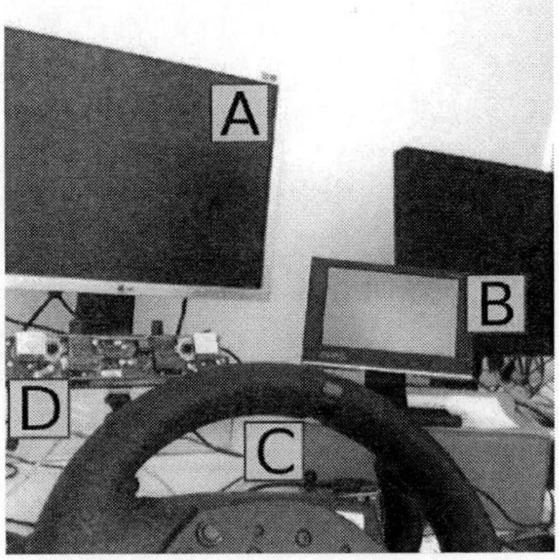

Figure 6: Experiment setup. A) Main screen B) Navigation screen C) steering wheel D) eye tracker

a separate 7" monitor (B). The driving simulator was controlled by means of a steering wheel (C), along with a pair of brake and acceleration pedals. We recorded user eye movements using a Tobii IS-Z1 table-mounted eye tracker (D). The generated instructions were converted to speech using MARY, an open-source text-to-speech system (Schröder and Trouvain, 2003), and played back on loudspeakers.

The task of the user was to drive the car in the virtual environment towards a given destination; spoken instructions were presented to them as they were driving, in real time. Using the steering wheel and the pedals, users had full control over steering angles, acceleration and braking. The driving speed was limited to 30 km/h, but there were no restrictions otherwise. The driving simulator sent the NLG system a message with the current position of the car (as GPS coordinates) once per second.

Each user was asked to drive three short routes in the driving simulator. Each route took about four minutes to complete, and the travelled distance was about 1 km. The number of episodes per route ranged from three to five. Landmark candidates were sufficiently dense that the Virtual Co-Pilot used landmarks to refer to all decision points and never had to fall back to the metric distance strategy.

There were three experimental conditions, which differed with respect to the spoken route instructions and the use of the navigation screen. In the baseline condition, designed to replicate the behavior of an off-the-shelf commercial car nav-

	All Users		Males		Females	
	B	VCP	B	VCP	B	VCP
Total Fixation Duration (seconds)	4.9	**3.5**	**2.7**	4.1	7.0	**2.9***
Total Fixation Count (N)	21.8	**15.4**	**13.5**	16.5	30.0	**14.3***
"The system provided the right amount of information at any time"	**3.9**	2.9	**4.2***	3.3	**3.5**	2.5
"I was insecure at times about still being on the right track."	**2.3**	3.2	**1.9***	2.8	**2.6**	3.5
"It was important to have a visual representation of route directions"	4.3	**4.0**	4.2	4.2	4.3	**3.7**
"I could trust the navigation system"	3.6	**3.7**	**4.1**	3.7	3.0	**3.7**

Figure 8: Mean values for gaze behavior and subjective evaluation, separated by user group and condition (B = baseline, VCP = our system). Significant differences are indicated by *; better values are printed in boldface.

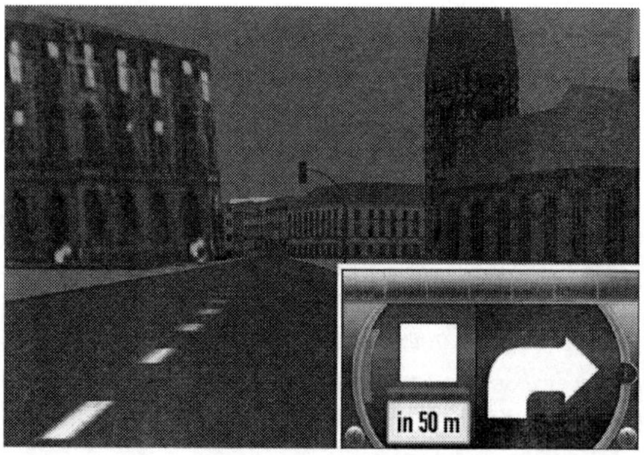

Figure 7: Screenshot of a scene in the driving simulator. Lower right corner: matching screenshot of navigation display.

igation system, participants were provided with spoken metric distance-to-turn navigation instructions. The navigation screen showed arrows depicting the direction of the next turn, along with the distance to the decision point (cf. Fig. 7). The second condition replaced the spoken route instructions by those generated by the Virtual Co-Pilot. In a third condition, the output of the navigation screen was further changed to display an icon for the next landmark along with the arrow and distance indicator. The three routes were presented to the users in different orders, and combined with the conditions in a Latin Squares design. In this paper, we focus on the first and second condition, in order to contrast the two styles of spoken instruction.

Participants were asked to answer two questionnaires after each trial run. The first was the DALI questionnaire (Pauzié, 2008), which asks subjects to report how they perceived different aspects of their cognitive workload (general, visual, auditive and temporal workload, as well as perceived stress level). In the second questionnaire, participants were state to rate their agreement with a number of statements about their subjective impression of the system on a 5-point unlabelled Likert scale, e.g. whether they had received instructions at the right time or whether they trusted the navigation system to give them the right instructions during trials.

5.2 Results

There were no significant differences between the Virtual Co-Pilot and the baseline system on task completion time, rate of driving errors, or any of the questions of the DALI questionnaire. Driving errors in particular were very rare: there were only four driving errors in total, two of which were due to problems with left/right coordination.

We then analyzed the gaze data collected by the table-mounted eye tracker, which we set up such that it recognized glances at the navigation screen. In particular, we looked at the *total fixation duration* (TFD), i.e. the total amount of time that a user spent looking at the navigation screen during a given trial run. We also looked at the *total fixation count* (TFC), i.e. the total number of times that a user looked at the navigation screen in each run. Mean values for both metrics are given in Fig. 8, averaged over all subjects and only male and female subjects, respectively; the "VCP" column is for the Virtual Co-Pilot, whereas "B" stands for the baseline. We found that male users tended to look more at the navigation screen in the VCP condition than in B, although the difference is not statistically significant. However, female users looked at the navigation screen significantly fewer times ($t(5) = 3.2, p < 0.05$, t-test for dependent samples) and for significantly shorter amounts of time ($t(5) = 3.2, p < 0.05$) in the VCP condition than in B.

On the subjective questionnaire, most questions yielded no significant differences (and are not reported here). However, we found that female users tended to rate the Virtual Co-Pilot more positively than the baseline on questions concerning trust in the system and the need for the navigation screen (but not significantly). Male users found that the baseline significantly outperformed the Virtual Co-Pilot on presenting instructions at the right time ($t(5) = 2.7, p < 0.05$) and on giving them a sense of security in still being on the right track ($t(5) = -2.7, p < 0.05$).

5.3 Discussion

The most striking result of the evaluation is that there was a significant reduction of looks to the navigation display, even if only for one group of users. Female users looked at the navigation screen less and more rarely with the Virtual Co-Pilot compared to the baseline system. In a real car navigation system, this translates into a driver who spends less time looking away from the road, i.e. a reduction in driver distraction and an increase in traffic safety. This suggests that female users learned to trust the landmark-based instructions, an interpretation that is further supported by the trends we found in the subjective questionnaire.

We did not find these differences in the male user group. Part of the reason may be the known gender differences in landmark use we mentioned in Section 2. But interestingly, the two significantly worse ratings by male users concerned the correct timing of instructions and the feedback for driving errors, i.e. issues regarding the system's real-time capabilities. Although our system does not yet perform ideally on these measures, this confirms our initial hypothesis that the NLG system must track the user's behavior and schedule its utterances appropriately. This means that earlier systems such as CORAL, which only compute a one-shot discourse of route instructions without regard to the timing of the presentation, miss a crucial part of the problem.

Apart from the exceptions we just discussed, the landmark-based system tended to score comparably or a bit worse than the baseline on the other subjective questions. This may partly be due to the fact that the subjects were familiar with existing commercial car navigation systems and not used to landmark-based instructions. On the other hand, this finding is also consistent with results of other evaluations of NLG systems, in which an improvement in the objective task usefulness of the system does not necessarily correlate with improved scores from subjective questionnaires (Gatt et al., 2009).

6 Conclusion

In this paper, we have described a system for generating real-time car navigation instructions with landmarks. Our system is distinguished from earlier work in its reliance on open-source map data from OpenStreetMap, from which we extract both the street graph and the potential landmarks. This demonstrates that open resources are now informative enough for use in wide-coverage navigation NLG systems. The system then chooses appropriate landmarks at decision points, and continuously monitors the driver's behavior to provide modified instructions in real time when driving errors occur.

We evaluated our system using a driving simulator with respect to driving errors, user satisfaction, and driver distraction. To our knowledge, we have shown for the first time that a landmark-based car navigation system outperforms a baseline significantly; namely, in the amount of time female users spend looking away from the road.

In many ways, the Virtual Co-Pilot is a very simple system, which we see primarily as a starting point for future research. The evaluation confirmed the importance of interactive real-time NLG for navigation, and we therefore see this as a key direction of future work. On the other hand, it would be desirable to generate more complex referring expressions ("the *tall* church"). This would require more informative map data, as well as a formal model of visual salience (Kelleher and van Genabith, 2004; Raubal and Winter, 2002).

Acknowledgments. We would like to thank the DFKI CARMINA group for providing the driving simulator, as well as their support. We would furthermore like to thank the DFKI Agents and Simulated Reality group for providing the 3D city model.

References

G. L. Allen. 2000. Principles and practices for communicating route knowledge. *Applied Cognitive Psychology*, 14(4):333–359.

C. Brenner and B. Elias. 2003. Extracting landmarks for car navigation systems using existing gis databases and laser scanning. *International archives of photogrammetry remote sensing and spatial information sciences*, 34(3/W8):131–138.

G. Burnett. 2000. 'Turn right at the Traffic Lights': The Requirement for Landmarks in Vehicle Navigation Systems. *The Journal of Navigation*, 53(03):499–510.

R. Dale, S. Geldof, and J. P. Prost. 2003. Using natural language generation for navigational assistance. In *ACSC*, pages 35–44.

B. Elias. 2003. Extracting landmarks with data mining methods. *Spatial information theory*, pages 375–389.

A. Gatt, F. Portet, E. Reiter, J. Hunter, S. Mahamood, W. Moncur, and S. Sripada. 2009. From data to text in the neonatal intensive care unit: Using NLG technology for decision support and information management. *AI Communications*, 22:153–186.

S. Kaplan. 1976. Adaption, structure and knowledge. In G. Moore and R. Golledge, editors, *Environmental knowing: Theories, research and methods*, pages 32–45. Dowden, Hutchinson and Ross.

J. D. Kelleher and J. van Genabith. 2004. Visual salience and reference resolution in simulated 3-D environments. *Artificial Intelligence Review*, 21(3).

A. Koller, K. Striegnitz, D. Byron, J. Cassell, R. Dale, J. Moore, and J. Oberlander. 2010. The First Challenge on Generating Instructions in Virtual Environments. In E. Krahmer and M. Theune, editors, *Empirical Methods in Natural Language Generation*. Springer.

N. Lessmann, S. Kopp, and I. Wachsmuth. 2006. Situated interaction with a virtual human – perception, action, and cognition. In G. Rickheit and I. Wachsmuth, editors, *Situated Communication*, pages 287–323. Mouton de Gruyter.

K. Lovelace, M. Hegarty, and D. Montello. 1999. Elements of good route directions in familiar and unfamiliar environments. *Spatial information theory. Cognitive and computational foundations of geographic information science*, pages 751–751.

K. Lynch. 1960. *The image of the city*. MIT Press.

R. Malaka and A. Zipf. 2000. DEEP MAP – Challenging IT research in the framework of a tourist information system. *Information and communication technologies in tourism*, 7:15–27.

R. Malaka, J. Haeussler, and H. Aras. 2004. SmartKom mobile: intelligent ubiquitous user interaction. In *Proceedings of the 9th International Conference on Intelligent User Interfaces*.

A. J. May and T. Ross. 2006. Presence and quality of navigational landmarks: effect on driver performance and implications for design. *Human Factors: The Journal of the Human Factors and Ergonomics Society*, 48(2):346.

P. E. Michon and M. Denis. 2001. When and why are visual landmarks used in giving directions? *Spatial information theory*, pages 292–305.

A. Pauzié. 2008. Evaluating driver mental workload using the driving activity load index (DALI). In *Proc. of European Conference on Human Interface Design for Intelligent Transport Systems*, pages 67–77.

M. Raubal and S. Winter. 2002. Enriching wayfinding instructions with local landmarks. *Geographic information science*, pages 243–259.

E. Reiter and R. Dale. 2000. *Building natural language generation systems*. Studies in natural language processing. Cambridge University Press.

D. M. Saucier, S. M. Green, J. Leason, A. MacFadden, S. Bell, and L. J. Elias. 2002. Are sex differences in navigation caused by sexually dimorphic strategies or by differences in the ability to use the strategies?. *Behavioral Neuroscience*, 116(3):403.

M. Schröder and J. Trouvain. 2003. The German text-to-speech synthesis system MARY: A tool for research, development and teaching. *International Journal of Speech Technology*, 6(4):365–377.

K. Striegnitz and F. Majda. 2009. Landmarks in navigation instructions for a virtual environment. *Online Proceedings of the First NLG Challenge on Generating Instructions in Virtual Environments (GIVE-1)*.

J. C. Stutts, D. W. Reinfurt, L. Staplin, and E. A. Rodgman. 2001. The role of driver distraction in traffic crashes. *Washington, DC: AAA Foundation for Traffic Safety*.

A. Tom and M. Denis. 2003. Referring to landmark or street information in route directions: What difference does it make? *Spatial information theory*, pages 362–374.

To what extent does sentence-internal realisation reflect discourse context? A study on word order

Sina Zarrieß **Jonas Kuhn**
Institut für maschinelle Sprachverarbeitung
University of Stuttgart, Germany
zarriesa,jonas@ims.uni-stuttgart.de

Aoife Cahill
Educational Testing Service
Princeton, NJ 08541, USA
acahill@ets.org

Abstract

We compare the impact of sentence-internal vs. sentence-external features on word order prediction in two generation settings: starting out from a discriminative surface realisation ranking model for an LFG grammar of German, we enrich the feature set with lexical chain features from the discourse context which can be robustly detected and reflect rough grammatical correlates of notions from theoretical approaches to discourse coherence. In a more controlled setting, we develop a constituent ordering classifier that is trained on a German treebank with gold coreference annotation. Surprisingly, in both settings, the sentence-external features perform poorly compared to the sentence-internal ones, and do not improve over a baseline model capturing the syntactic functions of the constituents.

1 Introduction

The task of surface realization, especially in a relatively free word order language like German, is only partially determined by hard syntactic constraints. The space of alternative realizations that are strictly speaking grammatical is typically considerable. Nevertheless, for any given choice of lexical items and prior discourse context, only a few realizations will come across as natural and will contribute to a coherent text. Hence, any NLP application involving a non-trivial generation step is confronted with the issue of soft constraints on grammatical alternatives in one way or another.

There are countless approaches to modelling these soft constraints, taking into account their interaction with various aspects of the discourse context (givenness or salience of particular referents, prior mentioning of particular concepts).

Since so many factors are involved and there is further interaction with subtle semantic and pragmatic differentiations, lexical choice, stylistics and presumably processing factors, theoretical accounts making reliable predictions for real corpus examples have for a long time proven elusive. As for German, only quite recently, a number of corpus-based studies (Filippova and Strube, 2007; Speyer, 2005; Dipper and Zinsmeister, 2009) have made some good progress towards a coherence-oriented account of at least the left edge of the German clause structure, the *Vorfeld* constituent.

What makes the technological application of theoretical insights even harder is that for most relevant factors, automatic recognition cannot be performed with high accuracy (e.g., a coreference accuracy in the 70's means there is a good deal of noise) and for the higher-level notions such as the information-structural focus, interannotator agreement on real corpus data tends to be much lower than for core-grammatical notions (Poesio and Artstein, 2005; Ritz et al., 2008).

On the other hand, many of the relevant discourse factors are reflected indirectly in properties of the sentence-internal material. Most notably, knowing the shape of referring expressions narrows down many aspects of givenness and salience of its referent; pronominal realizations indicate givenness, and in German there are even two variants of the personal pronoun (*er* and *der*) for distinguishing salience. So, if the generation task is set in such a way that the actual lexical choice, including functional categories such as determiners, is fully fixed (which is of course not always the case), one can take advantage of these reflexes. This explains in part the fairly high baseline performance of n-gram language models in the surface realization task. And the effect can indeed be taken much further: the discriminative training experiments of Cahill and Riester (2009) show how effective it is to systematically take advantage of asymmetry patterns in the morphosyntactic reflexes of the discourse notion of information status (i.e., using a feature set with well-chosen purely sentence-bound features).

These observations give rise to the question: in the light of the difficulty in obtaining reliable discourse information on the one hand and the effectiveness of exploiting the reflexes of discourse in the sentence-internal material on the other – can we nevertheless expect to gain something from adding sentence-external feature information?

We propose two scenarios for adressing this question: first, we choose an approximative access to context information and relations between discourse referents – lexical reiteration of head words, combined with information about their grammatical relation and topological positioning in prior sentences. We apply these features in a rich sentence-internal surface realisation ranking model for German. Secondly, we choose a more controlled scenario: we train a constituent ordering classifier based on a feature model that captures properties of discourse referents in terms of manually annotated coreference relations. As we get the same effect in both setups – the sentence-external features do not improve over a baseline that captures basic morphosyntactic properties of the constituents – we conclude that sentence-internal realisation is actually a relatively accurate predictor of discourse context, even more accurate than information that can be obtained from coreference and lexical chain relations.

2 Related Work

In the generation literature, most works on exploiting sentence-external discourse information are set in a summarisation or content ordering framework. Barzilay and Lee (2004) propose an account for constraints on topic selection based on probabilistic content models. Barzilay and Lapata (2008) propose an entity grid model which represents the distribution of referents in a discourse for sentence ordering. Karamanis et al. (2009) use Centering-based metrics to assess coherence in an information ordering system. Clarke and Lapata (2010) have improved a sentence compression system by capturing prominence of phrases or referents in terms of lexical chain information inspired by Morris and Hirst (1991) and Centering (Grosz et al., 1995). In their system, discourse context is represented in terms of hard constraints modelling whether a certain constituent can be deleted or not.

In the linearisation or surface realisation domain, there is a considerable body of work approximating information structure in terms of sentence-internal realisation (Ringger et al., 2004; Filippova and Strube, 2009; Velldal and Oepen, 2005; Cahill et al., 2007). Cahill and Riester (2009) improve realisation ranking for German – which mainly deals with word order variation – by representing precedence patterns of constituents in terms of asymmetries in their morphosyntactic properties. As a simple example, a pattern exploited by Cahill and Riester (2009) is the tendency of definite elements tend to precede indefinites, which, on a discourse level, reflects that given entities in a sentence tend to precede new entities.

Other work on German surface realisation has highlighted the role of the initial position in the German sentence, the so-called *Vorfeld* (or "prefield"). Filippova and Strube (2007) show that once the *Vorfeld* (i.e. the constituent that precedes the finite verb) is correctly determined, the prediction of the order in the *Mittelfeld* (i.e. the constituents that follow the finite verb) is very easy. Cheung and Penn (2010) extend the approach of Filippova and Strube (2007) and augment a sentence-internal constituent ordering model with sentence-external features inspired from the entity grid model proposed by Barzilay and Lapata (2008).

3 Motivation

While there would be many ways to construe or represent discourse context (e.g. in terms of the global discourse or information structure), we concentrate on capturing local coherence through the distribution of discourse referents in a text. These discourse referents basically correspond to the constituents that our surface realisation model has to put in the right order. As the order of referents or constituents is arguably influenced by the information structure of a sentence given the previous text, our main assumption was that infor-

(1) a. Kurze Zeit später erklärte ein Anrufer bei Nachrichtenagenturen in Pakistan , **die Gruppe Gamaa** bekenne sich.
Shortly after, a caller declared at the news agencies in Pakistan, that **the group Gamaa** *avowes itself.*

b. **Diese Gruppe** wird für einen Großteil der Gewalttaten verantwortlich gemacht , die seit dreieinhalb Jahren in Ägypten verübt worden sind .
This group *is made responsible for most of the violent acts that have been committed in Egypt in the last three and a half years.*

(2) a. **Belgien** wünscht, dass sich WEU und NATO darüber einigen.
Belgium *wants that WEU and NATO agree on that.*

b. **Belgien** sieht in der NATO die beste militärische Struktur in Europa .
Belgium *sees the best military structure of Europe in the NATO.*

(3) a. **Frauen** vom Land kämpften aktiv darum , ein Staudammprojekt zu verhindern.
Women *from the countryside fighted actively to block the dam project.*

b. Auch in den Städten fänden sich immer mehr **Frauen** in Selbsthilfeorganisationen zusammen.
Also in the cities, more and more **women** *team up in self-help organisations.*

mation about the prior mentioning of a referent would be helpful for predicting the position of this referent in a sentence.

The idea that the occurence of discourse referents in a text is a central aspect of discourse structure has been systematically pursued by Centering Theory (Grosz et al., 1995). Its most important notions are related to the realisation of discourse referents (i.e. described as "centers") and the way the centers are arranged in a sequence of utterances to make this sequence a coherent discourse. Another important concept is the "ranking" of discourse referents which basically determines the prominence of a referent in a certain sentence and is driven by several factors (e.g. their grammatical function). For free word order languages like German, word order has been proposed as one of the factors that account for the ranking (Poesio et al., 2004). In a similar spirit, Morris and Hirst (1991) have proposed that chains of (related) lexical items in a text are an important indicator of text structure.

Our main hypothesis was that it is possible to exploit these intuitions from Centering Theory and the idea of lexical chains for word order prediction. Thus, we expected that it would be easier to predict the position of a referent in a sentence if we have not only given its realisation in the current utterance but also its prominence in the previous discourse. Especially, we expected this intuition to hold for cases where the morpho-syntactic realisation of a constituent does not provide many clues. This is illustrated in Examples (1) and (2) which both exemplify the reiteration of a lexical item in two subsequent sentences, (reiteration is one type of lexical chain discussed in Morris and Hirst (1991)). In Example (1), the second instance of the noun 'group' is modified by a demonstrative pronoun such that its "known" and prominent discourse status is overt in the morpho-syntactic realisation. In Example (2), both instances of "Belgium" are realised as bare proper nouns without an overt morphosyntactic clue indicating their discourse status.

Beyond the simple presence of reitered items in sequences of sentences, we expected that it would be useful to look at the position and syntactic function of the previous mentions of a discourse referent. In Example (1), the reiterated item is first introduced in an embedded sentence and realised in the *Vorfeld* in the second utterance. In terms of centering, this transition would correspond to a topic shift. In Example (2), both instances are realised in the *Vorfeld*, such that the topic of the first sentence is carried over to the next.

In Example (3), we illustrate a further type of lexical reiteration. In this case, two identical head nouns are realised in subsequent sentences, even though they refer to two different discourse referents. While this type of lexical chain is described as "reiteration without identity of referents" by Morris and Hirst (1991), it would not be captured in Centering since this is not a case of strict coreference. On the other hand, lexical chains do not capture types of reiterated discourse referents that have distinct morpho-syntactic realisations, e.g. nouns and pronouns.

Originally, we had the hypothesis that strict corefence information is more useful and accurate for word order prediction than rather loose lexical chains which conflate several types of referential and lexical relations. However, the advantage of chains, especially chains of reiteration, is that they can be easily detected in any corpus text and that they might capture "topics" of sentences beyond the identity of referents. Thus, we started out from the idea of lexical chains and added corresponding features in a statistical ranking model for surface realisation of German (Section 4). As this strategy did not work out, we wanted to assess whether an ideal coreference annotation would be helpful at all for predicting word order. In a second experiment, we use a corpus which is manually annotated for coreference (Section 5).

4 Experiment 1: Realisation Ranking with Lexical Chains

In this Section, we present an experiment that investigates sentence-external context in a surface realisation task. The sentence-external context is represented in terms of lexical chain features and compared to sentence-internal models which are based on morphosyntactic features. The experiment thus targets a generation scenario where no coreference information is available and aims at assessing whether relatively naive context information is also useful.

4.1 System Description

We carry out our first experiment in a regeneration set-up with two components: a) a large-scale hand-crafted Lexical Functional Grammar (LFG) for German (Rohrer and Forst, 2006), used to parse and regenerate a corpus sentence, b) a stochastic ranker that selects the most appropriate regenerated sentence in context according to an underlying, linguistically motivated feature model. In contrast to fully statistical linearisation methods, our system first generates the full set of sentences that correspond to the grammatically well-formed realisations of the intermediate syntactic representation.[1] This representation is an f-structure, which underspecifies the order of constituents and, to some extent, their morphological realisation, such that the output sentences contain all possible combinations of word order permutations and morphological variants. Depending on the length and structure of the original corpus sentence, the set of regenerated sentences can be huge (see Cahill et al. (2007) for details on regenerating the German treebank TIGER).

[1]There are occasional mistakes in the grammar which sometimes lead to ungrammatical strings being generated, but this is rare.

The realisation ranking component is an SVM ranking model implemented with SVMrank, a Support Vector Machine-based learning tool (Joachims, 2006). During training, each sentence is annotated with a rank and a set of features extracted from the F-structure, its surface string and external resources (e.g. a language model). If the sentence matches the original corpus string, its rank will be highest, the assumption being that the original sentence corresponds to the optimal realisation in context. The output of generation, the top-ranked sentence, is evaluated against the original corpus sentence.

4.2 The Feature Models

As the aim of this experiment is to better understand the nature of sentence-internal features reflecting discourse context and compare them to sentence-external ones, we build several feature models which capture different aspects of the constituents in a given sentence. The sentence-internal features describe the morphosyntacic realisation of constituents, for instance their function ("subject", "object"), and can be straightforwardly extracted from the f-structure. These features are then combined into discriminative precedence features, for instance "subject-precedes-object". We implement the following types of morphosyntactic features:

- syntactic function (arguments and adjuncts)
- modification (e.g. nouns modified by relative clauses, genitive etc.)
- syntactic category (e.g. adverbs, proper nouns, phrasal arguments)
- definiteness for nouns
- number and person for nominal elements
- types of pronouns (e.g. demonstrative, reflexive)
- constituent span and number of embedded nodes in the tree

In addition, we also include language model scores in our ranking model. In Section 4.4, we report on results for several subsets of these features where "BaseSyn" refers to a model that only includes the syntactic function features and "FullMorphSyn" includes all features mentioned above.

For extracting the lexical chains, we check for any overlapping nouns in the n sentences previous to the current one being generated. We check

Rank	*Sentence and Features*
1	% **Diese Gruppe** wird für einen Großteil der Gewalttaten verantwortlich gemacht. *% This group is for a major part of the violent acts responsible made.* subject-<-pp-object, demonstrative-<-indefinite, overlap-<-no-overlap, overlap-in-vorfeld, lm:-7.89
3	% Für einen Großteil der Gewalttaten wird **diese Gruppe** verantwortlich gemacht. *% For a major part of the violent acts is this group responsible made.* pp-object-<-subject, indefinite-<-demonstrative, no-overlap-<-overlap, no-overlap-in-vorfeld, lm:-10.33
3	% Verantwortlich gemacht wird **diese Gruppe** für einen Großteil der Gewalttaten. *% Responsible made is this group for a major part of the violent acts.* subject-<-pp-object, demonstrative-<-indefinite, overlap-<-no-overlap, lm:-9.41

Figure 1: Made-up training example for realisation ranking with precedence features

proper and common nouns, considering full and partial overlaps as shown in Examples (1) and (2), where the (a) example is the previous sentence in the corpus. For each overlap, we record the following properties: (i) function in the previous sentence, (ii) position in the previous sentence (e.g. *Vorfeld*), (iii) distance between sentences, (iv) total number of overlaps.

These overlap features are then also combined in terms of precedence, e.g. "has_subject_overlap:3-precedes-no_overlap", meaning that in the current sentence a noun that was previously mentioned in a subject 3 sentences ago precedes a noun that was not mentioned before.

In Figure 1, we give an example of a set of generation alternatives and their (partial) feature representation for the sentence (1-b). Precedence is indicated by "<".

Basically, our sentence-external feature model is built on the intuition that lexical chains or overlaps approximate discourse status in a way which is similar to sentence-internal morphosyntactic properties. Thus, we would expect that overlaps indicate givenness, salience or prominence and that asymmetries between overlapping and non-overlapping entities are helpful in the ranking.

4.3 Data

All our models are trained on 7,039 sentences (subdivided into 1259 texts) from the TIGER Treebank of German newspaper text (Brants et al., 2002). We tune the parameters of our SVM model on a development set of 55 sentences and report the final results for our unseen test set of 240 sentences. Table 1 shows how many sentences in our training, development and test sets have at least one textually overlapping phrase in the previous 1–10 sentences.

We choose the TIGER treebank, which has no

# Sentences	% Sentences with overlap		
in context	Training	Dev	Test
1	20.96	23.64	20.42
2	35.42	40.74	35.00
3	45.58	50.00	53.33
4	52.66	53.70	58.75
5	57.45	58.18	64.58
6	61.42	57.41	68.75
7	64.58	61.11	70.83
8	67.05	62.96	72.08
9	69.20	64.81	74.17
10	71.16	70.37	75.83

Table 1: The percentage of sentences that have at least one overlapping entity in the previous n sentences

coreference annotation, since we already have a number of resources available to match the syntactic analyses produced by our grammar against the analyses in the treebank. Thus, in our regeneration system, we parse the sentences with the grammar, and choose the parsed f-structures that are compatible with the manual annotation in the TIGER treebank as is done in Cahill et al. (2007). This compatibility check eliminates noise which would be introduced by generating from incorrect parses (e.g. incorrect PP-attachments typically result in unnatural and non-equivalent surface realisations).

For comparing the string chosen by the models against the original corpus sentence, we use BLEU, NIST and exact match. Exact match is a strict measure that only credits the system if it chooses the exact same string as the original corpus string. BLEU and NIST are more relaxed measures that compare the strings on the n-gram level. Finally, we report accuracy scores for the *Vorfeld* position (VF) corresponding to the percentage of sentences generated with a correct *Vorfeld*.

S_c	BLEU	NIST	Exact	VF
0	0.766	11.885	50.19	64.0
1	0.765	11.756	49.78	64.0
2	0.765	11.886	50.01	64.1
3	0.765	11.885	50.08	63.8
4	0.761	11.723	49.43	63.2
5	0.765	11.884	49.71	64.2
6	0.768	11.892	50.42	64.6
7	0.765	11.885	50.01	64.5
8	0.764	11.884	49.78	64.3
9	0.765	11.888	49.82	63.6
10	0.764	11.889	49.7	63.5

Table 2: Tenfold-crossvalidation for feature model FullMorphSyn and different context windows (S_c)

Model	BLEU	VF
Language Model	0.702	51.2
Language Model + Context $S_c = 5$	0.715	54.3
BaseSyn	0.757	62.0
BaseSyn + Context $S_c = 5$	0.760	63.0
FullMorphSyn	0.766	64.0
FullMorphSyn + Context $S_c = 5$	0.763	64.2

Table 3: Evaluation for different feature models; 'Language Model': ranking based on language model scores, 'BaseSyn': precedence between constituent functions, 'FullMorphSyn': entire set of sentence-internal features.

4.4 Results

In Table 2, we report the performance of the full sentence-internal feature model combined with context windows from zero to ten. The scores have been obtained from tenfold-crossvalidation. For none of the context windows, the model outperforms the baseline with a zero context which has no sentence-external features. In Table 3, we compare the performance of several feature models corresponding to subsets of the features used so far which are combined with sentence-external features respectively. We note that the function precedence features (i.e. the 'BaseSyn' model) are very powerful, leading to a major improvement compared to a language model. The sentence-external features lead to an improvement when combined with the language-model based ranking. However, this improvement is leveled out in the BaseSyn model.

On the one hand, the fact that the lexical chain features improve a language-model based ranking suggests these features are, to some extent, predictive for certain patterns of German word order. On the other hand, the fact that they don't improve over an informed sentence-internal baseline suggests that these patterns are equally well captured by morphosyntactic features. However, we cannot exclude the possibility that the chain features are too noisy as they conflate several types of lexical and coreferential relations. This will be adressed in the following experiment.

5 Experiment 2: Constituent Ordering with Centering-inspired Features

We now look at a simpler generation setup where we concentrate on the ordering of constituents in the German *Vorfeld* and *Mittelfeld*. This strategy has also been adopted in previous investigations of German word order: Filippova and Strube (2007) show that once the German *Vorfeld* is correctly chosen, the prediction accuracy for the *Mittelfeld* (the constituents following the finite verb) is in the 90s.

In order to eliminate noise introduced from potentially heterogeneous chain features, we look at coreference features and, again, compare them to sentence-internal morphosyntactic features. We target a generation scenario where coreference information is available. The aim is to establish an upper bound concerning the quality improvement for word order prediction by recurring to manual corefence annotation.

5.1 Data and Setup

We carry out the constituent ordering experiment on the Tüba-D/Z treebank (v5) of German newspaper articles (Telljohann et al., 2006). It comprises about 800k tokens in 45k sentences. We choose this corpus because it is not only annotated with syntactic analyses but also with coreference relations (Naumann, 2006). The syntactic annotation format differs from the TIGER treebank used in the previous experiment, for instance, it explicitely represents the *Vorfeld* and *Mittelfeld* as phrasal nodes in the tree. This format is very convenient for the extraction of constituents in the respective positions.

The Tüba-D/Z coreference annotation distinguishes several relations between discourse referents, most importantly "coreferential relation" and "anaphoric relation" where the first denotes a relation between noun phrases that refer to the same entity, and the latter refers to a link between a pronoun and a contextual antecedent, see Naumann (2006) for further detail. We expected the coreferential relation to be particularly useful, as it cannot always be read off the morphosyntactic realisation of a noun phrase, whereas pronouns are almost always used in an anaphoric relation.

The constituent ordering model is implemented as a classifier that is given a set of constituents and predicts the constituent that is most likely to be realised in the *Vorfeld*.

The set of candidate constituents is determined from the tree of the original corpus sentence. We will assume that all constituents under a *Vorfeld* and *Mittelfeld* node can be freely reordered. Thus, we do not check whether the word order variants we look at are actually grammatical assuming that most of them are. In this sense, this experiment is close to fully statistical generation approaches. As a further simplification, we do not look at morphological generation variants of the constituents or their head verb.

The classifier is implemented with SVMrank again. In contrast to the previous experiment where we learned to rank sentences, the classifier now learns to rank constituents. The constituents have been extracted using the tool described in Bouma (2010). The final data set comprises 48.513 candidate sets of freely orderable constituents.

5.2 Centering-inspired Feature Model

To compare the discourse context model against a sentence-based model, we implemented a number of sentence-internal features that are very similar to the features used in the previous experiment. Since we extract them from the syntactic annotation instead of f-structures, some labels and feature names will be different, however, the design of the sentence-internal model is identical to the previous one in Section 4.

The sentence-external features differ in some aspects from Section 4, since we extract coreference relations of several types (see (Naumann, 2006) for the anaphoric relations annotated in the Tueba-D/Z). For each type of coreference link, we extract the following properties: (i) function of the antecedent, (ii) position of the antecedent, (iii) distance between sentences, (iv) type of relation. We also distinguish coreference links annotated for the whole phrase ("head link") and links that are annotated for an element embedded by the constituent ("contained link"). The two types are illustrated in Examples (4) and (5). Note that both cases would not have been captured in the lexical chain model since there is no lexical overlap between the realisations of the discourse referents.

	# VF	# MF
Backward Center	3.5%	5.1%
Forward Center	6.8%	6.8%
Coref Link	30.5%	23.4%

Table 4: Backward and forward centers and their positions

These types of coreference features implicitly carry the information that would also be considered in a Centering formalisation of discourse context. In addition to these, we designed features that explicitly describe centers as these might have a higher weight. In line with Clarke and Lapata (2010), we compute backward (CB) and forward centers (CF) in the following way:

1. Extract all entities from the current sentence and the previous sentence.
2. Rank the entities of the previous sentence according to their function (subject $<$ direct object $<$ indirect object ...).
3. Find the highest ranked entity in the previous sentence that has a link to an entity in the current sentence, this entity is the CB of the sentence.

In the same way, we mark entities as forward centers that are ranked highest in the current sentence and have a link to an entity in the following sentence.[2] In Table 4, we report the percentage of sentences that have backward and forward centers in the *Vorfeld* or *Mittelfeld*. While the percentage of sentences that realise a backward center is quite low, the overall proportion of sentences containing some type of coreference link is in a dimension such that the learner could definitely pick up some predictive patterns. Going by the relative frequencies, coreferential constituents have a bias towards appearing in the *Vorfeld* rather than in the *Mittelfeld*.

5.3 Results

First, we build three coreference-based constituent classifiers on their entire training set and compare them to their sentence-internal baseline. The most simple baseline records the category of

[2]In Centering, all entities in a given utterance can be seen as forward centers, however we thought that this implementation would be more useful.

(4) a. Die Rechnung geht an **die AWO**.
The bill goes to **the AWO**.

b. [Hintergrund der gegenseitigen Vorwürfe in **der Arbeiterwohlfahrt**] sind offenbar scharfe Konkurrenzen zwischen Bremern und Bremerhavenern.
Apparently, [the background of the mutual accusations at **the labour welfare***] are rivalries between people from Bremen and Bremerhaven.*

(5) a. Dies ist die Behauptung, mit der **Bremens Häfensenator** die Skeptiker davon überzeugt hat, [...].
This is the claim, which **Bremen's harbour senator** *used to convince doubters, [...].*

b. Für diese Behauptung hat **Beckmeyer** bisher keinen Nachweis geliefert. *So far,* **Beckmeyer** *has not given a prove of this claim.*

Model	VF
ConstituentLength + HeadPos	47.48%
ConstituentLength + HeadPos + Coref	51.30%
BaseSyn	54.82%
BaseSyn + Coref	56.21%
FullMorphSyn	57.24%
FullMorphSyn + Coref	57.40%

Table 5: Results from Vorfeld classification, training and evaluation on entire treebank

Model	VF
ConstituentLength + HeadPos	46.61%
ConstituentLength + HeadPos + Coref	52.23%
BaseSyn	54.63%
BaseSyn + Coref	56.67%
FullMorphSyn	55.36%
FullMorphSyn + Coref	57.93%

Table 6: Results from Vorfeld classification, training and evaluation on sentences that contain a coreference link

the constituent head and the number of words that the constituent spans. Additionally, in parallel to the experiment in Section 4, we build a "BaseSyn" model which has the syntactic function features, and a "FullMorphSyn" model which comprises the entire set of sentence-internal features. To each of these baseline, we add the coreference features. The results are reported in Table 5.

In this experiment, we find an effect of the sentence-external features over the simple sentence-internal baselines. However, in the fully spelled-out, sentence-internal model, the effect is, again, minimal. Moreover, for each baseline, we obtain higher improvements by adding further sentence-internal features than by adding sentence-external ones the accuracy of the simple baseline (47.48%) improves by 7.34 points through adding function features (the accuracy of BaseSyn is 54.82%) and by only 3.48 points through adding coreference features.

We run a second experiment in order to so see whether the better performance of the sentence-internal features is related to their coverage. We build and evaluate the same set of classifiers on the subset of sentences that contain at least one coreference link for one of its constituents (see Table 4 for the distribution of coreference links in our data). The results are given in Table 6. In this experiment, the coreference features improve over all sentence-internal baselines including the 'FullMorphSyn' model.

5.4 Discussion

The results presented in this Section consistently complete the picture that emerged from the experiments in Section 4. Even if we have high quality information about discourse context in terms of relations between referents, a non-trivial sentence-internal model for word order prediction can be hardly improved. This suggests that sentence-internal approximations of discourse context provide a fairly good way of dealing with local coherence in a linearisation task. It is also interesting that the sentence-external features improve over simple baselines, but get leveled out in rich sentence-internal feature models. From this, we conclude that the sentence-external features we implemented are to some extent predictive for word order, but that they can be covered by sentence-internal features as well.

Our second evaluation concentrating on the sentences that have coreference information shows that the better performance of the sentence-internal features is also related to their coverage. These results confirm our initial intuition that coreference information can add to the predictive power of the morpho-syntactic features in certain contexts. This positive effect disappears when sentences with and without coreferential constituents are taken together. For future work, it would be promising to investigate whether the positive impact of coreference features can be strengthened if the coreference annotation scheme is more exhaustive, including, e.g., bridging and event anaphora.

6 Conclusion

We have carried out a number of experiments that show that sentence-internal models for word order are hardly improved by features which explicitely represent the preceding context of a sentence in terms of lexical and referential relations between discourse entities. This suggests that sentence-internal realisation implicitly carries a lot of information about discourse context. On average, the morphosyntactic properties of constituents in a text are better approximates of their discourse status than actual coreference relations.

This result feeds into a number of research questions concerning the representation of discourse and its application in generation systems. Although we should certainly not expect a computational model to achieve a perfect accuracy in the constituent ordering task – even humans only agree to a certain extent in rating word order variants (Belz and Reiter, 2006; Cahill, 2009) – the average accuracy in the 60's for prediction of *Vorfeld* occupance is still moderate. An obvious direction would be to further investigate more complex representations of discourse that take into account the relations between utterances, such as topic shifts. Moreover, it is not clear whether the effects we find for linearisation in this paper carry over to other levels of generation such as tactical generation where syntactic functions are not fully specified. In a broader perspective, our results underline the need for better formalisations of discourse that can be translated into features for large-scale applications such as generation.

Acknowledgments

This work was funded by the Collaborative Research Centre (SFB 732) at the University of Stuttgart.

References

Regina Barzilay and Mirella Lapata. 2008. Modeling local coherence: An entity-based approach. *Computational Linguistics*, 34:1–34.

Regina Barzilay and Lillian Lee. 2004. Catching the drift: Probabilistic content models with applications to generation and summarization. In *Proceedings of HLT-NAACL 2004*, Boston,MA.

Anja Belz and Ehud Reiter. 2006. Comparing automatic and human evaluation of NLG systems. In *Proceedings of EACL 2006*, pages 313–320, Trento, Italy.

Gerlof Bouma. 2010. Syntactic tree queries in prolog. In *Proceedings of the Fourth Linguistic Annotation Workshop, ACL 2010*.

Sabine Brants, Stefanie Dipper, Silvia Hansen, Wolfgang Lezius, and George Smith. 2002. The TIGER Treebank. In *Proceedings of the Workshop on Treebanks and Linguistic Theories*.

Aoife Cahill and Arndt Riester. 2009. Incorporating information status into generation ranking. In *Proceedings of the Joint Conference of the 47th Annual Meeting of the ACL and the 4th International Joint Conference on Natural Language Processing of the AFNLP*, pages 817–825, Suntec, Singapore, August. Association for Computational Linguistics.

Aoife Cahill, Martin Forst, and Christian Rohrer. 2007. Stochastic Realisation Ranking for a Free Word Order Language. In *Proceedings of the Eleventh European Workshop on Natural Language Generation*, pages 17–24, Saarbrücken, Germany. DFKI GmbH.

Aoife Cahill. 2009. Correlating human and automatic evaluation of a german surface realiser. In *Proceedings of the ACL-IJCNLP 2009 Conference Short Papers*, pages 97–100, Suntec, Singapore, August. Association for Computational Linguistics.

Jackie C.K. Cheung and Gerald Penn. 2010. Entity-based local coherence modelling using topological fields. In *Proceedings of the 48th Annual Meeting of the Association for Computational Linguistics (ACL 2010)*. Association for Computational Linguistics.

James Clarke and Mirella Lapata. 2010. Discourse constraints for document compression. *Computational Linguistics*, 36(3):411–441.

Stefanie Dipper and Heike Zinsmeister. 2009. The role of the German Vorfeld for local coherence. In Christian Chiarcos, Richard Eckart de Castilho, and Manfred Stede, editors, *Von der Form zur Bedeutung: Texte automatisch verarbeiten/From Form to Meaning: Processing Texts Automatically*, pages 69–79. Narr, Tübingen.

Katja Filippova and Michael Strube. 2007. The german vorfeld and local coherence. *Journal of Logic, Language and Information*, 16:465–485.

Katja Filippova and Michael Strube. 2009. Tree Linearization in English: Improving Language Model Based Approaches. In *Proceedings of Human Language Technologies: The 2009 Annual Conference of the North American Chapter of the Association for Computational Linguistics, Companion Volume: Short Papers*, pages 225–228, Boulder, Colorado, June. Association for Computational Linguistics.

Barbara J. Grosz, Aravind Joshi, and Scott Weinstein. 1995. Centering: A framework for modeling the local coherence of discourse. *Computational Linguistics*, 21(2):203–225.

Thorsten Joachims. 2006. Training linear SVMs in linear time. In *Proceedings of the ACM Conference on Knowledge Discovery and Data Mining (KDD)*, pages 217–226.

Nikiforos Karamanis, Massimo Poesioand Chris Mellish, and Jon Oberlander. 2009. Evaluating centering for information ordering using corpora. *Computational Linguistics*, 35(1).

Jane Morris and Graeme Hirst. 1991. Lexical cohesion, the thesaurus, and the structure of text. *Computational Linguistics*, 17(1):21–225.

Karin Naumann. 2006. Manual for the annotation of in-document referential relations. Technical report, Seminar für Sprachwissenschaft, Abt. Computerlinguistik, Universität Tübingen.

Massimo Poesio and Ron Artstein. 2005. The reliability of anaphoric annotation, reconsidered: Taking ambiguity into account. In *Proc. of ACL Workshop on Frontiers in Corpus Annotation*.

Massimo Poesio, Rosemary Stevenson, Barbara di Eugenio, and Janet Hitzeman. 2004. Centering: A parametric theory and its instantiations. *Computational Linguistics*, 30(3):309–363.

Eric K. Ringger, Michael Gamon, Robert C. Moore, David Rojas, Martine Smets, and Simon Corston-Oliver. 2004. Linguistically Informed Statistical Models of Constituent Structure for Ordering in Sentence Realization. In *Proceedings of the 2004 International Conference on Computational Linguistics*, Geneva, Switzerland.

Julia Ritz, Stefanie Dipper, and Michael Götze. 2008. Annotation of information structure: An evaluation across different types of texts. In *Proceedings of the the 6th LREC conference*.

Christian Rohrer and Martin Forst. 2006. Improving Coverage and Parsing Quality of a Large-Scale LFG for German. In *Proceedings of the Fifth International Conference on Language Resources and Evaluation (LREC)*, Genoa, Italy.

Augustin Speyer. 2005. Competing constraints on vorfeldbesetzung in german. In *Proceedings of the Constraints in Discourse Workshop*, pages 79–87.

Heike Telljohann, Erhard Hinrichs, Sandra Kübler, and Heike Zinsmeister. 2006. Stylebook for the tübingen treebank of written german (tüba-d/z). revised version. Technical report, Seminar für Sprachwissenschaft, Universität Tübingen.

Erik Velldal and Stephan Oepen. 2005. Maximum entropy models for realization ranking. In *Proceedings of the 10th Machine Translation Summit*, pages 109–116, Thailand.

Behind the Article: Recognizing Dialog Acts in Wikipedia Talk Pages

Oliver Ferschke[‡]**, Iryna Gurevych**[†‡] **and Yevgen Chebotar**[‡]

† Ubiquitous Knowledge Processing Lab (UKP-DIPF)
German Institute for Educational Research and Educational Information

‡ Ubiquitous Knowledge Processing Lab (UKP-TUDA)
Department of Computer Science
Technische Universität Darmstadt

`http://www.ukp.tu-darmstadt.de`

Abstract

In this paper, we propose an annotation schema for the discourse analysis of Wikipedia Talk pages aimed at the coordination efforts for article improvement. We apply the annotation schema to a corpus of 100 Talk pages from the Simple English Wikipedia and make the resulting dataset freely available for download[1]. Furthermore, we perform automatic dialog act classification on Wikipedia discussions and achieve an average F_1-score of 0.82 with our classification pipeline.

1 Introduction

Over the past decade, the paradigm of information sharing in the web has shifted towards participatory and collaborative content production. Texts are no longer exclusively prepared by individuals and then shared with the community. They are increasingly created collaboratively by multiple authors and iteratively revised by the community.

When researchers first conducted surveys on professional writers in the 1980s, they found that the collaborative writing process differs considerably from the way individual writing is done (Posner and Baecker, 1992). In joint writing, the writers have to externalize processes that are otherwise not made explicit, like the planning and the organization of the text. The authors have to communicate *how* the text should be written and *what* exactly it should contain.

Today, many tools are available that support collaborative writing. A tool that has particularly taken hold is the *Wiki*, a web-based, asynchronous co-authoring tool. A unique characteristic of Wikis is the documentation of the edit history which keeps track of every change that is made to a Wiki page. With this information, it is possible to reconstruct the writing process from the beginning to the end. Additionally, many Wikis offer their users a communication platform, the Talk pages, where they can discuss the ongoing writing process with other users.

The most prominent example for a successful, large-scale Wiki is *Wikipedia*, a collaboratively created online encyclopedia, which has grown considerably since its launch in 2001, and contains a total of almost 20 million articles in 282 languages and dialects, as of Sept. 2011. As there is no editorial body that manages Wikipedia top-down, it is an open question how the huge online community around Wikipedia regulates and enforces standards of behavior and article quality. The user discussions on the article Talk pages might shed light on this issue and give an insight into the otherwise hidden processes of collaboration that, until now, could only be analyzed via interviews or group observations in experimental settings.

The main goal of the present paper is to analyze the content of the discussion pages of the Simple English Wikipedia with respect to the dialog acts aimed at the coordination efforts for article improvement. Dialog acts, according to the classic speech act theory (Austin, 1962; Searle, 1969), represent the meaning of an utterance at the level of illocutionary force, i.e. a dialog act label concisely characterizes the intention and the role of a contribution in a dialog. We chose the Simple English Wikipedia for our initial analysis, because we are able to obtain more representative results

[1] `http://www.ukp.tu-darmstadt.de/data/wikidiscourse`

by covering almost 15% of all relevant Talk pages, as opposed to the much smaller fraction we could achieve for the English Wikipedia. The long-term goal of this work is to identify relations between contributions on the Talk pages and particular article edits. We plan to analyze the relation between article discussions and article content and identify the edits in the article revision history that react to the problems discussed on the Talk page. In combination with article quality assessment (Yaari et al., 2011), this opens up the possibility to identify successful patterns of collaboration which increase the article quality. Furthermore, our work will enable practical applications. By augmenting Wikipedia articles with the information derived from automatically labeled discussions, article readers can be made aware of particular problems that are being discussed on the Talk page "behind the article".

Our primary contributions in this paper are: (1) an annotation schema for dialog acts reflecting the efforts for coordinating the article improvement; (2) the Simple English Wikipedia Discussion (SEWD) corpus, consisting of 100 segmented and annotated Talk pages which we make freely available for download; and (3) a dialog act classification pipeline that incorporates several state of the art machine learning algorithms and feature selection techniques and achieves an average F_1-score of .82 on our corpus.

2 Related Work

The analysis of speech and dialog acts has its roots in the linguistic field of pragmatics. In 1962, John Austin shifted the focus from the mere declarative use of language as a means for making factual statements towards its non-declarative use as a tool for performing actions. The speech act theory was further systematized by Searle (1969), whose classification of illocutionary acts (Searle, 1976) is still used as a starting point for creating dialog act classification schemata for natural language processing.

A well known, domain- and task-independent annotation schema is DAMSL (Core and Allen, 1997). It was created as the standard annotation schema for dialog tagging on the utterance level by the Discourse Resource Initiative. It uses a four-dimensional tagset that allows arbitrary label combinations for each utterance. Jurafsky et al. (1997) augmented the DAMSL schema to fit the peculiarities of the Switchboard corpus. The resulting SWDB-DAMSL schema contained more than 220 distinct labels which have been clustered to 42 coarse grained labels. Both schemata have often been adapted for special purpose annotation tasks.

With the rise of the social web, the amount of research analyzing user generated discourse substantially increased. In addition to analyzing web forums (Kim et al., 2010a), chats (Carpenter and Fujioka, 2011) and emails (Cohen et al., 2004), Wikipedia Talk pages have recently moved into the center of attention of the research community.

Viégas et al. (2007) manually annotate 25 Wikipedia article discussion pages with a set of 11 labels in order to analyze how Talk pages are used for planning the work on articles and resolving disputes among the editors. Schneider et al. (2011) extend this schema and manually annotate 100 Talk pages with 15 labels. They confirm the findings of Viégas et al. that coordination requests occur most frequently in the discussions.

Bender et al. (2011) describe a corpus of 47 Talk pages which have been annotated for authority claims and alignment moves. With this corpus, the authors analyze how the participants in Wikipedia discussions establish their credibility and how they express agreement and disagreement towards other participants or topics.

From a different perspective, Stvilia et al. (2008) analyze 60 discussion pages in regard to how information quality (IQ) in Wikipedia articles is assessed on the Talk pages and which types of IQ problems are identified by the community. They describe a Wikipedia IQ assessment model and map it to established frameworks. Furthermore, they provide a list of IQ problems along with related causal factors and necessary actions which has also inspired the design of our annotation schema.

Finally, Laniado et al. (2011) examine Wikipedia discussion networks in order to capture structural patterns of interaction. They extract the thread structure from all Talk pages in the English Wikipedia and create tree structures of the discussion. The analysis of the graphs reveals patterns that are unique to Wikipedia discussions and might be used as a means to characterize different types of Talk pages.

To the best of our knowledge, there is no work yet that uses machine learning to automati-

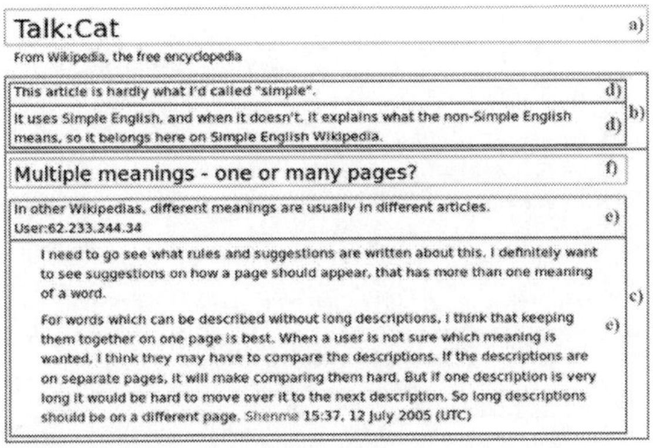

Figure 1: Structure of a Talk page: *a)* Talk page title, *b)* untitled discussion topic, *c)* titled discussion topic, *d)* unsigned turns, *e)* signed turns, *f)* topic title

cally classify user contributions in Wikipedia Talk pages. Furthermore, there is no corpus available that reflects the efforts of article improvement in Wikipedia discussions. This is the subject of our work.

3 Annotation Schema

The main purpose of Wikipedia Talk pages is the coordination of the editing process with the goal of improving and sustaining the quality of the respective article. The criteria for article quality in Wikipedia are loosely defined in the guidelines for *"good articles"*[2] and *"very good articles"*[3]. According to these guidelines, distinguished articles must be *well-written in simple English*, *comprehensive*, *neutral*, *stable*, *accurate*, *verifiable* and follow the Wikipedia *style guidelines*[4]. These criteria are the main points of reference in the discussions on the Talk pages.

Discourse analysis, as it is performed in this paper, can be carried out on various levels, depending on what is regarded as the smallest unit of the discourse. In this work, we focus on turns, not on individual utterances, as we are interested in a coarse-grained analysis of the discourse-structure as a first step towards a finer-grained discourse analysis. We define a *turn* (or contribution) as the body of text that is added by an individual contributor in one or more revisions to a single discussion topic until another contributor edits the page. Furthermore, a *topic* (or discussion) is the body of turns that revolve around a single matter. They are usually headed by a topic title. Finally, the *thread structure* designates the sequence of turns and their indentation levels on the Talk page. A structural overview of a Talk page and its constituents can be seen in Figure 1.

We composed an annotation schema that reflects the coordination efforts for article improvement. Therefore, we manually analyzed a set of thirty Talk pages from the Simple English Wikipedia to identify the types of article deficiencies that are discussed and the way article improvement is coordinated. We furthermore incorporated the findings from an information-scientific analysis of information quality in Wikipedia (Stvilia et al., 2008), which identifies twelve types of quality problems, like e.g. *Accuracy*, *Completeness* or *Relevance*. Our resulting tagset consists of 17 labels (cf. Table 1) which can be subdivided into four higher level categories:

Article Criticism Denote comments that identify deficiencies in the article. The criticism can refer to the article as a whole or to individual parts of the article.

Explicit Performative Announce, report or suggest editing activities.

Information Content Describe the direction of the communication. A contribution can be used to communicate new information to others (`IP`), to request information (`IS`), or to suggest changes to established facts (`IC`). The `IP` label applies to most of the contributions as most comments provide a certain amount of new information.

Interpersonal Describe the attitude that is expressed towards other participants in the discussion and/or their comments.

Since a single turn may consist of several utterances, it can consequently comprise multiple dialog acts. Therefore, we designed the annotation study as a multi-label classification task, i.e. the annotators can assign one or more labels to each annotation unit. Each label is chosen independently. Table 1 shows the labels, their respective definitions and an example from our corpus.

4 Corpus Creation and Analysis

The SEWD corpus consists of 100 annotated Talk pages extracted from a snapshot of the Simple En-

[2] http://simple.wikipedia.org/wiki/WP:RGA
[3] http://simple.wikipedia.org/wiki/WP:RVGA
[4] http://simple.wikipedia.org/wiki/WP:STYLE

Label	Description	Example
Article Criticism		
CM	Content incomplete or lacking detail	*It should be added (1) that voters may skip preferences, but (2) that skipping preferences has no impact on the result of the elections.*
CW	Lack of accuracy or correctness	*Kris Kringle is NOT a Germanic god, but an English mispronunciation of Christkind, a German word that means "the baby Jesus".*
CU	Unsuitable or unnecessary content	*The references should be removed. The reason: The references are too complicated for the typical reader of simple Wikipedia.*
CS	Structural problems	*Also use sectioning, and interlinking*
CL	Deficiencies in language or style	*This section needs to be simplified further; there are a lot of words that are too complex for this wiki.*
COBJ	Objectivity issues	*This article seems to take a clear pro-Christian, anti-commercial view.*
CO	Other kind of criticism	*I have started an article on Google. It needs improvement though.*
Explicit Performative		
PSR	Explicit suggestion, recommendation or request	*This section needs to be simplified further*
PREF	Explicit reference or pointer	*Got it. The URL is* `http://www.dmbeatles.com/history.php?year=1968`
PFC	Commitment to an action in the future	*Okay, I forgot to add that, I'll do so later tonight.*
PPC	Report of a performed action	*I took and hopefully simplified the "[[en:Prehistoric music—Prehistoric music]]" article from EnWP*
Information Content		
IP	Information providing	*"Depression" is the most basic term there is.*
IS	Information seeking	*So what kind of theory would you use for your music composing?*
IC	Information correcting	*In linguistics and generally speaking, when Talking about the lexicon in a language, words are usually categorized as 'nouns', 'verbs', 'adjectives' and so on. The term 'doing word' does not exist.*
Interpersonal		
ATT+	Positive attitude towards other contributor or acceptance	*Thank you.*
ATTP	Partial acceptance or partial rejection	*Okay, I can understand that, but some citations are going to have to be included for [[WP:V]].*
ATT-	Negative attitude towards other contributor or rejection	*Now what? You think you know so much about everything, and you are not even helping?!*

Table 1: Annotation schema for the dialog act classification in Wikipedia discussion pages with examples from the SEWD Corpus. Some examples have been shortened to fit the table.

glish Wikipedia from Apr 4th 2011.[5] Technically speaking, a Talk page is a normal Wiki page located in one of the Talk namespaces. In this work, we focus on article Talk pages and do not regard User Talk pages. We selected the discussion pages according to the number of turns they contain. First, we discarded all discussion pages with less than four contributions. We then analyzed the distribution of turn counts per discussion page in the remaining set of pages and defined three classes: (i) discussion pages with 4-10 turns, (ii) pages with 11-20 turns, and (iii) pages with more than 20 turns. We then randomly extracted 50 discussion pages from class (i), 40 pages from class (ii) and 10 pages from class (iii). This decision is grounded in the restricted resources for the human annotation task.

[5]The snapshot contains 69900 articles and 5783 Talk pages of which 683 contained more than 3 contributions.

Data Preprocessing Due to a lack of discussion structure, extracting the discussion threads from the Talk pages requires a substantial amount of preprocessing. Laniado et al. (2011) tackle the thread extraction by using text indentation and inserted user signatures as clues. We found these attributes to be insufficient for a reliable reconstruction of the thread structure.[6]

Our preprocessing approach consists of three steps: *data retrieval*, *topic segmentation* and *turn segmentation*. For retrieving the discussion pages, we use the *Java Wikipedia Library (JWPL)* (Zesch et al., 2008), which offers efficient, database-driven access to the contents of Wikipedia. We segment the individual Talk pages into discussions topics using the MediaWiki parser that comes with JWPL. In our corpus, the parser managed to identify all topic boundaries without any errors. The most complex preprocessing step is the turn segmentation.

First, we use the revision history of the Talk page to identify the author and the creation time of each paragraph. We use the *Wikipedia Revision Toolkit* (Ferschke et al., 2011) to examine the changes between adjacent revisions of the Talk page in order to identify the exact time a piece of text was added as well as the author of the contribution. We have to filter out malicious edits from the history, as they would negatively affect the segmentation process. We therefore disregard all edits that are reverted in later later revisions. In contrast to vandalism on article pages, this approach has proven to be sufficient to detect vandalism in the Talk page history.

Within each discussion topic, we aggregate all adjacent paragraphs with the same author and the same time stamp to one turn. In order to account for turns that were written in multiple revisions, we regard all time stamps within a window of 10 minutes[7] as belonging to the same turn, unless the page was edited by another user in the meantime. Finally, the turn is marked with the indentation level of its least indented paragraph. This information is used to identify the relationship between the turns, since indentation is used to indicate a reply to an existing comment in the discussion.

A co-author of this paper evaluated the acceptability of the boundaries of each turn in the SEWD corpus and found that 94% of the 1450 turns were correctly segmented. Turns with segmentation errors were not included in the gold standard.

[6]Viégas et al. (2007) reported that only 67% of the contributions on Wikipedia Talk pages are signed, which makes signatures an unreliable predictor for turn boundaries.

[7]We experimentally tested values between 1 and 60 minutes.

Annotation Process For our annotation study, we used the freely available MMAX2 annotation tool[8]. Two annotators were introduced to the annotation schema by an instructor and trained on an extra set of ten discussion pages. During the annotation of the corpus, the annotators were allowed to discuss difficult cases and could consult the instructor if in doubt. They had access to the segmented discussion pages within the MMAX2 tool as well as to the original Wikipedia articles and discussion pages on the web.

The reconciliation of the annotations was carried out by an expert annotator. In order to obtain a consolidated gold standard, the expert decided all cases in which the annotations of the two annotators did not match. Descriptive statistics for the label assignments of each annotator and for the gold standard can be seen in Table 2 and will be further discussed in Section 4.2.

Corpus Format We publish our SEWD corpus in two formats[9], the original MMAX format, and as XMI files for further processing with the *Apache Unstructured Information Management Architecture*[10]. For the latter format, we also provide the type system which defines all necessary corpus specific types needed for using the data in an NLP pipeline.

4.1 Inter-Annotator Agreement

To evaluate the reliability of our dataset, we perform a detailed inter-rater agreement study. For measuring the agreement of the individual labels, we report the observed agreement, Kappa statistics (Carletta, 1996), and F_1-scores. The latter are computed by treating one annotator as the gold standard and the other one as predictions (Hripcsak and Rothschild, 2005). The scores can be seen in Table 2.

The average observed agreement across all labels is $\bar{P_O} = .94$. The individual Kappa scores largely fall into the range that Landis and Koch (1977) regard as *substantial agreement*, while three labels are above the more strict .8 threshold for reliable annotations (Artstein and Poesio, 2008). Furthermore, we obtain an overall pooled Kappa (De Vries et al., 2008) of $\kappa_{pool} = .67$,

[8]http://www.mmax2.net

[9]http://www.ukp.tu-darmstadt.de/data/wikidiscourse

[10]http://uima.apache.org

Label	Annotator 1 N	Annotator 1 Percent	Annotator 2 N	Annotator 2 Percent	Inter-Annotator Agreement $N_{A_1 \cup A_2}$	P_O	κ	F_1	Gold Standard N	Gold Standard Percent
Article Criticism										
CM	183	13.4%	105	7.7%	193	.93	.63	.66	116	8.5%
CW	106	7.8%	57	4.2%	120	.95	.52	.55	70	5.1%
CU	69	5.0%	35	2.6%	83	.95	.38	.40	42	3.1%
CS	164	12.0%	101	7.4%	174	.94	.66	.69	136	9.9%
CL	195	14.3%	199	14.6%	244	.93	.73	.77	219	16.0%
COBJ	27	2.0%	23	1.7%	29	.99	.84	.84	27	2.0%
CO	20	1.5%	59	4.3%	71	.95	.18	.20	48	3.5%
Explicit Performative										
PSR	458	33.5%	351	25.7%	503	.86	.66	.76	406	29.7%
PREF	43	3.1%	31	2.3%	51	.98	.61	.62	45	3.3%
PFC	73	5.3%	65	4.8%	86	.98	.76	.77	77	5.6%
PPC	357	26.1%	340	24.9%	371	.97	.92	.94	358	26.2%
Information Content										
IP	1084	79.3%	1027	75.1%	1135	.89	.69	.93	1070	78.3%
IS	228	16.7%	208	15.2%	256	.95	.80	.83	220	16.1%
IC	187	13.7%	109	8.0%	221	.89	.46	.51	130	9.5%
Interpersonal										
ATT+	71	5.2%	140	10.2%	151	.94	.55	.58	144	10.5%
ATTP	71	5.2%	30	2.2%	79	.96	.42	.44	33	2.4%
ATT-	67	4.9%	74	5.4%	100	.96	.56	.58	87	6.4%

Table 2: Label frequencies and inter-annotator agreement. $N_{A_1 \cup A_2}$ denotes the number of turns that have been labeled with the given label by at least one annotator. P_O denotes the observed agreement.

which is defined as

$$\kappa_{pool} = \frac{\bar{P_O} - \bar{P_E}}{1 - \bar{P_E}} \quad (1)$$

with

$$\bar{P_O} = \frac{1}{L}\sum_{l=1}^{L} P_{O_l} \quad , \quad \bar{P_E} = \frac{1}{L}\sum_{l=1}^{L} P_{E_l} \quad (2)$$

where L denotes the number of labels, P_{E_l} the expected agreement and P_{O_l} the observed agreement of the lth label. κ_{pool} is regarded to be more accurate than an averaged Kappa.

For assessing the overall inter-rater reliability of the label set assignments *per turn*, we chose Krippendorff's Alpha (Krippendorff, 1980) using MASI, a measure of agreement on set-valued items, as the distance function (Passonneau, 2006). MASI accounts for partial agreement if the label sets of both annotators overlap in at least one label. We achieved an Alpha score of $\alpha = .75$. According to Krippendorff, datasets with this score are considered reliable and allow tentative conclusions to be drawn.

The CO label showed the lowest agreement of only $\kappa = .18$. The label was supposed to cover any criticism that is not covered by a dedicated label. However, the annotators reported that they chose this label when they were unsure whether a particular criticism label would fit a certain turn or not.

Labels in the interpersonal category all show agreement scores below 0.6. It turned out that the annotators had a different understanding of these labels. While one annotator assigned the labels for any kind of positive or negative sentiment, the other used the labels to express agreement and disagreement between the participants of a discussion.

A common problem for all labels were contributions with a high degree of indirectness and implicitness. Indirect contributions have to be interpreted in the light of conversational implicature theory (Grice, 1975), which requires contextual knowledge for decoding the intentions of a speaker. For example, the message

Is population density allowed to be n/a?

has the surface form of a question. However, the context of the discussion revealed that the author tried to draw attention to the missing figure in the article and requested it to be filled or removed. The annotators rarely made use of the context, which was a major source for disagreement in the study.

Another difficulty for the annotators were long discussion turns. While the average turn consists of 42 tokens, the largest contribution in the corpus is 658 tokens long. Turns of this size can cover multiple aspects and potentially comprise many different dialog acts, which increases the probability of disagreement. This issue can be addressed by going from the turn level to the utterance level in future work.

A comparison of our results with the agreement reported for other datasets shows that the reliability of our annotations lies well within the field of the related work. Bender et al. (2011) carried out an annotation study of social acts in 365 discussions from 47 Wikipedia Talk pages. They report Kappa scores for thirteen labels in two categories ranging from .13 to .66 per label. The overall agreement for each category was .50 and .59, respectively, which is considerably lower than our $\kappa_{pool} = .67$. Kim et al. (2010b) annotate pairs of posts taken from an online forum. They use a dialog act tagset with twelve labels customized for modeling troubleshooting-oriented forum discussions. For their corpus of 1334 posts, they report an overall Kappa of .59. Kim et al. (2010a) identify unresolved discussions in student online forums by annotating 1135 posts with five different speech acts. They report Kappa scores per speech act between .72 and .94. Their better results might be due to a more coarse grained label set.

4.2 Corpus Analysis

The SEWD corpus contains 313 discussions consisting of 1367 turns by 337 users. The average length of a turn is 42 words. 208 of the 337 contributors are registered Wikipedia users, 129 wrote anonymously. On average, each contributor wrote 168 words in 4 turns. However, there was a cluster of 16 people with ≥ 20 contributions.

Table 2 shows the frequencies of all labels in the SEWD corpus. The most frequent labels are *information providing* (IP), *requests* (PSR) and *reports of performed edits* (PPC). The IP-label was assigned to more than 78% of all 1367 turns, because almost every contribution provides a certain amount of information. The label was only omitted if a turn merely consisted of a discussion template but did not contain any text or if it exclusively contained questions.

More than a quarter of the turns are labeled with PSR and PPC, respectively. This indicates that edit requests and reports of performed edits are the main subject of discussion. Generally, it is more common that edits are reported after they have been made than to announce them before they are carried out, as can be seen in the ratio of PPC to PFC labels. The number of turns labeled with PSR is almost the same as the number of contributions labeled with either PPC or PFC. This allows the tentative conclusion that nearly all requests potentially lead to an edit action. As a matter of fact, the most common label adjacency pair[11] in the corpus is PSR→PPC, which substantiates this assumption.

Article criticism labels have been assigned to 39.4% of all turns. Almost half (241) of the labels from this class are assigned to the first turn of a discussion. This shows that it is common to open a discussion in reference to a particular deficiency of the article. The large number of CL labels compared to other labels from the same category is due to the fact that the Simple English Wikipedia requires authors to write articles in a way that they are understandable for non-native speakers of English. Therefore, the use of adequate language is one of the major concerns of the Simple English Wikipedia community.

5 Automatic Dialog Act Classification

For the automatic classification of dialog acts in Wikipedia Talk pages, we transform the multi-label classification problem into a binary classification task (Tsoumakas et al., 2010). We train a binary classifier for each label using the WEKA data-mining software (Hall et al., 2009). We use three learners for the classification task, a Naive Bayes classifier, J48, an implementation of the C4.5 decision tree algorithm (Quinlan, 1992) and SMO, an optimization algorithm for training support vector machines (Platt, 1998). Finally, we combine the best performing learners for each label in a UIMA-based classification pipeline (Ferrucci and Lally, 2004).

Features for Dialog Act Classification As features, we use all uni-, bi- and trigrams that occurred in at least three different turns. Furthermore, we include the time distance to the previous and the next turn (in seconds), the length of the current, previous and next turn (in tokens), the

[11] A label transition $A \rightarrow B$ is recorded if two adjacent turns are labeled with A and B, respectively.

position of the turn within the discussion, the indentation level of the turn and two binary features indicating whether a turn references or is referenced by another turn.[12] In order to capture the sequential nature of the discussions, we use the n-grams of the previous and the next turn as additional features.

Balancing Positive and Negative Instances Since the number of positive instances for each label is small compared to the number of negative instances, we create a balanced dataset which contains an equal amount of positive and negative instances. Therefore, we randomly select the appropriate number of negative instances and discard the rest. This improves the classification performance on every label for all three learners.

Feature Selection Using the full set of features, we achieve the following macro/micro averaged F_1-scores: 0.29 / 0.57 for Naive Bayes, 0.42 / 0.66 for J48 and 0.43 / 0.72 for SMO. To further improve the classification performance, we reduce the feature space using two feature selection techniques, the χ^2 metric (Yang and Pedersen, 1997) and the Information Gain approach (Mitchell, 1997). For each label, we train separate classifiers using the top 100, 200 and 300 features obtained by each feature selection technique and choose the best performing set for our final classification pipeline.

Indentation and *temporal distance to the preceding turn* proved to be the best ranked non-lexical features overall. Additionally, the *turn position within the topic* was a crucial feature for most labels in the criticism class and for PSR and IS labels. This is not surprising, because article criticism, suggestions and questions tend to occur in the beginning of a discussion. The two *reference* features have not proven to be useful. The relational information was better covered by the *indentation* feature. The subjective quality of the lexical features seems to be correlated with the inter-annotator agreement of the respective labels. Features for labels with low agreement contain many n-grams without any recognizable semantic connection to the label. For labels with good agreement, the feature lists almost exclusively contain meaningful lexical cues.

[12] A turn Y references a preceding turn X if the indentation level of Y is one level deeper than of X.

Label	Human	Base	Naive Bayes	J48	SMO	Best
CM	.66	.07	.68	.48	.66	.68
CW	.55	.01	.70	.20	.56	.70
CU	.40	.07	.66	.35	.59	.66
CS	.69	.09	.67	.67	.75	.75
CL	.77	.11	.70	.66	.73	.73
COBJ	.84	.04	.78	.51	.63	.78
CO	.20	.02	.61	.06	.39	.61
PSR	.76	.30	.72	.70	.76	.76
PREF	.62	.00	.76	.41	.64	.76
PFC	.77	.04	.70	.62	.73	.73
PPC	.94	.25	.74	.82	.85	.85
IP	.93	.74	.83	.93	.93	.93
IS	.83	.16	.79	.86	.85	.86
IC	.51	.06	.67	.32	.59	.67
ATT+	.58	.10	.61	.65	.72	.72
ATTP	.44	.03	.72	.25	.62	.72
ATT-	.58	.07	.52	.30	.52	.52
Macro	.65	.13	.70	.52	.68	.73
Micro	.79	.35	.74	.75	.80	.82

Table 3: F_1-Scores for the balanced set with feature selection on 10-fold cross-validation. *Base* refers to the baseline performance, *Best* to our classification pipeline.

Classification Results Table 3 shows the performance of all classifiers and our final classification pipeline evaluated on 10-fold cross validation. Naive Bayes performed surprisingly well and showed the best macro averaged scores among the three learners while SMO showed the best micro averaged performance. We compare our results to a random baseline and to the performance of the human annotators (cf. Table 3 and Figure 2). The baseline assigns the dialog act labels at random according to their frequency distribution in the gold standard. Our classifier outperformed the baseline significantly on all labels.

The comparison with the human performance shows that our system is able to reach the human performance. In most cases, the annotation agreement is reliable, and so are the results of the automatic classification. For the labels CU and CO, the inter-annotator agreement is not high. The comparably good performance of the classifiers on these labels shows that the instances do have shared characteristics. Human raters, however, have difficulties recognizing these labels consistently. Thus, their definitions need to be refined in future work.

To our knowledge, none of the related work on discourse analysis of Wikipedia Talk pages per-

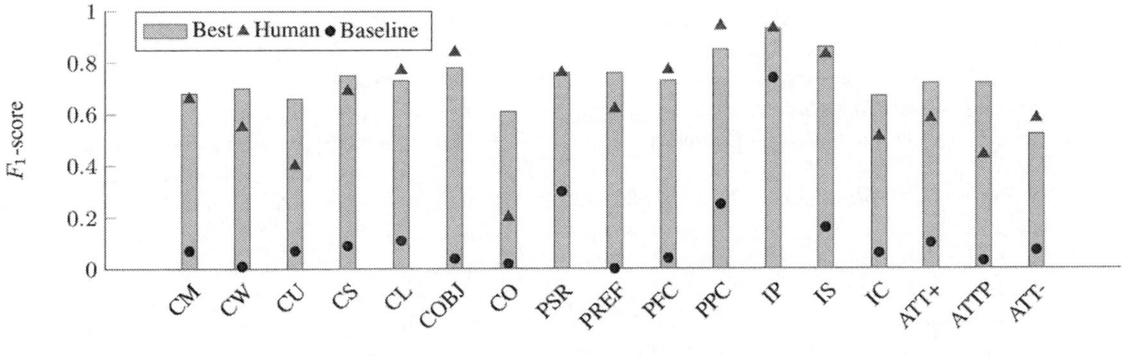

Figure 2: F_1-Scores for our classification pipeline (*Best*), the human performance and baseline performance.

formed automatic dialog act classification. However, there has been previous work on classifying speech acts in other discourse types. Kim et al. (2010a) use Support Vector Machines (SVM) and Transformation Based Learning (TBL) for the automatic assignment of five speech acts to posts taken from student online forums. They report individual F_1-scores per label which result in a macro average of 0.59 for SVM and 0.66 for TBL. Cohen et al. (2004) classify speech acts in emails. They train five binary classifiers using several learners on 1375 emails and report F_1 scores per speech act between .44 and .85. Despite the larger tagset, our classification approach achieves an average F_1-score of .82 and therefore lies in the top ranks of the related work.

6 Conclusions

In this paper, we proposed an annotation schema for the discourse analysis of Wikipedia discussions aimed at the coordination efforts for article improvement. We applied the annotation schema to a corpus of 100 Wikipedia Talk pages, which we make freely available for download. A thorough analysis of the inter-annotator agreement showed that the dataset is reliable. Finally, we performed automatic dialog act classification on Wikipedia Talk pages. Therefore, we combined three machine learning algorithms and two feature selection techniques to a classification pipeline, which we trained on our SEWD corpus. We achieve an average F_1-score of .82, which is comparable to the human performance of .79. The ability to automatically classify discussion pages will help to investigate the relations between article discussions and article edits, which is an important step towards understanding the processes of collaboration in large-scale Wikis. Furthermore, it will be the basis for practical applications that bring the hidden content of Talk pages to the attention of article readers.

Acknowledgments

This work has been supported by the Volkswagen Foundation as part of the Lichtenberg-Professorship Program under grant No. I/82806, and by the Hessian research excellence program "Landes-Offensive zur Entwicklung Wissenschaftlich-ökonomischer Exzellenz" (LOEWE) as part of the research center "Digital Humanities".

References

Ron Artstein and Massimo Poesio. 2008. Inter-Coder Agreement for Computational Linguistics. *Computational Linguistics*, 34(4):555–596, December.

John L. Austin. 1962. *How to Do Things with Words.* Clarendon Press, Cambridge, UK.

Emily M. Bender, Jonathan T. Morgan, Meghan Oxley, Mark Zachry, Brian Hutchinson, Alex Marin, Bin Zhang, and Mari Ostendorf. 2011. Annotating Social Acts: Authority Claims and Alignment Moves in Wikipedia Talk Pages. In *Proceedings of the Workshop on Language in Social Media*, pages 48–57, Portland, Oregon, USA.

Jean Carletta. 1996. Assessing Agreement on Classification Tasks: The Kappa Statistic. *Computational Linguistics*, 22(2):249–254.

Tamitha Carpenter and Emi Fujioka. 2011. The Role and Identification of Dialog Acts in Online Chat. In *Proceesings of the Workshop on Analyzing Microtext at the 25th AAAI Conference on Artificial Intelligence*, San Francisco, CA, USA.

William W. Cohen, Vitor R. Carvalho, and Tom M. Mitchell. 2004. Learning to Classify Email into "Speech Acts". In *Proceedings of the 2004 Conference on Empirical Methods in Natural Language Processing*, pages 309–316, Barcelona, ES.

Mark G. Core and James F. Allen. 1997. Coding dialogs with the DAMSL annotation scheme. In *Proceedings of the Working Notes of the AAAI Fall Symposium on Communicative Action in Humans and Machines*, pages 28–35, Cambridge, MA, USA.

Han De Vries, Marc N. Elliott, David E. Kanouse, and Stephanie S. Teleki. 2008. Using Pooled Kappa to Summarize Interrater Agreement across Many Items. *Field Methods*, 20(3):272–282.

David Ferrucci and Adam Lally. 2004. UIMA: An Architectural Approach to Unstructured Information Processing in the Corporate Research Environment. *Natural Language Engineering*, 10:327–348.

Oliver Ferschke, Torsten Zesch, and Iryna Gurevych. 2011. Wikipedia Revision Toolkit: Efficiently Accessing Wikipedia's Edit History. In *Proceedings of the 49th Annual Meeting of the Association for Computational Linguistics: Human Language Technologies. System Demonstrations*, pages 97–102, Portland, OR, USA.

Paul Grice. 1975. Logic and Conversation. In Peter Cole and Jerry L. Morgan, editors, *Syntax and Semantics*, volume 3. New York: Academic Press.

Mark Hall, Eibe Frank, Geoffrey Holmes, Bernhard Pfahringer, Peter Reutemann, and Ian H. Witten. 2009. The WEKA Data Mining Software: An Update. *SIGKDD Explorations*, 11:10–18.

George Hripcsak and Adam S. Rothschild. 2005. Agreement, the f-measure, and reliability in information retrieval. *Journal of the American Medical Informatics Association*, 12(3):296–298.

Dan Jurafsky, Liz Shriberg, and Debbra Biasca. 1997. Switchboard SWBD-DAMSL Shallow-Discourse-Function Annotation Coders Manual. Technical Report Draft 13, University of Colorado, Institute of Cognitive Science.

Jihie Kim, Jia Li, and Taehwan Kim. 2010a. Towards Identifying Unresolved Discussions in Student Online Forums. In *Proceedings of the NAACL HLT 2010 Fifth Workshop on Innovative Use of NLP for Building Educational Applications*, pages 84–91, Los Angeles, CA, USA.

Su Nam Kim, Li Wang, and Timothy Baldwin. 2010b. Tagging and linking web forum posts. In *Proceedings of the Fourteenth Conference on Computational Natural Language Learning*, CoNLL '10, pages 192–202, Stroudsburg, PA, USA.

Klaus Krippendorff. 1980. *Content Analysis: An Introduction to Its Methodology*. Thousand Oaks, CA: Sage Publications.

J. Richard Landis and Gary G. Koch. 1977. An Application of Hierarchical Kappa-type Statistics in the Assessment of Majority Agreement among Multiple Observers. *Biometrics*, 33(2):363–374, June.

David Laniado, Riccardo Tasso, Yana Volkovich, and Andreas Kaltenbrunner. 2011. When the Wikipedians Talk: Network and Tree Structure of Wikipedia Discussion Pages. In *Proceedings of the 5th International AAAI Conference on Weblogs and Social Media*, Dublin, IE.

Tom Mitchell. 1997. *Machine Learning*. McGraw-Hill Education (ISE Editions), 1st edition.

Rebecca Passonneau. 2006. Measuring Agreement on Set-valued Items (MASI) for Semantic and Pragmatic Annotation. In *Proceedings of the Fifth International Conference on Language Resources and Evaluation*, Genoa, IT.

John C. Platt. 1998. Fast training of support vector machines using sequential minimal optimization. In *Advances in Kernel Methods: Support Vector Learning*, pages 185–208, Cambridge, MA, USA.

Ilona R. Posner and Ronald M. Baecker. 1992. How People Write Together. In *Proceedings of the 25th Hawaii International Conference on System Sciences*, pages 127–138, Wailea, Maui, HI, USA.

Ross Quinlan. 1992. *C4.5: Programs for Machine Learning*. Morgan Kaufmann, 1st edition.

Jodi Schneider, Alexandre Passant, and John G. Breslin. 2011. Understanding and Improving Wikipedia Article Discussion Spaces. In *Proceedings of the 26th Symposium on Applied Computing*, Taichung, TW.

John R. Searle. 1969. *Speech Acts*. Cambridge University Press, Cambridge, UK.

John R. Searle. 1976. A classification of illocutionary acts. *Language in Society*, 5:1–23.

Besiki Stvilia, Michael B. Twidale, Linda C. Smith, and Les Gasser. 2008. Information Quality Work Organization in Wikipedia. *Journal of the American Society for Information Science*, 59:983–1001.

Grigorios Tsoumakas, Ioannis Katakis, and Ioannis P. Vlahavas. 2010. Mining multi-label data. In *Data Mining and Knowledge Discovery Handbook*, pages 667–685. Springer.

Fernanda Viégas, Martin Wattenberg, Jesse Kriss, and Frank Ham. 2007. Talk Before You Type: Coordination in Wikipedia. In *Proceedings of the 40th Annual Hawaii International Conference on System Sciences*, Waikoloa, Big Island, HI, USA.

Eti Yaari, Shifra Baruchson-Arbib, and Judit Bar-Ilan. 2011. Information quality assessment of community generated content: A user study of Wikipedia. *Journal of Information Science*, 37:487–498.

Yiming Yang and Jan O. Pedersen. 1997. A Comparative Study on Feature Selection in Text Categorization. In *Proceedings of the Fourteenth International Conference on Machine Learning*, pages 412–420, San Francisco, CA, USA.

Torsten Zesch, Christof Müller, and Iryna Gurevych. 2008. Extracting Lexical Semantic Knowledge from Wikipedia and Wiktionary. In *Proceedings of the 6th International Conference on Language Resources and Evaluation*, Marrakech, MA.

An Unsupervised Dynamic Bayesian Network Approach to Measuring Speech Style Accommodation

Mahaveer Jain[1], **John McDonough**[1], **Gahgene Gweon**[2], **Bhiksha Raj**[1], **Carolyn Penstein Rosé**[1,2]
1. Language Technologies Institute; 2. Human Computer Interaction Institute
Carnegie Mellon University
Pittsburgh, PA 15213
{mmahavee, johnmcd, ggweon, bhiksha, cprose}@cs.cmu.edu

Abstract

Speech style accommodation refers to shifts in style that are used to achieve strategic goals within interactions. Models of stylistic shift that focus on specific features are limited in terms of the contexts to which they can be applied if the goal of the analysis is to model socially motivated speech style accommodation. In this paper, we present an unsupervised Dynamic Bayesian Model that allows us to model stylistic style accommodation in a way that is agnostic to which specific speech style features will shift in a way that resembles socially motivated stylistic variation. This greatly expands the applicability of the model across contexts. Our hypothesis is that stylistic shifts that occur as a result of social processes are likely to display some consistency over time, and if we leverage this insight in our model,we will achieve a model that better captures inherent structure within speech.

1 Introduction

Sociolinguistic research on speech style and its resulting social interpretation has frequently focused on the ways in which shifts in style are used to achieve strategic goals within interactions, for example the ways in which speakers may adapt their speaking style to suppress differences and accentuate similarities between themselves and their interlocutors in order to build solidarity (Coupland, 2007; Eckert & Rickford, 2001; Sanders, 1987). We refer to this stylistic convergence as speech style accommodation. In the language technologies community, one targeted practical benefit of such modeling has been the achievement of more natural interactions with speech dialogue systems (Levitan et al., 2011).

Monitoring social processes from speech or language data has other practical benefits as well, such as enabling monitoring how beneficial an interaction is for group learning (Ward & Litman, 2007; Gweon, 2011), how equal participation is within a group (DiMicco et al., 2004), or how conducive an environment is for fostering a sense of belonging and identification with a community (Wang et al., 2011).

Typical work on computational models of speech style accommodation have focused on specific aspects of style that may be accommodated, such as the frequency or timing of pauses or backchannels (*i.e.*, words that show attention like 'Un huh' or 'ok'), pitch, or speaking rate (Edlund et al., 2009; Levitan & Hirschberg, 2011). In this paper, we present an unsupervised Dynamic Bayesian Model that allows us to model speech style accommodation in a way that does not require us to specify which linguistic features we are targeting. We explore a space of models defined by two independent factors, namely the direct influence of one speaker's style on another speaker's style and the influence of the relational gestalt between the two speakers that motivates the stylistic accommodation, and thus may keep the accommodation moving consistently, with the same momentum. Prior work has explored the influence of the first factor. However, because accommodation reflects social processes that extend over time within an interaction, one may expect a certain consistency of motion within the stylistic shift. Furthermore, we can leverage this consistency of style shift to identify socially meaningful variation without specifying ahead of time which particular stylistic elements we are focusing on. Our evaluation provides support for this hypothesis.

When stylistic shifts are focused on specific linguistic features, then measuring the extent of the stylistic accommodation is simple since a speaker's style may be represented on a one or two dimensional space, and movement can then be measured precisely within this space using simple linear functions. However, the rich sociolinguistic literature on speech style accommodation highlights a much greater variety of speech style characteristics that may be associated with social status within an interaction and may thus be beneficial to monitor for stylistic shifts. Unfortunately, within any given context, the linguistic features that have these status associations, which we refer to as *indexicality*, are only a small subset of the linguistic features that are being used in some way. Furthermore, which features carry this indexicality are specific to a context. Thus, separating the socially meaningful variation from variation in linguistic features occurring for other reasons is akin to searching for the proverbial needle in a haystack. It is this technical challenge that we address in this paper.

In the remainder of the paper we review the literature on speech style accommodation both from a sociolinguistic perspective and from a technological perspective in order to motivate our hypothesis and proposed model. We then describe the technical details of our model. Next, we present an experiment in which we test our hypothesis about the nature of speech style accommodation and find statistically significant confirming evidence. We conclude with a discussion of the limitations of our model and directions for ongoing research.

2 Theoretical Framework

Our research goal is to model the structure of speech in a way that allows us to monitor social processes through speech. One common goal of prior work on modeling speech dynamics has been for the purpose of informing the design of more natural spoken dialogue systems (Levitan et al., 2011). The practical goal of our work is to measure the social processes themselves, for example in order to estimate the extent to which group discussions show signs of productive consensus building processes (Gweon, 2011). Much prior work on modeling emotional speech has sought to identify features that themselves have a social interpretation, such as features that predict emotional states like uncertainty (Liscombe et al., 2005), or surprise (Ang et al., 2002), or social strategies like flirting (Ranganath et al., 2009). However, our goal is to monitor social processes that evolve over time and are reflected in the change in speech dynamics. Examples include fostering trust, forming attachments, or building solidarity.

2.1 Defining Speech Style Accommmodation

The concept of what we refer to as Speech Style Accommodation has its roots in the field of the Social Psychology of Language, where the many ways in which social processes are reflected through language, and conversely, how language influences social processes, are the objects of investigation (Giles & Coupland, 1991). As a first step towards leveraging this broad range of language processes, we refer to one very specific topic, which has been referred to as entrainment, priming, accommodation, or adaptation in other computational work (Levitan & Hirschberg, 2011). Specifically we refer to the finding that conversational partners may shift their speaking style within the interaction, either becoming more similar or less similar to one another.

Our usage of the term accommodation specifically refers to the process of speech style convergence within an interaction. Stylistic shifts may occur at a variety of levels of speech or language representation. For example, much of the early work on speech style accommodation focused on regional dialect variation, and specifically on aspects of pronunciation, such as the occurrence of post-vocalic "r" in New York City, that reflected differences in age, regional identification, and socioeconomic status (Labov, 2010a,b). Distribution of backchannels and pauses have also been the target of prior work on accommodation (Levitan & Hirschberg, 2011). These effects may be moderated by other social factors. For example, Bilous & Krauss (1988) found that females accommodated to their male partners in conversation in terms of average number of words uttered per turn. For example, Hecht et al. (1989) reported that extroverts are more listener adaptive than introverts and hence extroverts converged more in their data.

Accommodation could be measured either from textual or speech content of a conversation. The former relates to "what" people say whereas the latter to 'how' they say it. We are only interested in measuring accommodation from speech in this work. There has been work on convergence in text such as syntactic adaptation (Reitter et al., 2006) and language similarity in online communities (Huffaker et al., 2006).

2.2 Social Interpretation of Speech Style Accommodation

It has long been established that while some speech style shifts are subconscious, speakers may also choose to adapt their way of speaking in order to achieve social effects within an interaction (Sanders, 1987). One of the main motives for accommodation is to decrease social distance. On a variety of levels, speech style accommodation has been found to affect the impression that speakers give within an interaction. For example, Welkowitz & Feldstein (1970) found that when speakers become more similar to their partners, they are liked more by partners. Another study by Putman & Street Jr (1984) demonstrated that interviewees who converge to the speaking rate and response latency of their interviewers are rated more favorably by the interviewers. Giles et al. (1987) found that more accommodating speakers were rated as more intelligent and supportive by their partners. Conversely, social factors in an interaction affect the extent to which speakers engage in, and some times chose not to engage in, accommodation. For example, Purcell (1984) found that Hawaiian children exhibit more convergence in interactions with peer groups that they like more. Bourhis & Giles (1977) found that Welsh speakers while answering to an English surveyor broadened their Welsh accent when their ethnic identity was challenged. Scotton (1985) found that few people hesitated to repeat lexical patterns of their partners to maintain integrity. Nenkova et al. (2008) found that accommodation on high frequency words correlates with naturalness, task success, and coordinated turn-taking behavior.

2.3 Computational models of speech style accommodation

Prior research has attempted to quantify accommodation computationally by measuring similarity of speech and lexical features either over full conversations or by comparing the similarity in the first half and the second half of the conversation. For example, Edlund et al. (2009) measure accommodation in pause and gap length using measures such as synchrony and convergence. Levitan & Hirschberg (2011) found that accommodation is also found in special social behaviors within conversation such as backchannels. They show that speakers in conversation tend to use similar kinds of speech cues such as high pitch at the end of utterance to invite a backchannel from their partner. In order to measure accommodation on these cues, they compute the correlation between the numerical values of these cues used by partners.

In our work we measure accommodation using Dynamic Bayesian Networks (DBNs). Our models are learnt in an unsupervised fashion. What we are specifically interested in is the manner in which the influence of one partner on the other is modeled. What is novel in our approach is the introduction of the concept of an accommodation state, or relational gestalt variable, which essentially models the momentum of the influence that one partner is having on the other partner's speaking style. It allows us to represent structurally the insight that accommodation occurs over time as a reflection of a social process, and thus has some consistency in the nature of the accommodation within some span of time. The prior work described in this section can be thought of as taking the influence of the partner's style directly on the speaker's style within an instant as the floor shifts from one speaker to the next. Thus, no consistency in the manner in which the accommodation is occurring is explicitly encouraged by the model. The major advantage of consistency of motion within the style shift over time is that it provides a sign post for identifying which style variation within the speech is salient with respect to social interpretation within a specific interaction so that the model may remain agnostic and may thus be applied to a variety of interactions that differ with respect to which stylistic features are salient in this respect.

3 A Dynamic Bayesian Network Model for Conversation

Speech stylistic information is reflected in prosodic features such as pitch, energy, speaking rate etc. In this work, we leverage on several of these speech features to quantify accommodation. We propose a series of models that can be trained unsupervised from speech features and can be used for predicting accommodation. The models attempt to capture the dependence of speech features on speaking style, as well as the effect of persistence and accommodation on style. We use a dynamic Bayesian network (DBN) formalism to capture these relationships. Below we briefly review DBNs, and subsequently describe the speech features used, and the proposed models.

3.1 Dynamic Bayesian Networks

The theory of Bayesian networks is well documented and understood (Jensen, 1996; Pearl, 1988). A Bayesian network is a probabilistic model that represents statistical relationships between random variables via a directed acyclic graph (DAG). Formally, it is a directed acyclic graph whose nodes represent random variables (which may be observable quantities, *latent* unobservable variables, or hypotheses to be estimated). Edges represent *conditional* dependencies; nodes which are connected by an edge represent random variables that have a direct influence on one another. The entire network represents the joint probability of all the variables represented by the nodes, with appropriate factoring of the conditional dependencies between variables.

Consider, for instance, a joint distribution over a set of random variables $x_1, x_2, \cdots, x_n$, modeled by a Bayesian network. Let $\mathcal{V} = v_1, v_2, \cdots, v_n$ represent the set of n nodes in the network, representing the random variables $x_1, x_2, \cdots, x_n$ respectively. Let $\wp(v_i)$ represent the set of parent nodes of v_i, *i.e.* nodes in $\mathcal{V}$ that have a directed edge into a node v_i. Then, by the dependencies specified by the network, $P(x_i|x_1, x_2, \cdots, x_n) = P(x_i|x_j : v_j \in \wp(v_i))$. In other words, any variable x_i is directly dependent only on its parent variables, *i.e.* the random variables represented by the nodes in $\wp(v_i)$, and is independent of all other variables given these variables. The joint probability of $x_1, x_2, \cdots, x_n$ is hence given by

$$p(x_1, x_2, ..., x_n) = \prod_i p(x_i|x_{\pi_i}) \quad (1)$$

Where x_{π_i} represents $\{x_j : v_j \in \wp(v_i)$, *i.e.* the parents of x_i in the network. We note that not all of these variables need to be observable; often in such models several of the variables are unobservable, *i.e.* they are *latent*. In order to obtain the joint distribution of the observable variables the latent variables must be marginalized out. *I.e.* if $x_1, \cdots, x_m$ are observable and $x_{m+1}, \cdots, x_n$ are latent, $P(x_1, \cdots, x_m) = \sum_{x_{m+1}, \cdots, x_n} P(x_1, x_2, \cdots, x_n)$.

Dynamic Bayesian networks (DBNs) further represent time-series data through a recurrent formulation of a basic Bayesian network that represents the relationship between variables. Within a DBN a set of random variables at each time instance t is represented as a static Bayesian Network with temporal dependencies to variables at other instants. Namely, the distribution of a variable $x_{i,t}$ at time t is dependent on other variables at times $t - \tau$, $x_{j,t-\tau}$ through conditional probabilities of the form $Pr(x_{i,t}|x_{j,t-\tau})$. An example DBN, consisting of three variables (A, B and C), two of which have temporal dependencies is shown in Figure 1.

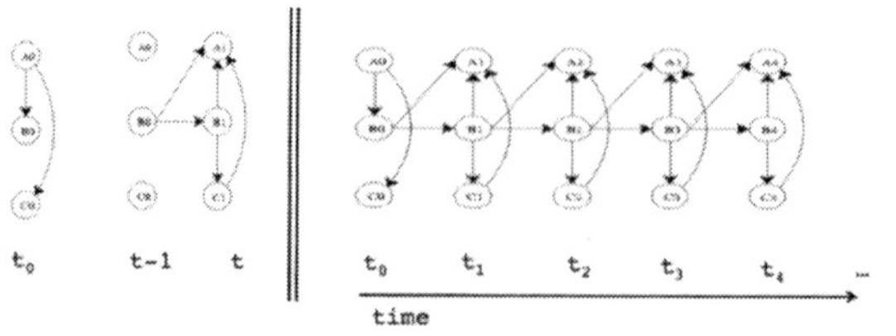

Figure 1: An example Dynamic Bayesian Network (DBN) showing the temporal relationship between three random variables (A,B and C). A is observered and dependent on two hidden variables B and C. Directed edges across time ($t - 1 \rightarrow t$) indicate temporal relationships between variables. In this example, the variables A_t and B_t are both dependent on B_{t-1} with the relationship defined through conditional distributions $P(A_t|B_{t-1})$ and $P(B_t|B_{t-1})$.

One benefit of the DBN formalism is that in addition to providing a compact graphical way of representing statistical relationships between variables in a process, the constrained, directed network structure also allows for simplified inference. Moreover, the conditional distributions associated with the network are often assumed not to vary over time, i.e. $Pr(x_{i,t}|x_{j,t-\tau}) = Pr(x_{i,t'}|x_{j,t'-\tau})$. This allows for a very compact representation of DBNs and allows for efficient Expectation-Maximization (EM) learning algorithms to be applied.

In the discussion that follows we do not explicitly specify the random variables and the form of the associated probability distributions, but only present them graphically. The joint distribution of the variables should nevertheless be obvious from the figures. We employ EM to learn the parameters of the models from training data, and the junction tree algorithm (Lauritzen & Spiegelhalter, 1988) to perform inference.

3.2 Speech Features

We characterize conversations as a series of spoken turns by the partners. We characterize the speech in each turn through a vector that captures several aspects of the signal that are salient to style. We used the OPENSmile toolkit (opensmile, 2011) to compute the features. Specifically, within each turn the speech was segmented into analysis windows of 50ms, where adjacent windows overlapped by 40ms. From each analysis window a total of 7 features were computed: voice probability, harmonic to noise ratio, voice quality , three measures of pitch (F_0, F_0^{raw}, F_0^{env}), and loudness. A 10-bin histogram of feature values was computed for each of these features, which was then normalized to sum to 1.0. The normalized histogram effectively represents both the values and the fluctuation in the features. For instance, a histogram of loudness values captures the variation in the loudness of the speaker within a turn. The logarithms of the normalized 10-bin histograms for the 7 features were concatenated to result in a single 70-dimensional observation vector for the turn. These 70 dimensional observation vectors for each turn of any speaker are represented in our model as o_t^i where t is turn index and i is speaker index.

3.3 Elements of the Models

In this section we formally describe the elements of our model.

Speaking Style State: These states represent the speaking styles of the partners in a conversation. We represent these states as s_t^i, where t represent turn index and i represents speaker index. These states are assumed to belong to a finite, discrete set $\mathcal{S} = \{s_1, s_2, \cdots, s_k\}$, *i.e.* $s_t^i \in \mathcal{S}\ \forall(i, t)$.

Accommodation State: An accommodation state represents the indirect influence of partners on each other in a conversation. In our present design, it can take a value of either 1 or 0. These states are represented as A_t, where t is turn index.

Observation Vector: The observation vectors are the feature vectors o_t^i computed for each turn.

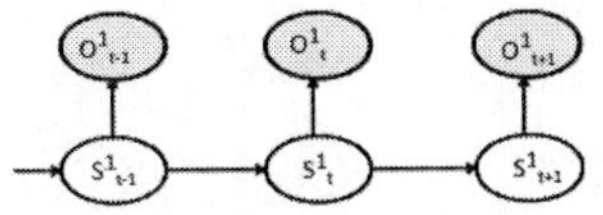

Figure 2: The basic generative model.

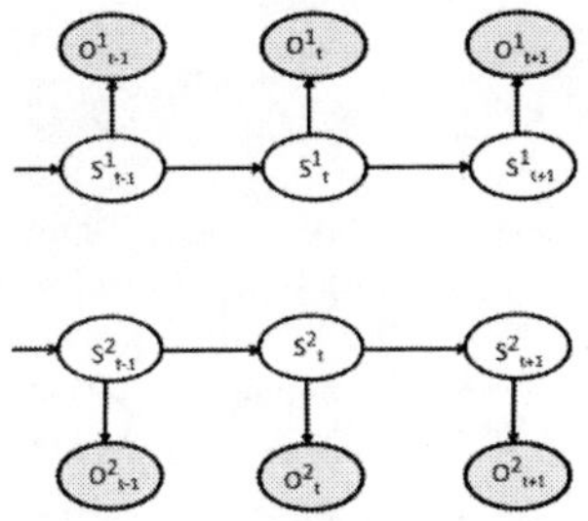

Figure 3: ISM: The dynamics of each speaker are independent of the other speaker.

3.4 Models for Accommodation

Our models embody two premises. First, a person's speech in any turn is a function of his/her speaking style in that turn. Second, a person's speaking style at any turn depends not only by their own personal biases, but also by their accommodation to their partner. We represent these dependencies as a DBN.

Our basic model to represent the generation of speech (i.e. speech features) by a speaker in the absence of other influences is shown in Figure 2. The speech features o_t^i in any turn depend only on the speaking style s_t^i in that turn. The style s_t^i in any turn depends on the style s_{t-1}^i in the previous turn, to capture the speaker-specific patterns of variation in speaking style. We note that this is a rather simple model and patterns of variation in style are captured only through the statistical dependence between styles in consequent turns.

We now build our models for accommodation on this basic model.

3.4.1 Style-based models

Our two first models assume that accommodation is demonstrated as a direct dependence of a person's speaking sytle on their partner's style. Therefore the models only consider speaking styles.

The Independent Speaker Model

Our simplest model for a conversation assumes

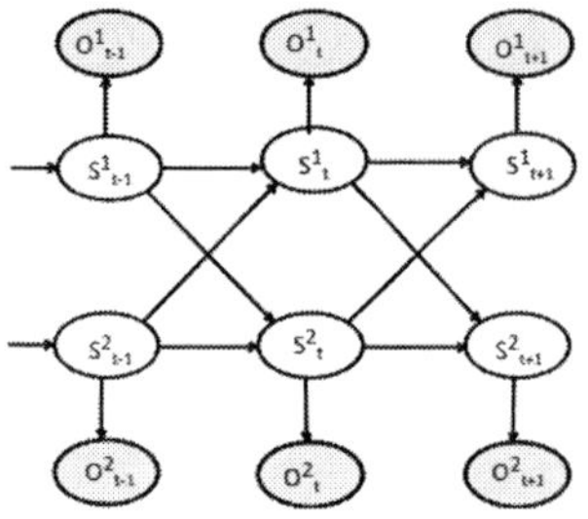

Figure 4: CSDM: A speaker's style depends on their partner's style at the previous turn.

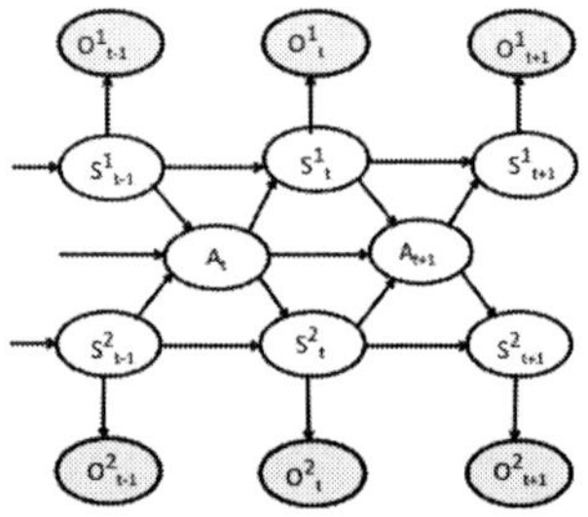

Figure 5: SASM: Both partners' styles depend on mutual accommodation to one another.

that each person's speaking style evolves independently, uninfluenced by their partner. The DBN for this is shown in Figure 3. We refer to this model as the *Independent Speaker Model* (ISM). Note that the set of values that the style states can take is common for both speakers. The speaking styles for the two speakers may be said to be confluent in any turn if both of them are in the same style state at that turn.

The Cross-speaker Dependence Model

Intuitively, in a conversation speakers are influenced by their partners' speaking style in previous turns. The *Cross-Speaker Dependence Model* (CSDM) represents this dependence as shown in the DBN in Figure 4. In this model a person's speaking style depends on both their own and their partner's speaking styles in the previous turn.

3.4.2 Accommodation state models

Accommodation state models assume that conversations actually have an underlying state of accommodation, and that speakers in fact vary their speaking styles in response to it. We models this through a binary-valued accommodation state that is embedded into the DBN. We posit two types of accommodation state models.

The Symmetric Accommodation State Model

In the *symmetric* accommodation state model

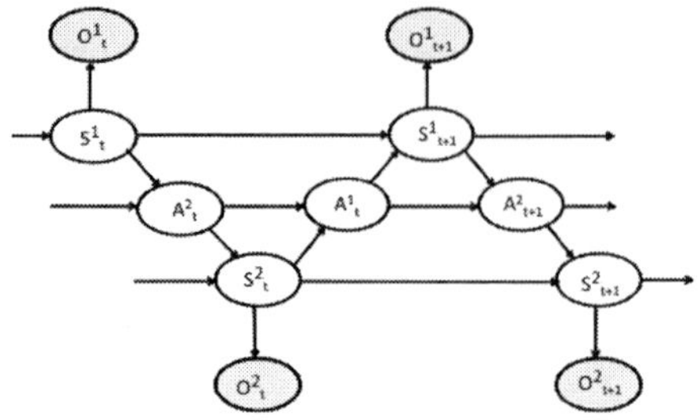

Figure 6: AASM: Accommodation state associated with every speaker turn

(SASM) we assume that accommodation is a jointly experienced characteristic of the conversation at any time, which enjoys some persistence, but is also affected by the speaking styles exhibited by the speakers at each turn. The accommodation at any time in turn affects the speaking styles of both speakers in the next turn. The DBN for this model is shown in Figure 5.

The Asymmetric Accommodation State Model

The *asymmetric* accommodation state model (AASM) represents accommodation as a speaker-turn-specific characteristic. In any turn, the accommodation for a speaker depends chiefly on their partner's most recent speaking style. The accommodation state can change after each speaker turn. Figure 6 shows the DBN for this model. Note that this model captures the asymmetric nature of accommodation, e.g. it may be the case that only one of the speakers is accommodating. For instance, if if $a_t^1 = 0$ and $a_t^2 = 1$, only speaker2 is accommodating but not speaker1.

3.4.3 Accommodated style dependence models

While accommodation state models explicitly models accommodation, they do not explicitly represent how it is expressed. In reality, accommodation is a process of convergence – an accommodating speaker's speaking style may be expected to converge toward that of their partner. In other words, the person's speaking style depends not only on whether they are accommodating or not, but also on their partner's style at the previous turn. *Accommodated style dependence models* explicitly represent this dependence.

The Symmetric Accommodated Style Dependence Model

The *Symmetric Accommodated Style Dependence Model* (SASDM) extends the SASM, to in-

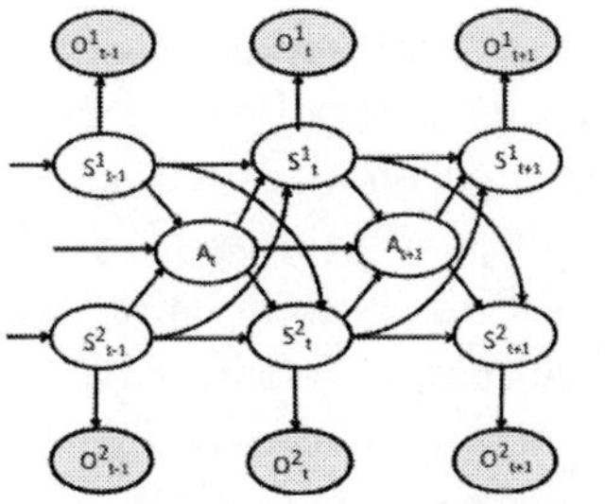

Figure 7: SASDM: A speaker's style depends both on mutual accommodation and the partner's style in the previous turn.

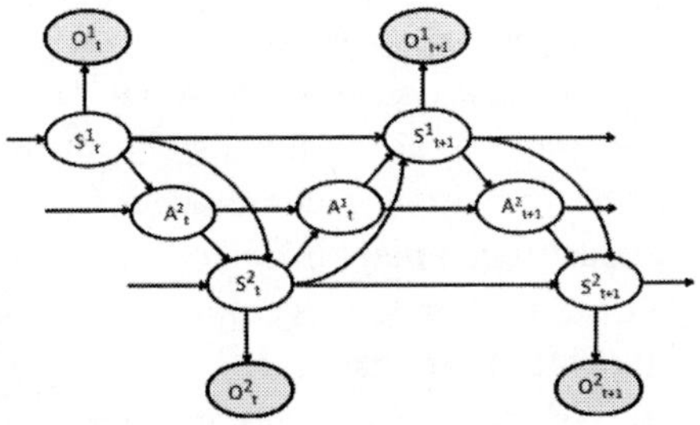

Figure 8: AASDM: The accommodation state associated with every speaker and a speaker's style depends on the partner's style.

dicate that a speaker's style in any turn depends both on accommodation and on their partner's style in the previous turn. Figure 7 shows the DBN for this model.

Asymmetric Accommodated Style Dependence Model

The *Asymmetric Accommodated Style Dependence Model* (AASDM) extends the AASM by adding a direct dependence between a speaker's style and their partner's style in their most recent turn. The DBN for this is shown in Figure 8.

3.5 Interpreting the states

We note that we have referred to the states in the models above as "style" states. In reality, in all cases, we learn the parameters of the model in an unsupervised manner, since the data we use to train it do not have either speaking style or accommodation indicated (although, if they were labeled, the labels could be employed within our models). Consequently, we have no assurance that the states learned will actually correspond to speaking styles. They can only be considered a *proxy* for speaking style. Nevertheless, if both speakers are in the same state, they can both be expected to be producing similar prosodic features, as represented in the observation vectors. It is hence reasonable to assume that they are both speaking in similar style. Similarly, the accommodation state cannot be expected to actually depict accommodation; nevertheless, it can capture the dependencies that govern when the two speakers are likely to be in the same state.

4 Evaluation

The model we have just described allows us to investigate two separate aspects of our concept of speech style accommodation. The first aspect is that style accommodation occurs as a local influence of one speaker's style on the other speaker's style, as depicted by direct links between style states. The second aspect is that although this is a local phenomenon, because it is a reflection of a social process that extends over a period of time, there will be some persistence of accommodation over longer periods of time, as characterized by the accommodation state. We presented two different operationalizations of the accommodation state above, namely Asymmetric and Symmetric.

Accommodation is a phenomenon that occurs within interactions between speakers; we can expect not to observe accommodation occurring between individuals that have never met and are not interacting. On average, then, we expect to see more evidence of speech style accommodation in pairs of individuals who are interacting (i.e., Real Pairs) than in pairs of individuals who are not interacting and have never met (i.e., Constructed Pairs). Thus, we may evaluate the extent to which our model is sensitive to social dynamics within pairs by the extent to which it is able to distinguish between true conversation between Real Pairs of speaker and synthetic conversation between Constructed Pairs. A similar experimental paradigm has been adopted in prior work on speech style accommodation (Levitan et al., 2011).

Hypothesis: Our hypothesis is that models that explicitly represent the notion that accommodation occurs over a span of time with consistency of momentum will achieve better success at distinguishing between Real Pairs and Constructed Pairs than models that do not.

Experimental Manipulation: Thus, using the model we have just described, we are able to test our hypothesis using a 2×3 factorial design in which one factor is the inclusion of direct links from the style of one speaker to the style of the other speaker, which we refer to as the DirectInfluence (DI) factor, with values True (T) and False (F), and the second factor is the inclusion of links from style states to and from Accommodation states, which we refer to as the IndirectInfluence (II) factor, with values False (F), Asymmetric (A), and Symmetric (S). The result of this 2×3 factorial design are the 6 different models described in Section 3, namely ISM (DI=False, II=False), CSDM (DI=True, II=False), SASM (DI=False, II=Symmetric), AASM (DI=False, II=Asymmetric), SASDM (DI=True, II=Symmetric), and AASDM (DI=True, II= Asymmetric).

Corpus: The success criterion in our experiment is the extent to which models of speech style accommodation are able to distinguish between Real Pairs and Constructed pairs. In order to set up this comparison, we began with a corpus of debates between students about the reasons for the fall of the Ottoman Empire. We obtained this corpus from researchers who originally collected it to investigate issues related to learning from conversational interactions (Nokes et al., 2010). The full corpus contains interactions between 76 pairs of students who interacted for 8 minutes. Within each pair, one student was assigned the role of arguing that the fall of the Ottoman empire was due to internal causes, whereas the other student was assigned the role of arguing that the fall of the Ottoman empire was due to external causes. Each student was given a 4 page packet of supporting information for their side of the debate to draw from in the interaction.

The speech from each participant was recorded on a separate channel. As a first step, we aligned the speech recordings automatically to their transcriptions at the word and turn level. After aligning the corpus at the word level, we identify the turn interval of each partner in the conversation. We use 66 of the debates out of the complete set of 76 for the experiments discussed in this paper. We had to eliminate 10 dialogues where the segmentation and alignment failed. For each of our models, we used the same 3 fold cross-validation.

Participants: Participants were all male undergraduate students between the ages of 18 and 25. In prior studies, it has been shown that accommodation varies based on gender, age and familiarity between partners. This corpus is particularly appropriate because it controls for most of these factors. Furthermore, because the participants did not know each other before the debate, we can assume that if accommodation happened, it was only during the conversation.

Real versus Constructed Pairs: In our analysis below, we compare measured accommodation between pairs of humans who had a real conversation and a constructed pair in which one person from that conversation is paired with a constructed partner, where the partner's side of the conversation was constructed from turns that occurred in other conversations. We set up this comparison in order to isolate speech style convergence from lexical convergence when we evaluate the performance of our model. The difference between the measured accommodation between real and constructed pairs is treated as a weak operationalization of model accuracy at measuring speech style accommodation.

For each of the 20 Real pairs in the test corpus we composed one Constructed Pair. Each Constructed Pair comprised one student from the corresponding Real Pair (i.e., the Real Student) and a Constructed Partner that resembled the real partner in content but not necessarily style. We did this by iterating through the real partner's turns, replacing each with a turn that matched as well as possible in terms of lexical content but came from a different conversation. Lexical content match was measured in terms of cosine similarity. Turns were selected from the other Real pairs. Thus, the Constructed Partner had similar content to the corresponding real partner on a turn by turn basis, but the style of expression could not be influenced by the Real Student. Thus, ideally we should not see evidence of speech style accommodation within the Constructed Pairs.

Experimental Procedure: For each of the four models we computed an Accommodation Score for each of the Real Pairs and Constructed Pairs. In order to obtain a measure that can be used to compute accommodation for all the models considered, we compute the accommodation value as the fraction of turns in a session where partners exhibited the same speaking style.

Results: In order to test our hypothesis we constructed an ANOVA model with Accommodation Score as the dependent variable and DirectInfluence, IndirectInfluence, RealVsConstructed as independent variables. Additionally we included the interaction terms between all pairs of inde-

	DI	II	Real $\mu(\sigma)$	Constructed $\mu(\sigma)$
SASDM	T	S	.54 (.23)	.44 (.29)
SASM	F	S	.54 (.23)	.44 (.29)
CSDM	T	F	.6 (.26)	.52 (.3)
ISM	F	F	.56 (.25)	.51 (.32)
AASM	F	A	.6 (.24)	.51 (.3)
AASDM	T	A	.61 (.24)	.48 (.3)

Table 1: Accommodation measured using different models. Legend: μ=mean, σ = standard deviation, DI = "Direct Influence", II = "Indirect Influence".

pendent variables. Using this ANOVA model, we find a highly significant main effect of the RealVsConstructed factor that demonstrates the general ability of the models to achieve separation between Real Pairs and Constructed Pairs; on average $F(1,780) = 18.22$, $p < .0001$.

However, when we look more closely, we find that although the trend is consistently to find more evidence of speech style accommodation in Real Pairs than in Constructed Pairs, we see differentiation among the models in terms of their ability to achieve this separation. When we examine the two way interactions between DirectInfluence and RealVsConstructed as well as between IndirectInfluence and RealVsConstructed, although we do not find significant interactions, we do find some suggestive patterns when we do the student T posthoc analysis. In particular, when we explore just the interaction between IndirectInfluence links, we find a significant separation between Real vs Constructed pairs for models with Accommodation states, but not for the cases where no Accommodation states are included. However, when we do the same for the interaction between DirectInfluence links and RealVsConstructed, we find significant separation with or without those links. This suggests that IndirectInfluence links are more important than DirectInfluence links. At a finer-grained level, when we examine the models individually, we only find a significant separation between Real and Constructed pairs with the model that includes both DirectInfluence and Symmetric IndirectInfluence links. These results suggest that Symmetric IndirectInfluence links may be slightly better than Asymmetric ones, and that combining DirectInfluence links and Symmetric IndirectInfluence links may be the best combination.

Based on this analysis, we find support for our hypothesis. We find that the model that includes Symmetric IndirectInfluence links and DirectInfluence links is the best balance between representational power and simplicity. The support for the inclusion of DirectInfluence links in the model is weaker than that of IndirectInfluence links, however. On a larger dataset, we may have observed stronger effects of both factors. Even on this small dataset, we find evidence that adding that structure improves the performance of the model without leading to overfitting.

5 Conclusions and Current Directions

In this paper we presented an unsupervised dynamic Bayesian modeling approach to modeling speech style accommodation in face-to-face interactions. Our model was motivated by the idea that because accommodation reflects social processes that extend over time within an interaction, one may expect a certain consistency of motion within the stylistic shift. Our evaluation demonstrated a statistically significant advantage for the models that embodied this idea.

An important motivation for our modeling approach was that it allows us to avoid targeting specific linguistic style features in our measure of accommodation. However, in our evaluation, we only tested our approach on conversations between male undergraduate students discussing the fall of the Ottoman Empire. Thus, while our evaluation provides evidence that we have taken a first important step towards our ultimate goal, we cannot yet claim that we have a model that performs equally effectively across contexts. In our future work, we plan to formally test the extent to which this allows us to accurately measure accommodation within contexts in which very different stylistic elements carry strategic social value.

Another important direction of our current research is to explore how measures of speech style accommodation may predict other important measures such as how positively partners view one another, how successful partners perform tasks together, or how well students learn together.

6 Acknowledgments

We gratefully acknowledge John Levine and Timothy Nokes for sharing their data with us. This work was funded by NSF SBE 0836012.

References

Ang, J., Dhillon, R., Krupski, A., Shriberg, E., & Stolcke, A. (2002). Prosody-based automatic detection of annoyance and frustration in human-computer dialog. In *Proc. ICSLP*, volume 3, pages 2037–2040. Citeseer.

Bilous, F. & Krauss, R. (1988). Dominance and accommodation in the conversational behaviours of same-and mixed-gender dyads. *Language and Communication*, **8**(3), 4.

Bourhis, R. & Giles, H. (1977). The language of intergroup distinctiveness. *Language, ethnicity and intergroup relations*, **13**, 119.

Coupland, N. (2007). *Style: Language variation and identity*. Cambridge Univ Pr.

DiMicco, J., Pandolfo, A., & Bender, W. (2004). Influencing group participation with a shared display. In *Proceedings of the 2004 ACM conference on Computer supported cooperative work*, pages 614–623. ACM.

Eckert, P. & Rickford, J. (2001). *Style and sociolinguistic variation*. Cambridge Univ Pr.

Edlund, J., Heldner, M., & Hirschberg, J. (2009). Pause and gap length in face-to-face interaction. In *Proc. Interspeech*.

Giles, H. & Coupland, N. (1991). *Language: Contexts and consequences*. Thomson Brooks/Cole Publishing Co.

Giles, H., Mulac, A., Bradac, J., & Johnson, P. (1987). Speech accommodation theory: The next decade and beyond. *Communication yearbook*, **10**, 13–48.

Gweon, G. A. P. U. M. R. B. R. C. P. (2011). The automatic assessment of knowledge integration processes in project teams. In *Proceedings of Computer Supported Collaborative Learning*.

Hecht, M., Boster, F., & LaMer, S. (1989). The effect of extroversion and differentiation on listener-adapted communication. *Communication Reports*, **2**(1), 1–8.

Huffaker, D., Jorgensen, J., Iacobelli, F., Tepper, P., & Cassell, J. (2006). Computational measures for language similarity across time in online communities. In *In ACTS: Proceedings of the HLT-NAACL 2006 Workshop on Analyzing Conversations in Text and Speech*, pages 15–22.

Jensen, F. V. (1996). *An introduction to Bayesian networks*. UCL Press.

Labov, W. (2010a). *Principles of linguistic change: Internal factors*, volume 1. Wiley-Blackwell.

Labov, W. (2010b). *Principles of linguistic change: Social factors*, volume 2. Wiley-Blackwell.

Lauritzen, S. L. & Spiegelhalter, D. J. (1988). Local computations with probabilities on graphical structures and their application to expert systems. *Journal of the Royal Statistical Society*, **50**, 157–224.

Levitan, R. & Hirschberg, J. (2011). Measuring acoustic-prosodic entrainment with respect to multiple levels and dimensions. In *Proceedings of Interspeech*.

Levitan, R., Gravano, A., & Hirschberg, J. (2011). Entrainment in speech preceding backchannels. In *Proceedings of the 49th Annual Meeting of the Association for Computational Linguistics: Human Language Technologies: short papers-Volume 2*, pages 113–117. Association for Computational Linguistics.

Liscombe, J., Hirschberg, J., & Venditti, J. (2005). Detecting certainness in spoken tutorial dialogues. In *Proceedings of INTERSPEECH*, pages 1837–1840. Citeseer.

Nenkova, A., Gravano, A., & Hirschberg, J. (2008). High frequency word entrainment in spoken dialogue. In *In Proceedings of ACL-08: HLT. Association for Computational Linguistics*.

opensmile (2011). http://opensmile.sourceforge.net/.

Pearl, J. (1988). *Probabilistic Reasoning in Intelligent Systems: Networks of Plausible Inference*. Morgan Kaufmann.

Purcell, A. (1984). Code shifting hawaiian style: childrens accommodation along a decreolizing continuum. *International Journal of the Sociology of Language*, **1984**(46), 71–86.

Putman, W. & Street Jr, R. (1984). The conception and perception of noncontent speech performance: Implications for speech-accommodation theory. *International Journal of the Sociology of Language*, **1984**(46), 97–114.

Ranganath, R., Jurafsky, D., & McFarland, D. (2009). It's not you, it's me: detecting flirting and its misperception in speed-dates. In *Proceedings of the 2009 Conference on Empirical Methods in Natural Language Processing: Volume 1-Volume 1*, pages 334–342. Association for Computational Linguistics.

Reitter, D., Keller, F., & Moore, J. D. (2006). Computational modelling of structural priming in dialogue. In *In Proc. Human Language Technology conference - North American chapter of the Association for Computational Linguistics annual mtg*, pages 121–124.

Sanders, R. (1987). *Cognitive foundations of calculated speech*. State University of New York Press.

Scotton, C. (1985). What the heck, sir: Style shifting and lexical colouring as features of powerful language. *Sequence and pattern in communicative behaviour*, pages 103–119.

Wang, Y., Kraut, R., & Levine, J. (2011). To stay or leave? the relationship of emotional and informational support to commitment in online health support groups. In *Proceedings of the ACM conference on computer-supported cooperative work*. ACM.

Ward, A. & Litman, D. (2007). Automatically measuring lexical and acoustic/prosodic convergence in tutorial dialog corpora. In *Proceedings of the SLaTE Workshop on Speech and Language Technology in Education*. Citeseer.

Welkowitz, J. & Feldstein, S. (1970). Relation of experimentally manipulated interpersonal perception and psychological differentiation to the temporal patterning of conversation. In *Proceedings of the 78th Annual Convention of the American Psychological Association*, volume 5, pages 387–388.

Learning the Fine-Grained Information Status of Discourse Entities

Altaf Rahman and **Vincent Ng**
Human Language Technology Research Institute
University of Texas at Dallas
Richardson, TX 75083-0688
{altaf,vince}@hlt.utdallas.edu

Abstract

While information status (IS) plays a crucial role in discourse processing, there have only been a handful of attempts to automatically determine the IS of discourse entities. We examine a related but more challenging task, *fine-grained* IS determination, which involves classifying a discourse entity as one of 16 IS *subtypes*. We investigate the use of rich knowledge sources for this task in combination with a rule-based approach and a learning-based approach. In experiments with a set of Switchboard dialogues, the learning-based approach achieves an accuracy of 78.7%, outperforming the rule-based approach by 21.3%.

1 Introduction

A linguistic notion central to discourse processing is *information status* (IS). It describes the extent to which a discourse entity, which is typically referred to by noun phrases (NPs) in a dialogue, is *available* to the hearer. Different definitions of IS have been proposed over the years. In this paper, we adopt Nissim et al.'s (2004) proposal, since it is primarily built upon Prince's (1992) and Eckert and Strube's (2001) well-known definitions, and is empirically shown by Nissim et al. to yield an annotation scheme for IS in dialogue that has good reproducibility.[1]

Specifically, Nissim et al. (2004) adopt a three-way classification scheme for IS, defining a discourse entity as (1) old to the hearer if it is known to the hearer and has previously been referred to in the dialogue; (2) new if it is unknown to her and has not been previously referred to; and (3) mediated (henceforth med) if it is newly mentioned in the dialogue but she can infer its identity from a previously-mentioned entity. To capture finer-grained distinctions for IS, Nissim et al. allow an old or med entity to have a *subtype*, which *subcategorizes* an old or med entity. For instance, a med entity has the subtype set if the NP that refers to it is in a set-subset relation with its antecedent.

IS plays a crucial role in discourse processing: it provides an indication of how a discourse model should be updated as a dialogue is processed incrementally. Its importance can be reflected in part in the amount of attention it has received in theoretical linguistics over the years (e.g., Halliday (1976), Prince (1981), Hajičová (1984), Vallduví (1992), Steedman (2000)), and in part in the benefits it can potentially bring to NLP applications. One task that could benefit from knowledge of IS is identity coreference: since new entities by definition have not been previously referred to, an NP marked as new does not need to be resolved, thereby improving the precision of a coreference resolver. Knowledge of *fine-grained* or *subcategorized* IS is valuable for other NLP tasks. For instance, an NP marked as set signifies that it is in a set-subset relation with its antecedent, thereby providing important clues for bridging anaphora resolution (e.g., Gasperin and Briscoe (2008)).

Despite the potential usefulness of IS in NLP tasks, there has been little work on *learning* the IS of discourse entities. To investigate the plausibility of learning IS, Nissim et al. (2004) annotate a set of Switchboard dialogues with such information[2], and subsequently present a

[1] It is worth noting that several IS annotation schemes have been proposed more recently. See Götze et al. (2007) and Riester et al. (2010) for details.

[2] These and other linguistic annotations on the Switchboard dialogues were later released by the LDC as part of the NXT corpus, which is described in Calhoun et al. (2010).

rule-based approach and a learning-based approach to acquiring such knowledge (Nissim, 2006). More recently, we have improved Nissim's learning-based approach by augmenting her feature set, which comprises seven string-matching and grammatical features, with lexical and syntactic features (Rahman and Ng, 2011; henceforth R&N). Despite the improvements, the performance on new entities remains poor: an F-score of 46.5% was achieved.

Our goal in this paper is to investigate *fine-grained IS determination*, the task of classifying a discourse entity as one of the 16 IS subtypes defined by Nissim et al. (2004).[3] Owing in part to the increase in the number of categories, fine-grained IS determination is arguably a more challenging task than the 3-class IS determination task that Nissim and R&N investigated. To our knowledge, this is the first empirical investigation of automated fine-grained IS determination.

We propose a *knowledge-rich* approach to fine-grained IS determination. Our proposal is motivated in part by Nissim's and R&N's poor performance on new entities, which we hypothesize can be attributed to their sole reliance on shallow knowledge sources. In light of this hypothesis, our approach employs *semantic* and *world* knowledge extracted from manually and automatically constructed knowledge bases, as well as *coreference* information. The relevance of coreference to IS determination can be seen from the definition of IS: a new entity is not coreferential with any previously-mentioned entity, whereas an old entity may. While our use of coreference information for IS determination and our earlier claim that IS annotation would be useful for coreference resolution may seem to have created a chicken-and-egg problem, they do not: since coreference resolution and IS determination can benefit from each other, it may be possible to formulate an approach where the two tasks can mutually bootstrap.

We investigate rule-based and learning-based approaches to fine-grained IS determination. In the rule-based approach, we manually compose rules to combine the aforementioned knowledge sources. While we could employ the same knowledge sources in the learning-based approach, we chose to encode, among other knowledge sources, the hand-written rules and their predictions directly as features for the learner. In an evaluation on 147 Switchboard dialogues, our learning-based approach to fine-grained IS determination achieves an accuracy of 78.7%, substantially outperforming the rule-based approach by 21.3%. Equally importantly, when employing these linguistically rich features to learn Nissim's 3-class IS determination task, the resulting classifier achieves an accuracy of 91.7%, surpassing the classifier trained on R&N's state-of-the-art feature set by 8.8% in absolute accuracy. Improvements on the new class are particularly substantial: its F-score rises from 46.7% to 87.2%.

[3]One of these 16 classes is the new type, for which no subtype is defined. For ease of exposition, we will refer to the new type as one of the 16 subtypes to be predicted.

2 IS Types and Subtypes: An Overview

In Nissim et al.'s (2004) IS classification scheme, an NP can be assigned one of three main types (old, med, new) and one of 16 subtypes. Below we will illustrate their definitions with examples, most of which are taken from Nissim (2003) or Nissim et al.'s (2004) dataset (see Section 3).

Old. An NP is marked is old if (i) it is coreferential with an entity introduced earlier, (ii) it is a generic pronoun, or (iii) it is a personal pronoun referring to the dialogue participants. Six subtypes are defined for old entities: identity, event, general, generic, ident_generic, and relative. In Example 1, *my* is marked as old with subtype identity, since it is coreferent with *I*.

(1) I was angry that he destroyed **my** tent.

However, if the markable has a verb phrase (VP) rather than an NP as its antecedent, it will be marked as old/event, as can be seen in Example 2, where the antecedent of *That* is the VP *put my phone number on the form*.

(2) They ask me to put my phone number on the form. **That** I think is not needed.

Other NPs marked as old include (i) relative pronouns, which have the subtype relative; (ii) personal pronouns referring to the dialogue participants, which have the subtype general, and (iii) generic pronouns, which have the subtype generic. The pronoun *you* in Example 3 is an instance of a generic pronoun.

(3) I think to correct the judicial system, **you** have to get the lawyer out of it.

Note, however, that in a coreference chain of generic pronouns, every element of the chain is assigned the subtype ident_generic instead.

Mediated. An NP is marked as med if the entity it refers to has not been previously introduced in the dialogue, but can be inferred from already-mentioned entities or is generally known to the hearer. Nine subtypes are available for med entities: general, bound, part, situation, event, set, poss, func_value, and aggregation.

General is assigned to med entities that are generally known, such as *the Earth*, *China*, and most proper names. Bound is reserved for bound pronouns, an instance of which is shown in Example 4, where *its* is bound to the variable of the universally quantified NP, *Every cat*.

(4) Every cat ate **its** dinner.

Poss is assigned to NPs involved in intra-phrasal possessive relations, including prenominal genitives (i.e., X's Y) and postnominal genitives (i.e., Y of X). Specifically, Y will be marked as poss if X is old or med; otherwise, Y will be new. For example, in cases like *a friend's boat* where *a friend* is new, *boat* is marked as new.

Four subtypes, namely part, situation, event, and set, are used to identify instances of bridging (i.e., entities that are inferrable from a related entity mentioned earlier in the dialogue). As an example, consider the following sentences:

(5a) He passed by the door of Jan's house and saw that **the door** was painted red.

(5b) He passed by Jan's house and saw that **the door** was painted red.

In Example 5a, by the time the hearer processes the second occurrence of *the door*, she has already had a mental entity corresponding to *the door* (after processing the first occurrence). As a result, the second occurrence of *the door* refers to an old entity. In Example 5b, on the other hand, the hearer is not assumed to have any mental representation of the door in question, but she can infer that the door she saw was part of Jan's house. Hence, this occurrence of *the door* should be marked as med with subtype part, as it is involved in a part-whole relation with its antecedent.

If an NP is involved in a set-subset relation with its antecedent, it inherits the med subtype set. This applies to the NP *the house payment* in Example 6, whose antecedent is *our monthly budget*.

(6) What we try to do to stick to our monthly budget is we pretty much have **the house payment**.

If an NP is part of a situation set up by a previously-mentioned entity, it is assigned the subtype situation, as exemplified by the NP *a few horses* in the sentence below, which is involved in the situation set up by *John's ranch*.

(7) Mary went to John's ranch and saw that there were only **a few horses**.

Similar to old entities, an NP marked as *med* may be related to a previously mentioned VP. In this case, the NP will receive the subtype event, as exemplified by the NP *the bus* in the sentence below, which is triggered by the VP *traveling in Miami*.

(8) We were traveling in Miami, and **the bus** was very full.

If an NP refers to a value of a previously mentioned function, such as the NP *30 degrees* in Example 9, which is related to *the temperature*, then it is assigned the subtype func_value.

(9) The temperature rose to **30 degrees**.

Finally, the subtype aggregation is assigned to coordinated NPs if at least one of the NPs involved is not new. However, if all NPs in the coordinated phrase are new, the phrase should be marked as new. For instance, the NP *My son and I* in Example 10 should be marked as med/aggregation.

(10) I have a son ... **My son and I** like to play chess after dinner.

New. An entity is new if it has not been introduced in the dialogue and the hearer cannot infer it from previously mentioned entities. No subtype is defined for new entities.

There are cases where more than one IS value is appropriate for a given NP. For instance, given two occurrences of *China* in a dialogue, the second occurrence can be labeled as old/identity (because it is coreferential with an earlier NP) or med/general (because it is a generally known entity). To break ties, Nissim (2003) define a precedence relation on the IS subtypes, which yields a total ordering on the subtypes. Since all the old subtypes are ordered before their med counterparts in this relation, the second occurrence of *China* in our example will be labeled as old/identity. Owing to space limitations, we refer the reader to Nissim (2003) for details.

3 Dataset

We employ Nissim et al.'s (2004) dataset, which comprises 147 Switchboard dialogues. We partition them into a training set (117 dialogues) and a test set (30 dialogues). A total of 58,835 NPs are annotated with IS types and subtypes.[4] The distributions of NPs over the IS subtypes in the training set and the test set are shown in Table 1.

	Train	(%)	Test	(%)
old/identity	10236	(20.1)	1258	(15.8)
old/event	1943	(3.8)	290	(3.6)
old/general	8216	(16.2)	1129	(14.2)
old/generic	2432	(4.8)	427	(5.4)
old/ident_generic	1730	(3.4)	404	(5.1)
old/relative	1241	(2.4)	193	(2.4)
med/general	2640	(5.2)	325	(4.1)
med/bound	529	(1.0)	74	(0.9)
med/part	885	(1.7)	120	(1.5)
med/situation	1109	(2.2)	244	(3.1)
med/event	351	(0.7)	67	(0.8)
med/set	10282	(20.2)	1771	(22.3)
med/poss	1318	(2.6)	220	(2.8)
med/func_value	224	(0.4)	31	(0.4)
med/aggregation	580	(1.1)	117	(1.5)
new	7158	(14.1)	1293	(16.2)
total	50874	(100)	7961	(100)

Table 1: Distributions of NPs over IS subtypes. The corresponding percentages are parenthesized.

4 Rule-Based Approach

In this section, we describe our rule-based approach to fine-grained IS determination, where we manually design rules for assigning IS subtypes to NPs based on the subtype definitions in Section 2, Nissim's (2003) IS annotation guidelines, and our inspection of the IS annotations in the training set. The motivations behind having a rule-based approach are two-fold. First, it can serve as a baseline for fine-grained IS determination. Second, it can provide insight into how the available knowledge sources can be combined into prediction rules, which can potentially serve as "sophisticated" features for a learning-based approach.

As shown in Table 2, our ruleset is composed of 18 rules, which should be applied to an NP in the order in which they are listed. Rules 1–7 handle the assignment of old subtypes to NPs. For instance, Rule 1 identifies instances of old/general, which comprises the personal pronouns referring to the dialogue participants. Note that this and several other rules rely on coreference information, which we obtain from two sources: (1) chains generated automatically using the Stanford Deterministic Coreference Resolution System (Lee et al., 2011)[5], and (2) manually identified coreference chains taken directly from the annotated Switchboard dialogues. Reporting results using these two ways of obtaining chains facilitates the comparison of the IS determination results that we can realistically obtain using existing coreference technologies against those that we could obtain if we further improved existing coreference resolvers. Note that both sources provide *identity* coreference chains. Specifically, the gold chains were annotated for NPs belonging to old/identity and old/ident_generic. Hence, these chains can be used to distinguish between old/general NPs and old/ident_generic NPs, because the former are *not* part of a chain whereas the latter are. However, they cannot be used to distinguish between old/general entities and old/generic entities, since neither of them belongs to any chains. As a result, when gold chains are used, Rule 1 will classify all occurrences of "you" that are not part of a chain as old/general, regardless of whether the pronoun is generic. While the gold chains alone can distinguish old/general and old/ident_generic NPs, the Stanford chains cannot distinguish any of the old subtypes in the absence of other knowledge sources, since it generates chains for *all* old NPs regardless of their subtypes. This implies that Rule 1 and several other rules are only a very crude approximation of the definition of the corresponding IS subtypes.

The rules for the remaining old subtypes can be interpreted similarly. A few points deserve mention. First, many rules depend on the string of the NP under consideration (e.g., "they" in Rule 2 and "whatever" in Rule 4). The decision of which strings are chosen is based primarily on our inspection of the training data. Hence, these rules are partly data-driven. Second, these rules should be applied in the order in which they are shown. For instance, though not explicitly stated, Rule 3 is only applicable to the non-anaphoric "you" and "they" pronouns, since Rule 2 has already covered their anaphoric counterparts. Finally, Rule 7 uses non-anaphoricity as a test of old/event NPs. The

[4]Not all NPs have an IS type/subtype. For instance, a pleonastic "it" does not refer to any real-world entity and therefore does not have any IS, and so are nouns such as "course" in "of course", "accident" in "by accident", etc.

[5]The Stanford resolver is available from http://nlp.stanford.edu/software/corenlp.shtml.

1. **if** the NP is “I” or “you” and it is not part of a coreference chain, **then**
   subtype := old/general
2. **if** the NP is “you” or “they” and it is anaphoric, **then**
   subtype := old/ident_generic
3. **if** the NP is “you” or “they”, **then**
   subtype := old/generic
4. **if** the NP is “whatever” or an indefinite pronoun prefixed by “some” or “any” (e.g., “somebody”), **then**
   subtype := old/generic
5. **if** the NP is an anaphoric pronoun other than “that”, or its string is identical to that of a preceding NP, **then**
   subtype := old/ident
6. **if** the NP is “that” and it is coreferential with the immediately preceding word, **then**
   subtype := old/relative
7. **if** the NP is “it”, “this” or “that”, and it is not anaphoric, **then**
   subtype := old/event
8. **if** the NP is pronominal and is not anaphoric, **then**
   subtype := med/bound
9. **if** the NP contains “and” or “or”, **then**
   subtype := med/aggregation
10. **if** the NP is a multi-word phrase that (1) begins with “so much”, “something”, “somebody”, “someone”, “anything”, “one”, or “different”, or (2) has “another”, “anyone”, “other”, “such”, “that”, “of” or “type” as neither its first nor last word, or (3) its head noun is also the head noun of a preceding NP, **then**
    subtype := med/set
11. **if** the NP contains a word that is a hyponym of the word “value” in WordNet, **then**
    subtype := med/func_value
12. **if** the NP is involved in a part-whole relation with a preceding NP based on information extracted from ReVerb’s output, **then**
    subtype := med/part
13. **if** the NP is of the form “X’s Y” or “poss-pro Y”, where X and Y are NPs and poss-pro is a possessive pronoun, **then**
    subtype := med/poss
14. **if** the NP fills an argument of a FrameNet frame set up by a preceding NP or verb, **then**
    subtype := med/situation
15. **if** the head of the NP and one of the preceding verbs in the same sentence share the same WordNet hypernym which is not in synsets that appear one of the top five levels of the noun/verb hierarchy, **then**
    subtype := med/event
16. **if** the NP is a named entity (NE) or starts with “the”, **then**
    subtype := med/general
17. **if** the NP appears in the training set, **then**
    subtype := its most frequent IS subtype in the training set
18. subtype := new

Table 2: Hand-crafted rules for assigning IS subtypes to NPs.

reason is that these NPs have VP antecedents, but both the gold chains and the Stanford chains are computed over NPs only.

Rules 8–16 concern med subtypes. Apart from Rule 8 (med/bound), Rule 9 (med/aggregation), and Rule 11 (med/func_value), which are arguably crude approximations of the definitions of the corresponding subtypes, the med rules are more complicated than their old counterparts, in part because of their reliance on the extraction of sophisticated knowledge. Below we describe the extraction process and the motivation behind them.

Rule 10 concerns med/set. The words and phrases listed in the rule, which are derived manually from the training data, provide suggestive evidence that the NP under consideration is a subset or a specific portion of an entity or concept mentioned earlier in the dialogue. Examples include “another bedroom”, “different color”, “somebody else”, “any place”, “one of them”, and “most other cities”. Condition 3 of the rule, which checks whether the head noun of the NP has been mentioned previously, is a good test for identity coreference, but since all the old entities have supposedly been identified by the preceding rules, it becomes a reasonable test for set-subset relations.

For convenience, we identify part-whole relations in Rule 12 based on the output produced by ReVerb (Fader et al., 2011), an open information extraction system.[6] The output contains, among other things, relation instances, each of which is represented as a triple, <A,rel,B>, where rel is a relation, and A and B are its arguments. To preprocess the output, we first identify all the triples that are instances of the part-whole relation using regular expressions. Next, we create clusters of relation arguments, such that each pair of arguments in a cluster has a part-whole relation. This is easy: since part-whole is a transitive relation (i.e., <A,$part$,B> and <B,$part$,C> implies <A,$part$,C>), we cluster the arguments by taking the transitive closure of these relation instances. Then, given an NP NP_i in the test set, we assign med/part to it if there is a preceding NP NP_j such that the two NPs are in the same argument cluster.

In Rule 14, we use FrameNet (Baker et al., 1998) to determine whether med/situation should be assigned to an NP, NP_i. Specifically, we check whether it fills an argument of a frame set up by a preceding NP, NP_j, or verb. To exemplify, let us assume that NP_j is "capital punishment". We search for "punishment" in FrameNet to access the appropriate frame, which in this case is "rewards and punishments". This frame contains a list of arguments together with examples. If NP_i is one of these arguments, we assign med/situation to NP_i, since it is involved in a situation (described by a frame) that is set up by a preceding NP/verb.

In Rule 15, we use WordNet (Fellbaum, 1998) to determine whether med/event should be assigned to an NP, NP_i, by checking whether NP_i is related to an event, which is typically described by a verb. Specifically, we use WordNet to check whether there exists a verb, v, preceding NP_i such that v and NP_i have the same hypernym. If so, we assign NP_i the subtype med/event. Note that we ensure that the hypernym they share does not appear in the top five levels of the WordNet noun and verb hierarchies, since we want them to be related via a concept that is not overly general.

Rule 16 identifies instances of med/general. The majority of its members are *generally-known* entities, whose identification is difficult as it requires world knowledge. Consequently, we apply this rule only after all other med rules are applied. As we can see, the rule assigns med/general to NPs that are named entities (NEs) and definite descriptions (specifically those NPs that start with "the"). The reason is simple. Most NEs are generally known. Definite descriptions are typically not new, so it seems reasonable to assign med/general to them given that the remaining (i.e., unlabeled) NPs are presumably either new and med/general.

Before Rule 18, which assigns an NP to the new class by default, we have a "memorization" rule that checks whether the NP under consideration appears in the training set (Rule 17). If so, we assign to it its most frequent subtype based on its occurrences in the training set. In essence, this heuristic rule can help classify some of the NPs that are somehow "missed" by the first 16 rules.

The ordering of these rules has a direct impact on performance of the ruleset, so a natural question is: what criteria did we use to order the rules? We order them in such a way that they respect the total ordering on the subtypes imposed by Nissim's (2003) preference relation (see Section 3), except that we give med/general a lower priority than Nissim due to the difficulty involved in identifying generally known entities, as noted above.

5 Learning-Based Approach

In this section, we describe our learning-based approach to fine-grained IS determination. Since we aim to automatically label an NP with its IS subtype, we create one training/test instance from each hand-annotated NP in the training/test set. Each instance is represented using five types of features, as described below.

Unigrams (119704). We create one binary feature for each unigram appearing in the training set. Its value indicates the presence or absence of the unigram in the NP under consideration.

Markables (209751). We create one binary feature for each markable (i.e., an NP having an IS subtype) appearing in the training set. Its value is 1 if and only if the markable has the same string as the NP under consideration.

Markable predictions (17). We create 17 binary features, 16 of which correspond to the 16 IS subtypes and the remaining one corresponds to a "dummy subtype". Specifically, if the NP un-

[6] We use ReVerb ClueWeb09 Extractions 1.1, which is available from `http://reverb.cs.washington.edu/reverb_clueweb_tuples-1.1.txt.gz`.

der consideration appears in the training set, we use Rule 17 in our hand-crafted ruleset to determine the IS subtype it is most frequently associated with in the training set, and then set the value of the feature corresponding to this IS subtype to 1. If the NP does not appear in the training set, we set the value of the dummy subtype feature to 1.

Rule conditions (17). As mentioned before, we can create features based on the hand-crafted rules in Section 4. To describe these features, let us introduce some notation. Let Rule i be denoted by $A_i \longrightarrow B_i$, where A_i is the condition that must be satisfied before the rule can be applied and B_i is the IS subtype predicted by the rule. We could create one binary feature from each A_i, and set its value to 1 if A_i is satisfied by the NP under consideration. These features, however, fail to capture a crucial aspect of the ruleset: the ordering of the rules. For instance, Rule i should be applied only if the conditions of the first $i-1$ rules are not satisfied by the NP, but such ordering is not encoded in these features. To address this problem, we capture rule ordering information by defining binary feature f_i as $\neg A_1 \wedge \neg A_2 \wedge \ldots \neg A_{i-1} \wedge A_i$, where $1 \leq i \leq 16$. In addition, we define a feature, f_{18}, for the default rule (Rule 18) in a similar fashion, but since it does not have any condition, we simply define f_{18} as $\neg A_1 \wedge \ldots \wedge \neg A_{16}$. The value of a feature in this feature group is 1 if and only if the NP under consideration satisfies the condition defined by the feature. Note that we did not create any features from Rule 17 here, since we have already generated "markables" and "markable prediction" features for it.

Rule predictions (17). None of the features f_i's defined above makes use of the predictions of our hand-crafted rules (i.e., the B_i's). To make use of these predictions, we define 17 binary features, one for each B_i, where $i = 1, \ldots, 16, 18$. Specifically, the value of the feature corresponding to B_i is 1 if and only if f_i is 1, where f_i is a "rule condition" feature as defined above.

Since IS subtype determination is a 16-class classification problem, we train a multi-class SVM classifier on the training instances using SVM^{multiclass} (Tsochantaridis et al., 2004), and use it to make predictions on the test instances.[7]

6 Evaluation

Next, we evaluate the rule-based approach and the learning-based approach to determining the IS subtype of each hand-annotated NP in the test set.

Classification results. Table 3 shows the results of the two approaches. Specifically, row 1 shows their accuracy, which is defined as the percentage of correctly classified instances. For each approach, we present results that are generated based on gold coreference chains as well as automatic chains computed by the Stanford resolver.

As we can see, the rule-based approach achieves accuracies of 66.0% (gold coreference) and 57.4% (Stanford coreference), whereas the learning-based approach achieves accuracies of 86.4% (gold) and 78.7% (Stanford). In other words, the gold coreference results are better than the Stanford coreference results, and the learning-based results are better than the rule-based results. While perhaps neither of these results are surprising, we are pleasantly surprised by the *extent* to which the learned classifier outperforms the hand-crafted rules: accuracies increase by 20.4% and 21.3% when gold coreference and Stanford coreference are used, respectively. In other words, machine learning has "transformed" a ruleset that achieves mediocre performance into a system that achieves relatively high performance.

These results also suggest that coreference plays a crucial role in IS subtype determination: accuracies could increase by up to 7.7–8.6% if we solely improved coreference resolution performance. This is perhaps not surprising: IS and coreference can mutually benefit from each other.

To gain additional insight into the task, we also show in rows 2–17 of Table 3 the performance on each of the 16 subtypes, expressed in terms of recall (R), precision (P), and F-score (F). A few points deserve mention. First, in comparison to the rule-based approach, the learning-based approach achieves considerably better performance on almost all classes. One that is of particular interest is the new class. As we can see in row 17, its F-score rises by about 30 points. These gains are accompanied by a simultaneous rise in recall and precision. In particular, recall increases by about 40 points. Now, recall from the introduc-

[7] For all the experiments involving SVM^{multiclass}, we set C, the regularization parameter, to 500,000, since preliminary experiments indicate that preferring generalization to overfitting (by setting C to a small value) tends to yield poorer classification performance. The remaining learning parameters are set to their default values.

		Rule-Based Approach						Learning-Based Approach					
		Gold Coreference			Stanford Coreference			Gold Coreference			Stanford Coreference		
1	Accuracy	66.0			57.4			**86.4**			78.7		
	IS Subtype	R	P	F	R	P	F	R	P	F	R	P	F
2	old/ident	77.5	78.2	77.8	66.1	52.7	58.7	82.8	85.2	**84.0**	75.8	64.2	69.5
3	old/event	98.6	50.4	66.7	71.3	43.2	53.8	98.3	87.9	**92.8**	2.4	31.8	4.5
4	old/general	81.9	82.7	82.3	72.3	83.6	77.6	97.7	93.7	**95.6**	87.8	92.7	90.2
5	old/generic	55.9	55.2	55.5	39.2	39.8	39.5	76.1	87.3	**81.3**	39.9	85.9	54.5
6	old/ident_generic	48.7	77.7	59.9	27.2	51.8	35.7	57.1	87.5	**69.1**	47.2	44.8	46.0
7	old/relative	55.0	69.2	61.3	55.1	63.4	59.0	98.0	63.0	**76.7**	99.0	37.5	54.4
8	med/general	29.9	19.8	23.8	29.5	19.6	23.6	91.2	87.7	**89.4**	84.0	72.2	77.7
9	med/bound	56.4	20.5	30.1	56.4	20.5	30.1	25.7	65.5	**36.9**	2.7	40.0	5.1
10	med/part	19.5	100.0	32.7	19.5	100.0	32.7	73.2	96.8	**83.3**	73.2	96.8	**83.3**
11	med/situation	28.7	100.0	44.6	28.7	100.0	44.6	68.4	95.4	79.7	68.0	97.7	**80.2**
12	med/event	10.5	100.0	18.9	10.5	100.0	18.9	46.3	100.0	**63.3**	46.3	100.0	**63.3**
13	med/set	82.9	61.8	70.8	78.0	59.4	67.4	90.4	87.8	**89.1**	88.4	86.0	87.2
14	med/poss	52.9	86.0	65.6	52.9	86.0	65.6	93.2	92.4	92.8	90.5	97.6	**93.9**
15	med/func_value	81.3	74.3	77.6	81.3	74.3	77.6	88.1	85.9	**87.0**	88.1	85.9	**87.0**
16	med/aggregation	57.4	44.0	49.9	57.4	43.6	49.6	85.2	72.9	78.6	83.8	93.9	**88.6**
17	new	50.4	65.7	57.0	50.3	65.1	56.7	90.3	84.6	**87.4**	90.4	83.6	86.9

Table 3: IS subtype accuracies and F-scores. In each row, the strongest result, as well as those that are statistically indistinguishable from it according to the paired t-test ($p < 0.05$), are boldfaced.

tion that previous attempts on 3-class IS determination by Nissim and R&N have achieved poor performance on the new class. We hypothesize that the use of shallow features in their approaches were responsible for the poor performance they observed, and that using our knowledge-rich feature set could improve its performance. We will test this hypothesis at the end of this section.

Other subtypes that are worth discussing are med/aggregation, med/func_value, and med/poss. Recall that the rules we designed for these classes were only crude approximations, or, perhaps more precisely, simplified versions of the definitions of the corresponding subtypes. For instance, to determine whether an NP belongs to med/aggregation, we simply look for occurrences of "and" and "or" (Rule 9), whereas its definition requires that not all of the NPs in the coordinated phrase are new. Despite the over-simplicity of these rules, machine learning has enabled the available features to be combined in such a way that high performance is achieved for these classes (see rows 14–16).

Also worth examining are those classes for which the hand-crafted rules rely on sophisticated knowledge sources. They include med/part, which relies on ReVerb; med/situation, which relies on FrameNet; and med/event, which relies on WordNet. As we can see from the rule-based results (rows 10–12), these knowledge sources have yielded rules that achieved perfect precision but low recall: 19.5% for part, 28.7% for situation, and 10.5 for event. Nevertheless, the learning algorithm has again discovered a profitable way to combine the available features, enabling the F-scores of these classes to increase by 35.1–50.6%.

While most classes are improved by machine learning, the same is not true for old/event and med/bound, whose F-scores are 4.5% (row 3) and 5.1% (row 9), respectively, when Stanford coreference is employed. This is perhaps not surprising. Recall that the multi-class SVM classifier was trained to maximize classification accuracy. Hence, if it encounters a class that is both difficult to learn *and* is under-represented, it may as well aim to achieve good performance on the easier-to-learn, well-represented classes at the expense of these hard-to-learn, under-represented classes.

Feature analysis. In an attempt to gain additional insight into the performance contribution of each of the five types of features used in the learning-based approach, we conduct feature ablation experiments. Results are shown in Table 4, where each row shows the accuracy of the classifier trained on all types of features except for the one shown in that row. For easy reference, the accuracy of the classifier trained on all types of features is shown in row 1 of the table. According to the paired t-test ($p < 0.05$), performance drops significantly whichever feature type is removed. This suggests that all five feature types are contributing positively to overall accuracy. Also, the *markables* features are the least important in the presence of other feature groups, whereas *mark-*

Feature Type	Gold Coref	Stanford Coref
All features	86.4	78.7
−rule predictions	77.5	70.0
−markable predictions	72.4	64.7
−rule conditions	81.1	71.0
−unigrams	74.4	58.6
−markables	83.2	75.5

Table 4: Accuracies of feature ablation experiments.

Feature Type	Gold Coref	Stanford Coref
rule predictions	49.1	45.2
markable predictions	39.7	39.7
rule conditions	58.1	28.9
unigrams	56.8	56.8
markables	10.4	10.4

Table 5: Accuracies of classifiers for each feature type.

able predictions and *unigrams* are the two most important feature groups.

To get a better idea of the utility of each feature type, we conduct another experiment in which we train five classifiers, each of which employs exactly one type of features. The accuracies of these classifiers are shown in Table 5. As we can see, the *markables* features have the smallest contribution, whereas *unigrams* have the largest contribution. Somewhat interesting are the results of the classifiers trained on the rule conditions: the rules are far more effective when gold coreference is used. This can be attributed to the fact that the design of the rules was based in part on the definitions of the subtypes, which assume the availability of perfect coreference information.

Knowledge source analysis. To gain some insight into the extent to which a knowledge source or a rule contributes to the overall performance of the rule-based approach, we conduct ablation experiments: in each experiment, we measure the performance of the ruleset after removing a particular rule or knowledge source from it. Specifically, rows 2–4 of Table 6 show the accuracies of the ruleset after removing the memorization rule (Rule 17), the rule that uses ReVerb's output (Rule 12), and the cue words used in Rules 4 and 10, respectively. For easy reference, the accuracy of the original ruleset is shown in row 1 of the table. According to the paired t-test ($p < 0.05$), performance drops significantly in all three ablation experiments. This suggests that the memorization rule, ReVerb, and the cue words all contribute positively to the accuracy of the ruleset.

Feature Type	Gold Coref	Stanford Coref
All rules	66.0	57.4
−memorization	62.6	52.0
−ReVerb	64.2	56.6
−cue words	63.8	54.0

Table 6: Accuracies of the simplified ruleset.

	R&N's Features			Our Features		
IS Type	R	P	F	R	P	F
old	93.5	95.8	94.6	93.8	96.4	95.1
med	89.3	71.2	79.2	93.3	86.0	89.5
new	34.6	71.7	46.7	82.4	72.7	87.2
Accuracy	82.9			91.7		

Table 7: Accuracies on IS types.

IS type results. We hypothesized earlier that the poor performance reported by Nissim and R&N on identifying new entities in their 3-class IS classification experiments (i.e., classifying an NP as old, med, or new) could be attributed to their sole reliance on lexico-syntactic features. To test this hypothesis, we (1) train a 3-class classifier using the five types of features we employed in our learning-based approach, computing the features based on the Stanford coreference chains; and (2) compare its results against those obtained via the lexico-syntactic approach in R&N on our test set. Results of these experiments, which are shown in Table 7, substantiate our hypothesis: when we replace R&N's features with ours, accuracy rises from 82.9% to 91.7%. These gains can be attributed to large improvements in identifying new and med entities, for which F-scores increase by about 40 points and 10 points, respectively.

7 Conclusions

We have examined the fine-grained IS determination task. Experiments on a set of Switchboard dialogues show that our learning-based approach, which uses features that include handcrafted rules and their predictions, outperforms its rule-based counterpart by more than 20%, achieving an overall accuracy of 78.7% when relying on automatically computed coreference information. In addition, we have achieved state-of-the-art results on the 3-class IS determination task, in part due to our reliance on richer knowledge sources in comparison to prior work. To our knowledge, there has been little work on automatic IS subtype determination. We hope that our work can stimulate further research on this task.

Acknowledgments

We thank the three anonymous reviewers for their detailed and insightful comments on an earlier draft of the paper. This work was supported in part by NSF Grants IIS-0812261 and IIS-1147644.

References

Collin F. Baker, Charles J. Fillmore, and John B. Lowe. 1998. The Berkeley FrameNet project. In *Proceedings of the 36th Annual Meeting of the Association for Computational Linguistics and the 17th International Conference on Computational Linguistics, Volume 1*, pages 86–90.

Sasha Calhoun, Jean Carletta, Jason Brenier, Neil Mayo, Dan Jurafsky, Mark Steedman, and David Beaver. 2010. The NXT-format Switchboard corpus: A rich resource for investigating the syntax, semantics, pragmatics and prosody of dialogue. *Language Resources and Evaluation*, 44(4):387–419.

Miriam Eckert and Michael Strube. 2001. Dialogue acts, synchronising units and anaphora resolution. *Journal of Semantics*, 17(1):51–89.

Anthony Fader, Stephen Soderland, and Oren Etzioni. 2011. Identifying relations for open information extraction. In *Proceedings of the 2011 Conference on Empirical Methods in Natural Language Processing*, pages 1535–1545.

Christiane Fellbaum. 1998. *WordNet: An Electronic Lexical Database*. MIT Press, Cambridge, MA.

Caroline Gasperin and Ted Briscoe. 2008. Statistical anaphora resolution in biomedical texts. In *Proceedings of the 22nd International Conference on Computational Linguistics*, pages 257–264.

Michael Götze, Thomas Weskott, Cornelia Endriss, Ines Fiedler, Stefan Hinterwimmer, Svetlana Petrova, Anne Schwarz, Stavros Skopeteas, and Ruben Stoel. 2007. Information structure. In *Working Papers of the SFB632, Interdisciplinary Studies on Information Structure (ISIS)*. Potsdam: Universitätsverlag Potsdam.

Eva Hajičová. 1984. Topic and focus. In *Contributions to Functional Syntax, Semantics, and Language Comprehension (LLSEE 16)*, pages 189–202. John Benjamins, Amsterdam.

Michael A. K. Halliday. 1976. Notes on transitivity and theme in English. *Journal of Linguistics*, 3(2):199–244.

Heeyoung Lee, Yves Peirsman, Angel Chang, Nathanael Chambers, Mihai Surdeanu, and Dan Jurafsky. 2011. Stanford's multi-pass sieve coreference resolution system at the CoNLL-2011 shared task. In *Proceedings of the Fifteenth Conference on Computational Natural Language Learning: Shared Task*, pages 28–34.

Malvina Nissim, Shipra Dingare, Jean Carletta, and Mark Steedman. 2004. An annotation scheme for information status in dialogue. In *Proceedings of the 4th International Conference on Language Resources and Evaluation*, pages 1023–1026.

Malvina Nissim. 2003. Annotation scheme for information status in dialogue. Available from `http://www.stanford.edu/class/cs224u/guidelines-infostatus.pdf`.

Malvina Nissim. 2006. Learning information status of discourse entities. In *Proceedings of the 2006 Conference on Empirical Methods in Natural Language Processing*, pages 94–102.

Ellen F. Prince. 1981. Toward a taxonomy of given-new information. In P. Cole, editor, *Radical Pragmatics*, pages 223–255. New York, N.Y.: Academic Press.

Ellen F. Prince. 1992. The ZPG letter: Subjects, definiteness, and information-status. In *Discourse Description: Diverse Analysis of a Fund Raising Text*, pages 295–325. John Benjamins, Philadelphia/Amsterdam.

Altaf Rahman and Vincent Ng. 2011. Learning the information status of noun phrases in spoken dialogues. In *Proceedings of the 2011 Conference on Empirical Methods in Natural Language Processing*, pages 1069–1080.

Arndt Riester, David Lorenz, and Nina Seemann. 2010. A recursive annotation scheme for referential information status. In *Proceedings of the Seventh International Conference on Language Resources and Evaluation*, pages 717–722.

Mark Steedman. 2000. *The Syntactic Process*. The MIT Press, Cambridge, MA.

Ioannis Tsochantaridis, Thomas Hofmann, Thorsten Joachims, and Yasemin Altun. 2004. Support vector machine learning for interdependent and structured output spaces. In *Proceedings of the 21st International Conference on Machine Learning*, pages 104–112.

Enric Vallduví. 1992. *The Informational Component*. Garland, New York.

Composing extended top-down tree transducers*

Aurélie Lagoutte
École normale supérieure de Cachan, Département Informatique
alagoutt@dptinfo.ens-cachan.fr

Fabienne Braune and **Daniel Quernheim** and **Andreas Maletti**
University of Stuttgart, Institute for Natural Language Processing
{braunefe,daniel,maletti}@ims.uni-stuttgart.de

Abstract

A composition procedure for linear and nondeleting extended top-down tree transducers is presented. It is demonstrated that the new procedure is more widely applicable than the existing methods. In general, the result of the composition is an extended top-down tree transducer that is no longer linear or nondeleting, but in a number of cases these properties can easily be recovered by a post-processing step.

1 Introduction

Tree-based translation models such as synchronous tree substitution grammars (Eisner, 2003; Shieber, 2004) or multi bottom-up tree transducers (Lilin, 1978; Engelfriet et al., 2009; Maletti, 2010; Maletti, 2011) are used for several aspects of syntax-based machine translation (Knight and Graehl, 2005). Here we consider the *extended top-down tree transducer* (XTOP), which was studied in (Arnold and Dauchet, 1982; Knight, 2007; Graehl et al., 2008; Graehl et al., 2009) and implemented in the toolkit TIBURON (May and Knight, 2006; May, 2010). Specifically, we investigate compositions of linear and nondeleting XTOPs (ln-XTOP). Arnold and Dauchet (1982) showed that ln-XTOPs compute a class of transformations that is not closed under composition, so we cannot compose two arbitrary ln-XTOPs into a single ln-XTOP. However, we will show that ln-XTOPs can be composed into a (not necessarily linear or nondeleting) XTOP. To illustrate the use of ln-XTOPs in machine translation, we consider the following English sentence together with a German reference translation:

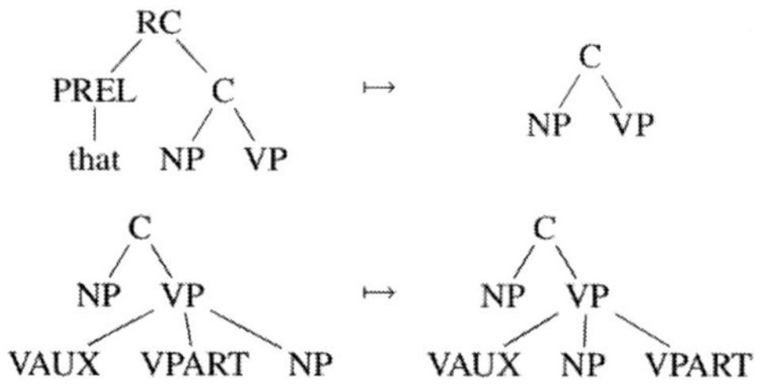

Figure 1: Word drop [top] and reordering [bottom].

The newswire reported yesterday *that the Serbs have completed the negotiations.*

Gestern [Yesterday] berichtete [reported] die [the] Nachrichtenagentur [newswire] *die* [the] *Serben* [Serbs] *hätten* [would have] *die* [the] *Verhandlungen* [negotiations] *beendet* [completed].

The relation between them can be described (Yamada and Knight, 2001) by three operations: drop of the relative pronoun, movement of the participle to end of the clause, and word-to-word translation. Figure 1 shows the first two operations, and Figure 2 shows ln-XTOP rules performing them. Let us now informally describe the execution of an ln-XTOP on the top rule ρ of Figure 2. In general, ln-XTOPs process an input tree from the root towards the leaves using a set of rules and states. The state p in the left-hand side of ρ controls the particular operation of Figure 1 [top]. Once the operation has been performed, control is passed to states p_{NP} and p_{VP}, which use their own rules to process the remaining input subtree governed by the variable below them (see Figure 2). In the same fashion, an ln-XTOP containing the bottom rule of Figure 2 reorders the English verbal complex.

In this way we model the word drop by an ln-XTOP M and reordering by an ln-XTOP N. The syntactic properties of linearity and nondeletion yield nice algorithmic properties, and the mod-

* All authors were financially supported by the EMMY NOETHER project MA / 4959 / 1-1 of the German Research Foundation (DFG).

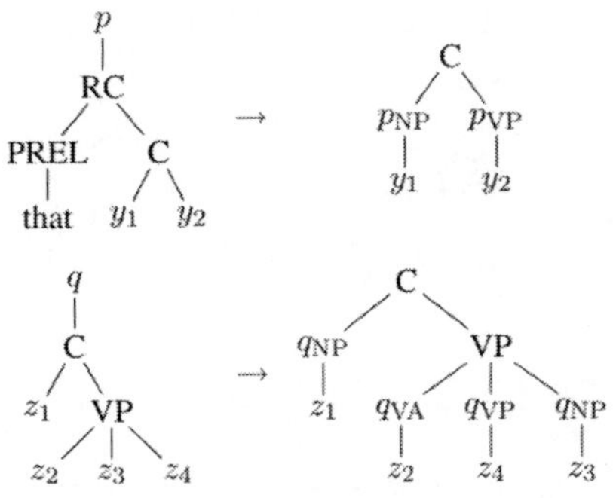

Figure 2: XTOP rules for the operations of Figure 1.

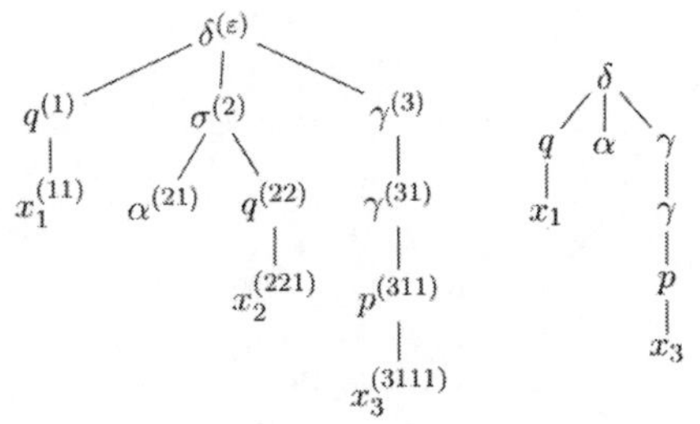

Figure 3: Linear normalized tree $t \in T_\Sigma(Q(X))$ [left] and $t[\alpha]_2$ [right] with $\mathrm{var}(t) = \{x_1, x_2, x_3\}$. The positions are indicated in t as superscripts. The subtree $t|_2$ is $\sigma(\alpha, q(x_2))$.

ular approach is desirable for better design and parametrization of the translation model (May et al., 2010). Composition allows us to recombine those parts into one device modeling the whole translation. In particular, it gives all parts the chance to vote at the same time. This is especially important if pruning is used because it might otherwise exclude candidates that score low in one part but well in others (May et al., 2010).

Because ln-XTOP is not closed under composition, the composition of M and N might be outside ln-XTOP. These cases have been identified by Arnold and Dauchet (1982) as infinitely "overlapping cuts", which occur when the right-hand sides of M and the left-hand sides of N are unboundedly overlapping. This can be purely syntactic (for a given ln-XTOP) or semantic (inherent in all ln-XTOPs for a given transformation). Despite the general impossibility, several strategies have been developed: (i) Extension of the model (Maletti, 2010; Maletti, 2011), (ii) online composition (May et al., 2010), and (iii) restriction of the model, which we follow. Compositions of subclasses in which the XTOP N has at most one input symbol in its left-hand sides have already been studied in (Engelfriet, 1975; Baker, 1979; Maletti and Vogler, 2010). Such compositions are implemented in the toolkit TIBURON. However, there are translation tasks in which the used XTOPs do not fulfill this requirement. Suppose that we simply want to compose the rules of Figure 2, The bottom rule does not satisfy the requirement that there is at most one input symbol in the left-hand side.

We will demonstrate how to compose two linear and nondeleting XTOPs into a single XTOP, which might however no longer be linear or nondeleting. However, when the syntactic form of the composed XTOP has only bounded overlapping cuts, post-processing will get rid of them and restore an ln-XTOP. In the remaining cases, in which unbounded overlapping is necessary or occurs in the syntactic form but would not be necessary, we will compute an XTOP. This is still an improvement on the existing methods that just fail. Since general XTOPs are implemented in TIBURON and the new composition covers (essentially) all cases currently possible, our new composition procedure could replace the existing one in TIBURON. Our approach to composition is the same as in (Engelfriet, 1975; Baker, 1979; Maletti and Vogler, 2010): We simply parse the right-hand sides of the XTOP M with the left-hand sides of the XTOP N. However, to facilitate this approach we have to adjust the XTOPs M and N in two pre-processing steps. In a first step we cut left-hand sides of rules of N into smaller pieces, which might introduce non-linearity and deletion into N. In certain cases, this can also introduce finite look-ahead (Engelfriet, 1977; Graehl et al., 2009). To compensate, we expand the rules of M slightly. Section 4 explains those preparations. Next, we compose the prepared XTOPs as usual and obtain a single XTOP computing the composition of the transformations computed by M and N (see Section 5). Finally, we apply a post-processing step to expand rules to reobtain linearity and nondeletion. Clearly, this cannot be successful in all cases, but often removes the non-linearity introduced in the pre-processing step.

2 Preliminaries

Our trees have labels taken from an alphabet Σ of symbols, and in addition, leaves might be labeled by elements of the countably infinite

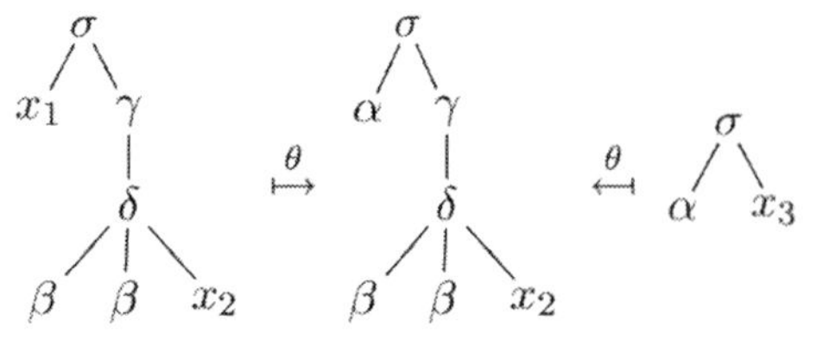

Figure 4: Substitution where $\theta(x_1) = \alpha$, $\theta(x_2) = x_2$, and $\theta(x_3) = \gamma(\delta(\beta, \beta, x_2))$.

set $X = \{x_1, x_2, \dots\}$ of formal variables. Formally, for every $V \subseteq X$ the set $T_\Sigma(V)$ of Σ-trees with V-leaves is the smallest set such that $V \subseteq T_\Sigma(V)$ and $\sigma(t_1, \dots, t_k) \in T_\Sigma(V)$ for all $k \in \mathbb{N}$, $\sigma \in \Sigma$, and $t_1, \dots, t_k \in T_\Sigma(V)$. To avoid excessive universal quantifications, we drop them if they are obvious from the context.

For each tree $t \in T_\Sigma(X)$ we identify nodes by positions. The root of t has position ε and the position iw with $i \in \mathbb{N}$ and $w \in \mathbb{N}^*$ addresses the position w in the i-th direct subtree at the root. The set of all positions in t is $\text{pos}(t)$. We write $t(w)$ for the label (taken from $\Sigma \cup X$) of t at position $w \in \text{pos}(t)$. Similarly, we use

- $t|_w$ to address the subtree of t that is rooted in position w, and
- $t[u]_w$ to represent the tree that is obtained from replacing the subtree $t|_w$ at w by $u \in T_\Sigma(X)$.

For a given set $L \subseteq \Sigma \cup X$ of labels, we let

$$\text{pos}_L(t) = \{w \in \text{pos}(t) \mid t(w) \in L\}$$

be the set of all positions whose label belongs to L. We also write $\text{pos}_l(t)$ instead of $\text{pos}_{\{l\}}(t)$. The tree $t \in T_\Sigma(V)$ is *linear* if $|\text{pos}_x(t)| \leq 1$ for every $x \in X$. Moreover,

$$\text{var}(t) = \{x \in X \mid \text{pos}_x(t) \neq \emptyset\}$$

collects all variables that occur in t. If the variables occur in the order $x_1, x_2, \dots$ in a pre-order traversal of the tree t, then t is *normalized.* Given a finite set Q, we write $Q(T)$ with $T \subseteq T_\Sigma(X)$ for the set $\{q(t) \mid q \in Q, t \in T\}$. We will treat elements of $Q(T)$ as special trees of $T_{\Sigma \cup Q}(X)$. The previous notions are illustrated in Figure 3.

A substitution θ is a mapping $\theta \colon X \to T_\Sigma(X)$. When applied to a tree $t \in T_\Sigma(X)$, it will return the tree $t\theta$, which is obtained from t by replacing all occurrences of $x \in X$ (in parallel) by $\theta(x)$. This can be defined recursively by $x\theta = \theta(x)$ for all $x \in X$ and $\sigma(t_1, \dots, t_k)\theta = \sigma(t_1\theta, \dots, t_k\theta)$

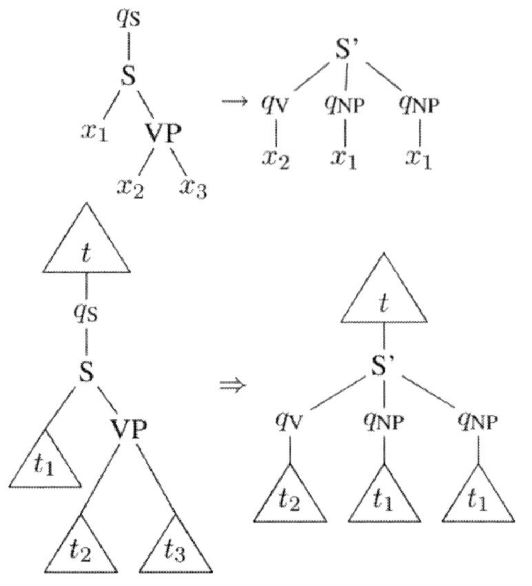

Figure 5: Rule and its use in a derivation step.

for all $\sigma \in \Sigma$ and $t_1, \dots, t_k \in T_\Sigma(X)$. The effect of a substitution is displayed in Figure 4. Two substitutions $\theta, \theta' \colon X \to T_\Sigma(X)$ can be composed to form a substitution $\theta\theta' \colon X \to T_\Sigma(X)$ such that $\theta\theta'(x) = \theta(x)\theta'$ for every $x \in X$.

Next, we define two notions of compatibility for trees. Let $t, t' \in T_\Sigma(X)$ be two trees. If there exists a substitution θ such that $t' = t\theta$, then t' is an *instance* of t. Note that this relation is not symmetric. A *unifier* θ for t and t' is a substitution θ such that $t\theta = t'\theta$. The unifier θ is a *most general unifier* (short: mgu) for t and t' if for every unifier θ'' for t and t' there exists a substitution θ' such that $\theta\theta' = \theta''$. The set $\text{mgu}(t, t')$ is the set of all mgus for t and t'. Most general unifiers can be computed efficiently (Robinson, 1965; Martelli and Montanari, 1982) and all mgus for t and t' are equal up to a variable renaming.

Example 1. Let $t = \sigma(x_1, \gamma(\delta(\beta, \beta, x_2)))$ and $t' = \sigma(\alpha, x_3)$. Then $\text{mgu}(t, t')$ contains θ such that $\theta(x_1) = \alpha$ and $\theta(x_3) = \gamma(\delta(\beta, \beta, x_2))$. Figure 4 illustrates the unification. □

3 The model

The discussed model in this contribution is an extension of the classical *top-down tree transducer*, which was introduced by Rounds (1970) and Thatcher (1970). The *extended top-down tree transducer with finite look-ahead* or just XTOP^{F} and its variations were studied in (Arnold and Dauchet, 1982; Knight and Graehl, 2005;

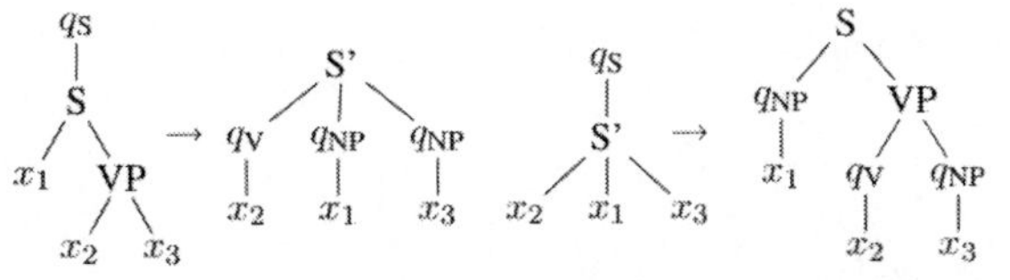

Figure 6: Rule [left] and reversed rule [right].

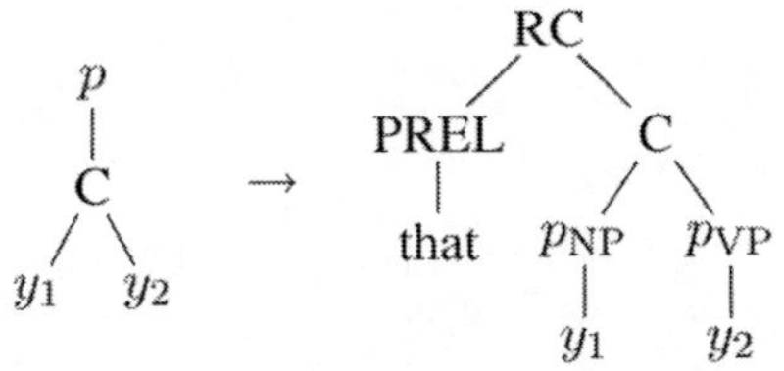

Figure 7: Top rule of Figure 2 reversed.

Knight, 2007; Graehl et al., 2008; Graehl et al., 2009). Formally, an *extended top-down tree transducer with finite look-ahead* (XTOP^{F}) is a system $M = (Q, \Sigma, \Delta, I, R, c)$ where

- Q is a finite set of *states*,
- Σ and Δ are alphabets of *input* and *output symbols*, respectively,
- $I \subseteq Q$ is a set of *initial states*,
- R is a finite set of (rewrite) *rules* of the form $\ell \to r$ where $\ell \in Q(T_\Sigma(X))$ is linear and $r \in T_\Delta(Q(\text{var}(\ell)))$, and
- $c\colon R \times X \to T_\Sigma(X)$ assigns a *look-ahead restriction* to each rule and variable such that $c(\rho, x)$ is linear for each $\rho \in R$ and $x \in X$.

The XTOP^{F} M is *linear* (respectively, *nondeleting*) if r is linear (respectively, $\text{var}(r) = \text{var}(\ell)$) for every rule $\ell \to r \in R$. It has *no look-ahead* (or it is an XTOP) if $c(\rho, x) \in X$ for all rules $\rho \in R$ and $x \in X$. In this case, we drop the look-ahead component c from the description. A rule $\ell \to r \in R$ is *consuming* (respectively, *producing*) if $\text{pos}_\Sigma(\ell) \neq \emptyset$ (respectively, $\text{pos}_\Delta(r) \neq \emptyset$). We let $\text{Lhs}(M) = \{l \mid \exists q, r\colon q(l) \to r \in R\}$.

Let $M = (Q, \Sigma, \Delta, I, R, c)$ be an XTOP^{F}. In order to facilitate composition, we define sentential forms more generally than immediately necessary. Let Σ' and Δ' be such that $\Sigma \subseteq \Sigma'$ and $\Delta \subseteq \Delta'$. To keep the presentation simple, we assume that $Q \cap (\Sigma' \cup \Delta') = \emptyset$. A *sentential form* of M (using Σ' and Δ') is a tree of $\text{SF}(M) = T_{\Delta'}(Q(T_{\Sigma'}))$. For every $\xi, \zeta \in \text{SF}(M)$, we write $\xi \Rightarrow_M \zeta$ if there exist a position $w \in \text{pos}_Q(\xi)$, a rule $\rho = \ell \to r \in R$, and a substitution $\theta\colon X \to T_{\Sigma'}$ such that $\theta(x)$ is an instance of $c(\rho, x)$ for every $x \in X$ and $\xi = \xi[\ell\theta]_w$ and $\zeta = \xi[r\theta]_w$. If the applicable rules are restricted to a certain subset $R' \subseteq R$, then we also write $\xi \Rightarrow_{R'} \zeta$. Figure 5 illustrates a derivation step. The *tree transformation computed by* M is

$$\tau_M = \{(t, u) \in T_\Sigma \times T_\Delta \mid \exists q \in I\colon q(t) \Rightarrow_M^* u\}$$

where $\Rightarrow_M^*$ is the reflexive, transitive closure of $\Rightarrow_M$. It can easily be verified that the definition of τ_M is independent of the choice of Σ' and Δ'. Moreover, it is known (Graehl et al., 2009) that each XTOP^{F} can be transformed into an equivalent XTOP preserving both linearity and nondeletion. However, the notion of XTOP^{F} will be convenient in our composition construction. A detailed exposition to XTOPs is presented by Arnold and Dauchet (1982) and Graehl et al. (2009).

A linear and nondeleting XTOP M with rules R can easily be reversed to obtain a linear and nondeleting XTOP M^{-1} with rules R^{-1}, which computes the inverse transformation $\tau_{M^{-1}} = \tau_M^{-1}$, by reversing all its rules. A (suitable) rule is reversed by exchanging the locations of the states. More precisely, given a rule $q(l) \to r \in R$, we obtain the rule $q(r') \to l'$ of R^{-1}, where $l' = l\theta$ and r' is the unique tree such that there exists a substitution $\theta\colon X \to Q(X)$ with $\theta(x) \in Q(\{x\})$ for every $x \in X$ and $r = r'\theta$. Figure 6 displays a rule and its corresponding reversed rule. The reversed form of the XTOP rule modeling the insertion operation in Figure 2 is displayed in Figure 7.

Finally, let us formally define composition. The XTOP M computes the tree transformation $\tau_M \subseteq T_\Sigma \times T_\Delta$. Given another XTOP N that computes a tree transformation $\tau_N \subseteq T_\Delta \times T_\Gamma$, we might be interested in the tree transformation computed by the composition of M and N (i.e., running M first and then N). Formally, the composition $\tau_M \,;\, \tau_N$ of the tree transformations τ_M and τ_N is defined by

$$\tau_M \,;\, \tau_N = \{(s, u) \mid \exists t\colon (s, t) \in \tau_M, (t, u) \in \tau_N\}$$

and we often also use the notion 'composition' for XTOP with the expectation that the composition of M and N computes exactly $\tau_M \,;\, \tau_N$.

4 Pre-processing

We want to compose two linear and nondeleting XTOPs $M = (P, \Sigma, \Delta, I_M, R_M)$ and

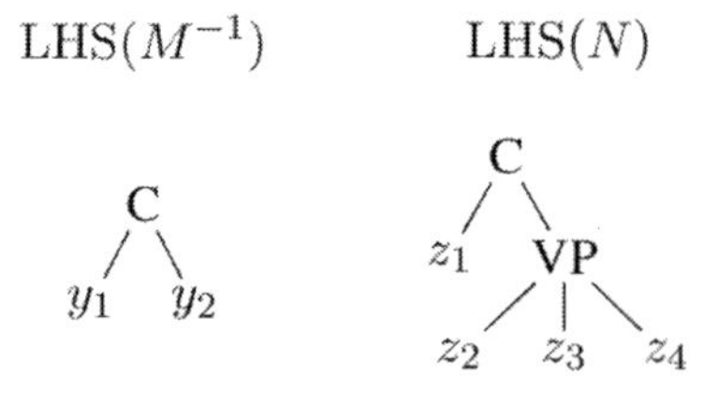

Figure 8: Incompatible left-hand sides of Example 3.

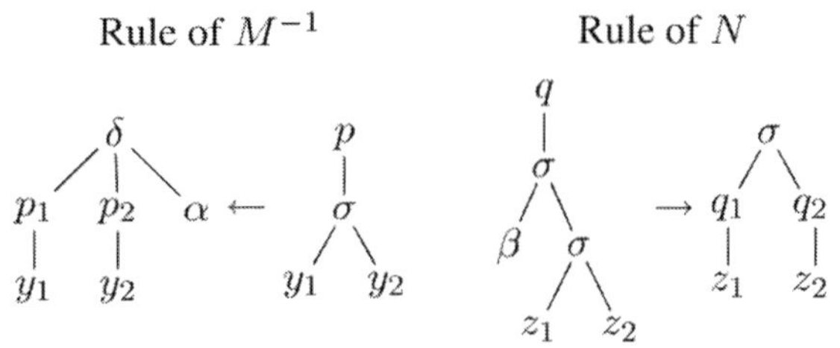

Figure 9: Rules used in Example 5.

$N = (Q, \Delta, \Gamma, I_N, R_N)$. Before we actually perform the composition, we will prepare M and N in two pre-processing steps. After these two steps, the composition is very simple. To avoid complications, we assume that (i) all rules of M are producing and (ii) all rules of N are consuming. For convenience, we also assume that the XTOPs M and N only use variables of the disjoint sets $Y \subseteq X$ and $Z \subseteq X$, respectively.

4.1 Compatibility

In the existing composition results for subclasses of XTOPs (Engelfriet, 1975; Baker, 1979; Maletti and Vogler, 2010) the XTOP N has at most one input symbol in its left-hand sides. This restriction allows us to match rule applications of N to positions in the right-hand sides of M. Namely, for each output symbol in a right-hand side of M, we can select a rule of N that can consume that output symbol. To achieve a similar decomposition strategy in our more general setup, we introduce a compatibility requirement on right-hand sides of M and left-hand sides of N. Roughly speaking, we require that the left-hand sides of N are small enough to completely process right-hand sides of M. However, a comparison of left- and right-hand sides is complicated by the fact that their shape is different (left-hand sides have a state at the root, whereas right-hand sides have states in front of the variables). We avoid these complications by considering reversed rules of M. Thus, an original right-hand side of M is now a left-hand side in the reversed rules and thus has the right format for a comparison. Recall that $\mathrm{Lhs}(N)$ contains all left-hand sides of the rules of N, in which the state at the root was removed.

Definition 2. The XTOP N is *compatible* to M if $\theta(Y) \subseteq X$ for all unifiers $\theta \in \mathrm{mgu}(l_1|_w, l_2)$ between a subtree at a Δ-labeled position $w \in \mathrm{pos}_\Delta(l_1)$ in a left-hand side $l_1 \in \mathrm{Lhs}(M^{-1})$ and a left-hand side $l_2 \in \mathrm{Lhs}(N)$. □

Intuitively, for every Δ-labeled position w in a right-hand side r_1 of M and any left-hand side l_2 of N, we require (ignoring the states) that either (i) $r_1|_w$ and l_2 are not unifiable or (ii) $r_1|_w$ is an instance of l_2.

Example 3. The XTOPs for the English-to-German translation task in the Introduction are not compatible. This can be observed on the left-hand side $l_1 \in \mathrm{Lhs}(M^{-1})$ of Figure 7 and the left-hand side $l_2 \in \mathrm{Lhs}(N)$ of Figure 2[bottom]. These two left-hand sides are illustrated in Figure 8. Between them there is an mgu such that $\theta(Y) \not\subseteq X$ (e.g., $\theta(y_1) = z_1$ and $\theta(y_2) = \mathrm{VP}(z_2, z_3, z_4)$ is such an mgu). □

Theorem 4. There exists an XTOP^{F} N' that is equivalent to N and compatible with M.

Proof. We achieve compatibility by cutting offending rules of the XTOP N into smaller pieces. Unfortunately, both linearity and nondeletion of N might be lost in the process. We first let $N' = (Q, \Delta, \Gamma, I_N, R_N, c_N)$ be the XTOP^{F} such that $c_N(\rho, x) = x$ for every $\rho \in R_N$ and $x \in X$.

If N' is compatible with M, then we are done. Otherwise, let $l_1 \in \mathrm{Lhs}(M^{-1})$ be a left-hand side, $q(l_2) \to r_2 \in R_N$ be a rule, and $w \in \mathrm{pos}_\Delta(l_1)$ be a position such that $\theta(y) \notin X$ for some $\theta \in \mathrm{mgu}(l_1|_w, l_2)$ and $y \in Y$. Let $v \in \mathrm{pos}_y(l_1|_w)$ be the unique position of y in $l_1|_w$.

Now we have to distinguish two cases: (i) Either $\mathrm{var}(l_2|_v) = \emptyset$ and there is no leaf in r_2 labeled by a symbol from Γ. In this case, we have to introduce deletion and look-ahead into N'. We replace the old rule $\rho = q(l_2) \to r_2$ by the new rule $\rho' = q(l_2[z]_v) \to r_2$, where $z \in X \setminus \mathrm{var}(l_2)$ is a variable that does not appear in l_2. In addition, we let $c_N(\rho', z) = l_2|_v$ and $c_N(\rho', x) = c_N(\rho, x)$ for all $x \in X \setminus \{z\}$.

(ii) Otherwise, let $V \subseteq \mathrm{var}(l_2|_v)$ be a maximal set such that there exists a minimal (with respect to the prefix order) position $w' \in \mathrm{pos}(r_2)$ with

Another rule of N

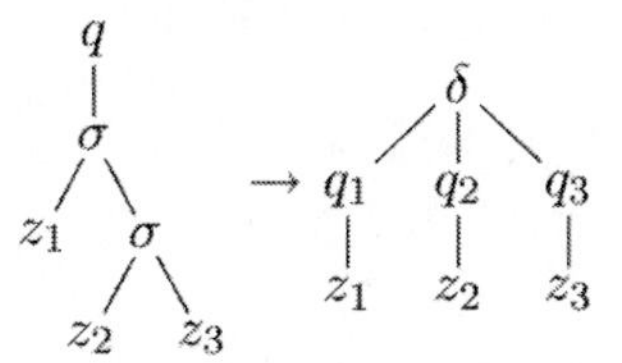

Figure 10: Additional rule used in Example 5.

$\text{var}(r_2|_{w'}) \subseteq \text{var}(l_2|_v)$ and $\text{var}(r_2[\beta]_{w'}) \cap V = \emptyset$, where $\beta \in \Gamma$ is arbitrary. Let $z \in X \setminus \text{var}(l_2)$ be a fresh variable, q' be a new state of N, and $V' = \text{var}(l_2|_v) \setminus V$. We replace the rule $\rho = q(l_2) \to r_2$ of R_N by

$$\rho_1 = q(l_2[z]_v) \to \text{trans}(r_2)[q'(z)]_{w'}$$
$$\rho_2 = q'(l_2|_v) \to r_2|_{w'} \ .$$

The look-ahead for z is trivial and otherwise we simply copy the old look-ahead, so $c_N(\rho_1, z) = z$ and $c_N(\rho_1, x) = c_N(\rho, x)$ for all $x \in X \setminus \{z\}$. Moreover, $c_N(\rho_2, x) = c_N(\rho, x)$ for all $x \in X$. The mapping 'trans' is given for $t = \gamma(t_1, \ldots, t_k)$ and $q''(z'') \in Q(Z)$ by

$$\text{trans}(t) = \gamma(\text{trans}(t_1), \ldots, \text{trans}(t_k))$$
$$\text{trans}(q''(z'')) = \begin{cases} \langle l_2|_v, q'', v'\rangle(z) & \text{if } z'' \in V' \\ q''(z'') & \text{otherwise,} \end{cases}$$

where $v' = \text{pos}_{z''}(l_2|_v)$.

Finally, we collect all newly generated states of the form $\langle l, q, v\rangle$ in Q_l and for every such state with $l = \delta(l_1, \ldots, l_k)$ and $v = iw$, let $l' = \delta(z_1, \ldots, z_k)$ and

$$\langle l, q, v\rangle(l') \to \begin{cases} q(z_i) & \text{if } w = \varepsilon \\ \langle l_i, q, w\rangle(z_i) & \text{otherwise} \end{cases}$$

be a new rule of N without look-ahead.

Overall, we run the procedure until N' is compatible with M. The procedure eventually terminates since the left-hand sides of the newly added rules are always smaller than the replaced rules. Moreover, each step preserves the semantics of N', which completes the proof. □

We note that the look-ahead of N' after the construction used in the proof of Theorem 4 is either trivial (i.e., a variable) or a ground tree (i.e., a tree without variables). Let us illustrate the construction used in the proof of Theorem 4.

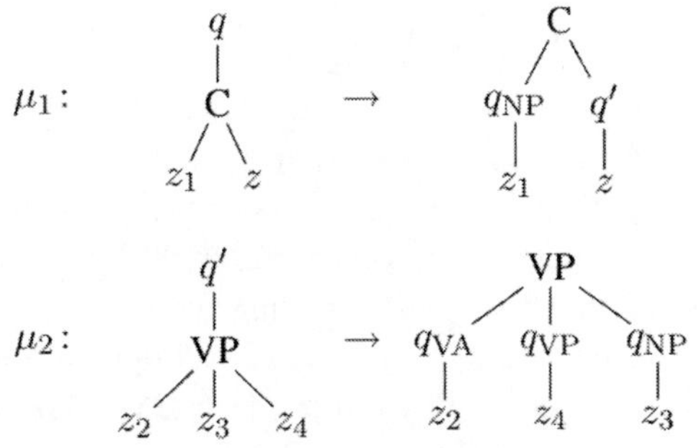

Figure 11: Rules replacing the rule in Figure 7.

Example 5. Let us consider the rules illustrated in Figure 9. We might first note that y_1 has to be unified with β. Since β does not contain any variables and the right-hand side of the rule of N does not contain any non-variable leaves, we are in case (i) in the proof of Theorem 4. Consequently, the displayed rule of N is replaced by a variant, in which β is replaced by a new variable z with look-ahead β.

Secondly, with this new rule there is an mgu, in which y_2 is mapped to $\sigma(z_1, z_2)$. Clearly, we are now in case (ii). Furthermore, we can select the set $V = \{z_1, z_2\}$ and position $w' = \epsilon$. Correspondingly, the following two new rules for N replace the old rule:

$$q(\sigma(z, z')) \to q'(z')$$
$$q'(\sigma(z_1, z_2)) \to \sigma(q_1(z_1), q_2(z_2)) \ ,$$

where the look-ahead for z remains β.

Figure 10 displays another rule of N. There is an mgu, in which y_2 is mapped to $\sigma(z_2, z_3)$. Thus, we end up in case (ii) again and we can select the set $V = \{z_2\}$ and position $w' = 2$. Thus, we replace the rule of Figure 10 by the new rules

$$q(\sigma(z_1, z)) \to \delta(q_1(z_1), q'(z), \overline{q_3}(z)) \qquad (\star)$$
$$q'(\sigma(z_2, z_3)) \to q_2(z_2)$$
$$\overline{q_3}(\sigma(z_1, z_2)) \to q_3(z_2) \ ,$$

where $\overline{q_3} = \langle \sigma(z_2, z_3), q_3, 2\rangle$. □

Let us use the construction in the proof of Theorem 4 to resolve the incompatibility (see Example 3) between the XTOPs presented in the Introduction. Fortunately, the incompatibility can be resolved easily by cutting the rule of N (see Figure 7) into the rules of Figure 11. In this example, linearity and nondeletion are preserved.

4.2 Local determinism

After the first pre-processing step, we have the original linear and nondeleting XTOP M and an XTOP^F $N' = (Q', \Delta, \Gamma, I_N, R'_N, c_N)$ that is equivalent to N and compatible with M. However, in the first pre-processing step we might have introduced some non-linear (copying) rules in N' (see rule ($\star$) in Example 5), and it is known that "nondeterminism [in M] followed by copying [in N']" is a feature that prevents composition to work (Engelfriet, 1975; Baker, 1979). However, our copying is very local and the copies are only used to project to different subtrees. Nevertheless, during those projection steps, we need to make sure that the processing in M proceeds deterministically. We immediately note that all but one copy are processed by states of the form $\langle l, q, v\rangle \in Q_l$. These states basically process (part of) the tree l and project (with state q) to the subtree at position v. It is guaranteed that each such subtree (indicated by v) is reached only once. Thus, the copying is "resolved" once the states of the form $\langle l, q, v\rangle$ are left. To keep the presentation simple, we just add expanded rules to M such that any rule that can produce a part of a tree l immediately produces the whole tree. A similar strategy is used to handle the look-ahead of N'. Any right-hand side of a rule of M that produces part of a left-hand side of a rule of N' with look-ahead is expanded to produce the required look-ahead immediately.

Let $L \subseteq T_\Delta(Z)$ be the set of trees l such that

- $\langle l, q, v\rangle$ appears as a state of Q_l, or
- $l = l_2\theta$ for some $\rho_2 = q(l_2) \to r_2 \in R'_N$ of N' with non-trivial look-ahead (i.e., $c_N(\rho_2, z) \notin X$ for some $z \in X$), where $\theta(x) = c_N(\rho_2, x)$ for every $x \in X$.

To keep the presentation uniform, we assume that for every $l \in L$, there exists a state of the form $\langle l, q, v\rangle \in Q'$. If this is not already the case, then we can simply add useless states without rules for them. In other words, we assume that the first case applies to each $l \in L$.

Next, we add two sets of rules to R_M, which will not change the semantics but prove to be useful in the composition construction. First, for every tree $t \in L$, let R_t contain all the rules $\overline{p}(l) \to r$, where $\overline{p} = p(l) \to r$ is a new state with $p \in P$, minimal normalized tree $l \in T_\Sigma(X)$, and an instance $r \in T_\Delta(P(X))$ of t such that

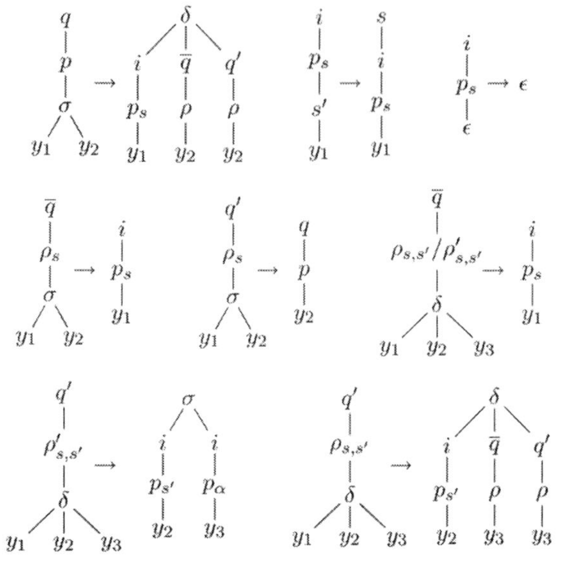

Figure 12: Useful rules for the composition $M' ; N'$ of Example 8, where $s, s' \in \{\alpha, \beta\}$ and $\rho \in P_{\sigma(z_2,z_3)}$.

$p(l) \Rightarrow^*_{M'} \xi \Rightarrow_{M'} r$ for some ξ that is not an instance of t. In other words, we construct each rule of R_t by applying existing rules of R_M in sequence to generate a (minimal) right-hand side that is an instance of t. We thus potentially make the right-hand sides of M bigger by joining several existing rules into a single rule. Note that this affects neither compatibility nor the semantics. In the second step, we add pure ε-rules that allow us to change the state to one that we constructed in the previous step. For every new state $\overline{p} = p(l) \to r$, let $\mathrm{base}(\overline{p}) = p$. Then $R'_M = R_M \cup R_L \cup R_E$ and $P' = P \cup \bigcup_{t\in L} P_t$ where

$$R_L = \bigcup_{t\in L} R_t \quad \text{and} \quad P_t = \{\ell(\varepsilon) \mid \ell \to r \in R_t\}$$

$$R_E = \{\mathrm{base}(\overline{p})(x_1) \to \overline{p}(x_1) \mid \overline{p} \in \bigcup_{t\in L} P_t\} \ .$$

Clearly, this does not change the semantics because each rule of R'_M can be simulated by a chain of rules of R_M. Let us now do a full example for the pre-processing step. We consider a nondeterministic variant of the classical example by Arnold and Dauchet (1982).

Example 6. Let $M = (P, \Sigma, \Sigma, \{p\}, R_M)$ be the linear and nondeleting XTOP such that $P = \{p, p_\alpha, p_\beta\}$, $\Sigma = \{\delta, \sigma, \alpha, \beta, \epsilon\}$, and R_M contains the following rules

$$p(\sigma(y_1, y_2)) \to \sigma(p_s(y_1), p(y_2)) \qquad (\dagger)$$

$$p(\delta(y_1, y_2, y_3)) \to \sigma(p_s(y_1), \sigma(p_{s'}(y_2), p(y_3)))$$
$$p(\delta(y_1, y_2, y_3)) \to \sigma(p_s(y_1), \sigma(p_{s'}(y_2), p_\alpha(y_3)))$$
$$p_s(s'(y_1)) \to s(p_s(y_1))$$
$$p_s(\epsilon) \to \epsilon$$

for every $s, s' \in \{\alpha, \beta\}$. Similarly, we let $N = (Q, \Sigma, \Sigma, \{q\}, R_N)$ be the linear and nondeleting XTOP such that $Q = \{q, i\}$ and R_N contains the following rules

$$q(\sigma(z_1, z_2)) \to \sigma(i(z_1), i(z_2))$$
$$q(\sigma(z_1, \sigma(z_2, z_3))) \to \delta(i(z_1), i(z_2), q(z_3)) \quad (\ddagger)$$
$$i(s(z_1)) \to s(i(z_1))$$
$$i(\epsilon) \to \epsilon$$

for all $s \in \{\alpha, \beta\}$. It can easily be verified that M and N meet our requirements. However, N is not yet compatible with M because an mgu between rules (†) of M and (‡) of N might map y_2 to $\sigma(z_2, z_3)$. Thus, we decompose (‡) into

$$q(\sigma(z_1, z)) \to \delta(i(z_1), \overline{q}(z), q'(z))$$
$$q'(\sigma(z_2, z_3)) \to q(z_3)$$
$$\overline{q}(\sigma(z_1, z_2)) \to i(z_1)$$

where $\overline{q} = \langle \sigma(z_2, z_3), i, 1 \rangle$. This newly obtained XTOP N' is compatible with M. In addition, we only have one special tree $\sigma(z_2, z_3)$ that occurs in states of the form $\langle l, q, v \rangle$. Thus, we need to compute all minimal derivations whose output trees are instances of $\sigma(z_2, z_3)$. This is again simple since the first three rule schemes ρ_s, $\rho_{s,s'}$, and $\rho'_{s,s'}$ of M create such instances, so we simply create copies of them:

$$\rho_s(\sigma(y_1, y_2)) \to \sigma(p_s(y_1), p(y_2))$$
$$\rho_{s,s'}(\delta(y_1, y_2, y_3)) \to \sigma(p_s(y_1), \sigma(p_{s'}(y_2), p(y_3)))$$
$$\rho'_{s,s'}(\delta(y_1, y_2, y_3)) \to \sigma(p_s(y_1), \sigma(p_{s'}(y_2), p_\alpha(y_3)))$$

for all $s, s' \in \{\alpha, \beta\}$. These are all the rules of $R_{\sigma(z_2,z_3)}$. In addition, we create the following rules of R_E:

$$p(x_1) \to \rho_s(x_1) \qquad p(x_1) \to \rho_{s,s'}(x_1)$$
$$p(x_1) \to \rho'_{s,s'}(x_1)$$

for all $s, s' \in \{\alpha, \beta\}$. □

Especially after reading the example it might seem useless to create the rule copies in R_l [in Example 6 for $l = \sigma(z_2, z_3)$]. However, each such rule has a distinct state at the root of the left-hand side, which can be used to trigger only this rule. In this way, the state selects the next rule to apply, which yields the desired local determinism.

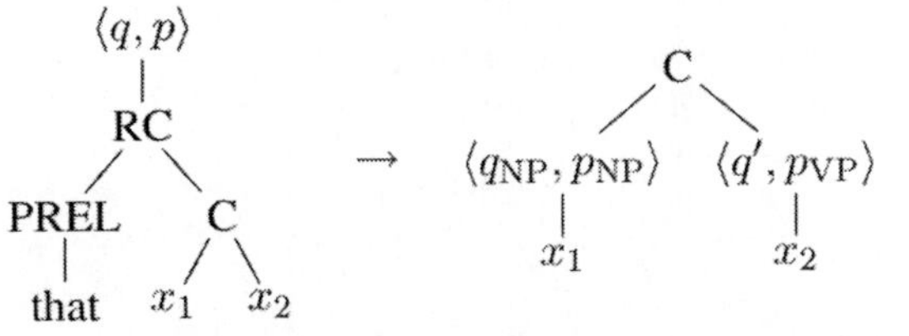

Figure 13: Composed rule created from the rule of Figure 7 and the rules of N' displayed in Figure 11.

5 Composition

Now we are ready for the actual composition. For space efficiency reasons we reuse the notations used in Section 4. Moreover, we identify trees of $T_\Gamma(Q'(P'(X)))$ with trees of $T_\Gamma((Q' \times P')(X))$. In other words, when meeting a subtree $q(p(x))$ with $q \in Q'$, $p \in P'$, and $x \in X$, then we also view this equivalently as the tree $\langle q, p \rangle(x)$, which could be part of a rule of our composed XTOP. However, not all combinations of states will be allowed in our composed XTOP, so some combinations will never yield valid rules.

Generally, we construct a rule of $M' ; N'$ by applying a single rule of M' followed by any number of pure ε-rules of R_E, which can turn states $\mathrm{base}(\overline{p})$ into $\overline{p}$. Then we apply any number of rules of N' and try to obtain a sentential form that has the required shape of a rule of $M' ; N'$.

Definition 7. Let $M' = (P', \Sigma, \Delta, I_M, R'_M)$ and $N' = (Q', \Delta, \Gamma, I_N, R'_N)$ be the XTOPs constructed in Section 4, where $\bigcup_{l \in L} P_l \subseteq P'$ and $\bigcup_{l \in L} Q_l \subseteq Q'$. Let $Q'' = Q' \setminus \bigcup_{l \in L} Q_l$. We construct the XTOP $M' ; N' = (S, \Sigma, \Gamma, I_N \times I_M, R)$ where

$$S = \bigcup_{l \in L} (Q_l \times P_l) \cup (Q'' \times P')$$

and R contains all normalized rules $\ell \to r$ (of the required shape) such that

$$\ell \Rightarrow_{M'} \xi \Rightarrow^*_{R_E} \zeta \Rightarrow^*_{N'} r$$

for some $\xi, \zeta \in T_\Gamma(Q'(T_\Delta(P'(X))))$. □

The required rule shape is given by the definition of an XTOP. Most importantly, we must have that $\ell \in S(T_\Sigma(X))$, which we identify with a certain subset of $Q'(P'(T_\Sigma(X)))$, and $r \in T_\Gamma(S(X))$, which similarly corresponds to a subset of $T_\Gamma(Q'(P'(X)))$. The states are simply combinations of the states of M' and N', of

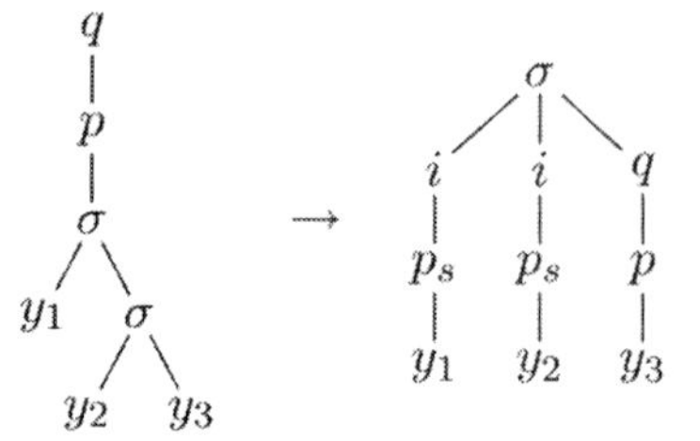

Figure 14: Successfully expanded rule from Example 9.

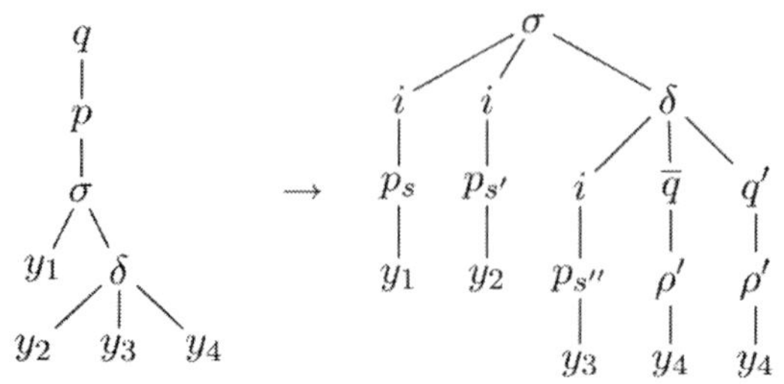

Figure 15: Expanded rule that remains copying (see Example 9).

which however the combinations of a state $q \in Q_l$ with a state $p \notin P_l$ are forbidden. This reflects the intuition of the previous section. If we entered a special state of the form $\langle l, q, v\rangle$, then we should use a corresponding state $p \in P_l$ of M, which only has rules producing instances of l. We note that look-ahead of N' is checked normally in the derivation process.

Example 8. Now let us illustrate the composition on Example 6. Let us start with rule (†) of M.

$$\begin{aligned} & q(p(\sigma(x_1, x_2))) \\ \Rightarrow_{M'}\ & q(\sigma(p_s(x_1), p(x_2))) \\ \Rightarrow_{R_E}\ & q(\sigma(p_s(x_1), \rho_{s',s''}(x_2))) \\ \Rightarrow_{N'}\ & \delta(i(p_s(x_1)), \overline{q}(\rho_{s',s''}(x_2)), q'(\rho_{s',s''}(x_2))) \end{aligned}$$

is a rule of $M' \,;\, N'$ for every $s, s', s'' \in \{\alpha, \beta\}$. Note if we had not applied the R_E-step, then we would not have obtained a rule of $M \,;\, N$ (because we would have obtained the state combination $\langle \overline{q}, p\rangle$ instead of $\langle \overline{q}, \rho_{s',s''}\rangle$, and $\langle \overline{q}, p\rangle$ is not a state of $M' \,;\, N'$). Let us also construct a rule for the state combination $\langle \overline{q}, \rho_{s',s''}\rangle$.

$$\begin{aligned} & \overline{q}(\rho_{s',s''}(\delta(x_1, x_2, x_3))) \\ \Rightarrow_{M'}\ & \overline{q}(\sigma(p_{s'}(x_1), \sigma(p_{s''}(x_2), p(x_3)))) \\ \Rightarrow_{N'}\ & q'(p_{s'}(x_1)) \end{aligned}$$

Finally, let us construct a rule for the state combination $\langle q'', \rho_{s',s''}\rangle$.

$$\begin{aligned} & q''(\rho_{s',s''}(\delta(x_1, x_2, x_3))) \\ \Rightarrow_{M'}\ & \overline{q}(\sigma(p_{s'}(x_1), \sigma(p_{s''}(x_2), p(x_3)))) \\ \Rightarrow_{R_E}\ & \overline{q}(\sigma(p_{s'}(x_1), \sigma(p_{s''}(x_2), \rho_s(x_3)))) \\ \Rightarrow_{N'}\ & q(\sigma(p_{s''}(x_2), \rho_s(x_3))) \\ \Rightarrow_{N'}\ & \delta(q'(p_{s''}(x_1)), \overline{q}(\rho_s(x_2)), q''(\rho_s(x_2))) \end{aligned}$$

for every $s \in \{\alpha, \beta\}$. □

After having pre-processed the XTOPs in our introductory example, the devices M and N' can be composed into $M \,;\, N'$. One rule of the composed XTOP is illustrated in Figure 13.

6 Post-processing

Finally, we will compose rules again in an effort to restore linearity (and nondeletion). Since the composition of two linear and nondeleting XTOPs cannot always be computed by a single XTOP (Arnold and Dauchet, 1982), this method can fail to return such an XTOP. The presented method is not a characterization, which means it might even fail to return a linear and nondeleting XTOP although an equivalent linear and nondeleting XTOP exists. However, in a significant number of examples, the recombination succeeds to rebuild a linear (and nondeleting) XTOP.

Let $M' \,;\, N' = (S, \Sigma, \Gamma, I, R)$ be the composed XTOP constructed in Section 5. We simply inspect each non-linear rule (i.e., each rule with a non-linear right-hand side) and expand it by all rule options at the copied variables. Since the method is pretty standard and variants have already been used in the pre-processing steps, we only illustrate it on the rules of Figure 12.

Example 9. The first (top row, left-most) rule of Figure 12 is non-linear in the variable y_2. Thus, we expand the calls $\langle \overline{q}, \rho\rangle(y_2)$ and $\langle q', \rho\rangle(y_2)$. If $\rho = \rho_s$ for some $s \in \{\alpha, \beta\}$, then the next rules are uniquely determined and we obtain the rule displayed in Figure 14. Here the expansion was successful and we could delete the original rule for $\rho = \rho_s$ and replace it by the displayed expanded rule. However, if $\rho = \rho'_{s',s''}$, then we can also expand the rule to obtain the rule displayed in Figure 15. It is still copying and we could repeat the process of expansion here, but we cannot get rid of all copying rules using this approach (as expected since there is no linear XTOP computing the same tree transformation). □

References

André Arnold and Max Dauchet. 1982. Morphismes et bimorphismes d'arbres. *Theoretical Computer Science*, 20(1):33–93.

Brenda S. Baker. 1979. Composition of top-down and bottom-up tree transductions. *Information and Control*, 41(2):186–213.

Jason Eisner. 2003. Learning non-isomorphic tree mappings for machine translation. In *Proc. ACL*, pages 205–208. Association for Computational Linguistics.

Joost Engelfriet, Eric Lilin, and Andreas Maletti. 2009. Composition and decomposition of extended multi bottom-up tree transducers. *Acta Informatica*, 46(8):561–590.

Joost Engelfriet. 1975. Bottom-up and top-down tree transformations—A comparison. *Mathematical Systems Theory*, 9(3):198–231.

Joost Engelfriet. 1977. Top-down tree transducers with regular look-ahead. *Mathematical Systems Theory*, 10(1):289–303.

Jonathan Graehl, Kevin Knight, and Jonathan May. 2008. Training tree transducers. *Computational Linguistics*, 34(3):391–427.

Jonathan Graehl, Mark Hopkins, Kevin Knight, and Andreas Maletti. 2009. The power of extended top-down tree transducers. *SIAM Journal on Computing*, 39(2):410–430.

Kevin Knight and Jonathan Graehl. 2005. An overview of probabilistic tree transducers for natural language processing. In *Proc. CICLing*, volume 3406 of LNCS, pages 1–24. Springer.

Kevin Knight. 2007. Capturing practical natural language transformations. *Machine Translation*, 21(2):121–133.

Eric Lilin. 1978. *Une généralisation des transducteurs d'états finis d'arbres: les S-transducteurs*. Thèse 3ème cycle, Université de Lille.

Andreas Maletti and Heiko Vogler. 2010. Compositions of top-down tree transducers with ε-rules. In *Proc. FSMNLP*, volume 6062 of LNAI, pages 69–80. Springer.

Andreas Maletti. 2010. Why synchronous tree substitution grammars? In *Proc. HLT-NAACL*, pages 876–884. Association for Computational Linguistics.

Andreas Maletti. 2011. An alternative to synchronous tree substitution grammars. *Natural Language Engineering*, 17(2):221–242.

Alberto Martelli and Ugo Montanari. 1982. An efficient unification algorithm. *ACM Transactions on Programming Languages and Systems*, 4(2):258–282.

Jonathan May and Kevin Knight. 2006. Tiburon: A weighted tree automata toolkit. In *Proc. CIAA*, volume 4094 of LNCS, pages 102–113. Springer.

Jonathan May, Kevin Knight, and Heiko Vogler. 2010. Efficient inference through cascades of weighted tree transducers. In *Proc. ACL*, pages 1058–1066. Association for Computational Linguistics.

Jonathan May. 2010. *Weighted Tree Automata and Transducers for Syntactic Natural Language Processing*. Ph.D. thesis, University of Southern California, Los Angeles.

John Alan Robinson. 1965. A machine-oriented logic based on the resolution principle. *Journal of the ACM*, 12(1):23–41.

William C. Rounds. 1970. Mappings and grammars on trees. *Mathematical Systems Theory*, 4(3):257–287.

Stuart M. Shieber. 2004. Synchronous grammars as tree transducers. In *Proc. TAG+7*, pages 88–95.

James W. Thatcher. 1970. Generalized^2 sequential machine maps. *Journal of Computer and System Sciences*, 4(4):339–367.

Kenji Yamada and Kevin Knight. 2001. A syntax-based statistical translation model. In *Proc. ACL*, pages 523–530. Association for Computational Linguistics.

Structural and Topical Dimensions in Multi-Task Patent Translation

Katharina Wäschle and **Stefan Riezler**
Department of Computational Linguistics
Heidelberg University, Germany
{waeschle,riezler}@cl.uni-heidelberg.de

Abstract

Patent translation is a complex problem due to the highly specialized technical vocabulary and the peculiar textual structure of patent documents. In this paper we analyze patents along the orthogonal dimensions of topic and textual structure. We view different patent classes and different patent text sections such as title, abstract, and claims, as separate translation tasks, and investigate the influence of such tasks on machine translation performance. We study multi-task learning techniques that exploit commonalities between tasks by mixtures of translation models or by multi-task meta-parameter tuning. We find small but significant gains over task-specific training by techniques that model commonalities through shared parameters. A by-product of our work is a parallel patent corpus of 23 million German-English sentence pairs.

1 Introduction

Patents are an important tool for the protection of intellectual property and also play a significant role in business strategies in modern economies. Patent translation is an enabling technique for patent prior art search which aims to detect a patent's novelty and thus needs to be cross-lingual for a multitude of languages. Patent translation is complicated by a highly specialized vocabulary, consisting of technical terms specific to the field of invention the patent relates to. Patents are written in a sophisticated legal jargon ("patentese") that is not found in everyday language and exhibits a complex textual structure. Also, patents are often intentionally ambiguous or vague in order to maximize the coverage of the claims.

In this paper, we analyze patents with respect to the orthogonal dimensions of topic – the technical field covered by the patent – and structure – a patent's text sections –, with respect to their influence on machine translation performance.

The topical dimension of patents is characterized by the International Patent Classification (IPC)[1] which categorizes patents hierarchically into 8 sections, 120 classes, 600 subclasses, down to 70,000 subgroups at the leaf level. Table 1 shows the 8 top level sections.

A	Human Necessities
B	Performing Operations, Transporting
C	Chemistry, Metallurgy
D	Textiles, Paper
E	Fixed Constructions
F	Mechanical Engineering, Lighting, Heating, Weapons
G	Physics
H	Electricity

Table 1: IPC top level sections.

Orthogonal to the patent classification, patent documents can be sub-categorized along the dimension of textual structure. Article 78.1 of the European Patent Convention (EPC) lists all sections required in a patent document[2]:

> "A European patent application shall contain:
>
> (a) a **request for the grant** of a European patent;

[1] http://www.wipo.int/classifications/ipc/en/

[2] Highlights by the authors.

(b) a **description** of the invention;

(c) one or more **claims**;

(d) any **drawings** referred to in the description or the claims;

(e) an **abstract**,

and satisfy the requirements laid down in the Implementing Regulations."

The request for grant contains the patent title; thus a patent document comprises the textual elements of title, description, claim, and abstract.

We investigate whether it is worthwhile to treat different values along the structural and topical dimensions as different tasks that are not completely independent of each other but share some commonalities, yet differ enough to counter a simple pooling of data. For example, we consider different tasks such as patents from different IPC classes, or along an orthogonal dimension, patent documents of all IPC classes but consisting only of titles or only of claims. We ask whether such tasks should be addressed as separate translation tasks, or whether translation performance can be improved by learning several tasks simultaneously through shared models that are more sophisticated than simple data pooling. Our goal is to learn a patent translation system that performs well across several different tasks, thus benefits from shared information, but is yet able to address the specifics of each task.

One contribution of this paper is a thorough analysis of the differences and similarities of multilingual patent data along the dimensions of textual structure and topic. The second contribution is the experimental investigation of the influence of various such tasks on patent translation performance. Starting from baseline models that are trained on individual tasks or on data pooled from all tasks, we apply mixtures of translation models and multi-task minimum error rate training to multiple patent translation tasks. A by-product of our research is a parallel patent corpus of over 23 million sentence pairs.

2 Related work

Multi-task learning has mostly been discussed under the name of multi-domain adaptation in the area of statistical machine translation (SMT). If we consider domains as tasks, domain adaptation is a special two-task case of multi-task learning. Most previous work has concentrated on adapting unsupervised generative modules such as translation models or language models to new tasks. For example, transductive approaches have used automatic translations of monolingual corpora for self-training modules of the generative SMT pipeline (Ueffing et al., 2007; Schwenk, 2008; Bertoldi and Federico, 2009). Other approaches have extracted parallel data from similar or comparable corpora (Zhao et al., 2004; Snover et al., 2008). Several approaches have been presented that train separate translation and language models on task-specific subsets of the data and combine them in different mixture models (Foster and Kuhn, 2007; Koehn and Schroeder, 2007; Foster et al., 2010). The latter kind of approach is applied in our work to multiple patent tasks.

Multi-task learning efforts in patent translation have so far been restricted to experimental combinations of translation and language models from different sets of IPC sections. For example, Utiyama and Isahara (2007) and Tinsley et al. (2010) investigate translation and language models trained on different sets of patent sections, with larger pools of parallel data improving results. Ceauşu et al. (2011) find that language models always and translation model mostly benefit from larger pools of data from different sections. Models trained on pooled patent data are used as baselines in our approach.

The machine learning community has developed several different formalizations of the central idea of trading off optimality of parameter vectors for each task-specific model and closeness of these model parameters to the average parameter vector across models. For example, starting from a separate SVM for each task, Evgeniou and Pontil (2004) present a regularization method that trades off optimization of the task-specific parameter vectors and the distance of each SVM to the average SVM. Equivalent formalizations replace parameter regularization by Bayesian prior distributions on the parameters (Finkel and Manning, 2009) or by augmentation of the feature space with domain independent features (Daumé, 2007). Besides SVMs, several learning algorithms have been extended to the multi-task scenario in a parameter regularization setting, e.g., perceptron-type algorithms (Dredze et al., 2010) or boosting (Chapelle et al., 2011). Further variants include different formalizations of norms for parameter regularization, e.g., $\ell_{1,2}$ regularization

(Obozinski et al., 2010) or $\ell_{1,\infty}$ regularization (Quattoni et al., 2009), where only the features that are most important across all tasks are kept in the model. In our experiments, we apply parameter regularization for multi-task learning to minimum error rate training for patent translation.

3 Extraction of a parallel patent corpus from comparable data

Our work on patent translation is based on the MAREC[3] patent data corpus. MAREC contains over 19 million patent applications and granted patents in a standardized format from four patent organizations (European Patent Office (EP), World Intellectual Property Organization (WO), United States Patent and Trademark Office (US), Japan Patent Office (JP)), from 1976 to 2008. The data for our experiments are extracted from the EP and WO collections which contain patent documents that include translations of some of the patent text. To extract such parallel patent sections, we first determine the longest instance, if different kinds[4] exist for a patent. We assume titles to be sentence-aligned by default, and define sections with a token ratio larger than 0.7 as parallel. For the language pair German-English we extracted a total of 2,101,107 parallel titles, 291,716 parallel abstracts, and 735,667 parallel claims sections.

The lack of directly translated descriptions poses a serious limitation for patent translation, since this section constitutes the largest part of the document. It is possible to obtain comparable descriptions from related patents that have been filed in different countries and are connected through the patent family id. We extracted 172,472 patents that were both filed with the USPTO and the EPO and contain an English and a German description, respectively.

For sentence alignment, we used the Gargantua[5] tool (Braune and Fraser, 2010) that filters a sentence-length based alignment with IBM Model-1 lexical word translation probabilities, estimated on parallel data obtained from the first-pass alignment. This yields the parallel corpus listed in table 2 with high input-output ratios for claims, and much lower ratios for abstracts and descriptions, showing that claims exhibit a natural parallelism due to their structure, while abstracts and descriptions are considerably less parallel. Removing duplicates and adding parallel titles results in a corpus of over 23 million parallel sentence pairs.

	output	de ratio	en ratio
abstract	720,571	92.36%	76.81%
claims	8,346,863	97.82%	96.17%
descr.	14,082,381	86.23%	82.67%

Table 2: Number of parallel sentences in output with input/output ratio of sentence aligner.

Differences between the text sections become visible in an analysis of token to type ratios. Table 3 gives the average number of tokens compared to the average type frequencies for a window of 100,000 tokens from every subsection. It shows that titles contain considerably fewer tokens than other sections, however, the disadvantage is partially made up by a relatively large amount of types, indicated by a lower average type frequency.

	tokens		types	
	de	en	de	en
title	6.5	8.0	2.9	4.8
abstract	37.4	43.2	4.3	9.0
claims	53.2	61.3	5.5	9.5
description	27.5	35.5	4.0	7.0

Table 3: Average number of tokens and average type frequencies in text sections.

We reserved patent data published between 1979 and 2007 for training and documents published in 2008 for tuning and testing in SMT. For the dimension of text sections, we sampled 500,000 sentences – distributed across all IPC sections – for training and 2,000 sentences for each text section for development and testing. Because of a relatively high number of identical sentences in test and training set for titles, we removed the overlap for this section.

Table 4 shows the distribution of IPC sections on claims, with the smallest class accounting for

[3]http://www.ir-facility.org/prototypes/marec

[4]A patent kind code indicates the document stage in the filing process, e.g., A for applications and B for granted patents, with publication levels from 1-9. See http://www.wipo.int/standards/en/part_03.html.

[5]http://gargantua.sourceforge.net

around 300,000 parallel sentences. In order to obtain similar amounts of training data for each task along the topical dimension, we sampled 300,000 sentences from each IPC class for training, and 2,000 sentences for each IPC class for development and testing.

A	1,947,542
B	2,522,995
C	2,263,375
D	299,742
E	353,910
F	1,012,808
G	2,066,132
H	1,754,573

Table 4: Distribution of IPC sections on claims.

4 Machine translation experiments

4.1 Individual task baselines

For our experiments we used the phrase-based, open-source SMT toolkit Moses[6] (Koehn et al., 2007). For language modeling, we computed 5-gram models using IRSTLM[7] (Federico et al., 2008) and queried the model with KenLM (Heafield, 2011). BLEU (Papineni et al., 2001) scores were computed up to 4-grams on lowercased data.

	Europarl-v6		MAREC	
	BLEU	OOV	BLEU	OOV
abstract	0.1726	14.40%	**0.3721**	3.00%
claim	0.2301	15.80%	**0.4711**	4.20%
title	0.0964	26.00%	**0.3228**	9.20%

Table 5: BLEU scores and OOV rate for Europarl baseline and MAREC model.

Table 5 shows a first comparison of results of Moses models trained on 500,000 parallel sentences from patent text sections balanced over IPC classes, against Moses trained on 1.7 Million sentences of parliament proceedings from Europarl[8] (Koehn, 2005). The best result on each section is indicated in **bold** face. The Europarl model performs very poorly on all three sections in comparison to the task-specific MAREC model, although the former has been learned on more than three times the amount of data. An analysis of the output of both system shows that the Europarl model suffers from two problems: Firstly, there is an obvious out of vocabulary (OOV) problem of the Europarl model compared to the MAREC model. Secondly, the Europarl model suffers from incorrect word sense disambiguation, as illustrated by the samples in table 6.

source	steuerbar	leitet
Europarl	taxable	is in charge of
MAREC	controllable	guiding
reference	controllable	guides

Table 6: Output of Europarl model on MAREC data.

Table 7 shows the results of the evaluation across text sections; we measured the performance of separately trained and tuned individual models on every section. The results allow some conclusions about the textual characteristics of the sections and indicate similarities. Naturally, every task is best translated with a model trained on the respective section, as the BLEU scores on the diagonal are the highest in every column. Accordingly, we are interested in the runner-up on each section, which is indicated in **bold** font. The results on abstracts suggest that this section bears the strongest resemblance to claims, since the model trained on claims achieves a respectable score. The abstract model seems to be the most robust and varied model, yielding the runner-up score on all other sections. Claims are easiest to translate, yielding the highest overall BLEU score of 0.4879. In contrast to that, all models score considerably lower on titles.

	test			
train	abstract	claim	title	desc.
abstract	*0.3737*	**0.4076**	**0.2681**	**0.2812**
claim	**0.3416**	*0.4879*	0.2420	0.2623
title	0.2839	0.3512	*0.3196*	0.1743
desc.	0.32189	**0.403**	0.2342	*0.3347*

Table 7: BLEU scores for 500k individual text section models.

The cross-section evaluation on the IPC classes (table 8) shows similar patterns. Each section

[6]`http://statmt.org/moses/`
[7]`http://sourceforge.net/projects/irstlm/`
[8]`http://www.statmt.org/europarl/`

is best translated with a model trained on data from the same section. Note that best section scores vary considerably, ranging from 0.5719 on C to 0.4714 on H, indicating that higher-scoring classes, such as C and A, are more homogeneous and therefore easier to translate. C, the Chemistry section, presumably benefits from the fact that the data contain chemical formulae, which are language-independent and do not have to be translated. Again, for determining the relationship between the classes, we examine the best runner-up on each section, considering the BLEU score, although asymmetrical, as a kind of measure of similarity between classes. We can establish symmetric relationships between sections A and C, B and F as well as G and H, which means that the models are mutual runner-up on the other's test section.

The similarities of translation tasks established in the previous section can be confirmed by information-theoretic similarity measures that perform a pairwise comparison of the vocabulary probability distribution of each task-specific corpus. This distribution is calculated on the basis of the 500 most frequent words in the union of two corpora, normalized by vocabulary size. As metric we use the $\mathcal{A}$-distance measure of Kifer et al. (2004). If $\mathcal{A}$ is the set of events on which the word distributions of two corpora are defined, then the $\mathcal{A}$-distance is the supremum of the difference of probabilities assigned to the same event. Low distance means higher similarity.

Table 9 shows the $\mathcal{A}$-distance of corpora specific to IPC classes. The most similar section or sections – apart from the section itself on the diagonal – is indicated in **bold** face. The pairwise similarity of A and C, B and F, G and H obtained by BLEU score is confirmed. Furthermore, a close similarity between E and F is indicated. G and H (electricity and physics, respectively) are very similar to each other but not close to any other section apart from B.

4.2 Task pooling and mixture

One straightforward technique to exploit commonalities between tasks is pooling data from separate tasks into a single training set. Instead of a trivial enlargement of training data by pooling, we train the pooled models on the same amount of sentences as the individual models. For instance, the pooled model for the pairing of IPC section B and C is trained on a data set composed of 150,000 sentences from each IPC section. The pooled model for pairing data from abstracts and claims is trained on data composed of 250,000 sentences from each text section.

Another approach to exploit commonalities between tasks is to train separate language and translation models[9] on the sentences from each task and combine the models in the global log-linear model of the SMT framework, following Foster and Kuhn (2007) and Koehn and Schroeder (2007). Model combination is accomplished by adding additional language model and translation model features to the log-linear model and tuning the additional meta-parameters by standard minimum error rate training (Bertoldi et al., 2009).

We try out mixture and pooling for all pairwise combinations of the three structural sections, for which we have high-quality data, i.e. abstract, claims and title. Due to the large number of possible combinations of IPC sections, we limit the experiments to pairs of similar sections, based on the $\mathcal{A}$-distance measure.

Table 10 lists the results for two combinations of data from different sections: a log-linear mixture of separately trained models and simple pooling, i.e. concatenation, of the training data. Overall, the mixture models perform slightly better than the pooled models on the text sections, although the difference is significant only in two cases. This is indicated by highlighting best results in **bold** face (with more than one result highlighted if the difference is not significant).[10]

We investigate the same mixture and pooling techniques on the IPC sections we considered pairwise similar (see table 11). Somehow contradicting the former results, the mixture models perform significantly worse than the pooled model on three sections. This might be the result of inadequate tuning, since most of the time the MERT algorithm did not converge after the maximum number of iterations, due to the larger number of features when using several models.

[9]Following Duh et al. (2010), we use the alignment model trained on the pooled data set in the phrase extraction phase of the separate models. Similarly, we use a globally trained lexical reordering model.

[10]For assessing significance, we apply the approximate randomization method described in Riezler and Maxwell (2005). We consider pairwise differing results scoring a p-value smaller than 0.05 as significant; the assessment is repeated three times and the average value is taken.

train	test A	B	C	D	E	F	G	H
A	*0.5349*	0.4475	**0.5472**	0.4746	0.4438	0.4523	0.4318	0.4109
B	0.4846	*0.4736*	0.5161	**0.4847**	**0.4578**	**0.4734**	0.4396	0.4248
C	**0.5047**	0.4257	*0.5719*	0.462	0.4134	0.4249	0.409	0.3845
D	0.47	0.4387	0.5106	*0.5167*	0.4344	0.4435	0.407	0.3917
E	0.4486	0.4458	0.4681	0.4531	*0.4771*	0.4591	0.4073	0.4028
F	0.4595	**0.4588**	0.4761	0.4655	0.4517	*0.4909*	0.422	0.4188
G	0.4935	0.4489	0.5239	0.4629	0.4414	0.4565	*0.4748*	**0.4532**
H	0.4628	0.4484	0.4914	0.4621	0.4421	0.4616	**0.4588**	*0.4714*

Table 8: BLEU scores for 300k individual IPC section models.

	A	B	C	D	E	F	G	H
A	*0*	0.1303	**0.1317**	0.1311	0.188	0.186	0.164	0.1906
B	**0.1302**	*0*	0.2388	**0.1242**	**0.0974**	**0.0875**	0.1417	0.1514
C	**0.1317**	0.2388	*0*	0.1992	0.311	0.3068	0.2506	0.2825
D	**0.1311**	0.1242	0.1992	*0*	0.1811	0.1808	0.1876	0.201
E	0.188	0.0974	0.311	0.1811	*0*	**0.0921**	0.2058	0.2025
F	0.186	**0.0875**	0.3068	0.1808	**0.0921**	*0*	0.1824	0.1743
G	0.164	0.1417	0.2506	0.1876	0.2056	0.1824	*0*	**0.064**
H	0.1906	0.1514	0.2825	0.201	0.2025	0.1743	**0.064**	*0*

Table 9: Pairwise $\mathcal{A}$-distance for 300k IPC training sets.

train	test	pooling	mixture
abstract-claim	abstract	**0.3703**	**0.3704**
	claim	0.4809	**0.4834**
claim-title	claim	**0.4799**	**0.4789**
	title	**0.3269**	**0.328**
title-abstract	title	**0.3311**	**0.3275**
	abstract	0.3643	**0.366**

Table 10: Mixture and pooling on text sections.

train	test	pooling	mixture
A-C	A	**0.5271**	**0.5274**
	C	**0.5664**	0.5632
B-F	B	**0.4696**	0.4354
	F	**0.4859**	0.4769
G-H	G	**0.4735**	**0.4754**
	H	0.4634	**0.467**

Table 11: Mixture and pooling on IPC sections.

A comparison of the results for pooling and mixture with the respective results for individual models (tables 7 and 8) shows that replacing data from the same task by data from related tasks decreases translation performance in almost all cases. The exception is the title model that benefits from pooling and mixing with both abstracts and claims due to their richer data structure.

4.3 Multi-task minimum error rate training

In contrast to task pooling and task mixtures, the specific setting addressed by multi-task minimum error rate training is one in which the generative SMT pipeline is not adaptable. Such situations arise if there are not enough data to train translation models or language models on the new tasks. However, we assume that there are enough parallel data available to perform meta-parameter tuning by minimum error rate training (MERT) (Och, 2003; Bertoldi et al., 2009) for each task.

A generic algorithm for multi-task learning can be motivated as follows: Multi-task learning aims to take advantage of commonalities shared among tasks by learning several independent but related tasks together. Information is shared between tasks through a joint representation and in-

test	tuning individual	pooled	average	MMERT	MMERT-average
abstract	**0.3721**	0.362	0.3657*+	**0.3719**+	0.3685*+
claim	0.4711	0.4681	**0.4749***+	**0.475***+	0.4734*+
title	0.3228	0.3152	**0.3326***+	0.3268*+	**0.3325***+

Table 12: Multi-task tuning on text sections.

test	tuning individual	pooled	average	MMERT	MMERT-average
A	0.5187	0.5199	**0.5213***+	0.5195	0.5196
B	0.4877	0.4885	0.4908*+	0.4911*+	**0.4921***+
C	**0.5214**	0.5175	0.5199*+	**0.5218**+	0.5162*+
D	**0.4724**	**0.4730**	**0.4733**	**0.4736**	**0.4734**
E	0.4666	0.4661	**0.4679***+	0.4669+	**0.4685***+
F	0.4794	0.4801	0.4811*	**0.4821***+	**0.4830***+
G	0.4596	0.4576	**0.4607**+	**0.4606**+	**0.4610***+
H	0.4573	0.4560	**0.4578**	**0.4581**+	**0.4581**+

Table 13: Multi-task tuning on IPC sections.

troduces an inductive bias. Evgeniou and Pontil (2004) propose a regularization method that balances task-specific parameter vectors and their distance to the average. The learning objective is to minimize task-specific loss functions l_d across all tasks d with weight vectors w_d, while keeping each parameter vector close to the average $\frac{1}{D}\sum_{d=1}^{D} w_d = w_{\text{avg}}$. This is enforced by minimizing the norm (here the ℓ_1-norm) of the difference of each task-specific weight vector to the avarage weight vector.

$$\min_{w_1,\ldots,w_D} \sum_{d=1}^{D} l_d(w_d) + \lambda \sum_{d=1}^{D} \|w_d - w_{\text{avg}}\|_1 \quad (1)$$

The MMERT algorithm is given in figure 1. The algorithm starts with initial weights $w^{(0)}$. At each iteration step, the average of the parameter vectors from the previous iteration is computed. For each task $d \in D$, one iteration of standard MERT is called, continuing from weight vector $w_d^{(t-1)}$ and minimizing translation loss function l_d on the data from task d. The individually tuned weight vectors returned by MERT are then moved towards the previously calculated average by adding or subtracting a penalty term λ for each weight component $w_d^{(t)}[k]$. If a weight moves beyond the average, it is clipped to the average value. The process is iterated until a stopping criterion is met, e.g. a threshold on the maximum change in the average weight vector. The parameter λ controls the influence of the regularization. A larger λ pulls the weights closer to the average, a smaller λ leaves more freedom to the individual tasks.

```
MMERT(w^(0), D, {l_d}_{d=1}^D):
for t = 1, ..., T do
  w_avg^(t) = 1/D Σ_{d=1}^D w_d^(t-1)
  for d = 1, ..., D parallel do
    w_d^(t) = MERT(w_d^(t-1), l_d)
    for k = 1, ..., K do
      if w[k]_d^(t) - w_avg^(t)[k] > 0 then
        w_d^(t)[k] = max(w_avg^(t)[k], w_d^(t)[k] - λ)
      else if w_d^(t)[k] - w_avg^(t)[k] < 0 then
        w_d^(t)[k] = min(w_avg^(t)[k], w_d^(t)[k] + λ)
      end if
    end for
  end for
end for
return w_1^(T), ..., w_D^(T), w_avg^(T)
```

Figure 1: Multi-task MERT.

The weight updates and the clipping strategy can be motivated in a framework of gradient descent optimization under ℓ_1-regularization (Tsuruoka et al., 2009). Assuming MERT as algorithmic minimizer[11] of the loss function l_d in equation 1, the weight update towards the average follows from the subgradient of the ℓ_1 regularizer. Since $w^{(t)}_{\text{avg}}$ is taken as average over weights $w_d^{(t-1)}$ from the step before, the term $w^{(t)}_{\text{avg}}$ is constant with respect to $w_d^{(t)}$, leading to the following subgradient (where $\text{sgn}(x) = 1$ if $x > 0$, $\text{sgn}(x) = -1$ if $x < 0$, and $\text{sgn}(x) = 0$ if $x = 0$):

$$\frac{\partial}{\partial w_r^{(t)}[k]} \lambda \sum_{d=1}^{D} \left\| w_d^{(t)} - \frac{1}{D} \sum_{s=1}^{D} w_s^{(t-1)} \right\|_1$$
$$= \lambda \ \text{sgn}\left(w_r^{(t)}[k] - \frac{1}{D} \sum_{s=1}^{D} w_s^{(t-1)}[k] \right).$$

Gradient descent minimization tells us to move in the opposite direction of the subgradient, thus motivating the addition or subtraction of the regularization penalty. Clipping is motivated by the desire to avoid oscillating parameter weights and in order to to enforce parameter sharing.

Experimental results for multi-task MERT (**MMERT**) are reported for both dimensions of patent tasks. For the IPC sections we trained a pooled model on 1,000,000 sentences sampled from abstracts and claims from all sections. We did not balance the sections but kept their original distribution, reflecting a real-life task where the distribution of sections is unknown. We then extend this experiment to the structural dimension. Since we do not have an intuitive notion of a natural distribution for the text sections, we train a balanced pooled model on a corpus composed of 170,000 sentences each from abstracts, claims and titles, i.e. 510,000 sentences in total. For both dimensions, for each task, we sampled 2,000 parallel sentences for development, development-testing, and testing from patents that were published in different years than the training data.

We compare the multi-task experiments with two baselines. The first baseline is individual task learning, corresponding to standard separate MERT tuning on each section (**individual**). This results in three separately learned weight vectors for each task, where no information has been shared between the tasks. The second baseline simulates the setting where the sections are not differentiated at all. We tune the model on a pooled development set of 2,000 sentences that combines the same amount of data from all sections (**pooled**). This yields a single joint weight vector for all tasks optimized to perform well across all sections. Furthermore, we compare multi-task MERT tuning with two parameter averaging methods. The first method computes the arithmetic mean of the weight vectors returned by the individual baseline for each weight component, yielding a joint average vector for all tasks (**average**). The second method takes the last average vector computed during multi-task MERT tuning (**MMERT-average**).[12]

Tables 12 and 13 give the results for multi-task learning on text and IPC sections. The latter results have been presented earlier in Simianer et al. (2011). The former table extends the technique of multi-task MERT to the structural dimension of patent SMT tasks. In all experiments, the parameter λ was adjusted to 0.001 after evaluating different settings on a development set. The best result on each section is indicated in bold face; * indicates significance with respect to the individual baseline, + the same for the pooled baseline. We observe statistically significant improvements of 0.5 to 1% BLEU over the individual baseline for claims and titles; for abstracts, the multi-task variant yields the same result as the baseline, while the averaging methods perform worse. Multi-task MERT yields the best result for claims; on titles, the simple average and the last MMERT average dominate. Pooled tuning always performs significantly worse than any other method, confirming that it is beneficial to differentiate between the text section sections.

Similarly for IPC sections, small but statistically significant improvements over the individual and pooled baselines are achieved by multi-task tuning and averaging over IPC sections, excepting C and D. However, an advantage of multi-task tuning over averaging is hard to establish.

Note that the averaging techniques implicitly benefit from a larger tuning set. In order to ascertain that the improvements by averaging are not

[11]MERT as presented in Och (2003) is not a gradient-based optimization techniquem, thus MMERT is strictly speaking only "inspired" by gradient descent optimization.

[12]The aspect of averaging found in all of our multi-task learning techniques effectively controls for optimizer instability as mentioned in Clark et al. (2011).

test	pooled-6k	significance
abstract	0.3628	<
claim	0.4696	<
title	0.3174	<

Table 14: Multi-task tuning on 6,000 sentences pooled from text sections. "<" denotes a statistically significant difference to the best result.

simply due to increasing the size of the tuning set, we ran a control experiment where we tuned the model on a pooled development set of $3 \times 2,000$ sentences for text sections and on a development set of $8 \times 2,000$ sentences for IPC sections. The results given in table 14 show that tuning on a pooled set of 6,000 text sections yields only minimal differences to tuning on 2,000 sentence pairs such that the BLEU scores for the new pooled models are still significantly lower than the best results in table 12 (indicated by "<"). However, increasing the tuning set to 16,000 sentence pairs for IPC sections makes the pooled baseline perform as well as the best results in table 13, except for two cases (indicated by "<") (see table 15). This is due to the smaller differences between best and worst results for tuning on IPC sections compared to tuning on text sections, indicating that IPC sections are less well suited for multi-task tuning than the textual domains.

test	pooled-16k	significance
A	0.5177	<
B	0.4920	
C	0.5133	<
D	0.4737	
E	0.4685	
F	0.4832	
G	0.4608	
H	0.4579	

Table 15: Multi-task tuning on 16,000 sentences pooled from IPC sections. "<" denotes a statistically significant difference to the best result.

5 Conclusion

The most straightforward approach to improve machine translation performance on patents is to enlarge the training set to include all available data. This question has been investigated by Tinsley et al. (2010) and Utiyama and Isahara (2007). A caveat in this situation is that data need to be from the general patent domain, as shown by the inferior performance of a large Europarl-trained model compared to a small patent-trained model.

The goal of this paper is to analyze patent data along the topical dimension of IPC classes and along the structural dimension of textual sections. Instead of trying to beat a pooling baseline that simply increases the data size, our research goal is to investigate whether different subtasks along these dimensions share commonalities that can fruitfully be exploited by multi-task learning in machine translation. We thus aim to investigate the benefits of multi-task learning in realistic situations where a simple enlargement of training data is not possible.

Starting from baseline models that are trained on individual tasks or on data pooled from all tasks, we apply mixtures of translation models and multi-task MERT tuning to multiple patent translation tasks. We find small, but statistically significant improvements for multi-task MERT tuning and parameter averaging techniques. Improvements are more pronounced for multi-task learning on textual domains than on IPC domains. This might indicate that the IPC sections are less well delimitated than the structural domains. Furthermore, this is owing to the limited expressiveness of a standard linear model including 14-20 features in tuning. The available features are very coarse and more likely to capture structural differences, such as sentence length, than the lexical differences that differentiate the semantic domains. We expect to see larger gains due to multi-task learning for discriminatively trained SMT models that involve very large numbers of features, especially when multi-task learning is done in a framework that combines parameter regularization with feature selection (Obozinski et al., 2010). In future work, we will explore a combination of large-scale discriminative training (Liang et al., 2006) with multi-task learning for SMT.

Acknowledgments

This work was supported in part by DFG grant "Cross-language Learning-to-Rank for Patent Retrieval".

References

Nicola Bertoldi and Marcello Federico. 2009. Domain adaptation for statistical machine translation with monolingual resources. In *Proceedings of the 4th EACL Workshop on Statistical Machine Translation*, Athens, Greece.

Nicola Bertoldi, Barry Haddow, and Jean-Baptiste Fouet. 2009. Improved minimum error rate training in Moses. *The Prague Bulletin of Mathematical Linguistics*, 91:7–16.

Fabienne Braune and Alexander Fraser. 2010. Improved unsupervised sentence alignment for symmetrical and asymmetrical parallel corpora. In *Proceedings of the 23rd International Conference on Computational Linguistics (COLING'10)*, Beijing, China.

Alexandru Ceauşu, John Tinsley, Jian Zhang, and Andy Way. 2011. Experiments on domain adaptation for patent machine translation in the PLuTO project. In *Proceedings of the 15th Conference of the European Assocation for Machine Translation (EAMT 2011)*, Leuven, Belgium.

Olivier Chapelle, Pannagadatta Shivaswamy, Srinivas Vadrevu, Kilian Weinberger, Ya Zhang, and Belle Tseng. 2011. Boosted multi-task learning. *Machine Learning*.

Jonathan Clark, Chris Dyer, Alon Lavie, and Noah Smith. 2011. Better hypothesis testing for statistical machine translation: Controlling for optimizer instability. In *Proceedings of the 49th Annual Meeting of the Association for Computational Linguistics (ACL'11)*, Portland, OR.

Hal Daumé. 2007. Frustratingly easy domain adaptation. In *Proceedings of the 45th Annual Meeting of the Association for Computational Linguistics (ACL'07)*, Prague, Czech Republic.

Mark Dredze, Alex Kulesza, and Koby Crammer. 2010. Multi-domain learning by confidence-weighted parameter combination. *Machine Learning*, 79:123–149.

Kevin Duh, Katsuhito Sudoh, and Hajime Tsukada. 2010. Analysis of translation model adaptation in statistical machine translation. In *Proceedings of the International Workshop on Spoken Language Translation (IWSLT'10)*, Paris, France.

Theodoros Evgeniou and Massimiliano Pontil. 2004. Regularized multi-task learning. In *Proceedings of the 10th ACM SIGKDD conference on knowledge discovery and data mining (KDD'04)*, Seattle, WA.

Marcello Federico, Nicola Bertoldi, and Mauro Cettolo. 2008. IRSTLM: an open source toolkit for handling large scale language models. In *Proceedings of Interspeech*, Brisbane, Australia.

Jenny Rose Finkel and Christopher D. Manning. 2009. Hierarchical bayesian domain adaptation. In *Proceedings of the Conference of the North American Chapter of the Association for Computational Linguistics - Human Language Technologies (NAACL-HLT'09)*, Boulder, CO.

George Foster and Roland Kuhn. 2007. Mixture-model adaptation for SMT. In *Proceedings of the Second Workshop on Statistical Machine Translation*, Prague, Czech Republic.

George Foster, Pierre Isabelle, and Roland Kuhn. 2010. Translating structured documents. In *Proceedings of the 9th Conference of the Association for Machine Translation in the Americas (AMTA 2010)*, Denver, CO.

Kenneth Heafield. 2011. KenLM: faster and smaller language model queries. In *Proceedings of the EMNLP 2011 Sixth Workshop on Statistical Machine Translation (WMT'11)*, Edinburgh, UK.

Daniel Kifer, Shain Ben-David, and Johannes Gehrke. 2004. Detecting change in data streams. In *Proceedings of the 30th international conference on Very large data bases*, Toronta, Ontario, Canada.

Philipp Koehn and Josh Schroeder. 2007. Experiments in domain adaptation for statistical machine translation. In *Proceedings of the Second Workshop on Statistical Machine Translation*, Prague, Czech Republic.

Philipp Koehn, Hieu Hoang, Alexandra Birch, Chris Callison-Birch, Marcello Federico, Nicola Bertoldi, Brooke Cowan, Wade Shen, Christine Moran, Richard Zens, Chris Dyer, Ondrej Bojar, Alexandra Constantin, and Evan Herbst. 2007. Moses: Open source toolkit for statistical machine translation. In *Proceedings of the ACL 2007 Demo and Poster Sessions*, Prague, Czech Republic.

Philipp Koehn. 2005. Europarl: A parallel corpus for statistical machine translation. In *Proceedings of Machine Translation Summit X*, Phuket, Thailand.

Percy Liang, Alexandre Bouchard-Côté, Dan Klein, and Ben Taskar. 2006. An end-to-end discriminative approach to machine translation. In *Proceedings of the joint conference of the International Committee on Computational Linguistics and the Association for Computational Linguistics (COLING-ACL'06)*, Sydney, Australia.

Guillaume Obozinski, Ben Taskar, and Michael I. Jordan. 2010. Joint covariate selection and joint subspace selection for multiple classification problems. *Statistics and Computing*, 20:231–252.

Franz Josef Och. 2003. Minimum error rate training in statistical machine translation. In *Proceedings of the Human Language Technology Conference and the 3rd Meeting of the North American Chapter of the Association for Computational Linguistics (HLT-NAACL'03)*, Edmonton, Cananda.

Kishore Papineni, Salim Roukos, Todd Ward, and Wei-Jing Zhu. 2001. Bleu: a method for automatic evaluation of machine translation. Technical Report IBM Research Division Technical Report, RC22176 (W0190-022), Yorktown Heights, N.Y.

Ariadna Quattoni, Xavier Carreras, Michael Collins, and Trevor Darrell. 2009. An efficient projection for $\ell_{1,\infty}$ regularization. In *Proceedings of the 26th International Conference on Machine Learning (ICML'09)*, Montreal, Canada.

Stefan Riezler and John Maxwell. 2005. On some pitfalls in automatic evaluation and significance testing for MT. In *Proceedings of the ACL-05 Workshop on Intrinsic and Extrinsic Evaluation Measures for MT and/or Summarization*, Ann Arbor, MI.

Holger Schwenk. 2008. Investigations on large-scale lightly-supervised training for statistical machine translation. In *Proceedings of the International Workshop on Spoken Language Translation (IWSLT'08)*, Hawaii.

Patrick Simianer, Katharina Wäschle, and Stefan Riezler. 2011. Multi-task minimum error rate training for SMT. *The Prague Bulletin of Mathematical Linguistics*, 96:99–108.

Matthew Snover, Bonnie Dorr, and Richard Schwartz. 2008. Language and translation model adaptation using comparable corpora. In *Proceedings of the Conference on Empirical Methods in Natural Language Processing (EMNLP'08)*, Honolulu, Hawaii.

John Tinsley, Andy Way, and Paraic Sheridan. 2010. PLuTO: MT for online patent translation. In *Proceedings of the 9th Conference of the Association for Machine Translation in the Americas (AMTA 2010)*, Denver, CO.

Yoshimasa Tsuruoka, Jun'ichi Tsujii, and Sophia Ananiadou. 2009. Stochastic gradient descent training for ℓ_1-regularized log-linear models with cumulative penalty. In *Proceedings of the 47th Annual Meeting of the Association for Computational Linguistics (ACL-IJCNLP'09)*, Singapore.

Nicola Ueffing, Gholamreza Haffari, and Anoop Sarkar. 2007. Transductive learning for statistical machine translation. In *Proceedings of the 45th Annual Meeting of the Association of Computational Linguistics (ACL'07)*, Prague, Czech Republic.

Masao Utiyama and Hitoshi Isahara. 2007. A Japanese-English patent parallel corpus. In *Proceedings of MT Summit XI*, Copenhagen, Denmark.

Bing Zhao, Matthias Eck, and Stephan Vogel. 2004. Language model adaptation for statistical machine translation with structured query models. In *Proceedings of the 20th International Conference on Computational Linguistics (COLING'04)*, Geneva, Switzerland.

Not as Awful as it Seems: Explaining German Case through Computational Experiments in Fluid Construction Grammar

Remi van Trijp
Sony Computer Science Laboratory Paris
6 Rue Amyot
75005 Paris (France)
remi@csl.sony.fr

Abstract

German case syncretism is often assumed to be the accidental by-product of historical development. This paper contradicts this claim and argues that the evolution of German case is driven by the need to optimize the cognitive effort and memory required for processing and interpretation. This hypothesis is supported by a novel kind of computational experiments that reconstruct and compare attested variations of the German definite article paradigm. The experiments show how the intricate interaction between those variations and the rest of the German 'linguistic landscape' may direct language change.

1 Introduction

In his 1880 essay, Mark Twain famously complained that *The awful German Language* is the most "slipshod and systemless, and so slippery and elusive to grasp" language of all. A brief look at the literature on the German case system seems to provide sufficient evidence for instantly agreeing with the American author. But what if the German case system were not the accidental by-product of diachronic changes as is often assumed? Are there linguistic forces that are not yet fully appreciated in the field, but which may explain the German case paradigm?

This paper demonstrates that there indeed are such forces through a case study on German definite articles. The experiments 'reconstruct' deep language processing models for different variants of this paradigm, and show how the 'linguistic landscape' of German has allowed its speakers to reduce their definite article system without loss in efficiency for processing and interpretation.

2 The Problem of German Case

German articles, adjectives and nouns are marked for gender, number and case through morphological inflection, as illustrated for definite articles in Table 1.

Case	SG-M	SG-F	SG-N	PL
NOM	*der*	*die*	*das*	*die*
ACC	*den*	*die*	*das*	*die*
DAT	*dem*	*der*	*dem*	*den*
GEN	*des*	*der*	*des*	*der*

Table 1: German definite articles.

The system is notorious for its *syncretism* (i.e. the same form can be mapped onto different functions), a riddle that has fascinated many formal and historical linguists looking for explanations.

2.1 Historical Linguistics

Studies in historical linguistics and grammaticalization often propose the following three forces to explain syncretism (Heine and Kuteva, 2005, p. 148):

1. The formal distinction between case markers is lost through phonological changes.
2. One case takes over the functional domain of another case and replaces it.
3. A case marker disappears and its functions are usurped by another marker.

Syncretism is thus considered as the *accidental* by-product of such forces, and German case syncretism is typically analyzed according to these lines (Barðdal, 2009; Baerman, 2009, p. 229). However, these forces are not explanatory: they only describe *what* has happened, but not *why*.

Another problem for the 'syncretism by accident' hypothesis is the fact that the collapsing of case forms is not randomly distributed over the whole paradigm as would be expected. Hawkins (2004, p. 78) observes that instead there is a systematic tendency for 'lower' cells in the paradigm (e.g. genitive; Table 1) to collapse before cells in 'higher' positions (e.g. nominative) do so.

2.2 Formal Linguistics

Many hidden effects of verbal linguistic theories can be uncovered through explicit formalizations. Unfortunately, formal linguists also typically distinguish between 'systematic' and 'non-systematic' syncretism when analyzing German case. For instance, in his review of a number of studies on German (a.o. Bierwisch, 1967; Blevins, 1995; Wiese, 1996; Wunderlich, 1997), Müller (2002) concludes that none of these approaches is able to rule out accidental syncretism.

There is however one major stone that has been left unturned by formal linguists: processing. Most formal theories, such as HPSG (Ginzburg and Sag, 2000), assume a strict division between 'competence' and 'performance' and therefore represent linguistic knowledge in a purely declarative, process-independent way (Sag and Wasow, 2011). While such an approach may be desirable from a 'mathematical' point of view, it puts the burden of efficient processing on the shoulders of computational linguists, who have to develop more intelligent interpreters.

One example of the gap between description and computational implementation is *disjunctive feature representation*, which became popular in feature-based grammar formalisms in the 1980s (Karttunen, 1984). Disjunctions allow an elegant notation for multiple feature values, as illustrated in example 1 for the German definite article *die*, which is either assigned nominative or accusative case, and which is either feminine-singular or plural. The feature structure (adopted from Karttunen, 1984, p. 30) represents disjunctions by enclosing the alternatives in curly brackets ({ }).

(1)
$$\left[\begin{array}{ll} \text{AGREEMENT} & \left\{\begin{array}{l} \left[\begin{array}{ll}\text{GENDER} & f\\ \text{NUM} & sg\end{array}\right] \\ \left[\text{NUM}\ \ pl\right]\end{array}\right\} \\ \text{CASE} & \left\{nom\ acc\right\}\end{array}\right]$$

However, it is a well-established fact that disjunctions are computationally expensive, which is illustrated in the top of Figure 1. This Figure shows the search tree of a small grammar when parsing the utterance *Die Kinder gaben der Lehrerin die Zeichnung* ('the children gave the drawing to the (female) teacher'), which is unambiguous to German speakers. As can be seen in the Figure, the search tree has to explore several branches before arriving at a valid solution. Most of the splits are caused by disjunctions. For example, when a determiner-noun construction specifies that the case features of the definite article *die* (nominative or accusative) and the noun *Kinder* ('children'; nominative, accusative or genitive) have to unify, the search tree splits into two hypotheses (a nominative and an accusative reading) even though for native speakers of German, the syntactic context unambiguously points to a nominative reading (because it is the only noun phrase that agrees with the main verb).

It should be no surprise, then, that a lot of work has focused on processing disjunctions more efficiently (e.g. Carter, 1990; Ramsay, 1990). As observed by Flickinger (2000), however, most of these studies implicitly assume that the grammar representation has to remain unchanged. He then demonstrates through computational experiments how a different representation can directly impact efficiency, and argues that revisions of the grammar for efficiency should be discussed more thoroughly in the literature.

The impact of representation on processing is illustrated at the bottom of Figure 1, which shows the performance of a grammar that uses the same processing technique for handling the same utterance, but a different representation than the disjunctive grammar. As can be seen, the alternative grammar (whose technical details are disclosed further below) is able to parse the German definite articles without tears, and the resulting search tree arguably better reflects the actual processing performed by native speakers of German.

2.3 Alternative Hypothesis

The effect of processing-friendly representations on search suggests that answers for the unsolved problems concerning case syncretism have to be sought in performance. This paper therefore rejects the processing-independent approach and explores the alternative hypothesis, following

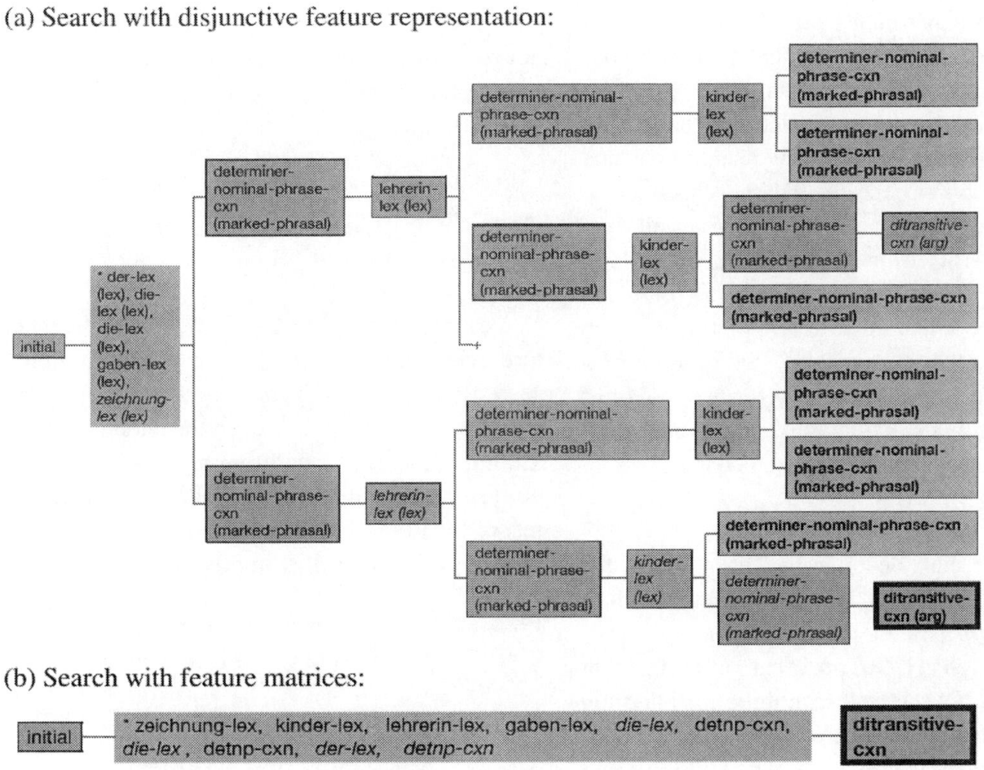

Figure 1: The representation of linguistic information has a direct impact on processing efficiency. The top figure shows a search tree when parsing the unambiguous utterance *Die Kinder gaben der Lehrerin die Zeichnung* ('The children gave the drawing to the (female) teacher') using disjunctive feature representation. The bottom figure shows the search tree using distinctive feature matrices. Labels in the boxes show the names of the applied constructions; boxes with a bold border are successful end nodes. Both grammars have been implemented in Fluid Construction Grammar (FCG; Steels, 2011, 2012a) and are processed using a standard depth-first search algorithm (Bleys et al., 2011) and general unification (*without* optimization for particular types or data structures; Steels and De Beule, 2006; De Beule, 2012). The utterance is assumed to be segmented into words. Interested readers can explore the Figure through an interactive web demonstration at `http://www.fcg-net.org/demos/design-patterns/07-feature-matrices/`.

Steels (2004, 2012b), that grammar evolves in order to optimize communicative success by dampening the search space in linguistic processing and reducing the cognitive effort needed for interpretation, while at the same time minimizing the resources required for doing so. More specifically, this paper explores the following claims:

1. The German definite article system can be processed as efficiently as its Old High German predecessor, which had less syncretism.
2. The presence of other grammatical structures have made it possible to reduce the definite article paradigm without increasing the cognitive effort needed for disambiguating the argument structures that underly German utterances.
3. The decrease of cue-reliability of case for disambiguation encourages the emergence of competing systems (such as word order).

The hypothesis is substantiated through computational experiments that reconstruct three different variants of the German definite article system (the current system, its Old High German predecessor, Wright, 1906; and the Texas German dialect system, Boas, 2009a,b) and compare their performance in terms of processing efficiency and cognitive effort in interpretation.

3 Operationalizing German Case

An adequate operationalization of German case requires a bidirectional grammar (for parsing and production) and easy access to linguistic processing data. All experiments reported in this paper have therefore been implemented in Fluid Construction Grammar (FCG; Steels, 2011, 2012a), a unification-based grammar formalism that comes equipped with an interactive web interface and monitoring tools (Loetzsch, 2012). A second advantage of FCG is that it features *strong* bidirectionality: the FCG-interpreter can achieve both parsing and production using the same linguistic inventory. Other feature structure platforms, such as the lkb-system (Copestake, 2002), require a separate parser and generator for formalizing bidirectional grammars, which make them less suited for substantiating the claims of this paper.

3.1 Distinctive Feature Matrix

German case has become the litmus test for demonstrating how well a feature-based grammar formalism copes with multifunctionality, especially since Ingria (1990) provocatively stated that unification is not the best technique for handling it. People have gone to great lengths to counter Ingria's claim, especially within the HPSG framework (e.g. Müller, 1999; Daniels, 2001; Sag, 2003), and various formalizations have been offered for German case (Heinz and Matiasek, 1994; Müller, 2001; Crysmann, 2005). However, these proposals either do not succeed in avoiding inefficient disjunctions or they require a complex double type hierarchy (Crysmann, 2005).

The experiments in this paper use a more straightforward solution, called a *distinctive feature matrix*, which is based on an idea that was first explored by Ingria (1990) and of which a variation has recently also been proposed for Lexical Functional Grammar (Dalrymple et al., 2009). Instead of treating case as a single-valued feature, it can be represented as an array of features, as shown for the definite article *die* (ignoring the genitive case for the time being):

(2) die: $\left[\text{CASE} \begin{bmatrix} \text{nom} & ?nom \\ \text{acc} & ?acc \\ \text{dat} & - \end{bmatrix}\right]$

The `case` feature includes a paradigm of three cases (`nom`, `acc` and `dat`), whose values can either be '+' or '–', or left unspecified through a variable (indicated by a question mark). The two variables `?nom` and `?acc` indicate that *die* can potentially be assigned nominative or accusative case, the value '–' for dative means that `die` cannot be assigned dative case. We can do the same for *Kinder* ('children'), which can be nominative or accusative, but not dative:

(3) Kinder: $\left[\text{CASE} \begin{bmatrix} \text{nom} & ?nom \\ \text{acc} & ?acc \\ \text{dat} & - \end{bmatrix}\right]$

As demonstrated in Figure 1, disjunctive feature representation would cause a split in the search tree when unifying *die* and *Kinder*. Using a feature matrix, however, the choice between a nominative and accusative reading can simply be postponed until enough information from the rest of the utterance is available. Unifying *die* and *Kinder* yields the following feature structure:

(4) die Kinder: $\left[\text{CASE} \begin{bmatrix} \text{nom} & ?nom \\ \text{acc} & ?acc \\ \text{dat} & - \end{bmatrix}\right]$

3.2 A Three-Dimensional Matrix

The German case paradigm is obviously more complex than the examples shown so far. Let's consider Table 1 again, but this time we replace every cell in the table by a variable. This leads to the following feature matrix for the German definite articles:

Case	SG-M	SG-F	SG-N	PL
?NOM	*?n-s-m*	*?n-s-f*	*?n-s-n*	*?n-pl*
?ACC	*?a-s-m*	*?a-s-f*	*?a-s-n*	*?a-pl*
?DAT	*?d-s-m*	*?d-s-f*	*?d-s-n*	*?d-pl*
?GEN	*?g-s-m*	*?g-s-f*	*?g-s-n*	*?g-pl*

Table 2: A distinctive feature matrix for German case.

Each cell in this matrix represents a specific feature bundle that collects the features case, number, and person. For example, the variable `?n-s-m` stands for nominative singular masculine. Note that also the cases themselves have their own variable (`?nom`, `?acc`, `?dat` and `?gen`). This allows us to single out a specific dimension of the matrix for constructions that only care about case distinctions, but abstract away from gender or number. Each linguistic item fills in as much information as possible in this case matrix. For example, Table 3 shows how the definite article *die* underspecifies its potential values and rules out all other options through '–'.

Case	SG-M	SG-F	SG-N	PL
?NOM	–	*?n-s-f*	–	*?n-pl*
?ACC	–	*?a-s-f*	–	*?a-pl*
–	–	–	–	–
–	–	–	–	–

Table 3: The feature matrix of *die*.

The feature matrix of *Kinder* ('children'), which underspecifies for nominative, accusative and genitive, is shown in Table 4. Notice, however, that the same variable names are used for both the column that singles out the case dimension as for the column of the plural feature bundles.

Case	SG-M	SG-F	SG-N	PL
?n-pl	–	–	–	*?n-pl*
?a-pl	–	–	–	*?a-pl*
–	–	–	–	–
?g-pl	–	–	–	*?g-pl*

Table 4: The feature matrix of *Kinder* ('children').

Unification of *die* and *Kinder* can exploit these variable 'equalities' for ruling out a singular value of the definite article. Likewise, the matrix of *die* rules out the genitive reading of *Kinder*, as illustrated in Table 5.

Case	SG-M	SG-F	SG-N	PL
?n-pl	–	–	–	*?n-pl*
?a-pl	–	–	–	*?a-pl*
–	–	–	–	–
–	–	–	–	–

Table 5: The feature matrix of *die Kinder*.

Argument structure constructions (Goldberg, 2006), such as the ditransitive, can then later assign either nominative or accusative case. The main advantage of feature matrices is that linguistic search only has to commit to specific feature-values once sufficient information is available, so the search tree only splits when there is an actual ambiguity. Moreover, they can be handled using standard unification. Interested readers can consult van Trijp (2011) for a thorough description of the approach, as well as a discussion on how the FCG implementation differs from Ingria (1990) and Dalrymple et al. (2009).

4 Experiments

This section describes the experimental set-up and discusses the experimental results.

4.1 Three Paradigms

The experiments compare three different variants of the German definite article paradigm.

Standard German. The Standard German paradigm has been illustrated in Table 1 and its operationalization has been shown in section 3.2. The paradigm has been inherited without significant changes from Middle High German (1050-1350; Walshe, 1974) and features six different forms.

Old High German. The Old High German paradigm is the direct predecessor of the current paradigm of definite articles. It contained at least twelve distinct forms (depending on which variation is taken) that included gender distinctions in plural (Wright, 1906, p. 67). It also included one definite article that marked the now extinct instrumental case, which is ignored in this paper. The variant of the Old High German paradigm that has been implemented in the experiments is summarized in Table 6.

Case	Singular		
	M	F	N
NOM	*dër*	*diu*	*daȥ*
ACC	*dën*	*die*	*daȥ*
DAT	*dëmu*	*dëru*	*dëmu*
GEN	*dës*	*dëra*	*dës*
	Plural		
	M	F	N
NOM	*die*	*deo*	*diu*
ACC	*die*	*deo*	*diu*
DAT	*dēm*	*dēm*	*dēm*
GEN	*dëro*	*dëro*	*dëro*

Table 6: The Old High German definite article system.

Texas German. The third variant is an American-German dialect called Texas German (Boas, 2009a,b), which evolved a two-way case distinction between nominative and oblique. This type of case system, in which the accusative and dative case have collapsed, is also a common evolution in the Low German dialects (Shrier, 1965). The implemented paradigm of Texas German is shown in Table 7.

Case	SG-M	SG-F	SG-N	PL
NOM	*der*	*die*	*das*	*die*
ACC/DAT	*den*	*die*	*den*	*die*

Table 7: The Texas German definite article system.

4.2 Production and Parsing Tasks

Each grammar is tested as to how efficiently it can produce and parse utterances in terms of cognitive effort and search (see section 4.3). There are three basic *types* of utterances:

1. Ditransitive: NOM – Verb – DAT – ACC
2. Transitive (a): NOM – Verb – ACC
3. Transitive (b): NOM – Verb – DAT

The argument roles are filled by noun phrases whose head nouns always have a distinct form for singular and plural (e.g. *Mann* vs. *Männer*; 'man' vs. 'men'), but that are unmarked for case. The combinations of arguments is always unique along the dimensions of number and gender, which yields 216 unique utterance types for the ditransitive as follows:

	NOM.S.M	V	DAT.S.M	ACC.S.M
	NOM.S.M	V	DAT.S.F	ACC.S.M
(5)	NOM.S.M	V	DAT.S.N	ACC.S.M
	NOM.S.M	V	DAT.PL.M	ACC.S.M
			etc.	

In transitive utterances, there is an additional distinction based on animacy for noun phrases in the Object position of the utterance, which yields 72 types in the NOM-ACC configuration and 72 in the NOM-DAT configuration. Together, there are 360 unique utterance types. As can be gleaned from the utterance types, the genitive case is not considered by the experiments, as the genitive is not part of basic German argument structures and it has almost disappeared in most dialects of German (Shrier, 1965).

In production, the grammar is presented with a meaning that needs to be verbalized into an utterance. In parsing, the produced utterance has to be analyzed back into a meaning. Every utterance is processed using a full search, that is, all branches and solutions are calculated.

The experiments exploit types because there are three different language systems, hence it is impossible to use a single, real corpus and its token frequencies. It would also be unwarranted to use different corpora because corpus-specific biases would distort the comparative results. Secondly, as the experiments involve models of *deep* language processing (as opposed to stochastic models), the use of types instead of tokens is justified in this phase of the research: the first concern of precision-grammars is descriptive adequacy, for which types are a more reliable source. Obviously, the effect of token frequency needs to be examined in future research.

4.3 Measuring Cognitive Effort

The experiments measure two kinds of cognitive effort: syntactic search and semantic ambiguity.

Search. The search measure counts the number of branches in the search process that reach an end node, which can either be a possible solution or a dead end (i.e. no constructions can be applied anymore). Duplicate nodes (for instance, nodes that use the same rules but in a different order) are not counted. The search measure is then used as a 'sanity check' to verify whether the three different paradigms can be processed with the same efficiency in terms of search tree length, as hypothesized by this paper. More specifically, the following conditions have to be met:

1. In production, there should only be one branch.
2. In parsing, search has to be equal to the semantic effort.

The single branch constraint in production checks whether the definite articles are sufficiently distinct from one another. Since there is no ambiguity about which argument plays which role in the utterance, the grammar should only come up with one solution. In parsing, the number of branches has to correspond to 'real' semantic ambiguities and not create additional search, as argued in section 2.2.

Semantic Ambiguity. Semantic ambiguity equals the number of possible interpretations of an utterance. For instance, the utterance *Der Hund beißt den Mann* 'the dog bites the man' is unambiguous in Modern High German, since *der Hund* can only be nominative singular-masculine, and *den Mann* can only be accusative masculine-singular. There is thus only one possible interpretation in which the dog is the biter and the man is being bitten, illustrated as follows using a logic-based meaning representation (also see Steels, 2004, for this operationalization of cognitive effort):

(6) Interpretation 1:

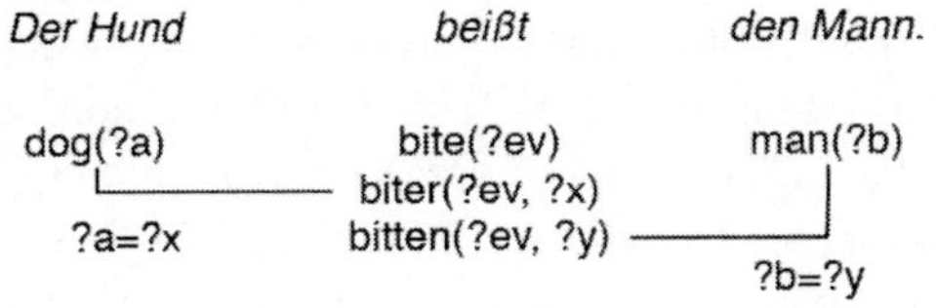

However, an utterance such as *die Katze beißt die Frau* 'the cat bites the woman' is ambiguous because *die* has both a nominative and accusative singular-feminine reading:

(7) a. Interpretation 1:

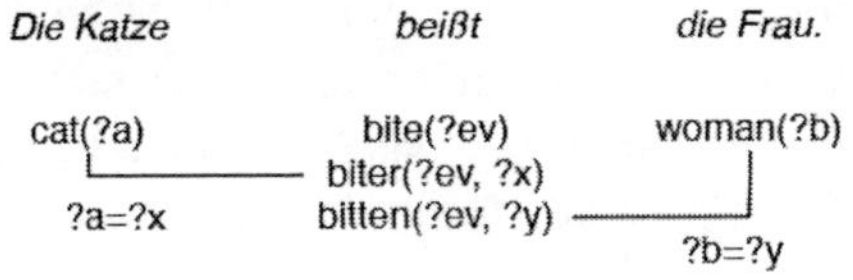

b. Interpretation 2:

Here, German speakers are likely to use word order, intonation and world knowledge (i.e. cats are more likely to bite a person than the other way round) for disambiguating the utterance.

4.4 Experimental Parameters

The experiments (E1-E4) concern the cue-reliability of the definite articles for disambiguating event structure. In all experiments, the different grammars can exploit the case-number-gender information of definite articles, and also the gender and number specifications of nouns, and the syntactic valence of verbs. For instance, the noun form *Frauen* 'women' is specified as plural-feminine, and verbs like *helfen* 'to help' are specified to take a dative object, whereas verbs like *finden* 'to find' take an accusative object. In other experiments, different combinations of grammatical cues become available or not:

Cue	E1	E2	E3	E4
SV-agreement		+		+
Selection restrictions			+	+

SV-agreement restricts the subject to singular or plural nouns, and semantic selection restrictions can disambiguate utterances in which for example the Agent-role has to be animate (e.g. in perception verbs such as *sehen* 'to see'). All other possible cues, such as word order, are ignored.

5 Results

5.1 Search

In all experiments, the constraints of the *search measure* were satisfied: every grammar only required one branch per utterance in production, and the number of branches in parsing never exceeded the number of possible interpretations. In terms of search length, more syncretism therefore does not automatically harm efficiency, provided that the grammar uses an adequate representation. Arguably, the smaller paradigms are even more efficient because they require less unifications to be performed.

5.2 Semantic Ambiguity

Now that it has been ascertained that more syncretism does not harm processing efficiency, we can compare cue-reliability of the different paradigms for semantic interpretation.

Ambiguous Utterances. Figure 2 shows the number of ambiguous utterances in parsing (in %) per paradigm and per set-up. As can be seen, the Old High German paradigm (black) is the most reliable cue in Experiment 1 (E1; when SV-agreement and selection restrictions are ignored) with 35.56% of ambiguous utterances, as opposed to 55.56% for Modern High German (grey) and 77.78% for Texas German (white).

When SV-agreement is taken into account (E2), the difference between Old and Modern High German becomes smaller, with both paradigms offering a reliability of more than 70%, while Texas German still faces more than 70% of ambiguous utterances.

Ambiguity is even more reduced when using semantic selection restrictions of the verb (set-up

E3). Here, the difference between Old and Modern High German becomes trivial with 4.44% and 6.94% of ambiguous utterances respectively. The difference with Texas German remains apparent, even though its ambiguity is cut by half.

In set-up E4 (case, SV-agreement and selection restrictions), the Old and Modern High German paradigms resolve almost all ambiguities, leaving little difference between them. Using the Texas German dialect, one utterance out of five remains ambiguous and requires additional grammatical cues or inferencing for semantic interpretation.

Number of possible interpretations. Semantic ambiguity can also be measured by counting the number of possible interpretations per utterance. A non-ambiguous language would thus have 1 possible interpretation per utterance. The average number of interpretations per utterance (per paradigm and per set-up) is shown in Table 8.

Paradigm	E1	E2	E3	E4
Old High German	1.56	1.22	1.04	1.03
Modern High German	1.56	1.28	1.07	1.04
Texas German	2.84	2.39	1.36	1.22

Table 8: Average number of interpretations per utterance type.

The Old High German paradigm has the least semantic ambiguity throughout, except in Experiment 1 (E1). Here, Modern High German has the same average effort despite having more ambiguous utterances. This means that the Old High German paradigm provides a better coverage in terms of construction types, but when ambiguity occurs, more possible interpretations exist.

6 Discussion

The experiments compare how well three different paradigms of definite articles perform if they are inserted in the grammar of Modern High German. The results show that, in isolation, Old High German offers the best cue-reliability for retrieving who's doing what to whom in events. However, when other grammatical cues are taken into account, it turns out that Modern High German achieves similar results with respect to syntactic search and semantic ambiguity, with a reduced paradigm (using only six instead of twelve forms).

As for the Texas German dialect, which has collapsed the accusative-dative distinction, the amount of ambiguity remains more than 20% using all available cues. One verifiable prediction of the experiments is therefore that this dialect should show an increase in alternative syntactic restrictions (such as word order) in order to make up for the lost case distinctions. Interestingly, such alternatives have been attested in Low German dialects that have evolved a similar two-way case system (Shrier, 1965). Modern High German, on the other hand, has already recruited word order for other purposes (such as information structure; Lenerz, 1977; Micelli, 2012), which may explain why the current paradigm has been able to survive since the Middle Ages.

Instead of an accidental by-product of phonological and morphological changes, then, a new picture emerges for explaining syncretism in Modern High German definite articles: German speakers have been able to reduce their case paradigm without loss in processing and interpretation efficiency. With cognitive effort as a selection criterion, subsequent generations of speakers found no linguistic pressures for maintaining particular distinctions such as gender in plural articles. Especially forms whose acoustic distinctions are harder to perceive are candidates for collapse if they are no longer functional for processing or interpretation. Other factors, such as frequency, may accelerate this evolution, as also argued by Barðdal (2009). For instance, there may be less benefits for upholding a case distinction for infrequent than for frequent forms.

If case syncretism is not randomly distributed over a grammatical paradigm, but rather functionally motivated, a new explanatory model is needed. One candidate is *evolutionary linguistics* (Steels, 2012b), a framework of cultural evolution in which populations of language users constantly shape and reshape their language in response to their communicative needs. The experiments reported here suggest that this dynamic shaping process is guided by the 'linguistic landscape' of a language. For instance, the presence of grammatical cues such as gender, number and SV-agreement may encourage paradigm reduction. However, reduction may be the start of a self-enforcing loop in which the decreasing cue-reliability of a paradigm may pressure language users into enforcing the alternatives to take on even more of the cognitive load of processing.

The intricate interactions between grammati-

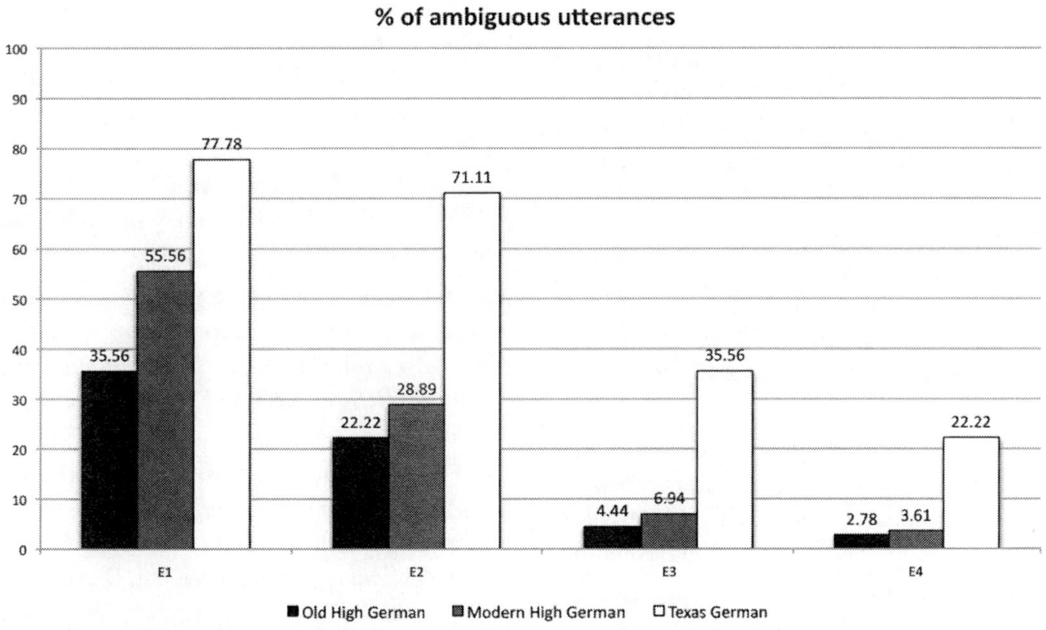

Figure 2: This chart shows the number of ambiguous utterances per paradigm per E(xperimental set-up) in %.

cal systems also requires more sophisticated measures. A promising extension of this paper could lie in an information-theoretic approach to language (Hale, 2003; Jaeger and Tily, 2011), which has recently explored a set of tools for assessing linguistic complexity, processing effort and uncertainty. Unfortunately, only little work has been done on morphological paradigms so far (see e.g. Ackerman et al., 2011), and the approach is typically applied in stochastic or Probabilistic Context Free Grammars, hence it remains unclear how the assumptions of this field fit into models of deep language processing.

7 Conclusions

More than 130 years after Mark Twain's complaints, it seems that the German language is not that awful after all. Through a series of computational experiments, this paper has proposed a different explanation for German case syncretism that answers some of the unsolved riddles of previous studies. First, the experiments have shown that an increase in syncretism does not necessarily lead to an increase in the cognitive effort required for syntactic search, provided that the representation of the grammar is processing-friendly. Secondly, by comparing cue-reliability of different paradigms for semantic disambiguation, the experiments have demonstrated that Modern High German achieves a similar performance as its Old High German predecessor using only half of the forms in its definite article paradigm.

Instead of a series of historical accidents, the German case system thus underwent a systematic and "performance-driven [...] morphological restructuring" (Hawkins, 2004, p. 79), in which linguistic pressures such as cognitive effort decided on the maintenance or loss of certain distinctions. The case study makes clear that formal and computational models of deep language understanding have to reconsider their strict division between competence and performance if the goal is to *explain* individual language development. This paper proposed that new tools and methodologies should be sought in evolutionary linguistics.

Acknowledgements

This research has been conducted at the Sony Computer Science Laboratory Paris. I would like to thank Luc Steels, director of Sony CSL Paris and the VUB AI-Lab of the University of Brussels, for his support and feedback. I also thank Hans Boas, Jóhanna Barðdal, Peter Hanappe, Manfred Hild and the anonymous reviewers for helping to improve this article. All errors remain of course my own.

References

Farrell Ackerman, James P. Blevins, and Robert Malouf. Parts and wholes: Implicative patterns in inflectional paradigms. In J.P. Blevins and J. Blevins, editors, *Analogy in Grammar: Form and Acquisition*, pages 54–81. Oxford University Press, Oxford, 2011.

Matthew Baerman. Case syncretism. In Andrej Malchukov and Andrew Spencer, editors, *The Oxford Handbook of Case*, chapter 14, pages 219–230. Oxford University Press, Oxford, 2009.

J. Barðdal. The development of case in germanic. In J. Barðdal and S. Chelliah, editors, *The Role of Semantics and Pragmatics in the Development of Case*, pages 123–159. John Benjamins, Amsterdam, 2009.

Manfred Bierwisch. Syntactic features in morphology: General problems of so-called pronominal inflection in German. In *To Honour Roman Jakobson*, pages 239–270. Mouton De Gruyter, Berlin, 1967.

James Blevins. Syncretism and paradigmatic opposition. *Linguistics and Philosophy*, 18:113–152, 1995.

Joris Bleys, Kevin Stadler, and Joachim De Beule. Search in linguistic processing. In Luc Steels, editor, *Design Patterns in Fluid Construction Grammar*. John Benjamins, Amsterdam, 2011.

Hans C. Boas. Case loss in Texas German: The influence of semantic and pragmatic factors. In J. Barðdal and S. Chelliah, editors, *The Role of Semantics and Pragmatics in the Development of Case*, pages 347–373. John Benjamins, Amsterdam, 2009a.

Hans C. Boas. *The Life and Death of Texas German*, volume 93 of *Publication of the The American Dialect Society*. Duke University Press, Durham, 2009b.

David Carter. Efficient disjunctive unification for bottom-up parsing. In *Proceedings of the 13th Conference on Computational Linguistics*, pages 70–75. ACL, 1990.

Ann Copestake. *Implementing Typed Feature Structure Grammars*. CSLI Publications, Stanford, 2002.

Berthold Crysmann. Syncretism in german: A unified approach to underspecification, indeterminacy, and likeness of case. In Stefan Müller, editor, *Proceedings of the 12th International Conference on Head-Driven Phrase Structure Grammar*, pages 91–107, Stanford, 2005. CSLI Publications.

Mary Dalrymple, Tracy Holloway King, and Louisa Sadler. Indeterminacy by underspecification. *Journal of Linguistics*, 45:31–68, 2009.

Michael Daniels. On a type-based analysis of feature neutrality and the coordination of unlikes. In *Proceedings of the 8th International Conference on HPSG*, pages 137–147, Stanford, 2001. CSLI.

Joachim De Beule. A formal deconstruction of Fluid Construction Grammar. In Luc Steels, editor, *Computational Issues in Fluid Construction Grammar*. Springer Verlag, Berlin, 2012.

Daniel P. Flickinger. On building a more efficient grammar by exploiting types. *Natural Language Engineering*, 6(1):15–28, 2000.

Jonathan Ginzburg and Ivan A. Sag. *Interrogative Investigations: the Form, the Meaning, and Use of English Interrogatives*. CSLI Publications, Stanford, 2000.

Adele E. Goldberg. *Constructions At Work: The Nature of Generalization in Language*. Oxford University Press, Oxford, 2006.

John T. Hale. The information conveyed by words in sentences. *Journal of Psycholinguistic Research*, 32(2):101–123, 2003.

John A. Hawkins. *Efficiency and Complexity in Grammars*. Oxford University Press, Oxford, 2004.

Bernd Heine and Tania Kuteva. *Language Contact and Grammatical Change*. Cambridge University Press, Cambridge, 2005.

Wolfgang Heinz and Johannes Matiasek. Argument structure and case assignment in german. In John Nerbonne, Klaus Netter, and Carl Pollard, editors, *German in Head-Driven Phrase Structure Grammar*, volume 46 of *CSLI Lecture Notes*, pages 199–236. CSLI Publications, Stanford, 1994.

R.J.P. Ingria. The limits of unification. In *Proceedings of the 28th Annual Meeting of the ACL*, pages 194–204, 1990.

T. Florian Jaeger and Harry Tily. On language 'utility': Processing complexity and communicative efficiency. *WIREs: Cognitive Science*, 2(3):323–335, 2011.

L. Karttunen. Features and values. In *Proceedings of the 10th International Conference on Computational Linguistics*, Stanford, 1984.

Jürgen Lenerz. *Zur Abfolge nominaler Satzglieder im Deutschen*. Narr, Tübingen, 1977.

Martin Loetzsch. Tools for grammar engineering. In Luc Steels, editor, *Computational Issues in Fluid Construction Grammar*. Springer Verlag, Berlin, 2012.

Vanessa Micelli. Field topology and information structure: A case study for German constituent order. In Luc Steels, editor, *Computational Issues in Fluid Construction Grammar*. Springer Verlag, Berlin, 2012.

Gereon Müller. Remarks on nominal inflection in German. In Ingrid Kaufmann and Barbara Stiebels, editors, *More than Words: A Festschrift for Dieter Wunderlich*, pages 113–145. Akademie Verlag, Berlin, 2002.

Stefan Müller. An HPSG-analysis for free relative clauses in german. *Grammars*, 2(1):53–105, 1999.

Stefan Müller. Case in German – towards and HPSG analysis. In Tibor Kiss and Detmar Meurers, editors, *Constraint-Based Approaches to Germanic Syntax*. CSLI, Stanford, 2001.

Allan Ramsay. Disjunction without tears. *Computational Linguistics*, 16(3):171–174, 1990.

Ivan A. Sag. Coordination and underspecification. In Jongbok Kom and Stephen Wechsler, editors, *Proceedings of the Ninth International Conference on HPSG*, Stanford, 2003. CSLI.

Ivan A. Sag and Thomas Wasow. Performance-compatible competence grammar. In Robert D. Borsley and Kersti Börjars, editors, *Non-Transformational Syntax: Formal and Explicit Models of Grammar*. Wiley-Blackwell, Oxford, 2011.

Martha Shrier. Case systems in German dialects. *Language*, 41(3):420–438, 1965.

Luc Steels. Constructivist development of grounded construction grammars. In Walter Daelemans, editor, *Proceedings 42nd Annual Meeting of the Association for Computational Linguistics*, pages 9–19, Barcelona, 2004.

Luc Steels, editor. *Design Patterns in Fluid Construction Grammar*. John Benjamins, Amsterdam, 2011.

Luc Steels, editor. *Computational Issues in Fluid Construction Grammar*. Springer, Berlin, 2012a.

Luc Steels. Self-organization and selection in cultural language evolution. In Luc Steels, editor, *Experiments in Cultural Language Evolution*. John Benjamins, Amsterdam, 2012b.

Luc Steels and Joachim De Beule. Unify and merge in Fluid Construction Grammar. In P. Vogt, Y. Sugita, E. Tuci, and C. Nehaniv, editors, *Symbol Grounding and Beyond.*, LNAI 4211, pages 197–223, Berlin, 2006. Springer.

Remi van Trijp. Feature matrices and agreement: A case study for German case. In Luc Steels, editor, *Design Patterns in Fluid Construction Grammar*. John Benjamins, Amsterdam, 2011.

M. Walshe. *A Middle High German Reader: With Grammar, Notes and Glossary*. Oxford University Press, Oxford, 1974.

Bernd Wiese. Iconicity and syncretism. on pronominal inflection in Modern German. In Robin Sckmann, editor, *Theoretical Linguistics and Grammatical Description*, pages 323–344. John Benjamins, Amsterdam, 1996.

Joseph Wright. *An Old High German Primer*. Clarendon Press, Oxford, 2nd edition, 1906.

Dieter Wunderlich. Der unterspezifizierte Artikel. In Karl Heinz Ramers Dürscheid and Monika Schwarz, editors, *Sprache im Fokus*, pages 47–55. Niemeyer, Tübingen, 1997.

Managing Uncertainty in Semantic Tagging

Silvie Cinková and **Martin Holub** and **Vincent Kríž**
Charles University in Prague, Faculty of Mathematics and Physics
Institute of Formal and Applied Linguistics
{cinkova|holub}@ufal.mff.cuni.cz
vincent.kriz@gmail.com

Abstract

Low interannotator agreement (IAA) is a well-known issue in manual semantic tagging (sense tagging). IAA correlates with the granularity of word senses and they both correlate with the amount of information they give as well as with its reliability. We compare different approaches to semantic tagging in WordNet, FrameNet, PropBank and OntoNotes with a small tagged data sample based on the Corpus Pattern Analysis to present the *reliable information gain* (RG), a measure used to optimize the semantic granularity of a sense inventory with respect to its reliability indicated by the IAA in the given data set. RG can also be used as feedback for lexicographers, and as a supporting component of automatic semantic classifiers, especially when dealing with a very fine-grained set of semantic categories.

1 Introduction

The term *semantic tagging* is used in two divergent areas:

1) recognizing objects of semantic importance, such as entities, events and polarity, often tailored to a restricted domain, or

2) relating occurrences of words in a corpus to a lexicon and selecting the most appropriate semantic categories (such as *synsets, semantic frames, wordsenses, semantic patterns* or *framesets*).

We are concerned with the second case, which seeks to make lexical semantics tractable for computers. Lexical semantics, as opposed to propositional semantics, focuses the meaning of lexical items. The disciplines that focus lexical semantics are lexicology and lexicography rather than logic. By semantic tagging we mean a process of assigning semantic categories to target words in given contexts. This process can be either manual or automatic.

Traditionally, semantic tagging relies on the tacit assumption that various uses of polysemous words can be sorted into discrete senses; understanding or using an unfamiliar word be then like looking it up in a dictionary. When building a dictionary entry for a given word, the lexicographer sorts a number of its occurrences into discrete *senses* present (or emerging) in his/her mental lexicon, which is supposed to be shared by all speakers of the same language. The assumed common mental representation of a words meaning should make it easy for other humans to assign random occurrences of the word to one of the pre-defined senses (Fellbaum et al., 1997).

This assumption seems to be falsified by the interannotator agreement (IAA, sometimes ITA) constantly reported much lower in semantic than in morphological or syntactic annotation, as well as by the general divergence of opinion on which value of which IAA measure indicates a reliable annotation. In some projects (e.g. OntoNotes (Hovy et al., 2006)), the percentage of agreements between two annotators is used, but a number of more complex measures are available (for a comprehensive survey see (Artstein and Poesio, 2008)). Consequently, using different measures for IAA makes the reported IAA values incomparable across different projects.

Even skilled lexicographers have trouble selecting one discrete sense for a concordance (Krishnamurthy and Nicholls, 2000), and, more to say, when the tagging performance of lexicographers and ordinary annotators (students) was compared, the experiment showed that the mental representations of a word's semantics differ for each group (Fellbaum et al., 1997), and cf. (Jorgensen, 1990). Lexicographers are trained in considering subtle differences among various uses of a word, which ordinary language users do not reflect. Identifying a semantic difference between uses of a word and deciding whether a difference is important enough to constitute a separate sense means presenting a word with a certain degree of *semantic granularity*. Intuitively, the finer the granularity of a word entry is, the more opportunities for interannotator disagreement there are and the lower IAA can be expected. Brown et al. proved this hypothesis experimentally (Brown et al., 2010). Also, the annotators are less confident in their decisions, when they have many options to choose from (Fellbaum et al. (1998) reported a drop in subjective annotators confidence in words with 8+ senses).

Despite all the known issues in semantic tagging, the major lexical resources (WordNet (Fellbaum, 1998), FrameNet (Ruppenhofer et al., 2010), PropBank (Palmer et al., 2005) and the word-sense part of OntoNotes (Weischedel et al., 2011)) are still maintained and their annotation schemes are adopted for creating new manually annotated data (e.g. MASC, the Manually Annotated Subcorpus (Ide et al., 2008)). More to say, these resources are not only used in WSD and semantic labeling, but also in research directions that in their turn do not rely on the idea of an inventory of discrete senses any more, e.g. in *distributional semantics* (Erk, 2010) and *recognizing textual entailment* (e.g. (Zanzotto et al., 2009) and (Aharon et al., 2010)).

It is a remarkable fact that, to the best of our knowledge, there is no measure that would relate granularity, reliability of the annotation (derived from IAA) and the resulting information gain. Therefore it is impossible to say where the optimum for granularity and IAA lies.

2 Approaches to semantic tagging

2.1 Semantic tagging vs. morphological or syntactic analysis

Manual semantic tagging is in many respects similar to morphological tagging and syntactic analysis: human annotators are trained to sort certain elements occurring in a running text according to a reference source. There is, nevertheless, a substantial difference: whereas morphologically or syntactically annotated data exist separately from the reference (tagset, annotation guide, annotation scheme), a semantically tagged resource can be regarded both as a corpus of texts disambiguated according to an attached inventory of semantic categories and as a lexicon with links to example concordances for each semantic category. So, in semantically tagged resources, the data and the reference are intertwined. Such double-faced semantic resources have also been called *semantic concordances* (Miller et al., 1993a). For instance, one of the earlier versions of WordNet, the largest lexical resource for English, was used in the semantic concordance SemCor (Miller et al., 1993b). More recent lexical resources have been built as semantic concordances from the very beginning (PropBank (Palmer et al., 2005), OntoNotes word senses (Weischedel et al., 2011)).

In morphological or syntactic annotation, the tagset or inventory of constituents are given beforehand and are supposed to hold for all tokens/sentences contained in the corpus. Problematic and theory-dependent issues are few and mostly well-known in advance. Therefore they can be reflected by a few additional conventions in the annotation manual (e.g. where to draw the line between particles and prepositions or between adjectives and verbs in past participles (Santorini, 1990) or where to attach a prepositional phrase following a noun phrase and how to treat specific "financialspeak" structures (Bies et al., 1995)). Even in difficult cases, there are hardly more than two options of interpretation. Data manually annotated for morphology or surface syntax are reliable enough to train syntactic parsers with an accuracy above 80 % (e.g. (Zhang and Clark, 2011; McDonald et al., 2006)).

On the other hand, semantic tagging actually employs a different tagset for each word lemma. Even within the same part of speech, individual words require individual descriptions. Possible similarities among them come into relief ex post rather than that they could be imposed on the lexicographers from the beginning. When assigning senses to concordances, the annotator often has to select among more than two relevant options. These two aspects make achieving good IAA much harder than in morphology and syntax tasks. In addition, while a linguistically educated annotator can have roughly the same idea of parts of speech as the author of the tagset, there is no chance that two humans (not even two professional lexicographers) would create identical entries for e.g. a polysemous verb. Any human evaluation of complete entries would be subjective. The maximum to be achieved is that the entry reflects the corpus data in a reasonable granular way on which annotators still can reach reasonable IAA.

2.2 Major existing semantic resources

The granularity vs. IAA equilibrium is of great concern in creating lexical resources as well as in applications dealing with semantic tasks. When WordNet (Fellbaum, 1998) was created, both IAA and subjective confidence measurements served as an informal feedback to lexicographers (Fellbaum et al., (1998), p. 200). In general, WordNet has been considered a resource too fine-grained for most annotations (and applications). Navigli (2006) developed a method of reducing the granularity of WordNet by mapping the synsets to senses in a more coarse-grained dictionary. A manual, more coarse-grained grouping of WordNet senses has been performed in OntoNotes (Weischedel et al., 2011). The OntoNotes 90 % solution (Hovy et al., 2006) actually means such a degree of granularity that enables a 90-%-IAA. OntoNotes is a reaction to the traditionally poor IAA in WordNet annotated corpora, caused by the high granularity of senses. The quality of semantic concordances is maintained by numerous iterations between lexicographers and annotators. The categories 'right'–'wrong' have been, for the purpose of the annotated linguistic resource, defined by the IAA score, which is—in OntoNotes—calculated as the percentage of agreements between two annotators.

Two other, somewhat different, lexical resources have to be mentioned to complete the picture: FrameNet (Ruppenhofer et al., 2010) and PropBank (Palmer et al., 2005). While WordNet and OntoNotes pair words and word senses in a way comparable to printed lexicons, FrameNet is primarily an inventory of *semantic frames* and PropBank focuses the *argument structure* of verbs and nouns (NomBank (Meyers et al., 2008), a related project capturing the argument structure of nouns, was later integrated in OntoNotes).

In FrameNet corpora, content words are associated to particular semantic frames that they evoke (e.g. *charm* would relate to the *Aesthetics* frame) and their collocates in relevant syntactic positions (arguments of verbs, head nouns of adjectives, etc.) would be assigned the corresponding *frame-element* labels (e.g. in *their dazzling charm*, *their* would be The Entity for which a particular gradable Attribute is appropriate and under consideration and *dazzling* would be Degree). Neither IAA nor granularity seem to be an issue in FrameNet. We have not succeeded in finding a report on IAA in the original FrameNet annotation, except one measurement in progress in the annotation of the Manually Annotated Subcorpus of English (Ide et al., 2008).[1]

PropBank is a valency (argument structure) lexicon. The current resource lists and labels arguments and obligatory modifiers typical of each (very coarse) word sense (called *frameset*). Two core criteria for distinguishing among framesets are the semantic roles of the arguments along with the syntactic alternations that the verb can undergo with that particular argument set. To keep low granularity, this lexicon—among other things—does usually not make special framesets for metaphoric uses. The overall IAA measured on verbs was 94 % (Palmer et al., 2005).

2.3 Semantic Pattern Recognition

From corpus-based lexicography to semantic patterns

The modern, corpus-based lexicology of 1990s (Sinclair, 1991; Fillmore and Atkins, 1994) has had a great impact on lexicography. There is a general consensus that dictionary definitions need to be supported by corpus examples. Cf. Fellbaum (2001):

"For polysemous words, dictionaries [...] do not say enough about the range of possible contexts that differentiate the senses. [...] On the other hand, texts or corpora [...] are not explicit about the word's meaning. When we first encounter a new word in a text, we can usually form only a vague idea of its meaning; checking a dictionary will clarify the meaning. But the more contexts we encounter for a word, the harder it is to match them against only one dictionary sense."

[1] Checked on the project web www.anc.org/MASC/Home 2011-10-29.

The lexical description in modern English monolingual dictionaries (Sinclair et al., 1987; Rundell, 2002) explicitly emphasizes contextual clues, such as typical collocates and the syntactic surroundings of the given lexical item, rather than relying on very detailed definitions. In other words, the sense definitions are obtained as syntactico-semantic abstractions of manually clustered corpus concordances in the modern corpus-based lexicography: in classical dictionaries as well as in semantic concordances.

Nevertheless, the word senses, even when obtained by a collective mind of lexicographers and annotators, are naturally hard-wired and tailored to the annotated corpus. They may be too fine-grained or too coarse-grained for automatic processing of different corpora (e.g. a restricted-domain corpus). Kilgarriff (1997, p. 115) shows (the *handbag* example) that *there is no reason to expect the same set of word senses to be relevant for different tasks* and that *the corpus dictates the word senses* and therefore 'word sense' *was not found to be sufficiently well-defined to be a workable basic unit of meaning* (p. 116). On the other hand, even non-experts seem to agree reasonably well when judging the similarity of use of a word in different contexts (Rumshisky et al., 2009). Erk et al. (2009) showed promising annotation results with a scheme that allowed the annotators graded judgments of similarity between two words or between a word and its definition.

Verbs are the most challenging part of speech. We see two major causes: *vagueness* and *coercion*. We neglect ambiguity, since it has proved to be rare in our experience.

CPA and PDEV

Our current work focuses on English verbs. It has been inspired by the manual Corpus Pattern Analysis method (CPA) (Hanks, forthcoming) and its implementation, the Pattern Dictionary of English Verbs (PDEV) (Hanks and Pustejovsky, 2005). PDEV is a semantic concordance built on yet a different principle than FrameNet, WordNet, PropBank or OntoNotes. The manually extracted *patterns* of frequent and normal verb uses are, roughly speaking, intuitively similar uses of a verb that express—in a syntactically similar form—a similar event in which similar participants (e.g. humans, artifacts, institutions, other events) are involved. Two patterns can be semantically so tightly related that they could appear together under one sense in a traditional dictionary. The patterns are not senses but syntactico-semantically characterized prototypes (see the example verb *submit* in Table 1). Concordances that match these prototypes well are called *norms* in Hanks (forthcoming). Concordances that match with a reservation (metaphorical uses, argument mismatch, etc.) are called *exploitations*. The PDEV corpus annotation indicates the norm-exploitation status for each concordance.

Compared to other semantic concordances, the granularity of PDEV is high and thus discouraging in terms of expected IAA. However, selecting among patterns does not really mean disambiguating a concordance but rather determining to which pattern it is most similar—a task easier for humans than WSD is. This principle seems particularly promising for verbs as words expressing events, which resist the traditional word sense disambiguation the most.

A novel approach to semantic tagging

We present the *semantic pattern recognition* as a novel approach to semantic tagging, which is different from the traditional word-sense assignment tasks. We adopt the central idea of CPA that words do not have fixed senses but that regular patterns can be identified in the corpus that activate different conversational implicatures from the meaning potential of the given verb. Our method draws on a hard-wired, fine-grained inventory of semantic categories manually extracted from corpus data. This inventory represents the maximum semantic granularity that humans are able to recognize in normal and frequent uses of a verb in a balanced corpus. We thoroughly analyze the interannotator agreement to find out which of the highly semantic categories are useful in the sense of information gain. Our goal is a dynamic optimization of semantic granularity with respect to given data and target application.

Like Passonneau et al. (2010), we are convinced that IAA is specific to each respective word and reflects its inherent semantic properties as well as the specificity of contexts the given word occurs in, even within the same balanced corpus. We accept as a matter of fact that interannotator confusion is inevitable in semantic tagging. However, the amount of uncertainty of the

<table>
<tr><th>No.</th><th>Pattern / Implicature</th></tr>
<tr><td>1</td><td>[[Human 1 | Institution 1] ^ [Human 1 | Institution 1 = Competitor]] submit [[Plan | Document | Speech Act | Proposition | {complaint | demand | request | claim | application | proposal | report | resignation | information | plea | petition | memorandum | budget | amendment | programme | ...}] ^ [Artifact | Artwork | Service | Activity | {design | tender | bid | entry | dance | ...}]] (({to} Human 2 | Institution 2 = authority)^({to} Human 2 | Institution 2 = referee)) ({for} {approval | discussion | arbitration | inspection | designation | assessment | funding | taxation | ...})
[[Human 1 | Institution 1]] presents [[Plan | Document]] to [[Human 2 | Institution 2]] for {approval | discussion | arbitration | inspection | designation | assessment | taxation | ...}</td></tr>
<tr><td>2</td><td>[Human | Institution] submit [THAT-CL|QUOTE]
[[Human | Institution]] respectfully expresses {that [CLAUSE]} and invites listeners or readers to accept that {that [CLAUSE]} is true}</td></tr>
<tr><td>4</td><td>[Human 1 | Institution 1] submit (Self) ({to} Human 2 | Institution 2)
[[Human 1 | Institution 1]] acknowledges the superior force of [[Human 2 | Institution 2]] and puts [[Self]] in the power of [[Human 2 | Institution 2]]</td></tr>
<tr><td>5</td><td>[Human 1] submit (Self) [[{to} Eventuality = Unpleasant] ^ [{to} Rule]]
[[Human 1]] accepts [[Rule |Eventuality = Unpleasant]] without complaining</td></tr>
<tr><td>6</td><td>[passive]
[Human| Institution] submit [Anything] [{to} Eventuality]
[[Human 1|Institution 1]] exposes [[Anything]] to [[Eventuality]]</td></tr>
</table>

Table 1: Example of patterns defined for the verb *submit*.

"right" tag differs a lot, and should be quantified. For that purpose we developed the *reliable information gain* measure presented in Section 3.2.

CPA Verb Validation Sample

The original PDEV had never been tested with respect to IAA. Each entry had been based on concordances annotated solely by the author of that particular entry. The annotation instructions had been transmitted only orally. The data had been evolving along with the method, which implied inconsistencies. We put down an annotation manual (a momentary snapshot of the theory) and trained three annotators accordingly. For practical annotation we use the infrastructure developed at Masaryk University in Brno (Horák et al., 2008), which was also used for the original PDEV development. After initial IAA experiments with the original PDEV, we decided to select 30 verb entries from PDEV along with the annotated concordances. We made a new semantic concordance sample (Cinková et al., 2012) for the validation of the annotation scheme. We refer to this new collection[2] as VPS-30-En (Verb Pattern Sample, 30 English verbs).

We slightly revised some entries and updated the reference samples (usually 250 concordances per verb). The annotators were given the entries as well as the reference sample annotated by the lexicographer and a test sample of 50 concordances for annotation. We measured IAA, using Fleiss's kappa,[3] and analyzed the interannotator confusion manually. IAA varied from verb to verb, mostly reaching safely above 0.6. When the IAA was low and the type of confusion indicated a problem in the entry, the entry was revised. Then the lexicographer revised the original reference sample along with the first 50-concordance sample. The annotators got back the revised entry, the newly revised reference sample and an entirely new 50-concordance annotation batch. The final multiple 50-concordance sample went through one more additional procedure, the *adjudication*: first, the lexicographer compared the three annotations and eliminated evident errors. Then the lexicographer selected one value for each concordance to remain in the resulting one-value-per-concordance gold standard data and recorded it into the gold standard set. The adjudication pro-

[2] This new lexical resource, including the complete documentation, is publicly available at http://ufal.mff.cuni.cz/spr.

[3] Fleiss's kappa (Fleiss, 1971) is a generalization of Scott's π statistic (Scott, 1955). In contrast to Cohen's kappa (Cohen, 1960), Fleiss's kappa evaluates agreement between multiple raters. However, Fleiss's kappa is *not* a generalization of Cohen's kappa, which is a different, yet related, statistical measure. Sometimes, the terminology about kappas is confusing in the literature. For a detailed explanation refer e.g. to (Artstein and Poesio, 2008).

tocol has been kept for further experiments. All values except the marked errors are regarded as equally acceptable for this type of experiments. In the end, we get for each verb:

- an entry, which is an inventory of semantic categories (patterns)
- 300+ manually annotated concordances (single values)
- out of which 50 are manually annotated and adjudicated concordances (multiple values without evident errors).

3 Tagging confusion analysis

3.1 Formal model of tagging confusion

To formally describe the semantic tagging task, we assume a target word and a (randomly selected) corpus sample of its occurrences. The tagged sample is $\mathcal{S} = \{s_1, \ldots, s_r\}$, where each *instance* s_i is an occurrence of the target word with its context, and r is the sample size.

For multiple annotation we need a set of m annotators $\mathcal{A} = \{A_1, \ldots, A_m\}$ who choose from a given set of semantic categories represented by a set of n semantic tags $\mathcal{T} = \{t_1, \ldots, t_n\}$. Generally, if we admitted assigning more tags to one word occurrence, annotators could assign any subset of $\mathcal{T}$ to an instance. In our experiments, however, annotators were allowed to assign just one tag to each tagged instance. Therefore each annotator is described as a function that assigns a single member set to each instance $A_i(s) = \{t\}$, where $s \in \mathcal{S}$, $t \in \mathcal{T}$. When a pair of annotators tag an instance s, they produce a set of one or two different tags $\{t, t'\} = A_i(s) \cup A_j(s)$.

Detailed information about interannotator (dis)agreement on a given sample $\mathcal{S}$ is represented by a set of $\binom{m}{2}$ symmetric matrices $C_{ij}^{A_k A_l} = |\{s \in \mathcal{S} \mid A_k(s) \cup A_l(s) = \{t_i, t_j\}\}|$, for $1 \leq k < l \leq m$, and $i, j \in \{1, \ldots, n\}$. Note that each of those matrices can be easily computed as $C^{A_k A_l} = C + C^T - I_n C$, where C is a conventional confusion matrix representing the agreement between annotators A_k and A_l, and I_n is a unit matrix.

Definition: *Aggregated Confusion Matrix* (ACM)

$$C^\star = \sum_{1 \leq k < l \leq m} C^{A_k A_l}.$$

Properties: ACM is symmetric and for any $i \neq j$ the number $C_{ij}^\star$ says how many times a pair of annotators disagreed on two tags t_i and t_j, while $C_{ii}^\star$ is the frequency of agreements on t_i; the sum in the i-th row $\sum_j C_{ij}^\star$ is the total frequency of assigned sets $\{t, t'\}$ that contain t_i.

An example of ACM is given in Table 2. The corresponding confusion matrices are shown in Table 3.

	1	1.a	2	4	5
1	85	8	2	0	0
1.a	8	1	2	0	0
2	2	2	34	0	0
4	0	0	0	4	8
5	0	0	0	8	6

Table 2: Aggregated Confusion Matrix.

Our approach to exact tagging confusion analysis is based on probability and information theory. Assigning semantic tags by annotators is viewed as a random process. We define (categorical) random variable T_1 as the outcome of one annotator; its values are single member sets $\{t\}$, and we have mr observations to compute their probabilities. The probability that an annotator will use t_i is denoted by $p_1(t_i) = \Pr(T_1 = \{t_i\})$ and is practically computed as the relative frequency of t_i among all mr assigned tags. Formally,

$$p_1(t_i) = \frac{1}{mr} \sum_{k=1}^{m} \sum_{j=1}^{r} |A_k(s_j) \cap \{t_i\}|.$$

The outcome of two annotators (they both tag the same instance) is described by random variable T_2; its values are single or double member sets $\{t, t'\}$, and we have $\binom{m}{2}r$ observations to compute their probabilities. In contrast to p_1, the probability that t_i will be used by a *pair* of annotators is denoted by $p_2(t_i) = \Pr(T_2 \supseteq \{t_i\})$, and is computed as the relative frequency of assigned sets $\{t, t'\}$ containing t_i among all $\binom{m}{2}r$ observations:

$$p_2(t_i) = \frac{1}{\binom{m}{2}r} \sum_k C_{ik}^\star.$$

We also need the conditional probability that an annotator will use t_i given that *another* annotator has used t_j. For convenience, we use the notation $p_2(t_i \mid t_j) = \Pr(T_2 \supseteq \{t_i\} \mid T_2 \supseteq \{t_j\})$.

	A_1 vs. A_2						A_1 vs. A_3						A_2 vs. A_3				
	1	1.a	2	4	5		1	1.a	2	4	5		1	1.a	2	4	5
1	29	1	1	0	0	1	29	2	0	0	0	1	27	2	0	0	0
1.a	0	1	0	0	0	1.a	1	0	0	0	0	1.a	2	0	1	0	0
2	0	1	11	0	0	2	0	0	12	0	0	2	1	0	11	0	0
4	0	0	0	2	0	4	0	0	0	1	1	4	0	0	0	1	4
5	0	0	0	3	1	5	0	0	0	0	4	5	0	0	0	0	1

Table 3: Example of all confusion matrices for the target word *submit* and three annotators.

Obviously, it can be computed as

$$\begin{aligned} p_2(t_i \mid t_j) &= \frac{\Pr(T_2 = \{t_i, t_j\})}{\Pr(T_2 \supseteq \{t_j\})} \\ &= \frac{C^\star_{ij}}{\binom{m}{2} r \cdot p_2(t_j)} = \frac{C^\star_{ij}}{\sum_k C^\star_{jk}}. \end{aligned}$$

Definition: *Confusion Probability Matrix* (CPM)

$$C^p_{ji} = p_2(t_i \mid t_j) = \frac{C^\star_{ij}}{\sum_k C^\star_{jk}}.$$

Properties: The sum in any row is 1. The j-th row of CPM contains probabilities of assigning t_i given that *another* annotator has chosen t_j for the same instance. Thus, the j-th row of CPM describes *expected tagging confusion* related to the tag t_j.

An example is given in Table 3 (all confusion matrices for three annotators), in Table 2 (the corresponding ACM), and in Table 4 (the corresponding CPM).

	1	1.a	2	4	5
1	0.895	0.084	0.021	0.000	0.000
1.a	0.727	0.091	0.182	0.000	0.000
2	0.053	0.053	0.895	0.000	0.000
4	0.000	0.000	0.000	0.333	0.667
5	0.000	0.000	0.000	0.571	0.429

Table 4: Example of Confusion Probability Matrix.

3.2 Semantic granularity optimization

Now, having a detailed analysis of expected tagging confusion described in CPM, we are able to compare usefulness of different semantic tags using a measure of the information content associated with them (in the information theory sense). Traditionally, the amount of self-information contained in a tag (as a probabilistic event) depends only on the probability of that tag, and would be defined as $I(t_j) = -\log p_1(t_j)$. However, intuitively one can say that a good measure of usefulness of a particular tag should also take into consideration the expected tagging confusion related to the tag. Therefore, to exactly measure usefulness of the tag t_j we propose to compare and measure similarity of the distribution $p_1(t_i)$ and the distribution $p_2(t_i \mid t_j)$, $i = 1, \ldots, n$. How much information do we gain when an annotator assigns the tag t_j to an instance? When the tag t_j has once been assigned to an instance by an annotator, one would naturally expect that *another* annotator will *probably tend* to assign the same tag t_j to the same instance. Formally, things make good sense if $p_2(t_j \mid t_j) > p_1(t_j)$ and if $p_2(t_i \mid t_j) < p_1(t_i)$ for any i different from j. If $p_2(t_j \mid t_j) = 100\,\%$, then there is full consensus about assigning t_j among annotators; then and only then the measure of usefulness of the tag t_j should be maximal and should have the value of $-\log p_1(t_j)$. Otherwise, the value of usefulness should be smaller. This is our motivation to define a quantity of *reliable* information gain obtained from semantic tags as follows:

Definition: *Reliable Gain* (RG) from the tag t_j is

$$RG(t_j) = \sum_k -(-1)^{\delta_{kj}} p_2(t_k|t_j) \log \frac{p_2(t_k|t_j)}{p_1(t_k)}.$$

Properties: RG is similar to the well known Kullback-Leibler divergence (or information gain). If $p_2(t_i \mid t_j) = p_1(t_i)$ for all $i = 1, \ldots, n$, then $RG(t_j) = 0$. If $p_2(t_j \mid t_j) = 100\,\%$, then and only then $RG(t_j) = -\log p_1(t_j)$, which is the maximum. If $p_2(t_i \mid t_j) < p_1(t_i)$ for all i different from j, the greater difference in probabilities, the bigger (and positive) $RG(t_j)$. And vice versa, the inequality $p_2(t_i \mid t_j) > p_1(t_i)$ for all i different from j implies a negative value of $RG(t_j)$.

Definition: *Average Reliable Gain* (ARG) from the tagset $\{t_1, \ldots, t_n\}$ is computed as an expected value of $RG(t_j)$:

$$ARG = \sum_j p_1(t_j) RG(t_j)$$

Properties: ARG has its maximum value if the CPM is a unit matrix, which is the case of the absolute agreement among all annotators. Then ARG has the value of the entropy of the p_1 distribution: $ARG_{max} = H(p_1(t_1), \ldots, p_1(t_n))$.

Merging tags with poor RG

The main motivation for developing the ARG value was the optimization of the tagset granularity. We use a semi-greedy algorithm that searches for an "optimal" tagset. The optimization process starts with the fine-grained list of CPA semantic categories and then the algorithm merges some tags in order to maximize the ARG value. An example is given in Table 5. Tables 6 and 7 show the ACM and the CPM after merging. The examples relate to the verb *submit* already shown in Tables 1, 2, 3 and 4.

Original tagset			Optimal merge		
Tag	f	RG	Tag	f	RG
1	90	+0.300	1 + 1.a	96	+0.425
1.a	6	−0.001			
2	36	+0.447	2	36	+0.473
4	8	−0.071	4 + 5	18	+0.367
5	10	−0.054			

Table 5: Frequency and Reliable Gain of tags.

	1	2	4
1	94	4	0
2	4	34	0
4	0	0	18

Table 6: Aggregated Confusion Matrix after merging.

	1	2	4
1	0.959	0.041	0.000
2	0.105	0.895	0.000
4	0.000	0.000	1.000

Table 7: Confusion Probability Matrix after merging.

3.3 Classifier evaluation with respect to expected tagging confusion

An automatic classifier is considered to be a function c that—the same way as annotators— assigns tags to instances $s \in \mathcal{S}$, so that $c(s) = \{t\}$, $t \in \mathcal{T}$. The traditional way to evaluate the accuracy of an automatic classifier means to compare its output with the correct semantic tags on a *Gold Standard* (GS) dataset. Within our formal framework, we can imagine that we have a "gold" annotator A_g, so that the GS dataset is represented by $A_g(s_1), \ldots, A_g(s_r)$. Then the classic accuracy score can be computed as $\frac{1}{r}\sum_{i=1}^{r} |A_g(s_i) \cap c(s_i)|$. However, that approach does not take into consideration the fact that some semantic tags are quite confusing even for human annotators. In our opinion, automatic classifier should not be penalized for mistakes that would be made even by humans. So we propose a more complex evaluation score using the knowledge of the expected tagging confusion stored in CPM.

Definition: Classifier evaluation *Score* with respect to tagging confusion is defined as the proportion $Score(c) = S(c)/S_{max}$, where

$$\begin{aligned} S(c) &= \frac{\alpha}{r}\sum_{i=1}^{r} |A_g(s_i) \cap c(s_i)| + \\ &+ \frac{1-\alpha}{r}\sum_{i=1}^{r} p_2(c(s_i) \mid A_g(s_i)) \\ S_{max} &= \alpha + \frac{1-\alpha}{r}\sum_{i=1}^{r} p_2(A_g(s_i) \mid A_g(s_i)). \end{aligned}$$

	$\alpha = 1$		$\alpha = 0.5$		$\alpha = 0$	
Verb		Score		Score		Score
halt	1	0.84	2	0.90	4	0.81
submit	2	0.83	1	0.90	1	0.84
ally	3	0.82	3	0.89	5	0.76
cry	4	0.79	4	0.88	2	0.82
arrive	5	0.74	5	0.85	3	0.81
plough	6	0.70	6	0.81	6	0.72
deny	7	0.62	7	0.74	7	0.66
cool	8	0.58	8	0.69	8	0.53
yield	9	0.55	9	0.67	9	0.52

Table 8: Evaluation with different α values.

Table 8 gives an illustration of the fact that using different α values one can get different results when comparing tagging accuracy for different words (a classifier based on bag-of-words approach was used). The same holds true for comparison of different classifiers.

3.4 Related work

In their extensive survey article Artstein and Poesio (2008) state that word sense tagging is one of the hardest annotation tasks. They assume that making distinctions between semantic categories must rely on a dictionary. The problem is that annotators often cannot consistently make the fine-grained distinctions proposed by trained lexicographers, which is particularly serious for verbs, because verbs generally tend to be polysemous rather than homonymous.

A few approaches have been suggested in the literature that address the problem of the fine-grained semantic distinctions by (automatic) measuring sense distinguishability. Diab (2004) computes sense perplexity using the entropy function as a characteristic of training data. She also compares the sense distributions to obtain sense distributional correlation, which can serve as a "very good direct indicator of performance ratio", especially together with sense context confusability (another indicator observed in the training data). Resnik and Yarowsky (1999) introduced the communicative/semantic distance between the predicted sense and the "correct" sense. Then they use it for evaluation metric that provides partial credit for incorrectly classified instances. Cohn (2003) introduces the concept of (non-uniform) misclassification costs. He makes use of the communicative/semantic distance and proposes a metric for evaluating word sense disambiguation performance using the Receiver Operating Characteristics curve that takes the misclassification costs into account. Bruce and Wiebe (1998) analyze the agreement among human judges for the purpose of formulating a refined and more reliable set of sense tags. Their method is based on statistical analysis of interannotator confusion matrices. An extended study is given in (Bruce and Wiebe, 1999).

4 Conclusion

The usefulness of a semantic resource depends on two aspects:

- reliability of the annotation
- information gain from the annotation.

In practice, each semantic resource emphasizes one aspect: OntoNotes, e.g., guarantees reliability, whereas the WordNet-annotated corpora seek to convey as much semantic nuance as possible. To the best of our knowledge, there has been no exact measure for the optimization, and the usefulness of a given resource can only be assessed when it is finished and used in applications. We propose the *reliable information gain*, a measure based on information theory and on the analysis of interannotator confusion matrices for each word entry, that can be continually applied *during* the creation of a semantic resource, and that provides automatic feedback about the granularity of the used tagset. Moreover, the computed information about the amount of *expected tagging confusion* is also used in evaluation of automatic classifiers.

Acknowledgments

This work has been supported by the Czech Science Foundation projects GK103/12/G084 and P406/2010/0875 and partly by the project EuroMatrixPlus (FP7-ICT-2007-3-231720 of the EU and 7E09003+7E11051 of the Ministry of Education, Youth and Sports of the Czech Republic).

We thank our friends from Masaryk University in Brno for providing the annotation infrastructure and for their permanent technical support. We thank Patrick Hanks for his CPA method, for the original PDEV development, and for numerous discussions about the semantics of English verbs. We also thank three anonymous reviewers for their valuable comments.

References

Roni Ben Aharon, Idan Szpektor, and Ido Dagan. 2010. Generating entailment rules from FrameNet. In *Proceedings of the ACL 2010 Conference Short Papers.*, pages 241–246, Uppsala, Sweden.

Ron Artstein and Massimo Poesio. 2008. Inter-coder agreement for computational linguistics. *Computational Linguistics*, 34(4):555–596, December.

Ann Bies, Mark Ferguson, Karen Katz, Robert MacIntyre, Victoria Tredinnick, Grace Kim, Mary Ann Marcinkiewicz, and Britta Schasberger. 1995. Bracketing guidelines for treebank II style. Technical report, University of Pennsylvania.

Susan Windisch Brown, Travis Rood, and Martha Palmer. 2010. Number or nuance: Which factors restrict reliable word sense annotation? In *LREC*, pages 3237–3243. European Language Resources Association (ELRA).

Rebecca F. Bruce and Janyce M. Wiebe. 1998. Word-sense distinguishability and inter-coder agreement. In *Proceedings of the Third Conference on Empirical Methods in Natural Language Processing (EMNLP '98)*, pages 53–60. Granada, Spain, June.

Rebecca F. Bruce and Janyce M. Wiebe. 1999. Recognizing subjectivity: A case study of manual tagging. *Natural Language Engineering*, 5(2):187–205.

Silvie Cinková, Martin Holub, Adam Rambousek, and Lenka Smejkalová. 2012. A database of semantic clusters of verb usages. In *Proceedings of the LREC '2012 International Conference on Language Resources and Evaluation*. To appear.

Jacob Cohen. 1960. A coefficient of agreement for nominal scales. *Educational and Psychological Measurement*, 20(1):37–46.

Trevor Cohn. 2003. Performance metrics for word sense disambiguation. In *Proceedings of the Australasian Language Technology Workshop 2003*, pages 86–93, Melbourne, Australia, December.

Mona T. Diab. 2004. Relieving the data acquisition bottleneck in word sense disambiguation. In *Proceedings of the 42nd Annual Meeting of the ACL*, pages 303–310. Barcelona, Spain. Association for Computational Linguistics.

Katrin Erk, Diana McCarthy, and Nicholas Gaylord. 2009. Investigations on word senses and word usages. In *Proceedings of the Joint Conference of the 47th Annual Meeting of the ACL and the 4th International Joint Conference on Natural Language Processing of the AFNLP*, pages 10–18, Suntec, Singapore, August. Association for Computational Linguistics.

Katrin Erk. 2010. What is word meaning, really? (And how can distributional models help us describe it?). In *Proceedings of the 2010 Workshop on GEometrical Models of Natural Language Semantics*, pages 17–26, Uppsala, Sweden, July. Association for Computational Linguistics.

Christiane Fellbaum, Joachim Grabowski, and Shari Landes. 1997. Analysis of a hand-tagging task. In *Proceedings of the ACL/Siglex Workshop*, Somerset, NJ.

Christiane Fellbaum, J. Grabowski, and S. Landes. 1998. Performance and confidence in a semantic annotation task. In *WordNet: An Electronic Lexical Database*, pages 217–238. Cambridge (Mass.): The MIT Press., Cambridge (Mass.).

Christiane Fellbaum, Martha Palmer, Hoa Trang Dang, Lauren Delfs, and Susanne Wolf. 2001. Manual and automatic semantic annotation with WordNet.

Christiane Fellbaum. 1998. *WordNet. An Electronic Lexical Database*. MIT Press, Cambridge, MA.

Charles J. Fillmore and B. T. S. Atkins. 1994. Starting where the dictionaries stop: The challenge for computational lexicography. In *Computational Approaches to the Lexicon*, pages 349–393. Oxford University Press.

Joseph L. Fleiss. 1971. Measuring nominal scale agreement among many raters. *Psychological Bulletin*, 76:378–382.

Patrick Hanks and James Pustejovsky. 2005. A pattern dictionary for natural language processing. *Revue Francaise de linguistique applique*, 10(2).

Patrick Hanks. forthcoming. *Lexical Analysis: Norms and Exploitations*. MIT Press.

Aleš Horák, Adam Rambousek, and Piek Vossen. 2008. A distributed database system for developing ontological and lexical resources in harmony. In *9th International Conference on Intelligent Text Processing and Computational Linguistics*, pages 1–15. Berlin: Springer.

Eduard Hovy, Mitchell Marcus, Martha Palmer, Lance Ramshaw, and Ralph Weischedel. 2006. OntoNotes: the 90% solution. In *Proceedings of the Human Language Technology Conference of the NAACL, Companion Volume: Short Papers*, NAACL-Short '06, pages 57–60, Stroudsburg, PA, USA. Association for Computational Linguistics.

Nancy Ide, Collin Baker, Christiane Fellbaum, Charles Fillmore, and Rebecca Passoneau. 2008. MASC: The Manually Annotated Sub-Corpus of American English. In *Proceedings of the Sixth International Conference on Language Resources and Evaluation (LREC'08)*, pages 28–30. European Language Resources Association (ELRA).

Julia Jorgensen. 1990. The psycholinguistic reality of word senses. *Journal of Psycholinguistic Research*, (19):167–190.

Adam Kilgarriff. 1997. "I don't believe in word senses". *Computers and the Humanities*, 31(2):91–113.

Ramesh Krishnamurthy and Diane Nicholls. 2000. Peeling an onion: The lexicographer's experience of manual sense tagging. *Computers and the Humanities*, 34:85–97.

Ryan McDonald, Kevin Lerman, and Fernando Pereira. 2006. Multilingual dependency analysis with a two-stage discriminative parser. In *Proceedings of the Tenth Conference on Computational Natural Language Learning CoNLLX 06*, pages 216–220. Association for Computational Linguistics.

Adam Meyers, Ruth Reeves, and Catherine Macleod. 2008. NomBank v 1.0.

G. A. Miller, C. Leacock, R. Tengi, and R. T. Bunker. 1993a. A semantic concordance. In *Proceedings of ARPA Workshop on Human Language Technology*.

G. A. Miller, C. Leacock, R. Tengi, and R. T. Bunker. 1993b. A semantic concordance. In *Proceedings of ARPA Workshop on Human Language Technology*.

Roberto Navigli. 2006. Meaningful clustering of senses helps boost word sense disambiguation performance. In *Proceedings of the 21st International Conference on Computational Linguistics and 44th Annual Meeting of the ACL*, pages 105–112, Sydney, Australia.

Martha Palmer, Dan Gildea, and Paul Kingsbury. 2005. The proposition bank: A corpus annotated with semantic roles. *Computational Linguistics Journal*, 31(1).

Rebecca J. Passonneau, Ansaf Salleb-Aoussi, Vikas Bhardwaj, and Nancy Ide. 2010. Word sense annotation of PolysemousWords by multiple annotators. In *LREC Proceedings*, pages 3244–3249, Valetta, Malta.

Philip Resnik and David Yarowsky. 1999. Distinguishing systems and distinguishing senses: New evaluation methods for word sense disambiguation. *Natural Language Engineering*, 5(2):113–133.

Anna Rumshisky, M. Verhagen, and J. Moszkowicz. 2009. The holy grail of sense definition: Creating a Sense-Disambiguated corpus from scratch. Pisa, Italy.

Michael Rundell. 2002. *Macmillan English Dictionary for advanced learners*. Macmillan Education.

Josef Ruppenhofer, Michael Ellsworth, Miriam R. L. Petruck, Christopher R. Johnson, and Jan Scheffczyk. 2010. *FrameNet II: Extended Theory and Practice*. ICSI, University of Berkeley, September.

Beatrice Santorini. 1990. Part-of-Speech tagging guidelines for the penn treebank project. *University of Pennsylvania 3rd Revision 2nd Printing*, (MS-CIS-90-47):33.

William A. Scott. 1955. Reliability of content analysis: The case of nominal scale coding. *Public Opinion Quarterly*, 19(3):321–325.

John Sinclair, Patrick Hanks, and et al. 1987. *Collins Cobuild English Dictionary for Advanced Learners 4th edition published in 2003*. HarperCollins Publishers 1987, 1995, 2001, 2003 and Collins A–Z Thesaurus 1st edition first published in 1995. HarperCollins Publishers 1995.

John Sinclair. 1991. *Corpus, Concordance, Collocation*. Describing English Language. Oxford University Press.

Ralph Weischedel, Martha Palmer, Mitchell Marcus, Eduard Hovy, Sameer Pradhan, Lance Ramshaw, Nianwen Xue, Ann Taylor, Jeff Kaufman, Michelle Franchini, Mohammed El-Bachouti, Robert Belvin, and Ann Houston. 2011. OntoNotes release 4.0.

Fabio Massimo Zanzotto, Marco Pennacchiotti, and Alessandro Moschitti. 2009. A machine learning approach to textual entailment recognition. *Natural Language Engineering*, 15(4):551–582.

Yue Zhang and Stephen Clark. 2011. Syntactic processing using the generalized perceptron and beam search. *Computational Linguistics*, 37(November 2009):105–151.

Parallel and Nested Decomposition for Factoid Questions

Aditya Kalyanpur, Siddharth Patwardhan, Branimir Boguraev, Jennifer Chu-Carroll and **Adam Lally**
IBM T. J. Watson Research Center
Yorktown Heights, NY 10598, USA
{adityakal,siddharth,bran,jencc,alally}@us.ibm.com

Abstract

Typically, automatic Question Answering (QA) approaches use the question in its entirety in the search for potential answers. We argue that decomposing complex factoid questions into separate facts about their answers is beneficial to QA, since an answer candidate with support coming from multiple independent facts is more likely to be the correct one. We broadly categorize decomposable questions as *parallel* or *nested*, and we present a novel question decomposition framework for enhancing the ability of single-shot QA systems to answer complex factoid questions. Essential to the framework are components for *decomposition recognition*, *question rewriting*, and *candidate answer synthesis and re-ranking*. We discuss the interplay among these, with particular emphasis on decomposition recognition, a process which, we argue, can be sufficiently informed by lexico-syntactic features alone. We validate our decomposition approach by implementing the framework on top of a state-of-the-art QA system, showing a statistically significant improvement over its accuracy.

1 Introduction

Question Answering (QA) systems for factoid questions typically adopt a "single-shot" approach for the task. Single-shot QA implicitly assumes that the question contains a single nugget of information (as in Example (1)).

(1) *In which city are the headquarters of GE located?*

To answer the question, these approaches attempt to locate the factual information (the location of GE's headquarters) in their underlying resources. Largely a legacy of the nature of TREC questions (Voorhees, 2002), this tactic works in most cases where the assumption holds that a question is focused upon a single fact, and support for it may be found in a single resource.

Our work deals with more complex factoid questions, specifically ones containing multiple facts related to the correct answer. Because such facts may be independent of each other, they may well reside in different resources—and thus outside of the scope of a single-shot search query.

(2) *Which company has origins dating back to the 1870s and became the first U.S. company to have 1 million stockholders?*

Example (2) shows a question with two facts about its answer (a company): its origins date back to the 1870s, and it became the first in U.S. to have 1 million stockholders. We turn to *question decomposition* to leverage the separate facts within the question, using them to garner support for the correct answer from independent sources of evidence. Our hypothesis is that the more independent facts support an answer candidate, the more likely it is to be the correct answer.

We focus here on decomposition applied to improving the quality of QA over a broad set of *factoid* questions. In contrast to most work on decomposition to date, which tends to appeal to discourse and/or semantic properties of the question (Section 2), we exploit the notion of a fact to view decomposition as circumscribed largely by the syntactic shape of questions. Facts are entity-relationship expressions, where the relation may be an N-ary predicate. Most informative, and thus useful, facts are those that contain at least one named entity (including temporal or locative expressions).

The particular relationship between independent facts in any given question leads us to categorize "decomposable" questions broadly into two types: *parallel* and *nested.* Examples (2) above and (3) below are parallel decomposable: sub-questions can be evaluated independently of one another. In contrast, nested questions require their decompositions to be processed in sequence, with the answer to an 'inner' sub-question plugged into the 'outer'. In Example (4), the inner sub-question is marked in brackets; its answer, "cirrhosis", then leads to an outer question *"In the treatment of cirrhosis, which drug reduces portal venous blood inflow"*, the answer to which is also the answer to the original question.

(3) *Which 2011 tax form do I fill if I need to do itemized deductions and I have an IRA rollover from 2010?*

(4) *In the treatment of [a condition that causes bleeding esophageal varices], which drug reduces portal venous blood inflow?*

Questions like these are found in domains such as medical, legal, etc., as they tend to arise in more dynamic QA system setting. Independently of domain and type, however, they share a common characteristic: if a search query is constructed from all the facts collectively describing the answer, it is likely to 'flood' the system with noise, and confuse the identification of potential answer-bearing passages. The notion of decomposition thus goes hand in hand with that of recursively applying a QA system to the individual facts (sub-questions), followed by suitable re-composition of the candidate answer lists for the sub-questions.

This paper presents a novel decomposition approach for such questions. We discuss the particular strategies for recognizing and typing decomposable questions, and the subsequent processing of sub-questions, and their candidate answer lists, in ways which can improve the performance of an existing state-of-the-art QA system.

2 Related work

A variety of approaches to QA cite 'decomposition', in the context of addressing question complexity. In most work to date, however, "complex" refers to questions requiring non-factoid answers: e.g. multiple sentences or summaries of answers (Lacatusu et al., 2006), connected paragraphs (Soricut and Brill, 2004), explanations and/or justification of an answer (Katz et al., 2005), lists (Hartrumpf, 2008) or lists of sets (Lin and Liu, 2008), and so forth.

In the literature, we find descriptions of processes like *local decomposition* and *meronymy decomposition* (Hartrumpf, 2008), semantic decomposition using *knowledge templates* (Katz et al., 2005), *question refocusing* (Hartrumpf, 2008; Katz et al., 2005), and *textual entailment* (Lacatusu et al., 2006) to connect, through semantics and discourse, the original question with its numerous decompositions. In general, such processes are not limited to using only lexical material explicitly present in the question: a constraint we place upon our decomposition algorithms in order to retain the ability to do open-domain QA.

Closer to our strategy are notions like the syntactic decomposition of Katz et al. (2005), and the temporal/spatial analysis of Saquete et al. (2004) and Hartrumpf (2008). Still, our approach differs in at least two significant ways. We offer a principled solution to the problem of the final combination and ranking of candidate answers returned from multiple decompositions, by means of training a model to weigh the effects of decomposition recognition rules. We also note that spatial and temporal decomposition are just special cases of solving nested decomposable questions.

The closest similarity our fact-based decomposition has with an established approach is with the notion of asking additional questions in order to derive constraints on candidate answers (Prager et al., 2004). However, the additional questions there are generated through knowledge of the domain, making that technique hard to apply in an open domain setting. In contrast, we developed a domain-independent approach to question decomposition, in which we use the question context alone in generating queriable constraints.

3 Fact-based Decomposition

Enhancing a single-shot QA system with a capability for incremental solving of decomposable questions requires recognizing that a question is decomposable, and engaging in a staged processing of its sub-question parts. Whether parallel or nested, the system needs to identify the multiple facts, and configure itself as appropriate. Figure 1 shows our fact-based decomposition "meta"-framework ("meta", as it builds on top of an existing QA system). It comprises four main components as illustrated in the figure.

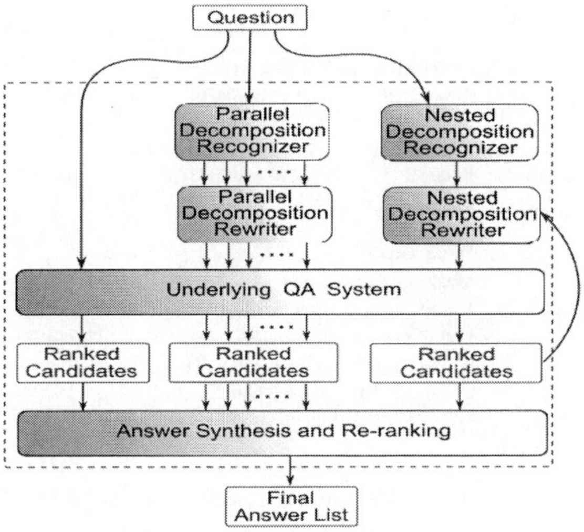

Figure 1: Fact-based decomposition framework

Decomposition Recognizers analyze the input question and identify decomposable parts using a set of predominantly lexico-syntactic cues (Section 4). *Question Rewriters* re-write the sub-questions found by the recognizer, retaining key contextual information (Section 5.1). *Underlying QA System* generates, for any factoid question, a ranked list of answer candidates, each with a *confidence* corresponding to the probability of the answer being correct. *Answer Synthesis and Re-ranking* is a placeholder for the particular process which tries to combine ranked candidate answers obtained to the original question with solutions for the decomposed facts into a uniform ranked answer list. In general, different combination functions may be appropriate for different types of decomposable questions. Thus, for the classes of parallel and nested questions, our decomposition strategies (described in Sections 5.2 and 5.3) defer to an Answer Merger. Other combination functions may be required for e.g. selecting from or aggregating over lists; cf. Hartrumpf's operational decomposition (2008), or Lin and Liu's multi-focus questions (2008); see also the special questions solving techniques of (Prager et al.,).

We use a particular QA system (Ferrucci et al., 2010) as base. However, any system can be plugged into our meta-framework, as long as: it can solve factoid questions by providing answers with confidences reflecting correctness probability; and it maintains context/topic information for the question separately from its main content.

Parallel and nested processing are distinct: note the two different pathways in the figure, multiple parallel facts submitted to the base QA system vs. inner-outer sub-question pairs, processed via a feedback loop. The base system is invoked on the full question, *and* on its decompositions.

4 Decomposition Recognizers

The primary goal in decomposing questions is to identify facts involving the entity being asked for (henceforth the focus), simpler than the full question and solvable independently (Section 1). Most question decomposition work (Section 2) tends to defer to semantic, discourse, and other domain-specific information; in contrast, we recognize decomposable questions primarily on the basis of their syntactic shape. This is important for our claim that the decomposition framework outlined in Section 3 is generally applicable to multiple QA tasks and system configurations.

In our work, we use a dataset of factoid question/answer pairs from Jeopardy!,[1] a popular TV quiz show in the US. The data is particularly challenging, not least for the broad domain it covers and the complex language used. In addition to making for an excellent test-bed for open-domain QA, the data offers a wide choice of questions which require decomposing.

4.1 Decomposition Patterns

Our analysis of complex decomposable questions highlights numerous syntactic cues that are reliable indicators for decomposition, and it is predominantly such cues we exploit for driving the recognition and typing of decomposable questions. A set of recognition patterns can be formulated in terms of fine-grained lexico-syntactic information, expressed over the predicate-argument structure (PAS) for the syntactic parse of the question. We identify three major categories of configurationally-based patterns: *independent subtrees*, *composable units* and *segments with qualifiers*. These are general, in the sense that they capture relationships between configurational properties of a question and its status with respect to decomposability. The specific rules implementing the patterns may, or may not, have to be modified as, for instance, there may be a style change, or a shift in the syntactic analysis framework of the base QA system, to a different parser;

[1] `http://www.jeopardy.com.`

Independent Subtrees		
(1.P) Parallel		
clause	*Its original name meant "bitter water" and it was made palatable to Europeans after the Spaniards added sugar*	**Fact #1**: Its original name meant "bitter water" **Fact #2:** It was made palatable to Europeans after the Spaniards added Sugar
complementary	*"American Prometheus" is a biography of this physicist who died in 1967*	**Fact #1**: this physicist who died in 1967 **Fact #2**: "American Prometheus" is a biography of this physicist
(1.N) Nested		
coincidental	*When "60 Minutes" premiered, this man was U.S. President*	**Inner Fact**: When "60 Minutes" premiered **Outer Fact**: When this man was president
based-on	*A controversial 1979 war film was based on a 1902 work by this author*	**Inner Fact**: A controversial 1979 war film **Outer Fact**: film was based on a work by this author
named-for	*Article of clothing named for an old character who dressed in loose trousers in commedia dell'arte*	**Inner Fact**: an old character who dressed in loose trousers in commedia dell'arte **Outer Fact**: Article of clothing named for character
Composable Units		
(2.P) Parallel		
verb-args	*He launched his lecturing career in 1866 with a talk later titled "Our fellow savages of the Sandwich Islands"*	**Fact #1**: He launched his lecturing career in 1866
focus-mod	*"The Mute" was the working title of this 1940 novel by a female author*	**Fact #1**: this 1940 novel by a female author
triple	*His rise began when he upset Robert M. La Follette, Jr. in a 1946 Senate primary*	**Fact #1**: he upset Robert M. La Follette, Jr.
(2.N) Nested		
explicit-link	*To honor his work, this man's daughter took the name Maria Celeste when she became a nun in 1616*	**Inner Fact**: To honor his work, [this] daughter took the name Maria Celeste, when . . . **Outer Fact**: this man's daughter
descriptive-np	*The word for this congressional job comes from a fox-hunting term for someone who keeps the hunting dogs from straying*	**Inner Fact**: a fox-hunting term for someone who keeps the hunting dogs from straying **Outer Fact**: The word for this congressional job comes from term
Segments with Qualifiers		
(3.P) Parallel		
qualifier	*Winning in 1965 and 1966, he was the first man to win the Masters golf tournament in 2 consecutive years*	**Fact #1**: he was the first man to win the Masters golf tournament in 2 consecutive years

Table 1: Decomposition Rule Sets

such implementations do not affect our analysis of *syntactically-cued* decomposition recognition.

Table 1 shows example decompositions within pattern categories; note that within a category, typically there are rule sets for parallel and nested decomposition types.[2]

Independent Subtrees A good source of independent sub-questions within a question is in clauses likely to capture a unique piece of information about the answer, distinct from the rest of the question. Relative or subordinate clauses (not in a superlative or ordinal context; see **Segments with Qualifiers** below) are examples of independent subtrees and are indicative of parallel decomposition. PAS configurations that connect such subtrees to the focus are generally good indicators of a sub-question: cues to "break off" a subtree from the question as a decomposable fact.

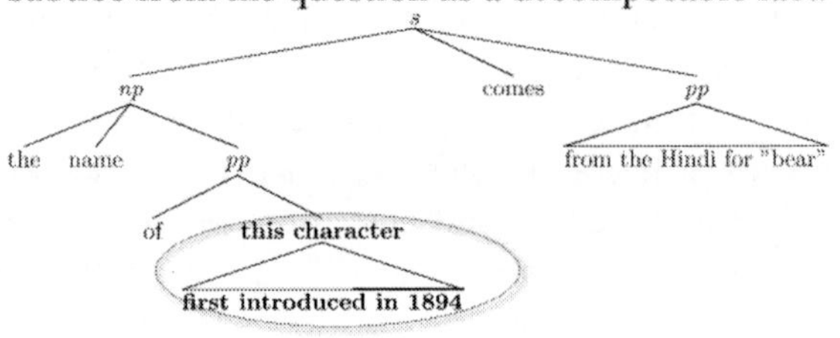

For example, the subtree fragment circled is an independent fact (in brackets) identified within the larger question "*The name of [this character, first introduced in 1894], comes from the Hindi for 'bear'*". This category also includes rules using conjunctions as decomposition points (at various levels of the syntactic parse), as in Example (3) earlier (Section 1).

Parallel decomposition of this type is captured in two rule sets, *clause* and *complementary*, which differ primarily in that 'complementary' rules attempt to derive two separate sub-questions, while the 'clause' rules attempt to locate independent

[2]In the data we use, questions are posed in a declarative format, with stylized marking of question focus. This should not detract from referring to them as 'questions'.

sub-questions in the original question. Examples in Table 1/Row (1.P) illustrate this distinction.

For nested decomposition, we have three rule sets: *coincidental*, *based-on* and *named-for*. These use lexical cues to detect specific semantic relations within the question that could indicate nestedness. For instance, the 'coincidental' rules identify sub-questions resolving a temporal link with the focus of the original question. The 'based-on' and 'named-for' rules detect sub-questions where the answer to the original question is based on or named for the answer to the inner sub-question (Table 1/row (1.N)). Note that in different domains, different relations may correlate with nestedness, for instance, *disease-causes-symptom* in a medical setting; cf. Example (4) in Section 1. The general pattern would still apply, even if we need different rule(s) to implement it.

Configurational information is used to determine whether the question exhibits parallel or nested decomposition profile. Thus the syntactic contour of Example (3) shows that two clauses characterize the same entity (the focus): a clear indicator that the sub-questions are parallel. Conversely, *"A controversial 1979 war film was based on a 1902 work by this author"* exhibits a very different set of configurational properties. There are two underspecified entities (including the focus), both characterized as head-plus-modifiers syntactic units; however, there is no 'sharing' of the separate characterizations (facts) via a common head. This indicates nestedness: the inner sub-question is the one around the underspecified, but non-focus, element (*"a controversial 1979 war film"*); the outer is *"[film] was based on a 1902 work by this author"*.

Another cue for nested questions is a sub-tree labeled by a temporal subordinate conjunction, or a subordinate clause, away from the focus-enclosing top level of the question and itself underspecified. Such analysis will motivate the question *"When "60 Minutes" premiered, this man was U.S. president"* to be solved first for the temporal expression, *"When did "60 Minutes" premiere?"*, followed by *"Who was U.S. President in 1968?"*.

Composable Units An alternate strategy for identifying sub-questions is to "compose" a fact by combining elements from the question. In contrast to the previous category, the 'Composable Units' rules combine separate parts of the PAS into a fact. For instance, a sub-question can be created by associating the focus head with its premodifiers and postmodifiers. If the premodifiers and postmodifiers are sufficiently specific, we obtain reasonably independent sub-questions, with parallel-decomposable behavior.

Three parallel decomposition rule sets are defined in this category: *verb-args*, *focus-mod* and *triple* (see Table 1/row (2.P)). The rules in 'verb-args' "compose" a fact from the verb and its arguments (subject, object, PP complements). The 'focus-mod' rules combine the head of the focus NP with its modifiers to generate a sub-question. Similar to 'verb-args' are 'triple' rules, which create less constrained sub-questions (in that the composition always links only two of the arguments to the underlying predicate, e.g. subject-verb-object or subject-verb-complement).

Here also, a particular configuration around the focus may indicate a question requiring nested processing. For nested, the Composable Units category has two rule sets: *explicit-link* and *descriptive-np* (Table 1/row (2.N)).

In contrast to questions where modifiers of the focus can be cues for parallel decomposition (i.e. the 'focus-mod' rules above), the 'explicit-link' rules detect nested decomposition, signaled by the focus itself being a modifier. For example, in *"To honor his work, this man's daughter took the name Maria Celeste when she became a nun in 1616"*, the focus (*"this man"*) is a determiner to an underspecified node (*"daughter"*). Traversing the tree without descending to the level of the focus would "carve out" an inner sub-question itself focused on that underspecified node (*"daughter"*): see Table 1/row (2.N).

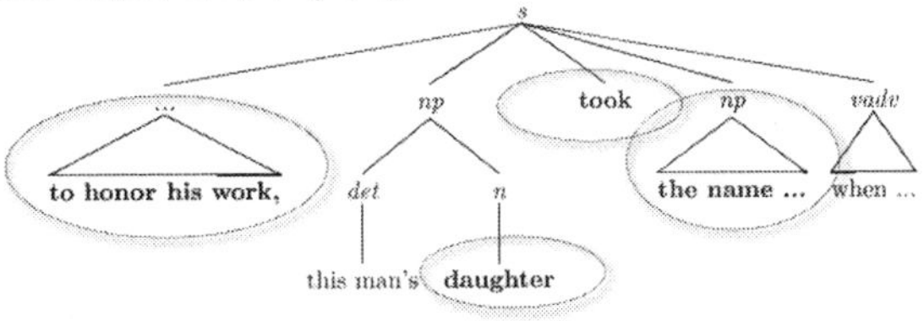

The 'descriptive-np' rule set finds 'parenthetical' descriptions of underspecified nouns in the primary question, as in e.g. *"This arboreally named area was made famous by [a prince in the region noted for impaling enemies on stakes]"*: the nested-decomposable nature of this question is captured in the descriptive phrase (in square brackets) functioning as an inner sub-question.

Segments with Qualifiers This category of rules covers cases where the modifier of the focus is a relative qualifier, such as "*the first*", "*only*", "*the westernmost*". In such cases, information from another clause is usually required to "complete" the relative qualifier: consider e.g. the incomplete "*the third man*" vs. the fact "*the third man ... to climb Mt. Everest*") To deal with these cases, rules in this category combine the characteristics of Composable Units with those of Independent Subtrees rules. We "compose" the relative qualifier, the focus (along with its modifiers) and the attached supporting clause "subtree" to generate this type of rules. As illustrated in row (3.P) of Table 1, for parallel decomposition our rule set covers sub-questions expressed as superlatives. We do not have any rules of this type for the nested case.

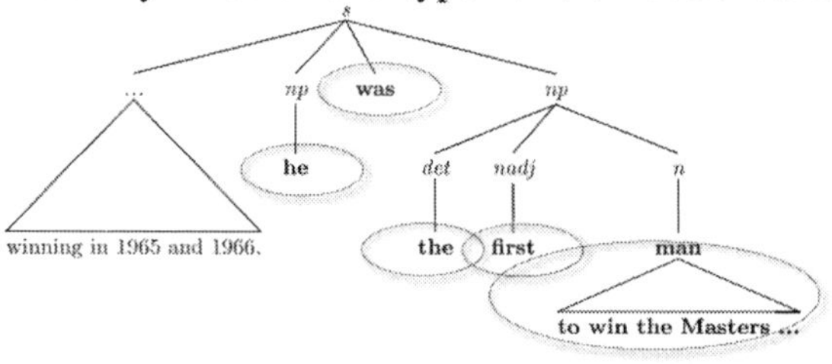

4.2 Decomposition Filters

All three pattern categories above rely only on a syntactic analysis of the question; this is delivered by the English Slot Grammar (ESG) parser (McCord, 1989). When rules fire, they also identify question segments proposed as sub-questions.

Not surprisingly, the rules over-generate; to mitigate against that, we apply several heuristic filters to the proposed sub-questions. The filters discard sub-questions that do not contain either a named entity, a quoted string, or a time or date expression (these are detected by the ESG parser). Additionally, we discard sub-questions that almost completely overlap the entire question or a sub-question from a prior rule. A partial priority order is imposed on rule application, based on intuitions of how informative the facts generated by a rule are; this order is reflected on a per-type basis in Table 1: e.g. within type (2.P) we prefer *verb-args* to *triple* since the latter tends to produce less constrained facts than the former.

5 Using Decomposition

In essence, decomposition recognition informs two processes. According to the question type, parallel or nested, the appropriate pathway in the framework (Figure 1) needs to get instantiated; before sub-questions are submitted to the base QA system, they may need augmentation to facilitate the recursive system invocation. The answer sets obtained from sub-questions processing need then to be analyzed and rationalized, to determine the final answer to the original question.

5.1 Question Re-Writing

For parallel decomposition, the goal is to solve the original question Q by solving sub-questions independently and combining results appropriately. For example, consider the Jeopardy! question

(5) HISTORIC PEOPLE: *The life story of this man who died in 1801 was chronicled in an A&E Biography DVD titled "Triumph and treason"*

We get two decompositions:[3]

Q_1: *This man who died in 1801*

Q_2: *The life story of this man was chronicled in an A&E Biography DVD titled "Triumph and treason"*

Submitting sub-questions—unmodified—to the base QA system raises at least two problems. Sub-questions are often much shorter than the original question, and in many cases no longer have a unique answer. Moreover, some of the information from the original question that was dropped in a sub-question may be relevant contextual cues that the QA system needs to come up with the correct answer. Q_1 above illustrates these problems: it does not have a unique answer, and suffers from a recall problem (the correct answer is not in the candidate answer list of the base system when it considers this sub-question alone).

Our solution is to insert contextual information into the sub-questions. In a two-step process for a sub-question Q_i, we obtain the set of all named entities and nouns (ignoring stopwords) in the original question text outside of Q_i, and we insert these keywords into the original question category. In Jeopardy! questions, the category field is the context/topic information which the underlying QA system needs in order to use the decomposition framework, as stated in Section 3. In general, a QA system may derive such information in a variety of ways, e.g. by exploiting the problem description in a technical assistance QA setting, or a patient's medical history,

[3] Jeopardy! questions also contain category information, which further contextualizes the search for the answer.

in a medical QA setting. What is important here is that the base system treat such information differently from the question itself. Rewriting takes advantage of this differential weighting to ensure that the larger context of the original question is still taken into account when evaluating a sub-question, albeit with less weight.

The re-written Q_1/Q_2 for Example (5) are:

(5-1) HISTORIC PEOPLE (A&E BIOGRAPHY DVD "TRIUMPH AND TREASON"): *This man who died in 1801*

(5-2) HISTORIC PEOPLE (1801): *The life story of this man was chronicled in an A&E Biography DVD titled "Triumph and treason"*

The keywords are inserted in parentheses, to ensure a clear separation between the original category terms and the context terms added. Other systems may need a different re-writing tactic.

The above re-writing technique is used for both parallel and nested decomposable questions. For the nested case, there is an additional re-writing step that needs to be done – after solving the inner question, we need to substitute its answer into the outer when solving for it. Thus the first example in Table 1/row(1.N) would have its inner focus *"When '60 Minutes' premiered"* replaced with *"In 1968"* creating the outer question *"In 1968, this man was U.S. President"* whose solution is the answer to the original question.

5.2 Answer Re-Ranking: Parallel

The base QA system will process the re-written category/sub-question pairs, and will produce a set of ranked candidate lists with confidences. These need to be combined into a final answer list for the original question, accounting for information across all sub-question candidate lists.

One way to produce a final score for each candidate answer is simply to take the product of the scores returned by the QA system for each of the sub-questions. This assumes that the sub-questions are typically independent and that the QA system produces a confidence which corresponds to the probability of the answer being correct. However, even if the sub-questions are independent, question re-writing breaks this assumption as it brings information from the remainder of the question into the sub-question context. Also, the sub-questions are generated by decomposition rules that have varying precision and recall, and thus should not be weighted equally.

Feature Name	Description
Orig. Top Answer	Binary feature signaling whether candidate was top answer to non-decomposed question
Orig. Confidence	Confidence for candidate answer to non-decomposed question
# Facts Matched	Number of sub-questions which have candidate answer in top 10
Rule-verb-args Rule-clause Rule-qualifier Rule-focus-mod Rule-complementary Rule-triple	Features corresponding to the rules sets used in parallel decomposition – each feature takes a numeric value, which is the confidence of the QA system on a fact identified by the corresponding rule set

Table 2: Features in Parallel Re-ranking Model

Finally, if the sub-questions are not of a good quality (e.g. due to a bad parse), we need a fallback to the original question, which implies that the confidence for the candidate answer for the entire question should also be considered when making a final decision. Consequently, we use a machine-learning model to combine information across sub-question answer confidences, with features capturing the above information (Table 2).

In case a candidate answer is not in the answer list of the full question or any of the decomposed sub-questions, the corresponding feature value is set to *missing*. If a rule generates multiple sub-questions, its corresponding feature value for the candidate answer is set to the sum of the confidences obtained for that answer across all sub-questions. The model is trained using Weka's (Witten and Frank, 2000) logistic regression algorithm with instance weighting.

5.3 Answer Re-Ranking: Nested

Nested questions decompose into inner/outer question pairs. The task is to solve the inner question first, substitute the answer obtained, based on its confidence, into the outer, and solve that for the final answer. This is contingent upon selecting answers to the inner question which might profitably be plugged into the outer; substituting incorrect answers will only lead to noisy final answers, with negative impact to overall accuracy.

We rely on the ability of the underlying QA system to produce meaningful confidences for its answers, and only consider the top answer to the inner question for substitution into the outer—if its confidence exceeds some threshold.

Finally, the answers to the outer question need to be related to the full question answer list, to produce the final ranked answers. For answer re-ranking, we use the following heuristic selection strategy: we compute the aggregate confidence of the answer obtained through decomposition as the product of the inner-question answer confidence and the outer-question answer confidence, and compare this value with that of the top answer confidence to the entire question selecting the higher confidence one as our final answer. Note that this re-ranking is different from the one used in parallel decomposition where we combine results from multiple sub-questions into a single confidence.

6 Evaluation

6.1 Evaluation Data

As we discuss question decomposition in the context of Jeopardy! data (Section 4), our test set contains only Final Jeopardy! (FJ) questions. They are often long and complex, with multiple facts or constraints that need to be satisfied. Also, they are typically much harder to answer than regular Jeopardy! questions both for humans and for our base QA system. The test set comprises close to 3000 FJ questions, broken into 1138 for training, 517 for development and 1269 questions for testing (as blind data).

6.2 Experiments

The decomposition rules (Section 4) and re-ranking parameters (Sections 5.2, 5.3) were defined and tuned on the development set. The final re-ranking model was trained over the training set, using the features described in Section 5.2, and logistic regression with instance re-weighting. The results of applying the decomposition rules followed by the re-ranking model to the 1269 test questions are shown in Table 3. The baseline is the performance of the underlying QA system used in our meta-framework without any decomposition components, applied to the same test set.

We evaluated separately the impact of our question re-writing strategy (Section 5.1) that maintains contextual information from the original question into the sub-questions. For this purpose, we altered our algorithm to issue the sub-question text as-is, using the original category, and re-trained and evaluated the resulting model again on the test set. The results are also shown in Table 3.

In the table, PB refers to Parallel Baseline, and NB to Nested Baseline; both are results from running the underlying QA system without any decomposition capabilities. PD and ND refer to Parallel and Nested Decomposition systems respectively and QR refers to question re-writing. Separate experiments determined end-to-end accuracy for the different system configurations, with respect to the entire test set, and accuracy over the decomposable questions subsets of the test set.

QA System	End-to-End Accuracy	Decomposable Q Accuracy
PB	635/1269 (50.05%)	339/598 (56.68%)
PD−QR	634/1269 (49.96%)	338/598 (56.52%)
PD+QR	**643/1269 (50.66%)**	**347/598 (58.02%)**
NB	635/1269 (50.05%)	129/255 (50.58%)
ND+QR	**640/1269 (50.43%)**	**134/255 (52.54%)**

Table 3: Evaluating Decomposition

We do not offer separate analysis of decomposition recognition. Manual creation of decomposition standard is highly non-trivial, largely due to the numerous alternative ways to decompose a question, and synthesize unique facts from the segments. Indeed, this is precisely the motivation for weighting the decomposition rules in a trained re-ranking model (Section 5.2). Given this, we are interested only in measuring the impact of decomposition on end-to-end QA performance.

6.3 Discussion of Results

The results in Table 3 show that the parallel decomposition rules were able to decompose a large fraction of the test set (598 out of 1269 questions: 47%). Interestingly, the performance of the baseline QA system on the decomposable set was 56.6%, which is 6% higher than the overall performance over the entire test set. One reason for this result would be that parallel decomposable questions typically contain a lot more information (more than one fact or constraint that the answer must satisfy) about the same answer, and the system in some cases is able to exploit this redundancy—such as when one fact is strongly associated with the correct answer and there is evidence supporting this in the sources.

A different, important result is that using the decomposition algorithm without question re-writing did not show impact over the baseline. This highlights the importance of contextual information for QA. On the other hand, when using re-writing to maintain context (Section 5.1), our parallel decomposition algorithm was able to achieve a gain of 1.4% on the parallel decomposable question set, which translated to an end-to-end gain of 0.6%.

Separately, the table shows that roughly a fifth (255 out of 1269 questions) of the entire test set were recognized as nested decomposable. Again, interestingly, the performance of the baseline QA system on the nested decomposable set was roughly the same as the overall performance (and much lower than the parallel decomposable cases). The likely explanation here is that nested questions require solving for an inner fact first, and it is the answer to this, which often provides the necessary missing information required to find the correct answer: this makes nested questions much harder to solve than parallel decomposable ones with their multiple independent facts. Our nested decomposition algorithm using the heuristic re-ranking approach (Section 5.3) was able to achieve a gain of 2% on the nested decomposable question set, which translated to an end-to-end gain of 0.4%.

The aggregate impact of parallel *and* nested decomposition was a 1.5% gain in accuracy on the decomposable set, and a 1% gain on end-to-end system accuracy (in our case the questions that are classified as parallel or nested form disjoint sets).

To put these results in perspective, we emphasize that the baseline QA system represents state-of-the-art in solving Jeopardy! questions. The FJ questions, which exclusively comprise our test data, are known to be harder than regular Jeopardy!: qualified Jeopardy! players' accuracy on this kind of questions is 48%,[4] and the underlying QA system has an accuracy close to 51% on previously unseen FJ questions. A gain of 1% end-to-end on such questions, therefore, represents a strong improvement. Also, using the statistical McNemar's test (McNemar, 1947), we found the net end-to-end impact to be statistically significant at a 99% confidence interval.

Finally, we note that our error analysis of the test questions shows a wide variety of reasons for their failures beyond question decomposition. To further improve the system on this test set would require advances beyond deciding whether to take a single-shot or decomposable approach to questions, which is beyond the scope of this paper.

[4]Calculated over historical games data, from J-archive (`http://www.j-archive.com`).

7 Conclusion

In this paper, we presented a general-purpose decomposition framework for answering complex factoid questions, which consists of three components: 1) a decomposition recognizer, which identifies the subparts of a decomposable question, 2) a question re-writer, which composes new sub-questions from the identified subparts, taking into account context from the original question, and 3) an answer synthesis and re-ranking component, which synthesizes and ranks final answers based on candidate answers to the sub-questions. Additionally, this framework leverages an underlying factoid QA system for producing answers to the sub-questions. Any QA system that can associate confidence scores with its answers and can make distinctions between the question and the context in which the question should be interpreted can be adopted in this decomposition framework.

We applied our decomposition framework to address two broad classes of complex factoid questions, parallel and nested decomposition questions. These are distinguished by how the identified sub-questions related to each other, which in turn affects how the candidate answers to the sub-questions are combined to form the final answers. In order to maintain generality and facilitate domain adaptation, the rule-based patterns for decomposition recognition leverage syntactic characteristics of the question that are indicative of sub-question boundaries. To optimally leverage these patterns, a machine learning model was trained to properly weigh the possibly overlapping, and occasionally conflicting, patterns.

We demonstrated the impact of our question decomposition approach on a state-of-the-art factoid QA system. On a test set of 1269 Final Jeopardy! questions, 47% of the question were found to be parallel decomposable and 20% were nested decomposable. Overall, the system achieved a statistically significant gain of 1.5% in accuracy on these questions, further increasing the system's lead over human Jeopardy! players' performance on these questions.

Given that factoid (and, often, complex) questions are typically found in several real world domains (e.g. medical, legal, technical support), we expect our decomposition framework to have broad impact, both in open- and specialized-domain QA.

References

D. Ferrucci, E. Brown, J. Chu-Carroll, J. Fan, D. Gondek, A. Kalyanpur, A. Lally, J. W. Murdock, E. Nyberg, J. Prager, N. Schlaefer, and C. Welty. 2010. Building Watson: An Overview of the DeepQA Project. *AI Magazine*, 31(3):59–79, Fall.

S. Hartrumpf. 2008. Semantic Decomposition for Question Answering. In *Proceedings of the 18th European Conference on Artificial Intelligence*, pages 313–317, Patras, Greece, July.

B. Katz, G. Borchardt, and S. Felshin. 2005. Syntactic and Semantic Decomposition Strategies for Question Answering from Multiple Sources. In *Proceedings of the AAAI Workshop on Inference for Textual Question Answering*, pages 35–41, Pittsburgh, PA, July.

F. Lacatusu, A. Hickl, and S. Harabagiu. 2006. The Impact of Question Decomposition on the Quality of Answer Summaries. In *Proceedings of the Fifth Language Resources and Evaluation Conference*, pages 1147–1152, Genoa, Italy, May.

C.J. Lin and R.R. Liu. 2008. An Analysis of Multi-Focus Questions. In *Proceedings of the SIGIR 2008 Workshop on Focused Retrieval*, pages 30–36, Singapore, July.

M. McCord. 1989. Slot Grammar: A System for Simpler Construction of Practical Natural Language Grammars. In *Proceedings of the International Symposium on Natural Language and Logic*, pages 118–145, Hamburg, Germany, May.

Q. McNemar. 1947. Note on the Sampling Error of the Difference Between Correlated Proportions or Percentages. *Psychometrika*, 12(2):153–157.

J. Prager, E. Brown, and J. Chu-Carroll. Special Questions and Techniques. Submitted to *IBM Journal of Research and Development*, Special Issue on DeepQA.

J. Prager, J. Chu-Carroll, and K. Czuba. 2004. Question Answering by Constraint Satisfaction: QA-by-Dossier with Constraints. In *Proceedings of the 42nd Annual Meeting of the Association for Computational Linguistics*, pages 574–581, Barcelona, Spain, July.

E. Saquete, P. Martínez-Barco, R. Muñoz, and J. Vicedo. 2004. Splitting Complex Temporal Questions for Question Answering Systems. In *Proceedings of the 42nd Annual Meeting of the Association for Computational Linguistics*, pages 566–573, Barcelona, Spain, July.

R. Soricut and E. Brill. 2004. Automatic Question Answering: Beyond the Factoid. In *Proceedings of the Human Language Technology Conference of the North American Chapter of the Association for Computational Linguistics*, pages 57–64, Boston, MA, May.

E. Voorhees. 2002. Overview of the TREC 2002 Question Answering Track. In *NIST Special Publication 500-251: The Eleventh Text REtrieval Conference (TREC 2002)*, Gaithersburg, MD, November.

I. Witten and E. Frank. 2000. *Data Mining - Practical Machine Learning Tools and Techniques with Java Implementations*. Morgan–Kaufmann, San Francisco, CA.

Author Index